Footprint

chile

The travel guide

Handbook 2002

Toby Green

"I can see how puzzling a country can be that starts at the frozen South Pole and stretches upwards to salt mines and deserts where it hasn't rained for eons."

Pablo Neruda, *Memoirs*

Chile Handbook
Third edition
© Footprint Handbooks Ltd 2001

Published by Footprint Handbooks
6 Riverside Court
Lower Bristol Road
Bath BA2 3DZ. England
T +44 (0)1225 469141
F +44 (0)1225 469461
Email discover@footprintbooks.com
Web www.footprintbooks.com

ISBN 1 903471 05 2
ISSN 1363-741X
CIP DATA: A catalogue record for this
book is available from the British Library

Distributed in the USA by
Publishers Group West

Neither the black and white nor
coloured maps are intended to have
any political significance.

Every effort has been made to ensure
that the facts in this Handbook are
accurate. However, travellers should still
obtain advice from consulates, airlines
etc about current travel and visa
requirements before travelling. The
authors and publishers cannot accept
responsibility for any loss, injury or
inconvenience however caused.

Credits

Series editors
Patrick Dawson and Rachel Fielding

Editorial
Editor: Stephanie Lambe
Maps: Sarah Sorensen

Production
Typesetting: Richard Ponsford, Emma
Bryers, Leona Bailey, Davina Rungasamy
and Jo Morgan
Maps: Robert Lunn, Claire Benison and
Angus Dawson
Colour maps: Kevin Feeney and
Robert Lunn
Proof reading: Carol Franklin and
Elizabeth Barrick
Cover: Camilla Ford

Design
Mytton Williams

Photography
Front cover: Still Pictures/
Brigitte Marcon-Bios
Back cover: Chris Barton
Inside colour section: BBC Natural
History Unit Picture Library,
Eye Ubiquitous, gettyone Stone, Image
Bank, James Davis Travel Photography,
Robert Harding Picture Library, South
American Pictures, Travel Ink

Print
Manufactured in Italy by LEGOPRINT

Chile

PERU

BOLIVIA

PARAGUAY

ARGENTINA

Pacific Ocean

Atlantic Ocean

Arica
Parque Nacional Lauca
Salar de Surire
Iquique
Calama
San Pedro de Atacama
Antofagasta
Copiapó
La Serena
Viña del Mar
Valparaíso
□ SANTIAGO
Curicó
Talca
Concepción
Chillán
Temuco
Lake District
Lago Llanquihue
Puerto Montt
Parque Nacional Fray Gorge
Castro
Chiloé
Chaitén
Puerto Aisén
Coyhaique
Parque Nacional Laguna San Rafael
Puerto Natales
Punta Arenas
Tierra del Fuego
Ushuaia
Puerto Williams

Falkland Islands

N

0 km 200
0 miles 200

Contents

Left: Pelicans crossing? Awaiting the fishermen's catch at Arica's harbour.

4

Right: *A homage to the ancestors – one of the 600 or so huge moai on Easter Island.*

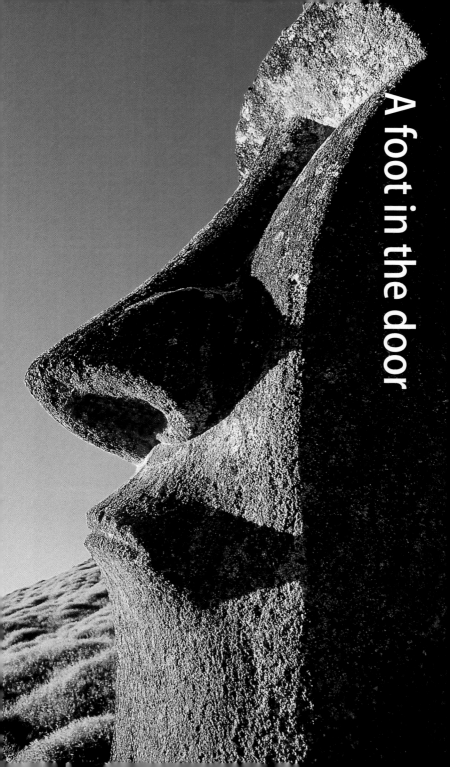

A foot in the door

6

Right: the old and the new, Santiago.
Below: the peaks of Torres del Paine National Park.

Above: The Valle de la Luna, so-called because the surreal landscape of dunes and salt is supposed to resemble a moonscape, with Volcano Licancabur in the distance.
Right: Check mate – chess in Santiago's Plaza de Armas.
Next page: Don't put your foot in it! – Crossing a crevasse in the icecap around the summit of Volcano Villarrica, Lake District.

Highlights

With an almost comical geographical shape, virtually every climate imaginable, and the recent political earthquake of the Pinochet affair to compliment its geological shudders, Chile is a country which in recent years has forced the world to sit up and take notice.

It is most often for its serenity and natural beauty that visitors are attracted to Chile. **In a microcosm** Travelling from north to south, and with only a little exertion, it is possible to see the highest geyser, the driest desert and one of the highest lakes in the world; a flowering desert; schools of dolphins; the Andes; forests of monkey puzzle trees; temperate rainforest; the Patagonian ice-field; and the glaciers of Tierra del Fuego and the islands near Cape Horn. The more vigorous can climb active volcanoes where the crater bubbles away beneath them, gallop horses along wild and empty beaches, ski in some of South America's finest mountain resorts, go whitewater rafting, canoeing or kayaking, and trek in one of the world's finest national parks, Torres del Paine in Patagonia.

Yet while the country wears its beautiful scenery on its sleeve, peel away the layers of **Highs of** urban life and an equally intriguing animal lurks below. Though Chile is perhaps more **metropolitan** 'European' than some of its Andean neighbours, it possesses some of the most fasci- **life** nating cities in South America. Santiago is a sophisticated capital with a vibrant cultural life tucked away, including an underground rock scene and some of South America's most experimental modern artists. The nearby port city of Valparaíso, meanwhile, was recently described by Brian Keenan as 'a Venice waiting to be discovered'; with its warrens of streets and brightly painted houses, it is a place where it is possible to spend weeks and not even scratch the surface. To the south, Chillán has wonderful galleries and museums which give an insight into the heartland of Chile, while Iquique – the driest city on earth – gives a sense of life on a forbidding frontier.

While the Quechua and Aymará peoples of Bolivia and Peru are perhaps more famous **Mapuche** outside the continent, it was Chile's Mapuches who provided the fiercest resistance to **to Moai** the Spanish. In fact, it was only following the advent of the breech-loading rifle in the second half of the 19th century that the Mapuches were finally forced to submit to Santiago. The region around Temuco in the south gives plenty of opportunities to see the fierce pride of the Mapuches in their heritage, and to understand something of their tragic history. Meanwhile, to confirm the strength of the indigenous cultures of Chile, it is only necessary to look westwards to Easter Island, where the mysterious *moai* figures have fascinated anthropologists for decades. This unique Polynesian culture provides an intriguing counterbalance to the prevailing mix of the European and the Amerindian which makes Chile such a distinctive South American country.

But just in case you are still doubtful that Chile is anything more than a European coun- **Doubts &** try disguised as a South American one, it is only necessary to take a short boat trip to **witches** the island of Chiloé, in the south of country. Here the islanders have an entire mythology all of their own, including goblins, ghost ships, mermaids and witches, who fly to the graveyards at night and eat the bodies of the recently interred.

Right: translucent icebergs in the sea, with the Laguna San Rafael Glacier in the background, Patagonia.
Below: A welcome sight after a steep climb, Laguna Amarga, Torres del Paine National Park.

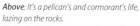

Above: It's a pelican's and cormorant's life, lazing on the rocks.
Right: the highest geysers in the world at El Tatio.
Next page: desert road in the Atacama.

The desert and the deep blue sea

Few countries in the world have quite such a split geographical personality as Chile. It is often possible to glimpse the high Andes from the Pacific Ocean, and indeed, from Valparaíso, the country's most important port, you can even see as far as Aconcagua over in Argentina. Hemmed in by some of the world's thickest temperate rainforests to the south, and by the Atacama desert to the north, the extremes are complete. But while the Andes and the forests are perhaps most famous outside Chile, the desert and the ocean have an equally important role in the national psyche.

The Atacama, with its endless space, the geoglyphs that are legacies of pre-Hispanic **A deserted** civilizations, and the pristine skies which are home to the world's most important **delight** observatories, is a world in itself. The desert's emptiness, and the intermingling of the old world with the new, have led to some of the most enduring aspects of ancient and modern Chilean culture: these range from the legend of the Inca princess La Tirana, which spawned the country's biggest religious fiesta, to the political militancy which arose among the nitrate mines in the early 20th century, and played a big part in forging Salvador Allende's Popular Unity government of 1970-1973 – later to be overthrown by Augusto Pinochet.

From the ugly desert hill that rises behind Arica, in the north, to the cliffs of Cape Horn, **Bandits &** in the south, the ocean affects Chileans deeply, as source of some of the country's **bounties** worst dangers and greatest riches. On the negative side, first come the English pirates, such as Drake and Cavendish, who laid waste to the young Spanish settlements. Then there is the more perennial danger of *maremotos*, the terrible tidal waves which occur once every century or so – in 1835, the *maremoto* completely destroyed Talcahuano; in 1960, it was Ancud's and Puerto Saavedra's turns to be ruined. And yet, the sea is also the source of Chile's wonderful seafood – with such a bewildering array of shellfish and larger fish always on offer, Chileans cannot but love the sea.

At the heart of the sea, and the contradictions – midway between the southern **Order &** forests and the northern deserts – is Valparaíso, which, like Chilean geography, is a **anarchy** contradiction in itself. The city ranges from being ordered and well-to-do by the port, to chaotic and anarchic in the hills above. Perhaps inevitably, it was in this uniquely atmospheric city that the symbols of Chilean political extremes were both born and raised in the early years of the 20th century: Salvador Allende, and Augusto Pinochet.

Poetry and motion

A nation With such a remarkable geography and an enduring sense of isolation, it is perhaps no
of poets surprise that poetry has flourished here. In Gabriela Mistral and Pablo Neruda, Chile has
produced two Nobel Prize-winning poets – a remarkable tally for a small and comparatively poor nation. The poetic output is not limited to the urbane; neither Mistral nor
Neruda were from large cities or privileged families, and Chileans have a saying that
there is a poet hidden under every stone. Even in remote rural areas it is possible to find
small poetry groups, or woodcutters and other *campesinos* who will have verses to
read to travellers. It is both a privilege and a chastening reminder of the power and
value of literature to come across rural workers scrawling out unpretentious verses in
dog-eared exercise books.

Neruda himself was fascinated by the sea, two of his three houses in the country
were on the coast, where the poet could sit in a garret high above the shore and
watch the waves roll in endlessly from across the Pacific. By contrast, Mistral was
brought up in the fertile Elqui Valley near La Serena, surrounded by the snows of the
high Andes and the barren slopes leading up to them. In these two great poets, something of the essence of Chile emerges. Whether living by the sea or surrounded by the
mountains, natural beauty poured out of the soul of Chile and into these men. With
forests, mountains, lakes, geysers and deserts, it is perhaps fitting that one of the
world's strongest poetic traditions should still be found here.

'The English of There is much more to Chile than the superficial veneer of European culture which the
South America' visitor sees in Santiago. Yet, when it comes to cultural characteristics, some Chileans
look in an unlikely direction for the roots of their most enduring features: '*Somos los
ingleses de Sudamérica*', they will tell you – 'We are the English of South America'.
The roots of this surprising assertion cut to the heart of much of what it means to be
Chilean. Inaccessible for centuries, except by sea or over the passes of the high Andes,
they have developed a highly distinct and slightly isolationist identity: an insularity and
indomitable national pride which means that they can empathize all too easily with a
place such as England. This 'Englishness' manifests itself in all sorts of surprising ways:
Chilean tea is known as *once*, the Spanish for 11 – supposedly a hangover from English
'elevenses'; they may often possess an old-fashioned courtesy and ceremoniousness
which hark back to stereotyped versions of the Victorian Englishman; and the Chilean
navy is modelled on English lines. Of course, this is not really Englishness at all, but a
highly developed national identity that is all its own. In a country of paradoxes, where
the mountains can be seen from the sea and deserts give way to glaciers, perhaps it is
the ultimate paradox that, with the forces of such a vast continent so easily apparent in
the soaring Andes, Chileans came to look on their own country almost as an island like
that small and distant country on the other side of the world.

Left: you might find yourself out on a limb while travelling in the Atacama Desert.
Below: araucarias or monkey puzzle trees – the national tree, these have been growing around the Lake District area for over 200 million years.

Above: one of Chile's more popular stretches of coast, Algarrobo's beach.
Left: the 17th-century Iglesia San Pedro in San Pedro de Atacama, one of the centres of occupation during the Spanish colonial period.
Next page: rural calm at Rilan on the mysterious island of Chiloé.

Essentials

2

Essentials

Planning your trip

Chileans say that, when God had almost completed the act of creation, there was a little of everything left – so God threw it all down in a narrow strip of land and called it Chile. The pride is justifiable, for this is a fantastically diverse country. With such variety, this volume makes no attempt to be prescriptive. There are, though, a number of places which stand out for the visitor. A word of advice is try not to do too much: you will get more out of your travels by covering a small area properly than by flitting from one place to another.

Where to go

Any list of such destinations would have to include Chilean Patagonia, notably the mountains and eerie blue glaciers of the **Parque Nacional Torres del Paine**, one of the great parks of the world. At the other end of the country is the small town of **San Pedro de Atacama**, an unlikely oasis in the middle of one of the world's driest deserts, set near geysers, volcanoes and saltflats. Lying between the two is the green island of **Chiloé**. Visiting Chiloé in 1835, Charles Darwin found that the rolling hills reminded him of England. Chiloé has changed little since and, with its rich mythology and close-knit agricultural communities, it still evokes a bygone age. Just north of Chiloé is the **Lake District**, where the lakes, volcanoes, forests and waterfalls offer some of Chile's most picturesque scenery.

If you have more time, the **Parque Nacional Lauca**, situated in the far north, is serenity personified, with volcanoes and a rich variety of birdlife set near one of the world's highest lakes. Further south lies the city of **La Serena**, with its long beaches and old Spanish colonial architecture. Near the capital, Santiago, is the main port, **Valparaíso**, where the maze of alleyways teetering above the Pacific give the city a feel quite unlike any other in South America. And **Santiago** itself is a thriving metropolis, close to ski resorts, beaches and fine walking country.

Meanwhile – in case that does not already sound enough to fill your time – the whole length of Chile's central coast is dotted with secluded beach resorts and deserted cliff-top tracks climbing above the ocean. **Lago Lanalhue** and the **Sierra de Nahuelbuta**, south of Concepción, receive far fewer visitors than the lakes further south, but are almost as dramatic. The **Camino Austral** is sparsely inhabited, and its forests and waterfalls bear comparison to any in the Lake District. Two final suggestions would be the **Juan Fernandez Islands** (where Alexander Selkirk, Defoe's model for *Robinson Crusoe*, was marooned for almost five years) and **Easter Island**, with its famous archaeological heritage – both of which are easily reached from Santiago by plane.

So much choice can be confusing for the visitor. Hemmed in by an ocean, the Atacama Desert and the Andes, Chileans say that they are at 'the end of the world'. When combined with the country's shape, these geographical barriers rule out circular routes within the country – the choice therefore comes down to whether to go north or south.

If time is limited, and you are travelling in the Chilean summer (December to March), **The south** you may want to focus on the southern part of the country. A two-week visit to the south could include a few days in the Lake District, followed by three days in Chiloé and four days in the far south (this itinerary to include flights from Santiago to Puerto Montt and from Puerto Montt to Punta Arenas). Travellers with more time could easily add another two weeks in the south, spending extra time in the Lake District – perhaps including a boat trip across the lakes to Bariloche in Argentina – and adding a journey down the Camino Austral to Coyhaique, and a boat trip, either between Puerto Montt and Puerto Natales, or to visit the glacier at Laguna San Rafael.

The north Most travellers in northern Chile visit the oasis town of San Pedro de Atacama. A brief trip to the north could also include a few days in the Parque Nacional Lauca, reached by bus from Arica, and a stopover in La Serena. Although the long distances would once again involve some air travel, bus journeys would be required and would give a good impression of the Atacama Desert. Those with more time could visit the world's largest open cast copper mine at Chuquicamata, the beaches and ghost towns near Iquique, or the Salar de Surire salt lake in the *altiplano* highlands.

Other options While the above suggestions include the most popular destinations for visitors to Chile, those with several months available will find their travel plans equally busy. Since over one third of Chileans live in Santiago, it is a shame to avoid the capital completely. Those who enjoy nightlife and/or urban living will thrive here, though it is best to try to avoid the incapacitating heat of summer and the worst days of the winter smog. Nearby, Valparaíso is perhaps the most interesting city in Chile, while the summit of the Cerro La Campana offers some of the best views in the whole country. The beach resorts north and south of Valparaíso are attractive and busy in summer. There are also many beaches on the coast near the Central Valley. The Central Valley itself, passed over by most travellers, is the best place to visit if you want to understand rural life in Chile.

When to go

When planning your trip you should take into account the time of year. In high summer (January-February) most options are open to you, though the *altiplano* (the high plain of the Andes east of the Atacama) can experience heavy rain. It is also worth bearing in mind that many destinations are busy with Chilean and Argentine tourists at this time, especially in the far south, and bus fares and hotel prices are higher. During the winter months of June, July and August many services in the south of the country are closed and transport links reduced, but the north is a good option and the skiing season is in full swing. Probably the ideal seasons for a visit are spring (October-November) and autumn (March-April) when many facilities in the south are open, but less crowded, and temperatures in the northern and central regions are lower.

Tours and tour operators

In the UK *Austral Tours*, 20 Upper Tachbrook Street, London SW1V 1SH, T0207-2335384,
& Ireland F2335385, www.latinamerica.co.uk Specialist company with a wide range of special activity holidays. *Condor Journeys and Adventures*, 1 Valley Rise, Mill Bank, Somerby Bridge, HX6 3EG, T01422-822068, F825276, www.condorjourneys-adventures.com *Cox & Kings Travel*, St James Court, 45 Buckingham Gate, London, T0207-8735001. *Destination South America*, 51 Castle Street, Cirencester, Glos, GL7 1QD, T01285-885333, www.destinationsouthamerica.co.uk Tailor-made tours. *Exodus Travels*, 9 Wier Road, London SW12 0LT, T020-87723822, www.exodus.co.uk Experience in adventure travel. *Hayes & Jarvis*, 152 King Street, London W6 0QU, T0208-2227844. Long established operator. Offers tailor-made itineraries as well as packages. *Journey Latin America*, 12-13 Heathfield Terrace, Chiswick, London W4 4JE, T0208-7478315, F7421312, wwwjourneylatinamerica.co.uk Long established company, running escorted and bespoke tours throughout the region, and offering a wide range of flight options. *Last Frontiers*, Fleet Marston Farm, Aylesbury, Buckinghamshire HP18 0QT, T01296-658650, www.lastfrontiers.co.uk *Passage to South America*, Fovant Mews, 12a Noyna Road, London SW17 7PH, T0208-7678989. Wide range of tailor-made packages throughout the region including the lost kingdom of the Incas. *Pura Aventura*, 18 Bond Street, Brighton, East Sussex BN11 1RD, T01273-676712, F676774, enquiries@pura-aventura.com

Small Chilean specialist with a wide range of organised and tailor-made tours. *South American Experience*, 47 Causton Street, Pimlico, London SW1P 4AT, T0207-9765511, F9766908. Apart from booking flights and accommodation, also offer tailor-made trips. *STA Travel*, Priory House, 6 Wrights Lane, London W8 6TA, T08701-600599 or T0161-8307413 for Northern telesales. *Trailfinders*, 194 Kensington High Street, London W8 7RG, T0207-9383939.

In North America *Discover Chile Tours*, 7325 Flagler St, Miami, Florida 33144. T(local)305-2665827, F2662801, T(toll-free)1-800-826-4845, www.discover-chile.com *4th Dimension Tours*, 9495 SW 72nd St, Ste 8280, Miami, FL 33173, T1-800-3430020, www.4thdimension.com Specialist South American operator doing tailor-made and bespoke itineraries. *International Expeditions*, 1 Environs Park, Helena, AL35080, USA, T1-800-6334734, www.internationalexpeditions.com Travel company specializing in nature tours. *Ladatco Tours*, 3006 Aviation Ave, Suite 4C, Coconut Grove, FL33133, T305-8548422, T1-800-3276162, F305-2850504, www.ladatco.com Based in Miami, run 'themed' explorer tours based around the Incas, mysticism etc. *Mila Tours*, T1-800-3677378, F1-847-2492772, www.milatours.com Arrange a wide range of tours from rafting to photography. *Mountain Travel Sobek*, 6420 Fairmount Ave, El Cerrito, CA 94530, T(toll-free)1-888-MTSOBEK or T1-510-527 8100, www.mtsobek.com A specialist in Chile, with a wide range of tours on offer. *Myths and Mountains*, Incline Village, NV, T1-800-6706984/7775-8325454, F1-775-8324454, www.mythsandmountains.com Educational tour operator offering cultural, wildlife and environmental trips. *South American Explorers Club*, 126 Indian Creek Road, Ithaca, New York 14850, USA, T(USA)607-2770488, F2776122. Can give good advice. *Wilderness Travel*, 1102 Ninth St, Berkeley, CA 94710-1211, T510-5582488 or toll-free

on T1-800-3682794, www.wildernesstravel.com Does trips worldwide, including very good tours of Patagonia.

Australian Andean Adventures, 33 Imperial Arcade, Pitt Street Mall, Sydney, T02-92351889, anna@andeanadventures.com The specialists in trekking in South America for Australia. *South America Travel Centre*, 104 Hardware St, Melbourne, T03-96425353, www.satc.com.au Does good, individual tailor-made trips to Chile.

In Australia & New Zealand

Finding out more

The **Tourism Promotion Corporation of Chile** is at Antonio Bellet 77, Oficina 602, Providencia, Santiago, T2350105, F2362166. On the Internet, there are a great many sites about Chile which surfers may wish to explore, but note that you may have to weed out the sites related to chile peppers. Three useful sites specifically covering the whole of Chile are www.visitchile.org; www.sernatur.cl; and www.gochile.cl A site geared specifically to Patagonia is www.chileaustral.com while www.rapanui.cl deals exclusively with Easter Island. Other sites dealing with specific locations in Chile include: www.pucon.com; www.valparaisochile.cl (the best map of the city available); www.chiloeisland.cl and www.chiloeweb.cl There are plenty of sites providing more specific information. Reservations for many hotels in Chile (particularly upmarket ones) can be made at www.chile-hotels.com Those wanting to enjoy the outdoors will want to look at www.chile-outdoors.cl and surfers will be interested in www.surf.cl There is up-to-date information on environmental issues at www.greenpeace.cl while www.desaparecidos.org/chile and www.remember-chile.org give background on the Pinochet years and the human rights situation.

Essentials

Using a search engine such as www.google.com will provide many more. Two sites of general interest on Latin America are the Latin American Travel Advisor (see below) and **El Planeta Platica: Eco Travels in Latin America**, edited by Ron Mader, www.txintinet.com/mader/ecotravel/schools

The **Latin American Travel Advisor** offers a travel information service including a comprehensive quarterly newsletter (free sample available), country reports sent by email or fax, and a wide selection of travel maps. Individual travel planning assistance is also offered to subscribers. Credit card payment is required for fax or mail orders. Contact PO Box 17-17-908, Quito, Ecuador; USA and Canada toll-free F888-2159511, International F593-2562566, www.amerispan.com/lata/

Language

See also page 559 for a list of useful words & phrases. See individual town and city directories for language schools

Though English is understood in many major hotels, tour agencies and airline offices (especially in Santiago), travellers are strongly advised to learn some Spanish before setting out. The Chilean pronunciation of Spanish, very quick and lilting, with final syllables cut off, can present difficulties to the foreigner. Chileans have a wide range of unique idioms which other Latin Americans find difficult to understand, let alone non-Spanish speakers. Visitors may want to buy *How to Survive in the Chilean Jungle* by John Brennan and Alvaro Taboada, a handbook for English speakers on Chilean colloquialisms and slang available in bookshops in Santiago. In rural areas of the IX Region and in the interior of the I and II Regions travellers will encounter indigenous languages – Mapudungu, the Mapuche language, in the south; Aymará in the north – but some people will usually speak Spanish.

Disabled travellers

Chileans are usually very courteous, and disabled travellers will be helped and assisted where possible. The 1992 census found that 288,000 citizens said that they had some form of disability, but the **National Fund for the Handicapped** (**FONDIS**) estimates that the actual number is closer to one million. Congress passed a law in 1994 to promote the integration of people with disabilities into society, and **FONDIS** has a US$1.5 mn budget. However, the disabled still suffer some forms of legal discrimination; for example, blind people cannot become teachers or tutors. Although the law now requires that new public buildings provide access for the disabled, the new *Linea 5* subway line has no facilitated access for the disabled. However, more expensive hotels usually have facilities for the disabled, and reserved parking for the disabled is becoming more common than it was in the past.

Useful organisations include: in the UK – **Disability Action Group**, 2 Annadale Ave, Belfast BT7 3JH, T01232-491011, with information about access for disabled travellers abroad; in the US – **Directions Unlimited**, 720 N Bedford Rd, Bedford Hills, NY 10507, T914-2411700, a tour operator specialising in tours for the disabled; in Australia and New Zealand – **Disabled Persons' Assembly**, PO Box 10, 138 The Terrace, Wellington, New Zealand, T04-4722626, with lists of tour operators and travel agencies catering for the disabled.

Gay and lesbian travellers

In a macho culture, it is no surprise that there is quite a lot of homophobia in Chile, and gay and lesbian travellers should be aware that derogatory jokes about homosexuals (especially men) are widespread. Having said that, attitudes are beginning to loosen up. A mine of information is the website www.gaychile.com where you can make gay/lesbian-friendly hotel reservations and seek out gay/lesbian-friendly shops and establishments up and down the country. There is a specialist travel agency for gays and lesbians in Chile called *Novellus*, Almirante Pastene 7, Of 54, Providencia, Santiago: T02-2518547, novellus@tempotravel.cl Locations of gay/lesbian friendly hotels, bars and restaurants are listed throughout the book.

Student travellers

If planning to study in Chile for a long period it is essential to get a student visa in advance: you obtain this by contacting a Chilean consulate (you will be asked for proof of affiliation to a Chilean university). Student cards can be obtained from Providencia 2594, Local 421 and cost US$8, photo and proof of status required. Student cards (local or international) must carry a photograph if they are to be of any use for discounts.

If you are in full-time education you are entitled to an International Student Identity Card, which is distributed by student travel offices and travel agencies in 77 countries. The ISIC gives you special prices on all forms of transport, and access to a variety of other concessions and services. To find the location of your nearest ISIC office contact: The ISIC Association, Box 9048, 1000 Copenhagen, Denmark T45-33939303. If you are a holder of an ISIC card and get into trouble, you can make a reverse charges call to the helpline on T44-20-8762-8110. If travelling with a student card, it is always worth asking for discounts for museum entry and bus tickets.

Travelling with children

Chile is a good place for travelling with children as there are few health risks and children are very popular. Travelling with children presents no special problems – in fact the path is often smoother for family groups. Officials tend to be more amenable where children are concerned, and even thieves and pickpockets seem to have retained the traditional respect for families – they may leave you alone because of it!

There is little point in taking a baby buggy as the roads are either very rough or very busy away from town centres

However, a lot of time can be spent waiting for **transport**. Although train journeys are easier, as they allow more scope for moving about, there are few of these in Chile. On bus journeys, if the children are good at amusing themselves, or can readily sleep while travelling, the problems can be considerably reduced. If your child is of an early reading age, take reading material with you as it is difficult and expensive to find. A bag of, say, 30 pieces of Duplo or Lego can keep young children occupied for hours. On all long-distance buses you pay for each seat – there are no half-fares. Shorter trips tend to be more crowded, and it is cheaper, if less comfortable, to seat small children on your knee. In city and local excursion buses, small children generally do not pay a fare, but are not entitled to a seat when paying customers are standing. On sightseeing tours you should always bargain for a family rate – often children can go free. All civil airlines charge half for children under 12. Note that a child travelling free on a long excursion is not always covered by the operator's travel insurance; it is advisable to pay a small premium to arrange cover.

Food can be a problem if the children are not adaptable. It is easier to take biscuits, drinks, bread etc with you on longer trips than to rely on meal stops, where the food may not be to taste. Avocados are safe, easy to eat and nutritious; they can be fed to babies as young as six months and most older children like them. A small immersion heater and jug for making hot drinks is invaluable.

In all **hotels**, try to negotiate family rates. If charges are per person, always insist that two children will occupy one bed only, therefore counting as one tariff. If rates are per bed, the same applies. In either case you can almost always get a reduced rate at cheaper hotels.

Women travellers

Chile presents no special problem to women travellers. Most Chileans are courteous and helpful. However, the following tips are all useful, and have been supplied by women (although most apply also to any single traveller).

When you set out, err on the side of caution until your instincts have adjusted to the customs. If you can befriend a local woman, you will learn a great deal. Unless actively avoiding foreigners like yourself, don't go too far from the beaten track; there is a very definite 'gringo trail' which you can join. This can be helpful when looking for safe accommodation, especially if arriving after dark (which is best avoided). Remember that a taxi at night can be as dangerous as wandering around on your own. At borders dress as smartly as possible. Buses are much easier than trains for a person alone; on major routes your seat is reserved and your bags are locked in the hold.

Women may, though, be subject to much unwanted attention. To help minimize this, do not wear suggestive clothing. Some readers advise not flirting. By wearing a wedding ring and carrying a photograph of your 'husband' and 'children' you may dissuade an aspiring suitor. If politeness fails, do not feel bad about showing offence and departing. When accepting a social invitation, make sure that someone knows the address and the time you left. Ask if you can bring a friend (even if you do not intend to do so). A good rule is always to act with confidence, as though you know where you are going, even if you do not. Someone who looks lost is more likely to attract unwanted attention.

Working in the country

It is not difficult to find work as a foreigner in Chile. The most obvious opening is as a teacher of English as a foreign language; even for those without the appropriate TEFL qualification, such work can be found, especially in Santiago, but also in bigger cities such as Viña del Mar, Concepción and La Serena. The best paid work for English language teachers is almost invariably private, one-to-one tuition, mainly found through word of mouth (although it may be worth placing an advertisement in *El Mercurio* as well); otherwise, rates are much lower.

Opportunities for work are not limited to language teaching. There is considerable scope for volunteers seeking work in Chile, both in inner cities and on environmental projects. Many foreign companies also have offices in Chile, and those with appropriate skills and experience may find work through approaching their offices direct (usually in Santiago). Perhaps most options exist for engineers or those in financial services. There is a large expatriate community in Santiago, and it may also be worthwhile visiting their favourite haunts, particularly *The Phone Box Pub* (Providencia 1670,

Santiago; Metro Manuel Montt), and asking around.

The main obstacle to anyone seeking to work in Chile is the problem of obtaining and maintaining a working visa. All sorts of extraordinary pieces of paper may be asked for (one woman was asked for her grandfather's birth certificate when trying to open a bank account) – and, at the very least, you will need proof of employment and proof of need before the visa is issued.

Business people face no special problems when doing business in the country, although they are best advised to enter on a tourist visa to avoid some of the problems mentioned above. It is also recommended to carry a good supply of business cards, as the first thing which many business people will do at a meeting is ceremoniously present you with their card.

An organisation which may be of help to travellers wishing to work is: *Earthwatch*, 126 Bank Street, South Melbourne, Victoria 3205, Australia, T03-96826828, organising volunteer work on scientific and cultural projects around the world (and associated offices in Oxford, UK; see the website at www.earthwatch.org). There are numerous other organisations offering volunteer work for foreigners, especially in the UK, where these include *The Project Trust*, The Hebridean Centre, Isle of Coll, Argyll PA78 6TE, T01879-230441, www.projecttrust.org.uk and *Raleigh International*, 27 Parsons Green Lane, London SW6 4HZ, T0207-3718585, www.raleigh.org.uk

Before you travel

Getting in

Visas are required by citizens of Cuba, Guyana, Haiti, Kuwait; all African and Middle-Eastern countries except Israel, Morocco, South Africa and Tunisia; all Asian and Pacific countries except Fiji, Indonesia, Japan, Malaysia, Singapore, Tonga and Turkey; former Communist countries except for Croatia, the Czech Republic, Estonia, Hungary, the Slovak Republic, Slovenia and Yugoslavia. A passport valid for at least six months and tourist card only are required for entry by all other foreigners, except for citizens of Argentina, Brazil, Colombia, Paraguay and Uruguay, who require national identity cards only. Ninety day visa-extensions (costing US$100) can be obtained from the *Ministerio del Interior* (Extranjería) in Santiago or from any local *gobernación* (government) office. The procedure is often time-consuming, and may include providing proof of funds and having an international record check. To avoid hours of queuing, and excessive punctiliousness when you are finally dealt with, you are advised to obtain extensions from small provincial offices rather than from Santiago – every provincial capital has a *gobernación*. If you must get the extension in Santiago, arrive at Extranjería before 7.30 am and consider bringing lunch. If you wish to stay longer than 180 days as a tourist, it is easier to make a short trip into Argentina, or Peru if near Arica, and return with a new tourist card, rather than to apply for a visa. There are entry taxes at all borders for nationals of Mexico (US$15), Australia (US$30), Canada (US$55) and the USA (US$61) – the tax to be paid in dollars.

Documents
Regulations change frequently, so it is imperative to check visa requirements before travel

Tourist cards These are valid for 90 days, except for nationals of Belize and Costa Rica (valid for 30 days) and Greece and Indonesia (valid for 60 days). They are handed out as a matter of routine at immigration offices at major land frontiers and Chilean airports. Onward tickets are officially required for entry but these are rarely asked for. Tourist card holders are not allowed to change their status to enable them to stay on in employment or as students: to do this you need to obtain a visa from a Chilean consulate. Holders of a residency visa may, though, exit and re-enter as tourists. On arrival you may be asked where you are staying in Chile – just give the name of any hotel.

It is essential that you keep the tourist card safe, since you must surrender it on departure

Essentials

Chilean embassies and consulates overseas

Argentina, Tagle 2762, Capital Federal (1425) Buenos Aires, T54-11-48027020, F48045927, echilear@tournet.com.ar

Australia, 10 Culgoa Circuit, O'Malley Act 2606, PO Box 69, Monaro Crescent Act 2603, Canberra, T61-2-62862430, F62861289, echileau@dynamite.com.au

Belgium, 40 Rue Montoyer, 1000 Brussels, T32-2-2801620, F2801481. embachile.belgica@skynet.be

Bolivia, Consulado General, Avda Hernando Siles 5873, Esq. Calle 13, Sector Obrajes, La Paz. T591–2-783018, F785046, cgchilp@ceibo.entelnet.bo

Brazil, Ses-Avda Des Nacoes, q. 803, Lote 11, CEP 70.407-900, Brasília, T55-61-3225781, F3222966, echilebr@nutecnet.com.br

Canada, 50 O'Connor Street, Suite 1413, Ottawa, Ontario K1P 6L2, T1-613-2354402, echileca@embachile-canada.com

Colombia, Calle 100 Nro 11 B-44, Apartado Aereo 90061, Santa Fe de Bogotá, T57-1-2147990, F6193863, echileco@colomsat.net.co

Denmark, Kastelsvej 15, 3rd Floor, 2100 Copenhagen, T45-35385834, F35384201, embassy@chiledk.dk

Ecuador, Juan Pablo Sanz 3617 y Amazonas, 4 Piso, Edificio Xerox, Quito, T593-2-249403, F444470, embchile@andinanet.net

Finland, Erottajankatu 11- 00130 Helsinki, T358-9-6126780, F61267825, echilefi@kolumbus.fi

France, 64 Bd de la Tour Maubourg, 75007 Paris, T33-1-47054661, F45511627, cgparifr@aol.com

Germany, Mohrenstrasse 4244, 10117 Berlin, T49-30-726203, F726603, echile_alemania@nikocity.de

Israel, Havakook No 7, Tel Aviv 63505, T972-3-6020131, F6020133, echileil@inter.net.il

Italy, Via Po No 23, 00198 Roma, T39-6-844091, F8841452, echileit@flashnet.it

Japan, Nihon Seimei Akabanebashi Bldg 8F, 3-1-14 Shiba, Minato-ku, Tokyo 105, T81-3-34527561, F34524457, embajada@chile.or.jp

Netherlands, Mauritskade 51, 2514 HG, The Hague, T31-70-3123640, F3616227, echilenl@euronet.nl

New Zealand, 1-3 Willeston St, Willis Corroon House 7th Floor, PO Box 3861, Wellington, T64-4-4716270, F4725324, consulnz@prochinz.co.nz

Norway, Meltzers Gate 5, 0257 Oslo, T47-22445496, F22442421, embchile@online.no

Peru, Avda Javier Prado Oeste 790, San Isidro, Lima, T51-1-2212221, F2211258, emchile@terra.com.pe

South Africa, Campus Centre (Volkskas Bank Building) 5th floor, 1102 Burnett St, Cm. Hilda, Hatfield 0181, Pretoria, T27-12-3421527, F3421658, cile@iafrica.com

Spain, Rafael Calvo 18–5º D, 28010 Madrid, T34-91-3190763, F3193278, cgmadres@interbrook.net

Sweden, Vasagatan No 36, Stockholm, T46-8-4060640, F4060355, cgestose@swipnet.se

Switzerland, Eigerplatz 5, 12 Piso, 3007 Berne, T41-31-3710745, F3720025, echilech@swissonline.ch

Turkey, Resit Galip Cad. Hirfanli Sok. 14/1-3, GOP Ankara, T90-312-4473418 F90-312-4474725, echiletr@mbox.marketweb.net.tr

UK, 12 Devonshire Street, London, W1N 2DS, T44-171-5801023, F44-171-4365204, cglonduk@congechile.demon.co.uk

US, 1732 Massachusetts Ave NW, Washington DC 20036, T1202-7851746, F8875579, embassy@embassyofchile.org

Venezuela, Av Venezuela, Edifcio Venezuela, Piso 3, Oficina 31, El Rosal, Caracas, T58-2-9531485, F58-2-9920614, congechiccs@cantv.net

Passport Remember that it is your responsibility to ensure that your passport is stamped in and out when you cross frontiers. The absence of entry and exit stamps can cause serious difficulties: seek out the proper immigration offices if the stamping process is not carried out as you cross. The vast majority of crossings, though, are trouble-free.

Finally, on a general note, Chilean officials are very document-minded, but also often exceptionally hospitable and helpful. In remote areas, you should make it a matter of course to register your documents where there are *carabineros* (police) – not only as a matter of courtesy, but also since they are a mine of information about local conditions and may be able to help with finding accommodation and transport. Although identity checks are uncommon, you should always carry your passport in a safe place about your person, or, if not going far, leave it in the hotel safe. If staying for a while, it is worth registering at your embassy or consulate. Then, if your passport is stolen, the process of replacing it is simplified and speeded up. Keeping photocopies of essential documents, including your flight ticket, and some additional passport-sized photographs, is recommended.

Insurance It is vital to take out fully comprehensive travel insurance (including medical insurance) for the duration of your stay overseas. There are numerous companies offering travel insurance, including many of the high street travel agents. As well as full medical insurance (including evacuation by air ambulance where necessary), it is important to check that you are covered for any special activities you may do: most policies exclude so-called dangerous sports (this even includes, in some cases, trekking). Also, many policies have a limit of cover per item, so, if you are taking something valuable and want it fully insured, you may need to pay extra.

If you do have the misfortune to be robbed (or even just to lose something), you need to make a report to the police and get a police certificate within 24 hours before you will be able to make a successful claim on your insurance. Note also that every policy will have an excess which you will have to pay yourself, and that this varies from policy to policy. There is no substitute for reading the small print of a policy before signing up to it.

Duty free & export allowance Some 500 cigarettes, 100 cigars, 500 g of tobacco, three bottles of liquor, and all articles of personal use, including vehicles, radios, portable tape recorders, cameras, personal computers, and similar items. Unlike neighbouring countries, Chile's agricultural sector is free of many diseases, and so fruit, vegetables, meat, flowers and milk products may not be imported; these will be confiscated at all borders, where there are thorough searches. This applies even to those who have had to travel through Argentina in the far south to get from one part of Chile to another. There are internal customs checks for all travellers going south from Region I in the far north. This is mainly to inspect for duty-free goods from Iquique; but fruit, vegetables, meat, flowers and milk products will also be confiscated.

Vaccinations Before you travel make sure the medical insurance you take out is adequate. Have a check-up with your doctor, if necessary, and arrange your immunisations well in advance. Try ringing a specialist travel clinic if your own doctor is unfamiliar with health in the region. No vaccinations are demanded by immigration officials in Chile, but you would do well to be protected by vaccination against typhoid, polio, both hepatitis A and B, and tetanus. It is also advisable to know your blood group. There is no malaria in Chile.

Essentials

What to take

Take twice as much money as you think you might need & half the clothes

Everybody has their own list but here are a few suggestions that might help you with your packing for your trip to Chile. As far as clothing is concerned be prepared for the desert heat and mountain snow. You'll need fully waterproof clothing (essential for the south at any time of year); very warm clothes for the highlands and far south; light clothing for the summer; a sarong is very useful – it can be used as a skirt, curtain, bedsheet, towel etc; a sun hat; a pair of strong shoes/boots and a pair of sandals (outside Santiago size 10½/44 are very hard to find).

Other items that you might want to take (especially budget travellers) include air cushions for slatted seats, inflatable travel pillow for neck support, a small first-aid kit and handbook, earplugs and airline-type eye mask to help you sleep in noisy and poorly curtained hotel rooms, a sheet sleeping-bag and pillow-case, a clothes line, a nailbrush (useful for scrubbing dirt off clothes as well as off oneself), a universal plug, a Swiss Army knife, an alarm clock or watch and a torch. If you use an electric shaver, take a rechargeable type. Remember not to throw away spent batteries containing mercury or cadmium; take them home to be disposed of, or recycled properly. There is no point in bringing extensive supplies of basic toiletries, as these are readily available.

Useful medicaments are given on page 64 but added to these are pre-moistened wipes (such as Wet Ones) and toilet paper – cheap hotels and restaurants do not supply it.

Money

Currency

The unit is the peso, its sign is $. Notes are for 500, 1,000, 2,000, 5,000, 10,000 and 20,000 pesos (this last almost never seen outside Santiago), and coins for 1, 5, 10, 50, 100 and 500 pesos. Inflation is low. Travellers to rural areas should carry supplies of 500 and 1000-peso notes; higher denominations are difficult to change. Official exchange rates for many currencies are quoted in *La Tercera*. Rates are best in Santiago.

Exchange

ATMs The easiest way to obtain cash in Chile is by using automatic telling machines (ATMs). These are situated at the major banks and often in other locations, especially in shopping malls, bus stations, at the larger supermarkets and at most Esso petrol stations. ATMs operate under the sign *Redbanc*; both Cirrus (Mastercard) and Plus (Visa) are accepted for daily transactions of up to US$400. A full list of *Redbanc* machines in Chile is listed by town at www.redbanc.cl.

Credit cards Visa, Mastercard and Diners' Club are readily accepted (*Bancard*, the local card, is affiliated to both Mastercard and Visa), but American Express is less useful. Credit card use does not usually incur a commission or higher charge in Chile, but in parts of Argentina commission of 10% is often charged. In shops, identification is usually necessary to use credit cards; places accepting Visa and Mastercard usually display a 'Redcompra' sticker in the window. In case of loss or theft of your card make sure that you carry the phone numbers necessary to report this – make a photocopy of the numbers and keep them in a safe place. Some travellers have reported problems with their credit cards being frozen by their bank when a charge is incurred in a foreign country. To avoid this problem, notify your bank before departure that you will be making charges in Chile (and other countries, where applicable). To avoid charges from your bank, top up your credit card account with sufficient cash before departure. If you will need to make very expensive one-off purchases, you may want to specify that your daily spending limit should not be applied to the amount by which your account is in credit – although this will prove dangerous if your card is stolen.

Exchange rates: September 2001

US$1	680	*DM1*	290
UK£1	920	*Dutch guilder 1*	259
Aus $1	345	*French franc 1*	87
Can $1	437	*Spanish peseta 100*	345
NZ $1	277	*Italian lira 1,000*	293
Yen 100	555		

Travellers' cheques Outside Santiago, exchange of travellers' cheques has become more difficult in most towns apart from Arica, Antofagasta and Puerto Montt. In Santiago, *American Express Bank*, Andres Bello 2711, Piso 9, will change their travellers' cheques to dollars without commission.

Cash US dollars are widely accepted by banks and *casas de cambio*, but rarely by shops and establishments other than hotels. Dollar bills are often scrutinized carefully and rejected if torn or marked in any way. Before changing check whether any commission is charged. Outside Santiago, currencies other than the US dollar are rarely accepted. If crossing to Argentina take some low value US dollar bills: the Argentine peso is par with the dollar and dollars are widely accepted (although change from dollars will be given in Argentine pesos).

Casas de cambio In many cities and towns changing cash and/or travellers' cheques is simpler and quicker at *casas de cambio* (exchange shops) than banks. Exchange rates vary and are not necessarily better than at the banks, so shop around.

A recommended method of transferring money is, before leaving your home country, to find out which local bank is correspondent to your bank at home. Then, when you need funds, telex your own bank and ask them to telex the money to the local bank (confirming by fax). Give exact information to your bank of the routing number of the receiving bank. Funds can be received within 48 banking hours. Otherwise, money can be sent within minutes by a friend back home through Western Union (Santiago number: T02-6968807); if collecting money in a city with more than one Western Union agent, you can go to any one of them to receive the money. **Transferring money**

Prices for food and other consumables tend to rise in proportion to the distance of a place from Santiago (being highest in Arica and Punta Arenas), although accommodation is cheaper outside the capital. In Santiago itself, Las Condes and Providencia are much more expensive than the rest of the city. **Cost of travelling**

You should budget on a minimum of US$20 per week per person for basic accommodation, food and overland transport. Chile is more expensive than much of South America, although it is cheaper than Argentina. Cheap accommodation in Santiago costs over US$8 per person, while north and south of the capital *alojamiento* in private houses (bed, breakfast and often use of kitchen) costs US$7-10 per person (bargaining is possible). *Colaciones* can be had for about US$2-3 in most places. Bus fares are reasonable (around US$2.50 per 100 km). Southern Chile is more expensive from 15 December to 15 March.

The minimum wage in Chile is approximately US$180 per month, while the wage for relatively senior office workers may be around US$600-700 per month. This is low considering the general cost of living in the country. The cost of accommodation or rent is higher in Santiago than elsewhere – around US$150 per month for a basic two-room **Cost of living** unfurnished flat in Santiago, and half that in the provinces. Many office workers eat out for lunch, and basic meals can usually be had for US$1.50 or US$2. City bus fares are US$0.50 in Santiago, less in the provinces. Someone living in Santiago and earning a reasonable salary (by Chilean standards) will find that they have little spare change at the end of the month, and that holidays and weekends away are a definite luxury. Electrical goods are more expensive in Chile than in Europe or North America, except in the duty-free shopping areas of Iquique and Punta Arenas.

Getting there

Air

From UK & Ireland Flights from the UK take 16-20 hours, including a change of plane. It is impossible to fly directly to Santiago from London or Dublin. Connections will have to be made on one of the following routes: *British Airways*, connecting through *LanChile* in Buenos Aires (four per week); *Air France* via Paris (three per week); *LanChile* and *Iberia* via Madrid (each daily); *Lufthansa* via Frankfurt (six per week); *SwissAir* via Zurich (four per week); *Avianca* via Bogotá (three per week); *Varig* via Rio or São Paolo (daily).

From North America Flights from Miami take nine hours; from New York 12 hours. To Santiago: *American Airlines*, *LanChile* and *United Airlines* all fly daily from Miami direct. Also from Miami, *LanPeru* fly via Lima. *LanChile* also has daily flights from New York and Los Angeles (via Mexico City and Lima) with onward connections to Boston, Chicago, Dallas, San Francisco and Washington. *Delta* fly from Dallas to Santiago three times a week. *Lacsa* (via Mexico City, San José and Lima) and *Mexicana* (via Mexico City and Bogotá) also fly from Los Angeles and Miami to Santiago. From Canada, *LanChile* offers connections with sister airlines from Vancouver to Los Angeles and thence to Santiago, or from Toronto to New York and on to Santiago.

From Australia & New Zealand *LanChile* flies once or twice a week, depending on season, between Tahiti (making connections from Japan, Australia and New Zealand) and Santiago; they stop over at Easter Island. *Air New Zealand* and *LanChile* have a co-sharing agreement on weekly flights between Auckland, Sydney and Santiago. For excursion fares between Australia/New Zealand and Chile, the stopovers at Easter Island now carry a surcharge of about US$125.

From Europe & Israel There are direct flights from many European destinations to Santiago. From Paris with *Air France* (three per week); from Madrid with *Iberia* and *LanChile* (each daily); from

www.journeylatinamerica.co.uk **GO**

JOURNEY LATIN AMERICA

BRITAIN'S FOREMOST LATIN AMERICAN SPECIALIST

20 YEARS SINCE 1980

 Flights only

 Escorted Groups

 Tailor-made Tours

 Cruises

 Insurance

 Brochures

 Active Adventure

Search: Favourites ▶ ▲

Amazon
Angel Falls
Atacama
Antarctica
Galapagos
Iguassu
Machu Picchu
Pantanal
Patagonia
Rio ▼

Rafting
Hiking
Kayaking
Biking
Riding

Search: Regions ▶ ▲
Argentina
Bolivia
Brazil
Caribbean ▶
Central America ▶
Chile
Colombia
Ecuador
Mexico
Peru
Uruguay
Venezuela ▼

FULLY BONDED
ATOL
ABTA
IATA
AITO 2828

JOURNEY LATIN AMERICA

12-13 Heathfield Terrace Chiswick **LONDON W4 4JE** **020 8747 8315** Fax 020 8742 1312

28-30 Barton Arcade 51-63 Deansgate **MANCHESTER M3 2BH** **0161 832 1441** Fax 0161 832 1551

Frankfurt with *Lufthansa* (six per week) and *LanChile* (daily); from Zurich with *SwissAir* (four per week); from Lisbon with *Varig* via Rio or São Paolo (daily); from Rome with *Varig* via São Paolo. From Israel, connections are best made in Europe.

From Africa From South Africa it is possible to connect to Santiago through Rio de Janeiro or São Paolo on *South African Airways* (twice weekly from Johannesburg). *Varig* has flights from some African destinations connecting to Santiago through São Paolo, including *Luanda* (Angola), *Maputo* (Mozambique) and *Sal* (Cape Verde).

Within Latin America To Santiago: From **Buenos Aires** (about 75 per week) by *LanChile*, *Aerolíneas Argentinas*, *Air France*, *SwissAir*, *American*, or *Avianca* (many depart at the same time, check carefully). From **Córdoba** (two daily) and **Mendoza** (two daily), both by *LanChile*. From **Montevideo** (eight weekly) by *LanChile* and *Pluna*. From **Asunción** (four a week) with *Lapsa*. From **Rio de Janeiro** with *Iberia* (four weekly), *LanChile* (two daily), or *Varig* (three daily). From **São Paulo** non-stop by *LanChile* (three daily), *Varig* (four daily). From **La Paz** (five weekly) by *Lloyd Aéreo Boliviano* (*LAB*) and daily with *LanChile* (*LAB* also from Cochabamba and Santa Cruz, *LanChile* three a week from Santa Cruz). From **Caracas**, *LanChile* (two weekly) and *Viasa* (two weekly). From **Lima** (23 per week) by *LanPeru*, *Lacsa*, *United* and *LanChile* (*LanChile* also flies daily to **Arequipa** and **Cuzco** through its sister airline *LanPeru*). From Bogotá (nine weekly) by *Avianca*, *Mexicana* and *LanChile*. From **Ecuador**, *LanChile*, *Tame* and *Saeta* non-stop from Guayaquil (*Saeta* and *Tame*'s flights start in Quito). There are also two weekly flights from **Havana** with *LanChile* and *Cubana*; six flights weekly from **Mexico City** with *Mexicana* and *LanChile* and two weekly from **Cancún** with *LanChile*.

To other Chilean destinations: There are flights to **Arica** and **Iquique** from La Paz and Santa Cruz by *LAB* and *LanChile*, and to **Antofagasta** from Santa Cruz with *LanChile*. *TAM* also has direct flights connecting Iquique to Asunción in Paraguay. *LanChile* flies to **Santiago** from Port Stanley on the Falkland (Malvinas) Islands via Punta Arenas and Río Gallegos. There are also two weekly flights to **Puerto Montt** from Bariloche and Neuquén (with *TAN*).

Airlines normally allow 30 kilos of luggage without surcharge for first class and 20 kilos for business and economy classes; but these limits are often not strictly enforced when it is known that the plane is not going to be full. If you know you are over the limit, arrive early. Weight limits for internal flights are often lower; best to enquire beforehand.

General tips

Essentials

The very busy seasons are 7 December to 15 January and 10 July to 10 September. If you intend travelling during those times, book as far ahead as possible. Between February to May and September to November special offers may be available. It is generally cheaper to fly from London rather than a point in Europe to Latin American destinations; fares vary from airline to airline, destination to destination and according to time of year. In the low season it may be possible to get a return flight from London to Santiago for as little as £450 (plus over £50 airport departure taxes), but in the high season this may rise to £650 return. Prices are comparable for flights from the US, but from Australia and New Zealand they may rise to £1000 return or more. Most airlines offer discounted fares of one sort or another on scheduled flights. These are not offered by the airlines direct to the public, but through agencies who specialize in this type of fare.

Prices & discounts
If you buy discounted air tickets always check the reservation with the airline concerned to make sure the flight still exists

In the UK Specialist agencies include *Austral Tours*, 20 Upper Tachbrook St, London SW1V 1SH, T0207-2335384. *Council Travel*, 28a Poland Street, London, W1V 3DB, T0207-4377767, www.destinationsgroup.com *Cox & Kings Travel*, St James Court, 45 Buckingham Gate, London, T0207-8735001. *Hayes & Jarvis*, 152 King Street, London W6 0QU, T0208-2227844. *Last Frontiers*, Fleet Marston Farm, Aylesbury, Buckinghamshire, HP18 0PZ, T01296-658650. *Journey Latin America*, 12-13 Heathfield Terrace, Chiswick, London W4 4JE, T0208-7478315. *Passage to South America*, Fovant Mews, 12a Noyna Road, London SW17 7PH, T0208-7678989. *South American Experience*, 47 Causton Street, Pimlico, London SW1P 4AT, T0207-9765511. *STA Travel*, Priory House, 6 Wrights Lane, London W8 6TA, T08701-600599 or T0161-830 4713 for northern telesales. *Trailfinders*, 48 Earl's Court Road, London, W8 6EJ, T0207-9383366. *Usit Campus*, 52 Grosvenor Gardens, London SW1 0AG, T0897-2401010, www.usitcampus.co.uk Student/youth travel specialists. Also check out websites such as **www.cheapflights.com**; **www.flynow.com**; **www.dialaflight.com**

In the US and Canada *Air Brokers International*, 323 Geary Street, Suite 411, San Francisco, CA 94102, T01-800-883273, www.airbrokers.com Specialist on RTW and Circle Pacific tickets. *Airtech*, 588 Broadway, Suite 204, New York, NY 10012, T212-219 7000, www.airtech.com *Council Travel*, 205E 42nd Street, New York, NY 10017, T1-800-COUNCIL, www.counciltravel.com Student/budget agency. *Discount Airfares Worldwide On-line*, www.etn.nl/discount.htm A hub of consolidator and discount agent links. *Exito Travel*, 1212 Broadway Suite 910, Oakland CA 94618, T(toll-free)1-800-6554053, www.exitotravel.com *Ladatco Tours*, 2220 Coral Way, Miami, Florida 33156 T305-8548422. *STA Travel*, 10 Downing St, New York, NY 10014, T(toll-free)1-800-777-0112. *Travel CUTS*, 234 College Street, Toronto, ON M5T 1P7, T(toll-free)1-866-246 9762, www.travelcuts.com, and in many other Canadian cities. Other online agents are **www.priceline.com**, **www.cheaptickets.com**, **www.travelocity.com** and **www.expedia.com**

In Australia and New Zealand *Anywhere Travel*, 345 Anzac Parade, Kingsford, Sydney, T02-96630411. *Budget Travel*, 600 Hurtsmere Road, Takapuna, Box 336620, Auckland, T09-4861081. *Destinations Unlimited*, 13 Clyde Road, PO Box 35573, Browns Bay, T09-4785042. *Flight Centres*, 82 Elizabeth Street, Sydney, T02-92353522 or 350 Queen Street, Auckland, T09-3584310. Also in many other Antipodean cities. *STA Travel*, T1300-360960, www.statravel.com.au 702 Harris St, Ultimo, Sydney. Also in other major cities and towns. *Travel.com.au*, 80 Clarence Street, Sydney, T02-92901500, www.travel.com.au

Other fares fall into three groups and are all on scheduled services

Excursion (return) fares Restricted validity eg seven to 90 days. Carriers are introducing flexibility into these tickets, permitting a change of dates on payment of a fee.

Yearly fares May be bought on a one way or return basis. Some airlines require a specified return date, changeable upon payment of a fee. If staying for a whole year, you may find that the airline is not yet booking return flights that far ahead – in that case it may be possible to secure one free change of date on your ticket, even if buying through a discount operator. To leave the return completely open is possible for an extra fee. You must fix the route (some of the cheapest flexible fares now have six months' validity). If you foresee returning home at a busy time, such as Christmas or August, a booking is advisable on any type of open return ticket.

Student (or under 26) fares Do not assume that student tickets are the cheapest; though they are often very flexible, they are usually more expensive than excursion or yearly fares. Some airlines are flexible on the age limit, others strict.

For people intending to travel a linear route and return from a different point from that which they entered, there are Open Jaw fares, available on student, yearly, or excursion fares. Many of these fares require a change of plane at an intermediate point, and a stopover may be permitted, or even obligatory, depending on schedules. Simply because a flight stops at a given airport does not mean you can break your journey there – the airline must have traffic rights to pick up or set down passengers between points A and B before it will be permitted. This is where dealing with a specialized agency (like *Journey Latin America*) will really pay dividends. On multi-stop itineraries, the specialized agencies can often save clients hundreds of pounds.

Road

Good roads connect Santiago with Mendoza, and Osorno and Puerto Montt with Bariloche, in Argentina; there is also a reasonable road between Arica and La Paz, Bolivia, and a good road from Arica to Tacna, Peru (all of these routes are served by bus services). Less good road connections north and south of Santiago are described in the book. Travelling to or from Argentina anywhere north of Mendoza is likely to be an adventure you will not forget in a hurry. Note that any of the passes across the Andes to Argentina can be blocked by snow from April onwards (including the main Mendoza crossing, where travellers are occasionally stranded at the border posts).

Sea

Enquiries regarding passages should be made through agencies in your own country, or through John Alton of *Strand Cruise and Travel Centre*, Charing Cross Shopping Concourse, The Strand, London WC2N 4HZ, T0207-8366363, F4970078. Also in London: *The Cruise People*, 88 York Street, W1H 1DP, T0207-7232450 (reservations T0800-526313). In the USA, contact *Freighter World Cruises*, 180 South Lake Ave, Pasadena, CA 91101, T818-4493106, or *Traveltips Cruise and Freighter Travel Association*, 163-07 Depot Road, PO Box 188, Flushing, NY 11358, T800-8728584.

Train

Chile is linked by rail from Calama to Uyuni and Oruro in Bolivia. See page 220 for full details.

Touching down

Airport information

Aeropuerto Arturo Merino Benitez handles both international and domestic flights. It is located 26 km northwest of the centre of Santiago at Pudahuel. Domestic and international flights leave from the same terminal. Procedures at customs (*aduana*) are quick and efficient. Facilities include banks (with ATMs), fast food outlets, a Sernatur tourist information office which offers an accommodation booking service, a *casa de cambio* for changing money near the baggage reclaim area and several car hire offices. Left luggage is US$2.50 per item per day (rates are much worse than in the city centre). Outside customs there are kiosks for bus and taxi companies serving Santiago, as well as car hire companies. Passengers are approached by people offering taxi and bus services as they emerge from the customs area.

Frequent **bus** services between the airport and the city centre are operated by two companies: *Tur Bus*, who leave from Moneda y San Martín, in the centre, every ½ hour

Essentials

Touching down

Business hours Banks: 0900-1400, but
closed on Saturday. **Government offices:**
This varies. Some are open from 1000 to 1230
only (the public is admitted for a few hours
only); but gobernaciónes in the provinces are
usually 0900-1230 and 1400-1700.
Businesses: 0830-1230, 1400-1800 (Monday
to Friday). **Shops** (Santiago): 1030-1930, but

0930-1330 Saturday.
Official time GMT minus four hours;
minus three hours in summer. Clocks go an
hour forward from mid-September or
October to early March.
Voltage 220 volts AC, 50 cycles.
Weights and measures The metric
system is used.

(US$2.50); **Centropuerto**, T6019883, first from centre 0600, last from airport 2230, US$2.50 leaving from Metro Los Héroes. Return tickets are cheaper than two singles. These buses leave from outside international and domestic terminals; en route to the airport, the buses pick up at Plaza Los Héroes (near the yellow Linea 2 metro sign); Estación Central and Terminal Santiago. Do not confuse these buses with the bus marked *Aeropuerto*. This stops 2 km short of the airport.

Minibus services between the airport and hotels/other addresses in the city are operated by four companies which have offices in the airport: **Transfer**, T7777707, **Delfos**, T6011111, **Turismo Bar-C** and **Navett**, T6956868. These charge US$5 to/from the city centre, US$7 to/from Las Condes. For transport to the airport book the previous day.

There is a **taxi** office inside the international terminal. Taxi to/from centre US$17, to/from Providencia US$20. Agree fare beforehand.

Airport departure information Check-in time for international flights is two hours, one hour for domestic flights. Some airlines will perform check-in at their offices in the city the previous day, after which they require you to be at the airport 45 minutes only before departure. Remember that airlines require you to reconfirm bookings on international flights 72 hours in advance. Taxis to the airport are cheaper if flagged down in the street rather than booked by phone or from a hotel. International terminal information T6901900/6018758; flight information T6763149/6763297.

Airport departure tax 7,500 pesos, or US$18.25 for international flights; US$9 for domestic flights (credit cards not accepted). There is a tourist tax on single air fares of 2%, and 1% on return fares beginning or ending in Chile; also a sales tax of 5% on all transport within Chile. All these taxes are usually included in the price of the ticket when bought by the traveller.

Tourist information

The national secretariat of tourism, **Sernatur**, has offices throughout the country (addresses are given in the book). The head office is at Av Providencia 1550, Santiago, T2362420, F2518469. City offices provide town maps, leaflets and much useful information. See pages 58 and 72 for useful organizations and their publications. **Ancient Forest International**, Box 1850, Redway, CA 95560, T/F707-3233015, USA, can be contacted regarding Chilean forests. For general information on travel in the region, see the Latin American Travel Advisor, page 24.

How big is your footprint?

It is often assumed that tourism only has an adverse impact on the environment and local communities at the more excessive end of the travel industry, as seen along the Spanish coast or in Bali. However travellers can have an impact, no matter how few in number they may be, where local people may be unused to their conventions or lifestyles and natural environments may be very sensitive. Here are a few tips:

■ *Where possible choose a destination, tour operator or hotel with a proven ethical and environmental commitment. If in doubt ask.*

■ *Spend money on locally produced goods and services and use common sense when it comes to bargaining – your few dollars saved may be a day's salary to others. See also page 57.*

■ *Use water and electricity carefully – travellers may receive preferential supply while the needs of local people are overlooked.*

■ *Protect wildlife and other natural resources – don't buy souvenirs or goods made from wildlife unless they are clearly sustainably produced and are not protected under CITES legislation. The establishment of national parks etc involves the creation of rules and guidelines for visitors; these should always be followed.*

■ *Always ask before taking photographs or videos of people.*

■ *Try and stay in local, rather than foreign owned, accommodation – the economic benefits for host communities are far greater – and there are far greater opportunities to learn about local culture.*

■ *Many Chileans are distressingly prone to throwing their litter away wherever it suites them; in this case, travellers should not do as the 'Romans' do.*

Local customs and laws

Remember that politeness – even a little ceremoniousness – is much appreciated. **Courtesy** Men should always remove any headgear and say "permiso" when entering offices, and be prepared to shake hands; always say "Buenos días" (until midday) or "Buenas tardes" and wait for a reply before proceeding further. Remember that the traveller from abroad has enjoyed greater advantages in life than most Chilean minor officials, and should be friendly and courteous in consequence. Never be impatient, and do not criticize situations in public: the officials may know more English than you think (especially when it comes to swearwords) and they can certainly interpret gestures and facial expressions. You should be aware that the stereotype of the corrupt Latin American official does not apply in Chile, and most officials are scrupulously honest.

Politeness should also be extended to street traders; saying "No, gracias" with a smile is better than an arrogant dismissal. Bargaining is not as commonplace in Chile as in some other South American countries, and very low offers will be seen as contemptuous, even in markets. Begging is rare outside Santiago. Whether you give money to beggars is a personal matter, but locals may provide an indication of whether people are begging out of genuine need. In Santiago, beggars get onto buses and sing or sell tiny religious calendar cards – Santiaguinos are often generous towards them. There are occasions where giving away food in a restaurant may be appropriate, but first inform yourself of local practice.

In restaurants 10% and a few pesos in bars and soda fountains. A tip of US$0.50 per **Tipping** piece of luggage is appropriate for railway and airport porters. Cloakroom attendants and cinema usherettes about US$0.20. Taxi drivers are not tipped.

Essentials

Prohibitions   There are several types of police. *Carabineros* (green uniforms) handle all tasks except immigration. *Investigaciones* (in civilian dress) are the detective police who deal with everything except traffic. *Policia Internacional,* a division of *Investigaciones,* handle immigration. Chilean police are very proud of their office, and you should never offer an official a bribe.

Clothing   Urban Chileans are very fashion conscious. You should dress reasonably smartly in the towns and cities: scruffiness will make things needlessly difficult. People tend to dress smartly at nightclubs in urban centres – Santiago, Viña del Mar, La Serena and Iquique being particularly swish. Away from the cities, though, and in areas where there are many foreign tourists, people are less concerned about such matters.

Safety

While Chileans will delight in building up the prowess of Chilean thieves to nervous visitors, Chile is generally a safe country to visit. Police stations in rural areas very rarely have people in their one cell. Like all major cities, though, Santiago and Valparaíso do have a crime problem. Avoid the *poblaciones* (shanty towns) of Santiago – especially Pudahuel and parts of the north (such as Conchali) – if going alone or recently arrived. In central Santiago and some of the hills of Valparaíso the following suggestions are particularly applicable.

Keep all documents secure; hide your main cash supply in different places or under your clothes – you may wish to use extra pockets sewn inside shirts and trousers, pockets closed on the outside with a zip or safety pin, moneybelts (best worn below the waist rather than outside or at it or around the neck), neck or leg pouches, a thin chain for attaching a purse to your bag or under your clothes, or elasticated support bandages for keeping money and cheques above the elbow or below the knee. Keep cameras in bags, preferably with a chain or wire in the strap to defeat the slasher; take spare spectacles; don't wear expensive watches or jewellery. If you wear a shoulder bag in a market, carry it in front of you. At the same time, avoid exhibiting paranoia, as this is a clear sign to any thief that you are carrying valuables. Walking confidently, but without excessive speed, is a sure way of showing that you are at home in a place – even if you are not.

Look out for tricks intended to distract your attention or separate you from your possessions. One common ruse in large city centres is 'the mustard trick': the victim is sprayed with mustard, ketchup or some other substance, apparently accidentally, and an accomplice offers sympathy and helps to clean your jacket, removing your wallet at the same time.

Be wary of plainclothes police; insist on seeing identification and on going to the police station by main roads. Do not hand over your identification, or money – which police should not need to see anyway, until you are at the station. On no account take them directly back to your lodgings. Be even more suspicious if the police officer seeks confirmation of status from a passer-by. If someone tries to extract a bribe from you, insist on a receipt. If attacked, remember your assailants may well be armed, and try not to resist.

It is best, if you can trust your hotel, to leave any valuables you don't need in the safe deposit there when sightseeing locally. Always keep an inventory of what you have deposited. If you lose valuables, always report to the police and note details of the report for insurance purposes.

Where to stay

In most parts of Chile accommodation is plentiful and finding a room to suit your budget should be easy. During the summer holiday months of January and February,

Hotel price codes

LL over US$150 *Top of the range hotels, mainly in Santiago. Have all amenities.*

L US$100-150 *Very luxurious business-style hotels.*

AL US$66-99 *Good city hotels and resort hotels. Usually very good sometimes with gym, pool, restaurants.*

A US$46-65 *Applies often to upper-range hotels in small cities and smaller resorts. Has most facilities.*

B US$31-45 *Mid-range hotels in cities, with many mod-cons. Usually with bath and TV.*

C US$21-30 *Comfortable smaller hotels with few luxuries, but decent facilities. Rooms are often small.*

D US$16-20 *Lower end hotels in small*

towns, or very expensive hospedajes.

E US$12-15 *Applies mainly to hospedajes in expensive resorts. Will have good breakfasts and facilities.*

F US$7-11 *The bulk of hospedajes come into this category. This range is very variable, but often excellent. Prices given throughout the book are per person.*

G US$4-6 *Applies mainly to hospedajes in remote parts of the country, or to dormitory accommodation in resorts. Again prices given throughout the book are per person.*

H US$3 and under *Only applies to a very few albuergues (youth hostels) in summer, and a couple of basic, ramshackle places in the North . Prices given are per person.*

Essentials

rooms can be more scarce – especially in upmarket hotels in the more popular holiday venues of the south. This is also true during Easter, and at the time of the Independence Day holidays in mid-September.

The term 'hotel' implies an expensive establishment. Top class hotels are available in Santiago and major cities, but elsewhere choice is more limited. *Hosterías* tend to be in rural areas and may have many of the facilities of a hotel; the terms *hostal*, *residencial* and *hospedaje* usually refer to a small family-run establishment with limited facilities and services. A motel, especially if it is situated on the outskirts of a city, is likely to rent rooms by the hour unless it is described as a *motel turístico*: usually the name or sign outside will indicate what type it is. In the south, many families offer bed and breakfast, which may be advertised by a sign in the window. People here often meet buses to offer rooms, but the quality of the rooms offered is variable.

Single rooms can be difficult to find and almost as expensive as double rooms (except in the *hospedajes* in the south, where prices are usually per person; you may have to share your room, though). Accommodation is more expensive in Santiago than in most other parts of the country. Prices also tend to be higher the further south you go from Puerto Montt, as well as in some northern cities such as Antofagasta. In tourist areas, prices rise in the high season (January/February, plus any local festivity), but off-season you can often bargain for a lower price, though you will usually have to be staying for two or more days to be successful: ask politely for a discount (*descuento*).

On hotel bills service charges are usually 10%. Value Added Tax (known as IVA) at 18% is charged on hotel bills and should be included in any price quoted in pesos. Whether VAT is charged on meals and other services on the bill seems to depend on the policy of the management. VAT and service charges do not apply in cheaper establishments. The government waives the VAT charge for hotel bills paid in dollars (cash or travellers' cheques) but only for hotels which have an agreement *(convenio)* with the government on this. As a result larger hotels (but few other establishments) can offer you much lower tariffs if you pay in dollars than those advertised in pesos.

Naturally you should establish clearly in advance what is being included in the price rather than relying on prices posted or services claimed on notices in the reception area. Many hotels have restaurants serving lunch and dinner; few budget places have this facility. Most *hospedajes* offer breakfast, which usually consists of instant coffee or tea with bread and jam. An increasing number of cheaper establishments offer kitchen facilities, but if you are relying on these you should check them out first. Most establishments will not allow you to wash and dry clothes in your room, but some offer facilities for you to do your own laundry. Many hotels have parking facilities, though in large cities this may be a few blocks from the hotel itself. Motorcycle parking is widely available.

In larger cities, the cheapest and often the nastiest hotels tend to be situated around bus terminals. If you arrive late and are just passing through they may be okay. Better quality accommodation is often, but not always, found near the main plaza. Taxi drivers are sometimes useful sources of information about accommodation, but, especially in tourist centres, they may also try to take you to a place where they know they will get a commission. Note also that even small villages often have someone who rents out a room for a very reasonable price; ask around.

Reception areas in hotels can be very misleading, so it is a very good idea to see the room before booking. Hoteliers often try to offload their least desirable rooms first. If you are shown a dark room without a window, ask if they have rooms with a window. In large cities the choice may be between an inside room without a window (*ventana*) and a room with a window over a noisy street. Many middle range establishments have two or more categories of room: with private bathroom (*con baño privado*) and without (*con baño compartido*) so it is often worth asking whether there is anything cheaper than the price initially quoted.

Many hotels, restaurants and bars have inadequate water supplies. Almost without exception used toilet paper should not be flushed down the pan, but placed in the receptacle provided. This applies even in expensive hotels. Failing to observe this custom will block the pan or drain, a considerable health risk. If you are concerned about the hygiene of the facility, put paper on the seat. Remember to carry toilet paper with you, as cheaper establishments as well as restaurants, bars, etc frequently do not supply it.

Camping Camping is not always cheap at official sites. A common practice is to charge US$10 for up to five people, with no reductions for fewer than five; however, if a site is not full, owners will often give a pitch to a single person for around US$4. Camping Gaz International stoves are recommended, since green replaceable cylinders are available in Santiago (white gas – *benzina blanca* – is available in hardware shops; for good value try the *Sodimac* or *Tricot* chains of DIY stores). Cheap gas stoves can be bought in camping shops in Santiago and popular trekking areas. *Copec* run a network of 33 'Rutacentros' along Ruta 5 which have showers, cafeterias and offer camping. Free camping is available at many filling stations. Campsites are very busy in January and February. *Turistel* publish an annual guide which lists campsites.

Camping wild is easy and safe in remote areas of the far south and in the *cordillera* north of Santiago. However in much of central and central-southern Chile the land is fenced off, and it is often necessary to enter a farm or smallholding and ask permission to camp on someone's land. In Mapuche and Aymará communities it is both courteous and advisable to make for the primary school (if there is one) or some other focal point of a village to meet prominent members of the community first. Camping wild in the north is difficult, though, because of the absence of water.

Albuergues (youth hostels) All over the south of Chile, *albuergues* spring up in summer. These are usually schools earning extra money by renting out floor space. They are very cheap (rarely more than US$3-4 per person) and are excellent places to meet young Chileans. Do not go to them if you want a good night's sleep, though; guitars often play on into the small hours. There is no need for an International Hostelling card to stay in *albuergues*, but there is rarely much in the way of security either. In addition to the *albuergues*, there are official youth hostels throughout Chile; average cost about US$5-8 per person. The Hostelling International card is usually readily accepted. A Chilean YHA card costs US$5. Hostelling International card costs US$15. These can be obtained from the **Asociación Chilena de Albergues Turísticos Juveniles** (ACHATJ), Hernando de Aguirre 201, Oficina 602, T2333220, achatj@hostelling.co.cl, together with a useful guidebook of all youth hostels in Chile, *Guía Turística de los Albergues Juveniles*.

Getting around

Internal transport is usually straightforward. Most of Chile is linked by one road, the paved Pan-American Highway (or Panamericana) – marked on maps as Ruta 5 – which runs from the Peruvian frontier south to Puerto Montt and the island of Chiloé. However, some of the most popular destinations in Chile lie to the south of Puerto Montt, and travelling to this part of the country requires careful planning. Though much of this area can be reached by the Camino Austral – a gravel road marked on maps as Ruta 7 – bus services here are far less reliable than elsewhere in the country. Furthermore, the Camino Austral is punctured by two ferry crossings, and there is no direct overland route from here to the far south. The only overland routes to the far south are through Argentina, with alternatives by sea and air from Puerto Montt. Ferries provide vital links in this region, notably those linking Chiloé with Puerto Montt and Chaitén for the Camino Austral; Puerto Montt with Puerto Chacabuco (and Coyhaique); and Puerto Montt with Puerto Natales in the far south.

Major domestic air routes

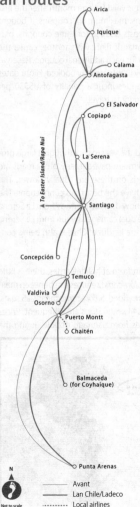

Air

Travellers with very limited time to spare should consider flying. Air travel can offer fantastic views stretching from the Andes to the sea, but the disadvantage, of course, is that it reduces your knowledge of the bits in between. Both *LanChile* (www.lanchile.cl) and *Ladeco* (www.ladeco.cl) (owned by *LanChile*) fly between Santiago and major cities. Until July 2001, the budget airline *Aerocontinente* provided much cheaper fares than *LanChile* or *Ladeco* – however, its planes were then impounded and its executives arrested on charges of drug running and money laundering. A new budget airline may soon surface, but at the time of

Needless to say for the best views of the Andes sit on the left flying south and the right flying north

You have to confirm domestic flights at least 24 hrs before departure

writing there is no alternative to *LanChile* or *Ladeco*. Several smaller airlines serve the south. Details of most flights are given in the book.

Book several months in advance for flights to Easter Island in January and February; if flying from Australia or New Zealand, note that some airlines offer a free stopover at Easter Island. Check with the airlines for matrimonial, student and other discounts. Both *LanChile* and *Ladeco* sell cut-price tickets with up to 50% off either as part of special promotions or to standby passengers, though the availability of standby fares is often denied. Passengers travelling to Chile with *LanChile* can obtain reductions on subsequent internal flights. Note that with some fares it may be cheaper to fly long distance than take a *salón cama* bus, and also that flight times may be changed without warning – always double check.

Visit Chile Airpass
The fares of Aerocontinente are often cheaper than those you will get with this airpass

LanChile sells a **Visit Chile Airpass** which can be used on all *LanChile* routes within Chile with the exception of Easter Island. The airpass can only be purchased abroad at the same time as a transatlantic ticket to Chile. It is valid for one month after the first coupon has been used. Minimum three coupons, maximum six coupons. If bought with a *LanChile* transatlantic flight the airpass costs US$250 for three coupons, plus US$50 per extra coupon. If bought with a transatlantic flight with another carrier the pass costs US$350 for three coupons plus US$80 for each additional coupon. Reservations should be made well in advance since many flights are fully booked. Flight dates can be altered without penalty, but route changes incur a penalty of US$30 per change. A refund (minus 10%) can be obtained prior to travel.

Road

About half of the 79,593 km of roads can be used the year round, though a large proportion is unimproved and only about 11,145 km are paved. Many other roads are described as *ripio* (gravel and/or stones). Speeds on these are usually slower. The region round the capital and the Central Valley have the best road connections. The main road is the Panamericana (Ruta 5), which is now dual carriageway from La Serena to Los Angeles; the plan is eventually to make the dual carriageway run from La Serena to Puerto Montt. A paved coastal route running the length of Chile is also being constructed, which should be ready by 2007.

Bus
Since there is lots of competition between bus companies, fares may be bargained lower, particularly just before departure; there is no need to reserve far in advance out of season

Buses are frequent, and on the whole good. Apart from at holiday times, there is little problem getting a seat on a long-distance bus. *Salón-cama* services run between main cities; *TurBus* and *Pullman Bus* are highly recommended. *Salón-cama* means 25 seats, *semi-cama* means 34 and *salón-ejecutivo* means 44 seats. Stops are infrequent. Prices are highest between December-March and fares from Santiago double during the

The price of a ticket

The following is intended to provide an idea of single bus fares from Santiago. Fares given are for standard services; other services such as salón-cama and semi-cama are more expensive. Lower fares than those shown are often available, but much higher fares are charged in summer (January-February) and during the Independence celebrations in September. Prices quoted are in dollars.

Northbound		**Southbound**	
La Serena	13	Talca	7
Copiapó	18	Temuco	15
Antofagasta	32	Valdivia	17
Iquique	38	Puerto Montt	20
Arica	40	Ancud	25
		Castro	25

Independence celebrations in September. Students and holders of Hostelling International cards may get discounts, which vary in amount, but these are not usually available in high season; discounts are also often available for return journeys. Most bus companies will carry bicycles, but may ask for payment; on *TurBus* payment is mandatory. Note that buses tend to be punctual, arriving and leaving when they say they will. Avoid back seats near the toilet due to smell and the disruption of passing passengers.

The best way of sending luggage around Chile is by "Encomienda" – your package is taken by bus from terminal to terminal and stored for up to one month at the destination (*TurBus* can deliver to an address). This is great if you only need camping or cold weather gear for, say, Torres del Paine – you can Encomienda bags when you don't need them, and pick them up when you do.

Documents Always carry your passport and driving licence. According to the Chilean Ley de Tránsito, foreign drivers need only their national driver's licence, but the *carabineros* will only accept an international driver's licence (in the north especially). To avoid problems, obtain one before leaving home. Car drivers also require a *Relaciones de pasajeros* document, available at borders, and must present the original registration document of their vehicle, as must motorcyclists. In the case of a car registered in someone else's name, carry a notarized letter of authorization.

Car
Carabineros (police) are strict about speed limits. Turistel maps mark police posts; make sure you are not speeding when you pass them

Taking a vehicle into Chile If you wish to take a vehicle into South America officially any one of the following three documents is required but in practice, none is asked: a *carnet de passages* issued by the **Fedération Internationale de l'Automobile** (FIA – Paris), a *carnet de passages* issued by the **Alliance Internationale de Tourisme** (AIT-Geneva), and the *Libreta de Pasos por Aduana* issued by the **Féderación Interamericana de Touring y Automóvil Clubs** (FITAC). The *carnet de passages* is available only in the country where the vehicle is registered. In the UK it can be obtained from the **RAC** and **AA**. In the USA the **AAA** seems not to issue the *carnet*, although the HQ in Washington DC may give advice. It is available from the **Canadian Automobile Association** (1775 Courtwood Crescent, Ottawa, K2C 3JZ, T613-2267631, F2257383) from whom full details may be obtained.

Buying a vehicle in Chile It is possible to buy a vehicle through an agent in Chile, which is an easier option for foreign nationals than trying to buy a car direct. This will usually involve a 'buy-back' guarantee. Bear in mind that you will be responsible for repairs, maintenance and road taxes; prices also tend to be higher than buying direct. Reports of the efficiency of companies offering this service are mixed. All Chilean cars have to undergo an annual technical revision ('*revision técnica*') to ensure road-worthiness; the month when this is due will be shown on a sticker on the windscreen. If your vehicle fails the technical revision you are given one month to carry out repairs. Technical revisions can be carried out in any of the larger cities; it is worth enquiring locally about the best centres as standards vary. If hiring a car, or buying through an agent with buy-back arrangements, check when its technical revision is due and who is responsible for it. In most cases it will be the hire company. Note also that all Chilean car taxes are payable in March each year; again, check who is responsible for paying tax. Failure to keep the tax up to date can lead to trouble with the police.

Car hire is an increasingly popular way of travelling in Chile, although it tends to reduce your contact with Chileans

Car hire Many agencies, both local and international, operate in Chile. Vehicles may be rented by the day, the week or the month, with or without unlimited mileage. Rates quoted do not normally include insurance or 18% VAT. Make sure you know what the insurance covers, in particular third party insurance. Often this is only likely to cover small bumps and scratches. Ask about extra cover for a further premium. If you are in a major accident and your insurance is inadequate, your stay in Chile may well be prolonged beyond its intended end. A small car, with unlimited mileage costs about US$500 a week in high season, a pick-up much more. In some areas rates are much lower off-season. At peak holiday times, eg Independence celebrations, car hire is very difficult. Shop around, there is much competition. Note that the *Automóvil Club de Chile* has a car hire agency (with discounts for members or affiliates) and that the office may not be at the same place as the Club's regional delegation. If intending to leave the country in a hired car, you must obtain an authorization from the hire company, otherwise you will be turned back at the frontier. When leaving Chile this is exchanged for a quadruple form, one part of which is surrendered at each border control. If you plan to leave more than once you will need to photocopy the authorization.

Insurance This is obligatory and can be bought at borders. It is getting increasingly difficult to insure against accident, damage or theft in the country of origin and it is very expensive to insure against accident and theft. If the car is stolen or written off you will be required to pay very high import duty on its value. Get the legal minimum cover, not expensive, as soon as you can, because if you should be involved in an accident and are uninsured, your car could be confiscated. If anyone is hurt, do not pick them up (you may become liable). Seek assistance from the nearest police station or hospital if you are able to do so.

See page 72 which gives more details of maps & guide books

Information and maps Members of foreign motoring organizations may join the *Automóvil Club de Chile*, Av Vitacura 8620, Santiago, T02-2125702, F2295295 (US$58 per three months) and obtain hotel discounts. Road maps are available at the Santiago headquarters, or other regional offices. Several individual maps provide greater detail than the Club's road atlas.

Fuel Gasoline (sold in litres) costs the equivalent of US$2.85 per US gallon (US$3.35 per imperial gallon); it becomes more expensive the further north and further south you go. Unleaded fuel, 93 octane, is available at many service stations in the major cities. Unleaded 95 and 97 octane are less common. Diesel fuel is widely available, and much cheaper. While *Esso* service stations usually accept credit cards, others may not do – always ask beforehand. When driving in the south (on the Camino Austral particularly), and in the desert north, always top up your fuel tank and carry spare fuel. Car hire companies may not have fuel cans. These are obtainable from some supermarkets but not from service stations. The standard of facilities in service stations is generally good.

Preparation Preparing your own car for the journey is largely a matter of common sense: obviously any part that is not in first class condition should be replaced. It's well worth installing extra heavy-duty shock absorbers (such as Spax or Koni) before starting out. Tyres need to be hard-wearing (avoid steel belt). Fit tubes on 'tubeless' tyres, since air plugs for tubeless tyres are hard to find, and if you bend the rim on a pothole, the tyre will not hold air. Take spare tubes, and an extra spare tyre. For car and motorcycle tyres try Calle Serranos 32, Santiago, reported to be the best stock in South America. Also take spare plugs, fanbelts, radiator hoses and headlamp bulbs; even though local equivalents can easily be found in cities, it is wise to take spares for those occasions late at night or in remote areas when you might need them. You can also change the fanbelt after a stretch of long, hot driving to prevent wear (eg after 15,000 km/10,000 miles). If your vehicle has more than one fanbelt, always replace them all at the same time (make sure you have the necessary tools if doing it yourself). If your car has sophisticated electrics, spare 'black boxes' for the ignition and fuel injection are advisable, plus a spare voltage regulator or the appropriate diodes for the alternator, and elements for the fuel, air and oil filters if these are not a common type. (Some drivers take a spare alternator of the correct amper-age, especially if the regulator is incorporated into the alternator.) Dirty fuel is a frequent problem, so be prepared to change filters more often than you would at home: in a diesel car you will need to check the sediment bowl often, too. An extra in-line fuel filter is a good idea if feasible (although harder to find, metal canister type is preferable to plastic), and for travel on dusty roads an oil bath air filter is best for a diesel car. For driving on gravel (*ripio*) roads, especially the Camino Austral, a good windscreen protector should be fitted: primitive versions are often of wire mesh. Because of the number of *ripio* roads outside the main cities a normal street car is of limited use in Chile; the Chevrolet LUV is a popular choice and is widely used throughout Chile. It is wise to carry a spade, jump leads, tow rope and an air pump. Fit tow hooks to both sides of the vehicle frame. A 12 volt neon light for camping and repairs will be invaluable. Spare fuel containers should be steel and not plastic, and a siphon pipe is essential for those places where fuel is sold out of the drum. Take a 10 litre water container for self and vehicle. In Santiago car parts available from many shops on Calle 10 de Julio.

The ripio (gravel) usually requires a 4WD; buen ripio should be OK for ordinary cars

Security Some drivers may wish to use a heavy chain and padlocks to chain doors shut and to lock the clutch or accelerator to the steering wheel, fit security catches on win-dows, and remove interior window winders (so that a hand reaching in from a forced vent cannot open the window); however, Chile is much safer than most South American countries, and these devices are as likely to attract thieves to your booty as to deter them (as well as inducing paranoia in the traveller). Nothing is foolproof; anything on the out-side – wing mirrors, spot lamps, motifs etc – may be stolen. Wheels should be secured by locking nuts. Remove all belongings and leave the empty glove compartment open when the car is unattended. Be sure to note down key numbers and carry spares of the most important ones (but don't keep all spares inside the vehicle).

Safety Driving at night is not recommended; be especially careful on major roads into and out of cities in the early evening because people tend to cross the highway with-out warning.

Taxis usually have meters and can be engaged either in the street or by phoning, though they tend to be more expensive when booked from a hotel; taxis show a mini-mum fare on a large sticker in the windscreen, and increments (usually per 100 m) below. Agree beforehand on fares for long journeys out of city centres or for special excursions. Taxi drivers may not know the location of streets away from city centres. *Colectivos* (collective taxis) operate on fixed routes (identified by numbers and destina-tions) and are a good way of getting about cities. *Colectivos* have fixed charges, which

Colectivos & taxis
A 50% surcharge is applied after 2100 & on Sunday. There is no need to give a tip unless some extra service is performed

Essentials

Essentials

increase at night and weekends and which are usually advertised in the front wind-screen. They are flagged down on the street corner (in some cities such as Puerto Montt there are signs). It is best to take small change as the driver takes money and offers change while driving. *Colectivos* also operate on some interurban routes (especially in the north), leaving from a set point when full. On interurban routes they compete favourably with buses for speed but not for comfort.

Cycling   At first glance a bicycle may not appear to be the most obvious vehicle for a major journey, but given ample time and reasonable energy it is certainly one of the best. It can be ridden, carried by almost every form of transport from an aeroplane to a canoe, and lifted across your shoulders over short distances. Cyclists can be the envy of travellers using more orthodox transport, since they can travel at their own pace, explore more remote regions and meet people who are less commonly in contact with tourists.

Choosing a bicycle   Unless you are planning to restrict your journey almost exclusively to paved roads – when a high quality touring bike such as a Dawes Super Galaxy would suffice – a mountain bike is strongly recommended, preferably with front suspension to combat the rough roads. Good quality mountain bikes (and the cast iron rule is never to skimp on quality) are incredibly tough and rugged, with low gear ratios for difficult terrain, wide tyres with plenty of tread for good road-holding, cantilever brakes, and a low centre of gravity for improved stability. Although imported spares are available in the larger cities, locally manufactured parts are of a lower quality and rarely last. Buy everything you possibly can before you leave home.

Bicycle equipment   A small but comprehensive tool kit (to include chain rivet and crank removers, a spoke key and possibly a block remover), a spare tyre and inner tubes, a puncture repair kit with plenty of extra patches and glue, a set of brake blocks, brake and gear cables and all types of nuts and bolts, at least 12 spokes (best taped to the chain stay), a light oil for the chain (eg Finish-Line Teflon Dry-Lube), tube of waterproof grease, a pump secured by a pump lock, a Blackburn parking block (a most invaluable accessory, cheap and virtually weightless), a cyclometer, a loud bell, and a secure lock and chain.

Luggage and equipment   Strong and waterproof front and back panniers are a must. When packed these are likely to be heavy and should be carried on the strongest racks available. Poor quality racks have ruined many a journey for they take incredible strain on unpaved roads. A top bag cum rucksack (eg Carradice) makes a good addition for use on and off the bike. A Cannondale front bag (or any other bar bag) is good for maps, camera, compass, etc. 'Gaffa' tape is excellent for protecting vulnerable parts of panniers and for carrying out all manner of repairs. All equipment and clothes should be packed in plastic bags to give extra protection against dust and rain. (Also protect all documents from sweat; carry them in plastic sealed bags when they are close to the body.) Always take the minimum of clothing. It's better to buy extra items en route when you find you need them. Always keep one set of dry clothes, including long trousers, to put on at the end of the day. The incredibly light, strong, waterproof and wind resistant goretex jacket and overtrousers are invaluable.

Useful tips   Wind, not hills, is the enemy of the cyclist. Try to make the best use of the times of day when there is little; mornings tend to be best but there is no steadfast rule. Take care to avoid dehydration. In northern Chile, where supplies of water are scarce between towns, be sure to carry an ample supply. For food, carry the staples (sugar, salt, dried milk, tea, coffee, porridge oats, raisins, dried soups, etc) and supplement these with whatever local foods can be found in the markets. Give your bicycle a thorough daily check for loose nuts or bolts or bearings. See that all parts run smoothly. A good chain should last 2,000 miles, 3,200 km or more but be sure to keep it as clean as possible – an old toothbrush is good for this – and to oil it lightly from time to time. Remember that thieves are attracted to towns and cities, so when sight-seeing, try to leave your bicycle somewhere secure. Country people tend to be more honest and are usually friendly and very inquisitive. However, don't take unnecessary risks. In more remote regions dogs can be a threat; carry a stick or some small stones to frighten them off. Traffic on the Pan-American Highway is a nightmare; it is usually far more rewarding to keep to the smaller roads if they exist. Most towns have a bicycle shop of some description, but it is best to do your own repairs and adjustments whenever possible. Most cyclists agree that the main danger comes from other traffic. A rearview mirror has been frequently recommended to forewarn you of vehicles which are too close behind. You also need to watch out for oncoming, overtaking vehicles, unstable loads on trucks, protruding loads etc. Make yourself conspicuous by wearing bright clothing and a helmet.

The **Expedition Advisory Centre**, administered by the Royal Geographical Society, 1 Kensington Gore, London SW7 2AR, has published a useful monograph entitled *Bicycle Expeditions*, by Paul Vickers, (1990) which is available direct from the Centre. In the UK there is also the *Cyclist's Touring Club*, CTC, Cotterell House, 69 Meadrow, Godalming, Surrey, GU7 3HS, T01483-417217, cycling@ctc.org.uk for touring, and technical information.

The machine It should be off road capable: a good choice would be the BMW R80/100/GS for its rugged and simple design and reliable shaft drive, but a Kawasaki KLR 650s, Honda Transalp/Dominator, or the ubiquitous Yamaha XT600 Tenere would also be suitable. A road bike can go most places an off road bike can go at the cost of greater effort.

Motorcycling
People are generally very amicable to motorcyclists

Preparations Fit heavy duty front fork springs and the best quality rebuildable shock absorber you can afford (Ohlins, White Power). Fit lockable luggage such as Krausers (reinforced luggage frames) or make some detachable aluminium panniers. Fit a tank bag and tank panniers for better weight distribution. A large capacity fuel tank (Acerbis), +300 mile/480 km range is essential if going off the beaten track. A washable air filter is a good idea (K&N), also fuel filters, fueltap rubber seals and smaller jets for high altitude Andean motoring. A good set of trails-type tyres as well as a high mudguard are useful. Get to know the bike before you go, ask the dealers in your country what goes wrong with it, and arrange a link whereby you can get parts flown out to you. If riding a chain driven bike, a fully enclosed chaincase is useful. A hefty bash plate/sump guard is invaluable.

Spares Reduce service intervals by half if driving in severe conditions. A spare rear tyre is useful but you can buy modern tyres (see above). Take oil filters, fork and shock seals, tubes, a good manual, spare cables (taped into position), a plug cap and spare plug lead. A spare electronic ignition is a good idea, try and buy a second-hand one and make arrangements to have parts sent out to you. A first class tool kit is a must and, if riding a bike with a chain, then a spare set of sprockets and an 'o' ring chain should be carried. Spare brake and clutch levers should also be taken as these break easily in a fall. Parts are few and far between, but mechanics are skilled at making do and can usually repair things. Castrol oil can be bought everywhere and relied upon. Take a puncture repair kit and tyre levers. Find out about any weak spots on the bike and improve them. Get the book for international dealer coverage from your manufacturer, but don't rely on it. They frequently have few or no parts for modern, large machinery. Recommended mechanics are given in the book.

Clothes and equipment A tough waterproof jacket, comfortable strong boots, gloves and a helmet with which you can use glass goggles (Halcyon) which will not

Essentials

scratch and wear out like a plastic visor. The best quality tent and camping gear that you can afford and a petrol stove which runs on bike fuel is helpful.

Security Try not to leave a fully laden bike on its own. An Abus D or chain will keep the bike secure. A cheap alarm gives you peace of mind if you leave the bike outside a hotel at night. Most hotels will allow you to take the bike inside. Look for hotels that have a courtyard or secure parking and never leave luggage on the bike overnight or whilst unattended.

Documents Passport, International Driving Licence, bike registration document are necessary. Riders fare much better with a *carnet de passages* than without it.

Hitchhiking Hitchhiking is relatively easy and safe, and when a lift does come along it is often in the shape of an exhilarating open-air ride in the back of a pick-up truck. In some regions – especially in the south – traffic is sparse; however, while roads in places like Tierra del Fuego rarely see more than two or three vehicles per day, these are likely to stop. Drivers will sometimes make hand-signals if they are only going a short distance beyond – this is not a rude gesture.

Sea

Reservations are essential for the ferries in high summer In the south of Chile, maritime transport is very important. Vital routes are, from north to south: Puerto Montt to Chiloé (many daily); Puerto Montt to Chaitén (three times weekly in summer) and Puerto Chacabuco (twice weekly); Puerto Montt to Puerto Natales (twice weekly in summer); Quellón to Chaitén (four weekly in summer, less in winter); Quellon to Puerto Chacabuco (once weekly); Punta Arenas to Porvenir (five times weekly); Punta Arenas to Puerto Williams (twice monthly). The main operators are *Transmarchilay* and *Navimag*. Details of all routes and booking information are given under the relevant chapters in the book.

Train

There are 4,470 km of line, of which most are state owned. Most of the privately owned 2,130 km of line are in the northern deserts where only one line, from Calama to Uyuni, Oruro and La Paz (Bolivia) carries passengers. The main passenger service south from Santiago runs to Temuco, and the journey is recommended as more tranquil than the Panamericana, and between Santiago and Chillán it is faster than the bus; President lagos has promised to return the train to its original terminus, Puerto Montt, by 2009. There are also suburban passenger trains around Santiago and inland from Valparaíso. The **Ferrocarriles del Estado** publish an annual *Guía Turística*, available in various languages from the larger stations.

Trains in Chile are moderately priced, but dining car food is expensive. There is a 15% discount on return tickets and a 10% discount for senior citizens aged 60 or over. There is a railway information office at Universidade de Chile metro station, level 1, T6883284, for all lines except for Calama-Oruro. English is spoken.

Keeping in touch

Communications

Internet The rise of the Internet café is inexorable, in Chile as elsewhere. Whereas four years ago you would have been lucky to find one in each large city, there is now competition in most tourist centres. Prices range from US$0.80-US$3 per hour. Addresses are given in the book.

The postal system is usually efficient. Airmail takes around a week from the UK. Seamail takes eight to 12 weeks. There is a daily airmail service to Europe. Poste restante only holds mail for 30 days, then returns it to sender. The *Lista de Correo* in the Central Post Office in Santiago is good and efficiently organized, but letters are kept separately for men and women so envelopes should be marked Sr or Sra/Srta. Letters to Europe/North America US$0.60, aerogrammes US$0.55. To register a letter costs US$0.75. Surface mail rates for parcels to Europe: less than one kilo US$14; one to three kilos US$18; 10 kilos US$30.

Post

National and international calls have been opened up for competition. There are eight main companies (known as *carriers)* offering competing rates, which are widely advertised. Though this sounds confusing, it is simple to operate and does mean that domestic and international phone rates are among the cheapest in South America. Callers choose companies by dialling an access code before the city code, see the inside front cover. For international calls you dial the company code, then 0, then country code. Ask which carrier has the best links with the country you wish to call (eg for making collect calls); for instance *CTC* is good for phoning Germany. The cheapest call centres tend to be *CTC* and small private centres operating as independents.

Telephone
Individual area codes are given under each town or city

Telephone boxes can be used to make local and long-distance calls, for making collect calls and receiving calls. It is cheapest and easiest to make national and international calls from a company office; national calls cost around US$0.10 per minute. To call mobiles, use phone boxes (US$0.25/0.30/minute). Telephone boxes have been programmed to direct calls via one carrier: to make a local call, simply dial the number you require and pay the rate charged by the carrier who owns the booth. To make an inter-urban call, dial '0' plus the area code (DDD) and the number; if you wish to select a carrier, dial its code, then the area code (leaving out '0'), then the number. To make an international call from a carrier's booth without choosing a different company, dial '00' before the country code. Yellow phones accept only 50 peso coins. Blue phones accept pre-paid phone cards costing 5,000 pesos (*tarjeta telefónica*); available from kiosks. On phone cards, only the time of the call is charged rather than the normal three minutes minimum. There are special phones for long-distance domestic calls which accept Mastercard and Visa credit cards. *Entel* has strategically-placed, self-dialling phones, which are white. Users press a button and are instantly connected with the operator from their own country. Booths taking *CTC* cards are more widespread than others.

Media

Santiago daily papers *El Mercurio* (centre-right, a heavyweight broadsheet), *La Nación* (liberal-left), *La Segunda* (middle-market tabloid), *La Tercera* (more serious tabloid), *La Quarta* (salacious and gossip-mongering), *Las Últimas Noticias* and *La Hora*. Look out for *The Clinic*, a satirical weekly named after the London hospital in which General Pinochet was arrested in 1998. *News Review*, a weekly in English is published on Fridays, US$1.35, on sale at selected kiosks; address: Casilla 151/9, Santiago, T2361423, F2362293; newsrevi@mcl.cl Recent international newspapers can be bought at kiosks on the *Paseo Ahumada* in Santiago. Magazines published weekly include *Hoy*, *Qué Pasa*, *Ercilla*, *Rocinante* (art, culture, society).

Newspapers & magazines

Radio
Compact or miniature portables are recommended, with digital tuning and a full range of short wave bands, as well as FM, long and medium wave

South America has more local and community radio stations than practically anywhere else in the world; a short wave (world band) radio offers a practical means to brush up on the language, sample popular culture and absorb some of the richly varied regional music. International broadcasters such as the **BBC World Service** (on 17.8h or 15.19 MHz), the **Voice of America**, **Boston (Mass)-based Monitor Radio International** (operated by *Christian Science Monitor* on 15.30 or 9.755 MHz) and the Quito-based Evangelical station, **HCJB**, keep the traveller abreast of news and events, in both English and Spanish. In small regional centres, the local radio station is a very effective medium for sending a message to someone else in the area; go to the studio and make the request in person.

Television
TV channels include **TVUC** (Universidad Católica) on Channel 13, the leading station; **TVN** (government operated) on Channel 7; **Megavisión** (private) on Channel 9 and **La Red** (private) on Channel 4. Soap operas (*teleseries*) and soccer constitute the most popular programmes. Soap operas are usually entertaining, and may have a historical or political slant – they are widely discussed, and run in six-month cycles.

Food and drink

Food

The main meals are breakfast (*desayuno*), lunch (*almuerzo*) and dinner (*cena*). Lunch is eaten any time from 1200 to 1500, and dinner before 2000-2300. *Las onces* (literally elevenses) is the name given to a snack usually including tea. In cafés and restaurants this is served at around 1700, but many Chileans also call their evening meal *once*. Breakfast usually consists of bread, butter and jam, served with coffee or tea. Lunch tends to be the main meal of the day, and by law restaurants have to serve a cheaper fixed price meal at lunch time; this is often called *la colación* or *el menu*. In more expensive places, this may not be referred to on the menu. When ordering from the menu note that vegetables, other than potatoes, are not usually included in the price quoted for main dishes.

Cuisine
For some basic vocabulary related to food, see page 559

Chile's cuisine is varied and often delicious. The Mediterranean climate of the central regions is perfect for growing a wide variety of fruit and vegetables – avocados are especially delicious. The semi-tropical climate of northern Chile supplies mangoes, papayas, *lúcumas* and *chirimoyas* (custard apples). The lush grasslands of the south are ideal for dairy and beef farming as well as for growing apples, cherries, plums and (in the far south) rhubarb. Local markets in central and southern Chile are full of beautiful fruit and vegetables at very reasonable prices.

Although Chilean cuisine is mostly rooted in the Spanish tradition, it has also been influenced by the immigrant groups who have settled in the country. The pastry making skills of the Germans have produced '*onces Alemanas*', a kind of high tea with *küchen*. *Pan de Pascua*, a traditional Christmas fruit loaf, also derives from Germany. Those who suffer from high blood pressure are advised, where possible, to cook their own food, as Chilean cuisine tends to have a high salt content.

Seafood Perhaps the most outstanding ingredient, though, is the seafood. Although there are good fish restaurants in Santiago, and fine seafood can be found at the Mercado Central, naturally the best seafood and fish is found on the coast. The excellent fish restaurants between Playa Ancha and Concón, near Valparaíso, are popular with *Santiaguinos*. Almost every port on the Chilean coast has a small market or a row of seafood restaurants where excellent seafood can be eaten very cheaply; in smaller harbours, it is often possible to eat with the fishermen. Most of these seafood

Empanadas de pino

Although other fillings are used nowadays for empanadas, the traditional filling is pino, a mixture of meat, onions, and spices. Most Chilean families have their own recipes: this one was kindly supplied by Manuel and Ximena Fernández.

Ingredients (to make 20 empanadas)
Pastry 1 kg flour; 125 g margarine, butter or lard; 1 level spoonful salt; cold water.
Filling 600 g meat, chopped into small pieces (or lean minced meat); 2 large onions; 4 or 5 tsp cooking oil; teaspoon each of cumin, black pepper and chilli powder; 1 tsp paprika; 3 cloves garlic, finely chopped; salt to taste; 4 hard boiled eggs; 1 tsp flour; 20 black olives; 40 raisins.

Method
Pastry In a bowl mix the flour and margarine, add salt (dissolved in ½ a cup water), gradually add more water to make soft but consistent pastry and leave it for at least one hour, then knead it for 10 minutes, before replacing it in the bowl and leaving it covered with a clean cloth.
Filling Heat the cooking oil in a large frying pan or pot, then add the onion and fry for about eight minutes. Add spices and

salt, then fry for two minutes. Add meat and fry for 15 minutes, stirring continuously, until the onions are crystal-like and softly cooked. Add the flour, lower the heat and simmer for five minutes. Leave overnight. Shell the eggs and cut into five long pieces.

Making the empanadas
Divide the pastry into 20 pieces, then roll each piece into a thin round shape. On one 'hemisphere' of each piece of pastry place the following: one piece of egg; one heaped teaspoon of the filling; a couple of raisins and an olive. Carefully paint the rim of each piece of pastry with water, then fold the empty 'hemisphere' over to enclose the filling; press the rim down. You should now have a semicircular turnover: paint the outer rim again with water and fold it again towards the centre of the empanada.

  Bake them in a preheated oven (200°C). After about five minutes reduce the heat to 150°C and bake for a further 14 minutes until the empanadas are nicely browned. To improve their appearance paint the empanadas with a thin coat of cold water as soon as you remove them from the oven.

  Serve hot with Chilean red wine.

Essentials

restaurants receive their supplies of fish and shellfish from local fishing boats which land their catch every morning in the harbours. Watching the unloading at a port such as Talcahuano can be fascinating. If you have the courage to bargain you may be able to pick up some delicious, fresh fish from the boats or from the stalls along the harbour; whole crates of shellfish go for a few dollars.

  In the north, great seafood can be had at Caleta Hornos, north of La Serena, and at Huasco. In the centre and south the best seafood is to be had at Valparaíso, Constitución, Talcahuano, Angelmo at Puerto Montt and on Chiloé – at Angelmo and on Chiloé you should try the famous *curanto*, a stew of shellfish, pork, chicken and other ingredients. Beware of eating seafood in the far south because of the poisonous '*marea roja*', see page 447.

  The most popular fish are *merluza* (a species of hake but inferior to European hake), *congrio* (ling), *corvina* (bass), *reineta* (a type of bream), *lenguado* (sole) and *albacora* (sword fish). *Merluza*, which is usually fried, is an inexpensive fish, found in ordinary restaurants. *Congrio* is very popular, particularly delicious served as *caldillo de congrio*, a soup containing a large *congrio* steak. *Albacora* is a delicious fish, available mainly in quality restaurants. *Ceviche*, fish marinated in lemon juice, is usually made with *corvina*.

  There is an almost bewildering array of shellfish. Look out for *choritos* (mussels), *ostiones* (scallops), *ostras* (oysters) and *erizos* (sea-urchins). Prawns are known as *camarones*. Chile's most characteristic products are the delicious *machas, picorocos* and *locos*, which are only found in these seas. *Machas a la parmesana* are *machas* prepared in their shells with a parmesan cheese sauce, grilled and served as a starter, or as a canapé with *pisco sour*. *Picorocos* (giant barnacles), which are normally boiled or steamed in white wine, are grotesque but have a very intense taste: it may be very disconcerting to be presented with a plate containing a rock with feathery fins but it is well worth taking up the challenge of eating it. *Locos* are the most popular Chilean mollusc, but because of overexploitation its fishing is frequently banned. This situation has led to an extensive illegal trade, both nationally and internationally, with *locos* being exported illegally to parts of Asia (especially Japan). The main crustaceans are *jaiva* (crab), *langosta* (lobster) and the local *centolla*, an exquisite king crab from the waters of the south.

Packages of dried seaweed, particularly *cochayuyo* (which looks like a leathery thong), are sold along coastal roads. Both *cochayuyo* and *luche* are made into a cheap, nutritious stew with vegetables, and eaten with potatoes or rice; these dishes are rarely available in restaurants. Until recently salmon was available only in the south where the rivers and lakes are full of 'wild' salmon that has escaped from farms. It is now farmed extensively in the south and can be found on menus in many parts of the country.

Specialities Away from seafood, savoury Chilean dishes tend to be creative. Specialities include *humitas* (mashed sweetcorn mixed with butter and spices and baked in sweetcorn leaves), *pastel de papas* (meat pie covered with mashed potatoes), and *cazuela de vacuno* (meat stew with pumpkin, potato, coriander and a twist of lemon – the most common everyday dish). In central and southern Chile stews with beans (*porotos*) are common. A typical (and unhealthy) dish from Valparaíso is the *chorillana*: chips covered with sliced steak, fried onions and scrambled eggs. A very typical dish is *cazuela de ave* (a nutritious stew containing chicken, potatoes, rice, and maybe onions and green peppers); best if served on the second day. *Valdiviano* is another stew, common in the south, with beef, onion, sliced potatoes and eggs. *Pastel de choclo* is a casserole of meat and onions with olives, topped with polenta, baked in an earthenware bowl. *Prieta* is a blood sausage stuffed with cabbage leaves. *Bistek a lo pobre* (a poor man's steak) can be just the opposite: it is a steak topped by two fried eggs, mashed potatoes, onions and salad. A *paila* can take many forms (the *paila* is simply a kind of dish), but the commonest are made of eggs or seafood. In the north, *paila de huevos* (two fried eggs with an *hallulla*) is common for breakfast. *Paila chonchi* is a kind of bouillabaisse.

Snacks Among the many snacks sold in Chile, the most famous are *empanadas*, pastry turnovers made either *de pino* (with meat, onions, egg and an olive) or *de queso* (with cheese). The quality of *empanadas* varies: many are full of onions rather than meat. In the south there are *empanadas* filled with seafood, which are delicious and usually better value. Sandwiches are fairly substantial: the *chacarero* contains thinly sliced steak and salad; *barros lucos have* steak and grilled cheese; and *barros jarpas* have grilled cheese and ham. *Completos* are the cheapest and most popular snacks, betraying the German influence on everyday food: these are hot dogs served with plenty of extras, including mustard, choukrut, tomatoes, mayonnaise and *aji* (chilli sauce). An *Italiano* is a *completo* with avocado and without the choukrut. Avocado is very popular at family *onces*, mashed up and served on bread. Bread itself is plentiful and cheap, and comes in pairs of fluffy rolls (*maraquetas*) or as a crisper slim roll (*hallullas*).

Desserts Chileans tend to have a very sweet tooth, and their desserts can be full of *manjar* (caramelised condensed milk). Central Santiago has many ice cream stands doing a roaring trade.

Those on a budget will want to stick to the cheaper eateries, where simple and very tasty meals can be had at a very reasonable price; a *colación* need not cost you more than US$2-3. The cheapest restaurants in urban areas tend to be by the transport terminals and markets or, in coastal areas, by the port. These restaurants may well have a wide choice of food for very reasonable prices, and often there is very little difference in the quality of the food between cheaper and more expensive places – the main differences being the service and the elegance (or pretensions) of the surroundings. More expensive places will, though, have a wider range of starters and desserts, which are often non-existent in cheaper eateries. The focal point for café life in towns is the plaza, in which there will typically be a number of slightly upmarket cafés, where people tend to have a beer and snacks, but rarely go for a full meal. If you are travelling in small villages off the beaten track, it is usually possible to find someone who will cook for you – ask around. Among the cheaper eating places are the *casinos de bomberos* (firemen's canteens) in most towns. Fire stations are not paid for by the state, and firemen are all voluntary. Eating at a casino helps fund their work, and the food is usually cheap and good.

Eating out
Waiters are referred to as garzón and never, as in some other parts of South America, as mozo

Vegetarians Although there are vegetarian restaurants in major cities, vegetarians will find that their choice of food is severely restricted, especially in smaller towns and away from tourist areas. To confuse matters, '*carne*' is understood to mean red meat, so vegetarians should explain which foods they cannot eat rather than saying '*Soy vegetariano*' ('I'm a vegetarian') or '*No como carne*' ('I don't eat meat'). Asking if a dish has meat in it is likely to lead to disaster; or chicken, at the very least. To make matters worse, most white bread is made with lard (*manteca*); ask first. There are fewer problems for vegetarians if they can cook for themselves, and they may be best off looking for accommodation which has cooking facilities.

It is certainly much more economical to eat in than out in Chile, especially if you shop in markets, where fruit and vegetables can be absurdly cheap. For non-perishable supplies, though, supermarkets are very good, and they are now ubiquitous in decent-sized towns up and down the country. In large villages there will always be one or two smaller stores with many things that you might want, although little in the way of fruit and vegetables.

Eating in

Drink

While Argentine cafés have excellent real coffee, if you ask for coffee in many places in Chile you will get a cup of boiling water and a tin of instant coffee – even in quite high class restaurants. There are espresso bars in major cities, such as *Café Haiti*, *Café Brasil* and *Dino*. Elsewhere specify *café-café, espresso*. Tea is usually served with neither milk nor lemon. The soluble tea should be avoided. If you order '*café*, or *té, con leche*', it will come with all milk; to have just a little milk in either, ask for a *cortado*. After a meal, instead of coffee, try an *agüita* – hot water in which herbs such as mint, or aromatics such as lemon peel, have been steeped. A wide variety of refreshing herbal teas is available in sachets.

Chilean wines are excellent, and even the cheapest ones are very drinkable. The best are from the central areas. The bottled wines are graded, in increasing excellence, as *gran vino, vino especial* and *vino reservado*. Champagne-style wines are also cheap and good (especially those from the Casablanca area). Even quite good wine is commonly sold in litre cartons, which are cheaper than bottles. Beer is cheap but hardly for connoisseurs; draught lager is known as *Schop*, and is drinkable; also try *Cristal Pilsener* (nationwide; not bad), or *Royal Guard* in the central regions, *Kunstmann* (very good) around Valdivia, and *Escudo Austral* and *Polar* in the south. *Malta*, a dark beer, is

For more on wine, see page 547

Essentials

Pisco sour

Most Chileans have their own recipe for this famous drink. Here is one...

Ingredients *1 litre of pisco (at least 35° and a good brand); half a litre of water; 250 ml of lemon juice; one to two medium-sized cups of sugar (to taste); ½ tsp egg white.*

Method *Either put all the ingredients in a cocktail mixer with ice and shake up, or put them in the fridge, and then liquidize. What is important in making pisco sour is the balance between the ingredients; once the mixing is done you can add extra sugar, pisco or lemon to taste. The egg white is purely for presentation.*

recommended for those wanting a British-type beer; however, there are different breweries, and the *Malta* north of Temuco is more bitter than that to the south. European-style lager is brewed by HBH, a company which began life in Temuco and which has bars in Santiago. European beers are increasingly available. As with wine, a deposit is required for beer bottles (about US$0.50); it may be worth buying some bottles and using them to exchange for new bottles up and down the country, as bottled beers are cheaper than cans.

The most famous spirit is *pisco*, made with grapes, usually drunk with lemon or lime juice as *pisco sour* (see box and page 56). *Pisco* is also often mixed with coca cola or sprite. *Pisco* is graded in strength from 30-46°; paradoxically, the stronger brands are much more pleasant and easy to drink. Recommended brands of *pisco* are *Alto del Carmen* and *Capel*; avoid the ironically named *Pisco Control*, especially at 30°. Good gin is produced. Reasonably good brandy, *anís* and crème de menthe are all bottled in Chile. Rum is very cheap and tends to lead to poisonous hangovers. *Manzanilla* is a local liqueur, made from *licor de oro* (like Galliano); *crema de cacao*, especially Mitjans, has been recommended. Two delicious drinks are *vaina*, a mixture of brandy, egg and sugar and *cola de mono*, a mixture of *aguardiente*, coffee, milk and vanilla served very cold at Christmas. With the wide variety of fruits in Chile, there are many seasonal fruit liqueurs which are delicious – *eguindado*, made from cherries, is particularly recommended. *Chicha* is any form of alcoholic drink made from fruit; *chicha cocida* is three-day-old fermented grape juice boiled to reduce its volume and then bottled with a tablespoonful of honey. Cider (*chicha de manzana*) is popular in the south. *Chicha fresca* is plain apple juice. *Mote con huesillo*, made from wheat hominy and dried peaches, is very refreshing in summer.

With such a wide range of inexpensive alcoholic drinks on offer, Chile does have quite a severe alcoholism problem, especially on Chiloé and in the far south. There are numerous bars in every town, and often many bars even in small villages; finding one to suit your purpose (however sober or otherwise it may be) is rarely a problem.

Shopping

What to buy There is an excellent variety of handicrafts: woodwork, pottery, copperware, leatherwork, Indian woven goods including rugs and ponchos. However, many of the goods sold in main handicraft markets are from elsewhere in South America, in some cases with the country of origin labels cut off; if going on a wider South American tour, these goods are almost always cheaper in the northern Andean countries. Among the most interesting purchases will be jewellery made with the semi-precious lapis lazuli stone, found only in Chile and Afghanistan. There are also less well known stones unique to Chile (such as the *combarbalita*, found around Combarbalá, near Illapel), and many fine jewels and knick-knacks (such as paperweights) made with stones such as onyx.

People returning home may find that they buy typical Chilean foods or drinks: *pisco*, *aji Chileno* or *manjar*, for instance.

Tips Bargaining is rare in Chile, and often seen as impolite. You can't try the usual 'offer a half, go up to two thirds' formula, and will often do well to knock more than the equivalent of US$1 off the asking price. The past decade has seen the growth of mall culture, especially in Santiago; Las Condes is brimful of malls (such as Parque Arauco), to which families descend en masse at weekends. VAT is 18%.

Entertainment and nightlife

Chile's centre for cultural and nocturnal entertainment is, naturally, Santiago. Here both visitors and residents will find their diaries can get frenetically full.

Santiago & around Bohemian nightlife in Santiago centres around *Barrio Bellavista*, below Cerro San Cristóbal, where clubs do not really get going until after 1, and the streets are crowded with night birds until after 5 in the morning. It is best to just turn up and go with the flow, as there are countless **bars** and **clubs** here, all with something to offer. More upmarket clubs are in the Providencia and *Barrio Alto* areas of Santiago – these tend to be expensive and posy. There are, though, good (but expensive) bars throughout the whole Providencia district, particularly on Calle Suecia (near Pedro de Valdivia). Away from the streets, parties have similar norms throughout the country: arrive much before 11.30 and you will be the first person there – and don't worry about getting home, as you will probably be up until the first morning buses run.

Santiago also has a thriving cultural scene, with numerous small **theatres**, arts' **cinemas** and a pulsating underground **music scene** (especially big in 'progressive rock'); the university campuses are good sources of information for these areas.

Going to watch a **football** match at one of the big stadia – Universidad Católica in Lo Barnechea, Colo Colo off Vicuña Mackenna or Universidad de Chile in the Estadio Nacional – is highly recommended.

Elsewhere Away from the capital, the scene is understandably less busy. Cities renowned for being lively are Iquique, Viña del Mar and La Serena, but everywhere – even very small towns and villages – has a *discoteca*. At these, the norms are usually fairly standard: they do not get going until after midnight, people tend to dance in couples (although not in Santiago), and the music is a mixture of mainstream Latin American and North American rock music, with occasional popular salsa and merengue. The cities with the biggest cultural scenes are those with a significant student population, particularly Concepción and La Serena; but even here, **cinemas** tend to show only the latest Hollywood blockbusters (usually with subtitles, not dubbed).

Holidays

1 January: New Year's Day
Easter: Holy Week (two days)
1 May: Labour Day; *21 May:* Navy Day
15 August: Assumption
First Monday in September: Day of National Unity; *18, 19 September:* Independence Days
12 October: Columbus Day
1 November: All Saints Day
8 December: Immaculate Conception; *25 December:* Christmas Day.

Essentials

Special interest travel

Chile might well have been designed for adventure tourism. In a country where you can often see the Andes from the coast, you are never more than a few hours' drive away from mountains, so a wide range of adventure activities can be practised year-round. In the high summer month of January, for instance, although Parinacota volcano in the north is shrouded in cloud, the Torres del Paine in Patagonia enjoy their main season. Some destinations possess unusual versatility – the mountain resorts near Santiago are famous for their skiing, but they are also good for mountain biking and trekking in high summer.

The infrastructure for 'soft' adventure tourism, such as a half-day's rafting on a Grade 3 river (quite a thrill), or a day spent climbing a volcano, is quite good. The Lake District is particularly strong for this. Agencies in centres such as Pucón, Puerto Varas and Puerto Montt organize combinations of activities, many for one day but some for longer durations. Parapenting and hang-gliding can be organized from Santiago, although there is a parapenting centre at the Antillanca ski resort. Santiago is well placed for short trips, especially for horse riding in the central *cordillera* and visits to the ski resorts nearby. Some of the world's top rafting and fishing is also easily accessible.

'Tougher' adventure tourism, often involving camping at high altitudes, is also possible. Chile offers boundless opportunities for well-equipped independent adventurers: the best way to see the Atacama Desert is in your own or rented four-wheel drive vehicle; and a mountain bike is the best form of transport on the Camino Austral. It is important to check the experience of agencies offering expeditions to remote areas.

Organizations
See also further reading on page 72

Among the organizations involved in adventure tourism several deserve special mention: **CATA** (Consejo de Autoregulación de Aventura), Arzobispo Casanova 3, Providencia, Santiago, T7358034, F7772375, is an organization formed by the more reputable agencies to try (with mixed success) to regulate adventure tourism to ensure safety and exclude 'cowboy' operators. It works closely with CONAF. **CONAF** (Corporación Nacional Forestal), Presidente Bulnes 291, piso 1, Santiago, T02-3900126, regulates adventure activities within the national parks, following CATA's written guidelines on matters such as the experience required of guides, types of activity provided, size of groups and safety requirements. CONAF's staff are dedicated and knowledgeable, and are usually extremely helpful in the parks themselves. CONAF also publishes a number of leaflets and has documents and maps about the national park system that can be consulted or photocopied in its Santiago office; but these are not very useful for walking. **Sernatur** (the National Tourist Board) has a separate section specializing in providing information on adventure tourism and ecotourism located within its head office in Santiago: Av Providencia 1550 (Casilla 14082), T02-2361416, TxSERNA CL 240137.

Climbing

Types of climbing
There are four distinct terrains for climbing in Chile: each poses different problems

Rock climbing is not organized on a national basis, though **ENAM** (Escuela Nacional de Montaña de Santiago) runs courses in rock climbing as well as ice climbing. Adventure tourism agencies are beginning to offer rock climbing activities. The three granite towers in the Parque Nacional Torres del Paine are the best known and most difficult climbs, but they are in such demand that a climbing fee is levied – the only place where this occurs in Chile. On the shores of Lago Todos Los Santos there are very high cliffs (800 m) at the eastern end and at Cerro Picada (800 m) on the northwest shore.

Chile has high mountains such as Tupungato and Ojos del Salado which rival the Argentine peak of Aconcagua for climbers. Like the latter they pose few technical difficulties, but the weather can be vicious and the altitude should be taken very seriously. Moreover, Ojos del Salado is not easily accessible.

Park life

Chile has an excellent network of protected and well-maintained natural areas, covering seven million hectares. These areas are divided into national parks, forest reserves, natural monuments and natural sanctuaries; distinctions which are of little importance to the visitor. Most of these areas have public access and details of the majority are given in the text. Camping areas are usually clearly marked; wild camping is discouraged and frequently banned.

The first forest reserve was the Reserva Forestal Malleco, created in 1907, and the first national park was the Parque Nacional Vicente Pérez Rosales, founded in 1926. The expansion of the system has been based on two desires: preserving natural resources which may be under threat, and creating easy public access to areas of outstanding beauty.

All of these protected areas are managed by CONAF (the Corporación Nacional Forestal), a dependency of the Ministry of Agriculture. The address of CONAF's head office in Santiago is given on page 58. It maintains an office in each of the regions of the country and kiosks in some natural areas and other locations. It publishes an illustrated guide to the parks and maps of the major protected areas which can be obtained from its head office and from some regional offices, the addresses of which are given in the text. CONAF publishes a useful little book on native trees, Arboles nativas de Chile, Guía de Reconocimiento, by Claudio Donoso Zegers (1983).

By contrast some of the most important high altitude ice climbs are easily reached from Santiago: the Loma Larga and Plomo massifs are two to three hours drive from the capital. The Federación de Andinismo can advise on the better known and more difficult climbs such as El Plomo, El Altar and El Morado, though it is less useful for information of mountains further afield and its offices are often closed.

Volcanoes provide the fourth type of climbing. There are hundreds to choose from, ranging from the high altitude Parinacota in the far north and remote Licancábur on the Bolivian frontier near San Pedro, to the chain of much lower cones in the Lake District and along the Camino Austral. Some of these, such as Puntiagudo and Corcovado with their precipitous plugs, are difficult climbs. The easiest and most popular are Villarrica and Osorno, though CONAF rightly controls access to these because the crevasses are hazardous. Osorno, with its seracs and ice caves is a more attractive climb, but Villarrica has the dubious advantage of being more active and hiring guides is much cheaper. Note that Osorno and Villarrica are still not easy climbs, and even well-equipped and experienced climbers have suffered fatal accidents on them.

The southern bank of the Río Petrohué offers many fantastic canyons for climbing. Nearby Aquamotion have fixed rope ladders in the canyon of the Río Leon, 30 minutes by boat from Petrohué on the southern shore of Lago Todos Los Santos.

Permission must be obtained from the **Dirección de Fronteras y Límites**, piso 5, **Formalities** Ministerio de Relaciones Exteriores, Bandera 52, Santiago, T6714210, F6971909, to climb some mountains in frontier areas, notably Ojos del Salado and Parinacota. Preferably apply three months in advance; Chilean embassies abroad can help. In addition, some mountains, such as Torres del Paine and Volcàn Osorno require climbers to have climbing permits – further information from the Federación de Andinismo (see below).

Mountain rescue services are provided by the **Cuerpo de Socorro Andino**, based in Santiago, and by rescue groups in popular climbing areas: if organizing a climb register with them, often at the entry control to the mountain and with the local carabineros. Away from the popular areas you are on your own, which can also be one of Chile's main attractions.

Further **Federación de Andinismo de Chile**, Almte Simpson 77A, Santiago, T02-2220888,
information F2226285, in theory open daily but frequently closed especially in January/February
(high season), has a small museum (1100-1330, 1700-2000, free) and library (weekdays
except Wednesday 1930-2100). The shop in the foyer sells climbing guides and equipment and is often open when the office is closed. **Escuela Nacional de Montaña**
(ENAM), at same address, T02-2220799, holds seminars and conferences on climbing,
runs rock and ice climbing courses and qualification courses for guides in Santiago and
elsewhere. Also administers the *Carnet de La Federación de Chile*, a climbing card which
is often required to climb mountains especially where CONAF control access. The
carnet can be renewed through CONAF offices.

Trekking

Chile offers limitless possibilities for both short and long treks in vastly differing landscapes: a one-day hike to the Valle de la Luna near San Pedro de Atacama is half a continent away from the famous week-long circuit of the Parque Nacional Torres del Paine.
Over 1,000 km of new hiking opportunities have been opened up by the building of
the Camino Austral, though the heavy rainfall in this area can be a drawback.

Within the national parks there are often short two-to three-hour sign-posted
nature trails, starting from a visitor's centre, where, in season, there are sometimes lectures, usually only in Spanish, on flora and fauna and other highlights of the park.

Skiing

Sernatur produces Chile's major international ski resorts lie in the Andes near Santiago and are described
a leaflet on all in the text, but skiing is possible from Santiago to Punta Arenas.
Chilean ski resorts Skiing elsewhere is mostly on the volcanoes to the south of Santiago, although
back-country ski-mountaineering is quite possible on the volcanoes of the northern
altiplano where a guide is essential and expertise required. The larger resorts in the
south are Termas de Chillán, Villarrica/Pucón and Antillanca, all of which have accommodation on or near the slopes. There are, however, alternatives to these: many suitable volcanoes close to towns have a small base lodge and a lift which functions at
weekends or peak periods (eg Antuco near Los Angeles; Llaima and Lonquimay further
south). Here prices tend to be very reasonable and basic equipment rental is usually
possible in the nearest town. Hitching is often the only form of transport, though it is
sometimes possible to arrange transport with the local *Club Andino*. After all the effort
to reach the snow, the atmosphere is happy-go-lucky and the skiing is great.

In the southern resorts skiing is for the laid-back and adventurous only. Snow conditions tend to become more slushy the further south you go. Lift systems are not the
most modern, fast or well-maintained, piste preparation is mediocre and the weather
is often more rainy than snowy. Despite all these disadvantages skiing on an active
volcano looking down onto five huge lakes, as is the case at Villarrica/Pucón, is a
memory which will truly last a lifetime.

Mountain biking

Mountain biking is a popular activity, particularly on descents from the Continental
Divide and from *refugios* on volcanoes such as Antillanca and Osorno. Touring the
length of the Camino Austral by mountain bike is also popular; mountain bikers might
also wish to explore coastal areas anywhere between Valparaíso and Puerto Montt. In
resorts such as Pucón and San Pedro, reasonable quality mountain bikes can be hired
(prices from US$8 per half day). The best place in Santiago for bikes is Calle San Diego,
south of the Alameda.

Rafting and kayaking

Over 20 rivers between Santiago and Tierra del Fuego are excellent for white water rafting. Apart from the Maipo, which is the most easily accessible from Santiago, the main ones are the Cachapoal, Teno, Claro, Maule and Biobío; the Trancura, Fuy, Bueno, Rahue and Petrohué; the Yelcho, Futaleufú; Corcovado, Palena and Baker and the Serrano and Tyndall. One of the most beautiful rivers is the Río Petrohué, which flows between the Osorno and Calbuco volcanoes with lush temperate rainforest along its banks. The Río Biobío, Chile's most famous river for rafting, is in decline: one dam has already been built and the completion of a second, due in 1997, will mark the end of a great rafting river. Some expert rafters have long maintained that the Biobío was, in any case, inferior to the Río Futaleufú. This river, east of Chaitén, will inevitably become known as one of the great Grade 5 rafting rivers in the world.

Rafting is generally well organized and equipment usually of high quality. Access to the headwaters of most rivers is easy. Many agencies, particularly in Santiago, Pucón and Puerto Varas, offer half-day trips to Grade 3 rivers for beginners, US$40-69 per person. Rafts should ideally carry six people and certainly no more than seven plus guide. If you do fall in, do not panic – guides are expert at picking you out again.

The most attractive waters for sea kayaking are around the islands off eastern Chiloé or around Hornopirén, in the fjords of the sheltered Gulf of Ancud. Very adventurous and experienced sea kayakers will be tempted by the prospect of circumnavigating the island of Cape Horn in the far south. The highlight for lake kayaking is the annual open competition on Lago Llanquihue, involving five stages totalling 310 km around the lake shore. Kayaks can be hired from *Oceanic*, Santiago (F2325539) and *Kayak Equipment*, San Vicente de Paul 5831, *La Reina*, Santiago (T/F2775288) and *Canoas Tours*, Rosario 1305, Puerto Varas (T233587). Courses are available at the *Chiloé Sea Kayaking Centre* near Dalcahue and are bookable through *Altué Expeditions* in Santiago.

Other water sports, such as diving and surfing, are generally practised in northern Chile. An exception is Pichilemu, a resort three hours to the south-west of Santiago, which is famous for surfing.

Sailing and yachting

Sailing, both wind and motor powered, is popular. Protected harbours, yacht clubs and racing fleets can be found at most sizeable coastal towns. There are regattas on Lago Llanquihue and Villarrica every Saturday, racing Lasers, Vagabonds and catamarans: there are also more important annual regattas. The biggest regatta is the biennial event in January (even years) from Puerto Montt around the coast of Chiloé. Sailing is best south of Puerto Montt. You should allow at least a week to begin to do justice to Chiloé and the islands off its eastern shore. Three weeks or more are required to reach the glaciers of Laguna San Rafael.

Chartering A variety of sail and power boats can be chartered from *MDS Charters* in Puerto Montt (address under Puerto Montt). Most charters are skippered: unusually good sailing credentials are required for a bareboat charter. For the really adventurous a dozen or more sailing yachts are based in Ushuaia/Puerto Williams: these are blue water sailing yachts doing charters to Cape Horn and Antarctica. They advertise in sailing magazines and are often booked a year in advance.

Yacht facilities There are three travel lifts in Valdivia, among them a 35-tonne lift and complete yacht repair facility at the modern Awolplast boatyard. The Valdivia yacht club often has slips available. At Puerto Montt Marina del Sur is a brand new marina with 65 slips, showers and laundry: a new hydraulic lift with a tidal grid (with 25 ft tides) is also available.

Essentials

Sailing through the southern channels

With over 4000 km of coastline, Chile is a great destination for sailors. The real Mecca for cruising boats is along the coast from Puerto Montt to Cape Horn through the beautiful green wooded areas of Chiloé, the Archipiélago de los Chonos and the mazy channels of Patagonia. There is probably no better way to see this spectacular part of South America than by yacht during the summer months.

These archipelagos provide some of the finest and most challenging sailing in the world. In general the navigation and the weather conditions become more difficult as you go south. The sailor's supreme challenge is, of course, western Tierra del Fuego and Cape Horn. To the east of the southern tip of Tierra del Fuego is Staten Island (Islas de los Estados), another challenging destination. Anyone who can take their boat this far south is already among a hardy but slowly growing band of experts, some of whom now cross the formidable Drake Straits south of the Cape, normally in January or February, to cruise to Antarctica.

For lesser mortals a much friendlier region is the archipelago of Chiloé, just south of Puerto Montt, at approximately 42°S, a region dotted with populated islands. The sailing, especially in January-March, is tough but sporty, rather than dangerous. These waters, shown on charts as the Gulf of Ancud and the Gulf of Corcovado, are completely protected by Chiloé from the giant swells of the southern Pacific. The weather is at best unsettled and even locals get it wrong. Strong winds can suddenly die to a flat calm; burning sun may be wiped out by squalls of rain and even hail – and that's during summer.

Tides of 6 to 8 m mean strong rips; shoals are frequent, but usually well marked on charts – 'usually' meaning that special care is needed around the smallest islands, especially on the mainland side. It's rare to be out of sight of land and you mostly know where you are to within 100 m or so, even without electronics,

The best harbours on Chiloé are, from north to south, Quemchi, Mechuque, Quehui, Castro, Queilén and Quellón. When the weather is fine, there are spectacular views across to the cone of the Corcovado Volcano. Fuel for outboard motors is usually available at Quemchi, Castro, Chonchi and Queilén. Water generally has to be brought aboard in jerry cans filled from a friendly householder's kitchen tap. Connections to shore electricity do not exist and, indeed, the smaller islands only have power themselves for an hour or two at night, The larger islands have at least a couple of general stores; but much better to stock up in Puerto Montt or Castro. The same applies for recharging batteries.

Budget minded sailors can pick up a mooring at the Club Náutico. South of Puerto Montt there are no marina facilities. Complete re-provisioning can be carried out in Puerto Montt, Castro, Puerto Aisén, Puerto Natales and Ushuaia; odds and ends can be found at Melinka and Puerto Aguirre, but fuel and other supplies are virtually unobtainable between Puerto Aguirre and Puerto Natales.

Navigation The yachting season runs from November to March in these southern waters. South of 45S the weather is significantly worse than at corresponding latitudes in the northern hemisphere. Reasonably accurate weather forecasts are provided by the Chilean Navy and are updated twice daily: they are broadcast over HF radio by voice and weatherfax map. Complete chart portfolios are stocked at the Navy administration offices in Puerto Montt and Puerto Williams. Individual charts cost US$23 each and are generally superior to the US charts. A high quality colour chart atlas containing 28 cm by 43 cm reductions of the entire Chile chart portfolio was published in 1997.

First past the post

January Chiloé/Puerto Montt Regatta *(every two years, next 2002)*. International Rally of Kayaking, *Lago Llanquihue, 310 km, five stages*. Regatta, *Lago Villarrica and* Pentathlon, *Lago Todos Los Santos/Petrohué*.

January/February International Triathlon, *Pucón*.

February International windsurfing contest *(slalom and speed categories)*, Lago Llanquihue, *incorporating a rafting, canoeing and kayaking competition on Río Petrohué*. Rafting Open, *Pucón,*

beginners and experts categories

March National Rodeo *competition in Rancagua, last week of March*.

April International Mountain Bike Competition, *Antillanca. Cycling Tour of Chile*.

September Horseracing on beach in *Parque National Chiloé (Chepu sector) and kayaking and canoeing races on Río Chepu*.

October International Surfing Competition, *Pichilemu*.

Fishing

The lakes and rivers of Regions IX (Araucanía), X (Los Lagos) and XI (Aisén) offer great opportunities for fishing, especially trout (rainbow, brown and fario) and salmon (coho and chinook); Lago Blanco on Tierra del Fuego is also a good destination for fishers. The season runs from 15 November to the first Sunday in May except on Lago Llanquihue where it starts on 15 September. A licence is required whether for one day or a longer period: licences are usually obtained from the local Municipalidad, though some tourist offices also sell them. Organized fly fishing with a guide can be expensive: trolling and spinning are the more widely practised methods. *Overfishing is generally not a problem*

Sea fishing is popular between Puerto Saavedra in the IX Region and Maullín in the X Region: the main centres are Mehuín, the coast from Niebla to Curiñanco near Valdivia, Maicolpué, Llico and Maullín itself, where salmon may be caught in the sea.

The Lake District is popular for trout fishing. Both rainbow and fario trout are found in all the major lakes; the largest fish are found in Lago Llanquihue, while Lago Todos Los Santos, on which very few boats are permitted, is noted for quantity. Apart from the main lakes, Lago Maihue and Lagunas El Toro, El Encanto and Paraíso (all in the Parque Nacional Puyehue) have been recommended. In the southern Lake District the main rivers for salmon fishing include the Ríos Pescado, Petrohué, Puelo, Maullín and, on Chiloé, the Chepu and Pudeto.

The greatest fishing area in Chile lies along the Camino Austral: Lago Yelcho and the Ríos Futaleufú and Palena are important areas for fly fishing, while further south the rivers and lakes around Coyhaique offer some of the best fishing in the world. Santiago and Valparaíso residents fish at the mountain resort of Río Blanco.

For details on licences and local conditions, contact the Asociación de Pesca y Caza, or Sernap, San Antonio 427, piso 8, Santiago, open Monday-Friday 0900-1400. Check with Sernatur on closed seasons. Fishing equipment can be bought from *Pesca Mundo Caza*, Benavente y M Rodríguez, Puerto Montt, *Winkler Deportes*, Antonio Varas 841, Puerto Montt and *Lagollan*, San José 315, Puerto Varas. **Further information**

Horseriding

Horse treks are organized in Santiago, in the Lake District and on Chiloé, and in numerous remote areas of the south. One of the best places for hiring and riding horses is along the west coast of Chiloé; expect to pay US$5 per hour. South of Santiago there is *The biggest danger to riders is from cars and trucks*

more of an equine culture than further north, but some of the best riding country is to the north and east of Santiago, where the narrow tracks over mountain passes provide spectacular terrain. Saddles are narrow and covered with sheepskins, but Argentine saddles are wider and tend to be more comfortable. A good horse costs from US$350 upwards; anything cheaper is likely to be a nag. The best horses are to be found in the area around Osorno. In rural areas, everyone will know who has horses for sale; if arriving at a city ask in a vet's for help in finding a reputable seller of horses. Horse sales are frequent in Puerto Montt's livestock market; horses are sold by weight. A good saddle costs at least US$300 (including tack). Pack-saddles cost a similar price; when buying a pack-saddle, make sure that the wooden cross is not cut low, as these press on the horse's withers and lead to sores. Saddlebags (*alforjas*) can be made up in saddlers (*talabarterías*) for about US$40 – make sure that the stitching is strong as they are liable to rip. A bale of hay (which should give fodder to two horses for one day) costs about US$4, and oats cost about US$0.25 per kilo.

Health

For anyone travelling overseas, health is a key consideration. With the following advice and precautions you should keep as healthy as you do at home. Most visitors return home having experienced no problems at all apart from some travellers' diarrhoea. There are no hard and fast rules to follow; you will often have to make your own judgement on the healthiness or otherwise of your surroundings. There are English (or other foreign language) speaking doctors in most major cities. Your embassy representative will often be able to give you the name of local reputable doctors, and most of the better hotels have a doctor on standby. If you do fall ill and cannot find a recommended doctor, try the Outpatient Department of a hospital – private hospitals are usually less crowded and offer better standards of care.

Checklist Sunglasses designed for intense sunlight; suntan cream with a high protection factor, especially if travelling to the far south; insect repellent containing DET for preference; travel sickness tablets; tampons; condoms; contraceptives; water sterilizing tablets; anti-infective ointment eg Cetrimide; dusting powder for feet etc containing fungicide; antacid tablets for indigestion; sachets of rehydration salts plus anti-diarrhoea preparations; painkillers such as Paracetamol or Aspirin; antibiotics for diarrhoea etc; a first aid kit containing a few sterile syringes and needles and disposable gloves. The risk of catching hepatitis etc from a dirty needle used for injection is negligible, but some may be reassured by carrying their own supplies – available from camping shops and airport shops.

Before travelling

Take out medical insurance. Make sure it covers all eventualities, especially evacuation to your home country by a medically equipped plane. Obtain a spare glasses prescription, a spare oral contraceptive prescription (or enough pills to last) and, if you suffer from a chronic illness (such as diabetes, high blood pressure, ear or sinus troubles, cardio-pulmonary disease or nervous disorder) arrange for a check up with your doctor, who can at the same time provide you with a letter explaining the details of your disability in English and if possible Spanish. If you are on regular medication, make sure you have enough to cover the period of your travel.

Children More preparation is probably necessary for babies and children than for an adult and a little more care should be taken when travelling to areas where health services are more basic. Children can become ill more rapidly than adults (on the other hand they often recover more quickly). Diarrhoea and vomiting are the most common problems, so take the usual precautions, but more intensively. Breastfeeding is best and most convenient for babies, but powdered milk is generally available and so are baby foods. Papaya, bananas and avocados are all nutritious and can be cleanly prepared. Children get dehydrated very quickly in hot countries and can become drowsy and uncooperative unless cajoled to drink water or juice plus salts. Upper respiratory infections, such as colds, catarrh and middle ear infections are also common and if your child suffers from these normally take some antibiotics against the possibility. Outer ear infections after swimming are also common and antibiotic eardrops will help. Wet wipes are always useful and sometimes difficult to find as, in some places, are disposable nappies.

Vaccination & immunization Vaccination against the following diseases is recommended: **Typhoid** This is a disease spread by the insanitary preparation of food. A number of new vaccines against this condition are now available; the older TAB and monovalent typhoid vaccines are being phased out. The newer, eg Typhim Vi, cause fewer side effects, but are expensive. For those who do not like injections, there are now oral vaccines; **Hepatitis** This is less of a problem for travellers than it used to be because of the development of two extremely effective vaccines against the A and B form of the disease. A combined hepatitis A and B vaccine covers both diseases; **Tuberculosis** This disease is on the increase worldwide, and travellers should ensure that they are protected against it by arranging a BCG test before departure; **Other vaccinations** Might be considered in the case of epidemics eg meningitis. There is an effective vaccination against rabies which should be considered by all travellers, especially those going to remote areas or if there is a particular occupational risk, eg veterinarians.

Further information Further information on health risks abroad, vaccinations etc, may be available from a local travel clinic. If you wish to take specific drugs with you – such as antibiotics – these are best prescribed by your own doctor. More detailed or more up-to-date information than local doctors can provide are available from various sources. In the UK there are hospital departments specializing in tropical and subtropical diseases in London, Liverpool, Birmingham and Glasgow. In the USA the local Public Health Services can give such information and information is available centrally from the Centre for Disease Control (CDC) in Atlanta, T404-3324559.

There are additional computerized databases which can be assessed for destination-specific up-to-the-minute information. In the UK there is MASTA (Medical Advisory Service to Travellers Abroad), T0906-8224100 and *Travax* (Glasgow, T0141-9467120, ext 247, www.axl.co.uk/scieh). Other information on medical problems overseas can be obtained from *Travellers' Health: How to stay healthy abroad*, (Oxford University Press 1992; reprinted with amendments 1999, £7.99) by Dawood, Richard (Editor). We strongly recommend this revised and updated edition, especially to the intrepid traveller heading for the more out of the way places. General advice is also available in the UK in *Health Information for Overseas Travel* published by the Department of Health and available from HMSO, and *International Travel and Health* published by WHO, Geneva.

On the road

Medicines It is no longer possible to buy all drugs in pharmacies without a prescription (although getting the contraceptive pill does not require one). Note also that, with those brands that are available over the counter, pharmacists will often try to palm you off with the most expensive brand, rather than much cheaper (and chemically identical) local brands. Many drugs and medicines are manufactured under licence from American or

European companies, so the trade names may be familiar to you. While you do not have to carry a whole chest of medicines with you, remember that the shelf life of some items, especially vaccines and antibiotics, is markedly reduced in hot conditions. Buy your supplies at the better outlets, where there are refrigerators, even though they are more expensive; check the expiry date of all preparations you buy. Immigration officials occasionally confiscate scheduled drugs (Lomotil is an example) if they are not accompanied by a doctor's prescription.

Intestinal upsets Although the thought of catching a stomach bug worries visitors to Latin America, this is rarely a severe problem in Chile, where standards of hygiene and sanitation are generally reasonable. Travellers' diarrhoea and vomiting is due, most of the time, to food poisoning, usually passed on by the insanitary habits of food handlers. As a general rule the cleaner your surroundings and the smarter the restaurant, the less likely you are to suffer. Drinking water is rarely the culprit. Sea water or river water is more likely to be contaminated by sewage and so swimming in such dilute effluent can also be a cause.

Avoid uncooked, undercooked, partially cooked or reheated meat, fish, eggs, raw vegetables and salads, especially when they have been exposed to flies. Stick to fresh food that has been cooked from raw just before eating, and make sure you peel fruit yourself. Wash and dry your hands before eating. Shellfish eaten raw are risky and at certain times of the year some fish and shellfish concentrate toxins from their environment and cause various kinds of food poisoning. See in particular the warning about *marea roja* under Punta Arenas. Heat treated milk (UHT), pasteurized or sterilized, is available in Chile, as is pasteurized cheese. On the whole matured or processed cheeses are safer than the fresh varieties; unpasteurized milk from whatever animal can be a source of food poisoning germs, tuberculosis and brucellosis. This applies equally to ice cream, yoghurt and cheese made from unpasteurized milk, so avoid these home-made products – the factory-made ones are probably safer. Tap water is generally safe in most places in Chile. Stream water, if you are in the countryside, can be contaminated by communities living higher in the mountains. Filtered or bottled water is usually available and safe.

Infection with various organisms can give rise to diarrhoea. They may be viruses, bacteria, eg Escherichia coli (probably the most common cause worldwide), protozoal (such as amoebas and giardia), salmonella and cholera. The diarrhoea may come on suddenly or rather slowly and may or may not be accompanied by vomiting or by severe abdominal pain and the passage of blood or mucus (when it is called dysentery). How do you know which type you have caught and how to treat it? If you can time the onset of the diarrhoea to the minute ('acute') then it is probably due to a virus or a bacterium and/or the onset of dysentery. The treatment in addition to rehydration is Ciprofloxacin 500 mg every 12 hours; the drug is now widely available and there are many similar ones. If the diarrhoea comes on slowly or intermittently ('sub-acute') then it is more likely to be protozoal. Antibiotics such a Ciprofloxacin will have little effect. These cases are best treated by a doctor, as is any outbreak of diarrhoea continuing for more than three days. Sometimes blood is passed in amoebic dysentery and for this you should certainly seek medical help. If this is not available then the best treatment is probably Tinidazole (Fasigyn) one tablet four times a day for three days. If there are severe stomach cramps, the following drugs may help but are not very useful in the management of acute diarrhoea: Loperamide (Imodium) and Diphenoxylate with Atropine (Lomotil). They should not be given to children.

Any kind of diarrhoea, whether or not accompanied by vomiting, responds well to the replacement of water and salts, taken as frequent small sips, of some kind of rehydration solution. Rehydration sachets can usually be bought in Chile, but take a supply from home in case. If you have no such sachets, you can make your own rehydration solution by adding ½ a teaspoonful of salt (3½ g) and four tablespoonfuls of sugar (40 g) to a litre of boiled water. Try to avoid the anti-diarrhoeal pills which are sold ("stoppers"); these do not cure diarrhoea, they only delay its symptoms for a period. Such pills should only really be taken if a long journey is unavoidable. Thus the linchpins of treatment for diarrhoea are rest, fluid and salt replacement, antibiotics such as Ciprofloxacin for the bacterial types and special diagnostic tests and medical treatment for the amoeba and giardia infections. Salmonella infections and cholera, although rare, can be devastating diseases and it would be wise to get to a hospital as soon as possible if these were suspected. Fasting, peculiar diets and the consumption of large quantities of yoghurt have not been found useful in calming travellers' diarrhoea or in rehabilitating inflamed bowels. Oral rehydration has, on the other hand, especially in children, been a life saving technique and should always be practised, whatever other treatment you use. As there is some evidence that alcohol and milk might prolong diarrhoea they should be avoided during and immediately after an attack. If it continues day after day seek medical advice.

Constipation is also common, probably induced by dietary change, inadequate fluid intake in hot places and long bus journeys. Simple laxatives are useful in the short-term and bulky foods such as maize, beans and plenty of fruit are also useful.

Travelling to high altitudes can cause medical problems, all of which can be prevented if care is taken. In Chile, these problems are mainly encountered when visiting the Parque Nacional Lauca in the far north, especially on day trips from Arica. **High altitude**

On reaching heights above about 3,000 m, heart pounding and shortness of breath, especially on exertion are a normal response to the lack of oxygen in the air. A condition called acute mountain sickness (*soroche* in South America) can also affect visitors. It is more likely to affect those who ascend rapidly, eg by plane, and those who over-exert themselves. *Soroche* takes a few hours or days to come on and presents itself with a bad headache, extreme tiredness, sometimes dizziness, loss of appetite and frequently nausea and vomiting. Insomnia is common and is often associated with a suffocating feeling when lying in bed. Keen observers may note their breathing tends to wax and wane at night and their face tends to be puffy in the mornings. Anyone can get this condition and past experience is not always a good guide.

The treatment of acute mountain sickness is simple – rest, painkillers, (preferably not aspirin based) for the headache and anti-sickness pills for vomiting. Oxygen is actually not much help, except at very high altitude. Various local panaceas – Coramina glucosada, Effortil, Micoren are popular and *mate de coca* (an infusion of coca leaves widely available and perfectly legal) will alleviate some of the symptoms.

To prevent the condition: on arrival at places over 3,000 m have a few hours rest in a chair and avoid alcohol, cigarettes and heavy food. If the symptoms are severe and prolonged, it is best to descend to a lower altitude and to re-ascend slowly or in stages. If this is impossible because of shortage of time or if you are going so high that acute mountain sickness is very likely, then the drug Acetazolamide (Diamox) can be used as a preventative and continued during the ascent. There is good evidence of the value of this drug in the prevention of *soroche*, but some people do experience peculiar side effects. The usual dose is 500 mg of the slow release preparation each night, starting the night before ascending above 3,000 m.

The air is also excessively dry at high altitude and you might find that your skin dries out and the inside of your nose becomes crusted. Use a moisturiser for the skin and some vaseline wiped into the nostrils. Some people find contact lenses irritate because of the dry air. It is unwise to ascend to high altitude if you are pregnant, especially in the first three months, or if you have a history of heart, lung or blood disease, including sickle cell.

A more unusual condition can affect mountaineers who ascend rapidly to high altitude – acute pulmonary oedema. Residents at altitude sometimes experience this

Essentials

Essentials

when returning to the mountains from time spent at the coast. This condition is often preceded by acute mountain sickness and comes on quite rapidly with severe breathlessness, noisy breathing, cough, blueness of the lips and frothing at the mouth. Anybody who develops this must be brought down as soon as possible, given oxygen and taken to hospital.

A rapid descent from high places will make sinus problems and middle ear infections worse and might make your teeth ache. Lastly, don't fly to altitude within 24 hours of scuba diving. You might suffer from 'the bends'.

Heat & cold The north of Chile is extremely hot and dry. Full acclimatization to high temperatures takes about two weeks. During this period it is normal to feel a bit apathetic, especially if the relative humidity is high. Drink plenty of water, use salt on your food and avoid extreme exertion. Tepid showers are more cooling than hot or cold ones.

The burning power of the sun, especially at high altitude, is phenomenal. Always wear a wide-brimmed hat and use some form of suncream lotion on untanned skin. You need suntan lotions designed specifically for the tropics or for mountaineers or skiers, with protection factors of 15 and upwards. Glare from the sun can cause conjunctivitis, so wear sunglasses – especially on beaches, where high protection factor sunscreen should also be used.

Remember that, especially at high altitude, there can be a large and sudden drop in temperature between sun and shade and between night and day, so dress accordingly. Warm jackets or woollens are essential after dark at high altitude. Loose cotton is still the best material when the weather is hot. It can also be extremely cold and wet the further south you go, so take appropriate clothing. In the south and at high altitude the ultra-violet rays of the sun are particularly strong, so do not forget your hat and sun protection cream; take these with you even if the day is overcast – a sudden clear spell of two hours may be enough to burn you severely.

Insects These are mostly a nuisance rather than a serious hazard and, if you try, you can prevent yourself entirely from being bitten. Sleep off the ground and use a mosquito net or some kind of insecticide.

You can also use insect repellents, most of which are effective against a wide range of pests. The most common and effective is diethyl metatoluamide (DEET). DEET liquid is best for arms and face (care around eyes and with spectacles – DEET dissolves plastic). Aerosol spray is good for clothes and ankles and liquid DEET can be dissolved in water and impregnated into clothes and mosquito nets. Some repellents now contain DEET and Permethrin insecticide. Impregnated wrist and ankle bands can also be useful. Although mosquitoes are not usually a problem, and there is no malaria in Chile, travellers to rural areas of the north should use repellents to protect themselves against the *vinchuca* bug (see below).

If you are bitten or stung, itching may be relieved by cool baths, antihistamine tablets (care with alcohol or driving) or mild corticosteroid creams, eg hydrocortisone (great care: never use if any hint of infection). Careful scratching of all your bites once a day can be surprisingly effective (but do not do this if *vinchucas* are suspected). Calamine lotion and cream have limited effectiveness and antihistamine creams are not recommended – they can cause allergies themselves.

Bites which become infected should be treated with a local antiseptic or antibiotic cream such as Cetrimide, as should any infected sores or scratches.

Hanta virus This virus, transmitted by mice, produces haemorrhaging and lung problems: some estimate that 50% of those infected in the Americas have died as a result. There is no vaccine; the faster that medical attention is obtained, the more likely that recovery will occur. The virus is contracted either by breathing air contaminated by the excrement, urine or saliva of infected field mice or by eating food contaminated in this way. It can also be contracted by handling infected field mice or as a result of a bite. Early symptoms are similar to those of 'flu: fever, headache, aching limbs, vomiting. These are followed by high temperature and difficulty in breathing. Guidelines issued by the Chilean Ministry of Health advise people on measures to avoid attracting mice into their homes, for example by storing food in sealed containers and by disposing of rubbish properly. The virus is not resistant to the heat of the sun, detergents or disinfectants. While the risk to most travellers is minimal, you should avoid staying in accommodation which is dirty or using dirty and badly maintained campsites. If camping, you should use a tent with a proper floor. Although most of the cases in Chile have occurred in the Lake District, the virus has now spread northwards well into the central valley, so travellers should be cautious anywhere south of Santiago.

A very common intensely itchy rash, prickly heat is avoided by frequent washing and by wearing loose clothing. It is cured by allowing skin to dry off through use of powder and spending two nights in an air-conditioned hotel!   **Prickly heat**

Other risks and more serious diseases

Rabies is fatal once the first symptoms have emerged. It is endemic throughout Latin America, so avoid dogs that are behaving strangely and cover your toes at night from the vampire bats, which also carry the disease. If you are bitten by a domestic or wild animal, do not leave things to chance: scrub the wound with soap and water and/or disinfectant, try to have the animal captured (within limits) or at least determine its ownership, where possible, and seek medical assistance at once. The course of treatment depends on whether you have already been satisfactorily vaccinated against rabies – seek medical advice before buying a vaccine. If you have been vaccinated, then some further doses of vaccine are all that is required. Human diploid vaccine is the best, but expensive: other, older kinds of vaccine, such as that derived from duck embryos may be the only types available. These are effective, much cheaper and interchangeable generally with the human derived types. If not already vaccinated then anti-rabies serum (immunoglobulin) may be required in addition. It is important to finish the course of treatment whether the animal survives or not.   **Rabies**

AIDS (locally *SIDA*) is increasing but is not wholly confined to the well known high risk sections of the population, ie homosexual men, intravenous drug abusers and children of infected mothers. Heterosexual transmission is now the dominant mode and so the main risk to travellers is from casual sex. The same precautions should be taken as with any sexually transmitted disease. The AIDS virus (HIV) can be passed by unsterilized needles which have been previously used to inject an HIV positive patient; check that needles have been properly sterilized or disposable needles have been used. If you wish to take your own disposable needles, be prepared to explain what they are for. The risk of receiving a blood transfusion with blood infected with the HIV virus is greater than from dirty needles because of the amount of fluid exchanged. Supplies of blood for transfusion should now be screened for HIV in all reputable hospitals, so again the risk is very small indeed. If you feel you have been put at risk, the only way to be sure is to have a blood test for HIV antibodies on your return to a place where there are reliable laboratory facilities. Test results only become positive some three months after the virus has been contracted.   **AIDS**

The main symptoms are pains in the stomach, lack of appetite, lassitude and yellowness of the eyes and skin. Medically speaking there are two main types. The less serious, but more common is Hepatitis A for which the best protection is the careful preparation of food, the avoidance of contaminated drinking water and scrupulous attention to toilet hygiene. The other, more serious, version is Hepatitis B which is acquired usually as a   **Hepatitis**
You should have a shot before leaving and have it repeated every six months

Essentials

sexually transmitted disease or by blood transfusions. It can less commonly be transmitted by injections with unclean needles and possibly by insect bites. The symptoms are the same as for Hepatitis A. The incubation period is much longer (up to six months compared with six weeks) and there are more likely to be complications.

Animal bites
It is best to rely on local practice in these cases, because the particular creatures will be known about and appropriate treatment can be given

Chile is said to be one of the few countries in the world with no poisonous snakes. Spiders (including black widows) and scorpions pose more of a threat. If you are unlucky (or careless) enough to be bitten by a venomous snake, spider, scorpion or sea creature, try to identify the creature, but do not put yourself in further danger. Snake bites in particular are very frightening, but in fact rarely poisonous – even venomous snakes bite without injecting venom. What you might expect if bitten by a poisonous creature are: fright, swelling, pain and bruising around the bite and soreness of the regional lymph glands, perhaps nausea, vomiting and a fever. Signs of serious poisoning would be the following symptoms: numbness and tingling of the face, muscular spasms, convulsions, shortness of breath and bleeding. Victims should be got to a hospital or a doctor without delay. Commercial snake bite and scorpion kits are available, but usually only useful for the specific type of snake or scorpion for which they are designed. Most serum has to be given intravenously so it is not much good equipping yourself with it unless you are used to making injections into veins.

When treating a snake, spider or scorpion bite reassure and comfort the victim frequently. Immobilize the limb with a bandage or a splint or by getting the person to lie still. Do not slash the bite area and try to suck out the poison because this sort of heroism does more harm than good. It is now possible to buy a pump-suction kit (such as Aspivenin) which, if used immediately, can remove as much as 50% of the injected venom. If you know how to use a tourniquet in these circumstances, you will not need advice; if you are not experienced, do not apply a tourniquet.

Chagas' Disease (South American Trypanosomiasis)

This is a chronic disease, very rarely caught by travellers and difficult to treat. It is transmitted by the simultaneous biting and excreting of the Reduvid bug (known as the *vinchuca* in Chile); when a person scratches the bite, the disease enters the bloodstream. Somewhat resembling a small cockroach, the *vinchuca* lives in poor adobe houses with dirt floors often frequented by opossums. If you cannot avoid such accommodation, sleep off the floor with a candle lit, use a mosquito net, keep as much of your skin covered as possible and use DEET repellent or a spray insecticide. If you are bitten overnight (the bites are painless) do not scratch them – it is this which spreads the disease – but wash thoroughly with soap and water. Travellers to rural areas of northern Chile should note that *vinchucas* are prevalent in some areas – seek local advice.

On your return

If you have had attacks of diarrhoea it is worth having a stool specimen tested in case you have picked up amoebas. If you have been living rough, blood tests may be worthwhile to detect worms and other parasites. Report any untoward symptoms to your doctor and tell the doctor exactly where you have been and, if you know, which diseases you may have been exposed to.

The above information has been compiled for us by Dr David Snashall, who is presently Senior Lecturer in Occupational Health at the United Medical Schools of Guy's and St Thomas' Hospitals in London and Chief Medical Adviser to the British Foreign and Commonwealth Office. He has travelled extensively in Central and South America, worked in Peru and in East Africa and keeps in close touch with developments in preventative and tropical medicine.

Further reading

Chatwin, Bruce, *In Patagonia* (1977), Pan. A modern classic for those visiting the far south, although concentrates mainly on Argentina. **Darwin, Charles**, *The Voyage of the Beagle* (1989), Penguin. Still fascinating reading of the great naturalist's voyage and adventures from Cape Horn to Copiapó in the 1830s. **Giménez Hutton, Adrian**, *La Patagonia de Chatwin* (1999), Editorial Sudamericana. Interesting Argentine perspective on Chatwin and Patagonia (both Argentine and Chilean). **Green, Toby**, *Saddled with Darwin* (2000), Phoenix House. The author of this book retraces Darwin's route in South America on horseback. **Keenan, Brian and McCarthy, John**, *Between Extremes*, (2000), Black Swan. The two friends from Lebanon travel together again, this time through Chile. **Lucas Bridges, E**, *Uttermost Part of the Earth* (1948), Hodder & Stoughton. Brilliant and beautiful account of his adventurous life in Tierra del Fuego with the Yámana and Ona peoples; the classic text on Tierra del Fuego. **Pilkington, John**, *An Englishman In Patagonia* (1991), Century. Heavily critical of Chatwin. **Souhami, Diana**, *Selkirk's Island* (2001), Weidenfeld & Nicolson. The extraordinary story of Alexander Selkirk and his island, inspirations for Robinson Crusoe and for the community of San Juan Bautista on modern-day Isla Robinson Crusoe. **Swale, Rosie**, *Back to Cape Horn* (1988), Fontana. Swale tells of her epic journey from Antofagasta to Cape Horn on horseback. **Wheeler, Sara**, *Travels in a Thin Country* (1994), Little, Brown & Co. Lively account of the author's six-month stay in Chile.

Chilean fiction is examined in more detail in the Background section. A selection of those in English translation includes the following: **Allende, Isabel**, The doyenne of modern Chilean letters. Her books include: *The House of the Spirits* (1994), Black Swan.

SADDLED
WITH
Darwin
by
TOBY
GREEN

A journey
through South
America on
horseback

"Funny, erudite,
charming"
Eric Newby

7.99 Paperback

WEIDENFELD
& NICOLSON

Brilliant, evocative, allegorical magical-realist account taking the reader through 20th century Chilean history. *Of Love and Shadows* (1988), Black Swan. Painful story about a journalist uncovering evidence of military atrocities under the military regime. *Paula* (1996), Flamingo. A beautiful "letter" written from Allende to her daughter, who is stuck in a coma after a car accident, taking in the modern history of Chile and Allende's emotional roots. **Donoso, José**, *The Garden Next Door*, (1994), Grove Press. Evocative novel which deals with the ageing process of a couple in Spain. *The Obscene Bird of the Night* (1995), Grove Press. Donoso's most famous, experimental novel, which gained him international acclaim across Latin America. **Dorfman, Ariel**, *Death and the Maiden* (1996), Nick Hern Books. Subtle, moving tale of torture and resistance, an allegory for the state of Chile. *The Nanny and the Iceberg* (1999), Sceptre. Cross-cultural story of Chile and North America told with Dorfman's usual eloquence. **Skármeta, Antonio**, *Il Postino, the postman* (1996), Bloomsbury.

Travelogues

Fiction

Beautiful novel about the relationship between Neruda and his postman while the poet is in exile in Italy, made into a famous film. *Watch Where the Wolf is Going* (1991), Readers' International. Another novel in Skármeta's trademark style of eloquence and emotional honesty.

Adventure sports

Mantellero, Alberto, *Una Aventura Navegando Los Canales del Sur de Chile*, a guide to sailing the southern coast, with maps. **Biggar, John**, *The High Andes*, (1996), Castle Douglas, Kirkudbrightshire. Andes contains three chapters with information on Chilean peaks. **CONAF**, *Guía de Parques Nacionales y Otras Areas Silvestres Protegidas de Chile*, US$12, a very useful guide to the main parks containing information on access, camping sites, flora and fauna. They also publish *Chile Forestal*, a monthly magazine with articles on the parks and ecological issues. **Fagerstrom, René Peri**, *Cuentos de la Carretera Austral*, on the Camino Austral. *Regata*, a monthly sailing magazine. Climbers will find *Cumbres de Chile*, two books with accompanying tapes, each covering 20 peaks, of interest.

Specialist & academic texts

Almarza V, Claudio, *Patagonia* (Punta Arenas: GeoPatagonia). A book of photographs, with text, on the region. **Cárdenas Saldivia, Umiliana**, *Casos de Brujos de Chiloé* (1989), Editorial Universitaria. Fascinating tales of witchcraft on Chiloé. **Clissold, Stephen**, *Chilean Scrapbook* (1952), The Cresset Press. Gives an evocative historical picture of Chile, region by region. **Collier, S, and Sater, WF**, *A History of Chile 1808-1994* (1996), Cambridge University Press. Examination of Chile's recent history. **Coña, Pascal**, *Memorias de un Cacique Mapuche* (1930), publisher unmarked. An account of Mapuche traditions and history by a Mapuche chief in his 70s. **Constable, Pamela, and Valenzuela, Arturo**, *Chile: A Nation of Enemies* (1991), Norton. Excellent on the Pinochet years. **Montecino, Sonia**, *Historias de Vida de Mujeres Mapuches* (1985), Centro de Estudios de la Mujer. Interviews with Mapuche women giving a real insight into their lives. **O'Shaughnessy, Hugh**, *Pinochet: The Politics of Torture* (2000), Latin American Bureau. Informed and up-to-date analysis of the whole Pinochet affair. **Read, Jan**, *The Wines of Chile* (1994), Mitchell Beazley. A gazetteer of the vineyards and wineries of Chile, ideal for the discerning specialist. **Spooner, MH**, *Soldiers In A Narrow Land* (1994), University of California Press. A readable account of the Pinochet dictatorship by a North American journalist resident in the country at the time. **Wearne, Philip**, *Return of the Indian*: Conquest and Revival in the Americas (1996), Cassell/Latin America Bureau. Information on the Mapuches within the entire Amerindian context. *The South American Explorer*, the journal of the *South American Explorers Club*, regularly publishes articles on Chile (126 Indian Creek Road, Ithaca, New York 14850, USA). Issues 22 (August 1989) and 31 (May 1992) both had features on Easter Island. Other titles on Easter Island will be found in that chapter.

Maps & guidebooks

The *Turistel* guides are very useful for roads and town plans, but not all distances are exact. It is published annually in three parts, *Norte*, *Centro*, and *Sur*, (in Spanish only) as well as a separate volume listing campsites. It contains a wealth of maps covering the whole country and neighbouring tourist centres in Argentina. It is well worth getting, particularly for those with their own transport. Each volume costs around US$10, but buying the whole set is better value; they are available from bookshops and from newspaper kiosks in the centre of Santiago. The publisher is Turiscom, Av Santa Maria 0120, Providencia, Santiago, T3658800, F3658801, turiscom@chilesat.net Sernatur publishes a *Guía Turística*/Tourist Guide in Spanish and English, good maps, useful text, free.

A good map of Santiago is the *Plano de Santiago*, published annually by Publiguías, Av Santa María 0792, Providencia, Santiago; this contains sectional maps of the city and a street index. Publiguías also publish a *Guía Comercial y Profesional de Providencia*. A series of maps of the major tourist areas is published by Mapas JLM, Gral del Canto 105 T/F2364808; these are sold at newpaper kiosks and elsewhere. Geophysical and topographical maps (US$11) are available from Instituto Geográfico Militar, at the main office Dieciocho 369, T6987278, open 0900-1800 Monday-Friday (0800–1400 January/February). The Instituto Geográfico has published a *Guía Caminera*, with roads and city plans (available only at IGM offices, not 100% accurate). The Biblioteca Nacional, Moneda 650, has an excellent collection of IGM maps, sections of which can be photocopied, particularly useful for climbing. CONAF publishes a series of illustrated booklets in Spanish/English on Chilean trees, shrubs and flowers, recommended, as well as *Juventud, Turismo y Naturaleza*, which lists national parks, their facilities and the flora and fauna of each. Bird-lovers will appreciate *Guía de Campo de Las Aves de Chile*, by B Araya and G Millie. A recommended series of general maps are published by *International Travel Maps* (ITM), 345 West Broadway, Vancouver, V5Y 1P8, Canada, T604-8793621, compiled with historical notes, by the late Kevin Healey.

Film

Without doubt, Ricardo Larrain's *La Frontera* (1991) is one of the best Chilean films ever made. The film, about an internal exile sent to the south of Chile during the Pinochet years is wonderfully humane and evocative, capturing the character of Chile and the troubled times it lived through in the 1970s and 1980s. Gustavo Graef Marino's *Johnny Cien Pesos* (1993) is another internationally successful film, using a bank robbery to make wider points about Chilean society. Aldo Francia's *Valparaíso Mi Amor* (1969) is an older film which masterfully evokes the intriguing atmosphere of Valparaíso. The film *Missing* was made by Costa-Guaras from a book by Thomas Hauser. A dramatic, harrowing portrait of the chaos following the coup in 1973, the story of two American journalists who disappeared at that time. See also the section on film on page 544.

Essentials

The Santiago Region

3

The Santiago Region

If you are flying into Chile, you will probably arrive in Santiago. No one can deny that the Chilean capital has a dramatic setting, with peaks over 5000 m high visible on clear days. They are most dramatic just after rainfall in winter, when the smog clears and the new snows glisten. With its many parks, interesting museums, glittering high-rises and boutiques, Santiago bursts with possibilities.

As far as entertainment goes, there are popular scenes in everything from techno to progressive rock, via bohemian hang-outs and most of the bits in between. Certainly, those who spend an extended period of time in Santiago soon find plenty of things to do at night and in the weekends.

The region near the capital is in many ways a microcosm of the country as a whole. Not only are the resorts on the coast less than two hours away, but the city is within easy reach of the best ski resorts in South America, which are also great spots for weekend hikes in summer. Meanwhile, the area south of Santiago is perhaps the best wine-producing area in Chile, and autumn, when the grapes are being harvested, is a particularly good time to visit the vineyards.

Background

Geography This region can be divided into three: to the east are the peaks of the Andes; to the west is the coastal range; and between is the Central Valley, much of which is between 600 and 1,000 m above sea level. On the eastern edge of the Central Valley lies Santiago, its more affluent suburbs spreading east into the foothills of the Andes.

Some of the highest peaks in the Andes lie in this region; just over the border in Argentina, Aconcagua is the highest mountain in the world outside Asia, rising to 6,964 m. There is a mantle of snow on all the high mountains, beginning at around 4,000 m, while the lower slopes are covered with dense forests. Between the forest and the snowline there are pastures; during the summer, cattle are driven up to these pastures to graze. The coastal range is lower here than in the northern desert but still reaches over 2,000 m in places.

Three river systems flow west from the Andes across the Central Valley, cutting their way through the Coastal Range through narrow gorges. In the north the Río Aconcagua – which rises in Argentina – flows into the sea north of Valparaíso. Further south, the Río Maipo flows south of Santiago, reaching the Pacific near San Antonio; its most important tributary is the Río Mapocho, the river on which Santiago is situated.

The population density of the area around Santiago is over 300 per sq km, though it is much lower in the valleys around Los Andes.

Santiago

Phone code: 02
Colour map 3, grid B3
Population: 5 mn
Altitude: 600 m

Attractively situated in the Central Valley, Santiago has grown to become the fifth largest city in South America, as well as the political, economic and cultural capital of Chile. The city is crossed from east to west by the long-suffering Río Mapocho, into which most of the city's sewage is dumped; the magnificent chain of the Andes provides a more appropriate natural landmark, and one that is impossible to miss.

It is easy to see Santiago as just another westernised Latin American city, but, away from the centre and wealthier suburbs, the reality is more complicated. Street vendors are often newly arrived from rural areas, many living in appalling villas misérias on the city's outskirts (Pudahuel, in the west, is an especially chastening barrio for those who claim that "poverty does not exist in Chile"). Some barrios in the south of the city even have a higher concentration of Mapuche people than the Mapuche heartlands of the south.

If just passing through, Santiago is unlikely to be the highlight of your trip to Chile – it can take a while to get a real feeling for the city's pulse. However it does still warrant a visit of a few days. On top of its setting and nightlife, there are excellent museums, and the contrast with the rest of the country is stark; over a third of Chileans live in Gran Santiago, so, if you want to understand the country you are visiting, Santiago is a must.

Ins and outs

Getting there
See page 110 for further details
International and domestic flights arrive at the Aeropuerto Arturo Merino Benitez at Pudahuel, 26 km northwest of the city centre. If you are arriving by bus there are 4 bus terminals, all located close to each other, just west of the city centre and not far from

the train station. The train station and bus terminals are all situated along the Av O'Higgins, the main east-west avenue through the city and within easy reach of Line 1 of the city metro.

Note that the city's main avenue, Av O'Higgins, is almost always referred to as the Alameda and that Plaza Baquedano, one of the city's main squares, is almost always known as Plaza Italia (in both instances, this book follows suit). Most of the more expensive accommodation is situated in the city centre or further east in the neighbourhoods of Providencia and Las Condes. Most budget accommodation is located in the city centre or further west in the vicinity of the bus terminals. Although parts of the centre can be conveniently explored on foot, you will need to master the city's transport system, which is, on the whole, well organised, even if crowded and slow in peak periods. Good city maps available from CTC phone company offices.

Getting around *See page 111 for a map of the Santiago metro*

Servicio Nacional de Turismo (Sernatur – the national tourist board), Av Providencia 1550 (Casilla 14082), T2361416, TxSERNA CL 240137. Between metros Manuel Montt and Pedro de Valdivia, next to Providencia Municipal Library. Open Mon-Fri 0845-1900, Sat 0900-1800, Sun 1000-1500. English and German spoken. Maps (road map US$1.50), many brochures and posters are available. Good notice board. Kiosk on Ahumada near Agustinas (erratic opening times). Information office also at the airport, open 0900-2100 daily. **Municipal Tourist Board**, Casa Colorada, Merced 860, T336700, offers walking tours of the city, Wed 1500, or from kiosk on Paseo Ahumada, good free booklet on historical buildings of the city available in English and Spanish, *Historical Heritage of Santiago: A Guide for Tourists*. Many tourist offices outside Santiago are

Tourist offices *See also page 71 for more information on maps and guide books*

The Santiago Region

Santiago orientation

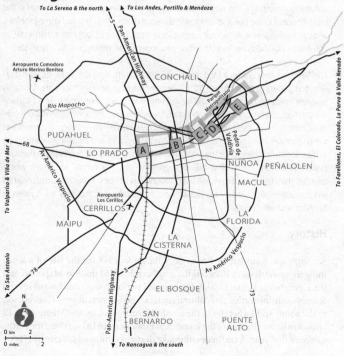

To La Serena & the north ↗   ↖ To Los Andes, Portillo & Mendoza

Aeropuerto Comodoro
Arturo Merino Benitez

CONCHALÍ

Río Mapocho

Parque
Metropolitano

PUDAHUEL

68

LO PRADO

Pedro de
Valdivia

NUÑOA   PEÑALOLEN

MACUL

Aeropuerto
Los Cerillos

CERRILLOS

MAIPU

LA
FLORIDA

LA
CISTERNA

EL BOSQUE

SAN
BERNARDO

PUENTE
ALTO

To Valparaíso & Viña del Mar ←

To San Antonio ↙   78

Av América Vespucio

Pan-American Highway

5

Av América Vespucio

73

To Farellones, El Colorado, La Parva & Valle Nevado →

N

0 km   2
0 miles   2

↓ To Rancagua & the south

The Santiago Region

 Arriving at night

Santiago's airport is perfectly safe if you arrive in the early hours, but you will not find any public transport to/from the city at this time. There will, however, be taxis, which you could use, although you could also arrange a radio taxi in advance (see page 112 for

address). There are official airport taxis, which are probably safest if arriving late. All reputable hotels have someone on duty all night – book ahead, and let them know that you are arriving late (they may also help you fix up a radio taxi).

closed in winter, so stock up on information here. Excellent road maps (US$2.50) and information may be obtained from the *Automóvil Club de Chile*, Vitacura 8620, T2125702, F2295295 (Metro Pedro de Valdivia then bus to Vitacura, or a US$6 taxi ride from the centre), which also gives discounts to members of affiliated motoring organizations; open Mon-Fri 0845-1815, Sat 0900-1300, very helpful. **CONAF** (Corporación Nacional Forestal), Presidente Bulnes 291, piso 1, T3900126, publishes a number of leaflets and has documents and maps about the national park system that can be consulted or photocopied (not very useful for walking). **CODEFF** (Comité Nacional Pro-Defensa de la Fauna y Flora), Bilbao 691, Providencia, T2510262, can also provide information on environmental questions.

Security Like all large cities, Santiago has problems of theft. However, it has to be said that these tend to be exaggerated by Santiaguinos. While the central area is frequented by pickpockets and bagsnatchers (who are often well-dressed) – operating mostly on the Metro, around the Plaza de Armas, near Cerro Santa Lucía and around the restaurants in Bellavista – these are easily avoided with a little common sense, and the biggest risk is in unwittingly entering a dangerous *barrio* away from the centre. Parts of Pudahuel in the west, Conchalí in the north, and Macul in the south have a big drug and crime problem, and can be dangerous. At night, it is best to take a public bus (*micro*) rather than a taxi, as you will be watched over by your fellow passengers; alternatively, call for a radio taxi.

Climate The Santiago area enjoys a Mediterranean climate, with long dry summers and daytime temperatures rising to over 30°C, when the heat can be uncomfortable. Rainfall is heaviest in autumn and winter, and almost unknown in summer: long spells of rain are uncommon, storms being heavy and brief. Snowfall is rare, though frost is not uncommon; note, though, that houses in Santiago rarely have central heating, so you will feel the cold more in winter. There is usually less wind in spring and autumn, making smog a more serious problem over the city (forecast levels of smog are published in the daily papers). Pollution levels vary; the west and the old 'city centre' are much worse affected than the more expensive areas around Las Condes. Pollution is usually at its worst in Jul, exacerbated by the lack of wind, and by the wet and cold. It is lightest in Sep/Oct, and after rainfall.

History

Santiago was founded by Pedro de Valdivia in 1541 on the site of a small indigenous settlement between the southern bank of the Río Mapocho and the Cerro Santa Lucía. During the colonial period it was only one of several Spanish administrative and cultural centres; also important were Concepción to the south and La Serena in the north. Nevertheless, by 1647 there were 12 churches in the city, but of these only San Francisco (1618) survived the earthquake of that year. A further earthquake destroyed most of the city in 1730.

Smog

While Santiago's smog is not too bad in spring, summer and autumn, those who arrive here during winter are often in for an unpleasant shock. Once on Chilean soil, it does not take more than half an hour for your throat to begin to choke and your eyes to begin to water with what is one of Santiago's biggest problems – smog. In 2001, Santiago was rated the eighth most polluted city in the world. Of course, when Pedro de Valdivia founded the city in 1541, between the coastal mountains and the Andes, it must have seemed like a perfect site; he could never have imagined that the city would one day engulf the valley, and that the mountains would become a serious problem.

The principal reason for Santiago's high levels of pollution is that it lies in a bowl, encircled by mountains, meaning that the pollution is trapped. This, combined with the centralisation of Chilean industry in Santiago, the fact that many buses are not equipped with catalytic converters, and the teeming cars which choke the city's highways, all conspire to create a problem that cannot easily be resolved. But it is a serious issue – asthma rates are high, and occasionally some older people die during the winter emergencias, when things get very bad.

Over the years, all sorts of solutions have been proposed. A team of Japanese scientists once even suggested blowing up the part of the Andes nearest the city, so that the pollution could also be blown away. Each day, cars whose number plates end in one of two digits are prohibited from circulating. But the fact remains that until the Chilean government finds a process by which population and industry can be dispersed more widely throughout the country, the problem is likely to remain.

Following independence the city became more important. In the 1870s, under the *Intendente* Benjamín Vicuña MacKenna, an urban plan was drafted, the Cerro Santa Lucía was made into a public park and the first trams were introduced. As the city grew at the end of the 19th century, the Chilean élite, wealthy from mining and shipping, built their mansions west of the centre around Calle Dieciocho. One of these families were the Cousiños (see box, page 90), who built the Palacio Cousiño and later donated this and what became the Parque O'Higgins to the city. Expansion east towards Providencia began in 1895. Until the 1930s, much of the city centre had colonial buildings in the style of Quito or Lima, but expansion and modernisation meant that these were gradually replaced. In the latter part of the 20th century, like most Latin American capital cities, Santiago spread rapidly – especially so since the 1950s. Many older Santiaguinos who live in areas that are now relatively central tell how, when they first arrived in the city, they lived right on the outskirts. In general, the more affluent moved east into new neighbourhoods in the foothills of the Andes, and poorer neighbourhoods were established to the west of the centre.

Sights

The centre of the old city lies between the Río Mapocho and the Alameda. From the **Plaza Italia** in the east of the city's central area, the Mapocho flows to the northwest and the Alameda runs to the southwest. From Plaza Italia, Calle Merced runs due west to the **Plaza de Armas**, the heart of the city which lies five blocks south of the Mapocho.

The Santiago Region

Around the Plaza de Armas The shadiness and tranquillity of the Plaza de Armas has been disturbed by a recent remodelling of the square. Some of the taller trees were stripped away to make way for new stonework, but most Santiaguinos are unhappy with the barer plaza that has resulted. On the eastern and southern sides of the Plaza de Armas there are arcades with shops; on the northern side is the post office and the Municipalidad; and on the western side the cathedral and the archbishop's palace. The **cathedral**, much rebuilt, contains a recumbent statue in wood of San Francisco Javier, and the chandelier which lit the first meetings of Congress after independence; it also houses an interesting museum of religious art and historical pieces (see below). In the **Palacio de la Real Audiencia**, on the northern side is the Museo Histórico Nacional (see below). A block west of the cathedral is the **former Congress** building now occupied by the Ministry of Foreign Affairs (the new Congress building is in Valparaíso). Nearby are the law courts. At Merced 864, a few metres east of the Plaza de Armas, is the **Casa Colorada**, built in 1769, the home of the Governor in colonial days and then of Mateo de Toro, first President of Chile. It is now the Museum of the History of Santiago. From the Plaza de Armas, **Paseo Ahumada** runs south to the Alameda, four blocks away. Ahumada is a pedestrianised street, and is the commercial heart of the centre. This is always an interesting place to come for a stroll, especially at night, when those selling pirated CDs or playing the three-card trick mix with evangelist preachers and satanists. One block south of the Plaza de Armas, Ahumada crosses **Calle Huérfanos**, which is also pedestrianized and presents a similar spectacle.

Four blocks north of the Plaza de Armas is the interesting **Mercado Central**, at 21 de Mayo y San Pablo. The building faces the Parque Venezuela, on which is the Cal y Canto metro station, the northern terminus of Line 2, and, at its western end, the former **Mapocho Railway Station**, now a cultural centre; the Mercado is the best place to come in Santiago for seafood (see page 98). If you head east from Mapocho station, along the river, you pass through the Parque Forestal (see page 88), before coming back to Plaza Italia.

Along the Alameda The Alameda runs through the heart of the city for over 3 km. It is 100 m wide, choked full of *micros*, taxis and cars day and night, and ornamented with gardens and statuary: the most notable are the equestrian statues of generals O'Higgins and San Martín; the statue of the Chilean historian Benjamín Vicuña MacKenna who, as mayor of Santiago, beautified Cerro Santa Lucía (see page 87); and the great monument in honour of the battle of Concepción in 1879.

The eastern end of the Alameda is at Plaza Italia, where there is a statue of General Baquedano and the Tomb of the Unknown Soldier. From here the Alameda skirts, on the right, Cerro Santa Lucía, and on the left, the Catholic University. Beyond the hill the Alameda goes past the neo-classical **Biblioteca Nacional** on the right, which also contains the national archives. Beyond, on the left, between Calle San Francisco and Calle Londres, is the oldest church in Santiago: the red-walled church and monastery of **San Francisco** (1618). Inside is the small statue of the Virgin which Valdivia carried on his saddlebow when he rode from Perú to Chile. Near the church cloisters is the Museo de Arte Colonial. South of San Francisco is the Barrio París-Londres, built in 1923-29, now restored and pedestrianized. Two blocks north of the Alameda on Calle Agustinas is the **Teatro Municipal**. ■ *Guided tours Tue 1300 to 1500 and Sun 1100 to 1400 hours, US$3.* A little further west along the Alameda, is the **Universidad de Chile**; the **Club de la Unión**, an exclusive social club founded in 1864, is almost opposite (the current building dates

24 hours in the city

First, make sure it's a Saturday! Assuming you are staying in the centre, get up early and walk down to Calle San Diego for breakfast. After breakfast, walk on down San Diego to the Iglesia de los Sacrementinos – Santiago's answer to Sacré Coeur – and then west through gardens until you reach the Palacio Cousiño in time for the first tour at 0930. This extraordinary building (see box, page 90) gives a real insight into the lives, customs and belief systems of the Chilean aristocracy, and the opulence to which the upper classes became accustomed. Once the tour has finished stroll to Toesca metro and head a few stops south to Franklin on Line 2. Here you will find swarms of people all making their way to the Bío Bío market. This market will show you how most of Santiago lives, and the contrast with Palacio Cousiño gives a real insight into the contradictions within Chilean society.

When you start feeling hungry, head back to Franklin Metro and take the train north to the Terminus of Line 2 at Cal y Canto. On the opposite side of the Mapocho river is the central market, where you will find the best seafood restaurants in Santiago. The choice is so wide that it will probably be difficult to pick one out of the many, especially with half a dozen touts following you around, but don't be put off – take your time, make your own choice, and sit down and enjoy some of the best shellfish the world has to offer, washed down with a glass of sauvignon blanc.

After lunch, it's time to remind yourself that Santiago has one of the most dramatic settings of any of the world's major cities. Cross back over the Mapocho river, and stroll east towards the conical hill of Cerro San Cristóbal. If it's summer, the heat may be making you feel a little tired by now – if so, you could go up the hill on the funicular railway. If you are lucky, and it is a clear day, you will have an unforgettable view of the Andes, almost unimpeded by the smog which stifles the city below – this is most likely just after rainfall. Here you can stroll through lanes that are lined with trees and a world away from the clutter of the city. There are even swimming pools and wine tasting is possible. Towards dusk, have a drink in the café near the funicular railway station and watch the sun go down over the coastal mountain range, lighting up the snows of the Andes.

After dark, go back down the hill by funicular railway (it's not advisable to walk now). Now it's time to sample Santiago's nightlife. Return to the foot of Cerro San Cristóbal, where you will be in Barrio Bellavista. Here you can take your pick of any one of dozens of excellent (and expensive) restaurants, before going out to one of the area's buzzing salsotecas. These don't really get going until midnight, and you'll usually find that you don't leave much before 5.

Most people will probably head back to their hotel for some sleep after this. You can spend your Sunday a la Chilena – sleeping until the early afternoon, and then going for a stroll in one of the city's many parks, such as the Quinta Normal, along with everyone else.

from 1925) – here wonderful meals are served at exorbitant prices. Nearby, on Calle Nueva York, is the **Bolsa de Comercio** (public viewing of the trading is permitted; passport essential).

One block further west there are three plazas: the Plaza de la Libertad to the north of the Alameda, the Plaza Bulnes in the centre, and the Plaza del Libertador O'Higgins to the south. To the north of the Plaza de la Libertad, hemmed in by the skyscrapers of the Centro Cívico, is the **Palacio de la Moneda** (1805), the Presidential Palace containing historic relics, paintings and sculpture, and the elaborate Salón Rojo used for official receptions (guided visits only with written permission from the Dirección Administrativa – three weeks' notice required). Although the Moneda was damaged by air attacks during the military coup of 11 September 1973 it has been fully restored. In front of the Palace is the statue of former President Arturo Alessandri Palma. (Ceremonial changing of the guard every other day, 1000.) Four blocks south of the Plaza del Libertador O'Higgins is a park, Parque Almagro, notable for the **Iglesia de los Sacramentinos**, a gothic church loosely designed in imitation of Sacré Coeur in Paris, which is best viewed from near Palacio Cousiño against the backdrop of the cordillera.

The Alameda continues westwards across the Panamericana towards the impressive railway station (Estación Central or Estación Alameda), which is surrounded by several blocks of market stalls. On the northern side of the

Santiago centre

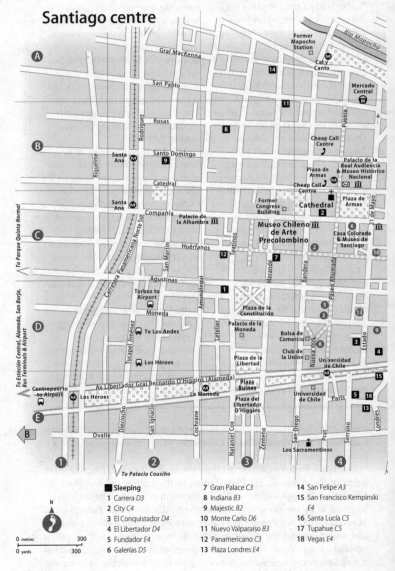

■ Sleeping	7 Gran Palace *C3*	14 San Felipe *A3*
1 Carrera *D3*	8 Indiana *B3*	15 San Francisco Kempinski
2 City *C4*	9 Majestic *B2*	*E4*
3 El Conquistador *D4*	10 Monte Carlo *D6*	16 Santa Lucía *C5*
4 El Libertador *D4*	11 Nuevo Valparaíso *B3*	17 Tupahue *C5*
5 Fundador *E4*	12 Panamericano *C3*	18 Vegas *E4*
6 Galerías *D5*	13 Plaza Londres *E4*	

0 metres 300
0 yards 300

Alameda is the Barrio Brasil (see below), a tranquil area in which many of the houses are brightly painted. Opposite Estacíon Central is the **Planetarium,** US$4.50. On Avenida Matucana, running north from here, is the very popular **Parque Quinta Normal** (see page 89). About six blocks west of the Estación Central are the major bus terminals.

This historic part of the city lies immediately to the west of the Panamericana, and was the first area to be colonised by Santiaguinos away from the centre, at the end of the 18th century. The area is rich in colonial architecture, and is also a centre for nightlife, with many underground bars, clubs and restaurants and

Barrio Brasil

Santiago's most radical shop, *La Lunita*, stocking feminist books and Santiago's only gay monthly, *Lambda News*.

The heart of the *barrio* is the **Plaza Brasil**, easily reached by walking straight up Calle Concha y Toro from Metro República. This is a narrow cobblestone street that passes elegant old stone homes in Rococo and German Gothic styles, and eventually reaches the plaza, shaded by palms, lime trees and silk cottons. Just west of the Plaza, on Compañia, is the **Basilica del Salvador**, a striking yellow and rose coloured church built between 1870 and 1872, with stained glass and a statue of the Virgen del Carmen – in 1981, a thief made off with the statue, but hastily returned it the next day after an earthquake rocked the city. A little further along Compañia is the **Iglesia Preciosa Sangre**, a bright red church of neo-classical design, with impressive reliefs and twin towers. You could then walk one block north to Catedral, where there are some fine old buildings with tall double windows, wooden balconies and stone pallisades.

Between the Parque Forestal, Plaza Baquedano and the Alameda is the **Lastarria** neighbourhood (Universidad Católica metro). For those interested in antique furniture, objéts d'art and old books, the area is worth a visit, especially the **Plaza Mulato Gil de Castro** (Calle Lastarria 305). Occasional shows are put on in the square, on which are the Museo Arqueológico de Santiago in a restored house, a bookshop (*Librería Latinoamericana*), handicraft and

Lastarria & Bellavista

● **Eating**
1 Acuario *E5*
2 Café Brasil *D5*
3 Café Caribe *D4*
4 Café Colonial *C4*
5 Café Haiti *D4*
6 Chez Henry *C4*
7 Da Carla *B5*
8 El 27 de Nueva York *D4*
9 El Naturista *D4*
10 El Vegetariano *C4*
11 Ikabaru *C4*
12 Lung Fung *D5*
13 Salon de Té Cousiño *D4*

The Santiago Region

antique shops, an art gallery, the Instituto de Arte Contemporáneo and the *Pergola de la Plaza* restaurant. Nearby, on Calle Lastarria, are the **Jardín Lastarria**, a cul-de-sac of craft and antique shops (No 293), *Gutenberg, Lafourcade y Cía*, an antiquarian bookseller (No 307), the Ciné Biógrafo (No 131) and, at the corner with Calle Merced, the Instituto Chileno-Francés (see page 116).

Santiago's bohemian face is most obvious in the **Bellavista** district, on the north bank of the Río Mapocho from Plaza Baquedano at the foot of **Cerro San Cristóbal** (see page 88). This is the main focus of nightlife in the old city, and the area around Pío Nono and López de Bello hums and buzzes, especially at weekends. In the bars you can see everything from live Cuban music to local imitations of Georges Brassens, while eating options ranging from Italian trattoria to sushi through to West African palm-nut stew. There are also theatres, entertainments, art galleries and craft shops specialising in lapis lazuli.

Providencia   East of Plaza Italia, the main east-west axis of the city becomes known as **Avenida Providencia**, which heads out towards the residential areas, including Las Condes, at the eastern and upper levels of the city. It passes through the neighbourhood of Providencia, the upmarket commercial centre of Santiago. This is a busy area of shops, offices and smart restaurants, mostly congregated around Pedro de Valdivia and Los Leones metro stations; the national offices

Bellavista

Sleeping	Eating	
1 Crowne Plaza	1 Casa en el Aire	6 El Otro Sitio
2 Hostal Del Parque	2 Cava de Dardignac	7 El Rincón Español
3 Monte Carlo	& Zen	8 Eladio
4 Posada del Salvador	3 Cipriani	9 Evelyn
5 Presidente	4 Dulcería Las Palmas	10 Gatopardo
6 Principado	5 El Antojo Gaugin	11 HBH Bar

of Sernatur, the national tourist board, are located here. Calle Suecia, near Los Leones, is the focal point for nightlife in this part of the city, with over a dozen 'pubs' offering European beers on tap, Tex-Mex food and live music.

At Metro Tobalaba, Avenida Providencia becomes **Avenida Apoquindo**, which carries on over Avenida Amérigo Vespuccio – Santiago's ring road – and out towards the exclusive neighbourhoods of Las Condes, Lo Curro and La Dehesa. Anyone who is anyone in Chilean society lives in this part of the city, and here you will find walled residential compounds, houses with servants and several brand new cars, and very expensive American-style shopping centres such as Parque Arauco or Alto Las Condes.

Las Condes

Parks and gardens

Situated in the *barrio* of La Recoleta, just north of the city centre, this cemetery contains the mausoleums of most of the great figures in Chilean history and the arts, including Violeta Parra, Victor Jara and Salvador Allende. There is also an impressive monument to the victims of the 1973-90 military government; their names, ages and dates of detention or disappearance are listed in two sections: those who disappeared and those executed for political reasons. The cemetery can be reached by any Recoleta bus from Calle Miraflores.

Cementerio General

12 Il Siciliano
13 La Bodega de Julio
14 La Divina Comida
15 Les Assasins
16 Libro Café
    Mediterraneo
17 Michelle's
18 San Fruttuoso
19 Venezia
20 Viejo Verde
╫╫╫╫ Funicular railway

Near the heart of the city, bounded by Calle Merced to the north, Avenida O'Higgins to the south, Calles Santa Lucía and Subercaseaux, is a cone of rock rising steeply to a height of 70 m called Cerro Santa Lucía. The Cerro can be scaled from the Caupolicán esplanade, on which, high on a rock, stands a statue of that Mapuche leader, but the ascent from the northern side of the hill – where there is an equestrian statue of Diego de Almagro – is easier. There are striking views of the city from the top, reached by a series of stairs, where there is a fortress, the Batería Hidalgo (the platform of which is its only colonial survival – the building is closed). The Cerro closes at 2100; visitors must sign a register at the entrance, giving their ID card number. It is best to descend the eastern side, to see the small Plaza Pedro Valdivia with its waterfalls and statue of Valdivia. The area is famous, at night, for its gay community and necking couples. Travellers should beware of thieves here, although with the new need to register ID cards security in the area has been tightened up.

Cerro Santa Lucía
On clear days you can see across to the Andes; even on smoggy days, the view of the sunset is good

The Santiago Region

Parque Balmaceda Also known as Parque Gran Bretaña, this lies east of Plaza Baquedano and is one of the more attractive parks in Santiago, with well laid-out gardens and fountains. The Museo Tajamares del Mapocho is here, see page 91.

Parque de la Paz This new peace park stands on the site of Villa Grimaldi, the most notorious torture centre during the Pinochet regime. The Irish missionary, Sheila Cassidy, has documented the abuses which she underwent when imprisoned without trial in this place. The walls are daubed with human rights' graffiti, and the park makes a moving and unusual introduction to the conflict which has eaten away at the heart of Chilean society for the past 30 years. ■ *Getting there: take a metro to Tobalaba, and then any bus marked Peñalolén heading south down Tobalaba. Get off at the junction of Tobalaba y José Arrieta, and then walk 5 mins up Arrieta towards the mountains.*

Parque Forestal This lies due north of Santa Lucía hill and immediately south of the Mapocho. Its layout is very attractive, but the proximity of many busy roads means that few people stroll here for long. The Museo Nacional de Bellas Artes is in the wooded grounds and is an extraordinary example of neo-classical architecture, details below.

Parque Metropolitano The sharp, conical hill of **San Cristóbal**, forming the Parque Metropolitano, to the northeast of the city, is the largest and most interesting of the city's parks and, on a clear day, provides excellent views over the city and across to the Andes. There are two sectors, sector Cumbre on Cerro San Cristóbal and, further east, sector Tupahue. There are two entrances: west from Pío Nono in Bellavista and east from Pedro de Valdivia Norte. ■ *Daily 0900-2100, vehicles, US$3.* When the weather is good, the walk up the access road from Bellavista is very pleasant, providing unexpected views of distant and little-visited northern parts of the city. On Cerro Cumbre (300 m) there is a colossal statue of the Virgin, which is floodlit at night; beside it is the astronomical observatory of the Catholic University which can be visited on application to the observatory's director. Near the Bellavista entrance is the **Jardín Zoológico**, which has a well-cared for collection of animals. ■ *Tue-Fri 1000-1300, 1500-1800, Sat, Sun and holidays 1000-1800, US$2.*

Further east in the Tupahue sector there are terraces, gardens, and paths; in one building there is a good, expensive restaurant (*Camino Real*, T2321758) with a splendid view from the terrace, especially at night, and an **Enoteca**, or exhibition of Chilean wines from a range of vineyards. You can taste one of the six 'wines of the day', US$1.50 per glass, and buy if you like, though prices are higher than in shops. Nearby is the Casa de la Cultura which has art exhibitions and free concerts at midday on Sunday. There are two good swimming pools: one at Tupahue (US$7); the other, Antilen (US$10) has a fine panoramic view over the city; it can be reached from the road that branches off north from below the Enoteca. East of Tupahue are the Botanical Gardens, with a collection of Chilean native plants, guided tours available. ■ *Daily 0900-1800.*

■ *Getting there: by funicular every few mins to Cerro San Cristóbal from Plaza Caupolicán at the northern end of Calle Pío Nono, 1000-2000 Mon-Fri, 1000-2000 Sat and Sun, US$1.50 return, US$1 one way. By teleférico from Estación Oasis, Av Pedro de Valdivia Norte via Tupahue to San Cristóbal near the funicular's upper station, 1430-1830 Mon, 1030-1830 Tue-Fri, 1030-1900 at weekends, US$3 combination ticket available with the funicular. An open bus operated by the teleférico company runs to San Cristóbal and Tupahue from the Bellavista entrance with the same schedule as the teleférico itself. The teleférico* *does not operate in winter; to reach Tupahue take the funicular or a taxi either from the Bellavista entrance (much cheaper from inside the park as taxis entering the park have to pay entrance fee), or from Metro Pedro de Valdivia. Alternatively you could walk from Metro Pedro de Valvivia, 1 km.*

This lies about 10 blocks south of the Alameda. It has a small lake, playing fields, tennis courts, a swimming pool (open from 5 December), an open-air stage for local songs and dances, a discothèque, the racecourse of the *Club Hípico*, and an amusement park, *Fantasilandia* (■ *Adults US$9, children US$7, unlimited rides, open at weekends only in winter, and not when raining*). There are kite-flying contests on Sundays, and during the independence celebrations around 18 September there are many good *peñas*. There is also a group of about 20 good, typical, restaurants, some craft shops, the Museo del Huaso, an aquarium and a small insect and shellfish museum at El Pueblito. Cars are not allowed in the Parque. It is reached by Metro Line 2 to Parque O'Higgins station or by bus from Parque Baquedano via Avenida MacKenna and Avenida Matta.

Parque O'Higgins

Situated north of the Estación Central on Avenida Matucana y Diego Portales, the Quinta Normal was founded as a botanical garden in 1830. It is a pleasant park which gets very crowded on Sundays with families and the street entertainers who vie with one another to get their pesos. The park contains four museums, details of which are given below.

Parque Quinta Normal

The Santiago Region

Museums

Biblioteca Nacional has temporary exhibitions of books, book illustrations, documents, posters. Many concerts and lectures, entry is often free. ■ *Free. Mon-Fri 1000-1400, 1530-1830, Sat 1000-1400. Moneda 650.* **Museo Chileno de Arte Precolombino**, in the former Real Aduana, one of the best museums in Chile, has a representative exhibition of objects from the pre-Columbian cultures of Central America and the Andean region. Highly recommended. ■ *US$2.50, students free, Sun free. Booklet, US$0.35. Tue-Fri 1000-1800. Sat, Sun and holidays 1000-1400, casmchap@ctcinternet.cl, Bandera 361.* **Museo de Arte Colonial**, beside Iglesia San Francisco, has displays of religious art. One room has 54 paintings of the life of St Francis; in the cloisters is a room containing Gabriela Mistral's Nobel Prize medal; also a collection of locks. ■ *US$1.50. Tue-Sat 1000-1300 and 1500-1930, Sun and holidays 1000-1400, some information in English. T6398737. Londres 4.* **Museo de Santiago** covers the history of Santiago from the Conquest to modern times, with excellent displays and models, and guided tours. ■ *US$2, students free. Booklet, US$0.35. Tue-Sat 1000-1800, Sun and holidays 1100-1400. Casa Colorada, Merced 860.* **Museo Histórico Nacional**, in the former Palacio de la Real Audiencia, covers the period from the Conquest until 1925, interesting model of colonial Santiago. ■ *US$0.80, free on Sun. Tue-Sat, 1000-1730, Sun and holidays 1000-1400. Plaza de Armas 951.* **Palacio Cousiño**, five blocks south of the Alameda, is a large mansion in French rococo style. The luxury is incredible: watch out for the chandelier made with 13,000 pieces of crystal and the superb Italian staircase built using 20 different types of marble; also for the "*indiscretos*", three-seater armchairs designed for courting couples and a chaperone. The upper storey was damaged by fire in 1968. Note the family monogram on the curtains, mirrors and doors. Owned by the Municipalidad, the Palacio is used for official receptions but is open as a museum. A visit is

Central
Almost all museums are closed on Mon, 1 Nov and Good Friday. A visit to Palacio Consiño is a must

From coal to wine: The Cousiño dynasty

A small group of families have dominated much of Chilean history since independence, their surnames often recurring as politicians, writers and entrepreneurs. One of the most important of these in the 19th century was the Cousiño family, with its interests ranging from mining to vineyards. Matías Cousiño (1810-63), the founder of the family's fortunes, began his working life in Copiapó, where he helped build the Caldera to Copiapó railway (1848) and became chief assistant to the silver magnate, Carlos Goyenechea. After the deaths of his first wife and Goyenechea, Matías Cousiño married Goyenechea's widow, becoming one of the wealthiest men in Chile. The family fortune was secured when Luis, Matías Cousiño's only son by his first marriage, married the only daughter of Goyenechea, Isadora.

Matías Cousiño later played an active role in politics and was elected to Congress, but it is as the founder of the first major coal mine in Chile at Lota in 1852 that he is best remembered. Lota became the biggest coal mine in Chile and, until the entry of US capital into the copper industry, the Compañia Minera de Lota was the largest company in the country, largely due to the efforts of four generations of the family. After Matías's death, Luis and Isadora extended the family's fortunes and founded the country's leading newspaper, El Mercurio. Luis's son, Carlos, founded the first cement company in Chile and built the

first hydroelectric plant. In the 1880s the family pioneered plantation forestry and modern porcelain and glass manufacture.

Mindful of the need to announce their wealth to the world, Luis and Isadora hired a French architect to design the Palacio Cousiño in Santiago. Luis died of tuberculosis in 1873 aged 38, leaving Isadora, a widow at the age of 37, to oversee its completion. Furnished with tapestries, antiques and pictures imported from France, the palace startled Santiago society with its great luxury and its advanced technology, including its own electricity generators and the first lift in the country. Much of the palace remains intact with its original furnishings, and a visit is recommended. Isadora's other great project was the famous park in Lota. Here, overlooking the mine and the town whose workers had contributed so much to the family fortunes, she oversaw the cultivation of plants from all over the world.

One of Luis's other achievements was the transformation of the family's vineyards, Cousiño Macul, on the eastern outskirts of Santiago and among the oldest in the country, which had been purchased by Matías in 1856. Luis imported cuttings from France and engaged French architects to design cellars to the best contemporary standards. It is, however, said that Isadora never permitted the serving of anything but French wine in the Palacio Cousiño. It was perhaps fitting that her death, in 1899, occurred in Paris.

highly recommended. See also box on page 90. ■ US$2.40. Calle Dieciocho 438. Guided tours only, in Spanish and English. It is best to get there in time for the first tour of the morning/afternoon, as late arrivals are rushed through to catch up. Visitors are provided with cloth bootees to protect the floors. Tue-Fri 0930-1330, 1430-1700 (last tour at 1600), Sat, Sun and holidays 0930-1330. **Palacio de la Alhambra** is a national monument sponsored by the Society of Arts. It stages exhibitions of paintings as well as having a permanent display. ■ Mon-Fri 1100-1300, 1700-1930. T6890875. Compañía 1340.

In Barrio Quinta Normal **Museo de la Solidaridad**, in a beautiful listed building with a cobbled patio and palm trees with nesting birds, houses a collection of over 400 art works produced by Chilean and foreign artists in support of the Unidad Popular government and in opposition to the Pinochet dictatorship. Artists include Alexander

Calder, Joan Miró, Oswaldo Guayasamin and Roberto Matta. There are also videos of interviews (in Spanish) with survivors of the 1973 coup. Information sheet in English. Highly recommended. Good café serving cheap set lunch. ■ *US$0.80. Tue-Sun 1000-1900. T6814954 Herrera 360, www.mssa.cl*

Museo Ferroviario contains the former Presidential stagecoach and 13 steam **In Parque** engines built between 1884 and 1953 including a rare surviving Kitson-Meyer. **Quinta Normal** ■ *US$1.20, free to those over 60, photography permit, US$2. Tue-Fri 1000-1800, Sat-Sun 1100-1900.* **Museo Nacional de Historia Natural**, founded in 1830 and one of Latin America's oldest museums, with exhibitions on Chile's flora and fauna. Housed in an impressive neoclassical building, housing exhibitions on zoology, botany, mineralogy, anthropology, ethnography and aeology. ■ *US$0.80. Tue-Sat 1000-1730, Sun and holidays 1100-1830.* **Museo Artequín**, is nearby on Avenida Portales 3530, in the Chilean pavilion built for the 1889 Paris International Exhibition, containing prints of famous paintings and activities and explanations of the techniques of the great masters. Recommended. ■ *US$1. Tue-Fri 0900-1700; Sat, Sun and holidays 1100-1800.*

La Chascona is the house of the poet Pablo Neruda and now headquarters of **In Lastarria** the Fundación Pablo Neruda. This is really three houses, built on a steep hill- **& Bellavista** side and separated by gardens. ■ *T7778741, fneruda@ctcinternet.cl US$2 guided visits only, English guides can be booked (see page 154). Daily except Mon 1000-1300, 1500-1800. F Márquez de la Plata 0192.* **Museo Arqueológico de Santiago**, in Plaza Mulato Gil de Castro, has temporary exhibitions of Chilean archaeology, anthropology and pre-Columbian art. ■ *Free. Mon-Fri 1000-1400, 1530-1830, Sat, 1000-1400. Lastarria 307.* **Museo Benjamín Vicuña MacKenna** records the life and works of the 19th-century Chilean historian and biographer who became one of Santiago's most important mayors. It also has occasional exhibitions. ■ *Tue-Sat 0930-1330 and 1400-1800. US$0.80. Av V MacKenna 94.* **Museo Nacional de Bellas Artes**, in the Parque Forestal, has a large display of Chilean and foreign painting and sculpture; contemporary art exhibitions are held several times a year. ■ *US$0.80. Tue-Sun 1000-1845.* In the west wing of the building is the **Museo de Arte Contemporáneo**. ■ *US$0.80.* **Museo Tajamares del Mapocho**, Parque Balmaceda, has an exhibition of the 17th- and 18th-century walls built to protect the city from flooding by the river, and of the subsequent canalization. Also houses temporary exhibition of photographs. ■ *Mon-Fri 0900-1400 and 1500-2100. Av Providencia 222.*

Acuario Municipal at Local 9, T5565680. ■ *Small charge. Daily 1000-2100.* **In Parque** **Museo de Insectos y Caracoles**, Local 12, has a collection of insects and shell- **O'Higgins** fish. ■ *Daily 1000-1930.* **Museo del Huaso** houses a small, interesting collection of *criollo* clothing and tools. ■ *Free. Mon-Fri 1000-1700, Sun and holidays 1000-1400. T5561927.*

Museo Aeronáutico, Camino a Melipilla 5100, Cerrillos Airport, has dis- **Other** plays on space exploration, and is worth a visit. ■ *Tue-Sun 1000-1700, free.* **museums** **Museo de la Escuela Militar** has displays on Bernardo O'Higgins, the Conquest and the Pacific War. ■ *Mon-Fri 0830-1330 and 1500-1730. Los Militares 4500, Las Condes.* **Museo Ralli** is an excellent museum with a collection of works by modern European and Latin American artists, including Dali, Chagall, Bacon and Miró. Recommended. ■ *Free. Tue-Sun 1000-1600. Closed in summer. Sotomayor 4110, Vitacura.*

Galleries

There are art galleries on Avenida Nueva Costanera and Alonso de Cordova, Vitacura, in the Barrio Alto. Here, four or five private galleries showcase contemporary Chilean and Latin American art. All galleries are within a couple of blocks of each other and make a worthwhile visit as a whole. Try **Galeria Tomas Andreu**, Avenida Nueva Costanera 3731, T222 89952, **Galeria de Arte Isabel Aninat**, Alonso de Cordoba 3053, T263 2729, **AMS Marlborough**, Avenida Nueva Costanera 3723, T228 8696. These galleries are usually open Tuesday to Friday 1000-1400 and 1600-2000, Saturday 1000-1400, Monday 1600-2000.

Excursions

Maipú is a suburb 10 km southwest of Santiago where a monument marks the site of the Battle of the Maipú, 5 April 1818, which resulted in the final defeat of the Spanish royalist forces in mainland Chile. Nearby is the interesting **National Votive Temple of Maipú**, of fine modern architecture and stained glass (best viewed from the inside), on the site of a temple which was originally built in 1818 on the orders of Bernardo O'Higgins to commemorate the battle – the walls of the old temple stand in the forecourt, having fallen into ruin with successive earthquakes. Pope John Paul II gave a mass here on his visit to Chile in 1987. ■ *Daily 0800-2100, also daily mass at 1830, 1730 Sat, 1000-1400, 1600-2000 Sun and religious holidays.* The **Museo del Carmen**, attached, which contains carriages, furniture, clothing and other

Providencia

Sleeping
1 Aloha
2 Orly
3 Park Plaza
4 Posada del Salvador
5 Presidente
6 Santa María
7 Torremayor

Eating
1 A Pinch of Pancho
2 Bistro Maestro
3 Brannigan's Pub
4 Café Villa Real

0 metres 200
0 yards 200

colonial and later items, is also interesting. ■ *Mon-Fri 1000-1300 and 1500-1800, Sat-Sun 0900-1300 and 1500-1800. Getting there: bus from Teatinos y O'Higgins, 45 mins.*

Essentials

Sleeping

Check if breakfast and 18% tax is included in the price quoted (if foreigners pay in US$ cash or with US$ travellers' cheques, the 18% VAT should not be charged; if you pay by credit card, there is often a 10% surcharge). There is very little good accommodation under US$20 per person. A website offering a hotel booking service for Santiago and the rest of Chile is **hotelschile.com**

■ *on maps pages 84, 86, 96 and 100*
Price codes: see inside front cover

L *Park Plaza*, Ricardo Lyon 207, T2336363, F2336668, bookings@parkplaza.cl Good. **Providencia**
L *Sheraton San Cristóbal*, Santa María 1742, T2335000, F2236656, guest@ stgusheraton.cl 5-star, best in town, good restaurant, good buffet lunch, and all facilities. Also *Sheraton Towers*. Slightly cheaper. **AL** *Aloha*, Francisco Noguera 146, T2332230, F2332494. Helpful, good restaurant. **AL** *Lyon*, Ricardo Lyon 1526, T2257732, F2258697, hotelyoon@gmr.met With breakfast, small, intimate, good value, also has annex **B** with breakfast. **AL** *Orly*, Pedro de Valdivia 27, metro Pedro de Valdivia, T2318947, F2520051, www.orlyhotel.com Small, comfortable, convenient location, good. Also smaller and cheaper rooms, small café attached with cheap food. **AL** *Presidente*, Eliodoro Yáñez 867, almost at Providencia, T2358015, F2359148,

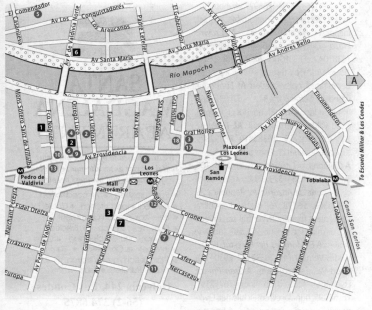

5 Carousel	9 El Huerto	13 La Pizza Nostra	16 Phone Box Pub
6 Cafetto	10 Gatsby	14 Mr Ed	& Café El Patio
7 Centre Catalá	11 Kimomo	15 Oradia	17 Red Pub
8 Copelia	12 La Mía Pappa		18 River Pub

The Santiago Region

info@presidente.cl Good value and good location. **AL** *Santa María*, Santa María 2050, T2326614, F2316287, hotelsantamaria@entelchile.net 3-star, excellent, friendly, small, good breakfast, other meals. Mixed reports as to value for money. **AL** *Torremayor*, Ricardo Lyon 322, T2342000, F2343779, gciatorre@entelchile. net Clean, modern, good service, good location. **A** *Posada del Salvador*, Eliodoro Yáñez 893, T2360991, F2518697. **C** *Hostal Parada*, Grau Flores 168, T4606640. Spacious, clean. **C** *Res Providencia*, Vicuna MacKenna 92B, T2220533 (Metro Baquedano). With bath, quiet. **C** *Res Manuel Montt*, M Montt 628, T2358048 (Metro Manuel Montt). Kitchen and laundry facilities, garden, meals.

Las Condes
See map, page 100

Las Condes **LL** *Hyatt Regency Santiago*, Av Las Condes 4601, T2181234, F2182279, info@hyatt.cl Superb, beautifully decorated, large outdoor pool, gymnasium, Thai restaurant. Highly recommended. **LL** *Radisson Royal*, Av Vitacura 2610, T2036000, F2036001, radisson@radisson.ia 5-star, excellent. **L** *Manquehue*, Esteban Dell'Orto 6615, T/F2128862, hotel@hotelmanquehue.com Very good with new wing and new pool, 4-star. **AL** *Montebianco*, Isidora Goyenechea 2911, T2325034, F2330420, montebia@entelchile.net Small, smart motel. **AL** *Santa Magdalena Apartments*, office: Helvecia 244, Las Condes, T3746875/6, www.santamagdalena.cl Apartment rental 1 block from metro stations, a/c. **A** *Parinacota*, Av Apoquindo 5142, T2126366, F2205386, hotelparinacota@bellsouth. cl 4-star, small, all services, no pool.

Centre **LL** *Carrera*, Teatinos 180, T6982011, F6721083, hotel.carrera@chilnet.cl Art-deco lobby, slightly faded grandeur, historical location opposite Moneda Palace, rooftop pool and restaurant (good buffet lunch), most expensive in Santiago, outstanding, 5-star. **L** *Galerías*, San Antonio 65, T6384011, F6395240, galerias@ entelchile.net Large rooms, good location, good breakfast, 5-star. **L** *Hostal del Parque*, Merced 294, opposite Parque Forestal, T6392694, F6392754, hotelhos. tade002@chilnet.cl Comfortable, quiet, friendly. Recommended. **AL** *Crowne Plaza*, O'Higgins 136 (the Alameda), T6381042, F6330960. All facilities, spacious, a/c (book through travel agent for better rates), noisy location. **AL** *Fundador*, Paseo Serrano 34, T/F6322566, hotelfundador@hotelfundador.cl Helpful, good value, charming staff. **AL** *Tupahue*, San Antonio 477, T6383810, F6392829, tupahue@chilnet.cl Comfortable.

A *Chilhotel*, Cirujano Guzmán 103, T2640643, F2641323, chilhotel@chilnet. cl **A** *Conde de Anzúrez*, Av República 25, T6996368, F6718376. Metro República, convenient for airport, central station and bus terminals, clean, helpful, safe, luggage stored. **A** *El Marqués del Forestal*, Ismael Valdés Vergara 740, T6333462, F6394157. Good value, apartments. **A** *Gran Palace*, Huérfanos 1178, 10th floor, T6712551, F6951095, hgpalace@entelchile.net Overpriced, good restaurant. **A** *Imperio*, O'Higgins 2876 (the Alameda), T6897774, F6892916, with breakfast, parking, convenient for bus terminals, gloomy.

A *Libertador*, O'Higgins 853 (the Alameda), T6394212, F6337128, info@hotellibertador.cl Helpful, stores luggage, good restaurant, bar, roof-top pool. Recommended. A *Majestic*, Santo Domingo 1526, T6958366, F6974051, hotelmajestic@entelchile.net With breakfast, pool, Indian restaurant, English spoken. Recommended. A *Monte Carlo*, Subercaseaux 209, T6391569, F6335577, info@hotelmontecarlo.cl At foot of Santa Lucía in quiet street, modern, restaurant, stores luggage. Recommended. A *Panamericano*, Rosa Rodriguez 1314, T6723060, F6964992, hotelpanamericano @hotmail.com Run down, unwelcoming to backpackers, serves popular business lunch between 1230 and 1530. A *Principado*, Vicuña MacKenna 30, 1 block south of Plaza Baquedano, T2228142, F2226065. Full facilities. A *Vegas*, Londres 49 T6322498, F6325084, hotelvegas@123click.cl Very convenient for centre. A-B *Lira*, Lira 314, T2222492, F6343637, htlira@entelchile.net Excellent.

B *Du Maurier*, Moneda 1510, quiet. Recommended. B *Ducado*, Agustinas 1990, T6969384, F6951271. With breakfast. Clean, quiet at back, nice area just west of the Panamericana. Secure parking. Recommended. B *Hostal Quito*, Quito 36, T6399918, F6397470, hquito@hotelquito-chile.cl Without breakfast, central, also apartments. B *Hostal Río Amazonas*, Rosas 2234, T6984092, F6719013. With breakfast and bath, internet, good value. B *Plaza Londres*, Londres 75, T6333320, F6640086. With breakfast, cable TV, quiet. B *Santa Lucía*, Huérfanos 779, Piso 4, T6398201, F6331844, santalucia@terra.cl Garage 2 blocks away, clean, comfortable, good, small, quiet restaurant. B *Tokio*, Almte Barroso 160, Metro Los Héroes, T6714516, F6984500. Helpful, friendly, good breakfast, manager speaks English and Japanese, lovely garden, good value, but does not accept credit cards. Recommended. C *Res Alemana*, República 220 (no sign), T6713668, F6712388, residencial.alemana@usa.net Metro República, with bath, D without, clean, with breakfast, pleasant patio, central,

The Santiago Region

heating on request, good cheap meals available. Recommended. **C** *Res Londres*, Londres 54, T/F6382215, unico54@ctcinternet.cl Near San Francisco Church, former mansion, large old-fashioned rooms and furniture, a few singles at **F**, no heating, English spoken, very popular, frequently recommended, usually full, book ahead. **C** *Santa Victoria*, Santa Victoria 06, T2220031, F6345753. Quiet, small, safe, family run. Recommended. **C-D** *París*, Calle París 813, T6640921, F6394037, www.hotelparis.cl With bath, quiet, clean, good meeting place, good value, luggage store. Recommended.

C *España*, Morandé 510, T6966066. With bath, hot water, clean, run down. **D**, Huérfanos 2842, T6825475. Kitchen, laundry, dormitory accommodation. **D** *Olicar*, San Pablo 1265, T6983683. Cooking facilities, quiet, clean. **E** pp *San Patricio*, Catedral 2235, T6954800. With bath, **F** pp without, with breakfast, clean, safe, friendly, hot showers, quiet location in Barrio Brasil, good value. **F** pp *Indiana* (no sign), Rosas 1339, T6880008/6982899, hostal_indiana@hotmail.com Very basic, kitchen facilities, friendly, internet US$2-3 per hr. **F** pp *Nuevo Valparaíso*, Morandé y San Pablo, T6715698. Simple, central, erratic hot water, poor beds, safe, basic, use of kitchen (no utensils), cable TV, popular, good meeting place. **F** pp *Res del Norte*, Catedral 2207, T6969251. Without bath, with breakfast, friendly, safe, clean, large rooms, credit cards accepted. **F** pp *Res Gloria*, Latorre 447, T6988315. Including breakfast, clean, popular, meals, difficult to use kitchen, Metro Toesca. Recommended. **F** pp *Res San Antonio*, Ismael Vargas Vergara 780, T6384607, ressnant@ctcinternet.cl Good place, decent value. **F** pp *Santo Domingo*, Santo Domingo 735, T/F6396733, sto.dgo@ctcreuna.cl Cleanish, basic, gloomy.

West of the centre
Convenient for bus terminals and Estación Central

C *Hostal Americano*, Compania 1906, T/F6981025, hostal@mi.terra.cl Shared bathrooms, breakfast not included (US$2 extra), clean, safe, friendly atmosphere. **C** *Res Mery*, Pasaje República 36, off 0-100 block of República, T6968883, m.mardones@entelchile.net Big green building down an alley, hot showers, quiet, good value. Recommended. **D** *Alojamiento Diario*, Salvador Sanfuentes 2258 (no sign), T6992938. With bath, **F** dormitory accommodation. Kitchen facilities. **D** *Amigos de Todo el Mundo*, Calle Libertad 371, T6817638, F6981474. With breakfast, "good accommodation in comfortable family guest houses", discounts for longer stays. **E** pp

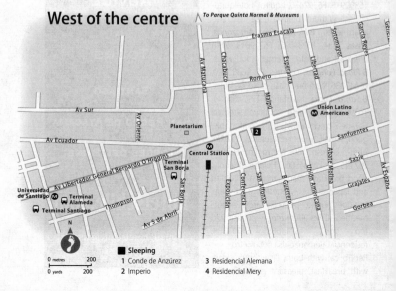

West of the centre

Sleeping
1 Conde de Anzúrez
2 Imperio
3 Residencial Alemana
4 Residencial Mery

Hostal Internacional Letelier, Cumming 77, T9656861. Internet, without breakfast, also Spanish classes. **F** pp *Res Vicky*, Sazie 2105, T6984507. Kitchen and laundry facilities, good dormitory accommodation, good beds. **F** pp *SCS Habitat*, San Vicente 1798, T6833732, F6843848. English spoken, helpful and informative, hot showers, laundry facilities, cycle rental, maps and camping equipment sold/rented, safe parking for cycles and motorbikes, frequently recommended. On north side of Alameda opposite bus terminals: **F** pp *Federico Scoto 130*, T7799364. Use of phone and fax, good meals, cooking facilities, hot water, large rooms, clean, good meeting place. Recommended.

There are many hotels on Morandé, Gral MacKenna, San Martín and San Pablo in the centre, but this is the red light district. Several on Gral MacKenna 1200 block, all very basic, including **F** pp *Res Sur*, Ruiz Tagle 055, T7765533. Clean, meals available. Same owner has *Bernal*, Bernal del Mercado, T7762679. Good. **F** pp *Res Wilson*, Jota Beche 225, T7764073. **F** pp *San Felipe*, No 1248, T6714598. Cheap laundry service, kitchen, noisy (2nd floor quieter), luggage stored, cable TV. Recommended. **Near Mapocho Station**

Travellers can find good accommodation in comfortable family guesthouses through *Amigos de Todo el Mundo*, Av Pdte Bulnes, Paseo, 285, dept 201, Casilla 52861 Correo Central, T6726525, F6981474. Run by Sr Arturo Navarrete, prices from US$16 with breakfast, other meals extra, monthly rates available, also transport to/from airport. Recommended. *Marilú Cerda*, Rafael Cañas 246 C, Providencia, T2355302, F3639154, tradesic@intermedia.cl and *Urania Cerda*, Boccaccio 60, Las Condes, T/F2012922, uraniae@hotmail.com Both offer bed and breakfast (**C** pp), comfortable, no credit cards, friendly, good beds, English and French spoken. Warmly recommended. **C** pp *Antonio & Ana Saldivia*, including breakfast. Guillermo Tell 5809, La Reina (a long way from the centre, near Las Condes), T2266267. Dinner on request US$6 per head including wine, hospitable. **D** *Ceclia Parada*, Llico 968, T5229947, F5216328. One block from Metro Departamental, laundry service, gardens, quiet. **E** pp *Rodrigo Sauvageot*, Gorbea 1992, dpto 113, T6722119. With breakfast, reservation essential. **F** pp *Sra Lucía*, Catedral 1029, piso 10, dept 1001, T6963832. Central, friendly, safe, cooking facilities, overpriced, basic. **F** pp *Sra Marta*, Amengual 035, Alameda Alt 4.400, T7797592. *Metro Ecuador*, good, hospitable, kitchen facilities, motorcycle parking. **Staying with families**

The Santiago Region

Estate agents handle apartments, but often charge half of the first month's rent as commission, while a month's rent in advance and 1 month's deposit are required. Recommended apartments are *Edificio San Rafael*, Miraflores 264, T6330289, F2225629. US$30 a day single, US$46 a day double, minimum 3 days, longer periods discounted. *Tempo Rent*, Santa Magdalena 116, T2311608, F3340374, tempo.rent@chilnet.cl Nancy Lombardo, MacIver 175, of 42, T6382009, F6330210, offers apartments with 1, 2 or 3 bedrooms, fully furnished. For private rentals, see the classified ads in *El Mercurio* – where flats, homes and family *pensiones* are listed by district – or in *El Rastro* (weekly), or try the notice board at the tourist office. Rates for 2-bed furnished apartments start at around **Longer stays**

Staying with a family is an economical and interesting option for a few months

US$200 per month, or US$130 if unfurnished. Note that you cannot install a phone line unless you have permanent Chilean residence; you may need to get a friend to put the line in their name.

Youth hostels The Chilean Youth Hostel association, the **Asociación Chilena de Albergues Turisticas Juveniles** (ACHATJ), has its offices at Hernando de Aguirre 201, of 602, T2333220, achatj@hostelling.co.cl (Worth getting a list of YH addresses around the country as these change.) Hostels in the capital include **F** pp *Cienfuegos 151*, T6718532 (5 mins from Metro Los Héroes), modern, clean, satellite TV, no cooking facilities, cafeteria, laundry facilities, parking, unwelcoming.

Camping 'Wild' camping on the Farellones road near the river or south of Santiago near Puente Alto. At Km 25 south of city on Panamericana, Esso garage offers only a vacant lot near highway. Excellent facilities about 70 km from Santiago at Laguna de Aculeo, called *Club Camping Maki*. Includes electricity, cold water, swimming pool, boat mooring, restaurant, but only available to members of certain organizations. An alternative site is *El Castaño* camping (with casino), 1 km away, on edge of lake. Very friendly, café sells fruit, eggs, milk, bread and kerosene, good fishing, no showers, water from handpump.

Eating

• *on maps pages 86, 92 and 100* Luxury hotels have computerized information on the more expensive restaurants, particularly useful if you are not sure what to eat. There is also an excellent guide to the more exclusive restaurants at www.emol.com, *El Mercurio*'s online entertainment guide.

Centre **Mid-range** *Acuario*, Paris 817. Excellent seafood and attentive service, good value set lunch. Highly recommended. *Chez Henry*, on Plaza de Armas. Expensive restaurant and delicatessen. Also has a delicatessen at O'Higgins 847. Very popular. Highly recommended. *Congreso*, Catedral 1221. Good meat and wines, popular at lunchtime. *Da Carla*, Maclver 577. Italian food, good, expensive. *San Marco*, 2 doors away, better still. *El Lugar de Don Quijote*, Morandé y Catedral. Bar/restaurant, parilladas, good wines, popular, good. *El 27 de Nueva York*, Nueva York 027, a stone's throw from the Alameda. International cuisine, good and varied menu. *Faisan d'Or* on Plaza de Armas. Good *pastel de choclo*, pleasant place to have a drink and watch the world go by. *Fra Diavolo*, París 836 (near *Res Londres*). Lunches only, excellent food and service, popular. *Guimas*, Huérfanos y Teatinos. Good, reasonable prices, good value *almuerzo*. *Guo Fung*, Moneda 1549. Good oriental food, central location. Good Indian restaurant inside *Hotel Majestic*, Santo Domingo 1526. *Les Assassins*, Merced 297. French, very good. Highly recommended. *Lung Fung*, Agustinas 715. Delicious oriental food, pricey, large cage in the centre with noisy parrots. *Omar Khayyam*, Peru 570. Arab specialities. *Restaurant Tragaluz*, Constitución 124, T738 2011. Good Chilean food, not cheap.

For excellent cheap seafood meals make for the Mercado Central (by Cal y Canto metro; lunches only), or at the Vega Central market on the opposite bank of the Mapocho **Cheap** *Bar Central*, San Pablo 1063. Popular, noisy, good specialities, good value. Recommended. *Bar Nacional No 1*, Huérfanos 1151 and *Bar Nacional No 2*, Bandera 317. Good restaurants, popular, local specialities. *Bella China*, Compania 2280, large portions of oriental food. Next door to No 2 is *El Rápido*, specialises in empanadas, cheap, quick service, popular. *Círculo de Periodistas*, Amunátegui 31, piso 2. Unwelcoming entrance, good value lunches. Recommended. *Mermoz*, Huérfanos 1048. Good for lunches. *Nuria*, Agustinas y Maclver. Wide selection. *Torres*, O'Higgins 1570. Traditional bar/restaurant, good atmosphere, live music at weekends. Cheap lunches are served in a large underground *comedor Pavo Real*, Estado 33 (just off O'Higgins), self-service, good value, US$5.

Seriously cheap Those on a budget should make straight for Calle San Diego, south of the Alameda, where there are the following: *Las Tejas*, No 234, lively, rowdy crowd, very cheap cocktails and drinks such as Pisco Sour and *pipeño*, excellent *cazuelas* and other typical dishes. *Masticón*, No 152, good service, excellent value, popular, wide range. *Sena*, No 145, good cocktails, good value, wide range. Those who can afford a little more should try *La Caleta de Don Beno*, No 397, excellent *parrilladas*, also seafood, popular, recommended. At No 260 is a Peruvian restaurant with live salsa music on Fri and Sat nights. Another option is the *Tercera Compañia de Bomberos*, Vicuña Mackenna 097, near the junction with Diagonal Paraguay, very cheap, recommended.

Mid-range *El Citta*, Cumming 635, Barrio Brasil. Good meat dishes. **Kitchen**, Rancagua 036, near Vicuña Mackenna, 3 blocks south of Plaza Italia. Excellent mixture of Greek and vegetarian, very popular, highly recommended. **Cheap** *La Máquina*, Calle Seminario, Metro Salvador. Nice atmosphere, music in the evening.

Near the centre

Mid-range *El Rincón Español*, just off Rosal. Spanish, good, reasonably priced, try the paella. Next door is *El Bar Escondida*, a small but pleasant bar. *Gatopardo*, Lastarria 192. Good value. Highly recommended. *La Pergola de la Plaza* in Plaza Mulato Gil de Castro. **Cheap** *Café Universitario*, Alameda 395 y Subercaseaux (near Sta Lucía). Good, cheap *almuerzos*, lively at night, separate room for lovers of rock videos, very pleasant.

Lastarria

This is one of the liveliest places to come out and eat at night, with many excellent and costly restaurants. **Expensive** *Cava de Dardignac*, Dardignac 0191. Portuguese cuisine with live fado music at night. *El Antojo Gaugin*, Pío Nono 069. Good *brochetas a la plancha*. *El Otro Sitio*, López de Bello 053. Peruvian, excellent food, good service, elegant. *Il Siciliano*, Dardagnac y Constitución. High class pasta and seafood. *La Divina Comida*, Purísima 093. Italian with 3 rooms – Heaven, Hell and Purgatory. Highly recommended. *Le Coq au Vin*, No 0110. French, excellent cuisine, reasonably priced. Recommended. *Nuevo Cipriani*, Pinto Lagarrigue 195. Italian, elegant atmosphere, very expensive, top class. *Off the Record*, López de Bello 153. Period design, nice atmosphere, cheaper set lunch. *San Fruttuoso*, Mallinckrodt 180. Italian, elegant. Recommended. *Zen*, Dardignac 175. Sushi restaurant. Recommended. **Mid-range** *Aji Verde*, Constitución 284. Specializes in Chilean food, open for lunch. *Eladio*, Pío Nono 251. Argentine cuisine, good steaks, bingo. *La Tasca Mediterránea*, Purísima 163. Extensive menu including fish, seafood, good value, good food. Recommended. *Michelle's*, Arzobispo 0615. Bistro with excellent seafood and fish dishes, recommended. *Venezia*, Pío Nono y Lopez de Bello. Huge servings, good value.

Bellavista
See map, page 86. Most restaurants are closed for lunch in Bellavista

Expensive *Centro Catalá*, Av Suecia 428 near Lota. Good, quiet street, nice décor, cheaper set lunch. On Av Providencia *Lomit's*, No 1980. Good, attentive service. *Salvaje*, No 1177. Excellent international menu, open-air seating, good value lunches. Warmly recommended. **Mid-range** *A Pinch of Pancho*, Gral del Canto 45. Seafood and fish specialities, very good. *Bistro Maestro*, Las Urbinas y Providencia, Russian food, good. *El Rincón Brasileiro*, M Montt 116. *Eladio*, 11 de Septiembre 2250, piso 5. Reasonably priced, good meat dishes. *Gatsby*, Providencia 1984. American food, as-much-as-you-can-eat buffet and lunch/dinner, also coffees and snacks, open till 2400, tables outside in warm weather, good. *La Pez Era*, Providencia 1421. Seafood, smart but reasonably priced.

Providencia
See map, page 92

Italian **Expensive**: *Cafetto Restaurant*, Pedro de Valdivia 030, next to *Hotel Orly*. Specialises in haute cuisine, very smart. *Da Renato*, Mardoqueo Fernández 138. (Metro Los Leones). Good. *La Pizza Nostra*, Av Las Condes 6757. Pizzas and good Italian food, real coffee, pricey. Also at Av Providencia 1975 and Luis Thayer Ojeda 019. *Valerio*, Apoquindo 4300, also Coronel Pereira 139. Smart, good wines, not cheap. **French** All expensive: **Carousel**, Los Conquistadores 1972. Fine cuisine, exceptionally smart, nice garden, very expensive. **El Giratorio**, 11 de Septiembre 2250, piso 16. Good food eaten while the whole city rotates outside your window. Recommended. **Oradia**, Tobalaba 477. Celebrated, very expensive. For cheaper French-style food, try **Au Bon Pain**, 11 de Septiembre 2263. 'The French bakery café', salads, sandwiches, real coffee, also at Miraflores 235, El Bosque Norte 0181 and elsewhere. **Oriental** *Oriental*, M Montt 584. One of the best Chinese in Santiago, expensive. **Bin-Xiang**, M Montt 155. Mid-range Chinese. **Jardín de Bambú**, Salvador 1827. Mid-range Vietnamese.

Las Condes **On Vitacura** Expensive: *Cuerovaca*, El Mañío 1659, T2468936. Serves fantastic tender steaks, both Argentinian and Chilean cuts. Highly recommended. **El Madroñal**, No 2911, T2336312. Excellent, Spanish cuisine, one of the best restaurants in town, booking essential. **Mid-range**: *Delmónico*, No 3379. Excellent, reasonably priced. *Jabri*, No 6477. Arab cuisine. **Le Fournil**, Vitacura 3841 (T2280219) opposite *Cuerovaca*. Excellent French bakery and restaurant. Particularly popular at lunch time. Also *Praga*, No 3917. Czech. **On Isadora Goyenechea** *La Cascade*, No 2930. French, expensive, long established, closed Sun. *München*, No 204. German. Pricey but recommended. *Pinpilinpausha*, No 2900. Good. **On El Bosque Norte** Very many expensive restaurants on this street, near Tobalaba metro. **Expensive**: *Coco Loco*, No 0215. Fish, seafood, good. *El Club*, No 0380

Many first class restaurants, including grills, Chilean cuisine (often with music), French cuisine and Chinese. This area tends to be more expensive than central restaurants

The Santiago Region

Las Condes

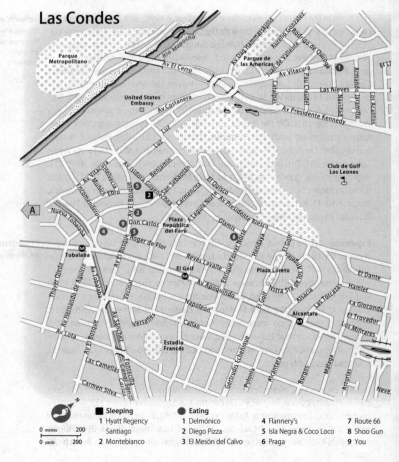

Sleeping	Eating		
1 Hyatt Regency Santiago	1 Delmónico	4 Flannery's	7 Route 66
2 Montebianco	2 Diego Pizza	5 Isla Negra & Coco Loco	8 Shoo Gun
	3 El Mesón del Calvo	6 Praga	9 You

0 metres 200
0 yards 200

(approximately). Popular, very smart, good. *El Mesón del Calvo*, seafood speciality, El Bosque Norte y Roger de Flor. *Isla Negra*, expensive, next door to Coco Loco, seafood a speciality. **Mid-range**: *Diego Pizza*, El Bosque Norte, y Don Carlos. Friendly, good cocktails, popular. Recommended. *"You"*, No 036. Japanese restaurant, Sushi, good.

Oriental Expensive: *Benyarong*, Américo Vespucio Norte 2970. Thai. *Sakura*, Vitacura 4111. Excellent sushi. Recommended. *Shoo Gun*, Enrique Foster Norte 172. Japanese. *Taj Mahal*, Isadora Goyenechea 3215 (Metro El Golf), T2323606. Indian, expensive but excellent. **Mid-range**: *The Wok House*, Vitacura 4355 T2074757. Good Chinese food, takeaway available. **Seafood** *Mare Nostrum*, La Concepción 281. *Puerto Marisko*, Isadora Goyenechea 3471. Good.

Cheap Budget travellers should make the *almuerzo* their main meal. For cheap meals in the evening try the *fuentes de soda* and *schoperias* scattered around the centre. Cheap lunches are served in the casino of the Universidad de Chile, Blanco Encalada 2186, next to Parque O'Higgins, Mon-Fri 1215-1415, except Jan-Mar.

Elsewhere

Centro Comercial
Lo Castillo

Centre All expensive: *Los Adobes del Argomedo*, Argomedo 411 y Lira. Good Chilean food, floor show (Mon-Sat) includes cueca dancing, salsa and folk. *El Villorio*, San Antonio 676, T6335605. Meat specialities. **Providencia** *Circulo Libanes*, Santa María 1880, T2332688. *García Lorca*, Guardia Vieja 109, T2339677. Spanish cuisine. **Bellavista** *Cipriani*, Ernesto Pinto Lagarrigue 195, T7350630. Italian food.

Restaurants with floor show

Expensive *El Huerto*, Orrego Luco 054, Providencia, T2332690. Recommended. Open daily, live music Fri and Sat evenings, varied menu, very good, popular. *El Viejo Verde*, López de Bello 94, Bellavista, excellent vegetarian food. **Mid-range** *Café El Patio*, Providencia 1652, next to *Phone Box Pub*, tofu and pasta as well as fish dishes, nice sandwiches, popular. **Cheap** *El Naturista*, Moneda 846, excellent, closes 2100. *El Vegetariano*, Huerfanos 827, Local 18, popular, good juices. *Kimomo*, Providencia 1480, tofu, miso soup, good snacks, reasonably priced. *Natural Green*, Huerfanos 1188, T3609689, also at Puente 689, Local 314. *Unicornio*, Plaza Lyon, Local 49.

Vegetarian restaurants

Centre For good coffee in the centre try *Café Caribe* and *Café Haití* on Paseo Ahumada, institutions among Santiago's businessmen and good places to see the people who make Chile tick – also branches throughout the centre and in Providencia. Another good coffee bar is *Café Ikabaru*, Huerfanos 709, popular,

Cafés
Note that almost all hotel bars are closed on Sun

The Santiago Region

intimate. *Bon Bon Oriental*, Merced 345. Superb Turkish coffee, savouries and cakes. *Café Colonia*, MacIver 133. Splendid variety of cakes, pastries and pies, fashionable and pricey, excellent. Recommended. *Café Paula*, several branches, eg Estado at entrance to Galería España, excellent coffee and cake, try the *café helado* (coffee with ice cream and cream), good breakfast, pricey, also on San Antonio opposite the Teatro Municipal. *Café Santos*, Av Providencia 2236 and other branches. Popular for excellent '*onces*' (afternoon tea). *New York Café* , Moneda y Tenderine. Helpful staff, good coffee. *Salón de Té Cousiño* , Cousiño 107. Good coffee, snacks and *onces*, very popular, not cheap. *Tip-Top Galetas*. Recommended for freshly baked biscuits, branches throughout the city. **Bellavista and Lastarrria** *Café de la Dulcería Las Palmas*, López de Bello 190. Good pastries and lunches. *Cafetería La Nona*, Pío Nono 099. Real coffee, good *empanadas* and cakes, fresh fruit juices. Recommended. *Empanatodos*, Pío Nono 153. Serves 25 different types of *empanadas*. *Green*, Constitución 042. Excellent healthy sandwiches and snacks. **Providencia** *Salón de Té Tavelli*, Drugstore precinct, No 2124. **Snacks and ice cream** Several good places on Av Providencia include *Copelia*, No 2211, *Bravissimo*, No 1406, *El Toldo Azul*, No 1936. In the centre try *Gelato's*, Agustinas 941. Very good.

Entertainment

Some of the restaurants and cafés which have shows are given above For all entertainment, nightclubs, cinemas, restaurants, concerts, the *El Mercurio Online* website has listings and a good search feature. Look under the *tiempo libre* section of the site: www.emol.com   Listings in weekend newspapers, particularly *El Mercurio* and *La Tercera*, and in *Santiago What's On*.

Lively areas to head for are the following: **Bellavista**, good selection of varied restaurants, bars, discos and *salsotecas*, reasonable prices (Metro Baquedano); **Avenida Suecia and General Holley**, smarter, recently remodelled and much of it pedestrianized, lots of bars and some restaurants and discos (Metro Los Leones); **El Bosque Norte**, chic bars and expensive restaurants for the Chilean jetset (Metro Tobalaba); **Barrio Brasil**, a number of bars and restaurants dotted around the Plaza Brazil and on Avenidas Brazil and Cumming, popular with Chilean students (Metro República); **Plaza Nuñoa**, a goodly number of bars dotted around the Plaza in the middle-class suburb of Nuñoa.

Bars **Bellavista** *HBH Bar*, Purísima y López de Bello. Good beer, good atmosphere. *La Bodega de Julio*, Constitución 256. Cuban staff and Cuban cocktails, excellent live music and dancing possible, very popular, free entry before 2300, very good value. Highly recommended. *La Casa en el Aire*, López de Bello 125. Pleasant, intimate atmosphere, live music (ask them to turn it down). Recommended. *La Chimenea*, Pje Principe de Gales 90. Hidden away up stairs in a small street in the close to the centre of downtown, an atmospheric and slightly dingy pub serving meals during the day. No airs and graces, but lively. *Libro Café Mediterraneo*, popular with students, lively, expensive, on Mon nights a local man does good Georges Brassens impressions, entrance US$4.50 charged to hear him. *Restaurant/Pub Evelyn*, Purísima 282. Austrian beers on tap, good atmosphere, not cheap.

Nuñoa *HBH Bar*, Irrarázaval y Macul. Popular, good beer. *La Batuta*, on George Washington near the plaza. Live jazz, very popular. *Las Lanzas*, Plaza Nuñoa. Popular, crowded.

Providencia Many including *Flannery's Irish Geo Pub*, Encomenderos 83. Irish pub, serving Guinness on draft, good lunches, popular among *gringos* and Chileans alike. *Golden Bell Inn*, Hernando Aguirre 27. Popular with expatriates. *Phone Box Pub*, Providencia 1670, T496627. Very popular with expats, serves numerous European beers

Huevón, Señor?

If you spend any time in Chile, it is almost impossible not to come across 'huevón'. This versatile word is unique to Chilean Spanish, and is used by all classes of society – literally meaning 'big egg', it is used to describe a person, and is by turns an expression of endearment ('mate', 'buddy') and a slang expression of disgust ('idiot', 'fool'), and is used equally often in both senses. In some conversations, virtually every other word may seem to be huevón.

Confusion arises for the visitor because of the similarity of huevón to 'huevo', the Spanish word for egg. Legend has it that an expatriate living in Santiago a few years ago made the mistake of ordering a sandwich with huevón rather than huevo – the waiter was so overcome that he had

to finish his shift early. The hilarity with which mistakes of this sort are greeted can be made to work to the visitor's advantage, however: tell any friend that you have been to the shop to buy huevón and your friendship will be secured for life (once the laughter has died down).

The use of huevón is symptomatic of the distinctiveness of Chilean Spanish, which has an unusually wide range of idioms and slang not used elsewhere in Latin America. Those spending any length of time in Chile, or who are serious about getting to grips with Chilean Spanish, should get hold of a copy of How to Survive in the Chilean Jungle by John Brennan and Alvaro Taboada (Ventriloc Dolmen Editores, 2001), a comprehensive handbook of Chilean colloquialisms.

The Santiago Region

including Pilsener Urquell, and canned British beers including Newcastle Brown Ale, Beamish Stout and Old Speckled Hen, a good place to go if you are missing home. On Suecia: **Brannigan Pub**, No 35. Good beer, live jazz, lively. **Louisiana River Pub**, Suecia y General Holley. Live music; **Mr Ed**, No 155; **Red Pub**, No 29. **Café Mistral**, C Arzobispo 0635, T7776173. Owned by French mountain-climber, free climbing wall, internet.

Las Condes *Country Village*, Av Las Condes 10680. Open Mon-Sat from 2000, Sun from lunch onwards, live music Fri and Sat. Next door is **Santa Fe**, No 10690. *Tex-Mex*, with **T'Quila Bar** next door. Excellent margaritas. Further east on Av Las Condes at Paseo San Damián are several popular bar-restaurants including **Tequila**. **Morena Pizza and Dance Bar**, No 0120. Nice dance floor, good sound system, live music at weekends, happy hour before 2200.

Bellavista *Bogart*, López de Bello 34. Rock music. **Caribbean**, López de Bello 40. Reggae. **Club 4-40**, Sta. Filomena 081, named after popular singer Juan Luis Guerra's backing group from the Dominican Republic, live Cuban music, packed at weekends. Recommended. **Disco Salsa**, Pío Nono 223. Good atmosphere, also salsa dance classes downstairs. **Emmanuelle**, Andrés Bello 2857. Shows at 0100 and 0300. **La Otra Puerta**, Pío Nono 348. Lively *salsoteca* with live music. Recommended. **Peña Nano Parra**, San Isidro 57. Good folk club, cheap. **Tu Tu Tanga**, Pío Nono 127. Busy at night, cheap, good value. See also **La Bodega de Julio** (under Bars above). **Las Condes and Providencia** These can be very expensive, up to US$20 or more to get in. **Club Tucán Salsoteca**, Pedro de Valdivia 1783. Caters to lovers of Brazilian rhythms. **Enigma**, Av Las Condes 9179. **Gente**, Av Apoquindo 4900. **Heaven**, Recoleta 345. Thu, Fri, Sat 2330-0500, entry US$12 per person. **Ilé Habana**, Bucaré just off Suecia. Bar with salsa music, often live, and a good dance floor. **Las Uracas**, Vitacura 9254, US$15 but free before 2300 if you eat there. Many more, mainly in the Providencia and Las Condes areas.

Nightclubs
Clubs in Bellavista are cheaper and more downmarket generally than those in Providencia

Seats cost US$4-6 with reductions on Wed (elsewhere in the country the day varies). Some cinemas offer discounts to students and over 60s (proof required). 'Ciné Arte'

Cinemas

(quality foreign films) is very popular and 7 cinemas specialize in this type of film: *Casa de Extensión Universidad Católica*, Av B O'Higgins 390, T6351994. *Cine Arte Normandie*, Tarapacá 1181, T6972979. Varied programme, altered frequently, films at 1530, 1830 and 2130 daily, students half price. *El Biógrafo*, Lastarria 181, T6334435. **Las Condes and Providencia** *AIEP*, Miguel Claro 177, T2649698, *Espaciocal*, Goyenechea y Vitacura, *Lo Castillo*, Candelaría Goyenechea 3820, T2461562 and *Tobalaba*, Av Providencia 2563, T2316630, full details are given in the press. Try also *Goethe Institut* (address below). There are many mainstream cinemas showing international films, usually in original English with Spanish subtitles. Multiplex centres at *Cinemark Alto Las Condes*, Av Kennedy 9001, T6002463, *Showcase Parque Arauco*, Av Kennedy 5413, T2247707, both attached to respective shopping malls. Good guide to daily cinema across the city in the 2 free newspapers, *La Hora* and *tmg*, which are given out at metro stations early on weekday mornings. **Centre** *Cinehoyts Huérfanos*, Huérfanos 735, T6641861, *Cinehoyts San Agustín*, San Antonio 144, T6329566, *Cinehoyts Estación Central*, in the shopping mall next to the train station.

Festivals During **Nov** there is a free art fair in the Parque Forestal on the banks of the Río Mapocho, lasting a fortnight. In **Oct** or **Nov** there is a sumptuous flower show and an annual agricultural and industrial show (known as *Fisa*) in Parque Cerrillos. Religious festivals and ceremonies continue throughout **Holy Week**, when a priest ritually washes the feet of 12 men. The image of the Virgen del Carmen (patron of the Armed Forces) is carried through the streets by cadets on **16 Jul**.

Theatres *Teatro Municipal*, Agustinas y San Antonio, stages international **opera**, concerts by the Orquesta Filarmónica de Santiago, and the Ballet de Santiago, throughout the year; on Tue at 2100 there are free operatic concerts in the Salón Claudio Arrau; tickets range from US$7 for a very large choral group with a symphony orchestra, and US$8 for the cheapest seats at the **ballet**, to US$70 for the most expensive opera seats. Some cheap seats are often sold on the day of concerts. *Teatro Universidad de Chile*, Plaza Baquedano, is the home of the Orquesta y Coro Sinfónica de Chile and the Ballet Nacional de Chile. There are a great number of theatres which stage **plays** in Spanish, either in the original language or translations, eg *Abril*, Huérfanos 786, *Camilo Henríquez*, Amunátegui 31, *Centro Arrayán*, Las Condes 14891, *El Galpón de los Leones*, Av Los Leones 238, *El Conventillo*, Bellavista 173, *La Comedia*, Merced 349. Four others, the *California*, Irarrázaval 1546, *Humoresque*, San Ignacio 1249, *Opera*, Huérfanos, and *Picaresque*, Recoleta 345, show mostly Folies Bergères-type revues. *Santiago Stage* is an English-speaking amateur drama group. Outdoor **rock** concerts are held at the *Estadio Nacional*, Av Grecia, at the *Teatro Teletón*, Rosas 325 (excellent sound system), and elsewhere. Events are listed in *El Mercurio* and *La Tercera*.

Free classical concerts are sometimes given in San Francisco church in summer; arrive early for a seat

Shopping

There are many shopping areas in Santiago. The shops in the centre and to the north of the Plaza de Armas are cheaper and more downmarket than the countless arcades and boutiques strung along Providencia, especially near Av Ricardo Lyon. Specialist shops tend to be grouped together, eg bikes and second-hand books on San Diego, new bookshops on Providencia, opticians on Mac Iver, Lapis Lazuli in Bellavista.

Many stalls on Paseo Ahumada/ Huérfanos sell overseas newspapers and journals

Bookshops There are many bookshops in the Pedro de Valdivia area on Av Providencia. Much better value but with a smaller selection are the bookshops on the shopping mall at Av Providencia 1114-1120. *Books*, Providencia 1652, Local 5, in a courtyard beside the Phone Box Pub and Café El Patio. Wide selection of English-language books for sale or exchange, English spoken. *Feria Chilena del Libro*, Huérfanos 623, largest bookstore in

Book prices are very high compared with Europe, even for second-hand books

Santiago, good for travel books and maps; also in Drugstore precinct, Providencia 2124. *LOM Ediciones*, Estación Mapocho. Sells a stock of literature, history, sociology, art and politics from its own publishing house. Also a bar, and attached a reading room with recent Chilean newspapers and magazines (Mon-Fri 1000-2000; Sat 1000-1400). *Librería Eduardo Albers*, Vitacura 5648, Las Condes, T2185371, F2181458 (Spanish, English and German – good selection, cheaper than most, helpful, also German and Swiss newspapers). *Librería Chile Ilustrado*, Providencia 1652 local 6, T2358145, chileil@tnet.cl, next door to *Books*, specializes in books (nearly all in Spanish) relating to Chile, particularly flora and fauna, history and anthropology. *Librería Inglesa*, Huérfanos 669, Local 11, Pedro de Valdivia 47, Vitacura 5950, Providencia 2653, www.libreriainglesa.cl T2319970. Sells only books in English, good selection, sells the *South American Handbook*. *Librería Lila*, Providencia 1652, Local 3. Mind/body/spirit specialists, best in Santiago for this field. *Librería Universitaria*, Av O'Higgins 1050, T6951529, F6956387. Particularly for books in Spanish. *South American Way*, Av Apoquindo 6856, Las Condes, T2118078. Sells books in English. Those looking for cheap English-language books should also try the many second-hand book kiosks on San Diego between Eleuterio Ramirez and Condor, 4 blocks south of Plaza Bulnes, next to the Iglesia de los Sacramentinos, or *Drago* second hand books, Rosas 3260 near the Parque Quinta Normal. For French language books: *Apostrophes*, Merced 324, specialize in French publications including literature. *Librairie Française*, books and newspapers, Estado 337. As well as the antiquarian bookshop mentioned above in the Lastarria district, there are other good antiquarian bookshops on Merced around the corner from Lastarria, eg *América del Sur Librería Editorial*, No 306, *Libros Antiguos El Cid*, No 344.

Harry Müller, Ahumada 312, Oficina 402. Good, quick and inexpensive. Recommended. Speaks German and English. For Minolta and Canon repairs, *TecFo*, Nueva York 52, piso 2, T6952969. Recommended. Many developers on Ahumada offer 24-hrs service of varying quality (some develop, but do not mount, slides, slow service). *Black Box*, Pérez Valenzuela 1503 (Metro Manuel Montt). Highly recommended. *Moretto*, Merced 753. Recommended as cheap and good. *Prontofoto*, Ahumada 264, T6721981. Good quality developing and printing. *Tecnofoto*, Ahumada 131, piso 7, Oficina 719, T6725004. Recommended as quick and efficient. For camera batteries and other spares try *Fotocenter*, Ahumada y Huérfanos. *Carmen Pérez Gúzman*, MacIver 148. Good quality, helpful, some English spoken.	**Camera repairs & film**

Standard camping gas cartridges can be bought at *Fabri Gas*, Bandera y Santo Domingo, or *Unisport*, Av Providencia 2503. Other equipment for camper-vans from *Bertonati Hnos*, Manuel Montt 2385. Climbing equipment at *La Cumbre*, Apoquindo 5258, Las Condes, T2209907, la_cumbre@email.com For tent repairs, *Juan Soto*, Silva Vildosola 890, Paradero 1, Gran Avenida, San Miguel, T5558329. Camping goods from *Club Andino* and *Federación de Andinismo* (see page 109); expensive because these articles are imported. *Industria Yarur*, Rosas 1289 y Teatinos, T6723696. Good value for money, discounts available. *Outdoors & Travel*, Encomeneros 206, Las Condes, T3357104. For wide range of imports and locally made goods. *Patagonia*, Helvecia 210, Providencia, T3351796 (Tobalaba metro). Good range of clothing and equipment, comparatively expensive. For packs also try Sr Espinosa, San Martín 835. Repair of camping stoves at *Casa Italiana*, Tarapacá 1120. For second-hand equipment try Luz Emperatriz Sanhuela Quiroz, Portal de León, Loc 14, Providencia 2198 (Metro Los Leones).

Camping equipment

The Santiago Region

Handicrafts

Those wishing to spend a reasonable amount of money buying good quality crafts may wish to travel to Pomaire (see page 118), where goods from all over Chile are for sale at cheaper prices than those in Santiago

The biggest craft market in Chile is now the **Plaza Artesanos de Manquehue**, on Av Manquehue Sur, block 300-600, just off Apoquindo in Las Condes. A good range of modern Chilean crafts from ceramics to textiles, a pleasant central piazza, and places where the artisans can be seen working on wood, silver, glass and so on. Although more expensive than, for instance, the market in Santa Lucía, this is a good and attractive place to come; take any bus east from Providencia or Escuela Militar which goes via 'Apoquindo'. Others include the following: **Aldea de Vitacura**, Vitacura 6838, T7353959, 1000-2000. *El Almacén Campesino*, Purísima 303, Bellavista, co-operative association in an attractive colonial building. Sells handicrafts from all over Chile, including attractive Mapuche weavings, wood carvings, pottery and beautiful wrought copper and bronze. Prices similar to those in Temuco. Ask about shipping. *Chile Vivo*, Dardignac 15, Barrio Bellavista, T7350227, chilevivo@latinmail. com Shopping centre with café, handicraft shop, internet, art gallery and jewellery workshop. *Prisma de los Andes*, Santo Domingo 1690 (Metro Santa Ana), T6730540. A women's social project, sells distinctive high quality textiles made in the organization's co-operative workshops (which can be visited). The gemstone lapis lazuli can be found in a few expensive shops in Bellavista but is cheaper in the arcades on south side of the Plaza de Armas and in the *Centro Artesanal Santa Lucía* (Santa Lucía metro, south exit) which also has a wide variety of woollen goods, jewellery, etc. Try also *Marita Gil*, Los Misioneros 1991, Pedro de Valdivia Norte, T2326853, F2322520. A cheaper craft market is next to the bridge of Pio Nono in Bellavista, best at weekends. *Amitié*, Av Ricardo León y Av Providencia (Metro Los Leones). *Dauvin Artesanía Fina*, Providencia 2169, Local 69 (Metro Los Leones) have also been recommended. *Cema-Chile* (Centro de Madres), Portugal 351 and at Universidad de Chile metro stop, and *Artesanía Chilena*, Estado 337, *Artesanías de Chile*, Varas 475, *Artesanía Popular Chilena*, Av Providencia 2322 (near Los Leones metro) and *Manos Chilensis*, Portugal 373, all have a good selection of handicrafts. *Talleres Solidarios*, de la Barra 456. Small selection. Antique stores in Plaza Mulato Gil de Castro and elsewhere on Lastarria (Merced end). Beside and behind the Iglesia de los Dominicos, on Av Nueva Apoquindo 9085 in Las Condes, is *Los Graneros del Alba*, or *El Pueblo de Artesanos*, open daily except Mon, 1130-1900. All types of ware on sale, classes given in some shops, interesting. *Restaurant El Granero* is here. To get there, take a No 326 or 327 bus from Av Providencia, marked 'Camino del Alba'. Get out at the children's playground at the junction of Apoquindo y Camino del Alba, at the foot of the hill leading up to the church, and walk up.

Maps

Automóvil Club de Chile, Vitacura 8620, sell route maps of Chile, 7 in total. US$6 each or US$3 each if affiliated to motor organization. *Instituto Geográfico Militar*, Dieciocho 369 (near Metro Toesca), T4608222, has detailed geophysical and topographical maps of the whole of Chile, very useful for climbing. Expensive (about US$11 each), but Biblioteca Nacional, Alameda 651, T3605200, has copies and will allow you to photocopy parts of each map. *Mapas*, Gral del Canto 105, Oficina 1506, Providencia, T2364808, jmattassi@interactiva.cl sells comprehensive maps of the whole of Chile. Some specialize in marking trekking routes, especially in National Park Areas where maps are produced in conjunction with CONAF. US$6 each. Purchase direct from small office on 15th floor of highrise just off Providencia, Mon-Fri 1000-1330 and 1430-1700.

Music

Biggest chain is *Feria del Disco* on Paseo Ahumada, and in numerous malls, who often sell tickets for rock concerts. Also *Musimundo* has 2 megastores, Huérfanos 930 (complete with listening stations) and Providencia 2266.

Opticians

Those needing to have a new set of glasses made up should head for MacIver 0-100 block, where there are many opticians to choose from, and prices are lower than comparable rates in Europe or North America.

El Mundo del Vino, Isidora Goyenechea 2929, T2448888. *The Wine House*, Vitacura **Wine**
2904, Mall Parque Arauco, local 333. *Vinopolis*, El Bosque Norte 038 and Pedro de
Valdivia 036. Mon-Fri 0900-2300, Sat 1000-2300, Sun 1000-2200. Exclusively Chilean
wines. Good selection and various prices. Also at airport.

The **Bío Bío** flea market on Calle Bío Bío (go to Metro Franklin and follow the crowds) is **Markets**
every Sat and Sun morning. This is the largest and cheapest flea market in the city, and
sells everything from spare parts for cars and motorbikes to secondhand furniture.
Those trying to do up a new flat on the cheap, a car on the hoof, or who are simply
interested in sharing a street with tens of thousands of others, should find their way
here. Santiaguinos say that if there was a market for souls, someone would be selling
them off at cost price in the Bío Bío. The *Mercado Central*, between Puente y 21 de
Mayo by the Río Mapocho (Cal y Canto metro) is brilliant for seafood, with many places
to eat cheaply, Don Agusto is recommended; otherwise an excellent range of goods,
but quite expensive; there is a cheaper market, the *Vega Central*, on the opposite bank
of the river. There are other craft markets in an alleyway, 1 block south of Av O'Higgins
between A Prat and San Diego, as well as on the 600 to 800 blocks of Santo Domingo
(includes pieces from neighbouring countries) and at Pío Nono y Av Santa María,
Bellavista. The shopping arcade at the Central Station is good value, likewise the street
market outside. There is a good outside fruit market at Puente 815, by *Frutería
Martínez*. There is an antique fair on Sun (1000-1400) in the summer and a Fiesta de
Quasimodo on the first Sun after Easter at Lo Barnechea, 30 mins by bus from Santiago.
For cheap secondhand clothes (especially good for winter clothes for travellers), the
following are recommended: many shops on Bandera esp 600 block; *S'tylo*, San Diego
y Copiapó; *Troya*, Local 392A, Pje Agustin Edwards, Compañia 1000-block, 1 block
from the Plaza de Armas.

The new Mall del Centro, on Calle Rosas 900-block, just north of the Plaza de Armas, has **Shopping**
brought mall culture to the centre of Santiago. The next most convenient is *Plaza* **malls**
Vespucio at the terminus of Metro line 5, Bellavista de La Florida. Generally open 7 days
a week 1000-2100. There are also 3 large shopping centres east of the centre in Las
Condes: *Apumanque*, at Apoquindo y Manquehue; *Parque Arauco*, on Av Kennedy,
north of Metro Escuela Militar; and (the largest and most modern) *Centro Comercial
Alto Las Condes*, further east on Av Kennedy, open 1000-2200.

Sports

For parts and repairs the only place to go is Calle San Diego, south of the Alameda. The **Bicycles**
800 and 900 blocks have scores of bicycle shops, with spare parts, new models and
repairs all offered at prices much cheaper than you will find in Providencia or Las
Condes. *Importadora Caupolicán*, San Diego 863, T6972765, F6961937. Wide range,
helpful, has been recommended; also *Bicicletas Wilson*, No 909; *El Supermercado de
las Bicicletas*, No 921, good stock; *Terrabike*, No 896, does repairs. *Luis Cabalin*, at
Coquimbó 1114, T6984193, is good for maintenance and repairs.

Bowling Center, Av Apoquindo 5012. Ten-pin bowling, lots of alleys. Recommended. **Bowling**

Saturday in summer at the snooty *Club Príncipe de Gales*, Las Arañas 1901, right by the **Cricket**
junction of Bilbao and Vespuccio. US$5, membership not required (just tell the door-
man you are there for the cricket), lots of drinks included in the price.

The 3 biggest clubs in Santiago are *Colo Colo* who play at the Estadio Monumental **Football**
(reached by any bus to Puente Alto; tickets from Cienfuegos 41, T6883244),

The Santiago Region

Football in Chile

Football arrived in Chile towards the end of the 19th century, courtesy of the British. The role of British workers – most of whom were employed in the construction of the railway system – is reflected in the names of several of the leading teams, notably Santiago Wanderers (who are based in Valparaíso), Everton (based in Viña) and Rangers (based in Talca). The game's popularity grew rapidly; by the 1940s most large towns boasted their own team and stadium. In 1962, Chile's importance as a soccer nation was recognised internationally when she hosted the World Cup, and the national side finished third. The quarter final between Chile and Italy became known as the 'Battle of Santiago', one of the most vicious games in the sport's history (Chile won 2-1).

Whilst Chilean football may not enjoy the worldwide recognition given to Argentina and Brazil, there is no doubt that Chileans follow 'the beautiful game' with as much passion as their illustrious neighbours. Chile played well in the qualifying round for the 1990 World Cup, and the decisive match saw them having to draw in Brazil to go through – losing 1-0, the Chilean goalkeeper, 'El Condor' Rojas, collapsed with blood falling from his cheek, claiming to have been hit by a missile from the crowd, and the Chilean team walked off in protest. However it later emerged that Rojas had cut himself with a razor blade, and Chile were disqualified and banned from the 1994 World Cup. Chile's performance in the 1998 World Cup – when they reached the last 16 – was thus a source of great national pride, but, in truth, the 1998 adventure was somewhat typical of Chilean football, as the national side flattered for a moment (being only eight minutes away from an unlikely victory against Italy in their first match), before going out 4-1 to Brazil; the last time a Chilean side reached the final of the Copa Libertadores (the South American club championship) was in 1993, when Universidad Católica somewhat let things slip by losing 5-1 to Sao Paolo in the away leg of the final, before waking up belatedly and winning the home leg 2-0.

The local season starts in March and runs through the winter to November, with a six-week break in the winter. Most of the support (and money) goes to the big three clubs, all based in Santiago: Universidad de Chile (known as 'La U'), Colo-Colo and Universidad Católica (which tends to be favoured by the well-off). The greatest rivalry is between La U and Colo-Colo (who are also known as Los Indios, as their strip carries an image of the great Mapuche leader after whom they were named). The most fervent supporters of the former are known as los de abajo (the underdogs), while those of the former are called la garra blanca (the white claw). Colo Colo were the most consistently successful team through the 1980s and 1990s, winning the Copa Libertadores in 1991 (the only time a Chilean club has done so), although in recent years "La U" have become much stronger.

A visit to a match, especially if it is either a clásico (local derby) or an international game, is an unforgettable experience. Watching football is still very much a family affair and the supporters dance, sing and wave their team colours beneath a nonstop rain of confetti, fireworks and coloured smoke. Tickets cost around US$5 (reductions for women and students in some parts of the ground). If you decide to visit the Estadio Nacional, the home of La U where international matches are played, find a space high up on the terraces and you will be able to watch the sun set over the mountains behind Santiago.

Universidad de Chile (Campo de Departes, Nunoa, T2392793) who play at the Estadio Nacional (Av Grecia 2001, T2388102), and Universidad Católica who play at San Carlos de Apoquindo (reached by bus from Metro Escuela Militar, tickets from Andrés Bello 2782, Providencia, T2312777).

In the centre: *Gimnásio Alicia Franché*, Moneda 1481, T6961681. Aerobics and fitness classes (women only). Another at Huérfanos 1313, T6711562. In Providencia: *Sesame*, Los Leones 2384. With pool, aerobics. Highly recommended.

Gymnasium

Club Hípico, Blanco Encalada 2540. Racing every Sun and every other Wed afternoon (moves to Viña del Mar, Jan-Mar), worthwhile even if only to watch dusk fall over the Andes, entry to main stand US$6, card of up to 18 races. Also at the Hipódromo Chile every Sat afternoon; pari-mutuel betting. Betting is a growing industry, with increasing numbers of *Teletrak* betting shops around the city.

Racecourses

The 2 main climbing areas near Santiago are the Grupo Loma Larga near the Cajón del Maipo and the Grupo Plomo near the ski resort of La Parva. For details of climbing in these areas, see pages 121 and 124. For ski resorts in the Santiago area see page 119. *Club Andino de Chile*, Enrique Foster 29. Ski club (open 1900-2100 on Mon and Fri). *Federación de Andinismo de Chile*, Almte Simpson 77A (T2220888, F2226285). Open daily, see page 60. It has the addresses of all the mountaineering clubs in the country and has a mountaineering school. *Club Alemán Andino*, El Arrayán 2735, T2425453. Open Tue and Fri 1800-2000, May-Jun. Equipment hire at *La Cumbra Ltda*, Av Apoquindo 5258, T678 4285, la_cumber@email.com Dutch proprietors very helpful, good climbing and trekking equipment. *Mountain Service*, Santa Magdelena 75, T2343439, F2343438, www.mountainservice.cl English spoken, tents, stoves, clothing, equipment rental. Recommended. *Panda Deportes*, Paseo Las Palmas 2217 (Metro Los Leones), T2321840. **Transport** to the ski resorts of Farellones, El Colorado, La Parva and Valle Nevado is operated by *Skitotal*, Av Apoquindo 4900, oficina 40-42, T2460156, who also rent equipment, organize accommodation, lessons. English, German spoken.

Skiing & climbing
Equipment hire is much cheaper in Santiago than in ski resorts. For detailed information on skiing near Santiago see pages 119-122

Tupahue, large pool with cafés, entry US$7; 2 for the price of 1 on Wed, and *Antilen*, US$10 both on Cerro San Cristóbal. Open daily in summer except Mon 1000-1500 (closed Apr-Oct). There are 2 pools in the Parque O'Higgins (one for children), summer only, T5569612, US$4. Olympic pool in Parque Araucano (near Parque Arauco Shopping Centre, closest Metro Escuela Militar), open Tue-Sat 0900-1900, Nov-Mar.

Swimming pools

As well as other martial arts at *Raul Tou-Tin*, Irarrázaval 1971, T2048082, F3641769.

Tai Chi

Santiago Tennis Club; also, *Club de Tenís Jaime Fillol*, Rancho Melnichi, Par 4. There are municipal courts in Parque O'Higgins; the national stadium, *Estadio Nacional* (Av Grecia con Av Marathon) has a tennis club which offers classes.

Tennis

Tour operators

All Travels, Huérfanos 1160, Local 10, T6964348. Good for flight tickets. *Asatej Student Flight Centre*, Hernando de Aguirre 201, Of 401, T3350395, F3350394, chile@asatej.com.ar For cheap flights and youth travel, also tours, car rental, ISIC cards, medical insurance and hotels. Recommended. *Blanco*, Pedro de Valdivia near Av Providencia. Good for flight information and exchange. *Cascada Expediciones*, Orrego Luco 040, Providencia, T2342274, www.cascada-expediciones.com Specialize in activity tours in remote areas. *Eurotur*, Huérfanos 1160, Local 13, www.eurotur.com For cheap air tickets to Europe. *Passtours*, Huérfanos 886, Of 1110, T6393232, F6331498, www.finam.cl/passtour Many languages spoken, helpful. Recommended. *Patagonia Connection SA*, Fidel Oteíza 1921, Of 1006, Providencia (Metro Pedro de Valdivia), T2256489, F2748111, info@patagoniaconnex.cl For cruises to Patagonia. *Rapa-Nui*, Huérfanos 1160. Specializes in trips to Easter Island. *Selectours*, Agencia de Viajes, Las Urbinas 95, Providencia, T2520201, F2342838. *Southern Cross*

The Santiago Region

Adventure, Jose Miguel de la Barra 521, T/F6396591, www.scadventure.com Branch office also at Toconao 544, San Pedro de Atacama. Offers mountaineering, biking, horseriding, trekking, high altitude archaeology, visits to volcanoes, fishing in the Andes. English, French, German and Spanish speaking guides, camping gear provided. **Turismo Cocha** (American Express representatives with mail service), Av El Bosque Norte 0430, Casilla 191035, Providencia, Metro Tobalaba, T2301000, www.cocha.com **Turismo Grace**, Victoria Subercaseaux 381, T6933740. Good service. **Turismo Tajamar**, Orrego Luco 023, Providencia, T3368000. Good for flights, helpful. Recommended. **USIT Andes** Av 11 de Septiembre 2305, Local 13, T3351415, hvergara@usitandes.cl Student travel agency. **VMP Ltda**, Huérfanos 1160, Local 19, T/F6967829, for all services. Many languages spoken, helpful. Recommended. **Wagons-Lits Cook**, Carmencita, Providencia, T2330820. Recommended.

Local tours *Ace Turismo*, O'Higgins 949, T6960391. City tour, US$12 for ½ day. *Maysa*, Paseo Ahumada 6, Of 43, T/F6964468. Good tours of wine bodegas and Valparaíso, US$30. *Nicole Aventuras*, T/F2256155, T8241277 (mob), wwwfis.puc.cl/~gtarrach/avenic Excursions in Santiago region, including wildlife and glacier tours.

Adventure tours & trekking *Altue Expediciones*, Encomenderos 83, piso 2, Las Condes, T2321103, F2336799, altue@entelchile.net For wilderness trips including tour of Patagonia and sea-kayaking in Chiloé. *Sportstours*, Moneda 970 Piso 14 T5495200, www.sportstour.cl German-run, helpful, 5-day trips to Antarctica (offices also at Hotels *Carrera* and *San Cristóbal*). Climbing and adventure tours in the Lake District and elsewhere: *Andina del Sud*, Bombero Ossa 1010, piso 3, Of 301, T6971010, F6965121. *Antu Aventuras*, Casilla 24, Santiago, T2712767, Tx440019, RECAL CZ. *Azimut 360*, Arzobispo Casanova 3, Providencia, T7358034, F7772375, www.azimut.cl Low prices. Adventure and eco-tourism throughout Chile, Aconcagua base camp services and mountaineering expeditions. Highly recommended. *Mountain Service*, Paseo Las Palmas, 2209 (Metro Los Leones), T2330913. Recommended for climbing trips. *Patagonia Chile*, Constitución 172, Bellavista, T351871. Offer mountain trips, river rafting, trekking. *Racies*, Plaza Corregidor Zañartu 761. Cultural tours, including Robinson Crusoe Island and Antarctica, T/F6382904. *Turismo Cabo de Hornos*, Agustinas 814, Of 706, T6338481, F6338486. For *DAP* flights and Tierra del Fuego/Antarctica tours. *Turismo Grant*, Huérfanos 863, Oficina 516, T6395524. Helpful, English spoken. For skiing in the Santiago area see page 119. *Turismo Joven*, Av Suecia Norte 0125, T2329946, F3343008, turjoven@mailent.rdc.cl Youth travel services for young people and students for travel, studies, leisure with links in Latin America and worldwide.

Transport

Local **Bus** In Santiago, buses are known as *micros*, with each *micro* displaying its particular route on a board in the window. Over the past decade, the system has progressed from one of utter chaos (in which buses could stop anywhere at all and no routes were numbered) to a curious combination of chaos and efficiency. Now routes are all numbered and, on most main roads, buses will only stop at bus stops. On the Alameda, Providencia and Apoquindo, different bus stops serve different destinations (eg Pudahuel, Las Condes, Maipú) – these destinations are clearly marked on the stops. The chaos is provided by the new ticket machines. Theoretically, on getting onto the bus, you are supposed to put exact change into the machine to get a printed ticket, but in practice any one of three things may happen: you may do this; you may give the money to the driver who will then arrange a printed ticket; or you may give the money to the driver who will give you a paper ticket of the type that were used before the machines were brought in. Whatever happens, the driver will expect you to be expecting his particular way of doing things. The fare is approximately US$0.50, but there are frequent rises.

Santiago metro

The Santiago Region

Car hire Prices vary a lot so shop around first. *Hertz*, *Avis*, *Budget* and others available from airport. *ANSA*, Irarrázaval 4369, T2762551. *Avis* at San Pablo 9900, T6019757. Poor service reported. *Full Famas*, Diego Portales 506, T258060. *Hertz*, Costanera Andrés Bello 1469, T6010477, at *Hotel Hyatt* T2455936. Has a good network in Chile and cars are in good condition. *Seelmann*, Las Encinas 3057, T398849. Also *Automóvil Club de Chile* car rental, Marchant Pereira 122, Providencia, T2744167, discount for members and members of associated motoring organizations. A credit card is usually asked for when renting a vehicle. As in most cities of its size, traffic and pollution are major problems: driving in the city is restricted according to licence plate numbers; each day, plates ending in one of two digits are prohibited from circulating (prohibited registration numbers are published in the press).

Tax of 18% is charged but usually not included in price quoted. If possible book a car in advance

Colectivo Collective taxis, which operate on fixed routes between the centre and the suburbs, are a convenient form of transport. They carry destination signs and route numbers. Fares vary, depending on the length of the journey, but are usually between US$0.75 and US$1.50. Higher fares at night.

Metro Line 1 of the underground railway system runs west-east between San Pablo and Escuela Militar, under the Alameda, Line 2 runs north-south from Cal y Canto to Lo Ovalle. The connecting station is Los Héroes. Line 5 runs north-south from Santa Ana on Line 2, via Baquedano on Line 1 to La Florida – work is under way to extend this line west to the Parque Quinta Normal (due to be completed in 2002). The trains are fast, quiet, and very full. The first train is at 0630 (Mon-Sat), 0800 (Sun and holidays), the last about 2245. Fares vary according to time of journey; there are 2 charging periods: high 0715-0900, 1800-1930, US$0.55; low all other times, US$0.40. The simplest solution is to buy a *boleto valor*, US$4.70, a charge card from which the appropriate fare is deducted; there are often queues for the ticket office, but bigger stations also have ticket machines. Metrobus services (blue buses, fare US$0.40) connect the metro

See map above

stations of Lo Ovalle, San Pablo, Las Rejas, Pilar del Granso, Cal y Canto, Salvador and Escuela Militar with outlying parts of Gran Santiago.

Motorcycle Small BMW workshop, Av San Camilo 185, Sr Marco Canales. BMW car dealer Frederic, Av Portugal, has some spares. Also tyre shops in this area. BMW riders can also seek help from the *carabineros* who ride BMW machines and have a workshop with good mechanics at Av Rivera 2003.

Taxi Taxis (black with yellow roofs) are abundant, and not expensive, with a minimum charge of US$0.50, plus US$0.10 per 200 m. Taxi drivers are permitted to charge more at night, but in the daytime check that the meter is set to day rates. Taxis are more expensive at bus terminals and from taxi ranks outside hotels – best to walk a block and flag down a cruising taxi. Avoid taxis with more than 1 person in them, especially at night. For journeys outside the city arrange the charge beforehand. The private taxi service which operates from the bottom level of *Hotel Carrera* has been recommended (same rates as city taxis), as has **Radio Taxis Andes Pacífico**, T2253064/2888; similarly **Rigoberto Contreras**, T6381042, ext 4215, but rates are above those of city taxis.

Long distance

Air For details of the Aeropuerto Arturo Merino Benitez, see page 37. For domestic flights from Santiago see under relevant destinations.

On Fri evening, when night departures are getting ready to go, the terminals are murder

Bus There are frequent, and good, interurban buses to all parts of Chile. Prices are much lower outside the peak summer season. You should always book ahead in Jan and Feb but, at other times of year departures are so frequent that it is usually possible to just turn up and go. Check if student rates are available (even for non-students), or reductions for travelling same day as purchase of ticket; it is worth bargaining over prices, especially shortly before departure and out of the summer season. Also take a look at the buses before buying the tickets (there are big differences in quality among bus companies); ask about the on-board services, as many companies offer drinks for sale, or free, and luxury buses have meals and wine, colour videos and headphones. Reclining seats are common and there are also *salón cama* sleeper buses. Fares from/to the capital are given in the text.

Bus terminals There are 4 terminals, all located close to each other near the city centre: **Terminal Alameda**, which has a modern extension with a shopping centre called Mall Parque Estación, O'Higgins 3712 (Metro Universidad de Santiago), T27071500, several Redbanc ATMs and internet. This has the best left luggage facilities in the city, and is a good choice as two of the best companies, *Tur Bus* and *Pullman Bus*, leave from here (serving all main destinations from Arica to Puerto Montt), and there are also *Pullman del Sur* buses to pretty and less frequented parts of the central valley, eg Chanco (US$7), Iloca (US$5.20). **Terminal Santiago**, O'Higgins 3878, T3761755, 1 block west of Terminal Alameda (Metro Universidad de Santiago) and sometimes referred to as the 'Terminal del Sur'. This terminal is used by services to and from the south, as well as buses to Valparaíso and Viña del Mar; it is the only terminal with services to Punta Arenas (48 hrs), and is also the centre for international services (see below). There is a Redbanc ATM. **Terminal San Borja**, O'Higgins y San Borja, T7760645, 1 block west of Estación Central, 3 blocks east of Terminal Alameda (Metro Estación Central). There are buses to destinations in the Santiago area such as Melipilla and most of the coastal towns (these are very frequent), some services to Valparaíso and Viña del Mar, and many companies serving northern Chile. Booking offices are arranged according to destination. The entrance is, inconveniently, located through the shopping centre next to the station, and is not immediately apparent from the Alameda. **Terminal Los Héroes**, T4200099, on Tucapel Jiménez, just north of the

Alameda (Metro Los Héroes). A smaller terminal with 8 companies, but useful destinations such as Vicuña with Diamantes de Elqui and Chiloé with Cruz del Sur. Note also that some long distance bus services also call at Las Torres de Tajamar, which is much more convenient if you are planning to stay in Providencia. *Tur Bus* also has a booking office in the centre at Bulnes 96, T6973541, and a centre on Av Apoquindo for those beginning their journeys in Las Condes.

To Argentina There are frequent services through the Cristo Redentor tunnel to Mendoza, 6-7 hrs, US$13, many companies, eg *Ahumada* (recommended), *Andesmar, CATA, TAC* (recommended), *Tas Choapa*, departures around 0800, 1200 and 1600, touts approach you in Terminal Santiago. Also *Tur Bus* services from the Terminal Alameda. Most of these services continue on to **Buenos Aires**, US$40, 24 hrs. There are also *colectivos* to **Mendoza** from the Terminal Santiago, US$20, 5 hrs, *Chi-Ar Ltda* is recommended (they pick up from hotels), shorter waiting time at customs. Companies in the Terminal Santiago have connections to many other cities: *Andesmar* to **Bahía Blanca**, US$50, change in Mendoza, 24 hrs; *Tur Bus, Tac* and *Tas Choapa* direct to **Córdoba**, US$28, 18 hrs (*El Rápido* not recommended); to **San Juan**, *TAC, Tas Choapa*, US$20. If going to destinations such as **Bariloche** or **Neuquén** in Argentine Patagonia, it is better to travel south to Temuco or Osorno and connect there.

Almost all international buses leave from the Terminal Santiago

To **Montevideo** (Uruguay), most involving a change in Mendoza, eg *Tas Choapa*, 27 hrs, including meals. To **São Paulo** and **Rio de Janeiro** (Brazil), *Chilebus* and *Pluma*, Tue, Thu, Sat, US$100, 72 hrs. To **Asunción** (Paraguay), 4 a week, 28 hrs, US$70. The biggest company serving Andean destinations is the Peruvian company *Ormeño* in Terminal Santiago, whose buses leave on Tue and Fri at 0900 to **Lima** (Peru), where connections are made to **Guayaquil** and **Quito** (Ecuador), **Cali** and **Bogotá** (Colombia) and **Caracas** (Venezuela) – buses are good and comfortable and there are meal stops. To **Lima**, 51 hrs, US$70 (it is cheaper to take a bus to Arica, a *colectivo* to Tacna (US$4), then bus to Lima); to **Guayaquil**, 80 hrs, US$120; to **Quito**, 88 hrs, US$130; to **Cali**, 4½ days, US$170; to **Bogotá**, US$185, 5 days; to **Caracas**, US$200, 7 days. Those heading for Bolivia are best advised to travel to one of the northern cities and then go by frequent bus from Iquique or Arica, or via the weekly train from Calama.

Hitchhiking To **Valparaíso**, take Metro to Pajaritos and walk 5 mins to west – no difficulty. Alternatively, take bus 'Renca Panamericana' from MacIver y Monjitas. To hitch **south**, take *Buses del Paine* from outside the Terminal San Borja as far as possible on the highway to the toll area, about US$1, 75 mins. To hitch **north** is not easy, but take blue Metrobus marked 'Til-Til' (frequent departures from near the Mercado Central as far as the toll bridge (*peaje*), 40 mins, US$1), then hitch from just beyond the toll-bridge; you may be better off getting a bus north to the town of La Calera, 2 hrs, and trying from there. To **Buenos Aires** (and Brazil) take a bus to Los Andes (*Buses Los Andes* leave from Tucapel Jimenez y Moneda, behind the Terminal Los Héroes), then go to *Copec* station on the outskirts (most trucks travel overnight).

Train There are no passenger trains to northern Chile, Valparaíso or Vína del Mar. The line runs south to Rancagua, San Fernando, Curicó, Talca, Linares, Parral and Chillán, thereafter services go to **Concepción** and **Temuco**. The line south from Temuco to Puerto Montt is scheduled to be reopened by 2006. There are 6 trains daily to Chillán (first 0830, last 2230, US$6), 1 daily to Temuco (2000, US$8 *económico*, US$12 *salón*, US$25 sleeper), and 1 daily to Concepción (2230, US$6 *económico*, US$9.50 *salón*, US$17 sleeper). *Expreso* services do not have sleepers; some *rápidos* do (in summer *rápidos* are booked up a week in advance). *Dormitorio* carriages were built in Germany in the 1930s, bunks (comfortable) lie parallel to rails, US-Pullman-style (washrooms at

All trains leave from Estación Central at Alameda O'Higgins 3322

Only posing officer!

On 4 March 1997, London's Financial Times *reported: "Chilean Police stopped 49 motorists in Santiago for using cellular phones while driving, only to find that a third were pretending to talk on fake phones."*

each end, one with shower-bath – often cold water only); an attendant for each car; bar car shows 3 films – no cost but you must purchase a drink ticket in advance. There is also a newer, *gran dormitorio* sleeping car (1984), with private toilet and shower, US$10 extra for 2. Recommended. Also a car-transporter service to Chillán and Temuco. Trains are still fairly cheap and generally very punctual, although 1st class is generally more expensive than buses; meals are good though expensive. Cycles can be carried, but check in advance. There are family and senior citizen discounts. No student discounts. Trains can be cold and draughty in winter and spring. There are also frequent local *Metrotren* services south to Rancagua. Booking offices: Alameda O'Higgins 853 in *Galería Hotel Libertador*, Local 21, T6322801, Mon-Fri 0830-1900, Sat 0900-1300; or Metro Escuela Militar, Galería Sur, Local 25, T2282983, Mon-Fri 0830-1900, Sat 0900-1300; Estación Central, open till 2230, T6895718/6891682. Left luggage office at Estación Central. A steam train runs tourist services between Santiago and Los Andes, a 5-hr journey, T6985536 for details.

Check shipping schedules with shipping lines rather than Sernatur **Shipping** *Navimag*, Av El Bosque Norte 0440, Of 1103, T4423120, for services from Puerto Montt to Puerto Natales and vice versa. *Transmarchilay*, Agustinas 715, Of 403, T6325100, for services between Chiloé and the mainland and ferry routes on the Camino Austral. *M/n Skorpios*, Augusto Leguía Norte 118, Las Condes, T2311030, F2322269, for luxury cruise out of Puerto Montt to Laguna San Rafael. *Transmarchilay* also sail to the Laguna San Rafael in summer. *Patagonia Connection SA*, Fidel Oteíza 1921, Of 1006, Providencia (Metro Pedro de Valdivia), T2256489, F2748111, for services Puerto Montt-Coyhaique/Puerto Chacabuco-Laguna San Rafael.

Directory

Airline offices *Ladeco/LanChile*, sales office: Américo Vespuccio 901, T600-5622000/6613000 (Ladeco), and several other offices, including at Paseo Estado Y Huérfanos and in the Centro Comercial Alto Las Condes. Also: *Aeroflot*, Guardia Vieja 255, Oficina 1008, T3310244. *Aero Perú*, Fidel Oteiza 1953, piso 4, T2742023. *Air France*, Alcantara 44, piso 6, Las Condes, T2909330, F2909340. *American*, Huérfanos 1199, T6790000. *British Airways*, Isidora Goyenechea 2934, Oficina 302, T3308600, airport T6010721. *Continental*, Nueva Tajamar 481, T2044000. *Ecuatoriana*, A de Fuenzalida 047, piso 2, Of 8, T3639442. *Iberia*, Bandera 206, piso 8, T8701000. *Italia and KLM*, San Sebastián 2839, Oficina 202, T2330011 (sales), T2330991 (reservations). *LACSA*, Dr Barros Borgoño 105, piso 2, T2355500. *Lufthansa*, Moneda 970, piso 16, T6301000. *South African Airlines*, Santa Magdalena 75, Of 411, T3353272. *Swissair*, Barros Errázuriz 1954, Oficina 810, T2442888. *United*, El Bosque Norte 0177, T3370000. *Varig*, El Bosque Norte 0177, piso 9, T3320618, T6395976. *Viasa*, Tenderini 82, piso 6, T6393922, T6951290.

Banks *Banks open from 0900 to 1400, but close on Sat* Official daily exchange rates are published in *El Mercurio* and *La Nación*. Some *casas de cambio* reduce their rates slightly when banks are closed. There is never a problem in finding a Redbanc ATM. Banks doing exchange: *American Express*, Andrés Bello 2711, piso 9, T3506700 (Metro Tobalaba) (Turismo Cocha, Av El Bosque Norte 0430, T2301000, Providencia, for travel information and mail collection). No commission, poor rates (better to change TCs into dollars – no limit – and then into pesos elsewhere). *Banco de Chile*, Ahumada 251. Demands the minimum of formalities, but may charge commission. *Citibank*, Av Providencia 2653 and branches elsewhere in the city. Thomas

Cook/Mastercard agent is **Turismo Tajamar**, Orrego Luco 023, T3368000. For Cirrus ATMs go to **Banco Santander** and **Banco de Santiago** and other banks with Redbanc sign. Visa at **Corp Banca**, Huérfanos y Bandera, but beware hidden costs in 'conversion rate', and **Banco Santander**, Av Providencia y Pedro de Valdivia. No commission. For stolen or lost Visa cards go to **Transbank**, Huérfanos 770, piso 10. **Casas de Cambio** (exchange houses). In centre: mainly situated on Agustinas and Huérfanos. **Afex**, Moneda 1140. Good rates for TCs. **Alfa**, Agustinas 1052. **Cambios Andino**, Ocho, Agustinas 1062. **Cambios Manquehue**, Huérfanos 1160, Local 5 (Galeria Alessandri). **Exprinter**, Bombero Osso 1053. Good rates, low commission, cambios. **Inter**, Andrés de Fuenzalida 47, Providencia. **Intermundi**, Moneda 896. In Providencia: several around Av Pedro de Valdivia, eg at Gral Holley 66. Good rates. **Casa de Cambio Blancas**, opposite Hotel Orly on Pedro de Valdivia, and **Mojakar**, Pedro de Valdivia 072. **Bataex**, Pedro de Valdivia 042. **Cambios Azul**, Galeria Las Palmas 2209, Local 034, Pedro de Valdivia. **Guínazu**, Pedro de Valdivia 048. All major currencies can be bought or sold. Some casas de cambio in the centre open Sat morning (but check first). Most casas de cambio charge 3% commission to change TCs into dollars. Always avoid street money changers (particularly common on Ahumada and Agustinas): they will show you a figure that is fractionally more than the going rate, before pulling any one of a number of tricks, eg using the MR button on calculators to do a false calculation giving much less than you should have, asking you to accompany them to somewhere obscure; the passing of forged notes and muggings are reported.

Internet Check out www.netcafeguide.com/chile **In the centre**: **Anditel**, Bandera y Catedral, 1 block from the Plaza de Armas, US$1.50 per hr, quiet. **c@fe.com**, O'Higgins 0145 (near Plaza Italia), good snacks, US$2.50 per hr. **Cybercafe**, Santa Lucía 0120, next to Instituto Chileno-Británico, US$1.20 per hr. **Internet Virtual**, Santo Domingo 1091, US$1.50 per hr, also very cheap call centre. **Sonnets Ltda.**, Londres 043, T6644725, US$2 per hr, tea, coffee, book exchange, owner speaks Spanish, English, Dutch and German, helpful, friendly atmosphere. **In Bellavista**: **Ciberia**, Pío Nono 015, US$1.20 per hr. **In Barrio Brasil**: **463@café**, Av Brasil 463. **Cybercafe**, Cienfuegos 161 (near junction with Moneda, just west of Panamericana), US$0.80 per hr, cheapest in Santiago. **ES Computación**, Salvador Sanfuentes 2352, T6887395, nine@ctc.internet.cl (Metro Republica), US$2.50 per hr, helpful staff. **In Providencia**: Near Metro Manuel Montt General del Canto y Providencia, US$1.30 per hr. **Near Metro Pedro de Valdivia**: **easy@net**, Ricardo Lyon y Providencia, US$1.50 per hr. **Near Metro Tobalaba**: **Café Phonet**, San Sebastián 2815, US$2 per hr, also very cheap international phonecalls. There is also access at the Terminal de Buses Alameda, in the CTC telefónica office on the lower floor of the attached shopping gallery.

Commun-ications

Post office: Plaza de Armas (0800-1900), poste restante well organized (though only kept for 30 days), passport essential, list of letters and parcels received in the hall of central Post Office (one list for men, another for women, indicate Sr or Sra/Srita on envelope). Also has philatelic section, 0900-1630 (if there are long queues at the main counters you can come here to buy your stamps and save yourself 10 mins). Also sub offices in Providencia at Av 11 de Septiembre 2092, Manuel Montt 1517, Pedro de Valdivia 1781, Providencia 1466, and in Estación Central shopping mall. These open Mon-Fri 0900-1800, Sat 0900-1230. If sending a parcel, the contents must first be checked at the post office. Paper, tape etc on sale. Open Mon-Fri 0800-1900, Sat 0800-1400.

Telephone: The cheapest call centres are on Calles Bandera, Catedral and Santo Domingo, all near the Plaza de Armas. International calls from here are half the price of the main company offices: to the US, US$0.30 per min, to Europe, US$0.40 per min, eg at Catedral 1033 and Santo Domingo 1091. Main offices: **Compañía de Teléfonos de**

Chile (Telefónica), Moneda 1151. Closed Sun. *ENTEL*, Huérfanos 1133. Mon-Fri 0830-2200, Sat 0900-2030, Sun 0900-1400, calls cheaper 1400-2200. Fax upstairs. Fax also available at CTC offices, eg *Mall Panorámico*, 11 de Septiembre, 3rd level (phone booths are on level 1). There are also CTC phone offices at some metro stations including *La Moneda, Escuela Militar, Tobalaba, Universidad de Chile* and *Pedro de Valdivia* for local, long-distance and international calls.

Cultural **International communities** *British Chamber of Commerce*, Av Suecia 155-C,
centres Providencia, Casilla 536, T2314366. *British Council*, Av Eliodoro Yáñez 832, near Providencia, T2361199. The British community maintains the *British Commonwealth Society* (old people's home etc), Av Alessandri 557, T2238807, and the interdenominational Santiago Community Church, at Av Holanda 151 (Metro Tobalaba), Providencia, which holds services every Sun at 1045. There is also the *Instituto Chileno Británico de Cultura*, Santa Lucía 124, T6382156. 0930-1900, except 1330-1900 Mon, and 0930-1600 Fri, has English papers in library (also in Providencia, Darío Urzúa 1933, and Las Condes, A. Vespucio 631), runs language courses. *Instituto Chileno Alemán de Cultura*, Goethe-Institut, Esmeralda 636, T6399418 – *German Chamber of Commerce*, Ahumada 131. *Instituto Chileno Francés de Cultura*, Merced 298, T6335465. In a beautiful house. *Instituto Chileno Israeli de Cultura*, E Yañez 2342, T2094624. *Instituto Chileno Japones de Cultura*, Alcantara 772, T2071896. *Instituto Chileno Italiano de Cultura*, Triana 843, T2360712. *Instituto Chileno Norteamericano de Cultura*, Moneda 1467, T6963215. Good for US periodicals, cheap films on Fri. Also runs language courses and free Spanish/English language exchange hours (known as Happy Hours) which are a good way of meeting people. (Ask also about Mundo Club which organizes excursions and social events.) *Instituto Chileno Suizo de Cultura*, San Isidro 171, T6385414, chilenosuizo@tie.cl Courses in Spanish, French, German and English taught by native speakers, computer courses, internet access, café, library, art gallery, accommodation can be arranged. *Instituto Chileno de Cultura Hispánica*, Providencia 927. **Local cultural societies** *Instituto Cultural del Banco del Estado de Chile*, Alameda 123. Regular exhibitions of paintings, concerts, theatrical performances. *Instituto Cultural de Providencia*, Av 11 de Septiembre 1995 (Metro Pedro de Valdivia). Art exhibitions, concerts, theatre, circus performances, well worth checking out the programme. *Instituto Cultural Las Condes*, Av Apoquindo 6570, near beginning of Av Las Condes. Also with art exhibitions, concerts, lectures, etc.

Embassies & **Embassies** *Argentina*, Miraflores 285, T6331076. *Australia*, Gertrudis Echeñique
consulates 420, T2285065. 0900-1200. *Austria*, Barros Errázuriz 1968, piso 3, T2234774. *Belgium*, Av Providencia 2653, depto 1103, T2321070. *Bolivia*, Av Santa María 2796, T2328180 (Metro Los Leones). Open 0930-1400. *Brazil*, Alonso Ovalle 1665, piso 15, T6982496. *Canada*, Nueva Tajamar 481, Torre Norte, Piso 12, T3629660. *Denmark*, Jacques Cazotte 5531, Vitacura, T2185949. *Finland*, Alcantara 1100, Of. 201, T2634947. *France*, Condell 65, T2251030. *Germany*, Agustinas 785, piso 7 y 8, T6335031. *Israel*, San Sebastian 2812, piso 5, T7500500. *Italy*, Clemente Fabres 1050, T2259439. *Japan*, Av Ricardo Lyon 520, piso 1, T2321807. *Netherlands*, Las Violetas 2368, T2236825. Open 0900-1200. *New Zealand*, El Golf 099, Of. 703, T2909802. *Norway*, San Sebastian 2839, T2342888. *Panamá*, Lota 2257, T2311641. *Peru*, Av Andrés Bello 1751, T2356451 (Metro Pedro de Valdivia). *South Africa*, Av 11 de Septiembre 2353, Edif San Román, piso 16, T2312862. *Spain*, Av Andres Bello 1895, T2352755. *Sweden*, 11 de Septiembre 2353, Torre San Ramón, piso 4, Providencia, T2312733, F2324188. *Switzerland*, Av Vespucio Sur 100, piso 14 (Metro Escuela Militar), T2634211. Open 1000-1200 (Metro Tobalaba). *UK*, El Bosque Norte 0125 (Metro Tobalaba), Casilla 72-D, T3704100, F3704160. Will hold letters, open 0900-1200. *USA*, Av Andrés Bello 2800, T2322600, F3303710.

Consulates Contact the embassies except for the following: *Argentina*, Vicuña MacKenna 41, T2226947, F2226853. Australians need a letter from their embassy to get an Argentinian visa here, open 0900-1400 (visa US$25, free for US citizens); if you need a visa for Argentina, get it here or in the consulates in Concepción, Puerto Montt or Punta Arenas, there are no facilities at the borders. *United States*, T710133. Merced 230 (visa obtainable here). *Brazil*, MacIver 225, piso 15. Mon-Fri 1000-1300, US$10 (visa takes 2 days). Take passport, 2 photos, ticket into and out of Brazil, photocopy of first 2 pages of passport, tickets, credit card and Chilean tourist card. *Paraguay*, Huérfanos 886, Of 514, T6394640. Open 0900-1300 (2 photos and copy of 1st page of passport required for visa).

Medical services

Dentist *Antonio Yazigi*, Vitacura 3082, Apto 33, T2087962/2085040. English spoken. Recommended. *Dr Torres*, Av Providencia 2330, Depto 23. Excellent, speaks English. **Hospitals** Emergency hospital at Marcoleta 377 costs US$60. If you need to get to a hospital, it is better to take a taxi than wait for an ambulance. For yellow fever vaccination and others (but not cholera), *Hospital San Salvador*, J M Infante 551, T2256441. Mon-Thu 0800-1300, 1330-1645; Fri 0800-1300, 1330-1545. Also *Vaccinatoria Internacional*, Hospital Luis Calvo, MacKenna, Antonio Varas 360. *Clínica Central*, San Isidro 231, T2221953. Open 24 hrs, German spoken. *Clínica Alemana*, Vitacura 5951, Las Condes. German and some English spoken (bus 344 from centre), mixed reports – often highly recommended, but also allegations of sexual assualt by one of the members of staff. Cheapest hospital is the public *Hospital de Urgencia*, Portugal 125, from US$125. **Emergency pharmacy** Portugal 155, T382439. **Physician** *Dr Sergio Maylis*, T2320853. 1430-1900.

Language schools

AmeriSpan Unlimited has an affiliated school in Santiago, details from PO Box 40513, Philadelphia, PA 19106, USA, T2159854522, F2159854524, info@amerispan. com *Carolina Carvajal*, T/F381000, ccarvajal@interactiva.cl Spanish taught to individuals and small groups, intensive/business courses offered. *Centro de Idiomas Bellavista*, Crucero Exeter 325, Barrio Bellavista, T7375102, F7357651, www.cib.in.cl *Escuela de Idiomas Violeta Parra*, Ernesto Pinto Lagarrigue 362A, Recoleta-Barrio Bellavista, T/F7358240, vioparra@chilesat.net Courses aimed at budget travellers, information programme on social issues, arranges accommodation and visits to local organizations and national parks. *Instituto Chilena de la Lengua*, Miraflores 590, piso 2, Of 4, T/F6643114, www.cmet.net/ichil *Natalislang Language Centre*, Vicuña Mackenna 06, piso 7, Of 4, T/F2228721, info@natalislang.com 2-week courses are recommended as good value. *Top Language Services*, Huérfanos 886, oficina 1107, T/F6390321, offers Spanish in groups and individually, accommodation organized. Many private teachers, includes Carolina Carvajal, Miraflores 113, depto 26, T3810000. Highly recommended. Patricia Vargas Vives, José Manuel Infante 100, oficina 308, Providencia, T2442283. Qualified and experienced (US$12.50 per hr). Lucía Araya Arévalo, Puerto Chico 8062, Villa Los Puertos, Pudahuel, T2360531 (after 1800). Speaks German and English. *Pacifica*, Guillermo Acuña 2884, Providencia, T2055129, F3437802, pacifica@netline. cl Anglo-Chilean agency offering cultural programmes to students. Will also find accommodation with families and arrange Spanish classes either in language schools or with private teachers, minimum 1 month, US$70 commission charged.

Laundry

Cheapest wet-wash in the centre is probably *Lavandería Lola*, Av Ricardo Cumming y Monedo. Very busy so get there before 1100, US$4.50 per load. Other wet-wash places in the centre: at Agustinas 1532, also *Nataly*, another at Bandera 572, at Catedral y Amunátegui and *Lava Fácil*, Huérfanos 1750. Mon-Sat 0900-2000, US$4 per load. There are plenty of dry-cleaners, eg Merced 494. Nearby, just south of Metro Universidad Católica, there are several, including *American Washer*, Portugal 71, Torre 7, local 4. US$3, open 0900-2100 including Sun, can leave washing and collect it later, also at Monjitas 650. Wet-wash laundries in Providencia including *Laverap*, Av

The Santiago Region

 English language teaching: no longer a gold mine

An increasing number of private language institutes offer English language classes. Many of the difficulties involved in teaching in these are highlighted by Russell Trounce, a teacher in Santiago:

"Most of these institutes are small and new but they have no classes for teachers. If they do have classes they pay woeful salaries, and you can easily be replaced because there are so many teachers seeking work. If you arrive in Santiago these days expecting to pick up easy work teaching English, then you may easily be disappointed. In addition, the institutes are becoming more fussy and require native speakers with experience, teachers who are clean-cut and well-dressed, and teachers who have residency, or are at least prepared to stay six months. The major institutes won't even look at foreigners who are illegal. Beware of some institutes who take 20%

income tax off your wages (10% is normal). The pay is poor: if you wish to be paid between US$2.50 and US$3 after tax per hour then go for it. Santiago is now an expensive city to live in and US$3 won't buy you a decent meal. I would warn travellers not to come here with too many illusions about teaching English: it takes time to establish yourself as a foreigner and you have to be extremely patient."

Work permits can only be obtained by teachers themselves, not by the institutes. We have also received reports of more unscrupulous institutes employing teachers with 90-day tourist visas and 'discovering' as this expires that the teacher is not entitled to work, at which point it is difficult to obtain unpaid wages. English language teachers seeking work should apply in mid-February/early March with a full CV and photo.

Providencia 1600 block, Manuel Montt 67; **Marva**, Carlos Antúñez 1823 (Metro Pedro de Valdivia), wash and dry US$8; Av Providencia 1039, full load, wet wash, US$5, 3 hrs. At the corner of Providencia and Dr Luis Middleton there are several self-service dry cleaners (Metro Pedro de Valdivia, 11 de Septiembre exit).

Places of worship *American Presbyterian Church*, Iglesia San Marcos, Av Manquehue Norte 1320, Los Hualtatas. Service in English Sun 0915. *Anglican Church*, Holanda 151. Service 1030. *Synagogues*, Tarapacá 870, T393872, and Las Hortensias 9322, T2338868; also on Ricardo Lyon, 5 blocks south of Providencia.

Useful addresses **Immigration** *Ministerio del Interior*, Departamento de Extranjería, Teatinos 950 (near Estación Mapocho), T6744000, for extension of tourist visa or any enquiries regarding legal status. Open Mon-Fri 0900-1200. They can give you the information you need, but to get the paperwork done you will then have to go round the back of the building and queue. The office to which this queue leads is open from 0900-1300. Make sure you are in the queue before 0800 and take a good book.

Around Santiago

Pomaire
Colour map 3, grid B3

The shops at the far (north) end of the street are as low as half the price of those at the entrance to the town

A small town 65 km west of Santiago, Pomaire is in a charming setting, surrounded by tall hills dotted with *algarrobo* bushes and covered in green grass. The town is famous for its ceramic work made from dark clay. The main street is brimful with shops selling the traditional dark clay pots and kitchenware, as well as diverse *artesanía* from all over Chile, including fine basketwork from the central valley and some lovely items made from the *combarbalita* stone from the north. There are probably few better places in Chile in which to buy general souvenirs and presents (although bargaining is not really entered into); pottery can be bought and the artists can be observed at work, before visitors retire to any one of numerous restaurants serving traditional dishes such as *humitas* and *pastel de choclo*.

Transport From Santiago take the Melipilla bus from San Borja behind Estación Central metro station, every few minutes, US$1 each way, Rutabus 78 goes on the motorway, 1 hr, other buses via Talagante take 1 hr 25 mins. Alight at the side road to Pomaire, 2-3 km from town; from here there are *colectivos* and *micros* every 10-15 mins (there are also *colectivos* linking Pomaire and Melipilla) – this route is easier than taking one of the infrequent direct buses from Santiago to Pomaire. En route, delicious *pastel de choclo* can be obtained at *Restaurant Mi Ranchito*.

The vineyards

The Maipo Valley is considered by many experts to be the best wine producing area of Chile. Several vineyards in the Santiago area can be visited, and this makes a good excuse to get away from the smog.

Cousiño-Macul, Av Quilin 7100, on the eastern outskirts of the city, offers tours Mon-Fri at 1100 in English and Spanish, phone first T2841011, vtaparticular@cousinomacul.cl Free, wine tasting US$2 per glass for good wines, US$1 per glass for new wines. Take either bus 390 from Alameda or bus 391 from Merced, both marked direction Peñalolén.

Concha y Toro, Virginia Subercaseaux 210, Pirque, near Puente Alto, 40 km south of Santiago, T8217069, rpublicas@conchaytoro.cl Give short tours (Spanish, English, French, German, Portuguese), Mon-Fri at 1030 and 1600 (Spanish) and 1130 and 1500 (English), Sat 1100 (Spanish) and 1000 and 1200 (English). Reserve 2 days in advance, cost US$4, wines US$1 per glass. Take the metro to La Florida, then catch Metrobus 74 to Pirque and ask the driver to let you off by the vineyard, or alternatively take the *colectivo* from Plaza Baquedano, US$2.50.

Undurraga, Santa Ana, 34 km southwest of Santiago, T3722800, sproduccion@undurraga.cl Also permits visits but with prior reservation 2 days in advance only, 1000-1600 on weekdays, free (tours given by the owner-manager, Pedro Undurraga). Take a Talagante bus from the Terminal San Borja to the entrance.

Viña Santa Rita, Padre Hurtado 0695, Alto Jahuel, Buin, 45 km south of Santiago on the Camino a Padre Hurtado, T3622520, rrivas@santarita.cl Good tour in English and Spanish, US$6, reserve 3 days in advance, Tue-Fri at 1030, 1130, 1215 and 1630, Sat and Sun at 1230 and 1530. Get a bus direct to Alto Jahuel from Terminal San Borja, bus company T7760645.

Ski resorts

There are six main ski resorts near Santiago, four of them around the mountain village of Farellones, 32 km east of the capital. All have modern lift systems, international ski schools, rental shops, lodges, mountain restaurants and first aid facilities. The season runs from June to September/October, weather permitting, although some resorts have equipment for making artificial snow. Many professional skiers from the northern hemisphere come here to keep in practice during the northern summer. Altitude sickness can be a problem, especially at Valle Nevado and Portillo: avoid over-exertion on the first day or two.

Colour map 3, grid B3

Ins & outs   Buses from Santiago to **Farellones**, **El Colorado**, **La Parva** and **Valle Nevado** are run in the ski season by *Ski Total*, Av Apoquindo 4900, Edificio Omnium, oficinas 40-42, T2466881, leaves from outside their offices, 4 blocks from Escuela Militar Metro, daily from 0800 in season, essential to book in advance, US$9 return. *Manzur Expediciones*, T7774284, leave for Farellones, El Colorado, Valle Nevado, Lagunillas and Portillo on Wed, Sat and Sun at 0830 from Metro Baquedano in central Santiago. It is easy to hitch from the junction of Av Las Condes/El Camino Farellones (YPF petrol station in the middle); take a Barnechea bus from C Merced. Except in bad weather, **Portillo** is easily reached by taking any bus from Santiago or Los Andes to Mendoza; you may have to hitch back (best done from the Chilean *aduana*).

Farellones   The first ski resort built in Chile, it is situated on the slopes of Cerro Colorado at 2,470 m and is reached by road in under 90 minutes. Now it is more of a ser-
Beautiful views for 30 km across 10 Andean peaks and incredible sunsets   vice centre for the three other resorts, but it provides affordable accommodation, has a good beginners area and is connected by lift to El Colorado. Perhaps the most popular resort for residents of Santiago, it is busy at weekends; it has several large restaurants. Daily ski-lift ticket, US$30; a combined ticket for all four resorts is also available, US$40-50 depending on season. One-day excursions are available from Santiago, US$5; enquire Ski Club Chile, Goyenechea Candelaria 4750, Vitacura (north of Los Leones Golf Club), T2117341.

Sleeping and eating   AL *La Cornisa*, T2207581, half board. **AL** *Motel Tupungato*, Candelaria Goyenechea 4750, Santiago, T2182216. **AL** *Posada de Farellones*, T2013704. Highly recommended. **B** pp *Refugio Club Alemán Andino* (address on page 109). Hospitable, good food.

El Colorado   Some 8 km further up Cerro Colorado along a very circuitous road, El Colorado has a large but expensive ski lodge at the base, offering all facilities, and a mountain restaurant higher up. There are nine lifts giving access to a large intermediate ski area with some steeper slopes. *La Cornisa* and *Cono Este* are two of the few bump runs in Chile. This is a good centre for learning to ski. Lift ticket US$37.

Sleeping and eating   L *Colorado Apart Hotel*, Av Apoquindo 4900, Oficina 43, Santiago, T2460660, F2461447. **L** *Edificio Los Ciervos* and *Edificio Monteblanco*, in Santiago, San Antonio 486, Oficina 151, T2335501, F2316965.

La Parva   Situated nearby at 2,816 m, La Parva is the upper class Santiago weekend
In summer, this is a good walking area. A good trail leads to the base of Cerro El Plomo which can be climbed   resort with 12 lifts, 0900-1730. Accommodation is in a chalet village and there are some good bars in high season. Although the runs vary, providing good intermediate to advanced skiing, skiers face a double fall-line. Not suitable for beginners. Connections with Valle Nevado are good. Lift ticket US$40; equipment rental US$10-15 depending on quality.

Sleeping and eating   L *Condominio Nueva Parva*. Good hotel and restaurant, reservations in Santiago: Roger de Flor 2911, T2121363, F2208510. Three other restaurants.

Valle Nevado   Owned by Spie Batignolles of France, this was the site of the 1993 Pan American winter games. It is 16 km from Farellones and offers the most modern ski facilities in Chile. "One has to imagine a deluxe hotel complex high up in the mountains with nothing else around" (Josselyn van der Pol and Leandro Yáñez). Although not to everyone's taste, it is highly regarded and efficient.

Climbing opportunities in the Grupo Plomo

Situated northeast of Santiago, this group lies near the ski resort of La Parva. The main peaks are La Parva itself (4,070 m), El Plomo (5,430 m), Paloma (4,930 m) and El Altar (5,222 m). El Plomo is not particularly difficult and is often used as an acclimatization climb before tackling Aconcagua or Ojos del

Salado. It was the southernmost Inca sacrificial peak and the ruins near the summit are in good condition. Allow three to four days: ice axe and crampons essential. El Altar is one of the hardest climbs in Chile; particularly difficult is the rarely scaled south face, grade 5.9 on loose rock.

There are 25 runs accessed by eight lifts. The runs are well prepared and are suitable for intermediate level skiers and beginners. There is a ski school and excellent heliskiing is offered. Lift ticket US$30 weekdays, US$42 weekends.

Sleeping and eating LL *Valle Nevado*, T2060027, F2080695, www.vallenevado. com *Puerta del Sol*, T6980103, F2080695. *Condominium Mirador del Inca*, T6980103 (Santiago 2060027), 6 restaurants. *Casa Valle Nevado*, Gertrudis Echeñique 441, T2060027, F2288888.

Situated at 2,855 m, Portillo lies 145 km north of Santiago and 62 km east of Los Andes near the customs post on the route to Argentina. One of Chile's best-known resorts, Portillo lies near the Laguna del Inca, 5½ km long and 1½ km wide; this lake, at an altitude of 2,835 m, has no outlet, is frozen over in winter, and its depth is not known. It is surrounded on three sides by accessible mountain slopes. From *Tío Bob's* there are magnificent views of the lake and surrounding area and condors may be spotted from the terrace. The runs are varied and well prepared, connected by 12 lifts, two of which open up the off-piste areas. This is an excellent family resort, with a very highly regarded ski school, and there are some gentle slopes for beginners near the hotel. The major skiing events are in August and September. Cheap packages can be arranged at the beginning and out of season. Lift ticket US$35, equipment hire US$22.

Portillo

There are boats for fishing in the lake; but beware the afternoon winds, which often make the homeward pull three or four times as long as the outward pull. Out of season this is another good area for walking, but get detailed maps before setting out. Mules can be hired for stupendous expeditions to the glacier at the head of the valley or to the Cerro Juncal, to the pass in the west side of the valley.

The Santiago Region

Sleeping L *Hotel Portillo*. Cinema, nightclub, swimming pool, sauna and medical service, on the shore of Laguna del Inca. Accommodation ranges from lakefront suites, full board, fabulous views, to family apartments, to bunk rooms without or with bath (much cheaper, from **C** up), parking charges even if you go for a meal, self-service lunch, open all year, minibus to Santiago US$50 each. Reservations, Roger de Flor 2911, T2313411, F2317164, Tx440372 PORTICZ, Santiago. **AL** *Hostería Alborada*, includes all meals, tax and service. During Ski Week (last in Sep), about double normal rate, all inclusive. Reservations, Agencia Tour Avión, Agustinas 1062, Santiago, T726184, or C Navarro 264, San Felipe, T101-R. Cheaper accommodation can be found in Los Andes but the road is liable to closure due to snow.

Eating Cheaper than the hotels are *Restaurant La Posada* opposite *Hotel Portillo*, open evenings and weekends only. Also *Restaurant Los Libertadores* at the customs station 1 km away.

Lagunillas Lagunillas lies 67 km southeast of Santiago in the Cajón del Maipo, 17 km east of San José de Maipo (see page 123 for transport to San José de Maipo), along a beautiful *ripio* road clinging to a chasm with stunning views of the far reaches of the Andes. In winter, the *carabineros* insist that drivers have snowchains, and rent them out at US$6. Accommodation in the lodges of the *Club Andino de Chile* (bookings may be made at Ahumada 47, Santiago). Tow fee US$20; lift ticket US$25; long T-bar and poma lifts; easy field. Being lower than the other resorts, its season is shorter, but it is also cheaper.

Santuario de la Naturaleza Yerba Loca Situated 45 km northeast of Santiago and reached by Route G21 (paved) towards Farellones, this park was founded in 1973. It covers 39,000 ha of the valley of the Río Yerba Loca, ranging in altitude between 900 and 5,500 m. Park administration is at Villa Paulina, 4 km north of Route G21, reached by a dirt road. From here a four-hour walk leads north to Casa de Piedra Carvajal, which offers fine views. Further north are two hanging glaciers, La Paloma and El Altar. Native tree species include the mountain olive. Birdlife includes eagles and condors. ■ *Getting there: colectivos with Taxis Transarrayán Ltda. Leave from Plaza San Enrique in Lo Barnechea (take any bus for Barnechea from Alameda or Providencia), T3216285. Sep-Apr, US$3. No accommodation. Maps and information available from CONAF in Santiago.*

Termas de Colina
Colour map 3, grid B3
Altitude: 915 m
43 km N of Santiago

This is an attractive, popular spa in the mountains. **AL** *Hotel Termas de Colina*, T/F8440990, has modern, expensive thermal baths, a beautiful swimming pool (closed Friday) US$6, formal restaurant; facilities open to public, crowded at weekends. ■ *Getting there: take a bus from Terminal de Buses Colina, Av La Paz 302 (40 mins), then another to the military base 1½ km from town. From here a rough road leads through beautiful countryside 6 km; last return bus at 1900. On the walk to the hotel do not take photos or even show your camera when passing the military base. Taxi from Colina to the hotel, US$5.*

The small towns in the Aconcagua Valley to the north – San Felipe, Jahuel and Los Andes – are described on page 125.

Reserva Nacional Río Clarillo
Colour map 3, grid B3

Some 45 km south of Santiago, this park is reached by paved road via San Bernardo and Pirque. The park covers 10,185 ha and is situated in the *precordillera* at between 850 and 3,000 m. It offers excellent views of the higher mountains, and of the surprisingly green pastures of the foothills. ■ *Getting there: bus from Puente Alto to El Principal, US$2.50, 1 hr. Administration at entrance, 2 km southeast of El Principal. Open all year.*

Cajón del Maipo

This rugged and surprisingly green valley, southeast of Santiago, provides an easy escape from the smog and bustle of Santiago. It is lined by precipitous mountains, and the snows of the high Andes can easily be seen. There are many interesting and beautiful sidetracks, eg to Lagunillas (see above) or Los Maiténes, and the upper reaches of the valley around El Volcán and Baños Morales are amazingly deserted, considering the proximity of Santiago. The road into the valley runs east from Puente Alto via Las Vizcachas, where the most important motor racing circuit in Chile is located, towards **San José de Maipo.** About 10 km east of Las Vizcachas is the *Restaurant El Calipso*, reputed to be one of the best restaurants in the country. The mountain town of **Melocotón** is 6 km south of San José de Maipo, and **San Alfonso** is 4 km further on. The walk from San Alfonso to the *Cascada de las Animas* is pleasant; ask permission to cross the bridge at the campsite (see below) as private land is crossed.

A visit here is highly recommended, particularly for those living in Santiago, it offers a welcome release from the city

The Santiago Region

San José F *Alojamento Inesita*, Comercio 301. Good, excellent chips. **Camino a Lagunillas A** *Cabañas Pura Vida*, T2084234, Km 4 from San José on the Lagunillas road, beautiful spot in a fantastic gorge, swimming pool, completely calm and off the beaten track, highly recommended. **Melocotón C** *Millahue*, T/F8899006. **San Alfonso C** *Posada Los Ciervos*, Camino al Volcan 31411, T/F8611581. With breakfast, **A** full board, good. **D** *Res España*. Clean, comfortable, restaurant. Also others. Campsite at the *Comunidad Cascada de las Animas*, T2517506. Also rents cabins (**C** for 4, hot water, cooking equipment etc) sauna, horseriding. Mid-range eateries include: *Restaurant El Campito*, Camino al Volcán 1841. Very good. Also on the road between Puente Alto and San José, *El Rancho del Ché*, in El Canelo, excellent Argentine meat and *La Petite France*, nearer San José, good French food, not cheap. Cheaper are *Restaurant La Isidora*, on the plaza in San José, smart, good, meat dishes and *Casino de Bomberos*, Comercio 1900-block, in San José.

Sleeping & eating

Buses leave Santiago from Metro Parque O'Higgins, Av Norte-Sur, or west side of Plaza Ercilla, every 15 mins to **San José**, US$1, 2 hrs; or else take Linea 5 metro to Bellavista de la Florida and wait for the bus on Av Vicuña Mackenna. *Línea 27 colectivos* also run from the plaza in Puente Alto as far as **San Alfonso**.

Transport

Cajón del Maipo

The Santiago Region

 Climbing opportunities in the Grupo Loma Larga

This massif, located around 100 km southeast of Santiago, lies just north of the Parque Nacional El Morado and is reached via Baños Morales. The main peaks are El Morado (5,060 m), Meson Alto (5,297 m), San Francisco (4,940 m), Arenas (4,400 m), the Mirador del Diablo and Cerro Unión.

Cerro Morado, on the northern edge of the national park, is one of the most difficult climbs in Chile; the south face climb to the southern summit (5,000 m) is particularly arduous involving 1,000 m of vertical climbing, grade 9, on rock and ice.

Around San Alfonso The road continues up the valley and divides 14 km southeast of San Alfonso. One branch forks northeast and runs via Embalse El Yeso to **Termas del Plomo**, Km 33, thermal baths with no infrastructure, very poor road (four-wheel drive essential) but stunning scenery. The other branch continues and climbs the valley of the Río Volcán. At **El Volcán** (1,400 m), 21 km from San Alfonso, there are astounding views, but little else; one or two small stores, but bring food from Santiago. It is possible to cross the river and camp wild on the far side, surrounded by giant rock walls and a real sense of isolation. If visiting this area or continuing further up the mountain, be prepared for military checks: passport and car registration numbers may be taken. From El Volcán the road (very poor condition) runs 14 km east to **Lo Valdés**, a good base for mountain excursions. Nearby are warm natural baths at **Baños Morales**, open from October, US$2. This is a wonderful area to come and get away from it all, and it is possible to spend days here exploring the paths that lead into the high mountains (this is the old southerly horse trail linking Santiago and Mendoza, and there is still a path over into Argentina). Some 12 km further east up the mountain is **Baños Colina** (not to be confused with Termas de Colina, see above) with hot thermal springs, free of cost and horses for hire. This area is popular at weekends and holiday times, but is otherwise deserted.

Sleeping and eating Lo Valdés B pp *Refugio Alemán Lo Valdés*, T2207610. Stone-built chalet accommodation, full board, own generator, good food. Recommended. **Baños Morales A** *Cabañas Corre Caminos*, Estero Morales 57402, T/F6992002, daniellapiccoli@hotmail.com Sleeps 4, comfortable. **D** pp *Hostería Baños* Morales, Balneario Villa del Valle. Nice set up. **E** pp *Res Los Chicos Malos*, T2885380. Comfortable, fresh bread, good meals. Free campsite. **F** *Residencial Pensión Diaz*, Río Maipo s/n, T8611496. Basic, friendly. **Baños Colina E** pp *Res El Tambo*, full board, restaurant, also camping. No shops so take food (try local goats cheese).

On weekdays hitching from San José is possible on quarry trucks

Transport Bus From Metro Parque O'Higgins, to **El Volcán** and to **Baños Morales** 1 bus daily, leaves Parque O'Higgins at 1200 (San José at 1345), returns at 1745; buy return on arrival to ensure seat back. Between Baños Morales and Baños Colinas you may be able to arrange a lift on one of the tour buses which run in summer.

Parque Nacional El Morado Situated north of Baños Morales, the park covers an area of 3,000 ha of the valley of the Río Morales, including the peaks of El Morado (5,060 m) and El Mirador del Morado (4,320 m), and El Morado glacier. It is in an exceptionally secluded and beautiful place, well worth making the effort to reach. ■ *Administration near the entrance, just north of Baños Morales. Park open Oct-Apr. US$2.*

From Santiago to Argentina

The route across the Andes via Los Andes and the Redentor tunnel is one of the major crossings to Argentina. Route 5 runs north of Santiago through the rich Aconcagua Valley, known as the Vale of Chile. The road forks at the Santuario de Santa Teresa, the west branch going to San Felipe, the east branch going to Los Andes and Mendoza.

Before travelling check on weather and road conditions beyond Los Andes. For buses on this route see page 113

The capital of Aconcagua Province, San Felipe is an agricultural and mining centre with an agreeable climate. Part of the Inca highway has recently been discovered in the city; previously, no traces had been found further south than La Serena. **Curimón**, 3 km southeast of San Felipe, is the site of the Convento de Santa Rosa de Viterbo (1727) which has a small museum attached. A paved road (13 km) runs north from San Felipe to the old town of **Putaendo**; in its church there is an 18th-century baroque statue of Christ. Accommodation is provided at **B** *Hostería San Felipe*, Merced 204, T510508, F513356.

San Felipe
Phone code: 034
Colour map 3, grid A3
Population: 42,000
96 km N of Santiago

Situated high in the *cordillera*, Termas de Jahuel lies 18 km by road northeast of San Felipe. The mountain scenery includes a distant view of Aconcagua. **L** *Termas de Jahuel*, T511240, has a thermal pool and tennis courts.

Termas de Jahuel
Altitude: 1,190 m

Some 16 km southeast of San Felipe, Los Andes is situated in a wealthy agricultural, fruit farming and wine-producing area, but is also the site of a large car assembly plant. It is a good place for escaping from Santiago and a convenient base for skiing at nearby Portillo. There are monuments to José de San Martín and Bernardo O'Higgins in the Plaza de Armas, and a monument to the Clark brothers, who built the Transandine Railway to Mendoza (now disused). There are good views from El Cerro de la Virgen, reached by a trail from the municipal picnic ground on Independencia (one hour).

Los Andes
Phone code: 034
Colour map 3, grid B3
77 km N of Santiago

Sleeping and eating A *Baños El Corazón*, at San Esteban 2 km north of Los Andes, T421371. Full board, swimming pool, thermal baths extra, take bus *San Esteban/El Cariño* (US$0.50). **A** *Plaza*, Esmeralda 367, T421929. Good, restaurant expensive. **D** *Central*, Esmeralda 278, T421275. Reasonable and very friendly (excellent bakery opposite, try the *empanadas*). **D** *Alameda*, Argentina 576, T422403. Without bath, clean, good rooms. **F** *Estación*, Rodríguez 389, T421026, without breakfast, basic. Cheap restaurant. **G** *Res Maruja*, Rancagua 182. Clean. **G** *Valparaíso*, Sarmiento 160. Clean.

Transport Bus Terminal is 1 block east of the Plaza de Armas. To **Mendoza** (Argentina), *Tas Choapa*, *Fenix Pullman Norte*, *Cata* and *Ahumada*. (Any of these will drop passengers off for Portillo, US$6.) **Hitchhiking** It is very difficult to hitchhike over the Andes, and Spanish is essential; try on trucks from Aduana building in Los Andes.

Directory Banks ATMs at banks on the Plaza de Armas. *Cambio Inter* at *Plaza Hotel*. Good rates, changes TCs. **Communications Telephone**: *CTC*, O'Higgins 405. **Useful addresses** *Automovil Club de Chile*, Chacabuco 33, T422790.

The road to Argentina follows the Aconcagua Valley for 34 km until it reaches the village of Río Blanco (1,370 m), where the Ríos Blanco and Juncal meet to form the Río Aconcagua. There is a fish hatchery with small botanical garden at the entrance to the Andina copper mine. East of Río Blanco the road climbs until Juncal where it zigzags steeply through a series of 29 hairpin bends at the top of which is the ski resort of Portillo (quite a sight from the top), see pages 120- 121.

Río Blanco

The Santiago Region

Sleeping and eating *Hostería Luna*, T421026, 4 km west of Río Blanco. Good value, clean, helpful, good food. *Hostería Guardia Vieja*, 8 km east of Río Blanco. Expensive but untidy, campsite. See page 121 for services in Portillo.

Transport Saladillo buses run hourly from Los Andes; from Santiago, Ahumada, at 1930 daily, direct, 2 hrs, US$2.

Border with Argentina: Los Libertadores

The Redentor tunnel, 4 km long, is open 24 hours from September to May, 0700-2300 from June to August, toll US$3. Cyclists are not allowed to cycle through but there is no-one to stop you on the Chilean side. Note that this pass is closed after heavy snowfall, when travellers are occasionally trapped at the customs complex on either side of the border.

Above the tunnel is the old pass, used before the tunnel was built. Above the pass at 3,854 m is the statue of *El Cristo Redentor* (Christ the Redeemer), which was erected jointly by Chile and Argentina in 1904 to commemorate King Edward VII's decision in the boundary dispute of 1902. It is completely dwarfed by the landscape. The old road over the pass is in a very poor state, especially on the Chilean side, and is liable to be blocked by snow even in summer. When weather conditions permit, the statue can be reached on foot from **Las Cuevas**, a modern settlement on the Argentine side (4½ hours up, two down). There are also 12-hour excursions to the statue from Mendoza.

Customs & immigration The Chilean border post is at Portillo. Bus and car passengers are dealt with separately. If entering Chile, there may be long delays during searches for fruit, meat and vegetables, which may not be imported into Chile. Remove all camera film to your hand luggage as it is not X-rayed. *Casa de Cambio* in customs building in Portillo. In Argentina, Ingeniero Roque Carranza, 13 km from the tunnel.

Into Argentina Just beyond Argentine customs and immigration is **Puente del Inca**, a sports resort named after the natural bridge which crosses the Río Mendoza. The bridge, apparently formed by sulphur-bearing hot springs, is 19 m high, has a span of 21 m and is 27 m wide. At the resort are *Hostería Puente del Inca* and *Residencial Vieja Estación* (much cheaper), as well as camping, transport to Mendoza and information and access for climbing **Aconcagua** (6,959 m), the highest mountain peak on earth outside Asia.

Some 17 km further east is **Punta de Vacas**, from where there is a good view of Tupungato (6,550 m). The only town of any size between the frontier and Mendoza is **Uspallata** with hotels and transport links, from where two roads lead to Mendoza: the paved, southern branch of Route 7, via Porterillos and Cacheuta; and the unpaved, northern branch via Villavicencio.

4

Valparaíso and Viña del Mar

Valparaíso and Viña del Mar

The coastal strip west of Santiago is one of the most popular destinations for regional tourists. Midway along the coast is Viña del Mar, one of the most famous resorts in South America, and awash with Argentines and Chileans strutting their stuff in summer. Near Viña are other popular resorts such as Concón and Horcón, while there is also a whole host of more secluded spots on the beaches near here, including Zapallar to the north and Quintay to the south. While the beaches are attractive, the water is very cold, and swimming is dangerous because of a heavy undertow.

The place that makes this part of Chile really worth visiting is Valparaíso, Chile's most important port and the most beguiling city in the country. Valparaíso is really two cities – the flat, ordered area by the port known as El Plán, and the chaotic, waspish cerros, in which most porteños (people from Valparaíso) live. It is possible to spend weeks exploring the alleyways of the cerros, where packs of dogs lie sunning themselves, brightly painted houses pile on top of one another, and half forgotten passageways head up and down the hills, offering fantastic views of the Pacific, the city, and – on a clear day – right over to the snowcapped cordillera. Nearer by is the lumpy summit of the Cerro La Campana, a high hill between the coast and the central valley which offers some of the best views in Chile, and can be climbed in a day. South of Valparaíso, towards the mouth of the Río Maipo, are a number of other centres, including Algarrobo – perhaps the most affluent resort along this coast – and Isla Negra, a village famous as the site of Pablo Neruda's home, the place in which the Nobel laureate gathered his collection of objets d'art from his journeys around the world.

Background

History This was one of the earliest areas settled by the Spanish, the lands being assigned to prominent conquistadores during the 16th century. For most of the colonial period this region was an important exporter of wheat and other foodstuffs to Peru. During the 19th century Valparaíso rose to become one of the most important ports on the Pacific coast of South America, but there were few other large centres of population along this coastline until the 1880s, when the fashion for holidaying near the sea spread from southern Europe. Viña del Mar was established in 1880 and several other resorts followed between 1880 and 1900: Algarrobo, Cartagena, Las Cruces, Zapallar and Papudo, all owing part of their popularity to the building of railway lines linking them to the capital. Although the influence of European resorts can still be seen in some of the buildings, especially in Viña del Mar and Zapallar, most of the older buildings have not withstood earthquakes and bulldozers.

Economy This area is one of the major economic centres of the country and its third most important industrial area. Valparaíso and San Antonio are important ports, between them handling much of the country's trade. Other facilities include an oil terminal and copper refinery at Quintero, an oil refinery at Concón and important chemical industries in Viña del Mar. The region is also a major producer of agricultural products, particularly soft fruit such as grapes and peaches. Its population is over 90% urban.

Climate This coastline enjoys a Mediterranean-style climate; the cold sea currents and coastal winds produce much more moderate temperatures than in Santiago and the central valley. Rainfall is moderate in winter and the summers are dry.

Valparaíso

Phone code: 032
Colour map 3, grid B2
Population: 345,000
116 km W of Santiago

Sprawling over a crescent of 42 hills that rear up from the sea, Valparaíso – the capital of Región V and seat of the Chilean parliament until 2002 – is a one-off. Unlike all other Chilean cities, the main residential areas are not divided into regimented blocks; here there is little order in the progression of streets from one point to another, and the urban chaos is mirrored in the bohemian and slightly anarchic sense of the cerros. Here you will find a 'monument to the urinal', a graveyard from which all the corpses were shaken out during a severe earthquake, many legends of ghosts and spirits, and grandiose houses and mansions mingling with some of Chile's worst slums. Valparaíso is all about contradictions – the fact that both Salvador Allende and Augusto Pinochet were born and raised here expresses this fact more eloquently than anything else, but the oppositions can also be seen in, for instance, the flat plan against the cerros; the sea against the views of Aconcagua; and the city's wealth set against its poverty. With all these conflicts, it is natural that the city should blend as one into Chile's most famous resort, Viña del Mar.

Ins and outs

Getting there
See page 142 for further details
There are inter-urban buses to Valparaíso from every major Chilean city (even including connections through to Punta Arenas), and it makes an interesting change to most travellers' itineraries to get a bus to Valparaíso instead of Santiago. Valparaíso also has connections through to Mendoza, Córdoba, Buenos Aires, and as far as Rio de Janeiro.

Things to do ★

- Enjoy the architectural anarchy of the hills of Valparaíso.
- Climb Cerro La Campana for some of the best views in Chile.
- Stroll down to San Antonio's fort to watch the catch being unloaded.
- Enjoy some of the best cuisine in Chile at one of Concón's many restaurants.
- Sun yourself along with the rich and famous on the beach at Viña del Mar.

Getting around To go anywhere between Plaza Aduana and Av Argentina, you should never have to wait more than 30 secs – buses with a "Pedro Montt" sign are cheaper but slower (the faster ones say "Errazuriz"). Buses to Cerro Alegre and the top of Cerro Concepción leave from Plazuela Ecuador (Nos 142 and D3). If you are going to Viña or one of the nearby towns to the north, catch a *micro* from Errazuriz or Brasil; *colectivos* to Viña leave from the same place. Taxis seldom use their meters, but are generally reasonable, and, if there are 3 or 4 of you, sharing a taxi can be cheaper than taking a *colectivo*. If you want to get up the *cerros*, taxis and *colectivos* usually wait around at the bottom of each *cerro*; otherwise, you can use the *ascensores* (lift) – sometimes you pay on entrance, sometimes on exit. Going uphill is slightly more expensive, but they are very cheap, and generally cost only US$0.10-0.20.

Tourist offices In the Municipalidad building, Condell 1490, Of 102. Open Mon-Fri 0830-1400, 1530-1730. Kiosks at bus terminal (good map available), helpful, open 0900-1300, 1530-1930 (closed Thu, Mar-Nov), Muelle Prat, open Nov-Mar 1030-1430, 1600-2000, and in Plaza Victoria, open 1030-1300, 1430-2000 Nov-Mar.

History

Founded in 1542, Valparaíso became, in the colonial period, a small port used for trade with Peru. It was raided at least seven times during the colonial era by pirates and corsairs, including Drake. The city prospered from independence more than any other Chilean town. It was used in the 19th century by commercial agents from Europe and the US as their trading base in the southern Pacific, and became a major international banking centre as well as the key port for shipping between the northern Pacific and Cape Horn. *El Mercurio de Valparaíso*, the oldest newspaper in South America, was first published here in 1827; the original office is in an interesting building located half a block from the Ascensor Turi and the Turi Clock Tower.

The city's decline was the result of two factors: the development of steam ships which stopped instead for coaling at Punta Arenas and Concepción, and the opening of the Panama Canal in 1914. Since then it has declined further owing to the development of a container port in San Antonio, the shift of banks to Santiago and the move of the middle classes to nearby Viña del Mar. Little of the city's colonial past survived the pirates, tempests, fires and earthquakes of the period, but a remnant of the old colonial city can be found in the hollow known as El Puerto, grouped round the low-built stucco church of La Matriz. Most of the principal buildings date from after the devastating earthquake of 1906, which was so severe that the modern area on which the *plan* and the port have been built quite literally rose from the sea at this point – until 1906, the ocean had lapped at the feet of the *cerros* (further serious earthquakes occurred in July 1971 and in March 1985). While the city has constantly been rebuilt, some impression of its 19th-century glory can be gained from the banking area of the lower town and from the mansions of wealthy merchants.

The No 9

The Camino Cintura (Avenida Alemania) is the only road which connects all the hills above Valparaíso; it affords constantly changing views, perhaps the best being from Plaza Bismarck. No 9 'Central Placeres' bus gives a fine scenic drive over the hills to the port.

Sights

There are two completely different cities. The lower part, known as **El Plan**, is the business centre, with fine office buildings on narrow streets that are strung along the edge of the bay and cluttered with buses. Above, covering the hills, or *'cerros'*, is a fantastic agglomeration of buildings in every conceivable style. Part of the charm of the *cerros* is that there is no order to speak of. It is as if every individual bought a plot of land and decided to build just as they saw fit, and the result is a unique hotchpotch of size and style and colour. Spanish colonial mansions lie side by side with adobe shacks and neo-classical monoliths. The buildings seem literally to tumble down the slopes; **Cerro Concepción** and **Cerro Alegre** are currently being considered for UNESCO World Heritage Site status.

Superb views over the bay are offered from most of the *cerros*, each *cerro* having a unique view. It is enjoyable to spend an afternoon exploring the hills. However lost you might feel, a few minutes walk down hill will lead you to *El Plan*. The poorer and rougher districts tend to be those furthest from the

Valparaíso

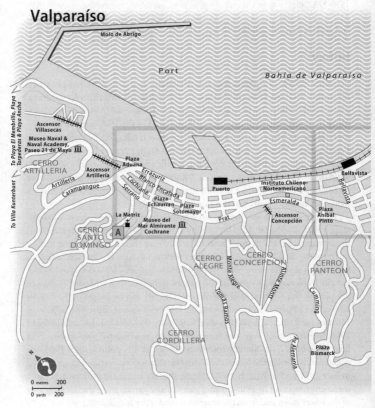

centre. The lower and upper cities are connected by steep winding roads, flights of steps and 15 *ascensores* or funicular railways dating from the period 1880-1914. The most unusual of these is **Ascensor Polanco** (entrance from Calle Simpson, off Avenida Argentina a few blocks southeast of the bus terminal), which is in two sections, the first of which is a 160 m horizontal tunnel through the rock, the second a vertical lift to the summit on which there is a *mirador*, or viewpoint. Note that the lower entrance is in an area which can be unsafe: do not go alone and do not take valuables.

The old heart of the city is the **Plaza Sotomayor**, dominated by the former **Intendencia** (Government House), now the seat of the admiralty, be careful when crossing the plaza, which at first sight appears pedistrianized, but is infact criss-crossed by busy roads. Opposite is a fine monument to the 'Heroes of the Battle of Iquique', which is also a mausoleum housing the bodies of all who fought in the battle. Visitors are allowed inside on 21 May of each year (the anniversary of the battle), following the massive procession of the armed forces through the city. While excavating under Plaza Sotomayor in order to build a new underground car park, parts of Valparaíso's original **old quay** were uncovered – they can be viewed from above ground through the glass ceiling, although the glass tends to mist up. The modern passenger quay is one block away from Plaza Sotomayor (handicraft shops on quay are expensive and poor quality), and nearby is the **railway station**, from which passenger services run on the metropolitan line to Viña del Mar and Limache.

Look out for the bronze plaques on the ground illustrating the movement of the shoreline over the centuries

Valparaíso and Viña del Mar

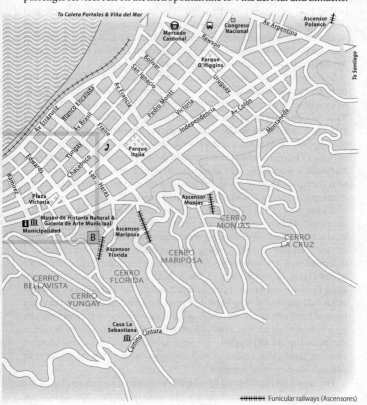

+++++++ Funicular railways (Ascensores)

Neruda on Valparaíso

"The hills of Valparaíso decided to dislodge their inhabitants, to let go of the houses on top, to let them dangle from cliffs that are red with clay, yellow with gold thimble flowers, and a fleeting green with wild vegetation. But houses and people clung to the heights, writhing, digging in, worrying, their hearts set on staying up there, hanging on, tooth and nail, to each cliff. The port is a tug-of-war between the sea and nature, untamed on the cordilleras. But it was man who won the battle little by little. The hills, and the sea's abundance gave the city a pattern, making it uniform, not like a barracks, but with the variety of spring, its clashing colours, its resonant bustle. The houses became colours: a blend of amaranth and yellow, crimson and cobalt, green and purple."
Pablo Neruda, Memoirs, Penguin, 1978.

In the evening the station is a gathering place for chess players; join in if your Spanish and chess are up to it.

The harbour is worth a visit on Saturday mornings to watch the fishing vessels unload their catch. Tell the gatekeeper you want to buy fish or you may be refused entry. The streets of El Puerto run on either side from Plaza Sotomayor. Calle Serrano runs northwest for two blocks to the Plaza Echaurren, a tree-lined square with a picturesque fountain and a sizeable population of local drunks. Near Plaza Echaurren stands the church of **La Matriz**, built in 1842 on the site of the first church in the city. This area can be dangerous at night; it is unadvisable to seek accommodation around here. Further northwest, along Bustamante, lies the Plaza Aduana named after the former customs building from where there is an *ascensor* to the bold hill of **Cerro Artillería**, crowned by the huge Naval Academy and a park.

Southeast of Plaza Sotomayor calles Prat, Cochrane and Esmeralda run through the old banking and commercial centre to Plaza Aníbal Pinto, around which are several of the city's oldest bars. Further east is the Plaza de la Victoria with the Plaza Simon Bolívar just north and the Cathedral on its east side; south of the Plaza on Cerro Bellavista is the **Museo al Cielo Abierto** (see box opposite). East of Plaza de la Victoria, reached by following Pedro Montt, is Plaza O'Higgins, which is dominated by the imposing new **Congreso Nacional**, a monolithic arch in neo-fascist style, thoroughly out of keeping with the rest of the city – with the congress soon to return to Santiago, the municipality are in a quandary as to what to do with the construction.

To the west of **Cerro Artillería** the Avenida **Playa Ancha** runs to the municipal stadium, seating 20,000 people, on Cerro Playa Ancha, home of local team Santiago Wanderers; *porteños* call the commune of Playa Ancha an "independent republic", owing to its reputation for self-sufficiency and independence. The buildings on Avenida Gran Bretaña are a good example of the eccentric architecture of Playa Ancha. Avenida Altamirano runs along the coast at the foot of Cerro Playa Ancha to **Las Torpederas**, a picturesque bathing beach. The **Faro de Punta Angeles**, on a promontory just beyond Las Torpederas, was the first lighthouse on the west coast; you can get a permit to go up. On another high point on the other side of the city is the **Mirador de O'Higgins**, the spot at which the Supreme Dictator exclaimed, on seeing Cochrane's liberating squadron: "On those four craft depends the destiny of America".

The New Year is celebrated by a superb 40-minute firework display on the bay, which is best seen from the *cerros*. The locals take supper and champagne to celebrate from vantage points around the bay.

El Museo al Cielo Abierto

Opened in 1992, this open air museum was the result of an initiative of the Universidad Católica de Valparaíso. Seventeen of Chile's leading contemporary artists were invited to present sketches for the large-scale murals which can be seen on the outside walls of buildings on Cerro Bellavista. The circuit starts at the foot of a steep flight of steps leading up from Calle Aldunate, one block south of Plaza Victoria. Murals can be seen at regular intervals as you climb to Pasaje Guimera. A further climb brings you to the top of Ascensor Espíritu Santo. Another series of murals appears as you continue along Calle Rudolph and then along Calle Ferrari which runs back down to Calle Aldunate. Look out in particular for the large (6 m by 3 m) mural by Chile's most famous contemporary artist Roberto Matta, situated just before you reach the Ascensor Espíritú Santo; a typical example of his later work with sharp-toothed gape-jawed monsters hurtling through space. The walk is delightful in itself. Though the other artists may be less well known internationally, this unusual collection should not be missed.

Museums

Casa de Lukas is dedicated to the work of the most famous Chilean caricaturist. Lukas (real name Renzo Pecchenino) was one of Chile's leading cartoonists. Originally from Italy, he spent most of his life in Valparaíso. The museum holds a permanent exhibition dedicated to his work giving a humorous insight into the political and social history of Valparaíso and Chile. Worth a visit. ■ *Paseo Mirador Gervasoni 448, Cerro Concepcion. Tue-Sun, summer 1100-2200, winter 1030-1400, 1530-1830. At the top of the ascensor.*

Casa La Sebastiana is the former house of Pablo Neruda, now housing an art gallery and showing his eccentric tastes to the full (see also his house at Isla Negra below). There is a small café in the garden, with fine views. ■ *US$2.50, Tue-Fri students half-price. Tue-Fri 1030-1410, 1530-1800. Sat, Sun, festivals, 1030-1800. In summer, Tue-Sun 1030-1850. Ferrari 692, off Av Alemania, Altura 6900 on Cerro Florida, T256606. Getting there: bus O from Av Argentina, US$0.30, or colectivo from Plazuela Equador, US$0.60.*

Museo de Historia Natural is in the 19th-century Palacio Lyon, Condell 1546. ■ *US$1. Tue-Fri 1000-1300, 1400-1800, Sat 1000-1800, Sun 1000-1400.* Also in the same building is the **Galería de Arte Municipal**. ■ *Mon-Sat 1000-1900, free.*

Museo del Mar Almirante Cochrane, Merlet 195, Cerro Cordillera, houses a collection of naval models built by local Naval Modelling Club, good views over port. ■ *Free. Tue-Sun 1000-1800. Getting there: take Ascensor Cordillera from Calle Serrano, off Plaza Sotomayor, to Cerro Cordillera; at the top, Plazuela Eleuterio Ramírez, take Calle Merlet to the left.*

Museo Municipal de Bellas Artes, with Chilean landscapes and seascapes and some modern paintings, is housed in Palacio Baburizza. The building is closed until the end of 2002 for refurbishment, but, if possible, a visit is highly recommended. If you are lucky, you may be able to see the whole of this interesting rococo mansion; the games room, drawing room, shower and servants' quarters provide an interesting insight into the contrasting lifestyles of the early part of the 20th century. ■ *Tue-Sun 1000-1800. Free. Paseo Yugoslavo, www.museobaburriza.cl Getting there: take Ascensor El Peral from Plaza Justicia, off Plaza Sotomayor.*

Valparaíso and Viña del Mar

Museo Naval, in the old Naval Academy, documents naval history 1810-80, and includes exhibitions on Chile's two naval heroes, Lord Cochrane and Arturo Prat. ■ *US$1. Tue-Sun 1000-1730. Paseo 21 de Mayo (on Cerro Artillería). Getting there: take Ascensor Artillería from Plaza Aduana.*

Tours Launches run trips around the harbour from Muelle Prat, 30 minutes, US$2, a pleasant view of the city, recommended. Beware that groups of foreign tourists are liable to be overcharged. Other boats can be hired for fishing. Don't photograph naval ships or installations.

Excursions

Reserva Nacional Peñuelas Reserva Nacional Peñuelas covers 9,260 ha surrounding the artificial Lago Peñuelas. The park, which is covered by pine and eucalyptus forest, is situated southeast of Valparaíso near the main road to Santiago (Route 68). Access is permitted for walking and fishing. Administration is at the park entrance, about 30 km from Valparaíso, 95 km from Santiago. ■ *US$2, buses between Valparaíso and Santiago pass the entrance.*

Plaza Aduana to Cerro Concepción

Sleeping		Eating
1 Brighton	5 Sr Juan Carrasco	1 Bar Inglés
2 Casa Aventura	6 Templemann	2 Bote Salvavidas
3 Garden	Apartments	3 La Colombina
4 Reina Victoria		4 La Costeñita

0 metres 100
0 yards 100

This is the least known of the villages on the central littoral (there are seldom **Quintay** direct buses from Santiago) and also one of the most picturesque and attractive. In its heyday, the former whaling station employed over 1,000 workers, mostly from Chiloé, but now only the fishermen remain. Try the local speciality – *caldillo de congrio* – at any of the cheap restaurants on the bay, then visit the whaling station. ■ *Tue-Sun 0900-1800, US$0.50.* Most people ignore the threatening sign warning you not to climb up to the lighthouse. If you take the risk, the view is worth the short climb – sit on the rocks and watch the sunset. Quintay has two beaches, the larger of which is being overrun by a housing development. The other, Playa Chica, is accessed via an unsignposted route through a eucalyptus wood, entry by the *carabineros* – deserted off-season, it is wonderfully relaxing. ■ *Getting there: take a* colectivo *from behind the bus terminal in Valparaíso – they don't go until full, but if in a hurry you may pay for the extra seats.*

Laguna Verde, 18 km south of Valparaíso, is a picturesque bay for picnics, **Laguna Verde** reached by a dusty walk over the hills. There is **F** *Posada Cruz del Sur*, while *Casa Gener*, **G**, offers bed, breakfast and hot showers, but is owned by the

5 La Playa
6 Le Filou Montpellier
7 Los Porteños
8 Turri

----- Cerros Alegre &
Concepción walking tour
Steep hillside
╫╫╫╫ Funicular railways (Ascensores)

Valparaíso and Viña del Mar

Valparaíso and Viña del Mar

 A walking tour of Cerros Alegre and Concepción

This is one of the best ways to view Valparaíso. From the Plaza de la Justicia a narrow passage (marked Museo de Bellas Artes) leads south to Ascensor El Peral, which has recently been renovated. At the top end of the Ascensor, turn left along Paseo Yugoslavo which offers superb views over the bay. On your right on the corner of Monte Alegre is the Palacio Baburrizza, formerly the residence of the nitrate barons, Ottorino Zanelli and Pascual Baburrizza, now housing the Museo de Bellas Artes.

The red and white mansion further along Monte Alegre on your left is now the Art Faculty of the University of Playa Ancha. At the end of the block turn left into Calle Leighton to reach a fork in the road, over which towers an unusual building, four storeys high and 3 m wide. Opposite is a passage, the Pasaje Bavestrello; at the other end of this turn left, cross Calle Urriola and climb the steps into Pasaje

Galves. Take the first passage on your right (Pasaje Templeman) and you will emerge into Calle Templeman. About 50 m along this to the left is the Anglican church of San Pablo, built in 1858, which has organ recitals every Sunday at 1230. From here follow Templeman one block further northeast, turn right onto Calle Abtao and you will reach the Iglesia Luterano (1897) from the base of which there are fine views over the cerros. From the east end of the church follow Paseo Atkinson round (more fine views) and then turn right into Calle Papudo and right again into Calle Templeman. At the northeast end of Templeman is the Paseo Gervasoni, from where you can return to the lower city via the Ascensor Concepción. Before doing this, however, take a look around the Casa de Lukas, which houses an exhibition of paintings of Valparaíso and cartoons, the work of Renzo Peccenino Lukas.

---

electricity generating company whose staff have first claim to rooms. Camping is also possible at *Camping Los Olivos* with good facilities, well run and friendly. ■ *Buses can be caught from Pedro Montt via Playa Ancha.*

Essentials

Sleeping
■ *on maps, page 136 and 142*
Price codes:
see inside front cover

El Plan A *Puerta de Alcalá*, Piramide 524, T227478, F745642, www.chileinfo.cl/puertadealcalahotel Probably the best hotel here. Has everything you would expect of a hotel in this bracket together with a decent if expensive restaurant. **B** *Lancaster*, Chacabuco 2362, T217391, F230216, somewhat surprisingly the only hotel to be officially given starred status. The quality is OK, but the hotel's location is more notable for its rent-boys than its views. **C** *Austral*, Las Heras 622, T216306, F230352. Without breakfast, kitchen facilities, central **F** pp without bath. **C** *Condell Pasaje*, Pirámide 557, T212788, F254704. Without breakfast, comfortable, clean, central, television, no singles. Under same management is **C** *Prat*, Condell 1443, T253081, F213368. Comfortable rooms, central, good restaurant with good value *almuerzo*. **C** *Hostal Kolping*, Vergara y Independencia, Valdes Vergara 622, T216306, F230352, without bath, pleasant, quiet, good value, one of the best hotels near the bus terminal. **C** *Reina Victoria*, Plaza Sotomayor 190, T212203. **D** on top floors, without bath, with breakfast, noisy, dingy, run down and with only a single bathroom on each floor, poor beds, overpriced, don't be fooled by the façade.

F *Castillo family*, 12 de Febrero 315, T220290, T096347239 (mob), family accommodation, hot showers, good local knowledge. **F** *Garden*, Serrano 501, T252776. Friendly, large rooms, gloomy and run down but central, use of kitchen. **F** *María Pizarro*, Chacabuco 2340, Casa No 2, T230791. Clean, lovely rooms, central, quiet, kitchen. Highly recommended, although in a somewhat seedy street. Also her neighbour,

Elena Escobar, Chacabuco 2340, Casa No 7, T214193, same price. Recommended. **F** *Res Eliana*, Av Brasil 2146, T250954, large old house, without breakfast. Recommended, in a slightly rough area. **F** *Res El Rincon Universal*, Argentina 825, T/F235184. With breakfast, laundry, study, cable TV and internet access, a good, reasonably priced alternative in the *plan* – the area can be a little intimidating at night, though. **F** *Sra Mónica Venegas*, Av Argentina 322, Casa B, T215673, 2 blocks from, bus terminal, often booked up. Recommended. **F** *Sra Silvia*, Pje La Quinta 70, Av Argentina, 3 blocks from Congress, T216592. Clean, quiet, kitchen facilities. Recommended, but not the safest area at night. Youth hostel office at Edwards 695, piso 3, will extend membership; hostel in Viña del Mar.

Los Cerros Cerro Alegre: **F** *Arcoiris*, Cirilo Armstrong, Pasaje 6, Casa 2, T09-4304394, arcoirischile@yahoo.com Near the police station, safe area, 1 room only rented out, good breakfast, balcony with great views, friendly, English spoken. Recommended. **F** *Casa Aventura*, Pasaje Galvez 11, off Calle Urriola, Cerro Alegre, T/F755963, casatur@ctcinternet.cl In restored traditional house, with good breakfast, German and English spoken, Spanish classes offered, good value tours given, helpful, friendly, informative, kitchen facilities. Highly recommended. **Cerro Concepción**: **B** *Brighton*, Paseo Atkinson 151, T223513, F598802, brighton-valpo@entelchile.net Bills itself as a typical building in an historic part of Valparaíso, a fact which riles some locals – the building is barely 5 years old! Good views, good rooms and service, live tango and bolero music in the bar at weekends. **B** *Templemann Apartments*, Pierre Loti 65, T257067, T09-5194811, F221205, chantalderementeria@hotmail.com Fully equipped, stylish, self-contained apartments sleeping 3-4, one uses an old weaving loom as table and has a wardrobe painted Mondrian style, good if you want a little peace away from the gringo trail. Recommended. **F** *Sr Juan Carrasco*, Cerro Abtao 668, Cerro Concepción, T210737. **Playa Ancha**: **F** *Villa Kunterbunt*, Av Quebrada Verde 192, T288873. Lovely building, fine views, with breakfast, very friendly, Chilean-German run, garden, English and German spoken. Highly recommended. Bus 1, 2, 5, 6, 17, 111, N, *colectivo* 150, 151, 3b all pass by. **Also**: **F** *Res Dinamarca*, Dinamarca 539, T259189, unfortunately located between the cemetery and the old prison (from Plazuela Ecuador – just south of Condell y Bellavista – take any micro marked 'Cárcel'; or climb 10 mins up Av Ecuador). With breakfast, clean, good value, parking, not near restaurants, not the safest area at night.

Expensive *Bote Salvavidas*, Muelle Prat s/n, piso 2. Seafood restaurant overlooking the port. *Caleta Portales*, Av España s/n, T625814, www.restaurantcaletaportales.cl Good seafood restaurant on the road to Viña. *Club Español*, Brasil 1589. Fine Spanish cuisine, elegant surroundings. *Club Valparaíso*, Condell 1190, piso 10. International cuisine, exclusive. *Coco Loco*, Blanco 1781, pisos 21 y 22, T227614. Plush revolving restaurant 70 m above the bay. *La Colombina*, Paseo Yugoslavo 15, Cerro Alegre, T236254/236226, lacolombina@entelchile.net Fish and seafood, good wines, fine views, reasonable food but a bit of a tourist trap. Also owns *Apolo 77* tour agency (see below). *Turri*, Templemann 147, on Cerro Concepción, T259198. Good food and service, wonderful views, lovely place.

Eating
● *on maps, page 136 and 142*

Mid-range *Bar Inglés*, Cochrane 851 (entrance also on Blanco Encalada). Historic bar dating from the early 1900s; a chart shows the ships due in port. Good food and drink, traditional, not cheap. Recommended. *Cinzano*, Plaza Aníbal Pinto 1182. The oldest bar in Valparaíso, also serving food. Flamboyant live music at weekends, noted for tango performances but no dancing by guests allowed. Service can be awful. *Club Alemán*, O'Higgins y Bellavista. Good German food. *Hamburg*, O'Higgins 1274. Owned by an elderly German emigré, right-wing military memorabilia abounds. The food is

Valparaíso and Viña del Mar

Lord Cochrane

Lord Thomas Alexander Cochrane (1775-1860), born into a Scottish aristocratic family, began his career in the British navy during the Napoleonic Wars, rising rapidly as an officer, fighting a duel with a French officer in Malta and later being captured by the French and ransomed. He was elected to Parliament in 1806 as MP for Honiton and in 1807 as MP for Westminster. Although he had never been on good terms with his naval superiors, his use of the House of Commons to accuse the naval commander, Lord Gambier, of incompetence, led to his downfall. Gambier was court-martialled and acquitted; Cochrane was retired on half-pay and spent the next three years exposing corruption and abuses in the navy. His links with a financial scandal in 1814 provided his enemies with an opportunity for revenge: he was dismissed from the navy, expelled from Parliament and sentenced to 12 months' imprisonment (he escaped and was recaptured).

Recruited for the armed forces by the Chilean agent in London, he quickly became friendly with O'Higgins and was put in command of the new republic's navy, a few ill-equipped vessels which relied on foreign

adventurers for experienced sailors. With this fleet Cochrane harassed the Spanish-held ports along the Chilean coast; his audacious storming of the fortresses of Corral, San Carlos and Amargos led to the capture of the key Spanish base of Valdivia. Later that year Cochrane transported San Martin's troops along the Pacific coast to invade Peru, but his relations with San Martin were poor and he became very critical of the latter's cautious strategy. Afterwards he continued to attack Spanish shipping in the Pacific, in 1822 sailing as far north as Mexico.

In 1823 the new government of Brazil appointed him to head its navy in the struggle for independence from Portugal. Once again leading a motley collection of boats manned largely by foreigners, Cochrane drove a Portuguese fleet from Bahia and pursued it back to Portugal. In 1825 he fell out with the Brazilian government and returned to Britain. Two years later he volunteered to help the Greeks in their struggle for independence from Turkey. He was reinstated in the British navy in 1832, was promoted to Rear-Admiral and spent much of the rest of his life promoting developments in the use of steam power in shipping.

apparently good. *La Costeñita*, Blanco 86. Good seafood restaurant. *La Playa*, Serrano 567. Another old time bar, similar to *Bar Inglés*, but with slightly more snooty staff. *Los Porteños*, Valdivia 169 and Cochrane 102. Perennial favourite for fish and shellfish, terse service but good food. *Pekin*, Pudeto 422. One of the best Chinese restaurants. *Pizza Roma*, Plaza Aníbal Pinto. Frozen bases, overpriced, but the locals seem to like it. *Sancho Panza*, Yungay 2250. Parrillada, popular. At Caleta Membrillo, 2 km northwest of Plaza Sotomayor, there are several good fish restaurants including *Club Social de Pescadores*, Altamirano 1480, good, and *El Membrillo*.

Cheap *Ave Cesár*, P Montt 1776. Fast food, good. *Bambú*, Pudeto 450, Mon-Sat 1000-1800, vegetarian. *El Domino*, Cumming 67. Traditional *porteño* restaurant serving *empanadas*, *chorillanas* and the like. Recommended. *Gioco*, Molina 586-B. Lunch only, excellent value vegetarian set lunches with fruit juices. Highly recommended. *La Puerta del Sol*, Montt 2033. Traditional Chilean dishes, great chips served outside. *Le Filou Montpellier*, Almte Montt 382. French-run, Sat menu very popular and deservedly so. *Marco Polo*, Pedro Montt y Gen Cruz. Delicious cakes, good Italian, good value *almuerzo*, if you want to be sick, try one of their giant completos – a week's worth of calories in a bun.

Seriously cheap Many on Pedro Montt and behind the bus station. Also on the 2nd floor of the market (off Plaza Echaurren), where the portions are large (closed in the evenings), eg **Anita's** – mixed reports, **Sandrita**, excellent *paila marina*, friendly, recommended. Others include **Empanadas Famosas's de Adali**, S Donoso 1379-81. Best *empanadas* in Valparaíso, and **Mi Casa**, Chacabuco 2811, cheap standard behind the bus terminal.

Cafés *Bogarín*, Plaza Victoria. Great juices, sandwiches. **Café do Brasil**, Condell 1342. Excellent coffee, juices, sandwiches. **Color Café**, Papudo 526, Cerro Concepción, T746136, T09-230247 (mob). Cosy, eclectic, arty café with a wide selection of teas and real coffee, fresh juice, good cakes, snacks and all-day breakfasts, regular live music, art exhibits, local art and craft for sale. **Pan de Magia**, Almte Montt 738 y Templemann, Cerro Alegre, T09-4268626. Cakes, cookies, and by far the best wholemeal bread in town. **Riquet**, comfortable, expensive, good coffee and breakfast. Recommended. **Hesperia**, Victoria 2250, a classic old-time coffee emporium, the internet annexe makes a strange contrast. **Westfalia**, Cochrane 847. Coffee, breakfasts, vegetarian lunches.

Bars Good bars at **Cinzano** and **Bar Ingles** (see above), in **Hotel Brighton** (wonderful views, live music at weekends 2300 to 0400) and in Centro Cultural Valparaíso. There are many bars on Subida Ecuador, but be careful which ones you go into, as in some of them you risk being eaten alive (only enter **El Muro** and **La Viuda** if you are into methylated spirits and the sordid elements of life): the following 2 are recommended – **Émile Dubois**, smart and popular with the well-to-do, and **Leo Bar**, which has great live music. Others in Valparaíso: **Bar Para So**, Errázuriz 1042, cover charge after midnight only, excellent live music. **Bar Roma**, situated in Playa Ancha, is the unofficial drinking hole of the crazier students of the university down the street. Don't be surprised if your bags are searched on your way in – to stop you smuggling in beer – and, men, if there is a hole in the ground where the urinal ought to be then the students have smashed it (a regular occurrence). Despite all this, the atmosphere is relaxed and friendly; if you have something you want to get off your chest, you can write it on the wall. **Liberty**, Almte Rivero 9, Plaza Echaurren. A real dingy old-timers' bar, where you can see local characters drinking and singing all day. Good cheap food is served.

Entertainment It is worth checking out www.granvalparaiso.com for the latest listings information

Cinema *Cinehoyts*, Pedro Montt 2111, T594709, but better choice in Viña. Also see under Instituto Chileno-Norteamericano de Cultura, page 144.

Discos *Cosmonova*, Pedro Montt 1195; Escape, in Galería of *Hotel Prat*, subsuelo; Gioko, Las Heras 304. Hadobar Pub, Plaza Anibal Pinto 1175. Latin and rock, every night except Thu. **La Piedra Feliz**, Errázuriz 1054. Everything from jazz to salsa, bossanova and tango depending on the evening, contains 3 areas, each with different décor, a large pub, a live music area, and a dance floor, entrance US$8. **Proa Al Canaveral**, Errázuriz 304. Good seafood restaurant downstairs, pleasant bar upstairs with dancing from 0100, poetry reading on Thu, Latin pop music, naval memorabilia. **Valparaíso Eterno**, Almirante Senoret 150. Three floors each hosting a different singer or band, including performers from Brazil and Peru, live music only at weekends, performances start about 2300 hrs, US$2 cover charge and cheap drinks, open till 0400.

Galleries Occasional exhibitions at the following galleries, all free: *Arte de Valparaíso*, Condell 1550, T220062. Mon-Sat 1000-1900. *Corporación de Valparaíso*, Esmeralda 1051, T597380. Mon-Fri 0930-1900. *Leonardo da Vinci*, Independencia 1978, T255511. Mon-Sat 0900-1300 and 1600-2000.

Valparaíso and Viña del Mar

Shopping   The fruit and veg market on Av Argentina, Wed and Sat, is colourful and well worth a visit – on Sun, there is a flea market here. There is a large antique market around Plaza O'Higgins on Sun mornings. *Emporio Echaurren*, Plaza Echaurren. A delicatessen which stocks the unlikeliest of provisions – if you are hankering after Coleman's mustard or mint sauce, this is the place to come. **Bookshops** *CHAOS*, on Pedro Montt by the bus terminal. An excellent new and second-hand bookshop. *Librería Universitaria*, Esmeralda 1132. Good selection of regional history; many others. **Department stores** *Falabella* and *Ripley*, both on Plaza Victoria.

Tour operators   *Apolo 77*, Pasaje Apolo 60C, Cerro Alegre, T592446, F235126.
Several companies Colombin@CTCReuna.cl Offer city tours on foot and by bus as well as railway trips
offer city tours on foot between Baron and Puerto stations in a restored 1930s carriage, minimum 20 passengers. *Casa Aventura* (see under sleeping) offers a good value tour of the historic parts of the city. *Valparaíso Mágico*, T/F911972, US$24 to US$50 per person depending on the tour, overpriced.

Transport   **Local Ascensores**: US$0.25. **Bus**: Buses and modern electric buses, US$0.35 within city limits. **Car hire**: *Bert Rent A Car*, Victoria 2681, T254842. *Colón Rent a Car*, Colón

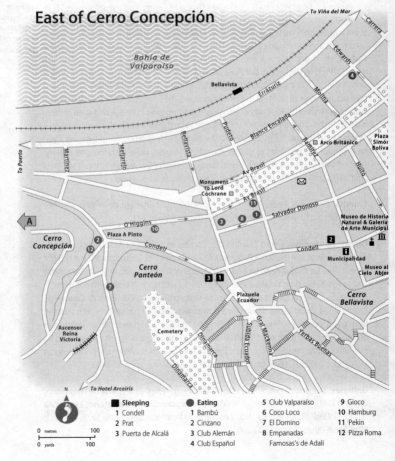

East of Cerro Concepción

Sleeping	Eating		
1 Condell	1 Bambú	5 Club Valparaíso	9 Gioco
2 Prat	2 Cinzano	6 Coco Loco	10 Hamburg
3 Puerta de Alcalá	3 Club Alemán	7 El Domino	11 Pekin
	4 Club Español	8 Empanadas Famosas's de Adali	12 Pizza Roma

2581, T256529. *Suzuval*, Colón 2537, T255505. **Taxi**: More expensive than Santiago. *Colectivos*, which pick up and set down passengers anywhere en route, operate along the same routes as buses and offer a cheap and quick form of transport. **Train**: Regular service on Merval, the Valparaíso metropolitan line between Valparaíso, Viña del Mar, Quilpué and Limache, to Viña del Mar every 15-30 mins, US$0.50, 15-min journey. *El Porteño* tourist train (sometimes with steam locomotive) runs on Sun, 1 Jan-28 Feb and on most public holidays.

Long distance Bus: Terminal Pedro Montt y Rawson, 1 block from Av Argentina; plenty of buses between terminal and Plaza Sotomayor. Excellent and frequent service to **Viña del Mar**, 25 mins, US$0.45 from Plaza Aduana, passing along Av Errázuriz; *colectivos* to Viña US$0.50. To **Santiago**, 2 hrs, shop around, frequent (book on Sat to return to the capital on Sun); buses to north and south are very frequent – to **Chillán**, US$10, 8 hrs; to **Concepción**, 11 hrs, US$12; to **Puerto Montt**, 17 hrs, US$18; to **Punta Arenas**, Buses Norte (Wed and Thu at 1800), US$60; to **La Serena**, 8 hrs, US$10; to **Calama**, US$35; to **Arica**, US$40, Fénix *salón cama* service, US$50. To **Argentina**: to **Mendoza**, 3 companies, 6-7 hrs, US$15, *Pluma* continue on to Buenos Aires, Florianopolis, Sao Paolo and Rio (Tue, Fri and Sun); to **Córdoba**, *Tas Choapa*, US$30, daily. Buses serving more local destina-

To Hotel Lancaster

Plaza de la Victoria

Cerro Bellavista

Ascensor Espíritu Santo

·········· Route around Museo
Al Cielo Abierto
⊢⊢⊢⊢⊢⊢ Funicular railways (Ascensores)

tions include Lago Peñuelas, leaving every 15 mins for Isla Negra, San Antonio and Llolleo (US$2.75); *La Porteña* and *Sol del Pacifico* every half-hour to Cabildo, via Quintero and La Ligua (US$3). *La Porteña* and *Intercomunal* also have buses north to Pichidangui and Los Vilos (several daily, *Intercomunal* continuing on to Illapel and Salamanca), although it may be easier to catch any bus to La Calera from Errázuriz/Brasil (every few minutes) and make a connection there. **Hitchhiking**: To Santiago is easy from the service station on Av Argentina. **Motoring**: Route 68, the main road to Santiago, passes through 2 tunnels, toll of US$3.25 paid at the first which is 51 km southeast of Valparaíso, but this can be avoided by turning off onto the old road over the mountains about 1 km before the tunnel; the toll is unavoidable on the return journey. There is another toll further east, 56 km west of Santiago. **Shipping**: For shipping services from Valparaíso to the Juan Fernández Islands, see the the Chilean Pacific Islands chapter.

Airline offices *Air France*, Cochrane 667, Of 603, T213249. *American*, Esmeralda 940, Of 61, T257777. *Continental*, Pje Ross 149, Of 205, T745600. *Iberia*, Blanco Encalada 838, piso 2, T256009. *Ladeco/LanChile*, Esmeralda 1048, T251441. *United*, Urriola 87, piso 3, T216569.

Directory

Valparaíso and Viña del Mar

Banks Banks open 0900 to 1400, but closed on Sat. Many Redbanc ATMs on Blanco and Prat, and also one in the bus terminal. Good rates at *Banco de Crédito e Inversiones*, Cochrane 820 and *Banco de Santiago*, Prat 816. Casas de Cambio: *Andino*, Esmeralda 970. *Ascami*, Esmeralda 940. *Exprinter*, Prat 887 (the building with the clocktower at junction with Cochrane). Good rates, no commission on TCs, open Mon-Fri 0930-1400, 1500-1800. *Gema Tour*, Esmeralda 940. *Inter Cambios*, Errázuriz esq Plaza Sotomayor. Good rates. *New York*, Prat 659. Best rates for cash. *Prat*, Prat 847. When cambios are closed, street changers operate outside Inter Cambios.

Communications Internet: *@rob' Art Café*, Edwards 625, US$1.50 per hr (cheaper for students). *Café Bell@vista*, Bellavista 463, loc 201. *Color Café*, Calle Papudo 526, 2 blocks from upper station of Ascensor Turi (see above). *Cybervalparaíso*, Condell 1217, loc 215 (Galería O'Higgins). *Prat*, Condell 1443, Of 24, on the ground floor of the *Hotel Prat* building. **Post office**: North side of Pedro Montt, between San Ignacio & Bolivar. **Telecommunications**: The cheapest call centres are all around the bus terminal, eg on Calle Rawson. Also: *CTC*, Esmeralda 940 or Pedro Montt 2023. *Entel*, Condell 1491. *VTR Telecommunications*, Cochrane 825.

Cultural centres *Centro Cultural de Valparaíso*, Esmeralda 1083, T216953. Open daily 1400-2000, exhibitions, concerts, theatre and other activities. *Instituto Chileno-Norteamericano*, Esmeralda 1069. Shows foreign films occasionally.

Consulates *Argentina*, Blanco 890, Of 204, T250039. *Belgium*, Prat 827, Piso 12, T213494. *Bolivia*, Serrano 579, T259906. *Brazil*, Blanco 951, Piso 2, T217856. *Denmark*, Errazuriz 940, T213942. *Ecuador*, Blanco Encalada 1623, oficina 1740, T222167. *Germany*, Blanco 1215, Of 1102, T250039. *Guatemala*, Blanco 1199, Local 4, T255214. *Norway*, Freire 657, T252219. *Panama*, Cochrane 813, oficina 307, T213592. *Peru*, Blanco Encalada 1215, oficina 1402, T253403. *Spain*, Brasil 1589, piso 2, T685860. *Sweden*, Casilla 416-V, T256507. *UK*, Blanco 1190, piso 5, T/F213063.

Medical services Dentist: *Dr Walther Meeden Bella*, Condell 1530, Depto 44, T212233.

Laundry *Las Heras 554*, good and cheap. *Lavanda Café*, Almirante Montt 454. Enjoy a coffee while you wait for your clothes. US$2.50 wash, US$2.30 dry, full service US$1 extra.

Security Robbery is increasingly common, in El Puerto and around the *ascensores*, especially on Cerro Santo Domingo. Also beware that Calle Chacabuco (on which some of hotels are located) is the pick-up point for local rent boys, and that the area around Plaza Echaurren is dangerous at night. Beware of the mustard trick (see page 40).

Useful addresses *YMCA (Asociación Cristiana de Jóvenes)*, Blanco Encalada 1117. *YWCA (Asociación Cristiana Feminina)*, Blanco 967. *Valparaíso Seamen's Institute*, Blanco Encalada 394.

From Valparaíso to Argentina Route 62 runs through Viña del Mar, climbs out of the bay and goes through **Quilpué**, Km 16, 1½ km east of El Retiro, a popular inland resort with medicinal springs and a municipal zoo. It crosses a range of hills and reaches the Aconcagua Valley at **Limache**, a sleepy market town, 40 km from Valparaíso. Route 62 joins Route 60 just before **Quillota**, a fruit growing centre (**B** *Balneario El Edén*, 5 km north, cabins for rent, up to six people, very good restaurant in an old estate building, T311963, F312342, good swimming), continuing to La Calera, Km 88, where it joins the Pan-American Highway;

turn southeast and east for Llaillay, San Felipe, Los Andes and the Redentor tunnel to Mendoza.

Parque Nacional La Campana

Situated north of Olmué (8 km east of Limache), the park covers 8,000 ha and includes Cerro La Campana (1,828 m) which Darwin climbed in 1835 and Cerro El Roble (2,200 m). The park is divided into three main sections, the *sectores Granizos* and *Cajón Grande* – from which the Cerro La Campana is climbed – and the *sector Ocoa*, the location of the main concentration of Chilean palms (*kankán*), now found in natural woodlands in only two locations in Chile. There are wonderful views from the top of the Cerro La Campana; about 300 km of the highest part of the Andes can be seen (including Aconcagua), as well as the rugged outlines of the central *cordillera* losing themselves in the haze to the north, the Pacific Ocean to the west, and the gentler scenes of the southern hills.

Cerro La Campana is best climbed from the Granizos entrance (see below). Entering the park, a path leaves the road to the left just past the CONAF *guardería*, and climbs steeply through forest, fording a clear, rushing stream and giving increasingly fine views of the Andes until reaching a camping area (two hours from the *guardería*). From here the path is well marked, but becomes more testing; after passing a plaque dedicated by the British community to Charles Darwin on the anniversary marking the centenary of his visit, it climbs over loose rock to a pass to the northeast, before doubling back and rising over rocks (where scrambling and a little very basic climbing is required) to the summit. A fair amount of agility is required – visitors without much climbing and scrambling experience may wish to seek advice or take a guide. Take food and drink. Allow a whole day to go up and down from Olmué, although those in training can ascend and descend in around seven hours. It is also possible to ascend from Quillota, but this route is more difficult and definitely requires guides.

In Olmué there are places to stay in all price categories: eg *El Copihue*, **A**, Diego Portales 2203, T441544, hcopihue@chilesat.net; *Sarmiento*, T442838, Blanco Encalda 4689, **E**; *La Alondra*, Grabizo 8459, T441163, **F**. It is also possible to camp in all sectors of the park, with advance reservations to be made on T44342. Entrance costs US$2 per person. There are 3 entrances: at Granizos, 5 km east of Olmué (local bus or *colectivo* from Limache to the entrance; Limache is reached by frequent buses from Valparaíso and Viña del Mar); at Cajón Grande, reached by unpaved road which turns off the Olmué-Granizos road; and at Palmar de Ocoa to the north reached by unpaved road (10 km) leading off the Pan-American Highway between Hijuelas and Llaillay. There is no public transport to this part of the park, although there is a service from Viña del Mar to within 1 km of the entrance (US$1, 1 hr).

Essentials

Viña del Mar

Nine kilometres northeast of Valparaíso via Route 68, which runs along a narrow belt between the shore and precipitous cliffs, is Viña del Mar, one of South America's leading seaside resorts. Viña is famous throughout Chile as the home of an annual international music festival which takes place in February, during which the entire country is kept on tenterhooks by gyrating stars from various parts of Latin America; the festival used to bring in some top names, but this is no longer the case, and to be truthful, neither the festival nor Viña are as wonderful as

Phone code: 032
Colour map 3, grid B2
Population: 304,203

Chileans like to make out. This is the only place in Chile where road signs are in English as well as Spanish, and much of the city feels like suburban North America. That said, with a pleasant beach and shady parks and avenues, Viña is a nice enough city to visit, especially if you have some pesos to burn, making an interesting contrast to nearby Valparaíso.

Ins & outs
See page 149 for further details

Getting there There are inter-urban buses to Viña del Mar from many Chilean cities. The city also has daily connections through to Mendoza in Argentina. **Getting around** There are frequent *micros* linking Viña and Valparaíso, going from the Plaza. *Colectivos* also serve this route, and to many of the destinations in the further reaches of the town. There are also many buses to nearby places on the coast. Taxis are plentiful and usually reasonably priced. **Tourist offices** *Sernatur*, Valparaíso 507, Of 303, T882285. Municipal office on the corner of Plaza Vergara. Arrangements may be made at the municipal tourist office for renting private homes in the summer season. *Automóvil Club de Chile*, 1 Norte 901, T689509.

Sights

The older part of Viña del Mar is situated on the banks of a creek, the Marga Marga, which is crossed by bridges. Around Plaza Vergara and the smaller Plaza Sucre to its south are the **Teatro Municipal** (1930) and the exclusive **Club de Viña**, built in 1910. The municipally owned **Quinta Vergara**, formerly the residence of the shipping entrepreneur Francisco Alvarez, lies two blocks south. The grounds are superb and include a double avenue of palm trees; it is here that the music festival takes over in February (tickets from the Municipalidad). The **Palacio Vergara**, in the gardens, houses the Museo de Bellas Artes and the Academia de Bellas Artes. Part of the grounds is a children's playground, and there is an outdoor auditorium where concerts and ballet are performed in the summer months.

Further west on a headland overlooking the sea is **Cerro Castillo**, the president's summer palace; its gardens can be visited. Just north, on the other side of the Marga Marga, is the **casino**, built in the 1930s and set in beautiful gardens. ■ *US$5, jacket and tie for men required, open all year.*

North are the main beaches, Acapulco and Las Salinas, but south of Cerro Castillo is Caleta Abarca, also popular. Beaches may be closed due to pollution. The coastal route north to Reñaca provides lovely views over the sea. East of the centre is the **Valparaíso Sporting Club** with a racecourse and playing fields. North of here in the hills are the Granadilla Golf Club and a large artificial lake, the **Laguna Sausalito**, which has an excellent tourist complex with swimming pools, boating, tennis courts, sandy beaches, water skiing, restaurants. ■ *US$2.50, children under 11, US$1.75.* Nearby is the Estadio Sausalito, home to Everton soccer club. ■ *Getting there: take colectivo No 19 from Calle Viana.*

Museums

Museo de la Cultura del Mar, in the Castillo Wolff, on the coast near Cerro Castillo, contains a collection on the life and work of the novelist and maritime historian, Salvador Reyes. ■ *Tue-Sat 1000-1300, 1430-1800, Sun 1000-1400, T625427.* **Museo de Bellas Artes** is in the Palacio Vergara. ■ *US$0.50. Tue-Sun 1000-1400, 1500-1800, T680618.* **Palacio Rioja** was built in 1906 by a prominent local family and is now used for official municipal receptions. The ground floor is preserved in its original state. Recommended. ■ *Tue-Sun 1000-1400, 1500-1800. Quillota 214. T689665.* **Museo Sociedad Fonk** is an archaeological museum, with objects from Easter Island

and the Chilean mainland displayed, including Mapuche silver. ■ *US$1. Tue-Fri 1000-1800, Sat-Sun 1000-1400. Calle 4 Norte 784.*

Jardín Botánico Nacional was formerly the estate of the nitrate magnate Pascual Baburizza and is now administered by CONAF. The garden lies 8 km southeast of the city. Covering 405 ha, it contains over 3,000 species from all over the world and a collection of Chilean cacti; pretty, but the species are not labelled. ■ *US$1. Getting there: take bus 20 from Plaza Vergara.*

Excursions

Essentials

There are a great many more places to stay in addition to those listed here, including private accommodation (**E-F** pp). Out of season furnished apartments can be rented through agencies (with commission). In season it is cheaper to stay in Valparaíso and commute to the beaches around Viña. Note that during the music festival in Feb, accommodation is almost impossible to find.

Sleeping
■ *on map*
Price codes:
see inside front cover
There are many
hotels in AL-B range,
some with beach

LL-L *Gala*, Arlegui 273, Local 10, T686688, F689568, galahotel@webhost.cl Excellent, all mod-cons. **AL** *Albamar*, San Martín 419, T975274, F970720. Tastefully decorated. **AL** *Alcázar*, Alvarez 646, T685112, F884245, hotelalcazar@chile.ia.cl Good restaurant, 4 star. **AL** *Cap Ducal*, Marina 51, T626655, F665471, old mansion charm, good restaurant. **AL** *José Francisco Vergara*, Dr von Schroeders 367, T626022, F660474. Has cabañas for up to 5. **AL** *Miramar*, Caleta Abarca, T62677, 5 stars. **AL** *San Martín*, San Martín 667, T689191, F689195. **A** *Genross*, Paseo Monterrey 18, T661711, genrosshotel@hotmail.com Located

Viña del Mar

■ Sleeping	9 Gala	17 Residencial	4 Casino Chico
1 Albamar	10 José Francisco	Magallanes	5 Machitún Ruca
2 Alcázar	Vergara	18 Residencial Remanso	6 Pizzería
3 Alejandra	11 Miramar	19 Residencial Villarica	Mama Mía
4 Andalue & Flavia	12 Offenbacher Hof	20 San Martín	7 Punto Verde
Restaurant	13 Quinta Vergara		8 Raul
5 Balia	14 Residencial Blanchart	● Eating	9 Samoiedo
6 Cap Ducal	15 Residencial Capric	1 Africa	
7 El Escorial	16 Residencial Helen	2 Alster	
8 Español	Misch	3 Armandita	

N
Not to scale

Valparaíso and Viña del Mar

in a beautiful old mansion, clean airy rooms with bath, garden patio and sitting room, very friendly and informative, English spoken, highly recommended. **A** *Quinta Vergara*, Errázuriz 690, T685073, F691978, hotelquinta@hotmail.com Clean, friendly, large rooms, beautiful gardens. Recommended.

B *Andalue*, 6 Poniente 124, T684147, F684148, with breakfast, central, recommended. **B** *Español*, Plaza Vergara 191, T/F685145, large rooms, run down. **B** *Petit Palace*, Paseo Valle 387, T/F663134. Small rooms, good, central, quiet. **B** *Offenbacher Hof*, Balmaceda 102, T621483, F662432. Clean, friendly. Recommended. **B** *Alejandra*, 2 Poniente 440, T974404. With shower and breakfast (**C** in low season). **B** *Balia*, von Schroeders 36, T976307, F680724, parking, overpriced. **C** *El Escorial*, 2 places: one at 5 Poniente 114, the other at 5 Poniente 441, T975266. With breakfast, shared bath, clean, central. **C** *Res France*, Montaña 743, T685976. Clean, safe, helpful. **C** *Res Helen Misch*, 1 Poniente 239, T971565, F972135. **C** *Res Magallanes*, Arlegui 555, T685101. With breakfast, clean, mixed reports. **C** *Res Remanso*, Av Valparaíso 217, T689057. Without bath, with breakfast. **C** *Res Victoria*, Valparaíso 40, T977370. With bath, with breakfast, clean, central. **C** *Res Villarica*, Arlegui 172, T881484, F942807. Good, friendly, without bath.

D *Res Agua Santa*, Agua Santa 34. Basic, hot shower. **D** *Res Capric*, von Schroeder 39, T978295. With bath and breakfast, TV, special rates for YHA members. **D** *Res Caribe*, Von Schroeders 46, T976191, with bath, small rooms, inconsistent hot water supply. **D** *Res de Casia*, Von Schroeder 151, T971861. **D** *Res Tajamar*, Alvarez 884, T882134. Opposite railway station, old-fashioned, central, huge rooms, full of character. **E** pp *Res Blanchart*, Valparaíso 82A, T974949. Clean, with breakfast, hot water, good service. **E** pp *Res Patricia*, Agua Santa 48.

Camping *Camping Reñaca*, Santa Luisa 401, east of centre, expensive, dirty, also *cabañas*. *Reñaca Center*, in town centre on river bank, T833207, good facilities, US$30 per site. **Youth hostels** **F** pp *Res La Montaña*, Agua Santa 153, T622230. with breakfast, other meals available, dingy, unhelpful, dirty bathroom, no cooking facilities, also family rooms.

Reñaca **L** *Cabañas Don Francisco*, Torreblanca 75, T834802, helpful, only available in week-long bookings. **AL** *Montecarlo*, V. MacKenna 136, T830397, very modern, comfortable. Several motels. Accommodation here is much cheaper out of season.

Eating **Expensive** *Alster*, Valparaíso 225. Smart, but you pay for it. *Cap Ducal* (hotel). Seafood, elegant. *Casino Chico*, Valparaíso y von Schroeders. Fish, seafood. *Flavia*, 6 Poniente 121, good Italian food, good service, good desserts and wine selection. **Mid-range** *Africa*, Valparaíso 324. Extraordinary façade, very good. *Armandita*, San Martín 501. *Parrilla*. Large portions, good service. *Colonial*, at *Hotel Español*. *El Encuentro*, San Martín y 6 Norte. Fish, very good. *Kumei*, Valparaíso between Von Schroeders and Ecuador, best set lunches in town, wide selection, good. *La Mía Pappa*, Italian, good lunches and evening buffets. *Las Gaviotas*, 14 Norte 1248. Chilean meat dishes, not expensive, live music. *Machitún Ruca*, San Martín 529. Excellent. *Pau San*, Quinta 122. Chinese. *Pizzería Mama Mía*, San Martín 435. Good, reasonably priced. *Raul*, Valparaíso 533. Live music. *Samoiedo*, Valparaíso 637. Confitería, grill and restaurant. **Cheap** The *Escuela de Hotelería y Turismo*, on the road to Valparaíso, T625799, has a good fixed price lunch menu. **Vegetarian** *Punto Verde*, Arlegui 346, Local A. Expensive. **Cafés** *Café Big Ben*, Valparaíso 469. Good coffee, good food.

Reñaca **Expensive**: *Hotel Oceanic*, Av Borgoño, T830006. Very good. *Rincón Marino*, Av Borgoño 17120. Good seafood. **Mid-range**: *El Pancho* , Av Borgoño 16180.

Excellent seafood and service. Also *El Ciervo*, Av Central y Segunda, bar/cafe, live music in evenings. Recommended.

Bars *Barlovento*, 2 Norte with 5 poniente, is THE designer bar in Viña, set over 3 floors with a lovely roof terrace, serves great pizzas and Kunstmann beer. **Cinemas** *Cine Arte*, Plaza Vergara 42. Also a multiplex in the shopping mall on Libertad (see below under shopping). **Discos** Several including *Cocodrilo*, south of town; *Kamikaze* and *Neverland* east of town; and *Twister*, Av Borgoño. *La Grua*, an old cargo crane, has been converted into a centre with many bars and clubs, very popular, beach location, good views. **Galleries** *Palacio Carrasco*, Libertad 250, T269708, Mon-Fri 0930-1300 and 1400-1830, Sat 1000-1330, free. *Sala de Arte Viña del Mar*, Arlegui 683, T680633, Mon-Sat 100-1400 and 1500-2000, Sun 1000-1300, free.

Entertainment

El Roto, **20 Jan**, in homage to the workers and peasants of Chile.

Festivals

Market At intersection of Av Sporting and river, Wed and Sat. There is a huge new mall on Libertad between 14 and 15 Norte, open till 11 pm.

Shopping

Bowling is now available in the shopping mall on Libertad (see above under shopping). **Paragliding** is taught in nearby Maitencillo (see below) by *Parapente Aventura* T2330349, www.parapente.cl Cost of single tandem flight is US$70. Course of 13 classes costs US$500.

Sport

Local Car hire: *Euro Rent-A-Car*, in *Hotel O'Higgins*, clean cars, efficient. *Hertz*, Quillota 766, T971625/6389918. **Car mechanic**: Luis Vallejos, 13 Norte 1228. Recommended.

Transport

Long distance **Air**: *Ladeco*, Santiago-Viña del Mar (to naval airfield near Concón), several daily, US$15. **Bus**: Terminal 2 blocks east of Plaza Vergara at Av Valparaíso y Quilpué. To **Santiago**, US$3-4, 2 hrs, frequent, many companies, heavily booked in advance for travel on Sun afternoons, at other times some buses pick up passengers opposite the train station; to **La Serena**, 6 daily, 8 hrs, US$10, to **Antofagasta**, 20 hrs, US$35, to **Temuco**, 12 hrs, US$14, to **Mendoza** (Argentina) *El Rápido*, *Fenix* and *TAC*, US$16, 8 hrs, all leave daily at 0830. Buses north from Valparaíso for destinations such as La Calera, La Ligua, Cabildo, Pichidangui and Los Vilos all pass through Viña, and can be caught on the Plaza. **Train**: Services on the Valparaíso Metropolitan line (Merval) stop at Viña (details under Valparaíso).

Banks Many *casas de cambio* on Arlegui including *Afex*, No 641 (open 0900-1400 Sat). *Cambio Norte*, No 610. *Cambio Andino*, No 644. Also in the tourist office. Many Redbanc ATMs on Libertad near 7 and 8 Norte, and also on Valparaíso (but note that this is not the safest area at night). Western Union money transfer, *Libertad 715* (also has DHL). **Communications** **Internet**: www.multimania.com/ruevalparaiso *Etnía Com*, Valparaiso 323, T711841. Internet less than US$1 per hr. Also at *Valparaíso 196*, T690529. **Telephone**: *CTC*, Valparaíso 628. Global *Telecommunications/Entel*, 15 Norte 961. **Cultural centres** **Casa Italia** (cultural centre, consulate, restaurant), Alvarez 398. **Instituto Chileno – Aleman de Cultura**, Goethe Haus, Alvarez 2950, T/F677249. **Instituto Chileno-Británico de Cultura**, 3 Norte 824, T971061. **Instituto Chileno-Francés de Cultura**, Alvarez 314, T685908. **Instituto Chileno – Norteamericano de Cultura**, 2 Oriente 335, T/F686191. **Places of worship** St Peter's (Anglican) and Union (Presbyterian) churches have English language services on Sun mornings.

Directory

Valparaíso and Viña del Mar

Resorts north of Viña del Mar

North of Viña del Mar the coast road runs through Las Salinas, a popular beach between two towering crags, Reñaca and Cochoa, where there is a large sea-lion colony 100 m offshore, to Concón. There is also a much faster inland road, between Viña del Mar and Concón. As this area comprises coastal communities, the Fiesta de San Pedro (the patron saint of fishermen) on 29 June, is understandably an important event.

Concón

Colour map 3, grid B2
18 km north of
Viña del Mar

Concón lies on the southern shore of a bay at the mouth of the Río Aconcagua. The town claims to be the oldest settlement in Chile, having been founded by Pedro de Valdivia in 1541, prior to his arrival at what is now Santiago. Concón is famous for its restaurants, and is rightly known as the culinary capital of the V region. An oil refinery (not visible from the beaches) causes occasional pollution, but the area is very popular among Santiaguinos, who often come here for the weekend. A series of six beaches stretches along the bay between Caleta Higuerilla at the western end and La Boca at the eastern end. These beaches include Playa Amarilla (good for sunbathing), Playa Higuerillas (lots of shells, very peaceful), Playa Los Lilenes (by the sand dunes), and Playa La Boca itself, which is excellent for beach sports.

There is a helpful tourist office, annexed to the municipal museum at Calle Maroto 1030, www.concon_online.com, maps available.

Sleeping   *Hostería Edelweiss*, Av Borgoño 19200, T814043, F903600. Modern *cabañas*, clean, comfortable, sea views, including breakfast, excellent food in attached restaurant, German spoken. Recommended. Several motels. **A** *Concón*, T814212, F813855. **A** *Internacional Playa Amarilla*, T811915, F814042. **B** *Cabañas Los Romeros*, T813671. **B** *Cabañas Río Mar*, T/F814644. Many other *cabañas* in the **A-B** price range. **Camping** *Matagua*, 3 km north, T811415, well equipped but very expensive, also *cabañas*.

Eating   Look out for good seafood *empanadas* at bars. **Caleta Higuerilla** The following are all
Both Caleta   excellent and recommended. All fall into the expensive/mid-range category. On Av
Higuerilla and   Borgoño: *Albátros*, No 21295; *Aqui Jaime*, No 21303; *Bellamar*, No 21505; *Don Chico*, No
La Boca are   21410; *Edelweiss*, No 19200; *Vista al Mar*, No 21270, T812221. Cheaper restaurants are to
renowned for   be found in Alto Higuerillas, where the following 'picadas' have been converted by the fish-
their restaurants ermen into good value restaurants, all recommended: *La Cava de Franz*, San Pedro 345; *La*
Seafood is the name of *Picá de Juan Segura*, Illapel 15; *La Picá El Horizonte*, San Pedro 120; *La Picá Los Delfines*,
the game here   San Pedro 130. **La Boca** *La Perla del Pacifico*, Borgoño 25007, excellent, expensive. *La Picá de Emeterio*, Borgoño 25069, mid-range; *Las Deliciosas*, Borgoño 25370, mid-range.

Directory   **Communications**: *Call centre* at Maroto y Pedro de Valdivia. **Tour operators:** It is possible to hire horses (US$3 per 30 mins) and kayaks at *Río Aconcagua*, on Playa La Boca.

Quintero   Another 23 km north of Concón, Quintero is a fishing town situated around a
Colour map 3, grid B2 rocky peninsula with 16 small beaches, all of varying character and quality. There is a path running along the north side of the peninsula, and a good view of the sunset over the ocean from the Cueva del Pirata (at the western end of the path). Good fishing and windsurfing are available at Playas Loncura and Ritoque to the north of the town, while horses can be hired on Playa Albátros. On the north shore of the bay at Las Ventanas stand a power station and

copper processing plant. Note that there are many touts and beggars in the high season, when the atmosphere is a little tense.

Sleeping and eating **AL** *Yachting Club*, Luis Acevedo 1736, T/F931557. **B** *Isla de Capri*, 21 de Mayo 1299, T930939. Pleasant, sea views. **B** *Res Brazilian*, 21 de Mayo 1336, with breakfast, large windows but no view, clean, well maintained, warm seawater baths for US$6. **C** *Monaco*, 21 de Mayo 1530, T930939. Run down but interesting, good views. Lots of *residenciales*.

Many cheap seafood restaurants down by the harbour

Entertainment *Disco Paladium*, 21 de Mayo 1500.

Set back in a cove surrounded by cliffs, Horcón, also known locally as Horcones, is a pleasant small village, mainly of wooden houses. Although overcrowded in season, the rest of the year it is a charming place, populated by fishermen and artists, with a tumbledown feel unlike the more well-to-do resorts to the north and south; sadly, a condominium development is underway on the northern side of the harbour, which will surely take away some of the secluded charm that is apparent for most of the year . To the south across the headland is the Playa Cau Cau, down a steep flight of log steps – more of a scramble than a walk. The reward, a sandy, frequently deserted tree-lined cove.

Horcón
Colour map 3, grid A2

On the beach cheap and unusual jewellery and trinkets are sold

Sleeping and eating **B** *El Ancla*, *cabañas*, pleasant, serves good food. **B-C** *Cabañas Arancibia*, T796169. With bath, **D** without, pleasant gardens, good food, friendly. Recommended. Also rooms in private houses. No campsite but camping possible at private houses. **D** *Juan Esteban*, Pasaje Miramar, Casa 2, T796056, T09-4384388, www.geocities.com/jestebanc Also **F** pp, English, Portuguese, Italian spoken, nice terrace with view. Recommended. Also fully equipped *cabañas*, **B** for 4 people. Eateries include: *Bahía*, mid-range, good food, nice. *El Ancla*, recommended. *Reina Victoria*, cheap, good. Good food at *Roly Schop* serves good *empanadas*. *Santa Clara*, try the *chupe de mariscos* and *pastel de jaivas*. Recommended.

Seafood lunches with the catch of the day, sold at any number of stalls on the seafront, are recommended. Drinking alcohol on the beach is forbidden – and enforced by the carabineros.

Sports *Parapente Aventura*, T09-233-0349, parapent@cix.cl Offer paragliding, US$70 per flight, and paragliding courses, US$500.

Maitencillo, 19 km north of Las Ventanas, is an upmarket resort consisting mainly of chalets. There is a wonderful long beach which is frequented mainly by well-to-do Santiaguinos; the sea here is notorious for its strong undercurrents. Just to the south is the tourist complex of Marbella, which has a hotel, conference centre, restaurants, golf course, tennis courts, pools.

Maitencillo

Sleeping and eating There is **B** *Cabañas Hermansen* and several other hotels, eg Regina, T771030, F771293, **B** pp. *Bar Rest La Canaste*, Mediterranean, Moroccan, elegant, expensive, worth every peso. *Bar Tsunami*, mid-range. *Café Entre Rojas* has good drinks and snacks.

Entertainment There are 2 discos in Maitencillo, both of them swish and expensive.

Sports Cycle hire from *Cabañas Hermansen* (see above). Surfing classes and biplane tours (US$35 for 20 mins) available from *Café Entre Rojas* (see above).

A fashionable resort with a lovely beach, Zapallar is an expensive place 33 km north of Las Ventanas. A hint of its former glory is given by a number of fine mansions along Avenida Zapallar. At Cachagua, 3 km south, a colony of

Zapallar
Colour map 3, grid A2

penguins on an island may be viewed from the northern end of the beach; take binoculars.

Accommodation is very expensive especially in the centre where it is very sparse

Sleeping and eating **L** *Isla Seca*, T741224, F741228, islasec@ctcinternet.cl Small, pool, very expensive suites (**LL**), good restaurant. **AL** *César*, T741259. Very nice but expensive. **B** *Hostal Villa Real*, large rooms, with breakfast. Recommended. **B** *Residencial Villa Alicia*, Moises Chacón 280, T741176, good, one of the cheapest. No campsite. The restaurant, *Isla Seca*, also Marisquería Chringuita, expensive, has excellent, seafood. *Restaurant César* (different management from hotel), on seafront, good and reasonable prices. Cheap eateries include *La Culebra* and *Los Troncos*. There are also good and cheap restaurants in Cachagua, to the south, such as *Natón* (has disco).

Sports Donkeys and horses may be hired in Cachagua. Also *Biplane Tours*, T771699, T09-7420548. Diving courses are available in Zapallar for US$300, including equipment.

Papudo
Population: 2,500
Colour map 3, grid A2

Ten kilometres further north is this site of a naval battle in November 1865 in which the Chilean vessel *Esmeralda* captured the Spanish ship *Covadonga*. Following the arrival of the railway Papudo rivalled Viña del Mar as a fashionable resort in the 1920s but it has long since declined. Among the buildings surviving from that period is the Casa Rawlings, now the Casa de la Cultura. There are two fine beaches, which are empty except at weekends in summer and weekdays at holiday times.

Sleeping **A** *Carande*, Chorrillos 89, T791103, F791118, best. **B** *Moderno*, F Concha 150, T711496. **B** *De Peppino*, No 609, T791108. **C** pp *Armandini*, F Concha 525, full board. **C** *Res Donde Tito*, Chorrillos 149, T791096, with breakfast. **D** *Res Valencia*, Chorrillos 107. **D** *Res La Plaza*, Chorrillos 119. Many more.

Eating *Cava del Mar*, international cuisine, pricey. *Gran Azul*, expensive seafood. *La Abeja*, mid-range. *Don Rota*, cheap seafood.

Entertainment **Bars**: *Bethania*, Irarrazaval s/n. *La Bahía*, Cochrane 49. **Discos**: *Disco "help"* , from techno to salsa, Glorias Navales 409.

Transport **Bus** From Valparaíso and Viña del Mar: to **Concón** bus 9 or 10 (from Av Libertad between 2 and 3 Norte in Viña), US$0.50; to **Quintero** and **Horcón**, *Sol del Pacífico*, every 30 mins, US$1, 2 hrs; to **Zapallar** and **Papudo**, *Sol del Pacífico*, 4 a day (2 before 0800, 2 after 1600), US$3.

Resorts south of Valparaíso

This cluster of resorts stretches along the coast from the mouth of the Río Maipo north towards Valparaíso. Although road links with the latter are poor, there are two good routes from Santiago, one leading from the main Santiago-Valparaíso highway to Algarrobo and the other, Route 78, direct to San Antonio.

San Antonio

Phone code: 035
Colour map 3, grid B2
Population: 74,742

Situated near the mouth of the Río Maipo 112 km south of Valparaíso, San Antonio is a container port and commercial centre for this part of the coast. It has a fishing port and fishmeal plants and is the terminal for the export of copper brought by rail from the large mine at El Teniente, near Rancagua. Many people come here to buy fish and seafood, and a visit to the port just after the catch has been unloaded is an interesting experience. The town was badly damaged by the 1985 earthquake. There is a museum, the Museo Municipal de Ciencias Naturales y Arqueología. ■ *Mon-Fri 0900-1300, 1500-1900. Av Barros Luco.*

Nearby to the south are two resorts: Llolleo, 4 km, famous for the treatment of heart diseases, and 7 km further Rocas de Santo Domingo, the most attractive and exclusive resort in this area with 20 km of beaches and a golf course; even in high season it is not very crowded.

San Antonio B *Jockey Club*, 21 de Mayo 202, T211777, F212922. Best, good views, restaurant. **D** *Colonial*, Pedro Montt 196. **Llolleo D** pp *Oriente*, Inmaculada Concepción 50, T32188. *Res El Castillo*, Providencia 253, T373821. **Santo Domingo A** *Rocas de Santo Domingo*, La Ronda 130, T444356, F444494, clean, friendly, restaurant, cable TV, good breakfast included in price. No cheap accommodation – try Llolleo. | **Sleeping & eating**

Bus To **Valparaíso**, Lago Peñuelas every 15 mins, *Pullman Bus*, every 45 mins, until 2000, US$2; to **Santiago**, *Pullman Bus*, every 20 mins, US$2. | **Transport**

Eight kilometres north of San Antonio, Cartagena is the biggest resort on this part of the coast. A quieter place than San Antonio, it is filled with fish restaurants and ice cream shops, and has lovely views sweeping north around the bay towards Isla Negra. In the early years of this century it was a fashionable summer retreat for the wealthy of Santiago; a number of mansions survive, notably the Castillo Foster overlooking the bay. The centre lies around the Plaza de Armas, situated on top of the hill. To the south is the picturesque Playa Chica, overlooked by many of the older hotels and restaurants; to the north is the Playa Larga. Between the two a promenade runs below the cliffs; high above hang old houses, some in disrepair but offering spectacular views. Cartagena is a very popular resort in summer, but out of season especially it is a good centre for visiting nearby points of interest; there are many hotels, and bus connections are good. | **Cartagena**
Colour map 3, grid B2
Population: 10,318
For more information on Cartagena, look at www.cartagena-chile.cl

Sleeping and eating C *Biarritz*, Playa Chica 196, T/F450476. **D** *Violeta*, Condell 140, T234093, swimming pool, good views. **E** pp *Res Carmona*, Playa Chica, T450485. Small rooms, basic, clean, good value. **F** *El Estribo*, just off Plaza de Armas, with breakfast, basic, cheap comedor. **F** *Residencial Patye*, Alacalde Cartagena 295, T450569, nice spot, good value.

The road to Algarrobo runs north along the coast through several small resorts including **Las Cruces**, **El Tabo** and **El Quisco**, a small fishing port with two beautiful white beaches (crowded during Chilean holidays). Just south of Las Cruces is **Laguna El Peral**, a nature reserve which protects a wide range of aquatic birds including black-necked swans. ■ *Sep-Apr 0900-1400, 1500-1800 daily; May-Aug 0900-1300, 1400-1800 daily.* | **North of Cartagena**

Sleeping and eating Las Cruces C *La Posada*, T21280. With bath and breakfast, good birdwatching. **El Tabo** C *Hotel El Tabo*, T33719. Good. *Motel El Tabo*, T212719. Next door (overfull in Jan-Feb), 2 cheap and basic campsites. **El Quisco** (accommodation generally expensive). A *Motel Barlovento*, T471030, 3-star. Residenciales 100-200 m from beach in C range, for example *Res Oriental*, T471662. With breakfast, good, clean, hot water. **E** pp *Cabañas del Irlandés Volador*, Aguirre 277, T473464.

D *Cabañas Pozo Azul*, Capricornio 234, T471401. Southeast of town, quiet. D *Res Julia*, Aguirre 0210, T471546. Very clean, quiet, good value. Recommended. Several on Dubournais (main street) including C *Gran Italia*, No 413, T/F481631. Good beds, pool. Recommended. D *El Quisco*, No 166, T481923. With breakfast, clean, open weekends only, with excellent seafood restaurant.

Isla Negra
Colour map 3, grid B2

Four kilometres south of El Quisco in the village of Isla Negra is the beautifully restored Museo-Casa Pablo Neruda. Bought by Neruda in 1939 this house, overlooking the sea, was his writing retreat in his later years. It contains artefacts gathered by Neruda from all over the world. Neruda and his last wife Mathilde are buried here, and the café specialises in Neruda's own recipes. There is definitely a strong sense of the poet in the house, and a visit is recommended, although some Chileans feel that the Fundación Pablo Neruda is profiteering by having the admission prices so high – Neruda was, after all, a communist. ■ *Guided tours in Spanish, English or French (see also Neruda's Santiago house, La Chascona, page 91, and La Sebastiana, page 135), summer: Tue-Sun 1000-2000; rest of year: Tue-Fri 1000-1400, 1500-1800, US$4, students US$1.50, T035-461284 for opening hours or to book English guide (US$5).*

The celebrated 1994 film *Il Postino* was based on Antonio Skármeta's novel *Ardiente Paciencia*, which is set in Isla Negra during the last years of Neruda's life. Skármeta himself adapted the book for the cinema in 1983, but after the 1994 success the novel was retitled *El Cartero de Neruda* (Neruda's Postman).

Sleeping and eating B *Hostería Santa Elena*, T213439. Beautiful building and location, restaurant, some rooms damp and gloomy. F *Casa Azul*, Av Santa Luisa, T461154. With breakfast, kitchen and living room, English spoken, camping. Recommended.

Transport Bus From Santiago: *Pullman Bus* service from Terminal Alameda, frequent in summer, US$8 return; also regular services by *Robles* and other companies from Terminal Sur. Tours from Santiago, departing at 0900 from Plaza de Armas (Compañia y Ahumada), cost US$20 and include seaside resorts, T2322574.

Algarrobo
Colour map 3, grid B2

In summer there are boat tours round the island from the jetty

North of Cartagena by 29 km, Algarrobo is the largest resort north of Cartagena and the most chic, with its large houses, yacht club and marina. Its shallow waters and sheltered bay ensures that sea temperatures here are much warmer than at most other resorts in central Chile. Conveniently located for Santiago, it was, in the 1960s, the retreat of politicians – both Salvador Allende and Eduardo Frei had summer residences here. Algarrobo remains one of the most popular spots on the central coast, as there are good beaches with fishing, surfing and sailing all available – the population of 4,000 is swamped by 100,000 summer visitors. From Playa Canelo there are good views of pelicans and boobies in a seabird colony on an offshore island (no entry).

Sleeping and eating A *Costa Sur*, Alessandri 2156, T481151. A *Uribe*, behind Costa Sur, T481035. Pleasant, quiet. C *Res Vera*, Alessandri 1521, T481131. With breakfast, good. F *Res San José*, Av Principal 1598, T481131. Basic, no hot water.

Transport Bus To Santiago, Pullman Bus, every 20 mins, 2 hrs, US$3, stopping in Cartagena and the resorts along the coast (but not San Antonio). Services to San Antonio by *Empresa de Buses San Antonio* (frequent, last bus around 2000) and *Empresa Robles*.

From Santiago to La Serena

5

From Santiago to La Serena

This is a little-known part of Chile, stretching 500 km from Santiago north to La Serena and the fertile Elqui Valley. While some of the coastal towns are popular, the interior between La Ligua and Vicuña is almost universally overlooked. Yet here there are rich rewards for those prepared to rough it and take a few risks – one of the world's highest concentrations of petroglyphs, spectacular mountainsides speckled different colours by the rich mineral deposits, and desolate tracks winding through some of Chile's best high mountain scenery.

The largest resort is La Serena, the usual centre for visiting the pisco distilleries of the Elqui Valley. This valley is one of the world's most important astronomical centres, with four observatories, including one built especially for visitors – it is also the focal point of Chile's new age movement, and was the birthplace of Nobel laureate Gabriela Mistral. South of La Serena is the lively city of Ovalle, an ideal centre for forays into the cordillera and for visiting the Parque Nacional Fray Jorge, a temperate rainforest which survives in this dry region due to the sea mists that hang almost constantly over its hills.

Background

History Archaeological finds indicate that the river valleys were inhabited at an early stage in prehistory. The Molle culture arose contemporaneously with the rise of Christianity in Europe – sharing links with northern Argentina, the Molle people produced intricate ceramics and worked with copper. They were superseded by the Diaguitas, who crossed the Andes around AD 900 and settled throughout the area. The pre-Hispanic peoples left their mark throughout the area with many petroglyphs (rock carvings).

Soon after the arrival of the Spanish and the foundation of Santiago, Pedro de Valdivia attempted to secure control over northern Chile by founding La Serena in 1544. With the arid climate and the more testing living conditions, the indigenous people were less numerous than the Mapuches in the south, and, despite a few setbacks for the Spanish, they were soon subjugated and wiped out. Throughout the colonial period, La Serena dominated the rest of the region; although small, it was the only city in the north and its leading families had close ties to the main Spanish landowners in the other valleys. After independence the area became an important mining zone, producing large amounts of silver, copper and gold.

Geography Stretching north from the Río Aconcagua to the Río Elqui, this area is a transitional zone between the fertile heartland and the northern deserts. North of the Aconcagua the Andes and the coastal *cordillera* merge in a spectacular lattice of mountains, and are crossed by river valleys separated by high ridges. North of La Ligua, the Pan-American Highway follows the coastline, which is relatively flat, passing many beautiful coves, alternatively rocky and sandy, with good surf, though the water is very cold. The valleys of the main rivers – the Choapa, Limarí and Elqui – are green oases; the land is intensively farmed using irrigation to produce fruit and vegetables. Elsewhere the vegetation is characteristic of semidesert (dry scrub and cactus), except in those areas where sea mists provide sufficient moisture to support temperate rainforest.

Climate Rainfall is rare, and occurs only in winter. Temperatures are relatively stable, with little seasonal variation, especially on the coast where the average temperature is 14°C, morning mists are common and humidity is high; the interior is dry, with temperatures averaging 16-17°C. Note that in inland towns such as Illapel and Combarbalá it gets very cold at night, especially in winter.

Economy Despite the dry climate agriculture is important, employing over a third of the labour force. Much of the region's industry is linked to its agricultural produce, notably the distilling of *pisco* from grapes; by law, only grapes grown in the regions of Copiapó and Coquimbo can be used to make *pisco*. There are large fish-meal and processing plants in Coquimbo. Mining is also important: among the major mines are El Indio, inland from La Serena, the biggest gold producer in Chile as well as a source of copper, and El Romeral, north of La Serena, the most important iron ore deposit in the country. Quartz and the semi-precious stones lapis lazuli and combarbalita are also mined.

★

Things to do

- Take in the biggest independence day celebrations in Chile – La Pampilla in Coquimbo, a week of constant revelry in September.
- Visit the incongruous Parque Nacional Fray Jorge, a temperate rainforest amid semi-desert that survives owing to dense fogs.
- Budding astronomers and those who are simply curious will want to visit at least one of the observatories near La Serena.
- Explore and imagine the pre-Hispanic past of the Diaguitas and Molle people, whose petroglyphs are etched poignantly into the area's beautiful mountainsides.
- Relax on a beach – get away from it all in places such as La Herradura, Tongoy and Pichidangui.

North to the Elqui Valley

The first stretch of the Pan-American Highway from Santiago is inland through green valleys with rich blue clover and wild artichokes. North of La Ligua it follows the coast, and the first intimations of the northern deserts appear.

Los Vilos

Los Vilos is a former mineral port, now a small seaside resort. Set in a wide bay, it is a peaceful, windswept place, disturbed mainly by the noise of kelp gulls and of the waves. There are several attractive plazuelas on the costanera, where there are stone benches from which you can watch the fishing boats bobbing in the sea; the water is cold for bathing, and the hotels are most popular among fishermen. Offshore are two islands reached by frequent launches: Isla de Los Huevos, situated in the bay, and, 5 km south, Isla de Los Lobos where there is a colony of seals. There is a tourist office at Caupolicán 278, summer only. **Pichidangui**, 26 km south, is a popular resort on a rocky peninsula with a beautiful beach to the north. **Los Molles**, 10 km south of Pichidangui, is a fishing village where many wealthy residents of Santiago have their summer homes. Nearby are the Puguén blow holes (US$1, free off-season) and the Piscina Los Molles, a natural swimming pool.

*Phone code: 053
Colour map 3, grid A2
Population: 9,422
216 km north of
Santiago*

C *Cabañas El Conquistador*, Caupolicán 200 block, T541663, with bath and big break-fast, TV and refrigerator in very nice rooms, pleasant patio, sauna, friendly, worth bargaining off season, excellent value, highly recommended. **C** *Lord Willow*, Hostería s/n, T541037, Santiago T02-8572930. Overlooking beach and harbour, interesting collection of old firearms, with breakfast and bath, pleasant, friendly, parking, weekend disco next door. **F** *Bellavista*, Rengo 020, T541073. With breakfast, bath and TV in carpeted rooms, hot water, sea views, clean, no curtains, recommended. Two more **F** residenciales on Caupolicán, *Drake*, No 435, and *Turismo*, No 437. **G** *Res Angelica*, Caupolicán 627. Cold, lumpy beds, central, basic. The *American Motel* is right on the highway, Km 224, **B**, T541020, and is a convenient stopping place between Viña del Mar or Santiago and La Serena, good value. There are several other motels here as well. Also camping at *Campomar*, near centre, F541049, **G**, and *cabañas*.

Sleeping

In Pichidangui A *Motel Pichidangui*, Francis Drake s/n, T531114, F02-2097449. Swimming pool. **C** *Cabañas Del Bosque*, El Bosque s/n, T531123. Recommended. **F** *Hostería Puquen*, 2 Poniente s/n, T531104. Attractive, good value. Various other hotels

From Santiago to La Serena

and *pensiones* in every price range. Camping at *El Bosque de Pichidangui*, T531030, **F** per site, and *Bahía Marina de Pichidangui*, T531120, sports facilities, *cabañas*. **In Los Molles** *Cabañas Los Molles*, F791787. *Cabañas Lourdes*, T02-5589778.

Eating

Restaurants in Pichindangui tend to be pricey, although there is a food shop

Mid-range *Alisio*, Caupolicán 298. Seafood and fish, good value. *Restaurant Turistico Costanera*, on Purén, good views over ocean, good meals and choice of wines, nice warm bread. Also serves cheap menu. **Cheap and seriously cheap** All the following serve supercheap menus and cheap special orders; seafood is the order of the day: *El Rey de la Paila Marina* and *El Rey de la Paila Marina Vileña*, both on Purén. There are countless places on the seafront, such as *Restaurant Crucero del Amor*. *Pastelería/Heladería Roma*, Caupolicán 712, excellent cakes and ice creams, very helpful owners both speak fluent English.

Entertainment

Pubs *Piel Morena*, Rengo s/n, summer only. **Discos** *Dino's Disco*, on Caupolicán, popular with locals. *Zone Beach*, Rengo 086, popular in summer.

Shopping

In the evenings there is a craft market at Caupolicán y Purén selling relatively cheap woollens and semi-precious stones.

Transport

Bus The main companies serving Los Vilos are *Pullman Bus* and *Tas Choapa*, both with 5 buses daily to *Santiago* (US$4) and *La Serena* (US$4.75), as well as frequent buses to *Illapel* (US$0.80) and *Salamanca* (US$1.60). There is only 1 bus daily Pichidangui-Santiago, but north-south buses (for example *Inca Bus*) on the Highway pass Los Vilos and Pichidangui.

Directory

Communications Post office: On Lincoyán. **Telephone:** *ENTEL* office at Caupolicán 873. **Dentist** *Juan Rubio*, Lautaro 435, T541683. **Film** *Caupolicán 667*. Also at *Rengo y Lautaro*.

Illapel

Phone code: 053
Colour map 3, grid A3
Population: 18,900
287 km north of Santiago

Illapel is surrounded by barren hills, and there are good views of the *cordillera* to the east. It is a poor town which depends on mining in the surrounding mountains, and heavy trucks continually lumber in and out on the road north to/from Combarbalá. While Illapel is not wildly interesting in itself, there is wonderful mountain country in the surrounding area, best explored by the adventurous or those with their own transport.

Ins & outs
Exchange is not possible in Illapel, and there are no Redbanc ATMs

Getting there Illapel is easily reached by regular buses from Los Vilos, taking an hour and costing US$0.80. From Los Vilos, a paved road turns off the Panamericana and climbs steeply up to a pass, from which there are staggering views of the Andes and the Choapa River. There are also many daily buses from both Santiago and La Serena and other destinations as far north as Calama. **Getting around** Illapel is a small town, and can be easily covered on foot; there are *colectivos* for those who require them.

The lives of the *pilquineros* (independent miners) in the nearby hills provide a sobering illustration of the lifestyle which miners in the north of Chile have endured since colonial times. The workers drag rocks from the mine-face in rusting wheelbarrows, living without power, fresh water or even public transport, and many of them die tragically young from lung cancer or chagas disease. If you do go up into these areas, bring gifts (such as cigarettes) and humility in abundance.

There is a small archaeological museum in the Casa de la Cultura, next to the Library, Valdivieso y Constitución, just off the Plaza de Armas, with a bizarre and disordered collection of arrowheads, jewellery, pottery, miners' boots and newspapers so dusty you almost choke. ■ *Mon-Fri 0900-1300 and 1400-1800, free.* There is no tourist office (although you could try in the Municipalidad on the Plaza), but there is a very helpful CONAF office at Vicuña Mackenna 093, 0830-1730.

Reserva Nacional Las Chinchillas

The reserve, 15 km north, is reached along a paved road passing impressive mountains speckled with cacti and minerals. The reserve covers 4,229 ha and protects the last remaining colony of chinchillas in this region. The chinchillas and six related species can be viewed from behind two-way mirrors. Accommodation is available in well-equipped *cabañas*, **F**, with kitchen facilities, and there is a campsite, **G**. ■ *Daily from 0900-1700 (until 1800 in summer). US$2.50. Getting there: by 2003 there may be public transport along the road heading for Combarbalá, but at present the best way to visit is to hire a taxi, costing approximately US$20.*

Sleeping

B *Diaguitas*, Constitución 276, T/F522587, noisy, swimming pool. **B** *Domingo Ortíz de Rozas*, Ignacio Silva 241, T/F522127, 3-star, all mod cons, attractive spot. **B/C** *Los Tilos*, Ignacio Silva 45, with bath, breakfast and TV, friendly, small rooms, overpriced. **D** *Alameda*, Ignacio Silva 20, T522355, cheaper rooms **F** pp, with bath and TV, without breakfast, friendly, clean, nice patio with lemon and orange trees, cheap laundry service, recommended. **D** *Americano*, Carrera 128, nice courtyard, with breakfast, bath and TV. **E** *Londres*, Mackenna 21, T211906, basic, quiet, friendly, worth bargaining. **F** pp *Regalona*, Buín 583, dirty, basic, overpriced. **G** *Pensión María Elena*, Esmeralda 54, best of the cheapies, very basic but warm and friendly.

From Santiago to La Serena

Illapel

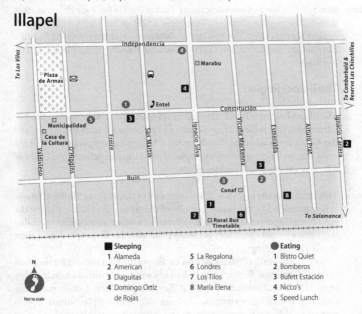

■ Sleeping		**● Eating**
1 Alameda	5 La Regalona	1 Bistro Quiet
2 American	6 Londres	2 Bomberos
3 Diaguitas	7 Los Tilos	3 Bufett Estación
4 Domingo Ortíz	8 María Elena	4 Nicco's
de Rojas		5 Speed Lunch

N
Not to scale

Eating **Mid-range** *Bistro Quiet*, Constitución 200 block, smart, fills up at weekends. *Bufett Estación*, Buín 452, smartest in town, smart, good food. *Nicco's*, Ignacio Silva 219. Good pizzas, fancy décor, vegetarian options. **Seriously cheap** *Bamby Restaurant*, Constitución 340, chicken and chips, not wonderful. *Casino de Bomberos*, Buín 590, incredibly friendly, excellent value, good views of the town, highly recommended. *Speed Lunch*, Constitución 160, friendly, some vegetarian possibilities (ask for lentils), not as bad as it sounds. Good bread and cakes at *Luz My Pan*, San Martín, opposite the bus station.

Entertainment **Disco** *Pub Marabú*, Ignacio Silva 260, at weekends, salsa and merengue, popular, US$3 with free drink.

Shopping Shopping centre *La Catedral* at Constitución 455. *Supermercado Las Naranjas*, Independencia 104.

Tour operators *Turismo Libuca*, Independencia 099, T522155, specialises in tours of the south for those from Illapel, but can arrange visits to Las Chinchillas.

Transport The bus station is at San Martín, on the 200 block. Illapel is best served by *Pullman Bus*, which has services to **Santiago** (US$4.75) and **La Serena** (US$5.20). *Intercomunal* have 4 buses daily to **Viña** and **Valparaíso**, (US$5.20). Buses to rural destinations leave from Independencia y Ignacio Silva; the timetables are posted at the greengrocer's at the bottom end of Ignacio Silva, but the buses do not leave from here. Bus companies take advantage of the remoteness of the Choapa Valley and double their prices for the stretch from Illapel to Los Vilos on the Panamericana, as set against the journey from Los Vilos to Illapel – unfortunately, those travelling by bus have no alternative means of leaving the area.

Directory **Banks** No exchange. **Communications** Post office: On the Plaza de Armas, does Western Union money transfers. **Telephone**: *ENTEL* at San Martín y Constitución. Another phone centre at Constitución 161. **Dentist** *Vicuña Mackenna 183*, T521010. **Hospital** *Independencia s/n*, T522312. **Laundry** *Alondra*, Ignacio Silva 370, only one in town.

The Illapel Region

The Illapel Region is largely ignored by travellers, yet it has some worthwhile attractions. This is the narrowest part of Chile between Arica and Aysén, and the Andes are nowhere as close by as here. Valleys carve right up towards the snowline, and there are many examples of pre-Hispanic petroglyphs for those who take the trouble to find them.

Salamanca This small, friendly town lies 32 km southeast of Illapel along the Río Choapa. It is surrounded by the dusty foothills of the Andes, and halfway along the road from Illapel is the Los Cristales Pass, from which there are views of distant snowy mountains. There is a shady plaza where craftspeople display their goods in the evenings.

Some 2 km north of Salamanca on the Illapel road is a turning for the small town of **Chalinga**, formerly an Indian encampment, with a church dating from 1750 (ask at the nearby convent if entry is possible). A dusty road continues from Chalinga up into the Chalinga valley, passing plantations of pisco grapes, prickly pears, fruit orchards and irrigated vegetable patches before heading up into barren mountain scenery. Here there are campsites, including one at **Zapallar**. The teacher at the school at Zapallar has made a study of the petroglyphs of the surrounding area – of which there are many – and may be able to help interested parties seek them out. There are one or two rural buses daily from Salamanca to these mountain communities, as well as *colectivos* to Chalinga.

Sleeping B *Hostal Vasco*, Bulnes 120, T551119, with bath and breakfast, swimming pool. G *Residencial O'Higgins*, O'Higgins 430, breakfast extra, friendly, clean, basic, patio.

Eating Seriously cheap *El Americano*, O'Higgins y M de Montepio, good lunches, also has information on the surrounding area. *Restaurant Crillón*, on the Plaza on Calle M de Montepio, friendly, excellent value almuerzos, serves Grolsch. *Restaurant Salamanca*, Echavarría 340, seafood and meat, clean. There are cheap ice creams at a shop next to ENTEL on the plaza.

Entertainment Disco *El Area*, Bulnes 240. **Holy Week** is a big event at Salamanca, with horse races *à la Chilena* and costumed processions through the town.

Transport Bus company offices on O'Higgins. Two buses an hour to Illapel from 0800 to 1800, US$0.80, as well as *colectivos*. These buses either continue north to La Serena or south to Santiago.

Directory Communications Post office: Bulnes, on the Plaza. **Telephone:** *CTC Veronica*, Salamanca, on the plaza. *ENTEL*, M de Montepio y Bulnes, on the plaza.

North of Illapel, a paved road leads 15 km north to **Reserva Nacional Las Chinchillas** (see page 161). After Las Chinchillas the asphalt disappears, the mountainsides close in – red, purple and white with minerals, and covered with cacti. The bad road climbs the Cuesta El Espino to a height of over 2000 m, from which there are unforgettable views of the multicoloured mountains and the white snows of the Andes. A much worse road – suitable for riders and cyclists only – branches off at the junction for Las Chinchillas and follows the old railway track on an even more remote and dramatic route to Combarbalá, via mining settlements at Farellón Sánchez and Matancillas. Eventually it rejoins the main road below Cuesta El Espino, and reaches the small town of Combarbalá, 73km north of Illapel.

Illapel to Combarbalá

Combarbalá is set in a dusty bowl surrounded by mountains. The town is famous as the home of the combarbalita, a semi-precious stone that was declared the National Stone of Chile in 1993. However, the town is little known, even to Chileans – in 2001 the Senatur office in Santiago told a caller to "phone the appropriate embassy" when aksed about Combarbalá. The combarbalita is similar in appearance to marble and is found nowhere else in the world. A craft centre is presently being built on the outskirts of the town, and will be well worth a visit from those with a serious interest in handicrafts. The Asociación de Artesanos is on the Plaze de Armas.

Combarbalá

Sleeping and eating There is basic accommodation, G at *Residencial La Golondrina*, Chacabuco y Libertad. Pizzas at *Crup-Chup's*.

Transport At present there is no transport from Illapel to Combarbalá. However, the road is due to be paved by 2003, when public transport services should commence. For now, buses serve mainly from Ovalle (see page 166), or with *Buses Combarbalá* from Santiago, La Calera, La Ligua and Los Vilos.

Mineral heaven

If you are at all interested in geology, you could spend months in this part of Chile and still not be satisfied. The mountains of the cordillera here are brimful of minerals that are easily visible to the naked eye. Near Combarbalá the colours are white and red, showing that the combarbalita – a marble-type rock found nowhere else in the world is nearby; in the high mountains inland from Ovalle is one of the world's two mines of the brilliant blue stone, lapis lazuli; while at Andacollo, you may have your only chance in Chile to see small-scale gold mining in operation, though the numbers of miners working here has declined rapidly in recent years.

Miners in these areas often work independently, and they are known as pilquineros. They process their findings in two types of small mills. The larger independent miners use the trapiche, which consists of two heavy vertical wheels in a container half filled with water. As the ore is ground between the wheels, the mineral sticks to mercury which is spread on the sides of the container. The other type of mill, the maray, resembles a large mortar and pestle and is hand driven. Both the trapiche and the maray are rented by the miner to process their own ore, the rent being paid as a share of the ore.

Ovalle

Phone code: 053
Colour map 2, grid C1
Population: 53,000
Altitude: 200 m

Situated inland in the valley of the Río Limarí – a fruit-growing and mining district – this lively town is a focal point for the numerous communities in the surrounding mountains. Surrounded by dusty hills which are lined with vines for pisco grapes and orchards of avocado trees, it gets busy on market days, when local campesinos throng around the market area. It is famous for its talabarterías (saddleries), and for its products made of locally mined lapis lazuli.

Ins & outs
See page 166 for further details

Getting there Ovalle is easily reached by regular buses: north from La Serena up to 20 per day, US$2.50 (and also from destinations as far north as Arica); south from Illapel (US$3) and Santiago (US$7), numerous. **Getting around** Ovalle is quite a large town, although the central part can be easily covered on foot; most *colectivos* leave from the Ariztía avenue.

Sights
Market days are Monday, Wednesday, Friday and Saturday, till 1600; the market, *feria modelo*, is on Benavente. The **Museo del Limarí** is housed in the old railway station, Covarrubias y Antofagasta, and has displays of petroglyphs and a good collection of Diaguita ceramics and other artefacts. ■ *Tue-Fri 0900-1300, 1500-1900, Sat and Sun 1000-1300, US$1.* There is a tourist information kiosk on the Plaza de Armas.

Excursions
Embalse La Paloma, the largest reservoir in Chile, is 26 km southeast. On the northern shore is the small town of **Monte Patria** with a pisco distillery which can be visited. Nearby accommodation is available at the *Hotel Hacienda Juntas*, **A**. It stands in 90 ha of vineyards, has spectacular views and a swimming pool. From Monte Patria, a paved road leads to Chilecito and Carén. At **Carén** is the Parque Ecológico La Gallardina, containing a beautiful collection of roses and other plants and flowers amid the dry mountains. ■ *US$1.50 (US$2.20 at weekends), T726009. Getting there: hourly buses from Ovalle to Carén, leaving from the rural bus terminal, continuing on to Tulahuén, from which a bad track leads to the lapis lazuli mine.*

Monumento Nacional Valle del Encanto, about 22 km southwest of Ovalle, is one of the most important archaeological sites in northern Chile. Artefacts from hunting peoples from over 2,000 years ago have been found, but the most visible remains date from the Molle culture (700 AD). There are over 30 petroglyphs as well as great boulders, distributed in six sites. Camping facilities. ■ *US$1. All year round 0800-1800. Getting there: no local bus service; you must take a southbound long distance bus and ask to be dropped off – 5 km walk to the valley; flag down a bus to return.*

Termas de Socos, situated 35 km southwest of Ovalle on the Pan-American Highway, is a very popular resort among Chileans. There are fine thermal springs, US$5, a good hotel (**L**, T 02-6816692, Casilla 323) and a campsite (**F** per tent, but bargain) nearby. ■ *Getting there: bus US$2.*

Essentials

A *Hotel Turismo*, Victorio 295, T623258, F623536, parking, modern, friendly. **B** *Gran Hotel*, Mackenna 210 (entrance through Galería Yagnam), T621084, F624122, yagnam@terra.cl Decent rooms, bargain, ask to be away from the main road. **B** *Hotel Americana*, Mackenna 169, T620159, F620722, friendly, small rooms, overpriced. **D** *Roxy*, Libertad 155, T620080. Constant hot water, big rooms, clean, friendly, patio, *comedor*. Highly recommended. **F** *Hotel Venecia*, Libertad 261, T09-7635928. Clean, safe, friendly. Recommended. **F** *Res Socos*, Socos 22, T629856. Clean, quiet, family run, breakfast extra. Recommended. For cheaper accommodation there is **G** *Res Lolita*, Independencia 274, without bath, basic, short-stay, noisy, bad beds, not recommended. Several other cheap *residenciales* in Calle Socos (short stay).

Sleeping
■ *on map*
Price codes:
see inside front cover

Mid-range *Bavaria*, MacKenna 161, usual range of sandwiches and main dishes. *Club Social Arabe*, Arauco 255. Spacious glass-domed premises, limited selection of Arab dishes, good but not cheap. **Cheap** *Club Comercial*, Aguirre 244 (on plaza).

Eating
● *on map*

Ovalle

Sleeping
1 Americana
2 Gran
3 Lolita
4 Residencial Socos
5 Roxy
6 Turismo
7 Venecia

Eating
1 Bavaria
2 Café Haiti
3 Club Comercial
4 Club Social Arabe
5 D'Oscar
6 El Quijote
7 Lucerna
8 Yum Yum

Not to scale

Open Sun. *El Quijote*, Arauco 294. Intimate atmosphere, good seafood, inexpensive, Ovalle's 'bohemian' hang out. *La Bocca Restaurant*, Benavente 110, specializes in shellfish. Two good seafood restaurants on Victoria 400-block by the market. **Seriously cheap** Good value *almuerzos* at *Casino La Bomba*, Aguirre 364, run by fire brigade. *Restaurant Lucerna*, Independencia 339 (opposite the market), opens early for breakfast, popular, interesting place doubling as a doss house for *campesinos*. Next door is *Las Tejas*, of a similar ilk.

For drinks and snacks try *Café Caribe Express*, V MacKenna 241. *Café Haiti*, Victoria 307, opens early for breakfast. *D'Oscar Bar*, Plaza de Armas, good real coffee, open late. *Yum Yum*, MacKenna 21. Good, cheap, lively. For cakes try *Pastelería Josti*, Libertad 427; mouthwatering cakes also at *Panadería Victoria*, Mackenna 060.

Entertainment   **Disco** *Eskla Discotheque*, Mackenna 100-block, often has live music. **Cinema** *Cine Cervantes*, Centro Comercial G Corral, on the plaza.

Shopping   *Supermercado La Italiana*, Libertad 200-block. For articles made of lapis lazuli try Sr Wellington Vega Alfaro; his workshop, on the northern outskirts, is difficult to reach without transport, T620797. There are many *talabarterías* on Benavente, near the *feria modelo*.

Transport   Ovalle is a small city, but confusingly it has 2 bus terminals: the **Terrapuerto Limarí** (next to the *feria modelo* near Benavente 500-block) and the **Terminal Media Luna** (by the rodeo ring on Ariztía Oriente). The Terrapuerto Limarí is by far the more important: it is the only one used by all major companies, and most buses using the Terminal Media Luna stop there after leaving from the Terrapuerto Limarí. Buses to **Santiago**, many, mostly in mid-morning or late at night, 6½ hrs, US$7; to **La Serena**, 20 a day, 1½ hr, US$2.50, *Horvitur* and *Via Elqui*; to **Antofagasta** (US$18) and **Arica** (US$30), mostly at night, *Tur Bus*, *Pullman Bus*, *Fenix Norte*. Rural buses – of which there are many – leave from a terminal outside the *feria modelo*, next to the Terrapuerto Limarí.

Directory   **Banks** Many Redbanc ATMS on the plaza, including *Banco de Chile* and *Banco Santander*. **Communications** Internet at *Big D@ddy* in the Centro Comercial Jofre, Mackenna 200-block, local 21. Also at *Chilesat* in the same Centro Comercial. **Post office**: On Mackenna on the Plaza de Armas. **Telephone**: *CTC*, Victoria y Vicuña Mackenna, on the Plaza. **Cycle repairs** *Cycles Penna*, Benavente 360. **Useful address** The **Automóvil Club de Chile** is at Libertad 144, T620011 – very helpful, overnight parking.

Around Ovalle

Parque Nacional Fray Jorge   This park, a UNESCO Biosphere Reserve, covers 9,959 ha and contains original temperate rainforests, which contrast with the otherwise barren surroundings. Receiving no more than 113 mm of rain a year, the forests survive because of the almost constant fog and mist covering the hills, the result of the discharge of the warm waters of the Río Limari into the cold waters of the Pacific. The increasingly arid climate of this part of Chile has brought the habitat under threat, and hence visits are closely controlled by CONAF – visitors should take particular care to leave no trace of their visit behind them.
■ *Getting there: situated 90 km west of Ovalle and 110 km south of La Serena at the mouth of the Río Limarí, the park is reached by a dirt road leading off the Pan-American Highway. The entrance and administration are at Km 18, from where it is 10 km further to the summit of the coastal hills (known as the Altos de*

Talinay) which rise to 667 m. Round trip in taxi from Ovalle, US$30, Abel Olivares Rivera, T053-620352. Recommended.

Essentials US$2.50, open Sat, Sun and public holidays only, 0900-1600, last departure 1800. Visits are closely controlled owing to risk of fire. Basic accommodation is available in an old hacienda, **F** pp; there is also 1 *cabaña* sleeping 5 people (**B**), which may be hired. There are 2 campsites, one is at the administration centre, T053-620058. Waterproof clothing essential. Scientific groups may obtain permission to visit from The Director, CONAF, Cordóvez 281, La Serena, T211124.

Some 47 km northeast of Ovalle at an altitude of 1,350 m, this park contains petrified tree trunks and archaeological remains, including a vast cave, comparable to the Cueva Milodón outside Puerto Natales, with remnants of ancient roof paintings. Gigantic rock formations can be seen on the surrounding mountains. Encouraged by the local mayor, a bright green model of a dinosaur has been erected here. Sure to be a magnet for groups of local schoolchildren, the dinosaur is supposed to be the north's answer to the sloth in the Milodon Cave near Puerto Natales, but as yet it is too early to claim that Jurassic Park has come to Pichasca. ■ *0800-1800. US$3. Getting there: reached by a mostly paved road which runs from Ovalle through to Vicuña (see below). Daily buses from Ovalle to Hurtado pass the turn off (to San Pedro) about 42 km from the city (bus times under Hurtado, page 168). From here it is 3 km to the park and about 2 km further to sites of interest.*

Monumento Natural Pichasca

Valley of the Limarí

From Ovalle, a road leads 77 km northeast, following the course of the Río Limarí to the village of Hurtado. The route passes the Recoleta Reservoir, and then follows the valley, where fat horses graze on alfalfa, vines with pisco grapes are strung out across what flat land there is, and the glades are planted with orchards of orange and avocado trees.

The road is paved as far as Samo Alto; shortly after is the turn-off for the Monumental Natural Pichasca (see above), and then the village of **Pichasca**, where basic accommodation is available at the *Restaurant Flor del Valle*, **H**, which also serves cheap meals. Just beyond Pichasca there are several plantations, and rickety wooden suspension bridges cross to the far side of the Río Limarí. It is a further 32 km to Hurtado, and the road continues winding along the side of the valley, with the Andes now easily visible at the head of the valley.

At **Vado Morrillos**, 4 km before Hurtado, is the *Hacienda Los Andes*, T053-1982106, www.haciendalosandes.com **C** per person for bed and breakfast. It is a new centre for horseriding excursions in the area, set in a very pretty location. There is also a 7 km nature trail. All the rooms have a private bath and there is a sauna and a jacuzzi that overlooks the river. The Hacienda is run by a German/Austrian couple with previous experience of running horseback trips, English and German spoken. Camping is also available, **G** including hot shower. Horseriding tours from one to three days are offered in the surrounding mountains, starting at US$80. If coming by bus to the hacienda, ask the driver to let you off at the bridge at Vado Morrillos – the entrance to the hacienda is just before the bridge on the right.

The road continues on to **Hurtado**, a village set at 1,300 m. Excellent accommodation is available with Sra Orieta, **F**, on the main street, near the church, with wonderful breakfast, very friendly. There is an interesting collection of ancient riding spurs, stirrups and Spanish padlocks in the hospedaje, and Sra Orieta's son, Lucho, is very knowledgeable about the area, and can lead visitors on climbs of Cerro Gigante (2,825 m), and to petroglyphs and the site of a Diaguita cemetery. Near Hurtado is the only petroglyph in Chile depicting the sun, hinting at possible links to the Incas.

Valley of the Limarí

The extremely adventurous may consider continuing from Hurtado into **Argentina** (permission must be sought from the *carabineros* in Hurtado). It is three days on horse to the pass into Argentina (4,229 m); near the pass are the corrals of El Ternero, where a wall built by pre-Hispanic peoples climbs up into the snows. On the far side of the frontier, the path descends to the Laguna de los Patos, where the Argentines have a police post. However, it is then a further 7-10 days by horse to the nearest settlement in Argentina, and there is no road. It may be possible to find guides for this trip in the village of Las Breas, 22 km beyond Hurtado, where there is a small restaurant. An easier option than the above is to continue from Hurtado north to Vicuña in the Elqui Valley, only 46 km away (similarly, those coming from the north could continue south from Vicuña to Hurtado). This is a desolate road; there is very little traffic and no public transport, but pick-ups can be hired in Hurtado to make the trip to Vicuña for US$20-25.

Transport *Buses M&R*, T053-1982121, T09-8220320, have an erratic schedule linking Ovalle and Hurtado. On Ovalle's market days (Mon, Wed, Fri, Sat) 3 buses leave Hurtado between 0600 and 0630; on Tue and Thu the buses leave Hurtado at 1000 and 1015, on Sun at 1230 and 1245. From Ovalle, there are three buses to Hurtado on market days (1200, 1230 and 1500), except for Sat, when there is just one bus at 1400. On Tue and Thu, buses leave Ovalle at 1615 and 1645, on Sun at 1700 and 1730. The fare is US$2.

To Andacollo The good road inland between Ovalle and La Serena makes an interesting contrast to Ruta 5, the Pan-American Highway, with a fine pass and occasional views of snowcapped Andes across cacti-covered plains and semi-desert mountain ranges. Some 61 km north of Ovalle a side road runs 44 km southeast, with the last 20 km being very bad, to Andacollo.

Andacollo
Colour map 2, grid C1
Population: 10,216
Altitude: 1,050 m

Situated in a gorge, Andacollo has been a mining centre since before the arrival of the Spanish (see box on page 164). Ruins of mines and waste tips dot the area. Two mines, one copper and one gold, still operate and there are many independent mines and *trapiches*, small processing plants, which can be visited; the gold has, however, begun to run out, and in recent years many miners have moved away. Andacollo, however, is more famous as one of the great pilgrimage sites in Chile. In the enormous **Basilica** (1893), 45 m high and with a capacity of 10,000, is the miraculous Virgen del Rosario de Andacollo. Nearby is the **Templo Antiguo**, smaller and dating from 1789. There is a museum, **Museo de Andacollo**, which is open daily 0900-1300, 1500-1830. There are no hotels, but some *pensiones*. During the festival private houses rent beds and some let you pay for a shower. The tourist office on the Plaza de Armas can arrange tours to the Basilica and to mining operations.

Festivals The *Fiesta Grande* from **23-27 Dec** (most important day 26 Dec) attracts 150,000 pilgrims from northern Chile. The ritual dances date from a pre-Spanish past. Transport is available from La Serena and Ovalle but 'purists' walk (torch and good walking shoes essential). Two villages are passed on the route, which starts on the paved highway, then goes along a railway track and lastly up a steep, dusty hill. There is also a smaller festival, the *Fiesta Chica* on the first Sun of **Oct**.

Transport From **Ovalle** *colectivo*, US$2; bus, US$1.40. From La Serena, yellow *colectivos* run from Calle Domeyko.

The Elqui Valley

A dramatic cleft in the heart of the mountains, the Elqui Valley is home to two of the north's most important cities, Coquimbo and La Serena. Inland, you will find scintillating starlit nights, ashram communities and isolated villages in the mountains.

Getting there The cities of Coquimbo and La Serena are easily reached by countless buses from both north and south, from any one of more than 10 companies. By air there are several flights daily from Santiago to Copiapó, Antofagasta and Calama via La Serena. **Getting around** La Serena and Coquimbo are linked by frequent buses that pass down Av Francisco de Aguirre in La Serena before travelling along the Panamericana; the fare is US$0.45. Taxis are plentiful and inexpensive.

Ins & outs

From Santiago to La Serena

Coquimbo

On the same bay as La Serena and only 84 km from Ovalle, Coquimbo is a port of considerable importance. It has one of the best harbours on the coast and several major fish-processing plants. The city is strung along the north shore of a peninsula. Most of the commercial life is centred on three streets which run between the port and the steep hillside on which are perched many of the poorer houses. On the south shore of the peninsula lies the suburb of Guayacán, with an iron-ore loading port, a steel church designed by Eiffel, an English cemetery and the huge cross erected to mark the millennium. In 1981 heavy rain uncovered 39 ancient burials of humans and llamas which had been sacrificed. A small museum has been built in the Plaza Gabriela Mistral to exhibit these.

Phone code: 051
Colour map 2, grid C1
Population: 122,000

  Coquimbo was used during the colonial period as a port for La Serena, attracting attention from English pirates including Francis Drake, who visited in 1578. A statue to Drake was erected in the city in 1998. Legends of buried treasure at Bahía la Herradura de Guayacán persist. From these small beginnings Coquimbo grew into a city in the 19th century, when it and the separate centre of Guayacán became important in the processing of copper. By 1854 there were two large copper foundries in Coquimbo and in 1858 the largest foundry in the world was built in Guayacán. Today, the city depends on the port for its vitality and economic solvency; there is a tourist kiosk on the Plaza de Armas. Travellers should beware that Coquimbo has a reputation for theft.

  In summer it is possible to take boat trips around the harbour and to Punta Lobos; regular departures, US$3. The **Cruz del Tercer Milenio** is an 83-m high cross marking the top of the hill behind Coquimbo; it is possible to climb the cross for a charge of US$1.50.

Nearby is **La Herradura**, 2½ km from Coquimbo, which has the best beaches and numerous *cabañas* and restaurants. Also nearby is a resort complex called *Las Tacas*, with beach, swimming pool, tennis, flats. At **Totoralillo**, 12 km south, there are good beaches, ideal for swimming.

Sleeping
■ *on map*
Price codes:
see inside front cover

Accommodation
is cheaper than
La Serena

C *Lig*, Aldunate 1577, T311171, F313717. Comfortable, friendly, with breakfast, over-priced, near bus terminal. **D** *Iberia*, Lastra 400, T312141, F326307, with bath, **E** without. Friendly. Recommended. **D** *Prat*, Bilbao y Aldunate, T/F311845. Comfortable, with breakfast, pleasant. **F** *Hotel Vegamar*, Las Heras 403, T311773, shared bath, basic. Several hotels in La Herradura, including **D** *La Herradura*, Av La Marina 200, T/F261647, with bath, restaurant attached. **Camping** *Camping La Herradura*, T263867, F261312, mac-food@ctcinternet.cl **F** for up to 5 people.

Eating
● *on map*

There are many good
seafood restaurants
at the municipal
market, Melgarejo
entre Bilbao y
Borgoño

According to the tourist office in La Serena, the best seafood is to be had at Coquimbo, not La Serena; it is especially cheap in the market. **Expensive/mid-range** *Sal y Pimienta del Capitán Denny*, Aldunate 769, one of the best, pleasant, old fashioned, mainly fish cooked in best Chilean style. **Mid-range** *Crucero*, Valera. Excellent. *La Picada*, Costanera near statue of O'Higgins. Excellent, good pebre. *Mai Lai Fan*, Av Ossandón 1. Excellent Chinese. Recommended. **Cheap** *La Bahía*, Pinto 1465. Excellent, good value. *La Barca*, Ríos y Varela. Modest but good.

Festivals
Coquimbo lays host to *La Pampilla*, by far the biggest independence day celebrations in Chile. Between 200-300,000 people come from all over the country for the fiesta, which lasts for a week. Things get going on **14 Sep**, and the partying does not stop

Coquimbo

To Guayacán, La Herradura & Santiago

0 metres 200
0 yards 200

■ Sleeping
1 Iberia   3 Prat
2 Lig   4 Punta del Este

● Eating
1 La Bahía
2 Sol y Pimienta del Capitán Denny

until **21 Sep**. It costs a nominal US$1.50 to gain access to the area where the main dancing tents are to be found, as well as much typical Chilean food and drink. One must pay to enter the *peñas*, but there also free communal areas, and big bands such as Illapu and La Ley have played here in recent years, as well as *cumbia* bands from Argentina and Colombia.

Bus Terminal at Varela y Garriga. To **La Serena**, every few mins, US$0.30. To **Guanaqueros**, US$0.80, 45 mins, and to **Tongoy**, US$1, 1 hr, with Ruta Costera, frequency varies according to day (more on Sun) and season. *Colectivos* to Guanaqueros US$1.40; to Tongoy US$1.70.

Transport

Communications Internet: *Aldunate 1196*, US$1.50/hr, open until 2330. Telephone: *CTC*, Aldunate 1633. **Exchange** *Cambios Maya*, Portales 305. Also many Redbancs in the centre.

Directory

Resorts south of Coquimbo

Guanaqueros, 37 km south, is a fishing village on the southern coast of a large bay, east of the village is a 10-km long beach. There is the clean and simple **D** *La Bahía* or **C** (for three people) *Cabañas Bahia Club*, T051-395819, F395818, camping1@entelchile.net, also camping, with kitchens, on the waterfront. Recommended. *Camping Oasis* on the beach, T395319, **D** per site.

Guanaqueros

Fifty kilometres south is an old fishing port occupying the whole of a small peninsula. It is now a rapidly growing resort and well worth a visit: the Playa Grande to the south is 14 km long; the Playa Socos to the north is 4 km in length.

Tongoy

Sleeping A/B *Hosteria Tongoy*, Costanera 10, T051-391203, F391900. **A-B** *Yachting Club*, Costanera 20, T051-391154, T391259. Good. **C** *Panorámico*, Mirador 455, T391944. Includes breakfast, all rooms with view of bay and fishing boats, excellent, clean, friendly. Several basic *residenciales*, including **F** *Res La Bahía*, Urmeneta Sur 95, T051-391244.

Eating Try the *marisquerías* near the fishing port, excellent value. *Restaurant El Buque*, Puesto 17 on seafront, near fishing harbour. Fish and meat with superb sauces, good service. Highly recommended.

La Serena

La Serena is the capital of Región IV and is one of the most attractive cities in northern Chile. Built on a hillside 2 km inland from the Bahía de Coquimbo, the city is famous for its numerous churches, and the centre is made up of white buildings of neo-colonial style; beneath this façade, however, La Serena has a more ancient history, and residents claim often to stumble across indigenous burial sites in their back yards. The city has rapidly become a major tourist centre, being popular for its long sandy beach and its proximity to the Elqui Valley – it is full of Argentines in January and Chileans in February.

Phone code: 051
Colour map 2, grid C1
Population: 120,000
473 km N of Santiago

The main tourist office is that of **Sernatur** in Edificio de Servicios Públicos (next to the post office on the Plaza de Armas), T/F225199, serna04@entelchile.net Open Mon-Fri 0845-1830 (0845-2030 in summer), Sat-Sun 1000-1400 (1000-1400 and 1600-2000 in summer), very helpful. Kiosks at bus terminal (summer only) and at Balmaceda y Prat

Tourist offices
See pages 169 and 177 for transport details

González Videla and the Plan Serena

The present-day layout and architectural style of La Serena have their origins in the 'Plan Serena' drawn up in 1948 on the orders of Gabriel González Videla, a native of the city. Born in 1898 González Videla was a lawyer, diplomat and Radical party politician who was elected President of Chile in 1946 as a result of deal with the Communist and Liberal parties. Once elected, he claimed to have discovered a left-wing plot, outlawed the Communist party and had many of its members imprisoned. The poet Pablo Neruda, a member of the Communist party, was understandably scathing, describing him as "an irresponsible and frivolous clown" and "a contemptible creature" with "an insignificant but twisted mind". It should be added that it was González Videla's government which gave the vote to women.

Eager to leave his mark on his native city, González Videla ordered the drafting of an urban plan. Under this, Avenida Francisco de Aguirre was modernized and the Pedro de Valdivia gardens, west of the city, were built. All new buildings in the centre were to be in Californian colonial style, though his regulation has since been modified permitting the construction of some modern buildings.

(open in theory Mon-Sat 1100-1400, 1600-1900), helpful. **Automóvil Club de Chile**, E de la Barra 435, T225279.

History   La Serena was founded by Juan de Bohón, aide to Pedro de Valdivia, in 1544, destroyed by Diaguita Indians in 1546 and rebuilt by Francisco de Aguirre in 1549. The city was sacked by the English pirate Sharpe in 1680. In the colonial period it was the main staging-post on the route north to Peru; many of the religious orders built churches and convents here providing accommodation for their members. In the 19th century the city grew prosperous from copper-mining; the neoclassical mansions of successful entrepreneurs from this period can still be seen. The characteristic neo-colonial style architecture of the centre dates from the 1950s, when the city was remodelled under the instructions of President Videla (see box).

Sights

Around the attractive Plaza de Armas are most of the official buildings, including the post office, the **cathedral**, built in 1844 and featuring a carillon which plays every hour, and the **Casa González Videla**, the great man's residence from 1927 to 1977, which now houses the Museo Histórico Regional, see below. There are 29 other churches, several of which have unusual towers. **San Francisco**, Balmaceda y de La Barra, built 1586-1627, has a baroque façade and faces a small plaza with arcades. **Santo Domingo**, half a block southwest of the Plaza de Armas, built 1755 with a clock tower dating from 1912, is fronted by a small garden with statues of sea-lions. **San Augustín**, Cantournet y Rengifo, originally a Jesuit church, dates from 1755 but has been heavily modified.

Opposite San Augustín at Cienfuegos y Cantournet is **La Recova**, the market, which includes a large display of handicrafts and, upstairs, several good seafood restaurants. One block west of the Plaza de Armas is the **Parque Pedro de Valdivia**, with the **Parque Japonés** just south of it. ■ *US$1.25. 1000-2000.*

Buccaneers of the Chilean coast

Sir Francis Drake was one of the first Europeans to commit piracy along the west coast of South America but his example was soon widely followed. By the second half of the 17th century free-booting renegades – mostly the English, French and Dutch – were roaming the South Seas preying on Spanish coastal towns and shipping in the hope of getting rich quick.

Basil Ringrose has a special place amongst these desperadoes because he left a fascinating first-hand account of his activities. Towards the end of 1679 he set out, under the command of a Captain Sharp, to take and plunder what Ringrose describes as the "vastly rich town of Arica". On finding the Spanish defence of Arica too strong to overcome, however, they had to continue south to nearby Hilo where they managed to land and occupy the sugar factory. The besieged Spaniards agreed to supply Ringrose and his comrades "four score of beeves" on condition they didn't burn the sugar factory to the ground. After several days of waiting for the "beeves" to arrive the pirates began to smell a rat and decided to burn the factory down regardless and retreated to their ship. It was as well they did because they had no sooner re-embarked than they saw 300 Spanish horseman advancing on their encampment. But Ringrose was still impressed by Hilo, describing it as "a valley very pleasant being all over set with figs, olives, oranges, lemons, and lime trees, and many other fruits agreeable to the palate". What Ringrose most remembered Hilo for, however, was its "good chocolate" of which they "had plundered some small quantity".

After the double disappointment of Arica and Hilo, the pirates continued south to the Bay of Coquimbo where they discovered the city of La Serena, "most excellent and delicate, and far beyond what we could expect in so remote a place". Ringrose was particularly impressed by the town's seven churches which he and his companions hoped to loot, but again news of their activities preceded them and the Spaniards had already removed the churches' treasures. Instead they "found strawberries as big as walnuts and very delicious to the taste".

From Santiago to La Serena

Avenida Francisco de Aguirre, a pleasant boulevard lined with statues and known as the **Alameda**, runs from the centre to the coast, terminating at the **Faro Monumental**, a neo-colonial mock-castle, US$0.50. A string of beaches stretch from here to Peñuelas, 6 km south, linked by the Avenida del Mar. Many apartment blocks, hotels, *cabañas* and restaurants have been built along this part of the bay.

Museo Histórico Casa Gabriel González Videla, in the Casa González **Museums** Videla on the Plaza de Armas, includes several rooms on the man's life. ■ *US$0.80. Tue-Sat 0900-1300, 1600-1900, Sun 1000-1300. Ticket also valid for Museo Arqueológico.*

Museo Arqueológico has an outstanding collection of Diaguita and Molle Indian exhibits, especially of attractively decorated pottery. Some exhibits from Easter Island. Poor labelling of items. ■ *US$0.80. Tue-Sat 0900-1300, 1600-1900, Sun 1000-1300. Cordóvez y Cienfuegos, muarse@entelchile.net*

Museo De Arte Religiosa, in the San Francisco church, which includes the funeral mask of Gabriela Mistral.

Museo Mineralógico Ignacio Domeyko, in the University of La Serena (for geologists). ■ *Free. Mon-Fri 0930-1230. A Muñoz 870.*

Essentials

Sleeping
■ *on map*
*Price codes:
see inside front cover
The tourist office in
the bus terminal is
helpful and has
accommodation
information*

Accommodation in town centre is expensive and prices are much higher in Jan and Feb. Route 5 from La Serena to Coquimbo is lined with cheaper accommodation, from hotels to *cabañas*, and restaurants. There are also hotels and other types of accommodation along Av del Mar. There are no buses along this road, but it's only 500 m off Route 5.

AL *Costa Real*, Av de Aguirre 170, T221010, F221122, www.regiondecoquimbo.cl /costareal, 5-star, restaurant, bar, pool, conference centre. **AL** *Los Balcones de Aragón*, Cienfuegos 289, T212419, F211800, parking, breakfast, modern. **AL** *Pucará*, Balmaceda 319, T211966, F211933, with bath and breakfast, modern, clean, helpful, quiet. **A** *Francisco de Aguirre*, Córdovez 210, T222991, F228506, www.chile-hotels. com/faguirre 4-star, with breakfast, shower, good rooms, reasonable restaurant. **A** *Mediterráneo*, Cienfuegos 509, Casilla 212, T/F225837. Includes good breakfast. Recommended. **A/B** *Berlín*, Córdovez 535, T222927, F223575. Clean, safe, efficient, good value. Recommended. **A/B** *Casablanca*, Vicuña 414, T/F213070, 3-star.

B *El Escorial I*, Colón 617, T224793, F221433. Good, reasonably priced, with breakfast and mod cons. **B** *Londres*, Córdovez 550, T214673. With bath, **C** without, restaurant, old fashioned. **C** *Alameda*, Av de Aguirre 452, T213052. Run down, clean and comfortable. **C** *Brasilia*, Brasil 555, T225248, F221922. Friendly, small rooms, overpriced. **C** *El Pacífico*, E de la Barra 252, T225674. Quiet. **C** *Hostal Santo Domingo*, Andres Bello 1067, T212718. With breakfast. Highly recommended. **C** *Lido*, Matta 547, T213073. Hot water, clean, friendly. **D** *Edith González*, Los Carrera 889, T221941/224978, with bath, **E** without. Cooking and laundry facilities. Recommended. **D** *El Cobre*, Colón y Matta, T221457. Large rooms, clean. **D** *Hostal Croata*, Cienfuegos 248, T/F224997. With bath, **E** without, with breakfast, laundry facilities, cable TV, patio, hospitable, excellent value. Recommended. **D** *Res Chile*, Matta 561, T211694. Basic, without bath, small rooms, clean, hot water morning only, overpriced. **D** *Res La Japonesita*, Muñoz 218, T213039. With breakfast. **D** *Res Suiza*, Cienfuegos 250, T216092. With bath and breakfast, good beds, excellent value. Highly recommended. **D** *Rosa Canto*, Cantournet 976, T213954. Kitchen, comfortable, family run, good value. Recommended. **D** *San Juan*, Balmaceda 827. Clean, central.

F *Amuñategui 315*, with bath, kitchen facilities, patio, good beds. Recommended. **F** *Backpacker Lodging*, El Santo 1058, T227580. Kitchen facilities, central, camping. **F** *Casa Alejandro Muñoz*, Brasil 720, T211619. Accommodation in family home in old part of town, hot showers, good breakfast, beautiful garden, English and French spoken, friendly atmosphere. Recommended. **F** *Casa de Huéspedes*, including breakfast. El Santo 1410, T213557. Convenient for bus terminal, hot water, cable TV, clean, friendly. Recommended. **F** *Casa Valentina*, Brasil 271, T2213142, fampintz@hotmail.com Good information on the area, hot showers, kitchen facilities, patio, laundry service, English and German spoken. Recommended. **F** *Casona de Cantournet*, Vicuña 414, T217162, F213070. With bath, huge rooms in old mansion, comfortable. **F** *Celia Rivera*, Las Rojas 21, T215838. Near terminal, use of kitchen, clean, friendly. **F** *Gabriela Matus*, Juan de Dios Peni 636, T211407. **F** *Gregoria Fernández*, Andrés Bello 979A, T224400. Highly recommended. Clean, friendly and very helpful, good beds, 3 blocks from terminal, excellent breakfast, fills up quickly so book ahead, good local information; if full she will divert you to her mother's house, also good but less convenient for the bus station. Next door is **F** *Raquel Pereira*, Andrés Bello 979B, T222419. Dormitory accommodation, with breakfast. **F** *Hostal Joffre*, Rgto Coquimbo 964 (entre Pení y Amuñátegui), T222335, hostaljofre@hotmail.com Available for use by visitors. With bath and breakfast, good beds, garden, near bus terminal, recommended, tours of Elqui arranged, Hector is best guide. **F** *Las Rojas 26*, Kitchen facilities, basic, family run, camping. **F** *Res El Loa*, O'Higgins 362, T210304. Without bath, with breakfast, good inexpensive home cooking, friendly, good value. **F** *Res Lorena*, Cantournet 850, T223330. Quiet, pleasant. **F** *Res Lorena/Carvajal*, Av Santo 1056,T/F224059. Family home, kitchen facilities, central camping. **F** *Res Petit*, de la Barra 586, T212536. Hot water. **G** *Maria Pizarro*, Las Rojas 18, T229282. Very welcoming, laundry facilities, camping, very helpful. Recommended repeatedly.

Youth hostel **F** *Res Limmat*, Lautaro 914, T/F211373. With breakfast, central, patio, tours offered, English and German spoken, Hostelling International reduction. Recommended.

Motels and cabañas **A** *Cabañas Los Papayos*, Gonzalez Videla, Huertos 66/67, 2 km south of city (*Vista Hermosa* bus), T294153, F293233, **C** out of season, 2 bedroom cabins, pool, gardens. Recommended. **B** *Motel/Cabañas El Palmar*, Av del Mar 5700, T247983, F231576. **A/B** *Cabañas de Turismo*, Av del Mar 1000, T212453. **A/B** *Canto del Agua*, Av del Mar 2200, T216630, F241767. Very good, pleasant *cabañas*, also apartments.

From Santiago to La Serena

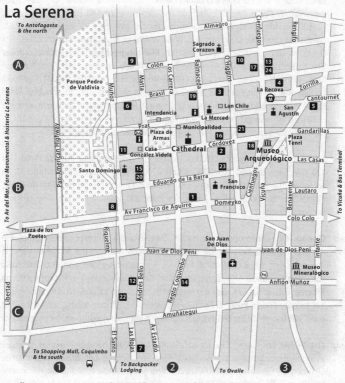

La Serena

Not to scale

■ **Sleeping**
1 Alameda *B2*
2 Berlín *B2*
3 Brasilia *A2*
4 Casa Alejandro Muñoz *A3*
5 Casablanca *A3*
6 Casa Valentina *A2*
7 Celia Rivera & María Pizarro *C2*
8 Costa Real *B1*
9 El Cobre *A2*
10 El Escorial I *A3*
11 Francisco de Aguirre *B2*
12 Gregoria Fernández & Raquel Pereira *C2*
13 Hostal Croata *A3*
14 Hostal Joffre *C2*
15 Lido *B2*
16 Londres *B2*
17 Los Balcones de Aragón *A3*
18 Mediterráneo *B3*
19 Pucará *A2*
20 Residencial Chile *B2*
21 Residencial El Loa *B3*
22 Residencial Lorena/Carvajal *C2*
23 Residencial Petit *B2*
24 Residencial Suiza *A3*

A/B *Hostal Del Mar*, Cuatro Esquinas 0680 (near beach), T22559. Also apartments, clean, friendly. **A/B** *La Fuente*, Av del Mar 5665, T245755, F541259. Apartments, cable TV, parking, very good. Several more motels along Av del Mar. **A/B** *Les Mouettes*, Av del Mar 2500, T225665, F226278. Good restaurant, includes breakfast. Recommended.

Camping Three sites south of La Serena: *Antares*, Los Pescadores 4655, T/F243753, **D** for up to 6 people, at Peñuelas; *Sole di Mare*, Peñuelas Vega Sur, T312531, on seafront, fully equipped, **F** *Hipocampo*, Av del Mar, 4 km south, T/F241316, **F**, reached by Coquimbo bus (get off at Colegio Adventista). English spoken. Also *Maki Payi*, 153 Vegas Norte, T213628, 5 km north of La Serena, near sea, friendly, also *cabañas*. Recommended.

Eating
Eating tends to be expensive in La Serena – Coquimbo is cheaper

For good fish lunches (mid-range/ cheap) try the restaurants on the upper floor of the Recova market where you will be immediately assailed by numerous waiters. The quality of restaurants, especially on Av del Mar, varies considerably; often many dishes on the menu are not available. **Mid-range** *Bavaria*, E de la Barra 489. International menu, excellent service, nice place. *Ciro's*, Av de Aguirre 431, T213482. Old fashioned, good lunch. Recommended. *Donde El Guatón*, Brasil 750. Parrillada, paradise for meat eaters, expensive. *El Cedro*, Prat 572. Arab cuisine, expensive. *La Mía Pizza*, O'Higgins 360, T215063. Italian, good value, (branch on Av del Mar 2100 in summer, T212232). *Pastissima Limitado*, O'Higgins 663. Wide variety of pizzas, delicious pancakes, not cheap, live music and dancing at weekends. **Mid-range/cheap** *Club Social*, Córdovez 516, 1 piso. Unpretentious but excellent value. *D'Carlo*, Córdovez 516. Good fish, seafood, reasonably priced, good value. *Diavoletto*, Prat 565 and O'Higgins 531. Fast food, popular. *Mai Lai Fan*, Cordóvez 740. Good Chinese, reasonably priced, *almuerzo*. *Plaza Royal*, Prat 465. Light meals and snacks, pleasant. Recommended. *Qahlûa*, Balmaceda 655. Good fish, seafood, popular, cheap. *Taiwan*, Cantournet 844. Cantonese, good quality, reasonably priced. For ice cream, make for *Bravissimo*, Balmaceda 545.

Cafés & bars *Bocaccio*, Prat y Balmaceda. Good cakes, modern, smart, popular. *Café del Patio*, Prat 470, café, bar with pub (Tijuana Blues) from 2100 with live music to the early hours. On Sat, offers The Beatles Club from 2300. Also tour agency (see below). *Café do Brasil*, Balmaceda 461. Good coffee. *Tahiti*, Córdovez 540, local 113. Real coffee, pastries. Recommended.

Entertainment **Cinema** *Cine Centenario*, Córdovez 399. There is also a multiplex cinema complex in the Mall Plaza (see below under shopping). **Discos** Most on the Av del Mar and in Peñuelas, such as: *B-Cool*, Av 4 Esquinas s/n, recommended and *Pub-Discosalsa Kamanga*, Costanera 4785, university crowd, fun, recommended. In town, try *Afroson Taberna*, Balamceda 824, salsa and frequent live music, good food, good meeting place, fun, recommended. **Pubs** *El Faro*, Av del Mar y Av Francisco Aguirre, a bit pricey but good. *VIP*, Edo de la Barra 645, popular night spot, intimate atmosphere. Recommended.

Shopping *Cema-Chile*, Los Carrera 562, for handicrafts. *La Recova* handicraft market, not bad, though many items imported from Peru and Bolivia. *Las Brisas* supermarket, Cienfuegos y Córdovez, open 0900-2200, very good. *Rendic* supermarket, Balmaceda 561. Open 0900-2300, good. There is also a big new shopping mall, the *Mall Plaza*, on the Panamericana next to the bus station.

Sports *Gimnasio GFU*, Amunátegui 426, T222420. *Vitalia*, Córdovez 756, T221939. There is a horse racing track at Peñuelas, and also a new golf club north of the city.

Tour companies *Gira Tour*, Prat 689, T223535, giratour@ctcinternet.cl *Ingservitur*, Matta 611, T/F220165, ingsvtur@ctcreuna.cl Guided tours to Valle del Encanto, Fray Jorge,

Andacollo, Isla Chañaral, Valle del Elgui and to observatories. *Intijalsu Tours*, Matta 621, T/F217945, www.intijalsu.cv.cl Specially trained guides and telescopes in a mobile observator.y *Valle Mar*, Los Carrera 594, T213784. *Talinay Adventure Expeditions* and *Inca Travel*, both at *Café del Patio* (address above), offer a range of local tours including Valle del Elqui, also trekking and climbing. Approximate tour prices: Valle del Elgui US$30, Parque Nacional Fray Jorge US$35, Tongoy US$28, city tour US$11.

Local Buses: City buses US$0.25. **Car hire**: *Avis*, Av de Aguirre 063, T227171; *Budget*, Balmaceda 3820, T297916; *Daire*, Balmaceda 3812, T293140, recommended, good service; *Hertz*, Av de Aguirre 0225, T212166/226171, prices range from US$65 to US$110 per day; *La Florida*, at airport, T271947. Cheapest is *Gala*, Balmaceda 1785, T221400. **Cycle repairs**: *Mike's Bikes*, Av de Aguirre 004, T224454. Sales, hire, repairs, English spoken, helpful. **Motorcycle spares**: *Tonino Motos*, Balmaceda 1461, T223628. **Taxis**: *Colectivos* operate on fixed routes throughout city. City taxis US$0.75 and US$0.20 every 200 m. • **Transport**

Long distance Air: Aeropuerto La Florida, 5 km east of the city, T271812. *Ladeco* flies to **San Juan**, Argentina; summer only. To **Santiago** and **Copiapó**, *Lan Chile*. Air transfer company to the airport, T295058.

Bus: Terminal, El Santo y Amunátegui (about 8 blocks south of the centre). Buses daily to **Santiago**, several companies, 7-8 hrs, US$9-12 (*Pullman Bus*, *semi cama*, US$20); to **Arica**, US$25, 20 hrs; to **Calama**, US$17, 16 hrs; to **Vallenar**, 3 hrs, US$4. To **Valparaíso**, 7 hrs, US$10; to **Caldera**, 6 hrs, US$9; to **Antofagasta**, 12 hrs, several companies, US$13, and to **Iquique**, 17 hrs, US$20; to **Vicuña**, *Via Elqui/Megal Bus*, every ½ hr, 1 hr, US$1.75; also collective taxis from Domeyko y Balmaceda, US$2.50; the buses continue to **Pisco Elqui**, US$2.50, last one at 2000; to **Coquimbo**, bus No 8 from Av Aguirre y Cienfuegos, US$0.30, every few mins; also *colectivos* from Av de Aguirre y Balmaceda.

Airline offices *Ladeco and LanChile*, Melgarejo 1086, T315099, also an office in the Mall Plaza. • **Directory**

If heading north note that La Serena is the last place to change TCs before Antofagasta

Banks *Corp Banca*, O'Higgins 529, Visa. ATMs at *Banco Santander*, Córdovez 351; *Banco Sud Americano*, Córdovez 699; *Banco Santiago*, Balmaceda 1015; *Banco de Chile*, Prat 481; *Banco BHIF*, Prat 528; *Banco BCI*, Prat 614; also at the *Las Brisas* supermarket. **Casas de Cambio**: *Intercam*, E de la Barra 435B, Prat 515. Changes TCs, 3 in the Caracol Colonial, Balmaceda 460, including *Cambio Fides*. Good rates, changes TCs (*Gira Tour*, Prat 689, basement, building closed 1400-1600), and *Cambios La Serena*.

Communications Internet: *Cyber-Bazaar 2000*, Fco de Aguirre 343-A. *Cybercafe*, Cordovez 285 y Matta, T212187. *Ingservitur*, Matta 611, T/F220165, US$1.50/hr. *Shalom*, Fco de Aguirre 343, US$3.20 per hr. Also at *The Electric Net*, Domeyko 560, T212224. **Telephones**: Long distance calls from Cordóvez 446 and La Recova market. *Entel*, Prat 571. CTC administration on Plaza de Armas sells *Turistel*. **Cultural centres** *Centro Latino-Americano de Arte y Cultura*, Balmaceda 824, T229344. Offers music and dance workshops, art gallery, handicraft workshops, also *Taverna Afro Son* (see under Discotheques). *Instituto Chileno-Francés de Cultura*, Cienfuegas 632, T224993. Library, French courses, films etc. *Nueva Acropolis*, Benavente 692, T21214. Lectures, discussions, free entry.

Laundry *La Universal*, Balmaceda 851, also Av de Aguirre 411 and Colón 560. *Laverap*, Av de Aguirre 447. *Nevada*, Los Carrera y Av de Aguirre. *Ro-Ma*, Los Carrera 654.

Observatories

It is critical to reserve all tours in advance, up to three to four months ahead in holiday periods

The clear skies and dry atmosphere of the valleys around La Serena have led to the area becoming one of the astronomical centres of the world (see box, page 179). There are four observatories. Travel agents in La Serena and Coquimbo including *Ingservitur, Gira Tour* and *Turismo Cristóbal*, receive tickets from the observatories and arrange tours to two of them, El Tololo and La Silla (to El Tololo US$22 per person). If you can arrange tickets directly with the observatory, taxi drivers will provide transport; one recommended as cheap and good is Cecilia Cruz, T222529, T09-5510579 (mob), US$63 to La Silla. Some visitors to the observatories complain that they do not get as much of an insight as they had expected. Bear in mind that trained astronomers have to reserve years in advance to use the equipment, and that a day tour will not be the beginning of your astronomical career – it will, though, give you a window onto the workings of some of the most important telescopes on earth.

El Tololo Situated at 2,200 m, 87 km southeast of La Serena in the Elqui valley, 51 km south of Vicuña, this belongs to Aura, an association of US and Chilean universities. It possesses what was until recently the largest telescope in the southern hemisphere (diameter 4 m), six others and a radio telescope. ■ *Open to visitors by permit only every Sat 0900-1200, 1300-1600; for permits (free) write to Casilla 603, La Serena, T051-205200, F205212, then pick your permit up before 1200 on the day before (the office is at Colina Los Pinos, on a hill behind the new university – personal applications can be made here for all three observatories). During holiday periods apply well in advance; at other times it is worth trying for a cancellation the day before. They will insist that you have private transport; you can hire a taxi, US$33, but you will require the registration number when you book. Motorcycles are, apparently, not permitted to use the access road.*

La Silla Located at 2,400 m, 156 km northeast of La Serena, this belongs to ESO (European Southern Observatory), financed by eight EU countries, and comprises 14 telescopes. ■ *Sat except in Jul and Aug, 1430-1730. Registration in advance in Santiago essential (Alonso de Córdoba 3107, Santiago, T02-2285006) or write to Casilla 567, La Serena, T224527. Getting there: from La Serena it is 120 km north along Route 5 to the turn-off (D Posada La Frontera, cabañas), then another 36 km.*

Las Campanas This observatory is at 2,510 m, 162 km northeast of La Serena, 30 km north of La Silla. Belonging to the Carnegie Institute, it has five telescopes and is altogether a smaller facility than the other two. ■ *Sat 1430-1730. For permit, write to Casilla 601, La Serena, T224680. Getting there: follow Route 5 to the same junction as for La Silla, take the turning for La Silla and then turn north after 14 km. La Silla and Las Campanas can be reached without private transport by taking any bus towards Vallenar (2 hrs, US$4) getting out at the junction (desvío) and hitching from there.*

Mamalluca Situated at 1,500 m, 6 km north of Vicuña, this new observatory was built specifically for the public. The first telescope, diameter 30 cm, was donated by El Tololo. There is a multimedia centre and cafeteria. Visits daily at 2000, 2200 and 2400, US$6 plus transport US$4 per person. Booking from the office at Gabriela Mistral 260, T411352, obser_mamalluca @yahoo.com Advance booking strongly recommended.

The clear skies of northern Chile

Astronomy favours clear skies and remoteness from sources of dust or artificial light and northern Chile, with its large expanses of uninhabited desert and its dry atmosphere, has become one of the great astronomical centres of the world. In the Elqui Valley alone there are no fewer than four observatories, one of them purposely built for visitors to the region. The other three were built by international organizations with important backing from Europe or the US. One, La Silla, is owned by European Southern Observatory (ESO), which is financed by the governments of Belgium, Denmark, France, Germany, Italy, The Netherlands and Sweden. There is also a small Swiss telescope on the site. The other two are El Tololo, which belongs to a consortium of US and Chilean universities, and Las Campanas, which is owned by the Carnegie Institute. All of these welcome visitors but visitors are not allowed to use the telescopes; for visitor arrangements see text. The fourth observatory, however, Mamalluca, financed partly by the Municipalidad of Vicuña and built specifically for the public, offers night-time visits and provides an opportunity to view the southern skies from the vantage point of the Elqui Valley.

Away from the Elqui the great powers of the world of astronomy continue to expand their operations in northern Chile. A new observatory was opened by ESO in March 1999 at Cerro Paranal, 120 km south of Antofagasta: known as the VLT ('very large telescope'), it includes what is claimed to be the most powerful telescope in the world, with a power equivalent to a normal telescope with a diameter of 200 m. The VLT is capable of picking out items on the moon as small as 1 m long; when the lenses arrived at the port of Antofagasta, the entire centre of the city had to be closed down to allow them to be transported to their final destination. Planning is now under way on an even larger project at Chajnantor, over 5,000 m up in the Andes; this giant observatory, with over 100 radio telescopes, is being financed by ESO along with the governments of the UK, the US and Japan.

These new developments are not without controversy. Construction of Cerro Paranal was held up by local landowners, who refused to renounce rights to permit mining activity on their land (which would threaten the observatory with increased dust). Eventually this forced the Chilean government to introduce new legislation to permit it to buy out the landowners.

Upper Elqui Valley

The valley of the Río Elqui is one of the most attractive oases in this part of northern Chile. There are mines, orchards, orange groves and vineyards. The road up the valley is paved as far as Varillar, 24 km beyond Vicuña, the capital of the valley. Except for Vicuña, most of the tiny towns have but a single street.

The valley is the centre of pisco production: of the nine distilleries in the valley, the largest is Capel in Vicuña. Huancara, a delicious liqueur introduced by the Jesuits, is also produced in the valley. The Río Elqui has been dammed east of **El Molle**, 30 km east of La Serena. This has forced the relocation of five small towns in the valley, and has also led to an increase of winds in the valley according to locals.

Vicuña

This small, clean, friendly, picturesque town was founded in 1821 and is 66 km east of La Serena. On the west side of the plaza is the Municipalidad, built in 1826 and topped in 1905 by a medieval-German-style tower – the Torre

Phone code: 051
Colour map 2, grid C2
Population: 7,716

The Elqui Valley in the words of its poet

"It is a heroic slash in the mass of mountains, but so short as to be little more than a green-banked torrent, yet small as it is one comes to love it as perfect. It contains in perfection all that man could ask of a land in which to live: light, water, wine and fruit. And what fruit! The tongue which has tasted the juice of its peaches and the mouth which has eaten of its purple figs will never seek sweetness elsewhere.

The people of the Elqui take remarkable

pride in their green soil. Whenever there is a hump, a ridge or bare patch without greenery, it is because it is naked rock. Wherever the Elquino has a little water and three inches of soil, however poor, he will cultivate something: peaches, vines or figs. That the leafy, polished vines climb only a little way up the mountainsides is because if they were planted higher, they would wither in the pitiless February sun."

Gabriela Mistral, quoted in Jan Reed, The Wines of Chile, Mitchell Beazley, 1994.

Bauer – prefabricated in Germany and imported by the German-born mayor of the time. Inside the Municipalidad is a gallery of past local dignitaries. Also on the plaza are the Iglesia Parroquial, dating from 1860 and the tourist office. There are good views from Cerro La Virgen, north of town.

The distillery does not operate on Sunday

The **Capel Pisco** distillery is 1½ km east, to the right of the main road; guided tours (in Spanish) are offered in December-February. ■ *Free. Dec-Feb, every day, 1000-1800. No booking required.* The new observatory of Mamalluca is 6 km north of Vicuña. For details see above.

Museo Gabriela Mistral contains manuscripts, books, awards and many other details of the poet's life. Next door is the house where the poet was born. ■ *US$1, students half price. Mon-Sat 1000-1900, Sun 1000-1800. Gabriela Mistral 759.* **Museo Entomológico** has over 3,000 insect species displayed. ■ *US$0.50, Mon-Sun 1000-2100 in summer; in winter, Mon-Fri 1030-1330 and 1530-1930, Sat-Sun 1030-1900. Calle Chacabuco.* **Solar de los Madariaga** is a former residence containing artefacts belonging to a prominent local family. ■ *US$0.80, visits Jan-Mar only, Mon-Fri 1000-1900. Gabriela Mistral.*

Vicuña

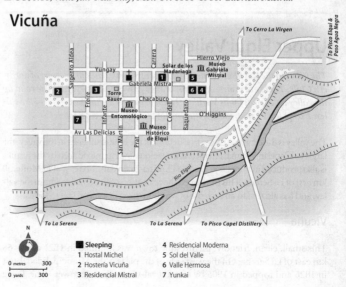

■ **Sleeping**
1 Hostal Michel
2 Hostería Vicuña
3 Residencial Mistral
4 Residencial Moderna
5 Sol del Valle
6 Valle Hermosa
7 Yunkai

Pisco

The national strong spirit of Chile is pisco, a liquor made from grapes and known until the late 19th century as aguardiente de vino. Under a law of 1985 defining its demarcation, the term pisco is reserved for a spirit produced and bottled in regions III and IV and made entirely by the distillation of wine grown in these regions. Although the Elqui Valley is the heartland of the pisco industry – the climate and soil being ideally suited to the cultivation of grapes with a high sugar-content – vines for pisco *are grown in the valleys of rivers throughout these two regions, from the Río Copiapó in the north to the Río Choapa in the south.*

After crushing and pressing, the juice is fermented and then distilled, before being aged four to 12 months in large oak barrels, stronger spirits spending more time in the wood: it is then diluted with water to the appropriate strength. There are four grades of strength: selección (30°); especial (35°); reservado (40°) and gran pisco (46°).

A *Hostería Vicuña*, Sgto Aldea 101, T411301, F411144. Swimming pool, tennis court, excellent restaurant, parking. **B/C** *Cabañas Yunkai*, O'Higgins 72, T411195, F411593. *Cabañas* for 4/6 persons, pool, restaurant. **C** *La Elquina*, O' Higgins 65, T411317. Lovely garden, laundry and kitchen facilities. **D** *Valle Hermoso*, Gabriela Mistral 706, T/F411206. Clean, comfortable, parking. Recommended. **F** *Sol del Valle*, Gabriela Mistral 743. With breakfast, hot water, TV, vineyard, restaurant, swimming pool. **F/G** *Residencial Restaurant Mistral*, Gabriela Mistral 180, T411278. Gardens very run down, basic, hot water, clean. In Valle Murillas **Camping** *Gabriela Mistral 152*, T09-4286158. **G**, hot showers, kitchen. *Camping y Piscina Las Tinajas*, east end of Chacabuco, swimming pool, restaurant.

Sleeping
■ *on map*
Price codes:
see inside front cover

Mainly on Gabriela Mistral *Club Social de Elqui*, at No 435. Very good, attractive patio, good value *almuerzo*, real coffee. *Halley*, at No 404. Good meat dishes, mid-range, swimming pool (US$5 entry). *Mistral*, at No 180. Very good, popular with locals, good value *almuerzo*. *Yo Y Soledad*, No 364. Inexpensive, good. *Pizzería Virgos*, on plaza, mid-range.

Eating

Bus To **La Serena**, about 10 a day, most by *Via Elqui/Megal Bus*, first 0800, last 1930, 1 hr, US$1.75, *colectivo* from Plaza de Armas US$2.50; to **Santiago** via La Serena, *Via Elqui*; to Pisco Elqui, 4 a day, *Vía Elqui* and *Frontera Elqui*, 1 hr, US$2.

Transport

From Santiago to La Serena

The valley

From Vicuña a *ripio* road runs south via Hurtado (Km 46), Pichasca (Km 85), and the Monumento Natural Pichasca to Ovalle (Km 120). The main road through the Elqui Valley continues east another 18 km to **Rivadavia** where the ríos Turbio and Claro meet. Here the road divides, the main route (Route 41) winding through the mountains to the Argentine frontier at Agua Negra (see below). At Juntas there is a turning to Baños del Toro and the Mina el Indio, which can be visited only with a permit (obtainable from Compañía Minería del Indio, Baño Industrial Piñuelas, La Serena).

The other branch of the road runs through Paihuano (camping) to **Monte Grande**, where the schoolhouse in which Gabriela Mistral lived and was educated by her sister is now a museum. The poet's tomb is situated 1 km out of town. To get there, take a bus from the plaza in Vicuña. Here the road forks, one branch leading to El Colorado. Along this road are several Ashram places, some of which welcome visitors; camping allowed.

Pisco Elqui, with a population of 500, is situated 2 km south of Monte Grande along the other branch of the road. It is an attractive town situated around a shady plaza with two pisco plants outside town. The one opposite the plaza offers free tours and tastings; the vineyards themselves are now covered by nets to protect them from the winds caused by the new dam.

Sleeping In Pisco Elqui **C** *Carillón*, A Prat s/n. Pool, also *cabanas*. **C** *El Tesoro del Elqui*, T/F451958. *Cabañas*, pleasant gardens, German spoken. **C** *El Elqui*, O'Higgins s/n. Hot shower, good restaurant. Recommended. Not always open. **F** *Hostería de Don Juan*. With breakfast, fine views, noisy. **Camping** *Sol de Barbosa*, T451102, **G** per site. Showers, open all year. **H** *El Olivo*, T451970. Small restaurant, pool, excellent facilities. Well-stocked supermarket 1 block from the plaza. In Valle Murillas, 3km west of Hurtado, **C** *Hacienda Los Andes*, t053-1982106, www.haciendalosandes. com Run by Manuela and Clark, bed and breakfast, horseriding colonial-style, English spoken, outdoor activities.

Transport Buses to La Serena, US$2.50, 6 a day, via Vicuña.

Directory **Useful information** *CODEFF*, the environmental organization, has an office on the outskirts of town.

Border with Argentina **Paso Agua Negra** (4,775m) is reached by good unpaved road from Rivadavia, 18 km east of Vicuña. Chilean immigration and customs are at Juntas, 84 km west of the frontier, 88 km east of Vicuña. They are open 0800-1700. There is basic accommodation at Huanta (Guanta on many maps) Km 46 from Vicuña, **H**, clean, ask for Guillermo Aliaga. Huanta is the last chance to buy food. No public transport beyond Rivadavia. El Indio mine transport may give lifts to Juntas, although the mine may be forced to close in the coming few years because of pollution concerns.

North of La Serena

6

From La Serena, the shrubs and cacti of the semi-desert stretch north as far as the mining and agroindustrial centre of Copiapó. Beyond this city, the Atacama Desert begins. The main population centres are in the valleys of the ríos Huasco, Copiapó and Salado, which are oases of olive groves and vineyards, but the most important economic activity is mining, especially around Vallenar and inland at El Salvador.

Though much of this region appears lifeless and of limited interest to visitors, the area around Vallenar is famous for the flowering of the desert following the rare occasions on which there is heavy rainfall; the upper reaches of the Huasco valley are beautiful and tranquil, and make a good resting point en route to/from the Atacama, while the port of Huasco itself has excellent seafood. There are also three national parks: one, the Parque Nacional Pan de Azúcar, protects areas which are home to a wide range of marine life; the second, the Parque Nacional Llanos de Challe, safeguards the habitat of one of the very rare flowers which buds with rainfall; and the third, the Parque Nacional Tres Cruces, covers extensive areas of salt flats northeast of Copiapó. East of the Parque Nacional Tres Cruces is the Paso San Francisco, a border crossing into Argentina; near the pass are some of the highest peaks in the Andes, though most are best tackled from Argentina.

Background

History Although small groups of Spanish settlers took over the fertile lands in the Huasco and Copiapó valleys in the 16th century, no towns were founded in this area until late in the colonial period. Even the valleys were sparsely populated until the 19th century when the development of mining led to the creation of the ports of Caldera, Chañaral and Huasco, and encouraged the building of railways between the mines and the ports.

Geography This part of the country can be divided into two: between the Río Elqui and the Río Copiapó the transitional semidesert zone continues; north of the Copiapó the Atacama desert begins. East of Copiapó the Andes divide: between the eastern range (Cordillera de Claudio Gay) and the western range (Cordillera de Domeyko) is a basin which collects the waters from the Andes but allows no escape. Here there are salt flats, the most extensive being the Salar de Pedernales. The eastern range rises to some of the highest peaks in Chile: Ojos del Salado (6,879 m/6,864 m – see page 196), Incahuasi (6,610 m), Tres Cruces (6,330 m) and San Francisco (6,020 m). The valleys of the three main rivers, the ríos Huasco, Copiapó and Salado, form oases in this barren landscape.

Climate On the coast, temperatures are moderated by the sea; mist is common in the mornings. Inland temperatures are higher by day and cooler by night. Rainfall is sparse and occurs in winter only. Amounts decrease as you go north: average annual rainfall in Vallenar is 64 mm, while in Copiapó it is 28 mm. Drivers should beware of high winds and blowing sand north of Copiapó. Note that in Vallenar and the upper valleys of the Copiapó and Huasco it gets cold at night, especially in winter.

Economy Mining is a major economic activity: one of the largest state-owned **copper mines** is at El Salvador, and over 50% of all Chilean iron ore is mined around Vallenar. Other minerals include gold and silver. Agriculture is mainly limited to the river valleys; the Copiapó valley is an important producer of grapes, while the lower Huasco valley is Chile's biggest olive-growing area. Fishing, centred on Caldera, and on a smaller scale, Chañaral and Huasco, is also important.

To Vallenar

It is 218 km north from La Serena to Vallenar, through a sparsely populated district usually bypassed by travellers. Thirty-five kilometres north of La Serena is **Caleta Hornos**, an impoverished fishing village with several restaurants where excellent seafood is served in three cheap restaurants (*locos* are sometimes available). The Panamericana then climbs to an arid plateau; 21 km beyond Caleta Hornos is a turning eastwards to **La Higuera**, a small town which once thrived from the iron ore mine at El Tofo on the opposite side of the valley.

El Tofo was once one of the largest iron ore mines in the world, and the mine stacks can clearly be seen from the Panamericana, as can the eerie eucalyptus trees on top of the hill, kept alive by the coastal fog. Only the guardian of the mine lives here now, but it is worth driving up to El Tofo to see the ghost town and for the spectacular views down to the coast.

Sixteen kilometres north of the turn-off for El Tofo, a road heads westwards from the Panamericana, sign-posted for **Punta de Choros**. This *ripio* road leads through a rugged dry river valley for 20 km before reaching the

Things to do ★

- Take a boat trip among dolphins, penguins and the sea-lions in the Reserva Nacional Pinguino de Humboldt.
- When it rains go to the desert around Vallenar and witness the blooms with a kaleidoscopic assortment of flowers, whose buds lie dormant in the sand waiting for moisture. An unforgettable sight.
- Explore the high mountain valleys in the Andes, such as the Tránsito Valley.
- Drink pisco at Alto del Carmen and Horcón Quemado; their distilleries in the upper Huasco Valley near Vallenar produce Chile's best liqueur.

small village of Los Choros Bajos, where the main activity is growing olives; the groves of olive trees provide a beautiful green backdrop to the harshness of the desert. There is a restaurant serving basic meals here, but it is better to continue a further 22 km to Punta de Choros, the departure point for visiting the **Reserva Nacional Pinguino de Humboldt**. This reserve consists of three islands: Chañaral, Choros and Damas. It was founded to preserve the coast's marine life, as there are many penguins, sea-lions and dolphins, as well as the wonderful birdlife. The combination of this and the coast's rugged isolation means that visits will not be quickly forgotten.

Essentials At Punta de Choros, you can stay at *Cabañas Los Delfines*, Pilpilen s/n, sitio 33, T09-6396678, **C** for up to 6 people. Isla Damas is the only island at which it is possible to disembark, and here camping is allowed, but before visiting or camping on the island you must seek permission from CONAF in Punta de Choros (T051-272798); there is a toilet on Isla Damas but no drinking water, and entrance to the island costs US$2.50. To visit the reserve, you can hire a boat with the local fishermen (around US$70 for up to 10 people).

There is no public transport to Punta de Choros, but tours are available from La Serena; traffic on the road to/from the Panamericana is relatively frequent, especially at weekends, so hitching is possible. The Panamericana continues north from the turning to Punta de Choros, passing several small mining towns. At Domeyko, 165 km north of La Serena, a *ripio* road leads west to the coast and the small *caleta* at Chañaral. From Domeyko it is 57 km to the Huasco Valley.

The Huasco Valley

This valley is an oasis of olive groves and vineyards. It is rugged and spectacular, somewhat reminiscent of the Cajón del Maipo near Santiago. At Alto del Carmen, 39 km east of Vallenar, the valley divides into the Carmen and Tránsito valleys. There are pisco distilleries at Alto del Carmen and San Félix, both of which have basic residenciales. A sweet wine known as Pajarete is also produced.

Ins & outs **Getting there** The Huasco Valley's main town is Vallenar, which is easily reached by regular buses from both north and south. **Getting around** There are *colectivos* in Vallenar, which may be useful for those with heavy luggage making their way to the bus terminals (catch them on Serrano).

Vallenar

Phone code: 051
Colour map 2, grid B2
Population: 42,725
194 km north of
La Serena

The chief town of the Huasco valley, Vallenar was founded in 1789. Its original name was San Ambrosio de Ballenary, to mark the birthplace in Ireland of Ambrosio O'Higgins. The town is centred on a pleasant Plaza de Armas, in which all the benches are made of the marble extracted from Chile's purest source of marble, which lies in the Tránsito valley. **Museo del Huasco** contains historic photos and artefacts from the valley. Opposite is the northernmost Chilean palm in the country. ■ *US$0.70. Tue-Fri 1500-1800. Sgto Aldea 742.* Tourist information is available from the Municipalidad on the Plaza de Armas, and from a kiosk on the Panamericana.

Excursions
Freirina, 36 km west, is easily reached by *colectivo*. Founded in 1752, Freirina was the most important town in the valley, its prosperity based upon the nearby Capote goldmine and on later discoveries of copper. On the main plaza are the Municipalidad (1870) and the Santa Rosa church (1869). There is no accommodation.

Sleeping
■ *on map*
Price codes:
see inside front cover

A *Hostería de Vallenar*, Ercilla 848, T614379, F614358, hotval@ctc.cl Excellent, pool, parking, worth bargaining, good breakfast, *Hertz* car hire office. **B** *Cecil*, Prat 1030, T614071, F614400. With bath and hot water, swimming pool, modern, clean. Recommended. **B/C** *Hostal Real Quillahue*, Plaza de Armas 70, T/F619992. With breakfast, modern, friendly. Recommended. **C** *Hostal Camino del Rey*, Merced 943, T/F613184. Clean, cheaper rooms without bath, friendly, good value. Recommended. Worth bargaining for longer stays. **D** *Vall*, Aconcagua 455, T613380. With breakfast and bath, friendly, parking, good value. **F** *Residencial Mary 2*, Ramirez 631. With private bath, friendly. **F** *Viña del Mar*, Serrano 611, T611478. Clean, *comedor*, nice rooms. Highly recommended. **G** *Res La Oriental*, Serrano 720, T613889. Pleasant, friendly, cheap meals, decent value. There are several *residenciales*.

Vallenar

Buses to Carmen
& Tránsito Valleys

To Copiapó & Route 5 north

Marañón

Merced

Aconcagua

Vallejos

Ambrosio

Santiago

Brasil

Colchagua

Alonso de Ercilla

Ramírez

Municipalidad

Prat

To Bus Stations (4 blocks)

Serrano

Verdaguer

Faez

Sargento Aldea

Museo
del Huasco
To Huasco & Route 5
south to La Serena

Sleeping		
1 Camino del Rey	6 Vall	3 Corona del Inca
2 Cecil	7 Viña del Mar	4 La Pica
3 Hostería de Vallenar		5 Shanghai
4 Mary 2	**Eating**	
5 Residencial Oriental	1 Bavaria	
	2 Bocato	

0 metres 100
0 yards 100

North of La Serena

The flowering of the desert

The average annual rainfall of this region declines as you travel northward: in Vallenar it is 65 mm, in Copiapó 20 mm. In most years the semi-desert appears to support only bushes and cacti and these become sparser as you continue north. However, in years of heavier than usual winter rainfall, this semi-desert breaks into colour as dormant seeds and bulbs germinate and produce blankets of flowers, while insects which normally hide underground emerge to enjoy the foliage.

The most recent years in which this desierto florido 'flowering of the desert' has occurred include 1983, 1987, 1991 and 1997. On the latter occasion a record 76 mm of rain fell in the space of 15 hours on 12 June; by July and August much of the region was covered with expanses of green; by September and October expanses of different colours could be seen in unexpected places.

Although the first traces of the desierto florido can be seen as far south as La Ligua and Los Molles, it is particularly worth seeing around Vallenar. From La Serena northwards, the Pan-American Highway is fringed with expanses of different colours: there are great stretches of violet Pata de Guanaco (Calandrinia longiscapa), yellow Corona del Fraile (Encelia canescens var oblongifolia) and blue Suspiro del Campo (Nolana paradoxa). Not all of these species can be seen at the same time: as the brief spring unfolds the colours change as new species push through to replace others.

Around Vallenar, however, the colours are more varied as different species compete to celebrate this infrequent coming of spring: the Pan-American Highway north of the city as far as Copiapó and the coastal road north of Huasco are both recommended for a prime view. For guided tours, contact Roberto Alegría, T613865, Vallenar. For information, contact the tourist office in Vallenar.

Eating Aficionados of Chile's seafood may want to take a trip to Huasco (next page) for lunch; the journey takes only 45 mins, and Huasco has some of Chile's best seafood. **Mid-range** *Bavaria*, Serrano 802. Cafetería, Santiago 678. Good class restaurant, attentive service. *Pizza Il Boccato*, Plaza de Armas. Good coffee, good food, popular. **Cheap** *Corona del Inca*, Prat 900-block in local set aside from road. Cheap meals, good cocktails. *Shanghai*, Ramírez 1267. Chinese. **Seriously cheap** *La Pica*, Brasil y Faez. Good, serves meals, cocktails and seafood. Other cheap places along south end of Av Brasil.

Entertainment **Pubs** *Billboard Pub*, Prat 920. Popular with locals. It is also worth checking out the *Centro Cultural Vallenar*, Vallenar y Colchagua, for any events they may be putting on.

Tour operators *Airazu*, Colchagua 792A, T619807.

Transport **Bus** *Tur Bus*, Merced 561. *Pullman Bus* is opposite. Next door is the bus terminal, from which *TasChoapa* and *Flota Barrios* depart. To **Copiapó**, US$4, 2 hrs; to **Chañaral**, US$8, 5 hrs; to **La Serena**, US$4, 2 hrs. Buses to **Junta de Valeriano** (Tránsito Valley) and **San Félix** (Carmen Valley), as well as the intermediate points such as Alto del Carmen, leave from Marañon 1289; buses leave at 0730, 1100, 1430, 1630, 1730.

Directory **Banks** *Banco de Chile*, Prat 1010, with ATM. *BCI*, Prat y Brasil. *Corpbanca*, Prat 1070, with ATM, exchanges dollars. **Communications** Internet: At Prat 862. *ENTEL* on Prat 1000-block. **Laundry** *Lavaseco Rodier*, Verdaguer y Ramirez. **Medical emergencies** *Consulta Médico y Laboratorio Clinico*, Pje Nicolas Naranjo 341, T616012.

North of La Serena

Huasco Situated at the mouth of the river, Huasco lies 56 km west of Vallenar. West of the town is a terminal for loading iron ore from Algarrobal, 52 km north of Vallenar. Destroyed by an earthquake in 1922, Huasco is a modern town with a large beach which is popular in summer. The port is interesting, as the fishermen unload their catches and hundreds of pelicans hover, waiting to snatch the fish that slip off the crates into the sea; but the best reason to come to Huasco is undoubtedly the seafood.

Sleeping and eating **B** *Hostería Huasco*, Craig y Carrera Pinto, T531026. Parking, conference room, with TV and all mod cons. **F** *Residencial San Fernando*, Pedro de Valdivia 176, T531726. Parking, restaurant. **Camping** *Tres Playitas*, 12 km north along the coastal road towards Carrizal Bajo. Also in Huasco near the post office, US$2 per site. *Restaurant Escorial*. Best. Many cheap seafood restaurants near port, highly recommended.

Carrizal Bajo North of Huasco a *ripio* road leads north to the small *caleta* of Carrizal Bajo, where there is a seafood restaurnt. Carrizal Bajo is the best place from which to visit the **Parque Nacional Llanos de Challe**, a national park set up to preserve the habitat of the *garra de león* flower during the rare occasions when the desert is in bloom. For those with their own transport, beautiful tracks follow the coastline north of Carrizal Bajo, passing a series of small *caletas* en route to Caldera, including the beautiful beach at Puerto Viejo, near Copiapó.

Alto del Carmen East of Vallenar a paved road leads 39 km east to Alto del Carmen, the site of the distillery of one of the best piscos in Chile. The road clings to arid hillsides sprinkled with cacti and *maitén* bushes, passing the Santa Juana Reservoir, which was created following the damming of the Huasco in 1995 and has transformed agriculture in the area. The valley is filled with grapevines for pisco, and by groves of pepper and eucalyptus trees.

At Alto del Carmen, the road forks: left for the **Tránsito Valley**, right for the **Carmen Valley**. The Tránsito Valley is wilder and gets further into the heart of the mountains, while the Carmen Valley is greener and more populous: both valleys are unlikely clefts in the rocky Andes, and reward the traveller who is prepared to make the effort to get to know them. The Tránsito Valley, 20 km beyond Alto del Carmen, has marble mines; the village of El Tránsito (where there is a cheap, small restaurant) is a further 10 km on. The Carmen Valley is 25 km from Alto del Carmen to San Félix, the largest town of the valley, and site of the distillery for Horcón Quemado pisco.

Sleeping Alto del Carmen: **G** *Residencial Supermercado*, basic, friendly, meals served. **San Félix**: **G** *Residencial San Félix* and **G** *Pensión Fortuna*. There is no accommodation in the Tránsito Valley, but camping wild is easy.

Transport There are 6 buses daily from Vallenar to Alto del Carmen and on to either the Tránsito or Carmen valleys – for details see under Vallenar, transport.

The Copiapó Valley

From Vallenar it is 148 km north to Copiapó, the largest city of the valley of the Río Copiapó, which is generally regarded as the southern limit of the Atacama desert. This valley is a surprisingly green cleft in the desert, and is an oasis of farms, vineyards and orchards about 150 km long.

Getting there The Copiapó Valley's main centre is Copiapó, which is easily reached by regular buses from both north and south. There are several daily flights serving Copiapó from Santiago and La Serena, continuing on to El Salvador. **Getting around** There are many *colectivos* and public buses in Copaipó, which may be useful for those heading for some of the out-of-town sites such as the Santuario de la Candelaria; the fare for buses is US$0.30.

Ins & outs

Copiapó

The capital of Región III, Atacama, Copiapó is an important mining centre with a big mining school. Founded in 1744, Copiapó became a prosperous town after the discovery in 1832 of the third largest silver deposits in South America at Chañarcillo. The wealth from Chañarcillo formed the basis of the fortunes of several famous Chilean families – most notably, the Cousiños (see box, page 90) – and helped finance the first railway line in South America, linking Copiapó to Caldera (1851). Although quite a poor city in itself, Copiapó's economy thrives on the large numbers of lone miners who descend to the city in order to seek distraction and spend their pay cheques. On cool summer nights people flock to the pleasant, shady Plaza de Armas to flirt and watch the world going by.

Phone code: 052
Colour map 2, grid B2
Population: 100,000

The Sernatur office is at Los Carrera 691, on the north side of Plaza de Armas, T212838, serna03@entelchile.net and it is extremely helpful. There is a CONAF office at Juan Martinez 55, T210282.

Several of Copiapó's churches will appeal to lovers of religious architecture, most of them dating from the silver boom that followed the growth of Chañarcillo. The **cathedral**, on Plaza Prat, dating from 1851, was designed by William Rogers. **San Francisco**, five blocks west of the Plaza, built in 1872 (the nearby convent is from 1662), is a good example of a 19th-century construction using Pino Oregano and Guayaquil cane. **Belén**, at Infante near Yerbas Buenas, a colonial Jesuit church, was remodelled in 1856, and can be visited (*Mon-Fri 1630-1830*). The **Santuario de la Candelaria**, 3 km southeast of the centre, is the site of two churches, the older built in 1800, the other in 1922; inside the latter is the Virgen de la Candelaria, a stone image discovered whole in the Salar de Maricunga by the muleteer Mariano Caro in 1780. The wealth of the 19th-century mining families is reflected in the **Villa Viña de Cristo**, built in Italian renaissance style, 1½ km north of the centre on Calle Freire. At Matta y O'Higgins there is a monument to Juan Godoy, the muleteer, who, in 1832, discovered silver at Chañarcillo. The Norris Brothers steam locomotive and carriages used in the inaugural journey between Copiapó and Caldera in 1851 can be seen at the Universidad de Atacama about 2 km north of the centre on Calle Freire; also at the university is an example of an old *trapiche* (see box, page 164).

Sights

North of La Serena

Museums **Museo Mineralógico**, Colipí y Rodríguez, one block east of Plaza Prat, is the best museum of its type in Chile. The museum possesses a collection of weird, beautiful minerals from Chile, and pieces also from Asia, Europe and North America. There is also a decent set of fossils. There is an unfortunate lack of narrative or explanation, but a visit is highly recommended nevertheless, and it is extraordinary how, although there are minerals from all over the world, the most colourful and/or striking are almost always Chilean. ■ *US$0.80. Mon-Fri 1000-1300, 1530-1900, Sat 1000-1300.*

Museo Regional del Atacama contains collections on local history, especially from the 19th century up to the time of the War of the Pacific; it is also notable for its collection of artefacts from the Huentelauquén people, thought to have flourished 10,000 years ago. ■ *US$1 (free on Sun). Mon 1400-1745, Tue-Fri 0900-1745, Sat 1000-1245, 1500-1745, Sun 1000-1245. Atacama y Rancagua, murea@entelchile.net*

Museo Ferroviario is in the old railway station on Calle Ramirez, west of the centre, but it opens only sporadically. It has photos and artefacts from the railway age.

Excursions **Centro Metalúrgico Incaico** is a largely reconstructed Inca bronze foundry, 90 km up the Copiapó valley by paved road. There is no accommodation in the nearby villages of Villa Hermoso, Las Juntas or Los Loros, which was the site of a clinic for pulmonary diseases at the beginning of the 20th century, attended by the rich from Santiago. ■ *Getting there: by public transport take Casther bus, 0845, to Valle del Cerro, US$1.30, 2 hrs and get off at Valle Hermoso (foundry is 1-km walk from main road). Return buses pass about 1400 and 1600.*

South of Copiapó, about 59 km on the Pan-American Highway, is a signpost for the turning to the ghost town and former silver mine of **Chañarcillo**,

Copiapó

■ Sleeping		● Eating
1 Archi	11 Montecatini I	1 Bavaria
2 Chagall	12 Palace	2 Chifa Hao Hwa
3 Corona del Inca	13 Residencial Benbau	3 Don Elias
4 Diego de Almeida	14 Residencial Casagrande	4 La Pizza di Tito
5 El Sol, Residencial	15 Residencial Chañarcillo	5 Quincho
Rodríguez & Residencial	16 Residencial Cristi	
Nuevo Chañarcillo	17 Residencial Rocío	
6 España	18 Residencial Torres	
7 Hostería Las Pircas	19 Rocca d'Argento	
8 Inti	20 San Francisco de la Selva	
9 La Casona		
10 Miramonti		

0 metres 200
0 yards 200

along a very poor road. When Chañarcillo was at its peak, the town had a population of 7,000; the mine was closed in 1875, but the tips have been reworked and this has destroyed much of the ruins. Now that the silver has gone, only a few goatherds live here.

Sleeping
■ *on map*
Price codes:
see inside front cover

AL *Diego de Almeida*, Plaza Prat, T/F212075, dalmeida@tnet.cl Cable TV, good restaurant, spacious bar, pool. **AL** *Hostería Las Pircas*, Copayapu 095, T213220, F211633, hostería.laspirca@chilnet.cl Bungalows, nice rooms, pool, good breakfast and good restaurant. **AL** *Miramonti*, Freire 731, T/F210440, miramont@entelchile.net All facilities. **A** *Chagall*, O'Higgins 760, T213775, F211527, chagall@ctcinternet.cl Modern, comfortable, central. **A** *La Casona*, O'Higgins 150, T217278, lacasona@entelchile.net Clean, friendly, good modern art in the lounge, nice rooms (but ask to be off the road), worth bargaining. Recommended. Tours organized. **B** *Hotel Copa de Oro*, Infante 530, T211309, F217604. Big rooms with all mod cons. **B** *Hotel Rocca d'Argento*, Maipú 580, T/F211191. Modern but soulless. **B** *Hotel San Francisco de la Selva*, Los Carrera 525, T217013, F213255, hosanco@entelchile.net Nice rooms, central, with breakfast, modern cafetería/bar. **B** *Inti Hotel*, Freire 180, T/F217756. Nice modern rooms, friendly. **B/C** *Corona del Inca*, Las Heras 54, T217019, F213831. With breakfast, big rooms, friendly, quiet, good value, worth bargaining. No restaurant. **B/C** *España*, Yerbas Buenas 571, T/F217198. With breakfast, friendly, small rooms, a little overpriced. **B/C** *Montecatini I*, Infante 766, T211363, F217021, hotelmontecatini@123click.cl Large rooms set around beautiful green courtyard with hibiscus, pool, helpful, best value in the more expensive price bracket. **B/C** *Palace*, Atacama 741, T212852. Comfortable, good breakfast, parking, central, nice patio. **C** *El Sol*, Rodriguez 550, T/F215672. With breakfast, parking, small rooms with cable TV, quiet, overpriced.

F *Hotel Archi*, Vallejos 111, T/F212983. Without bath, ugly setting, convenient for bus terminal. **F** *Res Chacabuco*, O'Higgins 921, T213428. More expensive with bath. Near bus terminal, quiet, clean. **F** *Res Chañarcillo*, O'Higgins 804, T212284. With breakfast, central, parking, decent rooms. **F** *Res Nuevo Chañarcillo*, Rodríguez 540, T212368. Pleasant lounge, small rooms, more expensive with bath. **F** *Res Rocío*, Yerbas Buenas 581, T215360. More expensive with bath, good value, clean, attractive patio. Recommended. **F** *Res Torres*, Atacama 230, T240727. Without bath, hot water, friendly, quiet. Recommended.

G *Res Benbau*, Rodriguez 541, T217634. Basic rooms but the best value of the many *residenciales* on this part of Calle Rodriguez. **G** *Res Casagrande*, Infante 525, T244450. With breakfast, friendly, with TV in big rooms, set in a beautiful old house with bougainvillaea in the courtyard, excellent value. Highly recommended. **G** *Res Cristi*, Maipú 739, T219650. Friendly, simple rooms, good beds, decent choice. **G** *Res Rodríguez*, Rodríguez 528, T212861. Basic, poky rooms, good *comedor*. Several cheap places, **G**, around local bus terminal.

Eating
● *on map*

Mid-range *Bavaria*, Plaza Prat. Pricey restaurant upstairs, cafeteria downstairs (open 0800 for breakfast), salon de té around the corner in Los Carrera. *El Corsario*, Atacama 245. Good food in shaded patio, reasonably priced. Recommended. *La Carreta*, Av Copayapu. Parrillada, expensive. *Nuevo Resaurante Quincho*, Atacama 109. Good range of meat, dancing on Fri and Sat.

Cheap *Don Elias*, Los Carrera y Yerbas Buenas. Excellent seafood, very popular. Highly recommended. *Kaliffa*, cheap, good value, clean and smart. *La Pizza di Tito*, Infante y Chacabuco. Pizzas with good fillings, sandwiches, cheap *almuerzos*. *Tebuk*, in the Cosmocentro Plaza Real. Self service, good range, reasonably priced, good views

North of La Serena

The churches of Copiapó

The 'Age of Silver', which followed the discovery of Chañarcillo, has left an unmistakable if subtle mark on the architecture of Copiapó's churches. New building materials, brought in to build railway stations and bridges, were used on houses and churches. Chief among these materials was Pino Oregano: neither a pine nor from Oregon (it is native to northern California), it offered the size and strength of timber required for the new buildings. Guayaquil cane, a type of large diameter bamboo from the Ecuadorean coast, was also introduced: sliced lengthways and flattened, it made strips of light fibre which could be used to make thin walls. At the same time, builders and carpenters from Britain and the United States, attracted by opportunies in railway and mine development, employed their skills on the new buildings of the city.

Church building in Copiapó was influenced by all these factors: architects such as the Englishman William Rogers designed churches which are generally recognized as reflecting English neoclassicism. Particularly noticeable is the design of the tower, positioned in the centre of the church and decorated with columns and wooden cornices. Built of wood and using strips of Guayaquil cane covered with clay, in an almost rainless climate, they have withstood earthquakes to become the oldest buildings in Copiapó.

overlooking Plaza Prat. *Y Se Llama Perú*, O'Higgins 12. Genuine Peruvian cuisine, lively atmosphere, live music at night. Warmly recommended. **Seriously cheap** *Benbow*, Rodriguez 543. Good value *almuerzo*, extensive menu. Recommended. *Lucerna*, O'Higgins 520. Excellent *porotos*, popular with locals. Recommended. *Willy Beer*, Maipú 386. Restaurant/bar, very cheap almuerzo, popular with locals. Several *chifas* (Chinese) including *Chifa Hao Hwa*, at Colipí 340 and Yerbas Buenas 334. There are good cakes at *Panadería La Industrial*, O'Higgins 984.

Cafés *Café Haiti*, Cosmocentro Plaza Real 215. Real coffee, snacks, overlooks Plaza Prat, popular meeting place. *El Bramador*, Paseo Julio Aciares (part of Casa de la Cultura). Real coffee, good meeting place. Recommended.

Entertainment **Discos/pubs** *La Tabla*, Los Carrera y Salas. Good pub, very popular with locals. The best disco is *El Sótano*, on the Panamericana Norte on the way out of town. **Cinemas** *Alhambra*, Atacama 455.

Festivals The *Fiesta de la Candelaria* begins on the first Sunday in February and lasts for 9 days. Up to 50,000 pilgrims and 3,000 dancers congregate from all over the north of Chile to this, one of the more important religious festivals of Chile.

Shopping *Cosmocentro Plaza Real*, on the east side of Plaza Prat, with cafés and restaurants; on the ground floor is a good bookshop, *Andres Bello*. *Supermercado Super Atacama*, Los Carrera 400-block. On Plaza Prat, at the corner of Colipi y Los Carrera, is a stall selling exquisite minerals from the Atacama – recommended.

Tour operators *Azimut 360*, Arzobispo Casanova 3, Providencia, Santiago, T2-7358034, F7772375, www.azimut.cl Adventure and ecotourism, mountaineering expeditions to Ojos de Salado and Incahuasi. *Holovet Travel*, Infante 971, T/F214185. *Turismo Atacama*, Los Carrera 716, T212712, F217357. *Turismo Cobre*, O'Higgins 640, T/F211072, sells air tickets and arranges regional tours.

Local Car hire: *Avis*, Peña 102, T/F213966. *Budget*, Freire 466, T218802. *Flota* **Transport**
Verschae, Luis Flores y Copayapu, T227898. *Hertz*, Copayapu 173, T213522. **Cycle**
repairs: *Bicicleteria Biman*, Las Carrera 998A, T217391. Sales, repairs, parts.
Recommended.

Long distance Air: Chamonate Airport, 12 km north (taxi US$10). *LanChile*, daily
to/from Santiago, also to El Salvador. For a transfer to the airport call T231488. **Bus**: The
main terminal is 3 blocks southwest of centre on Freire y Chacabuco. To **Santiago**
12 hrs, US$15; to **La Serena** 5 hrs, US$6.50; to **Antofagasta** US$13, 8 hrs; to **Calama**
US$17, 11 hrs. Note that *Pullman Bus* have their own terminal next door, where there
is a good left luggage store. Although main companies serve Caldera, the cheapest
buses are with *Buses Recabarren*, every half-hour, leaving from the street one block
west from the main bus terminal; *colectivos* to Chañaral also leave from this point.

Airline offices *Ladeco/LanChile*, Colipí 484, T213512, F217224, airport T214360. **Directory**
Banks *Cambio Fides*, Atacama 541, Galeria Coimbra local 3, 2 piso. Mon-Fri 1000-1400,
1600-1900 (closed Sat/Sun). *Banco Concepción*. Cash advance on Visa. *Finandes*, Colipí
484. Mastercard agent. *Corp Banca*, Chacabuco 481 (on plaza), visa agent; next door is
BCI, with a Redbanc – other Redbancs in the Plaza Real shopping centre and at the
Banco de Chile, O'Higgins y Colipi. **Communications** Internet: *Cybercafe Zona Virtual*,
Rodriguez/Colipi, T240308, www.zonavirtual.cl *Terra*, Chacabuco 380, US$1.80 per hr.
Post office: Los Carrera y Colipi, on Plaza Prat. Open Mon-Fri 1000-1400, 1600-2000.
Telecommunications: *Entel*, Colipí 484. *CTC*, O'Higgins 531. **Cultural centres** *Casa de
la Cultura*, Plaza Prat. In a colonial-style mansion, with a gallery devoted to plastic arts;
also organizes workshops. Film shows once a week. An annex houses the *Café El
Bramador*, theatre productions and recitals. **Dentist** *Eduardo Cáceres*, Salas 385,
T211902. **Film and camera equipment** *Foto Master*, Chacabuco 355. **Hospital** *Los
Carrera s/n*, T212023. **Laundry** *Lavandería Añañucas*, Chañarcillo 612.

The Argentine frontier can be crossed at Paso San Francisco (4,726 m) which is **East of**
situated just north of **Ojos del Salado**, considered to be the third highest peak in **Copiapó**
the Americas, see box. Its height is now thought to be 6,864 m, though the Chil- **to Paso San**
ean IGM map gives its height as 6,879 m. The pass can be reached from Copiapó **Francisco**

The route to Argentina via the Paso de San Francisco

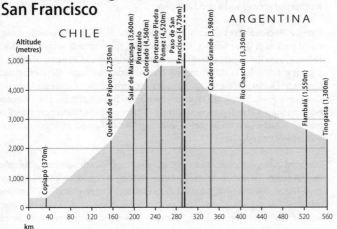

Climbing Ojos del Salado

Ojos del Salado, the highest active volcano in the world, is best climbed between January and March, though ascent is possible between November and April. In November, December and April it can be hit by the Invierno Boliviano, a particularly nasty weather pattern coming from the northeast. Temperatures have been known to drop to -40°C with high winds up to 150 km per hour.

Access is by a road turning off the main Chile-Argentina road at Hostería Murray (burned down). Base camp for the climb is at the old Argentine frontier post (4,500 m). There are two refugios: Refugio Atacama (four to six beds) at 5,100 m and Refugio Tejos (better, 12 beds) at 5,750 m. The spur to the former is not easy to find, but with a

high clearance four-wheel drive vehicle you can drive to the refugio. From the latter it is 10-12 hours' climb to the summit, approx grade three. The climb is not very difficult, except the last 50 m, which is moderate climbing on rock to the crater rim and summit. There is little or no snow: water is available at Hostería Murray but it may be advisable to carry it from Copiapó. Large quantities must be taken on the ascent. Guides and equipment can be hired in Copiapó: try Rubén E Rubilan Cortes, O'Higgins 330, T216535 or Patricio Ríos, T212714 (US$450-600).

Permits are required: obtainable free from the Dirección de Fronteras y Límites in Santiago (Bandera 52, 4º piso, T6714110, F6971909), taking two to three days to issue.

by three roads, all poor *ripio*, and by a *ripio* road which runs south and east from El Salvador. All these routes meet up near the Parque Nacional Tres Cruces (see below). The road from El Salvador meets the main road from Copiapó near the Salar de Maricunga, 96 km east of Paso San Francisco. The other two routes from Copiapó are branches off the main one: the first forks off 10 km east of the Pan-American Highway and runs south through the Quebrada San Miguel to reach the Laguna del Negro Francisco in the southernmost sector of the Parque Nacional Tres Cruces before turning north; the second runs through the Quebrada de Paipote and then through the northernmost sector of the park. Travellers taking either of these alternatives en route for Argentina will need to deviate north to pass through the Chilean immigration post at the Salar de Maricunga. Paso San Francisco lies 104 km east of the Salar de Maricunga by a *ripio* road which runs along the southern shore of Laguna Verde, where there are thermal springs and a good campsite.

Parque Nacional Tres Cruces Extending over 59,082 ha, this newly desig- nated park is in three sectors: the largest part, the northern sector, includes Laguna Santa Rosa and parts of the Salar de Maricunga, an expanse of salt flats covering 8,300 ha at 3,700 m; the central sector includes Cerro Ciénaga Redondo (5,190 m); the southernmost sector covers the area around Laguna del Negro Francisco, a salt lake covering 3,000 ha at 4,200 m. The lakes are home to some 47 bird species, including all three species of flamingo, as well as guanacos and vicuñas. The park is stunningly beautiful and, owing to its isola- tion, rarely visited.

Essentials The park administration is just beyond the Chilean border post at the Salar de Maricunga, on the route to Quebrada Paipote, and is open 0830-1230 and 1400-1800. Entrance costs US$4 (US$2.20 for Chileans). There are two CONAF *refugios*, one southeast of Laguna Santa Rosa and the other southeast of Laguna del Negro Francisco, with bunk beds, heating, electric light and hot water, **F** pp. There are no public transport connections.

Paso San Francisco Although officially open all year, this crossing is liable to closure after snow in winter. Call T052-238032 for reports of the road's condition. On the Argentine side a poor road, described as "quite some washboard", continues to Tinogasta. It is suitable only for 4-WD vehicles. Customs are near the Salar de Maricunga, 100 km west of the frontier, open 0900-1900; US$2 per vehicle charge for crossing Sat, Sun and holidays. The Argentine border post is at Fiambalá, 210 km beyond the border, open 0700-1900, although there is also a police post at La Gruta, 24 km beyond the frontier.

Border with Argentina

There are two alternative routes north: west to Caldera and then north along the coast to Chañaral, 167 km; and the inland route, known as the Inca de Oro, via Diego de Almagro and then west to meet the Pan-American Highway near Chañaral, 212 km.

North from Copiapó

Caldera

Situated 73 km northwest of Copiapó, Caldera is a port and terminal for the loading of iron ore. In the late 19th century it was a major railway engineering centre, but there are few reminders of this era; the **Iglesia de San Vicente** (1862) on the Plaza de Armas was built by English carpenters working for the railway company.

*Phone code: 052
Colour map 2, grid B2
Population: 12,000*

Bahía Inglesa, 6 km south of Caldera and 6 km west of the Pan-American Highway, is popular with Chileans for its beautiful, white sandy beaches and unpolluted sea. It is very expensive and can get crowded January-February and at weekends. It was originally known as Puerto del Inglés after the visit in 1687 of the English pirate, Edward Davis.

Caldera B *Hostería Puerta del Sol*, Wheelwright 750, T315205, F315507. *Cabañas* with kitchen, all mod cons, laundry service, view over bay. B *Portal del Inca*, Carvallo 945, T315252. *Cabañas* with kitchen, English spoken, restaurant not bad, order breakfast on previous night. C *Costanera*, Wheelwright 543, T/F316007. Takes credit cards, simple rooms, friendly. F *Res Millaray*, Cousiño 331, T315528, on main plaza. Friendly, good value, basic. Also D *Restaurant Hospedaje Mastique*, Panamericana Norte Km 880, outside Caldera. Cabin accommodation, hot showers, breakfast included, comfortable. **Bahía Inglesa** B *Los Jardines de Bahía Inglesa*, Av Copiapó, T315359. *Cabañas*, open all year, good beds, comfortable. C *El Coral*, Av El Morro, T315331. Also *cabañas*. Overlooking sea, good seafood, open all year. *Camping Bahía Inglesa*, Playa Las Machas, T315424, **C** per site. Fully equipped *cabañas* for up to 5 persons. C *cabañas*, Playa Paraíso, T315363, F315507. On beach, solar heating. Recommended.

Sleeping

Caldera Mid-range: *Charles*, Ossa Cerda. Slow service. *El Pirón de Oro*, Cousiño 218. Good but not cheap. **Cheap**: *Miramar*, Gana 090, at pier. Good seafood.

Eating

Bus To **Copiapó** (US$1 with *Buses Recabarren*; more expensive with other companies) and **Santiago**, several daily; to **Antofagasta**, US$11, 7 hrs; to travel north, it may be better to take a bus to **Chañaral** (Inca-bus US$2), then change. Hourly buses between Bahía Inglesa and Caldera, US$0.30; *colectivos* US$1.

Transport

North of La Serena

The Salado Valley

It is 93 km north from Caldera to Chañaral, the port of the valley of the Río Salado. Until Chañaral, there are some vestiges of vegetation in the desert, but thereafter there is nothing but unremitting pampa until Antofagasta. The course of the Río Salado itself is always dry, and the valley is less fertile and prosperous than the Copiapó or Huasco valleys.

Chañaral

Phone code: 052
Colour map 2, grid B2
Population: 12,000
968 km N of Santiago

This is a small, sad town with wooden houses perched on the hillside; there is a beautiful and often deserted beach just beyond the Panamericana. In its heyday, Chañaral was the processing centre for ore from the nearby copper mines of El Salado and Las Animas, but those mines have declined, and the town now ekes out a living processing the ores from other mines in the interior. Stone walkways climb steeply up the desert hills behind the main street, Merino Jarpa, reaching platforms where there are many stone benches from which to watch the sea; behind the benches are religious murals daubed with the graffiti of impoverished, angry urban youth.

The **Museo de Historia Natural** is at Buín 818, with exhibits on the mineralogy, hydrobiology and entomology of the region; interesting for naturalists. ■ *Mon-Fri 0900-1300 and 1530-1900, free.*

There is a kiosk with tourist information on the Panamericana, at the south end of town, in summer.

Sleeping & eating

B *Hostería Chañaral*, Müller 268, T480055, F480554. Very spacious and attentive, excellent restaurant in beautiful dining room, pool room, parking. Recommended. **C** *Nuria*, Costanera 302, T480903. Breakfast, parking, friendly, but a little basic and overpriced. Worth bargaining. **D** *Carmona*, Costanera 402, T480522. With bath and TV, friendly, decent value. **F** *Hotel Jiménez*, Merino Jarpa 551, T480328. Without bath, friendly, patio with lots of birds, clean rooms, good beds, modern shared bathrooms, good value restaurant, convenient for Pullman Bus. Recommended. **F** *Residencial Sutivan*, Comercio 365, T489123. More expensive rooms with bath, very friendly, clean, nice rooms, excellent value. Highly recommended. Also arranges tours to Pan de Azúcar. **G** *La Marina*, Merino Jarpa 562. Basic, many parakeets.

Restaurant Nuria, Yungay y Buín, on the Plaza. Not bad, open at night, cheap. *Rincón Porteño*, Merino Jarpa 567. Good and inexpensive. *Restaurante de los Pescadores*, in La Caleta. Good fish, clean, cheap. Recommended. There are a couple of cheap stalls serving coffee and sandwiches early in the morning, next to the *Pullman Bus* terminal.

Festivals

On the night of **15 Jul**, the people of Chañaral celebrate the *Fiesta of the Virgen del Carmen* (the same festival for which the fiesta at La Tirana is so famous, see page 251). This is a much scaled-down version of La Tirana, but there is still much drumming and dancing around the plaza. The religious groups are dressed in elaborate costumes, and vie with one another for the loudest band and the most complex dance; it is really quite moving to watch this poor, proud town manifest its faith.

Tour operators

Chango Turismo, Panamericana Norte s/n, T480484. Offers transfers to the Parque Nacional Pan de Azúcar. Tours of the park are also offered by *Residencial Sutivan* (see above).

Bus No main terminal. *Pullman Bus* terminal at Los Baños y Costanera, *Tur Bus* at Merino Jarpa 858. Frequent services to **Antofagasta** US$10 *semi cama*, 5 hrs, and **Santiago** US$18. To Copiapó, US$3; *colectivos* to Copiapó leave from Merino Jarpa y Los Baños, US$5, best to leave early in the morning.

Transport

Banks Poor rates for cash in *BCI* on the plaza. Nowhere to change TCs, and no Redbanc ATMs. In summer, there is money exchange offered at the ironmonger's, at the junction of Consuelo y Merino Jarpa. **Communications** *CTC*, Merino Jarpa 506, and *ENTEL* on Merino Jarpa 700-block, next to the municipal health centre.

Directory

North of Chañaral is this park, consisting of the Isla Pan de Azúcar, containing Humboldt penguins and other sea birds, and some 43,754 ha of coastal hills rising to 800 m. The park is home to 103 species of birds as well as to guanacos and foxes. A sea-lion colony can be observed by following the signs marked 'loberías' from the park entrance. Fishermen near the CONAF office offer boat trips round Isla Pan de Azúcar to see the penguins, US$20, though these are sometimes visible from the mainland. There are fines for driving in 'restricted areas' of the park. There are beaches, which are popular at weekends in summer.

Parque Nacional Pan de Azúcar
After rain in some of the gullies there are tall alstroemerias of many colours

Essentials Two entrances: north by good secondary road from Chañaral, 28 km to Caleta Pan de Azúcar; from the Pan-American Highway 45 km north of Cañaral, along a side road 20 km (road in parts deep sand and very rough, 4-WD essential). CONAF office in Caleta Pan de Azúcar with an exhibition room, Mon-Sun 0830-1800. Maps are available here; park entry US$4 (US$2.20 for Chileans), camping **E** per site, no showers, take all food (tap water is sold by the bottle); there are also 2 *cabañas* (reservations, T213404). Taxi from Chañaral US$25, or hitch a lift from fishermen at sunrise.

Some 67 km from Chañaral on the El Salvador road is the smaller mining town of Diego de Almagro. Twelve kilometres north of Diego de Almagro, on a mining track through the desert, is the interesting project of the Pampa Austral. Here, Codelco, the state mining company, have used some of the water resulting from the process of extracting copper from nearby mines to irrigate the desert, producing a 4-ha extension of plantations in the middle of the desert *pampa*.

Diego de Almagro

A modern town, built near one of the biggest copper mines in Chile, El Salvador lies 120 km east of Chañaral in the valley of the Río Salado, reached by a road which branches off the Pan-American Highway 12 km east of Chañaral. All along the valley there are people extracting metal ore from the water by building primitive settling tanks. In El Salvador here is *Camino del Inca*, **AL**, El Tofo 330, T475252, F475207 and **C**, *Hostería El Salvador*, Potrerillos 003, T475749.

Further east, 60 km by unpaved road is the **Salar de Pedernales**, salt flats 20 km in diameter and covering 30,000 ha at an altitude of 3,350 m where pink flamingos can be seen.

El Salvador
Phone code: 052
Colour map 2, grid A2

Transport Air: *Lan Chile* from Santiago and Copiapó. **Bus**: *Pullman Bus* daily to Santiago, Copiapó and Chañaral.

Situated 25 km off the Pan-American Highway and 146 km north of Chañaral, Taltal is the only town between Chañaral and Antofagasta, a distance of 420 km. Along Avenida Prat are several wooden buildings dating from the late 19th century when Taltal prospered as a mineral port of 20,000

Taltal
Phone code: 055
Colour map 2, grid A2

North of La Serena

people, exporting nitrates from 21 mines in the area. The town is now a fishing port with a mineral processing plant. There is an archaeological museum on Avenida Prat. North by 72 km is the Quebrada El Médano, a gorge with ancient rock-paintings along the upper valley walls.

Sleeping and eating C *Hostal del Mar*, Carrera 250, T/F611612. Modern, comfortable. C *Hostería Taltal*, Esmeralda 671, T611625, F611173. Excellent restaurant, good value *almuerzo*. C *Verdy*, Ramírez 345, T611105. With bath. **F** without. Clean, spacious, restaurant. Recommended. Opposite is **F** *Taltal City*, Ramirez 348, T611440. Clean, without bath. **F** *San Martín*, Martínez 279, T611088, F268159. Without bath, good *almuerzo*. Eateries include *Club Social Taltal*, Torreblanca 162. Excellent, good value, mid-range. The former club of the British community, with poker room, billiard table and ballroom; and *Caverna*, Martínez 247. Good, cheap seafood.

Transport Bus: To **Santiago** 2 a day; to **Antofagasta** *Pullman Bus* and *Tur Bus*, US$5. There are many more bus services from the Pan-American Highway (taxi US$8).

7

Antofagasta, Calama and San Pedro

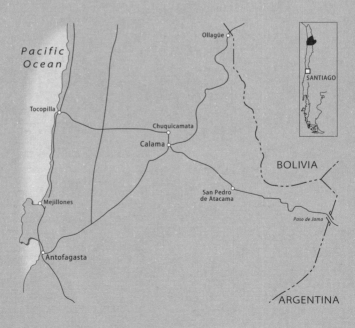

This desolate region is one of the most striking for visitors to Chile. The Atacama Desert is punctuated by small oases in the all-encompassing yellowness; clefts of green such as the beautiful Quebrada de Jerez, near Toconoa, or the Alto Loa, in which the lifelessness of the desert seems impossible. The main cities are Antofagasta and Calama, both of which are service centres for the mining industry which dominates the region's economy. Calama is the departure point for the sole remaining passenger train service in northern Chile, the "tren de la muerte" to Uyuni and Oruro in Bolivia. Most visitors, though, make first for San Pedro de Atacama, an ancient centre of civilisation in the region since well before the Spanish conquest, and the centre for excursions to spectacular desert landscapes such as the Valle de la Luna and the Salar de Atacama, as well as to the El Tatio Geysers. San Pedro is home to one of the north's most important archaeological museums, and excursions can also be made over the frontier into Bolivia to the Salar de Uyuni and to two beautiful lakes, Laguna Colorada and Laguna Verde.

Background

History Before the Spanish conquest, this part of Chile was populated both on the coast and inland. The Chango people fished in the Pacific from boats made from the pelts of sea-lions. They traded fish with the peoples of the interior, from whom they bought coca leaves and quinoa (the staple grain before the arrival of those from Europe); from around the first century AD, there is evidence of an extensive network of paths and trade routes crossing the desert, linking the coastal areas between Taltal and the estuary of the Río Loa with the *altiplano* of Chile, Argentina and Bolivia.

Until the arrival of the Incas in around 1450, the most important inland civilization was that of the Atacameños, based in the area around San Pedro de Atacama. The Atacameños are believed to have arrived around 9000 BC, and, over the course of the millennia, they managed to arrive at an accommodation with the incredibly harsh terrain in which they lived. After the arrival of the Incas, the Atacameños adapted their cultural rituals to suit their new masters.

The first Spanish expedition arrived in 1536, led by Diego de Almagro. Four years later, Pedro de Valdivia took San Pedro de Atacama and the fort at Quitor, and thereafter the Spanish and the Atacameño peoples enacted the familiar and tragic pattern of subjugation and extinction. San Pedro was the colonial centre, but by the end of the colonial era the Spanish had established urban settlements only here and in Chiu Chiu. At independence most of the region became part of Bolivia, though the frontier with Chile was ill-defined. Before the War of the Pacific deprived her of this coastal territory, Bolivia established several towns along the coast, notably Cobija (1825), Mejillones (1841), Tocopilla (1843) and Antofagasta (1872). Nevertheless, by 1875 the total population of the region was under 10,000. After the War of the Pacific the territory passed to Chile; the exploitation of nitrates led to a population increase, construction of railways and ports and Antofagasta's growth into one of Chile's most important cities.

Geography The Atacama Desert stretches 1,255 km north from the Río Copiapó to the Chilean frontier with Peru. The Cordillera de la Costa, at its highest in this region (the highest peak is Cerro Vicuña, 3,114 m), runs close to the coast, an inhospitable and spectacular cliff face rising sheer from the waters to a height of from 600 m to 900 m. Below this cliff, on the edge of the Pacific is a ledge on which are situated the city of Antofagasta, some smaller towns and a road connecting them. In the eastern branch of the Andes several peaks rise to around 6,000 m: Llullaillaco (6,739 m), Socompa (6,051 m), Licancábur (5,916 m), Ollagüe (5,863 m). The western branch of the Andes ends near Calama. In between these two ranges the Andean Depression includes several salt flats, including the Salar de Atacama and the smaller Salar de Ascotán.

Although there are small streams around San Pedro de Atacama, the only river in this part of Chile is the Río Loa, the longest river in the country. It has been dammed at Conchi to provide irrigation for several oases around Calama. The river reaches the sea barely 2 m wide, testament to the great struggle fought by the water to get this far.

Things to do ★

- Take in La Portada – the arch near Antofagasta – famous throughout the country.
- Visit the mine at Chuquicamata – the sense of enormity of the process makes for a very interesting trip.
- See the geysers of El Tatio – set at over 4,000 m, they are the highest geysers in the world.
- For adventurous and well-equipped trekkers and mountain climbers, choose from any one of many volcanoes and remote routes through the *altiplano*. The Volcán Láscar, active and smoking, is very popular.
- One of the most memorable elements of this region is the contrast between the desert and some beautiful green oases – the Quebrada de Jerez, near Toconao, and the Río Loa, near Lasana, are both recommended for this.

Climate

As elsewhere in northern Chile, there are major differences between the climate of the coast and that of the interior. The coast is frequently humid and cloudy; *camanchaca*, a heavy sea mist caused by the cold water of the Humboldt current, is common in the morning, and, in spite of the fact that this is one of the driest places in the world, it can seem that it is about to rain at any moment. In the interior the skies are clear day and night, leading to heat by day and extreme cold by night. The temperatures on the coast are fairly uniform; in the interior there is often a great difference in the temperature between day and night; the winter nights are often as cold as -10°C, and colder in the high *altiplano*. Strong winds, lasting for up to a week, are common in the interior, especially, it is said, around the full moon. Between December and March there are often violent storms of rain, snow and hail in the *altiplano*, a phenomenon known as *invierno altiplánico* (highland winter) or *invierno boliviano* (Bolivian winter).

Economy

Mining is much the most important economic activity. The region includes large copper mines at Chuquicamata, Mantas Blancas, La Escondida and La Exótica, as well as new reserves at Zaldívar and El Abra and smaller-scale operations along the road between Antofagasta and Tocopilla. María Elena produce nitrates and iodine from the Salar del Miraje, while the Salar de Atacama and the Salar de Ascotán contain respectively the world's largest known deposits of lithium and borax. Fishing is a major industry: the three main ports are Antofagasta, Mejillones and Tocopilla; there are 24 fish processing plants. Other industries include the manufacture of explosives at Calama and of cement at Antofagasta. Agricultural activity is limited by the lack of water and poor soils. Apart from tropical fruit production on the coast south of Antofagasta, agriculture is limited to inland areas around the Río Loa and its tributaries.

The main towns, Antofagasta and Calama, account for 87% of the population of the area, 98.8% of which is urban. Other urban centres have few economic activities not associated with the mining companies. Life in the area is artificial. Water has to be piped for hundreds of kilometres to the cities and the mining towns from the Cordillera; all food and even all building materials have to be brought in from elsewhere.

Antofagasta, Calama and San Pedro

Antofagasta

Phone code: 055
Colour map 1, grid C1
Population: 225,316
699 km south of Arica

Situated on the edge of a bay, Antofagasta is the largest city in northern Chile and the fourth largest in the country. It is not a terribly attractive place, although the combination of the tall mountains and the ocean is dramatic. The city's economy depends on the enormous mine at La Escondida in the interior, where 8,000 people work, doing week-long shifts at the mine before spending a week in the city; the city's port also acts as the processing point for the copper from La Escondida and Chuquicamata. As well as being the capital of the Region II, Antofagasta is also an important commercial centre and the home of two universities.

Ins and outs

Getting there
See page 211 for further details

Antofagasta is served by many regular buses from both north and south. All major companies serving the north stop here, and there are frequent flights with Ladeco and LanChile south to Santiago, and north to Calama, Iquique and Arica.

Getting around

Antofagasta is one of Chile's largest cities, and you may need to take some of the *colectivos* or buses to get to more out-of-the-way places, particularly the discos and bars to the south and the university campuses. Specific details are given in the text for these destinations.

Tourist office

The tourist office is at Prat 384, in the intendencia on the Plaza Prat, T451818, serna_antof@entelchile.net Mon-Fri 0830-1300, Mon-Thu 1500-1930, Fri 1500-1930, very helpful. There is also a kiosk on Balmaceda near *Hotel Antofagasta* Mon-Fri 0930-1300, 1530-1930, Sat/Sun 0930-1300 kiosk at airport (open summer only). Automóvil Club de Chile, Condell 2330, T225332. CONAF at Argentina y Baquedano.

Climate

Apart from the lack of rain, the climate is pleasant; the temperature varies from 16°C in Jun and Jul to 24°C Jan and Feb, never falling below 10°C at night.

Sights

In the main square, **Plaza Colón** is a clock tower donated by the British community in 1910. It is a miniature of Big Ben with a carillon which produces similar sounds. Two blocks north of Plaza Colón, near the old port, is the former **Aduana**, built as the Bolivian customs house in Mejillones and moved to its current site after the War of the Pacific. Opposite are two other buildings, the former **Capitanía del Puerto** and the former **Resguardo Marítimo** (now housing DIGADER, the regional coordinating centre for sport and recreation). East of the port are the buildings of the **Antofagasta and Bolivia Railway Company** (FCAB) dating from the 1890s and beautifully restored, but still in use and difficult to visit. These include the former railway station, company offices and workers' housing. Just north of the port is the **Terminal de Pescadores**, where there are markets selling seafood, fruit and vegetables; there are half-hour tours of the port available from La Cabaña de Mario, s/n Anibal Pinto, US$3.50. Pelicans sit on the fish market roof and sea-lions swim in the harbour. The former main plaza of the **Oficina Vergara**, a nitrate town built in 1919 and dismantled in 1978, can be seen in the campus of the University of Antofagasta, 4 km south of the centre (Bus 3 or 4). Also to the south on a hill (and reached by Bus B) are the ruins of **Huanchaca**, a Bolivian silver refinery built after 1868 and closed in 1903. From below, the ruins resemble a fortress rather than a factory.

Museo Regional de Antofagasta, in the former Aduana, includes displays on the geology and natural history of the north, as well as sections on the War of the Pacific and the Nitrate Era. Explanations are in Spanish only. Recommended. ■ *US$1, children half-price. Tue-Sat 1000-1300, 1530-1830, Sun 1100-1400, museoantof@terra.cl Balmaceda y Bolívar.* **Museums**

Museo Geológico of the Universidad Católica del Norte is inside the university campus. ■ *Free. Mon-Fri 0900-1200, 1500-1800. Getting there: colectivo 3 or 33 from town centre, Gchong@socompa.ucn Av Angamos 0610.*

Museo del Ferrocarril a Bolivia has an interesting museum of the history of the Antofagasta-Bolivia railway, with photographs, maps, instruments and furniture. Reservations must be made 48 hours in advance. ■ *T206311, jlyons@fcab.cl Bolívar 255.*

Excursions

La Portada, 16 km north, has fantastic cliff formations which are the symbol of the Region II, and often seen on postcards up and down the country. From the main road it is 2 km to the beach which, though beautiful, is too dangerous for swimming. There is an excellent and expensive seafood restaurant, *La Portada*, and café, open lunchtime only. A number of bathing beaches are also within easy reach. ■ *Getting there: reached by minibuses from Latorre y Sucre (US$4 return), or any bus for Mejillones from the Terminal Centro. Taxis charge US$11. Hitching is easy.* **La Portada**

A windsurfers' paradise, Juan López, is 38 km north of Antofagasta. The sea is alive with birds, including Humboldt penguins, especially opposite Isla Santa María. There are a couple of hotels en route: *La Rinconada*, **A** for up to five people, T261139, 10 km from Juan López and *Hostería Sandokan*, **C**, T692031. If you have your own transport, follow the road out of Juan López to the beautiful cove at Conchilla. Keep on the track to the end at Bolsico. ■ *Getting there: buses go there at weekends in the summer only; there are also minibuses daily in summer from Latorre y Sucre.* **Juan López**

Chacabuco, 30 km north and just off the Pan-American Highway, is a large abandoned nitrate town, opened in 1924 and closed in 1938. Chacabuco was used as a concentration camp by the Pinochet government between 1973 and 1975. Workers' housing, the church, theatre, stores and the mineral plants can be visited. ■ *Getting there: hitch or take a bus from Antofagasta towards Calama, get off at the Carmen Alto junction and walk the last 4 km. There is a free guided tour in Spanish. It is essential to take water and set out early morning as you will probably be hitching back.* **Chacabuco**

The Very Large Telescope (see box, page 179) at **Cerro Paranal** can be visited. This is, at present, the most powerful telescope in the world, although a more powerful one is being built near La Serena. The site was chosen on a hill in the coastal *cordillera*, 132 km south of Antofagasta, as 350 clear nights a year were guaranteed. ■ *Open on the last 2 Sat in the month, between 1400-1700. Reservations are essential, call T055-281291, or else get details from Intitour (see below, under tour companies).* **Very Large Telescope**

Nitrates

The rise and fall of the nitrate industry played an important part in opening up the northern desert areas between Iquique and Antofagasta to human settlement. In the second half of the 19th century, nitrates became important in Europe and the US as an artificial fertilizer and for making explosives. The world's only known deposits of nitrates were in the Atacama Desert provinces of Antofagasta in Bolivia and Tarapacá in Peru. After the War of the Pacific, Chile gained control of all the nitrate fields, giving her a monopoly over world supply. Ownership was dominated by the British who controlled 60% of the industry by 1900. Taxes on the export of nitrates provided Chilean governments with around half their income for the next 40 years.

The processing of nitrates was labour intensive: at its height over 60,000 workers were employed. Using a combination of dynamite and manual labour, the workers dug the nitrate ore from the desert floor. It was then transported to nitrate plants known as oficinas, crushed and mixed with water, allowing pure nitrates to be extracted. The mining and refining processes were dangerous and cost many lives. Wages were relatively high, but workers were paid in special tokens valid only for the particular oficina in which

they worked. This not only meant that they had no means of leaving the oficina with ready cash, but also that they had to buy all their goods from the company stores which were, of course, controlled by the oficina.

The development of the Haber-Bosch process, a method of producing artificial nitrates in Germany during the First World War, dealt a severe blow to the nitrate companies and many mines closed in the 1920s. New techniques were introduced by the Guggenheim company, but the world depression after 1929 led to the collapse of demand for nitrates and with it the Chilean nitrate industry. Traces of the nitrate era can, however, still be seen: the mining ghost towns of Humberstone, near Iquique, and Chacabuco, north of Antofagasta, can be visited, as can Baquedano, the most important junction of the nitrate railways; most of the other oficinas are marked only by piles of rubble at the roadsides north of Antofagasta. Only one mine survives today, at María Elena; paradoxically, its future is secure, as the nitrates from the Atacama are believed to be much better for the soil than those created by the artificial process and demand has increased in recent years.

Essentials

Sleeping

■ on map
Price codes:
see inside front cover
Cheap hotels are
scarce and poor
quality.
The tourist office does
not maintain a list of
cheaper places

AL *Antofagasta*, Balmaceda 2575, T/F228811. Garage, pool, lovely view of port and city, good but expensive restaurant (bar serves cheaper snacks), with breakfast (discount for Automóvil Club members), beach, but rooms facing the city are noisy due to all night copper trains. **A** *Diego de Almagro*, Condell 2624, T269331, F251721. Good for the money but a bit tatty. **A** *Plaza*, Baquedano 461, T269046, F266803, hplaza@chilesat.net Pool, squash court, parking. TV, salon de té, pool, parking, recommended, exchange (see below), also has apartments.   **A** *Tatio*, Av Grecia 1000, T/F277602. Modern building, out of old town on the beach, good restaurant. **B** *Ancla Inn*, Baquedano 508, T224814, F261551, www.ancla.inn@entelchile.net **B** *Astore, Matta 2537*, T251611, F267439. All mod cons, friendly. **B** *Marsal*, Prat 867, T268063, F221733, marsalhotel@terra.cl Modern, very comfortable, Catalan owner, friendly, recommended. **B** *Nadine*, Baquedano 519, T227008, F265222. TV, bar, café, parking, etc. **B** *Parina*, Maipú, T223354, F266396. Modern, comfortable, friendly, restaurant, conference centre, good value. **B** *Sol del Horizonte*, Latorre 2450, T/F221886, hotelsoldelhorizonte@123click.cl Cable TV, bar, friendly, pleasant, good value, recommended.

C *Colón*, San Martín 2434, T261851, F260872. With breakfast, local phone calls free, quiet, clean. **C** *Costa Marfil*, Prat 950, T225569, F264806. With breakfast, friendly, English spoken. **C** *Dakota*, Latorre 2425, T251649. With breakfast and cable TV, friendly, popular, good value, recommended. **C** *San Marcos*, Latorre 2946, T251763, F221492. Modern, comfortable, parking, avoid rooms at the back (loud music), overpriced. **C** *San Martín*, San Martín 2781, T263503, F268159. With bath, TV, parking, clean, safe and friendly. **D** *Chillán*, Sucre 823, T227237. Friendly, with bath and breakfast. **D** *Ciudad de Avila*, Condell 2840, T/F221040. Very clean, TV, restaurant, excellent value. Warmly recommended. **D** *Frontera*, Bolívar 558, T281219. Without bath, poky rooms, basic, overpriced. **D** *Maykin*, Condell 3130, T/F259400. With bath, modern, helpful, good value. Recommended. **D** *Hostal del Norte*, Latorre 3162, T251265, F267161. Without bath, clean, comfortable, quiet.

F *Brasil*, Ossa 1978, T267268. Basic, dark. **F** *Rawaye*, Sucre 762, T225399. Very basic, hot water morning only, no towels. **F** *Res Aliro*, Ossa 2275, T410505, basic, overpriced. **F** *Res El Cobre*, Prat 749, T225162. Without bath, clean, dingy, unattractive. **F** *Res La Riojanita*, Baquedano 464, T226313. Friendly, basic, very helpful, noisy but recommended.

Camping To the south on the road to Coloso are: *Las Garumas*, Km 6, T247763 ext 42. **F** per site (bargain for lower price out of season), **C** for cabins (sleep 4); cold showers and beach (reservations Av Angamos 601, Casilla 606); wild camping on the beach nearby. *Rucamóvil*, Km 11, T223929. Open year-round, **E** per site.

Expensive *Club de la Unión*, Prat 474, 2 piso. Excellent *almuerzo*, good service, traditional atmosphere. Recommended. *Club de Yates*, on the *costanera* beside *Hotel Antofagasta*, exclusive, great seaviews and great seafood. *Marina Club*, Av Ejército 0909. Good fish and seafood dishes and a view, expensive but worth it.

Eating
● *on map page 210.*
*Note that many bars
and restaurants are
closed on Sun*

Antofagasta, Calama and San Pedro

Mid-range *Bavaria*, Ossa 2428. Excellent meat and German specialities, cheaper cafeteria downstairs, real coffee. *Chifa Pekín*, Ossa 2135. Chinese, smart, reasonable prices. *D'Alfredo*, Condell 2539. Pizzas, good. *El Arriero*, Condell 2644. Good service, cheaper set lunch, popular, live music. *Panda*, Condell y Baguedano. Self-service, eat all you can for US$8. *Pizzante*, Carrera 1857. Good pasta and seafood. *Puerto Caliche*, Ejercito 0809, excellent food and service. *Rincón Oriental*, Washington 2432. Excellent Cantonese, pricey, 'over the top' jolly atmosphere.*Tío Jacinto*, Uribe 922. Friendly, good seafood.

Cheap *Bundes Schop*, Latorre 2655, cheap, open late. Casa Vecchia, O'Higgins 1456. Good value. *Chicken's House Center*, Latorre 2660. Chicken, beef and daily specials, open till 2400. *La Yugoslava*, Matta 2341. Fast food, cheap *almuerzo*, snacks. *Oliver Café Plaza*, Plaza Colón. Self-service, modern, reasonably priced. Recommended.

Seriously cheap *La Selecta*, Sucre 720, basic food, but cheap and open for *cenas*. Many eating places in the market; above the market are several good places selling cheap seafood *almuerzos* and supercheap set lunches, including *El Mariscal* and *Toledo*. Good fish restaurants also in *terminal pesquero centro* and at *Caleta Coloso*, 8 km south.

Cafés It is difficult to find coffee or breakfast before 0900. For real coffee: *Café Bahía*, Prat 474, and *Café Caribe*, Prat 482. Open 0900. Or try *Café Haiti*, in galeria at Prat 482. Cafetería of *Hotel Nadine*, real coffee, pastries, ice cream. Recommended. *Chez Niko's*,

Antofagasta

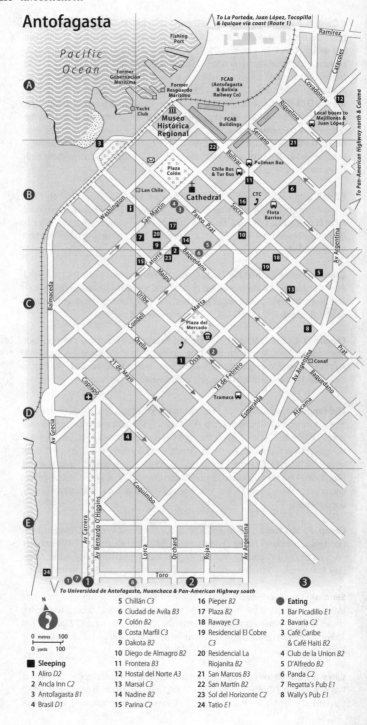

Sleeping
1 Aliro *D2*
2 Ancla Inn *C2*
3 Antofagasta *B1*
4 Brasil *D1*
5 Chillán *C3*
6 Ciudad de Avila *B3*
7 Colón *B2*
8 Costa Marfil *C3*
9 Dakota *B2*
10 Diego de Almagro *B2*
11 Frontera *B3*
12 Hostal del Norte *A3*
13 Marsal *C3*
14 Nadine *B2*
15 Parina *C2*
16 Pieper *B2*
17 Plaza *B2*
18 Rawaye *C3*
19 Residencial El Cobre *C3*
20 Residencial La Riojanita *B2*
21 San Marcos *B3*
22 San Martín *B2*
23 Sol del Horizonte *C2*
24 Tatio *E1*

Eating
1 Bar Picadillo *E1*
2 Bavaria *C2*
3 Café Caribe & Café Haiti *B2*
4 Club de la Union *B2*
5 D'Alfredo *B2*
6 Panda *C2*
7 Regatta's Pub *E1*
8 Wally's Pub *E1*

Ossa 1951. Bakery, *pastelería*, good pizzas, *empanadas* and bread. *Pastelería La Palmera*, Ossa 2297. Good cakes, pastries, bread. Good bread and cakes also at *Panadería El Sol*, Baquedano 785. Ice creams at *Heladería Latorre*, Baquedano y Latorre.

Bars *Bar Picadillo*, Av Grecia 1000, recommended, lively atmosphere, also good food. *Castillo Pub*, Pasaje Carrera 884. Live music, good food with good value *almuerzo*, good fun. Recommended. *Pub En Vivo*, O'Higgins 1998, often has live music, popular. *Wally's Pub*, Toro 982. British expat-style with darts and beer, closed Sun. **Discos** Because of Antofagasta's high student population, there is thriving nightlife here. *Club Happy*, *Entre Negros* and *La Terraza* all popular. Also try *Vox*, Comino y Coloso, popular. **Theatre** *Teatro Municipal*, Sucre y San Martín, T264919. Modern, state-of-the-art. *Teatro Pedro de la Barra*, Condell 2495. Run by University of Antofagasta, regular programme of plays, reviews, concerts etc, high standard, details in press.

Entertainment
Note that most of the most popular discotheques are south of the town in Balneario El Huascar. Take Micro 2 in Calle Matta to get there

Swimming *Olympic Swimming Pool*, Condell y 21 de Mayo. **Sauna** *Geyser*, Chillán 1245, T255278. Genuine sauna plus Turkish bath, hydromasssage, health suite. **Tennis** *Club de Tenis Antofagasta*, Av Angamos 906, T247756 for details of temporary membership.

Sports

29 Jun, *San Pedro*, patron saint of the fishermen: the saint's image is taken out by launch to the breakwater to bless the first catch of the day. On the last weekend of **Oct**, the foreign communities put on a joint festival on the seafront, with national foods, dancing and music.

Festivals

Galería de Arte Imagen, Uribe 485. Sells antiques including artefacts from nitrate plants. *Naturista*, Condell 2394, specializes in healthfood. **Bookshops** *Librería Andres Bello*, Condell 2421. Excellent selection. *Librería Universitaria*, Latorre 2515. Mainly technical books. Opposite is *Multilibro*, contemporary Latin American literature, also English language authors. Recommended. **Market** *Municipal market*, Matta y Uribe. Fish market is on Av Pinto. Next to it is the Feria Modelo O'Higgins, which has excellent fruit and vegetables as well as restaurants. **Supermarkets** *Korlaert*, on Ossa 2400-2500 block; *Las Brisas*, Baquedano 750, has an ATM; *Lider* on A Pinto, north of the fishing port; *Tricot*, Ossa 2450, has an ATM.

Shopping

Many including *Intitour*, Baquedano 460, T266185, F260882, intitour@entelchile.net English spoken. *Maerz*, run by Alex Joseph Valenzuela Thompson, Prat 831, Piso 2, Of 6, T243322, F259132, maerz@entelchile.net *Tatio Travel*, Washington 2513, T263532, F263532. English spoken, tours arranged for groups or individuals. Highly recommended. *Terra Expedition Tour*, Balmaceda 2575 (in *Hotel Antofagasta*), T/F223324. *Turismo Corssa*, San Martín 2769, T/F227675. Recommended. *Alex Joseph Valenzuela Thompson*, Atacama Wüstereisedienst, Apartado Postal 55, T243322, F259132. Offers to guide German speakers around the area.

Tour companies

Local *Car rental*: *Avis*, Balmaceda 2499, T221073. *Budget*, Balmaceda 2584, Of 6, T251745. *First*, Bolívar 623, T225777. *Hertz*, Balmaceda 2492, T269043. Offer city cars and jeeps (group D, Toyota Landcruiser) and do a special flat rate, with unlimited mileage. *IQSA*, Latorre 3033, T264675. **Car mechanic**: Andrés Ljubetic Romo, Atacama 2657, T268851. Recommended. **Cycle spares**: Rodrigo Baez Banda, Condell 3071, also repairs. *Cicles Miranda*, Matta 2795, T223867.

Transport

Long distance Air: Cerro Moreno Airport, 22 km north. Taxi to airport US$7, but cheaper if ordered from hotel. Airport transfer, Baquedano 328, T262727. *LanChile* and *Ladeco* fly daily to Santiago, Iquique and Arica.

No main terminal; each company has its own office in town, quite some distance from the centre

Bus: Buses for **Mejillones** and **Tocopilla**, operated by *Barrios*, *Pullman Bus*, *Tur Bus* and others, depart from the Terminal Centro at Riquelme 513. Minibuses to Mejillones leave from Latorre 2730. Bus company offices as follows: *Flota Barrios*, Condell 2682, T268559; *Géminis*, Latorre 3055, T251796; *Pullman Bus*, Latorre 2805, T262591; *Tur Bus*, Latorre 2751, T264487. To **Santiago**, 20 hrs (*Flota Barrios*, US$50, *cama* including drinks and meals); 30% reduction on *Inca*, *Tramaca*, and *Géminis* buses for students, but ask after you have secured a seat; many companies: fares US$35-40, book 2 days in advance. If all seats to the capital are booked, catch a bus to **La Serena** (11 hrs, US$15, or US$25 *semi cama*), or **Ovalle**, US$18 and re-book. To **Valparaíso**, US$30. To **Arica**, US$12, *Tur-Bus*, 13½ hrs. To **Chuquicamata**, US$5, frequent, 3 hrs. To **Calama**, several companies, US$4.50, 3 hrs; to **San Pedro de Atacama**, *Tur Bus* at 0630, or via Calama; to **Copiapó**, US$10; to **Iquique**, US$9, 6 hrs, frequent. **To Salta and Argentina** *Tur Bus*, Wed at dawn, change at Calama, via San Pedro, Paso Sico and Jujuy US$38. Immigration check at San Pedro de Atacama. Book in advance for this service, take food and as much warm clothing as possible. There is nowhere to change Chilean pesos en route; take small denomination dollar bills to use in Argentina.

Hitchhiking If hitchhiking on the coast road to Mejillones/Tocopilla try at the police checkpoint on the Mejillones road north of the city. If hitching south go to the police checkpoint/restaurant/gas station La Negra, about 15 km south of the city.

Train There are no passenger services from Antofagasta. The journey to Uyuni and Oruro in Bolivia starts from Calama (see page 220) – tickets from Tramaca, Uribe 936 or in Calama.

Directory **Airline offices** *Ladeco/LanChile*, Washington 2552, T265151, F222526. *LAB*, San Martín 2395, T/F260618.

It is impossible to change TCs south of Antofagasta until you reach La Serena

Banks Major banks around Plaza Colón including *Corp Banca*, visa agents. *Banco Santiago* and *Banco BCI*, all have ATMs. There are also ATMs at the *Tricot* and *Las Brisas* supermarkets. *Casas de Cambio* are mainly on Baquedano, such as *Ancla*, Baguedano 524. Open Mon-Fri 0900-1400, 1600-1900, Sat 0900-1400, poor rates (if closed try the ice cream shop next door). Several exchange agents in the shopping centre at Baquedano 482-498; nearby is also *Nortour*, Baquedano 474. *AFEX*, Latorre 668. Open Mon-Fri 0830-2000, Sat 0830-1400, better rates for TCs than Ancla.

Communications **Internet**: Cheapest is *Intitour* (see above, Tour companies), US$0.60/hr. Also try *Cybercafé*, Maipú y Latorre, US$1.30/hour, or *Sucre 671*, US$0.80/hr. **Post office**: on Plaza Colón. 0830-1900, Sat 0900-1300. **Telephones**: *CTC*, Condell 2529. *Entel Chile*, Condell 2451. On Sun, the only call centre to open is *CTC*, Condell 2750. **Consulates** **Argentina**, Blanco Encalada 1933, T220440. **France** and **Belgium**, Baquedano 299, T268669. **Bolivia**, Washington 2675, P 13, Of 1301, T225010. **Germany**, Pérez Zujovic 4940, T251691. **Holland**, Washington 2679, Of 902, T266252. **Italy**, Matta 1945, Of 808, T227791. **Spain**, Rendic 4946, T269596. **Cultural centres** Centro Cultural Nueva Acropolis, Condell 2679, T222144. Talks on Wed 2100, also Tai Chi, yoga, archaeological and philosophical discussions. **Instituto Chileno-Alemán de Cultura**, Bolívar 769, T225946. **Instituto Chileno-Norteamericano de Cultura**, Carrera 1445, T263520. **Customs agent** *Luis Piquimil Bravo*, Sucre 363, Of 28, T251789, F6385727. Excellent, fast service, efficient.

Laundry *Clean clothes*, G Lorca 271. *La Ideal*, Baguedano 660. *Laverap*, 14 Febrero 1802, efficient, not cheap. *París*, Condell 2455. Laundry and dry cleaning, expensive, charges per item.

This port stands on a good natural harbour protected from westerly gales by high hills. Until 1948 it was a major terminal for the export of tin and other metals from Bolivia. Remnants of that past include a number of fine wooden buildings: the Intendencia Municipal, the Casa Cultural, built in 1866, and the church, 1906, as well as the Capitanía del Puerto. Mejillones' life has been transformed in recent years by the project of building the largest port in South America here – the port will act as a link for Argentina, southern Brazil and Paraguay with the lucrative markets of the Asian Pacific Rim, and the large port buildings dominate the northern end of the town. Fishing remains important, however, and Mejillones comes alive in the evening when the fishermen prepare to set sail. The sea is very cold because of the Humboldt current.

Mejillones
Phone code: 055
Colour map 1, grid C1
Population: 5,500
60 km north of
Antofagasta

Sleeping and eating A *Costa Del Sol*, M Montt 086, T621590, 4-star, new. **B** *Paris*, Pje. Iquique 095, T623061, clean, modern, good. **F** *Res Elisabeth*, Alte Latorre 440, T621568. Friendly, basic, restaurant. **F** *Res Marcela*, Borgoño 150, T621464. With bath, pleasant. No campsite, but wild camping possible on the beach. Cheap eats at *Juanito*, Las Heras 241. Excellent *almuerzo*. *Sion-Ji*, Alte Latorre 718. Chinese, good value.

Directory Banks: There are two Redbanc ATMs in Mejillones.

North along the Pan-American Highway

The Highway continues north via Baquedano (Km 72) and Carmen Alto (Km 98), the turning to Calama. A turning 69 km north of Carmen Alto leads to **Pedro de Valdivia**, a nitrate town abandoned in 1996, which has been declared a National Monument and can be visited.

From Pedro de Valdivia a road runs north, parallel to the Pan-American Highway, crossing the Salar del Mirage to **María Elena**, the only nitrate town still functioning. The nitrate business is now seen as more profitable than during the half-century or more of doldrums endured by the region, as the nitrates extracted from the Atacama desert are thought to be better for the soil than the chemical version invented in the 1920s (see box, page 208). The Museo Arqueológico y Histórico on the main plaza has exhibits on pre-hispanic cultures. ■ *US$1*. There is the run down **F** *Residencial Chacance*, T632749, with nicer clean rooms around the corner at **E**. Cheap meals at the *Casino Social*. *Tur Bus* goes to Iquique from here taking six hours, US$6.

Some 22 km southeast of María Elena, part of the Pan-American Highway, is the **Balneario Chacance**, also known as the Parque El Loa, where bathing and camping are available on the banks of the Río Loa.

North of María Elena, the Pan-American Highway crosses the Tocopilla-Calama road 107 km north of Alto Carmen. Some 15 km further north there is accommodation at *Posada Los Arbolitos*, **F**, also *cabañas*, meals, no running water.

At **Quillagua**, Km 81, there is a customs post where all vehicles heading south are searched. Situated 111 km further north is the southernmost and largest section of the **Reserva Nacional Pampa del Tamarugal**; the other sections are further north, near La Tirana (see page 251) and 60 km north of Pozo Almonte (see page 220).

In the southern section are the **Geoglifos de Pintados**, about 400 figures of humans, animals and geometric shapes on the hillside 3 km west of the highway (see page 246). North of the Reserve are Pozo Almonte and the turn-off for Iquique.

There are two routes from Antofagasta north to Iquique along the Pan-American and the coastal road. The coastal route is more picturesque

Antofagasta, Calama and San Pedro

North along the coastal road

There is no fuel between Mejillones and Tocopilla

The coastal road, Route 1, is a beautiful alternative to the sterility that accompanies large stretches of the Panamericana. From Mejillones the road runs at the foot of 500 m cliffs, with constantly shifting views of the mountains and of the glistening ocean. Where the cliffs break down into jagged rocks on the shoreline, hundreds of cormorants can be seen swarming all over the pinnacles. Behind the mountains, the coastal sierra is extensively mined for copper, often by *pilquineros*, small groups of self-employed miners. There are larger mines, with the biggest concentration inland at Michilla, 107 km north.

Reminders of the area's mining past can be seen, principally at the ruins of **Cobija**, 127 km north, founded by order of Simón Bolívar in 1825 as Bolivia's main port. A prosperous little town handling silver exports from Potosí, it was destroyed by an earthquake in 1868 and again by a tidal wave in 1877 before losing out to the rising port of Antofagasta. Adobe walls, the rubbish tip right above the sea and the wreckage of the port are all that remains. The haunting ruins of the port of Gatico are at Km 144, just a little way beyond. About 4 km further north there is an amazing ransacked cemetery.

A very steep zigzag road winds up the cliffs to the mine at Mantos de la Luna about 152 km north of Antofagasta. At the top there are rather dead-looking groves of giant cactus living off the sea mist which collects on the cliffs. Wildlife includes foxes, or *zorros*.

There are good, weekend beach resorts at Hornitos, 88 km north of Antofagasta, and Poza Verde, 117 km north.

Tocopilla

Phone code: 055
Colour map 1, grid C1
Population: 24,574

This town is 187 km north of Antofagasta via the coast road, or 365 km via the Pan-American Highway. It has one of the most dramatic settings of any Chilean town, sheltering at the foot of 500-m high mountains that loom inland. There are some interesting early 20th-century buildings with wooden balustrades and façades. The plaza is an unlikely fiesta of palms and pepper trees amid the otherwise unremitting desert. Tocopilla is dominated by a thermal power station, which supplies electricity to the whole of northern Chile, and by the port facilities used to unload coal and to export nitrates and iodine from María Elena and Pedro de Valdivia. There are two good beaches: Punta Blanca 12 km south and Caleta Covadonga 3 km south, which has a swimming pool. There is also fine deep sea fishing if you can find a boat and a guide.

For a spectacular view, head up Baquedano as far as possible until you reach a stone stairway. Walking up this, you reach a minor road which climbs up behind the town, giving views of the cliffs to the north, the mountains reaching inland and the fishing boats bobbing up and down in the harbour.

Sleeping **C** *Atenas*, 21 de Mayo 1448, T/F813650. Good restaurant, overpriced. **C** *Bolívar*, Bolívar 1332, T812783, **F** without bath. Modern, helpful. Opposite on Bolívar is the *Sucre*, same ownership, same price. **C** *Chungará*, 21 de Mayo 1440, T811036. With all mod cons. **C** *Vucina*, 21 de Mayo 2069, T/F813088. Modern, good restaurant. **D** *Hotel Colonial*, 21 de Mayo 1717, T811621, F811940, with bath, breakfast and cable TV, friendly, helpful. **F** *Casablanca*, 21 de Mayo 2054, T813187. Friendly, helpful, good restaurant, good value. **G** *América*, Serrano 1243. Without bath, clean. **G** *Residencial Royal*, T/F 811488, 21 de Mayo 1988, helpful, basic, without breakfast or bath, parking. **H** *Hostal Central*, A Pinto 1241, huge rambling place like something out of a Hitchcock film, very basic, friendly, vast rooms, no hot water.

Mid-range Good meals in restaurants of *Hotel Bolívar*, *Hotel Vucina* and *Hotel Casablanca*. Also try *Bavaria*, Rodriguez 1280. Cafeteria, fine sea views from veranda. *Club de la Unión*, Prat 1354. Pleasant atmosphere. Good value *almuerzo*. *Echikhouse*, 21 de Mayo 2132. Good value 4-course *almuerzo*. *Luciano's Pizzas*, 21 de Mayo 1995. Fairly good. *Piero's Place*, 21 de Mayo 1395. Café-bar, lively, good music with video screen. Recommended. **Eating**

Cheap Three Chinese restaurants: *Chifa Fu Zhou Lou*, 21 de Mayo 1842, pleasant; *Chifa Jok San*, 21 de Mayo 1488; *Chifa Ji Kong*, 21 de Mayo 1848. *Los Dos Leones*, 21 de Mayo 1993. Sandwiches, good value *almuerzo*, popular with locals. *Pizzeria Vittorio*, good atmosphere, good value. Good seafood at *La Caleta* opposite the old wooden clock tower. At Caleta Covadonga: *Caleta Boy*, seafood. Recommended.

Seriously cheap *Restaurant Oasis*, 21 de Mayo 2072A, good value. Few places open early for breakfast, but *Restaurant El Chilenito*, Cienfuegos y 21 de Mayo, is the first up.

Discos/Pubs *Dreamy*, on Serrano, specialises in salsa and merengue, does classes. *Tequila Pub*, 21 de Mayo y Serrano, dancing Thu-Sat. **Entertainment**

Tocopilla

Basar e Artesano Lastato, 21 de Mayo y Washington, has varied crafts. Craft market on 21 de Mayo outside the post office. *Supermercado Colón*, Colón y 21 de Mayo. *Supermercado Loconómico*, Bolívar y Sucre. **Shopping**

Munditour, Sucre 1228, T813523, 09-540519. Mostly fixes up trips for locals to the south, but may be able to arrange things in the area. **Tour operators**

Bus No terminal. Bus offices all on 21 de Mayo, eg *Pullman Bus*, *Tur Bus*, *Barrios*, *Pullman Carmelita*. Few buses leave Tocopilla early in the morning for southern destinations, as they all have to arrive first from Iquique. Above companies serve the following destinations: **Antofagasta**, many daily, US$3, 2½ hrs; **Iquique**, 3 hrs, US$4, frequent. **Chuquicamata** and **Calama**, *Tur-Bus*, 2 a day, 3 hrs, US$5. All the above companies serve Santiago. **Transport**

Banks *Banco de Crédito e Inversiones*, Baquedano y Prat, has a Redbanc ATM machine. **Communications** Internet: At 21 de Mayo 1721, US$1.20/hr. **Post office**: At 21 de Mayo y A. Pinto. **Telephone**: CTC call centre nearby. Also ENTEL at 21 de Mayo 2066. **Directory**

Not to scale

Sleeping
1 América
2 Atenas
3 Bolívar
4 Casablanca
5 Chungará
6 Colonial
7 Hostal Central
8 Residencial Royal
9 Sucre
10 Vucina

Eating
1 Chifa Fu Zhou Lou
2 Club de la Unión
3 El Chilenito
4 Los Dos Leones
5 Luciano's Pizzas
6 Piero's Place
7 Pizzería Vittorio

Antofagasta, Calama and San Pedro

Routes north and east of Tocopilla The coastal road runs north from Tocopilla to Iquique, 244 km away, and is a highly recommended journey, offering views of the rugged coastline and tiny fishing communities. The customs post at Chipana-Río Loa (Km 90) searches all southbound vehicles for duty-free goods; this can take up to half-an-hour. Basic accommodation is available at **San Marcos**, a fishing village (Km 131). At **Chanaballita** (Km 184) there is a hotel, *cabañas*, camping, restaurant, shops. There are campsites at the former salt mining town of **Guanillos** (Km 126), **Playa Peruana** (Km 129) and **Playa El Aguila** (Km 160).

East of Tocopilla a good paved road climbs a steep and narrow valley 72 km to the Pan-American Highway. From here the road continues east across the Pan-American Highway to **Chuquicamata**: the first 62 km east of the Pan-American Highway is in good condition, the last part is very poor. Chuquicamata lies 16 km away from Calama, the main city of the interior.

Calama

Phone code: 055
Colour map 1, grid C2
Population: 121,300
Altitude: 2,265m
202 km NE of Antofagasta

Calama is a seedy city set in the oasis of the Río Loa, lightened by beautiful views of the volcanoes in the Ollagüe area. It is an expensive modern town which acts as a service centre for the large nearby mines of Chuquicamata and Radomiro Tomic. Initially a staging post on the silver route between Potosí and Cobija, Calama superseded San Pedro de Atacama in importance with the development of mining activities at Chuquicamata. Most travellers use Calama as the departure point for San Pedro de Atacama and the weekly train to Bolivia, but football fans will certainly want to make sure that their visit coincides with a home match of Cobreloa, perhaps the most successful Chilean football team outside Santiago in the past 20 years or so.

Ins and outs

Getting there
See page 219 for further details
Calama is easily reached by regular buses from Antofagasta, and by less frequent buses from Iquique and Arica, which often travel overnight. For those heading to Uyuni in Bolivia, there is a weekly train and 2 weekly buses. There is also 1 weekly bus to Salta in Argentina.

Getting around
The central part of Calama is relatively compact, and you should not need to take public transport. There are, though, many *colectivos*, most of which pick up on Abaroa or Vargas.

Tourist office
The Sernatur office is at Latorre 1689, T345345, calamainfotour@entelchile.net, map of town, helpful. Open Mon-Fri 0900-1300, 1430-1900. There is also the Automóvil Club de Chile, Av Ecuador 1901, T/F342770.

Sights

The central plaza of Calama is the 21 de Mayo, a shady spot in which to relax. The peach-coloured **Catedral San Juan Bautista** on the west side makes a pleasant contrast to the colours of the desert. On the northeastern side of the plaza, the pedestrian walkway of Ramirez continues two blocks east; on the second block, visitors will not be able to miss the bright red, phallic statue of **El Minero**, erected as a tribute to the bravery of the region's miners, but which can also be seen as an unlikely piece of kitsch in the Atacama.

On Avenida B O'Higgins, 2 km from the centre, is the **Parque El Loa**, which contains a reconstruction of a typical colonial village built around a reduced-scale reproduction of Chiu Chiu church. ■ *1000-1800 daily*. Nearby in the park is the **Museo Arqueológico y Etnológico**, with an exhibition of pre-hispanic cultural history. ■ *Tue-Sun 1000-1300, 1500-1930, US$0.40.* There is also the new **Museo de Historia Natural**, with an interesting collection on the *oficinas* and on the region's ecology and palaeontology. ■ *Wed-Sun 1000-1300, 1430-2000, US$0.65.*

Essentials

L *Lican Antai*, Ramírez 1937, T341621, hotellicanantai@terra.cl With breakfast, central, good service and good restaurant, TV. Recommended. **L-AL** *Hostería Calama*, Latorre 1521, T341511, hcalama@directo.cl Comfortable, good food and service. **L-AL** *Hotel Paradise Desert*, Ramirez 1867, T/F341618, paradise_hotel@hotmail. com Internet, more expensive rooms with jacuzzi, excellent views, nice terrace, good for business people. **AL** *Alfa*, Sotomayor 2016, T342496, hotelalfa@terra. cl Comfortable, good service. **AL** *Park*, Camino Aeropuerto 1392, T319900, F319901 (Santiago T233-8509). First class, pool, bar and restaurant. Recommended. **AL** *Quitor*,

Sleeping
■ *on map below*
Price codes:
see inside front cover

Calama

■ **Sleeping**	11 Hostal Internacional	● **Eating**
1 Alfa	12 Hostal Splendid	1 Bavaria
2 Atenas	13 Hostería Calama	2 Club Croata
3 Capri 1	14 John Kenny	3 Di Giorgio
4 Capri 2	15 Lican Antai	4 Los Adobes de
5 Casablanca	16 Los Andes	Balmaceda
6 Casa de Huéspedes	17 Mirador	5 Mariscal JP
7 Claris Loa	18 Olimpo	6 Nueva Chong Hua
8 El Loa	19 Palermo	7 Pollo Scout
9 Génesis	20 Paradise Desert	8 Pukará
10 Hostal Coco	21 Quitor	9 Tropicana

Antofagasta, Calama and San Pedro

Ramirez 2116, T341716, hotelquitor@terra.cl Central, pleasant, helpful. Good. **A** *El Mirador*, Sotomayor 2064, T/F340329, hotelelmirador@ hotmail.com With bath, good atmosphere, clean, helpful. Recommended. **A** *Olimpo*, Santa Maria 1673, T342367. Good. **B** *Casablanca*, Sotomayor 2160, T341938. Clean. **B** *John Kenny*, Ecuador 1991, T341430. Modern, clean, friendly, parking.

C *Atenas*, Ramirez 1945, T342666, F316399, with bath and cable TV, but small rooms, expensive laundry service, breakfast extra, overpriced. **C** *Genesis*, Granaderos 2148, T342841, cheaper double rooms, **E**, near Geminis bus terminal, clean. Recommended. **C** *Hostal Coco*, Sotomayor 2215, T310591. Clean, with private bathroom and breakfast, US$2 to store luggage. **D** *El Loa*, Abaroa 1617, T341963. English spoken. **D** *Hostal Internacional*, Velázquez 1976, T342927. Basic, overpriced. **D** *Hostal Splendid*, Ramirez 1960, T341841. Central, clean, friendly, hot water, often full, good.

F *Palermo*, Sotomayor 1889, T341283, friendly, dark, central. **F** *San Sebastián*, Pinto 1902, T343810. With bath, good beds, meals available, decent choice, family run. **G** *Capri I*, Vivar 1639, T342870. Basic, small rooms. **G** *Capri 2*, Ramirez 1880. Basic, safe. **G** *Casa de Huéspedes*, Sotomayor 2079. Poor beds, basic but reasonable, pleasant courtyard, clean, hot shower. **G** *Cavour*, Sotomayor 1841, T317392, simple, basic, friendly. **G** *Claris Loa*, Granaderos 1631, T319079. Clean, quiet. **G** *Los Andes*, Vivar 1920, T341073. Good beds, noisy.

Eating
● *on map*

Mid-range *Bavaria*, Sotomayor 2095. Good restaurant with cafeteria downstairs, real coffee, open 0800, very popular, also at Latorre 1935. *Los Adobes de Balmaceda*, Balmaceda 1504. Excellent meat. *Los Braseros de Hans Tur*, Sotomayor 2030, good ambience, good food. *Mariscal JP*, Félix Hoyos 2127. Best seafood in town, not cheap but worth it. *Mexico*, Latorre 1986. Genuine Mexican cuisine, fairly expensive, live music at weekends. **Mid-range/cheap** *Continental*, Vargas 2180. Good seafood and fish, cheaper than *Mariscal JP* but less charm. Best Chinese is *Nueva Chong Hua*, Abaroa 2006, good. Recommended by those in the know. Several places in this range on Abaroa along the side of the Plaza 23 de Marzo: *Club Croata*, excellent value 4-course *almuerzo*, good service; *D'Alfredo Pizzeria*, vast and uninviting but good pizzas and *almuerzos*; *Di Giorgio*; pizzas, good coffee, ice cream, fancy building with a nice outlook, opens 0900. Recommended; *Plaza Restaurant*, good *almuerzos*, opens early, good service. Recommended. **Cheap** *Lascar*, Ramirez 1917. Good value *almuerzo*. Recommended. *Nueva Victoria*, Vargas y Abaroa. Good inexpensive *almuerzos* and à la carte, popular with locals. Highly recommended. *Pollo Scout*, Vargas 2102, Clean, friendly, popular, reasonable. **Seriously cheap** *Pukará*, Abaroa 2054B, typical local food. Highly recommended. Fruit juices at *Jugo Camelot*, Abaroa 1968 and *Tropicana*, Sotomayor 2043.

Entertainment

Calama comes alive at night. In the plaza, teenagers get off with one another and Argentine backpackers down on their luck ponder their next move. The pedestrian walkways of Ramírez are awash with the young, the old, beggars, hippies and an old man winding a barrel organ and displaying a parakeet. **Bars** *Karka's Pub*, Latorre 1986B, swish, good. *Schoperia Ché Carlitos*, Abaroa 1901, central, popular. **Discos** All out of town on Av Circunvalación. There are over 10 of them. *Kamikaza*, very expensive, and *Vox* are both recommended. **Cinema** at Ramírez 1970.

Festivals

Calama's annual festival takes place between **6 Feb-24 Feb**, and is full of different activities and celebrations – recommended for those in the area.

The tren de la muerte from Calama to Oruro

The line between Calama and Oruro in Bolivia is the only section of the old Antofagasta and Bolivia railway line still open to passenger trains. It is a long, slow journey, theoretically taking 24 hours to Uyuni and 36 hours to Oruro (in reality often up to 48 hours), one of the world's great train journeys but uncomfortable in the extreme - if your idea of fun is standing still at a border post for up to 10 hours, this is the trip for you. The journey is very cold, both during the day and at night (-15°C). From Calama the line climbs to reach its highest point at Ascotán (3,960 m); it then descends to 3,735 m at Cebollar, skirting the Salar de Ascotán. Chilean customs are at Ollagüe, where there is a delay of five to six hours while an engine is sent from Uyuni. Immigration formalities are conducted on the train but passengers are required to disembark with their luggage, to be searched on the Bolivian side. There are money changers on the train but beware of forged notes. From the border the line runs to Uyuni, 174 km northeast, crossing the Salar de Chiguana and running at an almost uniform height of 3,660 m. Uyuni is the junction with the line south to the Argentine frontier at Villazón.

A personal account: " A few years back, I was travelling with two friends in Bolivia, and decided to take the famous train back from Uyuni to Calama. We were told that the train would arrive in Uyuni at 2300, so we sat in the waiting room until 0230, when the train finally arrived. The 'train' in fact consisted of several different sections, each heading in a different direction – some carriages only to Potosí, others on to Villazón, and only two carriages to Chile. After running frantically up and down in the freezing temperatures, we finally found the right carriage. However, we went nowhere until dawn, when the driver awoke and decided to continue. We reached Ollagöe at 1000, and then spent the entire day waiting there as the Chilean border guards methodically searched every bag of every passenger for contraband goods – Bolivians travel with a lot of bags, and so the train did not leave Ollagöe until 2000. As we pulled out, the Chilean border guard remarked that the train was ahead of schedule. It arrived in Calama at 0300 the next morning, when, of course, most of the hotels were shut." Toby Green

Shopping

Market on Antofagasta between Latorre and Vivar, selling fruit juices and crafts. Craft is also sold at a set of stalls on Latorre 1600-block. **Supermarkets** *Economico*, Grecia 2314; *El Cobre*, Vargas 2148.

Tour operators
The tourist office (see above) also offers tours of the area

Several agencies run 1-day and longer tours to the Atacama region, including San Pedro; these are usually more expensive than tours from San Pedro and require a minimum number for the tour to go ahead. Reports of tour quality are mixed – poorly maintained vehicles and poor guides. Those with positive recommendations including: *Azimut 360*, T/F333040, www.azimut.cl Tours to the Atacama Desert, mountaineering expeditions to Licanábur and Llullaillaco; *Colque Tours*, Calle Caracoles, T851109, F851446, colquetours@terra.cl 4WD tours of Andes and salt plains into Bolivia, good guides, well maintained vehicles, good food and accommodation; *Turismo Buenaventura*, T/F341882, buenventur@entelchile.net Recommended; *Turismo El Sol*, V Mackenna 1812, T340152, main office in San Pedro de Atacama; *Turismo Tujina*, Ramirez 2222, T/F342261.

Transport
Car hire is not readily available in San Pedro de Atacama

Local Car hire: *Avis*, Gallo 1985A, T319757; *Budget*, Granaderos 2925, T341076; *Hertz*, Latorre 1510, T341380; *IQSA*, O'Higgins 877, T310281. A 4-WD jeep (necessary for the desert) costs US$87-118 a day. Rates are sometimes much lower at weekends. A hired car, shared between several people, is an economic alternative for visiting the Atacama region. **Cycle spares** *Cicles Miranda*, Sotomayor 2271, T342769.

Long distance Air: *LanChile/Ladeco* to Santiago via Antofagasta, 5 daily, US$180. Taxi to town US$6 (courtesy vans from hotels *Calama, Alfa* and *Lican Antai*). Transport to airport also with Alberto Molina, T324834, US$3, recommended.

Bus: No main terminal, buses leave from company offices: *Tur Bus*, Ramirez y Balmaceda; *Pullman Bus*, Sotomayor 1808; *Géminis*, O'Higgins 078; *Kenny Bus*, Vivar 1954; *Flota Barrios*, Ramírez 2298. To **Santiago** 22-24 hrs, US$25 (*sálon cama* US$40); to **Arica**, usually overnight, US$9, 8 hrs, or change in Antofagasta; to **Valparaíso/Viña del Mar**, US$25; to **Iquique**, 8 hrs, via Chuquicamata and Tocopilla, US$7, most overnight, but *Tur Bus* have 1 early morning and 1 mid-afternoon service. To **La Serena**, usually with delay in Antofagasta, 15 hrs, US$17. To **Chuquicamata** (see below). To **San Pedro de Atacama**, *Tur Bus*, daily 0950, *Atacama 2000*, 3 a day from Abaroa y Antofagasta, *Frontera*, 9 a day from Antofagasta 2142, last bus 2030, US$1.50, 1½ hrs; to **Antofagasta**, 3 hrs, several companies, US$4. **To Argentina** *Tur Bus* services leave for **Salta** at 0915 on Weds, US$30, *Géminis* on Tue and Fri for US$32 (leaving from Pullman Bus Terminal), 22 hrs. **To Bolivia** *Buses Manchego* leave for Uyuni at midnight on Wed and Sun, US$10.50, also serving Ollague for US$5.25, T318466.

Train To Uyuni and Oruro (Bolivia), weekly service, Wed 2300 (in theory), US$10.50 to Uyuni, US$15 to Oruro, journey time to Oruro up to 48 hrs. Station closes for lunch 1300 to 1500, no luggage store. Book seats in advance (passport essential) from railway station after 1500 on the day of travel. Catch the train as early as possible: although seats are assigned, the designated carriages may not arrive; passengers try to occupy several seats to sleep on but will move if you politely show your ticket. Sleeping bag and/or blanket essential. Restaurant car serves cheap food and drinks, with waiter service; food is also available at Ollagüe. No heating on freight train to Ollague, and it gets very cold overnight. (See box, page 219.)

Remember that between October and March, Chilean time is 1 hour later than Bolivian

A freight train with 1 or 2 passenger cars attached leaves Calama for Ollagüe Saturday 2300, return departure unknown, check details beforehand, buy ticket a few hours before departure, US$5 one way, not crowded. Note that there is no connecting passenger train and riding on goods trains from Ollagüe into Bolivia is not allowed. No accommodation in Ollagüe.

Directory **Airline offices** *Ladeco/LanChile*, Latorre 1499, T341477/341494 and airport, T311331. **Banks** Rates are generally poor especially for TCs. *Corp Banca*, Sotomayor 2041. Visa, ATM. *Finandes*, Latorre 1763. Mastercard. Many Redbanc ATMs on Latorre and Sotomayor. **Casas de Cambio:** *Moon Valley Money Exchange*, Sotomayor 1960, and also another exchange at Sotomayor 1837. Also on Ramirez, next to Centro Comercial Gala, most open Sat. Try also shop at Ramírez 1434 and *La Media Luna* clothes store, Ramírez 1992 (poor rates). Poor rates for buying and selling Bolivian currency. **Communications** **Post office**: Granaderos y V Mackenna. 0830-1300, 1530-1830, Sat 0900-1230, will not send parcels over 1 kg. **Telecommunications:** *CTC*, Sotomayor 1825. *Entel*, Sotomayor 2027. **Internet**: *Centro Internet*, Vargas 2054, US$1.50/hr. *Cybercafé*, Vargas 2014, piso 2, T318925, US$1.50/hr. *Cybercafé Machi*, Vivar 1944. **Consulates** **Bolivia**, Sr Reynaldo Urquizo Sosa, Bañados Espinoza 2232, Apdo Postal 85, T341976. Open (in theory) 0900-1230 and 1530-1830 Mon-Fri, friendly, helpful. **Film** *Fuji Film* at Abaroa 1922. **Laundry** *Universal*, Vargas 2178 (cheapest). *Lavexpress*, Sotomayor 1887. Good, speedy.

Copper: Chilean red gold

Although copper was mined in Chile in pre-Inca times, it only became important after independence. For much of the 19th century Chile was the world's leading copper producer, until new technology helped the US overtake her in 1882. After 1900, US investment and technology led to increased Chilean copper production, exploiting low-grade deposits through the use of large-scale open cast mining (as at Chuquicamata) and using new methods for separating the ore.

Copper was soon at the heart of a close relationship between Chile and the US. During the First World War, US demand for copper for arms manufacturing led to a 400% growth in Chilean copper production; by 1918, US investors controlled 87% of Chilean copper. Among the American corporations were the Chile Exploration Company, American Smelting, Kennecott and Braden, but by the 1960s two companies, Kennecott and Anaconda, dominated.

During the 1950s the role of the US in the Chilean economy became a controversial issue in Chilean politics; US ownership of copper, which in 1970 accounted for 78.5% of Chilean commodity exports, was seen as a symbol of Washington's domination. The Christian Democrat government of Eduardo Frei (1964-70) met the calls for nationalization with what it called Chileanization: under this the state took a controlling 51% share of the large companies. Complete nationalization was promised by Popular

Unity in its 1970 election manifesto, but nationalization was popular not only on the left; many conservatives supported it as a way of reducing US influence. The nationalization bill of 1971 passed through the Chilean Congress with the support of all parties. The large mines were taken over completely and placed under the control of CODELCO-Chile (Corporación Nacional del Cobre de Chile), which became the largest copper mining and refining company in the world.

Although the Pinochet government of 1973-90 sold off most state-run industries to the private sector, CODELCO was not touched. However, since the 1980s new mining laws have encouraged private investment in new mines. This has led to the opening of large new private mines and an increase in Chilean copper output from 1.6 million to 2.2 million metric tonnes between 1990 and 1995. The biggest new mine is La Escondida, where production began in 1990 . The mine now produced an output of 800,000 a year, making it the world's leading mine. At Collahuasi, 330,000 metric tonnes a year is now produced. Although some of CODELCO's older mines are in decline, it too is opening new mines.

Since 1982, Chile has once again been the world's leading producer of copper. Despite the growth of new exports such as fruit and wine, copper is likely to remain of central importance to the Chilean economy, as it has been since the collapse of nitrates in the 1920s.

Chuquicamata

Sixteen kilometres north of Calama, Chuquicamata is the site of the world's largest open-cast copper mine, employing 8,000 workers and operated by Codelco, the state copper corporation. Although copper has been mined here since pre-Inca times, it was the Guggenheim brothers who introduced modern mining and processing techniques after 1911 and made Chuquicamata into the most important single mine in Chile. Chuquicamata is about to be changed forever, though, as the town which surrounds the mine is to be closed by 2003 and the families are being moved to Calama, leaving only a small historical centre for visitors (see box, page 222). This will make Chuquicamata the largest of the Atacama's long line of ghost towns.

Phone code: 055
Colour map 1, grid C2
Population: 12,722
Altitude: 2,800 m

A visit here is truly memorable

Antofagasta, Calama and San Pedro

The Death of Chuqui

The town of Chuquicamata has always been famous in Chile. Quite apart from the fact that the mine is responsible for a large part of Chile's GDP, miners at "Chuqui" are treated differently, with free healthcare in a special modern hospital in the town of Chuqui and arranged housing in the town by the mine. The decision to move all those living in Chuqui down to Calama is very sad for those who have grown up and lived in the town, and will have a severe impact on both the people of Chuqui and on nearby Calama.

Some 2,500 families are to be moved from Chuqui to Calama. New neighbourhoods are being built in Calama on the outskirts of the town, near the road to Chiu Chiu. The famous hospital has already been transferred to Calama, which will of course be of great benefit to the city. By 2003, the move is expected to be complete. The two reasons for the change are the reserves of copper lying beneath the town of Chuqui, and the risks of pollution for those living there. Certainly, anyone approaching Calama only has to look at the great cloud which hangs to the north to appreciate the dangers of pollution in Chuqui, but, nevertheless, the move and the death of the town are momentous and sad events in the history of the north of Chile.

A visit to the mine at Chuquicamata is highly recommended for the insight it gives into the industry which bankrolls Chile's economy. It also gives fantastic views of the desert *pampa* and the volcanoes to the east. Everything about the mine is huge: the pit from which the ore is extracted is 4 km long, 2 km wide and 630 m deep; the giant trucks, with wheels over 3 m high and tyres worth over US$6,000 each, carry 255-ton loads and work 24 hours a day since the pit is floodlit at night. In other parts of the plant 60,000 tons of ore are processed a day. Although the ore extracted is low grade, refined copper of 99.98% purity is produced. Since 1986 output has been over 500,000 tonnes a year, but the diggers are having to cut ever deeper into the desert, making the extraction process increasingly expensive. It is this which has fuelled the decision to move the people of Chuquicamata down to Calama, as this will enable Codelco to exploit the copper which is buried in the earth beneath the houses.

■ *Guided tours, by bus, in Spanish (also in English if enough people) leave from the office of Chuqui Ayuda (a local children's charity) near the entrance at the top end of the plaza, Mon-Fri 0945 (though less frequently in low season – tourist office in Calama has details), 1 hr, US$2.50 is requested as a donation to the charity; register at the office half-an-hour in advance; passport essential. No filming permitted. In order to get on the tour, the tourist office in Calama recommends that you catch a* colectivo *from Calama at 0800.*

Eating   Cheap lunches available at the *Club de Empleados* and at *Arco Iris* both facing the bus terminal – though these will both close when the town is shut down.

Transport   From Calama yellow *colectivos* (marked 'Chuqui') from the corner of the Plaza 23 de Marzo, US$0.75. Buses to **Arica** at 2200 (weekends at 2300), US$9, 9 hrs; to **Antofagasta**, US$5; to **Iquique**, US$7; to **Santiago**, US$26, 24 hrs.

North and east of Calama

Chiu Chiu was one of the earliest centres of Spanish settlement in the area. Set in the shadow of the Volcán San Pedro, it is a peaceful oasis village and a nice contrast to the bustle of Calama. In the glades nearby, horses graze on surprisingly lush grasses and the local people cultivate alfalfa. Chiu Chiu's plaza, fringed with pepper trees and opposite the church, is a nice place to while away a few hours. The church of **San Francisco**, dating from 1611, has roof beams of cactus and walls over 1 m thick – please leave a donation. Some 10 km distant on the road to Caspana is a unique, perfectly circular, very deep lake, called Chiu Chiu or Icacoia.

Essentials C*Hostal Chiu Chiu*, Esmeralda s/n, T326386, friendly and helpful. Mid-range meals can be had at the *Café Tambo* , which is a nice place with very old wooden furniture. There are *colectivos* to/from Calama with Línea 80, T362523, about 8 a day, US$2. To catch one, either ring ahead in Calama, or take the Línea 80 *colectivo* on Abaroa to the end of the line in Calama and then catch the next vehicle to Chiu Chiu.

From Chiu Chiu, the *ripio* road continues north towards Ollagüe. Just beyond the oasis, a small turning branches off the main road and follows the course of the Río Loa. Here the canyon is green with crops, and donkeys plough the earth – it seems like a secret valley. This area has been settled for millenia, and petroglyphs are clearly visible in the rocks on the right-hand side of the road heading towards the small hamlet of **Lasana**, 8 km north of Chiu Chiu, where there are striking ruins of a pre-Inca *pukará*, a national monument; drinks are on sale. If arranged in advance, the *colectivos* of Linea 80 will continue on to Lasana for an extra charge – you will have to book the return trip, or walk back to Chiu Chiu.

At **Conchi**, 25 km north of Lasana, the road crosses the Río Loa via a bridge dating from 1890; there is a spectacular view over the river from the bridge, but it is a military zone, so no photographs are allowed. Access to the river is by side tracks, best at Santa Bárbara. There is interesting wildlife and flower meadows and trout fishing in season. You can obtain a permit from Gobernación in Calama.

From Conchi a road branches east following the valley of the Río San Pedro, which has been a route for herders and silver caravans for centuries, to Inacaliri, from where a very poor road (four-wheel drive essential) runs south to Linzor and the geysers of El Tatio (see page 231). While there are several direct routes east from Chiu Chiu towards the geysers of El Tatio, only one is in good condition: just north of Chiu Chiu turn right off the Ollagüe road and continue until you reach a fork some 22 km east of Chiu Chiu. Take the right fork, ignoring the large sign pointing leftwards to El Tatio; this leads to a very bad track via Linzor. At Km 47 a track turns off north to Caspana. At about Km 65 the main road climbs steeply up the Cuesta de Chita. At about Km 80, branch left to Tatio; this branch meets the main Tatio-San Pedro road some 5 km further north.

Caspana is beautifully set among hills with a tiny church dating from 1641 and a museum with interesting displays on Atacameño culture. Basic accommodation is available. A poor road runs north and east of Caspana through valleys of pampas grass with llama herds to **Toconce**, which has extensive prehispanic terraces set among some interesting rock formations. At Toconce, a community tourism project has recently been set up, designed to help stem the flow of people moving away to an impoverished urban existence in Calama. Three rooms are available, and there is accommodation for up to 12 people, with full board. There are many archaeological sites nearby, and the area is ideal for hiking, with the Cerros Toconce, León and Paniri – all over 5,500 m – nearby. Further information on the project can be had from the tourist office in Calama, who may also help with arranging transport, or from toconce@mixmail.com, T321828. Given the fragility of these Andean communities, and that this is the community's first foray into tourism, please visit with as much sensitivity as possible. If visiting Toconce, it is also a good idea to check in with the *carabineros* in the plaza.

Twenty kilometres west of Toconce is **Ayquina**, in whose ancient church is enshrined the statue of the Virgin of Guadalupe. Her feast-day is 8 September, when pilgrims come from far and wide. There is day-long group dancing to Indian rhythms on flute and drum. Towards sunset the Virgin is carried up a steep trail to a small thatched shrine, where the image and the people are blessed before the dancing is renewed at the shrine and all the way back to the village. The poor people of the hills gather stones and make toy houses all along the route: miniatures of the homes they hope to have some day.

Six kilometres north of Ayquina are the lukewarm thermal waters of the **Baños de Turi** and the ruins of a 12th-century *pukará* which was the largest fortified town in the Atacama mountains. Southwest of Ayquina is **Cupo**, which has a *fiesta*, San José, on 19 March. Between this village and Turi is a large, ruined prehispanic settlement at **Paniri** with extensive field systems, irrigation canals (including aqueducts) and a necropolis. Some of the fields are still in use. The area around Cupo is one of the best for seeing the Atacama giant cactus (*Notocereus atacamensis*). Flamingos can be seen on the mudflats. The Vega de Turi is an important site for the llama and sheep herders, who believe it has curative properties. At several times in the year, especially September, herders from a wide area congregate with their flocks.

The route to Ollagüe
Do not deviate from the road, as the desert to the eastern side of the road is extensively covered by minefields

From Chiu Chiu a road runs to Ollagüe, 240 km north on the Bolivian border. The first section to Estación San Pedro is in poor condition, but from Estación San Pedro to Ascotán it is worse. There is a *carabinero* checkpoint at Ascotán, the highest point of the road at 3,900 m. North of Ascotán the road improves as it crosses the Salares de Ascotán and Ollagüe. Ask at Ascotán or Ollagüe about the conditions before setting out, especially in December and January or August. There are many llama flocks along this road, and flamingos on the *salares*. There is no petrol between Calama and Uyuni in Bolivia. If you are really short, try buying from the *carabineros* at Ollagüe or Ascotán, the military at Conchi or the mining camp at Buenaventura. The only real answer is to take enough.

Ollagüe

Colour map 1, grid B3
Population: 433
Altitude: 3,696 m

Situated 198 km north of Calama on the dry floor of the Salar de Ollagüe, Ollagüe is surrounded by a dozen volcanic peaks of over 5,000 m. It is a cold, dusty, windswept place, but nevertheless is remarkable for its sense of remoteness.

Five kilometres south of Ollagüe is the sulphur mining camp of Buenaventura, which is situated at an altitude of 5,800 m, only 150 m short of the summit of Ollagüe Volcano. Camping is possible, and there are amazing views over the volcanoes and salt flats. A road leads to the sulphur camp, but be wary of walking the route if not coming from Bolivia, as you will not yet be acclimatised for exercise at this altitude.

A 77-km spur railroad of metre gauge runs north from Ollagüe to the copper mines of Collahuasi, but these cannot be visited. A road runs west from Ollagüe to the sulphur mines, now closed, of Aucanquilcha, formerly the highest mine in the world at 5,300 m, where there are the ruins of an aerial tram system. From the mine you can scramble to the summit of Aucanquilcha, at 6,176 m, where there are superb views. A high clearance vehicle is needed to drive to the mine. An interesting excursion can be made north from Ollagüe to the village of **Coska** with its traditional agriculture and herds of llamas and alpacas.

At this altitude nights are cold, the days warm and sunny. Minimum temperature at Ollagüe is -20°C, and at Buenaventura mine, -37°C. There are only 50 mm of rain a year, and water is very scarce.

Sleeping There is nowhere to stay in Ollagüe, but police and border officials will help find lodgings. **Festivals** On **19 Jun** is the *Fiesta de San Antonio de Padua*, patron saint of Ollagüe, characterized by Quechua dancing and customs, such as the sacrifice of llamas. **Transport** Buses Manchego from Calama, US$5.25, 5 hrs, Wed, Sun at 2400; returns next day. Ollagüe can be reached by taking the Calama-Oruro train (see page 220) but, if you stop off, you will have to hitch back as the daily freight trains are not allowed to carry passengers. Hitching is difficult but the police may help you to find a truck.

Essentials
There is no fuel in Ollagüe

A poor road leads across the frontier and runs to Uyuni, 170 km east. Trucks take a more northerly route across the Salar de Uyuni. Motorists are warned against using this route into Bolivia. There is the danger of getting lost on the many tracks leading over the deserted salt lakes, no gasoline between Calama (Chile) and Uyuni, and little hope of help with a breakdown on the Bolivian side unless you don't mind waiting for perhaps a week. After rain the route is impassable and even experienced guides get lost. Maps give widely differing versions of the route. Where the road has been built up, **never** forsake it for the appealing soft salt beside it. The salt takes a person's weight but a vehicle breaks through the crust into unfathomable depths of plasticine mud below.

Into Bolivia
Immigration and customs open 0800-2000

At Paso Barros Arana (Km 58) there is an unpaved turning to the left which leads through interesting desert scenery to the small, mud-brick village of Río Grande. Look out for vicuñas and guanacos on the pass. The main road continues, and skirts the Cordillera de la Sal about 15 km from San Pedro. There are spectacular views of the sunset over to the Western Cordilleras. The old unpaved road to San Pedro turns off the new road at Km 72 and crosses this range through the Valle de La Luna (see Excursions below), but should only be attempted by four-wheel drive vehicles. This road is partly paved with salt blocks.

Calama to San Pedro de Atacama

San Pedro de Atacama

Situated 103 km by paved road southeast of Calama, San Pedro is an oasis town in the valley of the Río San Pedro. While San Pedro is now famous among visitors as the centre for excursions in this part of the Atacama, it was important as the centre of the Atacameño culture long before the arrival of the Spanish. There is a definite sense of history in the shady streets and the crumbling ancient walls which drift away from the town into the fields, and then into the dust. Owing to the clear atmosphere and isolation, there are wonderful views of the night sky after the electricity supply is switched off.

*Phone code: 055
Colour map 1, grid C3
Population: 2,824
Altitude: 2,436m*

No food, water or fuel along the Calama-San Pedro road

Getting there San Pedro can be reached by bus from Calama. There are 3 companies – *Atacama 2000*, *Frontera* and *Tur Bus* – and there are 12 buses a day in total to/from Calama. **Getting around** San Pedro is so small that there are no taxis or *colectivos*. **Tourist office** Sernatur has an office in the plaza, but it has little information and is rarely open. **Climate** Be prepared for the harsh climate and high altitudes of the interior. Gloves, a hat and a warm coat are essential for excursions from San Pedro, especially for the early morning trip to El Tatio. High factor sun cream and (again) a hat are necessary for the burning daytime sun.

Ins & outs
See page 230 for further details

Take plenty of water on any excursion

History

The main centre of the Atacameño culture which flourished in this region before the arrival of the Incas around 1450, San Pedro was defended by a *pukará* (fortress) at Quitor, 3 km north. The cultivable land around was distributed in 15 *ayllos* (socio-economic communities based on family networks) and irrigation channels were built. San Pedro was visited by both Diego de Almagro and Pedro de Valdivia and the town became a centre of Spanish colonial control; a mission was established in 1557. After independence the town became an important trading centre on the route between Cobija on the coast and Salta in Argentina, but the decline of Cobija and the rise of copper-mining led to San Pedro's replacement as an economic centre by Calama.

In the early 20th century, San Pedro's economy was based around mining, with salt mines in the Valle de la Luna (whose ruins are easily visible today) and sulphur mines in the high mountains. Since the 1970s, tourism has been of increasing importance, and the town is now dependent on the annual influx of Chilean and foreign visitors. However, travellers should be aware that tourism is a somewhat divisive issue in San Pedro. The tour companies are often run by outsiders, and the glut of travel agencies has led to a tenfold increase in rents in the past ten years; many of the local people still work in agriculture, having lower incomes than those who work with tourism, and, with 25 tour companies and not enough tourists to go round, there are dark (and doubtless somewhat exaggerated) rumours that some of these operations are fronts for money laundering and drug running, especially with Bolivia so close.

Sights

The **Iglesia de San Pedro**, dating from the 17th century, is supposedly the second oldest church in the country. It has been heavily restored and the tower was added in 1964. The roof is made of cactus; inside, the statues of Mary and Joseph have fluorescent light halos. Nearby, on the Plaza, is the **Casa Incaica**, the oldest building in San Pedro.

The Museo Arqueológico has the collection of Padre Gustave Paige, a Belgian missionary who lived in San Pedro between 1955 and 1980. It is now under the care of the Universidad Católica del Norte. One of the most important museums in northern Chile, it traces the development of pre-hispanic Atacameño society. It is well organized; the labels (in Spanish only) on displays are good and there is a comprehensive booklet in Spanish and English. Graham Greene observed "the striking feature of the museum is the mummies of Indian women with their hair and dresses intact dating from before the Conquest, and a collection of paleolithic tools which puts the British Museum in the shade". ■ *US$1.50, Mon-Fri 0900-1300, 1500-1900; Sat and Sun 1000-1200, 1500-1800, museospa@entelchile.net No heating: wear warm clothing.*

Excursions

For Toconao, the Salar de Atacama and the Geysers of El Tatio, all of which can be visited on tours from San Pedro, see below

Valle de la Luna is 12 km west, with fantastic landscapes caused by the erosion of salt mountains. The valley is crossed by the old San Pedro-Calama road. Although buses on the new road will stop to let you off where the old road branches off 13 km northwest of San Pedro (signposted to Peine), it is far better to travel from San Pedro on the old road, either on foot (allow three hours there, three hours back; no lifts), by bicycle or by car. The Valle is best seen at sunset, although with hundreds of fellow tourists nearby it is not a

Archaeology of the Atacama

From very early times, people settled along the northern coast of Chile, sustained by the food supply from the Pacific Ocean. Since about 7600 BC, fisherfolk and foragers lived in relatively large groups in permanent settlements, such as the Quebrada de Conchas, just to the north of Antofagasta. They fished with fibre nets, sometimes venturing inland to hunt for mammals.

About 2,000 years later the successors of these people, the 'Chinchorros', developed one of the deepest characteristics of Andean cultures, veneration for their ancestors. The role of the dead in the world of the living was vital to the earliest Andean people. As a link between the spiritual and the material world, the ancestor of each local kin group would protect his clan. The expression of these beliefs came in the form of veneration of the ancestors' bodies; sacrifices were made to them, funeral rites were repeated, and precious grave offerings were renewed. In the arid climate of the Atacama, the people observed how bodies were naturally preserved. The skilled practice of mummification was thus developed, over a period of 3,000 years, dedicated to preserving the dead as sacred objects and spiritual protectors.

Another major cultural practice of northern Chile was the use of hallucinogens. Grave remains found in the region, dating from about AD 1000, include leather bags containing organic powder, wooden tablets and snuffer tubes. The tablets and snuffers were often decorated with supernatural figures, such as bird-headed angels, winged humans, star animals and other characters familiar in altiplano cultures. Although the origins and function of taking hallucinogens is not known for certain (see page 515), it is thought that the practice may have been brought down to the coast by traders from the highlands. There were also 'medicine men' who travelled throughout the central and south central Andes dispensing the drugs and healing the sick. As with cures still practised in the Andes and Amazonia, it is possible that the drugs were taken as part of religious rituals, and often for a combination of spiritual and physical healing.

particularly peaceful place at this time. Take water, hat, camera and torch. Also consider spending the night to see the sunrise (take warm clothes and plenty of water). Agencies in San Pedro offer tours, departing 1530, returning 1900, US$4-6 per person, but make sure the agency departs in time for arrival in the Valle before sunset as they do not always do so. Tours usually include a visit to the **Valle de la Muerte**, a crevice in the Cordillera de la Sal near San Pedro, with all the rock walls red and contorted into fantastic shapes.

Three kilometres north of San Pedro along the river is the **Pukará de Quitor**, a pre-Inca fortress restored in 1981. The fortress, which covers 2.5 ha on a hillside on the west bank of the river, was stormed by the Spanish under Pedro de Valdivia, 1,000 defenders being overcome by 30 horsemen who vaulted the walls. The road to Quitor involves fording the river several times, until the Pukará comes into view on the hill on the left-hand side of the valley; there is a new plaza here, built as a homage to the indigenous people of the region, and set amid thorn trees. The road continues along the valley of the Río San Pedro as the canyon climbs further into the Atacama, passing a couple of small farmsteads sheltered by pepper trees where sheep graze in the desert sun. A further 4 km up the river there are ruins at Catarpe, which was the Inca administrative centre for this region. The ruins are on top of a hill on the east side of the valley, and are difficult to find without a guide – archaeological tours are offered in San Pedro.

Antofagasta, Calama and San Pedro

At **Tulor**, 12 km southwest of San Pedro, there is an archaeological site where parts of a village (dated 500-800 BC) have been excavated. The road is impassable to cars, but it is worth a visit on foot and you can sleep in two reconstructed huts, or take a tour, US$5. Nearby are the ruins of a 17th-century Spanish-style village, abandoned in the 18th century because of lack of water.

Essentials

San Pedro has electricity in the evening (until 2400), but take a torch (flashlight) for walking at night. *Residenciales* supply candles, but better to buy them in Calama beforehand. San Pedro is an expensive town and accommodation is particularly expensive in Jan and Feb when it may also be scarce. Drink bottled water as, owing to arsenic reserves in the desert, the local supply is not drinkable.

Sleeping L *Explora*, Av Américo Vespucio Sur 80, 5 piso, Santiago, T2066060, F2284655,
■ *on map* explora@entelchile.net Luxury full board and excursion programme, 3 nights, 4
Price codes: nights and 8 nights, advance booking only. L *Hostería San Pedro*, Solcor, T851011,
see inside front cover hsanpedro@chilesat.net Pool (residents only), petrol station, cabins, hot water, constant electricity, restaurant (good *almuerzo*) and bar. Accepts Amex but not TCs. L *Terrantai*, Tocopilla, T851140, F851032 (Casilla 10), terrantai@adex.cl Comfortable, but only offers all-inclusive packages, good restaurant. L *Tulor*, Atienza, T/F851248, tulor@chilesat.net Good service, swimming pool, heating, parking, laundry service, excellent restaurant. Recommended. **AL** *Kimal*, Atienza y Caracoles, T851159, F851030, kimal@entelchile.net Comfortable, nice living room, now expanding, excellent restaurant. A *El Tatio*, Caracoles, T851263, F851092, hoteleltatio@usa.net Comfortable, parking, small rooms, bargain off season, English spoken. **AL** *La Casa de Don Tomás*, Tocopilla, T851055, F851175, dontomas@rdc.cl Good accommodation, very pleasant inside, quiet, friendly, swimming pool, good restaurant. Recommended.

B *Casa Corvatsch*, on Le Paige, T/F851101, corvatsch@entelchile.net Many cheaper rooms **F** pp. Pleasant views, English/German spoken, usually recommended, but some mixed reports. B *Hostal Inti Kamac*, on Atienza, T851200. Pleasant veranda, with bath, friendly, good value. B *Hostal Takha-Takha*, Caracoles, T851038, or **F** pp for cheaper rooms. Pretty, lovely garden, nice patio, nice rooms. Camping **G** pp. Laundry facilities. B *Hotel Tambillo*, on Le Paige opposite Casa Corvatsch, T/F851078. Pretty, benches on the patio, 24-hr electricity and hot water, good value. B *Res Don Rául*, Caracoles, T851138. With bath and mod cons, small rooms, or **F** pp for basic rooms. B *Res Licancábur*, Toconao, T851007, **C** off-season, much cheaper rooms **F/G** pp, clean, nicely furnished, friendly, a little basic. **C** *Katarpe*, Atienza, T851033, katarpe@galeon.com Comfortable, quiet, nice patio, good value, friendly. Recommended. **C** *Res Juanita*, on the plaza, T851039. With bath, **F** without, hot water, run down, decent value, restaurant. **C** *Res Rayco*, Antofagasta, T851008. Basic, overpriced.

D *La Quinta Adela*, Toconao, with private bath, hot water, no breakfast, good but expensive. **F** *Casa de Nora*, Tocopilla, T851114. Family accommodation, simple rooms, lovely patio. Recommended. **F** *Hostal Edén Atacameño*, Toconao, T851154, no singles, basic, also camping **H**. **F** *Res Chiloé*, Atienza, T851017. Hot water, sunny veranda, good clean bathrooms, good meals, laundry facilities, good beds, luggage store, good value. **F** *Residencial Vilacoyo*, on Toconao, friendly, kitchen facilities. **G** *Res Florida*, Tocopilla, T851021. Without bath, basic, clean, quiet patio, hot water evenings only, laundry facilities, no singles.

Camping *Camping Kunza*, Antofagasta y Atienza, T851183, **G**, but disco next door at weekends. Also *Camping Los Perales*, **F**.

Mid-range *Adobe*, Caracoles. Open fire, watch the moon rise, good meeting place, loud music, small portions, "Greenwich Village/Islington in the Atacama", somewhat supercilious service. *Café Export*, Toconao y Caracoles, nice décor, vegetarian options, real coffee, English spoken, loud music. *Casa Piedra*, open fire, friendly service, also has a cheap menu, many of the waiters are musicians who, if in the mood, will play Inti Illimanni or Victor Jara songs on panpipes and *queñas* late at night, good food and cocktails, warmly recommended. *Hosteria San Pedro*, good value almuerzo. *La Casona*, Caracoles. Good food, vegetarian options, cheap lunchtime menu, large portions, interesting cubist-style paintings of the desert, popular, warmly recommended. *Tulor*, Atienza. First class pizzeria, also à la carte menu, real coffee. **Cheap** *Café El Viaje*, on Tocopilla in the Casa de la Arte, nice patio, good for vegetarians. *Flamenco*, Calama y Caracoles, friendly service, bad food. *Quitor*, Licancabur y Domingo Atienza, T851056. Good, basic food, inexpensive (3 courses for US$3). **Seriously cheap** *Tahira*, on Tocopilla, excellent value *almuerzo*, local dishes, friendly. **Cafés** *Café Tierra Todo Natural*, Caracoles. Excellent fruit juices, "the best bread in the Atacama", real coffee, yoghurt, much the best choice for breakfast, opens earliest.

Eating
● on map
Price codes:
see inside front cover

Few places are
open before 1000

San Pedro de Atacama

Antofagasta, Calama and San Pedro

N
Not to scale

Sleeping
1 Camping Kunza
2 El Tatio
3 Hostal Edén Atacameño
4 Hostal Inti-Kamac
5 Hostal Takha-Takha
6 Hostería San Pedro
7 Katarpe
8 Kimal
9 La Casa de Don Tomás
10 Residencial Chiloé
11 Residencial Don Rául
12 Residencial Florida
13 Residencial Juanita
14 Residencial Licancábur
15 Residencial Rayko
16 Residencial Vilacoyo
17 Tambillo
18 Terrantai
19 Tulor

Eating
1 Adobe & Casa Piedra
2 Café Export
3 El Viaje
4 Flamenco
5 La Casona
6 La Estaka
7 Todo Natural

Entertainment **Bars** *Estaka*, Caracoles. Lively watering hole after 2300, where the Chilean new age scene congregates. Also very good cuisine and service. Recommended. **Discos** *La Esquina del Sol*, Le Paige y Atienza, opens weekends, does not get going until after midnight.

Shopping There is a good craft market on the plaza. Also try *Bazar Shaman*, excellent cheap goods, friendly, on Le Paige opposite the church.

Sports **Climbing** Licancábur (5,916m) on the border with Bolivia can only be climbed from the Bolivian side, see box on page 232.

Tour companies San Pedro is awash with tour operators, and, with competition so stiff, prices are low. Approximate prices for tours as follows (although these may rise in season): Valle de la Luna US$4-6, Salar de Atacama US$8-10, Geysers of Tatio US$12-14, Altiplano Lakes (including Toconao and Salar de Atacama) US$25-30. The following advice should help those trying to pick through the minefield of operators: avoid cut-price operators and try to check out vehicles and guides before booking; report any complaints to the Municipalidad or to Sernatur; if in doubt, check through the book with travellers' complaints at the Municipalidad. Spanish-speakers may prefer to go with one of the smaller operators, as English-speaking tours with big companies such as *Cosmo Andino* and *Desert Adventure*, while excellent, often have 15-20 people on them in season, thus meaning that the experience of the vastness of the desert is somewhat watered down. There are about 25 agencies, but some are impermanent and/or open for only part of the year. One of the best is *Cosmo Andino Expediciones*, Caracoles, T/F851069, cosmoandino@entelchile.net English, French, German, Dutch spoken, good vehicles, good drivers, experienced guides, large numbers, excellent book exchange, highly recommended for non-Spanish speakers. Dutch owner Martin Beeris is very knowledgeable about the region. *Desert Adventures*, Caracoles S/N, T/F851067, deserts@ctcinternet.cl, offers excursions to all the major sites, modern fleet of vehicles, large numbers. *Labra Turismo*, Caracoles, T851137. English, German spoken, reliable, owner Mario Banchón an expert guide who accompanies trips, good for visiting the altiplano lakes. Recommended. Others include: *Atacama Inca Tour*, Plaza, T581034, F851062. Recommended but not always open. *Expediciones Corvatsch*, Tocopilla. Operated jointly by Res Corvatsch and Res Florida, good vehicles, casual service, offer discounts for package tours with accommodation. *Pachamama Tours*, Toconao, T851064. Open for part of the year. *Turismo Ochoa*, Caracoles y Toconao, oldest operator in San Pedro, knowledgeable local guides who are a bit taciturn, inexpensive. Horseback tours are operated by *La Herradura*, Tocopilla s/n, laherraduraatacama@hotmail.com, good local guides, repeatedly recommended. Mountain climbs are run by *Petro Pizza*, on Toconao, go to infrequently visited areas, also hire out mountain bikes, recommended. For tours to Bolivia the specialists are *Turismo Colque*, Caracoles, T851109, who offer tours across the frontier into Bolivia including 1-day tour to Laguna Verde (US$90 per person) and 3-day tours to Laguna Colorado and the Salar de Uyuni (see below); TCs, Visa and Mastercard all accepted, reliable, hires sleeping bags, recommended, has agencies in Uyuni and La Paz.

Transport **Bus** To **Calama**, *Tur Bus*, 1800, (continues to Antofagasta); *Frontera* 7 a day, US$1.50, 1½ hrs, first 0900, last 1900. Frequencies vary with more departures in Jan/Feb and some weekends, fewer out of season. Book in advance to return from San Pedro Sun evening. *Frontera* also run to Toconao, 4 daily, 1240, 1600, 1930, 2030, US$0.80, and to Peine, 1600, returns 0600 next day, US$2. Daily direct service to Antofagasta, 1100. *Tur Bus* and *Géminis* services from Calama to Salta (Argentina) stop in San Pedro; book in Calama, Iquique or Antofagasta. **Car hire** Some agencies

El Tatio

The highest geyser in the world, El Tatio was formed as a result of water percolating through the porous volcanic rock until it gets trapped above a layer of impermeable rock. Here it comes into contact with intensely hot rock and is heated. As there is little space for it to expand and boil, pressure builds up until, *eventually, the water explodes to the surface, rushing out through cracks and fissures. On the way up, the very hot water dissolves the silica and other minerals in the surrounding rock. In the cold dry air at the surface the boiling water evaporates, leaving behind tiny crystals of silica and chloride.*

in San Pedro may offer vehicle hire, but you should check vehicle condition and insurance very carefully as there are reports of accidents involving uninsured and badly serviced vehicles. It may be better to hire cars in Calama. **Cycle hire** *Pangea*, Tocopilla, T851111. Most reliable, has best mountain bikes, rental US$2 per hr, US$15 per day. Treks organized, very knowledgeable. Warmly recommended. Several other agencies offer cycle hire, check prices.

Directory

Banks No banks or ATMs. *Cambio Atacama*, Toconao. Open daily 1030-1800, rates posted outside, good rates for US$ cash, poor rates for TCs. Best not to try changing TCs in San Pedro; take cash. Best to bring Chilean pesos from Calama. **Communications** **Internet** in *Café Adobe* and also in *Café Étnico*, on Tocopilla. **Post office**: On Padre Le Paige, opposite Museo Archaeológico. **Telephone**: *CTC*, Caracoles y Toconoa. *Entel* on the plaza, open Mon-Fri 0900-2200, Sat 0930-2200, Sun 0930-2100. Fax for incoming calls 851052. **Laundry** Alana on Caracoles, near Atienza.

The geysers of El Tatio

At an altitude of 4,321 m, the geysers of El Tatio are a popular attraction. From San Pedro they are reached by a maintained road which runs northeast, past the **Baños de Puritama** (28 km), then on a further 94 km. The geysers are said to be at their best 0630-0830, though the spectacle varies: locals say the performance is best when weather conditions are stable. A swimming pool has been built nearby. There is a workers' camp which is empty apart from one guard, who will let you sleep in a bed in one of the huts, **H**, take food and sleeping bag. From here you can hike to surrounding volcanoes if adapted to altitude, although it is advisable to take a guide because of the dangers of minefields. There is no public transport and hitching is impossible. If going in a hired car, make sure the engine is suitable for very high altitudes and is protected with anti-freeze; four-wheel drive is advisable. If driving in the dark it is almost impossible to find your way: the sign for El Tatio is north of the turn off. People have been killed or seriously injured by falling into the geysers, or through the thin crust of the mud. Do not stand too close either, as the geysers may belch forth unexpectedly.

Tours

Agencies in San Pedro operate tours to El Tatio, departing 0330, arriving at the geysers 0700, US$12-14, including breakfast. These offer opportunities to swim in the hot thermal pool and to visit the Baños de Puritama on the return journey. Take warm clothing and swimming costume. Some agencies offer tours to El Tatio and on to Calama, via some of the small Andean villages in between.

Antofagasta, Calama and San Pedro

Climbing Licancábur

Licancábur, 5,916 m, on the border between Chile and Bolivia, can only be climbed from the Bolivian side; the Chilean side is mined.

Licancabur was a sacred site for the Incas, and focal point of three Inca paths that crossed the altiplano and the Salar de Atacama – remains have been found at 5,500 m. To climb the volcano from the Bolivian side, drive from Laguna Verde to the prehispanic pukará, about 15 km further southwest. From here you need to start out at 0500 at the latest; follow the

riverbed straight up and hold right to the ridge after about three hours' climbing; there are red flags to show you the way. After about five hours you will pass the grave of a tourist killed in 1989, a reminder that the mountain is dangerous. After about eight hours you reach a flat section; from here it is still 1½ hours to the summit. To descend, go straight down the riverbed, allowing at least four to five hours. Take plenty of water. Beware of falling rocks. Note that there is no rescue service.

South of San Pedro de Atacama

From San Pedro to Toconao, 37 km south, the paved road runs through groves of acacia and pepper trees. There are many tracks leading to the wells (pozos) which supply the intricate irrigation system. Most have thermal water but bathing is not appreciated by the local farmers. The groves of trees are havens for wildlife especially rheas (ñandu) and Atacama owls, and there are also some llamas.

Zapar About 4 km before Toconao, vehicle tracks head east across the sand to a hidden valley 2 km from the road where there is a small settlement called Zapar. Here are some well-preserved prehispanic ruins on the rocky cliffs above the cultivated valley. The sand is very soft and a four-wheel drive vehicle is essential.

Toconao
Colour map 1, grid C3
Altitude: 2,600 m

Unlike San Pedro, Toconao's economy is based on agriculture, not tourism

This village is on the eastern shore of the Salar de Atacama. All houses are built of bricks of white volcanic stone, which gives the village an appearance totally different from San Pedro. The 18th-century church and bell tower are also built of volcanic stone. East of the village is a beautiful gorge called the **Quebrada de Jerez**, which is almost unimaginably verdant, and filled with fruit trees and grazing cattle. At the bottom of the gorge a crystal-clear stream cuts down towards Toconao. ■ *US$0.80 is charged to the Quebrada de Jerez.* Nearby is the quarry where the stone *sillar* is worked; it can be visited. The stones sound like bells when struck. Worth visiting also are the vineyards which produce a unique sweet wine. There are basic *residenciales*, **G** accommodation is also offered at the *Restaurant Lascar*, which has good, simple food. Camping is possible along the Quebrada de Jérez. ■ *Getting there: 4 Frontera buses daily to/from San Pedro, US$0.80. One continues on to Peine at 1700.*

Salar de Atacama
The third largest expanse of salt flats in the world

South of Toconao is one of the main entrances to the Salar de Atacama, 300,000 ha in extent. Rich in minerals including borax, potassium and an estimated 40% of world lithium reserves, the Salar is home to the pink flamingo and other birds (though these can only be seen when lakes form in winter). The air is so dry that you can usually see right across the Salar. ■ *US$3.* Three areas of the Salar form part of the **Reserva Nacional de los Flamencos**, in seven sectors totalling 73,986 ha, administered by CONAF in San Pedro. The

Antofagasta, Calama and San Pedro

Salar is home to three of the world's five species of flamingos: Andean, Chilean and James. The flamingos live by eating algae and tiny shellfish that subsist in the small saline pools in the Salar. This food contains the chemical that turns them pink, hence, the pinker the flamingo, the older it is.

Tours Agencies in San Pedro offer excursions to Toconao and the Salar, returning via the Quebrada de Jérez, US$8-10 plus park entry, usual departure 1530, but note that the flamingos are best seen in the morning, so try to get a morning tour, or combine with visiting the altiplano lakes.

South of Toconao

From Toconao the road heads south through the villages of **Camar**, where handicrafts from cactus may be bought, and **Socaire**, which has llama wool knitwear for sale; the road is paved as far as Socaire. About 20 km south of Socaire, a rough road leaves the main route to the Paso Sico and climbs a hill to the beautiful **Laguna Miscanti**, a lake which is part of the Reserva Nacional Los Flamencos. Nearby is the **Laguna Miñiques**. The lakes are on the site of ancient Atacameño hunting grounds, and arrowheads can still be found. The shores are edged with whorls of salt crystals, and there are clear views of the volcanoes behind the lake, as well as fantastic views down to the Salar. '*Miscanti*' means 'toad' in Aymará, and the lake used to be rich in toads. In the 1940s and 1950s, Americans working in Chuquicamata came here to fish, and

South of San Pedro de Atacama

Minefields: Beware

An indication of the nature of General Augusto Pinochet's geopolitics in the 1970s and 1980s is given by the numerous minefields which were placed along Chile's border with Bolivia and northern Argentina at that time. The minefields were put down to forestall possible invasion from Chile's neighbours, which was then perceived to be a very real threat. For foreign visitors in the new millennium, the consequence is that it is very unwise to make any lone forays into the altiplano without a knowledgeable local guide. Minefields are known to affect the new Parque Nacional Llullaihaico and the Chilean side of Volcan Licancabur, to give just two examples – and there may be other areas which are not known about. Always ask first before heading off into the northern wilderness.

trout were put into the lake as a result. This led to the decline of the population of toads – today there are none left. After the turning to the lakes, the road goes on to the mine at Laco, with one poor stretch below the mine, before proceeding to the Paso de Sico, which has replaced the higher, more northerly Guaytiquina pass, at 4,295 m, also spelt Huaytiquina, to Argentina.

Ten kilometres south of Toconao the old road branches east towards Guaytiquina. In a deep *quebrada* below Volcán Láscar is the small agricultural settlement of **Talabre**, with terracing and an ancient threshing floor. Above the *quebrada* is an isolated, stone-built cemetery. Large flocks of llamas graze where the stream crosses the road below the Láscar Volcano at 5,154 m. After a steep climb, you reach the **Laguna Lejía** at 4,190 m, where flamingos abound. You then pass through the high plains of **Guaytiquina** (4,275 m), where only a few herdsmen are found. This crossing is not open for road traffic to Argentina.

South from Toconao by 67 km, on a road that runs along the eastern edge of the Salar de Atacama, is the attractive village of **Peine**, which is the site of the offices of the lithium extraction company. It is worth asking if the company's access road can be used to visit the Salar de Atacama's spectacular salt formations. There is also a thermal pool where you can swim. Woollen goods and knitwear are made here and there is a daily bus by *Frontera* from San Pedro (see page 230). To the east of the village lies a group of beautifully coloured hills, whose colours are more vibrant at sunset, with good views over the Salar de Atacama. A path leads across these hills to Socaire; allow two days. Other villages worth visiting include Tilomonte and Tilopozo, south and west of Peine.

From Peine a road (64 km) crosses the Salar de Atacama; it joins a road which runs from San Pedro down the west side of the Salar and continues south to **Pan de Azúcar**, an abandoned railway station. Here it meets the paved road which leads from the Pan-American Highway, 50 km south of Antofagasta via La Escondida, a modern copper mine with an output of copper higher than any other mine in the world, to Socompa on the Argentine border. Between Pan de Azúcar and Socompa (poor road) is Monturaqui, the source of the green onyx which is much used for carving in northern Chile.

Parque Nacional Llullaillaco This recently created park covers 263,000 ha and includes Cerro Llullaillaco at 6,739 m, the second highest peak in Chile, as well as three other peaks over 5,000 m: Cerro de la Pena at 5,260 m, Guanaqueros, 5,131 m, and Aguas Calientes, 5,070 m. The park is inhabited by large numbers of guanacos and vicuñas. Access is via a poor road which turns off south from the La Escondida-Socompa road at Imilac, 10 km east of La Escondida. Visits by arrangement only with CONAF in Antofagasta, owing to the dangers of minefields in the area.

Border crossings from San Pedro

There are three crossings; the best is the most northerly, the **Paso de Jama** at 4,200 m, 165 km southeast of San Pedro, which is reached by a paved road that runs via the Salar de Tara which forms a sector of the Reserva Nacional de los Flamencos. The main alternative to this, **Paso de Sico** at 4,079 m, lies further south, 207 km southeast of San Pedro, and is reached by a poor road which runs via Toconao and Socaire (see above, page 233). This pass has replaced the higher **Paso de Guaytiquina** at 4,275 m. The most southerly crossing is **Paso de Socompa**, 3,865 m, which is reached by a poor road from Pan de Azúcar (see page 234).

Border with Argentina

Immigration There is a Chilean immigration and customs post at Paso Socompa, open 0800-2000. Chilean immigration and customs formalities for Paso de Jama and Paso de Sico are dealt with in San Pedro de Atacama, open 0900-1200, 1400-1600. Incoming vehicles are searched for fruit and dairy products.

Transport If crossing by private vehicle check road conditions with the *carabineros* and at immigration in San Pedro as these crossings are liable to be closed by heavy rain in summer and blocked by snow in winter. For bus services from Antofagasta, Calama and San Pedro to Jujuy and Salta, see above. If hitching try the immigration post in San Pedro; Spanish is essential.

Into Argentina On the Argentine side of the border all these roads link up and continue to San Antonio de los Cobres (where Argentina customs and immigration formalities take place) and Salta. Transport using the Paso de Jama crossing usually follows a more northerly alternative via Susques, where there is accommodation, and Jujuy. The most southerly route via Paso de Socompa is perhaps the most spectacular, crossing salt flats and wide expanses of desert, but this route is virtually unused.

The route to Argentina via the Paso de Jama

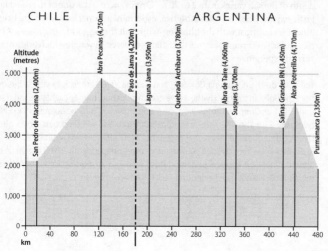

Border with Bolivia There are two crossings, the more northerly of which, via Ollagüe, is described above (see page 225). The more southerly crossing is at **Hito Cajones**, 45 km east of San Pedro via a poor road which turns off the paved road towards Paso de Jama at La Cruz, 8 km southwest of the frontier. Laguna Verde (see below) is 7 km north of Hito Cajones.

Immigration Chilean immigration and customs are in San Pedro, open 0900-1200, 1400-1600. Incoming vehicles are searched for fruit, vegetables and dairy products.

Transport There is no public transport: do not be tempted to hitch to the border as you risk being stranded without water or shelter at sub-zero temperatures. The most practicable method of crossing this border is with a tour from San Pedro (see below).

Into Bolivia: the Salar de Uyuni

East of San Pedro, on the border with Bolivia, lies the Licancábur Volcano (5,916 m) which can be climbed only from the Bolivian side, see box. The climbing season is all year except January-February. At the foot of the volcano on the Bolivian side is **Laguna Verde** (4,400 m), which extends over 17 sq km; its wind-lashed waters are an impressive jade, the result, it is said, of magnesium, or calcium carbonate, or lead, or arsenic. There is a *refugio* near the lake (US$2, small, mattresses, running water). Further north is the equally impressive **Laguna Colorada** (4,278 m) which covers 60 sq km; its flaming red waters are the result of the effects of the wind and afternoon sun on the micro-organisms which live in it (up to midday the water is pretty normal in colour). The water is less than a metre deep but the mud is very soft. The shores are encrusted with borax, which provides an arctic white contrast with the waters of the lake. The pink algae in the lake provide food for the rare James flamingos, which live here along with the more common Chilean and Andean flamingos. Some 40 other bird species can also be seen. Further north still, north of Ollagüe, is the **Salar de Uyuni**, the largest and highest salt lake in the world, an increasingly popular attraction for visitors. Situated at an altitude of 3,650 m and covering 9,000-12,000 sq km (depending on who you believe), the Salar is twice as big as the Great Salt Lake in the United States. The depth of the salt varies from 2 to 20 m. Driving across it is one of the most fantastic experiences in South America, especially in June/July when the bright blue skies contrast with the blinding-white salt (bring good sunglasses). After particularly wet rainy seasons the Salar is covered in water, which adds to the surreal experience.

Tours The Salar de Uyuni, Laguna Colorada and Laguna Verde are usually visited by tours from the Bolivian town of Uyuni, where accommodation, money exchange and transport to La Paz, Oruro and Potosi are all available. However, Turismo Colque in San Pedro (see page 230) also offers this tour from San Pedro and will drop passengers off for Uyuni, although some report that to see the colour changes on Laguna Colorada the trip is best done from Uyuni. If you intend to travel independently in this region do not underestimate the dangers of getting stuck without transport or accommodation at this altitude. Do not travel alone and seek full advice in advance.

Iquique, Arica and the Far North

8

Iquique, Arica and the Far North

PERU

Parque
Nacional
Lauca

Arica

Putre

SANTIAGO

Reserva Nacional
Las Vicuñas

Salar
de Surire

BOLIVIA

Parque Nacional
Volcán Isluga

Colchane

Pacific
Ocean

Mamiña

Iquique

Pozo
Almonte

La Tirana

Pica

The far north of Chile is equally as forbidding as the region around Antofagasta and Calama. North of the attractive city of Iquique, transport arteries head inland into the desert pampa. There is a definite sense of antiquity here in the few oases and settlements which are sprinkled across the Atacama; the profusion of geoglyphs are testament to the fact that, wherever there is water, people have been living for millennia. These geoglyphs of peoples now vanished, and the countless ghost towns of former nitrate oficinas, both stand witness to the harshness and fragility of life in the region.

Further inland still, towards the altiplano, are some beautiful spots. Mamiña and Pica are two thermal springs resorts near Iquique, each of them remarkable for their tranquillity. There are four national parks in the high Andes, the northernmost of which – the Parque Nacional Lauca – offers some of the most stunning scenery in Chile, with snow-capped volcanoes, a necklace of high lakes, lava fields and varied birdlife: it is easily reached from Arica, Chile's northernmost city, along the international road to Bolivia. Near Parque Nacional Lauca are small Andean villages such as Visviri and Parinacota, where most people speak Aymará and Spanish remains a foreign language, and three more remote national parks.

Background

History   As elsewhere in northern Chile, there was a widespread and highly developed network of pre-Hispanic cultures. The geoglyphs at sites such as Pintados and Tiliviche are thought to have been markers for caravans of traders making their way from the *altiplano* to and from the coast. Circles marked in the hillsides signalled the presence of water. As with further south in the Antofagasta area, the coastal peoples traded furs and fish with the more highly developed cultures of the interior, maintaining links with Tiahuanaco and, later, the Incas.

Even after the Spanish conquest, the early Spanish settler population was small in numbers. Settlement was concentrated largely in the oases of the *sierra*, where the climate was easier and where malaria, the scourge of the coast, was not found. From an early date, Arica became one of the principle ports for the silver trade from Potosí, but the coast remained sparsely inhabited until the 19th century. At the time of independence the whole of this area became part of Peru as the provinces of Tarapacá and Arica, with the provincial capital at the now ruined city of Tarapacá, near Huara. The region became the focal point for the War of the Pacific (1879-1883), with decisive battles fought at Iquique on 21 May 1879, and at Angamos, near Mejillones, on 8 October of the same year. Chile's naval superiority enabled her troops to occupy Peruvian territory as far north as Lima, with the peace treaty being signed in 1883. After the War of the Pacific, the area as far north as Tacna came under Chilean control, and became the country's breadbasket following the sudden growth of the nitrate industry which followed soon after the war (see page 208).

With the poor conditions of workers in the nitrate mines, this far northern part of Chile was one of the first in which left-wing and trade unionist movements developed. In 1907, a group of miners from one of the nitrate *oficinas* was executed by the army in the Santa María school in Iquique when campaigning for the end of payment in *oficina* tokens instead of hard cash; the legacy of the far north's radicalism can be seen in the now infamous 'caravan of death' executed in seven northern cities by one of General Pinochet's henchmen in the days following the 1973 coup.

The region's borders were finally delineated in 1929: Tacna voted in a referendum to return to Perú, while Arica opted to remain Chilean. The collapse of the nitrate industry in the 1930s and 1940s was a regional crisis, but the quick growth of the fishing industry saved the area from disaster. With new mines such as Collahuasi recently having been opened, mining is of increasing importance.

Geography   The Atacama Desert extends over most of the Far North. The Cordillera de la Costa slowly loses height north of Iquique, terminating at the Morro at Arica: from Iquique northwards it drops directly to the sea and, as a result, there are few beaches along this coast. Inland, the central depression, the *pampa*, 1,000-1,200 m high, is arid and punctuated by salt flats south of Iquique. Between Iquique and Arica it is crossed from east to west by four gorges. East of the central depression lies the *sierra*, the western branch of the Andes, beyond which is a high plateau, the *altiplano* (3,500 m-4,500 m) from which rise volcanic peaks, the highest of which include Parinacota (6,350 m), Pomerape (6,250 m), Guayatiri (6,064 m), Acotango (6,050 m), Capurata (5,990 m), Tacora (5,988 m) and Tarapacá (5,825 m).

Northwards from Pisagua several rivers flow west from the *sierra*; the more northerly of these, the Ríos Lluta and San José, provide water for Arica. In the *altiplano* there are a number of lakes, the largest of which, Lago Chungará, is

Things to do

- Stay in Iquique and wander among its well preserved 19th-century architecture, built with the wealth of the nitrate era.
- Visit the ghost towns of Humberstone and Santa Laura, abandoned nitrate towns. At Santa Laura, the machinery used to crush the minerals is intact, while Humberstone maintains the original theatre and Olympic-size swimming pool.
- Take a thermal bath at the hot springs of Mamiña. This small Andean village is famous for the restorative powers of its waters.
- Be amazed by the geoglyphs carved in the desert by pre-Hispanic people at the Cerro Unitas, Pintados or Tiliviche, three of the best-known sites.
- Escape the modern world in the unforgettable, pristine natural environments of Isluga, Las Vicuñas or Surire national parks.

one of the highest lakes in the world. The main river draining the *altiplano*, the Río Lauca, flows eastwards into Bolivia.

Climate

The coastal strip and the *pampa* are permanently rainless; on the coast temperatures are moderated by the Pacific Ocean, but in the *pampa* variations of temperature between day and night are extreme, ranging between 30°C and 0°C. In the *sierra* temperatures are lower, averaging 20°C in summer and 9°C in winter. The *altiplano* is much colder, temperatures averaging 10°C in summer and -5°C in winter. Both the *sierra* and the *altiplano* are affected by storms of rain, snow and hail (*invierno boliviano*). Coastal regions receive *camanchaca* (sea mist).

Economy

Over 90% of the population of this area lives in the two coastal cities, Arica and Iquique. The sea provides the main source of wealth. Iquique is the principal fishing port in Chile, unloading 35% of the total national catch, and the city has important fish processing industries. Mining is much less important than in other parts of northern Chile, but silver and gold are mined at Challacollo and copper at Sagasca, near Tarapacá, while the new copper mine at Collahuasi has made a big difference to the region's economy. Fruit is grown in the Valle de Azapa, the oasis formed by the Río San José, and in the *sierra* around Pica. The Azapa valley also produces olives. Vegetables and alfalfa are grown in the oases of the *sierra*. Commerce is an important source of local employment: Arica benefits from its position as a port for Bolivian goods and its proximity to Peru, while Iquique is the site of a duty free zone.

Iquique

Iquique is the the capital of Región I (Tarapacá) and one of the main ports of northern Chile. The name of the town is derived from the Aymará word ique-ique, meaning place of 'rest and tranquillity'. The city is situated on a rocky peninsula at the foot of the high coastal mountain range, sheltered by the headlands of Punta Gruesa and Cavancha. Iquique is perhaps the most attractive city in northern Chile, with a well preserved collection of historical buildings in the centre whose brightly painted wooden façades make a surprising contrast to the lifeless desert and the grey coastal mist. The beach at Playa Cavancha is very popular in summer – in spite of the Humboldt Current, the water is almost warm – while surfers and other watersports enthusiasts make for the pounding waves of Playa Brava.

Phone code: 057
Colour map 1, grid B2
Population: 145,139
492 km north of
Antofagasta

Iquique, Arica and the Far North

Camels of South America

The llama, alpaca, guanaco and vicuña are all camelids, or South American camels, adapted for the mountainous terrain by having narrower feet than the desert forms of the species. There are estimated to be some 7.7 million camelids, over half of them in Peru. All four species can be seen in Chile, though three of these are only found in the north. The relationships between camelids is very confused: fertile offspring arise from matings between all of them. There is a long-held view that both the llama and the alpaca are descended from wild guanaco.

Guanaco, coffee coloured with a darker head and tail and weighing up to 55 kg, were once found throughout Chile except in rainforest areas. Both a grazer and browser, it lives in deserts, shrub land, savannah and occasionally on forest fringes. In many areas hunted to extinction, an estimated 20,000 now survive in the far north, especially in the Parque Nacional Lauca, in coastal areas between Antofagasta and Lago Rapel, and in parts of the far south such as the Parque Nacional Torres del Paine.

Vicuña, weighing up to 20 kg, are like half-sized guanaco, though with a yellower coat and coffee coloured head and tail. Hunted almost to extinction, there were only around 400 in Chile in 1970. Protection has increased their numbers to around 12,000, mainly in the far north at altitudes of 3,700-4,800 m.

Alpaca are domesticated animals, weighing 20-30 kg, but seeming to be much larger because of their wool. Colours vary between black, coffee coloured, mahogany, grey and white. An estimated 20,000 can be found in drier parts of the northern altiplano.

Llama are also domesticated and are usually found with alpacas. Larger than alpacas and weighing up to 55 kg, their wool varies in colour but is shorter than that of alpacas. They are found only in the area of their domestication, which first occurred around Lake Titicaca some 4,000-5,000 years ago. Used as pack animals, males can carry loads of up to 40 kg. There are some 40,000 in the Tarapacá and Antofagasta regions of Chile.

Ins and outs

Getting there
See page 248 for further details

Iquique is served by all major bus companies from the south and from Arica – most southbound buses take the coast road to Tocopilla. There are also daily buses up to Oruro and La Paz in Bolivia. *Ladeco* and *LanChile* fly south to Santiago, via Antofagasta, and north to Arica – some flights continue on to La Paz and Santa Cruz in Bolivia. There are also international flights with *TAM* to Asunción, Paraguay, for US$320 return.

Getting around The best way to get around in Iquique is by *colectivo*. Any car that looks like a taxi in fact serves as a *colectivo* unless it says '*sólo taxi*'. Tell the driver where you are going, and, if your destination can combine with that of other passengers, he will take you; if you are the first passenger, the driver will fit the journeys of subsequent passengers around your destination. The fare is US$0.50 (a little more late at night).

Tourist offices Sernatur, Serrano 145, Edif Econorte, 3 piso, Of 303, T427686, sernatur_iquiq@entelchile.net Mon-Fri 0830-1630, very helpful. Automóvil Club de Chile, Serrano 154, T426772.

History Although the site was used as a port in pre-hispanic times, it remained sparsely populated throughout the colonial period. Even in 1855, when Iquique had begun to export nitrates, the population was about 2,500. The nitrate trade transformed the city, bringing large numbers of foreign traders and creating a wealthy élite. Though partly destroyed by an earthquake in 1877, the city became the centre of this trade after its transfer from Peru to Chile at the end of the War of the Pacific.

Sights

In the centre of the old town is **Plaza Prat** with a clock tower and bell dating from 1877. On the northeast corner of the Plaza is the **Centro Español**, built in Moorish style by the local Spanish community in 1904. The ground floor is a restaurant, on the upper floors are paintings of scenes from Don Quixote and from Spanish history by the Spanish artist, Vicente Tordecillas. On the south side of the Plaza is the **Teatro Municipal**, built as an opera house in 1890; the façade features four women representing the seasons. Plaza Prat is currently (July 2001) a vast building site, as work is being undertaken to make an underground car park and to remodel the plaza; this work may not be completed until 2003. Three blocks north of the Plaza is the old **Aduana** (customs house) built in 1871; in 1891 it was the scene of an important battle in the Civil War between supporters of President Balmaceda and congressional forces. Part of it is now the **Naval Museum**. Five blocks east along Calle Sotomayor is the **Railway Station**, now disused, built in 1883 and displaying several old locomotives. Two blocks south of the railway station, on Bolívar, is the **cathedral**, painted bright yellow and blue and with interesting stained glass windows inside. On Amunátegui, behind the **Escuela Santa María** on Zégers, there is a memorial to the workers from the nitrate mines who were killed by the army while sheltering in the school during the strike of 1907. Along Calle Baquedano, which runs south from Plaza Prat, are the attractive former mansions of the 'nitrate barons'. Adorned with columns and balconies, and with impressive old doors, these buildings date from between 1880 and 1903 and were constructed from timber imported from California. The finest of these is the **Palacio Astoreca**, Baquedano y O'Higgins, built in 1903, subsequently the Intendencia and now a museum. Continuing in this direction and down towards the beach at **Playa Cavancha**, on Baquedano and on neighbouring streets such as Lynch and Obispo Labbé there are many beautiful old wooden houses painted blue, green, yellow, pink, with white columns and large wooden shutters and doors; this area is really worth exploring.

Those who enjoy walking may want to climb the large sand dune, **Cerro Dragón**, which rises behind Iquique and gives fantastic views of the city and the sea; take a *colectivo* to Chipana y La Tirana and then walk to the base of the hill.

Sea lions and pelicans can be seen from the harbour. There are cruises around the harbour from the passenger pier, US$2.50, 45 minutes, minimum 10-15 people.

Iquique is a major duty-free centre. The main Free Zone, the Zofri, lies north of town along Amunátegui: it is a giant shopping centre selling a wide range of duty-free imported products including electronic goods, new and used cars, motorcycles and good quality camping equipment. At Christmas, people come from all over Chile to do their shopping, as the Zofri is said to be cheaper than Punta Arenas' equivalent, the Zona Franca. ■ *1100 to 2100 Mon to Sat. Colectivo from the centre US$0.50.* Another duty-free zone, Mall Los Américas, has been opened south of the centre on Avenida Héroes de la Concepción. ■ *Limit on tax free purchases US$650 for foreigners, US$500 for Chileans. All vehicles travelling south from Iquique are searched for duty-free goods at Quillagua on the Pan-American Highway and at Chipana on Route 1, the coastal road.*

North the Nitrate King

In the history of northern Chile few people have played a more controversial role than John North, known in both Chile and Britain as the 'Nitrate King'. Born in Leeds in 1842, North arrived in Chile at the age of 24 and worked as a railway engineer in Caldera and Iquique. In 1875 he began supplying water to Iquique by boat from Arica. During the War of the Pacific North and his partner, John Harvey, bought large numbers of shares in the Peruvian nitrate companies of the Atacama at low prices. When, after the war, the Chilean government unexpectedly recognised ownership of the shares, North had acquired six nitrate mines and made a fortune. Some suggest that North and Harvey, a mining engineer employed by the Chilean government, had inside knowledge of the decision to recognise the shares.

North returned to London in 1882 and built a large empire of companies with interests in northern Chile. By 1889 he controlled 15 nitrate mines, four railway companies including the Nitrate Railways Company which monopolized rail transport around Iquique, the Bank of Tarapacá and London and the Nitrate Provisions Company, which supplied food to the nitrate oficinas. North's efforts to establish a monopoly over nitrate transport were opposed by President Balmaceda and, when the president came into conflict with the Chilean Congress in 1891, North provided £10,000 for the Congressional war effort which was to overthrow the President.

By this time North was a famous figure in London, spending ostentatiously on his business and society friends; his mansion at Avery Hill, Eltham, was the scene of great parties; he owned racehorses and sponsored other sports. In 1895 he stood for parliament as a Conservative, but was narrowly defeated. He died, of a heart attack, in May 1896 and his funeral was attended by huge crowds. By the time of his death nitrate stocks had gone into decline, but North had quietly sold most of his shares, shifting his wealth into coal mining in South Wales, gold mining in Australia, trams in Cairo, cement in Belgium and rubber plantations in the Congo.

Museums A visit to the **Museo Regional** is highly recommended. It has an excellent collection of pre-Hispanic artefacts (including several mummies). The archaeological section is very well set out and explained (Spanish only), tracing the development of pre-Hispanic civilizations in the region and containing an important ethnographical collection of the Isluga culture of the altiplano (circa 400 AD) and of contemporary Aymará cultures. There is also a section devoted to the Nitrate Era which includes a collection of the tokens in which the workers were paid by each *oficina*, a model of a nitrate *oficina* and the collection of the nitrate entrepreneur, Santiago Humberstone. ■ *Mon-Fri 0800-1300, 1500-1900, Sat 1030-1300, Sun (in summer) 1000-1300 and 1600-2000. Free. Baquedano 951.*

Palacio Astoreca has fine late 19th-century furniture and exhibitions of shells. ■ *US$0.60. Mon-Fri 1000-1300, 1600-1930, Sat 0930-1330, Sun 1100-1400. Baquedano y O'Higgins.*

Excursions **Humberstone**, a large nitrate town, now abandoned, at the junction of the Pan-American Highway and the road to Iquique. At its height in 1940 the town had a population of 3,700. Though closed since 1961, you can see the plaza, the church, a very well preserved theatre, the *pulpería* (company stores) and the Olympic-size swimming pool complete with grandstand (built of metal plating from ships' hulls). ■ *Visits possible 0900-1800, 'voluntary' donation of US$1.50 invited. Guided tours Sat-Sun. Leaflets available. For further information T751213.*

Nearby are the ruins of several other mining towns including **Santa Laura**, only 2 km from Humberstone. Santa Laura has the only nitrate processing plant still intact, and a small museum of the mine and the equipment used by the miners. ■ *Visits possible 1000-1800, further information on T751981.*

Iquique

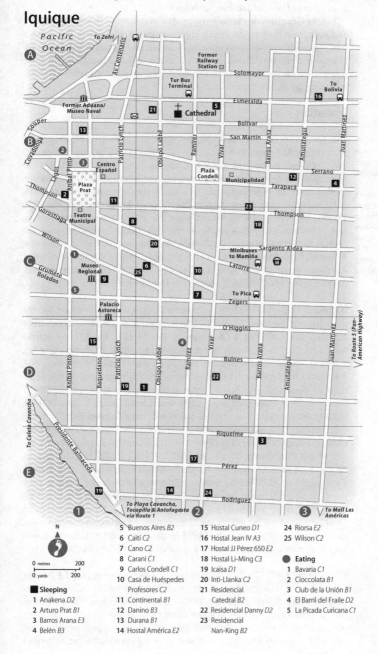

Sleeping
1 Anakena *D2*
2 Arturo Prat *B1*
3 Barros Arana *E3*
4 Belén *B3*

5 Buenos Aires *B2*
6 Caiti *C2*
7 Cano *C2*
8 Carani *C1*
9 Carlos Condell *C1*
10 Casa de Huéspedes Profesores *C2*
11 Continental *B1*
12 Danino *B3*
13 Durana *B1*
14 Hostal América *E2*

15 Hostal Cuneo *D1*
16 Hostal Jean IV *A3*
17 Hostal JJ Pérez 650 *E2*
18 Hostal Li-Ming *C3*
19 Icaisa *D1*
20 Inti-Llanka *C2*
21 Residencial Catedral *B2*
22 Residencial Danny *D2*
23 Residencial Nan-King *B2*

24 Riorsa *E2*
25 Wilson *C2*

● **Eating**
1 Bavaria *C1*
2 Cioccolata *B1*
3 Club de la Unión *B1*
4 El Barril del Fraile *D2*
5 La Picada Curicana *C1*

From Iquique take any bus to/from Arica, or a colectivo *for Pozo Almonte from Sgto Aldea y Barros Arana, US$2 (there is a phone for contacting taxi company for return journey, or you could probably flag down an Iquique-bound bus or minibus from the highway). Humberstone and Santa Laura can be visited on tours arranged by local agencies (see below).*

For the **Geoglifos de Pintados** (see page 254) take any bus south, US$2.50, and walk from the Pan-American Highway, then hitch back or flag down a bus. Many other sites around Iquique, including the Gigante del Atacama (see box, page 254), are difficult to visit without a vehicle. Hire a car and drive south along the Pacific coast to see sealions, fishing villages and old salt mines, including the ghost town of Guanillos.

Essentials

Sleeping
■ *on map*
Price codes:
see inside front cover

Accommodation is scarce in the weeks before Christmas as many Chileans visit Iquique to shop in the Zofri. At other times it is always worth bargaining

L-AL *Terrado*, Los Rieles 126, T437878, reservas@terrado.cl, sea views, most expensive, all mod-cons. **AL** *Gavina*, Balmaceda 1497, T413030, F411111, gavina@ctcinternet.cl Very exclusive, central. **AL** *Hostería Cavancha*, Los Rieles 250, T/F434800, hostcav@entelchile.net 4-star, expensive restaurant, pleasant inside but ugly exterior, south of city on the water's edge; outside is a giant chessboard. **AL** *Icaisa*, Orella 434, T412324, F428462, nice swimming pool, friendly, good. **AL-A** *Arturo Prat*, Plaza Prat, T411067, F423309, hap@entelchile.net 4-star, pool, health suite, expensive restaurant, tours arranged. **A** *Chucumata*, A Prat 850, T435050, F439733, reservas@ chucumata.tie.cl, bilious red colour, all mod-cons, a little soulless, near Playa Cavancha. **A** *Majestic Playa Brava*, Playa Brava 3115, T441068, F431039. With breakfast, good. **A-B** *Barros Arana*, Barros Arana 1330, T412840, F426709, hba@ctcreuna.cl Clean, modern, swimming pool, friendly, good value, recommended.

B *Anakena*, Orella 456, T/F510182, paoa@entelchile.net, nice old armchairs, friendly, good. **B** *Atenas*, Los Rieles 738, T431075. Pleasant, personal, good value, good service and food. Recommended. **B** *Cano*, Ramirez 996, T416597, F422032, hotelcano@ hotmail.com, big rooms, friendly, nice atmosphere, good value. **B** *Carani*, Latorre 426, T399999, F399998, smart, modern, helpful. **B** *Carlos Condell*, Baquedano 964, T/F3113027, hotel-carlos-condell@entelchile.net, friendly, in the historic centre, negotiable for longer stays, with parking and mod-cons. **B** *Riorsa*, Vivar 1542, T/F420153, friendly, modern, near beach, worth bargaining. **C** *Belén*, Tarapacá 1002, T421774, F413644, friendly, laundry service, in a bad area. **C** *Hostal Catedral*, T426372, Labbé 235, with bath, quiet, nice balcony, interesting building, also cheaper rooms **F**. **C** *Hotel Caiti*, Gorostiaga 483, T/F423038, pleasant, with bath breakfast and all mod cons, recommended. **C** *Inti-Llanka*, Obispo Labbé 825, T311104, F311105. Nice rooms, clean, helpful, good value. **C** *Playas*, Gral Hernán Fuenzalida 938, T423706. Small, friendly. **C** *Wilson*, Wilson 422, T423789, good sized rooms, with telephone and mod cons, worth bargaining. **D** *Danino*, Serrano 897, T417301, F443079, with breakfast, free local phone calls, clean, modern, good value. **D** *Hotel Buenos Aires*, Esmeralda 713, T/F413288, with breakfast and TV cable, clean, modern, helpful, convenient for Tur Bus, excellent value, also cheaper rooms **F** pp. **E** *Hostal JJ Pérez 650*, at JJ Perez 650, with breakfast, rooms with bath and cable TV, good value, simple and clean.

F *Continental*, Lynch 679, T429145. Small rooms, noisy, basic, overpriced. **F** *Durana*, San Martín 294, T410959. Central, hot water, friendly, breakfast included, recommended. **F** *Hostal Cuneo*, Baquedano 1175, T428654. Modern, clean, nice rooms, helpful, pleasant, good value. **F** *Hostal Jean IV*, Esmeralda 938, T/F510855, mespina@entelchile.net, with breakfast, clean, friendly, nice lounge and nice patio, with bath, convenient for buses to Bolivia, excellent value, highly recommended.

F *Hostal San Francisco*, Latorre 990, T427524. Clean, hot water, noisy. **F** *O'Higgins 963*, T422896, big rooms, good breakfast, recommended. **F** *Res Danny*, Vivar 1266, T390439, shared bath, with breakfast. **F** *Res Nan-King*, Thompson 752, T423311. Clean, small but nice rooms. **G** *Casa de Huéspedes Profesores*, Ramirez 839, T314692, inostrozaflores@entelchile.net, with breakfast, helpful, old building with lots of character, recommended. **G** *Hostal América*, Rodríguez 550, T/F427524. Near beach, shared bath, unhelpful. **G** *Hostal Li Ming*, Barros Arana 705, T421912, F422707, clean, simple, good value, small rooms, recommended.

Camping No site but wild camping possible on La Brava beach. **Equipment**: *Tunset*, in Zofri; *Lombardi*, Serrano 447.

Expensive At Caleta Cavancha – *Club Náutico*, Los Rieles s/n, seafood, exclusive, recommended. *El Sombrero*, Los Rieles 704. Quality fish and seafood cuisine, elegant setting, not cheap. *Otelo*, Valenzuela 775. Italian specialities, seafood, pricey. Also *Neptuno*, in Hostería Cavancha.

Eating
● *on maps*
Price codes:
see inside front cover

Mid-range *Bavaria*, Pinto 926. Expensive restaurant, reasonably priced café serving real coffee, snacks and *almuerzo*. *Casino Español*, Plaza Prat, good meals well served in beautiful building, expensive, "a good place to celebrate your birthday". *Club de la Unión*, Plaza Prat, roof terrace with panoramic views, open lunchtimes only, pricey but worth it. *Colonial*, Plaza Prat, fish and seafood, popular, good value. *El Barril del Fraile*, Ramírez 1181, good seafood, nice atmosphere. *Las Tejas de Barros Arana*, Barros Arana 684. Peruvian *parrillada*. *La Tarantella*, Tarapacá y Baquedano, small portions, Italian-style, smart, cheap *almuerzo*. *Pizzeria d'Alfredo*, Los Molles 2290 (Playa Brava). Large variety of pizzas, well-prepared pastas, not cheap, reasonably priced *almuerzo*. Beware of the expensive and poor value tourist restaurants on the wharf on the opposite side of Av Costanera from the bus terminal.

Cheap Several good, cheap and supercheap seafood restaurants can be found on the 2nd floor of the central market, Barros Arana y Latorre. Also try: *Bolivia*, Serrano 751. *Humitas* and *salteñas*. Recommended. *Compañía Italiana de Bomberos*, Serrano 520, authentic Italian cuisine, excellent value *almuerzo*, otherwise more expensive, recommended. *Esquis Schop*, Bolivar 446B, fruit juices, nice ambience, good. *La Picada Curicana*, Pinto y Zegers. Good local cuisine, good value *menu de la casa*. *San Lorenzo*, clean, good dishes, good value. Many Chinese *chifas* including *Win Li*, San Martin 439 and *Sol Oriental*, Martínez 2030 and 6 cheaper ones on Tarapacá 800/900 blocks.

Seriously cheap Many very cheap and not particularly salubrious restaurants along Barros Arana, near the market, eg *Schopería Las Tejas*, Barros Arana 680, good value.

Cafés Several excellent cafés in the centre including: *Cioccolata*, Pinto 487 (another branch in the Zofri), nice, good. *Splendid*, Vivar 795, good *onces*, inexpensive. *Salon de Té Ricotta*, Vivar y Latorre, very popular for *onces*, quite expensive. *Tropical*, at Baquedano y Thompson. Juices, snacks. Recommended. *Via Pontony*, Baquedano y Zegers. Also fruit juices and *empanadas*. Recommended. Good fruit juices at *Jugos Tarapacá*, Tarapacá 380.

Bars and pubs *Santa Fé*, Mall Las Américas, locales 10-11-193, Mexican, live music, great atmosphere, very popular, highly recommended. For late night food, drink, video entertainment, dancing: *Taberna Barracuda*, Gorostiaga 601, nice décor, nice atmosphere, recommended. **Discos** Most are out of the town on the road south to the airport. The *Hotel Gavina* has a good club on Fri and Sat nights, quite smart. The next

Entertainment

nearest to the city is *Pharo's*, Av Costanera Sur 3607, on Playa Brava, elaborate design, popular, good. Most popular of all is *La Caldera del Sabor*, playing salsa and merengue, dance classes, in Bajo Molle at the southernmost end of the city, open Thu-Sat. **Cinemas, casino and theatre** *Cine Tarapacá*, Serrano 202, shows foreign films. There is also a six screen cinema in Mall las Américas, T432500 for the programme. *Casino*, Balmaceda 2755. Open nightly, entry to salóns, US$1.50. Plays, ballet, dance and concerts in the Teatro Municipal. There are occasional recitals in the Cathedral.

Shopping Most of the city's commerce is in the two Free Zone centres. **Bookshops** Andrés Bello, Héroes de la Concepción 2855, excellent range.

Sports **Bathing** Beaches at Cavancha just south of town centre, good, and Huaiquique, reasonable, popular between Nov and Mar. Restaurants at Cavancha. Piscina Godoy, fresh water swimming pool on Av Costanera at Aníbal Pinto and Riquelme, open evening, US$1. **Fishing equipment** *Ferretería Lonza*, Vivar 738, T415587. *Ferretería La Ocasión*, Sgto Aldea 890. Fishing for broadbill swordfish, striped marlin, yellowfin tuna, oceanic bonito, Mar till end of Aug. **Golf** *Playa Blanca Club*, Bolívar 395, T413361. **Paragliding** Two hang-gliding clubs, *Altazar*, T431382, and *Manutara*, T418280; the cliffs directly behind Iquique are a great place from which to launch off down towards the coast, frequently recommended. **Surfing** Iquique offers some of the best surfing in Chile with numerous reel breaks on Playa Brava, south of the city, not for beginners. *Club de Surf* at Héroes de la Concepción 1939, T447070. **Tennis** *Club de Tenis Tarapacá*, Bulnes 140, T412489 for temporary membership.

Festivals See page 251 for the festival of the *Virgen del Carmen* in La Tirana, 70 km east of Iquique, **10-16 Jul**. There are also numerous other, smaller religious festivals – ask in Iquique's tourist office for more details.

Tour companies *Iquitour*, Lynch 563, T/F412415, tour to Pintados, La Tirana, Humberstone, Pica, etc, no English spoken, day tours start at US$20. *Viatours*, Baquedano 736, T/F417197, viatours@entelchile.net Tours are also offered by the *Hotel Arturo Prat*. There are many others; the tourist office maintains a list.

Transport **Local Car hire**: *Continental*, 18 de Setiembre 105, T441426. *Hertz*, A Pinto 1303, T510432. Airport office T407020. *IQSA*, Labbé 1089, T417068. *Jofamar*, Libertad 1156, T411639. *Procar*, Serrano 796, T413470, at airport T410920. **Motorcycle mechanic**: Sergio Cortez, *Givet*, Bolívar 684. Highly recommended. In the Zofri there is a wide range of motorcycle tyres. **Bicycles**, *Redolfi*, Latorre 786. Sales, parts, repairs. Try also the Zofri.

Long distance Air: Diego Aracena international airport, 35 km south at Chucumata. Taxi US$9.50; airport transfer, T310800, US$3.20, unreliable, if there are 3 or more passengers; it is just as cheap to get a taxi. National flights to Arica, Antofagasta and Santiago; international to Asunción, La Paz and Santa Cruz.

Bus: terminal at north end of Patricio Lynch (not all buses leave from here); *Tur Bu*s have their own terminal at Ramírez y Esmeralda, with a Redbanc ATM and a good luggage store; bus company offices are near the market on Sgto Aldea and Barros Arana. All southbound buses are stopped for a luggage check on leaving the duty free zone of Region I at Quillagua on the Pan-American Highway and at Chipana/Río Loa on the coastal Route 1. Inter-regional buses: To **Arica**, buses and *colectivos*, frequent, US$5, 4 hrs; to **Antofagasta**, US$9.50, 8 hrs. To **Calama**, 8 hrs, US$7. To **Tocopilla** along the coastal road, several companies, 3 hrs, US$4; to **La Serena**, 17 hrs, US$19; to **Santiago**,

27 hrs, several companies, US$30 (US$50 for *salón cama*). Buses within Region I: To **Colchane**, *Pullman Paloma*, leave daily at 2300 from Esmeralda y Juan Martínez, US$5. To **Pica**, *Pullman Chacón*, many daily, leave from Barros Arana opposite the market, also San Andrés and Santa Rosa, on Barros Arana. To **Mamiña**, *Transporte Tamarugal* and *Turismo Mamiña* both leave at 0800 from Barros Arana y Sargento Aldea, mini-buses, best to book the day before, US$4 one way. **International buses**: most bus companies for services to Oruro and La Paz are on Esmeralda, near the junction of Juan Martínez (note that some buses go via Arica and Tambo Quemado to La Paz, not via Colchane and Oruro). There are many companies, eg *Litoral Buses*, T423670, daily at 2200 to **Oruro**, US$8, US$12 to **La Paz**; *Salvador Buses* at 2300, same price; *Géminis* at the bus terminal to **La Paz** (Bolivia) via Oruro, more expensive. To **Oruro** via Colchane several companies including *Delta*, *Tata Sabaya* and *Comet*, all leave from Esmeralda y Juan Martínez around 2100-2300, bargain for a good price.

Airline offices *LanChile*, Tarapacá 465, T427600, and in the Mall Las Américas. Also: **Directory** *Iberia*, Vivar 630, T411878. *KLM*, Pinto 515, T423009. *LAB*, Serrano 442, T407015. **Banks** *Finandés*, Tarapacá 441, Mastercard. *Corp Banca*, Serrano 343, Visa. Numerous Redbanc ATMs in the centre. **Casas de Cambio**: *AFEX*, Serrano 396, changes TCs. *Cambio Cambio's*, Lynch 548, Local 1-2. *Wall Street*, in the Zofri, sells Amex TCs and changes them. Lots of ATMs in the Zofri. **Communications** Internet: *Fassher Internet*, Vivar 1497, piso 2, US$0.80/hr. Same price is *PC@NET Computación*, Vivar 1373. More central is *Obispo Labbé y Serrano*, US$1.50/hr. Post office: *Correo Central*, Bolívar 485, beware overcharging. Telephone: *CTC*, Serrano 620. *Entel*, Tarapacá 476. *Correos*, *CTC*, *Chilexpress*, *Chilesat* and *Entel* all have offices in the Plaza de Servicios in the Zofri. **Consulates** Bolivia, Gorostiaga 215, Departamento E, T421777. Mon-Fri 0930-1200. Holland, Manzana 11, Galpón 2, ZOFRI, T426074. Italy, Serrano 447, T421588. Peru, Zegers 570, T411466. Spain, Manzana 2, Sitio 5 y 9, ZOFRI, T422330. **Dentist** *Clinica Dental Lynch*, Lynch y Orella, T413060. **Hospitals** *Centro Médico*, Orella 433, T/F414396. Also hospital at *Héroes de la Concepción 502*, T415555. **Language schools** *Academia de Idiomas del Norte*, Ramírez 1345, T411827, F429343, idiomas@chilesat.net Swiss run, Spanish classes and accommodation for students. **Laundry** *Central Dry Clean*, Serrano 772; *Laverap*, San Martín 490 – both self-service laundries. Also *King Service Lavandería*, Thompson 666.

Around Iquique

Inland from Iquique there are several small towns which were the early cen-tres of Spanish colonial settlement, and are well worth visiting – less crowded than villages near Calama and Arica. The rainy season in this area is mainly in January.

Situated on the Pan-American Highway 5 km south of the turning to Iquique, **Pozo Almonte** Pozo Almonte was the main service centre for the nitrate fields of the area. The *Population: 5,400* **Museo Histórico Salitrero**, on the plaza, displays artefacts and photographs of the nitrate era. ■ *Mon-Fri 0830-1300 and 1600-1900*. There is *Hotel Anakana*, Comercio 053, T751201, F751621 and *Hostería Fauda*, on the northern outskirts, T751396, F751025, with a restaurant. *Estancia Inn* is on Calle Comercial.

Radioactive riches

The site of abundant thermal springs as well as a unique mud spring, Mamiña has been a popular health resort since the nitrate era. The thermal springs are classified as being radioactive, are rich in sodium, potassium, sulphur, chlorides and silicates, and are acknowledged to be valuable in treating ailments such as rheumatoid arthritis and sciatica as well as respiratory and digestive problems. The Los Chinos thermal mud bath is seen as valuable in the treatment of many skin diseases such as psoriasis. The bath contains radioactive mud with natural deposits of vegetal mineral mud activated by the fermentation of certain algae; the mud is allowed to dry on the skin after the bath and then washed off in one of the thermal springs.

Mamiña

Phone code: 057
Colour map 1, grid B2
Altitude: 2,750 m

General Pinochet is known to come here to relieve the aches and pains of old age

A very popular thermal springs resort, Mamiña is reached by a good paved road which runs 74 km east from Pozo Almonte. Situated on a ridge, this is a delightful and very friendly village, and would be an ideal place to relax for a few days after more strenuous activities in Bolivia or San Pedro. Mamiña has pre-Hispanic origins – the word means 'the girl of my eyes' in Aymará – and is inhabited mainly by people of Aymará origin; standing on the hill above the village, a circular geoglyph indicating the presence of water is clearly visible on the opposite side of the valley. The Aymará cultural centre, Kaspi-Kala, near the *Hotel Los Cardenales*, includes an artesanía workshop and a sales outlet. An Inca *pukará* stands on a hilltop 3 km east; the hilltop is marked by a white cross which can be seen from the village, although it may be best to go with a guide. There are also said to be the ruins of a pre-Hispanic settlement further down the valley towards the *pampa*. Legend has it that one of Mamiña's thermal pools cured an Inca princess. The church, built in 1632, is the only colonial Andean church in Chile with twin towers, each topped by a bell tower – the church can be climbed by steps at the side, and the bells in the tower are interesting for being linked together by a single rope. In the nitrate period its agreeable climate and its thermal springs made it a resort for the wealthy: the *Hotel Termas* dates from this period. There is also a mud spring, the Baño Los Chinos (■ *0930-1300*) and good accommodation.

Sleeping
All the following are recommended, and all have rooms with private bath and thermal water available. Prices are for full board; as there are so many hotels in Mamiña, it is always worth bargaining

B pp *Los Cardenales*, T438182, T09-5451091. 4-star, thermal baths, swimming pool with spring water, excellent cuisine in attractive restaurant, games room, lovely gardens and outlook, English, German spoken, delightful. Highly recommended. **B** pp *Refugio del Salitre*, T751203, F420330, secluded, pretty terrace, lovely views, swimming pool, nice rooms, games room, helpful, interesting older part where the top brass from the nitrate *oficinas* stayed, recommended. **C** pp *Bellavista*, T474506, secluded, aviary in garden, games room, friendly, good cooking (including vegetarian options), sun terrace, basic but good rooms, worth bargaining. **C** pp *La Coruña*, T09-5430360. Children half-price, good Spanish cuisine, games room, swimming pool, very friendly and helpful, lots of local knowledge, parking and cable TV, highly recommended. **C** pp *Hotel Kusy Tambo*, T420436, Casilla 621 Iquique, friendly, clean, modern, table tennis available, recommended. **C** pp *Llama Inn*, T419893. Pool tables, casino table, massage, terrace, friendly, cook will produce vegetarian meals if asked. Highly recommended.

Eating
Most hotels operate on a full board basis only. There are also the following eateries, all cheap: *Cafetería Ipla*, excellent fruit juices, vegetarian options. *Los Chacras de Pasquito*, cheap, clean, good. *Restaurant Cerro Morado*, good variety, traditional dishes including rabbit, good.

La Tirana

The legend of La Tirana is an intriguing mix of Andean traditions and Catholocism. It is said that, when Diego de Almagro made the first Spanish foray into Chile, one of his companions was an Inca princess. She was a fierce warrior who loathed everything to do with the Spanish, and escaped into the pampa *to wage war against them. She was so fierce that she became known as* La Tirana. *La Tirana's techniques were overthrown when she fell in love with Vasco de Almeyda, a Portuguese soldier enlisted by the Spanish, who persuaded her to convert to Christianity. When her companions discovered her treachery, both the Inca princess and the warrior were killed. The legend goes that a priest, coming some years later to the area to evangelise, discovered a cross on the spot where the couple had died, and built a church there.*

Today, the fiesta treads a fine line between commercialism and maintaining these hybrid traditions. The most

important day and night occur on 16 July, but for up to a week beforehand the town is awash with travelling salesmen who come from all over Chile, and sell everything that you could possibly need – clothes, music, bags, hats, cheap meals, ice creams and so on. At the same time, troupes of religious dancers and their accompanying brass bands come from as far away as Peru and Argentina to give homage to the Virgen del Carmen. Eclecticism is the order of the day: as well as traditional Andean groups, there are also dancers who imitate the Sioux Indians from North America, and the 'Ali Baba Christians' dancing with imitation wooden sphinxes. The noise is deafening, day and night, as the brass bands vie with one another to produce the greatest racket. There is even an office set up by the church to perform marriages, and one of the most touching sights at the fiesta is that of happy couples being carried towards the church, amid the dancing, music and the chaos.

Transport

Bus From Iquique: *Transportes Tamarugal*, Barros Arana 897, daily 0800, 1600, 2½ hrs, US$4, from Mamiña 0800, 1800. *Turismo Mamiña*, Latorre 779, Mon-Sat 0800-1600, also Sun 1600, 2½ hrs US$4, from Mamiña Tue-Sat 0830, Mon-Sat 1800.

Directory

Communications There are a couple of call centres on the plaza, and one supermarket (open only sporadically).

La Tirana
Population: 558
Altitude: 995 m

Situated 10 km east of the Pan-American Highway by a turning 9 km south of Pozo Almonte, La Tirana is famous for a religious festival to the Virgen del Carmen, held from 10 to 16 July (see box, page 251). This attracts some 150,000 pilgrims. Over 100 groups dance night and day, starting on 12 July. All the dances take place in the main plaza in front of the church; no alcohol is served. Accommodation is difficult to find, other than in organized campsites (take tent) which have basic toilets and showers, and through a few families who rent out rooms for over US$20 a night. There are two small museums: the Museo de la Virgen de La Tirana, which contains gifts to the virgin; and the Museo de La Tirana, which houses a collection of artefacts from the nitrate era. In ordinary times, buses from Iquique to Pica stop here; during the festival, virtually every taxi and *colectivo* in Iquique seems to be making 'special' trips to La Tirana, leaving from Sargento Aldea by the market, and some bus companies have direct services from Antofagasta and Arica.

Matilla
Altitude: 1,160 m

Some 38 km east of La Tirana, Matilla is an oasis settlement founded in 1760 by settlers from Pica. The village declined after 1912 when the waters of the Quebrada de Quisma were diverted to Iquique. The church (1887) is built of blocks of borax, and rears up from over the arid plain like a version of Sacré Coeur in the desert. Nearby is a **museum** in the Lagar de Matilla, used in the 18th century for fermenting wine. ■ *Daily 0900-1700. Key from the kiosk in the plaza.* There is accommodation in the *Complejo Turístico El Parabien*, T431645, which has fully furnished *cabañas* and a pool. Near Matilla an unpaved and rough road runs southwest to meet the Pan-American Highway.

Pica

Phone code: 057
Colour map 1, grid B2
Population: 1,767
Altitude: 1,325 m

Four kilometres northeast of Matilla, Pica was the most important centre of early Spanish settlement in this region. In colonial times it produced a famous wine sold as far away as Potosí. Most of the older buildings including the church date from the nitrate period when it became a popular resort. It is a leafy oasis, famous for its thermal baths and the fruit grown here – one of the highlights of a stay is drinking fresh fruit juices from any one of numerous stalls near the thermal springs of the Cocha Resbaladero, which lie about 1 km from the centre of the town. ■ *0700-2000 all year. US$2. Changing rooms, snack bar, beautiful pool.*

There is a small tourist information office opposite the Cocha de Resbaladero.

Sleeping

The hotels get full at weekends and at holidays, as well as during La Tirana – it is best to ring ahead.

Near the Cocha Resbaladero C *Hostal Suizo*, Ibañez 210, T741551. With bath, popular, modern, very comfortable. **F** *Hostal Casablanca*, Ibañez 075, T741410, friendly, comfortable, cooking facilities, parking. **F** *Res El Tambo*, Ibañez 68, T/F741041. Without bath, meals served, very popular, hospitable. Warmly recommended. **G** *Res Milton*, No 188 opposite entrance to thermal baths, T741105, with excellent breakfast, basic, friendly, good, canaries on patio. **In the town centre** **F** *Camino El Inca*, Esmeralda 014, T/F741008, with breakfast, shady patio, table football, good value, recommended. **F** *Hostería O'Higgins*, Balmaceda 6, T741524. With bath, modern. **F** *Los Emilios*, Cochrane 213, T/F741126. With bath and breakfast, friendly, nice lounge, small swimming pool, interesting old building with photos of the nitrate era, lovely patio, highly recommended. **F** *San Andrés*, Balmaceda 197, T741319. With bath and breakfast, basic but clean, good restaurant with cheap 4-course *almuerzos*. Cabañas: *Res El Tambo* (see above) **B**, sleeps 4. Also *Mirador de Pica*, Resbaladero, T741061, **B**, sleeps 6. *Miraflores*, in Ibañez, T741338, **B**, sleeps 3. *San José*, T741160, **B**, sleeps 5.

Eating

Mid-range *El Edén de Pica*, Riquelme 12. Best in town, speciality dishes, fine ice cream, lovely surroundings. *Los Naranjos*, Esmeralda y Barbosa, nice décor, good. **Cheap** Hotels *San Andrés* and *El Tambo* have good cheap restaurants. *La Mía Pappa*, Balmaceda. Good selection of meat and juices, attractive location near plaza. *La Palmera*, Balmaceda 115. Excellent *almuerzo*, popular with locals, near plaza. *La Viña*, Ibañez 70, by Cocha de Resbaladero. Good cheap *almuerzo*. **Seriously cheap** *Oasis*, on Balmaceda, by the plaza. Pica is famous for its *alfajores* filled with cream and honey, recommended; and you cannot leave without trying some of the fruit juices.

Transport

The first bus from Pica back to Iquique leaves at about 1100

Bus From Iquique operated by 3 companies: *Santa Rosa*, Barros Arana 777, daily 0830 and 0930, 2 hrs; from Pica 1700 and 1800, US$2.50; *San Andrés*, Sgto Aldea y Barros Arana, daily 0930, return departure 1800, US$2.50; *Pullman Chacón*, Barros Arana y Latorre, many daily, US$2.50.

From Iquique to the Bolivian border

At Huara, 33 km north of Pozo Almonte, a road turns off the Pan-American Highway and runs to Colchane, 173 km northeast on the Bolivian frontier. Some 13 km east of Huara, the road passes, on the right, the **Geoglifos de**

Geoglyphs

Found as far south as the Río Loa and as far north as the Río Azapa near Arica, as well as along the Peruvian coast as far as Nazca, geoglyphs or geoglifos are one of the most visible traces left by ancient civilizations in the Atacama. Dating from an estimated 1000-1400 AD, these designs were made on the rocks using two different techniques: by scraping away the topsoil to reveal different coloured rock beneath or by arranging stones to form a kind of mosaic. They exhibit three main themes: geometrical patterns; images of animals, especially camelids, birds and snakes; and humans, often holding or carrying instruments or weapons such as a bow and arrows. They are easily visible because they were intended to be seen. They are generally located on isolated hills in the desert, on the western slopes of the Cordillera de la Costa or on the slopes of quebradas (gorges).

Their significance is thought by some experts to be ritual, but the more current theory is that they were often a kind of signpost pointing out routes between the coast and the sierra. The largest site is at Pintados, 96 km south of Iquique, reached by turning off the Pan-American Highway towards Pica and then following a 4 km

track from which several panels can be seen, including representations of a large number of humans dressed in ponchos and feather head-dresses, as well as geometrical designs and representations of animals and birds. Though there are more sites, the most important of the others are the following: at Tiliviche, 127 km north of Iquique, some 600 m south of the Pan-American Highway, where, on the southern side of the quebrada, a 300 m panel can be seen representing a drove of llamas moving from the cordillera to the coast; at Cerro Rosita, 20 km north of Huara near the Pan-American Highway, where the 'Sun of Huara' (an Aymara sun emblem) is visible on the eastern side of the hill; and at Cerro Unitas, 15 km east of Huara, where geoglyphs are visible on the western and southern sides of an isolated hill. On the western slope of Cerro Unitas is the Gigante del Atacama or Giant of the Atacama, probably the most famous of all the images: 86 m high, this is a representation of an indigenous leader with a head-dress of feathers and a feline mask; to his left is a reptile, thought to link him to the earth god Pachamama, to his right is his staff of office.

Cerro Unitas, the most outstanding of which is the **Gigante del Atacama**, a human figure 86 m tall, reported to be the largest geoglyph in the world and best viewed from a distance.

At Km 23 a road branches off south to **Tarapacá**, settled by the Spanish around 1560 and capital of the Peruvian province of Tarapacá until 1855, now largely abandoned except for the Fiesta of the Virgen de la Candelaria on 2 and 3 February. The major historic buildings, the Iglesia de San Lorenzo and the Palacio de Gobierno, are in ruins. From Km 25 the road is unpaved. At **Chusmisa**, 3 km off this road at Km 77 there are thermal springs: the water is bottled and sold throughout northern Chile. Basic accommodation is available in the forlorn and windy border town of **Colchane**, four basic *residenciales*, all **G**. Some 6 km northwest of Colchane is the southern entrance to the Parque Nacional Volcán Isluga (see below page 268). Colchane livens up during the market, which takes place every other Saturday.

Transport Bus Colchane can be reached from Iquique by daily buses with *Pullman La Paloma* at 2300 from Esmeralda y Juan Martínez.

Colchane Open 0800-2000 daily. On the Bolivian side an unpaved road leads to Oruro, 233 km northeast.

From Iquique south towards Antofagasta South of Pozo Almonte, the Pan-American Highway runs to Quillagua, 172 km, where there is a customs post. All southbound vehicles including buses are searched. The road continues towards Antofagasta. At Km 24 the road runs through the largest section of the **Reserva Nacional Pampa del Tamarugal** (the other two sections are around La Tirana and north of Huara) which is administered by CONAF. Covering a total of 100,650 ha, the reserve includes plantations of tamaruga, a tree species adapted to the dry climate and saline soils. The **Geoglifos de Pintodos**, some 400 figures on the hillsides, representing humans, animals and birds as well as abstract designs, are situated some 3 km west of the Pan-American Highway, turn off at Km 43.

From Iquique north towards Arica

The Pan-American Highway runs across the Atacama Desert at an altitude of around 1,000 m, with several steep hills which are best tackled in daylight. At night, sea mist, *camanchaca*, can reduce visibility.

Huara Thirty three kilometres north of Pozo Almonte, Huara was once a town of 7,000 people (now 400), serving as a centre for the nearby nitrate towns but little evidence remains of that period apart from the railway station, which is a national monument. Nearby are the huge and impressive geoglyphs of Cerro Unita, see above. There is an interesting church and a small museum preserving a pharmacy from the nitrate era with all the cures and remedies which were then on offer. Basic accommodation is available in the *Restaurant Frontera*.

Pisagua At **Zapiga**, 47 km north of Huara there is a crossroads: one branch leads west for 41 km to Pisagua, formerly an important nitrate port, now a small fishing port. Several old wooden buildings here are national monuments including the Municipal Theatre (1892) and the Clock Tower (1887), but it is now largely abandoned. There are fish restaurants and it makes a pleasant stop for a meal. Pisagua was the site of a detention centre after the 1973 military coup: mass graves from that period were discovered near here in 1990. Accommodation is available in the friendly *Restaurant Acuario*, **G**. There is a campsite at the northern end of the beach.

Camiña A picturesque village in an oasis, Camiña lies 67 km east of Zapiga along a poor road (deep sand and dust).There is a basic *hostal* on the plaza, **F**. From here a terrible road runs to the **Tranque de Caritaya**, a dam 45 km further northeast which supplies water for the coastal towns and which is set in splendid scenery with lots of wildlife and interesting botany (especially *llareta*).

Continuing north At Km 57 north of Huara there is an interesting British cemetery dating from the 19th century: note the fine wrought-iron gates. Nearby from the highway there is a view of the **Geoglifos de Tiliviche** representing a group of llamas (signposted to left and easily accessible). Further north at Km 111, the **Geoglifos de Chiza** can be seen from the bridge which carries the Highway over the Quebrada de Chiza. At Km 172 a road runs east to **Codpa**, an agricultural community in a deep gorge with interesting scenery. From Codpa poor roads lead north and east through **Tignamar** and Belén to Putre.

A tiny village founded by the Spanish in 1625, Belén was on the silver route **Belén** between Potosí and the coast. It has two colonial churches: the older one, the Iglesia de Belén is one of the oldest (and smallest) churches in Chile; the other, the Iglesia de Carmen, dates from the 18th century. There are many pre-Hispanic ruins in the area, with 4 pukarás and a well-preserved stretch of the Camino del Inca. At Tignamar Viejo, an abandoned village 14 km south, there is another colonial church. Accommodation and food is available in Belén with María Martinez, General Lagos y San Martín. ■ *Getting there:* Buses La Paloma *(In Arica:* German Riesco *2071, T058-222710), leave Arica for Belén on Tuesdays and Fridays at 0645, US$3.*

Arica

Arica is the northernmost Chile in city, just 19 km south of the Peruvian border. *There is a distinct sense of the proximity of Peru, and the city itself is quite an attractive one, with long beaches and pleasant gardens, extensive networks of sand dunes nearby, and the hill known as the Morro de Arica rearing up behind the town.*

Phone code: 058
Colour map 1, grid A1
Population: 169,456

Ins and outs

Arica is a long way from most of Chile. All major bus companies serving the north make this their final stop, and buses take up to 30 hrs south to Santiago; there is also quite a wide-ranging bus service to villages in the sierra and the *altiplano.* Arica is a centre for connections to Bolivia and Peru, with frequent *colectivos* (and 2 daily trains) north to Tacna in Peru, and buses east to La Paz, Bolivia. *Ladeco* and *LanChile* fly south to Santiago via Iquique and Antofagasta, with some flights continuing on to La Paz and Santa Cruz in Bolivia.

Getting there
See page 261 for further details

Arica is quite a large city, and you may need to take some of the *colectivos* or buses to get to more out-of-the-way places, particularly the discos (many of which are on the road out to the Azapa Valley).

Getting around

The Sernatur office is at Prat 375, piso 2. Mon-Fri 0830-1300, 1500-1830, T232101. Very helpful, English spoken, good map, supplies list of tour companies. Automobile Club de Chile, Chacabuco 460, T252678. CONAF, MacKenna 820, T/F250570, Mon-Thu 0800-1300, 1400-1730, Fri 0800-1300, 1400-1630.

Tourist office

Background

During the colonial period Arica was important as the Pacific end of the silver route from Potosí. Independence as part of Peru and the re-routing of Bolivian trade through Cobija led to a decline from which the city recovered with the building of rail links with Tacna (1855) and La Paz (1913). The city came under Chilean control at the end of the War of the Pacific. The **Morro** in Arica was the site of an important Chilean victory over Peru on 7 June 1880.

Arica remains an important route centre and port; linked to the Bolivian capital La Paz now by road and an oil pipeline, it handles a large proportion of Bolivia's foreign trade. It is frequented for sea bathing by Bolivians, as well as by the locals. There are also road and rail connections with the Peruvian city of Tacna, 54 km north. There are large fishmeal plants and a car assembly factory. Regrettably there are indications that Arica is also becoming a key link in the international drugs trade.

A national obsession

It is impossible to spend much time in Chile without becoming aware of the fragility of the land beneath your feet. Earth tremors and violent quakes are a part of everyday life, and raising the matter with Chilean friends tends to lead to quick changes of the subject. While the northern section of this book was being researched in June 2001, an earthquake struck southern Peru at nearly 8 on the Richter Scale, killing many people, and also severely damaging the old buildings in the Arica and the new border post at Chacalluta.

Quite apart from the terror of the earthquakes, tremors really are common-place. These are most often felt at night, owing to the fact that everything is quieter. If sleeping, your first feeling may be that someone is gently shaking your bed and interfering with your dream. The vibrations of crockery and swaying flowers should

alert you that this is something more. Once the tremor has passed, dogs burst into frightened barks, thought to be because, owing to their more sensitive hearing, they can hear the creaks and groans of the earth below.

While it is likely that visitors passing through the region will experience nothing but tremors, they should be aware that a severe earthquake is expected in the Iquique/Arica region at some point in the next 10-15 years. There is no way of telling, at the beginning of a tremor, whether it will develop into a full-scale earthquake. If you are unfortunate enough to experience an earthquake, do not panic. Rushing outside into the street leaves you open to falling masonry and objects such as flower pots. The safest place to go really is beneath the lintels of doorways, as in the old wives' tale.

Sights

The city is centred around the **Plaza Colón**, on which stands the gothic-style cathedral of **San Marcos**, built in iron by Eiffel. Though small, it is beautifully proportioned and attractively painted. It was brought to Arica from Ilo in Peru as an emergency measure after a tidal wave swept over Arica in 1868 and destroyed all its churches; inside the cathedral is a Christ figure dating from the 12th century. Eiffel also designed the nearby **Aduana** (customs house) which is now the Casa de la Cultura. ■ *Mon-Sun 0830-2000.* Just north of the Aduana is the La Paz railway station; outside is an old steam locomotive (made in Germany in 1924) once used on this line. In the station is a memorial to John Roberts Jones, builder of the Arica portion of the railway. To climb the **Morro**, 110 m high, walk to the southernmost end of the Calle Colón, and then follow the pedestrian walkway up to the summit; there are fine views of the city. The **Museo Histórico y de Armas**, on the summit of the Morro, contains weapons and uniforms from the War of the Pacific. ■ *0830-2000. US$1.*

Excursions

A highly recommended excursion is up the Azapa Valley, a beautiful oasis east of Arica. At Km 12 is the **Museo Arqueológico San Miguel de Azapa**, part of the University of Tarapacá and well worth a visit. Set in a pleasant, shady part of the valley, the museum contains a fine collection of pre-Columbian weaving, pottery, woodcarving and basket work from the coast and the valleys as well as seven mummified humans from the Chinchorro culture (8,000-10,000 BC), the most ancient mummies yet discovered. Comprehensive explanations are provided by booklets in English, French, German and Spanish, loaned free at the entrance. ■ *0900-2000 (2 Jan-28 Feb), 1000-1800*

(1 Mar-31 Dec), closed 1 Jan, 1 May, 25 Dec. US$2, T224248, museo@uta.cl
Getting there: Take a yellow colectivo from P Lynch y Chacabuco, US$1.

In the forecourt of the museum are several boulders with pre-Columbian petroglyphs. On the road between Arica and San Miguel several groups of geoglyphs of humans and llamas can be seen to the south of the road. On the opposite side of the valley at San Lorenzo are the ruins of a *pukará* (pre-Inca fortress) dating from the 12th century.

In the nearby village of San Miguel, there is a very friendly supercheap restaurant serving good food and Peruvian Arequipeña beer. A good walk in the area is to climb the desert hill behind the valley, 45 minutes, giving wonderful views of the green oasis and the desolation beyond – running back down the hill takes 3 minutes and is an exhilarating experience.

To the **Lluta Valley**, north of Arica along Route 11, bus from MacKenna y Chacabuco: between Km 14 and Km 16, on the hillsides are the **Geoglifos de Lluta**, four groups of geoglyphs representing llamas and humans. The road continues through the Parque Nacional Lauca and on to Bolivia (see below).

Essentials

AL *Americano*, Lagos 571, T257752, F252150, servturi@entelchile.net Cable TV, sauna, gymnasium. **AL** *Arica*, San Martín 599, 2 km south on coast (frequent buses and *colectivos*), T254540, F231133. Lower rates off season, good value, excellent restaurant, tennis court, pool, lava beach (not safe for swimming). **AL** *Azapa*, Sánchez 660, Valle de Azapa, T244537, F244517. Attractive grounds, pleasant location, also cheaper *cabañas*, good restaurant. **AL** *El Paso*, Gen Velásquez 1109, T/F231965. Bungalow style, excellent restaurant, lovely gardens, tennis court, pool. **A-B** *Savona*, Yungay 380, T231000, F231606. Comfortable, 3-star, friendly, quiet. Highly recommended. **B** *Aragón*, Maipú 344, T/F252088. With breakfast. **B** *Concorde*, Velásquez 580, T252000, F230022. Busy popular restaurant, noisy, overpriced. **B** *King*, Colón 376, T232094, F251124, with bath, central. **B** *Motel Saucache*, Sanchez 027, Valle de Azapa, T/F241458. Fully equipped *cabañas*, sleeps 2 or 4. **B** *Plaza Colón*, San Marcos 261, T254424, F231244. Modern, comfortable. **B** *San Marcos*, Sotomayor 387, T232970, F251815. Three-star, comfortable, good value. **B** *Sol de Arica*, Avalos 2041, T246050, F246113. Sauna, jacuzzi, pool, recommended. **B** *Star Apart Hotel*, Av Consistorial y Ramón Carnicer, T214691, F211107. Fully furnished apartments. **B-C** *Amadís*, Prat 588, T/F232994. Central, modern. **C** *Diego de Almagro*, Sotomayor 490, T224444, F221240. With breakfast, helpful, comfortable, parking. Recommended. Stores luggage. **C** *Res Las Condes*, MacKenna y Maipú, kitchen facilities, hot showers, clean. **D** *Hostal Casa Mia Nona*, 21 de Mayo 660, T250597. With bath, without breakfast. **D** *Lynch*, Lynch 589, T251956, F231581, with bath.

F *Hostal Chez Charlie*, Paseo Thompson 236, T/F250057, latinor@entelchile.net, comfortable, without breakfast, good value, recommended. **F** *Hostal Jardín del Sol*, Sotomayor 848, T232795. With bath, with breakfast, comfortable, friendly, good value. Highly recommended. **F** *Hostal Sammy*, Lagos 1066. With breakfast. **F** *Res América*, Sotomayor 430, T254148, with bath. Clean, hospitable, good value. **F** *Res Blanquita*, Maipú 472, T232064, F250062. Clean, pleasant, good value. **F** *Res Caracas*, Sotomayor 867, T253688. Clean, with breakfast. **F** *Res Chillán*, Velásquez 749, T251677. Noisy, poor beds. **F** *Res Ecuador*, Juan Noé 989, T/F251934, with bath and breakfast, kitchen and laundry facilities, recently renovated, recommended. **F** *Res Leiva*, Colón 347, T/F232008. Without bath, French spoken, cooking facilities, cycle hire. **F** *Res Stagnaro*, Gallo 294, T231254, F256687. With breakfast, very good value, recommended. **F** *Sra Gloria Martinez*, Pasaje 7, No 1026, Población Juan Noé, T241971. Friendly, helpful.

Sleeping
■ *on map, page 258*
Price codes:
see inside front cover

In Jan-Feb the
municipality
supplies cheap basic
accommodation, ask
at the tourist office

Arica

To Airport, Pan-American Highway (North)
to Peru, Parque Nacional Lauca & Bolivia

Playa Chinchorro

Raúl del Canto

Buses to
Tacna

Diego Portales

Río San José

JA Ríos

To Poblado Artesanal & Pan-American Highway (South) to Azapa Valley

Gral Velásquez

Universidad
de Tarapacá

Independencia

Cemetery

J Waidelle

M Blanco Encalada

Av Santa María

Angamos

Salvo

Larco Herrera

Lastarria

Esmeralda

Av Vicuña Mackenna

A Latorre

Casino

Juan Noé

Parque
Brasil

Colectivos
to Tacna

Parque General C Ibáñez
del Campo

Chacabuco

O' Higgins

Av Costanera Norte

Maipú

Baquedano

16

23

20

18 de Septiembre

Buses to
Visviri

A Prat

Gral Velásquez

24

1

2   15

P Lynch

Gral Lagos

12

Bolivian
Consulate

San Martín

Arturo Gallo

5   3

9

19

Maximo Lira

P Montt

Thompson

Colón

4

21 de Mayo

3

M Blanco Encalada

Peruvian
Consulate

Bolognesi

18   8

11

25

Sotomayor

22

Sangra

4

14   6   10

13

Mercado
Central

San Marcos

Casa de la Cultura
(ex-Aduana)

Plaza
Colón

Cathedral

Yungay

Ejército

Harbour

7 de Junio

26

Plaza Vicuña
Mackenna

Morro

Museo
Histórico y
de Armas

El
Morro

Faldeos El Morro

Camino Al Morro

To Hotel Arica, La Lisera, Playa Brava & El Laucho Beaches

Sleeping		
1 Amadís	12 Lynch	22 Residencial Real
2 Aragón	13 Plaza Colón	23 Residencial Velásquez
3 Casa mía Nonna	14 Residencial América	24 Residencial Venecia
4 Central	15 Residencial Blanquita	25 San Marcos
5 Concorde	16 Residencial Chillán &	26 Savona
6 Diego de Almagro	several others in this	
7 El Paso	block	● Eating
8 Hostal Leiva	17 Residencial Ecuador	1 Bavaria
9 Hostal 18	18 Residencial Española	2 Don Floro
10 Jacora	19 Residencial Jardín del Sol	3 El Rey del Marisco
11 King	20 Residencial Madrid	4 Los Aleros del 21
	21 Residencial Nilda	

0 metres   200
0 yards   219

F *Sunny Days*, Tomas Aravena 161, T241058, run by New Zealander, English spoken, nice atmosphere, lots of information on the area, highly recommended. **G** *Res Española*, Bolognesi 340, T231703. Without breakfast, central, basic, quiet. Recommended. **G** *Res Madrid*, Baquedano 685, T231479. Without bath or breakfast, laundry, hot water, poor beds, good value, reductions for Hostelling International cards. **G** *Res Pacífico*, Velásquez 611, T230567, with breakfast, cooking facilities. **G** *Res Velásquez*, Velásquez 669, T231989. Basic, friendly, laundry facilities, cable TV. **G** *Res Venecia*, Baquedano 739, T252877. Spotless, hot water, small rooms, good value. Recommended. **H** *Res El Sur*, Maipú 516, T252457. Clean, cheap, but grim.

Camping Many sites at Villa Frontera, 15 km north including *Gallinazos*, T232373. Full facilities, pool. *El Refugio de Azapa*, 3½ km from Arica, T227545. At Playa Las Machas, 5 km north, no water or facilities. Free camping (no facilities) at Playa Chinchorro. Camping at Playa Corazones, 8 km south, (no water) is risky as there are reports of daylight mugging and robbery.

Mid-range *Bavaria*, Colón 613. Good restaurant, coffee and cakes. *Casanova*, Baquedano 397. Excellent but not cheap. *D'Aurelio*, Baquedano 369. Italian specialities, good pasta, seafood. *Don Floro*, V MacKenna 847. Good seafood and steaks, good service. Highly recommended. *El Arriero*, 21 de Mayo 385. *Parrillada*, also seafood and fish. Warmly recommended. *El Rey del Marisco*, Maipú y Colón. Excellent seafood, pricey, not always welcoming. *Las Tejas de Azapa*, Valle de Azapa Km 2, No 4301 *Parrillada*, seafood, pool, expensive. *Los Aleros del 21*, 21 de Mayo 736. Recommended for seafood and service. *Maracuyá*, San Martín 0321. Seafood, splendid location on the coast, pricey. More expensive Chinese restaurants include *Chin Huang Tao*, Lynch 317. Excellent, pricey but worth it; *Chifa Chin*, Patricio Lynch 224, with good value Chinese food, diners welcome to take away 'leftovers'.

Eating
● *on map*

Cheap *Acuario*, Muelle Turístico. Good food in fishy environment, good value *menu de casa*. *Cyclo*, Lynch 224. Seafood, pasta, reasonably priced. Recommended. *El Tambo*, in Poblado Artesanal, Hualles 2025. For lunches, folk music and dancing on Fri/Sat evenings. *Govinda*, Bolognesi 430. Vegetarian, good value lunches. *La Ciboulette*, Paseo Thompson 238. Good food, pleasant atmosphere, not expensive. Recommended. *La Jaula*, 21 de Mayo 293. Snacks, meals, not expensive. *Snack Suceso Inn*, 18 de Septiembre 250. Good set meal and coffee. *Yuri*, Maipú y Lynch. Good service, cheap lunches. Recommended. Cheaper Chinese restaurants include *Kau Chea*, 18 de Septiembre y Prat, good value, and *Shaolin*, 18 de Septiembre 601.

Seriously cheap *Capricho Latino*, 18 de Septiembre 250. Good value *almuerzo* *La Bomba*, Colón 357, at fire station. Good value *almuerzo*, friendly service. There are many cheap restaurants on Baquedano 600/700 blocks including *San Fernando*, No 601. Simple breakfast, good value *almuerzo*.

Cafés Three good places all on 21 de Mayo and offering real coffee and outdoor seating: *Caffelatte*, No 248. *Carlos Díaz León Snack Place*, No 388. *Di Mángo*, No 244. Juices, ice cream. Also *Mi Viejo*, Maipú 436. Cheap meals and snacks, and *Scala*, 21 de Mayo 201. Excellent fruit juices, real coffee.

Pubs *Carpaccio*, Velásquez 510. Restaurant and bar, live music from 2330 Wed-Sat. *France Tropicale Pub*, Baquedano 371. Open till dawn, live music weekends. French and English spoken. *Puerto Navarrón*, Paseo Bolognesi. Open till 0400, live music at weekends.

Bars

Iquique, Arica and the Far North

Entertainment **Cinemas** *Colón*, 7 de Junio 190, T231165. *Cine Arte*, at the Biblioteca Publíca on Yungay. **Music** Peña folklorica of Andean music in the Poblado Artesanal, Fri and Sat 2130. **Discos** *Avant Premier*, Santiago Flores 180 (taxi from centre US$5). *Soho*, Buenos Aires 209. For rock 'n' roll. *Sunset* and *Swing*, both 3½ km out of town in the Valle de Azapa. 2300-0430 weekends (taxi US$3). **Theatre** *Teatro Municipal de Arica*, Baquedano 234. Wide variety of theatrical and musical events, exhibitions. Recommended.

Sports **Bathing** Olympic pool in Parque Centenario, Tue-Sun; take No 5A bus from 18 de Septiembre (you need to buy a weekly ticket, available for purchase only on Thu mornings). The best beach for swimming is Playa Chinchorro, north of town (bus 24) but Playa Las Machas, further north, has strong currents. Buses 7 and 8 run to beaches south of town – the first two beaches, La Lisera and El Laucho, are both small and mainly for sunbathing. Playa Brava is popular for sunbathing but not swimming (dangerous currents). **Surfing** Good surfing at Playa Las Machas and Playa Chinchorro, north of the city, and at La Isleta and Playa Corazones, 9 km south along coast road (take bus or colectivo). **Golf** 18-hole course in Valle de Azapa, open daily except Mon. **Tennis** *Club de Tenis Centenario*, Av España 2640. Open daily. **Paragliding** is practised on the mountains overlooking the city. Contact Escuela Profesional de Parapente Termica, Av La Tirana 3441, Depto C-37, T/F450675.

Festivals In **Jan**, Arica hosts a miniature version of the *Festival de la Canción* famous in Viña del Mar, with performances by Andean musicians. **Jun** sees the annual festival of Arica and the national Cueca championships.

Shopping **Artesanía** *Feria Turística Dominical*, Sun market, on Chacabuco between Velásquez and Mackenna, good prices for llama sweaters. *Poblado Artesanal*, Plaza Las Gredas, Hualles 2825 (take bus 2, 3 or 7): expensive but especially good for musical instruments, open Tue-Sun 0930-1300, 1500-1930. **Markets** *Mercado Central*, Sotomayor y Sangra, recently renovated, fruit and vegetables, mornings only. Fruit, vegetables and old clothes market at Terminal del Agro at southeastern edge of town; take bus marked 'Agro' along 18 de Septiembre. Supermarkets at Baguedano y 18 de Septiembre, San Martín y 18 de Septiembre, Chacabuco y Lagos. **Cameras and film** *Profonor*, 18 de Septiembre y Lynch, recommended. Avoid *Megaclor* on 21 de Mayo for developing film.

Tour operators *AYCA Tour*, Covadonga 312, T/F240404. Archaeological and historical tours. *Ecotour Expediciones*, Bolognesi 460, T/F25000. *Globo Tour*, 21 de Mayo 260, T/F232909. Recommended for international flight bookings. *Kijo Tour and Travel*, Bolognesi 357, T/F232245. Good for international travel. *Latinorizons*, Bolognesi 449, T/F250007, latinor@entilchile.net Specializes in tours to Lauca National Park, recommended. *Parmacota Expeditions*, Bolognesi 475, T/F251309. *Transtours*, Bolognesi 421, T253927, F251675. *Turismo Daroch*, Bolognesi 360A, T/F254088. *Turismo Payachatas*, Sotomayor y Bolognesi, T/F256981 (in Santiago: 11 de Septiembre 2214, oficina 71, T/F231-1292). Most of these offer local tours and excursions to the *altiplano* at similar prices: city tour US$10; to Valle de Azapa US$12; to Parque Nacional Lauca one-day US$20, 2 days US$60 including accommodation; to Lauca and Isluga National Parks, 3 days US$180. Agencies pay up to 25% commission to hotels and *residenciales* which refer travellers; to get a lower price form a group of 5 or 6 travellers and negotiate direct with agencies. It is better to spend more than one day in the Lauca National Park, but if limited to a 1-day tour choose carefully. *Azimut 360*, Arzobispo Casanova 3, Providencia, Santiago, T2-7358034, F7772375, www.azimut.cl Tours to the Atacama Desert and mountaineering expeditions to Parinacota and Sajama.

Local Bicycles: *Bicicletas Wilson*, 18 de Sept 583. Repairs, parts, sales, ATB specialists. **Bus**: buses run from Maipú, US$0.25. **Colectivos**: run on fixed routes within city
limit, US$0.30 per person (US$0.50 per person after 2000). **Car hire**: *American*, Gen
Lagos 571, T/F257752; *Cactus*, Baquedano 635, Loc. 40, T257430, F258353. *GP*,
Copacabana 628, T252594, good reports. *Hertz*, Baquedano 999, T231487; *Klasse*,
Velásquez 760, Piso 2, Loc 25, T/F254498. For the Parque Nacional Lauca 4WD and
antifreeze are essential; if you wish to cross from the park into Bolivia you will need a
permit from the hire company. *Hertz* provides the most reliable vehicles but check
any rental vehicle for jack, lug wrench as well as the condition of both the fan belt
(often dry and cracked) and the spare tyre. Crossing to Tacna (Peru) with a hire car
can be difficult: Klasse can arrange the paperwork for this. **Motoring**: *Automóvil
Club de Chile*: Chacabuco 460, T252878, F232780. Car insurance at Dirección de
Tránsito; may insist on car inspection. Car service at *Shell*, Panamericana Norte 3456;
Esso, Portales 2462; *Autocentro*, Azola 2999, T241241. **Motorcycle repairs**: Pablo
Fernández Davils, El Salitre 3254, T212863, F212823.

Long distance Air: airport 18 km north of city at Chacalluta, T222831. Taxi to town
US$9, *colectivo* US$4-5 per person from Lynch y 21 de Mayo. Radiotaxis *Chacalluta*,
T254812, specialize in journeys to/from the airport. Flights: to **La Paz**, *LanChile/Ladeco*
and *LAB*; to **Santiago**, *Ladeco/LanChile* all via Iquique and Antofagasta. Book well in
advance. To **Lima**, *LanPerú* and others from Tacna (Peru), enquire at travel agencies
in Arica.

Bus Terminal (Rodoviario) northeast of centre at Av Portales y Santa María, T241390,
reached by many buses and *colectivos* including No 8 and 18 (US$0.20, or US$0.45), taxi
to centre US$2 (terminal tax US$0.25). All southbound luggage is carefully searched for
fruit prior to boarding and is then searched again at Cuya on the Pan-American Highway.
Bus company offices at bus terminal apart from the following: *Buses La Paloma*, Germán
Riesco 2071 (bus U from centre); *Humire*, P Montt 662, T206164; *Martínez*, 21 de Mayo
575, T232265; *Bus Lluta*, Chacabuco y V Mackenna. *Litoral*, Chacabuco 454, T254702;
Andes-Mar, Galerin Río San José, Av Santa María 2010, T 248200/232265. To
Antofagasta, US$12, 10 hrs; to **Calama** and **Chuquicamata**, 8 hrs, US$10, several com-
panies, all between 2000 and 2200; to **Iquique**, frequent, US$5, 4½ hrs, also *collectivos*,
several companies, all with offices in the terminal; to **Santiago**, 30 hrs, a number of com-
panies, for example *Carmelita*, *Ramos Cholele*, *Pullman Bus*, *Fénix* and *Flota Barrios*
US$35-40, also *salón cama* services, run by *Fichtur*, *Flota Barrios*, *Fénix* and others,
US$75 (most serve meals though these vary in quality; generally better on more expen-
sive services; student discounts available); to **La Serena**, 21 hrs, US$25-30; to **Viña del
Mar** and **Valparaíso**, US$40, also *salón cama* service, US$50. **International**: to **La Paz**,
Bolivia, *Humire*, Sun at 0800, US$11; *Geminis*, Mon, Wed, Fri 1000, US$15 without lunch;
ChileBus, US$15, daily at 1030; *Transalvador*, Tue, Thu, Fri, 0830, US$11, via border
towns of Chungará (Chile) and Tambo Quemado (Bolivia, very cold at border – take blan-
ket/sleeping bag, food, water and sense of humour), 8-10 hrs. See page 262 for buses
and *colectivos* to Tacna, Peru.

Car: It is illegal to take fruit and dairy products south of Arica: all vehicles are
searched at Cuya, 105 km south, and at Huara, 234 km south. **Service stations**
between the Peruvian border and Santiago can be found at: Arica, Huara, Iquique,
Pozo Almonte, Oficina Victoria, Tocopilla, Oficina María Elena, Chuquicamata,
Calama, Carmen Alto, Antofagasta, La Negra, Agua Verde (also fruit inspection post),
Taltal, Chañaral, Caldera, Copiapó, Vallenar, La Serena, Termas de Soco, Los Vilos, and
then every 30 km to capital.

Hitchhiking: Not easy to hitch south: try the Terminal del Agro off the Pan-American Highway (trucks leave Mon, Thu and Sat before 0700) and the *Copec* station opposite (reached by bus from Arica marked 'Agro' or *colectivo* No 8).

Directory **Airline offices** *Ladeco/LanChile*, 21 de Mayo 345, T251641, F252600. *Lloyd Aéreo Boliviano*, P Lynch 371, T216411. *National*, 21 de Mayo 417, T250001.

Banks Street money changers on 21 de Mayo and its junction with Colón, mainly operate outside normal banking hrs, accept TCs but at poor rates. *Banco Santander*, 21 de Mayo. Open 24 hrs. *Corp Banca*, Bolognesi 317. Visa. ATM. *Finandes*, 21 de Mayo 560. Mastercard. Many Redbanc ATMs. **Casas de Cambio**: for TCs *Marta Daguer*, 18 de Septiembre 330, slow service, very high commission, and *Yanulaque*, 21 de Mayo 175, Mon-Fri 0900-1400, 1600-2000, Sat 0930-1330. Most large hotels also change cash. Rates for TCs are generally poor. **Communications** Internet: *Biomar Technology*, Maipú 487. **Post office**: Prat 375. To send parcels abroad, contents must be shown to Aduana (1st floor of post office), Mon-Fri 0800-1200. Packaging sold but take your own tape. **Telephone**: *CTC*, Colón 430 and at 21 de Mayo 211. *Entel-Chile*, 21 de May 345. Open 0900-2200. *VTR Telecommunications*, 21 de Mayo 477 and Colón 301. Telex, fax, telegrams. **Consulates** Bolivia, 21 de Mayo 575, T231030. Peru, San Martín 220, T231020. Germany, 21 de Mayo 639, T231551. **Cultural centres** Instituto Chileno-Alemán de Cultura, Camino Azapa 3727. **Instituto Chileno – Británico de Cultura** (library open Mon-Fri 0900-1200, 1600-2100) has newspapers, Baquedano 351, T231960, Casilla 653. **Instituto Cultural Chileno Norteamericano**, San Marcos 581. **Medical services** Dentist: *Juan Horta Becerra*, Latorre 565, Of 202, T252497. Speaks English. *Rodrigo Belmar Castillo*, Latorre 565, Of 306, T252047. Hospital at 18 de Setiembre 1000, T232242. **Laundry** *Lavandería A Kilo*, Santa Isabel shopping centre. $6 per 5 kilos. *Lavandería La Moderna*, 18 de Septiembre 457. US$4 per kg, open Sat till 2200.

Border with Peru
Between October and March Chilean time is 1 hour later than Peruvian, 2 hours later October to February or March (varies annually)

Immigration at **Chacalluta** is open Sun-Thu 0800-2400, all 24 hrs Fri and Sat. A fairly uncomplicated crossing, although the customs complex was severely damaged by the earthquake of Jun 2001 (see box, page 256). If crossing by private vehicle drivers entering Chile are required to file a form, *Relaciones de Pasajeros* (4 copies; 8 if planning to return via this crossing), giving details of passengers, obtained from a stationery store in Tacna, or at the border in a kiosk near Customs. You must also present the original registration document for your car from its country of registration. The first checkpoints outside Arica on the road to Santiago also require the *Relaciones de Pasajeros* form. If you can't buy the form, details on a piece of paper will suffice, or you can get them at service stations. The form is not required when travelling south of Antofagasta. Crossing to Tacna with a hire car is difficult: make sure you have the correct papers. There are exchange facilities at the border, but better rates reported in Tacna.

Transport *Colectivos* run every 15 mins from the international terminal at Diego Portales 1002 to **Tacna**, US$3 per person, 1½ hrs, drivers take care of all the paperwork. 4 companies: *Chile Lintur*, Baquedano 796, T232048; *Chasquitur*, Chacabuco 320, T231376. San Marcos, Noé 321, T252528; *Colectivo San Remo*, Chacabuco 350, T251925. Bus from the terminal, US$2, also *Taxibus*, 2 hrly, US$4. The train service has been interrupted while repairs are carried out; the train station is on Maximo Lira, by the port, and, in normal times, a train leaves at 1000 and 2000, Mon-Fri, and at 1500 on Sat, US$1.50.

Into Peru **Tacna** is 36 km north of the border. The city was in Chilean hands from 1880 to 1929, when its citizens voted by plebiscite to return to Peru. There is a wide variety of hotels and restaurants as well as bus and air services to the rest of

Acclimatization for the Altiplano

Unless you are entering Chile from Bolivia, the high altitude of the altiplano encountered in the Parque Nacional Lauca presents specific health problems for the traveller to Chile. These should not be underestimated; anyone with circulation or respiratory problems would be advised to avoid the risks involved. Visitors to the park are advised to spend at least one night, preferably more, in Putre before moving on to higher altitudes. Drinking lots of water and/or mate de coca is also advised to compensate for the loss of body fluid caused by increased respiration and perspiration. You should, of course, take it easy, limiting exercise before you get that familiar headache associated with

soroche (altitude sickness), avoid smoking and take steps to get as much fresh air as possible, particularly if spending the night in a refugio. In popular refugios there can be six to 10 people breathing the same air all night in a small room: to avoid the 3 am headache which often develops in such conditions leave a window open and keep the water bottle nearby. Sleeplessness is a common first night problem but is not a cause for concern.

One-day trips to the park from Arica cannot really be recommended, either for health or for enjoyment: what should be a great trip amid incredible scenery can become an endurance exercise in a minibus full of passengers suffering from soroche.

Peru, and a tourist office at Avenida Bolognesi 2088, T3778. The Peruvian side of the border is open 0900-2200.

From Arica to Bolivia

Route 11 (paved to La Paz) turns off the Pan-American Highway 12 km north of Arica and runs via Putre and Parinacota through the Parque Nacional Lauca (see page 264) to the border at Chungará. This is the route followed by most transport to Bolivia, including buses and trucks. Estimated driving time to La Paz is 6 hours. Chilean immigration formalities are 7 km west of the border, open 0800-2000. Bolivian immigration and customs are at Tambo Quemado, just over the border (where there is a local barter market every other Fri). This is a relatively speedy crossing.

Via Chungará & Tambo Quemado
There are two routes from Arica to the Bolivian border

Transport There are 2 or 3 buses daily between Arica and La Paz; for details see under Arica. The Chungará frontier post is a good place for hitching to La Paz.

Into Bolivia The road to Oruro and La Paz (Route 108) passes through the **Parque Nacional Sajama**. This park covers 60,000 ha and contains the world's highest forest, consisting mainly of the rare Kenua tree which survives at altitudes of up to 5,200 m. The scenery is wonderful and includes views of three volcanos: Parinacota (6,342 m) and Pomerape (6,282 m) both of which are on the frontier, and Sajama (6,530 m), which is Bolivia's highest peak, but can be seen from the Lauca National park in Chile. Park administration is at Sajama village, 14 km off Route 108 (altitude 4,200 m) where there is also basic accommodation. There is also accommodation at Carahuara de Carangas, 111 km northeast of Tambo Quemado. The main Oruro-La Paz highway is reached at Patacamaya, 104 km south of La Paz, where there is basic accommodation and a Sunday market.

This route is unpaved and should not be attempted in wet weather. It follows the La Paz-Arica railway line to **Visviri** (altitude 4,069 m), which is 3 km from the Bolivian frontier and 12 km from Peru (no crossing). There are markets on Wednesday and Saturday

Via Visviri & Charalla

mornings and a Sun morning market is held from 0900 north of the town at the frontier of the 3 countries. There is no fuel or accommodation. Visviri can also be reached by road from Putre. Immigration office opens 0800-2000. Chilean formalities are at Visviri, Bolivian formalities are conducted at Charaña, 10 km east.

Transport *Humire* buses from Arica, Tue and Fri at 1030, US$6.50. From Visviri, you can take a jeep across the border to Charaña.

Into Bolivia In **Charaña,** immigration is behind the railway station. Accommodation is available at *Alojamiento Aranda* (**H**). There are two routes, both poor, from Charaña towards La Paz, both of which meet at Viacha. Buses to La Paz, US$4, 6 hrs, leave before 1000. Truck transport to La Paz leaves in the afternoon.

Parque Nacional Lauca

Colour map 1, grid A2
145 km east of Arica

Situated in the Andes and stretching from the entrance to the border with Bolivia, this park is one of the most spectacular national parks in Chile. Declared a Biosphere Reserve by UNESCO, it is renowned for its birdlife, but is equally remarkable for the extraordinary views of snow-capped volcanoes set against the backdrop of Lago Chungará, one of the world's highest lakes, and the profusion of vicuñas and vizcachas which live here. The brilliant quality of the light gives colours an intensity that is not easily forgotten, and there are many deserted tracks across the altiplano which provide a unique sense of the space and beauty of this remote corner of the world.

In & outs
See page 267 for further details

Access is easy as Route 11, the main Arica-La Paz road, runs through the park. From mid Dec to mid Mar, and during the rainy season and in Aug, when snowfall occurs, some roads in the park may be impassable; check in advance with CONAF or the *carabineros* in Arica or Putre. Maps are available from the Instituto Geográfico Militar in Santiago. Water in the park is not drinkable; drink bottled water.

The route
Often, when climbing the road from Arica, it may seem as though the weather is overcast; but vehicles soon gain altitude, climbing through the mist into a sort of lost world above, where the sky is a piercing blue colour, from which you gaze down at the grey clouds huddled in the valley as if looking into a different plane of reality. On the way from Arica at Km 90 there is a pre-Inca *pukará* (fortress) and a few kilometres further there is an Inca *tambo* (inn).

The park
The park covers 137,883 ha and includes a large lake, Lago Chungará, a system of smaller lakes, the lagunas Cotacotani, and lava fields. Ranging in altitude from 3,200 m to four peaks of over 6,000 m, Lauca brings significant risks of *soroche*, or altitude sickness; beware unless you are coming from Bolivia. Because of the extreme height, it is best to rise in stages, spending a night in Putre before going on to Lago Chungará; for this reason one-day tours from Arica are not the best way of seeing the park.

Putre
Population 1,200
Altitude: 3,500 m

Putre is a scenic Aymará village, 15 km west of the park entrance, which provides an ideal base for exploring and acclimatization. Situated at the base of Volcán Taapacá (Spanish name Nevadas de Putre, 5,824 m), it is surrounded by terracing dating from pre-Inca times which is now used for cultivating alfalfa and oregano. It has a church dating from 1670. The village is a good centre for hiking: an extensive network of trails lead to numerous villages in

Wildlife of Parque Nacional Lauca

Although the park lies very close to the lifeless Atacama desert, it receives more rain because of its altitude and the reward is a fairyland of volcanoes and highland lakes surrounded by brilliant green wetlands and vast expanses of puna grassland. The Río Lauca rises near Lago Chungará, then laces slowly through the park leaving marshy cushion bogs and occasional raceways and providing an array of habitats for the wildlife of the altiplano.

The camelids are the stars of the park; thousands of domesticated llamas and alpacas, as well as the dainty, graceful, wild vicuña which now number over 18,000. The charming viscacha, seemingly a long tailed rabbit, but in fact belonging to the chinchilla family, can be seen perched sleepily on the rocks, backside toward the morning sun. Pumas, huemules (deer), foxes, skunks and armadillos are the more elusive mammals, some nocturnal, occupying the more remote reaches.

Lauca birdlife is spectacular with more than 120 species either resident or migrant. Lago Chungará is home to more than 8,000 giant coots, their bright orange legs, never-ending nest building, and primordial cackling entertains all. In addition to coots, ducks and grebes, the wetlands provide a fine habitat for the puna plover, the rare diademed sandpiper plover, the puna ibis, Andean species of avocet, goose and gull, and an assortment of migratory shorebirds. Occasionally one can see three species of flamingoes at once, the Andean and the James (locally called parinas) and the more common Chilean flamingo. Trips through the drier grasslands can produce glimpses of the puna tinamou, always in groups of three, and the puna rhea, seen in October and November with 20 or 30 miniatures scooting along behind. Passerines occupy all the habitats in the park, some to 5,000 m and above nearly to the snowline. There are Sierra finches, black siskins, tit-spinetails, earthcreepers, miners, canasteros, cinclodes, new names for most birders. After all this, don't forget to look up! Andean condors, mountain caracaras, aplomado falcons, black chested buzzard eagles and buteo hawks have all been seen in the skies above.

the mountains, which provide great opportunities to explore for those with the necessary time and fitness. In the vicinity there are four archaeological sites with cave paintings up to 6,000 years old. Some 5 km east by trail (11 km by road) are the hot springs of Jurassi, with very hot water and a red mud bath. Note that weather can be poor in January and February, with fog and rain.

Parinacota From Putre the road continues to climb, and soon enters the park. At Parinacota (4,392 m), a small village of whitewashed adobe houses 26 km into the park, and 41 km from Putre, there is an interesting **17th-century church** – rebuilt 1789 – with frescoes, silver religious objects and the skulls of past priests. Senor Sipriano keeps the key: ask for him at the kiosks and make sure you leave a donation. Parinacota lay on two ancient trading routes, one from Potosí to Arica and the other from Belén into Bolivia. There is a small shop in Parinacota with basic supplies, and the CONAF office that administers the Lauca park is also here, 0900-1200 and 1230-1700, daily. Most of the handicrafts sold in Parinacota are from Bolivia or Peru: a better place to buy locally made products is **Chucuyo**, 36 km further east where local residents weave and knit from their own high quality alpaca wool. Buses Humire have buses on Tue and Fri from Arica to Parinacota at 1030, US$4.75.

Hikes From Parinacota an unpaved road runs to the Bolivian frontier at Visviri, 90 km further north (see above). **Cerro Guaneguane** (5,300 m) can be climbed from Parinacota; ask one of the villagers to accompany you as a guide (and pay them). There is also a path to the **Lagunas de Cotacotani**, a walk that would make a good day hike. CONAF maintains a nature trail which covers most plant and bird habitats, beginning at the CONAF pond in Parinacota and ending back in the village. Some 20 km southeast of Parinacota is **Lago Chungará**, one of the highest lakes in the world at 4,512 m, a must for its views of the Parinacota, Pomerape, Sajama and Guallatire volcanoes. Overlooking the lake there is a CONAF *refugio* and campsite; vicuñas, llamas and alpacas can be seen grazing nearby. From here it is 3 km to the Chilean passport control point and 10 km to the Bolivian frontier at Tambo Quemado.

Essentials

Sleeping and eating

Putre B *Hostería Las Vicuñas*, T/F228564. Half board, bungalow-style, heating, restaurant, does not accept TCs, US$ cash or credit cards. **F** *Res La Paloma*. Newly renovated, indoor parking, no heating, good food, friendly. **F** *Res Rosamel*. Clean, pleasant, hot water, restaurant. **G** *Res Oasis*. Basic, no showers, good food, very friendly. **Camping** Sra Clementina Caceres, blue door on Calle Lynch, allows camping in her garden, lunches served.

For all overnight stays in the park take a sleeping bag, food and candles Conaf refugios do not provide sheets or blankets

Inside the park Lagunillas: 10 km north of Parinacota on road to Visviri, turn left near lake. Sr Gumercindo Gutierrez provides accommodation, guide. **Chucuyo**: *Res Copihue de Oro*, 1 room, 4 beds, no showers, restaurant. *Res Doña Mati*, 1 room, 5 beds, no shower, restaurant. *Restaurant Los Payachatas*. All 3 restaurants serve tasty alpaca dishes. **Parinacota**: *Sra Francisca*, 3 beds, cooking facilities. *Uta Maillko* ('home of the condor' in Aymara), dormitory, home-cooked Aymara food. **E** pp *CONAF refugio*, many beds, cooking facilities, also camping **F** per site, reserve in Putre. **D** *Casa Barbarita*, T300013, F222735. 2 bedrooms, cooking facilities, heating, naturalist library. **Lago Chungará**: *CONAF Refugio*, 8 beds, wood stove, cooking facilities, camping, prices as in Parinacota, reserve in Putre.

Tour operators

Birding Alto Andino, Baquedano 299, T058-300013, offers specialist birding tours of the area and also walking tours along the Camino del Inca, English spoken, owner is an Alaskan biologist/naturalist, recommended. *Freddy Torrejón* offers accommodation and tours of the surrounding area, including Lago Chungará and the village of Parinacota, as well as trips to the more out of the way places, such as the Salar de Surire and ancient rock paintings; T/F58-253361, www2.gratisweb.com/losandeschileno/ or contact him at Gonzalo Cerda 1366, Arica.

Sports

Best season for climbing is August to November; avoid January to February

Mountain climbing: Arturo Gomez, who lives next to the Lipigas propane shop in Putre, is a climbing guide and local plant expert. Permits are required for climbing Parinacota, Pomerape, Taapacá and Guallatire volcanoes; these can be obtained from the Governor's office in Putre. The procedure is routine (passport required) but expect a delay of 1 or 2 days. To obtain permit in advance contact Departamento de Fronteras y Limites (DIFROL), Banderas 52, piso 5, Santiago, T6794200, listing the mountains you wish to climb.

Shopping

Putre has markets where bottled water, fresh bread, vegetables, meat, cheese and canned foods can be obtained. The *Cooperativo* on the plaza is usually cheapest. Fuel is available from the *Cali* and *Paloma* supermarkets, but is cheaper at *ECA*, next to the post office. Buy all food for the park in Putre. Sra Daria Condori's shop on Calle O'Higgins sells locally made *artesanía* and naturally coloured alpaca wool. Organically grown vegetables are available from Freddy Blanco, opposite the *Banco del Estado*.

Also *Turismo Taki*, located in Copaquilla, 45 km west of Putre, 100 km east of Arica: restaurant, camping site and excursions to nearby *pukarás*, Inca *tambo* and cemetery and the nearby Inca trail which connected the highlands with the coast, homemade bread, English and Italian spoken. One-day tours are offered by many agencies in Arica (see above), daily in season, according to demand at other times, US$20 with light breakfast and lunch; all one day tours make Parinacota their last stop. Longer tours are also available. You can leave the tour and continue on another day as long as you ensure that the company will collect you when you want (tour companies try to charge double for this). For 5 or more, the most economical proposition is to hire a vehicle in Arica but take at least 1 spare fuel can with a tightly fitting cap. While climbing from Arica stop several times to release excess pressure in fuel cans. For tyre repairs, ask for Andrés in Putre. If you wish to cross into Bolivia you will need written permission from the hire company.

Tour companies
See also under Putre

Bus *La Paloma* leave Arica daily at 0630 for Putre, US$2.75, returning from Putre at 1330. *Jurasi colectivos* leave Arica daily at 0700, picking up at hotels, T222813, US$5. **Hitchhiking** Hitching back to Arica is not difficult; you may be able to bargain with one of the tour buses. Trucks from Arica to La Paz rarely give lifts, but a good place to try is at the Poconchile control point, 37 km from Arica. Most trucks for Bolivia pass Parinacota between 0700-1100.

Transport

Banks Bank in Putre changes TCs, and cash to pesos, but commission on TCs is very high.

Directory

Reserva Nacional Las Vicuñas, Salar de Surire and Parque Nacional Volcán Isluga

These three parks, covering areas of the western range of the Andes south of Parque Nacional Lauca, are best visited from Arica or Putre as this permits acclimatization in Putre (Colchane and Enquelga, the alternatives, are too high). The route begins in the Parque Nacional Lauca at the dirt road (A235) which turns south off the Arica-La Paz highway 1 km past Las Cuevas and ends at Huara on the Pan-American Highway, near Iquique. There is no public transport on this route, and frequently no traffic of any sort passes for days on end between Las Cuevas and Isluga. The road is open all year round, but between January and March and in August it may be impassable because of deep mud and water, while bridges may be washed out. Four-wheel drive is essential; take sleeping bags and stock up on fuel, drinking water and food for emergencies.

Colour map 1, grid A2

Tours in this area, lasting two or four days, can be arranged in Putre

Although many maps show roads descending from the *altiplano* from Surire to the Pan-American Highway, and from Colchane to Camiña, do not be tempted to follow them. These roads are terrible in the dry season, dangerous and impassable in the rainy season; if stranded you could wait weeks for help to arrive. The only two safe routes between the *altiplano* and the Pan-American Highway are the international routes from Arica through Parque Nacional Lauca and from Huara to Colchane.

Split off from Parque Nacional Lauca in order to permit mining, this reserve, reached by Route A235, stretches across 209,131 ha, most of it rolling *altiplano* at an average altitude of 4,300 m. The reserve is bisected by the Río Lauca along which riverine vegetation alternates with puna tola/grasslands and many camelids can be seen. Keep an eye open for condors, rheas and migrating peregrine falcons. Mina Choquelimpie (not operating), one of the

Reserva Nacional Las Vicuñas

world's highest gold and silver mines, can be reached by a 7 km detour (clearly marked) off Route A235. Entrance to the park is free. There is accommodation for up to seven people at the park administration in **Guallatire** (imperative to reserve at least five days in advance on T058-250570, or it will be closed), a village 96 km south of Las Cuevas at the foot of the smoking Guallatire Volcano (6,060 m); the village has a lovely 17th-century *altiplano* church and a *carabinero* control post. At Km 139 the road reaches the Salar de Surire.

Sleeping and eating Sra Clara Blanca, an Aymaran weaver, offers overnight accommodation, food typical of the region, allows travellers to help with llamas and alpacas; house situated 1 km east off A235 and reached by turning 10 km after Chuquelimpie turnoff. *Restaurant Sanchez* (no sign), 1 block from *carabineros* in Guallatire, serves good lunch stews in an *altiplano* truckstop.

Monumento Natural Salar de Surire Situated at 4,300 m and covering 17,500 ha, the Salar de Surire is a drying salt lake with thermal springs and a year-round population of 12,000-15,000 flamingos of three species (nesting season is January). It is open all year, but see advice above. Access is by Route A235. Administration is in **Surire**, 45 km south of Guallatiri and 138 km south of Putre. About half of the salar is mined for borax; sometimes Surire may be reached by getting a ride in a borax truck from Zapahuira, a road junction at Km 100 on the road from Arica to La Paz; trucks run sporadically depending on rainfall and the drop-off point is on the mine side of the Salar, 30 km from the hot springs.

Sleeping and eating *CONAF refugio*, at Surire, 8 km past the borax mine, 15 beds and cooking facilities, advance booking at CONAF in Arica essential (see telephone number above). Campsite at Polloquere, 17 km south of Surire in the southeastern corner of the salar, no facilities, no water, **F** per site if CONAF check.

Parque Nacional Volcán Isluga
This park includes some of the best volcanic scenery of northern Chile

This park covers 174,744 ha at altitudes above 2,100 m. Although the lower parts of the park, at its southwestern end, lie in the hills of the precordillera, the heart of the park is situated between Laguna Aravilla with its flamingoes and the village of **Isluga**, where there is an 18th-century Andean church and bell tower. Route A235 crosses the park, from the northern entrance, 40 km south of Surire to the southern near Isluga. Northeast of Isluga under the smoking Volcán Isluga of 5,501 m is the village of **Encuelga**, where Aymaran weavers can be seen working in the sand behind wooden wind breaks. There are three other peaks over 5,000 m: Quimsachata (5,400 m), Tatajachura (5,252 m) and Latamara (5,207 m). Wildlife varies according to altitude; there are large numbers of camelids and birds but fewer camelids and rheas than in Parque Nacional Lauca.

Essentials Park administration is at Encuelga, but there are seldom *guardaparques* there. *CONAF refugio* in Encuelga, 6 beds and cooking facilities, reservation in Arica essential (see telephone number above). There are also several basic residenciales in Colchane, which lies 6 km south of the southern entrance (see above page 252).

The Central Valley

9

The Central Valley

Rancagua

Curicó

Talca

Constitución

Pacific Ocean

SANTIAGO

Chillán

Concepción

ARGENTINA

Los Angeles

The Central Valley is the heart of Chile. Stretching from just north of Santiago south to the Río Biobío, this wonderful region ranges from secluded tracks along the coast to the high Andes in the east, with the fertile valley itself in between. On clear days the snows of the mountains can easily be seen from the coast, reaching out across the woods, fields and vineyards in Chile's agricultural heartland. It is here that the most enduring images of Chilean village life can be found: huasos (cowboys) with their long spurs, green valleys with grazing horses, and whitewashed houses in colonial style, hinting at that bygone age before cars and motorbikes sounded the death knell for the horse.

The Central Valley

Background

History The peoples of the Central Valley did not prove as fierce as their Mapuche neighbours to the south. They were conquered by the Incas in about 1470, and this influenced what the Spanish found on their arrival. On his second visit to Chile Pedro de Valdivia led an expedition southwards, founding Concepción in 1550 and a further seven cities south of the Río Biobío. The Mapuche insurrection of 1598 and the Spanish defeat at Curalabo in 1599 led the Spanish to withdraw north of the Río Biobío and concentrate their colonial efforts in the central valley.

In the Central Valley, the land and inhabitants were divided up between the colonists. This was the origin of the hacienda which was to dominate social and economic life for at least 200 years. The hacienda was a self-contained unit, producing almost everything it needed. Until the 18th century there were no towns in the area, but from the 1740s the Spanish crown founded settlements in an attempt to increase its control, including San Fernando (1742), Curicó (1743), Talca (1742), Cauquenes (1742) and Linares (1755).

After independence the Río Biobío continued to be the southern frontier of white settlement until, in 1862, Colonel Cornelio Saavedra led an army south to build a line of 10 forts, each 4 km apart, between Angol and Collipulli. Following the occupation of the coast around Arauco in 1867 another line of forts was built across the Cordillera de Nahuelbuta. By 1881 the railway from Santiago had reached Angol, from where Chilean troops set out on the final campaign against the Mapuche.

Geography This section covers three of the administrative regions of Chile, Regions VI (O'Higgins), VII (Maule) and VIII (Biobío). The Central Valley is a wide depression located between the Andes to the east and the Cordillera de la Costa to the west. The Andes gradually lose height as they continue southwards, although there are a number of high peaks east of Rancagua: Alto de los Arrieros, 5,000 m, El Palomo, 4,986 m, Tingiririca, 4,280 m. The Coastal Range is low at under 500 m, but south of the Río Biobío it forms a range of high peaks known as the Cordillera de Nahuelbuta. Five major rivers cross the Central Valley: from north to south these are the Ríos Rapel, Mataquito, Maule, Itata and Biobío. Of these the Biobío, one of the longest rivers in Chile, is the most important.

Climate The northern parts of the Central Valley enjoy a Mediterranean climate, with a prolonged dry season, but with more rain than Santiago. In general, rainfall increases gradually from north to south, until around Concepción some rain falls in most months. The Central Valley itself receives less rain than the coastal mountains, but temperatures vary much more inland than in coastal areas.

Economy The Central Valley is the agricultural heartland of Chile, transformed in the past 30 years by the growth of commercial export agriculture: wheat, maize, rice, sugar, beans, vegetables and fruit are grown throughout this area, which also produces most of Chile's wine. Much local industry is based on these products: rice mills, sugar mills, vegetable oil refineries and wineries are important sources of employment. While commercial forestry is based around the Río Biobío, it is important throughout the Central Valley. Fishing is of less importance, except around the Río Biobío: the coastline between Dichato and Arauco saw an important growth in large scale fishing and fish-processing in the 1980s and early 1990s.

★

Things to do in the Central Valley

- Surf off the coast of Pichilemu, one of the best surfing beaches in Chile.
- Wine-taste in the vineyards around Santa Cruz and the Maule Valley.
- Visit any one of countless small resorts along the beautiful and largely deserted Pacific coast – Curanipe, Iloca and Lebu being favourites.
- Trek in the mountains near the resort of Vilches, east of Talca.
- Take in a rodeo in summer; the highlight being the National Rodeo championships in Rancagua at the end of March.

Concepción and the surrounding area constitute the second most important industrial area in Chile, partly as a result of the construction of the country's only steelworks at Huachipato in the 1950s and the development of major hydroelectric power plants along the Río Laja. Coal mining, however, which for many years was the mainstay of the coastal strip south of Concepción, went into decline in the 1980s and all the mines have now closed.

The Rapel Valley

The damming of the Río Rapel has created Lago Rapel, the largest artificial lake in Chile, and a very popular destination for Santiaguinos taking their summer holidays. There are numerous small and pleasant towns, and several large fundos (farms) south of the town of Rapel in an area of green hills and stunted thorn trees. Open roads by the coast have wonderful views of the high Andes east of Rancagua, while the beach at Pichilemu is one of the best in Chile for surfing.

Rancagua

The capital of VI Región, Libertador General Bernardo O'Higgins, Rancagua lies 82 km south of Santiago, on the Río Cachapoal. Founded in 1743, it is a service and market centre for a rich agricultural area.

Phone code: 072
Colour map 3, grid B3

Getting there Rancagua is accessible by bus and train from Santiago (both hourly). There are also connections to the towns further south, especially Talca, Chillán, Concepcíon, Temuco and Puerto Montt (several daily). **Getting around** While the centre of Rancagua is quite compact, some of the outlying *barrios* are quite a distance, and you may wish to take one of the numerous *colectivos*. **Tourist offices** Germán Riesco 277, T230413, F232297, sernatur_rancag@entelchile.net Helpful, English spoken. Also municipal office in the Municipalidad on the Plaza de los Héroes. *Automóvil Club de Chile*, Ibieta 09, T239930, F239907.

Ins & outs
See page 275 for further details

At the heart of the city is an attractive tree-lined plaza, the **Plaza de los Heroes** and several streets of single-storey colonial-style houses. In the centre of the plaza is an equestrian statue of O'Higgins. The double-spired cathedral, on the south side of the plaza was restored in the 1860s, the original building having been destroyed in the battle of Rancagua. The **Merced** church, one block north, several times restored, dates from 1758. The main commercial area lies along Avenida Independencia, which runs west from the plaza towards the bus and rail terminals.

Sights

The **Museo Histórico**, housed in a colonial mansion, contains collections of religious art and late 19th-century furniture. ■ *US$1, (Tue free), Tue-Fri*

The Central Valley

Coming of age as a cow

During the summer months rodeo is one of the most popular sports in central and southern Chile, second only to the inevitable: football. Teams (or colleras) of two riders on horseback compete throughout the season, culminating in the national championships in Rancagua at the end of March. Eliminatory rounds are held in Osorno, Temuco, San Carlos, San Fernando, Vallenar and Los Andes, but most small towns in central southern Chile have their own media lunas (stadia, with their own corrals and horseboxes), often used once a year only.

Rodeo owes its origins to the colonial period, when cattle roamed openly and were rounded up once annually to be identified and marked by their owners in a rodeo. Based on the traditional view that heifers need to be broken in, the modern sport of rodeo is a test of the ability of two horses and their riders to work together and control the cattle.

The event takes place inside a stockade of thick upright timbers; although now circular, this is known as a media luna (crescent) after the design of the early rings: at two points the walls of the ring are covered by padded sections, with a flag at either end of the section. Each collera competes by manoeuvring a heifer around the edge of the ring between the padded sections, stopping it at each padded section by pinning its hindquarters against the fence, before turning it in the opposite direction. This is done three times before the animal is released from the ring. Three judges give points (on a scale of one to seven) for skills of horsemanship and elegance. It is one of the principles of rodeo that no heifer should be put through this performance more than once; the event should come as a complete surprise.

Rodeo is a good opportunity to see traditional Chilean rural customs: the huasos (cowboys) in wide-brimmed hats, brightly coloured ponchos and the carved wooden stirrups which were common in the 19th century, the fine horses and the cuecas (traditional dances) which sometimes follow the event.

1000-1800, Sat, Sun 0900-1300. Estado y Ibieta, T/F221524, museo@chilesat.net There is also a **Casa de la Cultura**, at the corner of Milán and Cachapoal, directly south of Plaza de Los Héroes. ■ 0830-1330, 1500-1700, T230976. In the station there is a small gallery with paintings by local artists for sale.

Excursions The thermal springs of **Cauquenes** are 28 km east, reached by one of five daily
Charles Darwin buses with *Buses Termas* (US$1) or a *colectivo* from Rancagua market. There is
was a visitor to **A Hotel Termas de Cauquenes**, T899010, F899011, which serves excellent
Cauquenes in 1835 food. It has a chapel and gardens. A bath in the springs costs US$5, while massage is US$7.50 and a jacuzzi costs US$14. Some 5 km north of Cauquenes is the village of **Coya**, where the Chilean President has a summer residence.

Sleeping **AL** *Camino del Rey*, Estado 275, T239765, F232314. 4-star, full facilities, best.
■ *on map page 275* **AL-A** *Santiago*, Brasil 1036, T230860, F230822. Poorly maintained, friendly.
Price codes: **A-B** *Aguila Real*, Brasil 1045, T222047, F223002. With breakfast, cable TV, laundry, res-
see inside front cover taurant. **A-B** *Rancagua*, San Martín 85, T232663, F241155. Bath, quiet, clean, secure parking. Recommended. **C** *España*, San Martín 367, T230141, F234196. Bath, cheaper without, central, hot water, pleasant, clean. **C** *Portobello*, Bueras 30, F238800. **E** pp *Res Ahumada*, Mujica 125, T225892. Kitchen facilities, secure. Some 50 km south (22 km north of San Fernando) is *Hacienda Los Lingues*, see page 277.

Mid-range *Guy Restaurante*, Astorga 319. French food. *Le Gourmet*, Independencia | **Eating**
634, 5th floor. **Cheap** *Geo Algas*, Independencia 677, 2nd floor. Vegetarian. *La Cocina Artesanal*, O´Carrol 60. Traditional meat and seafood dishes. Also *Bravissimo*, Astorga 307, for ice cream, and *Lasagna*, west end of Plaza, for bread and *empanadas*.

Pubs *La Notta*, Illanes 303-A, with restaurant. *Pub Restaurant Puerto Girón*, Bueras | **Entertainment**
358. Both expensive. **Disco** *Varadero*, O'Carrol 1109. **Cinema** *Cine Rex*, Astorga 360.
Also at Independencia 591.

National Rodeo Championships, at the end of **Mar** in the Complejo Deportivo, north | **Festivals**
of the centre, US$10 per day (plenty of opportunities for purchasing cowboy items;
watch out for the fantastic spurs, much more important to horsemanship in Chile than
elsewhere in Latin America). *Festival del Poroto* (Bean Festival), **1-5 Feb**; beans are the
most important staple food for *campesinos* in the area.

Shopping Mall at Cuevas 483. Supermarket at *Hipermercado Independencia,* Av | **Shopping**
Miguel Ramírez 665.

Bus Main terminal at Doctor Salinas y Calvo just north of the market but most buses | **Transport**
for Santiago leave from terminal on O'Carrol. *Tur Bus* terminal at Calvo y O'Carrol. Many
services from further south stop on the Pan-American Highway, 2 km outside town.
Local: There are far too many local buses to list here, but destinations include **Lago
Rapel** with *Sextur* (T231342) or *Galbus* (T230640), US$2, every 20 mins; **Pichilemu**,
US$4 1-way, many companies; and **Termas Del Flaco** (US$12 return) with *Buses
Amistad* (T229358), booking required 2 days in advance. **Long distance**: Frequent
services to **Santiago**, US$3, 1¼ hrs. To **Valparaíso** and **Viña del Mar**, *Tur Bus*, US$6.
Viatur (T234502) have a nightly bus to **Valdivia, Osorno** and **Puerto Montt**
(US$15-17), and another to Chillán and Los Angeles (US$8); *Buses Lit* (T239800) also

Rancagua centre

To Pan-American Highway (North)

The Central Valley

Sleeping		Eating	
1 Aguila Real	4 Portobello	1 Bravissimo	4 Lasagna
2 Camino del Rey	5 Rancagua	2 Geo Algas	5 La Gourmet
3 España	6 Santiago	3 Guy Restaurante	

Not to scale

The battle of Rancagua

Rancagua was the scene of an important battle during the Wars of Independence. On 1-2 October 1814, Bernardo O'Higgins and his 1,700 Chilean patriots were surrounded in the centre of the town by 4,500 Royalist (pro-Spanish) troops. O'Higgins, who commanded his forces from the tower of the Merced church, managed to break out and escape. Following this defeat he was forced into exile in Argentina, while the Royalists re-established control over Chile. While in Argentina, O'Higgins met up with San Martín who led the invasion force across the Andes which resulted in the final defeat of Spanish forces in Chile. Plaques in the centre of Rancagua mark the sites of the battle and a diagram in the Plaza de los Héroes shows the disposition of the troops. The battle resulted in the destruction of most of the buildings around the Plaza.

have buses to the south. **Cycle** Spares at Gustavo Sepúlveda, Bueras 481, T241413. **Motoring** For car parts try *Aucamar*, Brasil 1177, T223594, and several others around Brasil 1100-1200, better selection and prices in Santiago. **Train** Mainline services **between Santiago and Chillán** stop here. Also regular services to/from **Santiago and San Fernando** on *Metrotren*, 1½ hrs, 10-19 a day, US$2. Station, T230361.

Directory **Airline offices** *Aerocontinente*, *Iberia*, *Lacsa* and *United Airlines*, Cuevas No 744, T220288 F237054. *LanChile* and *Ladeco*, Astorga 223B, T235573, F244392. **Banks** Exchange at *Cambios Afex*, Av Campos 363. For US$ cash. *Cambios Transafex*, Ramírez 655, open every day. Also several banks on Independencia. **Car hire** *Weber Rentacar*, Membrillar 40, Of 2, T226005. **Communications** Internet: *Ciber Space*, Alcázar 376.

Around Rancuagua

Lago Rapel Lago Rapel, southwest of Rancagua, is 40 km long and feeds the Rapel hydro-electric plant. Most facilities at this popular summer resort are on the east shore around El Manzano, the main town, while the tourist information office is in Las Cabras. There are watersports at Bahía Skorpios, including windsurfing, yachting, waterskiing and fishing.

Sleeping and eating **L-AL** *Punta Verde*, Bahía Skorpios, T591434, F591442, full facilities. **E** *Hostería Playa Llallauquén*, Llallauquén Viejo s/n, T561474 and many more. The eastern shore of the lake around El Manzano is lined with campsites (*Camping Punta Arenas*, 3 km north of El Manzano, basic, cheap).

El Teniente & Chapa Verde The El Teniente copper mine, one of the biggest in the country, lies 67 km east. Owned by Codelco, it can only be visited by prior arrangement with the company. Nearby, on a private road above El Teniente, is the small Chapa Verde ski resort, owned by Codelco, but open to the public in season. It can only be reached by mine-transport bus (from *Del Sol* shopping centre on the northern outskirts of Rancagua, daily 0900, weekends in season every 15 minutes between 0800 and 0930). Equipment can be hired, no accommodation, lift tickets US$18 weekdays, US$25 weekends, obtainable only from resort office in Del Sol shopping centre.

Situated 50 km southeast of Rancagua and 22 km from the Termas de **Reserva**
Cauquenes, the park covers 36,882 ha of the valley of the Río de los Cipreses at **Nacional Río**
altitudes ranging from 900 m to 4,900 m. Park administration is at the **de los Cipreses**
entrance at the north end of the park, T297505, entrance US$3. There is a
campsite at Los Maitenes, 12 km south of the entrance, **F** per site.

San Fernando

This town lies on the Río Tingiririca, 51 km south of Rancagua. Founded in *Phone code: 072*
1742, it is capital of Colchagua Province and a service town for this fertile val- *Colour map 3, grid B3*
ley. There is a small local museum, the **Casa Patronal de Lircunlauta**. *Population: 44,500*
■ *Closed Mon, US$2.50. Jiménez y Alameda.*

From San Fernando a road runs east towards the Cordillera and divides: the **Excursions**
southern branch of the road goes to the resort of **Sierra Bellavista**, a private
fundo where many Santiago businessmen have holiday houses, and where
there are rodeos in October and November. The northern branch, 75 km,
runs to the **Termas del Flaco** near the Argentine border, where there is a poor
campsite, *cabañas* and hotels. Thermal springs (*US$1.40*) are open only in the
summer when they attract large numbers of visitors. Some 500 m from the
Termas del Flaco are 'Las huellas de Dinosaurios', dinosaur footprints preserved in the rock, dating from over 120 million years ago. **Los Lingues** is a
private *hacienda*, 20 km northeast of San Fernando, where, it is said, the best
horses in Chile are bred. In 1984 Rosie Swale rode from Antofagasta to Caleta
Tortel with two horses lent to her by the owner of the hacienda, see page 71.
Visits can be arranged to the 17th-century house, a gift of the King of Spain.
One-day tours including transport, rodeo and lunch are available. There is
very expensive accommodation (*starting at US$250*) with an extra charge for
breakfast or full board. The *hacienda* is a member of the French Hotels et
Relais et Chateaux. Contact: Hacienda Los Lingues, Torre C de Tajamar, Of
205, Santiago, T235-2458/5446/7604, F235-7604.

On Av Rodríguez **B** *Español*, No 959, T711098. **B- C** *Imperio*, No 770, T714595. With **Sleeping**
bath, clean. **C** *Marcano*, No 968, T714759, F713943. **E** *Pérez*, No 1028, T713328. **& eating**
Without bath. All are cheap eateries: *Club Social San Fernando*, Rodríguez 787. Good
local food. *Restaurante La Carreta*, Rancagua 759. Traditional. *Rigoletto*, Rodríguez
751. Pizzas.

Bar *Pepe Cuervo Pub-Bar*, Costanera 1. **Disco** *Toscano Pub Disco*, Quechereguas **Entertainment**
966, Fri and Sat only.

Bus Many companies serving **Santiago** (US$2.50), including *Andimar* (T711817) and **Transport**
Pullman del Sur (T714076). To **Pichilemu** (US$2.50) with *Nilahue* (T711937) and
Galbus (T712983); to **Termas del Flaco** (US$8 return) with *Amistad* (T710348),
Andibus (T711817) and others. Lots of competition to the south, with services as far as
Chiloé (US$17) with *Cruz del Sur* (T710348), and most intermediate destinations with
Turbus (T712923) and *Buses Lit* (T711679). **Car hire** *Alvaro Arsenjoz*, España 928,
T/F712105. **Train** *Metrotren*, 10 daily to Santiago, station T711087.

Fifty kilometres southwest of San Fernando is this small town, from which **Santa Cruz**
excellent tours of the region's vineyards can be made on the Circuito del Vino
de Colchagua.

The Central Valley

Tours Half day and full day tours can be arranged at the Plaza de Armas 140, Of 6, T/F823199, rv@uva.cl 48 hrs notice required, English speaking guides, (US30-60 per person depending on tour and size of group). A full day tour takes in 2 vineyards, tasting 2 wines at each, lunch, museum visit. Half day tours are the same, but without lunch. The following may be visited independently: *Viña La Posada*, Rafael Casanova 570, Santa Cruz. Reservations are only required for weekend visits. Also accommodation (**AL**) and meals served. T822589, F822448, laposada@entelchile.net *Viña Pueblo Antiguo*, Florecio Valdés 236, Nancagua (half way between San Fernando and Santa Cruz). Reservations advised, meals served. T858296, F923712, www.puebloantiguo.com

Pichilemu

Many people come to Pichilemu for the nightlife, and there is a good atmosphere after dark

Pichilemu is a coastal resort with a great many hotels and *residenciales* lying 120 km west of San Fernando. It was founded by Agustín Ross Edwards, in the 19th century, in the style of a European resort. There are many beaches, including the Punta Los Lobos beach, where international surfing competitions are held. The former train station, made of wood in 1925, is a national monument. There is also a small museum, the **Museo del Niño Rural de Ciruelos**, with three rooms of interesting exhibits of remains from the pre-Hispanic cultures of the region. Fishing is good in nearby lakes.

Some distance before Pichilemu, many tracks branch off the road from San Fernando, southwards through quiet hill country towards Lago Vichuquén. Dry thorn trees gradually give way to more fertile land, there are the first signs of *copihues* and forests, and beautiful routes keep to ridges high above the valleys; recommended for cyclists, walkers and horseback riders.

Sleeping and eating C *Chile-España*, Ortúzar 255, T841270, F841314. **D** off season. Friendly, helpful, excellent restaurant, good value. **C** *Rex*, Ortúzar 124, T/F841003. Good breakfast, good value. Also *Cabañas Lugano*, Calle Santiago, T/F842200, clugano@ctcinternet.cl Cabin accommodation with TV, private bath and kitchen, various outdoor activities organized. **F** *Bahía*, Ortúzar 262. With breakfast, clean. **Camping** Campsites, US$15 per site, more expensive than *residenciales*.

Entertainment Bars *Bar Pub Pepe Cuervo*, Avda Costanera 1, with restaurant. **Discos** *Disco Club 127*, Angel Gaete 127. *Vivo*, Ross 136. *Fabrica*, Acevedo 125.

Transport *Andimar* and *Nilahue* buses to **Santiago**, 4 hrs, US$5.50.

The Mataquito Valley

The Río Mataquito, formed by the confluence of the Ríos Lontué and Teno, flows through the heart of Chilean wine country, reaching the Pacific at a wide and serene estuary near Iloca. It is a peaceful valley, and the coast is largely deserted; from the cliffs above, the Andes can clearly be seen.

Curicó

Phone code: 075
Colour map 3, grid C2
Population: 103,919
192 km to Santiago

Curicó, which means *black water* in the Mapuche language, lies between the Ríos Lontué and Teno, 54 km south of San Fernando. Founded in 1743, it is the only town of any size in the Mataquito Valley. A bustling town, it is the service centre for the region's vineyards, with good views towards the mountains and a friendly atmosphere after dark.

Getting there Curicó is easily accessible by bus from Santiago (many times daily). There are also some connections to the towns further south, especially Talca, Chillán, Temuco and Puerto Montt (several daily). **Getting around** While the centre of Curicó is quite compact, some of the outlying *barrios* are quite a distance away, and you may wish to take one of the numerous *colectivos*. **Tourist offices** In Gobernación Provincial on Plaza de Armas. Mon-Fri 0900-1330, 1600-1800, helpful, has street map. Automóvil Club de Chile, Chacabuco 759, T311156. CONAF, Gobernación Provincial building, piso 1, Plaza de Armas, open 0900-1430.

Ins & outs
See page 280 for further details

In the **Plaza de Armas**, which is surrounded by about 40 Cañarí Island Palms, there are lovely fountains with sculptures of nymphs, black-necked swans and a monument to the Mapuche warrior, Lautaro, carved from the trunk of an ancient beech tree. There is a steel bandstand, built in New Orleans in 1904, which is a national monument. On the western side of the plaza is the church of **La Merced**, which was badly damaged by an earthquake in 1986, and is slowly being restored. Five blocks east is the neo-gothic church of **San Francisco**, a national monument, which contains the 17th-century Virgen de Velilla, brought from Spain. At the junction of Carmen and Avenida San Martín is the imposing **Iglesia del Carmen**. To the east of the city is the Avenida Manso de Velasco, with statues of various

History

The Central Valley

Curicó

■ Sleeping	**9** Residencia Rahue	**5** El Fogón Chileno
1 Comercio	**10** Savoy	
2 Palmas Express	**11** Turismo	**Ⓢ Banks**
3 Prat		**1** Banco BCI
4 Residencia Alemana	**● Eating**	**2** Banco BHIF
5 Residencia Central	**1** American Bar	**3** Banco de Chile
6 Residencia Colonial	**2** Café-Bar Maxim	**4** Banco Santander
7 Residencia Ensueño	**3** Centro Italiano Club Social	**5** Banco Santiago
8 Residencia Montt	**4** Club de la Unión	

0 metres 50
0 yards 50

national heroes, and also a bust of Mahathma Gandhi. Nearby is **Cerro Condell** offering fine views of the surrounding countryside and across to the distant Andes; it is an easy climb to the summit, from where there are a number of walks. Tourist information can be obtained from the Municipality. **Torres wine bodega** is 5 km south of the city. To get there, take a bus for Molina from the local terminal or from outside the railway station and get off at Km 195 on the Pan-American Highway. ■ *0900-1230, 1500-1730, T310455. No organized tour, Spanish only, worth a visit.*

Sleeping
■ *on map*
Price codes:
see inside front cover

A *Palmas Express*, Membrillar 728, T320066, F321425. **A** *Turismo* (officially, Luis Cruz Martínez), Prat y Carmen, T310552, F310823. Modern, with breakfast, pleasant garden. **A-B** *Comercio*, Yungay 730, T310014, F317001. 3 star, clean. **D** *Res Rahue*, Peña 410, T312194. Basic, meals, hot water, annex rooms have no ventilation. **D** *Res Central*, Prat 669. Good value, but not in the centre. **D** *Res Ensueño*, Rodríguez 442, T312648. **D** *Res Montt*, M Montt 432, T312929. **D** *Savoy*, Prat 726. Basic. **E-F** pp *Res Alemana*, Yungay 98, T/F314462. **F** *Prat*, Peña 427, T311069. Pleasant patio with grapevines and fig trees, friendly, clean, hot water, laundry facilities, breakfast extra, parking. Recommended. **F** *Res Colonial*, Rodríguez 461, T314103. Clean, patio, friendly, with bath, **G** without.

Eating
● *on map*

Expensive/mid-range *Club de la Unión*, Plaza de Armas. Good, expensive, smart dress. **Mid-range** *American Bar*, Yungay 647. Real coffee, small pizzas, good sandwiches, pleasant atmosphere, open early morning to late evening including weekends. Recommended. *El Fogón Chileno*, M Montt 399. For meat and wines. *Los Cisnes*, Rodríguez 1186. Parilladas, cheaper *almuerzos*. **Cheap** *Café-Bar Maxim*, Prat 617. Light meals, beer and wine. *Centro Italiano Club Social*, Estado 531, good, cheap meals. There are several seriously cheap restaurants with varying standards of cleanliness outside the market on Calle Donoso. Also *Sant' Angelo*, Prat 430, for excellent patisserie.

Entertainment

Pubs *Bar Deportivo*, Montt 446. *Crazy Horse*, on Manso de Velazco. *Scram Pub*, Velazco 451.

Festivals

Mid Mar *Fiesta de la Vendimia* with displays on traditional wine making.

Shopping

Supermarket *Unimarc*, Estado 43.

Transport
There is a toll (US$3) on the Pan-American Highway south of Curicó

Bus Main bus terminal on Prat y Maipú. Local buses, including to coastal towns as well as some long distance services, from Terminal Plaza, Prat y Maipú. *Turbus* stop on M De Velazco; their office is also on M De Velazco, 1 block south. *Pullman del Sur* have their own terminal at Henríquez y Carmen. Many southbound buses by-pass Curicó, but can be caught by waiting outside town. To **Santiago** *Pullman del Sur*, frequent, 2½ hrs, US$5. To **Temuco**, *LIT* and *Tur Bus*, US$7. To **Llico**, *Buses Díaz*, US$3, 3 hrs. To **Iloca**, US$2, regular in summer. **Motorcycle spares** *Chaleco López Motos*, San Martín 171, T316191. **Train** Station is at the western end of Prat, 4 blocks west of Plaza de Armas, T310028. To/from **Santiago**, 5 a day, 2½ hrs, US$6 *salón*, US$4 *turista*. To/from **Chillán**, 4 a day, 3 hrs, US$7 *salón*, US$5 *turista*.

Directory
See map for locations of banks

Banks Major banks located around Plaza de Armas. *Casa de Cambio*, Merced 255, Local 106, no TCs. **Communications** Post office: Plaza de Armas. **Telephones:** Call centres are expensive in Curicó, but try *O'Higgins 877* or Prat 74. Also *CTC*, Peña 650-A. **Internet:** Carmen y Argomedo, *M y T Computación*, Peña 430, T/F319865, mytcompu@entelchile.net *Montt 440*, *Prat 291*, and *Yungay 665*. **Laundry** *Ecológico*, Yungay 411. *Lavacentro*, Yungay 437. Expensive, good.

The Central Valley

This park is in two sectors, one at Radal, 65 km east of Curicó, the other at Parque Inglés, 9 km further east. The most interesting sector is at Radal, where the Río Claro flows through a series of seven rock bowls (the *siete tazas*) each with a pool emptying into the next by means of a waterfall. The river then passes through a canyon, 15 m deep but only 1½ m wide, which ends abruptly in a cliff and a beautiful waterfall. There are several well-marked trails. ■ *Oct to Mar. US$2. Administration is in Parque Inglés.*

Area de Proteccíon Radal Siete Tazas

Sleeping and eating C *Hostería La Flor de la Canela*, at Parque Inglés, T491613. Breakfast extra, good food. Highly recommended. **Camping** Campsite near entrance dirty, US$1 pp, shop. Also *Camping Las Catas*, 2 km inside park, expensive, US$13 per site, no shop.

Transport Bus: Take a minibus to Molina, 26 km south, from Terminal Plaza, frequent. From Molina buses run to the Parque Inglés daily in summer, 4 a day, 3 hrs, US$2, last return 1700. Daily bus from Curicó in summer, 1330, 4½ hrs, returns 0745 (Sun 0700, returns 1900). Access by car is easy as the road through the park is paved.

From Curicó a road runs west through the small town of Licantén to the mouth of the Río Mataquito and the popular resort of Iloca. Some 5 km north of Iloca is Puerto Duao, a fishing village with a good campsite. Iloca is set in a wide bay with great views south along the coastline. There is a bridge across the Río Mataquito 6 km west of Licantén, leading to a road south along the coast to Pudú and the Río Maule, where a ferry crosses to Constitución.

Iloca

Sleeping and eating B *Hostería Iloca*, Besoain 260, T243508. B *Hotel Iloca*, Besoain 221, T887998. Breakfast, good views, run down. 35 km west of Curico on road to Hualañe and Iloca is *Hospedaje El Capricho del Corazón*, **D-E** pp, Swiss run, English, French, German spoken, tours arranged. Recommended. T09-6391086, Casilla 322, Curicó. **F** accommodation on Besoain: nos 161, 198, 222. **Camping** *La Puntilla*, T09-7415585, 2 km north, also *cabañas* **B** sleep 6. *El Peñon*, 6 km south. Reservations: T471026 or Santiago, T02-6336099.

Transport Bus: from Terminal Plaza in Curicó, every hour in summer, less frequently off season, US$2.50, 2 hrs.

Llico, north of Iloca, is a good resort for windsurfing, reached either by a coastal route or by an unpaved inland road which branches off at Hualañe, 74 km east of Curicó.

Llico

Sleeping and eating B *Hostería Atlántida 2000*, T400264, F312089, near beach. Small rooms, with breakfast. **D** *Hostería Llico*. **E** *Pensión Chile*. Clean, friendly, rooms with bath have hot water, cheap meals. **E** pp *Res Miramar*, Carrera Pinto 48, T400032. Good seafood restaurant, very small rooms but excellent, **C** pp with full board.

Transport Bus: from Terminal Plaza in Curicó, by *Bravo* and *Llomar* companies, both daily 1230 and 1540, also *Díaz*, Mon-Sat 1530, 3 hrs.

A large lake surrounded by pine forest, Lago Vichuquén lies 114 km west of Curicó, just east of Llico. It is in a calm spot, set in a bowl surrounded by pine woods. The nearby town of Vichuquén has some well-preserved colonial architecture – there is a small museum in a beautiful porticoed house in the centre of Vichuquén. A visit is recommended. ■ *US$1.50*. Lago Vichuquén is

Lago Vichuquén

The Central Valley

very popular with the wealthy and with watersports enthusiasts. Parts of the eastern shore of the lake are inaccessible by road, but there are full facilities on the western shore, particularly at Aquelarre.

Sleeping and eating **AL-A** *Hotel Playa Aquelarre*, T400018. Well-equipped, restful, good food. **A** *Brujas del Lago*, T400020. **Camping**: *Vichuquén*, on east shore, T400062. Full facilities. *El Sauce*, at north end of lake, F75400203. Good facilities.

Reserva Nacional Laguna Torca Situated just north of Lago Vichuquén, 120 km west of Curicó, this park, covering 604 ha, is a natural sanctuary for over 80 species of birds, especially blacknecked swans and other water fowl. ■ *Administration is 4 km east of Llico; campsite nearby. Getting there: take any bus from Curicó to Llico and get out near Administration. Sep-Apr.*

The Maule Valley

The Río Maule, 240-km long, flows from Laguna Maule in the Andes to the sea at Constitución. Its waters have been dammed east of Talca, providing power and creating Lago Colbún. The river itself is particularly beautiful near the coast at Constitución.

Talca

Phone code: 071
Colour map 3, grid C2
Population: 160,000
258 km to Santiago

Situated on the south bank of the Río Claro, a tributary of the Maule, Talca lies 56 km south of Curicó. The most important city between Santiago and Concepción, it is a major manufacturing centre and the capital of Región VII, Maule. Founded in 1692, it was destroyed by earthquakes in 1742 and 1928. Today it is a busy, dusty town, with a lively atmosphere day and night.

Ins & outs
See page 284 for further details

Getting there Talca is easily accessible by bus and train from Santiago (both many times daily). There are also frequent connections to the towns further south, especially Chillán, Concepción, Temuco and Puerto Montt (several daily). **Getting around** Talca is a sizeable city, and some of the *barrios* are quite a distance from the centre. Buses and *colectivos* ply to these areas from the centre, with their destinations marked in the window. **Tourist offices** Sernatur, 1 Poniente 1281, T233669, sernatur_talca@entelchile.net Open winter Mon-Fri 0830-1730; summer Mon-Fri 0830-1930. Automóvil Club de Chile, 1 Poniente 1267, T2232774.

Sights In the **Plaza de Armas** are statues looted by the Talca Regiment from Peru during the War of the Pacific. Just off the Plaza at 1 Norte y 2 Oriente is the **Museo O'Higginiano**, located in a colonial mansion which belonged to Juan Albano Pereira, tutor to the young Bernardo O'Higgins, who lived here between the ages of four and 10. The house was later the headquarters of O'Higgins' Patriot Government in 1813-14, before his defeat at Rancagua. In 1818 O'Higgins signed the declaration of Chilean independence here: the room Sala Independencia is decorated and furnished in period style. The museum also houses a collection of regional art. ■ *Tue-Fri, 1030-1300, 1430-1845, Sat/Sun 1000-1300. US$1.* About 8 km southeast is **Villa Huilquilemu**, a 19th-century *hacienda*, now part of the Universidad Católica del Maule, housing four museums, of religious art, handicrafts, agricultural machinery and wine. ■ *Tue-Fri 1500-1830, Sat 1600-1830, Sun 1100-1400. T242474. US$1. Getting there: reached by taking San Clemente bus. The*

Casino de Bomberos has a small museum room with two old fire engines, old firefighting equipment, and – for those with an interest in little known conflagrations – historical information on important fires in Talca's history.

AL-A *Plaza*, 1 Poniente 1141, T226150. Good commercial standard. **AL-A** *Terrabella*, 1 Sur 641, T/F226555. **A** *Inca del Oro*,1 Sur 1026, T239608, F239603. Fully equipped, conference room, sauna. **A** *Marcos Gamero*, 1 Oriente 1070, T223100, F224400. **B** *Cordillera*, 2 Sur 1360, T221817, F233078. Bath, **C** without, good breakfast. **B** *Hostal del Puente*, 1 Sur 407, T220930, F225448. Lovely gardens, English spoken, parking. **B-D** *Amalfi*, 2 Sur 1265, T225703. Old-fashioned, central, good breakfast. **C** *Hostal Balcones del Maule*, 2 Norte 830, T230503. **D** *Oriente*, 10 Oriente 940. **D** *Res Maule*, 2 Sur 1381, T220995. Without breakfast, overpriced. **F** *Casa Chueca*, including breakfast, all rooms with private bathrooms. Colonial style house with swimming pool, botanical garden, climbing wall, gym. Excellent restaurant, games room, tours organised, English, German, French, Portuguese and Swedish spoken. Dinner on request. Casilla 143, Correo Talca, Región VIII, Chile; T370096, F214226, casachueca@hotmail.com **F** *Hostal Alcázar*, 6 Oriente y 4 Norte, T233587, without bath, quiet, good value.

On the **Pan-American Highway** 8 km north of Talca is **A** *Cabañas Entre Ríos*, T223336, F220477. Very good value, excellent breakfast, pool, very helpful owner. Highly recommended. At **Pellarco**, 18 km northeast is **F** *Hosp Santa Margita*, T09-3359051, F71-299799 (Casilla 1104, Talca), Swiss-run, meals served, open Dec-Mar only, reservation advised.

Mid-range *Bavaria*, 1 Sur 1370. Real coffee at *Café Brasil*, Plaza de Armas, and at *Mi Sandwich*, nearby. **Cheap/seriously cheap** *Casino de Bomberos*, 2 Sur y 5 Oriente. Good value. Cheap lunches also at *Casino Sociedad de Empleados*, 1 Norte 1025, and *Casino Club Deportivo*, 2 Sur 1313.

Sleeping
■ *on map*
Price codes:
see inside front cover

Eating
● *on map*

The Central Valley

Talca

■ Sleeping
1 Amalfi
2 Cordillera
3 Hostal Alcázar
4 Hostal Balcones del Maule
5 Inca del Oro
6 Marcos Gamero
7 Oriente
8 Plaza
9 Residencial Maule
10 Terrabella

● Eating
1 Bavaria
2 Casino Club Deportivo
3 Casino de Bomberos
4 Casino Sociedad de Empleados

Ⓢ Banks
1 Banco BHIF
2 Banco de Chile
3 Banco Santander
4 Banco Santiago

Entertainment **Pub** *El Barril*, 1 Norte 1352. Nice atmosphere, live music Fri and Sat, snacks. **Cinema** 1 Sur 1271 and Sur 770. Arts cinema at 1 poniente 685.

Festivals Regional folklore festival during 1st week of **Jan**. There is also a Feria Regional de Folklore y Artesaniá, at Villa Cultural Huilquilemu during the last week in **Nov**. There is an important *huaso* festival, *Fiesta San Francisco*, **4 Oct**, in Huerta del Maule (southwest of Talca). Those with an interest in Chilean wine might enjoy the *Feria del Vino y la Viticultura* (TECVIN), 1st week in **Nov**.

Tour operators *Barlovento*, Santa Marta de Huechuraba 6480, www.chileoutdoors.net *Expediciones Rapel*, 1 Oriente 260, T09 8923625, bosque@123mail.cl Also *Leonardo Cáceres Rencoret*, T09 892 3625. Good mountain guide, works for CONAF.

Transport **Bus** Terminal at 12 Oriente y 2 Sur. To **Chillán**, frequent service, US$2; also every 20 mins to **Constitución**, 2 hrs, US$1.20. To **Puerto Montt**, US$14. To **Temuco**, US$12, 7 hrs. Many to Santiago, and direct to destinations as far north as Copiapó. Countless local services also; see specific entries for further details. **Cycle** Repairs at *Bicimotora Burgos*, 5 Oriente 1185. **Train** Station at 2 Sur y 11 Oriente, T226254. To **Santiago**, 5 a day, US$5. To **Talca** and **Chillán**, 3 a day. To **Temuco**, 1 a day. To **Concepción**, Sat and Sun only. To **Constitución**, 2 a day, US$2, 2½ hrs.

Directory **Banks** *Banco Santander*, 1 Sur y 4 Oriente. *Edificio Caracol*, Oficina 15, 1 Sur 898. For *See map for* US$ cash. **Communications** Post office: 1 Oriente s/n. **Telephones**: *CTC*, 1 Sur 1156 *locations of banks* and 1 Sur 835. **Internet**: *1 Poniente 1282*, opposite Sernatur. *2 sur 1661*, T216636, free, but reservation essential. *7 Oriente 1180*. **Laundry** *Lavaseco Donini*, 6 Oriente 1120. *Lavaseco Flash*, 1 Norte 995.

Around Talca

San Javier Just south of Talca, San Javier is a peaceful town in the middle of the wine-growing district of the Maule region, see page 287. *Hospedaje Los Patiperros* **G** without breakfast, **F** with breakfast, Avenida Chorrillos 1226, T/F322342. French run bed and breakfast, cheap, clean, with patio, quiet but near town centre, runs tours including visits to vineyards, mountain bikes, horse trekking, lospatiperros@yahoo.com

Linares Fifty-three kilometres south of Talca, Linares is a peaceful town with a distinctly *huaso* feel. It boasts the remarkable **Cathedral de San Ambrosio**, built between 1934 and 1967 in a Byzantine romantic style. On Letelier 572, in the middle of a row of colonial houses, is the **Museo de Arte y Artesania Nacional.** Here there are exhibits of local, military and prehistoric history, including a 2-ft long decorative curved spanner, and an exploded cannon. Also horsehair artefacts from the village of Rari, local paintings, petrified wood, old toys and everyday utensils. ■ *Tue-Fri 1000-1730, Sat 1000-1700, Sun 1200-1700, US$1, Sun free.* In the **Mercado Municipal**, Chacabuco 300, it is possible to buy horsehair art from Rari (ask at any of the artesanal stalls). Tourist information from the Gobernación and Municipalidad, both on plaza.

Sleeping **A** *Hotel Curapalihue*, Curapalihue 411, T/F73-212516. Breakfast and bath, TV in room, conference facilities. **A-B** *Hotel Turismo*, Manuel Rodríguez 522, T73-210636, F214128. Breakfast and bath, restaurant, TV in room. **C** *Hotel Real*, Freire 482, T/F73-210834. Bath, without breakfast, TV in room. **E** *Hotel Londres*, Chacabuco

512, T73-213727, F213720. Without bath and breakfast, also has single rooms at **F**. **F** *Hostal Linares*, Freire 442, T210695. With breakfast.

Eating Mid-range *Fay Chy*, Rodríguez 398, Chinese. *Las Parrillas de Linares*, Lautaro 350, Meat. **Cheap** *Estadio Español*, León Bustas 01242. Traditional food.

Entertainment Pubs *El Tablón*, Ibáñez y Chacabuco. *Refugio*, V. Letelier 480.

Tour operators *Achibueno Expediciones*, T375098, F214861, www.achibueno expediciones.cl 8 km southeast of Linares offer bespoke horseriding trips in the cordillera. Also **Carlos Alberto Espinoza**, Rodríguez 712, T216240, F219957, juridachibueno@ entelchile.net Tours on horseback and with 4-WD. Recommended, but quite expensive. Speaks English.

Transport Bus Terminal at Espinoza 530. Frequent buses to **Talca** (US$1) with many companies. Also to **Colbún** via Quinimávida and Panimávida, US$1. There is a cycle path much of the way between Linares and Panimávida. **Train** To Santiago 4 a day, 3¾ hrs, to Chillán 4 a day, 1¼ hrs. Station T216352.

Directory Banks *Banco A Edwards*, on plaza, and *Banco Santander*, Independencia 555. **Communications** Internet: Chacabuco 491. **Post office**, Rodríguez 610. **Telephone**: *Call centre*, Independencia 488A.

From Talca a road runs 175 km southeast along Lago Colbún and up the valley of the Río Maule, passing through some of the finest mountain scenery in Chile to reach the Argentine border at Paso Pehuenche. At the western end of Lago Colbún is the town of Colbún. From here another road leads south and west to join the Pan-American Highway at Linares. **Lago Colbún**

En route from Colbún is Panimávida, 5 km south of Colbún, where there are thermal springs. Artesanal goods are better and cheaper here than in Linares. While at Panimávida, try the local Bebida Panimávida, made from spring water, still or sparkling, flavoured with lemon or raspberry. The *Hotel Termas de Panimávida* is a once grand hotel now being restored – there is a feeling of decaying grandeur. In the grounds is a small fountain, where you can drink the sulphourous 'agua de la mona'. Further on towards Linares is Quinamávida, 12 km south of Colbún, where there are thermal springs, and an upmarket hotel. In the hotel there are thermal baths, Turkish baths, reflexology, and massage. T213887. **Panimávida**

Sleeping and eating AL *El Colorado*, on north shore of Lago Colbún, T/F221750. **C** pp *Posada Campesina*, at Quinamávida, T09-7520510. Rabones, Linares/Panimavida rd, T752-0510. Large *estancia* offering full board, forest trails, beaches, English spoken. Highly recommended. **Camping** There are several campsites east of Colbún on the south shore of Lago Colbún, including *Marina del Lago*, Km 11, T211743. *Marina del Condor*, Km 13, T211743. *El Mirador de Colbún*, Km 13, T213776. There are also 3 sites near Panimávida.

Transport Bus: To Lago Colbún, *Pullman del Sur*, 2 daily from Talca (US$1.40). Direct buses from Santiago's Terminal Sur to Quinamávida with *Buses Villa Prat*, T02-3761758.

Some 63 km east of Talca, Vilches is the starting point for the climb to the volcanoes Quizapu (3,050 m) and Descabezado (3,850 m). For walks on **Vilches**

The Central Valley

Descabezado Grande and Cerro Azul, ice axe and crampons needed, contact recommended guide Carlos Verdugo Bravo, Probación Brilla El Sol, Pasaje El Nickel 257, Talca (Spanish only).

Sleeping and eating AL *Hostería*, Vilches, T621463. With breakfast, use of kitchen, good food, *cabañas* **C** for 4 people, hospitable, pool, knowledgeable family (postal address: Casilla 876, Talca).

Transport 5 buses a day, US$1.80, 2-2½ hrs.

Reserva Nacional Altos del Lircay Situated just west of Vilches, this park covers 12,163 ha and includes peaks up to 2,228 m as well as several small lakes. Much of the park is covered with mixed forest including lenga, ñirre, coigüe, roble, raulí and copihue. Near the entrance are the administration and visitors centre; nearby are the Piedras Tacitas, a stone construction supposedly built by the indigenous inhabitants of the region, and the Mirador Del Indio from where there are fine views over the Río Lircay. There are also two good hikes: to Laguna del Alto, eight hours via a lagoon in a volcanic crater; to El Enladrillado, a high basalt plateau from which there are great views, 12 hours. ■ *US$1*.

Border with Argentina **Paso Pehuenche**, 2,553 m, is reached by unpaved road southeast from Lago Colbún. On the Argentine side the road continues to Malargüe and San Rafael. The border is open from December to March, 0800-2100, and from April to November, 0800-1900.

Constitución *Colour map 3, grid C2* Lying west of Talca at the mouth of the Río Maule, Constitución is reached by road (89 km) from San Javier and a narrow gauge railway line which offers fine views over the wooded Maule Valley. Founded in 1794, it is situated in a major commercial logging area; there are naval shipyards and a giant cellulose factory; fishing is also important. Its main attraction is as a seaside resort, which, in season is popular with Chileans. However, it has to be said that while the coast to the north is beautiful, there are few reasons for travellers to come to Constitución itself. The beach, an easy walk from the town, is surrounded by very picturesque rocks. There are good views from Cerro Mutrún, at the mouth of the river, access from Calle O'Higgins. A quiet track leads along the south bank of the Maule to a disused railway bridge over the river, 8 km east of Constitución; the bridge is open to vehicles, and has great views of the river valley and the bridge, recommended as a walk or drive.

Sleeping and eating AL-A *Hostería Constitución*, Echeverria 460, T671450, F673735. Best. **B** *Posada Colonial*, Blanco 390, T672887, F671335. **C** *Avendaño*, O'Higgins 681. Pleasant patio, restaurant, friendly, safe. **D** *Res Urrutia*, Freire 238. Breakfast, some rooms gloomy, laundry facilities. On Portales: **E** *Res Cristina*, No 368. Good. **E** *Res Santa Catalina*, No 320. There are many other *residenciales* on Freire 100-300 blocks, including *Res López*, No 153; *Res Familiar*, No 160; *Res Ramírez*, No 292, but book in advance from Jan to Mar.

Transport **Bus**: To Talca, *Empresa O'Higgins* and *Contimar*, frequent, 2 hrs, US$2. To Cauquenes, *Empresa Amigo*, 2½ hrs, US$2. **Train** To Talca, 2½ hrs, US$2, 2 a day.

South of Constitución A paved road runs from Constitución along the coast, through thick forest and past a large logging factory, via the small towns of **Chanco** and **Pelluhue** to **Curanipe**, 83 km south. Curanipe has a beautiful black sand beach. Both Pelluhue and Curanipe are popular for surfing.

La Ruta del Vino

*The Maule Valley is one of the largest wine-producing areas in Chile. Some 20 km south of Talca, in the vicinity of the small town of San Javier, is the **Ruta del Vino San Javier-Villa Alergre**, covering 23 vineyards which can be visited. Although transport is essential for visiting most, those near San Javier can be visited without it. A few have regular visiting hours which are given below; for the remainder advance notice is required. Further details can be obtained from the Municipalidad in San Javier.*

1	Alto de Pichivoque	T73-322696	**13**	J Bouchón	T73-372708
2	Balduzzi	T73-322138		(open Wednesday 1500-1700)	
	(open Monday-Saturday 0900-1900)		**14**	La Cabaña	T73-322437
3	Carta Vieja	T73-381612	**15**	Los Ciervos	T73-321053
	(open Wednesday 1700-1800)		**16**	Poxo de Oro	T73-346004
4	Comávida	T73-322696	**17**	Saavedra	T73-346006
5	Concha y Toro	T73-321767	**18**	San Clemente	T73-381474
6	Cooperativa Lancomilla	T73-322540		(open daily 0900-2000)	
7	Cremaschi	T73-372125.	**19**	Santa Beatriz	T73-321977
8	El Aromo	T71-242438	**20**	Santa Berta	T73-322478
9	El Durazno	T09-7513368	**21**	Santa Hilda	T73-321367
10	El Sauce	T09-7513142	**22**	Segú Ollé	T73-210078
11	Gabriel Court	T73-322299		(open Friday marnings)	
12	Guzmán	T73-328066	**23**	Tabontinaja	T73-375539

Tours to these and other vineyards from "circuito del vino del valle del Maule" in Calle Sargento Aldea 2491, San Javier, Mon-Fri 0915-1815, T/F323657, wineroute@entelchile.net One and two day circuits. 10-16 people, seven days' notice required.

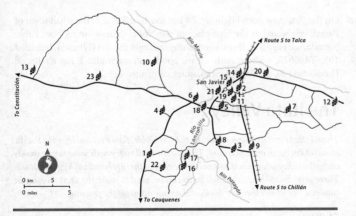

A small town with traditional colonial architecture, and the charming Iglesia San Ambrosia, Chanco has several bars that get busy at weekends. There is a pleasant 3 km walk to the coast and the unspoilt Playa Monolito (camping facilities). The land just north of Chanco is the prettiest in this area, with rolling hills and small farmsteads. Here there are two small parks. The Area Silvestre Laguna Reloca, 8 km north of Chanco, is a private park covering 245 ha. Some 130 bird species have been identified including flamingoes and black necked swans. ■ *Mon-Fri 1430-1800, Sat-Sun 0830-1800. Free.*

The Reserva Nacional Federico Albert, 1 km north of Chanco, covers 145 ha of dunes planted with eucalyptus and cypresses in experiments to control the shifting sands. It has a visitors centre and campsite. ■ *Apr-Nov 0830-1800, Dec-Mar 0830-2000. US$1.* This coast can also be reached by paved road from Parral via Cauquenes. Just north of this road, between Cauquenes and Chanco, is a park, the Reserva Nacional Los Ruiles, which covers 45 ha of native flora including the *ruil* (Nothofagus alessandri), an endangered species of southern beech. ■ *Dec-Mar 0830-2000, Apr-Nov 0830-1800, US$1. Buses from Constitución or Cauquenes.*

Pelluhue is more expensive than Curanipe, has lots of seafood restaurants and two discos

Sleeping Pelluhue B *Hostería Blanca Reyes*, Prat 615, T541061, F541022. Best. **C** *Hostal Casablanca*, Condell 1019, T541014. **E** *Pensión Rocas*, Condell 708, T541017, basic. **E** *Res La Playa*, Prat 510. Also lots of *cabañas*. **Curanipe** To the north of the town are *Cabañas Campomar*, **A** for up to 6 people, kitchen, good view, English spoken T541000, campomar@ctcinternet.cl **C** *La Bahía*, Comercio 438, T556066. **C** *Pacífico*, Comercio 509, T556016. Pleasant, clean. Several others, **F-G** , municipal campsite.

Transport Hourly buses from Talca to **Chanco**, **Curanipe** and **Pelluhue** with *Buses Bonanza* (US$3.50); also 3 daily with *Contimar* (US$3.50), and 10 daily with *Pullman del Sur* (US$2.50).

Cobquecura

From Curanipe a poorly maintained track leads 50 km through wild country to the small seaside town of Cobquecura. A tranquil, friendly town, it has a good beach, a pretty plaza, several good seafood restaurants and well pre-served colonial-style houses. There are two *residenciales*, **F**. About 5 km to the north is an impressive *portada* or arch in the cliffs. There are also a few good surfing beaches nearby.

Parral

On the Pan-American Highway, 88 km south of Talca, is the small town of Parral, celebrated as the birthplace of the Nobel Prize-winning poet Pablo Neruda, see page 542. If you need to stay the night there is **C** *Brescia*, Igualdad 195, T462675, without bath, clean, good restaurant and **E** *Res do Brasil*, Dieciocho 140, T462555, a clean, quiet, campsite.

The Itata Valley

The Río Itata and its longer tributary, the Río Ñuble, flow west reaching the Pacific some 60 km north of Concepción. This is a tranquil valley with some native woods along the valley sides near the mouth of the river at the tiny hamlet of Vegas de Itata. There is no bridge here, although boats can be hired to make the short crossing in summer – in winter the river swells and no one attempts the crossing.

Chillán

Phone code: 042
Colour map 3, grid C2
Population: 146,000
150 km south of Talca

Chillán is a busy but friendly place and one of the most interesting cities south of Santiago with several museums worth visiting. Pleasantly hot in summer, there is a shady plaza and numerous interesting churches, as well as a mural of the life of Bernardo O'Higgins. The city – filled with local *campesinos* on market days – smacks of the essence of the Central Valley.

Quinchamalí

Quinchamalí is one of the two most famous villages in Chile for producing black ceramic ware; the other, Pomaire, near Santiago, is much more influenced by tourism. Quinchamalí is a village of little houses hidden under large fruit trees; in these the women work with the clay while the men work on the land. Apart from items for domestic use, the women produce a wide range of other pieces including roosters, three legged pigs and

women with children but the most popular is perhaps the guitarrera (a woman playing the guitar). The clay is mixed with sand to make it porous and to prevent it breaking when it is heated; the mixture is worked in two halves which are then joined and allowed to dry. The characteristic white patterns are made by incising with an old needle before the piece is wrapped in straw and heated over an open fire.

Getting there Chillán is served by the railway from Santiago – there are several trains daily. The city is easily accessible by bus from Santiago (countless daily). There are also frequent connections to the towns further south, especially Concepcíon, Temuco and Puerto Montt (many daily). **Getting around** Chillán is an important city, and some of the outlying *barrios* and attractions are quite a distance from the centre. Buses and *colectivos* are numerous, with their destinations marked in the window. Taxis are most useful for arranging excursions out of the city. **Tourist offices** 18 de Sept 455, at side of Gobernación, T223272, left-hand gallery. Street map of city, leaflets on skiing, Termas de Chillán, etc. Automóvil Club de Chile, O'Higgins 677, T212550.

Ins & outs
See page 291 for further details

Chillan enjoys very warm weather in summer

Background

Founded in 1580 and destroyed by the Mapuche, the city has been moved several times. Following an earthquake in 1833, the site was moved slightly to the northwest, though the older site, now known as Chillán Viejo, is still occupied. Further earthquakes in 1939 and 1960 have ensured that few old buildings have survived. Chillán was the birthplace of Bernardo O'Higgins. Arturo Prat, Chile's naval hero, was born 50 km away at Ninhue. In 2003, the centenary year of the birth of the pianist Claudio Arrau, Chillán will be the American city of culture.

Sights

The city is centred around the Plaza O'Higgins. The modern cathedral, on the plaza, is designed to resist earthquakes. The **San Francisco** church, three blocks northeast of the Plaza, contains a **museum** of religious and historical artefacts. ■ *Tue-Sun 1600-1800, US$1.* Above the main entrance is a mural by Luis Guzmán Molina, a local artist, which is an interpretation of the life of San Francisco but placed in a Chilean context. The adjoining **convent** (1835) was a big centre for missionary work among the Mapuche. Five streets west of the Plaza is the neogothic **Iglesia Padres Carmelita**. Northwest of the Plaza O'Higgins, on the Plaza Héroes de Iquique, is the **Escuela México**, donated to the city after the 1939 earthquake. In its library are outstanding murals by the great Mexican artists David Alvaro Siqueiros and Xavier Guerrero which present allegories of Chilean and Mexican history. ■ *Daily 1000-1300, 1500-1830.* Three blocks further south is the **Museo Naval El Chinchorro**, Collin y I Riquelme, which contains naval artefacts and models of Chilean vessels. ■ *Tue-Fri 0930-1200, 1500-1730.*

In **Chillán Viejo**, southwest of the centre, there is a monument and park on the site of the birthplace of Bernardo O'Higgins; it has a 60 m long mural depicting his life (an impressive, but sadly faded, mosaic of various native stones), and a **Centro Histórico y Cultural**, with a gallery of contemporary

The Central Valley

paintings by regional artists. ■ *The park is open 0830-2000*. Half-way between the centre and Chillán Viejo on Avenida O'Higgins is the **Capilla San Juan de Dios**, a small chapel dating from 1791.

zTwo interesting publications on Chillán are: *Iconografía de Chillán, 1835-1939*, by Marco Aurelio Reyes (Universidad del Bío-Bío, 1989) which describes the history of Chillán up to the devastating 1939 earthquake with text, photographs and documents; and *Chillán me persigue*, by Luis Guzmán Molina, Sergio Hernández, Marco Aurelio Reyes and Norman Ahumada, which contains images of Chillán in drawings, poetry and prose (1995).

Excursion
See also the box

Quinchamalí is a small village 27 km southwest, at the halfway point of the new motorway between Chillán and Concepción. The village is famous for the originality of its crafts in textiles, basketwork, black ceramics, guitars and primitive paintings. These are all on sale in Chillán market. The village holds a handicraft fair in the second week of February, and there is also a *Museo Histórico Artesanal*.

Sleeping
● *on map*
Price codes:
see inside front cover

A *Hostal de la Avenida*, O'Higgins 398 y Bulnes, T230256. **A-B** *Isabel Riquelme*, Arauco 600, T213663, F211541. **A-B** *Paso Nevado*, Libertad 219, T237788, F237666. **B** *Quinchamalí*, El Roble 634, T223381, F227365. Central, quiet, clean, hot water, heated lounge. **B** *Rucamanqui*, Herminda Martín 590 (off Plaza de Armas), T222704, F217072. Clean, spartan. **B-C** *Cordillera*, Arauco 619, on Plaza de Armas, T215211, F211198. 3-star, small, good. **C** *Floresta*, 18 de Septiembre 278, T222253. Quiet, old fashioned, friendly. **C** *Libertador*, Libertad 85, T223255. Without breakfast, parking, clean, good. **C** *Ruiz de Gamboa*, O'Higgins 497, T221013. **C** *San Bartolemé*, El Roble 585, T226721. Bath, parking, run down. **D** *Claris*, 18 de Septiembre 357, T221980. Clean, friendly, run down, with bath (**F** pp without). **D** *Hostal 5 de Abril*, 5 de Abril y Constitución. Without bath. **D** *Res Su Casa*, Cocharcas 555, T223931. Clean, parking. **E** *Hostal Cañada*, Libertad 269, T234515. Without breakfast or bath. **E** *Chillán*, Libertad 85, basic. Near the central terminal on Constitución are **F** *Res Vem-Sau*, No 96, T210958, and **F** *Res Chi-Can*, No 34. Both basic and noisy. **F** *Sonia Segui*, Itata 288, T214879. Good beds, good breakfast, huge *almuerzo*, dirty bathrooms but recommended, friendly, noisy. Lots of *hospedajes*, **E/F** on Constitutión 1-300.

Eating
● *on map*

Mid-range *Arcoiris*, El Roble 525, vegetarian. *Café de París*, Arauco 666, with good bar and fine restaurant upstairs and *Café Europa*, Libertad 475. Recommended. *Fuente Alemana*, Arauco 661. *La Cosa Nostra*, Libertad 398, Italian cuisine, German and Italian spoken, very good and reasonably priced. In Chillán Viejo, *Los Adobes*, on Parque O'Higgins. Good food and service, reasonable prices. **Cheap** *Club Comercial*, Arauco 745. Popular at lunchtime, good value *almuerzo*, popular bar at night. Recommended. *Jai Yang*, Libertad 250. Good Chinese. O'Higgins y Libertad. Good value. *La Copucha*, 18 de Septiembre y Constitución. Inexpensive meals and sandwiches. *La Masc'a*, 5 de Abril 544. Excellent cheap meals, *empanadas de queso*, drinks. Recommended. Many seriously cheap restaurants around the Mercado Municipal. The Chillán area is well-known for its *pipeño* wine (very young) and its *longanizas* (sausages).

Entertainment

Cinema at Libertad 210.

Festivals

In Jan the *Encuentro International de Teatro* is held, with plays being performed in public spaces around the city. An annual wine festival, *Fiesta de la Vendemia*, is held in the 3rd week in **Mar**.

Large *Mercado y Ferio Municipal* at Riquelme y Marpón which sells regional arts and crafts. Nearby is a large modern shopping centre, Plaza El Roble, at El Roble y Riquelme. **Shopping**

Puelche, T224829, Trekking on horseback around Volcán Chillán. **Tour operator**

Bus Two long distance terminals: *Tur Bus*, *Línea Azul*, *Tas Choapa* and *LIT* all use central terminal at Brasil y Constitución. Other companies use the modern northern terminal at O'Higgins y Ecuador. Local bus terminal, Maipón y Sgto Aldea near the market. Buses to **Yumbel** and **Quinchamalí** (US$1, 30 mins), leave from here. To **Santiago**, US$7-11, 5½ hrs. To **Concepción**, *Tur Bus* and *Línea Azul* every 30 mins, 1¼ hrs, US$3. To **Curicó**, US$4. To **Tecumo**, US$5. **Motorcycle spares** *Roland Spaarwater*, Ecuador 275, T/F232334. **Train** Station, Brasil opposite Libertad, 5 blocks west of Plaza de Armas, T222424. To **Santiago**, 5 daily, 5½ hrs, *salón* US$7. **Transport**

Chillán

Sleeping	
1	Claris
2	Cordillera
3	Floresta
4	Hostal 5 de Abril
5	Hostal Cañada
6	Hostal de la Avenida
7	Isabel Riquelme
8	Libertador
9	Paso Nevado
10	Quinchamalí
11	Residencial Chi-Can
12	Residencial Su Casa
13	Residencial Vem-Sau
14	Rucamanqui
15	Ruiz de Gamboa
16	San Bartolemé
17	Sonia Segui

Eating	
1	Arcoiris
2	Café de París
3	Café Europa
4	Club Comercial
5	Fuente Alemana
6	Jai Yang
7	La Masc'a

The Central Valley

Violeta and the Parra family of Chillán

Violeta and Nicanor Parra were two of the 11 children of Nicanor and Clarisa Parra. The family was brought up in Chillán. Their father, Nicanor, was a music teacher, while their mother, Clarisa, was a seamstress who played the guitar and sang. Most of the children were artistic in some way. Violeta sang with her sister Hilda in Santiago bars for several years. She also worked in the circus. Another child, Nicanor, became a professor of maths and physics. His poetry is discussed elsewhere, as is that of Pablo de Rokha, who was a great friend of Violeta.

Together Violeta and de Rokha travelled the length of Chile and abroad collecting material for and promoting their idea of Chilean-ness. While de Rokha expressed himself in the lyrical epic, Violeta sang, wrote songs, made tapestries, ceramics, paintings and sculpture. All her work was based on a philosophy of helping those in need. In France she was recognized as a great artist and her works were exhibited in the Louvre in 1964, but at home recognition was only grudgingly given. Neruda called her 'Santa Violeta'; the Peruvian novelist Jose Maria Arguedas described her as 'the most Chilean of all Chileans I could possibly know, but at the same time the most universal of all Chile'.

In the 1960s she set up her La Carpa de la Reina *as a centre for popular art in the capital. It was here, in February 1967, that she committed suicide, her head resting on her guitar. The national grief at her funeral far outweighed the acclaim given her during her life. Her daughter Isabel was also a singer, as was her son, Angel, whose radical views prompted the military government to arrest him after the 1973 coup and imprison him in the Pisagua concentration camp.*

For Violeta, folklore was a form of class struggle. Her influence on a whole generation of Latin American folk singers was enormous and, without her, Salvador Allende would not have had the folkloric backing of Victor Jara, Inti-Illimani, Los Quilapayún and Angel and Isabel Parra themselves. After her death, her brother Nicanor had published Décimas, a sort of autobiography in verse, full of simple humanity.

Thanks to Life

I give thanks to life which has given me so much. It has given me two eyes, and when I open them I distinguish perfectly black from white,
and in the sky its starry depths
and in the crowds the man that I love.
I give thanks to life which has given me so much. It has given me hearing, which in all its breadth records night and day the crickets and canaries; hammers, turbines, barks and squalls,
and the tender voice of my beloved...
I give thanks to life which has given me so much. It has given me laughter and it has given me tears, so that I can tell good fortune from despair, the two materials which make up my song, and your song which is the same song and everyone's song which is my own song.

Directory **Banks** On the Plaza de Armas are *Banco BCI*, *Banco Santander* and *Banco de Chile* all with ATMs. There is also *Banco Sudamericano*, Arauco y El Roble. Poor rates. *Banco Santiago*, El Roble 580. *Corp Banca*, for Visa. Better rates than banks at *casa de cambio*, Constitución 550, or *Café de París* (ask for Enríque Schuler). **Communications** Internet: *Gateway*, Libertad 360, T238855, gateway3@CTCrenuna.cl *Planet Cybercafe*, Arauco 683, 2nd floor. **Post office**: in Gobernación building on Plaza de Armas. **Telephone**: *Entel*, 18 de Septiembre 746. *CTC*, Arauco 625. Also call centre at 5 de Abril 607.

Termas de Chillán

Situated 82 km east of Chillán by good road (paved for the first 50 km), 1,850 m up at the foot of the double-cratered Chillán volcano, are thermal baths and, above those, the largest ski resort in southern Chile. There are two open-air thermal pools, officially for hotel guests only, and a health spa with jacuzzi, sauna, mud baths etc. A few kilometres past the Termas de Chillán, there are natural hot mud baths, free of charge. The ski resort includes rental shops, restaurants, bars, ski school, first aid and nursery. Suitable for families and beginners and cheaper than centres nearer Santiago, Chillán has 10 ski lifts and 28 ski runs, the longest of which is 13 km in length. It offers nordic, alpine randonnée and heli-skiing. Weekly packages are available, but are not cheap. Lift pass is US$30 per day, US$20 for a half day. You can obtain information from Chillán Ski Centre, Barros Arana 261, or from Sociedad *Hotelera de Montaña y Turismo Somontur*, address below. Equipment can be hired also from the Chillán Ski Centre, for about US$25.

At Las Trancas on the road to the Termas, 70 km southeast of Chillán are **LL** *Gran Termas de Chillán*, T215977, 5-star, sports facilities, sauna, thermal pool and spa centre. **LL-L** *Pirigallo*, 3-star. Bookings for both via *Sociedad Hotelera de Montaña y Turismo Somontur*, Av Libertad 1042, Chillán, T223887, F223576, ventachi@termachillan.cl **AL** *Parador Jamón*, Pan y Vino, T373872, F220018. Arranges recommended horse riding expeditions. **AL** *Robledal*, T/F214407. **B** pp *Los Pirineos*, T293839. Several *cabañas* also available in the village. **Camping** 2 km from the slopes.

Sleeping & eating

Ski buses run from Libertador 1042 at 0800 and from Chillán Ski Centre, subject to demand, US$30 (including lift pass). Summer (Jan-mid Mar) bus service from **Anja**, 5 de Abril 594, Thu, Sat, Sun only, 0730, US$5 return, book in advance. Taxi US$30 one way, 1½ hrs. At busy periods hitching may be possible from Chillán Ski Centre.

Transport

The Biobío Valley

The Río Biobío flows northwest from the Andes to reach the sea near Concepción. At 407 km long, it is the second longest river in Chile. Its more important tributaries include the Ríos Laja, Duqueco and Renaico. Apart from Concepción and Talcahuano on the coast, the valley includes several other important cities, notably Los Angeles.

Concepción

The capital of Región VIII (Biobío), 15 km from the estuary of the Río Biobío, Concepción is the third biggest city in Chile. Although it is one of the country's major industrial centres, Concepción is not in itself a wildly beautiful or a fascinating place. Those staying for a long period or getting involved with students at the important university will find doors opening, but otherwise a visit to the port of Talcahuano, Chile's most important naval base (15 km north), is the highlight – here crowds of fishermen unload their catches of seafood before a seething mass of buyers, stevedores and old sea dogs snaffling molluscs as they are carried past.

Phone code: 041
Colour map 3, grid C1
Population: 210,000
516 km south of Santiago

Ins and outs

Getting there

The weather is very pleasant during the summer months, but From April to September the rain falls heavily

There are flights to Concepción from Santiago and Puerto Montt (several daily), 1 or 2 a day continuing on to Punta Arenas. Concepción is the transportation hub of the region, and there are also countless buses to and from Santiago, Temuco, Valdivia and Puerto Montt, as well as to and from other smaller destinations such as Cañete and Lota. To get to nearby destinations such as Dichato and Talcahuano, it is easiest to take a *colectivo*.

Getting around

Colectivos and buses abound; the destinations are signed in the window or on the roof. Fares are US$0.30 for buses, slightly more for *colectivos*.

Tourist offices

Aníbal Pinto 460 on Plaza de la Independencia, T227976. Information on the more expensive hotels and *residenciales*. Automóvil Club de Chile, O'Higgins 630, Oficina 303, T245884. For information and car hire (T222070). Codeff (Comité Nacional pro Defensa de la Fauna y Flora) Caupolicán 346, Of east, p 4, T226649.

History

Founded in 1550, Concepción became a frontier stronghold in the war against the Mapuche after 1600. Destroyed by an earthquake in 1751, it was moved to its present site in 1764. It suffered another destructive earthquake, followed by a tidal wave, in 1835; this quake was so severe that some cows, grazing on an island in the bay, were rolled into the sea.

Sights

In the centre is the attractive **Plaza de la Independencia**, where, in January 1818, Bernardo O'Higgins proclaimed the independence of Chile. Nearby are many of the official buildings including the modern cathedral, the Municipalidad and the Palacio de la Justicia. Southeast of the plaza is the **Parque Ecuador**, with the Galería de la Historia (see below). A few blocks north of the park is the Casa del Arte (see below). From the Parque Ecuador you can climb **Cerro Caracol**, to the south, from where there are views over the city and the river.

The *Galería de la Historia* is an audiovisual depiction of the history of Concepción and the region; upstairs is a collection of Chilean painting. ■ *Free. Mon 1500-1830, Tue-Fri 1000-1330, 1500-1830, Sat/Sun 1000-1400, 1500-1900.*

Museo de Arte Sagrado, contains many fine sacred Christian objects, including priests robes embroidered with gold, and a marble Christ. ■ *Tue-Fri 1000-1330, 1600-2000; Sat-Sun, 1100-1400. US$0.50. Caupolicán 441.*

The **Casa del Arte**, Roosevelt y Larena, contains the University art collection; the entrance hall is dominated by *La Presencia de América Latina*, by the Mexican Jorge González Camerena (1965), an impressive allegorical mural depicting Latin American history, famous throughout Chile and often depicted on postcards. Note especially the pyramid representing the continent's wealth, the figures of an armoured warrior and an Indian woman and the wounded cactus with parts missing, representing Mexico's defeat by the USA in 1845-1848. ■ *Free. Tue-Fri 1000-1800, Sat 1000-1600, Sun 1000-1300. Explanations are given free by University Art students.* There is another fine mural in the entrance hall of the railway station, *La Historia de Concepción* by Gregorio de la Fuente.

Excursions

Museo y Parque Hualpen, 16 km from Concepción, consists of a house built around 1885, which is now a national monument, and its gardens. The museum contains beautiful pieces from all over the world, recommended. Further west in the park, near the mouth of the Río Biobío, there are good opportunities for walking on the hills and several fine beaches including Playa Rocoto. ■ *Free. Tue-Sun 1000-1300, 1400-1900. Getting there: take a city bus to Hualpencillo from Freire, ask the driver to let you out then walk 40 mins, or hitch. You have to go along Av Las Golondrinas to the Enap oil refinery, turn left, then right (it is signed).*

Laguna San Pedro, on the far bank of the Río Biobío, has a beach and is where watersports are practised.

Essentials

A *Alborada*, Barros Arana 457, Casilla 176, T/F242144. Good. **A** *Alonso de Ercilla*, Colo Colo 334, T227984, F230053. Breakfast. Recommended. **A** *Concepción*, Serrano 512, T228851, F230948. Central, comfortable, heating, English spoken. Recommended. **A-B** *El Dorado*, Barros Arana 348, T229400, F231018. Comfortable, central, cafeteria, parking. **B** *Manquehue*, Barros Arana 790, p 8, T238348, F238350. Clean. Highly recommended. **B** *San Sebastián*, Rengo 463, T243412, F242710. With breakfast, parking. **B-C** *Ritz*, Barros Arana 721, T226696, F243249. Reasonable. **C** *Cecil*, Barros Arana 9, near railway station, T230667, with breakfast, clean, quiet. Highly recommended. **C** *Hostal Casablanca*, Cochrane 133, T226576. With bath, cheaper without, clean. **C** *Res Metro*, Barros Arana 464, T225305. Without bath, clean, poor showers. **C-D** *Res Antuco*, Barros Arana 741, flats 31-33, T/F235485. Recommended. This is entered via the Galería Martínez, as is **C** *Res San Sebastián*, Barros Arana 741, flat 35, T242710, F243412. Central, Hostelling International reductions. **D** *Res Central*, Rengo 673, T227309. A little rundown, with breakfast. **D** *Res Colo Colo*, Colo Colo 743, T227118. With breakfast. **F** *Pablo Araya*, Salas 643-C. **F** *Res O'Higgins*, O'Higgins 457, T228303. With breakfast, comfortable. **F** *Res Tiempo Libre*, Las Heras 646, T246525. Clean, also short stay. **F** *Silvia Uslar*, Edmundo Larenas 202, T227449. Good breakfast, quiet, clean, comfortable. Good budget accommodation is hard to find.

Sleeping
■ *on map, page 297*
Price codes:
see inside front cover

Expensive *Le Château*, Colo Colo 340. French, seafood and meat, closed Sun. *Rincón de Pancho*, Cervantes 469 (closed Sun). Excellent meat, also pasta and congrio, good service and ambience. **Mid-range** *Big Joe Saloon*, O'Higgins 808, just off plaza. Popular at lunchtime, open Sun evening, good breakfasts, vegetarian meals, snacks and pizzas. *El Rancho de Julio*, O'Higgins 36. Argentine *parrillada*. *Piazza*, Barros Arana 631, 2nd floor. Good pizzas. *Novillo Loco*, Portales 539. Traditional food. Good, efficient service. **Cheap** *Casino de Bomberos*, O'Higgins y Orompello, good value lunches. *Chicki*, Portales 531, Spanish. *Mar y Tierra*, Colo Colo 1182, seafood, fish. **Oriental** *Yiet-Xiu*, Angol 515. Good, cheap. *Chung Hwa*, Barros Arana 262.

Eating
● *on map*

Cafés and bars Several *fuentes de soda* and cafés on Caupolicán near the Plaza de Armas including: *Café El Dom*, No 415, and *Café Haiti*, No 515, both open Sun morning, good coffee, and the Fuente Alemana, No 654. Recommended. Other good cafes include *Café Colombia*, Aguirre Cerda, good coffee, good atmosphere; *Treinta y Tantos*, Prat 356, nice bar, good music, wide selection of *empanadas*, good breakfasts and lunches, recommended; and *La Capilla*, Vicuña MacKenna 769, good ponches, popular, crowded. Also *Nuria*, Barros Arana 736. Very good breakfasts and lunches, good value. *QuickBiss*, O'Higgins between Tuscapel and Castellón. Salads, real coffee, good service, good lunches. *Royal Pub*, O'Higgins 790. A posh snack bar. *Saaya 1*, Barros Arana 899. Excellent *panadería/pastelería/rotisería*. Highly recommended.

The Central Valley

From monkey-puzzles to woodchips

The Río Biobío is the heartland of Chilean commercial forestry. Timber is a major industry in the Bíobío region: there are four major cellulose plants in the Bíobío Valley, at La Laja, Concepción, Nacimiento and Mininco, as well as two more at Arauco on the coast. Chilean forestry owes its modern dynamism largely to a 1974 law which provided incentives for the development of the industry. Since 1974 over 1,000,000 ha of trees have been planted in Regions VII, VIII and IX, mostly Monterrey Pine (Pinus radiata), favoured for its fast growth and suitability for cellulose and construction timber. Climatic conditions for forestry are particularly favourable in the area inland from Arauco, which has a high number of days of optimal temperatures and humidity for the growth of the Monterrey Pine, though this is now being replaced by faster growing species of eucalyptus.

Forestry development is not limited to the Bíobío area: further south there are other signs of Chile's growing importance as a timber producer, for instance in the wood-chip mountains of Puerto Montt, testifying to Chile's becoming a great power in world timber production. However, environmentalists are increasingly voicing concern at the disappearance of native species, and have joined forces with farmers at highlighting the environmental damage produced by species such as the eucalyptus which extract most of the goodness from the soil, and plantations of pine which acidify the soil.

Entertainment   **Cinemas** Multiscreen cinemas in the Plaza del Trebol shopping centre. **Disco** *El Caríno Malo*, Barros Arana y Salas, bar, disco, live music, popular, not cheap.

Shopping   *Feria Artesanal*, Freire 757. *Galería Internacional*, Caupolicán y Barros Arana is worth a
Main shopping area is   visit (*El Naturista* vegetarian restaurant at local 22). The market has excellent seafood,
north of Plaza de   fruit and vegetables. *Las Brisas* supermarket, Freire y Lincoyán, and *Supermercado*
Armas   *Unimarc*, Chacabuco 70. There is a large modern shopping mall, the Plaza del Trebol north of the city (see also under cinemas) off the road to Talcahuano (near the airport). To get there, take any bus for Talcahuano.

Sports   **Country club** Pedro de Valdivia, outdoor swimming pool, tennis. **Horseracing** *Club Hípico*, north of the city on the road to Talcahuano. Race meetings Sun and holidays.

Tour operators   The following all do city tours and general local tours: *Aventuratur*, Ejército 599, T819634. *Ram*, T256161. *Viajes Publitur*, A Pinto 486, Of. 202, T240800. For those who want to go further afield, try *Alta Luz*, S Martín 586, Piso 2, T217727 (tours to national parks), *Chile Indomito Adventure*, Serrano 551 Of 3, T221618 (trekking in Reserva Nacional Ralco), or *South Expeditions*, O'Higgins 680, piso 2, Of 218D, T/F232290, rafting, horseriding, fishing and trekking expeditions, 1 and 2-day programmes. Student travel agency at *Usit Andes* Barros Arana 631, Local 31. T216608.

Transport   **Local Bicycle repairs**: *Martínez*, Maipú y Lincoyán, very helpful. **Car hire**: *Automóvil Club de Chile*, Caupolicán 294, T2250939. *Avis*, Chacabuco 726, T235837. *Budget*, Castellón 134, T225377. *Dollar*, at airport, T483661. *Full famas*, O'Higgins 1154, T248300, F242385, airport T094403300. *Hertz*, Prat 248, T230341.

Long distance Air: airport is north of the city, off the main road to Talcahuano. In summer, flights daily to and from Santiago (fewer in winter) and connections to Temuco, Puerto Montt and Punta Arenas. Airlines run bus services to the airport from their offices, leaving 1 hr before flight, US$2.50, also meet flights. Taxi US$8.

Bus: main long distance terminal, known as Terminal Collao, is 2 km east, on Av Gen Bonilla, next to athletics stadium. (To the city centre take a Bus marked 'Hualpencillo' from outside the terminal and get off in Freire, US$0.40, taxi US$4.) *Tur Bus*, Línea Azul and *Buses Bío Bío* services leave from Terminal Camilo Henríquez 2 km northeast of

Concepción

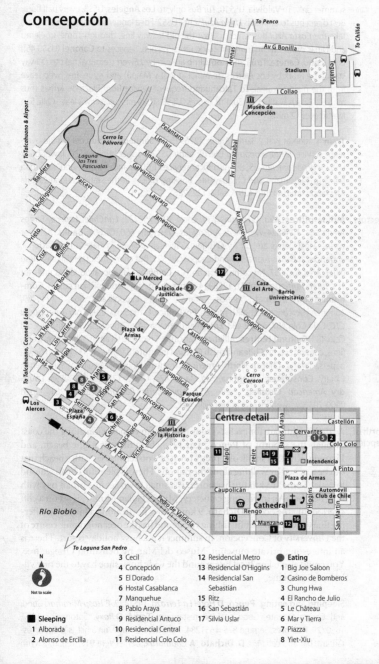

The Central Valley

N

Not to scale

Sleeping ■
1 Alborada
2 Alonso de Ercilla
3 Cecil
4 Concepción
5 El Dorado
6 Hostal Casablanca
7 Manquehue
8 Pablo Araya
9 Residencial Antuco
10 Residencial Central
11 Residencial Colo Colo
12 Residencial Metro
13 Residencial O'Higgins
14 Residencial San Sebastián
15 Ritz
16 San Sebastián
17 Silvia Uslar

Eating ●
1 Big Joe Saloon
2 Casino de Bomberos
3 Chung Hwa
4 El Rancho de Julio
5 Le Château
6 Mar y Tierra
7 Piazza
8 Yiet-Xiu

main terminal on J M García, reached by buses from Av Maipú in centre. To **Santiago**, 8½ hrs, US$12, 8 companies. To **Valparaíso**, 9 hrs, US$12 (most go via Santiago; check). *Estrella del Sur* have buses to **La Serena** and **Iquique**. To **Loncoche**, 7 hrs, US$6.50. To **Puerto Montt** several companies, US$15, about 12 hrs; to **Pucón** direct, 8 hrs, US$8, in summer only. To **Valdivia**, US$10, *Tur Bus* only; to **Los Angeles**, US$3, every half hour. Best direct bus to **Chillán** is *Línea Azul*, 2 hrs, US$2. For a longer and more scenic route, take the *Costa Azul* bus which follows the old railway line, through Tomé, Coelemu and Nipas on to Chillán (part dirt-track, takes 5½ hrs). Services to **Coronel** (US$0.45), **Lota, Lebu, Cañete, Tirúa** and **Contulmo** are run by *J Ewert* (terminal next to railway station on Prat), by Los Alerces (terminal at Prat y Maipú) and by Jeldres, who leave from the main terminal. To **Talcahuano** frequent service from Plaza de Armas (bus marked 'Base Naval'), US$0.30, 1 hr, express US$0.50, 30 mins; *colectivos* leave Calle San Martín every 2 mins.

Train: station at Prat y Barros Arana, T226925. To **Santiago**, Rápido del Bío Bío overnight service, 9 hrs, *económica* US$10; *salón* US$20, upper bunk US$30, lower bunk US$39; *departamento* US$80. Also local services to Laja and Yumbel, and suburban trains to Talcahuano and Chiguayante. Booking offices at the station and at Galería Alessandri, Aníbal Pinto 478, local 3, T225286.

Directory **Airline offices** *Alta*, O'Higgins 734, Local 19, T252732. *LanChile, Ladeco*, Barros Arana 560, T248824. *Aerolíneas Argentinas*, O'Higgins 650, Of 602. **Banks** ATMs at banks. Most banks are on Av O'Higgins. Several *cambios* in Galería Internacional, entrances at Barros Arana 565 and Caupolicán 521, but check their rates first as these differ. *Afex*, local 57. No commission on TCs. *Cambios Fides*, local 58. Good rates for TCs. *Inter-Santiago*, local 31, T228914. Banks charge high commission on Tcs. **Communications** **Internet**: Barros Arana 541, Caupolicán 567, T245409, admin@cyberconce.cl, English spoken. **Post office**: O'Higgins y Colo Colo. **Telephone**: *CTC*, Colo Colo 487, Angol 483. *Entel*, Barros Arana 541, Caupolicán 567, piso 2, Colo Colo 487. **Cultural centres** **Alliance Française**, Colo Colo y Lamas. Library, concerts, films, cultural events. **Chilean-British Cultural Institute**, San Martín 531 (British newspapers, library). **Chilean-North American Institute**, Caupolicán 301 y San Martín. Library. **Consulates** **Argentina**, San Martin 472, Of 52, T230257, F230995. **Laundry** *American Cleaning*, Freire 817. *Lavandería Radiante*, Salas 281. Open 0900-2030, very good. Also at Lincoyán 441.

North of Concepción A road (nightmare for cyclists) runs north from Concepción along the coast through the suburbs of **Penco** (Km 12), where there is a fine beach, and **Lirquén**, Km 15, a small, old, pretty town of wooden houses with a beach that can be reached by walking along the railway. There is plentiful cheap seafood for sale. **Tomé**, 13 km further north, is a small town set in a broad bay with long beaches. An interesting cemetery, Miguel Gulán Muñoz, is set on a cliff overlooking the ocean. **Dichato**, 9 km further north along a hilly road offering fine views, is a beautiful fishing village and has the oceanographic centre of the University of Concepción. In summer it is a busy holiday resort. There is an interesting private museum, Museo del Mar, by Benjamín Ortega, free. You could also take a local bus around the wide horseshoe bay to the tiny village of Cocholgüe.

Sleeping and eating **Penco** **D** *Hotel La Terraza*, T451422. **E** *Hosp Miramar*. Good, and Casino Oriente. Good seafood restaurant. **Tomé** **D** *Roxy*, Sotomayor 1077, T650729. **F** *Linares*, Serrano 875, T651284. 7 km before Tomé, on a hill, is El Edén, restaurant, bar and *cabañas*, **D**. **Dichato** **A** *Chamaruk*, Daniel Vera 912, T683022. With

Battles of Coronel and the Falklands, 1914

The British defeat at Coronel in November 1914, and their subsequent victory five weeks later in the Battle of the Falklands, were part of a general struggle to control the sea and thus influence the outcome of the First World War in Europe. At the outbreak of war, the British navy set up a network of cruiser squadrons around the world to protect allied shipping and to drive German merchant shipping from the seas. At Coronel a small British force made up of three elderly cruisers and an armed merchant cruiser met a German squadron, which, under Vice-Admiral Graf von Spee, was en route to Germany via Cape Horn. The British were outgunned and lost two of their four vessels, Good Hope which blew up, and Monmouth which sank.

On 8 December when von Spee reached Port Stanley in the Falklands he sighted a larger British force in the harbour, including two battlecruisers, Invincible and Inflexible, sent by the British to deal with the German

squadron. Von Spee attempted to flee. The ensuing battle was a series of duels which resulted in the sinking of four German vessels; the remaining one, Dresden, escaped and hid in Fiordo Leptepu, just north of Chaitén, until she was destroyed by the British in March 1915.

The Battle of the Falklands was the last sea battle decided purely by naval gunnery: henceforth submarines, torpedoes, mines and aircraft would also influence the outcome of naval warfare. Victory cleared the Pacific and South Atlantic of German shipping, an important part of the British strategy. Yet a questionmark remains over von Spee's decision not to attack the British vessels in harbour: faced with such a superior force his squadron was doomed, but it could have inflicted considerable damage on the port facilities and on the two battlecruisers which were relatively unmanoeuvrable in the confined space of Port Stanley harbour.

bath, **C** without, clean, pleasant. **B** *Kalifa*, Daniel Vera 813, T683027, F229019. With bath, restaurant. **B** *Manantial*, Aguirre Cerda 201, T683946. **D** *Chicki*, Ugalde 410, T683004. With bath, **E** without. **E** *Res Santa Inés*, República 540. Without bath; *albergue* in the school in summer, **G**. Eateries include: **Tomé**, *Munot*, Baquedano 1690, Swiss food. *Villa Marina*, Riquelme 55, traditional food; and in **Dichato** there are several seafood restaurants on P Aguirre Cerda 600 and 700 blocks.

Transport *Línea Azul* and *Costa Azul* buses from Concepción pass through all these villages, which can also be reached cheaply by *colectivo* (every 15-20 mins).

Situated at the neck of a peninsula, Talcahuano has the best harbour in Chile. It is Chile's main naval station and an important commercial and fishing port. In the naval base you can visit the **Huáscar**, a relic of the War of the Pacific. ■ *Tue-Sun 0900-1230, 1330-1730. US$1.50. Photography is permitted, but passports must be handed in at the main gate.* On Península Tumbes is **Parque Tumbes**, owned by Codeff: paths lead along the coast, there are no services and no admission charge. Details are available from the Codeff office in Concepción.

Talcahuano
Colour map 3, grid C1
Population: 244,000

Sleeping and eating **B** *De La Costa*, Colón 630, T545913. With breakfast. **B** *France*, Av Pinto 44, T542230, F548748. With breakfast. **C** *Res San Pedro*, Rodríguez 22, T542145. With breakfast. **F** without bath. **Mid-range**: *Club Talcahuano*, Colón 446, for meat. **Mid-range/cheap**: *El Alero de los Salvo*, Colón 3396. *Benotecas*, on seafront, a row of 4 restaurants sharing one window facing the harbour. Superb fish and seafood in each one, reasonable prices. Recommended. *Domingo Lara*, Aníbal Pinto 450. Seafood specialities, excellent. *La Aguada*, Colón 912. Shellfish dishes.

The market abounds with places serving fine seafood very cheaply

The Central Valley

The coastal route south of Concepción

South of the Río Biobío is the **Costa del Carbón**, until recently the main coal-mining producing area of Chile, linked with Concepción by two bridges over the Biobío. Between Concepción and Lota are the Laguna San Pedro Chica, which is good for swimming, and Laguna Grande, a watersports centre, just across the Río Biobío. The road is busy, noisy and polluted by trucks plying to and from the numerous local industries. Nearer Lota is the small Playa Negra with few people and black sand and Playa Blanca with white sand, which is bigger and more crowded. It has bars, cafés, many seafood restaurants and a free campsite. Both beaches are on the Bahía de Coronel.

Coronel Coronel, 29 km from Concepción, was the scene of a British naval defeat in 1914. The *Good Hope* and *Monmouth* were sunk by the *Scharnhorst* and a monument commemorating the defeat was erected in November 1989. The defeat was later avenged at the Battle of the Falklands/Malvinas with the destruction of the German squadron (see box).

Lota
Colour map 4, grid A1
Population: 52,000
42 km south of Concepción

Lota was, until recently, the site of the most important coal mine in Chile. Originally the property of the Cousiño family (see box, page 90), the mine closed in April 1997. The town was known to be one of the poorest in Chile even before the mine's closure; although the government has invested in retraining the miners and in trying to open up Lota to tourism, things have been a far greater struggle since, and there is much poverty and neglect.

The town is in two parts: Lota Alto, on the hill, is the original mining town, while Lota Bajo, below, is more recent. In the church on the main plaza you can see a virgin made of coal. Offshore is an island, Isla Santa María, which has basic accommodation and good beaches.

The **Parque de Lota**, covering 14 ha on a promontory to the west of the town, was the life's work of Isadora Cousiño. Laid out by English landscape architects in the 19th century, it contains plants from all over the world, ornaments imported from Europe, romantic paths and shady nooks offering views over the sea, and peafowl and pheasants roaming freely. The mansion which was Isadora's home during her stays in Lota was destroyed in the 1960 earthquake. ■ *1000-1800 daily, till 2000 in summer. US$2.50, no picnicking.* Near the entrance to the park is the **Museo Historíco de Lota**. ■ *1000-2000 Nov-Mar, 1000-1800 Apr-Oct. US$1.*

The **Coalmine**, the tunnels of which run almost entirely under the sea (the longest is 11 km) can be visited; at the entrance is a small **Museo Minero**. ■ *Guided tours led by former miners, daily 1000-1700, US$5, T870682.*

Sleeping and eating C *Angel de Peredo*, Alessandri 169, T876824. F *Res Roma*, Galvarino 233, T876257. Clean, friendly. *El Greco*, P Aguirre Cerda 422. Traditional food, cheap.

Transport Buses to **Concepción**, 1½ hrs, US$0.50. Many buses bypass the centre: catch them from the main road.

South of Lota South of Lota the road runs past the seaside resort of **Laraquete** where there are miles of golden sands. The road passes a large cellulose factory, and then at Carampangue, Km 64 south of Concepción, it forks: one branch running west to **Arauco**, the site of two cellulose factories; the other branch continues south, 52 km, to Tres Pinos, where there is a turning for Lebu. Twenty-four kilometres beyond Tres Pinos is the small town of **Cañete**.

Sleeping and eating Laraquete E *Laraquete*, on Gabriela Mistral (main street). Friendly, small rooms, poor bathrooms. **E** *Hostal La Quinta*, T571993. Helpful, basic, good breakfast. Several *residenciales* close to beach; campsite near beach. **Arauco** B *Hostería Arauco*, Esmeralda 80, T551131, F551100. C *Plaza*, Chacabuco 345, T551265. **F** without bath.

A fishing port and coal washing centre, Lebu lies at the mouth of the Río Lebu, 149 km south of Concepcíon, and is the capital of Arauco province. There are enormous beaches to both north and south, popular on summer weekends. About 3 km north at Playa Millaneco are caves with steep hills offering good walks and majestic views.

Lebu
Phone code: 041

Sleeping and eating A *Hostería Millaneco*, at Playa Millaneco, T511904, T/F511540. Offers *cabañas*, sleep 7, good restaurant. Recommended. **E** pp *Central*, Pérez 183, T/F511904. With bath, **F** without, clean, parking. Recommended. **E** *Gran* Pérez 309, T511939. With bath, **F** without, old fashioned, clean, *comedor*. **F** *Res Alcázar*, Alcázar 144. With breakfast, cold water, friendly.

Cañete is a small, friendly town on the site of the historic Fort Tucapel, where Pedro de Valdivia and 52 of his men were killed by Mapuche warriors in 1553. About 1 km south on the road to Contulmo, is the **Museo Mapuche Juan Antonio Ríos** in a modern building supposedly inspired by the traditional Mapuche *ruca*; displays include Mapuche ceramics and textiles. Behind the museum is a reconstruction of a *ruca*. ■ *0930-1230, 1400-1830, daily in summer, closed Mon in winter. US$1.25.*

Cañete
Phone code: 041
Colour map 4, grid A1

Sleeping and eating B *Hostería VIP's*, Av Bonilla, T/F611012. With breakfast. **C** *Nahuelbuta*, Villagrán 644, T611073. Clean, pleasant, parking. Cheaper without bath. **D** *Derby*, Mariñán y Condell, T611960. With bath, clean, basic, restaurant. **E** pp *Alonso de Ercilla*, Villagrán 641, T611974. With bath, clean. **E** *Comercio*, 7 de la Línea, T611218. Very pleasant. Recommended. **E** *Gajardo*, 7 de la Línea 817 (1 block from plaza). Without bath, old fashioned, friendly, pleasant. *Don Juanito*, Riquelme 151. Very good, friendly. Recommended by the locals, cheap. Real coffee at *Café Nahuel*, off the plaza.

Transport Bus Buses leave from 2 different terminals: *J Ewert*, *Inter Sur* and *Thiele* from Riquelme y 7° de la Línea; *Jeldres*, *Erbuc* and other companies from the Terminal Municipal, Serrano y Villagrán. To **Santiago**, *Inter Sur*, daily, 12 hrs; to **Purén**, US$1.50; sit on right for views of Lago Lanalhue; to **Concepción**, 3 hrs, US$3.50; to **Lebu** US$1.50; to **Angol** US$3.50; to **Tirúa**, *Jeldres*, frequent and *J Ewert*, 3 a day, 2 hrs, US$2.

Lago Lleulleu is a peaceful lake covering 4,300 ha. It lies 34 km south of Cañete; to get there, turn off at Peleco, Km 11. The lake offers sandy beaches, many opportunities for camping and fine views of the coastal mountain range, but there are few facilities.

Tirúa, at the mouth of the Río Tirúa, is 78 km south of Cañete. The beach is calm and deserted. There are three *hospedajes* all **F**, including *Residencial Elimar*, T894902. The island of **Mocha**, visited by Juan Bautista Pastenes in 1544 and later by Sir Francis Drake, lies 32 km offshore. Most of the island's 800 inhabitants live around the coast, the interior being forest. The main settlement is La Hacienda where accommodation is available with families.

Lago Lleulleu & Tirúa
The town, Tirúa, itself is unremarkable, but it lies near some wonderful country for walking and riding

The Central Valley

■ *Getting there: from Tirúa: ferry daily 0600, US$14; plane US$56 (ask the police to radio the plane which is based on Mocha). Buses run from Cañete to Tirúa.*

Lago Lanalhue Situated south of Cañete, Lago Lanalhue is surrounded by forested hills from which there has been extensive logging. Much less popular than the Lake District, this area offers good opportunities for walking. A road runs south from Cañete along the north side of the lake to Contulmo at its southern end. Access to the lake shore is restricted as much of it is private property. Playa Blanca, 10 km north of Contulmo, is a popular beach in summer (take any bus between Contulmo and Cañete). There are several *cabañas* on lakeshore. For further information on the area ask at the *Hostal Licahue* (see below). Tours are offered by *Lanalhue Turismo*, T09-6767695, www.lanalhueturismo.cl

Contulmo
Colour map 4, grid A2
Population: 2,000

This sleepy village at the foot of the Cordillera hosts a *Semana Musical* or music week in January. The wooden **Casa y Molino Grollmus**, 3 km northwest along the southern side of the lake, are well worth a visit. The house, dating from 1918, has a fine collection of every colour of *copihue*, the national flower, in a splendid garden. The mill, built in 1928, contains the original wooden machinery. From here the track runs a further 9 km north to the *Posada Campesina Alemana*, an old German-style hotel in a fantastic spot at the water's edge. The **Monumento Natural Contulmo**, 8 km south of the village and administered by CONAF, covers 82 ha of native forest.

Sleeping and eating D *Contulmo*, Millaray 116, T894903. With bath, **F** pp without, an attractive retreat, friendly and hospitable. Highly recommended. **F** *Central*, Millaray 131. T618089. Without bath, no sign, very hospitable. **On the lake**: **A** *Posada Campesina Alemana*, open Dec-Mar, poor beds, own generator, fish come to hotel steps, details from Millaray 135 in Contulmo. **B** pp *Hotel Licahue*, 4 km north towards Cañete, T09-8702822, Casilla 644, Correo Contulmo. With breakfast, also full board, attractively set overlooking lake, pool. Highly recommended. Also *cabañas*, **AL**, sleep 7, on far side of lake (connected by boat). *Hostería Lago Lanalhue*, reached from Tirúa road, on southern lakeside, T234981. **Camping** *Camping Elicura*, clean, US$6. Recommended. *Camping Playa Blanca*, clean. *Camping Huilquehue*, 15 km south of Cañete on lakeside.

Transport Bus: To **Concepción**, *Thiele*, US$4.50, 4 hrs; to **Temuco**, *Thiele* and *Erbuc*, US$4; to **Cañete**, frequent, US$1.

Purén Twenty kilometres further south, Purén is reached by crossing the Cordillera through dense forest (do this journey in daylight). Located in a major logging area, Purén was the site of a fortress built by Pedro de Valdivia in 1553 and destroyed soon after. It was a key stronghold of the Chilean army in the last campaign against the Mapuche (1869-1881) and there is a full-scale reconstruction of the wooden fort on the original site. There is **E** *Tur*, Dr Garriga 912, T793216 and *Central*, which is on the plaza. *Central* has excellent meals, but only lets rooms in the tourist season. **Lumaco**, 21 km southeast, is the site of a major Mapuche festival, the *Fiesta de Piedra Santa* (see box on page 306).

Los Angeles

Situated on the Pan-American Highway, Los Angeles is the capital of Biobío province. Founded in 1739 as a fort, it was destroyed several times by the Mapuche. Located between the rivers Laja and Biobío at the heart of a wine, fruit and timber-producing district, it has become an important agroindustrial centre and is a pleasant, expanding city, with a large Plaza de Armas. Most visitors find themselves here on their way to Parque Nacional Laguna de Laja.

Phone code: 043
Colour map 4, grid A2
Population: 114,000
110 km south
of Chillán

Getting there Los Angeles is easily accessible from north and south by bus; the most common destinations are Santiago, Puerto Montt and Concepción, but all intermediate destinations are also served. **Getting around** Los Angeles is not as big as some of the other cities of the central valley, and as a result it is not necessary to take public transport quite as often as in, say, Chillán or Talca. **Tourist offices** On Caupolicán close to Post office. CONAF, Ercilla 936. 0900-1300. Automóvil Club de Chile, Villagrán y Caupolicán, T322149.

Ins & outs
See page 304 for further details

There isn't much here in the way of sights. Colón is the main shopping street and there is a good daily market. Swimming is possible in the nearby Río Dueco, 10 minutes south by bus, US$0.80. The Museo de la Alta Frontera has some Mapuche silver and colonial artefacts. ■ *Mon–Fri 0815-1445, 1500-1830, free, Colón 195.*

A *Gran Hotel Müso*, Valdivia 222 (Plaza de Armas), T313183, F312768. Good restaurant open to non residents. **A** *Mariscal Alcázar*, Lautaro 385 (Plaza de Armas), T/F311725. **C** *Res Santa María*, Plaza de Armas. Hot shower, TV, friendly but run down and overpriced. **C** *Winser*, Rengo 138. Overpriced but clean and friendly. **D** *Mazzola*, Lautaro 579, T321643. With breakfast. There are several residenciales (**C-D** range) around Colo Colo and Almagra. **E** Private house at Caupolicán 651, large breakfast, good value. Opposite is another, also No 651, basic, cheaper. **E** pp *Res Winser*, Colo Colo 335, T323782, small rooms.

Sleeping
■ *on map*
Price codes:
see inside front cover

Eighteen kilometres north is **F** *Hospedaje El Rincón*, Panamericana Sur Km 494, Cruce La Mona 2 km east, T09-4415019, F043-317168, elrincon@cvmail.cl Beautiful property beside a small river, restful. South American and European cuisine, including vegetarian (**B** pp full board), tours arranged, Spanish classes, horse riding, rafting, English, French and German spoken, kitchen facilities. Antukelen, Camino Los Angeles-Santa Bárbara-Ralco, 62. 7 km southeast on the Alto Bío-Bío, reservations Siegfried Haberl, Casilla 1278, Los Angeles, T043-326097/09-4500210. Camping, US$15 per site, showers, German, English and French spoken, vegetarian food and other natural attractions; *cabañas*, natural therapy centre and excursions.

Mid-range *Bavaria*, Colón 357. Good. *Di Leone*, Av Alemania 606. Good lasagne. *El Arriero*, Colo Colo 235, T322899. Good *parrillas* and international dishes. *Rancho de Julio*, Colón 720. Excellent *parrilla*. **Cheap** *Julio's Pizzas*, Colón 542. Good.

Eating

The Central Valley

Tour operators *Senderos Chile Expediciones*, T09-7143958, trekking, mountain biking. *Strong Visión*, Caupolicán 506, T09-312295. Trekking, mountain biking, rafting, kayaking, bungee-jumping, fishing.

Transport **Bus** Long distance bus terminal on northeastern outskirts of town, local terminal at Villagrán y Rengo in centre (most services to Ralco and Santa Barbara). To **Santiago**, 9 hrs, US$12, *Ejecutivo* US$23. To **Viña del Mar** and **Valparaíso**, 10 hrs, US$14; to **Concepción**, US$2.50, 2½ hrs; to Valdivia, US$7; to Chillán, US$2.50. To **Temuco**, US$5, hourly; to **Curacautín**, daily at 0600, 3 hrs, US$4. **Motorcycle** Spares *Moto Stop*, Galvarino 487, T/F316987.

Directory **Banks** *Banco Santander*, Colón 500, Mastercard. *Corp Banca*, Colón 300, Visa. ATMs at banks and at supermarket at Av Alemaña 686. Banks are reluctant to change TCs or cash. Best rates at *Agencia Interbruna*, Caupolicán 350. **Communications** Post office: on Plaza de Armas. **Telephone**: *CTC*, on Colo Colo. *Entel*, Colo Colo 393.

Salto del Laja Salto del Laja, 25 km north of Los Angeles, is a spectacular waterfall where the Río Laja plunges 15 m over the rocks. Numerous tour groups stop here, and the place is filled with tourist kiosks selling pap; it is pretty nonetheless. There are several *cabañas*, and a supermarket. Boat trips are available in the Buenaventura, T09-4181247.

Sleeping and eating **AL** *Hostería Salto del Laja*, Casilla 562, Los Angeles, T321706, F313996. With fine restaurant, 2 swimming pools and chalet-type rooms on an island overlooking the falls. Nearby is **B** *Complejo Turístico Los Manantiales*, T/F314275. Also camping. Motels *El Pinar* and *Los Coyuches*.

Transport **Bus**: *Bus Biobío* from Los Angeles, US$1, 30 mins – frequent; to Chillán, frequent, US$2.

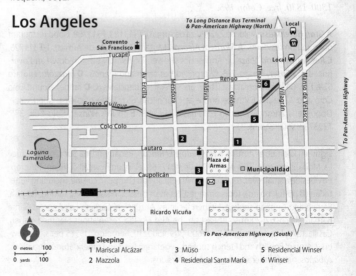

Los Angeles

To Long Distance Bus Terminal & Pan-American Highway (North)

Local

Convento San Francisco
Tucapel

Local

To Pan-American Highway

Av Ercilla
Mendoza
Valdivia
Rengo
Colón
Almagro
Villagrán
Manso de Velasco

Estero Quilque

Colo Colo

5

2

1

Lautaro

Laguna Esmeralda

3

Plaza de Armas

Municipalidad

Caupolicán

4

i

Ricardo Vicuña

N

0 metres 100
0 yards 100

To Pan-American Highway (South)

■ Sleeping
1 Mariscal Alcázar
2 Mazzola
3 Müso
4 Residencial Santa María
5 Residencial Winser
6 Winser

Parque Nacional Laguna de Laja

Covering 11,600 ha and situated 93 km east of Los Angeles by a road, paved for the first 64 km, which runs past the impressive rapids of the Río Laja, the park is dominated by the scree slopes of the Antuco Volcano (2,985 m), which is still active, and the glacier-covered Sierra Velluda. The valley below is green and wooded – very pleasant and sparsely visited, even in the high season. Passing the ski station, the road reaches the turquoise waters of the Laguna de la Laja, with a small pier and views of the Andes stretching towards Argentina; note, though, that it is a walk of several hours from the park entrance to the lake, and there is very little passing traffic. (The road continues to the Argentine border at Paso Pichachén; open October-April, depending on amount of snow.) The laguna was created by the damming of the Río de Laja by a lava flow. It is surrounded by stark scenery of scrub and lava. Trees include a few surviving araucarias. There are 47 species of birds including condors and the rare Andean gull. The visitors centre is 1 km from park administration (4 km from the entrance).

There is no clear path to the summit of Antuco. From the Refugio Digeder at 1,400 m allow about six hours to ascend; start out early (0500) to allow time for the descent, which is exhausting. The volcano slopes are made of black scorias blocks which are razor sharp, so wear good strong boots and take water; be warned that this sort of terrain is exhausting and can catch out those who are unaware of its severity.

Colour map 4, grid A

From the summit of Antuco Volcano – where there are sulphur fumes – are fine views over the Sierra Velluda and its glaciers and south to the smoking Villarrica Volcano

Antuco F *Hostería El Mirador*, without bath. There is a supermarket, *Santa Theresa*, Los Carrera 360. **Abanico** F *Hostería El Bosque*, restaurant, good campsite. **In the park** *Cabañas y Camping Lagunillas*, T321086 (or Caupolicán 332, Of 2, Los Angeles T043-231066) 50 m from the river, 2 km from park entrance. Open all year, cabins sleep 6, lovely spot among pine woods, restaurant, camping US$2.50 pp. Camping not permitted on lake shore. 21 km from the lake is the *Refugio Chacay* offering food, drink and bed (**B** , T043- 222651, closed in summer). 2 other *refugíos: Digeder*, **F**, 11 km from the park entrance and *Universidad de Concepción*, both on slopes of Antuco Volcano, for both T041-229054, Of O'Higgins 740. Nearby is the Club de Esquí de los Angeles with 2 ski-lifts, giving a combined run of 4 km on the Antuco Volcano (season, May-Aug).

Sleeping

In Antuco, most places are fully occupied by local workers.

For the Parque Nacional Laguna de Laja, take your own food as little is available in Abanico or inside the park

Take a bus from Los Angeles (*ERS Bus*, Villagrán 507) to Abanico then 4 km to park entrance. Alternatively take a bus to Antuco, US$1.35, 2 hrs, weekdays 5 daily, Sun/festivals 2 daily, then hitch the remaining 24 km to the park. US$1.50.

Transport

Angol

Situated at the confluence of the Ríos Rehue and Picolquén, Angol lies at the foot of the Cordillera de Nahuelbuta. Capital of the province of Malleco, it can be reached from the Pan-American Highway by roads from Los Angeles and Collipulli. Founded by Pedro de Valdivia in 1552, Angol was destroyed seven times by the Mapuche Indians.

The church and convent of **San Beneventura**, northwest of the attractive Plaza de Armas, built in 1863, became the centre for missionary work among the Mapuche. Worth visiting is **El Vergel**, 5 km southeast, founded in 1880 as an experimental fruit-growing nursery; it now includes an attractive park with a wide range of trees and the **Museo Dillman Bullock** with displays on archaeology and natural history. ■ *Mon-Fri 0900-1900, Sat-Sun 1000-1900. US$1. Getting there:* colectivo *No 2.* The tourist office is O'Higgins s/n, across bridge from bus terminal, T711255. Excellent. CONAF, Prat 191, piso 2, T711870.

Phone code: 045 Colour map 4, grid A2 Population: 39,000

Though of limited interest to travellers, it is the main base for visiting the Parque Nacional Nahuelbuta, further west

The Central Valley

Fiesta de la Piedra Santa

The ancient festival of the Holy Stone is celebrated every year on 20 January. The women dress in their traditional costumes, with colourful belts and silver jewellery. Each family carries a fowl which is sacrificed, covering the stone with blood, while they ask for favours or give thanks for favours received. A few drops of wine are also poured onto the stone before the rest is drunk. The stone is illuminated by hundreds of candles and crosses made of straw or grass are placed over the blood,

which sticks to them. Machis (shamans), surrounded by people from their communities, go up to the stone and, accompanied on their sacred instrument, the kultrung, they sing, dance and recite, while passing their knives over the diseased parts of the bodies of the sick. The festival continues through the night with singing, dancing, music and prayers.

Abridged and translated from Lengua y Costumbres Mapuches *by Orietta Appelt Martin, Imprenta Austral, Temuco, 1995.*

Sleeping & eating **B** *Club Social*, Caupolicán 498, T711103. With breakfast. **B** *Josanh-Paecha*, Caupolicán 579, T711771. With breakfast, clean, good food. **B** *Millaray*, Prat 420, T711570. With breakfast. **C** *Olimpia*, Lautaro 194, T711517. **D** pp La Posada, at El Vergel, T712103. Full board, clean, friendly. **D** *Res Olimpia*, Caupolicán 625, T711162. Good. **E** *Casa de Huéspedes*, Dieciocho 465. With breakfast, friendly. **E** *El Parrón*, O'Higgins 345, T711370. **E** *Vergara 651*, chaotic but cheap. **Camping** on the road to Parque Nacional Nahuelbuta west of the city are *Las Quilas*, Km 21 *El Manzano*, Km 20. **Eateries:** *Carloncho*, Lautaro 447. Popular with locals. *Flores*, Caupolicán 330. Both cheap.

Transport **Bus** Long distance terminal is at Chorrillos y Caupolicán. Local buses use Terminal Rural, Ilabaca y Lautaro. To **Santiago** US$6.50, **Los Angeles**, US$1.20, or **Collipulli**. To **Temuco**, Trans Bío-Bío, frequent, US$2.50. **Car hire** *Christopher Car*, Ilabaca 421, T/F715156.

Directory **Banks** *Banco Bice*, Chorrillas 364. *Banco Santander*, Lautaro 399.

Parque Nacional Nahuelbuta
Colour map 4, grid A2

Situated in the coastal mountain range at an altitude of 800-1,550 m, the park covers 6,832 ha of forest and offers views over both the sea and the Andes. There are some good walks. One to Piedra el Aguila at 1,158 m, 4 km west of visitors centre, where there is a *mirador* on top of a huge boulder. Another goes to Cormallín, 5 km north of visitors centre, from where you may continue to Cerro Anay, 1,402 m, and another *mirador*. ■ *Open all year (snow Jun-Sep).*

Although the forest includes many species of trees, the araucaria is most striking; with some over 2,000 years old, 50 m high and with trunks 2 m in diameter. There are also seven species of orchids. Animals include pudu, Chiloé foxes, pumas, kodkod, black woodpeckers and parrots. There is a visitors centre at Pehuenco, 5 km from the entrance.

Sleeping Camping Near visitors centre, US$9 – there are many free campsites along the road from *El Cruce* to the entrance. Also at Cormallín, no facilities.

Rough maps are available at the park entrance for US$0.25

Transport From Dec to Feb there is a direct bus to park entrance, Sun, 0800 from Angol, return 1700. Otherwise, take a bus to Vegas Blancas (27 km west of Angol) 0700 and 1600 daily, return 0900 and 1600, 1½ hrs, US$1.20, get off at *El Cruce*, from where it is a 7 km walk to park entrance (US$4.50). Access is also possible by dirt road from Cañete, 40 km west. . Between Jun and Sep, access is possible only by 4WD vehicles.

The Lake District

10

Extending from the Río Biobío south to the city of Puerto Montt, the Lake District is one of the most popular destinations for Chileans and visitors alike. The main cities are Temuco, Valdivia, Osorno and Puerto Montt, but the most attractive scenery lies further east where a string of lakes stretches down the western side of the Andes. Much of this region has been turned into national parks, and the mixture of forests, lakes and snow-capped volcanoes is unforgettable. Between Temuco and the Pacific coast, meanwhile, is the indigenous heartland of Chile, home to the largest Mapuche communities; here you will find traditional thatched houses (rucas) and communities still fiercely proud of their traditions, hinting at the sort of country that the first conquistadors might have found.

The major resorts include Pucón on Lago Villarrica and Puerto Varas on Lago Llanquihue. The cities of Temuco and Puerto Montt are also popular, the former for excursions into the Mapuche communities towards the coast, and the latter as a base for longer voyages south to Puerto Natales, Puerto Chacabuco and the San Rafael glacier, and east across the lakes and mountains to the Argentine resort of Bariloche.

The Lake District

Background

History After the Mapuche rebellion of 1598, Spanish settlement south of the Río Biobío was limited to Valdivia, although the Spanish had a right of way north from Valdivia along the coast to Concepción. At independence the only other Spanish settlement in this region was Osorno, refounded in 1796. The Chilean government did not attempt to extend its control into the Lake District until the 1840s. In 1845 all land south of the Río Rahue was declared the property of the state and destined for settlement; in 1850 Vicente Pérez Rosales was sent to Valdivia to distribute lands to arriving European colonists.

The southern Lake District was settled from the 1850s onwards, mainly by German immigrants. Further north Chilean troops began occupying lands south of the Biobío after 1862, but the destruction of Mapuche independence did not occur until the early 1880s when Chilean forces led by Cornelio Saavedra founded a series of forts in the area including Temuco (1881), Nueva Imperial (1882), Freire (1883) and Villarrica (1883). A treaty ending Mapuche independence was signed in Temuco in 1881.

White settlement in the area was further encouraged by the arrival of the railway, which reached Temuco in 1893, reducing the journey time from Santiago to 36 hours; the line was later extended to Osorno (1902) and Puerto Montt (1912).

Geography South of the Río Biobío both the Andes and the snowline are lower. The coastal range of mountains is also lower. The region between the cities of Temuco and Puerto Montt is one of the most picturesque lake regions in the world. There are 12 great lakes, and dozens of smaller ones, as well as imposing waterfalls and snowcapped volcanoes. This landscape has been created by two main geological processes: glaciation and volcanic activity. The main mountain peaks are volcanic: the highest are Lanín (3,747 m) and Tronador (3,460 m), both on the Argentine border. The most active volcanoes include Llaima and Villarrica, which erupted 22 and 10 times respectively in the 20th century.

Seven main river systems drain the Lake District, from north to south the ríos Imperial, Toltén, Valdivia, Bueno, Maullín, Petrohué and Puelo. The Río Bueno drains Lago Ranco and is joined by the ríos Pilmaiquén and Rahue, thus receiving also the waters of Lagos Puyehue and Rupanco: it carries the third largest water volume of any Chilean river. In most of the rivers there is excellent fishing.

Climate Rain falls all the year round, and more heavily further south. Rainfall decreases as you go inland: some 2,500 mm on the coast and 1,350 mm inland. Average daily temperatures in Valdivia are around 17°C in summer and 5°C in winter. In the national parks to the east night temperatures can drop as low as -10°C, even in summer. Beware if camping.

Out of season many facilities are closed. In season (from mid-December to mid-March), prices are high, and it is best to book well in advance, particularly for transport. Between mid-December and mid-January enormous horse-flies (*tábanos*) are a problem – do not wear dark clothes, especially black or navy blue.

Economy Agriculture is the most important sector of the local economy. Cereals, potatoes, beans and sugar beet are grown throughout the region; cattle and sheep farming are more important further south than around Temuco. The farms

Things to do in the Lake District

- Make the journey from Puerto Montt to Bariloche in Argentina, across the emerald waters of the Lago Todos Los Santos – which itself is overlooked by the Osorno Volcano and thick forests – and then through a narrow pass in the Andes.
- Go to the Parque Nacional Conguillio, the best place in Chile to see the famous *araucarias* (monkey puzzle trees), in the shadow of Volcan Llaima.
- Climb Volcan Villarrica, an active volcano where molten lava bubbles in the crate.
- Eat at Angelmo, a harbour near Puerto Montt, which has some of the best seafood in Chile (and, by extension, in the world).
- Spend a morning at Temuco's market. It is one of the biggest and most fascinating in Chile, filled with Mapuche men and women who have come by ox cart to the city to sell their produce.
- Take a trip to the old forts at Niebla and Corral, near Valdivia. South of Corral, a path follows the shore through wild forest clinging to cliffs above the ocean.

are mostly medium sized. Irrigation is unnecessary for agriculture. There is enough rainfall to maintain heavy forests, mostly of southern beech and native species, though increasingly of eucalyptus and other introduced varieties for the booming timber industry. Fishing is particularly important in the south of the region, where the growth of salmon farming is reflected in its presence on restaurant menus. Tourism is a mainstay in summer.

Industry has grown in importance in recent years, the main industries being connected to the region's produce, for example cereal mills, fish and meat processing plants, sugar beet plants, dairy processing and sawmills.

There are four main routes from the Lake District into Argentina: 1) From Pucón and Curarrehue to Junín de los Andes via Paso Tromen (see page 334). 2) From Panguipulli via Choshuenco and Lake Pirehueico to San Martín de los Andes via Paso Huahum (see page 340). 3) From Osorno and Entrelagos via the Parque Nacional Puyehue and Paso Puyehue to Bariloche (see page 354). 4) The Lakes Route, from Puerto Montt or Osorno via Ensenada, Petrohué and Lago Todos Los Santos to Bariloche (see page 367).

Crossing to Argentina

The Lake District

Temuco

At first sight, Temuco may appear a grey, forbidding place. However in reality it is a lively industrial and university town. For visitors, it is perhaps most interesting as a contrast to the more European cities in other parts of Chile. Temuco is proud of its Mapuche heritage, and it is this which gives it its distinctive character, especially around the market area. North and east of the city are three national parks and several hot springs. West of the city in the valley of the Río Imperial are the market towns of Nueva Imperial and Carahue and, on the coast, the resort of Puerto Saavedra.

Phone code: 045
Colour map 4, grid A2
Population: 225,000
Altitude: 107 m

Getting there There are several daily flights north to Santiago and Concepción, and south to Puerto Montt. Temuco is the transport hub for the Lake District, and the Municipal Bus station serves much of the Lake District, as well as the communities towards the coast. The city is also easily accessible by bus from Santiago (many daily).

Ins & outs
See page 316 for further details

The Mapuche

The largest indigenous group in southern South America, the Mapuche now live mainly in communities south of the Biobío. There are also reserves in the Argentine cordillera around Lago Nahuel Huapi. The name Mapuche is derived from the Mapuche for 'land' (mapu) and 'people' (che). They were known as Araucanians by the Spanish.

Never subdued by the Incas, the Mapuche successfully resisted Spanish attempts at conquest. At the time of the great Mapuche uprising of 1598 they numbered some 500,000, concentrated in the area between the Río Biobío and the Reloncaví estuary. After 1598 200 years of intermittent war were punctuated by 18 peace treaties; the 1641 Treaty of Quilín recognized Mapuche autonomy south of the Biobío. So great was the Mapuche threat considered to be that Concepción became the base of the only standing army in Spanish America.

Although tools and equipment were privately owned, the Mapuche held land in common, abandoning it when it was exhausted by repeated use. This relatively nomadic lifestyle helps explain their ability to resist the Spanish. Learning from their enemies how to handle horses in battle, they became formidable guerrilla fighters. They pioneered the use of horses by two men, one of whom handled the animal while the other was armed with bow and arrows. Horses also enabled them to extend their territory to the
eastern side of the Andes, reaching the Argentine pampas.

The conquest of the Mapuche was made possible by several developments: the building of railways; and new weapons, especially the breach-loading rifle (which had a similarly disquieting effect in Africa and Asia). The settlement of border disputes between Chile and Argentina enabled Argentine troops to occupy the border crossings while the Chilean army subjugated the Mapuche. Under the 1881 treaty, the Mapuches received 500,000 ha from the government, while 5,000,000 ha were kept for Chile.

The Mapuche were confined to reservations, most of which were situated near large estates for which they provided a labour force. By the 1930s, living in more than 3,000 separate reservations, the surviving Mapuche had become steadily more impoverished and more dependent on the government. The agrarian reforms of the 1960s provided little real benefit to the Mapuche since it encouraged individual landholding; indeed some communal lands were sold off. The military government made continued encroachments on Mapuche communities, which are certainly among the poorest in Chile. It is estimated that the Mapuche now occupy only about 1½% of the lands they inhabited at the time of the Spanish conquest, and July 2001 saw repeated clashes with the police over land rights.

There are also connections to the larger towns both north and south, especially Talca, Chillán, Concepción, Valdivia and Puerto Montt (many daily). **Getting around** Temuco is a large city, and there are *colectivos* and buses serving the outlying *barrios*. However, the centre is relatively compact, and few places are more than a ½-hr walk away in this area. **Tourist offices** Bulnes 586, T211969. Open 0830-2030, all week in summer, 0900-1200, 1500-1700 Mon-Fri in winter. Automóvil Club de Chile: Varas 687, T213949. CONAF: Bilbao 931, T234420.

Sights

Temuco is centred on the **Plaza Aníbal Pinto**, around which are the main public buildings including the cathedral and the municipalidad; the cathedral was destroyed by the 1960 earthquake, when most of the old wooden buildings in the city were also burnt down. On the plaza itself is a monument to La Araucanía featuring figures from local history. Nearby are fountains and a small Sala de Exposiciones, which stages exhibitions.

The produce market at Lautaro y Pinto is always crammed with people who have come from the countryside, and it is one of the most compelling markets in Chile; here you will find excellent cheap fruit and vegetables, and also local spices like Merquén – made from smoked chillies – and fish, grains, cheese, honey; there are many inexpensive bars and restaurants nearby, and the place is well worth a visit.

Temuco offers the opportunity to interact with Mapuche people at the market and to see *huasos* (cowboys) at the cattle auctions held on Thursday mornings in the stockyards on Calle Malvoa behind the railway station and at the Feria Agroaustral, just west of Temuco on the road to Nueva Imperial, on Friday from 1400 (take bus 4 from Calle Rodríguez). Traditional Mapuche spinning and weaving demonstrations are held at the **Casa de la Mujer Mapuche**, 283, where textiles made by a co-operative of 135 Mapuche weavers are sold, very good quality, but correspondingly expensive. ■ *Mon-Fri 0900-1300, 1500-1900*. There is also an Anglican church on Plaza Teodoro Schmidt.

North of the city is the **Monumento Natural Cerro Nielol** offering reasonable views. The hill has a one-way system for drivers – entry by Prat, exit by Lynch. There is an excellent visitors' centre run by CONAF and a fine collection of native plants in their natural environment, including the *copihue rojo*, the national flower. ■ *US$1*. Cerro Nielol was the site of the signing of the final peace treaty between the Chilean army and the Mapuche (1881); it was signed under La Patagua, a tree which can still be seen.

Museo de la Araucanía houses a well arranged collection devoted to the history and traditions of the Mapuche nation; also a section on German settlement. ■ *US$1. Mon-Fri 0900-1700, Sat 1100-1700, Sun 1100-1300. Alemania 084. Getting there: bus 1 from centre.* **Museums**

Parque Museo Ferroviario, 1 km north of centre, contains 15 railway engines under restoration, and eight passenger coaches. ■ *Tue-Sun 0900-1800. Av Barros Arana 1000.*

To get a flavour of the life of the Mapuches, it is well worth making a trip to **Chol Chol**, a dusty, friendly country town in the heart of Mapuche country, situated 30 km northwest of Temuco by unpaved road across rolling countryside. On a clear day it is possible to see five volcanoes. You will see people travelling by ox cart on the tracks nearby, and a few traditional round *rucas*. For an overnight stay and information, contact Sra Lauriza Norváez, Calle Luzcano s/n, who prepares meals, and is very helpful; there are also several cheap bars, as well as a small museum dedicated to Mapuche culture. ■ *Getting there: daily buses, laden with corn, vegetables, charcoal, animals as well as the locals, leave from Terminal Rural, Huincabus, 1 hr, 4 between 1100 and 1800, US$1.* **Excursions**

Nueva Imperial is a market town, 35 km west by a paved road, which follows the Río Imperial; cattle auctions are held here on Mondays and Tuesdays. From here the road continues to **Carahue**, where there is accommodation, a market, supermarkets and shops. This was the site of the Spanish colonial city of Imperial which was destroyed by the Mapuche. Further on is Puerto Saavedra, see page 317. see page 317 ■ *Getting there: reached by frequent buses from Temuco's rural bus station (see below, under transport).*

The Lake District

The 1960 earthquake

Southern Chile is highly susceptible to earthquakes: severe quakes struck the area in 1575, 1737, 1786 and 1837, but the tremor which struck around midday on 22 May 1960 caused extensive damage throughout Southern Chile and was accompanied by the eruption of four volcanoes. The resulting maremoto (tidal wave) was felt as far away as New Zealand and Japan.

Around Valdivia the land dropped 3 m, creating new lagunas along the Río Cruces to the north of the city. The maremoto destroyed all the fishing villages and ports between Puerto Saavedra in the north and Chiloé to the south. The earthquake also provoked several landslides. The greatest of these blocked the Río San Pedro near the point where it drains Lago Riñihue. The lake, which receives the waters of six other lakes, rose 35 m in 24 hours. Over the next two months all available labour and machinery was used to dig channels to divert the water from the other lakes and to drain off the waters of Lago Riñihue, thus averting the devastation of the San Pedro valley.

Essentials

Sleeping
■ on map, page 315
Price codes:
see inside front cover
Do not confuse
the streets Vicuña
MacKenna and
Gen MacKenna

LL-L *Terraverde*, Prat 0220, T239999, F239455, restera@panamericanahoteles.cl 5-star. **AL** *Nuevo Hotel de la Frontera*, Bulnes 726, T200400, F200401. With breakfast, excellent. **AL-A** *Bayern*, Prat 146, T276000, F212291. 3-star. Small rooms, clean, helpful. **A** *C'est Bayonne*, Vicuña MacKenna 361, T234119, F214915, netchile@entelchile.net With breakfast, small, modern, German and Italian spoken. **A** *Hotel Don Eduardo*, Bello 755, T214133, F215554, deduardo@ctcinternet.cl Parking, suites with kitchen, recommended. **B** *Hostal Chalet Alemán*, Varas 349, T/F212818. **B** *Luanco*, Aldunate 821, T/F213749. Apartments with kitchenette. **B** *Tierra del Sur*, Bulnes 1196, T/F232439. Pool, sauna. **B-C** *Continental*, Varas 708, T238973, F233830, continental@ifrance.com Popular with business travellers, old-fashioned building, old beds, excellent restaurant, the bar is popular with locals in the evening, cheaper rooms without bath. Recommended.

C *Espelette*, Claro Solar 492, T/F234805. Helpful, quiet. **D** *Alba Jaramillo*, Calbuco 583, near Av Alemania, T240042. With breakfast, clean. **D** *Blanco Encalada 1078*, T234447. Use of kitchen, friendly. Recommended. **D** *Bulnes 1006 y O'Higgins*. Good double rooms, hot water, above drugstore, ask for house key otherwise access limited to shop hours. **D** *Casa Blanca*, Montt 1306 y Zenteno, T212740. Good breakfast, friendly. **D** *Flor Acoca*, Lautaro 591. Hot water, breakfast, clean. **D** *Hosp Adriane Becker*, Estebáñez 881. Without bath, good breakfast, basic, friendly. **D** *Hospedaje La Araucaria*, Varas 552, T322820. **D** *Hostal Argentina*, Aldunate 864. With breakfast, hot water, clean. **D** *Las Heras 810*. Without breakfast, basic, clean. **D** *Rupangue*, Barros Arana 182. Hot shower, clean, helpful, good value. **D** *Sevilla*, Aldunate 153.

E *Casa Blanca*, Montt 1306 y Zenteno, T272667, F212740. Good breakfast and friendly, but dirty bathrooms and a little overpriced. **E** *Hosp Aldunate*, Aldunate 187, T213548. Friendly, cooking facilities, also **F** dormitory accommodation. **E** *Hospedaje 525*, T233982. Zenteno 525. Without breakfast, large rooms, clean, poor beds but good value. TV lounge. Smaller double rooms (**F**) including private bath. **E** *Oriente*, M Rodríguez 1146, T/F233232. Clean, recommended. **E** *San Martín 01760*, T246182. With breakfast, clean. **F** *Hosp Millaray*, Claro Solar 471. T645720. Simple, basic. Other private houses on this street. **F** *Res Temuco*, Zenteno 486, T211269. Friendly, clean, hot water, recommended. Accommodation in private houses, category **E-F**, can be arranged by tourist office. Other cheap residenciales and pensiones can be found in the market area.

Camping *Camping Metrenco*, on Pan-American Highway, Km 12.

Mid-range *Caletas Restaurante*, Bello y V. MacKenna, fish/seafood. *Centro Español*, Bulnes 483. *D'Angelo*, San Martín 1199. Good food, pleasant. *La Cumbre del Cerro Nielol* (dancing), on top of Cerro Nielol. *La Parrilla de Miguel*, Montt 1095, good for meat and wine, mid-expensive. *Pizzeria Madonna*, M Montt 670, good atmosphere, good pizzas, reasonably priced. **Cheap** *Ñam-Ñam*, Portales 802. Sandwiches etc, good. *Pront Rapa*, Aldunate 421. For take-away lunches and snacks, recommended. *Quick Biss*, Varas 765, fast food. *Restaurant del sur*, Portales 921, cheap, open 24hrs. *Restaurante Temedors*, San Martín 827, good value lunch. **Seriously cheap** For those on a budget, make for the market or the rural bus terminal, where there are countless restaurants serving very cheap set meals at lunch. *Humitas* are on sale in the street, while the Mercado Municipal has several butchers and restaurants, where there is fierce touting for business.

Eating

Temuco

The Lake District

■ Sleeping

1 Bayern
2 C'est Bayonne
3 Casa Blanca
4 Continental
5 Don Eduardo
6 Espelette
7 Flor Acoca
8 Hospedaje Aldunate
9 Hospedaje Millaray
10 Hospedaje 525
11 Hospedaje La Araucaria
12 Hostal Argentina
13 Hostal Chalet Alemán
14 Luanco
15 Nuevo Hotel de la Frontera
16 Oriente
17 Residencial Temuco
18 Sevilla
19 Terraverde
20 Tierra del Sur

● Eating

1 Centro Español
2 La Parrilla de Miguel
3 Ñam-Ñam
4 Pizzería Madonna
5 Pront Rapa
6 Quick Biss
7 Restaurant del Sur
8 Restaurante Temedors

Not to Scale

Cafés *Café Marriet*, Prat 451, Local 21. Excellent coffee. *Cafetería Ripley*, Prat y Varas. Real coffee. On Bulnes: *Della Maggio*, No 536. Real coffee and light meals. *Dino's*, No 360. Good coffee. *Il Gelato*, No 420. Delicious ice cream.

Entertainment **Pubs** *HBH Bar*, M Montt 847, European style lager. *Masquerito's Pub*, Bulnes 770. **Discos** *El Tunnel*, Caupolicán y M Blanco, restaurante bailables. *"Mr Jones"*, Bello 844, pub-cafe-disco. Pub-Disco *"banana bliss"*, Montt 1031. *Sol y Luna*, 10 km south on road to Pucón, 2400-0600. There is a **cinema** on the plaza.

Shopping **Bookshops** *Librería Alemana*, Montt 104. German proprietor also speaks English, books in English, German and Spanish. **Cameras** *Ruka*, Bulnes 394. Helpful, owner speaks German. **Crafts** Mapuche crafts and textiles are sold inside and around the Mercado Municipal at Aldunate y Portales. **Supermarket** *Frutería Las Vegas*, Matta 274. Dried fruit (useful for climbing/trekking). *Las Brisas*, Rodríguez 1100 block. *Santa Isabel*, Bulnes 279. *"Super"*, Rodríguez 1400 block. There is also Mall Temuco, a modern shopping centre north of city, bus 2, 7.

Tour companies *Turismo*, Claro Solar 988, T211278. *Turismo Nielol*, Claro Solar 633, T/F239497, offers towns to Parque Nacional Conquillo US$34, to Puerto Saavedra US$37, to Villarica volcano US$60. *Turismo Sur de América*, P De Valdivia 0413, T/F317777, myriamhernandez@latinmail.com *T&S Tour Operador*, Claro Solar 950, Of 404, T275445, F275446, tts@ctcreuna.cl

Transport **Local** **Car hire**: *Automóvil Club de Chile*, Varas 687, T248903 and at airport. *Budget*, Lynch 471, T214911, *Christopher Car*, Varas 522, T/F215988. *Dollar*, at airport, T336512. *Euro*, MacKenna 426, T210311, helpful, good value. *Hertz*, Las Heras 999, T235385, US$45 a day. *Puig*, Portales 779. *Fatum*, Varas 983, T234199. **Bicycle**: Parts at *Oxford*, Andrés Bello 1040, T211869. Repairs at Bulnes 228, Lautaro 1370, Portales 688. Also many on Balmaceda, nos. 1266, 1294 and 1448. **Motorbike**: Spares at *Terremoto*, Claro Solar 358, T312828, F312800.

Long distance **Air**: Manquehue Airport, 6 km southwest of city. *LanChile* and *Ladeco* to Santiago. *LanChile* and *Ladeco* to Osorno and Valdivia. *TAN* flies to Neuquén, Argentina.

Bus: new long distance terminal north of city at Pérez Rosales y Caupolicán – to get there, take buses 2 or 7 from the centre. Services to neighbouring towns leave from Terminal Rural, Pinto y Balmaceda or from bus company offices nearby: *Erbuc*, Miraflores y Bulnes; *JAC*, Balmaceda y Aldunate (*NarBus* and *Igi Llaima* offices opposite); *Tur Bus* on Lagos 500 block. To **Santiago** several companies, US$18, 9-11 hrs, most overnight. *Cruz del Sur*, 3 a day to **Castro**, 10 a day to **Puerto Montt** (US$8, 5½ hrs); to **Valdivia** US$3; to **Osorno** US$6; to **Concepción**, *Bío Bío*, US$5, 4½ hrs; to **Arica**, US$55 or US$70 *cama*; to **Antofagasta**, US$45; to **Chillán**, 4 hrs, US$4.50; to **Villarrica** and **Pucón** many between 0705 and 2045, 1½ hrs, US$3, and 2 hrs, US$3.50; to **Coñaripe**, 3 hrs, and **Lican Ray**, 2 hrs; to **Panguipulli**, *Power* and *Pangui Sur*, 3 hrs, US$3. *Pangui Sur* to **Loncoche**, **Los Lagos**, US$4, **Mehuín** in summer only; to **Curacautín**, *Erbuc*, US$2, 6 daily, 2 hrs. To **Lonquimay**, *Erbuc*, 4 daily, 4 hrs, US$3. *Narbus* to **Nueva Imperial, Carahue and Puerto Saavedra**, 6 a day, US$3; to **Laguna** Captren, *Erbuc*, Mon and Fri 1645, 4 hrs, US$3; to **Contulmo**, US$4, 2 hrs, **Cañete**, US$4 and **Lebú**, *Erbuc* and *Thiele*.

Bus to Argentina: *JAC* to **Junín de los Andes** (US$25), **San Martín de los Andes** (US$25) and **Neuquén** (US$30), Wed and Fri 0400; also Igi Llaima and San Martín 3 a week each. *Nar Bus* from Terminal Rural to **San Martín** and **Neuquén**, Mon-Fri (San Martín buses go via Villarrica and Pucón when the Tromen Pass is open); *Ruta Sur*, Miraflores 1151, to **Zapala** (US$22) and **Neuquén** (US$28), via Paso Pino Hachado, Wed and Sat 0400; *La Unión del Sud*, Miraflores 1285, same destinations Wed, Fri and Sat. *Fénix* to **Buenos Aires** and **Mendoza**; to **Bariloche** via Osorno, Tas Choapa, US$23, daily.

Train: the station is at Barros Arana y Lautaro Navarro, T233416. Ticket office at Bulnes 582, T233522, open Mon-Fri 0900-1300, 1430-1800, Sun 0900-1300 as well as at station. To **Santiago**: overnight service, daily 2000, 12 hrs. The dining car (built in the early 1930s) and the sleeping car (1929) were both made in Germany. Sleeping car has hot showers. Fares: *económica* US$11, *turista* US$13, *salón* US$18, *lower bunk* US$35, *upper bunk* US$28, *double compartment* US$75, restaurant car expensive. *There are no trains south of Temuco*

Airline offices *LanChile/Ladeco*, Bulnes 699, on Plaza, T211339. *TAN*, T210500. *Varig*, Bello 870, T213120. **Banks** ATMs at many banks on Plaza A Pinto: these include *Banco Santander, Banco Bice, Banco BCI, Banco Sud Americano, Banco de Chile*; also at the new JAC bus terminal. **Casas de Cambio:** *Christopher*, Prat 696, Oficina 419. *Comex*, Prat 471. *Inter-Santiago*, Bulnes 443, Local 2. *Turcamb*, Claro Solar 733. Also at Bulnes 667, Local 202, and at Prat 427; many cambios around the Plaza. All deal in dollars and Argentine pesos. **Communications** Internet: Gral. MacKenna 445. **Post office**: Portales 839. **Telephones:** *CTC*, A Prat just off Claro Solar and plaza. Open Mon-Sat 0800-2400, Sun and holidays 1030-2400. *Entel*, Bulnes 303. Daily 0830-2200. Also call centres at Lautaro 1311 and Montt 631. **Consulates** Netherlands, España 494. Honorary Consul, Germán Nicklas, is friendly and helpful. **Cultural Institutes** Instituto Chileno-Frances, Varas 736. Instituto Chileno-Norte Americano, Grl MacKenna 555; both institutes are always worth checking out for films and events. **Laundry** *Alba*, Zeneto 480, opposite the church, and at Aldunate 324, and Aldunate 842; also at Portales 1185, expensive. *Marva*, M Montt 415 and 1099. Mon-Sat 0900-2030. **Shipping Office** *Navimag office*, Bello 870. **Directory**

West of Temuco

Puerto Saavedra lies behind a sandspit south of the mouth of the Río Imperial. The most famous Chilean film in recent years, *La Frontera*, was filmed here. Founded in 1897 at the mouth of the river, the town was destroyed in 1960 by a *maremoto* (tidal wave); few people were killed as they saw the water draining from the bay (the warning sign of a *maremoto*). The impact of the *maremoto* on the local psyche and on folktales cannot be overestimated – said one man to the author, "We thought it was the end of the world, so we spent two months drunk on the hills until the water receded".

Puerto Saavedra
Population: 2,300
81 km west of Temuco

The centre of the town moved inland after the *maremoto*. There are now three distinct areas: the administrative centre of Puerto Saavedra, inland; Maule, 2 km south, is a fishing port with one poor *residencial* (this was the site of the town before 1960 – just beyond Maule is a track to the incredibly narrow sandspit which stretches several kilometres north to the mouth of the Río Imperial; beautiful beach and uninterrupted views of the ocean; this oddity in the coastline is a legacy of the *maremoto*); the third area is Boca Budi, a further 4 km south, a resort with an enormous beach.

From Puerto Saavedra a track leads north 2 km to a free ferry crossing over the Río Imperial to **Nehuentue**, on the north bank, where the ferry is based (if the ferry is on the other side of the river, shout until the ferryman hears you – he will cross). From here launches may be chartered up the Río Moncul to the pleasant tour of **Trovolhue**, four hours. From Nehuentue there are beautiful tracks leading north towards the town of **Tirúa**, 70 km away; the route is being widened by mechanical diggers (but still a long way from being completed), best travelled on horse or bicycle.

Sleeping Boca Budi: **A** *El Criollito*, T212583; *Lago Los Cisnes*, T251891; **F** *Sra Rita Sandoval Muñoz*, Las Dunas 01511. Lovely, knowledgeable. **Maule E** *Hosteleria Maule*, T634013. **Puerto Saavedra**: Two or three *pensiones*, **G**. **Camping** *Rayen Lafquen*, in Boca Budi, El Cisne, in Maule.

Transport Bus: To Temuco (Terminal Rural), *Nar Bus*, 3 a day, 3¼ hrs, US$2.50.

Lago Budi   The only inland saltwater lake in Chile, Lago Budi lies south of Puerto Saavedra. Over 130 species of water bird, including black necked swans, visit it. Although the lake is marked on maps as having an outlet to the sea, this is dried up for most of the year, when there is a continuous track along the expanses of sandy beach from Puerto Saavedra south to Porma and Toltén. This was the old right of way of the Spanish between Concepción and Valdivia before their final defeat of the Mapuches; wild and remote, it passes many isolated Mapuche communities.

On the east shore of Lago Budi, 40 km by road south of Carahue, is **Puerto Domínguez**, a picturesque little town famous for its fishing. On the west shore is Isla Huapi (also spelt Guapi), a peninsula with a Mapuche settlement (also known as Isla Huapi) of traditional thatched houses (*rucas*) and fine views of both the lake and the Pacific. Ideal for camping. Isla Huapi can be reached by ferry (*balsa*) either from about 10 km south of Puerto Saavedra or from Puerto Domínguez (see below). However, this is one of the poorest spots in Chile.

Sleeping Puerto Domínguez: **F** *Hostería Rucaleufú*, Alessandri 22. With good meals, clean, lake views. Highly recommended. **Camping** *Puaucho*, on Isla Huapi.

Transport Bus: to Puerto Domínguez from Temuco, 3 hrs. **Ferry**: The *Carlos Schalchli* ferry leaves Puerto Domínguez for Isla Huapi, Mon and Wed 0900 and 1700, returning 0930 and 1730, free, 30 mins.

East of Temuco

Thirty kilometres east of Temuco a paved road branches off the Pan-American Highway and runs east to the Argentine frontier at Pino Hachado, passing through Curacautín and providing access to several national parks; there is also paved access from Victoria, further north.

Curacautín   A small town situated on the Río Cautín, Curacautín lies 84 km northeast of
Phone code: 045   Temuco and 56 km southeast of Victoria (both roads paved). Its main indus-
Colour map 4, grid A2   try is forestry and there are several sawmills. It is a useful centre for visiting the nearby national parks and hot springs.

Sleeping and eating C *Plaza*, Yungay 157, T881256, main plaza. Restaurant good but pricey. **F** *Hostería Abarzúa*, T870011. Full board, **C**, camping. **F** *Res Rojas*, Tarapacá 249. Without bath, good meals. Recommended. **F** Rodríguez 705 (corner of plaza). With breakfast, clean, kitchen facilities. **F** *Turismo*, Tarapacá 140, T881116. Clean, good food, comfortable, best value. **Camping** *Trahuilco*, 3 km south. Expensive. *El Refugio* is a popular eating place.

A man with a mission

One of the more unusual European visitors to Southern Chile in the 19th century was Oréllie Antoine de Tounens, a native of Périgueux in the Dordogne. Reading explorers' accounts of South America inspired him to propose reuniting the 17 newly independent Spanish American states into a Monarchical Confederation with himself as king.

However, on arrival in South America in 1858, he decided instead to become King of the Mapuche. The widespread Mapuche belief that victory against the Chilean and Argentine governments would occur with the arrival of a new white chief meant that Antoine, an imposing figure with long black hair who wore a French coat and poncho and carried a curved sabre, was received better than might have been expected. Antoine's proposals for the new coat of arms, flag and constitution of Araucania or Nueva Francia appealed to Quilapán, one of the Mapuche chiefs, and Antoine was duly crowned. The Chilean government was less impressed: when Antoine led a band of armed Mapuche to the Río Biobío to negotiate a peace settlement, the Santiago authorities had him arrested. Antoine's claims that he merely intended to build schools and encourage education were rewarded with

a 10-year prison sentence. French diplomats attempted to secure his release on the grounds of insanity. Eventually a compromise was arranged: the court ruled that although sane now, Antoine had been insane at the time of his offences.

Back in France, Antoine wrote his memoirs. His attempts to find benefactors to finance another visit to his kingdom were unsuccessful, so he returned penniless. With the Chilean government offering a reward for his head he was forced to flee. Back in France he sold bonds to finance another expedition, but the Chilean government objected to his activities and he was tried for selling fraudulent bonds. His final attempt to return was cut short when he was recognized disembarking at Bahia Blanca and deported by the Argentine government. Holding court in France, he sold specially minted coins, but was excommunicated by the Pope. The French government then refused him the pension he claimed for services to his country of birth, and eventually his friends got him a job lighting street lamps. On his death in 1878 he left his crown to a cousin.

For more information see La Patagonia de Chatwin by Adrian Giménez Hutton.

The Lake District

Tour operator *Turismo Christopher*, Yungay 260, T882471.

Transport Bus: Terminal in the old railway station, west of the plaza on the main road. Buses to/from Temuco and Los Angeles. *Tur Bus*, 2 daily direct to Santiago. *Erbuc* buses continue to Malalcahuello and Lonquimay.

Termas de Manzanar

These indoor hotsprings are 17 km east of Curacautín. They cost US$5 and are open all year. The road passes the Salto del Indio (Km 13) a 60-m high waterfall, before which there is a turn-off to Laguna Blanca (25 km north, take fishing gear, ask *Sernatur* about trucks). Three kilometres beyond Manzanar is the Salto de la Princesa, a 50-m waterfall. ■ *Getting there: reached by bus from Temuco and Victoria.*

Sleeping and eating L-A *Termas de Manzanar*, T/F881200, termasmanzanar@ indecom.cl Also simple rooms with bath. **C** *Hostería Abarzúa*, T870011. Simple, friendly, also **E** without bath. **C** *Hostería La Rotunda del Cautín*, T351478, F881569. Food available in the hotels.

Termas de Tolhuaca The beautiful pine-surrounded Termas de Tolhuaca are 35 km to the northeast of Curacautín by ripio road, or 57 km by unpaved road from just north of Victoria; a high clearance four-wheel drive essential. The hot springs are open from November to April daily, and from May to October at weekends only.

Sleeping and eating **AL** *Termas de Tolhuaca*, T881164, F881211. With full board, includes use of baths and horseriding, very good. **F** *Res Roja*. Hot water, food, camping near the river, good.

Parque Nacional Tolhuaca
Open from Dec to Apr
This park, 2 km north of the Termas de Tolhuaca, covers 6,374 ha of the valley of the Río Malleco at altitudes of 850 to 1,830 m and includes the waterfalls of Malleco and Culiebra, and two lakes, Laguna Malleco and Laguna Verde. Superb scenery and good views of volcanoes from Cerro Amarillo. Park administration is near Laguna Malleco and there is a campsite nearby. ■ *Getting there: reached either from Curacautín via the Termas de Tolhuaca (route open all year) or by dirt road from the Pan-American Highway 5 km north of Victoria (4WD essential in winter and autumn). Bus from Victoria to San Gregorio (19 km from park entrance) Mon, Wed, Fri 1715, return same day 0645.*

Reserva Nacional Malalcahuello-Nalcas

Access is best from Malalcahuello and Lonquimay
Situated northeast of Curacautín, this 31,305 ha park lies on the slopes of the **Lonquimay Volcano** (2,865 m), and is much less crowded than the nearby Parque Nacional Conguillio.

In Malalcahuello, where most of the accommodation is (see below), there is a steam-powered carpenter's shop, and also three marked CONAF trails leaving from the CONAF centre near Malalcahuello. Near Lonquimay Village is Los Arenales, a new ski resort (season June – September) with four lifts going up to an altitude of 2,500 m.

Lonquimay Volcano began erupting on Christmas Day 1988. The new crater is called Navidad. **To climb Lonquimay**, access is made from Malalcahuello, 15 km south and halfway between Curacautín and Lonquimay town. From the ski lodge it is a one-hour walk to the base of the mountain. Walk towards the ski lift and from there head to the spur to the left. Allow four hours for the ascent, one hour for the descent. Information from the CONAF HQ on the main road at Malalcahuello. Crampons and ice-axe are essential. The headmaster at Malalcahuello school, Jose Córdoba, organizes tours and arranges horseriding trips; Sra Naomi Saavedra at *Residencial Los Sauces* also arranges lifts.

The reserve is also a popular centre for **fly-fishing**: Sr Jorge Vio, at the ski lodge, provides information and acts as guide, US$40 pp per day, including transport but not equipment.

Sleeping *Res Los Sauces*, **D** pp, full board, or **F** with use of kitchen, hot water, good value. *Suizandina*, **F-G**, Km 28 on Curacautín-Lonquimay road (3 km from Malalcahuello), T9-8849541, F881892, Casilla 44 Curacautín, www.suizandina.com Hostel with camping, hiking, horseriding, laundry, homebaked bread, English, German spoken, travellers cheques accepted, recommended. Also has more expensive double rooms, **A**. There is also a CONAF lodge. Accommodation is also available at the *Centro de Ski Lonquimay*, 10 km from the bus stop, **C** pp, with breakfast, full board also available, free camping, open all year, ski pass US$17.

In Lonquimay: **F** *Hospedaje Navidad*, Caupolicán 915, T891111. **F** *Hostal Lonquimay*, Pinto 500, T891324.

Bus *Erbuc* from Temuco, US$2 to Malalcahuello, 4 a day, 4 hrs, 5½ to Lonquimay town, US$3. There is accommodation in Lonquimay, but no public transport to the volcano. **Transport**

Parque Nacional Conguillio

Covering 60,833 ha, the park, situated 80 km east of Temuco, is one of the most *Colour map 4, grid A3* popular in Chile though it is deserted outside January and February and at weekends. In the centre is the **Llaima Volcano** (3,050 m), which is still active and can be climbed. There are two craters; the western crater was completely blown out in 1994 and it began erupting again in March 1996. There are two large lakes, Laguna Verde and Lago Conguillio, and two smaller ones, Laguna Arco Iris and Laguna Captrén. North of Lago Conguillio rises the snow-covered extinct volcano Sierra Nevada, the highest peak of which reaches 2,554 m.

Much of the park is covered in forests of southern beech but the park is also the best place in Chile to see araucaria forest which used to cover an extensive area in this part of the country (see page 325). Mature araucaria forest can be found around Lago Conguillio and on the slopes of Llaima. Other trees include cypresses, and *canelo* (winter's bark). Birdlife includes the condor, the black woodpecker and many waterfowl. Mammals include the marsupial *monito del monte*, pumas and *pudu*.

To climb Llaima, crampons and ice-axe are essential except in summer (ask first). Climb south from *Guardería Captrén*, avoiding the crevassed area to the left of the ridge and keeping to the right of the red scree just below the ridge. From the ridge it is a straight climb to the summit. Beware of sulphur fumes at the summit. Allow five hours to ascend, two hours to descend. Information on the climb is available from Sr Torres at *Guardería Captrén*.

Parque Nacional Conguillio

The Lake District

There is a range of **trails**, from 1 km to 22 km in length. Details are available from park administration or CONAF in Temuco. The route through the park from the south end is as follows: from the entrance, a 600-m trail to Río Truful-Truful canyon and waterfall; 8 km to Laguna Verde; 4 km to Laguna Arco Iris; 4 km to Laguna Conguillio; 6 km from Centro de Información Ambiental on Conguillio to Laguna Captrén; 10 km to park limits and *guardería*.

Llaima **ski resort**, one of the prettiest in Chile, is reached by a poor road from Cherquenco, 30 km west (high clearance vehicle essential).

The administration and information centre is open from November to June, at Laguna Arco Iris, Laguna Captrén and at Truful-Truful. Out of season administration is at the western entrance. There is a Visitors' Centre at Lago Conguillio, open December to March. CONAF run a series of free slide lectures during daytime and evenings and short guided walks for adults and children during the summer, covering flora and fauna, Volcán Llaima and other subjects; details from the visitors' centre. ■ *US$5.*

There are three **entrances**: the northern entrance is reached by *ripio* road which continues through the park from Curacautín, 28 km north (taxi from Curacautín, US$30); the southern entrance at Truful-Truful is reached by a *ripio* road from Melipeuco, 13 km southwest; the western entrance, near the Llaima ski resort (see above) is reached by *ripio* road from Cherquenco. It is then a two- to three-day hike around Volcán Llaima to Lago Conguillio, dusty, but beautiful views of Laguna Quepe, then on to the Laguna Captrén *guardería*.

Sleeping & eating

In the park, there is a campsite at Laguna Captrén, US$20 per site including firewood but no other facilities. Lago Conguillio has a campsite, US$20 per tent, hot water, showers, firewood. A cheaper campsite, *camping de mochileros*, US$5 pp; showers US$1, firewood US$2. *Cabañas* **A** summer only, sleep 6, gas stove, and café/shop but supplies are much cheaper in Temuco or Melipeuco. Book campsite with CONAF in the park; book *cabañas* with Jorge Lefenda/Sra Silvia Weisser, Alvisur, Pedro de Valdivia 0631, Temuco, T/F214363. In Melipeuco: **D** *Hosteria Hue-Telén*, Aguirre Cerda 1, Casilla 40, T/F581005 to leave message, good restaurant, free municipal campsite. **F** *Germania*, Aguirre 399, basic, good food. **F** *Pensión Hospedaje*, Aguirre 729, more spacious, recommended. Also *Camping Los Pioneros*, 1 km out of town on road to the park, hot water. *Restaurant Los Troncos*, Aguirre 352, recommended.

Transport

To the northern entrance: bus from Temuco Terminal Rural, *Nar Bus*, 5 daily, 0900-1830, 4 hrs, US$1.30, ask driver to drop you at the road fork, 10 km from park entrance, last back to Temuco at 1630. Bus from Curacautín to Laguna Captrén, *Erbuc*, Mon and Fri, 1730, summer only. To the western entrance: daily buses from Temuco to Cherquenco, from where there is no public transport to the park. Transport to the southern entrance can be arranged from Melipeuco (ask in grocery stores and *hospedajes*, US$25, one way). For touring, hire a 4-WD vehicle in Temuco. Several agencies in Temuco offer tours to the park, US$34, 1 day.

Border with Argentina

The pass, **Paso Pino Hachado**, of 1,884 m can be reached either by unpaved road, 77 km southeast from Lonquimay or by unpaved road 103 km east from Melipeuco. On the Argentine side this road continues to Zapala. Immigration and customs is at Liucura, 22 km west of the frontier, is open from December to March 0800-2100, April to November 0800-1900. Very thorough searches and two- to three-hour delays are reported. Buses from Temuco to Zapala and Neuquén use this crossing: see under Temuco.

The pass, **Paso de Icalma**, of 1,298 m is reached by *ripio* road, 53 km from Melipeuco. On the Argentine side this road continues to Zapala. Chilean immigration is open December to March 0800-2100, April to November 0800-1900.

Lago Villarrica

Wooded Lago Villarrica, 21 km long and about 7 km wide, is one of the most beautiful lakes in the region, with the snow-capped Villarrica Volcano (2,840 m) to the southeast. Visitors should note, though, that its resorts are among the most expensive in Chile (although those with the money will find them well worth the expense).

Villarrica

Pleasantly set at the extreme southwest corner of the lake, Villarrica can be reached by a paved road southeast from Freire, 24 km south of Temuco on the Pan-American Highway, or from Loncoche, 54 km south of Freire, also paved. Less significant as a tourist resort than nearby Pucón, it is also cheaper. Founded in 1552, the town was besieged by the Mapuche in the uprising of 1599: after three years the surviving Spanish settlers, 11 men and 13 women, surrendered. The town was refounded in 1882.

Colour map 4, grid B2
Population: 36,000
Phone code: 045

There is a small museum, the **Museo Histórico** containing a collection of Mapuche artefacts, at Pedro de Valdivia 1050 y Zegers. ■ *US$0.25, Mon-Sat 0900-1930, 1800-2200, Sun 1800-2200, reduced hrs in winter.* Next to it is the **Muestra Cultural Mapuche**, featuring a Mapuche *ruca* and stalls selling good quality handicrafts. The *costanera* offers good views of the volcano. For good views over the lake go south along Aviador Acevedo and then Poniente Ríos towards the *Hostería La Colina*.

The tourist office is at Valdivia 1070, T411162, F414261. Information and maps (open all day all week in summer).

AL-A *El Ciervo*, Koerner 241, T411215, F410925, elciervo@villaricanet.com 4-star. German spoken, beautiful location, pool. Recommended. **AL-B** *Hostería de la Colina*, Las Colinas 115, overlooking town, T411503, Casilla 382, aldrich@entelchile.net With breakfast, large gardens, good service, good restaurant. Highly recommended. **A** *Hostería Bilbao*, Henríquez 43, T411452. Clean, small rooms, pretty patio, good restaurant. **A** *Hotel y Cabañas El Parque*, 3 km east on Pucón road, Casilla 65, T411120, F411090, hotelparque@entelchile.net Lakeside with beach, tennis courts, with breakfast, good restaurant with set meals. Highly recommended. **A** *Hotel-Yachting Kiel*, Koerner 153, T411631. **D** off season, lakeside, clean, friendly, good. **A** *Villarrica*, Koerner 255, T/F411641. **A** *Yachting Club*, San Martín 802, T/F411191. **B** *Bungalowlandia*, Prat 749, T/F411635, bungalowlandia@villaricanet.com Cabañas, with *comedor*, good facilities. **B** *Cabañas Traitraico*, San Martín 380, T/F411064, 100 m from lake, sleep 6, TV, heating, kitchenette, parking.

C *Kolping*, Riguelme 399, T/F411388. Good breakfast, recommended. **D** *Rayhuen*, Pedro Montt 668, T411571. **E** *Fuentes*, Vicente Reyes 665, T411595, very basic, friendly, restaurant. **E** *Hosp Dalila Balboa*, San Martín 734, clean, cheap. **E** *La Torre Suiza*, Bilbao 969, T/F411213, zbinden@chilesat.net Excellent breakfast, kitchen and laundry facilities, camping, cycle rental, book exchange, German, English spoken, repeatedly recommended. **E** *Villa Linda*, Valdivia 678, T411392, hot water, clean, basic, cheap, good restaurant. **E** *Yandaly*, Henríquez 401, T411452, good, English spoken. **E** Several on

Sleeping
■ *on map*
Price codes: see inside front cover
Prices given are high season (Jan-Feb); off-season 30-40% lower

The Lake District

Muñoz 400 and 500 blocks including *Res Victoria*, Muñoz 530, cooking facilities. Nearby, **E** *Vicente Reyes 854*, T414457. Good breakfast, limited bathroom facilities. **F** *Hostería Las Rosas del Lago*, Julio Zegers 897, T411463. Clean and friendly. **F** *Sra Nelly*, Aviador Acevedo 725, T412299, hot water all day, good value, camping, recommended. Rooms in private homes, all **F**: several in Bilbao including Eliana Castillo, No

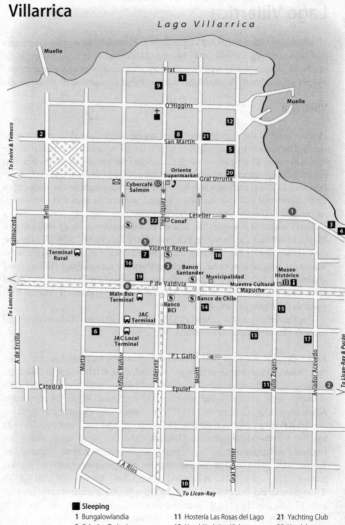

Villarrica

Lago Villarrica

The Lake District

■ **Sleeping**		
1 Bungalowlandia	11 Hostería Las Rosas del Lago	21 Yachting Club
2 Cabañas Traitraico	12 Hotel-Yachting Kiel	22 Yandaly
3 Camping du Lac	13 La Torre Suiza	
4 Camping Los Castaños	14 Rayhuen	● **Eating**
5 El Ciervo	15 Residencia San Francisco	1 El Rey de Mariscos
6 Eliana Castillo	16 Residencia Victoria	2 El Tabor
7 Fuentes	17 Señora Nelly	3 El Viejo Bucanero
8 Hospedaje Dalila Balboa	18 Vicente Reyes 854	4 Rapa Nui
9 Hostería Bilbao	19 Villa Linda	5 Travellers
10 Hostería de la Colina	20 Villarrica	6 Treffpunkt

The Monkey Puzzle Tree

The Araucaria Araucana, known in Chile as the araucaria *or* pehuén *and elsewhere called variously the Chilean pine, the umbrella tree, the parasol tree and the monkey puzzle tree, is the Chilean national tree. They have flourished in this area for 200 million years. Very slow growing, it can grow up to 40-m high; and live for 1,200 years. Though its natural habitat is on both sides of the Andes between 37° and 39° south, it is much more widespread in Chile than in Argentina. It was revered by the Mapuche, who ate its cones and its sharp leathery leaves. Some isolated trees are still seen as sacred by the Mapuche who leave offerings to the tree's spirit. The characteristic cones can weigh up to 1 kg so take care sitting underneath!*

537, clean, friendly; also in Koerner 300 block and O'Higgins 700 and 800 blocks. Urrutia 407, large breakfast, kitchen, clean; Matta 469, cooking facilities, clean. **Youth hostel F** *Res San Francisco*, Julio Zegers 646. Shared rooms.

Camping Many sites east of town on Pucón road, but these are expensive and it may be cheaper to stay in a *hospedaje*; those nearest to town are *El Edén*, T412772, 1 km southeast of centre, US$4 pp. Recommended. *Los Castaños*, T412330, US$11 per site, and *du Lac*, T210466, F214495. Quiet, but buy supplies at Los Castaños which is cheaper.

Expensive *El Tabor*, Epulef 1187, excellent but pricey. **Mid-range** *El Rey de Mariscos*, Letelier 1030. Good seafood. *Hotel Yandaly*, Henríquez 401. Good food. Recommended. *Rapa Nui*, Vicente Reyes 678. Good and cheap end of the range, closed Sun. *The Travellers*, Letelier 753. Varied menu, Asian food, bar, English spoken. *Treffpunkt*, Pedro de Valdivia 640, good. **Cheap** *El Viejo Bucanero*, Henríquez 552, good fixed price *almuerzo*, live music at weekends. *Café 2001*, Henríquez 379. Coffee and ice cream, good.

Eating
● *on map, page 324*

Festival Cultural Mapuche, with market, usually in second week of Feb. Enquire at the Santiago or Temuco tourist office.

Festivals

Karina Tour, Letelier 825, T412048. *Politur*, Henriquez 475, T414547. *Turismo Coñaripe*, P Montt 525, T411111. *Turismo Repu-Pehuén*, Pedro de Valdivia 565, T/F412065. Prices are about: Parque Nacional Villarrica US$13, Villarrica Volcano US$55, Valdivia US$25, Termas de Coñaripe US$22.

Tour companies

Bus Main terminal Pedro de Valdiva y Muñoz; *JAC* has 2 terminals of its own, the long-distance one is at Muñoz y Bilbao, local terminal for Pucón and Lican-Ray is opposite. Many other local services leave from the Terminal Rural, Matta y Vicente Reyes. Buses to **Santiago**, 10 hrs, US$18, several companies; to **Pucón**, both Vipu-Ray (main terminal) and *JAC*, services in summer every 30 mins, 40 mins journey, US$1; to **Puerto Montt**, US$9.40; to **Valdivia**, *JAC*, US$3.50, 5 a day, 2½ hrs; to **Lican-Ray** frequent services in summer, *JAC* and *Vipu-Ray*, US$1; to **Coñaripe** (US$1.50) and **Liquiñe** at 1600 Mon-Sat, 1000 Sun; to **Temuco**, *JAC*, US$3 every 30 mins in summer; to **Loncoche** (Route 5 junction for hitching), US$1.50. There are no direct buses to Panguipulli, go via Loncoche. To **Argentina**: Tue, Thu and Sat, *Empresa San Martín* (Muñoz 604) and Mon, Wed and Fri, *Igi-Llaima*, Pedro de Valdivia 611, US$20, 6 hrs, but if the Tromen pass is blocked by snow buses go via Panguipulli instead of Pucón.

Transport

Car hire *Christopher Car*, Pedro de Valdivia 1061, T/F413980. **Cycles** *Mora Bicicletas*, Körner 760, helpful.

The Lake District

Directory　**Banks** ATMs: at *Banco BCI*, Pedro de Valdivia y Alderete, *Banco de Chile*, Pedro de Valdiva y Pedro Montt, *Banco Santander*, Pedro de Valdiva 778. **Casa de Cambio**: *Carlos Huerta*, Muñoz 417. *Cristopher*, Valdivia 1061. Good rates for TCs. *Turcamb*, Henríquez 570. Poor rates for TCs. In general, rates are poor. **Communications** Internet: *Cybercafé Salmon*, Letelier y Henríquez. *New Yandaly*, Henríquez 401. **Post office**: Muñoz y Urrutia. Open Mon-Fri 0900-1300, 1430-1800. Sat 0900-1300. **Telephone**: *CTC*, Henríquez 544, Chilesat, Henriquez 473. *Entel*, Henriquez 440 and 575. **Laundry** *Lavacenter*, Alderete 770. *Lavandería y Lavaseco Villarrica*, Andrés Bello 348, T411449. *Todo Lavado*, Urrutia 669.

Pucón

Phone code: 045
Colour map 4, grid B2
Population: 8,000
26 km east of Villarrica

On the southeastern corner of the lake, Pucón is one of the most popular destinations in the Lake District, famous above all as a centre for visiting the Villarrica Volcano (2,840 m), which lies to the south. Built across the neck of a peninsula, it has two black sand beaches which are popular for swimming and watersports. Whitewater rafting is also offered on the nearby rivers and excursions can be made into the Parque Nacional Huerquehue which lies east of the town. The Pucón of today is very different from the town of 30 years ago. It is now a thriving tourist centre, full of Chileans in summer and gringos in the autumn. Neon signs are forbidden, and roadsigns and telephone kiosks are made of wood.

Ins & outs
See page 330 for further details

Getting there Pucón is served by 1 or 2 daily buses from Puerto Montt and Santiago in summer, and by more regular services from Temuco and Villarrica. **Getting around** Pucón is small enough to walk around on foot. Taxis are useful for out-of-town trips. **Tourist offices** Municipal Tourist Office, O'Higgins y Palguín. Provides information and sells fishing licences (US$1 per month). The local hotel association runs an information office at Caupolicán y Brasil.

Sights The main commercial centre lies between Avenida O'Higgins, the main avenue, and the *Gran Hotel Pucón*. From **La Península**, west of town, there are fine views of the lake and volcano as well as pony rides and golf. Getting here involves crossing private land; ask for permission at the entrance. There is also a pleasant walk, along the **Costanera Otto Gudenschwager**, starting at the northern end of Calle Ansorena and following the lakeside north. Just south of O'Higgins on Ansorena, there is a large handicraft market where you can occasionally see spinning and weaving in progress.

Excursions Excursions on the **lake** by launch are operated in summer from the landing stage at La Poza at the western end of O'Higgins. ■ *1500, 1900, US$4, 2 hrs.* Walk a couple of kilometres north along the beach to the mouth of the Río Pucón, with views of the volcanoes Villarrica, Quetrupillán and Lanín. There are boats to the mouth of the river from near the *Gran Hotel*, US$12, in summer only. To cross the Río Pucón: head east out of Pucón along the main road, then turn north on an unmade road leading to a new bridge; from here there are pleasant walks along the north shore of the lake to Quelhue and Trarilelfú, or northeast towards Caburga, see page 331, or up into the hills through farms and agricultural land, with views of three volcanoes and, higher up, of the lake.

There is also a privately managed site of **Cuevas Volcanicas** (volcanic caves), just east of Pucón. Here there are tunnels and a museum, as well as paths through the forest, expensive at US$10 pp, but a bad-weather option.

Essentials

Prices given below are Jan-Feb. Off-season rates are 20-40 % lower and it is often possible to negotiate. **LL** *Antumalal*, www.antumalal.com   2 km west, T441011, F441013. Very small, picturesque chalet-type, magnificent views of the lake, tennis court, lovely gardens, excellent, with meals, open year round, pool. **LL-L** *Del Lago*, Ansorena 23, T291000, F291200, sistcasino@entelchile.net   5 star, pool, health suite, casino, cinema. **LL-L** *Gran Hotel Pucón*, Holzapfel 190, T441001. Restaurant, disco, sports centre, shared with **L** *Condominio Gran Hotel* apartments. **L** *Interlaken*, Colombia y Caupolicán, T441276, F441242. Chalets, recommended, water skiing, pool, TCs changed (open Nov-Apr), no restaurant. **AL** *Munich*, Alderete 275, T/F442293. Modern, spacious, German and English spoken. **A** *Araucarias*, Caupolicán 243, T/F441286, araucari@cepri.cl Clean, comfortable, indoor pool. **A** *Gudenschwager*, Pedro de Valdivia 12, T/F441156, gudens@cepri.cl **A** *Hostería El Principito*, Urrutia 291, T441200. Good breakfast, clean, very friendly, recommended. **A** *La Palmera*, Alderete 435, T/F441083, palmera@ceprinet.cl **A** *La Posada Plaza-Pucón*, Valdivia 191, T/F441088, laposada@unete.com With bath, cheaper without, full board available, also spacious cabins (**C** low season). **A** *Oregón*, Fresia 260, T441977, F442433. Clean, good beds.

B *Kernayel*, 1 km east at Camino International 1510, T442164, F442170, kernayel@cepri.cl Apartments and *cabañas*, pool, comfortable. **C** *Hosp Del Montanés*, O'Higgins 472, T441267. Good value, clean, TV, central, restaurant. **C** *Hostería Milla Rahue*, O'Higgins 460, T441610. Clean, good inexpensive restaurant. **C** *La Tetera*, Urrutia 580, T/F441462, www.tetera.cl With bath and good breakfast with real coffee, German and English spoken, book swap, Navimag reservations, informative. Highly recommended. **C-D** *Hosp La Casita*, Palguín 555, T441712, lacasita@entelchile.net Clean, laundry and kitchen facilities, English and German spoken, large breakfast, garden, motorcycle parking, ski trips, Spanish classes, **E** off season. Recommended. **D** *Hostal Carlos Alfredo Richard*, Arauco 171, parque_huerquehue@ hotmail.com Central location, shared rooms, use of kitchen, internet, also at Parque Huerquehue (see below). **D** *Hostal O'Higgins*, O'Higgins 136, T441153, F441334. Clean, cooking facilities.

E *Familia Acuña*, Palguín 223 (ask at *peluquería* next door), without breakfast, hot water, kitchen and laundry facilities, dirty, good meeting place. **E** *Hostería école*, Urrutia 592, T/F441675, trek@ecole.cl With breakfast, no singles, also dormitory accommodation, **F** (sleeping bag essential), discount for Hostelling International Members, good vegetarian and fish restaurant, ecological shop, forest treks, rafting, biking, information, language classes, massage. **E** *Tr@vel Pucón*, Blanco Encalada 190, T/F444093, pucontravel@terra.cl English, German, French spoken, Spanish classes.

The following are all private houses, all **E** or **F**: On Lincoyán: *Hosp El Refugio*, No 348, T441347. With breakfast, good. *Hosp Sonia*, No 485, T441269. Use of kitchen, very noisy and crowded, meals, friendly. *Juan Torres*, No 445, T441248. Poor bathrooms, noisy, cooking facilities. No 630, friendly, clean. No 815, cooking facilities (information on climbing Villarrica). Nearby is *Casa Eliana*, Pasaje Chile 225, T441851. Kitchen facilities. Highly recommended. **F** *Adriana Molina*, No 312. With breakfast, clean, helpful. **F** *Casa de Mayra*, Palguín 695, T441511. Kitchen facilities. **F** *Casa Richard*, Paraguay 140. Basic but friendly, cooking facilities. Recommended. **F** *Hosp Arauco*, Arauco 272, T442223, without bath, **C** with, without breakfast, noisy. **F** *Hosp Graciela*, Pasaje Rolando Matus 521 (off Av Brasil). Comfortable rooms, good food. **F** *Hosp Los Castaños*, Colo Colo 440, T442180, kitchen facilities. **F** *Irma Villena*, Arauco 460. Clean, friendly. Recommended. **F** *Res Lincoyán*, Av Lincoyán, T441144,

Sleeping
■ *on map, page 328*
Price codes:
see inside front cover
High season (Dec-Feb) rooms may be hard to find.
There are plenty of alternatives (usually cheaper) in Villarrica

The Lake District

www.lincoyan.cl With bath, cheaper without, clean and comfortable. **F** *Roberto y Alicia Abreque*, Perú 170. Basic, noisy, popular, kitchen and laundry facilities, information on excursions. **G** *Casa de María*, General Urrutia 560, T443264. Double rooms, use of kitchen, good position, friendly. **G** *Hosp Irma*, Lincoyán 545, T442226. Cooking facilities, clean. **G** *Hosp Lucía*, Lincoyán 565, T441721. Friendly, quiet, garden, recommended, cooking facilities. **G** No 630, T441043. Kitchen facilities, good value. Many other families have rooms – look for the signs or ask in bars/restaurants.

Camping Buy supplies in Villarrica (cheaper). Sites near Pucón include: *Ainoha*, 12 blocks north on lakeside. *La Poza*, Costanera Geis 769, T441435. Hot showers, clean, quiet, good kitchen facilities, open all year. Recommended. **G** *Los Boldos*, Pasaje Las

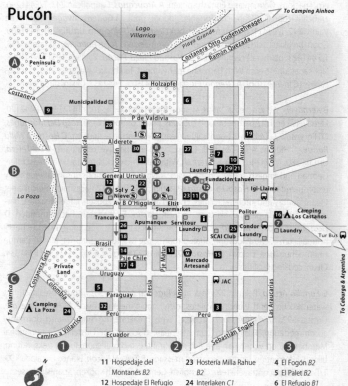

Pucón

■ Sleeping	11 Hospedaje del Montanés *B2*
1 Araucarias *B1*	12 Hospedaje El Refugio *B1*
2 Casa de María *B2*	13 Hospedaje Graciela *C2*
3 Casa de Mayra *C2*	14 Hospedaje Irma *C2*
4 Casa Eliana *C2*	15 Hospedaje La Casita *C2*
5 Casa Richard *C1*	16 Hospedaje Los Castaños *B3*
6 Del Lago *A2*	17 Hospedaje Lucía *C2*
7 Familia Acuña *B2*	18 Hospedaje Sonia *C2*
8 Gran Hotel Pucón *A2*	19 Hostal Carlos Alfredo Richard *B3*
9 Gudenschwager *A1*	20 Hostal O'Higgins *B1*
10 Hospedaje Arauco *B2*	21 Hostería ¡école! *B3*
	22 Hostería El Principito *B2*

23 Hostería Milla Rahue *B2*	4 El Fogón *B2*
24 Interlaken *C1*	5 El Palet *B2*
25 Irma Villena *C2*	6 El Refugio *B1*
26 Juan Torres *C2*	7 El Rincón de Los Castaños *B3*
27 La Palmera *B2*	8 La Buonatesta *B2*
28 La Posada Plaza-Pucón *B1*	9 La Terraza *B2*
29 La Tetera *B2*	10 Puerto Pucón *B2*
30 Munich *B2*	11 Tijuana *B2*
31 Oregón *B2*	12 Trabún *B2*
32 Roberto y Alicia Abreque *C1*	**⑤ Banks**
	1 Banco BCI *B2*
● Eating	2 Banco del Estado *B2*
1 Arabian *B2*	3 Banco de Chile *B2*
2 Coppa Kabana *B2*	4 Banco Santander *B2*
3 Coronado *B2*	

Rosas, east of town. *Los Castaños*, O'Higgins 870, **G**. Other sites west along Lago Villarrica, including *Saint John*, Km 7, T441165, casilla 154, **G**. *Millaray*, Km 7, T212336, campsite. Also several sites en route to the volcano including *L'etoile*, Km 2, T442188, in attractive forest; *Mahuida*, Km 6. On the road to Tromen Pass, *Cabañas El Dorado*, US$18 for 2, good site, poorly maintained. Cheaper sites en route to Caburga. Equipment at *Eltit Supermarket*, O'Higgins y Fresia. *Outdoors and Travel*, Lincoyán 361.

Expensive *En Alta Mar*, Urrutia y Fresia, fish, seafood, very good. *Puerto Pucón*, Fresia 251. Spanish, stylish. **Midrange** *Arabian*, Fresia 354-B, good Arab food. *El Fogón*, O'Higgins 480. Very good. *El Palet*, Fresia 295, T8134504. Authentic local food, clean, friendly service, reasonably priced. Recommended by local people. *El Refugio*, Lincoyán 348. Some vegetarian dishes, expensive wine. *El Rincón de Los Castaños*, Colo-Colo 450, Chilean food. *La Buonatesta*, Fresia 243. Good pizzeria. *Tijuana*, Fresia 303, Mexican. **Cheap** *Coppa Kabana*, Urrutia y Ansorena; *Coronado*, Urrutia 425; *La Terraza*, O'Higgins 323. Pleasant terrace, cheap lunches. *Trabún*, Palguin 348. **Cafés** For real coffee, *Café Brasil*, Fresia 477. *Café de la P*, O'Higgins y Lincoyán. *El Turista*, Fresia y Alderete. *Holzapfel Backerei*, Holzapfel 524. German café. Recommended. *La Tetera*, Urrutia 580. Wide selection of teas, good coffee, snacks, German spoken. Recommended. *Hostería école* (see under sleeping).

Eating
● *on map*
*See also
sleeping above*

*For vegetarians there
is a delicatessen at
O'Higgins y Fresia
serving fresh
vegetarian food*

Bars *Mamas and Tapas*, O'Higgins y Arauco. *Pub del Pelao*, O'Higgins y Alderete. *Pub for You*, Ansorena 370. English-style pub. *Disco For You*, 2 km east. Open all year (transport in summer from *Pub for You*). **Discos** At weekends in summer, there are discos 2-3 km east of town: *Kamikaze* and *La Playa*. Also *Club 77*.

Entertainment

Pucon Express, O'Higgins y Colo Colo, 24-hr supermarket.

Shopping

Aerial sports Paragliding, *Fabrice Pini*, Colo Colo 830, T09 4111072, US$50 for ½ hr; also offers hydrospeed watersports, US$20 for the morning. **Canoeing** Canoe trips on Río Liucura, by *Aguaventura expediciones*, Palguín 336, T444246, aguaventura@hotmail.com US$10 pp. French run, English spoken. **Fishing** Pucón and Villarrica are celebrated as centres for fishing on Lago Villarrica and on the beautiful Lincura, Trancura and Toltén rivers. Local tourist office will supply details on licences and open seasons etc. Guides include *Mario's Fishing Zone*, O'Higgins 581, T444259, www.pucon.com/fishing Expensive, but good guide, and *Off Limits*, Fresia 273, T441210, F441604, offlimitspucon@hotmail.com Fishing specialists, English spoken, offer fly-fishing excursions US$100 per day, maximum 3 persons. Also fishing boat excursions, from US$190 for 2 persons. Some other tourist agencies also offer trips. **Hiking** To the Cañi Forest Sanctuary, overnight hikes are recommended, see below. **Horseriding** Horse hire US$35 half day, US$55 full day, enquire at *La Tetera*. Also Centro de Turismo Ecuestre Huepil, T09-4534212, small groups, local excursions and 3-day trips to Argentina. See also *Rancho de Callabos* at Termas de Palguín, page 333. **Skiing** on the slopes of the Villarrica Volcano. **Watersports** Water-skiing, sailing, windsurfing at Playa Grande, the beach by *Gran Hotel* and La Poza beach end of O'Higgins (more expensive than Playa Grande, not recommended). Playa Grande: water-skiing US$10 for 15 mins, Laser sailing US$11 per hr, sailboards US$10 per hr, rowing boats US$4 per hr. **Whitewater rafting** Very popular on the Río Trancura, east of Pucón; many agencies offer trips (see below), Trancura Baja (basic) US$15; Trancura Alta (advanced) US$25. Three-day excursions are also offered to the Río Bío Bío (advanced), US$250 pp, with food, transport and equipment, Oct-Mar only.

Sports

On O'Higgins: *Politur*, No 635, T/F441373, turismo@politur.com *Servitour*, No 447, T441959. *Sol y Nieve* (esq Lincoyán, T/F441070, solnieve@entelchile.net). Previously

Tour companies

The Lake District

held in high esteem, with guides and equipment repeatedly recommended, but now some mixed reports about organization. *Sur Expediciones*, No 660, new but good. *Turismo Florencia*, No 480, T443026. Also *Hosteria école* (address above). Others include *Travelsur*, Fresia 285, T/F444135, www.travelsur.com All arrange trips to thermal baths, trekking to volcanoes, whitewater rafting, etc. Prices: whitewater rafting and riding, see above; climbing Villarrica, US$50, 12 hrs, equipment provided; mountain bike hire from US$3 per hr to US$12 per day, ski hire and transport to slopes US$20 pp. Tours to Termas de Huife, US$20 including entry. Shop around, prices vary at times, quality of guides and equipment variable. For falls, lakes and *termas* it is cheaper, if in a group, to flag down a taxi and bargain.

Transport **Local Bicycle hire**: *Taller el Pollo*, Palguin 500 block; *Trancura*, O'Higgins 261, US$10 per day; several other bike rental places in O'Higgins – shop around.Try also travel agencies, eg *Sol y Nieve*. **Car hire**: *Christopher Car*, O'Higgins 335, T/F449013. *Hertz*, Fresia 220, T441664, US$65 for cheapest car (including tax, insurance, and 200 km free); same prices per day at *Gran Hotel*. *Pucón Rent A Car*, Camino Internacional 1395, T441922, kernayel@cepri.cl *Sierra Nevada*, Palguín y O'Higgins, cars and 4x4s. Reasonably priced. **Taxi**: *Cooperative*, T441009, individual member Oscar Jara Carrasco, T411992 (home in Villarrica).

Long distance Bus: No municipal terminal – each company has its own terminal: *JAC*, Uruguay y Palguin. *Tur Bus*, O'Higgins 910, east of town. *Igi Llaima* and *Condor*, Colo Colo y O'Higgins. *LIT*, O'Higgins y Palguín. *Transportes Liucura*, O'Higgins 615. *JAC* has most services to **Villarrica**, every 15 mins, US$1. To **Valdivia**, US$4.50. To **Temuco** hourly, US$3, 2 hrs, *rápido* US$3.50, 1 hr; for **Puerto Montt** either go to Valdivia and change, or take the new service linking Pucon with Osorno and Puerto Montt, US$9.40, 6 hrs, every day at 1015 with *Tur Bus* all year. To Santiago, 10 hrs, US$18, many companies, *Power* cheapest (and least comfortable), overnight only; daytime go via Temuco; *cama* service by *Tur-Bus* and *JAC*, US$40. To Paillaco and Lago Caburga – see below. To Argentina: Buses from Temuco through to the Tromen Pass to Junín pass through Pucón, fares are the same as from Temuco.

Directory **Airlines** *LanChile* at Fresia 275. **Banks** ATMs: in *Banco Santander* and *Eltit Supermarket*, all on O'Higgins. Also at *Banco BCI*, Fresia y Alderete, and in casino. Several *casas de cambio* on O'Higgins. *Eltit* supermarket also changes TCs but best to change TCs before arriving as rates poor. **Communications** Internet: O'Higgins 555, some computers with Hebrew keyboards. **Post office**: Fresia 183. **Telephone**: *CTC*, Gen Urrutia 472. *Entel*, Ansorena 299. **Laundry** Urrutia 520; Palguín 460; Fresia 224; Colo-Colo 475 and 478, several others.

East of Lago Villarrica

Within easy reach of Villarrica and Pucón are two more lakes, two national parks and several hot springs. Although busy with Chilean tourists in summer, these are among the most dramatic spots in the Lake District, and well worth a visit for those in the area.

Parque Nacional Villarrica
Colour map 4, grid B2

This park, which covers 61,000 ha, stretches from Pucón to the Argentine border near Puesco. There are three sectors: Villarrica Volcano, Quetrupillán Volcano and the Puesco sector which includes the slopes of the Lanín Volcano on the Argentine frontier. Each sector has its own entrance and ranger station.

The **Villarrica Volcano**, 2,840 m high and still active, lies 8 km south of Pucón. At the summit you can look down into the crater at the molten lava below: beware of the sulphur fumes – take a cloth mask moistened with lemon juice. On exceptionally clear days you can see six other volcanoes.

It is possible to ski at the Pucón resort, owned by the *Gran Hotel Pucón*, situated on the eastern slopes of the volcano and reached by a badly maintained track, 35 minutes. A large modern base lodge offers equipment rental (US$15 per day, US$82 per week), ski instruction, first aid, restaurant and bar as well as wonderful views from the terrace. There are eight lifts, though rarely do more than two or three work. Lift tickets cost US$15-25 for a full day, depending on the season. The season is from July to November. Piste preparation is at best mediocre. Information on snow and ski lifts (and, perhaps, transport) from *Gran Hotel Pucón*. The snow is generally soft and good for beginners, though more advanced skiers can try the steeper areas.

Essentials Entry US$3.50. Due to accidents, access to the Villarrica volcano sector is restricted only to groups with a guide and to individuals who can show proof of membership of a mountaineering club in their own country. Several agencies offer excursions, US$40-50 (plus park entry) including guide, transport to park entrance and hire of equipment (no reduction for those with their own equipment), good boots, crampons and ice picks essential. Also take sunglasses, sun block and plenty of water. At the park entrance equipment is checked. Entry is refused if the weather is poor. Travel agencies will not start out if the weather is bad and some travellers have experienced difficulties in obtaining a refund: establish in advance what terms apply in the event of cancellation and be prepared to wait a few days. Bargain for group rates. Conditions permitting, groups may carry ski and snowboard equipment for the descent. For information on guides, see above under tour companies. Also Alvaro Martínez, Cristóbal Colón 430; Juan Carlos, at Oliva's *pensión*, or his pool room on main street. Recommended. Crampons, ice axe, sunglasses can be rented for US$4 per day from the *Taller El Pollo* bicycle shop (address above) and from tour agencies. There is a refuge without beds 4 km inside the park, insecure and in desperate need of renovation. Campsite with drinking water, toilets, below refuge.

Lago Colico

One of the less accessible lakes, Lago Colico lies north of Lago Villarica in a wild, remote setting. A road from Cunco runs east along the lake's northern shore leading to the northern tip of Lago Caburga, see below.

Sleeping A *Trailanqui*, on riverbank 20 km west of Lago Colico. Luxury, also suites, *cabañas* with kitchens, campsite (expensive), horseriding. Booking: *Trailanqui*, Portales 812A, Temuco, T/F045-214915. **Camping** 2 sites about half-way along north shore: *Quichelmalleu*, Km 22 from Cunco, T573187. *Ensenada*, Km 26, T221441.

Lago Caburga

A very pretty lake in a wild setting 25 km northeast of Pucón at an altitude of 700 m, Lago Caburga (spelt locally Caburgua) became famous as the setting for *Oro Verde*, one of Chile's most popular soap operas in recent years. It is unusual for its beautiful white sand beach (other beaches in the area are of black volcanic sand). The east and west shores of the lake are inaccessible to vehicles. The north shore can be reached by a road from Cunco via the north shore of Lago Colico. The village of Caburga, at the southern end, is reached by a turning off the main road from Pucón to Argentina 8 km east of Pucón. Rowing boats may be hired US$2 per hour. Just off the road from Pucón, Km 15, are the **Ojos de Caburga**, beautiful pools fed from underground, which are particularly attractive after rainfall. ■ *US$0.50.*

The Lake District

Sleeping and eating C *Hostería Los Robles*, 3 km from Caburga village, T236989. Lovely views, good restaurant; campsite, expensive in season, but cheap out of season. The southern end of the lake is lined with campsites. No shops, so take own food. East of the lake is **E** *Landhaus San Sebastián*, F443057. With bath and breakfast, good meals, laundry facilities, good walking base.

Transport *JAC* buses to Caburga, 4-6 daily; there are *colectivos* every 30 mins from Ansorena y Uruguay. Taxi day trips from Pucón, US$25 return. If walking or cycling, turn left 3 km east of Pucón (sign to Puente Quelhue) and follow the track for 18 km through beautiful scenery, recommended.

Parque Nacional Huerquehue
Colour map 4, grid B3

Located a short distance east of Lago Caburga, the park, covering 12,500 ha at altitudes of 700-2,000 m, includes steep hills, the highest of which is Cerro Araucano, and at least 20 lakes, some of them very small. Entrance and administration are near **Lago Tinguilco**, the largest lake, on the western edge of the park. From the entrance there is a well-signed track north up a steep hill to Lago Chico; there the track divides left to Lago Toro, right to Lago Verde. All three lakes are surrounded by trees and are very beautiful.

Essentials Park entrance is 7 km (3 uphill, 3 down, 1 along Lago Tinquilco) from Paillaco, which is reached by a *ripio* road which turns off 3 km before Caburga. Entry US$4. The park is open officially only Jan-Mar, but you can get in at other times. Adequate map available at entrance. Warden very helpful; people in the park rent horses and boats. Take your own food. Beware dogs along the paths to Lago Verde. There is a private car park, US$1, 1½ km along the track.

Camping is not allowed in the park

Sleeping At the park entrance there are 2 campsites, US$8. **D** pp *Hostal Carlos Alfredo Richard*, southwest shore of Lago Tinquilco, 2 km from park entrance, parque_huerquehue@hotmail.com Large rooms, private bathrooms with hot water, restaurant, breakfast included in price, rowboats for hire. **E** *Refugio Tinquilco*, 3½ km from park entrance, T02-7777673, F7351187, patriciolanfranco@entelchile.net also **C** double with bath, meals served, cooking facilities, heating. At the southern end of Lago

Lagos Villarrica, Caburga & Colico

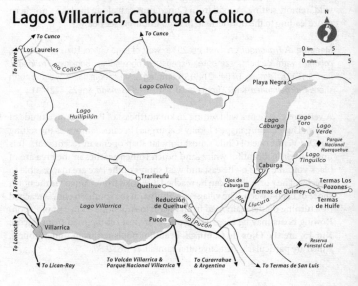

Tinquilco near the entrance, 2 German-speaking families, the Braatz and Soldans, offer accommodation, **F**, no electricity, food and camping (US$6); they also rent rowing boats on the lake. Nidia Carrasco Godoy runs a *hospedaje* in the park, T09-4432725. **F**, with breakfast, hot water.

Transport *JAC* bus from Pucón to inside the park, 1½ hrs, US$1, 3 daily in summer, 2 in winter. Tour agencies arrange transport for groups, US$8. Taxi US$34 return trip. Minibuses (no schedule) from Ansorena y Brasil.

South of the Huerquehue Park on a turning from the Pucón-Caburga road there are three sets of thermal baths.

Termas de Quimey-Co, about 29 km from Pucón, are new, less ostentatious or expensive than Huife. There is a campsite, two cabins and the hotel *Termas de Quimey-Co*, T045-441903. Termas de Huife, Km 33, has *Hostería Termas de Huife*, T441222. Costing US$12 in season, US$9 off season, it includes the use of one pool, modern, pleasant, picnicking not allowed. Termas los Pozones, Km 35, are very popular with travellers, six large pools, little infrastructure, US$5 per day, US$7 at night.

■ *Getting there: taxi from Pucón, US$23 return with taxi waiting, US$16 one way; Hostería Termas de Huife has its own transport and will pick people up from Pucón.*

Termas de Qimey-Co, de Huife & los Pozones

Situated south of Parque Nacional Huerquehue and covering 500 ha, this is a private nature reserve owned by the Fundación Lahuén. It contains 17 small lakes and is covered by ancient native forests of coigue and lenga and includes some of the oldest araucaria trees in Chile. From its highest peak, *El Mirador*, (1,550 m) there are panoramic views over neighbouring parts of Argentina and Chile, including four volcanoes: Lanín, Villarrica, Quetrupillán and Llaima.

Reserva Forestal Cañi

Essentials Tours with guide only, US$17 pp (take lunch), plus transport, also 2-day tour with basic overnight accommodation, US$34 pp. Contact **Fundación Lahuén**, Urrutia 477, Pucón, T/F441660, lahuen@interaccess.cl or *Hostería école* (see page 327). As the reserve is above the snowline, tours are normally restricted to summer, though visits in winter are sometimes possible.

To Argentina

From Pucón a road runs southeast along the southern bank of the valley of the Río Traniura to **Curarrehue** and the Argentine border. An unpaved road runs along the northern side of the valley to the **Termas de Menetue**, 21 km east of Pucón, where there are two thermal pools, US$9, and *cabañas*. At Km 18 on the Pucón-Curarrehue road there is a turning south 18 km (*ripio*) to the **Termas de Palguín**, US$6. There are many hikeable waterfalls in the area. For example at about 6 km from the turn-off for Termas de Palguín, Salto Palguín can be seen, but not reached. A further 2 km is Salto China, spectacular, entry US$1, restaurant, camping. Another 1 kilometre on is Salto del Puma and Salto del León, US$1.50 for both, each spectacular and 800 m from the Termas. From Termas de Palguín a rough dirt road runs south to Coñaripe.

E *Rancho de Caballos*, T441575. Restaurant with vegetarian dishes, laundry and kitchen facilities; also *cabañas* and camping, horseriding excursions US$50 per day, English, German spoken. Also **E** pp *Kila Leufu*, Km 20, Mapuche-run 'ethnotourism', T09-7118064. Basic but very friendly, English spoken, full board, also offers horseriding and mountain bike hire.

Sleeping

The Lake District

Transport From Pucón take Bus Regional Villarrica from Palguín y O'Higgins at 1100 to the junction (10 km from Termas); last bus from junction to the Termas at 1500, so you may have to hitch back. Taxi US$17.

Quetrupillán Near Palguín is the entrance to the Quetrupillán section of the Parque
area Nacional Villarrica. A high clearance vehicle is necessary; but horses are best. The treks in this sector of the park are not physically demanding and have good views. There is free camping and wonderful views over Villarrica Volcano and six other peaks. Palguin is also the starting point for a four- to five-day hike to Puesco, which offers great views over the Villarrica and Lanín volcanoes.

At Km 23 on the Curarrehue road a turning leads north to **Termas de San Luis**, from which it is 30 minutes' walk to Lago del León. For accommodation, there is the *Termas de San Luis*, T411388.

At Km 35 another turning leads north, 15 km, to the **Termas de Pangui**, where there are three pools beautifully situated in the mountains, US$10. C *Hotel Termas*, T045-442039, F442040, good vegetarian meals, English spoken, tents that sleep three, and transport from Pucón. Information from *Limay Tours* in Pucón.

From Curarrehue the road turns south to Puesco and deteriorates. It climbs via **Lago Quellelhue**, a tiny gem set between mountains at 1,196 m to reach the border at the Mamuil Malal or Tromen Pass.

The Lanín To the south of the pass rises the graceful cone of Lanín at 3,747 m. Although
Volcano extinct Lanín is geologically one of the youngest volcanoes in the Andes. It is
One of the world's climbed from the Argentine side. A four-hour hike from the Argentine cus-
most beautiful toms leads to the *refugio* at 2,400 m. The climb from here to the summit is not
mountains difficult but crampons and ice axe are needed.

Border with Cross into Argentina over **Paso Mamuil Malal** or **Tromen**. Once on the
Argentina Argentine side the road runs south to Junín de los Andes, San Martín de los
Daily bus from Pucón, Andes and Bariloche. Chilean immigration and customs is at Puesco, open
1800, 2 hrs, US$2. from December to March 0800-2100, and April to November 0800-1900.
To Pucón 0700

Sleeping Puesco A *Cabañas La Tranquera*, sleep 6, also dormitory **F**, restaurant, campsite. There is also a CONAF campsite at Puesco and another 5 km from the frontier near Lago Tromen, free, no facilities.

The Seven Lakes

This group of lakes, situated south of Lago Villarrica, provide a beautiful necklace of water, surrounded by thick woods, and with views of distant snows giving a picture-postcard backdrop. Six of the lakes lie in Chile, with the seventh, Lago Lacár, in Argentina. Five of the lakes empty their waters into Lago Panguipulli from where in turn they flow into Lago Riñihue. The three western lakes, Calafquén, Panguipulli and Riñihue, were created by glacial morraine forming a barrier across steep river valleys. After the final peace settlement of 1882 the area around these lakes was reserved for Mapuche settlements. The southernmost lake, Lago Riñihue, is most easily reached from Valdivia and Los Lagos and is dealt with in a later section (see page 347).

The legend of Lican-Ray

At the height of the wars between the Spanish and the Mapuche a young Spanish soldier lost the rest of his unit and strayed into the forests near Lago Calafquén. Suddenly he saw a beautiful young Mapuche woman drying her hair in the sun and singing. As he did not want to frighten her he made himself visible at a distance and began to sing along. Singing, smiling and exchanging glances, they fell in love. She called him Allumanche, which means white man in Mapuche, and, pointing to herself, indicated that her name was Lican Rayan, meaning the flower of magic stone. They began to live together near the lake.

Her father, Curtilef, a powerful and fearsome chief, feared she might be dead. One day a boy came to him and said: "Lican Rayan is alive. I have seen her near the lake with a white man but she is not a prisoner: it is clear they are in love".

Lican Rayan saw the warriors coming to look for her. Knowing her father she feared what might happen, so she

persuaded the soldier that they should flee. They escaped by riding on logs to one of the islands. There they felt safe, but they could not light a fire against the cold because the smoke would give them away. The weather grew cooler, the north wind blew and it rained heavily. After several days, unable to bear the cold and thinking that the warriors would have given up the search, they lit a fire. The smoke was spotted by Curtilef's men, so they fled to another island further away but again they were discovered and had to escape. This happened so many times that, although they were never caught, they were never seen again.

In the town of Lican-Ray, named after Curtilef's daughter, it is said that on spring afternoons it is sometimes possible to see a distant column of smoke from one of the islands, where Lican Rayan and the soldier are still enjoying their love of over 400 years.

Abridged and translated from Lengua Y Costumbres Mapuches by Orietta Appelt Martin, Imprenta Austral, Temuco, 1995.

The most northerly of the seven lakes, Lago Calafquén is a popular tourist destination, readily accessible by a paved road from Villarrica, along which there are fine views over Villarrica volcano. Wooded and dotted with small islands, the lake is reputedly one of the warmest and is good for swimming. Unpaved roads run round the lake.

Lago Calafquén
Colour map 4, grid B2

Lican-Ray

Situated 30 km south of Villarrica on a peninsula on the north shore, Lican-Ray is the major resort on the lake. It is named after a legendary Mapuche woman, see box on page 335.

There are two fine beaches, one on each side of the rocky peninsula. Boats can be hired (US$2 an hour) and there are catamaran trips. Although very crowded in season, most facilities close by the end of March. Some 6 km to the east is the river of lava formed when the Villarrica volcano erupted in 1971. There is a tourist office on the plaza, open daily in summer, from Monday to Friday off season.

Phone code: 045
Colour map 4, grid B2
Population: 1,700

Playa Chica A *Becker*, Manquel 105, T431156. **C** *Hosp Los Nietos*, Manquel 125, T431078. Without breakfast. **Playa Grande C** *Hostería Inaltulafquen*, Casilla 681, T431115, F410028. With breakfast and bath, English spoken, comfortable. **D** *Cabañas Cacique Vitacura*, Urrutia 825, sleep 2, also larger cabins, with kitchen (Santiago T2355302, F3639154, tradesic@intermedia.cl). **D** *Cabañas El Eden*, Huenuman 105. Sleep 6. **E** pp *Res Temuco*, G Mistral 515, T431130. Clean, without

Sleeping
Lots along north shore of Lago Calafquén towards Coñaripe

bath, with breakfast, good. *El Conquistador*, Cacique Millaqueo s/n. **Camping** Foresta, T211954, **B** for 6 persons, ½ km east of town. *Prado Verde*, T431161, 1 km east of town. 6 sites just west of town.

Eating *Café Ñaños*, Urrutia 105. Very good, reasonable prices, helpful owner. *Restaurant-Bar Guido's*, Urrutia 405. Good value.

Sports **Cycle hire** US$3 per hr. **Horseriding** *Corral Club de Huasos*, US$6 per hr, summer only. **Boat** Trips US$3 voyages in catamaran; also voyages to islands US$11 per hr.

Transport **Bus** No central terminal; buses leave from offices around plaza. Buses from Villarrica (1 hr, US$1, *JAC*), frequent in summer; in Jan-Feb, there are direct buses from Santiago (10 hrs, US$16, *Tur Bus*) and Temuco (US$3, *JAC*). To Panguipulli, Mon-Sat 0730.

Coñaripe

Phone code: 045
Colour map 4, grid B2
Population: 1,250

Lying 21 km southeast of Lican-Ray at the eastern end of Lago Calafquén, Coñaripe is another popular Chilean tourist spot. At first sight the village is dusty and nondescript, but its setting, with a black sand beach surrounded by mountains, is very beautiful. From here a road around the lake's southern shore leads to Lago Panguipulli (see below), 38 km west, and offers superb views over Villarrica volcano.

Sleeping and eating **E** *Antulafquen*, Entre Montañas, T317298. Homely. **F** *Hosp House*, with breakfast. Good meals. **Campsites** on both north and south sides of the lake, US$20 per site. Free camping on the beach. Also Isla Llancahue, campsite on an island in Río Llanchue, 5 km east, T317360, F317200, **G**, also caba*ñas*.

Transport **Bus** To **Panguipulli**, several a day, US$1.50; to **Villarrica** US$1.50.

The Seven Lakes

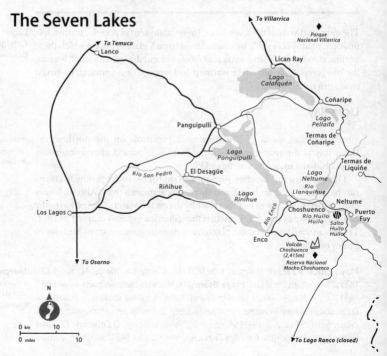

From Coñaripe a road runs southeast over the steep Cuesta Los Añiques offering views of **Lago Pellaifa**, a tiny lake with rocky surroundings covered with vegetation and a small beach. The **Termas de Coñaripe**, Casilla 603, Lican-Ray, T411407, at Km 16, 2 km from the lakeshore, has four pools, accommodation, restaurant, cycles and horses for hire. Further south at Km 32 are the **Termas de Liquiñe**, Casilla 202, Villarrica, T/F063-317377, **A** pp, full board, cabins, restaurant, hot pool, small native forest, tours offered. There is also accommodation in private houses, **F** pp. Nearby there are several other thermal springs, though these have little infrastructure. There are tours to Liquiñe from Lican-Ray in summer, US$17, 0830-1830 with lunch. About 8 km north of Liquiñe is a road going southwest (20 km) along the southeast shore of **Lago Neltume** to meet the Choshuenco-Puerto Fuy road (see below).

Southeast of Coñaripe

Paso Carirriñe is reached by unpaved road from Termas de Liquiñe. It is open 15 October to 31 August. On the Argentine side the road continues to San Martín de los Andes.

Border with Argentina

Lago Panguipulli

Covering 116 sq km, Lago Panguipulli, the largest of the seven lakes, is reached by paved road from Lanco on the Pan-American Highway or *ripio* roads from Lago Calafquén. A road leads along the beautiful northern shore, which is wooded with sandy beaches and cliffs. Most of the south shore is inaccessible by road.

Panguipulli

ARGENTINA

Paso Carirriñe

To Junín de los Andes

Lago Pirehueico

Parque Nacional Lanín

Puerto Pirehueico

Paso Huahum

To Junín de los Andes

Lago Lascar

San Martín de los Andes

Situated on a hillside in the northwest corner of the lake in a beautiful setting, Panguipulli is the largest town in the area. The town grew as a railway terminal and a port for vessels carrying timber from the lakesides. The streets are planted with roses: it is claimed that there are over 14,000. There is a tourist office in the plaza, open December-February only.

On Plaza Prat is the **Iglesia San Sebastián**, built in Swiss style with twin towers by the Swiss Padre Bernabé; its belltower contains three bells from Germany. From Plaza Prat the main commercial street, Martínez de Rozas, runs down to the lake. **Catamaran** trips are offered on the lake and excursions can be made to Lagos Calafquén, Neltume, Pirehueico and to the northern tip of **Lago Riñihue** at El Desagüe (see page 347). The road east to Coñaripe, on Lago Calafquén, offers superb views of the lake and of the Villarrica Volcano.

Phone code: 063
Colour map 4, grid B2
Population: 8,326

The site of a Mapuche settlement, Panguipulli is Mapuche for 'hill of pumas'

The Lake District

Sleeping
■ *on map*
Price codes:
see inside front cover

B *Hostal España*, O'Higgins 790, T311166, F311327, with breakfast. **B** *Hostería Quetropillán*, Etchegaray 381, T311348. Comfortable. **B** *Cabañas El Mirador*, Carrera Pinto s/n, T311106. **C** *Cabañas Tío Carlos*, Etchegaray 377, T311215, F311280. **D** *Res La Bomba*, J M Carrera y R Freire. Quiet, friendly. **E** *Hotel Central*, Valdivia 115, T311331. Clean, good breakfast. Recommended. **E** private house opposite *Quetropillán*. Clean, beautiful garden. **E** *Etchegaray 464*, for longer stays, clean, good breakfast. **E** *Hosp Familiar*, Los Ulmos 62, T311483. English, German spoken, kitchen facilities, helpful, good breakfast. **E** *Olga Berrocal*, JM Carrera 834. Small rooms. **E** *Sra Pozas*, Valdivia 251. Clean. **Youth Hostel** **F** *Albergue Juvenil*, Gabriela Mistral 1112, T311282, opposite bus terminal. **Camping** *Camping Lago Rinihue*, T461344, F461111, **E/F** per site. *El Bosque*, P Sigifredo 241, T311489. **F** per site, clean, hot water. Also 3 sites at Chauquén, 6 km southeast on the lakeside.

Eating

Didáctico El Gourmet, restaurant of professional hotel school. Excellent food and wine, pricey but high quality, open in school terms only. *Café Central*, M de Rozas 750. Good cheap lunches, expensive evening meals. Cheap restaurants in O'Higgins 700 block.

Sports

Fishing excursions on Lago Panguipulli are recommended: good locations include Puntilla Los Cipreses, 30 mins by boat; the mouth of the Río Huanehue, 11 km east of Panguipulli; and the mouth of the Río Niltre, on the east side of the lake. Boat hire US$3. Licences from the Municipalidad (Mon-Fri), Librería Colón, O'Higgins 528 (daily) or from the *Club de Pesca*. Good **rafting** opportunities: on the Río Fuy, grade 4-5; Río San Pedro, varying grades, and on the Río Llanquihue near Choshuenco.

Festivals

Last week of **Jan**, *Semana de Rosas*, with dancing and sports competitions.

Panguipulli

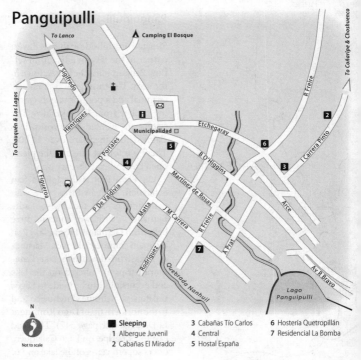

Sleeping
1 Albergue Juvenil
2 Cabañas El Mirador
3 Cabañas Tío Carlos
4 Central
5 Hostal España
6 Hostería Quetropillán
7 Residencial La Bomba

Not to scale

The Lake District

Bus Terminal at Gabriela Mistral y Portales. To **Santiago** daily, US$15. To **Valdivia**, fre-
quent (Sun only 4), several lines, 2 hrs, US$3. To **Temuco** frequent, Power and Pangui
Sur, US$2. To **Puerto Montt**, US$7. To **Calafquén**, 3 daily at 1200, 1545 and 1600. To
Choshuenco, **Neltume** and **Puerto Fuy**, *Buses La Fit* 1000, 1500, 1630 (Mon-Sat),
1800 (Sun); *Buses Huahum*, Mon-Sat 1130, 1530, also to Choshuenco and Neltume,
Mon-Fri 1900. US$3, 2½ hrs. To **Coñaripe** (with connections for Lican-Ray and
Villarrica), 6 daily Mon-Fri, 1 Sat, 1½ hrs, US$2. No direct buses to Villarrica.

Transport

Banks *Banco de Crédito e Inversiones*, *casa de cambio*, M de Rozas y Matta. Some
shops accept US$ cash. Rates poor, TCs not accepted anywhere.

Directory

On the Río Llanquihue, Choshuenco lies at the eastern tip of the lake. To the
south is the **Reserva Nacional Mocho Choshuenco** (7,536 ha) which
includes two volcanoes: Choshuenco (2,415 m) and Mocha (2,422 m). On
the slopes of Choshuenco the Club Andino de Valdivia has ski slopes and
three *refugios*. This can be reached by a turning from the road which goes
south from Choshuenco to Enco at the east end of Lago Riñihue (see
page 347). From Choshuenco a road leads east to Lago Pirehueico, via the
impressive waterfalls of **Huilo Huilo**, where the river channels its way
through volcanic rock before thundering down into a natural basin. The falls
are three hours' walk from Choshuenco, or take the Puerto Fuy bus and get off
at *Alojamiento Huilo Huilo*, Km 9 (1 km before Neltume) from where it is a
five-minute walk to the falls.

Choshuenco
Colour map 4, grid B2
45 km east of
Panguipulli

Sleeping and eating B *Pulmahue*, T211754, ext 224. 3 star. D *Choshuenco*, T224402
ext 214, run down. Clean, good meals. Various *hosterías*, including D *Hostería Rayen
Trai* (former yacht club), María Alvarado y O'Higgins. Good food, open all year. Recommended. D *Rucu Pillán*, San Martín 85, T224402, ext 220. **Camping** On the beach. **In
Neltume** D *Restaurant Robles*, without bath, good beds. F *Pensión Neltume*, meals.
At Huilo Huilo F *Alojamiento Huilo Huilo*. Basic but comfortable and well situated
for walks, good food. Highly recommended.

Transport Bus To Panguipulli 0645 and 0700.

Lago Pirehueico

Lago Pirehueico is a 36-km long, narrow and deep glacial lake, surrounded by
virgin *lingue* forest. It is beautiful, and largely unspoilt. There are, however,
plans to build a huge tourist complex in Puerto Pirehueico. There are no
roads along the shores of the lake.

Colour map 4, grid B2
21 km southeast of
Choshuenco

There are two ports on the lake: **Puerto Fuy** at the northern end and
Puerto Pirehueico at the southern end. These are linked by a ferry service, see
below. The two ports can be reached by a road from Neltume which links
Puerto Pirehueico and the Argentine border crossing at Paso Huahum. The
road south from Puerto Fuy around the Choshuenco volcano and through
rainforest to the Río Pillanleufú, Puerto Llolles on Lago Maihue and Puerto
Llifén on Lago Ranco, see below, one of the most beautiful in Chile, is privately owned and closed to all traffic.

Puerto Pirehueico and Puerto Fuy F *Hosp Pirehueico*. F *Restaurant Puerto Fuy*,
cold water, good restaurant. Beds also available in private houses. **Campsite** Free
camping on the beach in both Puerto Fuy and Puerto Pirehueico.

**Sleeping
and eating**

The Lake District

Transport
This is a beautiful ferry crossing

Bus Daily Puerto Fuy to Panguipulli, 3 daily, 3 hrs, US$3. There is also a daily service from Puerto Pirehueico via Paso Huahum to San Martín de los Andes in Argentina. **Ferry** The *Mariela* sails from Puerto Fuy across the lake to Puerto Pirehueico, 2-3 hrs, foot passengers US$1, cars US$23. To take vehicles reserve in advance at the *Hotel Quetropillán* in Panguipulli. **Schedule:** Nov/Dec and Mar/Apr from Pirehueico daily 1000, 1700, return 0700, 1400; Jan/Feb from Pirehueico daily 1000, 1530, 2000, return 0700, 1300, 1800; May-Oct from Pirehueico Mon-Sat 1000, 1500, no Sun service.

Border with Argentina

The **Paso Huahum** is 11 km southeast of Puerto Pirehueico. On the Argentine side the road leads along the north side of Lago Lacar to San Martín de los Andes, 47 km east, and Junín de los Andes. This crossing is usually open all year. Chilean immigration is open summer 0800-2100, winter 0800-2000.

Valdivia

Phone code: 063
Colour map 4, grid B2
Population: 110,000
839 km south
of Santiago

Surrounded by wooded hills, Valdivia is one of the most pleasant cities in southern Chile, a good place to rest after arduous treks in the mountains. With a high student population, it is also one of the best cities for meeting young Chilenos, who will be at the pulse of anything in the way of nightlife in the city. Valdivia lies at the confluence of two rivers, the Calle Calle and Cruces, which form the Río Valdivia. To the north of the city is a large island, Isla Teja, where the Universidad Austral de Chile is situated.

Ins and outs

Getting there
See page 344 for further details

There are daily flights north to Santiago, Concepción and Temuco, and south to Puerto Montt. The bus network is very wide, and there are numerous daily buses to Santiago and south to Puerto Montt, as well as to cities such as Temuco, Concepción and Chillán. By road access to the Panamericana is north to Loncoche (toll US$2.50) or south to Paillaco.

Getting around

Valdivia is quite sizeable, and there are *colectivos* and buses serving the outlying *barrios*. However, like many Chilean cities, the centre is relatively compact, and few places are outside walking distance, even across the river on the Isla Teja.

Tourist offices

Prat 555, by dock, T213596. Good map of region and local rivers, list of hotel prices and examples of local crafts with artisans' addresses. Helpful kiosk in bus terminal, mainly bus information. CONAF, Ismael Váldez 431, T218822. *Automóvil Club de Chile*, García Reyes 490, T250376. Also for car hire.

History

Valdivia was one of the most important centres of Spanish colonial control over Chile. Founded in 1552 by Pedro de Valdivia, it was abandoned

Valdivia centre

Sleeping
1 Palace
2 Pedro de Valdivia

Eating
1 Bar Olimpia
2 Café Haussmann
3 Dino
4 Entrelagos
5 Palace

Not to scale

as a result of the Mapuche insurrection of 1599 and the area was briefly occupied by Dutch pirates. In 1645 it was refounded as a walled city, the only Spanish mainland settlement south of the Río Biobío. The coastal fortifications at the mouth of the river also date from the 17th century. From independence until the 1880s Valdivia was an outpost of Chilean rule, reached only by sea or by a coastal route through Mapuche territory.

Sights

The city is centred around the tree-lined **Plaza de la República**, three blocks east of which is the river and the **Muelle Fluvial**, the dock for boats down the river. A pleasant walk is along the **Costanera** (Avenida Prat) which runs from Muelle Fluvial north, under the bridge to Isla Teja and round the bend in the river as far as the bus terminal. On **Isla Teja**, on the western bank of the river, there is a **botanical garden** and **arboretum** with trees from all over the world. West of the botanical gardens is the **Parque Saval**, which has beautiful flowers in November. ■ *US$0.50*.

Museo Histórico y Antropológico is beautifully situated in the former mansion of Carlos Andwandter, a leading German immigrant. Run by the University, it contains sections on archaeology, ethnography and German colonization. Next door, in the former Andwandter brewery, is the **Museo de Arte Moderno**. ■ *US$1.50. Tue-Sun, 1000-1300, 1400-1800*. **Museo de la Cathedral de Valdivia** has four centuries of Christian history. ■ *Tue-Sun 1000-1300, 1600-1900, in winter, Mon-Fri 1000-1300, 1600-1900, Sat 1000-1300. Independencia 514*.

Excursions

While the various rivers are navigable, and there are pleasant journeys by rented motor boat on the Ríos Futa and Tornagaleanes around the Isla del Rey, the most interesting excursions involve the historical sites of Niebla and Corral (see below). Boat trips can also be made around Isla Teja, offering views of birds and seals.

Santuario de la Naturaleza Río Cruces was flooded as result of the 1960 *maremoto*. There are lots of bird species are visible; tours by boat. *Isla del Río*, daily 1415, six hours, US$15 each.

The **Kunstmann Brewery**, just out of town on the Niebla road, offers tours of the brewery and its beer museum. There are meals. T292969, www.chilesur.com/kunstmann

Essentials

Sleeping

■ *on maps, pages 340 and 343*
Price codes: see inside front cover

Accommodation is scarce during Semana Valdiviana

LL-L *Puerto del Sur*, Los Lingues 950, Isla Teja, T224500, F211046, 5 star, very good. **AL** *Pedro de Valdivia*, Carampangue 190, T212931, F203888. With breakfast, good. **A** *Melillanca*, Alemania 675, T212509, F222740, with breakfast, modern. Recommended. **A** *Naguilán*, Gen Lagos 1927, T212851, F219130. Clean, quiet, pool, good restaurant. **A** *Palace*, Chacabuco y Henríquez, T213319, F219133. With breakfast, good, comfortable. **A** *Villa del Río*, España 1025, T216292, F217851. Restaurant expensive (try salmon in almond sauce), rents apartments with kitchen. **A** *Villa Paulina*, Yerbas Buenas 389, T/F216372. Clean, pool. **B** *Hosp Pérez Rosales*, Pérez Rosales 1037, T215607. With bath and breakfast, **E** pp without. Modern, small rooms, good beds, electricity supply can be uncertain as it shares a circuit with a welding business next door. **B** *Raitúe*, Gen Lagos 1382, T212503. **B-C** *Jardín del Rey*, Gen Lagos 1190, T218562, with breakfast. **C** *Hostal Centro Torreón*, P Rosales 783, T212622. With breakfast, old German villa, nice atmosphere, cable TV, parking. **C** *Hostal Esmeralda*,

A German influence

From 1849 to 1875 Valdivia was a centre for German colonization of the Lake District and a comparatively small number of German and Swiss colonists settled in the city, exerting a strong influence on architecture and on the agricultural methods, education, social life and customs of the area. They established most of the industries which made Valdivia an important manufacturing centre until the 1950s. According to an 1884 survey all the breweries, leatherworks, brickworks, bakeries, machine shops and mills in Valdivia belonged to families with German surnames.

"By the end of World War I, Valdivia was one of the most flourishing centres of German colonization in the South of Chile. Oh these earthy German gentleman farmers who dream and sing of their new world utopia before crackling fires of hawthorn and cinnamon wood, and toast it with fiery shots of homemade booze!

Cowboys, loggers, contractors, shipbuilders, industrialists, merchants; in half a century they turned the unruly, inhospitable country to the south into an exclusive society, firm and resilient. A rough-hewn frontier world, yet one of poetic beauty where the winter rains blur the outlines of smoking pine cabins along the riverbanks, the lakeshores, and the tumbling sea." (Fernando Alegría, Allende: A Novel, Stanford University Press, 1993).

Little of the architectural heritage of this period survived the 1960 earthquake, but the city's German heritage can still be seen in some of its best cafés and restaurants and in the names of its streets.

Esmeralda 651, T215659, with bath, **D** without bath, also *cabañas*, parking. **C** *Prat*, Prat 595, T222020. With good breakfast and bath, cable TV. **C** *Hosp Universitaria*, Serrano 985, T218775. Breakfast, kitchen facilities, family atmosphere, clean, cheap meals. Recommended. **C** *Villa Beauchef*, Beauchef 844, with bath and breakfast, **E** without.

D *Hosp Internacional*, García Reyes 660, T212015. With breakfast, clean, helpful, English and German spoken, use of kitchen. Recommended; also **F** without bath, *cabañas*. **E** Arauco 935. Clean, friendly. **E** pp, Baquedano 664, with breakfast (but avoid laundry service). **E** *Sra Paredes*, García Reyes 244. with breakfast, hot water. Recommended. **F** *Ana María Vera*, Beauchef 669, T218542. Clean, friendly, hot water, good breakfast. **F** Aníbal Pinto 1335, friendly and cheap. **F** Gen Lagos 874, T215946. With breakfast, old German house, pleasant family atmosphere. Recommended. **F** *Hosp Turístico*, Henríquez 745, T250086. Without bath, lovely villa in large gardens, friendly, large rooms, kitchen and laundry facilities, clean. Highly recommended. **F** *Hostal Arauco*, Arauco 869, T206013, with large breakfast, kitchen and laundry facilities. **F** *Hostal Cochrane*, Cochrane 595. With breakfast. **F** Picarte 2625, T216750, clean, German spoken, recommended. **F** Riquelme 15, T218909. With breakfast, friendly, clean, good value. **H** *Albergue Juvenil*, García Reyes s/n, off Picarte. Jan/Feb only.

Around the bus terminal On Picarte: **D** *Hostal Montserrat*, No 849, T215410. Without bath, with breakfast, poor beds. **F** *Hosp Elsa Martínez*, No 737, T212587. With breakfast, kitchen facilities, clean, friendly. Highly recommended. **F** *Hostal del 900*, No 953. With breakfast. **F** *Res Germanía*, No 873, T212405. With breakfast, without bath, poor beds, clean, German spoken, Hostelling International reductions. Several others. On A Muñoz, outside terminal: **F** No 345. With breakfast, clean, friendly. **F** No 353. Breakfast, hot water. Recommended. On Calle Anwandter: **C** *Hostal La Terraza* No 624, Casa 4, T212664. With breakfast, very comfortable, lovely views, parking. **C** *Hosp Andwandter*, No 601, T218587, with bath and breakfast, **E** without bath. **C-D** *Hostal Casagrande*, Andtwandter 880, T202035. With bath and breakfast, no singles, cable

TV. Attractive old house, laundry facilities. Recommended. **F** *Hosp Aredi*, No 624, Casa 2, T290450. With breakfast, friendly, good value, comedor.

Campsite *Camping Centenario*, in Rowing Club on España, **F** per tent, overlooking river. *Isla Teja*, T213584, lovely views over river.

Expensive *Restaurante Camino de Luna*, Prat s/n Costanera, floating restaurant – unique in Chile. **Mid range** *Cervecería Kunstmann* T292969, Camino Niebla s/n, German food, good beer. *Delicias*, Henríquez 372. Recommended for meals and cakes, real coffee (open Sun morning). *Palace*, Arauco y P Rosales. *Selecta*, Picarte 1093. Pleasant, excellent fish and meat, not cheap. *Shanghai* Andwandter y Muñoz. Pleasant Chinese. **Cheap** *Bar Olimpia*, Libertad 28. Always full, 24 hrs, good meeting point. *Cats Club*, Esmeralda 657, good food, salad bar, pleasant ambience. *Derby*, Henríquez 314, large portions, good value. *New Orleans*, Esmerelda 652, large portions. *Restaurant Volcán*, Caupolicán y Chacabuco, Pichangas, Cazuelas, great food at a good price. **Seriously cheap** There are plenty of very cheap restaurants down by the waterfront facing the boat dock, and in the market – the food is good.

Eating

Valdivia

Cafés For real coffee and sandwiches: *Café Express*, Picarte 764. Real coffee. *Café Haussmann*, O'Higgins 394. Good tea and cakes. *Dino*, Maipú y Rosales. *Entrelagos* Pérez Rosales 622. Ice cream and chocolates, expensive. *La Ultíma Frontera*, Perez Rosales 787 (in Centro Cultural 787), real coffee, homemade cakes etc. **Bakery** *La Baguette*, Libertad y Yungay. French-style cakes, brown bread. Repeatedly recommended.

Entertainment **Bars** *Bataclan*, Henriquez 326, live music. *El Cantino*, Andwandter 385, Brazilian bar/restaurant. *Fuerte de Pedro*, Caupolicán 337, cheap, new restaurant/bar. *La Bomba*, Caupolicán 337, old Valdivian bar, pleasant, empanadas. *Pub en el Clavo*, Alemania 209. *Tragobar*, Beauchef 620, great drinks, good music and ambience. **Cinema** In Chacabuco 300 block. *Cine Club UACH*, University campus, weekend shows (not in summer).

Sports **Clubs** *Santa Elvira Golf Club*, 9 holes. Tennis, sailing, motor, and rowing clubs like Phoenix on Teja Island. **Swimming** Indoor pool, Holzapfel y Las Tarrias, T220310, US$4, closed Mon.

Festivals *Semana Valdiviana*, in mid-Feb, culminates in *Noche Valdiviana* on the Saturday with a procession of elaboratedly decorated boats which sail past the Muelle Fluvial.

Shopping **Film** *Fotoquick Agfa*, Picarte 430. Fotoquideon, Picarte 417. For developing. *Kodak*, Picarte 382. **Supermarkets** *Hiper-Unico*, Arauco 697. *Las Brisas*, Henriquez 522 (on plaza). **Bookshops** *Librería Andrés Bello*, Independencia 635. *Librería/Centro Cultural 787*, Pérez Rosales 787, old mansion, hip bookstore, café, art exhibitions. *Librería Chiloé*, Caupolicán 410.

Tour companies *Asotur*, Libertad 23, T290491, asotur@entelchil.net *Outdoor Chile*, Quineo 636, Villa Rucahue, T253377, F255955, www.OutDoorsChile.com *Paraty Club*, Independencia 640, T215585. *Turismo Conosur*, Maipu 129, T212757. *Turismo Koller*, Martí 83, T255335, F250326, www.turismokoller.com *Turismo Los Notros*, O'Higgins 189, T210533. Several companies offer boat trips, eg *Catamaran Extasis* – US$30, or US$45 with dinner.

Transport **Local Car hire** *Autovald*, Henríquez 610, T212786. *Hertz*, Picarte 640, airport, T272273, T218316. *Turismo Méndez*, Gen Lagos 1335, T213205.

Long distance Air *LanChile* and *Ladeco* to/from Santiago every day via Temuco. **Bus** Terminal at Muñoz y Prat, by the river. To **Santiago**: several companies, 13 hrs, most services overnight, US$17 (*Tur Bus* good) *salón cama* US$40. ½-hourly to **Osorno**, 2 hrs, several companies, US$3. To **Llifén**, 4 a day, US$2.50. To **Panguipulli**, US$3, *Empresa Pirehueico*, about every 30 mins, US$3. Many daily to **Puerto Montt**, US$6, 3 hrs. To **Castro**, US$10, 7 hrs. To **Temuco**, US$3. To **Puerto Varas**, 2 hrs, US$6. To **Frutillar**, US$4. To **Villarrica**, by *JAC*, 6 a day direct, 2½ hrs, US$3.50, continuing to Pucón, US$4.50, 3 hrs. Frequent daily service to Riñihue via Paillaco and Los Lagos. **To Argentina**: to **Bariloche** via Osorno, 10 hrs, *Bus Norte*, US$20. To **Zapala**, *Igi-Llaima*, Mon, Thu, Sat, 2300, change in Temuco at 0200, arrive Zapala 1200-1500, depending on border, US$34. To **Mendoza**, *Fénix* and *Andesmar*.

Directory **Airline offices** *LanChile*, O'Higgins 386, T213042. *Ladeco*, Caupolicán 364, T213392. **Banks** There is a *Redbanc* in the Hyperunico Supermarket (see above). Banks: *Banco del Estado*, Camilo Henríquez 562 (huge commission on TCs). Good rates for cash at *Banco Santander*, P Rosales 585, *Corp Banca*, Picarte 370, Visa. Will change cash and TCs. *Banco*

Santiago, Arauco 149. Mastercard. *Turismo Cochrane*, Arauco 435. Casa de Cambio at Carampangue 325, T213305. *Turismo Austral*, Arauco y Henríquez, Galería Arauco. Accepts TCs. **Communications** Internet: *Cafe Phonet*, Libertad 127, with cafe, also very cheap call centre. *Centro Internet Libertad*, Libertad 7. *Internet Letelier 236*, of 202. There are also several internet on the plaza. **Telephone**: *CTC*, Independencia 628, T252700. *Entel*, Pérez Rosales 601, T225334. **Laundry** *Au Chic*, Arauco 436. *Lavazul*, Chacabuco 300. Slow. Coin laundry at *Lavamatic*, Schmidt y Picarte (Mon-Sat 0930-2030). *Manantial*, Henríquez 809, T217609. **Public showers** In the market, US$1.

Around the Río Valdivia

At the mouth of the Río Valdivia there are interesting and isolated villages which can be visited by road or by river boat. The two main centres are Niebla on the north bank and Corral opposite on the south bank. There is a frequent boat service between the two towns; south of Corral is remote, wild, forested country, very rarely visited.

Niebla is a resort with seafood restaurants and accommodation. In mid-February there is a *Feria Costumbrista*, with lots of good food including *pullmay asado* and *paila marina*. To the west is the Fuerte de la Pura y Limpia Concepción de Monfort de Lemus, on a promontory. Built in 1671 and partially restored in 1992, it has an interesting museum on Chilean naval history. ■ *US$0.75. Sun free, daily in summer 1000-1900, closed Mon in winter.* Tourist information and telephone office nearby.

Niebla
Colour map 4, grid B1
18 km west of Valdivia

About 6 km further round the coast is **Los Molinos**, a seaside resort set among steep wooded hills. There is a campsite and lots of seaside restaurants including *La Bahía* which has good food but it's not cheap.

Río Valdivia

The Lake District

Spanish forts in the Río Valdivia

The Spanish fortifications at the mouth of the Río Valdivia were among the strongest in the empire. Although dating from just after the reoccupation of the city in 1645, they were greatly strengthened after 1760, owing to fears that Valdivia might be seized by the British. The main forts were rebuilt in brick and stone using the latest techniques of European military engineering. Large numbers of cannon were used to control access to the estuary. In all there were 17 forts: the main ones to see are at Niebla, Corral, Isla Mancera,

Amargos and San Carlos. One other, San Luis de Alba de las Cruces, up the Río Cruces, can be visited by boat from Valdivia or by unpaved road from San José de la Mariquina.

These great fortifications were of little avail during the Wars of Independence: overnight on 2 February 1820 the Chilean naval squadron under Lord Cochrane seized San Carlos, Amargos and Corral and turned their guns on Niebla and Mancera which surrendered the following morning.

Sleeping and eating *Cabañas Fischer*, T282007, **B-C** per *cabaña*, camping. Worth bargaining out of season. **D** *Hostería Riechers*, T/F282043. **E** *Villa Santa Clara*, T282018 (Casilla 52, Valdivia), with breakfast, also *cabañas* **E** pp, cooking and laundry facilities. *Las Delicias*, T213566, a restaurant with 'a view that would be worth the money even if the food weren't good'. Also *cabañas* and camping. *Camping Rayen Quitral*.

Corral
Colour map 4, grid B1
Population 3,600
62 km west of Valdivia

Corral is the main port serving the city. The town is much quieter and more pleasant than Niebla. Visits can be made to the **Castillo de San Sebastian**, built in 1645; its 3-m wide walls were defended by a battery of 21 guns. Inside is a museum. In summer re-enactments of 18th-century battles in period costume are held, daily 1530 and 1730. The fort has a dilapidated, interesting atmosphere and horses are sometimes found grazing in the ramparts. Further north along the coast are the remains of two other Spanish colonial forts: the Castillo San Luis de Alba and the Castillo de San Carlos. The coastal walks west and south of Corral are splendid, along very isolated and forested roads above the ocean.

Sleeping and eating **E** *Hostería Los Alamos*, a delightful hideout for those seeking a quiet life. **F** *Res Mariel*, Tarapacá 36, T471290. Modern, clean, friendly, good value. On Isla Moncera: **C** *Hostería Mancera*, T/F216296, open Dec-Mar, depending on weather, no singles, phone first: water not drinkable.

Transport The tourist **boats** to Isla Mancera and Corral, offer a guided ½-day tour (US$20 with meals – cheaper without) from the Muelle Fluvial, Valdivia (behind the tourist office on Av Prat 555), 1330 daily. **Buses** to Niebla from Chacabuco y Yungay, Valdivia, roughly every 20 mins between 0730 and 2100, 30 mins, US$0.75 (continues to Los Molinos). Also *colectivos*.

Isla Mancera
In midstream, between Niebla and Corral is this small island, fortified by the Castillo de San Pedro de Alcántara, which has the most standing buildings. The island is a pleasant place to stopover on the boat trips, but it can get crowded when an excursion boat arrives.

Resorts further north

This small town, 42 km north of Valdivia, lies on the Río Cruces. From here an
unpaved road leads south along the river to the Castillo de San Luis de Alba
(22 km), a colonial fortification built in 1647 and largely rebuilt according to
the original plans.

Mehuin is a small, friendly resort and fishing port with a long beach. A clifftop
road (fantastic views north and south along the coastline) leads 6 km further
north to **Queule**, which has a good beach, but which is dangerous for bathing
at high tide because of undercurrents (bathing is safer in the river near the
ferry). From Queule, a pretty road leads north to Toltén; there are numerous
small ferry crossings to isolated Mapuche communities along the coast.

Sleeping A *El Nogal*, T/F451352. With bath and breakfast, good. **E** *Mehuín*, T219235,
not very inviting. **E** *Playa*, T451376 **F** *Hosp Marbella*, clean, cheapest. **Queule**: there
are two simple *residenciales*.

Transport Bus: from Valdivia, 2 hrs, US$2.

Covering 2,307 ha, this newly designated park in the coastal mountain range
protects an area of alerce forest (though a fire in 1975 destroyed some of the
forest which can be seen in the distance). There is a CONAF *guardería* and
refugio, from which a 3-km trail leads to a 3,500-year-old alerce. Entry is free.
Access is by a very poor road, 32 km *ripio*, 20 km unpaved, which runs northwest from La Unión (see page 347).

Lago Riñihue
Colour map 4, grid B2
93 km east of Valdivia

Lago Riñihue is the southernmost of the Seven Lakes. There is no road around
the northern edge of the lake and the road around the southern edge of the
lake from Riñihue to Enco is closed (except to jeeps in summer only), so
Choshuenco at the southeast end of Lago Panguipulli can only be reached by
road from Panguipulli or Puerto Fuy. **Riñihue**, a beautiful but very small and
isolated village at the western end of the lake, is worth a visit.

Sleeping and eating C *Hostería Huinca Quinay*, 3 km east of Riñihue, T461347,
F461406, *cabañas*, restaurant. **F** *Restaurant del Lago* (no meals). Campsite by the lake.
El Desague, 20 km south of Panguipulli. **C** *Riñimapu*, T311388. Comfortable, good
value, excellent food. *Vista Hermosa*, T/F311537.

Lago Ranco

One of the largest lakes, covering 41,000 ha, and starred with islands, this is
also one of the most accessible as there is a road round its edge, albeit terrible,
with lots of mud and animals, including oxcarts. However the road is worth
taking to see an older lifestyle, the beautiful lake, waterfalls and sunsets on the
distant volcanoes. It is better to travel anti-clockwise for the best views. To
descend the worst hills; if you are walking, beware of the numerous guard
dogs in the area. There is excellent fishing on the southern shore and several
hotels organize fishing expeditions.

From the north the lake can be reached from the Pan-American Highway
from Los Lagos or from a point 18 km south of Los Lagos, 11 km north of
Paillaco. These two roads join and meet the road around the lake some 5 km
west of Futrono. From the south access is from **La Unión** (*Hotel Club Alemán*,

Letelier 497, T322695) and **Río Bueno**, which are bypassed by the Pan-American Highway.

The main town on the northern shore is **Futrono** from where the road curves round the north of the lake to **Llifén**, Km 22, a picturesque place on the eastern shore. From Llifén, a visit can be paid to **Lago Maihue**, 33 km further east, the south shore of which is covered by native forests. From Llifén the road continues via the Salto de Nilahue (Km 14) to **Riñinahue**, Km 23, at the southeast corner of the lake and **Lago Ranco**, Km 47, an ugly little town on the south shore, which has a museum with exhibits on Mapuche culture. On the western shore is **Puerto Nuevo**, where there are watersports and fishing on the Río Bueno. Further north, 10 km west of Futrono is **Coique** with the best beach on the lake.

Sleeping & eating

There is only one (dismal) pace in Futrono to eat in the evening

Futrono C *Hostería Rincón Arabe*, T481262, F481330. **D** *Hosp Futronhue*, Balmaceda 90, T481265, good breakfast. **G** in the Casa Parroquial. **Llifén** **AL** *Huequecura*, Casilla 4, T09-6535450. Includes meals and fishing services, good restaurant. **B** *Hostería Chollinco*, 3 km out of town on the road towards Lago Maihue, T0638-202. Limited electricity, swimming pool. **C** *Hostería Lican*, T09-6535315, F Valdivia 218921. **Riñinahue** **A** *Hostería Riñinahue*, Casilla 126, T491379, organizes fishing expeditions. *Hostería El Arenal del Nilahue*. **Lago Ranco** *Parque Thule*, T491293. **C** *Hostería Casona Italia*, T491225. **C** *Hostería Phoenix*, T491226. *Residenciales*, houses to let in summer. **Puerto Nuevo** **AL** *Hotel Puerto Nuevo*, very good.

Camping There are campsites all around Lago Ranco as well as several on Lago Maihue, though many open in summer only and prices are high. At **Futrono**: *Nalcahue*, 1 km west, T481663, US$18 per site. *Bahía Las Rosas*, 1 km east, US$18 per site, Bahía Coique, 9 km west, T481264, autocamping, US$50 per site in summer, US$35 per site off season. At **Llifén**: Callejón Huequecura, 1 km south. Chollinco, 3 km east. At **Lago Maihue**: Puerto Llolles, at western end, no facilities. Maqueo, on eastern shore, US$18 per site. At **Riñinahue** Playa Ranquil, US$10 per site. At **Lago Ranco**: Camping Lago Ranco, US$15 per site,

Transport

Bus *Cordillera Sur* bus from Valdivia to Llifén, 2 daily, once Sun; from Osorno to Lago Ranco, *Empresa Ruta 5*, 6 daily.

Lagos Ranco & Maihue

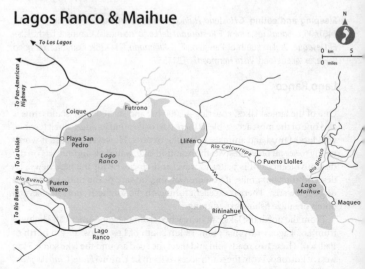

Osorno

Situated at the confluence of the Ríos Rahue and Damas, Osorno is a reasonable base for visiting the southern lakes. Founded in 1553, it was abandoned in 1604 and was refounded by Ambrosio O'Higgins and Juan MacKenna O'Reilly in 1796. It later became one of the centres of German immigration; their descendants are still of great importance in the area. But this is not really a touristic city, and is likely to be a place that you will pass through.

Phone code: 064
Colour map 4, grid B2
Population: 114,000
921 km south
of Santiago

Ins and outs

Osorno is a key crossroads for bus routes in southern Chile. Passengers heading for Bariloche, Neuquén, Coyhaique or Punta Arenas will pass through here before making for the Puyehue Pass into Argentina; buses tend to leave from Puerto Montt, and travellers from Santiago may well change buses here. There are also hourly local services to Puerto Montt, as well as frequent services north to Temuco and Valdivia.

Getting there
See page 351 for further details

Osorno is not one of the largest cities in Chile, and most of the places visitors are likely to visit are within easy walking distance. Taxis or *colectivos* may be useful for longer trips.

Getting around

CONAF at de Rosas 430, T234393. **Sernatur**, provincial government office, on Plaza de Armas, O'Higgins s/n, p 1, left, T234104. Municipal office in bus terminal and Kiosk on Plaza de Armas, both open Dec-Feb. *Automóvil Club de Chile*: Bulnes 463, T232269. Information and car hire.

Tourist offices

Sights

On the large **Plaza de Armas** stands the modern, concrete and glass cathedral, with many arches, repeated in the tower, itself an open, latticed arch with a cross superimposed. West of the centre on a bend overlooking the river is the **Fuerte María Luisa**, built in 1793, restored 1977, with only the river front walls and end turrets standing. East of the main plaza along Calle MacKenna are a number of late 19th-century wooden mansions built by German immigrants, now preserved as national monuments. ■ *Free tours of the city, Mon-Fri 1500 and 1700, Jan-Feb only. Book at municipal tourist office.*

Museo Histórico Municipal includes displays on natural history, Mapuche culture, refounding of the city and German colonization. ■ *Entrance in Casa de Cultura, US$1; Mon-Sun 1100-1900. Winter, Mon-Fri 0930-1730, Sat 1500-1800. Matta 809.* **Auto Museo Moncopulli**, 25 km east of Osorno on Route 215, is the best motor museum in Chile. Exhibits include a Studebaker collection from 1852 to 1966. There is also a 1950s-style cafeteria. ■ *1000-1900. T204200. Transport: bus to Entre Lagos from the Mercado Municipal terminal.*

Río Bueno, 30 km north, is celebrated for its scenery and for fishing. There is a Spanish colonial fort dating from 1777, situated high above the river and offering fine views. Frequent buses from the Mercado Municipal terminal. At **Trumao**, a river port on the Río Bueno, 22 km further west via La Unión, a launch may be taken to La Barra on the coast; leaves Wednesday and Saturday only at 0900, five hours, returns Thursday and Sunday at 0900, US$9 return, no service in winter.

Excursions

The Lake District

There are beaches at **Maicolpue**, 60 km west (*D Hostería Müller*, on the beach, clean, good service, recommended campsite) and **Pucatrihue** (*Hostería Incalcar*, summer only) which are worth a visit in the summer. ■ *Daily bus service from the Mercado Municipal terminal.*

Essentials

Sleeping
■ *on map*
Price codes:
see inside front cover

L-AL *Del Prado*, Cochrane 1162, T235020. Pool, garden, good meals, well-located, charming. **L-AL** *Waeger*, Cochrane 816, T233721, PO Box 802, F237080. 3-star, poor restaurant, comfortable. Recommended. **AL** *Mendoza*, Mackenna 1040, T237111, F237113, 4-star. **AL** *Rayantú*, Patricio Lynch 1462, T238114, F238116, 4-star. **A** *Gran Hotel Osorno*, O'Higgins 615, T233990, F239311. Cable TV, comfortable. **A** *Inter-Lagos*, Cochrane 515, T234695, F232581. With breakfast, garage, restaurant. **A** *Pumalal*, Bulnes 630, T243520, F242477. With breakfast, modern, airy, clean. **A** *Res Riga*, Amthauer 1058, T232945. Clean, pleasant. Highly recommended but heavily booked in season. **A-B** *Eduviges*, Eduviges 856, T/F235023. Spacious, clean, quiet, attractive, gardens, also *cabañas*. Recommended. **B** *Hostal Rucaitué*, Freire 546, T239922, F310617. With breakfast, cable TV, comfortable. **B** *Res Bilbao*, Bilbao 1019, T236755, F321111; and *Res Bilbao II*, MacKenna 1205, T/F242244. With breakfast, parking, restaurant. **C** *Millantué*, Errázuriz 1339, T242490, near bus terminal. With breakfast, parking. Dirty and overpriced. **C** *Res Hein*, Errázuriz 1757, T234116. Old-fashioned, spacious, family atmosphere.

Near terminal **E** *Amunátegui 520*. Good. **E** *Res Ortega*, Colón y Errázuriz. Parking, basic, clean, toilet facilities limited. **E** pp *Res Sánchez*, Los Carrera 1595, T232560.

Osorno

To Pan-American Highway

N
0 metres 100
0 yards 100

■ **Sleeping**
1 Amunátegui 520 *B3*
2 Colón 844 *B3*
3 Del Prado *C2*
4 Eduviges *B3*
5 Germania *C2*
6 Gran Osorno *B2*
7 Hospedaje de la Fuente *B3*
8 Hostal Rucaitué *B2*
9 Inter-Lagos *B2*
10 La Paloma *B3*
11 Mendoza *B2*
12 Millantué *B3*
13 Pumalal *B2*
14 Rayantú *B3*
15 Residencia Bilbao *B2*
16 Residencia Bilbao II *B3*
17 Residencia Carillo *A3*
18 Residencia Hein *B2*
19 Residencia Riga *C2*
20 Residencia San Diego *B3*
21 Residencia Sánchez *B3*
22 Waeger *B2*

● **Eating**
1 Chung Hwa *B2*
2 Dino's *B2*
3 La Paisana *B2*
4 Peter's Kneipe *C2*
5 Shangri-La *B2*

Shared bathrooms, use of kitchen, noisy, basic, friendly, with breakfast. Owners lock up at 2100. **E** *Germania*, Rodríguez 741. No hot water, cooking facilities. **F** *Anibal Pinto 1758*, with breakfast, T238024. **F** *Colón 844*. With breakfast. **F** *Hosp de la Fuente*, Los Carrera 1587. Basic, friendly. **F** *Res San Diego*, Los Carrera 1551, with breakfast. Private houses at Germán Hube, pasaje 1, casa 22, población Villa Dama, **F**, hot water, clean, use of kitchen. Recommended. **G** *Res Carillo*, Angulo 454. Basic, clean. *La Paloma*, Errázuriz 1599, basic. *Richmond*, Lastarria 530, basic. *Silvane*, Errázuriz y Lastarria, T234429. Fairly basic.

Camping Municipal site off Pan-American Highway near southern entrance to city, open Jan-Feb only, poor facilities, US$5 per site.

Mid-range *Dino's*, Ramírez 898, on the plaza. Restaurant upstairs, bar/cafeteria downstairs, good. *La Paisana*, Freire 530. Arab specialities. *Peter's Kneipe*, M Rodríguez 1039. Excellent German restaurant. *Shangri-La*, Ramon Freire 542, Local 16, Chilean and Nepalese cuisine, French, English spoken. Good food and service, pleasant atmosphere. Recommended. **Cheap** *Chung Hwa*, Matta 517, Chinese. Travels in bus terminal for cheap snacks. *Waldis*, on Plaza de Armas. Real coffee. Bakery at Ramírez 977. Good wholemeal bread.

Eating
● *on map*

Bars *El Fogón*, O'Higgins 533, and *La Pinte*, Freire 677.

Entertainment

Ekono Supermarket, Colón y Errázuriz. For fishing tackle try *Climet*, Angulo 603 and *The Lodge*, Los Carrera 1291, local 5. *Alta Artesanía*, MacKenna 1069, excellent handicrafts, not cheap. There is a new mall on Calle Freire 542 with 3 internet cafes and a bookshop, CM Books, which sells some English titles.

Shopping

Skiing *Club Andino*, O'Higgins 1073. For advice on possibilities.

Sports

Local Buses to Entre Lagos, Puyehue and Aguas Calientes leave from the Mercado Municipal terminal, 1 block west of the main terminal. To Entre Lagos frequent services in summer, *Expreso Lago Puyehue*, T234919, and *Buses Puyehue*, 45 mins, US$1, reduced service off-season; some buses by both companies also continue to Aguas Calientes (off-season according to demand) 2 hrs, US$2; in summer there are also services Maicolpué on the coast if demand is sufficient. **Car mechanic** at *Automotriz Amthauer*, Amthauer 1250. *Automotriz Salfa Sur SA*, Fco Bilbao 857.

Transport

Long distance Air: *LanChile/Ladeco* daily flights to Santiago, via Temuco. **Bus**: Main terminal 4 blocks from Plaza de Armas at Errázuriz 1400. Left luggage open 0730-2030, bus from centre, US$0.30. To **Santiago**, frequent, US$17, *semi cama* US$25, 16 hrs. To **Valparaíso** and **Viña del Mar**, *Tas Choapa*, US$21. To **Arica**, *Tas Choapa*, US$55. To **Concepción**, US$10. To **Temuco**, US$6. To **Panguipulli**, *buses Pirehueico*, 4 a day. To **Pucón** and **Villarrica**, *Tur Bus*, frequent, US$7. To **Valdivia**, frequent, 2 hrs, several companies, US$3, but *Igi Llaima* only US$1.80. To **Frutillar**, US$1.50, **Llanquihue**, **Puerto Varas** and **Puerto Montt** (US$3) services by Varmontt every 30 mins. To **Puerto Octay**, US$2, *Vía Octay* company 6 daily between 0815-1930 (return 0800-1930) Mon-Sat, 5 on Sun between 0800 and 2000 (4 return buses). To **Lago Ranco**, (town) 6 a day, *Empresa Ruta 5*, 2 hrs, US$2. To **Punta Arenas**, US$55, several each week.

Airline offices *LanChile*, Matta 862, T236688, *Ladeco*, MacKenna 1098, T236102. **Banks** ATMs at *Banco BCI*, MacKenna 801, *Banco Santiago*, MacKenna 787 (Visa). *Casas de cambio. Cambio Tur*, MacKenna 1004, T234846. *Turismo Frontera*, Ramírez 949, local 11 (Galería Catedral). If stuck try Travels bar in bus terminal. **Communications** Post

Directory

office: O'Higgins 645. Also telex. **Telephone**: Ramírez at central plaza and Juan MacKenna y Cochrane. **Internet**: *Chat-Mail MP3*, Patricio Lynch 1334. Also *Dream House*, Matta 510, opposite *Chung Hwa Restaurant*, *Pub Sa Tanca*, Patio Freire 542, local 18, and *Turismo Seis*, Patio Freire 542, local 8. **Laundry** Prat 678 (allow at least a day).

East of Osorno

From Osorno Route 215 runs east to the Argentine frontier at the Puyehue Pass via the south shore of Lago Puyehue, Anticura and the Parque Nacional Puyehue.

Lago Puyehue
Colour map 4, grid B2
47 km east of Osorno

Surrounded by relatively flat countryside, Lago Puyehue extends over 15,700 ha. The southern shore is much more developed than the northern shore which is accessible only by unpaved road from the western end. At the western end is **Entre Lagos** and the **Termas de Puyehue** are at the eastern end. ■ *US$3.50 outdoor pools, US$15 indoor pools, 0900-2000.*

Sleeping and eating Entre Lagos AL *Cabañas No Me Olvides*, T371633, with kitchen. **D** *Hosp Vista Hermosa*, with breakfast. **B** *Hostería Entre Lagos*, Ramírez 65, lake view, T371225. **E** *Villa Veneto*, Gral Lagos 602, T371203. **E** *Hosp Miraflores*, Ramírez 480, T371275, also *cabañas*. **C** *Hosp Millarey*, Ramírez 333, T371251. With breakfast, excellent, clean, friendly. *Jardín del Turista*, F371214. Very good restaurant, *cabañas*. *Pub del Campo*, F371220. Highly recommended restaurant.

On the southern lakeshore *Chalet Suisse*, Km 55 (Casilla 910, Osorno, T064-234073). Restaurant with excellent food. *La Valenciana*, Km 53, T09-6433133. **C** *Posada Puntillo*, at Shell station, Km 62. A *Motel Ñilque*, Santiago T09-647218, cabins, half-price May-Oct, fishing trips, watersports, car hire. **C** *Hostería Isla Fresia*, located on own island, T236951, Casilla 49, Entre Lagos. Transport provided.

At the Termas L *Gran Hotel Termas de Puyehue*, T232157, F371272 (cheaper May to mid-Dec). 2 thermal swimming pools (one indoors, very clean), theatre, conference centre, well maintained, meals expensive, in beautiful scenery, heavily booked Jan-Feb. Accommodation also in private house nearby, **E** pp, also full board.

Camping *Camping No Me Olvides*, Km 56. US$10. Also *cabañas*. *Playa Los Copihues*, Km 56.5 (hot showers, good), both on southern shore of Lake Puyehue. *Camping Playa Puyehue*, Km 75.

Transport Bus 2½ hrs, schedule under Osorno; buses do not stop at the lakeside (unless you want to get off at *Gran Hotel Termas de Puyehue* and clamber down), but continues to Aguas Calientes.

Parque Nacional Puyehue

Colour map 4, grid B2

Located east of Lago Puyehue and stretching to the Argentine frontier, this park covers 107,000 ha, much of it in the valley of the Río Golgol. On the eastern side are several lakes, including Lago Constancia and Lago Gris. There are two volcanic peaks: **Volcán Puyehue** (2,240 m) in the north (access via a private road US$2.50) and **Volcán Casablanca** (also called Antillanca, 1,900 m).

At **Aguas Calientes**, 4 km south of the Termas de Puyehue in a thickly forested valley, there is an open-air pool (dirty) with very hot thermal water beside the Río Chanleufú (where there is a campsite; US$4 pp). ■ *0830-1900, US$2, children US$1, Mon-Fri (in season only) 0830-1230, 1400-1800, Sat, Sun and holidays (all year) 0830-2030, US$6, children US$3.*

From Aguas Calientes the road continues 18 km southeast past three small lakes and through forests to **Antillanca** on the slopes of Volcán Casablanca. In winter a one-way traffic system operates on the last 8 km: up 0800-1200 and 1400-1730, down 1200-1400 and after 1730. This is a particularly beautiful section, especially at sunrise, with views over Lago Puyehue to the north and Lagos Rupanco and Llanquihue to the south, as well as the snow-clad peaks of Calbuco, Osorno, Puntiagudo, Puyehue and Tronador forming a semicircle. The tree-line on Casablanca is one of the few in the world made up of deciduous trees (*nothofagus* or southern beech). From Antillanca it is possible to climb Casablanca for even better views of the surrounding volcanoes and lakes, no path, seven hours' return journey, information from Club Andino in Osorno. On the south side of the volcano there are caves (accessible by road, allow five hours from *Hotel Antillanca*). There are few mammals but waterfowl are common on the lake and condors can be seen near the volcanoes.

Attached to the *Hotel Antillanca* is one of the smallest **ski** resorts in Chile; there are three lifts, ski instruction and first aid available. Piste preparation is unreliable. Skiing is not difficult but quality depends on the weather: though rain is common it often does not turn to snow.

In the Anticura section of the park, northeast of Aguas Calientes, are three waterfalls, including the spectacular 40-m wide **Salto del Indio**. Legend has it that an Indian, enslaved by the Spanish, was able to escape by hiding behind the falls. Situated just off the road, the falls are on a marked path through dense forest which includes a 800-year-old Coihue tree known as 'El Abuelo'.

Park administration is at Aguas Calientes; there is also a ranger station at Anticura. Leaflets on walks and attractions are available.

B *Hotel Antillanca*, T235114. Includes free mountainbiking and parapenting, at foot of Volcán Casablanca, excellent restaurant/café, with pool, sauna, friendly club-like **Sleeping and eating**

Lagos Puyehue & Rupanco

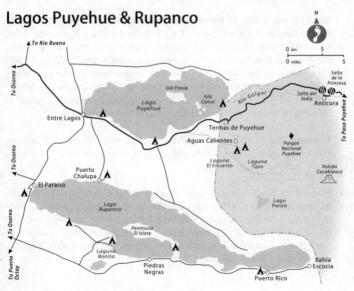

The Lake District

atmosphere. **Camping** *Chanleufu*, in Aguas Calientes. With hot water, US$25 per site, *cabañas* (**A** in season, **C** off season) T236988. A small shop – better to take your own food, and an expensive café. *Los Derrumbes*, 1 km from Aguas Calientes. No electricity, US$20 per site. CONAF *refugio* on Volcán Puyehue, but check with CONAF in Anticura whether it is open.

Transport   See under Osorno for buses. No public transport from Aguas Calientes to Antillanca; try hitching – always difficult, but it is not a hard walk.

Border with Argentina
This route is liable to closure after snow

Paso Puyehue is reached by the paved Route 215 from Osorno via Entre Lagos and Lago Puyehue. On the Argentine side the road continues to Bariloche. Chilean immigration is open second Sat in Oct-second Sat in Mar 0800-2100, otherwise 0800-1900. The Chilean frontier post is at Pajaritos, 4 km east of **Anticura**, which itself lies 22 km west of the border (Hostería y Cabañas Anticura; Camping Catrue). All luggage is passed through an X-ray machine. For private vehicles entering Chile, formalities are quick (about 15 mins), but includes a search for fruit, vegetables and dairy produce.

Transport   To Anticura, bus at 1620 from Osorno, 3 hrs. Several bus companies run daily services from Puerto Montt via Osorno to Bariloche along this route (see page 376). Although less scenic than the ferry journey across Lake Todos Los Santos and Laguna Verde (see page 365) this crossing is cheaper, reliable and still a beautiful trip.

Lago Rupanco
Colour map 4, grid B2

Popular for fishing

Lying south of Lago Puyehue and considerably larger, this lake covers 23,000 ha and is far less accessible and less developed for tourism than most of the other larger lakes. Access from the northern shore is via two unpaved roads which branch off Route 215. **El Paraíso**, at the western tip of the lake, can be reached by an unpaved road which runs south from Entre Lagos. A 40-km dirt road runs along the southern shore, via **Laguna Bonita**, a small lake surrounded by forest, and **Piedras Negras** to **Bahía Escocia** at the eastern end. From the south access is from two turnings off the road between Osorno and Las Cascadas.

Sleeping and eating El Paraíso *Hostería y Cabañas El Paraíso*, T236239. At **Piedras Negras** *Hostería El Islote*, 7 km east. **Bahía Escocia L** *Puntiagudo Lodge*, T/F731515, also **AL**, with breakfast, very comfortable, good restaurant, fly fishing, horseriding, boat excursions, highly recommended. *Bahía Escocia Fly Fishing*, Casillon 1312, Osorno, T/F064-371515, offers excursions (advance booking required). There is no accommodation on the northern shore. **Camping** *Puerto Chalupa*, on northern shore, T064-232680, F064-232741, US$28 per site. *Desague del Rupanco*, just south of El Paraíso, no facilities. Several on southern shore including at Puerto Rico.

Transport   Bus: From Osorno to Piedras Negras from either *Minimarket El Capricho*, MacKenna y Colón, or Estaión Viejo (old railway station), leaves 1645, 1545 on Sat, returns from Piedras Negras 0700.

Hacienda Rupanco   Situated southeast of Lago Rupanco and covering 47,000 ha, this hacienda, the largest milk-producer in Chile, invites day visitors and provides accommodation. Activities include horseriding, fishing, rafting, canoeing and sailing on Lago Rupanco. The main entrance is off the Osorno-Puerto Octay road. Accommodation **A** in comfortable houses, full board, also camping, open all year. T/F064-203000.

Lago Llanquihue

This lake is one of the highlights of the Lake District. Three snowcapped volcanoes can be seen across this sea of water: the perfect cone of Osorno (2,680 m), the shattered cone of Calbuco (2,015 m), and the spike of Puntiagudo (2,480 m), as well as, when the air is clear, the distant Tronador (3,460 m). On a clear night with a full moon, the snows reflect eerily in the lake and the peace and stillness are hard to match.

The second largest lake in Chile and the third largest natural lake in South America

The largest towns, Puerto Varas, Llanquihue and Frutillar are all on the western shore, linked by the Pan-American Highway. Although there are roads around the rest of the lake the eastern shore is difficult to visit without transport: from Puerto Octay the eastern lakeside, with the Osorno volcano on your left, to Ensenada is very beautiful, but the road is narrow with lots of blind corners, necessitating speeds of 20-30 kph at best in places (see below). There is almost no public transport on this section and hitching is very difficult.

Ins & outs
Camping wild and having barbecues are forbidden on the lake shore

Puerto Octay

Puerto Octay is a small town at the north tip of the lake set amid rolling hills, hedgerows, German-style farmhouses and views over the Osorno volcano. Founded by German settlers in 1851, the town enjoyed a boom period in the late 19th century when it was the northern port for steamships on the lake: a few buildings survive from that period, notably the church and the enormous German-style former convent. Since the arrival of railways and the building of roads, the town has declined.

Phone code: 064
Colour map 4, grid B2
Population: 2,000
56 km southeast of Osorno

Lago Llanquihue

The Lake District

About 3 km south along an unpaved road is the **Peninsula of Centinela** with accommodation, camping, a launch dock, bathing beaches, watersports. From the headland are fine views of the Osorno, Calbuco and Puntiagudo volcanoes; a very popular spot in good weather. ■ *Getting there: taxi US$2.50 one way*. The *Hotel Centinela*, idyllically situated, was built in 1913 as a summer mansion. Much less busy than Frutillar or Puerto Varas, Puerto Octay offers an escape for those seeking peace and quiet.

Museums Museo el Colono has displays on German colonization. ■ *Tue-Sun 1500-1900, Dec-Feb only. Independencia 591.* Another part of the museum, housing agricultural implements and machinery for making *chicha*, is just outside town on the road to Centinela.

Sleeping and eating C *Haase*, Pedro Montt 344, T391193. With breakfast, attractive old building. **D** *Hosp Fogón de Anita*, 1 km out of town, T391325. Good breakfast. **D** pp *Hotel Centinela*, T391326. Run down but with superb views, also *cabañas*, restaurant with grand minstrels' gallery and bar, open all year. After abdicating, British king Edward VIII stayed here with his paramour Mrs Simpson. **D** *Posada Gubernatis*, Santiago s/n, lakeside. Clean, comfortable. **E** *Hosp Raquel Mardorf*, Germán Wulf 712. With enormous breakfast, clean, comfortable, owners have *Restaurante La Cabaña* at No 713. Good. *Restaurante Baviera*, Germán Wulf 582. Cheap and good. **F** *Hosp La Naranja*, Independencia 361. Without bath, with breakfast, restaurant, good views. **F** *Hostería La Baja*, Casilla 116, T391269. Beautifully situated at the neck of the peninsula, with breakfast and bath. **F** *Zapato Amarilla*, 35-mins' walk north of town, T/F391575, www.zapatoamarillo.8k.com Good for backpackers, clean, use of kitchen, good breakfast with home-made bread, English and German spoken, friendly, bicycle and canoe rental, luggage storage, phone for free pick up from town. House has a grass roof. Recommended. **Camping** *El Molino*, beside lake. US$5 pp, clean, friendly, recommended. Municipal site on lakeside, US$15 per site, T391326.

Transport **Buses** to **Osorno** 7 a day, US$2. To **Frutillar** (1 hr, US$0.90), **Puerto Varas** (2 hrs) and **Puerto Montt** (3 hrs, every 30 mins, US$2) *Thaebus*. To **Las Cascadas** (see below) Mon-Fri 1700, return next day 0600. To **Ensenada** 0600, daily in season, less frequent out of season.

East of Puerto Octay From Puerto Octay the road runs along the eastern shore of the lake to Ensenada. At Km 10 is Playa Maitén, 'highly recommended, nice beach, marvellous view to the Volcán Osorno, no tourists'. Continue for another 24 km and you'll reach **Las Cascadas**, surrounded by picturesque agricultural land, old houses and German cemeteries. There are attractive waterfalls in a gorge.

Sleeping and eating *Centro de Recreación Las Cascadas*, T235377. **F** *Hostería Irma*, on lake, 2 km past Las Cascadas, run by Tres Marías. Attractive former residence, good food, very pleasant. Several farms on the road around north and east side of the lake offer accommodation, look for signs. Camping *Centro de Recreación Las Cascadas* and *Villa Las Cascadas* picnic area (free); at Playa Maitén. Recommended.

Frutillar

Lying about half-way along the western side of the lake, Frutillar is in fact two towns: Frutillar Alto, just off the main highway, and Frutillar Bajo, beautifully situated on the lakeside, 4 km away.

Frutillar Bajo is possibly the most attractive – and expensive – town on the lake; its feel is very much German, and a little snobbish. From its *costanera* there are superb views over the water with Volcan Osorno and Mount Tronador in the background. There is a large open-air chess board in the square outside the *Club Alemán*. At the northern end of the town is the **Reserva Forestal Edmundo Winckler**, run by the Universidad de Chile and extending over 33 ha, with a guided trail through native woods. Named after one of the early German settlers, it includes a very good collection of native flora as well as plants introduced from Europe.

Museo Colonial Alemán, set in spacious gardens, includes a watermill, which does not turn, replicas of two German colonial houses with furnishings and utensils of the period and a blacksmith's shop with personal engravings on horseshoes for US$5. It also has a *campanario*, which is a circular barn with agricultural machinery and carriages inside, as well as gardens and a handicraft shop. It is well worth a visit. ■ *Daily 1000-1930 summer, Tue-Sun 1000-1330, 1500-1800 winter, US$2.*

Colectivos run between the two towns, five minutes, US$0.50

Frutillar Bajo

North of Frutillar Bajo L *Salzburg*, T421589. Excellent restaurant, sauna, mountain bikes, arranges tours and fishing. **AL** *Hostal Cinco Robles*, Casilla 100, T421351. With breakfast, other meals on request, parking. **A-B** *3 Los Maitenes*, 3 km north, T/F339130, hosterialosmaool@chilnet.cl

Frutillar Bajo A *Casona del 32*, Caupolicán 28, T421369. Casilla 101. With breakfast, comfortable old house, central heating, English and German spoken. Recommended. **On Philippi: A** *Klein Salzburg*, No 663, T421201. **A** *Residenz/Café am See*, No 539. Good breakfast. **C** *Hosp El Arroyo*, No 989, T421560. With breakfast. Highly recommended. **C-D** *Hosp Costa Azul*, No 1175, T421388. Mainly for families, good breakfasts. **C** *No 451*, T421204, clean, good breakfast. **C** *Winkler*, No 1155, T421388. Discount to Hostelling International members, cabins, friendly. Recommended. **D** pp *Hosp Vivaldi*, No 851, T421382. Sra Edith Klesse, quiet, comfortable, excellent breakfast and lodging, also family accommodation. Recommended. **D** pp *Kaisersee Hause*, No 1333, T421387, **F** without bath. **D** *Las Rocas*, No 1235, T421397. With breakfast. **D** *Hosp Trayén*, No 963, T421346. Basic, clean. **E** pp *Nohelia*, Phillippi 615, T421310, with

Sleeping
on map, page 357
Price codes: see inside front cover

During the annual music festival accommodation should be booked well in advance; alternatively stay in Frutillar Alto or Puerto Varas

Sleeping
1 Casona del 32
2 Hospedaje Costa Azul
3 Hospedaje El Arroyo
4 Hospedaje Tía Clara
5 Hospedaje Trayén
6 Hospedaje Vivaldi
7 Kaisersee Hause
8 Klein Salzburg
9 Las Rocas
10 Nohelia
11 Pérez Rosales 451
12 Pérez Rosales 590
13 Residenz/Café am See
14 Winkler

● **Eating**
1 Andes
2 Casino de Bomberos
3 Club Alemán

German colonization in Llanquihue

The most important area of German agricultural colonization in Chile was around Lago Llanquihue. The Chilean government declared the area as destined for colonization in 1845, and appointed Vicente Pérez Rosales to encourage settlement. Rosales travelled to Lago Llanquihue in 1851 and tried to sail around the lake in a dugout; it sank and, though he swam to safety, his companion drowned.

To encourage settlement and help the new arrivals get started the government gave each adult male 75 cuadras of land plus an extra 12 cuadras for each son, a milking cow, 500 planks of timber, nails, a yoke of oxen, a year's free medical assistance and medicines and Chilean citizenship on request.

The first groups of German colonists arrived in the area in 1852: one group settled around Maitén and Puerto Octay, another helped found Puerto Montt. The lives of these early settlers were hard and the risks great: in cutting a path between Puerto Montt and Lago Llanquihue, two young settlers strayed from the others and were never seen again. Yet within 10 years the settlers had cleared much of the forest round the lake and soon they were setting up small industries. In 1880, when the offer to colonists ended, unsettled land was auctioned in lots of 400-800 ha. By then the lake was ringed by a belt of smallholdings and farms. The legacy of this settlement can be seen in the German-looking farmhouses around Puerto Octay and in many of the older buildings in Frutillar and Puerto Varas.

bath. **On Perez Rosales**: Also **D** No 590, excellent breakfast. Also *Hosp Tia Clara*, **F** pp, No 743, T421806, kitchen facilities, very friendly, good value. Recommended.

Services such as shopping are much better here than in Frutillar Bajo

Frutillar Alto E *Faralito*, Winkler 245. Hot water, cooking facilities (owner can be contacted at shop at Winkler 167, T421440). **F** *Hosp Juana Paredes*, Anibal Pinto y Winkler, T421407, recommended, also *cabañas*, **B**, sleep 5, parking. Several along Carlos Richter (main street), including **F** at No 245, T412546. Cheap accommodation in the school in Frutillar Alto (**G-H**), sleeping bag required.

Camping *Los Ciruelillos*, 2 km south, T339123. Most services. *Playa Maqui*, 7 km north of Frutillar, T339139. Fancy, expensive. Try also Sr Guido González, Casa 3, Población Vermont, T421385. **G**. Recommended.

Eating
● *on maps, pages 357 and*

Mid-range *Andes*, Philippi 1057, good set menus and à la carte. *Club Alemán*, Av Philippi 747. Good but not cheap, hostile to backpackers. *Selva Negra*, Varas 24 y Philippi, in a traditional German mill, with scores of toy witches hanging from the ceiling. Open 1100-2300. **Cheap/Seriously cheap** *Casino de Bomberos*, Philippi 1060. Upstairs bar/restaurant, best value, open all year, memorable painting caricaturing the firemen in action. **Cafés** Several German-style cafés and tea-rooms on Calle Philippi, eg *Salón de Te Frutillar*, No 775. Also *Der Volkladen*, O'Higgins y Philippi. Natural products, chocolates and cakes, natural cosmetics.

Festivals In late **Jan to early Feb** there is a highly regarded classical music festival.

Tour companies *Viajes Frutillar*, Richter y Alissandre in Alto Frutillar. Run tours.

Transport **Bus** to Puerto Varas (US$0.75) and **Puerto Montt** (US$1.25), frequent, *Varmontt* and *Full Express*. To Osorno, *Turismosur* 1¼ hrs, US$1.50. To **Puerto Octay**, *Thaebus*, 6 a day. Most buses leave from opposite the *Copec* station in Alto Frutillar. For **car** repairs, *Toirkens*, Los Carrera 1260, highly recommended.

The Lake District

Banks *Banco Santander*, on Phillippi, at the lakeside. *Redbanc* ATM taking Visa and other cards. **Communications Post office**: San Martín y Pérez Rosales, Mon-Fri 0930-1230, 1430-1800, Sat 0900-1230. **Telephone**: call centre at Phillippi 883. **Useful services** Toilet, showers and changing cabins for beach on O'Higgins. *Cema-Chile* shop, Phillippi y O'Higgins. **Directory**

Twenty kilometres south of Frutillar, Llanquihue lies at the source of the Río Maullín which drains the lake. The site of a large dairy processing factory, it is the least touristy town on the lake and offers uncrowded beaches and a cheaper alternative to Puerto Varas and Frutillar. There is a German-style beer festival at the end of January with German music. **Llanquihue** *Phone code: 065*

Sleeping A *Siete Lagos*, Errázurriz 132, T242020. **B** *El Cisne*, M Montt s/n, T242726. *Cabañas*. *Posada Alemana*, Errázuriz 517, T242629. Several *hospedajes*. **Camping** North of Llanquihue are Baumbach, Km 1, T242643, on lakeside, meals available. *Playa Werner*, Km 2, T242114, on lakeside. *El Totoral*, Km 8, T339123, also *cabañas*.

Puerto Varas

Situated on the southwestern corner of the lake, Puerto Varas is the commercial and tourist centre of Lago Llanquihue and a residential centre for Puerto Montt, 20 km to the south. In the 19th century, it was the southern port for shipping on the lake; it is now an expensive resort, popular with Argentine tourists. Despite the numbers of visitors, though, it has a friendly, compact feel, and is one of the best bases for exploring the southern Lake District, near centres for trekking, rafting, canyoning and fly fishing. *Phone code: 065 Colour map 4, grid C2 Population: 16,000*

Getting there Puerto Varas is served by many buses from Puerto Montt; there are also connections north to Osorno, and some on to Valdivia and Temuco. **Getting around** Puerto Varas is a small town, and easily navigable on foot. **Tourist office** On pier on lakefront, T237272, turismo@telsur.cl Jan-Feb: 0800-2200 every day, otherwise Mon-Sat 0800-2000. **Ins & outs** *See page 362 for further details*

Sights

Parque Philippi, on top of a hill, is a pleasant place to visit; walk up to *Hotel Cabañas del Lago* on Klenner, cross the railway and the gate is on the right. The views are a bit restricted by trees and the metal cross at the top is unattractive (so is the electric clock which, during daylight hours, chimes the quarter-hours in town). The centre lies at the foot of the hill, but the town stretches east along the lake to Puerto Chico where there are hotels and restaurants. The Catholic church, in monumental Baroque style, built by German Jesuits in 1918, is a copy of the church in Marieenkirche in the Black Forest; worth a visit. North and east of the **Gran Hotel Puerto Varas** (1934) are a number of German-style mansions dating from the early 20th century.

Excursions

Puerto Varas is a good base for trips around the lake. A paved road runs along the south shore to Ensenada on the southwestern corner of the lake. Two of the best beaches are Playa Hermosa, Km 7 and Playa Niklitschek, Km 8, where an entry fee is charged. **La Poza**, at Km 16, is a little lake to the south of Lago

The Lake District

Llanquihue reached through narrow channels overhung with vegetation. **Isla Loreley**, an island on La Poza, is very beautiful, frequent boat trips, US$1.50. A concealed channel leads from La Poza to yet another lake, the Laguna Encantada. At Km 21 there is a watermill being converted into a museum. For the continuation of this road to Ensenada and for transport between Puerto Varas and Ensenada, see below.

Essentials

Sleeping
■ on map page 361
Price codes:
see inside front cover

L *Colonos del Sur*, Del Salvador 24, T233369, F233394. Good views of the lake, decent rooms, good restaurant, tea-room. **L** *Los Alerces*, Pérez Rosales 1281, T233039. 4-star, with breakfast, new cabin complex, attractive. **AL** *Antonio Varas*, Del Salvador 322, T232375, F232352. Very comfortable. **AL** *Cabañas del Lago*, Klenner 195, T232291, F232707. On Philippi hill overlooking lake, superb views. Also self-catering *cabañas* sleeping 5 (good value for groups), cheaper rates in low season, heating, sauna. **AL** *Licarayén*, San José 114, T232305, F232955. Overlooking lake, comfortable, 'enthusiastically recommended'. Book in season, **C** out of season, clean, friendly, 'the perfect place for bad weather or being ill'.

There are many hotels all along lake front, but in high season they tend to be tourist traps **A** *Bellavista*, Pérez Rosales 60, T232011, F232013. Cheerful, recommended, restaurant, overlooking lake. **A** *Cabañas Amancay*, Walker Martínez 564. With breakfast, German spoken, sleep 4. Recommended. **A** *Cabañas Ayentemo*, Pérez Rosales 1297. Clean, comfortable, friendly, T/F232270. **A** *Del Bosque*, Santa Rosa 714, T232897, F236000. With breakfast, recommended. **A** *El Greco*, Mirador 134, T233388. Modern, good. **A** *Terrazas del Lago*, Pérez Rosales 1571, T/F232622, good breakfast, views over Osorno volcano, restaurant. **B** *Agatha Haus*, Route 5 on southern outskirts, very relaxed, German spoken. **B** *Hotel Loreley*, Maipo 911, T232226. Homely, quiet. Recommended. **B** *Motel Altué*, Pérez Rosales 1679, T232294. With breakfast. **C** *Hostal Chancerel*, Decher 400, T/F234221. Also offers tours. **D** pp, Andrés Bello 321. Nice atmosphere, good breakfast. **D** *Hosp Carla Minte*, Maipo 1010, T232880. With breakfast, cable TV, very comfortable. **D** pp *Hosp Las Carmelas*, Imperial y Rosario. Excellent, helpful, good meals, lends books including some in English. Highly recommended. **D** pp *Hostal Erika*, Maipa 0290, T233760. Also *cabañas*. **D** *María Schilling Rosas*, La Quebrada 752. Recommended.

E pp *Hospedaje AMAC*, San Bernardo 313, T234216. Apartment style accommodation, clean, comfortable, heating in lounge, TV, use of kitchen, hot water. **E** *Hosp Ellenhaus*, Walker Martínez 239, T233577. Kitchen and laundry facilities, luggage stored, lounge, hospitable, highly recommended. **E** *Hosp Imperial*, Imperial 0653, T232451. Clean, including breakfast, central, recommended. Several other family *hospedajes* on same street. **E** *Hosp Las Rosas*, Santa Rosa 560, T232770, new owner. **E** pp *The Outsider*, San Bernardo 318, T/F232910, www.campo-aventura.com With bath, real coffee, meals, friendly, comfortable, also horseback trekking, rafting, sea kayaking, climbing. German and English spoken. **E** *Res Alemana*, San Bernardo 416, T232419. With breakfast, without bath, clean. **E** pp *Rincón Aleman*, San Francisco 1004, T232087. **E** pp *Villa Germania*, Nuestra Sra del Carmen 873, T233162. Also *cabañas*.

F *Casa Azul*, Mirador 18, Calle Imperial, T232904, www.casaazul.net German/Chilean owners, homemade muesli for breakfast, kitchen facilities, good beds with duvets, internet, book exchange, English and German spoken, tours organised, friendly, helpful. Highly recommended. **F** *Colores del Sur*, Santa Rosa 318, T338588. Dormitory accommodation without breakfast, good meeting place. **F** *Compas del Sur*, Klenner 467, T232044, mauro98@telsur.net Chilean-Swedish run, kitchen facilities, internet, cable TV, breakfast with muesli and real coffee, friendly, helpful, German, English, Swedish spoken. **F** *Elsa Pinto*, Verbo Divino 427. Clean. **F** *Hosp Don Raúl*, Salvador 928, T234174. Laundry and cooking facilities, very friendly, garden with hammock, clean. Recommended. Camping by main road **G**. **F** *Maria Angélica Banda*, Del Salvador 1026. With breakfast, meals served. **F** *Pío Nono 474*, T233172. With breakfast.

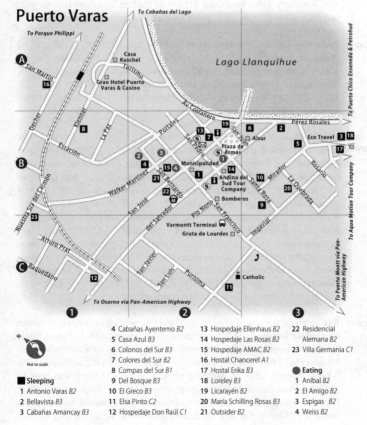

Puerto Varas

To Cabañas del Lago

To Parque Philippi

Lago Llanquihue

To Puerto Chico Ensenada & Petrohué

Casa Kuschel

Gran Hotel Puerto Varas & Casino

Av Costanera

Pérez Rosales

Portales

Alsur

Eco Travel

Plaza de Armas

Municipalidad

Andina del Sud Tour Company

Bomberos

Varmontt Terminal
Gruta de Lourdes

Catholic

To Osorno via Pan-American Highway

To Aqua Motion Tour Company

To Puerto Montt via Pan-American Highway

Not to scale

4	Cabañas Ayentemo *B2*
5	Casa Azul *B3*
6	Colonos del Sur *B3*
7	Colores del Sur *B2*
8	Compas del Sur *B1*
9	Del Bosque *B3*
10	El Greco *B3*
11	Elsa Pinto *C2*
12	Hospedaje Don Raúl *C1*
13	Hospedaje Ellenhaus *B2*
14	Hospedaje Las Rosas *B2*
15	Hospedaje AMAC *B2*
16	Hostal Chancerel *A1*
17	Hostal Erika *B3*
18	Loreley *B3*
19	Licarayén *B2*
20	María Schilling Rosas *B3*
21	Outsider *B2*
22	Residencial Alemana *B2*
23	Villa Germania *C1*

■ **Sleeping**
1 Antonio Varas *B2*
2 Bellavista *B3*
3 Cabañas Amancay *B3*

● **Eating**
1 Aníbal *B2*
2 El Amigo *B2*
3 Espigas *B2*
4 Weiss *B2*

The Lake District

Camping On south shore of Lago Llanquihue east of Puerto Varas: Km 7, *Playa Hermosa*, T Puerto Varas 338283, Puerto Montt 252223, fancy, US$23 per site, bargain off season. Recommended. Take own supplies. Km 8, *Playa Niklitschek*, T338352, full facilities. Km 10, *Los Troncos*, US$10 per site, no beach access. Km 20, *Playa Venado*.

Eating **Expensive** *Merlin*, Imperial 0605, T233105, F234300, www.merlinrestaurant.cl An excellent restaurant, one of the best in the Lake District. Highly recommended. **Mid-range** At the Puerto Chico end of Pérez Rosales are Dicorazzo, No 01071, recommended. *Espigas*, Martínez 417, local 3. Vegetarian. *Ibis*, No 1117. Expensive motel restaurants just beyond it aren't worth visiting, although service is friendly. **Cheap** *Aníbal*, Del Salvador y Santa Rosa, Italian, cheap, tasty. *Domino*, Del Salvador 450. Good, cheap. *Donde El Gordito*, downstairs in market, immense portions, no set menu, mixed reports. *El Amigo*, San Bernardo 240. Large portions, good value. Warmly recommended. *Restaurant La Olla*, San Bernado y Martinez, seafood, traditional Chilean food. Recommended. *Weiss*, San José 415. Good value, very good meat, seriously cheap. *Rancho Chico*, on San Francisco opposite the church, menus for US$300. **Cafés** *Café Danés*, Del Salvador 441. Good coffee and cakes. *Coffee Break*, San José 319, real coffee. *El Molino*, café next to an old water mill, on road to Ensenada 22 km east.

Shopping **Supermarkets** *Las Brisas*, Salvador 451. *VYH Meistur*, Walker Martínez. Good selection, reasonably priced. **Bookshop** *El Libro del Capitán*, Martiínez 417, book swap, large selection in German and English. **Chocolates** *Mamusia*, San José 316.

Sports **Cycle hire** *Thomas Held Expeditions*, Martínez 239, T/F311889. US$20 per day. *Travel Art*, Imperial 0661, T232198. Check equipment carefully. **Fishing** The area around Puerto Varas is popular for fishing. Licence (obligatory) obtainable from the Municipalidad. Fishing expeditions are organized by Quiroz Hnos, Estación 230, T233771, 235693. **Horse riding** *Cabañas Puerto Decher* at the Fundo Molino Viejo, 2 km north, T338033. Guided tours, horseriding, minimum 2 persons. See below.

Tour companies
Most tours operate in season only (1 Sep-15 Apr)
Alsur, Del Salvador 100, T/F232300, alsur@telsur.cl Rafting on Rió Petrohue. Good camping equipment, tours. *Andina del Sud*, Del Salvador 72, T232511. Operate 'lakes' trip to Bariloche, Argentina via Lago Todos los Santos, Peulla, Cerro Tronador (see under Puerto Montt, To Argentina), plus other excursions, good. Also *Eco Travel*, Av Costanera s/n, T233222. *Austral Explorations*, French/Chilean run, offers bike hire, white-water rafting and sea kayaking, San José 308, T346433, richard@whitewater.chile.ms, also has an internet café. *Aqua Motion*, San Pedro 422, T/F232747, paulina@aquamotion.cl rafting, trekking, mountain biking, fishing. Also ethnoastronomical tours based in La Serena, reservations best made 1 month ahead, clear weather vital. Outsider, *San Bernardo 318*, T232710, English and German spoken, offer 1, 3 and 10-day trips on horseback (see below under Cochamó). Several others. *Tranco Expeditions*, Santa Rosa 190. Imperial 0699, T/F232747, for trekking, rafting and climbing, Norwegian and English spoken, good equipment.

Transport **Bus** Varmontt terminal, San Francisco 500 block. To **Santiago**, *Varmontt, Igi Llaima, Cruz del Sur* and others, US$21, *semi cama* US$34, *cama* US$44. To **Puerto Montt**, 30 mins, *Varmontt* and *Full Express* every 15 mins, US$0.50; same companies, same frequency to Frutillar (US$0.75, 30 mins) and **Osorno** (US$3, 1 hr). To **Valdivia** US$6, 3 hrs to **Temuco**, US$8. To **Bariloche**, services from Puerto Montt stop here. For **Andina del Sud** via Lago Todas Los Santos, see under Puerto Montt. To **Cochamó** via Ensenada, 5 a day, US$2. Minibuses to **Ensenada** and **Petrohué** leave from San Bernardo y Martínez. **Car hire** *Adriazola Expediciones*, Santa Rosa 340, T233477. *Turismo Nieve*, Gramado 560, T346115.

Banks *Redbancs* at following: *BBV Banco Bhif*, San Pedro 326; *De Chile*, Salvador 201; **Directory**
Del Estado, Santa Rosa 414; *Santiago*, San José 291. Exchange also at *Banco Osorno*,
Del Salvador 399. Good rates. *Casas de cambio: Exchange Ltda*, Del Salvador 257, local
11. *Travel Sur*, San José 261, local 4. *Turismo Los Lagos*, Del Salvador 257 (Galería Real,
local 11). Open daily 0830-1330, 1500-2100, Sun 0930-1330, accepts TCs, good rates.
Camera and film *Foto Kodak*, on Del Salvador. *Foto Master*, San José 301. **Commu-
nications** Internet: *Ciber Service*, Salvador 264, local 6-A, and *George's*, San Ignacio
574; also at Gramado 560, piso 2, and San José 380, piso 2. See also *Austral
Expediciones*, above under tour companies. **Post office:** San José y San Pedro. Del Salvador y Santa Rosa. **Telephone:** *Bellsouth*, San Bernardo 555; *CTC*, Salvador 320; *del
Sur*, Del Salvador 314; *Entel*, San José 314. **Laundry** At Gramado 1090, or *Lavandería
Delfin*, Martínez 323, expensive. **Medical emergencies** Otto Bader 810, T346336.

Ensenada

Despite its lack of a recognizable centre, Ensenada is beautifully situated at the   *Phone code: 065*
southeast corner of Lago Llanquihue, almost beneath the snows of Volcán   *Colour map 4, grid C2*
Osorno. Before you reach Ensenada, coming from Puerto Varas, is the *Hotel*   *47 km east of*
El Pilar, **D/E** pp. *Cabañas* are situated away from the road with good views of   *Puerto Varas*
Volcan Osorno and good service. A good half-day trip from Ensenada itself is
to **Laguna Verde**, about 30 minutes from *Hotel Ensenada*, along a beautiful
circular trail behind the lake (take first fork to the right behind the information board), and then down the road to a secluded campsite at Puerto Oscuro
on Lago Llanquihue.

AL *Cabañas Brisas del Lago*, T212012. On beach, sleep 6, good restaurant nearby,   **Sleeping**
supermarket next door. Highly recommended. **AL** *Ensenada*, Casilla 659, Puerto
Montt, T/F212018. With bath, olde-worlde, good food (closed in winter), good view of
lake and Volcán Osorno, runs tours, hires mountain bikes (guests only). Also *hostal* in
the grounds, cooking facilities, much cheaper but not that cheap. **B** *Cabañas Villa
Ensenada*, T212070, sleeps 4. Bargain off season. **C** *Hosp Arena*, T212037. With breakfast. Recommended. **D** *Hosp Ensenada*, T338278. Very clean, excellent breakfast,
E off-season. Recommended. **D** *Hosp Opazo*, with breakfast, friendly. **F** *Hosp*, above
Toqui grocery. Cheapest in town, basic, quiet, hot water, use of kitchen, beach in the
back yard, recommended. About 2 km from town is **C** *Pucará*, also with good restaurant (the steaks are recommended). **E** pp *Ruedas Viejas*, T/F212050, for room, or **D** in
cabañas; about 1 km west from Ensenada, Hostelling International reductions, basic,
damp, hot water, restaurant. **Camping** *Montaña*, central Ensenada, **F**, per site, good
beach space. *Trauco*, 4 km west, T212033. Large site with shops, fully equipped,
US$4-9 pp. Also at Playa Larga, 1 km east of *Hotel Ensenada*, US$10 and at Puerto
Oscuro, 2 km north, US$8.

Canta Rana, recommended for bread and *kuchen*. *Ruedas Viejas*, the cheapest.   **Eating**
Donde Juanito, Km 44, excellent value cheap set lunch. Several shop selling basic
supplies. Most places closed off season, other than a few pricey shops – take your
own provisions.

Patagonia Adventures, T212030, F212031. *Southern Chile Expeditions*, T213030.   **Tour**
Guide: Ludwig Godsambassis, owner of *Ruedas Viejas*, who works for *Aqua Motion* in   **companies**
season, works independently as a trekking guide out of season and is very knowledgeable about flora and fauna.

The Lake District

Transport Minibuses run from Puerto Varas, frequent in summer. Buses from Puerto Montt via Puerto Varas to **Cochamó** also stop here. Hitching from Puerto Varas is difficult.

Directory **Communications** Internet at *Yessely*.

Volcán Osorno

Colour map 4, grid C2 The most lasting image of Lago Llanquihue is the near perfect cone of the Volcán Osorno, situated north of Ensenada on the eastern edge of the lake. Although the peak lies on the edge of the Parque Nacional Pérez Rosales, it is climbed from the western side which is outside the park. Access is via two roads which branch off the Ensenada-Puerto Octay road along the eastern edge of Lago Llanquihue: one at Puerto Klocker, 20 km south of Puerto Octay; the other 2 km north of Ensenada.

Weather permitting, *Aqua Motion* (address under Puerto Varas), organize **climbing expeditions** with a local guide, transport from Puerto Montt or Puerto Varas, food and equipment, US$150 pp, payment in advance (minimum group of two, maximum of six with three guides) all year, setting out from the *refugio* at La Burbuja. They check weather conditions the day before and offer 50% refund if climb is abandoned due to weather. From La Burbuja it is six hours to the summit. Only experienced climbers should attempt to climb right to the top, ice climbing equipment essential. CONAF checks equipment and only allow experienced climbers to continue.

"Unlike many other volcanoes Osorno has some interesting ice climbing on crevasse walls and between high seracs (although you avoid the technical stuff if you go on a tour). Best for this are the southern and southeastern slopes. There is a large ice cave on the north slope." Simon Harvey

Sleeping and eating There are three *refugios*, two of them south of the summit and reached from the southern access road: *La Burbuja*, the former ski-club centre 14 km north of Ensenada (1,250 m) and the *Refugio Teski Ski Club*, just below the snow line, **E** pp, meals served. On the northern slopes, 20 km east of Puerto Klocker is the *Refugio La Picada* (950 m), **E** pp.

Parque Nacional Vicente Pérez Rosales

Colour map 4, grid C2 *Established in 1926, this is the oldest national park in Chile, stretching east from Lago Llanquihue to the Argentine frontier. It contains a large lake, Lago Todos Los Santos and three major volcanic peaks: Osorno, Puntiagudo and Tronador. Several other peaks are visible, notably Casablanca to the north and Calbuco to the south. The park is covered in woodland, and is very beautiful; near the lake are the Saltos de Petrohué, impressive waterfalls on the Río Petrohué.*

Ins & outs Entrance to the park is free. CONAF office in Petrohué with a visitors' centre, small
See page 367 for museum and 3D model of the park. There is a *guardaparque* office in Puella. No maps of
transport details treks are available in the park. The park is infested by *tábanos* in Dec and Jan: cover up as much as possible with light coloured clothes which may help a bit. In wet weather many treks in the park are impossible and the road to Puerto Montt can be blocked.

The Lake District

Lago Todos los Santos is a long, irregularly shaped sheet of water. The waters are emerald green; the shores are deeply wooded and several small islands rise from its surface. Beyond the hilly shores to the east are several graceful snow-capped mountains, with the mighty Tronador in the distance. To the north is the sharp point of Cerro Puntiagudo, and at the northeastern end Cerro Techado rises cliff-like out of the water. The lake is fed by several rivers, including the Río Peulla to the east, the Ríos Techado and Negro to the north, and the Río Blanco to the south. At its western end the lake is drained by the Río Petrohue. The ports of **Petrohué** at its western and **Peulla** at its eastern ends are connected by boat. Sheltered from the winds, the lake is warm and is a popular location for water sports and swimming. Trout and salmon fishing are excellent in several parts including Petrohué. There are no roads round it and only people with houses on the lake are allowed boats on it. The only scheduled vessel on the lake is the Andino del Sud service with connections to Bariloche (Argentina), but private launches can be hired for trips. **Isla Margarita**, the largest island on the lake, with a lagoon in the middle of it, can be visited (in summer only) from Petrohué.

Lago Todos los Santos
The most beautiful of all the lakes in southern Chile

Petrohué, 16 km northwest of Ensenada, is a good base for walking tours around the foot of Volcàn Osorno, or for lookouts over it, eg Cerro Picada. Near the Ensenada-Petrohué road, 6 km west of Petrohué, is the **Salto de Petrohué**. The falls were formed by a relatively recent lava flow of hard volcanic rock. ■ *US$1.50. Near the falls is a snack bar; there are also 2 short trails, the* Sendero de los Enamorados *and the* Sendero Carileufú.

Petrohué

Parque Nacional Pérez Rosales & the lakes route to Argentina

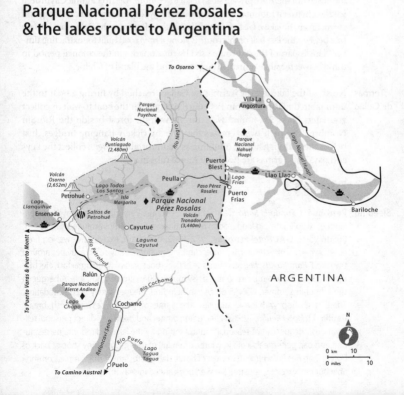

The Lake District

Reaching the top

Tronador, 3,460 m, offers many technical possibilities, with both easy and difficult stretches on the upper slopes. It is usually climbed from the Argentine side. There is no road on the Chilean side, so a three-day hike is required to go there and back. From Peulla, it is a 29-km walk along the pretty road to Puerto Frias; then a six to seven-hour hike south to Paso de las Nubes, on the east side of Tronador. Glaciers on the western (Chilean) slopes pose safety problems. There is a basic hut on the Chilean side.

Puntiagudo, 2,490 m, is the most distinctive peak in the Lake District, as a result of its sharp volcanic plug summit which is much steeper than the lower slopes. Only ever climbed a few times, it poses considerable climbing problems because of the 75-90° upper slopes and the very poor loose rock, though it may be easier in winter when there is more snow and ice. The southern side is the most difficult. Access is from the northern side of Lago Todos Los Santos or from the southern side of Lago Rupanco.

Peulla Peulla is a good starting point for hikes in the mountains. The *Cascadas Los Novios*, signposted above the *Hotel Peulla*, are a steep walk, but are stunning once you reach them. There is also a good walk to Laguna Margarita which takes four hours. Take water.

Cayutué On the south shore of Lago Todos Los Santos is the little village of Cayutué, reached by hiring a boat from Petrohué, US$30. From Cayutué (no camping on the beach but there are private sites) it is a three-hour walk to **Laguna Cayutué**, a jewel set between mountains and surrounded by forest. Here you can camp and swim. From the lake it is a five-hour hike south to Ralún on the Reloncaví Estuary (see below): the last half of this route is along a *ripio* road built for extracting timber. This is part of the old route used by missionaries in the colonial period to travel between Nahuel Huapi in Argentina and the island of Chiloé.

Termas de Callao North of the lake are the Termas de Callao, reached by hiring a boat to the uninhabited El Rincón from Petrohué. Arrange for the boat to wait or collect you later. "It is 3½-hours' walk through virgin forest beside the Río Sin Nombre. The path twice crosses the river by rickety hanging bridges. Just before the baths is a house, doubling as a comfortable *refugio*: collect the keys and pay. The Termas are two large Alerce tubs in a cabin."

Essentials

Sleeping **Petrohué** L *Fundo El Salto*, near Salto de Petrohué. Very friendly, run by New Zealanders, mainly a fishing lodge, good home cooking, fishing trips arranged. Casilla 471, Puerto Varas. **L-AL** *Hotel Petrohué*, T/F258042. With bath, excellent views, log fires, cosy; owner, Franz Schirmer, a former climbing guide, can advise on activities around the lake. **F** *Familia Küschel*, on other side of river (boat across). With breakfast, electricity only 3 hrs in evening, dirty (rats), noisy, poor value, camping possible. Albergue in the school in summer. CONAF office can help find cheaper family accommodation. There is a shop with basic supplies and some of the houses sell fresh bread. **Peulla** LL *Hotel Peulla*, T258041, including dinner and breakfast, direct personal reservations, cheaper out of season. Beautiful setting by the lake and mountains, restaurant and bar, poor meals, cold in winter, often full of tour groups (tiny shop at back of hotel). **E** pp *Res Palomita*, 50 m west of hotel. Half board, family-run, simple, comfortable but not spacious, separate shower, book ahead in season, lunches.

Petrohué Camping: at Petrohué on far side beside the lake, US$4 per site, no services (local fishermen will ferry you across, US$0.50). At Peulla, opposite CONAF office, US$1.50. Ask the commander of the military garrison at the beach nearest the hotel if you can camp on the beach; no facilities. Good campsite 1¾ hrs' walk east of Peulla. Small shop in Andino del Sud building in Petrohué but best to take your own food.

Camping wild and picknicking is forbidden at Petrohué; car parking US$2 per day

Boats The *Andino del Sud* catamaran between Petrohué and Peulla costs US$30 day return or one way (book in advance); it leaves Petrohué at 1030, Peulla at 1500 (not Sun, 2 hrs – most seating indoors, no cars carried, cycles free), commentaries in Spanish and English. Take own refreshments as those sold on board are very expensive. This is the only public service across the lake and it connects with the Andina del Sud tour bus between Puerto Montt and Bariloche (see page 375). However, it is no longer possible to get a day return from Petrohué to Peulla; you have to stay overnight in Peulla, which is expensive. Local fishermen make the trip across the lake and for a group this can be cheaper than the public service, allow 3½ hrs. If planning to go to Bariloche in stages, book through to Bariloche in Petrohué, not Peulla because onward connections from Peulla may be full and the accommodation is not so good there. **Minibuses** From Puerto Varas to Ensenada continue to Petrohué, frequent in summer.

Transport
It is impossible to do this journey independently out of season: there are buses only as far as Ensenada, little traffic for hitching and none of the ferries takes vehicles

The lakes route to Bariloche

This popular route from Puerto Montt to Bariloche, involving ferries across Lago Todos Los Santos, Lago Frías and Lago Nahuel Huapi, is outstandingly beautiful.

The journey is as follows: by bus via **Puerto Varas**, **Ensenada** and the **Petrohué falls** (20 minutes stop) to **Petrohué**, where there is a connection with catamaran service (1¾ hours) across **Lago Todos Los Santos to Peulla**. Lunch stop in Peulla two hours (lunch not included in fare: *Hotel Peulla* is expensive, see above for alternatives). Chilean customs are in Peulla, followed by a two-hour bus ride through the **Paso Pérez Rosales** to Argentine customs in **Puerto Frías**, 20-minute boat trip across **Lago Frías** to **Puerto Alegre** and bus (15 minutes) from **Puerto Alegre** to **Puerto Blest**. From Puerto Blest it is a beautiful one-hour catamaran trip along **Lago Nahuel Huapi** to **Puerto Panuelo**, from where there is a one-hour bus journey to Bariloche (bus drops passengers at hotels, camping sites or in town centre).

This journey is operated only by *Andino del Sud* (see page 375). Bus from company offices in Puerto Montt daily at 0800; the fare is US$110 one way. From 1 May to 30 Aug this trip is done over 2 days with overnight stay in Peulla, add about US$89 to single fare for accommodation in *Hotel Peulla*. Baggage is taken to *Hotel Peulla* automatically but for alternative accommodation see above. If you have time, buy the boat sections in Puerto Montt or Puerto Varas and do the rest of the trip yourself (though this will probably involve walking sections since there is little transport for hitching).

Essentials
The trip may be cancelled if the weather is poor; there are reports of difficulty in obtaining a refund

Paso Pérez Rosales, Chilean immigration is in Peulla, 30 km west of the frontier, open summer 0800-2100, winter 0800-2000.

Border with Argentina

Bariloche is a popular destination and centre for exploring the Argentine Lake District. Beautifully situated on the south shore of Lago Nahuel Huapi, the streets rise steeply along the edge of a glacial morraine. West of the city on the shores of the lake is the resort of Llao Llao, where the famous *Hotel Llao Llao* looks out over chocolate box scenery. Nearby are two ski resorts and boat excursions can be made on the lake and to other parts of the Argentine Lake

Into Argentina
Population 77,750

The Lake District

District. There is a wide range of accommodation as well as air and bus connections to Buenos Aires and other destinations in Argentina. For more complete details see the *Argentina Handbook* or the *South American Handbook*.

The Reloncaví Estuary

The Reloncaví Estuary situated east of Puerto Montt and south of the Parque Nacional Pérez Rosales, is the northernmost of Chile's glacial inlets. It is quiet and beautiful, often shrouded in mist and softly falling rain, but stunning nonetheless, and recommended for its sea lions, dolphins and its peace. It is relatively easily reached from Puerto Montt by a road which runs along the wooded lower Petrohué valley south from Ensenada and then follows the eastern shore of the estuary for almost 100 km to join the Camino Austral.

Ralún
Colour map 4, grid C2

A small village situated at the northern end of the estuary, Ralún is 31 km southeast from Ensenada by a poorly paved road. On the outskirts of the village there are **thermal baths**. ■ *US$2, reached by boat, US$2.50 across the Río Petrohué*. Ralún is the departure point for a five-hour walk north to **Laguna Cayutué** in the Parque Nacional Vicente Pérez Rosales, see above. There is a village shop and post office. A road branches off and follows the western side of the estuary south, 36 km to Lago Chapo, giving access at the eastern end to Parque Nacional Alerce Andino (see page 409).

Sleeping and eating A *Cabañas Ralún*, T/F(065)-278286. **B** *Cabañas Villa Margarita*, Santiago T2361817. **F** *El Encuentro*. **F** *Navarrito*, restaurant and lodging. **F** *Restaurant el Refugio*, rents rooms. **G** *Posada Campesino*, simple, clean, without breakfast, very friendly. *The Hotel Ralún*, T/F233457, at south end of the village, which burnt down in 1992, has *cabañas*, **L**, sleep 6.

Transport Bus from Puerto Montt, 5 a day, *Bohle*, between 1000 and 1930, 4 on Sat, return 0700-1830, US$2.50; also 2 a day with *Buses Fierro*.

Cochamó
Population: 1,000
Colour map 4, grid C2

Some 17 km south of Ralún along a poor *ripio* road, on the east shore of the estuary, Cochamó is a pretty village situated in a striking setting, with the estuary and volcano behind. There is a fine wooden church similar to those on Chiloé, dating from 1900, which has an intriguing wooden clock with wooden hands; inside the church is a highly unusual black statue of Christ. There is also a small, frequently deserted waterfront, where there are benches from which you can sit and watch the sea and volcano.

Sleeping and eating E *Hosp Maura*, JJ Molina 12, beautifully situated, good food. **E** *Cochamó*, T216212. Basic but clean, friendly, often full with salmon farm workers, good meals, recommended, and a large number of *pensiones* (just ask), eg **F** *Mercado Particular Sabin*, Catedral 20, next to *Hotel*. **F** *Hosp Edicar*, without bath, spacious, recommended. **F** *Restaurant Copihue*. **Camping** *Camping Los Castaños*, T216212 (Reservations Casilla 576, Puerto Montt). Eateries include: *Donde Payi* opposite church. *Reloncaví*, on the road down to the waterfront. On the seafront there is a cheap fish/seafood restaurant, which also hires out canoes, US$1 for 30 mins.

Legend of Cochamó

It is said that when the Jesuits were expelled from Chile, many hid in Ancud, later to make their way across the Gulf of Ancud and up the Reloncavi Estuary and *then overland via Cochamó to Bariloche. Along the way they buried the valuables they were carrying, including hoards of gold, silver and coins.*

Entertainment Bars *Copihue*, JJ Molina 08. **Disco** *La Ola* at weekends.

Sports Horseriding (trekking with packhorses) *Campo Aventura* (Casilla 5, Correo Cochamó) T/F232910, www.campo-aventura.com Offer accommodation at their base camp, 4 km south of Cochamó, where there is a signpost on road (**F** pp, kitchen, sauna, camping), and at their other base, a renovated mountain house in the valley of La Junta. Camping is also possible. Specialises in horseback and trekking expeditions along the Gaucho trail between the Reloncaví Estuary and the Argentine frontier, 2-10 days; good guides, spectacular scenery, highly recommended – US$97 pp per day all in. English, French and German spoken, "best breakfast in Chile"; they have their own cow, so very fresh milk, herb garden, good food using local produce, vegetarian also available, book exchange, "living Spanish" classes. Joint **sea kayaking-horseriding** trips organised with *Austral Exploraciones* in Puerto Varas.

The Gaucho Trail east to Paso León on the Argentine frontier was used in the colonial period by indians and Jesuit priests and later by gauchos. The route runs along Río Cochamó to La Junta, then along the north side of Lago Vidal, passing waterfalls and the oldest surviving Alerce trees in Chile at El Arco. It takes three to four days by horse, five to six days on foot, depending on conditions (best done December-March). From the border crossing at Paso León it is a three-hour walk to the main road to San Carlos de Bariloche. **Gaucho Trail**

Further south, on the south bank of the Río Puelo, Puelo is a most peaceful place (ferry crossing). Accommodation is available at one of the restaurants, **G**, and with families – try Roberto and Olivia Telles, simple, clean, no bath/shower, meals on request, or Ema Hernández Maldona; two restaurants. From here the road continues 36 km further southwest to Puelche on the Camino Austral. There is also a wild horsetrail over towards El Bolsón in Argentina – seek advice locally. **Puelo**
Colour map 4, grid C2

Transport Bus *Buses Bohle* from Puerto Montt, Sun 0900 and 1500 via Puerto Varas (departure 30 mins later), **Ensenada**, **Ralún** and **Cochamó**. Departures from Cochamó Mon-Sat 0745 and 1645, Sun 1100 and 1500. The bridge over the Río Puelo is due to be completed soon, at which point the project of paving the whole stretch from Ralún to Puelo will be begun in earnest. At present, when arriving at the riverbank from Cochamó, ask for Tito, who will take you to Don Rene´s farm in his motor boat (US$9), from where it is a pleasant 5-km walk to Puelo. **Boat** In summer boats sail up the Estuary from Angelmó. Tours from Puerto Montt US$30. Off season the *Carmencita* sails once a week, leaving Puelo Sun 1000 and Angelmó Wed 0900 (advisable to take warm clothes, food and seasickness pills if windy).

Puerto Montt

Phone code: 065
Colour map 4, grid C2
Population: 110,139

The capital of Región X (Los Lagos), Puerto Montt lies on the northern shore of the Seno de Reloncaví 1,016 km south of Santiago. The jumping-off point for journeys south to Chiloé and Patagonia, it is a busy modern city, a good place to rest for a few days before or after undertaking more gruelling adventures in the south. It was founded in 1853 on the site of a Mapuche community known as Melipulli, meaning four hills, as part of the German colonization of the area. Good views over the city and bay are offered from outside the Intendencia Regional on Av X Region.

Ins and outs

Getting there There are several daily flights north to Santiago, Concepción and Temuco, and south to
See page 376 for Coyhaique and Punta Arenas. Ferries serve Chaitén (4 times weekly) and Puerto
further details Chacabuco (4 times weekly), as well as the weekly service south to Puerto Natales. Puerto Montt is also the departure point for bus services south to Coyhaique and Punta Arenas, and for buses north to Santiago and all the intermediate cities.

Getting around Puerto Montt is quite a large city, and there are many *colectivos* and buses serving the *barrios* on the hill above the town. The cental area is down by the port, though, and everything here is within walking distance.

Tourist offices *Sernatur* office in Gobernación Provincial building on Plaza de Armas, daily in summer 0900-1300, 1500-1900, Mon-Fri in winter 0830-1300, 1400-1800. Ask for information on Chiloé as this is often difficult to obtain on the island. Sernatur is in the Intendencia Regional, Av Décima Región 480 (p 3), Casilla 297, T254580. Also kiosk on Plaza de Armas run by the municipality, open till 1800 on Sat, town maps available, but little information on other places. *Telefónica del Sur* and *Sernatur* operate a phone information service: dial 142 (cost is the same as a local call); dial 149 for chemist/pharmacy information; 148 for the weather; 143 for the news, etc. The service operates throughout the Tenth Region. CONAF: Ochogavia 458, but cannot supply details of conditions in national parks. Automóvil Club de Chile: Esmeralda 70,

Sights

The **Plaza de Armas** lies at the foot of steep hills, one block north of Av Diego Portales, which runs east-west parallel to the shore. Two blocks west of the square is the **Iglesia de los Jesuitas** on Calle Gallardo, dating from 1872, which has a fine blue-domed ceiling; behind it on a hill is the **campanario** (clock tower).

The little fishing port of **Angelmó**, 2 km west along Av Diego Portales, has become a tourist centre. It has many seafood restaurants and handicraft shops and is very popular with Chileans. Anyone in any doubt as to the dangers of deforestation, and the accompanying threat of global warming, need only make for Angelmó, where there is an enormous mountain of wood chips which is shipped off to Japan every week, and then replenished. ■ *Buses and colectivos Nos 2, 3 and 20 ply the route, US$0.30 each.*

Museo Regional Juan Pablo II documents local history. It has a fine collection of historic photos of the city; also memorabilia of the Pope's visit. ■ *1030-1800, US$1, Diego Portales 997 near bus terminal.*

The Poet and the Sea

"We sing to the sea"
At that time I was unaware,
Frankly, even of my own name,
I hadn't written my first poem,
Nor shed my first tear;
My heart was nothing more, nothing less
Than a forgotten kiosk in a square.
It so happened that one day my father
Was exiled to the South, to far off
Chiloé Island where the winter
Is like an abandoned city.
I left with him and without thinking we
arrived
In Puerto Montt one clear morning.
My family had always lived
In the Central Valley or in the mountains,
So that never, in our house, did we think
about
Or talk about the sea.
On this point I only knew what was taught
in public school...
We got down from the train among flags
And a solemn fiesta of bells
When my father took me by the arm
And turning his eyes to the white,

Free and eternal foam which navigates
In the distance towards some nameless
country,
Said to me as if uttering a prayer
In a voice which still rings in my ear:
"That, my boy, is the sea."...
I began to run, headlong,
As if desperate towards the beach
And for an unforgettable moment I stood
In front of that great lord of battles ...
How long our greeting lasted
I cannot put into words.
I can only add that on that day
The need and the anguish was born in my
mind
To create in verse what in wave after
wave
God created ceaselessly in my vision...
It is, in truth, that since the world began,
The voice of the sea has been in my being.

Translated from "se canta al mar", Nicanor
Parra, Obra gruesa (Santiago: Editorial
Andrés Bello, 1983), pages 18-20.

Excursions

The wooded **Isla Tenglo**, offshore from Puerto Montt and reached by launch from Angelmó (US$0.50), is a favourite place for picnics. There are magnificent views from the summit. The island is famous for its *curanto*, served by restaurants in summer. Boat trips round the island from Angelmó last for 30 minutes and cost US$8.

Chinquihue (the name means 'place of skunks'), west of Angelmó, has many seafood restaurants, oysters being a speciality.

East of Puerto Montt, **Chamiza**, up the Río Coihuin, has fine fishing. There is a polluted bathing beach with black sand at **Pelluco**, 2 km north along the coast (accommodation including *cabañas*; several good seafood restaurants and discotheques – see below) – take colectivo 13, but do not confuse with Pelluco Alto.

Isla Guar, an island in the Seno del Reloncaví, may be visited by boat from Angelmó harbour (1600, two hours). The boat returns from the other end of the island at 0730. The north shore is rocky. If you are lucky you can stay at the church, but it may be best to camp.

West of Puerto Montt the Río Maullin, which drains Lago Llanquihue, has some attractive waterfalls and good salmon fishing. At its mouth is the little fishing village of **Maullin**, founded in 1602 (B *Motel El Pangal*, 5 km away, T244). Southeast of here, on the coast, is Carelmapu. About 3 km away is an excellent beach, Playa Brava with *cabañas*. **Calbuco**, centre of the fishing industry (*Hotel Colonial*, T461546; several others; municipal campsite.

The Lake District

Restaurant San Rafael, recommended) is on an island linked to the mainland by a causeway. It has good scenery and can be visited direct by boat or by road (the old coast road from Puerto Montt is very beautiful).

South of Puerto Montt is the **Parque Nacional Alerce Andino** (see page 409).

Essentials

Sleeping
■ *on map, page 374*
Price codes:
see inside front cover

Accommodation is
expensive in season,
much cheaper
off season

L *O'Grimm*, Gallardo 211, T252845, F258600. With breakfast, cosy restaurant with occasional live music, central. **L** *Vicente Pérez Rosales*, Varas 447, T252571. With breakfast, some rooms noisy, excellent restaurant, seafood, fine views, tourist and climbing information. Recommended. **AL** *Colón*, Pedro Montt 65, T264290, F264293, good value. **AL** *Club Presidente*, Portales 664, T251666. 4-star, with breakfast, very comfortable, also suites. English spoken. Recommended. **AL** *Don Luis*, Urmeneta y Quillota, T259001, F259005. Heating, very good, good restaurant. **AL** *Viento Sur*, Ejército 200, T258701, F258700. 4-star, excellent, good restaurant, sauna, gym, excellent views. **AL-A** *Burg*, Pedro Montt y Portales, T253941. Modern, central heating, centrally located, good, interesting traditional food in restaurant. **A** *Le Mirage*, Rancagua 350, T255125, F256302. With breakfast, small rooms, clean.

B *Colina*, Talca 81, T T253502. Restaurant, bar, car hire, noisy. Recommended. **B** *Millahue*, Copiapó 64, T253829, F253817, and apartments at Benavente 959, T/F254592. With breakfast, modern, good restaurant. **B** *Montt*, Varas y Quillota, T253651. Also **C** without bath, clean, friendly, good value, good restaurant. Helpful. **C** *El Candil*, Varas 177, T253080. Run down. Also has **C** *Res Candil*, Illapel 87. Nearby. **C** pp *Hostal Pacífico*, J J Mira 1088, T256229. With bath, **D** pp without, with breakfast, cable TV, parking, comfortable. Recommended. **C** pp *Res Urmeneta*, Urmeneta 290, T253262. With bath, **D** pp without, clean, comfortable. Recommended. **D** *Res Embassy*, Valdivia 130, T253533. With bath, **F** without, clean, stores luggage. Recommended. **D** pp *Res La Nave*, Ancud y Varas, T253740. With bath, **F** without, clean, inexpensive restaurant.

Near the bus terminal **D** *Hosp Polz*, J J Mira 1002,T252851. With breakfast, clean, warm, good beds. Recommended. **E** pp *Res El Turista*, Ancud 91, T254767. With bath, with breakfast, noisy. **G** *Res El Talquino*, Pérez Rosales 114, T253331. Hot water, clean. The following are all **F**: *Casa Gladis*, Ancud y Mira. Dormitory style (but some double rooms), kitchen and laundry facilities, crowded; *Goecke 347*, T288954, without

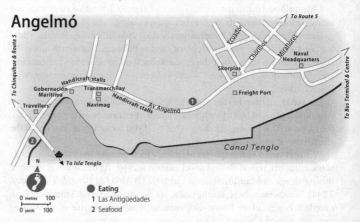

Angelmó

To Route 5
To Chinquihue & Route 5
Ecuador
Chorillos
Miraflores
Naval Headquarters
Skorpios
Handicraft stalls
Gobernación Marítima
Transmarchilay
Freight Port
Travellers'
Navimag
Handicraft stalls
Av Angelmó
To Bus Terminal & Centre
Canal Tenglo
N
To Isla Tenglo

0 metres 100
0 yards 100

● **Eating**
1 Las Antigüedades
2 Seafood

breakfast, helpful; *Goecke 245*, T258688, kitchen and laundry facilities; *Hosp Godoy*, Goecke 119, T266339, with breakfast, clean, cooking facilities, poor bathroom; *Res Central*, Lota 111, T257516. Clean, use of kitchen, good beds. Recommended. *Vista Hermosa*, Miramar 1486, T/F268001, without bath, quiet, helpful, fine views. *Walglad*, Ancud 112. With breakfast, clean, run down. **G** *Hosp Leticia* , Lota 132, T256316. With breakfast. Basic, safe, cooking facilities, hot showers. Recommended.

Near the Plaza de Armas **E** pp *Hosp Suizo*, Independencia 231, T/F252640. Attractive house, with breakfast, clean, German, Italian spoken, painting and Spanish classes. **E** *Res Calipso*, Urmeneta 127, T254554. Without bath, clean. Hostelling International discounts. **E** *Res La Alemana*, Egaña 82, T255092. With breakfast, German spoken, run down. The following are all **F** in Calle Huasco: *Hosp Frente al Mar*, no 6, T260126, with breakfast, kitchen, also *cabañas*. *No 16*, T254709. With breakfast, basic. *No 126*, friendly. Recommended. *No 130*, cooking facilities, home-made bread. Recommended. Also at *Antonio Varas 840*, basic, including breakfast and *Antonio Varas 770*, T254720, with breakfast.

E *Casa Haraldo Steffen*, Serrano 286, T253823. With breakfast, 15-mins' walk from centre, small clean rooms, run down, only 1 bathroom. **E** *Alda González*, Gallardo 552, T253334. With bath, **F** without, with breakfast, cooking facilities, English, German spoken, good value. **E** *Esmeralda*, Libertad 395, T255649. **E** *Aníbal Pinto 328*, with breakfast, popular, laundry facilities, 10-mins' walk from centre. Recommended. **E** *Balmaceda 300*, with breakfast, clean, friendly. **E** *Balmaceda 283*, clean, hospitable. **E** *Casa Patricia*, Trigal 361. Family run, clean, welcoming. **E** *La Familia*, Bilbao 380, T256514. Hot water, very clean, comfortable. **E** *Sra María Oyarzo*, Subida Miramar 1184, T259957. With breakfast, friendly, basic (no heating, hot water next door), clean, good beds. **E** *Vivar 1141*, T255039. With breakfast, hot water. **E** *Baquedano 247*, T252862. Friendly, clean. **F** *Casa Perla*, Trigal 312, T262104, casaperla@hotmail.com With breakfast, English spoken, helpful, friendly, meals, laundry, internet, pleasant garden. Spanish classes offered, good meeting place. Recommended. **F** *Hospedaje Erica*, Trigal 309, T259923. Kitchen facilities, TV, big bathroom, good views. **F** *Hosp Nina*, Crucero 1351, small twin rooms, nice kitchen, clean. **F** *Res Emita*, Miraflores 1281. With breakfast with home-made bread, clean, friendly, safe. **F** *Hostal Independencia*, Independencia 167, T277949, also Av Angelmo 2196, T257938, opposite Navimag terminal. Hostelling International reductions. **F** *Hostal Rocco*, Pudeto 233,T/F272897, Hostelrocco@hotmail.com Without bath, with breakfast, real coffee, English spoken, friendly atmosphere. **On Allende** *No 119*, T258638. Clean, friendly. Recommended. *Hosp Montesinos*, No 121, T255353. With breakfast, clean. Recommended. *El Forastero*, Colo Colo 1350, T263342. With good breakfast, very clean. *Albergue* in school opposite bus station, **G** sleeping bag on floor, cold showers, kitchen and laundry facilities, but no security, open 2 Jan-15 Feb only. **G** *El Tata*, Gallardo 621, floor space. Very basic, popular, packed in summer. Lots of *cabañas*, **E**, both on the outskirts of the city, eg *El Toqui*, Huasco 213, T255824; *Melipulli*, Libertad 610, T253325, and outside especially in *Pelluco*, eg Rucaray, T252395; *El Rincón de Gabriel*, T251293.

E is per person unless otherwise stated

Camping 'Wild' camping possible along the sea front. Several sites west of Puerto Montt: *El Ciervo*, 3 km west, good. **Camping Municipal** at Chinquihue, 10 km west (bus service). Open Oct-Apr, fully equipped with tables, seats, barbecue, toilets and showers, small shop, no kerosene. *Camping Anderson*, 11 km west, American run, hot showers, private beach, home-grown fruit, vegetables and milk products. *Camping Los Alamos*, T25667, 13 km west. Nice views, poor services, stray dogs, US$17 per site. *Camping Metri*, 30 km southeast on Caminó Austral, T251235. *Fierro bus*, US$2 per tent.

The Lake District

The Lake District

Eating

Look out for local specialities such as curanto and picoroco al vapor, a giant barnacle whose flesh looks and tastes like a crab

Expensive *Balzac*, Urmeneta y Quillota. Very good. *Centro Español*, O'Higgins 233. Expensive but very good. *Club Alemán*, Varas 264. Old fashioned, good food and wine. *Club de Yates*, Juan Soler s/n. Excellent, expensive seafood. **Mid-range** *Café Amsel* (in *Hotel Burg*), Pedro Montt y Portales. Superb fish, not cheap, real coffee. *Embassy*, Ancud 106. Very good, upper end of range. *Puerto Café*, Angelmó 2456 (above Travellers). Real coffee, vegetarian dishes, English spoken, recommended. **Cheap** *Café Real*, Rancagua 137. For *empanadas*, *pichangas*, *congrío frito*, and cheap lunches. *Costa de Reloncaví*, Portales 736. Good, moderate prices. *Dino*, Varas 550. Restaurant upstairs, snacks downstairs (try the lemon juice). *Don Pancho*, in old railway station. Good. *Plato's*, Portales 1014, Galería Comercial España. Cheap, good. *Restaurant de las Antigüedades*, Av Angelmo, attractive and unusual décor, real coffee, interesting menu. *Rincón Sureño*, Talca 86. Poor meat dishes, good fish. Cheap food at bus terminal (all credit cards accepted). For **seafood** enthusiasts, the only place to go is Angelmó, where there are many small seafood restaurants in the old fishing port, very popular, excellent food, lunches only, ask for *té blanco* (white wine – they are not legally allowed to serve wine).

Cafés *Café Alemana*, Rancagua 117. Real coffee, good. *Café Plaza*, Urmeneta 326, T295750. Good location, friendly, pool/billiards. Also in the Galería is *El Rinconcito*, a

Puerto Montt

To Residencial El Tata

To Pan-American Highway & Airport

Santa María
Ochagavía
Vergel
Crucero
Rengifo
Campanario
Jesuita
Benavente
Urmeneta
Paseo del Mar Shopping Mall
Av Diego Portales
Las Brisas Supermarket
Fullfresh Supermarket
Museo Juan Pablo II
Miramar

To Hotel Suizo

To Angelmó

Isla Tenglo

Seno del Reloncavi

0 metres 200
0 yards 200

N

Sleeping
1	Alda González	7	Don Luis	13	Millahue
2	Burg	8	Hospedaje Erica	14	Montt
3	Casa Gladis	9	Hospedaje Leticia	15	O'Grimm
4	Casa Perla	10	Hospedaje Polz	16	Residencial Central
5	Colina	11	Hostal Pacífico	17	Residencial El Talquino
6	Colón	12	Le Mirage	18	Residencial El Turista

good bar. *Asturias*, Angelmó 2448. Limited menu. Often recommended. **Pelluco** *Pazos*, T252552. Best curanto in Puerto Montt. Azzuro, T318989. Italian. Several other seafood restaurants. **Chinquihué** *Kiel*, T255010. Excellent, not cheap. *La Casona*, T255044.

Watch out – several of the 'bars' near the port and along Perez Rosales have more to them than meets the eye. **Discos** Several in Pelluco including *Cocodrilo* and *Black Hole*; also *Star*, on Route 5 north. **Casa del Arte Diego Rivera**, off Plaza de Armas. Temporary exhibitions, concerts, plays. **Entertainment**

Aerial Felix Oyarzo Grimm, owner of the *Hotel O'Grimm* can advise on possibilities, especially parachuting. **Fishing** Luis Wellman, at the *Hotel Don Luis* is very knowledgeable about fishing in the area. **Football** Stadium opposite Marina del Sur yacht club. **Gymnasium** Augusto Trautmann 1320, T254957. **Kayaking** *Kayaking Austral* offers guided sea kayaking, T09 6980951, or book through Casa Perla. **Sailing** 2 Yacht Clubs in Chinquihué: *Marina del Sur* (MDS), T/F251958. Modern, bar and restaurant, sailing courses, notice board for crew (*tripulante*) notices, *MDS Charters* office specializes in cruising the Patagonian channels. Charters US$2,200-8,500 per week depending on size of boat. *Club de Deportes Náuticas*, founded by British and Americans in 1940s, more oriented towards small boat sailing, windsurfing, watersports. **Rafting and water sports** *Alsur*, Antonio Varas 445, T/F287628. **Sports**

19 Residencial Embassy
20 Residencial La Nave
21 Residencial Urmeneta
22 Vicente Pérez Rosales
23 Viento Sur
24 Vista Hermosa

● Eating
1 Balzac
2 Café Real
3 Centro Español
4 Club Alemán
5 Embassy

Large modern shopping mall, *Paseo del Mar*, Talca y Antonio Varas; a large new mall is also being built on the seafront. Woollen goods and Mapuche-designed rugs can be bought at roadside stalls in Angelmó and on Diego Portales opposite the bus terminal. Prices are much the same as on Chiloé, but quality is often lower. **Camera** *Torres Color*, Rancagua III, for photo developing and repairs, efficient. **Supermarkets** *Las Brisas* and *Fullfresh* opposite bus terminal. Open 0900-2200 daily. **Bookshops** *Libros*, Diego Portales Portales 580. Small selection of English novels, also maps. **Electricals** *Dimarse*, Varas Y Chillan. Bulbs for maglite torches. **Shopping**

Andina del Sud, very close to central tourist kiosk, Varas 445, T257686. Sells a daily tour at 0830 (not Sun) to Puerto Varas, Parque Nacional V Pérez Rosales, Petrohué, Lago Todos los Santos, Peulla and back (without meals US$27, with meals US$37), and to other local sights, as well as skiing trips to the Osorno Volcano (see below for trip to Bariloche). *Cruce de Lagos*, www.crucedelagos.cl, an association of Chilean and Argentine companies **Tour operators**

The Lake District

offering cruises throughout the Andes. *Eureka Turismo*, Varas 449, T250412, F255146, helpful, German, English spoken. *Petrel Tours*, San Martín 167, oficina 403, T/F255558. Recommended. *Reloncaví*, Angelmó 2448, T288080, F288081. *Patagonia Verde*, Diego Portales 514. Mountaineering, fishing, trekking, horseriding. Many other agencies. Most offer 1-day excursions to Chiloé (US$20) and to Puerto Varas, Isla Loreley, Laguna Verde, and the Petrohué falls: these tours are much cheaper from bus company kiosks inside the bus terminal, eg Bohle, US$17 to Chiloé, US$11 to the lakes. Some companies, eg *Reloncaví*, also offer 2-day excursions along the Camino Austral to Hornopirén, US$76 including food and accommodation. *Travellers*, Av Angelmó 2456, Casilla 854, T262099, F258555, www.travellers.cl Open Mon-Fri 0900-1330,1500-1830, Sat 0900-1400 for booking for Navimag ferry to Puerto Natales, bespoke excursions, money exchange, flights, also sells imported camping equipment and runs computerized tourist information service, book swap ("best book swap south of Santiago"), map display, TV, real coffee, English-run. T252968. Information on the Parque Pumalin at Buin 356, T251911/255145.

Transport **Local Boat hire**: *Lucinda Cárdenas*, Manuel Montt Pasaje 7, Casa 134, Angelmó, for trips around the harbour or to Tenglo island. **Car hire**: *Automotric Angelmó*, Talca 79, cheap and helpful. *Automóvil Club de Chile*, Ensenada 70, T254776, and at airport. *Autovald*, Diego Portales 1330, T256355, cheap rates. Others are *Avis*, Urmeneta, 1037, T253307, and at airport. *Budget*, Gallardo 450, T254888 and at airport. *Dollar* (*Hotel Vicente Pérez Rosales*), Antonio Varas 447. *First*, Antonio Varas 447, T252036; *Formula Uno*, Santa María 620, T254125, highly recommended. *Full Famas*, Diego Portales 506, T258060, F259840, and airport, T263750, friendly, helpful, good value, has vehicles that can be taken to Argentina. *Hertz*, Antonio Varas 126, T259585, helpful, English spoken. *Travicargo*, Urmeneta 856, T257137. **Cycle repairs**: 3 on Urmeneta, none very well stocked, including *Oxford*, Urmeneta 908, T272960. **Motorcycle repairs**: Miguel Schmuch, Urmeneta 985, T/F258877.

Long distance Air: El Tepual Airport, 13 km northwest of town. *ETM* bus from bus terminal 1½ hrs before departure, US$2. *ETM* also run a minibus service to/from hotels, US$4 pp, T294292. Taxi to Puerto Varas, US$20. To **Santiago** at least 2 daily flights by *LanChile* and *Ladeco*. To **Balmaceda**, *LanChile* daily. To **Chaitén**, *Aeromet*, Mon-Fri 1200, US$40; also *Aerosur* and *Aero Vip*. To **Punta Arenas**, *LanChile* and *Ladeco* have many flights daily, fare US$105; in Jan, Feb and Mar you may be told that flights are booked up; however, cancellations may be available from the airport.

The Lake District

International flights To **Bariloche** and **Neuquén (Argentina)**, *TAN*, 2 a week, 40 mins. To **Port Stanley** (Falkland Islands/Islas Malvinas), from Santiago via Punta Arenas, *LanChile*, Sat, US$280, return next morning.

Bus Very crowded terminal on seafront at Diego Portales y Lota, has telephones, restaurants, *casa de cambio* left luggage (US$1.50 per item for 24 hrs). To **Puerto Varas** (US$0.50), **Llanquihue**, **Frutillar** (US$1.25) and **Osorno** (US$5) minibuses every few minutes, *Varmontt*, *Expreso Puerto Varas*, *Thaebus* and *Full Express*. To **Ensenada** and **Petrohué**, *Buses JM* at least 3 a day. To **Ralún**, **Cochamó** and **Puelo**, *Bohle* (5 a day via Puerto Varas and Ensenada; 2 to Puelo), *Fierro*, 2 a day. To **Pucón**, US$9.40, daily, 6 hrs. To **Santiago**, express, US$20, *cama* US$45, several companies including *Tur Bus*, very good, 14 hrs, *Tas Choapa Royal Class* US$32. To **Temuco** US$8, to **Valdivia**, US$6; **Concepción**, US$12. For services to **Chiloé**, see page 387. To **Punta Arenas**, *Austral*, *Turibus* and *Ghisoni*, between 1-3 times a week, approximately US$55 (bus goes through Argentina via Bariloche – take US$ cash to pay for meals etc in Argentina), 32-38 hrs. Book well in advance in Jan-Feb and check if you need a multiple-entry Chilean visa; also book any return journey before setting out. To **Coyhaique**, 2 a week with *Turibus* via Bariloche, US$46.

Buses to Argentina Via Osorno and the Puyehue pass. Daily services to **Bariloche**, US$18, 7-8 hrs, run by *Cruz del Sur*, *Rio de la Plata*, *Tas Choapa* and *Bus Norte*. *Tas Choapa* services also run to Mendoza, Buenos Aires, Montevideo and Rio de Janeiro. Out of season, services are reduced. Buy tickets for international buses from the bus terminal, not through an agency. Hitchhiking on this route is difficult. For the route to Argentina via Lago Todos Los Santos see below.

Book well in advance in Jan and Feb

Motoring When driving north out of Puerto Montt (or out of Puerto Varas, Frutillar, etc), look for signs to 'Ruta 5'.

Shipping offices: *Navimag* (Naviera Magallanes SA), Terminal Transbordadores, Angelmó 2187, T253318, F258540. *Skorpios*, Angelmó 1660 y Miraflores (Castilla 588), T252619, Tx370161 NATUK CL. *Transmarchilay Ltda*, Terminal Transbordadores, Angelmó 2187, T270416, F270415.

Airline offices *Don Carlos*, Quillota 127, T253219. *LanChile*, O'Higgins y Umeneta, T253141/253315. *Ladeco*, Benevente 350, T253002. *TAN*, T250071.

Directory

Banks ATMs at banks including *Banco Santiago*, Urmeneta 541. *Banco Santander*, Antonio Varas 501. Also at *Las Brisas* supermarket, in the *Fullfresh* supermarket opposite the bus terminal and in the Terminal Transbordadores. For Visa *Corp Banca*, Pedro Montt y Urmeneta. Good rates. Commission charges for TCs vary widely. *Casas de Cambio* Good rates at *Galería Cristal*, Varas 595. *Afex*, Portales 516. *La Moneda de Oro* at the bus terminal exchanges Latin American currencies (Mon-Sat 0930-1230, 1530-1800). *Turismo Los Lagos*, Varas 595, local 13. *Travellers*, travel agent in Angelmó (see above) has exchange facilities.

Communications Internet: Antonio Varas 629. Also *Latin Star*, Av Angelmo 1684, T310036, US$5 per hour, mail-latinstar@telsur.cl Offer cheap phone rates, phone cards, stamps, fax service, English spoken, helpful. *Mundo Sur*, at San Martín 232. Also at Angelmó 1724 and 2456. **Post office**: Rancagua 126. Open 0830-1830 (Mon-Fri), 0830-1200 (Sat). **Telephone**: Pedro Montt 114 and Chillán 98. *Entel*, Averas between Talca and Pedro Montt. There is also a cheap call centre at Rosales 148. **Consulates** Argentina, Cauquenes 94, piso 2, T253996, quick visa service. Germany,

The Lake District

Antonio Varas y Gallardo, piso 3, Oficina 306. Tue/Wed 0930-1200. **Spain**, Rancagua 113, T252557. **Netherlands**, Chorillos 1582, T253003.

Laundry Center Antonio Varas 700. *Lavatodo*, O'Higgins 231; *Narly*, San Martín 187, Local 6, laundry prices generally high (US$7 for 3 kg); *Nautilus*, Av Angelmó 1564, cheaper, good; *San Martín 232*; *Unic*, Chillán 149. *Yessil't*, Edif Caracol, Urmeneta 300. Service. **Medical services** At Seminario s/n, T261134.

Sea routes south of Puerto Montt

Puerto Montt is the departure point for several popular voyages along the coast of southern Chile. All sailings are from Angelmó. Shipping offices in Puerto Montt are listed above. All shipping services should be checked carefully in advance as schedules change frequently.

To Puerto Natales

See the colour map at the end of the book for ferry routes

One of the highlights of many journeys to Chile is the 1,460-km voyage between Puerto Montt and the southern port of Puerto Natales. Both the *M/V Edén* and the *M/V Magallanes* now make this journey – the *Magallanes* is a new ferry which takes cargo and is quicker than the *Edén*, allowing a stop at Puerto Chacabuco and direct ferry transport from Puerto Chacabuco to Puerto Natales. The route south is as follows: from Puerto Montt across the Seno Reloncavi and the Golfo de Ancud between the mainland and the large island of Chiloé, then south through the Canal Moraleda and the Canal Errázuriz, which separate the mainland from the outlying islands before sailing west through the Canal Chacabuco to Bahía Anna Pink and across the open sea and the infamous Golfo de Peñas (Gulf of Sorrows) to reach a series of channels, Canal Messier, Angostura Inglesa, Fiordo del Indio and Canal Kirke which provide one of the narrowest routes for large shipping in the world. Spectacular views of the wooded fjords, particularly beautiful at sunrise and sunset; a sense of desolate peace is everywhere except on board ship, which is filled with cows in transport containers mooing day and night and people having a good time (at night).

The only regular stop on this route is at the fishing village of **Puerto Edén** on Isla Wellington, one hour south of the Angostura Inglesa. This is a fishing village with three shops (scant provisions), one off-licence, one café, and an *hospedaje* for up to 20 people. The population is 180, plus five *carabineros* and the few remaining Alacaluf Indians. It is, though, the drop-off point for exploring Isla Wellington, which is largely untouched, with stunning mountains. If stopping here, take all food; maps (not very accurate) are available in Santiago. The fare is US$50 between Isla Wellington and Puerto Natales.

Both ferries sail this route once a week from 1 November to 30 April, departing from Puerto Montt on Mondays and Thursdays, returning on the same days from Puerto Natales. The voyage takes four days and three nights; the fare ranges from US$220 each economy (including meals) to US$792 each in various classes of cabin (also including meals); 10% discount on international student cards in cabin class only, fares 10-20% lower in March-April. Payment by credit card or foreign currency is generally not accepted. Economy class accommodation is basic and near the engine room, in 24-berth dormitories. Apart from videos, entertainment on board is limited. Economy class and cabin passengers eat the same food but in separate areas (economy class are very cramped). The food is variable (some say it is good, others disagree). This is a ferry which also carries cargo (including cattle and sheep) rather than a cruise liner; it is cheaper to fly and quicker to go by bus via

On board the Puerto Edén

"When the boat began loading there was a mild stampede, especially for us economy class (or dungeon class) passengers: we didn't want to end up in one of the top bunks, which require elaborate climbing equipment to reach and which give only 3 ins of headroom. There were two 24-occupant dungeon-class barracks, each equipped with two toilets and one shower, located at the very bottom of the ship, scattered alongside the engine room, the generator, the anchor-chain-dropping room and the rock-concert-amplifier-testing room. It was loud.

What did we do all day? Not much. The ship felt like an airport waiting room. People read, played cards, drank and slept. The scenery was indeed 'breathtakingly beautiful and rugged' but it was too windy and cold to stay outside for long, so we usually settled for glancing out of the ship's tiny windows. At Puerto Edén we were awakened by the release of the anchor which, in dungeon class, sounded as though it had been dropped through the ceiling. We weren't sure whether to wake up or abandon ship. Nearly 200 of us decided to go ashore. We each wore a bright orange life jacket so, naturally, we were easily identifiable to the locals who were eager to do business with us. After a few hours of stocking up on the requisite souvenirs, we went back and steeled ourselves for the rough sea crossing. The waves, relative to the boat's size, were not threatening, but they hit the boat directly on her port side and created an impressive nauseating effect. Some passengers took seasickness pills and wandered down to their rooms to pass out. Others drank wine or beer till this had the same effect.

Perhaps the highlight of the trip was a tug-o-war on the upper cargo deck against the crew. The passengers, who had spent too much time sitting around and too little time loading and unloading cargo ships, were trounced. Team gringo fared better, however, in the ensuing soccer match: adding to the excitement were the obstacles on the 'pitch': huge metal rivets every few metres and a 20 tonne freight elevator."

Argentina but the voyage is spectacular. Standards of service and comfort vary, depending on the number of passengers and weather conditions. Take seasickness tablets.

Booking Economy class can only be booked, with payment, through *Navimag* offices in Puerto Montt and Puerto Natales. Economy tickets are frequently sold on the day of departure when conditions in the *Navimag* office can be chaotic. Cabin class can be booked in advance through *Travellers* in Puerto Montt, through *Navimag* offices in Puerto Montt, Puerto Natales and Punta Arenas, or through *Cruceros Australis* (Navimag parent company) in Santiago. All of these have their own ticket allocation: once this is used up, they have to contact other offices to request spare tickets. Book well in advance for cabin class departures between mid-Dec and mid-Mar especially for the voyage south. Puerto Natales to Puerto Montt is less heavily booked. The ferries tend to be booked up to 2 weeks in advance in Feb but it is worth putting your name on the waiting list for cancellations.

Departures are frequently delayed – or even advanced – by weather conditions

The Lake District

Both *Navimag* and *Transmarchilay* operate regular sailings between Puerto Montt and Puerto Chacabuco, 80 km west of Coyhaique, taking 24 hours. Though beautiful, this voyage means that travellers miss out on the attractions of the Camino Austral. The Navimag ferry *M/N Evangelista* sails this route twice a week throughout the year except in January and February when it operates every four days. In January and February the vessel continues once a week from Puerto Chacabuco to visit Laguna San Rafael, 21-24 hour

To Puerto Chacabuco

excursion. Fares Puerto Montt-Puerto Chacabuco range from US$125-250 for first class, depending on which cabin and number of occupants, to US$145 for tourist class and US$40-70 for reclining seats (*butacas*). Return fares on the excursion to Laguna San Rafael from Puerto Montt are much higher, ranging from US$300 to US$1,000 first class return. It is slightly cheaper to sail from Puerto Montt to Laguna San Rafael and then disembark in Puerto Chacabuco. Vehicle charges between Puerto Montt and Puerto Chacabuco: cars US$150, motorcycles US$35, cycles US$20. The Transmarchilay ferry *El Colono* sails twice a week from Puerto Montt to Puerto Chacabuco, once every four days in January-February, also once a week in January-February from Puerto Chacabuco to Laguna San Rafael. Fares are similar to those on *Evangelistas*. For fares from Puerto Chacabuco to Laguna San Rafael on these services see under Puerto Chacabuco. These vessels have been described as "floating buses"; apart from those in cabins, passengers sleep in their seats and there is little space for luggage. There is a small canteen; long queues if the boat is full. Food is expensive so take your own.

To Laguna San Rafael The m/n *Skorpios 1* and *2* of Constantino Kochifas C leave Puerto Montt on Saturday at 1100 for a luxury cruise with stops at Puerto Aguirre, Melinka, Laguna San Rafael, Quitralco, Castro (each ship has a slightly different itinerary) and returns to Puerto Montt on Friday at 0800. The fare varies according to season, type of cabin and number of occupants: a double ranges from US$465 (low) to US$660 (high) on *Skorpios 1* and from US$770 (low) to US$1,100 (high) on *Skorpios 2*, which is the more comfortable of the two. It has been reported that there is little room to sit indoors if it is raining on *Skorpios 1*, but generally service is excellent, the food superb and at the glacier, you chip your ice off the face for your whisky. (After the visit to San Rafael the ships visits Quitralco Fiord where there are thermal pools and boat trips on the fiord.) In June 2001 Constantino Kochifas was said to just have launched *Skorpios 3* on this route as well.

Patagonia Connection SA, Fidel Oteíza 1921, Oficina 1006, Providencia, Santiago, T225-6489, F274-8111, operates *Patagonia Express*, a catamaran which runs from Puerto Chacabuco to Laguna San Rafael via Termas de Puyuhuapi, see page 415. Tours lasting 4 to 6 days start from Puerto Montt and include the catamaran service, the hotel at Termas de Puyuhuapi and the day excursion to Laguna San Rafael. High season is 20 December-20 March, low season, 11 September-19 December and 21 March-21 April. High season fares for a four-day tour from US$940, all inclusive, highly recommended.

Raymond Weber, Av Chipana 3435 Pasaje 4, T8858250, www.chilecharter.com, has two luxury sailing catamarans for charter to visit Golfo de Ancud and Laguna San Rafael.

Other routes The Navimag ferry *Alejandrina* sails to **Chaitén** (for the trip along the Camino Austral) Tuesday, Thursday, Saturday in summer, reduced service off season, 10-hour crossing. Fares: passengers US$22, *literas* US$33, cars US$100, cycles US$11. The Transmarchilary ferry *Pincoya* also sails this route on Friday 2200, as does Catamaranes del Sur on Monday, Wednesday and Friday at 0800, US$35, tickets through Patagonia Verde.

Río Negro The m/n *Bohemia* makes six day/five night trips from Puerto Montt to Río Negro, Isla Llancahué, Baños Cahuelmó and Fiordo Leptepu/Coman, US$545-720 pp depending on season (Antonio Varas 947, T254675, Puerto Montt).

Chiloé

11

382

Chiloé

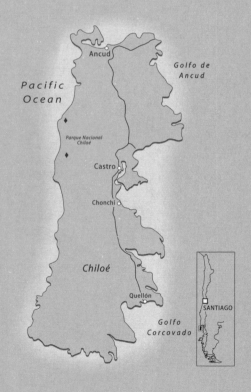

The mysterious archipelago of Chiloé is one of the most fascinating areas of Chile. With one main island and numerous islets, the area consists of patchworks of fields and thick forest set on rolling hills, and provides a lasting sense of rural calm. Here you are almost always within sight of the sea, with dolphins playing in the bay and, on a clear day, views across to the twisting spire of Corcovado Volcano on the mainland. A land of small fishing villages and farms, Chiloé is famous for its legends and rich mythology; here witches are said to fly around at night, identifiable as lights in the dark sky. Chiloé is equally well known for its painted wooden churches, some of them dating back to the late colonial period. In February and March most towns and villages celebrate their annual fiestas; traditional dishes such as curanto *are served, and there are rodeos and dancing, as well as much drinking of local chicha.*

Chiloé

Background

Officially known as Chiloé Grande, the main island of Chiloé is 250 km long and 50 km wide. The Cordillera de la Costa runs at low altitudes along the Pacific side of the island. South of Castro there is a gap in the range in which there are two connected lakes, Lago Huillinco and Lago Cucao. Thick forests cover most of the sparsely populated western and southern parts of the island. In summer the hillsides are covered with wheat fields and dark green plots of potatoes and the roads are lined with wild flowers. There are two main towns,

Chiloé

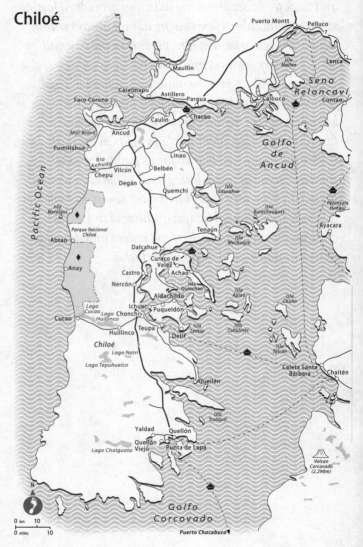

> ## Things to do in Chiloé
>
> - Gallop on horseback along the beach at Cucao.
> - Explore the thick forest at the northern end of the Parque Nacional Cucao.
> - Eat *curanto* and other specialities in the seafood restaurants by the port at Castro.
> - Visit any of the fascinating wooden churches based on the design of the Jesuits.
> - Explore the small islets between the main island of Chiloé and the mainland.
> - Join in the *fiestas* held at small towns throughout January and February.

Ancud and Castro, in which most of the 116,000 people live; there are also many fishing villages. East of the main island are several groups of smaller islands, where the way of life is even more peaceful.

History

The original Chilotes (inhabitants of Chiloé) were the Chonos, who were pushed south by the Huilliches, invading from the north. The first Spanish sighting was by Francisco de Ulloa in 1553; in 1567 Martín Ruiz de Gamboa took possession of the islands on behalf of Spain. The small settler population divided the indigenous population and their lands between them. The rising of the Huilliche after 1598 drove the Spanish out of the mainland south of the Río Biobío, isolating the 200 Spanish settlers on Chiloé. Following a violent earthquake in 1646, the Spanish population asked the Viceroy in Lima for permission to leave, but this was refused. Much of Chiloé's distinctive character derives from the following 200 years of separation from the mainstream of Spanish colonial development.

The islanders were the last supporters of the Spanish Crown in South America. When the Chilean parrtriot leaders rebelled, the Spanish Governor fled to the island and, in despair, offered it to Britain. George Canning, the British Foreign Secretary, turned the offer down; Chiloé finally surrendered to the patriots in 1826. Visiting less than a decade later, Charles Darwin still clearly distinguished Chiloé from the rest of Chile, saying that here the Andes were not nearly "so elevated as in Chile".

Throughout the 19th and the first part of the 20th century, Ancud was the capital of Chiloé. All that changed with the earthquake and *maremoto* (tidal wave) of 1960. This severely altered the landscape in Ancud, bringing petrified trees to the surface and causing forests to fall under water. The whole of the lower town was destroyed except for the cathedral, which was badly damaged, and then blown up rather than renovated – until then, this had been the second biggest cathedral in South America. The capital was then moved back to its former site of Castro, which is the only place in Chiloé that feels urban today. The *maremoto*, and the rivalry between Ancud and Castro which it spawned, have not entirely been forgotten.

Climate

The appalling climate of Chiloé is almost as legendary as the witches that are said to live there. The west coast has particularly vile conditions; it can rain for three weeks at a time. The sheltered east coast and the offshore islands are only a little drier. The whole archipelago is frequently wet, even in summer. Some of the best weather is in early December and late March. The main benefits of the climate are culinary. Because of the Humboldt current and the sheltered nature of the east coast, shellfish are available, fresh and delicious all year. Chiloé also has indigenous elephant garlic, which is used to make very tasty garlic sauce.

Chiloé

The Jesuits in Chiloé

The Jesuits arrived in Chiloé in 1608 and the first Jesuit residence was established four years later. Although in Chiloé they established few of the missions for which they became famous in Paraguay, at their expulsion in 1767 there were 79 churches on the island. The key to their influence lay in their use of fiscales, indigenous people trained to teach Christian doctrine and ensure that everyone observed religious duties. One fiscal was appointed for every 50 inhabitants. On 17 September each year, two missionaries set sail from Castro in small boats, taking with them statues of saints and other essential supplies. They spent the next eight months sailing round the islands, visiting all the parishes in a set order. In each parish they spent three days, carrying out weddings and baptisms, hearing confessions and reviewing the work of the fiscales.

Most of the old churches for which Chiloé is famous date from after the expulsion of the Jesuits, but some writers claim that their influence can still be seen, for example in the enthusiasm for education in the island, which has long boasted one of the lowest illiteracy rates in the world. Many villages, meanwhile, still have fiscales who are, by tradition, responsible for keeping the church keys.

Art and architecture The availability of wood and the lack of metals have left their mark on Chilote architecture. Some of the earliest of the island's churches were built entirely of wood, using wooden pegs instead of nails. These early churches often displayed German influence as a result of the missionary work of Bavarian Jesuits. Three notable features were the *esplanada* or porch which ran the length of the front of the church, the not-quite semi-circular arches and the central position of the tower directly above the door. In the 19th century the original design was often modified. Few of the oldest churches have survived fire, earthquakes and the weather, but there are still over 150 churches on the islands, and small villages almost invariably have churches with pretty cemeteries – in 2001 UNESCO declared them part of the patrimony of humanity.

The *rucas* (houses) of the indigenous population were thatched; throughout the 19th century thatch continued in widespread use. Two features of local architecture often thought to be traditional are in fact late 19th century in origin. The use of thin *tejuelas* (tiles) made from alerce wood was influenced by the German settlers around Puerto Montt; these tiles, which are nailed to the frame and roof in several distinctive patterns, overlap to form effective protection against the rain. *Palafitos* or wooden houses built on stilts over the water, were once popular in all the main ports, but are now mainly found just to the north of Castro, to the west of the Panamericana.

The islands are also famous for their traditional handicrafts, notably woollens and basketware, which can be bought in all the main towns and on some of the smaller islands, as well as in Puerto Montt.

Modern Chiloé Although fishing and agriculture remain mainstays of the economy, salmon farming has become important. Seaweed is harvested for export to Japan. Tourism provides a seasonal income for a growing number of people, especially in Castro. The relatively high birth rate and the shortage of employment in Chiloé have led to regular emigration. Chilotes have settled across Chile; they were prominent as shepherds in late 19th century Patagonia and are an important source of labour for the Argentine oil industry.

Chiloé's distinctive history and its maritime traditions are reflected in the strength of its unique folklore. There is widespread belief in a mermaid (*pincoya*), witches and a ghost ship, the *Caleuche*, which whisks ship-wrecked sailors aboard (see box on page 390). The witches are said to meet at caves near Quicavi, between Dalcahue and Quemchi; the *Caleuche* is said to transform itself into a log, brought ashore by its crew (who become birds) when it needs repairs. Legend has it that Chiloé's dead are rowed along the reaches of Lago Huillinco and Lago Cucao in a white ship, out into the Pacific. Further reading: *Casos de Brujos de Chiloé* by Umiliana Cárdenas Saldivia (1989, Editorial Universitaria), can be bought in Castro; *Chiloé, Manual del Pensamiento Mágico y Creencía Popular* by Renato Cárdenas and Catherine Hall (1989, El Kultrún).

This consists in staying with rural families in Chiloé, and sharing their way of life, whether it be farming, fishing with your hosts or neighbours, or simply staying with a real Chilote family. The host families are invariably friendly and welcoming. Locations of families offering agrotourism are mentioned in the text, and the stays are highly recommended as offering something fascinating and completely different; prices per person are all **E/F** with breakfast, **D/E** for half board, and **C** for full board. It is important to try to make reservations in advance – more information from Sernatur in Ancud or Castro. | **Agrotourism in Chiloé**

Ins and outs

A ferry service connects Quellón with Chaitén and the Camino Austral, but the main sea link is with Puerto Montt to the north: frequent vehicle ferry services are operated by several companies across the Chacao straits between Pargua, on the mainland (55 km southwest of Puerto Montt) and Chacao, on the island. The crossing takes half an hour, cars are US$11.40 one way (more expensive at night), foot passengers US$1, dolphins often follow the boat. | **Getting there** *For details of ferry services between Quellón and Chaitén see page 402*

Frequent bus services, which connect with ferry sailings, operate between Ancud and Castro, the main towns on Chiloé, and Puerto Montt. There are many local services as well, which are crowded, slow and often wet, but provide a good picture of life in rural Chiloé. It is possible to travel direct to many cities, including Santiago, Osorno, Valdivia, Temuco and Los Angeles. Inter-urban bus transport is dominated by *Cruz del Sur*, who also own *Trans Chiloé* and *Regional Sur* and, in Castro, operate from their own terminal. *Cruz del Sur* also operate their own ferries, which give priority over cars to *Cruz del Sur*. The only independent bus operator to the island is *Queilen Bus*. | **Getting around** *Mountain bikes and horses are ideal for travelling slowly through the more remote parts of the archipelago*

Chacao has a small, attractive plaza. Black necked swans arrive in summer. East of the port is Chacao Viejo, with a pretty church and old wooden houses. Some 2 km south, in Pulelo, Ariela Bahamonde and Amador Villagas offer agrotourism, where they still use traditional agricultural techniques and make preserves (T09-8842421, T09-824 6378). Just outside, on the road to Ancud, is a shop selling good smoked salmon. | **Chacao and around**

The Panamericana heads west to Ancud; just outside Chacao, a coastal roach branches south, towards Quemchi. En route is the small village of Hueihue, where fresh oysters can be bought, US$15 for 100. Further south, before Quemchi, is a small lake with model sailing boats.

Sleeping and eating in Chacao **F** *Hosp Angelino* and **F** *Pensión Chiloé*. **F** Restaurant and *hospedaje* at Freire 35. Also, eating at *Restaurant Pilón de Oro*, middle range, good Chilote fare.

Chiloé

Ancud

Phone code: 065
Colour map 4, grid C1
Population: 23,148

Situated on the northern coast of Chiloé 34 km west of the Straits of Chacao, Ancud lies on a great bay, the Golfo de Quetalmahue. It is a little less characterful than some of the other towns on the island, but is nevertheless a good centre for visiting the villages of northern Chiloé. There is a friendly small-town feel; everyone knows each other and everything happens in its own time. Tourism is slowly reviving Ancud's fortunes following the disaster of the maremoto in 1960.

Ins & outs
See page 392 for further details

Getting there Ancud is easily accessible from north and south. There are many buses south to Castro and Quellón (hourly), and also north to Puerto Montt. *Cruz del Sur* have buses continuing north to Valdivia, Temuco and Santiago (several daily). A bridge is planned linking Ancud to the mainland, but it is unlikely to be completed for some years yet. **Getting around** Ancud is big enough for you to want to take the occasional *colectivo*; there are many of these, with their destinations signed on the roof (fares are rarely over US$0.30). There are some buses serving outlying *poblaciones*, but it is unlikely that you will need to use these. **Tourist office** Sernatur, Libertad 665, T622665. Open Mon-Fri 0900-1300, 1430-1730.

Ancud

To Polvorín del Fuerte & Playa Arena Gruesa

To Long Distance Bus Terminal & Ruta 5 for Castro & Chacao

Bahía de Ancud

Transmarchilay
Municipalidad
Museo Regional

To Mar Brava, Pumillahue & Faro Corona

To Posada Cumelen Hotel, Ruta 5 for Castro & Chacao

N
Not to scale

Sleeping
1 Balai
2 Caleta Ancud
3 Elena Bergmann
4 Galeón Azul

5 Hospedaje Alinar
6 Hospedaje Capri
7 Hospedaje Miranda
8 Hospedaje O'Higgins
9 Hospedaje San José
10 Hospedaje Santander
11 Hostería Ahui
12 Hostería Ancud
13 Lacuy

14 Lluhay
15 Lydia
16 Madryn
17 Montserrat
18 Polo Sur
19 Pudeto 331
20 Residencial Germania
21 Residencial Weschler
22 San Bernardo

● Eating
1 Carmen
2 Coral
3 El Cangrejo
4 El Pinguinito
5 El Sacho
6 El Trauco
7 Jardín
8 La Pincoya

Chiloé

Curanto

Particularly associated with Puerto Montt and Chiloé, curanto is a very filling fish, meat and seafood stew, which is delicious despite the rather odd combination of ingredients. Though of prehispanic origins, it has developed by adding new ingredients according to new influences. In its original pre-conquest form, a selection of fish was wrapped in leaves and baked over hot stones in a hole – some specialists wonder if this way of cooking may have come from the Pacific islands, where pit baking is still practised. With the arrival of the Spanish, the dish was modified to include pork, chicken and white wine. Nowadays it is usually cooked in a large pan and is often advertised as pullmay, to distinguish it from the pit-baked form.

Sights

The port is dominated by the Fuerte San Antonio, the site of the Spanish surrender of Chiloé to Chilean troops in 1826. Close to it are the ruins of the Polvorín del Fuerte (a couple of cannon and a few walls; not spectacular). A kilometre north of the fort is a secluded beach, Arena Gruesa, where public concerts are held in summer. Some 2 km east is a Mirador offering good views of the island and across to the mainland. The small fishing harbour at Cochrane y Prat is worth a visit, especially in the evening when the catch is landed. On the road west, along the coast, you can see concrete pillars which are remnants of the old railway.

Near the Plaza de Armas is the **Museo Regional**, with an interesting collection on the early history of Chiloé as well as replicas of a traditional Chilote thatched wooden house and of the small sailing ship *Ancud* (which took an expedition from Ancud to claim the Straits for Chile, pipping the French to the post who arrived a day after). ■ *US$1. Summer daily 1100-1900, winter Tue-Fri 0900-1300, 1430-1830, Sat 1000-1330, 1430-1800. Good craft shop, café, student reductions, activities for children.*

Excursions **Faro Corona** is the lighthouse on Punta Corona, 34 km west along the beach, which, though unsuitable for swimming (absolutely freezing, quite apart from the dangerous currents), offers good views with interesting birdlife. There isn't much there so take something to eat and drink. ■ *Getting there: bus from Ancud 0645; return departure 1730.* South of Faro Corona is **Fuerte Ahuí**, an old fort with good views of Ancud. Near Faro Corona, at Guapilacuy, Juan Saldivia and Corina Huentelicán are part of the agrotourism network, making cheese, butter and preserves, T09-6539422.

Caulín is east of Ancud along the north coast where there are good beaches. The road goes along the beach and is only passable at low tide. Here, fresh oysters can be had at *Ostras Caulín*, T09-6437005, excellent, very fresh, served in any number of ways, but expensive/middle range. In Caulín you can see many black necked swans in summer, and flamingos in autumn – it is a beautiful place. There is also the **AL** *Hotel Caulín*, in whose gardens grow native Chilote trees.

El Trauco, La Fiura, La Sirena and El Calueche

Visitors to Chiloé should beware of these four unlikely mythological hazards. El Trauco *is – perhaps a little too conveniently – held to be responsible for unwanted pregnancies, especially among young girls. A small, ugly and smelly man who wears a small round hat made of bamboo and clothing of the same material, he usually carries a small stone hatchet, with which he is reputed to be able to fell any tree in three strokes. He spends much of his time haunting the forests, sitting on fallen tree trunks and weaving his clothes.*

El Trauco *specializes in seducing virgins. He uses his magic powers to give them erotic dreams while they are asleep; they wake and go to look for him in the forest and are seduced by his eyes. Despite his ugliness, he is irresistible and the girl throws herself on the ground. You should be careful not to disturb the Trauco while he is thus occupied: those who do so are immediately deformed beyond recognition and sentenced to die within 12 months.*

La Fiura, *a small ugly woman, lives in the forests near Hualdes, where she is reputed to bathe in the streams and waterfalls combing her hair with a crystal comb. Known as the indefatigable lover of bachelors, she attracts her victims by wearing colourful clothes. As the man approaches he is put to sleep by her foul breath. After* La Fiura *has satisfied her desire, the unfortunate man goes insane. Refusing her advances is no escape either: those who do so, whether animals or men, are so deformed that they become unrecognizable.*

La Sirena *and* El Caleuche, *on the other hand, are a dangerous double act for those travelling by sea. La Sirena is a mermaid who lies alluringly on rocks and entices sailors to their deaths. Once shipwrecked, sailors are whisked into the bowels of El Caleuche, the ghost ship that is said to patrol the channels of the archipelago. There have been reported sightings of the Caleuche by both the Chilean navy and merchant ships, and the author of this book has met several people on Chiloé who claim to have seen the Caleuche; but a word of warning was sounded by an old cynic in Castro: 'I knew a fisherman who used to walk along the beach shouting "I've seen La Sirena". All the other fishermen fled, and then he stole their fish.'*

Essentials

Sleeping
■ *on map, page 388*
Price codes:
see inside front cover

L ***Hostería Ancud***, San Antonio 30, T622340, F622350, www.hosteriancud.com Overlooking bay, wonderful views, attractive, very comfortable, friendly and helpful, restaurant, traditional Chilote carvings, conference room, English spoken, tours offered. **AL** ***Cabañas Las Golondrinas***, end of Baquedano at Arena Gruesa, T622823. Superb views, with kitchenette, overpriced. **AL** ***Galeón Azul***, Libertad 751, T622567, F622543. **AL** ***Lacuy***, Pudeto 219 near Plaza de Armas, T/F623019. With breakfast, restaurant. Recommended. **AL** ***Lydia***, Pudeto y Chacabuco, T622990, F622879. With bath, **B** without bath. Poor beds, small rooms, overpriced. **A** ***Montserrat***, Baquedano 417, T/F622957. With breakfast, clean, good views, small rooms. **A-C** ***Playa Gaviotas***, T09-4196288, some 6 km north on R5, Km1103. Indoor swimming pool and *cabañas* – **C** for 2 people, **B** for 4, **A** for 6, basic. **C** ***Hostería Ahui***, Costanera 906, T622415. With breakfast, modern, clean, good views, restaurant. **C** ***Hotel Balai,*** Pudeto 169, T/F622541, hotelbalai@entelchile.net With heating, laundry, parking, restaurant, cable TV, interesting local paintings, models and artefacts on display. Tours arranged. **C** ***Polo Sur***, Costanera 630, T622200. With bath, good seafood restaurant, not cheap, avoid rooms overlooking disco next door. **C** ***Res Germania***, Pudeto 357, T/F622214. With bath, **D** without, parking, comfortable, clean. **C** ***Res Weschler***, Cochrane 480, T622318. With bath, **E** without. Clean, view of bay. **D** ***Lluhay***, Cochrane 458, T/F622656, meals served, recommended. **D** *Madryn*, Bellavista 491, T622128. With bath, also meals, clean. **D** *Posada Cumelen*, Quintanilla No 5, just off Pudeto 600 block, T/F625677, www2.netexplora.com/cumelen Comfortable rooms, with bath, heating, laundry, good breakfast, free internet, bar, pool table, great views, friendly, tours arranged, highly recommended.

E *Caleta Ancud*, Bellavista 449. Good breakfast, good restaurant. **E** *Hosp Alinar*, Ramírez 348. Clean, hospitable. Recommended. **E** *Hosp Alto Bellavista*, Bellavista 449, T622384, **G** with sleeping bag on floor. **E** *Hosp Capri*, Ramírez 325. Good breakfast. **E** *Hosp Santander*, Sgto Aldea 69. With bath, **F** without, clean. **E** *Hosp O'Higgins 06*, T6222266, with breakfast, spacious, interesting objets d'art, near the sea, nice views, recommended, with bath, **F** without. **E** *Res MaCarolina*, La Torre 558, T622458. With breakfast. **F** *Elena Bergmann*, Aníbal Pinto 382. Clean, friendly, use of kitchen, parking. **F** *Errázuriz 442*. With breakfast, cold water. **F** *Hosp Blanca Vargas*, Blanco Encalada 579, T624343, with breakfast. **F** *Hosp Elisabeth Vargas*, Carreras 821, T622296, nice house, clean, friendly, kitchen facilities. **F** *Hosp Miranda*, Mocopulli y Errázuriz, with breakfast comfortable. **F** *Hosp Sra Marta*, Lautaro 988, with breakfast, TV, kitchen facilities, good beds, good views from some rooms, good breakfast, recommended. **F** *Hostal Chiloe*, O'Higgins 274, T622869, with bath, large doll collection. **F** *Lautaro 947*, T2980. Clean, friendly. **F** *Marcopulli 710 y Ramirez* (enter through restaurant), very friendly, living room full of plants and flowers, full breakfast, quiet. **F** *Posada del Mar*, Anibal Pinto 1030, T623548, F623199, posadadelmar13@hotmail.com With breakfast. **F** *Pudeto 331*, T622535. Without bath, old fashioned. Recommended. **F** *Sra Lucía*, San Martín 705. **F-G** *Aguilera 756*, good beds, nice bathroom. **F-G** *Hosp San José*, Pudeto 619. With breakfast, large rooms, very friendly, internet, information, good beds, recommended. **G** *Aníbal Pinto 1340*, with breakfast. **G** *San Bernardo*, Errázuriz 395, T622657; dormitories, clean. Several others on same street. In summer the school on Calle Chacabuco is used as an *albergue*, **H**.

Camping At Arena Gruesa beach, at north end of Baguedano are: *Arena Gruesa*, F623428. **D** per site, and *Chiloé*, T622961, F2363647, **D** per site. Playa Gaviotas, 5 km north, T09-6538096, also has *cabañas*. **C** per site. Playa Larga Huicha, 9 km north. **F** per site, hot water, electricity.

Mid-range *Coral*, Pudeto 346. Good, not cheap. *El Mirador Restaurant*, 2 km west of Ancud, excellent and entertaining dinners – the chef sings (but don't ask him to sing Victor Jara songs). Highly recommended, good pisco sours, traditional *curantos* baked in the ground with advance notice. Also on road road to west, *Patagonia Beef*, Argentinian restaurant, lots of meat as is implied. *Jardín*, Pudeto 263. Good local food, not cheap. *Kuranton*, Prat 94, good *curantos*, seafood. Good lunches at *Hotel Polo Sur*. **Cheap** *Carmen*, Pudeto 159. Chilean cooking, *pasteles*. *El Cangrejo*, Dieciocho 155. Seafood highly recommended. *El Timon*, Yungay y Allende, small, cheap, good value. *El Trauco*, Blanco y Prat. Seafood excellent. Highly recommended. *Hamburguería*, Av Prat. Much better than name suggests, good seafood. *La Pincoya*, on Prat next to harbour. Seafood. *Lydia*, Pudeto 254. Chilean and international. *Macaval*, Chacabuco 691. Mar y Velas, Serrano 2. Beautiful views, good food. Also *El Sacho*, Mercado Municipal, Local 7, huge portions, not fancy but very reasonable; several similar places in same arcade. **Seriously cheap** *El Pinguinito*, lunch only, good. Also look in the market area, where there are *colaciones*.

Eating
● *on map, page 388*
Excellent cheap seafood restaurants in the market area

Chiloé

Pubs *Retro's Pub*, Maipú 615, off Pudeto, good ambience, food (including for vegetarians), good cocktails. Open Mon-Fri 1100-0300, Sat 2000-0400, in summer, Sun 2000-0400. **Discos** *Disco 'grado 30'*, Pudeto 270; *Entre Locos*, Km 3 on Lechagua road.

Entertainment

Shopping Opposite *Hotel Polo Sur* on the coast is a small kiosk selling many different types of the local artesanal liqueur: *licor de oro*. Excellent wooden toys are made by Lucho Troncoso, Prat 342, T09-2639383.

Tour *Austral Adventures*, www.australadventures.com Small group tours of Chiloe Archi-
companies pelago and northern Patagonia (including Parque Pumalín), hiking or by sea, bilingual guides, US run, recommended. *Paralelo 42*, Prat 28, T2458, F2656. Recommended for tours to the Río Chepu area, including 2-day kayak trips, guide Carlos Oyarzun (also at *Res MaCarolina*). Recommended. *Turismo Ancud*, Pudeto 219, Galería Yurie, T2235, Tx297700, ANCD CL. Tours also available from the kiosk on the plaza.

Transport **Bus** Local buses leave from the Terminal Rural at Pedro Montt 538. Long distance ter-
minal on eastern outskirts at Av Prat y Marcos Vera, reached by bus 1 or Pudeto *colectivos*. To Santiago, *Cruz del Sur*, US$25, *salón cama* US$36, 24 hrs. To Castro, fre-
quent, 1½ hrs, *Cruz del Sur/Regional Sur*, US$2.50, *Queilén Bus* US$2. To Chonchi US$3. To Quellón, *Cruz del Sur/Regional Sur*, 11 daily, US$5. To Puerto Montt, 2 hrs, frequent services by *Cruz del Sur*, US$4.50, *Regional Sur*, US$4, and *Queilen Bus*, US$3.50. To Quemchi via Linao and the coast, dramatic road plunging up and down forested hills by the coast, 2 hrs, US$1.50. **Cycle hire** *Ramírez 311*, US$1/hr or US$5/day.

Directory **Banks** ATM at *Banco BCI* on Ramirez, 1 block up from the plaza. *Casa de Cambio* on Ramírez, 1 block up the hill from the Plaza de Armas. **Communications** Post office: on corner of Plaza de Armas at Pudeto y Blanco Encalada. **Telephone:** Plaza de Armas. Open Mon-Sat 0700-2200. Also *Pudeto 219*, ENTEL, with internet; *Los Carreras 823*.

Around Ancud

Pumillahue Pumillahue is 27 km southwest of Ancud, on the Pacific coast. About 10 km before Pumillahue is **Mar Brava**, a vast curved beach, deserted, and wonderful for horseriding. About 3 km away from Pumillahue there is a penguin col-
ony situated on an island looked after by the Otway Foundation, T315494, otwafund@ctcinternet.cl Tours with their guides in English and German are US$5, or with local fishermen (in Spanish with exaggerated hand gestures) for US$3.50. The penguins are there from November to February. The best time to see them is in the early morning or evening.

Sleeping and eating Between Mar Brava and the penguins is the imaginatively named *Pinguinland Cabañas*, **AL** for 5-7 people, clean, also rooms, **C** for 2, clean. Spectacular view if weather is good, expensive meals. T627193, pinguinland@hotmail.com

Transport Buses to Pumillahue and Mar Brava from Ancud Mon-Sat 0645, Mon-Fri 1200, Sat 1400, Mon-Fri 1600 with *Buses Mar Brava*.

Chepu Chepu, on the coast southwest of Ancud and reached along a poor *ripio* road, is famed for its river and sea fishing. It is a base for exploring the drowned forest and the waterways of the Río Chepu and its tributaries (a result of the 1960 *maremoto*). There is a wide range of birdlife here. It is also the entrance to the north part of the Parque Nacional Chiloé, see page 400. At **Río Anguay** (also known as **Puerto Anguay**) there is a camping site and *refugio*. From here it is a 1½-hour walk to Playa Aulén which has superb forested dunes and an extinct volcano.

Boat trips can be organized in Río Anguay to Laguna Coluco, one hour up the Río Butalcura (a tributary of the Río Chepu). Two-day trips, navigating the ríos Grande, Carihueco and Butalcura, usually start further inland and finish at Río Anguay. These can be arranged in Ancud. For fishing trips in the area, try Alphonso Bergara, T09-5170358.

This area also offers great opportunities for **horseriding** with long beaches for galloping. Try Sr Zuñipe or Sr Uroa (recommended), US$5 per hour (ask at the *refugio* in Río Anguay).

Agrotourism Armando Pérez and Sonia Díaz make cheese, have cattle and sheep and have good walks in the Chepu area. To get there from Ancud, travel 26 km south on Route 5, turn right (east) for 5 km to Coipomó, there turn left, and after 3½ km turn right. The farm is on the left after 2 km, T09-6539241.

Transport Access is along a dirt road from the Pan-American Highway, at a junction 26 km south of Ancud. Alternatively there is a wild 2-day coastal walk from Ancud: you can take the daily bus to Pumillahue (0645, return 1330) or hitch. The route is difficult to follow so take food for 3 days and wear light-coloured clothes in summer to protect against *tavanos*.

Ancud to Castro

There are two alternative routes – direct along the Pan-American Highway, crossing rolling hills, forest and agricultural land, or via the east coast along unpaved roads passing through small farming and fishing communities and offering a real insight into rural life in Chiloé. The two main towns along the coastal route, Quemchi and Dalcahue, can also be reached by roads branching off the Pan-American Highway.

Quemchi is a quiet town with long beaches. There are wooded islands in the bay; a short walk up the road north towards Linao leads to high ground from which there are views to the temperate rainforest on the mainland. Miniature boats are made in the village. Some 4 km from Quemchi is Isla Aucar, once linked by bridge (now ruined), where black necked swans can be seen. There is a small tourist information booth in the plaza.

Quemchi
Colour map 4, grid C1
Population: 2,000
56 km south of Ancud

Sleeping and eating G *Hosp El Embrujo*, Pedro Montt 431, T651262. G *Hosp La Tranquera*, Yungay 40, T651250. Without bath, basic. *Restaurant Centenario*, Bahamonde 360, good, cheap. About 4 km north of Quemchi, at Huite, Magali Miranda offers agrotourism, where she produces honey, milk, preserves, and smoked salmon, T09-6539245 or 09-5173731. Also in Huite, Guillermo Hernández and Bernarda Zúñiga are part of the agrotourism network, offering similar activities, T09-6539239 or T09-6450918. At Tubildad, 2 km north of Quemchi, Juan Dougnac and Evangelina Cordaro go salmon fishing, T691305.

The road from Quemchi to Dalcahue (50 km) passes many places which are of the essence of Chiloé. The road rises up and down steep forested hills, rich with flowers, past salmon farms and views of distant bays. Some 20 km from Quemchi is a turn-off to Quicaví, legendary as the home to the witches of Chiloé; a further few kilometres brings you to Tenaún, a beautiful village with a church dating from 1837, which is now a UNESCO world heritage site – trips to neighbouring islands are easy to arrange here. There are then numerous small communities with churches and views to the coast before you reach Dalcahue.

Quemchi to Dalcahue

Chiloé

Agrotourism María Soto and Manuel Vásquez, who make honey, *chicha* and preserves, T09-6539416/6476752; and Mirella Montaña and Guido Vásquez, who make butter, preserves, *chicha* and pastries, T09-6539423/6476750.

Dalcahue
Colour map 4, grid C1
Population: 3,000

Seventy-four kilometres south of Ancud via the Pan-American Highway, Dalcahue is more easily reached from Castro, 30 km further south. It is one of the main ports for boats to the offshore islands, including Quinchao and Mechuque (see below). The wooden church on the main square dates from the 19th century, and is a UNESCO world heritage site. The market is on Sunday, from 0700 to 1300. It has good quality goods, but bargaining is practically impossible, and in recent years it has become somewhat overrun with tourists; good *curantos*, though. There is a tourist kiosk in season. Sea kayaking is offered by *Altue Active Travel* from its sea kayaking centre, 3 km south of Dalcahue.

Sleeping and eating E-F *La Feria*, Rodríguez 17, T641293. Without bath, basic. **E-F** *Res Playa*, Rodríguez 9. Basic. **F** *Hosp Mary*, Tte Merino 10, T641260, also sells handicrafts. **F** *Hosp Puteman*, Freire 305, T330. Clean, basic. **F** *Res San Martín*, San Martín 1, T641207. Basic, clean, also meals. *Restaurant La Dalca*, Freire 502, serves good, cheap food. Recommended. Numerous small restaurants along the harbour and around the market with excellent and cheap seafood.

Transport Buses to Castro, hourly, 40 mins, US$1. Also *colectivos* to Castro and to Achao, US$1.50. There are buses along the road to Quemchi, several daily.

Quinchao
Colour map 4, grid C1
Population: 2,500

The island of Quinchao is a short ferry journey from Dalcahue. Passing the pretty village of Curaço de Veléz, you reach the main settlement, **Achao**, 25 km southeast of Dalcahue. This is a large fishing village serving the smaller islands offshore, with a boarding school attended by pupils from outlying districts. Its wooden church, built in 1730, is the oldest surviving church in Chiloé. Saved by a change of wind from a fire which destroyed much of the town in 1784, it is a fine example of Chilote Jesuit architecture. There is a small museum, US$1. With persistence and patience, boats can be found to take you from Achao to outlying islands, where facilities are basic, shops non-existent (but lodging can be had with families; ask around). A beautiful road leads 9 km south of Achao to the small village of Quinchao in a secluded bay at the foot of a hill. There is a fine church here; a religious festival is held on 8 December (Dia de la Virgén), when people come from all over Chiloé to watch as a huge model of the Virgin is carried with great reverence to the church. There is a tourist office in Achao, Serrano y Progreso, open only from December to March.

Sleeping and eating D *Plaza*, Plaza de Armas, T661283. With bath and breakfast, clean, good. **D-E** *Hosp Chilhue*, Zañartu 021. Without bath, with breakfast, clean. **E** *Hosp Achao*, Serrano 061, T661373. Without bath, good, clean. **E** *Hostería La Nave*, Prat y Aldea, T/F661219. With bath. **F** without bath, with breakfast, restaurant with fine views over bay. **F** *Hosp Sao Paulo*, Serrano 52. Basic, poor beds, hot water. For eating, *Arrayan*, Zañartu 19. *Restaurant Central*, simple, cheap, good. Good food at the *Hostería La Nave*. All restaurants are cheap.

Agrotourism There are two agrotourist options on Quinchao: at Huyar Bajo (turn left before Achao en route from Cura,o de Velez), Juan Guilquiruca and Luzmira Barrientos make butter, preserves and *chicha*, T09-7963697; at Matao, on the southeastern tip of the island, Ramiro and María Cárcamo make preserves and *chicha*, T09-6539424/6216548.

Transport *Arriagada* buses from Ancud, 5 daily. For bus services from Castro see page 398. From Dalcahue, frequent, free for pedestrians and cyclists.

The Chauques are a group of 16 islands, interconnected by sandbars which are crossable at low tide. The largest island Mechuque, east of Dalcahue, has one village and offers splendid walking country. Beautiful views of the mainland in good weather.

Mechuque & the Chauques Islands

Sleeping and eating Accommodation with the schoolteacher's son or with Sra Dina del Carmen Paillacar, **E**, good meals. Recommended. **Transport** Bus from Tenaún, departs Wed 1730, returns Thu, 2½ hrs, US$2.50 one way.

Castro

The capital of Chiloé, Castro lies 88 km south of Ancud on a fjord on the east coast. It is a small, friendly town, full of bars and seafood restaurants where Chilotes from remote regions sit drinking chicha, *eating* cazuela *and swapping tall stories. The centre is on a promontory, from which there is a steep drop to the port. Castro is the major tourist centre of the island.*

Phone code: 065
Colour map 4, grid C1
Population: 20,000

Getting there Castro is the transport hub for Chiloé. There are many buses north to Ancud and Puerto Montt and south to Quellón (hourly). *Cruz del Sur* have buses continuing north to Valdivia, Temuco and Santiago (several daily). Many buses serve the more isolated Chilote communities from the Municipal Bus Terminal. **Getting around** There are some *colectivos* and public buses serving the *barrios* high above the town near the *media luna*, but it is unlikely that you will need to use these. It is only a half-hour walk up to there in any case. **Tourist offices** Kiosk run by local hotels and agencies, on Plaza de Armas opposite cathedral. CONAF in Gamboa behind the Gobernación building.

Ins & outs
See page 398 for further details

Sights

On the Plaza de Armas is the large **cathedral**, unmissable in its bright lilac and orange, built by the Italian architect, Eduardo Provosoli, and dating from 1906. South of the Plaza on the waterfront is the **Feria Artesanal**, where local woollen articles such as hats, sweaters, gloves can be found, though many of the articles sold are imported from elsewhere in South America. Nearby are several *palafito* restaurants, built on stilts above the water. More *palafitos* can be seen on the northern side of town and by the bridge over the Río Gamboa. There are good views of the city from **Mirador La Virgen** on Millantuy hill above the cemetery.

Museo Regional on Esmeralda, one block south of the Plaza de Armas, contains history, folklore, handicrafts and mythology of Chiloé and photos of the effects of the 1960 earthquake. ■ *Summer Mon-Sat 0930-2000, Sun 1030-1300; winter Mon-Sat 0930-1300, 1500-1830, Sun 1030-1300.* **Museo de Arte Moderno** is in the Parque Municipal, about 3 km northwest of the centre. It is reached by following Calle Galvarino Riveros up the hill west of town, from where there are fine views. ■ *T632787, F635454. 1000-1900.*

Passing the Parque Municipal, Calle Galvarino Riveros becomes a small track heading out into the thick forests of the interior, with several small farmsteads – it's delightful. There is also a pleasant walk through woods and fields to

Excursions

Chiloé

Puntilla Ten Ten and the Peninsula opposite Castro. It is a two-hour round trip; turn off the Pan-American Highway, 2 km north of town. **Nercón**, 4 km south, has a wooden church which was restored in 1996.

Essentials

Sleeping
■ *on map*
Price codes:
see inside front cover

AL *Cabañas Pleno Centro*, Los Carrera 346, T635092, sleeps 2, also larger, with kitchen. **AL** *Gran Alerce*, O'Higgins 808, T632267, 4 km south of Castro. Heating, helpful, breakfast, also has *cabañas* and restaurant. **AL** *Hostería Castro*, Chacabuco 202, T632301, F635668. With breakfast, good restaurant, wonderful views. **AL** *Unicornio Azul*, Pedro Montt 228, T632359, F632808. Good views over bay, comfortable, restaurant, English spoken. **B** *Casa Kolping*, Chacabuco 217, T/F633273. **B** *Casita Española*, Los Carrera 359, T635186. Heating, TV, parking. Recommended. **B** *Chilhue*, Blanco Encalada 278, T632956. With bath, good. **B** *Motel Auquilda*, Km 2 north on the Pan-American Highway, T632458. **C** *Casa Blanca*, Los Carrera 308, T/F632726. With breakfast, without bath, clean, modern, warm, also *cabañas*, sleeps 5. **C** *Costa Azul*, Lillo 67, T632440. With bath, **D** without. Friendly. **D** *Hilton*, Ramírez 385. Good value, friendly, restaurant. **E** *Hosp Sotomayor*, Sotomayor 452, T632464. With breakfast, quiet, small beds. **E** *Los Carrera 658*, no sign, with breakfast, clean, friendly. Recommended. **E** *Res El Gringo*, Lillo 51. Without bath, good views, overpriced. **F** *Chacabuco 449*. Good beds, clean, quiet, friendly, water only warm. **F** *Eyzaguirre 469*. Comfortable. Recommended. **F** *Freire 758*. Breakfast, clean, good value. **F** *Hosp of Jessie Toro*, Las Delicias 287. With good breakfast, helpful, clean, spacious, good bathrooms, also *cabañas*. Recommended. **F** *Hospedaje América*, Chacabuco 215, T634364. Friendly, very good food – "our tourists arrive thin and leave fat" – cable TV, shared bathrooms, breakfast. **F** *Hosp Bellavista*, Barros Arana 151, clean, good views. **F** *Hosp El Mirador*, Barros Arana 127, T633795. Good breakfast, kitchen facilities, good views, very clean. **F** *Hospedaje El Molo*, Arana 140, T635026. 20-30 beds, use of kitchen. **F** *Hosp Llapui*, O'Higgins 657. Run down, with breakfast. **F** *Hosp Tonque*, Pasaje Díaz 170, T632773. Without breakfast, clean, hot water. **F** *Los Carrera 560*, T632472. Clean, hot water. **F** *María Zuñiga*, Barros Arana 140, T635026. With breakfast, clean, comfortable, cooking facilities, friendly, secure. Recommended. **F** *O'Higgins 415*, Dpto 41. Quiet, very clean, hot water. **F** *O'Higgins 765*. Clean, friendly. **F** *Res La Casona*, Serrano 488, above TV shop. With breakfast. Recommended. **F** *Los Carrera 785*, T632989, with good breakfast. **F** *Serrano 407*. Breakfast, friendly, warm water. **G** *Hosp Polo Sur*, Barros Arana 169, T635212. Cooking facilities, wonderful views, noisy. Basic, noisy accommodation Dec-Feb in the Gimnasio Fisical, Freire 610, T632766, **H**.

On the road to Chonchi AL *Cabañas Centro Turístico Nercón*, Km 5, T632985, with bath, hot water, heating, restaurant, tennis court. **A** *Cabañas Trayen*, Km 5, T633633. **B** off season, lovely views. **A** *Posada Alemana*, Km 5, noisy. **B** *Cabañas Llicaldad*, Km 6, T635080 (or Esmeralda 269, Castro), also camping.

San Martín B/C *Hostal Quelqún*, No 581, T632396. With bath, **F** without, heating, helpful. **E** *Res Mirasol*, No 815. Basic, friendly, noisy. **F** *Hosp Chiloé*, No 739. Breakfast, clean. Recommended. **F** *Hosp Guillermo*, No 700. Clean, cheap. **F** *Pensión Victoria*, No 747. Small rooms, clean, pretty. **F** *Res Capullito*, No 709. Clean, friendly, quiet. **G** *No 879*. With big breakfast, central, clean. Highly recommended. **G** *Lidia Low*, No 890. With good breakfast, warm showers, use of kitchen.

Camping *Pudu*, 10 km north on the Pan-American Highway, T/F632476, **F** per site. Also *cabañas*, hot showers, sites with light, water, children's games. Several sites along road south towards Chonchi including: Montpellier, Km 2; Santa Elba, Km 4; El Chilote, Km 4.5, **E** per site, also *cabañas*; Llicaldad, Km 6, T638188/635080, **E** per site.

Chiloé

Mid-range *Anadito* pub/restaurant, on Plaza – good. *Del Mirador*, on Plaza. Meat and seafood specialities. *Donde Eladio*, Lillo 97, same owner as Del Mirador, same menu. *Gipsy*, O'Higgins 548. Chinese. *La Playa*, Lillo 441, fish, meat, recommended. **Cheap and seriously cheap** Palafito restaurants near the Feria Artesanía on the waterfront offer good food and good value, including *Brisas del Mar* (mixed reports), *La Amistad* and *Rapu Nui. Chilo's*, San Martín 459. Good lunches. *Don Camilo*, Ramírez 566. Good food, not expensive. *El Curanto*, Lillo 67. Seafood including *curanto*. Recommended. *Sacho*, Thompson 213. Good sea views. Recommended. Also very cheap restaurant by the municipal bus terminal. **Cafés** *La Brújula del Cuerpo*, Plaza de Armas. Good coffee, snacks. *Stop Inn Café*, Prat y Chacabuco. Good coffee. In the market, try *milcaos*, fried potato cakes with meat stuffing.

Eating
● *on map*
*Breakfast before
0900 is difficult*

Hiper Beckna supermarket, Sargento Aldea y O'Higgins; good bakery. *Cema-Chile* outlet on Esmeralda, next to Museo Regional. The **Municipal Market**, Yumbel St, off Pilato Samuel Ulloa, has good fish and vegetables. There is also an **Artisans' Market** on the wharf with good quality woollens at reasonable prices. *Annay Libros*, Serrano 357, and *El Tren Libros*, Thompson 229, both sell books in Spanish on Chiloé, often cheaper than Santiago bookshops. Also *Libros Chiloé*, Blanco Encalada 204. Cassettes of typical Chilote music are widely available.

Shopping

Castro

Chiloé

Tour companies

The prices of tours are US$25 to Parque Nacional Chiloé, US$37 to Mechuque

Chiotours, Blanco 293, T639544, to Chiloé national park, Quinchao, Lemuy, Queilen, Castro, boat trips.*Turismo Isla Grande*, Thompson 241, Transmarchilay and Navimag agency. *Turismo Pehuén*, Blanco Encalada 299 y Esmeralda, T632361, F635254, pehuentr@entelchile.net *LanChile/Ladeco* agents. Horseriding excursions, trips to national park, penguins and islands. *Turismo Queilén*, Gamboa 502, T632776. Good tours to Chonchi and Chiloé National Park. Recommended. Local guide Sergio Márquez, Felipe Moniel 565, T632617, very knowledgeable, has transport.

Transport

There are 2 bus terminals. *Cruz del Sur* services depart from *Cruz del Sur* terminal, T632389 on San Martín behind the cathedral. Other services leave from the Municipal Terminal, San Martín, 600 block (2 blocks further north). Castro is the hub for services to rural communities, leaving mostly from the Municipal terminal. Frequent services to **Chonchi**, choose between buses (*Cruz del Sur, Queilén Bus* and others), minibuses and *colectivos* (from Ramirez y San Martín and Esmeralda y Chacabuco). *Arroyo* and *Ocean Bus* both run to **Cucao** for the **Parque Nacional Chiloé**, 1 a day off season, 6 daily in summer, US$2.20; avoid Fri, when the service is crowded with schoolchildren. To **Dalcahue** frequent services by *Gallardo* and *Arriagada*, also *colectivos* from San Martín 815. To **Tenaún**, daily 1200. To **Achao** (US$1.75) via **Dalcahue** and **Curaco de Vélez** (US$1.50), **Arriagada**, 4 daily, 3 on Sun, last return from Achao 1730. To **Puqueldón Gallardo**, Mon-Sat, 4 a day, US$1.50; to **Quellón**, *Cruz del Sur/Trans Chiloé*, frequent (US$2); to **Queilén**, *Queilen Bus*, 6 a day, US$2.50; to **Quemchi**, 1 a day, *Queilén Bus*. Frequent services to **Ancud** (1 hr) and **Puerto Montt** (3 hrs, US$4.50) by *Cruz del Sur, Trans Chiloé* and *Queilén Bus. Cruz del Sur* also run to **Osorno, Valdivia, Temuco, Concepción** and **Santiago**. *Bus Norte* to **Ancud, Puerto Montt, Osorno** and **Santiago** daily; to **Punta Arenas**, *Queilén Bus*, Mon, 36 hrs, US$60.

Directory

Airline offices *LanChile*, Blanco 209. *Ladeco* agency on Serrano, opposite *Hostería Castro*. **Banks** *Banco de Chile*, Plaza de Armas. ATM. Accepts TCs (at a poor rate). *BCI*, Plaza de Armas. Mastercard and Visa ATM. Better rates from *Julio Barrientos*, Chacabuco 286. Cash and TCs. **Communications** *Internet at O'Higgins 486*. US$7 per hour, charged by the minute. Open 0900 to 1300 and 1600 to 2200. Also at Cadesof Ltda, Gamboa 447, 2nd floor, and n@vegue, San Martín 309. **Phone office:** Latorre 289. *Entel*, O'Higgins between Sotomayor and Gamboa. Also private centres at *Latorre 275* and *Lillo 93*. **Post office**: on west side of Plaza de Armas. **Film** At *Blanco 360* or *Gamboa 450*. **Medical services** Doctor: Muñoz de Las Carreras, near police station. Surgery 1700-2000 on weekdays. Recommended. **Laundry** *Clean Centre*, Serrano 440. *Lavandería Adolfo*, Blanco Encalada 96. Quick, reasonably priced. *Lavaseco Unic*, Gamboa 594, T635766.

Castro to Quellón

The Pan-American Highway continues south to Quellón, the southernmost port in Chiloé. There are paved side roads to Chonchi and an unpaved one to Cucao. From Chonchi a road runs south to Queilen. This road, 7 km of which is paved, winds across forested hills, and is probably the most attractive on the island, especially in autumn; there are numerous sideroads leading to deserted beaches where you can walk for hours and hear nothing but the plashing of dolphins in the bays.

Chonchi

Phone code: 065
Colour map 4, grid C1
Population: 4,000
23 km south of Castro

A picturesque fishing village, Chonchi is a good base for exploring the island. Known as the *Ciudad de los Tres Pisos*, or 'the city built on three levels', it was, until the opening of the Panama Canal, a stopping point for sailing ships. In the years which followed it was the cypress capital of Chile: big fortunes were made and the grand timber mansions in the town date from this period. In the 1950s the town boomed as a free port, but in the 1970s it lost that status to Punta Arenas. Its harbour is now the supply point for the salmon farms almost as far south as Coyhaique. There is a kiosk with tourist information on the main plaza in summer.

On the plaza is the church, built in neo-classical style in 1880. From the plaza Calle Centenario, with several attractive but sadly neglected wooden mansions, drops steeply to the harbour. Fishing boats bring in the early morning catch which is carried straight into the nearby market. There is an 18th-century church at Vilopulli, 5 km north.

A *Posada Antiguo Chalet*, Gabriela Mistral, T671221. **B** in winter, charming, beautiful location, very good. **B** *Cabañas Amankay*, Centenario 421, T671367. Homely, kitchen facilities. Recommended. **D** *Huildin*, Centenario 102, T671388. Without bath, old fashioned, good beds, also *cabañas* **A**, garden with superb views, parking. **E** *Hosp Mirador*, Alvarez 198. With breakfast, friendly, clean. Recommended. **F** *Aguirre Cerda 160*. There are other *hospedajes* on Irarrazával, eg Nos 181, 189. **F** *Baker at Andrade 184*. Clean, friendly. **F** *Esmeralda by the Sea*, on waterfront 100 m south of the market, T/F671328, grady@telsur.cl (Casilla 79). With breakfast, attractive, welcoming, English spoken, kitchen facilities, cheap meals served, good beds, canoe and boat trips offered, also rents bicycles, information. Highly recommended. **F** *Res Turismo*, Andrade 299, T257. Without bath, with breakfast. **G** *Refugio Sra*, Fedima, Pedro Aquire Cerda 176. Own sleeping bag required, use of kitchen, friendly. Also *Cabañas América*, Pedro Jose Ondrade 159. **Camping** *Los Manzanos*, Aguirre Cerda y Juan Guillermo, T671263. **E** per site.

Mid-range *La Parada*, Centenario 133. Very friendly, good selection of wines, erratic opening hours. Recommended. **Cheap** *El Alerce*, Aguirre Cerda 106. Excellent value. *El Trébol*, Irarrazával 187. Good views over harbour. *La Quila*, Andrade 183. Cheap, good, popular with locals.

Bars *Club 88* bar/restaurant, on waterfront. **Discos** *Rockets Disco*, near *Copec* filling station, weekends, more often in summer. *La Semana Chonchina* is during the second week of **Feb**.

Handicrafts from *Opdech* (Oficina Promotora del Desarrollo Chilote), on the waterfront, and from the *parroquia*, next to the church (open Oct-Mar only). In the summer many artesanal stalls open, a speciality being traditional woollen clothes.

Bus Buses and taxis to **Castro**, frequent, US$0.75, from main plaza. To **Puerto Montt** US$5.50. Services to **Quellón** and **Queilén** from Castro and Puerto Montt and from Castro to **Cucao** also call here.

Banks *Nicolás Alvarez*, Centenario 429. Cash only. **Communications** Call centre: San Martín y Mistral.

Sleeping

Eating

Entertainment

Shopping

Transport

Directory

Chiloé

This island, covering 97 sq km, lies opposite Chonchi and offers many good walks along quiet unpaved roads through undulating pastures and woodland. From the ferry crossing a road runs east across the island to **Puqueldón**, the main settlement (built on a very steep hill down to the port). At Km 3 there is a fine 19th-century wooden church at Ichuac. From Puqueldón the road continues a further 16 km on a ridge high above the sea, passing small hamlets, with views of the water and the patchwork of fields. There are old churches at Aldachildo, 9 km east of Puqueldón, and at Detif, in the extreme south of the island.

Lemuy
Colour map 4, grid C1
Population: 4,200

Sleeping and eating F *Restaurant Lemuy* and *Café Amancay*. Both in Puqueldón, both clean, without bath, good, food served only in high season. Puqueldón also has a post office and a telephone centre. **Camping** *Los Isleños*, 1½ km from Puqueldón, T09-6548498. **Agrotourism** At Puchilco, 10 km beyond Puqeldón, Lidia and José Pérez make butter, preserves and *chicha*, T09-8842430/8998914/4440252.

Transport Bus 4 a day except Sun from Castro. **Ferry** Service from Puerto Huicha, 4 km south of Chonchi, approximately every ½ hrs, foot passengers free.

Queilen
Colour map 4, grid C1
46 km SE from
Chonchi

Queilen is a pretty fishing village with long beaches and a wooden pier. The beach by the port runs in a long finger-shaped peninsula which returns to the other side of the town. There are fine views of Tanqui Island across the straits, and of the mainland. If you'd like to stay the night there is the basic *Pensión Chiloé*, friendly, without bath, **G** and the friendly *Restaurant Melinka*. There is also accommodation in the big house beside the pier, **F**, and cheapish food at *Bar Restaurant El Refugio*. ■ *Getting there: buses to Castro, Queilen Bus, 6 a day, 4 on Sat, 3 on Sun, 2 hrs, US$2.50.*

Agrotourism Several options between Chonchi and Queilen, including Ernesto Gamín and Diana Bahamonde at Contuy, who make butter and *chicha* and have cattle and sheep, T09-6539206 or T09-6449262 – 28 km south of Chonchi, turn west, and travel a further 10 km. Also, at Dét ico, Manuel Pérez and Bertila Díaz make butter, cheese, honey and *chicha*, T02-9605558 – 4 km before Queilen turn right, and travel a further 6 km; the farm is by the football pitch.

Cucao

One of only two settlements on the west coast of Chiloé, Cucao lies 40 km west of Chonchi by *ripio* road. At Km 12 is Huillinco, a charming village on Lago Huillinco with an **F** per person *residencial* with good food, or stay at the Post Office. Cucao lies at the southern edge of the southern section of the Parque Nacional Chiloé. There is an immense 20-km long beach with thundering Pacific surf and dangerous undercurrents; this is one of the most dramatic places along the whole coast of Chile.

Sleeping and eating F *Casa Blanca*, T633040. With breakfast. F *Hosp Paraíso*, T633040. Friendly. F *Posada Cucao*, T633040. With breakfast, hot water, meals, friendly. **F** with full board or *demi-pension* at *Provisiones Pacífico* (friendly, good, clean, no hot water). Meals and good homemade bread. Recommended. **G** *Parador Darwin*, with breakfast, good food with vegetarian options, real coffee. Highly recommended. **Camping** Several campsites including *Parador Darwin*. Check prices carefully first. *Lago Mar*, 2 km east, T635552. US$12 per site. *Las Luminarias* sells excellent *empanadas de machas* (*machas* are local shellfish).

Transport Six buses a day from Castro via Chonchi in season, US$2.20, last departure 1600, reduced service off-season; hitching is very difficult.

Parque Nacional Chiloé

The park, which is in three sections, covers extensive areas of the wild and uninhabited western side of the island. Much of it is filled by temperate rainforest. The southern sector, 35,207 ha, is entered via a bridge 1 km north of Cucao, where there is an administration centre with limited information and a guest bungalow for use by visiting scientists; applications to CONAF via your embassy. In 1998 the bridge connecting Cucao and the park collapsed, but it has since been replaced. However, the second bridge, past the visitors centre, has been washed out – there is a boat service. You can take a car as far as the visitors centre, where there are decent camping facilities. ■ *US$2. Maps of the park are available. Refugios are inaccurately located.*

There are many wonderful walks. A path runs 3 km north from the administration centre to Laguna Huelde and then north a further 12 km to Cole Cole. From the path there are great views. Once you reach Río Anay you can wade or swim across the river to reach a beautiful, secluded beach from where you have a fantastic view of dolphins playing in the huge breakers. The journey can be made on horseback, US$40 a day, horses of varying tameness, taking nine hours for the round trip. There is a *refugio* at Cole Cole and camping. Take lots of water and your own food. The next *refugio* is at Anay, 9 km further north. There are several other walks but signposts are limited. Many houses in Cucao rent horses at US$2.50 per hour, US$22 per day. If you hire a guide you pay for his horse too. *Tavanos* are bad in summer so wear light coloured clothing.

Wildlife includes the Chiloé fox and pudu deer. There are over 110 species of birds including cormorants, gulls, penguins and flightless steamer ducks

■ *Getting there: for transport to northern sector see under Chepu, page 392; for southern sector see under Cucao. The third section, the small island of Metalqui, is not easily accessible.*

Quellón

The southernmost port in Chiloé, Quellón is the departure point for ferries to Chaitén. Most of the town's commercial activity lies along the attractive waterfront on Costanera Pedro Montt; however, there is not that much of interest here, and most people arriving here from the Camino Austral will

Phone code: 065
Colour map 5, grid A2
Population: 18,700
92 km S of Castro

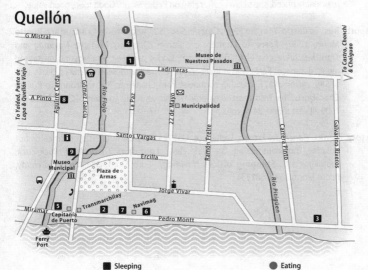

Quellón

To Castro, Chonchi & Chaiguao

To Yaldad, Punta de Lapa & Quellón Viejo

Museo de Nuestros Pasados

Municipalidad

Plaza de Armas

Capitanía de Puerto

Ferry Port

Museo Municipal

N

Not to scale

Chiloé

■ **Sleeping**
1 Club Deportes Turino
2 El Chico Leo
3 G Laris
4 La Pincoya
5 Las Brisas
6 Melimoyu
7 Playa
8 Residencial Esteban
9 Residencial Estrella del Mar

● **Eating**
1 Fogón Las Quilas
2 Los Suizos

want to press on northwards.

There are pleasant beaches nearby. Viejo, 4 km west, with an old wooden church, Punta de Lapa, 7 km west, and Yaldad, 9 km west along a pretty road over the hills. The launch Puerto Bonito sails three times daily in summer from the pier, to tour the bay passing Punta de Lapa, Isla Laitec and Quellón Viejo, US$12.50. A trip can also be made to Chaiguao,11 km east, where there is a small Sunday morning market. Horses can be hired US$2.50 per hour; kayaks with a guide, US$2.50 per hour.

In Quellón the **Museo de Nuestros Pasados**, Ladrilleros 225, includes reconstructions of traditional Chilote house and mill.

Sleeping ■ *on map*
Price codes:
see inside front cover

B *Melimoyu*, Pedro Montt 375, T681250. Clean, good beds, parking. **C** *El Chico Leo*, Pedro Montt 325. Without bath. **E** *Playa*, Pedro Montt 427, T68127. With breakfast, without bath. Clean. **F** *G Laris*, Pedro Montt 45, with breakfast. **F** *Hosp La Paz*, La Paz 370, T681207. With breakfast, hot water. **F** *La Pincoya*, La Paz 064, T681285. **F** *Res Esteban*, Aguirre Cerda 351, safe clean. **F** *Res Estrella del Mar*, Gómez García 248. Without bath, basic, poor value. **G** *Club Deportes Turino*, Ladrilleros y La Paz 024. Floor space and camping, cold water, kitchen facilities, basic. Open Dec-Feb only. **G** *Las Brisas*, Pedro Montt 555, T681413. Without bath, basic. The school becomes an *albuergue* in summer; **H** locals, **G** foreigners, dormitory accommodation. **At Punta de Lapa Camping** Five sites in Punta de Lapa. Also sites without services at Chaiguao and Yaldad. *Leo Man*, chalets and *cabañas*, and *Cabañas y Camping Las Brisas*. **Agrotourism** Near Quellón is Mercedes Vargas, who makes preserves and *chicha*. About 10 km north on Route 5 from Quellón, turn right at Candelaria; the farm is 2 km on the right, T09-6539213.

Eating **Mid-range** *Fogón Las Quilas*, La Paz 053, T206. Famous for lobster. Recommended. *Los Suizos*, Ladrilleras 399, Swiss cuisine, good. **Cheap** *El Coral*, 22 de Mayo. Good, reasonably priced, superb views. Rucantú on Pedro Montt. Good food, good value.

Transport **Bus** To **Castro**, 2 hrs, frequent, *Cruz del Sur*, US$3; also services to **Ancud** and **Puerto Montt** (US$7). **Ferry** To **Chaitén**: in summer (Dec-early Mar) the *Navimag* and *Transmarchilay* serve Chaitén, on the mainland, 4 per week; 5-hr crossing, off-season reduced service. Fares: passengers US$20-28, reclining seats (*literas*) US$30, cars US$88, cycles US$11. The ship continues from Chaitén to Puerto Montt. To **Puerto Chacabuco**: the *Transmarchilay* ferry *Pincoya* also sails to **Puerto Chacabuco** Sat 1900 all year round, 24 hr voyage.

Directory **Banks** *Banco del Estado*, Ladrilleros. US$12 commission on TCs, credit cards not possible, no commission on US$ cash. **Laundries** *Lavandería Ruck-Zuck*, Ladrilleras 392. **Shipping offices** *Navimag*, Pedro Montt 383. *Transmarchilay*, Pedro Montt 457, T681331.

Chiloé

The Camino Austral

12

The Camino Austral

For 1,000 km south of Puerto Montt, the laws of nature seem to be temporarily suspended. Before the opening of the Camino Austral (formerly the Carreterra Austral), this long stretch of country was largely inaccessible. It remains breathtaking. Deep tree-lined fjords penetrate into the heart of a land of spiralling volcanoes and glaciers, running beside rushing rivers and temperate rainforest rich with southern Chile's unique flora. The only town of any size, Coyhaique, lies in the valley of the Río Simpson. South of Coyhaique are Lago General Carrera, the largest lake in Chile, and the Río Baker, one of the longest rivers in the country. Further south still are the icefields of the Campo de Hielos Sur, which feed the magnificent glacier at Laguna San Rafael. Coyhaique enjoys good air connections with Puerto Montt and Santiago while, nearby, Puerto Chacabuco can be reached by ferry from Puerto Montt, Puerto Natales and Chiloé. The most appealing parts of this region, however, can only be visited by travelling along the Camino Austral.

The Camino Austral

Background

History The original inhabitants were Tehuelches (Tzónecas, or Patagones), who lived on the pampa hunting guanacos, *ñandúes* (rheas) and *huemules* (an indigenous deer, now almost extinct), and *alacalufes* (Kaweshour, or *canoeros*), who were coast dwellers living off the sea. (See pages 517 and 441.) There are some fine cave paintings in the vicinity of Lago General Carrera, for example at Cueva de la Guanaca, near Lago Lapparent, and Cueva de las Manos, on the Argentine side of the frontier near Chile Chico.

The Spanish called the region Trapalanda, but initially explored little more than the coast. This was the last territory to be occupied by the Chilean state after independence from Spain. In the late 19th century expeditions up the rivers led by George Charles Musters (1869) and Enríque Simpson Baeza (1870-72) were followed by a failed attempt to found a settlement at the mouth of the Río Palena in 1884. Fearing that Argentina might seize the territory, the Chilean government appointed Hans Steffen to explore the area. His seven expeditions (1892-1902) were followed by an agreement with Argentina to submit the question of the frontier to arbitration by the British crown.

Chile's first attempt to occupy the area was by granting concessions to three large cattle companies. One of these, on the Río Baker, was managed by E Lucas Bridges, of the Bridges family from Tierra del Fuego and author of *Uttermost Part of the Earth* (for more details, see *South* by AF Tschiffely). Until the 1920s there were few settlers; early pioneers settled along the coast and supplied themselves from Chiloé. The first estimate, in 1907, gave the population as 197. By 1920 this had risen to 1,660 and by 1930, 8,886 inhabitants were in the region. Although the first town, Balmaceda, was founded in 1917, followed by Puerto Aisén in 1924, the first road, between Puerto Aisén and Coyhaique, was not built until 1936. It was not until the 1960s when new roads were built and airstrips were opened that the integration of this region with the rest of the country began.

Geography
This is one of the most sparsely populated areas of Chile, with fewer than 100,000 inhabitants, most of whom live in Coyhaique or in nearby Puerto Aisén

South of Puerto Montt the sea has broken through the coastal *cordillerra* and drowned the central valley between the Andes and the coastal *cordillerra* – Chilote legend ascribes this fact to a war between two serpents, one good (on land) and one evil (in the sea). The higher parts of the coastal *cordillerra* form a maze of islands, stretching for over 1,000 km and separated from the coast by tortuous fjords.

The Andes are much lower than further north and eroded by glacial action: towards the coast they rise in peaks such as San Valentín (4,058 m), the highest mountain south of Talca; inland they form a high steppe around 1,000 m. To the south of Coyhaique are two areas of highland covered by ice, known as *campos de hielo* (icefields). The Campo de Hielo Norte, over 100 km from north to south and some 50 km from west to west, includes the glaciers San Rafael, San Quintin and Steffen. The Campo de Hielo Sur covers a larger area, stretching south from the mouth of the Río Baker towards Puerto Natales.

Five main rivers flow westwards: from north to south these are the Futaleufú or Yelcho, the Palena, the Cisnes, the Simpson or Aisén and the Baker. The latter, at 370 km, is the third longest river in Chile. Only the Cisnes and the Simpson are entirely in Chile, the other three being fed from Argentina. The three largest lakes in this region, Lago General Carrera, Lago Cochrane and Lago O'Higgins, are also shared with Argentina.

Things to do in the Camino Austral

- Visit the Parque Pumalin. Not only is it an area of outstanding beauty, it also gives an insight into what is widely regarded as one of the world's most important conservation projects.
- Sail on a cruise ship right up to the icebergs at the foot of the Laguna San Rafael.
- Trek, especially near Futaleufú in the north, and Chile Chico in the south.
- Take a ferry ride across the huge, deep blue expanse of Lago General Carrera, between Puerto Ibañez and Chile Chico.
- Mountain-bike along the whole length of the spectacular Camino Austral itself.

Climate
Jan and Feb are probably the best months for a trip here

There is no real dry season. On the offshore islands and along the coast annual rainfall is over 2,000 mm. Westerly winds are strong, especially in summer. Temperatures vary little between day and night. Inland on the steppe the climate is drier and colder.

Economy

Agriculture is limited by the climate and poverty of the soil. Potatoes and cereals are among the major crops, while sheep farming is more important than cattle. The shores of Lago General Carrera enjoy a warm microclimate which allows the production of fruit. Fishing remains important as a source of employment in the inland channels. Forestry plays a growing role in the economy: wood is used for construction and in towns such as Coyhaique is in such demand in winter for fuel that it costs as much as petrol. Zinc, lead and copper are mined, but of these only zinc is produced in major quantities. Manufacturing is mainly restricted to processing local agricultural produce.

The Camino Austral

Travelling along the Camino Austral is one of the greatest journeys Chile has to offer. The Camino is an unmade-up ripio road stretching over 1,000 km; watching the cloak of dust thrown up when hitching in the back of a pick-up, while taking in the forests, mountains and waterfalls, is an unforgettable experience. Much of the road passes through virgin temperate rainforest, from Puerto Montt to the small community of Villa O'Higgins. Beyond this, the icefields of the Campo de Hielo Sur prevent further construction.

Although the road has helped transform the lives of many people in this part of Chile, the motivation behind its construction was mainly geopolitical. Ever since independence, Chilean military and political leaders have stressed the importance of occupying the southern regions of the Pacific coast and preventing any incursion by Argentina. Building the Camino Austral was seen by General Pinochet as a means of achieving this task: a way of occupying and securing territory, just as colonization had been in the early years of the 20th century.

Begun in 1976, the central section of the Camino Austral, from Chaitén to Coyhaique, was opened in 1983. Five years later the northern section, linking Chaitén with Puerto Montt, and the southern section, between Coyhaique and Cochrane, were officially completed. Since then the work has been completed, taking the road south of Cochrane to Villa O'Higgins.

The road can be divided into three sections: Puerto Montt-Chaitén (242 km) with two or three ferry crossings; Chaitén-Coyhaique (435 km); and Coyhaique-Villa O'Higgins (582 km) with one ferry crossing. There is also a

The Camino Austral

Pudu

To see a pudu in the wild is a very rare experience. These miniature deer, approximately 40 cm tall and weighing only 10 kg, are ideally adapted to the dense undergrowth of the temperate rainforests of Chile and Argentina. Reddish-brown in colour (the males grow two short spiked antlers) the pudu is the smallest member of the deer family in the world. They scoot along on trail systems which weave around in the undergrowth, leaving behind minuscule 2 cm long cloven tracks. They are reported to live solitary lives, perhaps due to the dense habitat in which they live. Native to southern Argentina and Chile, the pudu is listed in Chile as vulnerable to extinction, largely due to habitat loss, but also because their unique appearance has led to poaching for zoos. The Camino Austral area is one of the best for trying to spot one.

branch which runs along the southern shore of Lago General Carrera to Chile Chico; one part of this was the most expensive to build as a route had to be cleared along the sheer rock face of the lake. The Puerto Montt-Chaitén section can only be travelled in summer, when the ferries are operating, but an alternative route, through Chiloé to Chaitén, exists year round. The plan is to have the road paved from Puerto Montt to Villa Cerro Castillo and Puerto Ibañez by 2005.

Most of the villages along the Camino are of very recent origin and consist of a few wooden houses, some of which offer accommodation and other services to travellers. Although tourist infrastructure is growing rapidly, motorists should carry adequate fuel and spares, especially if intending to detour from the main route, and should protect their windscreens and headlamps. Some sections of the road can be difficult or even impassable after heavy rainfall. Unleaded fuel is available as far south as Cochrane. Cyclists should note the danger of stones thrown up by passing vehicles; motorists should protect their windscreens for the same reason. See box on page 409 for further information on cycling the Camino Austral. Hitching is popular in season, but be prepared for long delays and allow at least three days from Chaitén to Coyhaique; south of Coyhaique, hitching is very difficult.

Puerto Montt to Chaitén

This section of the Camino Austral, 242 km long, passes two national parks and the private Parque Pumalin. The route includes two ferry crossings. This is perhaps the most inaccessible and secluded section of the whole Camino Austral. Beautiful old trees close in on all sides, the rivers and streams sparkle, and on (admittedly rare) clear days there are beautiful views across the Golfo de Ancud to Chiloé; those who travel this part of the road rate it very highly. Before setting out, it is imperative to check when the ferries are running and, if driving, make a reservation: do this at the *Transmarchilay* office in Puerto Montt, rather than in Santiago. The alternative to this section is by ferry from Puerto Montt or Quellón to Chaitén.

The road from Puerto Montt to La Arena will be paved by 2003 – half is paved already. The road heads west out of Puerto Montt, through Pelluco and follows the shore of the beautiful Seno Reloncaví passing the southern entrance of the Parque Nacional Alerce Andino, Km 40.

The Camino Austral on two wheels

Cycling the Camino Austral is highly recommended, but you need plenty of time to enjoy it. Going by bus is way too fast and hitching can be competitive in the high season, with up to 20 people trying to get a ride out of the same place. In emergencies or if you are pushed for time, it is fairly easy to catch a bus, although you may need to wait a day to make a connection, and buses charge extra for the bikes.

Stock up on provisions in major towns. Bread is generally available in small towns or houses en route. Free camping is fairly easy to find and water is easily available from small streams or by asking at nearby

houses. The road conditions of the Camino vary, but the uphill stretches (cuestas) are manageable. An especially rainy section is through the Parque Nacional Queulat. If it looks like raining here, try to head for the camping areas which have covered spaces for fires and picnic tables. The circuit around Lago General Carrera via Puerto Ibáñez and Chile Chico involves a ferry journey across the lake; the scenery is spectacular but there are some very challenging passes on the southern shore. If possible, travel from Cochrane towards Chile Chico to take advantage of the spectacular views of the Andes.

Situated between the Seno Reloncaví to the south and west and Lago Chapo to the northeast, this park covers 39,255 ha of steep forested valleys rising to 1,500 m, some 50 small lakes and many waterfalls. The park contains one of the best surviving areas of alerce trees, some over 1,000 years old, with the oldest estimated at 4,200 years. Wildlife includes *pudu*, pumas, *vizcachas*, condors and black woodpeckers. Lago Chapo (5,500 ha) feeds a hydroelectric power station at Canutillar, east of the park. There are four ranger posts: at Río Chaicas, Lago Chapo, Laguna Sargazo and at the north entrance. There are basic *refugios* at Río Pangal, Laguna Sargazo and Laguna Fría and camping sites at Río Chaicas and the north entrance. There is very little information at the ranger posts; a map is available from CONAF in Puerto Montt.

Parque Nacional Alerce Andino
Colour map 4, grid C2
Entry costs US$5; no camping inside the park boundaries

Transport There are 2 entrances: 2½ km from Correntoso (35 km west of Puerto Montt) at the northern end of the park and 7 km west of Lenca (40 km south of Puerto Montt) at the southern end. To the northern entrance: take *Fierro* or *Río Pato* bus from Puerto Montt to Correntoso (or Lago Chapo bus which passes through Correntoso), several daily except Sun, then walk. To the southern entrance: take any *Fierro* bus to Chaicas, La Arena, Contau and Hornopirén, US$1.50, getting off at Lenca sawmill, then walk (signposted).

Forty-six kilometres south of Puerto Montt (allow one hour), La Arena is the site of the first ferry, across the Reloncaví Estuary to Puelche. From Puelche there is a paved road north to Puelo (see page 369), from where transport can be found north to Cochamó and Ralún. ■ *Getting there: ferry, 30 mins, 10 crossings daily Dec-Mar, reduced service off season. Arrive at least 30 mins early to guarantee a place; buses have priority, cars US$5.*

La Arena
Colour map 4, grid C2

Also called Río Negro, Hornopirén lies 58 km south of Puelche at the northern end of a fjord and at the foot of the Hornopirén volcano. Although a branch of the Camino Austral runs round the edge of the fjord to Pichanco, 35 km further south, that route is a dead-end, and Hornopirén is the departure point for the second ferry, to Caleta Gonzalo. There is excellent fishing in the area and Hornopirén is a base for excursions to the Hornopirén volcano (1,572 m) and to Lago Cabrera which lies further north. At the mouth of the

Hornopirén
Colour map 4, grid C2
Population 1,100

Climbing volcanoes

The many volcanoes along the Camino Austral offer climbing opportunities of varying degrees of difficulty, though in this part of the country most climbs usually take only one or two days and there are no problems with soroche.

Corcovado (2,600 m), a beautiful mountain with a sharp summit situated 40 km south of Chaitén and visible from parts of Chiloé, is particularly difficult. Most are much easier; such as Volcán Yates, further north near Puelche.

fjord is **Isla Llancahué**, a small island with a hotel and thermal springs, which is reached by boat on a crossing which affords views of dolphins and fur seals (phone the hotel to arrange transport, US$25 one way shared between group).

Sleeping and eating **A** *Holiday Country*, O'Higgins 666, T263062. Restaurant, also *cabañas*. **A** *Termas de Llancahué*, T09-65-38345. Full board, good food, thermal pool. *Hornopirén*, Carrera Pinto 388, T255243 (Casilla 650, Puerto Montt). Highly recommended, also *cabañas*. Lots of other *cabañas*. **Camping** Good site next to the *Hostería Setca*, US$14 per site. Four more sites south of Hornopirén on the road to Pichanco.

Parque Nacional Alerce Andino

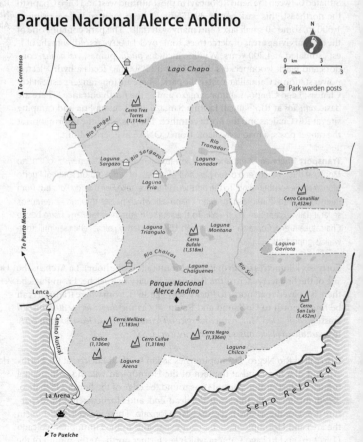

🏠 Park warden posts

Buses along the Camino Austral

Most of the buses which ply the Camino Austral are minibuses operated by small companies and often they are driven by their owners. Services are less reliable than elsewhere in Chile, and timetables change frequently as operators go out of business and new ones start up. Perhaps one of the major reasons for this is the cost of operating vehicles over the gravel and stone surfaces of the Camino Austral: *buses need regreasing after every return trip between Chaitén and Coyhaique; spare parts are expensive and have to be flown in from Puerto Montt; in summer tyres may have to be changed every month. Fuel is also more expensive than in other parts of Chile. Anxious to maintain rural services, the government offers subsidies on some routes, especially in winter, to maintain some transport network.*

Transport **Bus** *Fierro* daily 0800 and 1500 from Puerto Montt. There are no buses south from Hornopirén. **Ferry** In Jan-Feb only the Transmarchilay ferry *Mailen* sails daily from Río Negro to Caleta Gonzalo, 1500; return departures daily 0900. Fares: vehicles over 4 m US$88, under 4 m US$75, foot passengers US$11, cycles US$9. Advance booking required: there can be a 2-day wait. *Chaitur* (address under Chaitén) organize transport between the ferry port in Caleta Gonzalo and Chaitén to connect with ferry services.

Parque Nacional Hornopirén Lying just east of Hornopirén and covering 48,232 ha, this park includes the Yates volcano (2,187 m) as well as the basins of two rivers, the Blanco and the Negro. The park protects some 9,000 ha of alerce forest as well as areas of mixed native forest including lenga and coigue. From the entrance a path leads 8 km east up along the Río Blanco to a basic *refugio*. The entrance is 16 km by *ripio* road east of Hornopirén. It is free to enter.

Caleta Gonzalo Situated on the southern edge of the Fiordo Reñihue, Caleta Gonzalo is the base for visiting Parque Pumalin. From Caleta Gonzalo the Camino Austral runs through the park, climbing steeply before reaching two lakes, Lago Río Negro and Lago Río Blanco. The coast is reached at Santa Bárbara, 48 km south, where there is a black sand beach, good campsite and swimming. Do not camp close to the water.

Sleeping and eating There is a restaurant, *cabañas* and campsite as well as visitors centre and demonstrations of agricultural techniques in the region.

Parque Pumalin *Entrance to the park is free. Seen by many as one of the most important conservation projects in the world* Created by the US billionaire Douglas Tompkins, this private reserve extends over 320,000 ha and is in two sectors, one just south of the Parque Nacional Hornopirén and the other stretching south and east of Caleta Gonzalo to the Argentine border. Its purchase aroused controversy, especially in the Chilean armed forces, which saw it as a threat to national sovereignty; initially, Tompkins was frustrated by stonewalling from the Chilean government, but progress has been made and the park has now been given nature sanctuary status.

Covering large areas of the western Andes, most of the park is occupied by temperate rainforest. The park is intended to protect the lifestyles of its inhabitants as well as the physical environment. Tompkins has established a native tree nursery; within three years, he hopes to produce 100,000 saplings of native endangered species. There is also apiculture; in 2000, bee stations produced 30,000 kg of honey.

The Camino Austral

There are treks ranging from short trails into the temperate rainforest to hikes lasting for several days (these are very arduous). There are cabins (from **D** sleeping up to four); meals are extra. Camping is available at several sites from US$1 per person per night. Information, T/F02-7358034, www.pumalin.org There are also three marked trails into the park: to a waterfall, *Cascadas Escondidas*; to an area of very old alerce trees; and to Laguna Tronador.

Chaitén

Phone code: 065
Colour map 4, grid C2
Population: 3,258

The capital of Palena province, Chaitén is in a beautiful spot, with a forest-covered hill rising behind it, and a quiet inlet leading out into the Patagonian channels. The town is important as a port for ferries to Puerto Montt and Quellón, and is a growing centre for adventure tourism and fishing excursions. Visits are also possible to a sea-lion colony offshore on Isla Puduguapi. There are good views over the Corcovado Bay from Avénida Corcovado.

Sleeping
● *on map*

The ferry from Quellón is met by people offering accommodation

AL *Mi Casa*, Av Norte, T/F731285, on a hill offering fine views – recommended. Comfortable, sauna, gymnasium, restaurant, good value set meal. **A** *Brisas del Mar*, Corcovado 278, T731284, F731294. *Cabañas*, sleep 4. **B** *Schilling*, Corcovado 230, T731295. With breakfast, heating, restaurant. **C** *Los Colonos*, Juan Todesco 77. With bath, shabby, without breakfast. **D** *El Triángulo*, Juan Todesco y Corcovado, T731312. Without bath or breakfast. **D** *Hostería Llanos*, Corcovado 378, T731332. Without bath, with breakfast, good beds, unwelcoming. **E** *Res Astoria*, Corcovado 442, T731263. Without bath or breakfast, clean.
E *Sebastián*, Riveros 163, T731225, without bath, with breakfast. **E** *Hosp Watson*, Ercilla 580. Use of kitchen, clean, friendly.
F *Casa Rita*, Rivero y Prat. (**G** for floor space, **H** for camping), use of kitchen, clean, open all year, heating. Recommended. **F** *Hosp Ancud*, Libertad 105, use of kitchen, very friendly. **F** *Hosp Hogareño*, Pedro de Valdivia 129, T731413, with breakfast, meals. **F** *Hosp Recoba*, Libertad 432, T731390. With breakfast, clean, friendly, good meals.
F *Martín Ruiz*, Camino Austral 1 km north. With breakfast, friendly, nice views.
Camping *Los Arrayanes*, 4 km north, with hot showers and close to sea, good.

Eating
● *on map*

Mid-range *El Canasto del Agua*, decent food, Prat 65. **Cheap** *El Quijote*, O'Higgins 42. Bar, snacks. *Flamengo*, Corcovado 218. Popular with travellers. *Mahurori*, Independencia 141.

Sports

There is excellent fishing nearby, especially to the south in the ríos Yelcho and Futaleufú and in lagos Espolón and Yelcho. Fishing licences are sold at the Municipalidad.

Chaitén

To Camino Austral (north)

Ferry Port

Av Norte
Prat
Ercilla
Libertad
Juan Todesco
Banco del Estado
Transmarchilay
Municipalidad
O'Higgins
Plaza
Corcovado
Aguirre Cerda
Almirante Riveros
D'Portales
Carrera Pinto
P de Valdivia

To Camino Austral (south)

N

0 metres 100
0 yards 100

■ Sleeping
1 Brisas del Mar
2 Casa Rita
3 El Triángulo
4 Hospedaje Hogareño
5 Hospedaje Recoba
6 Hostería Llanos
7 Los Colonos
8 Mi Casa
9 Residencial Astoria
10 Schilling
11 Sebastián

● Eating
1 El Canasto del Agua
2 El Quijote
3 Flamengo

The Camino Austral

Chaitur, Calle Diego Portales 350, T/F731429, nchaitur@hotmail.com Excursions, **Tour operators**
trekking, horseriding, fishing, trips to Pumalin park, English spoken, friendly and helpful. Recommended. Opposite *Chaitur* is an office of the Parque Pumalín.

Air   Flights to Puerto Montt by *Aerosur*, *AeroVip* and *Aeromet* (daily 1200, 35 mins, **Transport**
US$40). *AeroVip* also fly to Castro. Bookings can be made through *Chaitur*.   *Fuel is available*

Bus   Terminal at O'Higgins 67. Minibuses are operated along the Camino Austral to
Coyhaique by several companies; in summer usually one daily, in winter 2 a week with
overnight stop in La Junta or Puyuguapi. Departures usually 0800-0900. *Chaitur* (details
below) acts as an agent for all these services. Or try *Buses Norte*, Libertad 432, T731390,
the only company based in Chaitén, with buses to Coyhaique (US$30) and intermediate
points such as La Junta and Puyuguapi. Minibuses usually travel full, so are unable to pick
up passengers en route. Hitching the whole route takes several days. It is recommended,
especially by pick-up truck, but there is a lot of competition and you must be prepared for
a day's wait if you find yourself out of luck. To **Futaleufú**, Mon-Sat 1530, Sun 1700, 5 hrs.

Sea   Service to Chonchi (Chiloé), a fascinating trip via the smaller islands off the coast,
8 hrs (including 1 hr stopover on an island), departures 0800, Wed, Sat, low season
(Oct-Dec, Mar-May), Tue, Thu, Sat, high season (Jan-Feb) US$15 low season, US$20
high season, bicycles US$10. Tickets from *Chaitur*. Ferry port about 1 km north of town.
To **Quellón**: In summer (Jan-early Mar) the **Navimag** ferry *Alejandrina* sails to Quellón,
on Chiloé, on Sun, US$20. *Transmarchilay* serve Quellón Mon, Wed and Fri, US$28. To
Puerto Montt: the *Navimag* ferry *Alejandrina* sails to Puerto Montt on Fri, US$24.
Transmarchilay also sail this route Mon, Wed and Thu, US$34, as does the new opera-
tor *Catamaranes del Sur* on Mon, Wed and Fri for US$35.

Banks   Exchange: *Banco del Estado*, O'Higgins y Libertad, charges US$10 for chang- **Directory**
ing TCs, *Redbanc* ATM. Rates in general are poor along the Camino Austral; change
money in Puerto Montt. **Shipping offices**   *Transmarchilay*, Corcovado 266, T731273.
Navimag, Carrera Pinto 108, T731570.

Chaitén to Coyhaique

*This section of the Camino Austral, 422 km long, runs through long stretches of
virgin rainforest, passing small villages, the perfectly still white waters of Lago
Yelcho, and the Parque Nacional Queulat, with its glaciers and waterfalls. Roads
branch off east to the Argentine frontier and west to Puerto Cisnes. Near
Coyhaique, the road passes huge open air tree cemeteries, testament to the depre-
dations of the early colonists.*

At Amarillo, 25 km south of Chaitén there is a turning to the **Termas de Ama- Amarillo**
rillo, 5 km west, which consist of two wooden sheds with a very hot pool *Colour map 5, grid A3*
inside, US$3, and an outdoor swimming pool. From here it is possible to hike
along the old trail to Futaleufú, four to seven days, not for the inexperienced, *There is superb*
be prepared for wet feet all the way. The trail follows the Río Michinmawida, *salmon fishing in*
passing the volcano of the same name, to Lago Espolón, see below. A ferry *the rivers, and the*
with a sporadic schedule crosses the lake, taking cargo only to Futaleufú. *local people are*
very friendly

Sleeping and eating   **B** *Termas de Amarillo*, at the Termas, T731326. Also camping
and *cabañas*. In the village: **B** *Hostería Galpones del Volcán*, T/F731605. **F** *Hosp Las
Rosas*. **F** *Res Marcela*, T264442. Also *cabañas*, camping.

The Camino Austral

Puerto Cárdenas
Colour map 5, grid A3

Situated 46 km south of Chaitén, Puerto Cárdenas lies on the northern tip of **Lago Yelcho**, a beautiful glacial lake on the Río Futaleufú surrounded by hills and the beautiful Yelcho glacier. The lake is frequented by anglers. At Puerto Cárdenas, there is forest on all sides; also a police post where you may have to register your passport. The *Isla Monita Lodge* offers packages for anglers and non-anglers on a private island in the lake, as well as fishing in many nearby locations; contact *Turismo Grant*, PO Box 52311, Santiago, T6395524, F6337133. Further south at Km 60, a path leads to **Ventisquero Yelcho**, a two-hour walk.

Sleeping and eating Two *residenciales* including **C** *Res Yelcho*. Clean, full board available. *Cabañas Yelcho en La Patagonia*, 7 km south on lakeshore, also camping, cafeteria. Also on the Lago Yelcho is *Cabanas CAVI*, a hotel with sauna, restaurant, video room, laundry. Six *cabañas* with private bathrooms, hot water, kitchen facilities. Camping with electricity, hot showers, drinking water, laundry facilities. Barbecue area, fishing boats for hire. Book via *Turismo Austral Ltda*, Santa Magdelena 75 of 902, Providencia, Santiago,T3341309, F3341328.

The route to Futaleufú and Argentina

Southeast of Chaitén the Argentine frontier is reached in two places, Futaleufú and Palena, along a road which branches off at **Villa Santa Lucía** (Km 81), where there are 30 houses, a military camp, one small shop and bread available from a private house. The road to the border is single track, *ripio*, passable in a regular car, but best with a good, strong vehicle; the scenery is beautiful. At **Puerto Ramírez**, Km 30, at the southern end of **Lago Yelcho** the road divides: the north branch runs along the valley of the Río Futaleufú to **Futaleufú** while the southern one continues to Palena. **Lago Espolón**, west of Futaleufú, reached by a turning 41 km northeast of Puerto Ramírez, is a beautiful lake in an area enjoying a warm microclimate: 30°C in the day in summer, 5°C at night. The lake is warm enough for a quick dip, but beware of the currents. There are *cabañas*, **E** per person, US$3.75 for a motor home, and a campsite. Aníbal, who owns the campsite, sells meat, bread, beer and soft drinks and will barbecue lamb. The Río Futaleufú and Lago Espolón provide excellent fishing, ask for the Valebote family's motorboat.

Sleeping and eating
Villa Santa Lucía Several places on main street: at No 7 (Sra Rosalía Cuevas de Ruiz, basic, meals available), No 13 (breakfast extra) and No 16 (not bad), all **G** , none has hot water. **Puerto Piedra** *Pensión Alexis*. Campsite nearby. **Puerto Ramírez** *Hospedaje Las Casas*. *Hostería Río Malito*. Rooms, camping, fishing. **Futaleufú** *Hostería Río Grande*, O'Higgins y Aldea, T258633, anexo 320. **D** *Continental*, Balmaceda 595, T258633, anexo 222. Basic, hot water, clean. Recommended. Cheap restaurant. **E** *Hosp Adolfo*, O'Higgins s/n, T258633, anexo 256. **E** *Hosp El Campesino*, Prat 107, T258633. **F** *Res Carahue*, O'Higgins 332, T258633. Very basic, kitchen facilities. **F** *Res Yamara*, O'Higgins s/n, without bath. Recommended. Several others, including *Skorpios* and *Café/Restaurant El Encuentro* (both recommended). **Palena** *La Frontera*, T741240. *Res La Chilenita*, T258633.

Tour operators
Futaleufú Expediciones, O'Higgins 397, Futaleufú, T/F258634. Organize rafting, canyoning, trekking and horseriding expeditions.

Transport
Air Airport 1 km east of Futaleufú. *Aerosur* flights from Chaitén to Futaleufú, Tue and Fri, US$62, Jan-Feb only. **Bus** To Chaitén daily, 5 hrs. To Puerto Montt via Argentina, Mon, Fri 0800, 13 hrs, US$35, *Transportes Cuchichi*, T731280.

Banks *Banco de Chile* in Futaleufú, changes US dollars and Argentine pesos.

Chilean immigration is at the frontier, at the bridge over the Río Grande, 8 km east of Futaleufú. To enter Chile continue from **Futaleufú** towards Puerto Ramírez, but outside Ramírez, take the right turn to Chaitén (left goes to Palena). If entering Chile change money in Futaleufú (poor rates). There is nowhere to change at the border. If entering Argentina pay the bus fare to Esquel in dollars and then change in Esquel. From Futaleufú a bus runs to the border, Mon and Fri 0900, 1800, US$3, 30 mins, from Balmaceda 419. From the Argentine side there are connecting services to Trevelin and Esquel. The Chilean immigration at Palena is 8 km west of frontier. *Expreso Yelcho* bus from Chaitén Tue, Thu, 0830, US$12, 5½ hrs.

Both crossings lead to **Trevelin**, which is 45 km east of Futaleufú, 95 km east of Palena. Trevelin is an offshoot of the Welsh Chubút colony on the Atlantic side of Argentine Patagonia. It has accommodation, restaurants, tea-rooms and a tourist office; features in Chatwin's *In Patagonia*.

At **Esquel**, 23 km northeast of Trevelin, there is a much wider range of services as well as transport connections for Bariloche and other destinations. Esquel is a base for visiting the Argentine Parque Nacional Los Alerces and for journeys on La Trochita, or the Old Patagonian Express.

From Villa Santa Lucía, the Camino Austral follows the Río Frío and then the Río Palena to La Junta, a drab, expensive village at the confluence of Río Rosselot and Río Palena, 151 km south of Chaitén. **Lago Rosselot**, surrounded by forest and situated in the **Reserva Nacional Lago Rosselot** (12,725 ha), 9 km east of La Junta, can be reached by a road which heads east, 74 km, to Lago Verde and the Argentine border. Border crossing at Lago Verde: summer 0730-2200; winter 0800-2000 to Las Pampas in Argentina. There is also a new road leading northwest from La Junta to Puerto Raúl Marín on the coast.

Sleeping and eating **A** *Hostal Espacio y Tiempo*, T314141, F314142, www.espacio-y-tiempo.cl Attractive garden with tables, also arranges tours. Restaurant, fishing expeditions. **F** *Café Res Patagonia*, Lynch 331, T314120. Good meals, small rooms, limited bathrooms. **F** *Res Copihue*, Varas 611, T314184. Without bath, good meals, changes money at very poor rates. **F** *Res Valdera*, Varas s/n, T314105. With breakfast and bath, very good value. At Lago Risopatrón there is a CONAF campsite.

Entertainment *Pub La Piramide*, Antonio Varas Sitio 8. Recommended.

Transport Fuel is available. *Buses Emanuel*, Manuel Montt, Esq Esmeralda, T314198, buses to Puerto Cisnes (Mon and Fri, US$6); also to Coyhaique (Tue and Sat, US$16) and Chaitén (Mon and Sat, US$10). Also *Transportes Lago Verde*, 3 weekly to Chaitén (US$10).

Puyuguapi

From La Junta the Camino Austral runs south along the western side of Lago Risopatrón, past several waterfalls, to Puyuguapi (also spelt Puyuhuapi), 45 km further south. Located in a beautiful spot at the northern end of the Puyuguapi Fjord, the village is tranquil and a good stopping place, about halfway between Chaitén and Coyhaique. It was founded by four Sudeten German families in 1935.

From Puyuguapi the road follows the eastern edge of the fjord along one of the most beautiful sections of the Camino Austral. There are views of the **Termas de Puyuhuapi**, a resort on the western edge of the fjord 18 km southwest of Puyuguapi and accessible only by boat: here there are several springs with 40°C water filling three pools near the beach. Baths cost US$15 per person, children under 12 US$10, take food and drink. This resort can be visited with four-and six-day tours run by *Patagonia Connection SA* (see pages 114 and 426).

Sleeping   **LL-AL** *Hotel Termas de Puyuhuapi* (price depends on season and type of room). Including use of baths and boat transfer to hotel, full board US$40 extra, good restaurant. Recommended. For reservations: *Patagonia Connection SA*, Fidel Oteíza 1921, Of 1006, Providencia, Santiago (Metro Pedro do Valdivia), T2236489, F2748111 or directly at the *Hotel Termas de Puyuhuapi*, T325103, F325117. Boat schedule from jetty, 2 hrs' walk from town, 0930, 1000, 1200, 1230, 1830, 1900, US$3 each way, 10 mins crossing. Transport to the hotel may be arranged independently via hydroplane from Puerto Montt. **A** *Cabañas Fiordo Queulat* (T067-233302). Recommended. **C/D** *Casa Ludwig*, on the road south, Av Otto Uebel 850, T/F325220, www.contactchile.cl/casaludwig Excellent, German spoken. Highly recommended. **C-D** *Hostería Alemana*, Otto Uebel 450, T325118. A large wooden house on the main road, owned by Sra Ursula Flack Kroschewski, comfortable. Highly recommended. **F** *Hosp El Pino*, Hamburgo s/n, T325117. Homemade bread, friendly. **F** *Hostería Elizabeth*, Llautured y Henríquez. With breakfast, clean, good meals. **F** *Sra Leontina Fuentes*, Llantureo y Circunvalación. Clean, hot water, good breakfast for US$1. There is a dirty campsite by the fjord behind the general store which is behind the service station.

Eating   *Café Rossbach* on the Costanera, with limited menu. Not cheap, excellent salmon; building in the style of a German Black Forest Inn. Also at *Restaurante Marili*, Otto Ubel s/n, cheaper option. There is 1 supermarket, the *Carretera Austral*, Otto Ubel s/n. There are also 2 bars.

Transport   **Bus** *Buses Norte*, O'Higgins 39, T325130, have buses to Chaitén (US$16) and Coyhaique (US$14), Mon, Wed and Fri at 1500.

Parque Nacional Queulat
Colour map 5, grid A3

Covering 154,093 ha of attractive forest around Puyuguapi, the park is, according to legend, the place where the rich Ciudad de los Césares once was. The Camino Austral passes through the park. In the north of the park is **Lago Risopatrón**; 24 km south of Puyuguapi is the beautiful **Ventisquero Colgante** (hanging glacier). ■ *US$3*. From here the Camino Austral climbs out of the Queulat valley through a series of hairpin bends offering fine views of the forest and several glaciers. Near the pass (500 m) is the Salto Pedro García waterfall. Some 5 km further on, near the southern entrance to the park, a path leads off to the Salto del Cóndor waterfall. Boat trips can be made on Lago Risopatrón. Administration is in the CONAF office in La Junta. There is an information centre near the Ventisquero Colgante.

Sleeping and eating   **LL** *Cabañas El Pangue*, north end of Lago Risopatrón, Camino Austral Norte, Km 240, Puyuhuapi, T/F325128, cpangue@entelchile.net Cabins sleep 4, private bathrooms, hot water, heating, telephone, parking, swimming pool, fishing trips, horseriding, mountain bikes. *Cabañas Lago Queulat*, on Seno Queulat. Campsite nearby, US$3.50. *Hospedaje*, 5 km north of the Ventisquero Colgante. CONAF campsites 12 km north of Puyuguapi on shores of Lago Risopatrón, and near the Ventisquero Colgante, cold water, basic. Reservations T067-212125.

Puerto Cisnes is an attractive settlement at the mouth of the Río Cisnes, reached by a 33-km road which branches west off the Camino Austral about 59 km south of Puyuguapi. The Río Cisnes, 160 km in length, is recommended for rafting or canoeing, with grand scenery and modest rapids except for the horrendous drop at Piedra del Gato. There is a 150 m cliff at Torre Bright Bank. Good camping in the forest.

There are good opportunities for fishing in the area – contact *German Hipp*, Costanera 51, T346587 or *Cabañas Río Cisnes*, Costanera 101, T346404. Traditional knitted clothes are made here too.

Puerto Cisnes
Colour map 5, grid A3
Population: 1,784

Sleeping and eating B *Manzur*, Dunn 75, T346453. *Cabañas.* D *Hostal Michay*, Mistral 112, T346462. *Pensión* at Carlos Condell y Dr Steffen. D, with breakfast, hot shower, friendly. **F-G** *Hostería El Gaucho*, Holmberg 140, T346514. With breakfast, dinner available, welcoming, hot water. All cheap: *El Guairao*, Piloto Prado 58. *K-Cos Café Restaurante*, Prat 270, good snacks. *Miramar*, Prat 465. *Restaurante Kiyipunch*, Mistral 558.

Transport To Coyhaique, *Transportes Terra Austral*, T346757, Mon-Fri 1430, US$14. Also on Sat at 1300, *Buses Norte*, T346440, US$12.

About 90 km south of Puyuguapi is Villa Amengual with a D *Hospedaje Christian* and *Café y Restaurante El Encanto*. At Km 92 a road branches west 104 km to the Argentine border via La Tapera. Chilean immigration is 12 km west of the frontier and is open daylight hours only. On the Argentine side the road continues to meet up with Route 40, the north-south road at the foot of the Andes.

The **Reserva Nacional Lago Las Torres** is 98 km south of Puyuguapi and covers 16,516 ha. It includes the wonderful Lago Las Torres, which offers good fishing and a small CONAF campsite – further information on fishing can be obtained from Turismo Lago Las Torres, 130 km Camino Austral Norte, T234242. Further south at Km 125 a road branches east to El Toqui where zinc is mined. From here the Camino Austral is paved.

Villa Mañihuales at Km 148 is near the **Reserva Forestal Mañihuales** (1,206 ha) where there is a huemul reserve. The forests were largely destroyed by forest fires in the 1940s, but the views are good. ■ *US$1*. There are A *Cabañas El Mirador*; F *Res Bienvenido*, clean, friendly, and with a restaurant; and F *Villa Mañihuales*, E Ibar 200, T234803. Friendly, with breakfast. There is a bus to Coyhaique every day except Sunday.

Rio Cisnes to Coyhaique

Coyhaique

Located 420 km south of Chaitén, Coyhaique lies in the broad green valley of the Río Simpson. The city is encircled by a crown of snowcapped mountains, and for a few hours after it has rained the mountainsides are covered in a fine layer of frost – a spectacular sight. Founded in 1929, it is the administrative and commercial centre of Región XI, and is the only settlement of any real size on the Camino Austral. It is quite a lively city, and some travellers may enjoy watching Coyhaique's only seamy side – hawkers peddling watches and cheap electronics to Argentinians in the cheaper bars. Coyhaique also provides a good base for hiking, skiing and fishing excursions in the area.

Phone code: 067
Colour map 5, grid B3
Population: 36,376

The Camino Austral

The price of settlement

In 1937, desperate to encourage settlement in this isolated region, the Chilean government passed a law offering settlers ownership of land provided it was cleared of forest. Of course, the people came – and smoke from the forest fires which followed could be seen from the Atlantic coast. The legacies of this dubious law are still *apparent to the visitor. Firstly, in the large expanses of burnt tree stumps to be seen, especially around the Río Palena and Mañihuales, and also in the shifting of the port facilities from Puerto Aisén to Puerto Chacabuco, as so much soil was washed into the rivers that the Río Aisén silted up, preventing vessels from reaching Puerto Aisén.*

Ins and outs

Getting there
See page 423 for further details
The most direct way into Coyhaique from Puerto Montt is to fly (flights often land at Balmaceda, 60 km south, where the airstrip is larger; there are 1 or 2 daily); buses from Puerto Montt have to take the route via Argentina, which is long and expensive (several weekly), and there are 1 or 2 weekly buses to Comodoro Rivadavia and south to Punta Arenas. Within Region XI, however, Coyhaique is the transport hub. There are minibuses north to Chaitén (several daily in summer) and south to Cochrane (several weekly), as well as minibuses connecting with the ferry at Puerto Ibañez for Chile Chico (5 weekly).

Getting around Coyhaique is small enough that it can quite easily be covered on foot; taxis are only useful for out-of-town excursions.

Sights

Coyhaique is an administrative town. It is a pleasant enough place, but there are few reasons to stay here long; a visit to the tourist office will throw up many more attractions outside Coyhaique than in the town. The town itself is cen-tred around an unusual pentagonal plaza, on which stand the cathedral, the Intendencia and a handicraft market. The plaza was built in 1945, supposedly inspired by the Place de l'Étoile in Paris. Two blocks northeast of the plaza at Baquedano y Ignacio Serrano there is a monument to El Ovejero (the shep-herd). Further north on Baquedano is a display of old military machinery out-side the local regimental headquarters. Near the city, on the west bank of the Río Simpson, is the **Piedra del Indio**, a rock outcrop which, allegedly, looks like a face in profile. This is best viewed from the Puente Simpson.

Museo Regional de la Patagonia Central in the Casa de Cultura, Baquedano 310, has sections on history, mineralogy, zoology and archaeol-ogy as well as photos of the building of the Camino Austral. ■ *US$1. Tue-Sun 0900-2000 (summer), 0830-1730 (winter).*

Excursions Some 5 km northwest off the Camino Austral is **Reserva Nacional Coyhaique**, which covers 2,150 ha of forest (mainly introduced species). Park administration is at the entrance. There is a basic campsite at Laguna Verde and another at Casa Bruja, 4 km and 2 km respectively from the entrance, US$4, and a *refugio* 3 km from the entrance. ■ *US$1.*

Situated around the valley of the Río Simpson west of Coyhaique and crossed by the road to Puerto Aisén, the **Reserva Nacional Río Simpson** covers 40,827 ha, most of it steep forested valleys and curiously shaped rounded hills rising to 1,878 m. One of these, near the western edge of the park, is known as *El Cake Inglés*. There are beautiful waterfalls and good views of the river and very good fly fishing. Wildlife includes pudu, pumas and huemul as well as a variety of birds ranging from condors to several species of ducks. Administration is 32 km west of Coyhaique, just off the road; campsite near the turning to Santuario San Sebastián, US$5. ■ *Getting there: take any bus between Coyhaique and Puerto Aisen.*

Fishing opportunities can be found southwest, **Lagos Atrevesado** (20 km) and **Elizalde** (also yachting and camping), and southeast at **Lagos Frío**, **Castor** and **Pollux**. The **Monumento Natural Dos Lagunas**, 25 km east on the Coyhaique Alto road, is a small park which includes Lagos El Toro and Escondido, worth a visit. ■ *US$1. Camping US$12 per site.*

Essentials

The tourist office has a full list of all types of accommodation, but look out for notices in windows since any place with less than 6 beds does not have to register with the authorities. **L** *Hostería Coyhaique*, Magallanes 131, T231137. Four star, in large gardens. **AL-A** *Luis Loyola*, Prat 455, T234200. **A** *Los Ñires*, Baquedano 315, T232261, F233372. With breakfast, small rooms, comfortable, parking. **A** *San Sebastian*, Baquedano 496, T233427. Small. **B** *El Reloj*, Baquedano 444, T231108. With good restaurant, nice lounge, sells local products, English spoken. Recommended. **B** *Libanés*, Simpson 367, T234242, hlibanes@entelchile.net With television, phones, heating, laundry and cafe, several small lounges. **B-C** *Hostal Araucarias*, Vielmo 71, T232707. Large rooms, good view, rents cars. **C** *Hosp Lautaro*, Lautaro 532, T231852. Clean, comfortable, kitchen facilities, large rooms. **C** *Hostal Bon*, Serrano 91, T231189. With breakfast, friendly, clean, also *cabañas* **D**, good meals served. Highly recommended. **C** *Hostal San Cayetano*, No 829, T/F231555. With bath, also **D** without, cooking facilities, good. **C** *Hotel y Apart Hotel Austral*, Colón 203, T232522. Hot water, clean, English spoken, tours arranged, friendly. Recommended. **D** *Res Mónica*, Lillo 664, T234302. **E** *Hosp Lautaro*, Lautaro 532, T231852. Clean, comfortable, kitchen facilities, large rooms. **E** *Res Licarayen*, Carrera 33A, T233377 (Santiago T02-7431294). With bath and breakfast, no singles, rundown.

F *Hosp* at Baquedano 20, Patricio y Gedra Guzmán, T232520. Room in family home, use of kitchen, breakfast with homemade bread, bathroom and laundry facilities, by the river, wonderful views from garden, recommended. **F** *Hosp Pierrot*, Baquedano 130, T221315. Friendly, great view, internet access. Highly recommended. Also *cabaña* at back of house. **F** *Res Puerto Varas*, Serrano 168, T/F235931. Restaurant and bar, tatty. Several cheap places on Av Simpson, for example **F** *Hospedaje Natti*, No 417, T231047. Clean, very friendly, kitchen facilities. Highly recommended. **F** *Hosp Mundaca No 571*, friendly, breakfast extra, will heat up pre-prepared food. **F** at No 649. Many other **F**s, including: **F** *Casa Irene*, 12 de Octubre 503, with breakfast, kitchen and laundry facilities. **F** *Hospedaje Chiloé*, Baquedano 274, T235332. Small rooms, very good, also lets apartments. **F** *Hosp Lautaro*, Lautaro 269, T238116, with parking, English spoken, internet access, kitchen facilities. Recommended. **F** *Hosp Ogana*, Av Ogana Pasaje 8, 185, T232353, cooking facilities, with breakfast, camping, helpful, also *cabañas*, **C**, sleep 3. **F** *Los Cuatro Hermanos*, Colón 495, T232647. Without breakfast (more with), hot water, clean. **F** *Los Profesores*, Presidente Errazuriz y Arturo Prat. Good beds, good showers. **F** *Res Mónica*, Lillo 664, T234302. **F** *Pensión América*, 21 de Mayo 233. **F** *Sra Elba Araneda*, Colón 190. UIT breakfast. Other cheap places, **F** Baquedano 444; Cochrane 532, Colón 133, Colón 166, Colón 190. *Hosp Belén*, **F** with breakfast, **G** without. Friendly, comfortable, cooking facilities. Recommended. Simon Bolivár 616, T218517. Youth hostel in summer at one of the schools (it changes each year), **G** with

Sleeping
■ *on map, page 420*
Price codes:
see inside front cover

The Camino Austral

sleeping bag. Another *albuergue*, **F** *Albergue Las Salamandras*, 2 km south of town in attractive forest, T/F211865. Camping, kitchen facilities, winter sports and trekking, (Jun-Oct). Highly recommended.

Cabañas **AL** *Cabañas San Sebastián*, Freire 554, T231762. Sleeps 4. **B** *Cabañas Río Simpson*, T232183. Km 3, cabins for 4–9 people, fully equipped, horse hire, fishing, tours, with several tame alpacas. **B-C** *Cabañas La Pasarela*, T234520. Km 1.5. Good atmosphere, *comedor*. **D** *Cabañas Mirador*, Baquedano 848, T233191. Sleeps 8.

Sernatur in Coyhaique has a full list of all sites in XI Región

Camping There are many camping sites in Coyhaique and on the road between Coyhaique and Puerto Aisén, for example at Km 1, (*Camping Alborada*, US$10, T238868, hot shower), 24, 25, 35, 37, 41, 42 (*Camping Río Correntoso*, T232005. US$15 per site, showers, fishing, Automobile Club discount) and 43.

Coyhaique

To Hospedaje at Baquedano 20, Cabañas La Pasarela, Puerto Aisén & Camino Austral North

To Airport, Albergue Las Salamandras, Puerto Ibáñez & Camino Austral South

N
Not to scale

■ **Sleeping**
1 Cabañas San Sebastián *B2*
2 Casa Irene *B1*
3 El Reloj *A3*
4 Hospedaje 649 *C2*
5 Hospedaje Belén *C2*
6 Hospedaje Lautaro *C2*
7 Hospedaje Lautaro *C1*
8 Hospedaje Mundaca 571 *C2*
9 Hospedaje Pierrot *A3*
10 Hospedaje Natti *C2*
11 Hostal Bon *B3*
12 Hostería Coyhaique *B3*
13 Hotel y Apart Hotel Austral *B3*
14 Libanés *C2*
15 Los Cuatro Hermanos *C2*
16 Los Ñires *A3*
17 Luis Loyola *B2*
18 Pensión América *A2*
19 Residencial Licarayen *A2*
20 Residencial Mónica *C2*
21 Residencial Puerto Varas *B3*
22 San Sebastián *A3*

● **Eating**
1 Café Kalu *B2*
2 Café Oriente *B2*
3 Café Restaurant Histórico *B2*
4 Café Ricer *B2*
5 Cafetería Alemana *B2*
6 Casino de Bomberos *B2*
7 El Mastique *B2*
8 La Olla *B2*
9 Loberías de Chacabuco *B2*

The Camino Austral

The Huemul

The Andean huemul (Hippocamelus bisulcus) is a mountain deer native to the Andes of southern Chile and Argentina. Sharing the Chilean national crest with the Andean condor, the huemul (pronounced 'way-mool') is a medium-sized stocky cervid adapted to survival in rugged mountain terrain. Males grow antlers and have distinctive black face masks. Huemul tend to live in groups of two to five – usually a breeding pair accompanied by offspring. The rutting season peaks in February and March; females give birth to a single fawn in November or December.

Although it used to range from just south of Santiago to the Straits of Magellan, human pressures have pushed the huemul to the brink of extinction. Current numbers are estimated at 1,000-1,500. A small and dwindling group of 60 animals survive in the Nevados de Chillán in central Chile, their northernmost presence. The remaining known populations are scattered across the southern regions of Argentina and Chile.

The huemul is the focal point of both national and international conservation efforts, carried out primarily by CONAF and the Comite pro la Defensa de la Fauna y Flora de Chile (CODEFF). The current focus is on halting and reversing the decline in numbers in central Chile and on determining more precisely numbers and distribution further south.

The huemul is a shy animal which tends to avoid human contact. Your best chance of seeing them is in one of two reserves managed by CONAF: the Reserva Nacional Río Claro, which lies on the southeastern corner of the larger Reserva Nacional Río Simpson just outside Coyhaique, and the Reserva Nacional Tamango, near Cochrane. To visit either of these you will need to be accompanied by a warden: enquire first in Coyhaique or Cochrane to make sure someone is available.

Mid-range *Café Ricer*, Horn 48, T232920. Good food. *Casona*, Vielmo 77. Traditional food. Recommended. *La Olla*, Gen Prat 176, T234700. Spanish, excellent cuisine, not cheap, good value lunches. Highly recommended. *La Posada del Conejo*, Km 3 to Teniente Vidal, T238335. Popular. Recommended. *Loberías de Chacabuco*, Prat 386, T211917. Good seafood, slow service. **Cheap** *Café Restaurant Historico*, Horn 48 y 40 2o Piso, Plaza Coyhaique, T232920. Recommended. *Cafetería Alemana*, Condell 119. Excellent cakes and coffee, vegetarian dishes. Recommended. *Don Carlos*, Baquedano 315. Good value lunches. *El Reloj*, Bequedano 444. Uses all local ingredients, recommended. *El Quincho*, Km 6 on road to Pto Aisén. Good food. Recommended. *La Fiorentina*, on Prat. Cheap pizzas, good. *Litos*, Lautaro 147. **Seriously cheap** *Casino de Bomberos*, Gen Parra 365. Wide range, very good value. *El Mastique*, Bilbao 141. Good. Recommended. **Cafés** *Café Kalu*, Prat 402. Beer, snacks. *Café Oriente*, Condell 201 y 21 de Mayo. Good bakery, tea.

Eating
● *on map*

Most places, except the Casino de Bomberos, are closed on Sun evenings

Bars *Bar West*, Bilbao y 12 de Octubre. Western style. *Piel Roja*, Moraleda y Condell. Nice atmosphere, laid back, meals served, not cheap. Also recommended is *Pub El Cuervo*, Parra 72, good cocktails, snacks, relaxed. Perhaps the trendiest bar in Coyhaique is the *@bar*, Moraleda y Carrera. **Disco** *Disco Corhal*, Bilbao 125 and *Naranja discotheque*, Ogana 1203.

Entertainment

Excellent opportunities for **fishing** in the Coyhaique area. **Skiing** at El Fraile, 29 km southeast near Lago Frío: there are 5 pistes, 2 lifts, cafetería, equipment hire (season Jun to Sep).

Sports

The Camino Austral

Angler's paradise

Coyhaique is the greatest centre for fishing in Chile; each summer the international fishing fraternity converge on the town for the season which runs from 15 November to 15 April. Rivers range from the typically English slow chalk stream to the fast flowing Andean snowmelt torrents, requiring a variety of angling techniques. On the outskirts of Coyhaique, the spectacular Río Simpson teems with both Rainbow and Brown trout. The Simpson offers over 60 km of world class angling. It is renowned for its exciting evening hatches (sedge and mayfly) which take place throughout the season. Anglers will find that, pound for pound, these are some of the best fighting fish to be found anywhere. Catches in excess of five pounds are frequent and Rainbow trout weighing over 12 pounds have been landed.

Located near the Argentine border, a scenic one-hour drive from Coyhaique, the Río Nirehuao is a fly-fisher's dream. Throughout the season the Brown trout feed voraciously on grasshoppers and dragonfly. The easy wading and moderate casting distances make this river an all-time favourite.

South of Coyhaique the Río Baker offers anglers a unique fishing experience in its turquoise blue water. The Baker is huge and intimidating, as are its fish: rainbows up to 12 pounds lurk here and anglers regularly take fish in the four to seven pound range. The Río Cochrane, a tributary of the Baker, also holds large Rainbows and, if it were possible for a river to be clearer than 'gin-clear', this would be it. The Cochrane is mainly a 'sight-fishing' experience which requires skill, patience and an experienced guide.

Shopping
Food, especially fruit and vegetables, is more expensive than in Santiago

Brautigam, Horn 47. Fishing gear, camping. *Cema-Chile*, on plaza, between Montt and Barroso. *Feria de Artesanía* on the plaza. *Manos Azules*, Riquelme 435, recommended for artesanía. Supermarkets: *Central*, Magallanes y Bilbao. Open daily until 2230. *Multimas*, Prat y Lautaro, both open until 2300, and *Vyhmeister*, Lautaro y Cochrane, open until 2200.

Tour operators
Full list of specialist tour guides and fishing guides available from Sernatur, see below

Aerohein, Baquedano 500, T/F232772, aerohein@entelchile.net, offer air tours to Laguna San Rafael. *Alex Prior*, T234732. For fly fishing. *Andes Patagónico*, Horn 48, and 40, local 11. T/F216711. Trips to local lakes as well as Tortel, and historically based trips, also bespoke trips all year round. Good, but not cheap. Gives general tourist information. *Aventura*, Gen Parra 222, T234748. Offers rafting. *Baltazar Araneda*, offers a horseriding trip – 'Los tres Lagos' – Palomo, Azul and Desierto, US$240 for 4 days, US$300 for 5 per person. Recommended, T231047 or book through *Hospedaje Natti*. *Cabot*, Dussen 357, T/F230101, Cabot@entelchile.net Offer horseriding excursions to Cerro Castillo, (US$70, 2 days) and other tours. *Encounter Patagonia*, Colon 166, T215001, info@encounterpatagonia.com Small agency specializing in the XI Region, strong local contacts, ecologically aware, English speaking guide. Highly recommended. *El Puesto Expeditions*, Moraleda 299, T/F233785, elpuesto@entelchile.net, hiking, fishing, climbing. *Patagonia Travel Service*, Condell 149, T237795, offer fishing tours on Lago Riesco and near Puerto Chacabuco. *Turaustralis*, Moraleda 589, T/F239696, hsaldivia@hotmail.com Fishing, horseriding, bird watching, trips to the lakes, tours along the Camino Austral. *Turismo Aysén*, Barroso 626, T238036, F235294. Fishing, horseriding tours. *Turismo Prado*, address in Banks above and *Expediciones Coyhaique*, Portales 195, T/F232300, both offer tours of local lakes and other sights, arrange Laguna San Rafael trips, etc. *Prado* does historical tours and offers general tourist information, while *Expediciones* does fishing trips and excursions down the Río Baker. *Turismo Queulat*, 21 de Mayo 1231, T/F231441. Trips to Queulat glacier, adventure and nature tourism, fishing, etc. Tours only operate in season.

Sernatur, Bulnes 35, T231752, F233949, sernatur-coyhai@entelchile.net Very helpful. Municipal kiosk on the plaza. English spoken; bus timetables available. CONAF
office, Ogana 1060. Maps (photocopies of 1:50,000 IGM maps) from Dirección de
Vialidad on the plaza.

Tourist office

Local Bicycle hire: *Figón*, Simpson y Colón, T234616, check condition first, also sells
spares. Repairs at Bilbao 500 block, poor supply of spares but good service. *Motortech*,
Baquedano 131. Also Tomás Enríque, Madrid Urrea, Pje Foitzick y Libertad, T252132.
Bicycle spares from several shops on Simpson. **Car hire**: *AGS*, Av Ogana 1298, T235354,
F231511. *Automóvil Club de Chile*, Carrerra 333, T231649. Rents jeeps and other vehi-
cles. *Automundo AVR*, Bilbao 510, T231621. *Traeger-Hertz*, Baquedano 457, T231648.
Sur Nativo Renta Car at same address, T235500. *Turismo Prado*, 21 de Mayo 417,
T/F231271. Cars may be taken across Argentine border and may be returned to a differ-
ent office. Buy fuel in Coyhaique, several stations. **Taxi**: Fares 50% extra after 2100.
Colectivos congregate at Prat y Bilbao, standard fare US$0.50.

Transport
*If renting a car a 4-WD
is recommended for
Camino Austral*

Long distance Air: There are 2 airports. Tte Vidal, about 5 km southwest of town
(including a steep climb up and down to the Río Simpson bridge). Taxi US$5. This air-
port handles smaller aircraft. *Don Carlos* to Chile Chico (Mon-Sat, US$39), **Cochrane**
(Mon and Thu, 45 mins, US$70), and **Villa O'Higgins** (Mon and Thu, US$104), recommended only for those who like flying, with strong stomachs, or in a hurry. Also flights
with *San Rafael* to **Melinka** (Mon and Thu, US$20), **Tortel** (Wed, US$30) and **Quellón**
(Thu, US$19) – flights and prices for residents; foreigners may be taken if there is room.
Balmaceda, 56 km southeast of Coyhaique via paved road, 5 km from the Argentine
frontier at Paso Huemules. Balmaceda is used by *LanChile* and *Ladeco* for flights from
Santiago via Puerto Montt for **Coyhaique**. There are also flights by *Don Carlos* to **Chile
Chico**, Tue, Thu, Sat, US$41. Airlines run connecting bus services to/from Coyhaique
(leave Coyhaique 2 hrs before flight), US$2. Minibuses also operate, collecting/deliver-
ing to hotels, US$4.50, several companies including *Travell*, Parra y Moraleda,
T230010, *Transfer*, Lautaro 828, T233030. Taxi from airport to Coyhaique, 1 hr, US$6.
Car hire at airport, Río Baker, T272163.

Bus: Terminal at Lautaro y Magallanes but few buses use this; most leave from bus
company offices: *Bus Sur*, Terminal, T211460. *Don Carlos*, Subteniente Cruz 63,
T232981. *Giobbi*, Terminal, T232607. *Suray*, Prat 265, T238387. *Turibus*, Baquedano
1171, T231333. To/from **Puerto Montt**, via Bariloche, all year, *Turibus*, Tue and Sat
1700, US$46, with connections to Osorno, Valdivia, Temuco, Santiago and Castro,
often heavily booked. To **Punta Arenas** via Coyhaique Alto and Comodoro Rivadavia,
Bus Sur, Tue and Fri, 1600, US$50. To **Comodoro Rivadavia**, *Turibus*, Mon, Fri, also
Giobbi, Tue, Sat, from terminal, US$30, 12 hrs. To **Puerto Aisén** minibuses run every
45 mins, 1 hr journey, *Suray* and *Don Carlos*, US$2, with connections for Puerto
Chacabuco. There are daily buses to **Mañihuales**, *Trans Mañihuales* (daily 1700). To
Puerto Ibáñez on Lago Gen Carrera, *colectivos* (connect with *El Pilchero* ferry to Chile
Chico) from your hotel 0700, 3 hrs, book the day before, US$7; several operators includ-
ing *Colectivos Sr Parra*, T251073 (0700 Sat/Sun), *Minibus Don Tito*, T250280, daily, Sr
Yarnil, T250346, daily. Buses on the **Camino Austral** vary according to demand: north
to **Chaitén**, several companies including *Buses Norte*, General Parra 337, T232167, Tue,
Thu, Fri and Sun, and *Transportes Daniela*, Baquedano 1122, T231701, Mon, Wed, Sat,
approximately 12 hrs, US$30; in winter these stop overnight in La Junta. To **La Junta**,
Morales, T232216, Tue, Sat, US$13. To **Puerto Cisnes**, *Transportes Terra Austral*,
T254475, Mon-Fri, US$14. South to **Cochrane**, *Don Carlos* (US$20), Tue, Sat at 0830;
Acuario 13 (US$19), Wed, Fri, Sat at 1000; and *Los Ñadis* (US$19), Tue, Thu, Sun at 1100.
10-12 hrs. *Don Carlos* also has buses on Tue and Sat to **Cerro Castillo** (US$5), **Bahía
Muerta** (US$10), **Puerto Tranquilo** (US$11) and **Puerto Bertrand** (US$15).

*Full listing of bus
services from tourist
information*

The Camino Austral

Routes to Argentina: options are given below and under Balmaceda, Chile Chico and Cochrane. Many border posts close at weekends. If looking for transport to Argentina it is worth going to the local Radio Santa María, Bilbao y Ignacio Serrano, and leaving a message to be broadcast.

Directory **Airline offices** *Emperador*, Bilbao 222. *LanChile*, Gen Parra 215, T231188. **Banks** *Banco Santander*, Condell y 21 de Mayo. Mastercard ATM, no exchange. For dollars, TCs and Argentine pesos. *Turismo Prado*, 21 de Mayo 417, T/F231271, turismoprada@entelchile.net TCs accepted. Both the following 2 *casas de cambio* are recommended: *Casa de Cambio Emperador*, Bilbao 222 and *Lucia Saldivia*, Baquedano 285. **Books** Library on Cochrane, near plaza, good selection of videos on Chile and book exchange (mostly English and German). **Cameras and film** Several on both Condell and Prat. **Communications** Internet: *Ciber Patagonia*, 21 de Mayo 525, cheap, best. *Entel*, Prat 340. US$7 per hr charged per min. *Hechizos*, 21 de Mayo 460, cheap. **Post office**: Cochrane 202. Open Mon-Fri 0900-1230, 1430-1800, Sat 0830-1200. **Telephone**: office at Barroso 626. Open until 2200, opens on Sun about 0900. **Hospital** Calle Hospital 068, T233172. **Language schools** *Baquedano International Language School*, Baquedano 20, at *Hosp* of Sr Guzmán (see sleeping above), T232520, F231511, www.patagoniachile.cl/com/bils US$300 per week course including lodging and all meals, 4 hrs a day person-to-person tuition, other activities organized at discount rates. Friendly, informative, highly recommended. **Laundry** *Lavaseco Universal*, Gen Parra 55. QL, Bilbao 160. **Mechanics** *Automotores Santiago*, Calle Los Nires 811, T238330, T096406896 (mob). Motor mechanic, speaks English, can obtain spare parts quickly. **Shipping** *Transmarchilay*, 21 de Mayo 447, T231971, F232700. *Navimag*, Ibáñez 347, T233306, F233386. *Greenline*, T238947, services to Termas de Chiconal and Laguna San Rafael, charters. *Sotramin* (services on Lago General Carrera), Moraleda y Portales, T233515.

Border crossings to Argentina The **Coyhaique Alto** crossing is reached by a *ripio* road which runs east of Coyhaique. On the Argentine side the road leads through Río Mayo and Sarmiento to Comodoro Rivadavia on the Atlantic seaboard. Chilean immigration is at Coyhaique Alto, 43 km west of Coyhaique, 6 km west of the frontier, open May-Aug 0800-2000, Sep-Apr 0730-2200. For buses between Coyhaique and Comodoro Rivadavia see above.

The **Paso Huemules** crossing is reached by a paved road, Route 245, which runs southeast, 61 km from Coyhaique, via Balmaceda airport, which is 5 km west of the frontier. There is no accommodation at the frontier or at the airport and no public transport from the frontier to the airport. See above for transport from the airport to Coyhaique. On the Argentine side a *ripio* road runs via Lago Blanco (fuel) to join Route 40, 105 km west of Paso Huemules. Chilean immigration opens May-Jul 0800-2000, Sep-Apr 0730-2200.

The Camino Austral

Puerto Aisén

Puerto Aisén lies at the confluence of the rivers Aisén and Palos. Dating from the 1920s, the town grew as the major port of the region though it has now been replaced by Puerto Chacabuco, 15 km further down the river. There are few vestiges of the port left, just some boats high and dry on the river bank when the tide is out and the foundations of buildings by the river, now overgrown with fuchsias and buttercups. To see any maritime activity you have to walk a little way out of town to Puerto Aguas Muertas where the fishing boats come in.

The town is linked to the south bank of the Río Aisén by the Puente Presidente Ibañez, the longest suspension bridge in Chile. From the far bank a paved road leads to **Puerto Chacabuco**; a regular bus service runs between the two. The harbour is a short way from the town. There is a helpful tourist office in the Municipalidad, Prat y Sgto Aldea, 1 December to end-February only.

Phone code: 067
Colour map 5, grid B3
Population: 13,050

It is much here is much wetter than in Coyhaique: local wags say that it rains for 370 days a year. September to January are the driest months

There is a good walk along a minor road to **Laguna Los Palos**, 10 km north of Puerto Aisén. Calm, deserted and surrounded by forested hills it is recommended. En route is a bridge over a deep, narrow river, freezing cold but with potential for a bracing swim. **Lago Riesco**, 30 km south of Puerto Aisén, can be reached by unpaved road following the Río Blanco. In season the *Apulcheu* sails regularly to **Termas de Chiconal**, about one hour west of Puerto Chacabuco on the northern shore of the Seno Aisén, offering a good way to see the fjord, US$30, take own food.

Excursions

B *Hotel Caicahues*, Michimalonco 660, T335680. **D** *Res Aisén*, Serrano Montaner 37, T332725. Good food, clean, full board available. **E-F** *Res Serrano Montaner*, Montaner 471, T332574. Very pleasant and helpful. Recommended. **F** *Hotel Plaza*, O'Higgins 237, T332784. Without breakfast. **F** *Roxy*, Aldea 972, T332704. Friendly, clean, large rooms, restaurant. Highly recommended. **F** *Yaney Ruca*, Aldea 369, T332583. Clean, friendly. No campsite but free camping easy. **In Puerto Chacabuco AL** *Parque Turístico Loberías de Aisén*, Carrera 50, T234520. Accommodation overpriced, best food in the area, climb up steps direct from port for drink or meal overlooking boats and mountains before boarding ferry. Car hire available. **F** *Moraleda*, O'Higgins 82, T351155. Eating at *Café Restaurante Ensenada*, O'Higgins 302, mid-price. No other places to buy food or other services.

Sleeping
■ *on map, page 426*
Price codes:
see inside front cover
Can be hard to find, most is taken up by fishing companies in both ports

Mid-range En route from Coyhaique to Puerto Aisén are *Restaurante La Cascada*, Km 32, and *Restaurante International*, Km 41, Villa Los Torreones, both recommended. **Cheap** *Café Rucaray*, south side of Plaza de Armas. *Gastronomía Carrera*, Cochrane 465. Large, very good, popular.

Eating
● *on map, page 426*

Bars *Crazy Pub*, Aldea 1170; make your own mind up how 'crazy' it is. *Eko Pub*, T(Merino)998. There are a couple of smaller bars; one has a wildly sloping pool table. **Discos** *Dina's Discotheque*, Carrera 1270. *Pollo's Discotheque*, Caupolicán 265.

Entertainment

Local festival of folklore, 2nd week in **Nov**.

Festivals

Turismo Rucaray, T(Merino)848, T332862, rucaray@entelchile.net Recommended, internet access.

Tour operator

Bus To **Puerto Chacabuco**, *Don Carlos* and *Suray*, every ½-1 hr, US$1, frequent *colectivos*, US$0.50. To **Coyhaique**, *Don Carlos* minibuses, 8 a day, *Suray* minibuses every 45 mins-1 hr, both charge US$2, 1-hr journey.

Transport

For fares from Puerto Montt to Laguna San Rafael see under Puerto Montt

Ferry To Puerto Montt: Both the *Transmarchilay* ferry *El Colono* (US$48) and the *Navimag* ferry *Evangelistas* (US$40) sail to Puerto Montt via the Canal Moraleda once a week, 24 hrs, all year service. **To Quellón**: The *Transmarchilay* ferry *Pincoya* sails to Quellón on Chiloé via Melinka and Puerto Aguirre, Mon 1800, 24 hrs, US$14 all year service. There is also a *Navimag* service, 36 hrs including stops at many islands en route. No cabins, take own food and water. **To Puerto Natales**: The new boat *Magallanes*, which runs between Puerto Montt and Puerto Natales, now stops at Puerto Chacabuco, meaning it is now possible to sail direct to Puerto Natales – this route is likely to be extremely popular. **To Laguna San Rafael**: In Jan and Feb both *El Colono* and *Evangelistas* make an excursion from Puerto Chacabuco to Laguna San Rafael. Departures on Sat, return Sun, 21-24 hr voyage. Fares including food: *El Colono* suite US$640 per person; *butaca* US$210-295; *Evangelistas* suite US$750 per person, *literas* US$370, semi-*cama* US$200. *Patagonia Connection SA*, Fidel Oteíza 1921, Oficina 1006, Providencia, Santiago, T2256489, F2748111, operates *Patagonia Express*, a catamaran which runs from Puerto Chacabuco to Laguna San Rafael via Termas de Puyuhuapi, see page 380 for further details. **Shipping offices**: *Agemar*, Tte Merino 909, T332716, Puerto Aisén; *Navimag*, Terminal de Transbordadores, Puerto Chacabuco, T351111, F351192; *Transmarchilay*, Av O'Higgins s/n, T351144, Puerto Chacabuco. It is best to make reservations in these companies' offices in Puerto Montt, Coyhaique or Santiago (or, for Transmarchilay, in Chaitén or Ancud). For other trips to Laguna San Rafael, see below; out of season, they are very difficult to arrange, but try *Edda Espinosa*, Sgto Aldea 943. Boat information is posted at *Café Rucaray*.

Directory **Banks** *Banco de Crédito*, Prat. For Visa. *Banco de Chile*, Plaza de Armas. Only changes cash, not TCs. **Communications** Post office: on south side of bridge. **Telephone:** office on south side of Plaza de Armas, next to *Café Rucaray*. *ENTEL*, Libertad 408, has internet access.

Puerto Aisén

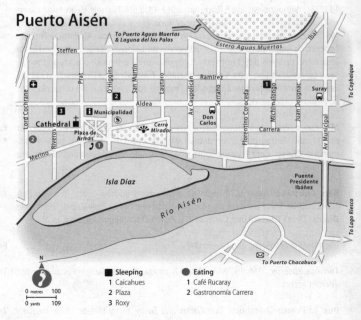

N

0 metres 100
0 yards 109

■ **Sleeping**
1 Caicahues
2 Plaza
3 Roxy

● **Eating**
1 Café Rucaray
2 Gastronomía Carrera

The Camino Austral

Lago General Carrera

Straddling the frontier with Argentina, Lago General Carrera is the second largest *Colour map 5, grid B3* lake in South America after Lake Titicaca. It is now reckoned to be the deepest lake in the continent; depth soundings in 1997 established its maximum depth as 590 m.

The lake is a beautiful azure blue; the Chilean end is surrounded by predominantly Alpine terrain and the Argentine end by dry pampa. To the north there are fine views of Cerro Castillo. The eruption of Volcán Hudson in 1991 (south of Chile Chico) polluted parts of the lake and many rivers, but the waters are now clear. The effects can still be seen in some places where there is a metre-thick layer of ash on the ground; this was a much greater disaster in Argentine Patagonia – prevailing winds blew the ash into the farmlands, blinding sheep and causing hundreds of thousands of them to die.

Getting there The main towns, Puerto Ibáñez on the north shore and Chile Chico on **Ins & outs** the south, are connected by a ferry, the *Pilchero*, but there are also 2, much longer, *See next page for* overland routes between Coyhaique and Chile Chico: through Argentina, or along the *further details* Camino Austral which runs west around the lake. **Getting around** Minibuses ply along the Camino Austral in summer, and some small 4-seater air taxis also link the small towns of the region. **Climate** The region prides itself in having the best climate in southern Chile, with some 300 days of sunshine; much fruit is grown as a result, especially around Chile Chico, where rainfall is very low for this area, and there is more of a similarity to Argentine Patagonia than to the rest of the Camino Austral region.

The principal port on the Chilean section of the lake, Puerto Ibáñez (officially **Puerto Ibáñez** Puerto Ingeniero Ibáñez) is reached by taking a branch road, 31 km long, *Colour map 5, grid B3* from Bajada Ibañez 97 km south of Coyhaique. There are some fine waterfalls, *Population: 828* the Salto Río Ibáñez, 6 km north.

Sleeping and eating **F-G** *Res Ibáñez*, Bertrán Dixon 31, T423227. Clean, warm, hot *Many shops and* water. Unnamed *hospedaje* at Bertrán Dixon 31. **F-G** *Vientos del Sur*, Bertrán Dixon *restaurants are* 282, T423208, cheap meals available, good. At Bajada Río Ibañez, **D** *Hostería Doña* *closed on Sun* *Amalia*, and **F** *Agroturismo Mary Sandoval*. Fuel (sold in 5 litre containers) available in Puerto Ibáñez at Luis A Bolados 461 (house with 5 laburnum trees outside). **Camping** Municipal campsite, T423234, US$7 per site, open Dec-Mar.

Transport Minibus **To Coyhaique**, 2½ hrs, US$7. There is a road to Perito Moreno, Argentina, but no public transport. **Ferry** The car ferry, *El Pilchero*, sails from Puerto Ibañez to **Chile Chico**, daily (except Sun) 1000, return departures 1700 daily except Sat (Sun 1200). Fares for cars US$45, for passengers US$4.40, 2¾-hrs crossing, motorbikes and bicycles US$8. Number of passengers limited to 70; arrive 30 mins before departure, reservations possible. This is a very cold crossing even in summer: take warm clothing. Buses and jeeps meet the ferry in Puerto Ibáñez for Coyhaique.

Around the lake

The Camino Austral has now been completed to its final destination at Villa O'Higgins. The section around the north and western sides of Lago General Carrera is reckoned by many people to be the most spectacular. A branch road along the southern shore of Lago General Carrera connects with the small town of Chile Chico near the Argentine frontier.

The Camino Austral

Reserva Nacional Cerro Castillo The Camino Austral runs southwest through the Reserva Nacional Cerro Castillo. Extending over 179,550 ha, this park is named after the fabulous **Cerro Castillo** (2,675 m) which resembles a fairytale castle with rock pinnacles jutting from a covering of snow. The park also includes Cerro Bandera (2,040 m) just west of Balmaceda and several other peaks in the northern wall of the valley of the Río Ibañez. There is a *guardería* at the northeastern end of the park near Laguna Chinguay and a CONAF campsite nearby, US$5 per site, T067-237070. At Km 83 the road crosses the Portezuelo Ibañez (1,120 m) and drops through the Cuesta del Diablo, a series of bends which offer fine views over the Río Ibañez.

Villa Cerro Castillo Villa Cerro Castillo, Km 98, 8 km beyond Bajada Ibañez (the turning for Puerto Ibañez) is a village in a narrow gorge, where there are two *residenciales* (one at Aguirre Cerda 35, **D**, with good mid-price meals) and a grocery store. Cheap meals also available at *Restaurante La Querencia*, O'Higgins s/n. There is a small local museum, 2 km south of Villa Cerro Castillo, open from December to March, 0900-1900. There is transport from Cerro Castillo to Coyhaique (US$7) through *Transportes Amin Ali*, O'Higgins s/n, T419200. Nearby is the **Monumento Nacional Manos de Cerro Castillo**, where traces of ancient rock paintings, estimated to be 10,000 years old, have been found.

The road climbs out of the valley, passing the aptly named Laguna Verde and the Portezuelo Cofré. It descends to the boggy Manso valley, with a good campsite at the bridge over the river – watch out for mosquitoes. This area was seriously affected by the ash from Volcán Hudson.

Lago General Carrera

Some 5 km off the Camino Austral at Km 203 is Bahía Murta, situated on the northern tip of the central 'arm' of Lago General Carrera. This village dates from the 1930s when it lived from exporting timber to Argentina via Chile Chico. From here the road follows the lake's western shore; the colour of the water is an unbelievable blue-green, reflecting the mountains which surround it and the clouds above.

Bahía Murta
Population: 600

Sleeping and eating F *Res Patagonia*, Pasaje España 64, T419601, very basic, without bath. **F-G** *Res Lago Gen Carrera*, Av 5 de Abril y Colombia, T419601. Excellent cheap meals, also has cabin with own store. Free camping by the lake, good views of Cerro Castillo.

This village, at Km 228 from Coyhaique, is where the buses stop for lunch: fuel is available at the ECA store from a large drum (no sign). Nearby is the unusual **Catedral de Mármol**, a peninsula made of marble, with caves which can be visited by boat – worth seeing. From Río Tranquilo, there is a new branch of the Camino Austral which heads northwest to Puerto Grosse on coast.

Río Tranquilo
Population: 400

Sleeping and eating D *Hostal Los Pinos*, 2 Oriente 41, T411576, family run, well maintained, good mid-price meals. Recommended. F *Cabañas Jacricalor*, 1 Sur s/n, T419500. F *Hostería Camino Austral*, 1 Sur 223, T419500. Mid-price/cheap meals. **Tour operator** *El Puesto Expediciones*, Lagos 258, T/F233785, elpuesto@entelchile.net

El Maitén, Km 279, lies at the southwestern tip of Lago General Carrera: here a road branches off west along the south shore of the lake towards Chile Chico, see below. South of El Maitén the Camino Austral becomes steeper and more bendy and in winter this stretch is icy and dangerous. Accommodation is available at *Mallín Colorado*, 2 km west, T2741807, F2042785, chile@patgonia-pacific.cl which has *cabañas*, adventure activities, horseriding, rafting, fishing, English and German spoken.

El Maitén

Puerto Bertrand, 5 km away, is a good place for fishing. Nearby is a sign to the Nacimiento del Río Baker: the place where the Río Baker is reckoned to begin. Beyond Puerto Bertrand the road climbs up to high moorland, passing the confluence of the Ríos Neff and Baker, before winding south along the east bank of the Río Baker to Cochrane. The scenery is splendid all the way; in the main the road is rough but not treacherous. Watch out for cattle on the road and take blind corners slowly.

Sleeping and eating in El Maitén LL *Hostería Campo Baker*, T411477, *cabañas*, sleeps five. Also *Doña Ester*, pink building, **F**, good. *Casa de Huéspedes*. Dormitory accommodation. One small shop. For excursions contact Jonathan Leidich, T411330, who lives on the edge of the lake, for rafting, horseriding and other activities, highly recommended. Fishing can be arranged at Puerto Bertrand through *Patagonia Baker Lodges*, Orillas del Río Baker, T411903 or *Río Baker Lodges*, T411499.

At Puerto Guadal, 10 km east of El Maitén, there are shops, places to stay and eat, a post office and petrol. This town is a centre for fishing which can be arranged through *Hacienda Tres Lagos*, Sector El Maitén, T411323, *Pasarela Lodges II*, Horn 47, Piso 2, T411425, or at *Playa Guadal*, 2 km from Puerto Guadal, T411443.

Puerto Guadal
Population: 500

Further east along the shore, just past the village of **Mallin Grande**, Km 40, the road runs through the Paso de las Llaves, a 30 km stretch carved out of the

Paso de las Llaves

The Camino Austral

The War of Chile Chico (1917)

Chile Chico dates from 1909 when Chilean settlers crossed from Argentina and occupied the land. In the previous year the Chilean government had granted 80,000 ha of land between Lago General Carrera and Lago Cochrane to cattle ranchers from *the Sociedad Explotadora Río Baker. In the showdown which followed the ranchers were driven out by the settlers, but it was not until 1931 that the Chilean government finally recognized the town's existence.*

rock-face overlooking the lake. This was the most expensive section of the Camino Austral. The road climbs and drops, offering wonderful views over the lake and over the icefields to the west. At Km 74 a turning runs to **Fachinal**. A further 8 km east there is an **open cast mine** which produces gold and other precious metals.

Chile Chico

Phone code: 067
Colour map 5, grid B3
Population: 3,757

A quiet, friendly but dusty town situated on the lake shore 122 km east of El Maitén, Chile Chico lies near the Argentine border. At the centre of a fruit growing region, it has an annual festival at the end of January. There is a small museum open in summer; outside is a boat which carried cargo on the lake before the opening of the new road along the southern shore of the lake. There are fine views from the Cerro de las Banderas at the western end of town. In the last week of January is the Festival Internacional de la Voz. There is a tourist office at the Municipalidad, O'Higgins 333 – ask here for help in arranging tours.

The country to the south and west of Chile Chico, with weird rock formations and dry brush-scrub, provides good walking terrain. The northern and higher peak of Cerro Pico del Sur (2,168 m) can be climbed by the agile from Los Cipres (beware dogs in farmyard). You will need a long summer's day and the 1:50,000 map. Follow the horse trail until it peters out, then navigate by compass or sense of direction until the volcano-like summit appears. After breaching the cliff ramparts, there is some scrambling and a 10 ft pitch to the summit, with indescribable views of the Lake and the Andes.

Twenty kilometres south of Chile Chico towards Lago Jeinimeni is the Cueva de las Manos, a cave full of Tehuelche paintings, the most famous of which are the *manos azules* (blue hands).

From the road, climb 500 m and cross Pedregoso stream. The path is difficult, and partly hidden. Recommended to take a guide.

Sleeping A *Austral*, O'Higgins 501, T411461, welcoming, very clean. Recommended. **C** *Res Aguas Azules*, Rodriguez 252, T411320. **C** *Ventura*, Carrera 29, T411311. Suites, modern. **D** *Casa Quinta No me Olvides/Manor House Don't Forget Me*, Camino Internacional s/n, without bath. Clean, cooking facilities, warm, camping. Recommended. Tours arranged to Lago Jeinimeni and Cueva de las Manos. **D** *Hostería de la Patagonia*, Camino Internacional s/n, T411337, F411414. Full board, clean, excellent food, English, French and Italian spoken, trekking, horseriding and white-water rafting organized (Casilla 91). Recommended. **E** *Hospedaje de Patagonia*, recommended, also camping. **F** *Hospedaje Alicia*, Ramon Freire 24. Single, double and three bed rooms, clean, use of kitchen. **F** *Hospedaje Transport Ales*, good beds, showers, cooking facilities, friendly atmosphere. **F** *Plaza*, O'Higgins y Balmaceda, T411510. Basic, clean. Recommended. **F** *Res Don Luis* , Balmaceda 175, T411384. Clean, meals available. **Camping** Free campsite at Bahía Jarra, 5 km from Chile Chico, then 12 km north. Also *Camping del Sol* at the eastern end of the town.

Mid-range *Cafetería Loly y Elizabeth*, Gonzalez 25, on the Plaza serves coffee and delicious ice cream and cakes. *Café Holiday*, Calle Gonzalez, good coffee, friendly. *Restaurante Aguas Azules*, Rodriguez 21. **Cheap** *Café Refer*, O'Higgins 416, *Café Wild West*, Gonzalez 111. Supermarket on B O'Higgins. **Eating**

Pub *Pub El Minero*, Carrera 205. Recommended. **Disco** *Zebra*, O'Higgins 750 Interior, the place to be seen in Chile Chico. **Entertainment**

Air *Don Carlos* to **Coyhaique** Mon, Wed, Fri, US$36; *Don Carlos* to **Balmaceda**, Tue, Thu, Sat, US$41. **Minibus** Along the south side of the lake to **Cochrane**, *Transportes Ales*, T411739, daily, US$20. To **Puerto Guadal**, Sr Sergio Haro Ramos, T411251, Wed, Sat, minibus service, US$10, *Transportes Ales*, 2 weekly (US$10), and *Transportes Seguel*, 2 weekly (US$9). **Transport** *See page 427 for ferry service to Puerto Ibañez and connecting minibus services to Coyhaique*

Banks Best to change money in Coyhaique or Argentina: dollars and Argentine pesos can be changed in small amounts at shops and cafés including *Café Loly y Elizabeth*, but at poor rates. **Camera and films** *Rene Villegas*, O'Higgins 424. **Car hire** *Jaime Acuña Vogt*, Grosse 150, T/F411553. **Fishing guide** Jaime Berrocal, O'Higgins 501, T/F 41146. **Hospital** Lautaro s/n, T411334. **Directory**

Situated south of Chile Chico, this park covers 160,000 ha and includes two lakes, Lago Jeinemeni and Lago Verde which lie surrounded by forests in the narrow valley of the Río Jeinemeni. There are impressive cliffs, waterfalls and small glaciers. Wildlife includes huemul deer, pumas and condors. Activities include fishing for salmon and rainbow trout, trekking and rowing. A good map is essential. Access is via an unpaved road which branches south off the road to Los Antiguos and crosses five rivers, four of which have to be forded. At Km 42 there is a small lake, Laguna de los Flamencos, where large numbers of flamingos can be seen. The park entrance is at Km 53; just beyond is a ranger station; 2 km further, at the eastern end of Lago Jeinemeni, there is a campsite and fishing area. ■ *US$1.50, Camping US$3. Take all supplies. The park is open all year but access may be impossible between Apr and Oct due to high river levels. Getting there: lifts may be possible from Chile Chico; try Juan Núñez, Hernán Trizzando 110, for a lift on a timber truck, or ask in the CONAF office.* **Reserva Nacional Lago Jeinimeni**

A road runs east from Chile Chico to the Argentine frontier 2 km east. From the frontier it is 5 km further to Los Antiguos. The immigration office is open Sep-Apr 0730-2200, May-Aug 0800-2000. Minibuses from Chile Chico to Los Antiguos are run by 3 companies, *Arcotrans*, T411358, *Jaime Acuña*, T411590 and *Transportes Padilla*, T411224, US$3 (payable in US$ or Argentine pesos only), 45 mins including formalities (once a day each company at weekends). **Border with Argentina**

Los Antiguos is also a fruit-growing town. There is an annual cherry festival in mid-January. Salmon fishing is also possible. There is accommodation. From here buses run weekdays to Comodoro Rivadavia via Perito Moreno, US$20, seven hours; there are also direct buses to Río Gallegos. **Into Argentina**

Perito Moreno, 67 km east of the frontier has a few hotels, a campsite, a restaurant and money exchange services. There is one flight a week Perito Moreno-Río Gallegos. About 120 km south is the famous **Cueva de las Manos**

The Camino Austral

where the walls of a series of galleries are covered with painted human hands and animals, 10,000 years old. All but 31 of the 800 hands are left-handed.

Cochrane

Colour map 5, grid C3
Population: 3,000
343 km south of Coyhaique

Sitting in a hollow on the northern banks of the Río Cochrane is Cochrane, a simple place, sunny in summer and good for walking and fishing. There is a small museum at San Valentín 555. ■ *Tue-Sun 0900-1300, 1500-1900.* The tourist office in the Plaza is open only in the summer. ■ *Mon-Sat 0900-1300, 1430-2000 – in winter go to the municipalidad, Esmeralda 398.*

Excursions can be made to **Lago Cochrane**, which straddles the frontier with Argentina (the Argentine section is called Lago Puerredón). The lake, which extends over 17,500 ha, offers excellent fishing. The views from the reserve are superb, over the town, the nearby lakes and to the Campo de Hielo Norte to the west; boats can be hired for US$12 per person. On the northern shores of the lake is the **Reserva Nacional Tamango**, which covers 6,925 ha of lenga forest and is home to one of the largest colonies of the rare huemal as well as guanaco, foxes and lots of birds including woodpeckers and hummingbirds. ■ *US$3. 0830-2100 Dec-Mar, 0830-1830 Apr-Nov. Guided visits to see the huemal, Tue, Thu, Sat, US$60 for a group of 6 people. Tourist facilities are rudimentary. Campsites at Los Correntadas, US$10 per site, also cabañas, and Los Coigües, US$13 per site, also cabañas. Details and booking through CONAF office on the main plaza (T422164).*

Sleeping
In summer it is best to book rooms in advance

A-B *Ultimo Paraíso*, Lago Brown 455, T522361. **C** *Hotel Wellmann*, Las Golondrinas 36, T522171. Hot water, comfortable, warm, good meals. Recommended. **D** *Res Rubio*, Tte Merino 4, T522173. Very good, breakfast included, lunch and dinner extra. **E** *Residencia Cero a Cero*, Lago Brown 464, T522158. With breakfast, welcoming, with bath. **F** *Café Rogery*, Tte Merino 502, *cabañas*, sleep 5, US$50 including breakfast (ie US$10), kitchen facilities. **F** *Hosp Cochrane*, Dr Steffens 451, T522377, good meals, camping. Recommended. **F** *Hospedaje Ernilda Cruzes*, clean, hot water. **F** *Hosp Paola*, Lago Brown 150, T522215, also camping. **F** *Res El Fogón*, San Valentín 651, T522240; its pub is the only eating place open in the low season. **F** *Res Sur Austral*, Prat 334, T522150. With breakfast, hot water, also good.

Eating
Mid-range/cheap *Café El Farolito*, Tte Merino 546. *El Arriero*, San Valentín 570, best in town. *Restaurante El Fogón*, San Valentín 651. *Restaurante Llanquihue*, Tte Merino 499. *Restaurant Rogeri*, Tte Merino 502.

Entertainment
Disco *Scala*, T Moreno 602. Recommended.

Sports
Horseriding Horses can be hired for excursions in the surrounding countryside. Try Don Pedro Munoz, T522244, F522245. **Canoeing** *Siesta Oppi*, a canoe shop, 3176 Neuenegg, Switzerland, T31-7419192, F7411215, organizes canoe trips in the area during Jan and Feb.

Tour operators
Red de Turismo Río Baker, San Valentin 438, T/F522646 trural@patagoniachile.cl *Samuel Smiol*, T522487. Offers tours to the icefields and mountains, English spoken. Excursions can also be arranged through Guillermo Paso, Transportes Los Ñadis. Fishing tours are available from *Hotel Ultimo Paraíso*.

Transport
Air Don Carlos to Coyhaique, Mon, US$65. **Bus** Company agencies: *Don Carlos*, Prat 344, T/F522150. Twice weekly to Coyhaique (US$15). *Los Ñadis*, Los Helechos 490,

T/F522196. Three weekly to Coyhaique (US$19), 3 weekly to Vagabundo (US$7), and 1 weekly to Villa O'Higgins (US$11). *Acuario 13*, Río Baker 349, T/F522143. Three weekly to Coyhaique (US$19), 4 weekly to Vagabundo (US$7) and 1 weekly to Villa O'Higgins (US$11). Petrol is available, if it hasn't run out, at the *Empresa Comercial Agrícola* (ECA) and at the *Copec* station.

Banks *Banco del Estado*, on the plaza, changes dollars. **Car hire** *Marcel Moya Diaz*, **Directory**
Dr Steffens 147, T522276. **Supermarket** *Melero*, Las Golondrinas 148.

Some 17 km north of Cochrane, a road through Villa Chacabuco and Paso **Into Argentina**
Roballos (78 km) enters Argentina (and continues to Bajo Caracoles). There
isn't any public transport and although the road is passable in summer it is
often flooded in spring. Summer 0730-2200, winter 0800-2000.

South of Cochrane

The final 224 km stretch of the Camino Austral from Cochrane to Villa
O'Higgins has now been completed – the final sector requires a ferry crossing
from Puerto Yungay to Río Bravo, daily 1000 hours and 1200 hours, return
1200 and 1400. At Km 45 from Cochrane there is a free *refugio*. From
Vagabundo, Km 98, where there is a *refugio* with four beds, boats sail regularly
down the Río Baker to Tortel. This is a beautiful trip through thick forest with
views of snow-capped mountains and waterfalls.

Tortel, a village built on a hill at the mouth of the river, has no streets, only **Tortel**
wooden walkways ('*no hay ni una bicicleta*'). It became famous in October
2000 as the place where Prince William of Britain spent three months working
for Operation Raleigh; it is also the place at which Rosie Swale ended her epic
horseback journey through Chile (see *Back to Cape Horn*, page 71). The village is still inaccessible by road, but a branch of the Camino Austral is being
built to Tortel which should be finished within two years, and the repercussions on the character of the place will be enormous. The main industries are
the trade in wood with Punta Arenas, and fishing for shellfish. From here you
can hire a boat to the spectacular **Ventisquero Jorge Montt**, five hours southwest, or to the **Ventisquero Steffens**, north on the edge of the Parque
Nacional San Rafael. On the Río Baker nearby is the Isla de los Muertos, which
is the site of the graves of some hundred Chilote workers who died here under
mysterious circumstances early in the 20th century.

Sleeping and eating Ask for Doña Berta Muñoz, **D** full board. "Expect fresh mutton
meals and if you are squeamish about seeing animals killed don't look out of the window when they butcher the two lambs a day on the front porch." **F** *Hospedaje
Costanera*, including breakfast, T/F234815. Clean, warm, attractive garden, open to
non-residents for breakfast, recommended. **F** Sergio Barrio, also **D** full board, good
food. **E/F**, *Casa Rural,* full board; **G** bed and breakfast. Free accommodation is also
available at the Centro Abierto, ask at the Municipalidad, T/F211876. *Café Celes Salom*,
basic cheap meals, disco every Sat, occasional visiting bands.

Transport Air Don Carlos to Coyhaique, Mon and Wed from Cochrane (US$65),
Tortel, Mon (US$91), and Villa O'Higgins, Wed (US$100). **Boat** From Vagabundo to
Tortel, Tue, Sun 1500, 3 hrs, US$2. From Tortel to Vagabundo, Tue, Sun 0900, 5 hrs
(upstream). There is also a boat once a fortnight from Tortel to Puerto Yungay. Charter
boats can be arranged through Viviana Muñoz or Hernán Ovando at the

The Camino Austral

Laguna San Rafael

The trip in the rowboat to the glacier is an awesome venture. At first it is fairly warm and easy to row. Gradually it gets colder when the wind sweeps over the glacier. It gets harder to row as small icebergs hinder the boat. Frequently somebody has to jump onto an iceflow and push the boat through. The glacier itself has a deep blue colour, shimmering and reflecting the light; the same goes for the icebergs,

which are an unreal, translucent blue. The glacier is very noisy; there are frequent cracking and banging sounds, resembling a mixture of gun shots and thunder. When a hunk of ice breaks loose, a huge swell is created and the icebergs start rocking in the water. Then great care and effort has to be taken to avoid the boat being crushed by the shifting icebergs; this is a very real danger.

Municipalidad, T/F211876. Prices to Ventisquero Jorge Montt, US$100 per person in a speedboat, 2 hrs, US$120 for lancha, 5 hrs. To Ventisquero Steffens, US$60 per person for speed boat (1 hr), $70 for lancha approximately 2½ hrs. To Puerto Yungay, US$110 return, 8 hrs, 6-10 passengers.

Directory Banks There is no bank in the village but a mobile bank comes by air twice per month. **Communications** Post office is open Mon-Fri 0830-1330, post leaves Tortel weekly by air. Telephone office, T234815. **Medical services** Medical centre staffed by doctors, nurses and dentists visiting monthly.

Villa O'Higgins Villa O'Higgins lies near the Argentine border at the northeastern end of an
Colour map 5, grid C3 'arm' of Lago O'Higgins which straddles the border (Lago San Martín in
Population: 500 Argentina). The town has spectacular views and mountains and glaciers are nearby. The people are very friendly, and there is still a frontier feel. On the lake are large numbers of icebergs which have split off the glaciers of the Campo de Hielo Sur to the west. Accommodation is available at the *Hospedaje Patagonia*, **D** per person without bath, T234813, and at *Donde El Diablo*, **E** per person without bath, T216927, serves food, pub, organizes tours. There are two restaurants, *Campo de Hielo Sur* and *Patagonia*. Boat trips are offered by Adolfo Güinao Velásquez. Fishing tours are arranged by Nelson Henriquez, Lago Cisnes 201. Horses can be hired. Tourist information from the Municipalidad, T211849.

Transport *Don Carlos* air taxi fly from **Balmaceda**, US$80, from **Cochrane**, US$50. There are also 2 weekly from **Cochrane** (see page 432).

Parque Nacional Laguna San Rafael

Laguna San Rafael is one of the highlights for many travellers to Chile. Situated west of Lago General Carrera and some 200 km south of Puerto Aisén, the *Ventisquero San Rafael* is one of many which flow off the giant Campo de Hielo Norte. About 45 km in length the glacier flows into the Laguna San Rafael which empties into the sea northwards via the Río Tempano. Towering 30 m above water level, the glacier carves small icebergs which are carried across the laguna and out through the Río Tempano. Around the shores of the laguna is thick vegetation and above are snowy mountain peaks.

Laguna San Rafael and the Campo de Hielo Norte are part of the Parque Nacional Laguna San Rafael, which extends over 1,740,000 ha. In the national park are puma, pudu, foxes, dolphins, occasional sea-lions and sea otters, and many species of bird. Walking trails are limited (about 10 km in all) but a lookout platform has been constructed, with fine views of the glacier.

Sadly, the glacier at Laguna San Rafael is rapidly disintegrating, and is thought to have only until 2011 before disappearing entirely. While this shrinkage is symptomatic of what has happened to many glaciers in Patagonia, including Perito Moreno in Argentina, some place the blame for the process on the waves created by tourist boats that go too close to the glacier, thereby creating a greater force of erosion against the ice. If the glacier is to be preserved, it is vital that travellers take a pro-active stance on this issue, and insist that the boats in which they travel to the park do not go too close to the glacier and further damage this fragile environment.

■ *Park entry fee is US$6. At the glacier there is a small ranger station which gives information; a pier and 2 paths have been built. One path leads to the glacier. The rangers are willing to row you out to the glacier in calm weather, a 3-hr trip.*

Transport
The only ways there are by plane or by boat

Air Taxis from Coyhaique by *Aerohein* and *Don Carlos* (addresses under Coyhaique), US$200 each if party of 5; some pilots in Puerto Aisén will fly to the glacier for about US$95 each, but many are unwilling to land on the rough airstrip. **Sea** The official cruises are: *Skorpios I* and *II* (see under Puerto Montt); *Navimag's Evangelistas* and *Transmarchilay's Colono* (see under Pto Chacabuco); *Patagonia Express,* a catamaran which sails from Puerto Montt to Laguna San Rafael via Termas de Puyuhuapi, in tours lasting 4-6 days (see page 416); *Iceberg Express,* a catamaran which offers 12-hr luxury cruises from Puerto Chacabuco; in Santiago, Av Providencia 2331, oficina 602, T3350580, F3350581. *Pamar,* Pacheco Altamirano 3100, T256220, Puerto Montt, Sep-Mar only; *Compañía Naviera Puerto Montt* has 2 vessels: the *Quellón,* with 6-day, 6-night tours to the Laguna from Puerto Montt via various ports and channels (US$900); Puerto Montt, Diego Portales 882, T/F252547; Puerto Chacabuco T351106. *Odisea* and *Visun,* motorized sailing boats, Dec to Mar, in Santiago, Alameda B O'Higgins 108, local 120, T6330883, in Puerto Aisén, Sgto Aldea 679, T332908, 6-day trips from Puerto Chacabuco to Laguna San Rafael. Various private yachts can be chartered in Puerto Montt for 6-12 passengers to Laguna San Rafael. Local fishing boats from Puerto Chacabuco/Puerto Aisén take about 18-20 hrs each way, charging the same as the tourist boats. Ask for Jorge Prado at the port (he takes a minimum of 7, more expensive than others); Andino Royas, Cochrane 129; Justiniano Aravena, Dr Steffen 703; Rodrigo Azúcar, Agemar office, T332716; or Sr Ocuña, ask at the port. These unauthorized boats may not have adequate facilities and may not be licensed for the trip.

The Camino Austral

The Far South

13

The Far South

A spectacular land of fragmenting glaciers and teetering icy peaks, southern Patagonia has a feel all its own. Although Chileans posted here will often say that they are a long way "from Chile", this is the country's most popular destination for visitors. The jewel in the crown is the Parque Nacional Torres del Paine, justifiably famous among travellers. With its glaciers, the exquisite turquoise hue of its lakes, thick forests of native trees, and three distinctive columns (the 'towers' after which the park is named), which point vertically like fingers from the Paine massif, Paine is a natural magnet for visitors from all over the world. Nearby, Punta Arenas is a European-style city with a lively Chilote community and various leftovers of the earlier English and Croatian influence. There are numerous other attractions, notably the glaciers which descend from Monte Balmaceda at the southern end of the Parque Nacional Bernardo O'Higgins. On the Argentine side of the frontier lies more spectacular scenery, notably the Perito Moreno Glacier and the mountainous area around Cerro Fitz Roy.

Things to do in the Far South

- Complete the 7-day trek in the Parque Nacional Torres del Paine passing fields of wild flowers, glaciers, mountains, forests, and white and turquoise lakes.
- Witness the creaking, heaving mass of Perito Moreno glacier in Argentina, where huge chunks of ice regularly break off into Lago Argentino.
- Trek in the area by Mount Fitz Roy, Argentine Patagonia – "anyone within 500 miles would be a fool to miss it".
- Ski near Punta Arenas, in one of the only places in the world where you can ski in sight of the sea.
- Take a boat trip along the Seno Última Esperanza to the glaciers at the bottom of one of the planet's largest icefields outside the polar regions, the *Campo de Hielos Sur*.
- Visit the penguins at Seno Otway, near Punta Arenas.

Background

History   Southern Patagonia was inhabited from the end of the ice ages, mainly by the Tehuelche people, who roamed from the Atlantic coast to the mountains. The first Europeans did not visit until the 16th century. When Magellan sailed through the Straits in 1520, their strategic importance was quickly recognized: soon Spanish naval and merchant ships were using the route, as were mariners from other countries, including Francis Drake on his world voyage (1578). However the route became less important after 1616 when the Dutch sailors Jacob le Maire and Cornelius van Schouten discovered a quicker route into the Pacific round Cape Horn.

At independence, Chile claimed the far southern territories along the Pacific coast. But little was done to carry out this claim until 1843 when, concerned at British activities in the area and at rumours of French plans to start a colony, President Bulnes ordered the preparation of a secret mission. The expedition, on board the vessel *Ancud*, established Fuerte Bulnes on a rocky point; the fort was abandoned in 1848 in favour of a new settlement 56 km north, which was called Punta Arenas. The development of sheep farming in Patagonia and on Tierra del Fuego (with the help of arrivals from the nearby Falkland Islands), and the importance of the Magellan Straits for international shipping, led to the rapid expansion of Punta Arenas at the end of the 19th century, when it took the first steps towards being the city that it is today.

Geography   Chilean southern Patagonia stretches south from the icefields of the *Campo de Hielos Sur* to the *Estrecho de Magallanes* (Straits of Magellan) which separate South America from Tierra del Fuego. The coastline is heavily indented by fjords; offshore are numerous islands, few of which are inhabited. The remnants of the Andes stretch along the coast, seldom rising above 1,500 m. Mountains above this altitude include the Cordillera del Paine (several peaks over 2,600 m) and Cerro Balmaceda (2,035 m). Most of the western coast is covered by thick rainforest, but further east is grassland, stretching into the arid Patagonian plateau across the Argentine frontier.

Together with the Chilean part of Tierra del Fuego, Isla Navarino and Chilean Antarctica, this part of Chile is administered as Región XII (Magallanes), whose capital is Punta Arenas. The whole region is sparsely populated. Although Región XII covers 17.5% of Chilean territory, its population is

The original Patagonians

The dry Patagonian plateau was originally inhabited by one principle indigenous group, the Tehuelches. The Tehuelches lived along the eastern side of the Andes as far north as modern-day Bariloche, and were hunters of guanaco and rheas. In the 18th century they began to domesticate the wild horses of the region and sailed down the Patagonian rivers to reach the Atlantic coast. They were very large: it is said that the name Patagonia originates from the Spanish qué patagón *('what a large foot') on discovering Tehuelche footprints in the sand. In the 18th and early 19th centuries, some Tehuelches had much intercourse with whalers, and were patronizingly described as 'semi-civilized'. For details of*

the indigenous groups further south and in the Patagonian fjords, see the chapter on Tierra del Fuego and page 549.

The granting by the Chilean government of large land concessions in the late 19th century, combined with Argentine President Julio Roca's wars of extermination against the Patagonian Indians in the 1870s, spelled the end for the Tehuelches. Hunted and persecuted, only a few survived diseases and the change of lifestyle. Towards the end of the 20th century, a belated sense of moral guilt arose among the colonizers, but it was too late to prevent the end of a way of life. A few isolated groups of Tehuelches remain in Argentine Patagonia.

around 171,000, under 1% of the Chilean total. Some 160,000 live in towns, most of them in Punta Arenas.

Climate People from Punta Arenas tell visitors that they often have four seasons in one day. Frequently, though, the only season appears to be winter. Strong, cold, piercing winds blow, particularly during the spring, when they may exceed 100 km per hour. These bring heavy rain to coastal areas, over 4,000 mm a year on the offshore islands. Further east the winds are much drier; annual rainfall at Punta Dungeness at the east end of the Straits of Magellan is only 250 mm. Along the coast temperatures are moderated by the sea: summer temperatures are more variable, though seldom rising above 15°C. In winter snow covers the country, except those parts near the sea, making many roads more or less impassable; there is little wind, however, and this means that tourism remains possible for most of the year. When travelling in this region, protection against the ultraviolet rays of the sun is essential at all times.

Economy Sheep farming remains important to the local economy; locally produced beef is mainly sold domestically. Potatoes are an important crop but, owing to the climate, most other vegetables are grown under cover. Forestry has become more important, but also controversial, as native forests are used for woodchips for export to Japan, Taiwan and Brazil. This is especially serious on Tierra del Fuego, where logging firms are in operation. Although oil production has declined as reserves have become depleted, large quantities of natural gas are now produced. About 33% of Chilean coal comes from large open cast coal mines on the Brunswick Peninsula, northwest of Punta Arenas; most of it is shipped to the thermal power stations of northern Chile. Tourism is growing rapidly, making an increasingly important contribution to the local economy.

The Far South

Punta Arenas

Phone code: 061
Colour map 7, grid B1
Population: 113,000

Capital of Región XII, Punta Arenas lies 2,140 km due south of Santiago. The city was originally named "Sandy Point" by the English, until adopting the hispanic equivalent. A centre for the local sheep farming and fishing industries, it is also the home of La Polar, the most southerly brewery in the world. Although it has expanded rapidly, Punta Arenas remains tranquil and pleasant. The climate and architecture give the city a distinctively northern European atmosphere, quite unlike anywhere else in Chile; it is also the only city in Chile where the sun rises over the sea and sets over land. The winter solstice is marked by a carnaval de invierno *(winter carnival) on the weekend closest to June 21st.*

Ins and outs

Getting there
See page 448 for further details

Punta Arenas is cut off from the rest of Chile. The only road connections are from Puerto Montt, via Bariloche, Comodoro Rivadavia and Río Gallegos (36 hrs; 1 or 2 daily buses in summer); it is quicker, and often cheaper, to take one of the many daily flights to/from Puerto Montt instead. Transport south to Tierra del Fuego is on the Melinka ferry to Porvenir (6 weekly) or, further north, at Punta Delgada (many daily) to Cerro Sombrero. Puerto Natales, 247 km north, is easily reached on a paved road (many buses daily).

Getting around
C Pedro Montt runs east-west, while C Jorge Montt runs north-south

Buses in Punta Arenas tend to go either north-south along the main Bulnes-Bories-Noguiera axis, or east-west up Independencia. In either case, Punta Arenas is not a huge city, and walking about is a pleasant way of getting to know it. Buses are plentiful and cheap: a taxi is only really necessary for out-of-town excursions.

Tourist offices

Sernatur, Waldo Seguel 689, Casilla 106-D, T241330. At the corner with Plaza Muñoz Gamero, 0830-1745, closed Sat and Sun. Helpful, English spoken. Kiosk on Colón between Bories and Magallanes, Mon-Fri 0900-1300, 1500-1900, Sat 0900-1200, 1430-1730, Sun (in the summer only) 1000-1230. *Turistel Guide* is available from kiosk belonging to *Café Garogha* at Bories 831. **CONAF**, Menéndez 1147, piso 2, T223841. Open Mon-Fri.

History

After its foundation in 1848, Punta Arenas became a penal colony modelled on Australia. In 1867 it was opened to foreign settlers and given free port status. From the 1880s it prospered as a refuelling and provisioning centre for steam ships and whaling vessels. It also became a centre for the new sheep *estancias* since it afforded the best harbour facilities. The city's importance was reduced overnight by the opening of the Panama Canal in 1914. Most of those who came to work in the *estancias* were from Chiloé, and many people in the city have relatives in Chiloé and feel an affinity with the island (the *barrios* on either side of the upper reaches of Independencia are known as Chilote areas); the Chilotes who returned north took Patagonian customs with them, hence the number of *maté* drinkers on Chiloé.

Sights

Around the attractive **Plaza Muñoz Gamero** are a number of former mansions of the great sheep ranching families of the late 19th century. See the **Palacio Sara Braun**, built between 1894 and 1905 with materials from

Europe; the Palacio now houses the *Hotel José Nogueira*, see below. In the centre of the plaza is a statue of Magellan with a mermaid and two Fuegian Indians at his feet. According to local wisdom, those who kiss the big toe of one of the Indians will return to Punta Arenas. Just north of the plaza on Calle Magallanes are the **Palacio Braun Menéndez** (see below) and the **Teatro Cervantes**, which is now a cinema: the interiors of both are worth a visit. Further north, at Av Bulnes 929, is the **cemetery**, one of the most interesting places in the city, with a **statue of Indicito**, the little Indian (now an object of reverence, bedecked with flowers, northwest side of the cemetery), cypress avenues, gravestones in many languages bearing testimony to the cosmopolitan provenance of Patagonian pioneers, and many memorials to pioneer families and victims of shipping disasters. ■ *0800-1800 daily*.

West of the Plaza Muñoz Gamero on Calle Fagnano is the **Mirador Cerro de La Cruz** offering a view over the city and the Magellan Straits complete with its various shipwrecks. Nearby on Waldo Seguel are two reminders of the British influence: the **British School** and **St James Church** next door. The **Parque María Behety**, south of town along 21 de Mayo, features a scale model of Fuerte Bulnes and a campsite, popular for Sunday picnics.

Museo Regional Salesiano Mayorino Borgatello covers the history of **Museums** indigenous peoples, sections on local animal and bird life, and other interesting aspects of life in Patagonia and Tierra del Fuego, excellent. ■ *In the Colegio Salesiano, Av Bulnes 374, entrance next to church, Tue-Sat 1000-1200 and 1500-1800, Sun 1500-1800, hours change frequently. US$2.*

Museo de Historia Regional Braun Menéndez is located in the opulent former mansion of Mauricio Braun, built in 1905. A visit is recommended. Part is set out as room-by-room regional history; the rest of the house is furnished. Guided tours are in Spanish only. ■ *Mon-Sat 1030-1700, Sun and festivals 1030-1400 (summer) and 1100-1300 (winter). US$1.50, children half-price, festivals free. Magallanes 949, off Plaza de Armas, T244216, museoregional1001@chilnet.cl Entry at rear on Navarro.*

The **Instituto de la Patagonia** houses the **Museo del Recuerdo**, T207056, an open-air museum with artefacts used by the early settlers, pioneer homes, and botanical gardens. ■ *Mon-Fri 0830-1130, 1430-1815, Sat 0830-1300. US$2, children free. Av Bulnes 01890, Km 4 north (opposite the university), T244216.*

Museo Naval y Marítimo, houses an exhibition of the maritime history of the area; interesting on shipping disasters. ■ *Tue-Sun 0930-1230, 1400-1700. US$1. Pedro Montt 981, T205479, terzona@armarda.cl*

Reserva Forestal Magallanes, 7 km west of town and known locally as the **Excursions** Parque Japonés, extends over 13,500 ha and rises to 600 m. Follow Independencia up the hill. About 3 km from the edge of town take the right turning for Río de las Minas. The entrance to the reserve is 2 km beyond; there you will find a self-guided nature trail through lenga and coigue trees, 1 km long, free leaflet (US$2).

The road continues through the woods for 14 km passing by several picnic sites. From the top end of the road a short path leads to a lookout over the **Garganta del Diablo** (Devil's Throat), a gorge with views over Punta Arenas and Tierra del Fuego. From here a slippery path leads down to the Río de las Minas Valley and then back to Punta Arenas. Administration at CONAF in Punta Arenas. *Turismo Pali Aike offers tours to the park, US$3.75 per person.*

The Far South

Essentials

Sleeping
■ *on map, page 446*
Price codes:
see inside front cover
Hotel prices are
substantially lower
during winter months
(April-September).
Most hotels include
breakfast in the
room price

LL *Cabo de Hornos*, Plaza Muñoz Gamero 1025, T/F242134, rescabo@panamericana hoteles.cl Recommended. **LL** *Finis Terrae*, Colón 766, T228200, F248124, finisterctcreuna.cl Modern, some rooms small, safe in room, rooftop café/bar with lovely views, English spoken, parking. **LL** *José Nogueira*, Bories 959, in former Palacio Sara Braun, T248840, F248832, nogueira@chileaustral.com Beautiful loggia, good food, parking, lovely atmosphere. Recommended. **L** *Isla Rey Jorge*, 21 de Mayo 1243, T248220, F222681, reyjorge@ctinternet.cl Modern, pleasant, pub downstairs. **L** *Los Navegantes*, Menéndez 647, T244677, F247545, hotelnavchilesat.net **L** *Tierra del Fuego*, Colón 716, T/F226200. Good breakfast, parking. Recommended. *Café 1900* downstairs.

AL *Apart Hotel Colonizadores*, Colón 1108, T244144, F226587. Clean, fully furnished apartments (for 2 to 5 people), 2 bedrooms, **AL**, discounts for long stay. **AL** *Hostería Yaganes*, Camino Antiguo Norte Km 7.5, T211600, F248052. *Cabañas* on the shores of the Straits of Magellan, nice setting. **AL** *Plaza*, Nogueira 1116, piso 2, T241300, F248613. Pleasant, good breakfast. **A** *Colonizadores*, 21 de Mayo 1690, T244144, F226587. **A** *Cóndor del Plata*, Colón 556, T247987, F241149. Excellent breakfast. **A** *Hostal Carpa Manzano*, Lautaro Navarro 336, T242296. Recommended. **A** *Hostal de la Avenida*, Colón 534, T247532. Good breakfast, friendly, safe. Recommended. **A** *Hostal de la Patagonia*, Croacia 970, T249970, F223670, ecopatagonia@entelchile.net cheaper without bath. **A** *Mercurio*, Fagnano 595, T/F242300, mercurio@chileaustral.com TV and phone, good restaurant and service. Recommended. **A-B** *Hostal Calafate*, Lautaro Navarro 850, T/F248415, calafate@entelchile.net with bath (**B** without), TV in room, internet US$3.75 per hr. Without bath, clean. **A-B** *Savoy*, Menéndez 1073, T241951, F247979. Pleasant rooms but some lack windows, good place to eat.

B *Hostal Del Estrecho*, Menéndez 1048, T/F241011, estrecho@chileanpatagonia.com With large breakfast and bath, central heating, cable TV (**C** without bath). **B** *Hostal Eduardo's*, Angamos 195, T227073, F241501, hostal_eduardo@chileaustral.com **B** *Hostal del Sur*, Mejicana 151, T227249, F222282, large rooms, excellent breakfast. Highly recommended. **B** *Hostal Rubio*, España 640, T226458, www.chileaustral.com/hostalrubio With bath, parking, laundry facilities, helpful. **B** *Monte Carlo*, Colón 605, T T222120, also **D** without bath, traditional, charming, good food. **B** *Ritz*, Pedro Montt 1102, T224422. Old, clean and cosy. Recommended (Bruce Chatwin stayed here: see his name in the guest book). **B-C** *Hostal Sonia Kuscevic*, Pasaje Darwin 175 (Angamos altura 550), T248543. Popular, Hostelling International discounts, with bath, breakfast, hot water, heating, parking.

C *Albatros*, Colón 1195, T223131. Without bath, good. **C** *Hosp Lodging*, Sanhueza 933, T221035. With bath (**E** without), clean, heating, modern. **C** *Hostal Paradiso*, Angamos 1073, T224212. With bath, breakfast, parking, use of kitchen. Recommended (**D** without bath). **C** *Hostal Patagonia*, Croacia 970, T249970, including breakfast and private bath. Kitchen facilities, laundry, tours arranged, friendly staff. **C** *Res Central*, No 1 España 247, T222315, No 2 Sanhueza 185, T222845. With bath (**D** without). Comfortable. **C-D** *Casa Dinka*, Caupolicán 169, T226056, F244292, fueguino@entelchile.net With breakfast, use of kitchen, noisy.

D *Hostal O'Higgins*, O'Higgins 1205, T225205, F243438. With breakfast, very clean. **D** *Lodging*, Sanhueza 933, T221035. With bath (**F** without), clean, heating, modern. **D** *Sra Carlina Ramírez*, Paraguaya 150, T247687. Motorcycle parking, meals, safe, quiet. Recommended. **E** *Hostal El Bosque*, O'Higgins 424, T221764, F224637. Breakfast included, use of kitchen, laundry facilities; **F** for shared room. **E** *Hostal O'Higgins*, O'Higgins 1205, T225205, F243438. With breakfast, very clean. **E** *The Pink House*, Caupolicán 99, T222436, pinkhouse@chileaustral.com With breakfast, clean (**F** without bath).

F *Alojamiento Prat*, Sgto Aldea 0520. Clean. Recommended. **F** *Hosp Nena*, Boliviana 366, T242411. Friendly, with large breakfast. **F** *Res Centenario*, Plaza Centenario 105, T225710, with breakfast. **F**, España y Boliviana, T247422. Without bath, clean, friendly, use of kitchen. **F** Sanhueza 750. Homely. Recommended. **F** *Res Roca*, Magallanes 888, T243903, without bath, clean. **F**, also at the Colegio Pierre Fauré, Bellavista 697, in Jan/Feb; cooking facilities, friendly, camping possible. Recommended. **F-G** *Alojamiento Golondrina*, Lautaro Navarro 182, T229708, kitchen facilities, meals served, English spoken, hot water, internet access, good large breakfast. Recommended. **F-G** *Lodging Manuel*, O'Higgins 648, T245441, F220567, without breakfast, internet access, laundry facilities, helpful. **F-G** *Res Independencia*, Independencia 374, T227572, independencia@chileaustral.com With breakfast, kitchen facilities, camping. **G** *Backpackers Lodging*, O'Higgins 646, T220567, without breakfast, helpful. **G** *Backpackers Paradise*, Carrera Pinto 1022, T222554, backpackers_paradise_ chile@yahoo.com dormitories, cooking facilities, limited bathroom facilities, good meeting place, luggage store, internet access. Recommended. **G** *Hospedaje Costanera*, Correa 1221, T240175, kitchen facilities, large breakfast, friendly, clean. **G** *Hospedaje Huala*, Maipú 851, T244244 kitchen facilities, laundry, book exchange. **G** *Hosp Tres Hermanos*, Angamos 1218, T225450. **G** *Miramar*, Errazuriz y Almte Senoret (entry on 1st floor). Friendly staff, good views over the bay. **G** *Unlimited Adventure Backpackers Hostel*, Balmaceda 545, drea_ms@yahoo.com kitchen, laundry facilities, cable TV, 24-hr hot water. Dormitory accommodation may also be available at the *Salvation Army Hostel*, Bellavista 577, **G**.

Accommodation available in many private houses, usually ask at tourist office

There are no campsites in or near the city

Expensive/Mid-range The hotels *Cabo de Hornos* (cheaper set lunch), *Los Navegantes* and *José Nogueira* all have excellent restaurants. *José Nogueira* has a lovely dining room.

Eating
● *on map, page 446*
Many eating places close on Sunday

Mid-range *Centro Español*, Plaza Muñoz Gamero 771, above Teatro Cervantes. Large helpings, limited selection, quite expensive. *El Estribo*, Carrera Pinto 762. Good grill, also fish. *El Mercado*, Mejicana 617, open 24 hrs, reasonably priced set lunch, expensive à la carte. *El Mesón del Calvo*, Jorge Montt 687. Excellent, seafood, lamb, small portions, pricey. Recommended. *Golden Dragon*, Colón 529. Chinese, expensive. *Quick Lunch Patagónico* Armando Sanhueza 1198, Esquina Errazuriz. Vegetarian, Mexican and Chinese food. *Sotitos*, O'Higgins 1138. Good service and cuisine, excellent. expensive. Recommended. *Yaganes*, Camino Antiguo Norte Km 7.5. Beautiful setting, weekend buffet. **Cheap** *Asturias*, Lautaro Navarro 967. Good food and atmosphere. *Bianco's Pizza*, Bulnes 01306. Excellent pizzas. Recommended. *Calypso*, Bories 817. Open Sun evening, busy at night, smoky, cheap. *Carioca*, Menéndez 600 y Chiloé. *Parrilla*, cheap lunches, snacks and beer, very friendly. *El Quijote*, Lautaro Navarro 1087. Good sandwiches and fish dishes. Highly recommended. *La Casa de Juan*, O'Higgins 1021. Spanish food. *La Terraza*, 21 de Mayo 1288. Sandwiches, *empanadas* and beer, cheap and good. *Lomit's*, Menéndez 722. Cheap snacks and drinks, open when the others are closed, popular with tourists. *Lucerna*, Bories 624. Excellent meat, reasonably priced, good. *Parrilla Apocalipsis*, Chiloé esq Balmaceda. *Restaurant Santino*, Colón 657, T220511. Good pizzas, large bar, good service.

Seriously cheap For economic set lunches several along Chiloé: *Los Años 60 The Mitchel*, No 1231. *Restaurant de Turismo Punta Arenas* , No 1280. Good, friendly.

The Far South

Recommended. Also serves beer and 26 varieties of sandwiches, open 24 hrs. *Kiosco Roca* (no sign), Roca 875. Early morning coffee. Cheap fish meals available at stalls in the *Cocinerías*, Lautaro Navarro south of the port entrance. Excellent *empanadas*, bread and pastries at *Pancal*, 21 de Mayo 1280. Also at *La Espiga*, Errázuriz 632. Excellent pastries at *Casa del Pastel*, Carrera Pinto y O'Higgins.

Seafood Lobster has become more expensive because of a law allowing only lobster pots. *Centolla* (king crab) is caught illegally by some fishermen using dolphin, porpoise and penguin as live bait. There are seasonal bans on *centolla* fishing to protect dwindling

Punta Arenas

To Patagonian Institute, Free Port, Airport, Puerto Natales & Ferry to Porvenir

To Fuerte Bulnes & Puerto del Hambre

Estrecho de Magallanes

N
Not to scale

Sleeping
1 Alojamiento Golondrina
2 Backpackers Paradise
3 Cabo de Hornos
4 Colegio Pierre Fauré
5 Hostal Carpa Manzano
6 Hostal de la Avenida
7 Hostal del Sur
8 Hostal Paradiso
9 Hostal Sonia Kuscevic
10 José Nogueira
11 Lodging Manuel
12 Mercurio
13 Pink House
14 Ritz
15 Sanhueza 750
16 Sra Carlina Ramírez
17 Tierra del Fuego

Eating
1 Asturias
2 Calypso
3 Centro Español
4 El Estribo
5 El Mercado
6 El Mesón del Calvo
7 El Quijote
8 Golden Dragon
9 La Casa de Juan
10 Lomit's
11 Los Años 60 The Mitchell
12 Lucerna
13 Parrilla Apocalipsis
14 Quick Lunch Patagónico
15 Sotitos
16 Turismo Punta Arenas

Buses
1 Austral
2 Fernández
3 Pingüino
4 Sur

stocks; do not purchase it out of season. At times *centolla* fishing is banned because the crabs can be infected with a disease which is fatal to humans. Visitors to Punta Arenas and the surrounding region should be especially wary of eating shellfish. In recent years the nearby waters have been affected by a *marea roja* (red tide) of poisonous algae. While the *marea roja* only affects bivalve shellfish, these molluscs can kill almost instantly. Mussels should not be picked along the shore of Punta Arenas – foreigners who have done this have died.

Pubs and bars *Bar Lunaticos*, 21 de Mayo 1262. Good fun, as the name implies. *El* **Entertainment** *Coral*, José Menéndez 844. *El Galeon*, 21 de Mayo 1243. *La Taberna del Club de la Unión*, Plaza Muñoz Gamero y Seguel. For drinks, more upmarket. *Makanudo*, Ovejero 474. Popular with locals. *Pub 1900*, Av Colón esq. Bories. **Disco** *Kamikaze*, Bories 655. *Laberinto*, Pedro Montt 951. *Borssalino*, Bories 587. *Cuervo*, José Menéndez 756. On the southern outskirts: *Torreones*, Km 5.5, T261985. *Millenium*, Km 7.5. To the north: *Drive-In Los Brujos*, Km 7.5, T212600. Note that anything called a 'nightclub' is infact a brothel.

Zona France Punta Arenas has certain free-port facilities; the Zona Franca is 3½ km **Shopping** north of the centre, on the right-hand side of the road to the airport. Cheap electrical goods are especially worth seeking out. Leather goods and sheepskin may also be worth having a look at, however the quality of most other goods is low and the prices little better than elsewhere. Open Mon-Sat 1030-1230, 1500-2000 (bus E or A from Plaza Muñoz Gamero; many *colectivos*; taxi US$3). **Handicrafts** At *Pingüi* Bories 404, (also stocks books on Tierra del Fuego, Patagonia and Antarctica). Also try *Artesanía Ramas*, Independencia 799, *Casa Diaz*, Bories 712/546. Chilean souvenirs at good prices, *Chile Típico*, Carrera Pinto 1015, and outdoor stalls at the bottom of Independencia, by the port entrance. Also *Talabartería Araucaria*, Magallanes 775. Saddlery and repairs to leather goods including rucksacks, helpful. **Cameras** Wide range of cameras but limited range of film, from Zona Franca. *Foto Sánchez,* Bories 768, for Fuji film and *Fotocentro*, Bories 789, for Agfa: all have same day print-processing service. **Chocolate** Punta Arenas is famous for the quality of its chocolate. Delicious handmade chocolate from *Chocolatería Tres Arroyos*, Bories 448, T241522. Also try *Chocolatería Regional Norweisser*, José Miguel Carrera 663. **Super-markets** *Abu Gosch*, between Magallanes and Bories north of Carrera Pinto. *Cofrima*, Lautaro Navarro 1293 y Balmaceda. *Cofrima 2*, España 01375. *Listo*, 21 de Mayo 1133. *Marisol*, Zenteno 0164. *Super Norte*, Salvador Allende y Chorillos.

Golf Nine-hole golf course 5 km south of town on road to Fuerte Bulnes. **Sports** **Skiing** Cerro Mirador, only 9 km west from Punta Arenas in the Reserva Nacional Magallanes, is one of the few places in the world where you can ski with a sea view; also a good 2-hr hike in summer, clearly marked and flora labelled. *Transtur* buses 0900 and 1400 from in front of *Hotel Cabo de Hornos*, US$3 return, taxi US$6. Daily lift-ticket, US$7; equipment rental, US$6 per adult. Mid-way lodge with food, drink and equipment. Season Jun to Sep, weather permitting. Contact the *Club Andino*, T241479, about crosscountry skiing facilities. Also skiing at Tres Morros. There is also a hippodrome north of the cemetery.

Arka Patagonia, Ignacio Carrera Pinto 946, T248167, F241504. All types of tours, raft- **Tour** ing, fishing, etc. El Conquistador, Menéndez 556, T222896. Recommended. *Turismo* **companies** *Aonikenk*, Magallanes 619, T228332. Recommended. *Turismo Aventour*, Nogueira 1255, T241197, F243354. English spoken, specializes in fishing trips, organize tours to Tierra del Fuego. *Turismo Comapa*, Independencia 840, T241437, F247514. Tours to Torres del Paine, Tierra del Fuego, also trips to the Falklands/Malvinas, charter boats to Cape Horn and Isla Magdalena. *Turismo Lazo*, Angamos 1366, T/F223771. Wide range

The Far South

of tours. Highly recommended. *Turismo Manuel*, O'Higgins 646; recommended. *Turismo Pali Aike*, Lautaro Navarro 1129, T223301. *Turismo Patagonia*, Bories 655 local 2, T248474, F247182. Specializes in fishing trips. *Turismo Pehoé*, Menéndez 918, T244506, F248052. Organizes tours and hotels, enquire here about catamaran services. *Turismo Runner*, Lautaro Navarro 1065, T247050, F241042. Adventure tours. *Turismo Viento Sur*, Fagnano 565, T/F225167, for camping equipment, fishing excursions, English spoken, good tours, recommended. Most organize tours to Torres del Paine, Fuerte Bulnes and *pingüineras* on Otway sound: shop around as prices vary. Sr Mateo Quesada, Chiloé 1375, T222662, offers local tours in his car, up to 4 passengers. *In-Tur* is an association of companies which aims to promote tourism in Chilean Patagonia. The members are *Arka Patagonia*, *Turismo Aventour*, *Turismo Pehoé*, *Turismo Runner*, *Aerovías DAP* and *Hostería Las Torres* (in the Parque Nacional Torres del Paine). The head office is at Errázuriz 840, p 2, Punta Arenas, T/F229049, which can be contacted for information. See below, for *In-Tur's* SIB bus to Torres del Paine.

Transport
All transport is heavily booked from Christmas through to March: advance booking strongly advised

Local   Car hire: You need a hire company's authorization to take a car into Argentina. *Paine Rent a Car*, Menéndez 631, T/F240852, try bargaining, friendly. *Hertz*, O'Higgins 987, T248742, F244729, English spoken; also at airport T210096. *Australmag*, Colón 900, T242174, F226916. *Automovil Club*, O'Higgins 931, T243675, F243097, and at airport. *Budget*, O'Higgins 964, T241696. *Internacional*, Sarmiento 790-B, T228323, F226334. Recommended. *Willemsen*, Lautaro Navarro 1038, T247787, F241083. Highly recommended. *Lubac*, Magallanes 970, T/F242023. *Todoauto*, España 0480, T212492, F212627. *First Rent a Car*, O'Higgins 949, T/F221601. *Emsa Rentacar*, Roca 1044, T/F229049. *Lotus Rentacar*, Mejicana 694, T228244, F241697. Repairs at *Automotores del Sur*, O'Higgins 850, T224153; *Automotriz Hoopers*, Boliviana y Chiloé, T241239; and *Centro automotriz Crisostomo*, Independencia 377, T243731. **Taxi**: Ordinary taxis have yellow roofs. *Colectivos* (all black) run on fixed routes, US$0.50 for anywhere on route. Reliable service from *Radio Taxi Austral*, T247710/244409. **Cycle parts**: *José Aguila Quezada*, Arauco 2675, T265399. **Motorcycle parts**: *Violic*, Sanhueza 285, T241606, also in the Zona Franca.

Long distance   Air: Carlos Ibáñez de Campo Airport, 20 km north of town (served by Punta Arenas-Puerto Natales buses). Bus service by *Buses Transfer* (address below) scheduled to meet flights, US$2.50. *LanChile*, *DAP* and *Ladeco* have their own bus services from town, US$2.50; taxi US$12. The airport restaurant is good. To **Puerto Montt**, with *Aerocontinente* (1 daily; US$75 one way) and *Ladeco/LanChile* (6 daily; US$105 one way). To **Santiago**, *LanChile* and *Ladeco* daily US$140, via Puerto Montt (sit on right for views). When no tickets are available, go to the airport and get on the standby waiting list. To **Porvenir**, *Aerovías DAP* 2/3 daily (US$30 one way), plus other irregular flights, with *Twin-Otter* and *Cessna* aircraft. To **Puerto Williams**, *Aerovías DAP* 3 times weekly (US$80 one way). Military flights approximately 2 a month to Puerto Montt US$30, information and tickets from airforce base at the airport, Spanish essential, T213559; need to book well in advance. It is very difficult to get space during the summer as all armed forces personnel and their families have priority over civilians. For flights to Puerto Williams, see page 498. **International services   To Argentina**: to Ushuaia, *Aerovías DAP* on Wed (US$120 one way). Reserve well in advance from mid-Dec to Feb. To Falkland Islands/Islas Malvinas, *LanChile*, Sat, US$230 (flies via Río Gallegos, Argentina, once a month).

Bus timetables are printed daily in La Prensa Austral

Bus   Company offices are: *Bus Sur* Menéndez 565, with *Austral Bus*. *Austral Bus*, Menéndez 565, T247139, T/F241708. *Buses Transfer*, J Menéndez 631, T220766. *Gesell*, Menéndez 556, T222896. *Los Carlos*, Plaza Muñoz Gamero 1039, T241321. *Pacheco*, Colón 900, T242174. *Pingüino* and *Fernández*, Sanhueza 745, T242313, F225984. *Tecni*

Austral, Lautaro Navarro 975, T223205. *Turbus*, Errázuriz 932, T/F225315. Buses leave from company offices. Services and frequencies change every year, so check on arrival – those below are for high season only. To **Puerto Natales**, 3 hrs, *Fernández* and *Transfer* (cheapest), *Buses Pacheco*, *Austral Bus*, and *Buses Sur*, each company has several every day, last departure 2000, US$4 one way, US$7.50 return, book in advance, buses will pick up at the airport. *In-Tur* runs a 2 daily circuit Punta Arenas-Puerto Natales-Torres del Paine in minibuses with snack, English-speaking guide and including national park entry. Service runs mid-Oct to mid-Apr. To **Coyhaique**, 20 hrs, *Buses Sur*, via Argentina, US$50. *Ghisoni* and *Austral* have services through Argentina to **Osorno**, **Puerto Montt** and **Castro**. Also *Cruz del Sur*, *Queilen Bus* and *Pacheco*. Fares to Puerto Montt or Osorno US$55 (cheaper off season) 36 hrs; to Castro US$67-83 (uncomfortable, not recommended); *Tur Bus* continues to **Santiago**, US$95 (cheaper in winter), 46 hrs. To **Río Gallegos**, Argentina, *Pingüino*, daily, 1245, return 1300; *Ghisoni*, 4 weekly, 1100; *Pacheco*, 5 weekly, 1130. All cost US$14 and take about 5 hrs. Services to Buenos Aires, *Pingüino*, via Río Gallegos, US$120. To **Río Grande**, *Pacheco* and *Tecni Austral* via Punta Delgada, buses most days, 8-10 hrs, US$20, heavily booked. To **Ushuaia** via Punta Delgada, 12-14 hrs, book any return at same time. *Tecni Austral*, Tue, Thu, Sat, Sun 0800, US$38; *Pacheco* Mon, Wed, Fri 0715, US$42.

Ferry For services to **Porvenir**, Tierra del Fuego, see page 484. For *Navimag* services Puerto Montt-Puerto Natales, see under Puerto Montt, page 378 (confirmation of reservations is advised). Visits to the beautiful fjords and glaciers of Tierra del Fuego are highly recommended. *Comapa* runs a fortnightly 22-hr, 320-km round trip to the fjord d'Agostino, 30 km long, where many glaciers come down to the sea. The luxury cruiser, *Terra Australis*, sails from Punta Arenas on Sat via Ushuaia and Puerto Williams; details from *Comapa*. Advance booking (advisable) from *Cruceros Australis* SA, Miraflores 178, piso 12, Santiago, T6963211, F331871. Government supply ships are recommended for the young and hardy, but take sleeping bag and extra food, and travel pills. For transport on navy supply ships to Puerto Williams and Cape Horn, enquire at **Tercera Zona Naval**, Lautaro Navarro 1150, but be prepared to be frustrated by irregular sailings and inaccurate information.

All tickets on ships must be booked in advance for Jan-Feb

To Antarctica Most cruise ships leave from Ushuaia. Other than asking in agencies for possible empty berths on the few cruise ships which call here, the only possibility is to ask at the Chilean navy (Tercera Zona Naval, see above). A letter of recommendation is helpful; Spanish is essential. The two naval vessels, the *Galvarino* and the *Lautaro*, charge US$80 pp per day; it may help to go to the port and try to talk to the Captain. There is no accurate schedule. Accommodation includes 4 meals a day (2 with meat), laundry facilities. Take twice as much film as you think you'll need.

During the voyage across the Drake Passage albatrosses, petrels, cormorants, penguins, elephant seals, fur seals, whales and dolphins can be sighted

To Argentina overland From Punta Arenas the route is north-east via Route 255 and Punta Delgada to the frontier at Kimiri Aike and then along Argentine Route 3 to Río Gallegos, an unappealing city (many buses). For routes to Calafate see page 456.

Airline offices *Aerovías DAP*, O'Higgins 891, T223340, F221693. Open 0900-1230, 1430-1930. *Ladeco*, Lautaro Navarro 1155, T241100, F223340. *LanChile*, Lautaro Navarro 999, T241232, F222366.

Directory

Banks *Banco BCI*, Errázuriz 799. *Banco Santander*, Magallanes 997, 24-hr access. *Banco Santiago*, on Plaza Muñoz Gamero, Visa. *Corbanca*, Magallanes 944. Most have ATMs. *Casas de cambio* open Mon-Fri 0900-1230, 1500-1900, Sat 0900-1230. Outside business hours try *Buses Sur*, Colón y Magallanes, kiosk at *Calypso Café*, Bories 817 and the major hotels (lower rates). Argentine pesos can be bought at *casas de cambio*.

Banks open Mon-Fri 0830-1400

Good rates at *Cambio Gasic*, Roca 915, Oficina 8, T242396. German spoken. *Kiosco Redondito*, Mejicana 613, in the shopping centre, T247369. *La Hermandad*, Lautaro Navarro 1099, T243991. Excellent rates, US$ cash for Amex TCs and credit cards. *Scott Cambios*, Colón y Magallanes, T227145. *Sur Cambios*, Lautaro Navarro 1001, T225656. Accepts TCs.

Communications Post office: Bories 911 y Menéndez. Mon-Fri 0830-1930, Sat 0900-1400. Telecommunications: For international and national calls and faxes (shop around as prices vary). *CTC*, Plaza Muñoz Gamero. Daily 0800-2200. *CTC*, Magallanes 922. Daily 0900-2030. *Entel*, Lautaro Navarro 957. Mon-Fri 0830-2200, Sat-Sun 0900-2200. *Telex-Chile/Chile-Sat*, Bories 911 and Errázuriz 856. Daily 0830-2200, also offers telex and telegram service. *VTR*, Bories 801. Closed Sat afternoon and Sun. For international calls and faxes at any hour *Hotel Cabo de Hornos*, credit cards accepted, open to non-residents. Internet: *Austrointernet Services*, Croacia 690, T/F229279/227971, US$4.75 per hr; *Backpackers Paradise*, Carrera Pinto 1022; *Canadian Language Institute*, O'Higgins y Carrera Pinto, US$5 per hr; *Ciber-Room Gon-Fish*, Croatia 1028. Internet at US$2.75 per hr before breakfast and US$3.60 later; *Cybercafe Austral*, Croatia 690; *Pialcomp*, Colón y Magallanes; also at *Tourist Centre*, Calle Independencia, US$5 per hr.

Consulates Argentina, 21 de Mayo 1878, T261912. Open 1000-1400, visas take 24 hrs, US$25. **Brazil**, Arauco 769, T241093. **Belgium**, Roca 817, Oficina 61, T241472. **Denmark**, Colón 819, Depto 301, T221488. **Finland**, Independencia 660, T247385. **Germany**, Pasaje Korner 1046, T241082, Casilla 229. **Italy**, 21 de Mayo 1569, T242497. **Netherlands**, Magallanes 435, T248100. **Norway**, Independencia 830, 2nd floor, T241052. **Spain**, Menéndez 910, T243566. **Paraguay**, Bulnes 0928 Dp14 p1, T211825. **Sweden**, Errazúriz 891, T224107. **United Kingdom**, Roca 924, T227221 (helpful; information on Falkland Islands). **Uruguay**, José Nogueira 1238, T241053.

Laundry *Lavaseco Josseau*, Carrera Pinto 766, T228413. *Lavasol*, the only self-service, O'Higgins 969, T243067. Mon-Sat 0900-2030, Sun (summer only) 1000-1800, US$6 per machine, wash and dry, good but busy.

Medical services Dentists: Dr Hugo Vera Cárcamo, España 1518, T227510. Recommended. Rosemary Robertson Stipicic, 21 de Mayo 1380, T22931. Speaks English. **Hospitals**: Hospital Regional Lautaro Navarro, Angamos 180, T244040. Public hospital, for emergency room ask for La Posta. Clínica Magallanes, Bulnes 01448, T211527. Private clinic, medical staff the same as in the hospital but fancier surroundings and more expensive; minimum charge US$45 per visit.

Shipping offices *Comapa* (Compañía Marítima de Punta Arenas), Independencia 830, T244400, F247514. *Navimag*, Independencia 830, T244400, F242003.

Around Punta Arenas

Fuerte Bulnes Fuerte Bulnes is a replica of the wooden fort erected in 1843 by the crew of the Chilean vessel *Ancud*; more remarkable for the peace than for the replica. It is 56 km south of Punta Arenas. Nearby is Puerto Hambre, with ruins of the church built by Sarmiento de Gamboa's colonists. This is a very beautiful area with views towards the towering ice mountains near Pico Sarmiento; it was of Puerto Hambre that Darwin wrote: "looking due southward...the distant channels between the mountains appeared from their gloominess to lead beyond the confines of this world". ■ *Getting there: tours by several agencies,*

Port Famine (Puerto Hambre)

In 1582 Felipe II of Spain, alarmed by Drake's passage through the Straits of Magellan, decided to establish a Spanish presence on the Straits. A fleet of 15 ships and 4,000 men, commanded by Pedro Sarmiento de Gamboa, was despatched in 1584. Before even leaving the Bay of Biscay, a storm arose and scattered the fleet, sinking seven ships and killing 800 people. Further depleted by disease, at length only three ships arrived, with 300 men on board. With his small force Sarmiento founded two cities: Nombre de Jesús on Punta Dungeness at the eastern entrance to the Straits and Rey Don Felipe near Puerto Hambre.

Disaster struck when their only remaining vessel broke its anchorage in a storm near Nombre de Jesús; the ship, with Sarmiento on board, was blown into the Atlantic. After vain attempts to re-enter the

Straits, Sarmiento set sail for Río de Janeiro where he organized two rescue missions: the first ended in shipwreck, the second in mutiny. Captured by English corsairs, Sarmiento was taken to England where he was imprisoned. Released by Elizabeth I, he tried to return to Spain via France, where he was jailed again. Until his death in 1608, Sarmiento besieged Felipe II with letters urging him to rescue the men stranded in the Straits.

When the English corsair Thomas Cavendish sailed through the Straits in 1587 he found only 18 survivors at Rey Don Felipe. With the English and Spanish at war, only one – Tomé Hernández – would trust Cavendish when he first arrived. A sudden spell of fine weather arose, and Cavendish set sail, leaving the rest to die. He named the place Port Famine.

US$9, but hitching is not difficult at weekends or in summer, as there are many holiday camps in the area.

At the intersection of the roads to Puerto del Hambre and Fuerte Bulnes, 51 km south of Punta Arenas, is a small monolith marking the Centro Geográfico de Chile, the midway point between Arica and the South Pole. Bypassing Fuerte Bulnes, the road continues past a memorial to Captain Pringle Stokes, Captain of the Beagle before FitzRoy, who committed suicide here in 1829. The road runs out 5 km further on at San Juan; there is no path on to Cape Froward – travellers have died attempting to reach this, the southernmost point of the continent of South America.

Reserva Forestal Laguna Parrillar About 25 km south of Punta Arenas, there is a fork in the road to the right; 27 km further on is the Parrillar reserve, covering 18,814 ha. This reserve has older forest than the Magallanes Reserve and sphagnum bogs. It is surrounded by snowcapped hills; very peaceful, excellent salmon trout fishing. There is a three-hour walk to the tree-line along poorly marked and boggy paths. There are fine views from the Mirador. Camping is forbidden (although possible in the wild in woods outside the Reserve), but there are sites for cooking on gas stoves. ■ *Getting there: no public transport, radio taxi US$60; hitching is virtually impossible.*

Seno Otway Seno Otway is the site of a colony of Magellanic penguins which can be visited from November to March. Rheas and skunks can also be seen; beautiful views across Seno Otway to the mountains to the north. It is 70 km from Punta Arenas. ■ *Getting there: tours by several agencies, US$12, entry US$4; taxi US$35 return.*

Isla Magdalena A small island, 25 km northeast, Isla Magdalena is the location of the **Monumento Natural Los Pingüinos**, a colony of 150,000 penguins.

The Far South

Deserted apart from the breeding season from November to January, the island is administered by CONAF. Magdalena is one of a group of three islands visited by Drake (the others are Marta and Isabel) whose men killed 3,000 penguins for food. ■ *Getting there: boat visits with* Comapa, *address above: Tue, Thu, Sat, 0800 (Dec-Feb), 2 hrs each way, with 2 hrs on the island, coffee and biscuits served, US$30, subject to cancellation if windy; full refund given. Recommended.*

To Puerto Natales From Punta Arenas a paved road runs 247 km north to Puerto Natales through forests of southern beech and prime pastureland for cattle grazing; this is the best area for cattle raising in Chile. Ñandus and guanacos can be seen en route. Fuel is available in Villa Tehuelches, 100 km north of Punta Arenas.

Sleeping Along this road are several hotels, including **C** *Hostería Río Verde*, Km 90, east off the highway on Seno Skyring, T311122, F241008. Private bath, heating. Stunning backdrop, utter calm, recommended; **AL** *Hostal Río Penitente*, Km 138, T331694. In an old *estancia*. Recommended; **C** *Hotel Rubens*, Km 183, T226916. Popular for fishing; and **A** *Hostería Llanuras de Diana*, Km 215 (30 km south of Puerto Natales), T248742, F244729 (Punta Arenas), T411540 (Puerto Natales). Hidden from road, beautifully situated. Highly recommended.

Puerto Natales

Phone code: 061
Colour map 6, grid B3
Population: 15,000
247 km north of
Punta Arenas

Puerto Natales lies between Cerro Dorotea (which rises behind the town) and the eastern shore of the Seno Ultima Esperanza (Last Hope Sound). It is the jumping-off place for the magnificent Balmaceda and Torres del Paine national parks and the place is used predominantly as a base for such trips. There are fine views over the Seno Ultima Esperanza to the Peninsula Antonio Varas. Tourism is now one of the most important industries, and the town has a prosperous if somewhat touristy atmosphere.

Ins & outs
See also page 456 for further detiails

Getting there Puerto Natales is easily reached by many daily buses from Punta Arenas, as well as on six daily buses from Río Turbio, Argentina (one or two of which begin in El Calafate). The town is also the terminus of the two ships, the *Puerto Edén* and *Magallanes*, who connect it to Puerto Montt and Puerto Chacabuco. **Getting around** Puerto Natales is not a large place, and taxis are only needed for journeys out of town. **Tourist office** There is a kiosk on the waterfront, Av Pedro Montt y Phillipi, T412125; information also at the Municipalidad, Bulnes 285, T411263. **CONAF**, O'Higgins 584.

Sights Founded in 1911, the town grew as an industrial centre. The biggest meatpacking factory in Patagonia was at Puerto Bories, 6 km north; though much of the old plant was destroyed by fire, the administration buildings and housing can be visited, and the colourful old steam train in the main square was used to take workers to the plant. Until recent years the town's prosperity was based upon employment in the coal mines of Río Turbio, nearby in Argentina.

Excursions
For excursions to the Torres del Paine and the Monte Balmaceda national parks, see below

A good walk is up to **Cerro Dorotea**, which dominates the town, with superb views of the whole Seno Ultima Esperanza. It can also be reached by any Río Turbio bus which is recommended, as the hill is farther off than it seems.

Monumento Nacional Cueva Milodón, 25 km north, is the end point of Bruce Chatwin's *In Patagonia*. The cave, a massive 50 m wide, 200 m deep and 30 m high, contains a plastic model of the prehistoric ground-sloth whose bones were found there in 1895; the plastic model "does not look as stupid as one might think". Evidence has also been found here of occupation by early Patagonian humans some 11,000 years ago. Nearby there is a visitors centre, summaries in English. There is free camping once the US$4 entrance fee has been paid. Buses J and B provice a regular service US$7.50; taxi US$18 return; or check if you can get a ride with a tour; both *Adventur* and *Fernández* tour buses to Torres del Paine stop at the cave.

Estancia Rosario offers lunches, horseriding, US$22 per person for three hours, and other activities, transport across the sound included. It is on the Peninsula Antonio Varas on the western side of the Seno Ultima Esperanza, T410836.

Essentials

LL *Costa Australis*, Pedro Montt 262, T412000, F411881. Modern, good views, popular cafeteria. Recommended. **L** *Juan Ladrilleros*, Pedro Montt 161, T411652, F412109. Modern, with bath, good restaurant, clean. Recommended. **L** *Martín Guisinde*, Bories 278, T412770, F412820. Pub, restaurant, modern. Recommended. **AL** *Glaciares*, Eberhard 104, T412189, F411452. New, snack bar. **AL** *Hostal Lady Florence Dixie*, Bulnes 659, T411158, F411943. Modern, friendly. Recommended. **AL** *Lago Sarmiento*, Bulnes 90, T411542. Good views, restaurant. **AL** *Palace*, Ladrilleros 209, T411134. Good food, overpriced. **AL** *Saltos del Paine*, Bulnes 156, T413608. Excellent. **AL-A** *Hostal Sir Francis Drake*, Phillipi 383, T/F411553. Good views, snack bar. Recommended. **A** *Lukovieks*, Ramirez 324, T411120, F412580, with breakfast, restaurant, helpful. **B** *Res Oasis*, Señoret 332, F411675. Comfortable, cable TV (**C** without bath). **C** *Blanquita*, Carrera Pinto 409. Quiet. Recommended. **C** *Concepto Indigo*, Ladrilleros 105, T413609, www.conceptoindigo.com also **E** dormitory accommodation, lovely views, rock climbing courses and tours, good meeting place, slide shows, pizzeria and vegetarian restaurant plus bar. Internet access. Recommended. **C** *Hostal Los Antiguos*, Ladrilleros 195 y Bulnes, T/F411488. Without bath, pleasant. **C** *Hostal Melissa*, Blanco Encalada 258, T411944. With bath. **C** *Hostal Reymar*, Baquedano 414, T/F411434, with breakfast, good restaurant. **C** *Natalino*, Eberhard 371, T411968. Clean and very friendly (tours to Milodón Cave arranged), parking. **C-D** *Hostal Puerto Natales*, Eberhard 250, T411098, huri@chileaustral.com Friendly, homemade jams, tours arranged. With bath.

E *Casa Cecilia*, Tomás Rogers 60, T/F411797, redcecilia@entelchile.net With bath, also **F** without bath, with breakfast, clean, cooking facilities, English, French and German spoken, kitchen facilities, heating, camping equipment rental, information on Torres del Paine, tours organized, credit cards accepted, internet access, airline tickets sold. Warmly recommended. **E** *Don Bosco*, Padre Rossa 1430. Good meals, pancakes for breakfast, use of kitchen, helpful. Recommended. Motorcycle parking, luggage store. **E** *Hostal Don Guillermo*, breakfast included, O'Higgins 657, T/F414506. Heating, clean, basic, restaurant and cooking facilities. **E** *Sra Bruna Mardones*, Pasaje Don Bosco 41 (off Philippi). Friendly, meals on request. **F** *Casa de familia Alicia*, M Rodríguez 283. With breakfast, clean, spacious, luggage stored, helpful. Recommended. **F** *Hosp Elsa Millán*, Sebastián El Cano 588, T414249. Good breakfast, homemade bread, dormitory-style, popular, hot water, warm, friendly, cooking facilities. Recommended. **F** *Hosp Laury*, Bulnes 222. With breakfast, cooking and laundry facilities, clean, warm, friendly. **F** *La Casona*, Bulnes 280, T412562. Clean, hot showers, heated lounge, including breakfast, helpful. **F** *Patagonia Adventure*, Tomás Rogers 179, T411028. Dormitory style, and private rooms, friendly, clean, use of kitchen, breakfast, English spoken, camping equipment for hire, book exchange. Recommended. **F** *Res Carahue*, Bulnes 370, T411339. With breakfast, laundry facilities, pleasant. **F** *Res Centro*, Magallanes

Sleeping
■ *on map, page 454*
Price codes:
see inside front cover
Most prices include breakfast

In season cheaper accommodation fills up quickly after the arrival of the Puerto Edén or Magallanes from Puerto Montt

The Far South

258A, T411996. With bath. **F** *Res El Mundial*, Bories 315, T412476. Use of kitchen, good value meals, luggage stored. Recommended. **F** *Res Gabriella*, Bulnes 317, T411061. Clean, good breakfast, helpful, luggage store. Recommended. **F** *Res La Florida*, O'Higgins 431, T411361. Luggage store, laundry facilities. **F** *Res Nataly*, O'Higgins 657. Dormitories. **F** *Res Temuco*, Ramírez 310, T411120. Friendly, reasonable, good food, laundry facilities, clean. **F-G** *Almirante Nieto*, Bories 206. Use of kitchen, dormitory accommodation, sleeping bag necessary, good meeting place, friendly. **F-G** *Bulnes*, Bulnes 407, T411307. With breakfast, good, laundry facilities, stores luggage. **F-G** *Los Inmigrantes*, Carrera Pinto 480. Good breakfast, clean, kitchen facilities, equipment rental, luggage store. Recommended. **F-G** *Res Sutherland*, Barros Arana 155. With bath, welcoming, clean, kitchen facilities.

G *Casa Teresa*, Esmeralda 463. Good value, warm, cheap meals, quiet, friendly. Recommended. Tours to Torres del Paine arranged. **G** *El Refugio*, O'Higgins 456, T414881. Youthful and lively place to stay. Offers tours. Internet access. **G** *Hosp La Chila*, Carrera Pinto 442, T412328. Use of kitchen, welcoming, laundry facilities, luggage store, bakes bread. Recommended. **G** *Hosp Gamma*, El Roble 650, T411420. Cooking and laundry facilities, evening meals, tours. **G** *Hosp María José*, Magallanes 646. Cooking facilities, helpful; luggage store, tours organised, tourist information. **G** *Res Asturias*, Prat 426, T412105, with breakfast, kitchen facilities, cosy. **G** *Res Dickson*, Bulnes 307, T411871. Good breakfast, clean, helpful, cooking and laundry facilities. Recommended. **G** *Res Lago Pingo*, Bulnes 808, T411026. Basic, with breakfast, laundry, use of kitchen, luggage stored, English spoken; similar at O'Higgins 70, 431 and Perito 443. **G** *Res Niko's*,

Puerto Natales

0 metres 200
0 yards 200

■ Sleeping
1 Blanquita *B2*
2 Casa Cecilia *A2*
3 Casa Teresa *B2*
4 Concepto Indigo *B1*
5 Costa Australis *B1*
6 Hospedaje La Chila *B2*
7 Hostal Lady Florence Dixie *B2*
8 Hostal Sir Francis Drake *A2*
9 Juan Ladrilleros *A1*
10 Los Inmigrantes *C2*
11 Martín Guisinde *B1*
12 Patagonia Adventure *B2*
13 Residencial Dickson *B1*
14 Residencial El Mundial *B1*
15 Residencial Gabriella *B2*
16 Residencial Niko's *C3*

● Eating
1 Andrés *B1*
2 Café Midás *B2*
3 Centro Español *B1*
4 Club Deportivo Natales *B1*
5 Cristal *B2*
6 Eden *B2*
7 El Marítimo *B1*
8 La Frontera *B3*
9 La Repizza *B2*
10 La Ultima Esperanza *B2*
11 Mari Loli *C3*
12 Tierra del Fuego *B1*

Ramirez 669, T412810, with breakfast, good meals, English spoken, also dormitory accommodation, recommended. **G** *Res Ritz*, Carrera Pinto 439, T412196. Full pension available, friendly. **G** *Tierra del Fuego*, Bulnes 23, T412138. Clean, parking, will store luggage, good.

North of Puerto Natales are: A *Cabañas Kotenk Aike*, 2 km north of town, T412581, F225935, sleep 4, very comfortable. **AL** *Cisne de Cuello Negro*, a former guesthouse for meat buyers at the disused meat packing plant, 5 km from town at Km 275 near Puerto Bories, T411498 (Av Colón 782, Punta Arenas, T244506, F248052). Friendly, clean, reasonable, excellent cooking. Recommended. **C** *Hotel 3 Pasos*, 40 km north, T228113. Simple, beautiful. In Villa Cerro Castillo, 63 km north. **B** *Hostería El Pionero*, T/F411646, anexo 722. With bath, country house ambience, good service, horses available for hire for Torres del Paine.

Hotels in the countryside open only in summer months: dates vary. For accommodation in the Torres del Paine area, see below

Mid-range *Centro Español*, Magallanes 247. Reasonable. *El Marítimo*, Pedro Montt 214. Seafood and salmon, good views, popular, slow service. *La Ultima Esperanza*, Eberhard 354. Recommended for salmon, seafood, enormous portions, not cheap but worth the experience. *Restaurant Eden*, Blanco Encalada 345. T/F414120. Specialises in *parilladas*, good lamb. **Cheap** *Andrés*, Ladrilleros 381. Excellent, good fish dishes, good service. *Café Midás*, Tomas Rogers 169, has book swap. *Cristal*, Bulnes 439. Good sandwiches and salmon, good value. *Don Alvarito*, Blanco Encalada 915. Hospitable. *La Frontera*, Bulnes 819. Set meals, good value. *La Repizza*, Blanco Encalada 294. Good value. *Mari Loli*, Baquedano 615. Excellent food, good value. *Melissa*, Blanco Encalada. Good coffee and sandwiches. *Tierra del Fuego*, Bulnes 29. Cheap, good, slow service, recommended. **Seriously cheap** Very cheap, decent meals at *Club Deportivo Natales*, Eberhard 332.

Eating
● *on map*

Pubs *El Bar de Ruperto*, Bulnes 371, good, English-run, cheap internet games, Guinness on draught, live music at weekends. *La Esquina*, Magallanes y Eberhard. Good bar. *Pub Tio Cacho*, Phillipi 553. **Discos** *Salsoteca Eclipse*, Ramírez 390. *Milodón*, Blanco Encalada 854.

Entertainment

Camping equipment *Patagonia Adventures*, Tomás Rogers 179. *Casa Cecilia*, Tomás Rogers 54. German, French and English spoken, imported gear, also for sale. Recommended. Check all equipment and prices carefully. Average charges, per day: tent US$6, sleeping bag US$3-5, mat US$1.50, raincoat US$0.60, also cooking gear US$1-2. Deposits required: tent US$200, sleeping bag US$100. Note that it is often difficult to hire walking boots. Camping gas is widely available in hardware stores, eg at Baquedano y O'Higgins and at Baquedano y Esmeralda. **Fishing** Tackle for hire at several places, including *Andes Patagónicos*, Blanco Encalada 226, T411594, US$3.50 per day for rod, reel and spinners; if you prefer fishing with floats, hooks, split shot, etc, take your own. Other companies up to 5 times as expensive. **Handicrafts** *Ñandu*, Eberhard 586. Popular. Also at Baquedano y Chorillos. **Shoe repairs** *París*, Miraflores between Blanco Encalada and Baquedano. **Supermarket** 24-hr supermarket Bulnes 300 block, markets good, food prices variable so shop around. Cheaper in Punta Arenas.

Shopping

Bigfoot Expediciones, Blanco Encalada 226-B, T414611, F414276, explore@bigfoot patagonia.com Sea kayaking and ice hiking trips arranged, recommended. *Knudsen Tours*, Blanco Encalada 284, T411531. Recommended. *GoToLatinTours.com*, T1-800254-7378, www.GoChileTours.com American based tour operator to South America offering personalized services. *Michay*, Baquedano 388, T411149 (Pedro Fueyo recommended). *Onas* and *Andescape*, Eberhard y Blanco Encalada, T412707, onas@chileauustral.com Tours of Paine and kayak trips; helpful. Servitur, Pratt 353,

Tour companies

The Far South

T411028. *Turismo Cabo de Hornos*, Pedro Montt 380. *Turismo Luis Díaz*, Blanco Encalada 189, T411654, for tours to Perito Moreno glacier (Argentina). *Turismo Tzonka*, Carrera Pinto 626, T411214. *Turismo Zaahj*, Prat 236. T412260, F411355. Recommended. Reports of the reliability of agencies, especially for their trips to Torres del Paine National Park, are very mixed. It is better to book tours direct with operators in Puerto Natales than through agents in Punta Arenas. Several agencies offer tours to the Perito Moreno glacier in Argentina, 1 day, US$70 without food or park entry fee, 14-hr trip, 2 hrs at the glacier. Take US$ cash or Argentine pesos as Chilean pesos not accepted.

Transport **Local Bicycle hire**: *Casa Cecilia* (see under sleeping) and for repairs: *El Rey de la Bicicleta*, Ramírez 540, good, helpful. **Car hire**: *Andes Patagónicos*, Blanco Encalada 226, T411728, US$85 per day including insurance and 350 km free. *Avis*, T410775. *Motor Cars*, Bulnes 659, T413806. *Ultima Esperanza*, Blanco Encalada 206, T410461. Hire agents can arrange permission to drive into Argentina, but this is expensive and takes 24 hrs to arrange. For repairs, Carlos González, a mechanic at Ladrilleros entre Bories y Eberhard, recommended.

Long distance Bus: to Punta Arenas, several daily, 3½ hrs, US$5. *Bus Fernández*, Eberhard 555, T411111, *Bus Sur*, Baquedano 534, T411325 and *Bus Transfer*, Baquedano 414, T421616. Book in advance. To **Coyhaique** via Calafate, *Urbina Tours*, 4 days, US$120 (Nov-Mar). For travel to Torres del Paine: *Andescape*, Eberhard 557, T/F412592. *JB*, Prat 258, T/F412824. *Fortaleza*, Prat 234, T/F410595. *Paori*, Eberhard 577, T/F411229.

To Argentina: to Río Gallegos direct, *Bus Sur*, US$14, and *El Pingüino*, US$14, no bus from either company on Mon; hourly to **Río Turbio**, *Lagoper* (Baquedano y Valdivia), *Turisur*, *Bus Sur*, *Cootra*, US$4, 2 hrs (depending on customs – change bus at border). To

Calafate, Buses *Cootra*, *Sur* and *Zaahj* bus, US$22, 7 hrs, reserve 1 day ahead. It is also possible to do a tour of the Perito Moreno glacier, US$56, or to be dropped in Calafate by the tour bus, US$39, in order to visit the glacier.

Ferry The *Navimag* ferry Puerto Edén sails every Fri in summer to Puerto Montt, less frequently off season (see page 378). The new M/V Magallanes also sails this route on Thu, stopping at Puerto Edén.

Airline offices *LanChile/Ladeco*, Tomás Roger 78. **Banks** *Banco Santiago*, Bulnes y Blanco Encalada. Mastercard and Visa, ATM. **Casas de cambio** *Cambio Stop*, Baquedano 380. Good for cash (also arranges tours). *Enio America*, Blanco Encalada 266 where Argentine pesos can be changed. Another two at Bulnes 683 and 1087 (good rates; also Argentine pesos). Others on Prat. Shop around as some offer very poor rates (better to change money in Punta Arenas); *Cambio Gasic* on Bulnes may be best. **Communications** Post office: Eberhard 417. Open Mon-Fri 0830-1230, 1430-1745, Sat 0900-1230. **Telephone**: *CTC*, Blanco Encalada 23 y Bulnes. Phones and fax: *Entel*, Baquedano y Bulnes, *Telefonica*, Blaco Encalada y Phillipi. **Internet**: *El Rincón de Tata*, Prat 236, also at Casa Cecilia, *Concepto Indigo*, Hosp María José (see under sleeping) and at Baquedano y O'Higgins. Access is very slow in Puerto Natales, as all calls are routed through Punta Arenas. **Laundry** *Lavandería Catch*, Bories 218, friendly service. *Liberty*, Bulnes 513. *Servilaundry*, Bulnes 513. *Tienda Milodón*, Bulnes. Or try *Sra María Carcamo* (at *Hosp Casa Teresa* at 1000-1200, 1800-2200). Good service, more expensive. **Shipping** *Navimag*: Pedro Montt 262 Loc B, Terminal Marítimo, T/F411421.

Directory
Poor rates for TCs, which cannot be changed into US$ cash

Often referred to as the **Parque Nacional Monte Balmaceda**, this park covers much of the *Campo de Hielo Sur* and the fjords and offshore islands further west. A three-hour boat trip from Puerto Natales up the Seno de Última Esperanza takes you to the southernmost section, around Monte Balmaceda (2,035 m). The boat passes the Balmaceda Glacier which drops from the eastern slopes of Monte Balmaceda. The glacier is retreating; in 1986 its foot was at sea level. The boat docks one hour further north at Puerto Toro, from where it is a kilometre walk to the base of the Serrano Glacier on the north slope of Monte Balmaceda. On the trip dolphins, sea-lions (in season), blacknecked swans, flightless steamer ducks and cormorants can be seen. The park is uninhabited but accommodation **L** is available at *Hosteria Balmaceda*, T220174, F243354.

Parque Nacional Bernardo O'Higgins
Colour map 6, grid B2
Take warm clothes, hat and gloves

Tours Three boats sail daily from Puerto Natales in summer and on Sundays only in the winter (minimum 10 passengers), when weather conditions may be better with less cloud and rain, US$55 (or US$50 cash). Book through *Casa Cecilia*, see under sleeping, or directly through *Turismo 21 de Mayo*, Ladrilleros 171, T/F411478, or through travel agencies, expensive lunch extra, take own food, drinks available on board. The trip can be combined with a visit to Torres del Paine. You have to pay full return fare on the boat and you need a permit from CONAF. There is a route from Puerto Toro along the Río Serrano to the Torres del Paine administration centre, 35 km, guided tours along this are available. It is also possible to travel from Puerto Toro along the Río Serrano by boat to the Paine administration centre, 4 hrs, US$60, details from *Casa Cecilia* in Puerto Natales.

Parque Nacional Torres del Paine

Colour map 6, grid B2
145 km northwest of
Puerto Natales

Allow a week to
10 days to see the
park properly

Covering 181,414 ha, this national park, a UNESCO Biosphere Reserve, is a must for its wildlife and spectacular scenery. Deriving from the Tehuelche word Paine, meaning 'blue', the park lies amid stunning surroundings, with constantly changing views of fantastic peaks, glaciers and icebergs, vividly coloured lakes of turquoise, ultramarine and grey, and quiet green valleys filled with wild flowers. In the centre of the park is a granite massif from which rise the Torres (Towers) and Cuernos (Horns) of Paine, oddly shaped peaks of over 2,600 m. The valleys are filled by beautiful lakes at altitudes of 50 m to 200 m above sea level.

Ins and outs

Getting there
See page 465 for
further details

The only practical way to get to Torres del Paine is with one of the many companies that leave Puerto Natales daily between 0630 and 0800. Getting around Most visitors will find that they get around on foot. However, there are minibuses between the CONAF administration and Guardería Laguna Amarga, as well as boats across Lago Pehoé.

Getting around Rangers keep a check on the whereabouts of all visitors: you are required to register and show your passport when entering the park or setting off on any hike.

Information There are entrances at Laguna Amarga, Lago Sarmiento and Laguna Azul. Entry for foreigners: US$13 (proceeds are shared between all Chilean national parks), climbing fees US$800. The park is administered by CONAF: the administration centre is in the south of the park at the northern end of Lago del Toro (0830-2000 in summer, 0830-1230, 1400-1830 off season). It provides a good slide show at 2000 on Sat and Sun and there are also excellent exhibitions on the flora and fauna of the park (Spanish and English), but no maps or written information to take away. There are 6 ranger stations (*guarderías*) staffed by rangers (*guardaparques*) who give help and advice and also store luggage (except at Laguna Amarga where they have no room).

Climate Snow may prevent access in the winter: warmest time is from Dec to Mar, although it can be wet and windy. The spring months of Oct and Nov are recommended for the wild flowers. In winter there can be good, stable conditions and well-equipped hikers can do some good walking. For information in Spanish on weather conditions phone the administration centre, T691931.

Background

There are 15 **peaks** above 2,000 m, of which the highest is Cerro Paine Grande (3,050 m). On the western edge of the park is the enormous *Campo de Hielo Sur* icecap; four main **glaciers** (*ventisqueros*) – Grey, Dickson, Zapata and Tyndall – branch off this and drop to the lakes formed by their meltwater. Two other glaciers, *Francés* and *Los Perros*, descend on the western side of the central *massif*.

The park enjoys a micro-climate especially favourable to **wildlife** and **plants**. There are 105 species of birds including 18 species of waterfowl and 11 birds of prey. Particularly noteworthy are condors, blacknecked swans, rheas, kelp geese, ibis, flamingos and austral parrakeets. The park is one of the best places on the continent for viewing guanacos and rheas. Apart from guanacos 24 other species of mammals can be seen including hares, foxes, skunks, *huemules* (a species of deer) and pumas (the last two only very rarely). Over 200 species of plants have been identified.

An impression of Torres del Paine

Torres del Paine is one of the most impressive mountain areas on Earth. Few places can compare to the 1,000-m vertical shafts of basalt with conical caps atop steep forested talus slopes. These are the remains of frozen magma in ancient volcanic throats, everything else having been eroded. As well as these spectacular mountains the surrounding forest, with turquoise lakes, glaciers and open

country, is truly magnificent.

Although few trees reach great size, several valleys are thickly forested and little light penetrates. The grassland is distinct from the monotony of the pampa and dispersed sclerophyl forest. A complex series of lakes and streams leads into fjords extending from the sea. These are another attraction; many are glacial fed (and thus very cold).

Torres del Paine has become increasingly popular with foreigners and Chileans alike: in 1996 it received 51,000 visitors, most during the summer months of January and February, which, if possible, should be avoided. Visiting the park in winter is increasingly popular as, although the temperature is low, there is little wind – many parts of the park are open all year round, as is *Hostería Las Torres*.

Numbers of visitors continue to rise. Despite the best efforts to manage this large influx of visitors rationally, the impact is starting to show. Litter has become a problem, especially around *refugios* and camping areas. Please take all your rubbish out of the park, and remember that toilet paper is also garbage.

Trekking

There are about 250 km of well marked trails. Visitors must keep to the trails: cross-country trekking is not permitted. It is vital not to underestimate the unpredictability of the weather (which can change in a few minutes), nor the arduousness of some of the stretches on the long hikes. Some paths are confusingly marked and it is all too easy to end up on precipices with glaciers or churning rivers awaiting below; be particularly careful in following the path at the Paso John Gadner on the *circuito*. Rain and snowfall are heavier the further west you go, and bad weather sweeps off the *Campo de Hielo Sur* without warning. It is essential to be properly equipped against cold, wind and rain. The only means of rescue are on horseback or by boat; the nearest helicopter is in Punta Arenas and high winds usually prevent its operation in the park.

The most popular trek is a circuit round the Torres and Cuernos del Paine: usually it is done anticlockwise starting from the Laguna Amarga *guardería*. From Laguna Amarga the route is north along the western side of the Río Paine to Lago Paine, before turning west to follow the lush pastures of the valley of the Río Paine to the southern end of Lago Dickson (it is possible to add a journey to the *campamento* by the Torres on Day 1 of this route); the land surrounding the refugio at Lago Dickson, which lies in front of an icy white lake with mountains beyond, is breathtaking. From Lago Dickson the path runs along the wooded valley of the Río de los Perros, past the Glaciar de los Perros, before climbing through bogs and up scree to Paso John Gadner (1,241 m, the highest point on the route), then dropping steeply through forest to follow the Grey Glacier southeast to Lago Grey, continuing to Lago Pehoé and the administration centre. There are superb views, particularly from the top of Paso John Gadner.

El Circuito
Although some people complete the route in less time, it normally takes 5 to 6 days

The Far South

In theory, lone walkers are not allowed on this route; camping gear must be carried. Some *campamentos* (eg by the Torres; *Campamento Paso*) do not have *refugios*. The circuit is often closed in winter because of snow. The longest lap is 30 km, between Refugio Laguna Amarga and Refugio Dickson (10 hours in good weather; two campsites on the way – Serón and Cairon), but the most difficult section is the very steep slippery slope from Paso John

Parque Nacional Torres del Paine

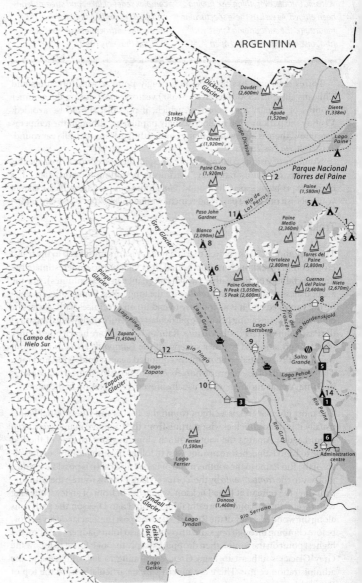

Gadner down to the *Campamento Paso* – the path is not well signed at the top of the Paso, and some people (including the author!) have got dangerously lost and ended up on the Grey Glacier itself. Although most people go anti-clockwise round the circuit, some advise doing it clockwise so that you climb to Paso John Gadner with the wind behind. The major rivers are crossed by footbridges, but these are occasionally washed away.

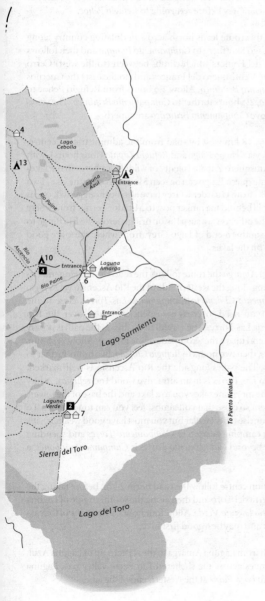

Sleeping
1 Explora
2 Hostería Estancia Lazo
3 Hostería Lago Grey
4 Hostería Las Torres
5 Hostería Pehoé
6 Posada Río Serrano

Refugios
1 Chileno
2 Dickson (Andescape)
3 Grey (Andescape)
4 Lago Paine
5 Lago Toro (Conaf)
6 Laguna Amarga
7 Laguna Verde
8 Los Cuernos
9 Pehoé (Andescape)
10 Pingo
11 Pudeto
12 Zapata

Camping
1 Campamento Británico
2 Campamento Caírón
3 Campamento Chileno
4 Campamento Italiano
5 Campamento Japonés
6 Campamento Las Guardas
7 Campamento Las Torres
8 Campamento Paso
9 Laguna Azul
10 Las Torres
11 Los Perros
12 Río Serrano
13 Serón
14 Lago Pehoé

Ranger stations (*guarderías*)

The Far South

The W

Allow 4 to 5 days. A popular alternative to El Circuito, this route can be completed without camping equipment as there is accommodation in refugios

This route combines several of the hikes described separately below. From *Refugio Laguna Amarga* the first stage runs west via *Hostería Las Torres* and up the valley of the Río Ascensio via *Refugio Chileno* to the base of the Torres del Paine (see below). From here return to the *Hostería Las Torres* and then walk along the northern shore of Lago Nordenskjold via *Refugio Los Cuernos* to *Campamento Italiano*. From here climb the Valley of the Río del Francés (see below) before continuing to *Refugio Pehoé*. From here you can complete the third part of the 'W' by walking west along the northern shore of Lago Grey to *Refugio Grey* and Glaciar Grey before returning to *Refugio Pehoé*.

Valley of the Río del Francés

From *Refugio Pehoé* this route leads north across undulating country along the western edge of Lago Skottberg to *Campamento Italiano* and then follows the valley of the Río del Francés which climbs between (to the west) Cerro Paine Grande and the Ventisquero del Francés and (to the east) the Cuernos del Paine to *Campamento Británico*. Allow 2½ hours from Refugio Pehoé to *Campamento Italiano*, 2½ hours further to *Campamento Británico*. The views from the *mirador* above *Campamento Británico* are superb.

To Lago Pingo

Allow about 5 hours

From *Guardería Grey*, 18 km west by road from the administration centre, follow the Río Pingo, via *Refugio Pingo* and *Refugio Zapata* (four hours), with views south over Ventisquero Zapata (plenty of wildlife, icebergs in the lake) to reach the lake. Ventisquero Pingo can be seen 3 km away over the lake. Two short signposted walks from Guardería Grey have also been suggested: one is a steep climb up the hill behind the ranger post to Mirador Ferrier from where there are fine views; the other is via a suspension bridge across the Río Pingo to the peninsula at the southern end of Lago Grey, from where there are good views of the icebergs on the lakes.

To the base of the Torres del Paine

About 6 hours

From *Refugio Laguna Amarga* the route follows the road west to *Hostería Las Torres*, before climbing along the western side of the Río Ascensio via *Refugio Chileno* and *Campamento Chileno* to *Campamento Las Torres*, close to the base of the Torres (you need to cross a suspension bridge over the Río Ascensio near Hostería Las Torres – be careful to do this, as the path is poorly marked and you can end up on the wrong side of the ravine). Allow 1½ hours to *Hostería Las Torres*, then two hours to *Refugio Chileno*, two hours further to *Campamento Torres*. The path alongside the Río Ascensio is well-marked, and the *Campamento Las Torres* is in an attractive wood (no *refugio*). A further 30 minutes up the morraine takes you to a lake and the base of the towers themselves – they seem so close that you almost feel you can touch them. To see the Torres lit by sunrise (spectacular but you must have good weather), it's well worth humping camping gear up to *Campamento Torres* and spending the night. One hour beyond *Campamento Torres* is *Campamento Japonés*, a good camping site.

To Laguna Verde

From the administation centre follow the road north 2 km, before taking the path east over the Sierra del Toro and then along the southern side of Laguna Verde to the *Guardería Laguna Verde*. Allow four hours. This is one of the easiest walks in the park and may be a good first hike.

To Laguna Azul & Lago Paine

Allow 8½ hours

This route runs north from Laguna Amarga to the western tip of Laguna Azul, from where it continues across the sheltered Río Paine valley past Laguna Cebolla to the *Refugio Lago Paine* at the western end of the lake.

A strong, streamlined, waterproof tent is essential if doing *El Circuito* (although you can hire camping equipment for a single night at most *refugios*). Also essential are protective clothing against wind and rain, strong waterproof footwear, compass, good sleeping bag and sleeping mat. You are not allowed to build fires in the park. In summer take shorts and sunscreen also. You are strongly advised to take all necessary equipment from Puerto Natales and not rely on availability at the Andescape *refugios*. Take your own food: the small shops at the Andescape *refugios* (see below) and at the *Posada Río Serrano* are expensive and have a limited selection. Note that rats and mice have become a major problem around camping sites and the free *refugios*. Do not leave food in your pack (which will be chewed through): the safest solution is to hang food in a bag on wire. Maps (US$6), are obtainable at CONAF offices in Punta Arenas or Puerto Natales but most are unreliable. One produced by *Cartographia Digital*, US$5, has been recommended as more accurate.

Equipment

Essentials

Hotels LL *Explora*, at Salto Chico on edge of Lago Pehoé, T411247. Ugly building but luxurious and comfortable, offering spectacular views, pool, gym, tours and transfer from Punta Arenas. Reservations: Av Américo Vespucci 80, piso 7, Santiago, T2066060, F2085479. **LL** *Hostería Lago Grey*, T/F227528. Good food, small rooms, on edge of Lago Grey. **L** *Hostería Pehoé*, T411390 (closed Apr-Oct), 5 km south of Pehoé ranger station, 11 km north of park administration, on an island with spectacular view across the Lake to Cerro Paine Grande and Cuernos del Paine, "a stunning location which is wasted", run down, overpriced. Reservations *Turismo Pehoé* in Punta Arenas. **L** *Hostería Las Torres*, head office Lautaro Navarro 1125, Punta Arenas, T226054, F222641. **AL** off season, good restaurant, English spoken, horse riding, transport from Laguna Amarga ranger station. Recommended. **AL** *Hostería Estancia Lazo*, on the eastern edge of the park, transport essential, (poor access road). Beautifully situated on Laguna Verde with spectacular views and good fishing, very friendly, comfortable, excellent food. Very highly recommended but an inconvenient base for visiting the park. Reservations *Operatur Patagónia*, Colón 822, T240513, F241153, Punta Arenas. **AL** *Posada Río Serrano*, **B** off season. An old *estancia*, run down and overpriced, some rooms with bath, some with shared facilities, breakfast extra, near park administration, with expensive but good restaurant and a shop (reservations advisable: run by *Turismo Río Serrano*, Prat 258, Puerto Natales, T410684). **B** *Hostería Lago Tyndall*, Expensive, cafeteria style restaurant, electricity during the day only, good views. Not recommended.

Sleeping
■ *on map, page 460*

Refugios G *Refugio Lago Toro*, near administration centre, run by CONAF, hot showers, cooking facilities, good meeting place, sleeping bag and mattress essential, no camping, open summer only – in the winter months another more basic (free) *refugio* is open near administration centre. The following are run by **Andescape** (for address see page 455): *Refugio Lago Pehoé*, on the northeast arm of Lago Pehoé, crowded, unfriendly. *Refugio Grey*, on the eastern shore of Lago Grey. Glacier walks including ice climbing US$50. *Refugio Lago Dickson*, *Refugio Los Chilenas*, in the valley of the Río Ascensio, recommended. *Refugio Los Cuernas*, on the northern shore of Lago Nordenskjold, good food, clean, recommended. All **E**, modern, closed in winter until 10 Sep, clean, with dormitory accommodation (sheets not provided), hot showers (US$2 for non-residents), cooking and laundry facilities, meals served, kiosk with basic food and other supplies, rental of camping equipment, campsite (**H**), advance booking advisable. **E** *Refugio Las Torres*, owned by *Hostería Las Torres*, meals served, kitchen facilities. In addition there are 6 free *refugios*: *Zapata*, *Pingo*, *Laguna Verde*, *Laguna Amarga*, *Lago*

Accommodation and meals in the Andescape refugios should be booked in advance in Puerto Natales (can also be booked by asking staff in one refugio to radio another)

The Far South

Paine and *Pudeto*. Most have cooking areas (wood stove or fireplace) but Laguna Verde and Pingo do not. These are in very poor condition.

Camping In addition to sites at the Andescape *refugios* there are the following sites: *Camping Serón* and *Camping Las Torres* (at *Hostería Las Torres)* both run by Estancia Cerro Paine. US$4, hot showers. *Camping Los Perros*, run by *Andescape*. **H**, shop and hot showers. *Camping Lago Pehoé* and *Camping Serrano*, both run by *Turismo Río Serrano* (address above). US$20 per site at former (maximum 6 persons, hot showers, beware mice) and US$15 per site at latter (maximum 6 persons, cold showers, more basic). *Camping Laguna Azul*, hot showers, **E** per site. Free camping is permitted in 7 other locations in the park: these sites are known as *campamentos*. The wind tends to increase in the evening so it is a good idea to pitch tents early (by 1600). Fires may only be lit at organized *camping* sites, not at *campamentos*. The *guardaparques* expect people to have a stove if camping. These restrictions should be observed as forest fires are a serious hazard. *Guardaparques* also require campers to have a trowel to bury their waste. Equipment hire in Puerto Natales (see above).

Boat trips From Refugio Lago Pehoé to *Refugio Pudeto*, US$15 one way daily, from Pudeto 1030, 1600, from Pehoé 1200, 1530, 1 hr; in high season it is essential to reserve in advance at the *refugios* at either end or at *Turismo Tzonka* in Puerto Natales. Off-season, radio for the boat from *Refugio Pehoé*.

Tour companies Before booking a tour check carefully on details and get them in writing: increasingly mixed reports of tours. Many companies who claim to visit the Grey Glacier only visit Lago Grey (you see the glacier in the distance). After mid-Mar there is little public transport and trucks are irregular. Several agencies in Puerto Natales including *Servitur*, *Knudsen*, *Zaahj*, *Scott Tours* and *Luis Díaz* offer 1-day tours by minibus, US$37.50 plus park entry; these give a good impression of the lower parts of the park, though you spend most of the day in the vehicle and many travellers would argue that you need to stay overnight to appreciate the park fully. José Torres of *Sastrería Arbiter* in C Bulnes 731, T411637, recommended as guide. *Enap* weekend tours in summer cost US$45 including accommodation and meals. *Buses Fernández* offer 2-day tours, US$132 and 3-day tours (which includes trip to the Balmaceda Glacier), US$177. *Onas Turismo* (for address see page 455) runs trips from the park down the Río Serrano in dinghies to the Serrano glacier and from there, on the tour boats to Puerto Natales, US$90 each all inclusive. Book in advance.

Bus *Andescape*, *Fortaleza*, *JB Buses*, and *Paori* (addresses above in Puerto Natales section) run daily bus services to the park from Puerto Natales leaving between 0630 and 0800. The normal route is via Laguna Amarga, but buses are presently entering the park at Guardería Lago Sarmiento as Guardería Laguna Armarga has been destroyed in an accident. Buses still leave the park at Laguna Armarga, though: return departures 1500 from administration centre, 1600 from Laguna Amarga, 2½ hrs journey to Laguna Amarga, 3 hrs to the administration centre, US$9 one way, US$16 open return (return tickets are not interchangeable between all different companies), from early Nov to mid-Apr. In normal times, buses will drop you at Laguna Amarga and pick you up at the administration centre for the return.

Transport
In high season book in advance. See also under Punta Arenas

For the daily *In-Tur* minibus service to Punta Arenas (in high season the buses fill quickly so it is best to board at the administration): all buses wait at Refugio Pudeto until the 1430 boat from *Refugio Lago Pehoé* arrives. Travel between 2 points within the park (eg Pudeto-Laguna Amarga), US$3. At other times services by travel agencies are dependent on demand: arrange return date with driver and try to arrange your return date to coincide with other groups to keep costs down. *Luis Díaz* has been recommended, about US$12, minimum 3 persons. In season there are minibus connections from Laguna Amarga to the *Hostería Los Torres* and from the administration centre to *Hostería Lago Grey*. To go from Torres del Paine to Calafate (Argentina) either return to Puerto Natales and catch a bus, or take a bus or hitch from the park to Villa Cerro Castillo border point (106 km south of the administration), cross to Paso Cancha de Carreras and try to link with the Río Turbio-Calafate bus schedule.

Car Hiring a pick-up from *Budget* in Punta Arenas is an economical proposition for a group (up to 9 people): US$415 for 4 days. If driving there yourself, the road from Puerto Natales is being improved: inside the park, the roads are narrow, bendy with blind corners; it takes about 3 hrs from Puerto Natales to the administration. Petrol available at Río Serrano, but fill up in case.

Horse hire *Baquedano Zamora*, Blanco Encalada 226, Puerto Natales, T/F412911 (or contact via the *Hostería El Pionero*, Cerro Castillo, T691932, anexo 722).

Puerto Natales to El Calafate (Argentina)

The small Argentine town of El Calafate, the base for visits to the Parque Nacional Los Glaciares, is a short distance from Puerto Natales and can easily be visited.

From Puerto Natales the Argentine frontier can be crossed at three points, all of which meet Route 40 which runs to El Calafate. These crossings are open, subject to weather conditions, 24 hrs a day from Sep to May, 0700-2300 Jun to Aug. **Paso Casas Viejas** This crossing, 16 km east of Puerto Natales, is reached by turning off Route 9 (the Punta Arenas road) at Km 14. On the Argentine side the road (*ripio*) runs east to meet Route 40, en route to Río Gallegos (or north to Calafate). This crossing is open all year. **Villa Dorotea** This crossing is reached by branching off Route 9, 9 km east of Puerto Natales and continuing north a further 11 km. On the Argentine side this road (*ripio*) continues north to Route 40 via Río Turbio. **Cerro Castillo** The most northerly of the three crossings, Cerro Castillo is reached by turning off the road north to Torres del Paine at Km 65. Chilean customs and immigration formalities are at Cerro Castillo; Argentine formalities are at Cancha Carrera, 2 km further east. Accommodation is available at Cerro Castillo at the *Hostería El Pionero* (details under Puerto Natales) and at 2 *hospedajes*. On the Argentine side of the frontier the road meets Route 40 in a very

Border with Argentina

The Far South

desolate spot – hitching may be possible, but this route is more feasible if you have your own transport.

Río Turbio
Phone code 02902
Population: 8,000

Only 30 km northeast of Puerto Natales, Río Turbio is the site of Argentina's largest coalfield. Little visited by travellers, it is a good centre for trekking and horseriding. There is a **tourist office** in the Municipalidad on Calle San Martín.

Visits can be made to **Mina Uno** (where the first mine was opened), to the south of the town, and to the present mining and industrial area, on the eastern outskirts, where there is a museum, the **Museo del Carbón**. ■ *Mon-Fri 0700-1200*. About 4 km south of town is **Valdelén**, a ski resort situated just inside the frontier on the slopes of Sierra La Dorotea.

Hotels almost always full

Sleeping and eating A *Hostería Capipe*, at Dufour 9 km west, T491240, F482930. A *Gato Negro*, T4921226, also **E**, dormitory accommodation. **E** *Hostería La Frontera*, an *albergue* at Valdelén. *Restaurant El Ringo*, near bus terminal, will shelter you from the wind.

Sports Skiing at Valdelén, with 6 *pistes*, is ideal for beginners. There is also scope for cross-country skiing nearby. Season runs from early Jun to late Sep, the *pistes* enjoying electric lighting to extend the short winter afternoons.

Transport Air: Airport 15 km southeast near 28 de Noviembre; taxi US$10. *LADE* flights to Río Gallegos. **Bus**: To **Puerto Natales**, 2 companies, US$4, regular. To **Calafate**, *Cootra* daily, 6 hrs, US$27. *Expreso Pingüino* runs daily at 0200 and *Tascsa/Quebek* at 0100 to **Río Gallegos**, 4 hrs, US$15. *LADE* flight to Río Gallegos once a week (airport 15 km from town, taxi US$10 per person).

El Calafate

There are two alternative routes. On clear days both offer fantastic views of Torres del Paine. The longest but easiest route runs north along Route 40 along beautiful valleys with flowers, woods and grazing horses, to Cancha Carrerra, the junction with the border crossing from Cerro Castillo, then following the Río Coyle to **La Esperanza**, Km 123, where it meets the main Calafate-Río Gallegos road, 161 km southeast of Calafate.

The shorter route continues northwards from Cancha Carrerra along a very poor, desolate *ripio* road, the continuation of Route 40, which turns off at Km 30 and runs northeast 70 km to meet the Calafate-Río Gallegos road at El Cerrito, 91 km southeast of Calafate. In winter both the Cerro Castillo crossing and this shorter route are closed. For public transport on this route see under Puerto Natales.

Accommodation along the route can be found at Fuentes del Coyle, 31 km east of Cerro Castillo, there is a small bar which rents out rooms and a hotel, **D**, cold, dirty, and at La Esperanza, **D**, *Restaurant La Esperanza*, bunk beds, with bath; also *cabañas* at the YPF service station.

El Calafate

Altitude: 225m
Phone code: 02902
Population: 4,000
312 km NW of
Río Gallegos

This little town is situated in a beautiful position on the southern shore of Lago Argentino, one of the largest lakes in Argentina. Mountains are everywhere. Founded in 1927, Calafate has grown rapidly as a tourist centre for the Parque Nacional los Glaciares, 50 km further west. Given the town's name, it is no surprise that the hills around abound with small calafate bushes.

The Calafate

Whoever eats the fruits of the Calafate, Berberis buxifolia, will return to Patagonia or so the story goes: whether they do or not, they are likely to have purple stained lips and fingers! This spiny, shiny leaved, hardy shrub grows to two metres in height and has single bright yellow/orange flowers dotted along its arching branches in spring. The deep purple grape-like edible berries are also found singly or in pairs. Also known as the Magellan barberry, its wood is used for making red dye.

Getting there Calafate is easily accessible from Puerto Natales in Chile (one or two buses daily in summer, less in winter) along a bone-breaking road north from Río Turbio, and along a smooth metalled road from Río Gallegos near the Atlantic coast (several buses daily). There are less good roads north to El Chaltén and Perito Moreno.

Ins and outs
See page 470 for further details

Getting around Calafate is so small that it's easy to get around the town on foot.

Tourist office In the bus terminal, info@calafate.com Hotel prices detailed on large chart at tourist office; has a list of taxis but undertakes no arrangements. Helpful staff. Oct-Apr 0700-2200 daily. For information on the Parque Nacional los Glaciares visit the park office, Mon-Fri 0800-1500, Libertador 1302, T491005.

Sights

There is a straightforward walk directly behind the town up a hill from which there are views of the silhouette of the southern end of the Andes, Bahía Redonda and Isla Solitaria on Lago Argentino. Just west of the town centre is Bahía Redonda, a shallow part of Lago Argentino where in winter you can ice skate and ski. At the eastern edge of Bahía Redonda is **Laguna Nimes**, a bird reserve where there are flamingos, black necked swans and ducks, recommended. There is scope for good hill walking to the south of the town, while Cerro Elefante, west of Calafate on the road to the Moreno glacier, is good for rock climbing.

Travel by road to the most interesting spots is limited and may require expensive taxis. Tours can be arranged at travel agencies, or with taxi drivers at the airport who await arrivals.

Excursions
For excursions to the Moreno glacier, Upsala Glacier and Fitz Roy, see below

Punta Gualicho, on the shores of Lago Argentino, some 15 km east of town (though less on foot when cutting across the pampa), has badly deteriorated painted caves. Several agencies run two-hour tours for US$16. The caves are on private property and may soon be closed to the public. There is an expensive entrance fee (US$7). On the same road, 12 km east of Calafate, on the edge of the lake are fascinating geological formations caused by erosion.

El Galpón, 21 km west, is an *estancia* offering visits from 1730 onwards which feature walks through a bird sanctuary where 43 species of birds have been identified, displays of sheep shearing and a barbecue as well as horseriding (visits at other times on request), transport arranged, English spoken; in Calafate T/F491793.

At **Lago Roca**, 40 km south, there is trout and salmon fishing, climbing, walking, and branding of cattle in summer. Good camping in wooded area and a restaurant.

The Far South

Essentials

Calafate is very popular in Jan-Feb, when booking all transport in advance is recommended and accommodation can be difficult to find. Credit cards are unwelcome, apart from at hotels, and high commissions are charged.

Sleeping

■ *on map, page 469*
Price codes:
see inside front cover
Many hotels are open
only from October to
April-May

LL *Los Alamos*, Moyano y Bustillo, T491145, F491186, posadalosalamos@ cotecal.com.ar Best, comfortable, very good food and service, extensive gardens, single-hole golf course. Recommended. **L** *El Mirador del Lago*, Libertador 2047, T/F491213, miradordellago@cotecal.com.ar Good accommodation, good restaurant (wines not recommended), better not to take half-board. **L** *Frai Toluca*, Calle 6 No 1016, T/F491773, fraitolucahotel@cotecal.com.ar good views, comfortable, restaurant; **L** *Hostería Kau-Yatun*, 25 de Mayo (10 blocks from town centre), T491059, F491260, kauyatun@cotecal.com.ar Many facilities, old *estancia* house, comfortable, restaurant and barbecues, horseriding tours with guides. **AL** *El Quijote*, Gob Gregores 1191, T491017, F491103, elquijote@cotecal.com/ar Recommended. **AL** *Kalken*, V Feilberg 119, T491073, F491036, hotelkalken@cotecal. com.ar With breakfast, spacious. **AL** *Michelangelo*, Espora y Gob Moyano, T491045, F491058, michelangelohotel@cotecal.com.ar With breakfast, modern, reasonable, good restaurant, accepts TCs (poor rates). **AL-A** *La Loma*, Roca 849, T491016, lalomahotel@cotecal.com.ar, with breakfast, modern, highly recommended, multilingual, restaurant, tea-room, spacious rooms, attractive gardens. **A** *ACA Hostería El Calafate*, 1° de Mayo, T491004, F491027. Modern, good view, open all year. **A** *Hostería Schilling*, Paradelo 141, T491453. With breakfast, nice rooms, poor beds.

B *Amado*, Libertador 1072, T491134, familiagomez@cotecal.com.ar Without breakfast, restaurant, good. **B** *Cabañas Del Sol*, Libertador 1956, T491439 (**D** in low season), good meals, highly recommended. **B** *Hosp Cerro Cristal*, Gob Gregores 989, T491088, helpful. Recommended. **B** *Hosp del Norte*, Los Gauchos 813, T491117. Open all year, kitchen facilities, comfortable, owner organizes tours. Highly recommended. **B** *Kapenke*, 9 de Julio 112, T491093. With breakfast, good beds. Recommended. **B** *Las Cabañitas*, V Feilberg 218, T491118, lascabanitas@cotecal.com.ar Cabins, hot water, kitchen and laundry facilities, helpful. Recommended. **B** *Los Lagos*, 25 de Mayo 220, T491170. Very comfortable, good value. Recommended. **B** *Paso Verlika*, Libertador 1108, T491009, F491279. With breakfast, good value restaurant. **B** *Upsala*, Espora 139, T491166, F491075. With breakfast, good beds. Recommended. **C** *Cabañas Nevis*, about 1 km from town towards glacier, Libertador 1696, T491180, for 4 or 8, lake view, full board good value. **D** *Youth Hostel Albergue del Glaciar*, Los Pioneros 251, T/F491243, www.glaciar.com Discount for ISIC or IYHA members, open mid-Sep to end-Apr, kitchen facilities, English, German, Italian spoken, internet, also rooms with bath (**B**) and sleeping bag space (**E**), *El Tempano Errante* restaurant with good value fixed menu and vegetarian options, booking service for hotels and transport throughout Patagonia. Recommended. Tour agency *Patagonia Backpackers*, runs tours to Moreno glacier (US$35 per person, good value) and elsewhere, free shuttle service from bus station, *Navimag* agents, book in advance in summer.

D-E *Hosp Alejandra*, Espora 60, T491328, without bath, good value, recommended; and airport, *Navimag* agents, book in advance in summer. **E** *Albergue Lago Argentino*, Campaña del Desierto 1050, T491423, F491139, near bus terminal, dormitory accommodation, limited bathrooms, kitchen facilities, helpful, **F** with sleeping bag. **E** *Hosp Buenos Aires*, Buenos Aires 296, 200 m from terminal, T491147, kitchen facilities, helpful, good hot showers, luggage store. **E** *Hosp Jorgito*, Gob Moyano 943, T491323. Without bath, basic, cooking facilities, heating, breakfast extra, often full. **E** *Hosp Los*

Dos Pinos, 9 de Julio 358, T491271. Dormitory accommodation, cooking and laundry facilities, also cabins **B**, and camping **F**, arranges tours to glacier, popular. **E** *Lago Azul*, Perito Moreno 83, T491419, only 2 double rooms. Highly recommended. Some private houses offer accommodation: these include Enrique Barragán, Barrio Bahía Redonda, Casa 10, T491325, **E**, recommended. **F** *Apartamentos Lago Viedma*, Paralelo 158, T491159, F491158. Hostel, 4 bunks to a room, cooking facilities. **F** *La Cueva de Jorge Lemos*, Gob Moyano 839, behind YPF station. Bunk beds, bathroom, showers, kitchen facilities, popular and cheap. If in difficulty, ask at tourist office from which caravans, tents (sleep 4) and 4-berth *cabañas* may be hired, showers extra.

In the Parque Nacional los Glaciares Some 40 km west of Calafate on the road to the Moreno glacier: **LL** *Los Notros*, T/F491437, www.lastland.com With breakfast, spacious, rooms with glacier views, recommended, transport from airport and other meals extra. In the far south of the park on the shores of Brazo Sur: **LL** *Estancia Helsingfors*, on the southern shore of Lago Viedma, T/F40966-20719. With breakfast, all other meals available, many treks, boat trips on Lago Viedma and flights over glaciers available, also riding, sheep-shearing, daily sailing across Lago Viedma, via Glaciar Viedma, at 0930 in summer. Recommended. **E** *La Leona*, T491418, 106 km north of Calafate near east end of Lago Viedma, without bath, camping.

For accommodation in El Chaltén in the northern part of the park see below

Camping Municipal campsite behind YPF service station, T491344, reservations off season T491829, **G**, hot water, security, bar, parillada, open 1 Oct-30 Apr; good meeting place. Three campsites in the park en route to the glacier: *Río Mitre*, near the park entrance, 52 km from Calafate, 26 km east of the glacier, **H** *Bahia Escondida*, 7 km east of the glacier, toilets and hot showers, crowded in summer, off season free but no water. Site at Arroyo Correntoso, 10 km east of the glacier, no facilities but nice location and lots of firewood. Take food to all three. *Lago Roca*, T499500, US$4, restaurant/

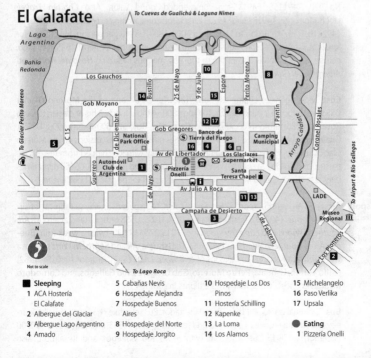

El Calafate

To Cuevas de Gualichú & Laguna Nimes

Lago Argentino

Bahía Redonda

To Glaciar Perito Moreno

Not to scale

To Lago Roca

The Far South

■ **Sleeping**
1 ACA Hostería El Calafate
2 Albergue del Glaciar
3 Albergue Lago Argentino
4 Amado

5 Cabañas Nevis
6 Hospedaje Alejandra
7 Hospedaje Buenos Aires
8 Hospedaje del Norte
9 Hospedaje Jorgito

10 Hospedaje Los Dos Pinos
11 Hostería Schilling
12 Kapenke
13 La Loma
14 Los Alamos

15 Michelangelo
16 Paso Verlika
17 Upsala

● **Eating**
1 Pizzería Onelli

confitería. *Ferretería Chuar*, Libertador 1242, sells white gas for camping. Another campsite is **Camping Río Bote**, 35 km, on road to Río Gallegos.

Eating **Expensive** *Michelangelo*, Espora y Gob Moyano, very expensive but magnificent steaks, trout, pastas. Recommended. *Paso Verlika*, Libertador 1108, small, 2 courses with wine US$16, credit cards 10% extra, good value. There is also an excellent restaurant at *Hotel Los Alamos*. **Mid-range** *La Loma* (address above), friendly, home food. *Mi Viejo*, Libertador 1111, *parrilla*. *Pizzería Casablanca*, Libertador y 25 de Mayo, good breakfasts. *Pizzería Onelli*, Libertador 1197, reasonable, stays open out of season. *Rick's Café*, No 1105. *Tenedor libre*, popular, US$11. **Cheap** Good value fixed price menu at Albergue del Glaciar (see under sleeping). Also *El Rancho*, 9 de Julio y Gob Moyano, large, cheap and good pizzas, popular, free video shows of the glacier. Highly recommended. Tea-rooms: *Bar Don Diego de la Noche*, Libertador 1603, lamb and seafood, live music, good atmosphere. *La Guanaconauta*, bar on Libertador. *Maktub*, Libertador 905, excellent pastries, pricey.

Festivals People flock to the rural show on **15 Feb** (*Lago Argentino Day*) from all over the vast Provincia de Santa Cruz. Many wear their finest *gaucho* clothes – *bombachas*, *espuelas* and wide-brimmed hats – and camp out with much revelry. There are dances, *asados* and *jineteadas* (rodeos – wild horses ridden by wild men). This is a highly recommended insight into Patagonia's 'wild west'. There are also barbecues and rodeos etc on *Día de la Tradición*, 10 Nov.

Tour companies
Many agencies, most of them along Libertador

Hielo y Aventura, No 935, T491053. Organizes 2-hr trek on glacier with champagne US$65. Recommended. *Interlagos*, No 1175, T491179, F491241. Tours to Moreno glacier, plenty of time allowed, provide cheapest transport to Fitz Roy (but double check return!), English- and Spanish-speaking guide. Highly recommended. *Los Glaciares*, No 920, T491158, F491159, recommended, good value. Also *Chaltén Travel*, Libertador 1177, T491833, T/F492212, rancho@cotecal.com.ar *Leutz*, 25 de Mayo 43, T492316. Daily excursion to Lago Roca 1000-1800, US$40 per person, plus US$22 for lunch at *Estancia Nibepo Aike*, and *Santa Cruz*, Campo del Desierto 1695, T493166, helpful. Several hotels also organise tours by minibus including *Hosp del Norte* and *Albergue del Glaciar*.

Cost Most agencies charge the same rates for excursions: to the **Moreno Glacier** US$35-40 for a trip leaving 0830, returning 1800, without lunch, 3 hrs at glacier; to **Lago Roca**, at 0930 return 1700, US$35; to **Cerro Fitz Roy**, at 0600 return 1900, US$50, **Gualicho caves**, 2 hrs, US$16. Several agencies offer walking excursions on the Moreno Glacier, usually finishing with champagne or whisky with ice chipped from the glacier; these include *Hielo y Aventura*, 1½ hrs, US$65 Jan-Feb and Holy Week, US$50 other times between 15 Oct and 15 Mar, plus US$15 for transport to the glacier, book ahead.

Transport
Mountain bikes can be hired from Bike Way, Espora 20, T492180, US$6 per hr, US$25 per day

Air Lago Argentino airport, 22 km east of town, has a paved runway suitable for jet aircraft. *Aerobus*, T492492, from airport to hotels US$5, US$8 return, stand at airport. *AR, Southern Winds* and *Lapa* (Av Libertador 1015, T491171) fly twice a week from **Buenos Aires**, *Southern Winds* via Bariloche. To **Ushuaia**, *AR* and *Southern Winds*, twice a week, the latter also to Río Gallegos once a week. *LADE* (Av Libertador 1080, T491262) to **Río Turbio**, **Ushuaia**, **Perito Moreno**, **Gob Gregores**, **Río Gallegos**, and **Comodoro Rivadavia** once a week. Many more flights in summer.

Bus Terminal on Roca, 1 block from Libertador. Bus schedule changes annually. Journey to **Ushuaia** requires 4 changes, and ferry, total cost US$43. *Interlagos* daily at 0900 (summer) or 0915 Tue, Thu, Sat (winter) to **Río Gallegos** and its airport; also

Tacsa/Quebek, 0300 and 0915 daily, and 1600 Mon, Fri, Sat, 4½ hrs, US$20-25. To **Río Turbio** with *Tacsa/Quebek*, 2 a day, US$24, 4 hrs. For **Buenos Aires** and northern destinations go to Río Gallegos and change (most departures in the evening). To **Bariloche**, along the beautiful and desolate Route 40, operated by *Almafuerte Travel*, 3 days with overnight stops in Puerto Moreno and Esquel, US$230, daily Jan/Feb, 3 times a week Oct-Dec, Mar, no service Apr-Sep, bookings through *Albuergue del Glaciar* and *Chaltén Travel* (T02962-493019), who also do buses to Perito Moreno (US$85) sometimes with a stop at Cueva de los Manos – book a week in advance. The Perito Moreno route is also done by *Padilla* (T491243).

To Chile *Cootra* to **Puerto Natales** via Río Turbio, daily, US$25, 6 hrs (advance booking recommended, tedious border crossing). *Bus Sur* (Tue, Sat 0800) and *Zaahj* (Wed, Fri, Sun 0800) run to **Puerto Natales** via Cerro Castillo (a simpler crossing), 4½-5 hrs, US$25. Travel agencies including *Albergue del Glaciar* run regular services in summer, on demand in winter, up to US$60, 5 hrs. These connect at Cerro Castillo with buses from Puerto Natales to Torres del Paine (Argentine pesos cannot be exchanged in Torres del Paine).

Taxi To **Río Gallegos**, 4 hrs, US$200 irrespective of number of people, up to 5.

Airline office *Kaiken*, 25 de Mayo 43, T492072, F491854. **Banks** Take cash as there are no *casas de cambio*, and high commission is charged on TCs. There are no ATMs. *Banco de la Provincia de Santa Cruz*, Libertador, 3% commission on TCs, 20% commission on Visa and Mastercard advances. *Banco de Tierra del Fuego*, on 25 de Mayo. *Bansud*, 25 de Mayo 34, changes TCs, no commission on Visa advances. Travel agencies such as *Interlagos* change notes; *YPF garage* and *Chocolate El Calafate* and some other shops give good rates for cash; *Albergue del Glaciar*, 5% commission on TCs; the *Scorpio* snack bar on Libertador is reported to give best rates. Many businesses add 10% for credit card transactions. Remember that US dollar notes are widely accepted. **Communications** Post office: on Libertador; postal rates much lower from Puerto Natales (Chile) and delivery times much quicker. **Telephone:** run by *Cooperativa Telefónica de Cafayate* (Cotecal), office at Espora y Gob Moyano, 0700-0100, also has internet (US$10 per hr), telex and fax facilities, all services expensive, collect calls impossible. **Laundry** *El Lavadero*, Libertador 1474, US$7 a load, also has internet access; also at *Hotel Cerro Cristal* (address above).

Directory

Parque Nacional Los Glaciares

This park, the second largest in Argentina, covers more than 660,000 ha. Over a third is covered by the hielos continentales, *giant ice fields which straddle the frontier with Chile. Of the 47 major glaciers which flow from the icefields, 13 descend into the park to feed two great lakes, Lago Argentino and Lago Viedma. The Río La Leona, flowing south from Lago Viedma, links the two lakes. There are also another 190 smaller glaciers that aren't even connected to the icefields. East of the icefields are areas of forest which eventually give way to Patagonian steppe. Here there are over 100 species of bird, among them being the condor, the patagonian woodpecker, the austral parakeet, the green-backed firecrown as well as blacknecked swans, Andean ruddy ducks and torrent ducks. Guanacos, grey foxes, skunks and rheas can be seen on the steppe while the endangered huemul inhabits the forest.*

The Far South

The advance and retreat of the Moreno Glacier

The Moreno Glacier is frequently said to be in retreat as a result of global warming. Though the glacier no longer blocks Brazo Rico on a three-yearly cycle, such statements must be treated with caution.

Glaciers are usually described by glaciologists as advancing, retreating or stable. However, even a retreating glacier will continue moving slowly forward; its frontage or snout retreats because it melts or breaks up at a faster rate than its forward movement. Though the Moreno glacier no longer behaves as it did until 1988, it is considered by glaciologists to be stable: its rates of forward movement and break-up are in a rough equilibrium.

One of the most puzzling things about glaciers is the way they change their behaviour. As far as is known, the Moreno glacier did not block Brazo Rico until 1917; according to early scientific studies its snout was 750 m away from the Magallanes Peninsula in 1900, a distance that had dropped to 350 m by 1908. In 1917 the small dam formed by the ice broke after a few weeks; the next time the glacier blocked the fjord was in 1934-5. Between this date and 1988 the glacier moved forward more vigorously; in 1939 when it reached the Magallanes Peninsula again, the waters in Brazo Rico rose nine metres and flooded coastal areas, leading to attempts by the Argentine navy to bomb it from the air. These failed but the waters eventually broke through. After 1939 the glacier reached the Peninsula about every three years until 1988. Its changed behaviour since then may be related to global warming, but we also need to know why the glacier started advancing so vigorously in the first place – one theory is that it was being pushed forward by an unknown glacier on the campo de hielos sur.

Ins and outs

Getting there
See page 478 for further details
There are 2 sections of the park – around the Perito Moreno glacier, and around Cerro Fitz Roy. To get to the former, most people take one of the minibuses that leave daily from El Calafate early in the morning. To get to the latter, there are daily buses to El Chalten.

Getting around
Once in a section of the park, most people walk, but to go from one part of the park to another, it is necessary to return to Calafate first and change buses.

Climate
Many facilities are closed off-season
The climate is variable, depending on altitude and season. The best time to visit is between Oct and Mar. Temperatures in summer reach 20-25°C and even 30°C on occasions – remember your sun block at all times. Rainfall ranges from 2,000 mm in the far west to 400 mm in the east, falling mainly between Mar and late May.

Information
Lighting fires and camping wild are prohibited throughout the park
The most popular sectors of the park are the southern area around Lago Argentino and the northern area around Cerro Fitz Roy. Access to the central sector, north of Lago Argentino and south of Lago Viedma, is difficult, and there are few tourist facilities though *estancias* such as *Helsingfors* and *La Cristina* offer accommodation and excursions. The *Helsingfors* offers boat trips to the Viedma Glacier.

Lago Argentino
The source of the Río Santa Cruz, one of the most important rivers in Patagonia, Lago Argentino covers some 1,400 sq km. At its western end there are two networks of fjords (*brazos*), fed by glaciers (*ventisqueros*). The major attraction in the park is the Perito Moreno glacier. Excursions also run to a group of four other glaciers further north, including the Upsala glacier.

Ventisquero Moreno

This glacier, 80 km west of Calafate, was until recently one of the few in the world still advancing. Some 250 km long, it reaches the water at a narrow point in one of the fjords, Brazo Rico, opposite Peninsula Magallanes. Five kilometres across and 60 m high, it used to advance across Brazo Rico,

Spectacular especially at sunset, the glacier is constantly moving and never silent

Parque Nacional Los Glaciares

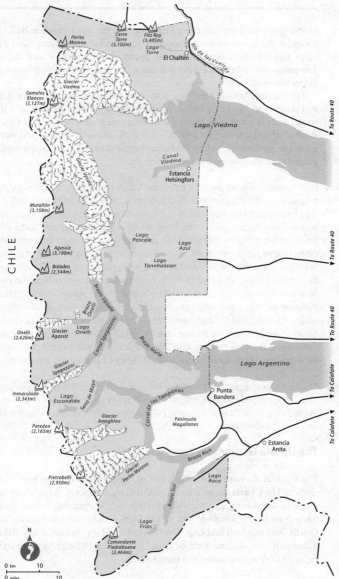

Beware: flying ice

"One or two of the tourists who ignore the prohibition signs and walk down to the rocks overlooking the channel in front of the glacier always get washed away every season. They all think it won't happen to them, but it does; 60 metres of ice break off *and hits the water just in front of them. But it isn't the water that kills them, it's the chunks of flying ice."*

Carlos Dupdez, Superintendent, Parque Nacional Los Glaciares, interviewed in the Buenos Aires Herald, *1 November 1997.*

blocking the fjord roughly every three years; as the water pressure built up behind it, the ice would break, reopening the channel and sending giant icebergs (*témpanos*) rushing down the appropriately named Canal de los Témpanos. Since February 1988 this has not occurred, possibly because of global warming.

The ice, with its vivid blue hues, is riven by crevasses; the noise as it cracks and strains can be clearly heard. As pieces break off and collapse into the water, there is a dull roar. From the viewing area it stretches back in a solid sheet of white towards the Chilean frontier. Wooden catwalks permit viewing; there is a fine of up to US$500 for leaving the catwalks. It is possible to join guided expeditions onto the glacier itself.

Tours
Take warm clothes, and food and drink

From Calafate there are buses by *Interlagos*, US$30 return. Many agencies also run minibus tours, US$30 return (plus US$5 park entry), leaving 0800 returning 1800, giving 3 hrs at glacier, book through any agency in Calafate, return ticket valid if you come back next day (student discount available). *Albergue del Glaciar* trips go out by a different route passing the *Estancia Anita* and have been repeatedly recommended; *Estancia Anita* was the site of a massacre of farmworkers during the failed Patagonian Revolution – Spanish speakers should consult *La Patagonia Rebelde* by Osvaldo Bayer for more details, as Chatwin's account in *In Patagonia* is a blatant piece of plagiarism of Bayer and riven with errors compounded by Chatwin's poor Spanish. Walking tours on the glacier are offered by several agencies in Calafate, see above. Taxis, US$80 for 4 passengers round trip. Out of season, trips to the glacier are difficult to arrange, but you can gather a party and hire a taxi (*Remise Taxis*, T491745, F491044). Ask rangers where you can camp out of season; there are no facilities except for a decrepit toilet block. It is possible to visit from Puerto Natales (Chile), which is cheaper than staying in Argentina.

Boat trips

Trips on the lake are organized by *Hielo y Aventura*, T491053, with large boats for up to 60 passengers: 'Safari Náutico', US$20, 1 hr offering the best views of the glacier; or 'Minitrekking', US$85, day trip including 2½-hr walk on the glacier. Recommended, but not for the fainthearted, take your own lunch.

The Upsala Glacier

The fjords at the northwestern end of Lago Argentino are fed by four other glaciers. The **Upsala** glacier is considered the largest in South America, 60 km long and, with a frontage 4 km wide and 60 m high. **Spegazzini**, further south, has a frontage 1½ km wide and 130 m high. In between are **Agassiz** and **Onelli**, both of which feed **Lago Onelli**, a quiet and very beautiful lake, full of icebergs of every size and sculpted shape, surrounded by beech forests on one side and ice-covered mountains on the other.

Tour boats from Punta Bandera, 50 km west of Calafate, visit the Upsala glacier, Lago Onelli and glacier (restaurant) and the Spegazzini glacier (check before going that access to the face of the Upsala glacier is possible), daily service in season on the catamaran *Serac*, US$90, or the motor boat *Nunatak* (slightly cheaper). The price includes bus fares and park entry fees. Bus departs 0730 from Calafate for Punta Bandera. 1 hr is allowed for a meal at the restaurant near Lago Onelli. Return bus to Calafate at 1930: a tiring day, it is often cold and wet, but memorable. *Upsala Explorer* organize tours for US$132, including food, 4WD trip, guided hikes around Estancia Cristina with amazing views of the glacier. Out of season it is extremely difficult to get to the glacier. Many travel agencies make reservations.

Tours
Pay in dollars and take food

Fitz Roy

In the far north of the park, 230 km north of Calafate at the western end of Lago Viedma is Cerro Fitz Roy (3,405 m), part of a granite massif which also includes the peaks of Cerro Torre (3,128 m), Poincenot (3,076 m), Egger (2,673 m), Guillaumet (2,503 m), Saint-Exupery (2,600 m), Aguja Bífida (2,394 m) and Cordón Adela (2,938 m). Clearly visible from a distance, Fitz Roy towers above

The Fitz Roy area

The Far South

Peaks in the Fitz Roy Range

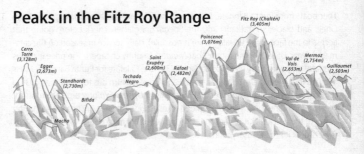

the nearby peaks, its sides normally too steep for snow to settle. Named after the captain of the *Beagle* who saw it from afar in 1833 (its Tehuelche name was El Chaltén), it was first climbed by a French expedition in 1952.

The area around the base of the massif offers fine walking opportunities (see below) and there are stupendous views: "anyone within 500 miles would be a fool to miss them". Occasionally at sunrise the mountains are briefly lit up bright red for a few seconds: this phenomenon is known as the *amanecer de fuego* ('sunrise of fire').

Hiking Trails around the base of the **Fitz Roy** massif are: **1)** Northwest from El Chaltén via a good campsite at Lago Capri, wonderful views, to Campamento Río Blanco, and nearby Campamento Poincenot, 2-3 hrs, from where a path leads up to Lago de los Tres (blue) and Lago Sucia (green), 2-3 hrs return from the camps. **2)** From Campamento Río Blanco a trail runs north along the Río Blanco and west along the Río Eléctrico via Piedra del Fraile (4 hrs) to Lago Eléctrico. At Piedra del Fraile, just outside the park, there are *cabañas* (**E** with hot showers) and campsite, US$5, plus expensive shop; from here a path leads south up Cerro Eléctrico Oeste (1,882 m) towards the north face of Fitz Roy, 2 hrs, tough but spectacular views. This route passes through private property: the owner allows you to walk through only. **3)** West from El Chaltén along the Río Fitz Roy to Laguna Torre, beautifully situated at Cerro Torre and fed by Glaciar Torre, 3 hrs. **4)** Southwest from El Chaltén along a badly marked path to Laguna Toro, 6 hrs, the southern entrance to the icefields. Do not stray from the paths. A map is essential, even on short walks. The park information centre has good information and provides photocopied maps of treks, but the best one is published by *Zagier and Urruty*, 1992, US$10; available in shops in Calafate and Chaltén. For trekking on horseback with guides: *Rodolfo Guerra*, T493020; *El Relincho*, T493007; *Albuergue Los Nires*, T493009. Prices: Laguna Capri US$20; Laguna Torre US$25; Río Blanco, Piedra del Fraile and Laguna Toro all US$30 each.

El Chaltén

Phone code: 02962 Northwest of Calafate by 230 km is this small village at the foot of Fitz Roy. It was founded in 1985 for military reasons to settle the area and pre-empt Chilean territorial claims, and still has something of a frontier feel about it. Growing rapidly as a centre for trekking and climbing, it also offers cross-country skiing opportunities in winter. Local trekking information is available from the national park office. The *Día de la Tradición* on 10 November is celebrated with gaucho events, riding and a barbecue (US$5).

Sleeping **L** *Hostería El Puma*, T493017, fitzroyexpediciones@infovia.com.ar With breakfast, comfortable, lounge with log fire. Recommended. **L** *La Aldea*, T493040, laldearg@internet.siscotel.com 5-bed apartments. **A** *Posada Lago del Desierto*, T493010, alessandra@arnet.com.ar good beds, *comedor*, Italian spoken, camping US$5. **B** *Fitz Roy Inn*, T493062, caltur@cotecal.com.ar with breakfast, restaurant, also **D** in shared cabins; opposite is **D** *Albergue Patagonia*, T461564, chalten1@hostels.org.ar Dormitory accommodation (**F**), kitchen and laundry facilities, TV and video, book exchange, accepts TCs, comfortable, Hostelling International discounts, mountain bike rental US$20 per day, reservations for local excursions (Lago del Desierto, Lago Viedma boat trip, ice trek on Cerro Torre glacier). Highly recommended. Next door is their restaurant *Bar de Ahumados*, regional specialities, homemade pastas, local ice cream. **B** *Estancia La Quinta*, 3 km from Chaltén, half-board, no heating, prepares lunch for trekkers. Recommended. **B** *La Base*, Av del Desierto, T493031. With bath, **D** shared room, nice atmosphere, kitchen facilities, video rental, hot water, heating, helpful. **D-E** *Albergue Rancho Grande*, T493005, rancho@cotecal.com.ar Small dormitories, good bathrooms, laundry and kitchen facilities, Hostelling International discounts, English, Italian, French, German spoken, highly recommended, reservations in *Chaltén Travel*, Calafate, T491833. **D** *Cabañas Cerro Torre*, T49306l, built for the Herzog film *El Grito de la Piedra*, cabins sleep 4/6, kitchenette. **D** *Cabaña de Miguel*, shared cabins. **D** *Casa de Piedra*, T493015, in shared cabins, also **AL** 4-bed cabins with bath, new restaurant, trekking guides (English, French and Italian spoken). **E** *Albergue Los Nires*, T493009, small dormitories, also camping, US$5. **E** *Despensa 2 de Abril*, one room, cheapest.

Camping *Camping Madsen* (free). *Ruca Mahuida*, T493018, very helpful, US$6, showers, stores gear, recommended; 2 free campsites. A stove is essential for camping as firewood is scarce and lighting fires is prohibited in campsites in the national park. Take plenty of warm clothes and a good sleeping bag. It is possible to rent equipment in El Chaltén, ask at park entrance. Equipment and cycles for hire at artésania shop on road to *Camping Madsen*, past Albergue Patagonia. All campsites in national park free, no toilets, please bury your waste. Hot showers available at *Albergue Patagonia* and *Confiteria La Senyera*, US$2.

Mid-range *Josh Aike*, excellent *confitería*, homemade food, beautiful building. Recommended. *La Senyera del Torre*, excellent bread. Use of shower US$2. Recommended. *The Wall Pub*, breakfasts and meals, interesting, shows videos of ascents of Fitz Roy and Cerro Torre.

Eating

Viento Oeste, T493021, rents and sells mountain equipment. There are several small shops selling food, gas and batteries (*Despensa 2 de Abril* is said to be cheapest) but buy supplies in Calafate (cheaper and more choice). Many places bake good bread. Fuel is available.

Shopping

Climbing Base camp for climbing Fitz Roy is Campamento Río Blanco (see above). Most of the peaks in the Fitz Roy massif are for very experienced climbers as is the Campo de Hielo Continental (Icefields) which mark the frontier with Chile (no access from Chile). Ask Sr Guerra about hiring animals to carry equipment. *Fitz Roy Expediciones*, in Chaltén, T493017, F491364, owned by experienced guide Alberto del Castillo, organizes adventure excursions including on the Campo de Hielo Continental, 8 hrs, US$75 including equipment, highly recommended, English and Italian spoken. For the icefields guides are essential; necessary gear is double boots, crampons, pickaxe, ropes, winter clothing; the type of terrain is ice and rock and you need to be in good condition. Permits for climbing are available at the national park information office.

Sports
The best time is mid-Feb to end-Mar; Nov-Dec is very windy; Jan is fair; winter is extremely cold

The park information centre provides photocopied maps of treks but the best is one published by *Zagier and Urruty*, US$10, available in shops in Calafate and Chaltén. For

Trekking

The Far South

trekking by horseback with guides: Rodolfo Guerra, T493020; El Relincho, T493007; Albergue Los Ñires, T493009. Prices: Laguna Capri US$20; Laguna Torre US$25, Río Blanco US$30, Piedra del Fraile US$30, Laguna Toro US$30.

Transport **Bus** Daily buses from **Calafate**, 4 hrs, US$25 one way. Run by *Chaltén Travel* and *Caltur*. Oct-Apr 0730, 0800, 0830, plus 1800, 1830, 1900 Dec-Feb, returning from El Chaltén 1700, 1730, 1800, plus 0500 (connection to Río Gallegos), 0700 and 0730, Dec-Feb; May-Sep 1 bus daily, Jun-Aug 1 bus every 3 days (ask at information centre). Best to book return before departure during high season. Day trips from Calafate involve too much travelling and too little time to see the area. Some agencies offer excursions, for example return travel by regular bus and 1 night accommodation US$79. Off season, travel is difficult: little transport for hitching. Agencies charge US$200 one way for up to 8 people, US$300 return. If you need a mechanic ask for Julio Bahamonde or Hugo Masias.

Lago del Some 37 km north of El Chaltén and surrounded by forests, this lake is reached
Desierto by an unpaved road which leads along the Río de las Vueltas via Laguna Condor, where flamingos can be seen. Earlier in the 1990s it was the site of a border dispute with Chile. A path runs along the east side of the lake to its northern tip, from where a trail leads west along the valley of the Río Diablo to Laguna Diablo. There is a campsite at the southern end of the lake and *refugios* at its northern end and at Laguna Diablo. Excursions from El Chaltén by *Chaltén Travel* daily in summer; daily boat trips on the lake on *Mariana* 1030, 1330, 1630, two hours, US$30 (details and booking, *Hotel El Quijote*, Calafate).

Tierra del Fuego

14

Tierra del Fuego

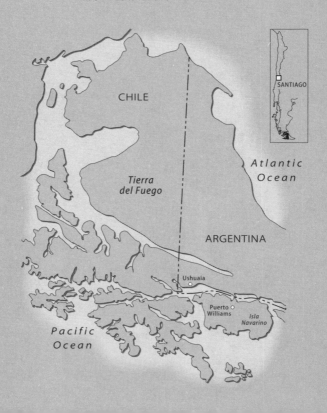

Tierra del Fuego really feels like the bottom of the world. The north is a desolate land of vast sheep farms; further south are mountains, icy blue glaciers, lakes, and forests which turn golden in the autumn. The island is now divided between Argentina and Chile; both are covered in this section, which also includes the Chilean island of Isla Navarino to the south. The main centre is the Argentine city of Ushuaia, which is a base for visiting the mountains and for boat trips along the Beagle Channel; travel in Chilean Tierra del Fuego is time-consuming, but provides an unforgettable adventure. On the southern shore of the Beagle Channel is Puerto Williams on Isla Navarino; to the south of Isla Navarino lies Cape Horn.

Background

History Human habitation of Tierra del Fuego dates back some 10,000 years; four indigenous groups inhabited the island until the early 20th century. The most numerous, the Onas (also known as the Selk'nam), were hunter-gatherers in the north, living mainly on guanaco and several species of rodents. The southeastern corner of the island was inhabited by the Haus or Hausch, also hunter-gatherers, of whom very little is known. The Yaganes or Yámanas lived along the Beagle Channel and on the islands further south. A seafaring people who lived mainly on seafood, fish and seabirds, they were physically smaller than the Onas, but with a strongly developed upper body for rowing long distances. The fourth group, the Alacalufe, lived in the west of Tierra del Fuego as well as in the Chonos Archipelago, surviving by fishing and hunting seals.

The first Europeans to visit the island came with the Portuguese navigator Fernão Magalhães (Magellan), who, in 1520, sailed through the channel that bears his name. The tradition is that, seeing fires lit on shore, Magellan and his crew called the place 'the land of fire' – Tierra del Fuego. But as a result of numerous maritime disasters, including the failure of Sarmiento de Gamboa's attempt at colonising the Straits in 1584, the indigenous population were left undisturbed for three centuries.

FitzRoy and Darwin's visits in 1832 and 1833 were a precursor to determined attempts to convert the Indian groups. Several disastrous missions followed; the first successful mission was established in 1869. In 1884, the Reverend Thomas Bridges founded a mission at Ushuaia. Bridges was the first European to learn the Yámana language, which eased his task. He soon had many Yámana settled around Ushuaia, and compiled his Yámana-English dictionary for the ease of conversion. After his visit, Charles Darwin had written that the Yámana language "barely deserves to be called articulate". But Yámana turned out to be an extraordinarily rich language – the dictionary had 32,000 words, and was not complete at the time of Bridges' death.

The work of the missionaries was disturbed by two developments: the discovery of gold and the growth of sheep farming. The Ona were attracted to the 'white guanacos' on their land and hunted them. The colonists responded by paying two sheep for each Indian that was killed (proof of their murder was provided by a pair of Indian ears). All Indian groups were further ravaged by epidemics of European diseases. In a desperate attempt to save the Ona, Salesian missionaries founded three missions in the Magellan Straits; but, stripped of their land, they lost their will to live – the last Ona died in 1999. The Hausch also became extinct. One old Yámana lady presently survives near Puerto Williams, and a handful of Alacalufe at Puerto Edén in the Chonos Archipelago.

Imprecision in the original colonial land division and the greed of the rush southwards led to border disputes between Argentina and Chile. These still rumble on today. The initial settlement of the dispute in 1883 was followed by a desire by both governments to populate the area by allocating large expanses of land for sheep farming. The main beneficiaries of this policy on Tierra del Fuego were the Menéndez and Braun families, already established in Punta Arenas.

Recommended reading on Tierra del Fuego: *Savage – The Life and Times of Jemmy Button* by Nick Hazelwood (Hodder & Stoughton, 2000). See also the reading list, page 71.

Things to do

- Fish on Lago Blanco – one of the remotest spots in the whole of Chilean Patagonia with some of the best fishing in Chile.
- Go to the Museo Martín Gusinde in Puerto Williams, a tribute to the lost peoples of Tierra del Fuego.
- Trek on Isla Navarino for the fantastic views of the forests and glaciers around.
- Cruise to Cape Horn – for the voyage through the icy, beautiful channels, and, on arrival, to stand on the cliff above the mist and waves with rain lashing into your face on the back of 100 km per hour winds.
- Take the southernmost train in the world in Ushuaia – a must for train buffs.
- Visit Estancia Harberton to get a sense of the endurance and bravery of the early pioneers to Tierra del Fuego.

Tierra del Fuego is separated from the South American mainland by the **Geography** Magellan Strait to the north; to the east is the Atlantic Ocean; the Beagle Channel to the south separates it from the southern islands; a complex network of straits divide it from the Pacific Ocean to the west.

The north of Tierra del Fuego is steppe, but further south the island is crossed from east to west by the continuation of the Andes; in the Argentine sector these rise to around 1,500 m, but in the Chilean part, in the far southwest, there are peaks of well over 2,000 m. The main rivers drain into the Beagle Channel and into Lago Fagnano, the largest lake on the island, which straddles the frontier between Chile and Argentina. There are numerous other lakes including Lagos Yehuín and Chapelmuth, just north of Lago Fagnano in Argentine territory, and Lagos Blanco, Chico and Lynch in Chilean territory.

The northern and southern parts of the island have contrasting vegetation: the steppe is sprinkled with grassland, while further south sub-Antarctic forests grow on hills up to about 600 m. Poorly drained low-lying areas in the south are covered with Sphagnum moss. Wildlife includes guanacos and red foxes; musk rats, beaver and rabbits have been introduced. In summer, wild geese and ducks can be seen; 150 bird species have been identified. The Bahía San Sebastián is an important area for migratory birds. Trout and salmon inhabit nearly all the lakes and rivers.

The island's climate is sub-Antarctic. In Ushuaia southwesterly winds prevail, **Climate** ranging from 15 km per hour to 100 km per hour. September to March are the windy months, while winter is normally calmer. In winter, average daily temperatures hover around zero but in summer they range from 15°C during the day to 5°C at night. Further north, in Río Grande, westerly winds blow up to 200 km per hour almost all year round; average temperatures range from -3°C to 2°C in winter and from 5°C to 15°C in summer. Rainfall is higher in Ushuaia than further north; in Río Grande most rain falls in summer and autumn.

Chilean Tierra del Fuego forms part of Región XII (Magallanes), the capital of **Government** which is Punta Arenas. Argentine Tierra del Fuego belongs to the Province of **& economy** Tierra del Fuego, Antártida y Las Islas del Atlántico Sur, the capital of which is Ushuaia. The population of the Argentine sector is around 70,000, most of whom live in the two towns of Río Grande and Ushuaia. Chilean Tierra del Fuego has a population of 7,000, most of whom live in Porvenir.

For many years the main economic activity of the northern part of the island was sheep farming, but Argentine government tax incentives to companies in the 1970s led to the establishment of new industries in Río Grande and Ushuaia and a rapid growth in the population of both cities; the subsequent withdrawal of incentives has produced increasing unemployment and migration. The island is the site of the smallest and most southerly oil refinery in the world in Argentine San Sebastián. Tourism is increasingly important in Ushuaia.

Ins and outs

Getting there **Air** Flights to and from the island are heavily booked in summer, especially in Jan. See under Porvenir. **Ferry** There are 2 crossings. **Punta Arenas to Porvenir**: the *Melinka* sails from Tres Puentes (5 km north of Punta Arenas, bus A or E from Av Magallanes, US$1; taxi US$3) at 0900 daily except Mon in season, less frequently off season, 2½ hr crossing (can be rough and cold; watch for dolphins), US$7 per person, US$10 per motorbike, US$44 per vehicle. Return from Porvenir 1500 (1700 Sun, no service Mon). Timetable dependent on tides and subject to change: check in advance. Reservations essential especially in summer (at least 24 hrs in advance for cars), obtainable from *Agencia Broom*, Bulnes 05075, T218100, F212126. The ferry company accepts no responsibility for damage to vehicles on the crossing. **Punta Delgada to Punta Espora**: this short crossing is via the *Primera Angostura* (First Narrows), 170 km northeast of Punta Arenas. There are several crossings a day; schedules vary with the tides. Pedestrians US$2.40, motorbikes US$6, US$20 per car one way. The ferry takes about 4 trucks and 20 cars; before 1000 most space is taken by trucks. There is no bus service to or from this crossing; but, if hitching, note that this is the principal route from Ushuaia north to mainland Argentina.

Getting around Throughout Tierra del Fuego the roads are narrow and gravelled. The exceptions are San Sebastián (Argentina)-Ushuaia, which is paved, and the road for about 50 km east of Porvenir, which is being widened. Fuel is available in Porvenir, Cerro Sombrero and Cullen (Chile), and Río Grande, Ushuaia and San Sebastián (Argentina).

Chilean Tierra del Fuego

Porvenir

Phone code: 061
Colour map 7, grid B1
Population: 4,500

Founded in 1894 as a port serving the sheep *estancias* of the island, Porvenir is the only town in Chilean Tierra del Fuego. It is quiet and pleasant. Many people are of Croatian descent; the signpost at the port marks the distance to Croatia. There is a small museum, the **Museo Fernando Cordero Rusque**, Samuel Valdivieso 402, with archaeological and photographic displays on the Onas, as well as sections on natural history and gold mining.

Sleeping **Porvenir** **AL** *Los Flamencos*, Tte Merino, T580049. Best. **C** *Central*, Phillippi 298, T580077. Hot water. **C** *España*, Croacia 698, T380160. Good restaurant with fixed price lunch. **C** *Hostal Patagonia*, Schythe 230, T580227. **C** *Res Los Cisnes*, Soto Salas 702, T580227. **C** *Rosas*, Phillippi, T580088. With bath, hot water, heating, restaurant and bar. Recommended. **F** *Miramar* Santos Mardones 366 (**E** with full board). Clean, friendly, heaters in rooms, hot water, good. **F** *Res Colón*, Damián Ríobó 198, T580108. Also full board.

Gold fever

The Tierra del Fuego Gold Rush began with Julio Popper. Popper settled in San Sebastián in 1887, where he founded the El Paramó mine. He died young in 1893, by which time his company had extracted 600 kilos of gold from El Paramó and from along the Beagle Channel. After his death, gold mining became a much larger scale business. But in 1909 the gold suddenly ran out. Despite its short life the gold rush had lasting consequences. Many prospectors came from North America and Europe hoping to get rich. The largest group were Croats from Dalmatia, then part of the Austrian Empire; many of their descendants still live in the area.

Elsewhere At Cerro Sombrero, 46 km south of Primera Angostura: **F** *Hostería Tunkelen*. Recommended. **G** *Pensión del Señor Alarcón*. Good, friendly. *Posada Las Flores*, Km 127 on the road to San Sebastián, reservations via *Hostal de la Patagonia* in Punta Arenas. *Refugio Lago Blanco*, on Lago Blanco, Punta Arenas T241197.

For accommodation at San Sebastián see below

Mid-range *Club Croata*, Senoret y Phillippi, good food but pricey. **Mid-range/ cheap** *Restaurante Puerto Montt*, Croacia 1169, for seafood, recommended. Many lobster fishing camps where fishermen will prepare lobster on the spot.

Eating

Air From Punta Arenas – weather and bookings permitting, *Aerovías DAP*, Of Foretic, T80089, Porvenir, fly 2 or 3 times daily, US$30 one way. Heavily booked so make sure you have your return reservation confirmed. **Bus** Two a week between Porvenir and Río Grande (Argentina), Tue and Sat 1400, 5 hrs, *Transportes Gessell*, Duble Almeyda 257, T580488 (in Punta Arenas: José Menéndez 556, T222896). US$20 heavily booked; Río Grande-Porvenir, Wed and Sun 0800. **Ferry** Porvenir is accessible by the *Melinka* ferry from Punta Arenas (6 weekly). Terminal at Bahía Chilota, 5 km west. From bus terminal to ferry, taxi US$6, bus US$1.50. **Hitchhiking** The road from Porvenir to Cameron and on to Lago Blanco has little traffic, but there are a few vehicles daily in summer. Waiting on a windswept plain for hours may not be to everyone's liking, but hitching is possible.

Transport

Exchange At *Estrella del Sur* shop, Santos Mardones. Remember that dollars are widely accepted in Argentina.

Directory

Cameron, the only other settlement of any size on the Chilean part of the island, lies 149 km southeast of Porvenir on the opposite shore of Bahía Inútil. About 90 km from Porvenir is a crossroads; north to San Sebastián, south to Cameron. Nearing Cameron the southern mountains loom ahead and the road passes secluded canyons and bays. There are a few farms (more before Cameron than after it). If hitching note that the road to Lago Blanco forks east just before Cameron; there is an abandoned police post here where stranded hitchhikers can keep warm. ■ *Getting there: to Cameron from Porvenir from Calle Manuel Señor, Mon and Fri 1700, US$10.*

Cameron & beyond

From Cameron a road runs southeast towards Estancia Vicuña. About 60 km from Cameron is an airfield. Some 40 km further east is a junction: north for San Sebastián and south for the farm of Sección Río Grande (7 km from the junction) and Estancia Vicuña (a further 35 km). The road climbs into the hills, through woods where guanacos hoot and run off into glades and the banks of red and purple moss. The south shores of **Lago Blanco** can be reached by cutting through woods from Sección Río Grande – superb views of the mountains surrounding the lake and the snows in the south – or from Estancia Vicuña. In the centre of the lake is Isla Victoria, with accommodation (see above). Beyond

Tierra del Fuego

Shipwrecked in the Magellan Straits

The Estrecho de Magallanes, 534-km long, is a treacherous sea passage with a long history of claiming victims. The hostile conditions are eloquently conveyed in the words of Sir John Narborough: "horrible like the ruins of a world destroyed by terrific earthquakes."

From the Atlantic end the first navigational problem facing sailors is simply the difficulty of entering the Straits against the fierce westerly gales which prevail. Once in the straits the dangers are far from over: many ships have fallen victim to the notorious Williwaws, winds with the ferocity of tornados which spring up from nowhere, or the vicious Pamperos, which blow off the land with enough force to capsize a vessel.

Though in 1520 Magellan succeeded in passing through the straits which bear his name, few others managed to do so in the years which followed: of 17 ships which attempted the passage in the early 16th century, only one, the Victoria, succeeded in reaching the Pacific and returning to Europe.

Twelve were lost near the eastern entrance and four returned in failure. The great attraction which drove these early navigators was the lure of a short route between Europe and the spices of the East. Once it was clear that there was no short route, it was still a useful way for Europeans to reach the rich Pacific ports of Peru and Chile without disembarking and crossing Mexico or Panama on foot or by mule.

Even with the development of advanced navigation techniques in the 19th century, losses continued: in 1869, for instance, the Santiago, an iron paddle steamer built in Glasgow and owned by the Pacific Mail line, went down off Isla Desolación at the western end with a cargo of gold and silver. While the Panama Canal now provides a shorter route between the Atlantic and Pacific Oceans, increases in ships' size mean that the Straits are still a busy shipping route. The most common cargo is now oil; casualties still occur with, of course, the added risk of environmental disaster from oil spillage.

Vicuña a horse trail leads across the Darwin Range to **Yendegaia**; very remote, only for the experienced, used almost exclusively by *carabineros* patrolling from Yendegaia. From there you must retrace your steps as you cannot get permission to cross the border to Ushuaia or get a Chilean exit stamp.

Border with Argentina
Argentine time is one hour ahead of Chilean time, March-October

The only legal crossing between the Chilean and Argentine parts of Tierra del Fuego is 142 km east of Porvenir. There are two settlements called San Sebastián, one on each side of the border, but they are 14 km apart; taxis may not cross. Going into Argentina make sure you get an entry stamp for as long as you require. **Sleeping B** *Hostería de la Frontera*, with bath. Basic accommodation in annex, **F**, sleeping bag essential, dirty.

Argentine Tierra del Fuego

Río Grande

Phone code: 02964
Colour map 7, grid B2
Population: 35,000

Situated 87 km south of San Sebastián, Río Grande lies on the southern edge of the Bahía San Sebastián. The largest settlement in Tierra del Fuego, it is a sprawling modern town in windy, dust-laden, sheep-grazing and oil-bearing plains. The *frigorífico* (frozen meat) plant and sheep shearing shed are among the largest in South America.

There is a small museum, the **Museo de Ciencias Naturales y História**, at El Cano 225. Tourist office at the Municipalidad, on Elcano, Monday-Friday. ■ *Tue-Fri 0900-1700. Sat-Sun 1500-2000.*

Salesian Missions

Founded in 1893 by José Fagnano, La Candelaria was one of three missions set up by the Salesians to try to protect the Onas of Tierra del Fuego from the gold prospectors and estancieros (sheep farmers). The first was established in Punta Arenas in 1886; the second, on Isla Dawson, two years later. The latter quickly *attracted over 1,000 Onas, shipped there by the estancieros. It was finally closed in 1920, by which time the anthropologist Martín Gusinde counted only 276 surviving Onas, most of them on an estancia owned by the Bridges family, see box on page 489.*

The Salesian Mission of **La Candelaria** is 11 km north along Route 3; has a historical museum housing a collection of Indian artefacts and also a natural history section. ■ *Mon-Sat 1000-1230, 1500-1900, Sun 1500-1900, US$1.50. Afternoon teas, US$3.* Nearby is the first parish church of Río Grande.

At **Estancia María Behety**, 18 km southwest, horses can be hired. **Refugio Dicky** is a private bird sanctuary covering 1,900 ha on Bahía San Sebastián.

AL *Atlántida*, Belgrano 582, T/F431914, said to be best, without breakfast, restaurant, parking. **AL** *Posada de los Sauces*, El Cano 839, T/F430868, with breakfast, good beds, comfortable, good restaurant, bar. Recommended. **A** *Federico Ibarra*, Rosales y Fagnano, T432485, with breakfast, good beds, large rooms, excellent restaurant. **A** *Isla del Mar*, Güemes 963, T/F422883, next to bus terminal, with breakfast. **A** *Los Yaganes ACA*, Belgrano 319, T430823, F423897, comfortable, good expensive restaurant. **B** *Hosp Noal*, Rafael Obligado 557, lots of bread and coffee for breakfast, cosy. Recommended. **B** *Res Rawson*, Estrada 750, T425503, F430352, cable TV, clean, poor beds. **B** *Villa*, San Martín 277, T422312, without breakfast, very warm. **C** *Hostería Antares*,

Sleeping
■ *on map*
Price codes: see inside front cover
Accommodation can be difficult to find if arriving at night

Río Grande

N
Not to scale

■ **Sleeping**

1 Atlántida	4 Hostería Antares	7 Posada de los Sauces
2 Federico Ibarra	5 Isla del Mar	8 Residencial Rawson
3 Hospedaje Noal	6 Los Yaganes	9 Villa

Tierra del Fuego

Echeverría 49, T421853. **Camping** *Club Naútico Ioshlelk-Oten*, Montilla 1047, 2 km from town on river. Clean, cooking facilities, camping inside heating building in cold weather. The gym has free hot showers for men, as has the ACA garage on the seafront.

Eating **Mid-range** *Club de Pesca*, El Cano, unsurprisingly, specialises in seafood; *Don Rico*, Belgrano y Pento Moreno, in ultra-modern building, interesting, closed Mon; *La Nueva Colonial*, Rosales 640, pizzeria, friendly. **Mid-range/cheap** *Rotisería CAI*, on Moreno, cheap, fixed price, popular with locals.

Festivals Local festivals are the *Trout Festival*, third Sun in **Feb**; *Snow Festival*, third Sun in **Jul**; *Woodsman Festival*, first week of **Dec**.

Shopping Food is cheaper than in Ushuaia. *La Nueva Piedmontesa*, Belgrano y Laserre, 24-hr food store; *Tia* supermarket, San Martín y Piedrabuena. Good selection. Fill up with gasoline here.

Festivals *Trout Festival*, 3rd Sun in Feb; *Snow Festival*, 3rd Sun in Jul; *Woodsman Festival*, 1st week of Dec.

Transport **Local Car hire**: *Rent-a-Car*, Belgrano y Ameghino, T422657. *Localiza*, at airport, T430482. **Mechanic** and VW dealer: *Viaval SRL*, Pento Moreno 927. **Long distance Air**: Airport 4 km west of town. Bus US$0.50. Taxi US$5. To **Buenos Aires** *Austral* and *Lapa* daily, 3½ hrs direct, otherwise in Río Gallegos. To **Ushuaia**, *LADE* also to **Río Gallegos**, 1 hr (book early in summer, 1 a week). **Bus** All buses leave from terminal, Elcano y Güemes. To **Porvenir**, Chile, 5 hrs, US$20, *Gesell*, Wed, Sun, 0800, meticulous passport and luggage control at San Sebastián. To **Punta Arenas**, Chile, via Punta Delgada, 10 hrs, *Pacheco*, Tue, Thu, Sat 0730, US$30, *Los Carlos*, Mon, Fri, 0700, same price. To **Ushuaia**, *Tecni Austral*, 3-4 hrs, 2 daily, US$15 and *Lider*, 4 daily, US$15,. Also *Tolkeyen*, US$20, 4 daily including at 1900 (which is supposed to connect with service from Punta Arenas, but there are earlier services; don't buy a through ticket Punta Arenas-Ushuaia). No buses to Río Gallegos. Very difficult to hitch to Porvenir or north into Argentina (try the truck stop opposite the bus terminal or the police post 7 km out of town). Hitching to Ushuaia is relatively easy in summer.

Directory **Airline offices** *Aerolíneas Argentinas/Austral*, San Martín 607, T422711. *Lapa*, San Martín 641, T432620. *LADE*, Laserre 425, T422968. **Banks** *Banco de la Nación Argentina*, San Martín 200. *Banco del Sud*, Rosales 241, cash advance on Visa. *Superkiosko*, Piedrabuena y Rosales, cash only. Exchange is difficult: buy Argentine pesos in Chile, or bring dollars. **Communications** Post office: Piedrabuena y Ameghino. **Laundry** *El Lavadero*, P Moreno y 9 de Julio. **Tour companies** *Yaganes*, San Martín 641, friendly and helpful.

Ushuaia

Phone code: 02901
Colour map 7, grid C2
Population: 30,000

The most southerly town in Argentina, and one of the most expensive, Ushuaia is 234 km southwest of Río Grande by a new road via Paso Garibaldi. Founded in 1884, it is situated on the northern shore of the Beagle Channel. Its streets climb steeply towards snow-covered Cerro Martial to the north. There are fine views across the Beagle Channel. The mainstays of the local economy are fishing and tourism.

Thomas and Lucas Bridges

An orphan from Bristol, Thomas Bridges was so named because he was found under a bridge with the letter T on his clothing. Bridges arrived in Tierra del Fuego from the Falkland Islands in 1871 with his wife, young daughter and his adoptive father, Reverend Despard. He remained when Despard left after a massacre of Christians by the Indians. Until his death in 1898, Bridges lived near the shores of the Beagle Channel, first at Ushuaia and then Harberton. Bridges devoted his life to his work with the Yámanas (Yaganes),

compiling an extensive dictionary of their language – there were 32,000 words in the dictionary, which was not complete at his death. Of his six children the most famous was Lucas (1874-1949), who, after spending his early life among the Yámanas and Onas and learning their languages, became an outspoken defender of their rights and an opponent of the early sheepfarmers. His memoirs, Uttermost Part of the Earth (1947), trace the tragic fate of the native population with whom he grew up.

Getting there It is not surprising that Ushuaia is hard to reach. By road, the only scheduled bus connection is the run up to Río Grande, or the direct connections to Punta Arenas. By far the easiest way in is by air, on the daily flights from Buenos Aires, Río Gallegos or Río Grande. **Getting around** Ushuaia is a relatively large town, and it may be worth taking taxis for some of the longer excursions. But everywhere within the central area is easily accessible by foot.

Ins & outs
See page 494 for further details

The old prison, **Presidio**, Yaganes y Gob Paz, at the back of the Naval Base, houses the **Museo Marítimo**, with models and artefacts from seafaring days, the **Museo Antártico** and, in the cells, the **Museo Penitenciario**, which details the history of the prison. ■ *Tue-Sun 1000-1300, 1500-2000. US$7, students US$5.* **Museo del Fin del Mundo**, Maipú y Rivadavia, has small displays on indigenous peoples, missionaries and first settlers, as well as natural history section (you can get an 'end of the world' stamp in your passport), recommended. ■ *Mon-Sun 1000-1300, 1500-1930. US$5, students US$3. T421863.* The building also contains an excellent library with helpful staff and a post office, open afternoons when the main one is closed. **Museo Fueguino**, Gob Godoy, interesting sections on indigenous peoples, videos and library, recommended. ■ *Daily 1100-1800. Free.*

Sights

The tourist office is said to be the 'best in Argentina' San Martín 674, T432000/1, F424550, www.tierradelfuego.org.ar It has literature in English, German and Dutch, helpful, English spoken. Large chart of hotels and prices and information on travel and staying at Estancia Harberton. Has noticeboard for messages. ■ *Mon-Fri 0830-2030, Sat and Sun 0900-2000.* **National Park Office**, on San Martín between Patagonia y Sarmiento, has a small map but not much information. The *ACA* office on Maipú also has maps and information.

Cerro Martial offers fine views down the Beagle Channel and to the north. It is about 7 km behind the town. Catch the chairlift (*Aerosilla*, US$5) by following Magallanes out of town, allow 1½ hours. Pasarela and Kaupen run minibus services, several departures daily in summer, US$5 return. There is skiing on the glacier in winter.

Harberton, 85 km east of Ushuaia, is the oldest *estancia* on the island. Run by descendants of its founder, Thomas Bridges, it offers guided walks through protected forest and refreshments are sold in the *Manacatush confitería*. Camping is possible. T422742. Access is from a dirt road which branches off

Excursions
Other excursions include: to the Parque Nacional Tierra del Fuego (see below); to the Río Olivio falls; to Lagos Fagnano and Escondido

Tierra del Fuego

☞ ## Estancia Harberton

In a land of superlatives, Harberton still stands out as special. The oldest estancia on Tierra del Fuego, it was built by Thomas Bridges in 1886 on a narrow peninsula overlooking the Beagle Channel. President Roca had given him the land for his work among the Yámana and for his help in rescuing victims of the numerous shipwrecks in the channel. Harberton is named after the Devonshire village where Bridges' wife Mary was born. The farmhouse was prefabricated by her carpenter father, and then assembled on a spot chosen by the Yámana Indians as the most sheltered. The English connection is still evident in the neat garden of lawns, shrubs and trees between the jetty and the farmhouse. Behind the buildings is a large vegetable garden, a real rarity on the island. Visitors will notice that there is much more wildlife around the estancia than in the Tierra del Fuego National Park.

Harberton is a working farm, run by Thomas Goodall, great-grandson of the founder. Visitors receive a conducted tour of the farm buildings and immediate surroundings: though there are guides, Thomas in his dungarees and horn-rimmed glasses, and his wife, Natalie, are usually also on hand. Natalie is an internationally recognized expert on whales and dolphins, which accounts for the whale jawbone arch over the garden entrance. Rounding off this beautiful and fascinating place, there is also a 'house of bones' where dolphin, whale and seal carcasses are cleaned and labelled for research, and entire skeletons displayed.

Route 3, 40 km east of Ushuaia and runs past Lago Victoria, then 25 km through forest before the open country around Harberton. Some parts of the road are bad; tiring driving which takes five hours there and back. Tours are offered by agencies in Ushuaia. By land they cost US$30 plus US$7 entrance; take your own food if not wishing to buy meals at the *estancia*. A track continues east along the channel through wild country towards very isolated *estancias*. For excursions to Harberton by boat see below.

Sea trips
The Beagle Channel can be rough but it is highly recommended

Trips to along the Beagle can be booked through most agencies. The main trips are: to the sea lion colony at Isla de los Lobos, two hours on the *Ana B*, US$35, four hours on the *Tres Marías*, US$40; to Lapataia Bay and Isla de los Lobos, five hours on the *Ezequiel MB*, US$35; to Isla de los Lobos and Estancia Harberton, six hours on the *Luciano Beta*, US$75, Tuesday, Thursday, Saturday; to Isla de los Lobos and the Isla Martillo Penguin colony, four hours on the *Luciano Beta*, US$60. Some tour agencies imply that their excursions to Harberton go to the *estancia* though in fact they only go to the bay; others go by inflatable launch from main boat to shore. Check thoroughly in advance. Food and drink on all boats is expensive, best to take your own.

Sleeping
■ *on map, page 492*
Price codes: see inside front cover

Prices double on 12 Dec and accommodation may occasionally be hard to find from Dec-Mar. The tourist office will help with rooms in private homes and with campsites. Accommodation, food and drink are all expensive. There is no youth hostel in Ushuaia. Hostel for sporting groups only at Haruwen Sports Complex.

On the road to the Martial Glaciar overlooking the city are: **LL *Las Hayas***, Km 3, T430710, F430719, lashayas@overnet.com.ar Colourful large rooms, pool, and **LL *del Glacier***, Km 3.5, T430640, F430636. Modern, casino, pool rooms, shuttle to/from *Hotel Albatros*. Also outside the city **L *Tolkeyen***, at Estancia Río Pipo 5 km from town, T422637, tolkeyen@tierradelfuego.org.ar With recommended restaurant *Tolkeyen* (see below). Others at **L** are ***Albatros***, Lasserre y Maipú, T430003, F430666, glaciar@

infovia.com.ar Modern, includes breakfast, good views; and *Ushuaia*, Laserre 933, 1 km north of town, T430671, F424217. With breakfast, restaurant, sauna. **L-AL** *Las Lengas*, Florencia 1722, T423366, F424599, laslengas@tierradelfuego.org.ar Superb setting, heating, good dining room. **AL** *Cabo de Hornos*, San Martín y Rosas, T422187, F422313, cabohornos@tierradelfuego.org.ar Comfortable, good value, often full, restaurant (residents only). **AL** *Canal Beagle*, Maipú y 25 de Mayo, T421117, F421120. *ACA hotel*, restaurant. **AL** *César*, San Martín 753, T421460, F432721, cesarhostal@infovia.com.ar Comfortable, including breakfast. Recommended. **AL** *Malvinas*, Deloqui 615, T/F422626. Without breakfast, pleasant, helpful, central heating. Recommended. **A** *Fernández*, Onachaga 72, T421192. With breakfast, good beds.

A *La Posada*, San Martín 1299, T433330, laposada@tierradelfuego.org.ar With breakfast, good. **A** *Posada Fin del Mundo*, Valdez 281, T434847, F424755. Family atmosphere. Recommended. **B** *Hostería Alakaluf*, San Martín 146, T436705, F431603. Without breakfast, quiet. **B** *Hostería América*, Gobernador Paz 1665, T423358, F431362. Without breakfast, modern. **B** *Maitén*, 12 de Octubre 140, T422745, F422733. Good value, 1 km from centre, no singles, 10% discount for ISIC and youth card holders. **B** *Mustapic*, Piedrabuena 238, Breakfast extra, poor beds, great views. **D** pp *Albergue de Mochilero*, 25 de Mayo 237, T436129, F431190, refmoch@satlink.com Small dormitories with kitchen facilities. **D** pp *Alojamiento Internacional*, Deloqui 395, T423483. Very basic, scruffy, dormitory, take sleeping bag, no security, good meeting place, changes money. **D** pp *Hosp Torres al Sur*, Gob Paz 1437, T430745, F437291, ushuaia@hostels.org.ar HI-affiliated, heating, good atmosphere, kitchen facilities, some long-term residents. **D** pp *Hostal Home*, Kayen 565. Comfortable, quiet. **D** pp *Kaisken*, Gob Paz 7, T436756, kaisken@tierradelfuego.org.ar Central, breakfast extra, helpful, discount for large groups, shared bath and kitchen, laundry service, internet. **E** pp *Casa Azul*, Las Primulas 283, Barrio Ecológico, T434769. Floor space. **E** pp *Casa de Alba*, Belakamain 247, T430473, www.lacasadealba.freeservers.com Good beds. Recommended. **F** *Violeta de la Montaña*, Belgrano 236, T421884. Large kitchen, helpful.

Accommodation in private homes **A** *Miguel Zapruscky*, Deloqui 271, T421316. **B** without bath, parking, kitchen, English spoken. Recommended. **B** *Familia Cárdenas*, 25 de Mayo 345, T421954. Without bath or breakfast, quiet. **D** pp *Familia Galeazzi*, Gdor Valdez 323, T423213, F432605, in pleasant suburb close to town. Bedrooms in house and 5-bed cabin in garden, excellent food. Highly recommended. **D** pp *María Navarrete*, 25 de Mayo 440, T423068. Without bath or breakfast (US$3 extra), hot water, laundry and cooking facilities. **D** pp *Posada de los Angeles*, Paz 1410, opposite *Torres al Sur*. Dormitories, good kitchen. **E** pp *Silvia Casalaga*, Gob Paz 1380 (Yellow Tower), T423202. Without bath, heating, breakfast extra, no sign. Recommended. List of private accommodation available from the tourist office. Many people offer rooms in private houses at the airport. No accommodation under US$10 per person.

List of private accommodation available from the tourist office. Many people offer rooms in private houses at the airport

At Lago Escondido **B** *Hostería Petrel*, 54 km north of Ushuaia, on the road to Río Grande (bus departs 0900, returns 1500, US$17 return, minimum 4 people), T433569. Trout fishing possible, boat rides, friendly staff. At Lago Fagnano **B** *Hostería El Kaiken*, T492208, 100 km north of Ushuaia on a promontory. Also **C** cheaper rooms and bungalows, good site.

Camping None in town. East of Ushuaia on Route 3 are: *Camping Río Pipo*, Ushuaia Rugby Club (Km 4) **G** per tent, friendly owners, use of kitchen, bus No 2 to centre. *Ushuaia Camping Municipal* (Km 8) **D/E** per tent, toilets, showers. *Camping del Solar del Bosque* (Km 14) **G**, hot showers. *Camping Río Tristen*, in the Haruwen Winter Sports complex (Km 36), T/F424058, **G** per tent, electricity, bar, restaurant. Inside the

Facilities at Kaiken and Petrel are open all year round. These inns are recommended for peace and quiet

Parque Nacional Tierra del Fuego (entry fee US$5) is **Camping Lago Roca**, 18 km from Ushuaia, at Lapataia, by forested shore of Lago Roca, with good facilities, dirty, showers (US$3), noisy, reached by bus Jan-Feb, small shop, cafeteria. **F Hain**, Tolhuin 3 km west on Lago Fagnano, T425951, hot water, clean, bar, restaurant, recommended. There are also 3 sites with no facilities: **Ensenada Camping** 14 km from Ushuaia; **Camping Las Bandurrias** and **Camping Laguna Verde**, both 21 km from Ushuaia.

Eating **Expensive** *Barcleit 1912*, Fadul 148. Cordon bleu cooking at reasonable prices. *Kaupé*, Roca 470. English spoken, excellent food and wine. Recommended. *Volver*, Maipú 37. Sea view, good food and service, not cheap. Best place to eat lamb is at *Tolkeyen*, 5 km from town. **Mid-range** *Barcito Ideal*, San Martín 393. Good, *tenedor libre* US$14, very popular with travellers. *Bidu Bar*, San Martín 898. Good music, lunches, good meeting place. *Café de la Esquina*, San Martín y 25 de Mayo. Nice view, pleasant, not cheap. *Los Amigos*, San Martín 130. Quick service, some cheaper dishes. *Mi Viejo*, Campos 758. Tenedor libre (self-service), good value. *Moustacchio*, San Martín 298. Good fish, good *tenedor libre*, expensive a la carte. **Mid-range/cheap** Good value set lunches at restaurant in *Ushuaia Shopping*, San Martín 788. Excellent home-made chocolate sold at a shop at San Martín 785. *Helados Massera*, San Martín 270-72. Good. The coffee bar at the airport is very expensive. Ask around for *centolla* (king crab) and *cholga* (giant mussels).

Entertainment A popular spot at night is the disco *Siglo* at 9 de Julio y Maipú. Other discos are *Barny's*, Antártida Argentina just off San Martín and *Garage*, San Martín 20; *El Ñaupe*, Gobernador Paz y Fadul. Bar with live music. **12 Oct**: Festival *Founding of Ushuaia*.

Ushuaia

■ Sleeping

1 Albatros	4 Canal Beagle	7 Hospedaje Torres al Sur
2 Albergue del Mochilero	5 César	8 Hostería Alakaluf
3 Cabo de Hornos	6 Fernández	9 Hostería América

Not to scale

Tierra del Fuego

Good boots at *Stella Maris*, San Martín 443. Bookshop at San Martín y 9 de Julio **Shopping** (Ushuaia Shopping). **Supermarkets** *Kelly*, San Martín y Onas, good selection, good climbing and trekking clothing at European prices, clean toilets. *La Anónima*, Rivadavia y Gob Paz. Things are expensive but there are some cheap imported goods, eg electrical equipment and cigarettes.

Sports centre on Malvinas Argentinas on west side of town (close to seafront). Ice skat- **Sports** ing rink at Ushuaia gymnasium in winter. Beachcombing can produce whale bones. **Fishing** Trout, season 1 Nov-31 Mar, licences US$20 per week, US$10 per day. Contact Asociación de Caza y Pesca at Maipú y 9 de Julio, which has a small museum. Fishing excursions to Lago Fagnano are organized by *Yishka*, Gobernador Godoy 115, T431535, F431230. **Skiing, hiking, climbing** Contact *Club Andino*, Fadul 5. **Skiing** A downhill ski run (beginner standard) on Cerro Martial. There is another ski run, Wallner, 3 km from Ushuaia, open Jun-Aug, has lights for night-skiing and is run by *Club Andino*. The area is excellent for cross-country skiing; *Caminante* organizes excursions 'off road'. Northeast of Ushuaia, 20 km, is Valle Tierra Mayor, a large flat valley with high standard facilities for cross country skiing, snow shoeing and snowmobiling; rentals and a cafeteria; bus in the morning and 1400 from *Antartur*, San Martín 638. The Haruwen Winter Sports complex is 36 km east on Route 3.

All agencies charge the same fees for excursions: Parque Nacional Tierra del Fuego, **Tour** 4 hrs, US$25; Lago Escondido, 5 hrs, US$30; Lagos Escondido and Fagnano, 8 hrs, **companies** US$45. With 3 or 4 people it is often only a little more expensive to hire a *remise* taxi (*Carlitos*, San Martín 989, T422222; *Bahía Hermosa*, Belakamain 334, T422233). The 2

largest agencies are: *Rumbo Sur*, San Martín 342, T422441/423085, F430499, rumbosur@satlink.com.ar Runs a range of tours on water and on land and offers a 2-day package to Calafate, US$150 including transport and hotel, good value. Also organises bus to ski slope, very helpful; and *Tolkeyen*, T422150, F430532, pretour@tierradelfuego.org.ar Recommended. Others include *Antartur*, Maipú 237, T423240, nunatak@tierradelfuego. org.ar Owns *Refugio Nunatak*, 10 km from town, walking tours arranged. *All Patagonia*, Juana Fadul 26, T430725, F430707, allpat@satlink.com Amex agent, packages to Cabañas del Martial. *Canal Fun*, Rivadavia 82, T437395, www.canalfun.com Offer a range of activities, riding, 4WD excursions. Recommended. *Turismo de Campo*, 25 de Mayo 76, T437351, F432419, info@turcampo. com *Estancia tourism*, horse riding and trekking. Recommended guide: Domingo Galussio, Intervú 15, Casa 211, 9410 Ushuaia, bilingual, not cheap (US$120), recommended. *Ushuaia Marina*, San Martín 788, T424058, www.ushuaiamarina.com.ar Trips in the yacht Callas in the Beagle Channel and as far as Antarctica.

10 Maitén   13 Ushuaia
11 Malvinas
12 Mustapic

Tierra del Fuego

Transport **Local** **Car hire**: *Tagle*, San Martín y Belgrano, T433084. Good, also *Río Grande*, Elcano 799, T422571, and *Localiza*, in *Hotel Albatros* and at airport. Recommended. T/F430663.

Long distance **Air**: Services are more frequent in high season; in winter weather often impedes flights. In the summer tourist season it is sometimes difficult to get a flight out: it may be worth trying Río Grande. *Aerolíneas Argentinas//Austral, Southern Winds* and *Lapa* to Buenos Aires via Río Gallegos, all year round, 3½ hrs direct. Airport tax for all internal flights except Río Gallegos is US$13. *LADE* to **Comodoro Rivadavia, Gob Gregores, Puerto** Deseado, Río Grande, San Julián and **Santa Cruz** once a week, and Río Gallegos. *AR, Lapa, Southern Winds* also to Calafate. *Southern Winds* to **Bariloche, Córdoba, Mendoza** and **Neuquén**. To **Punta Arenas**, *DAP* once a week, US$120 one way. At the airport ask around for a pilot willing to take you on a 30-min flight around Ushuaia, US$38 per person (best to go in evening when wind has dropped). Alternatively ask about flights at the tourist office in town. Aerial excursions over the Beagle Channel with local flying club, hangar at airport, 3-5 seater planes, 30 mins.

Bus To **Río Grande** 4 hrs, *Tecni Austral* (*Tolkar*, Roca 157, T423396/423304), and *Líder* (Gob Paz 921, T436421), both US$15, 2 a day, and *Tolkeyen Patagonia* (Maipú 237, T/F437073, pretour@tierradelfuego.org.ar), 4 a day US$20. To **Punta Arenas**, *Tecni Austral/Ghisoni*, Mon, Wed, Fri 0700, US$45, and *Tolkeyen/Pacheco*, Tue, Thu, Sat, 0800, 12 hrs, US$50, a comfortable and interesting ride via Punta Delgada. Both also have services through Porvenir. No through services to Río Gallegos (change at Río Grande but book connection in Ushuaia).

Hitching Trucks leave Ushuaia for the refinery at San Sebastián Mon-Fri. It is easy to hitch to Río Grande. A good place to hitch from is the police control on Route 3.

Shipping To **Puerto Williams** (Chile) there are no regular sailings. Yachts based at the *Club Náutico* carry charter passengers in summer, returning the same day (US$50-75 one-way); enquire at the club, most possibilities in Dec because boats visit Antarctica in Jan. Luxury cruises around Cape Horn via Puerto Williams are operated by the Chilean company, *Tierra Austral*, 7/8 days, US$1,260. To **Antarctica** Most tourist vessels to Antarctica call at Ushuaia and, space permitting, take on passengers. Enquire at *Rumbo Sur* or other agencies. All agencies charge similar price, US$2,200 per person for 8/9 day trip, though prices may be lower for late availability, which are posted in window of *Rumbo Sur*.

Train A Decauville gauge train for tourists runs along the shore of the Beagle Channel between the Fin del Mundo station west of Ushuaia and the boundary of the Parque Nacional Tierra del Fuego, 4½ km, 3 departures daily, US$26 (tourist), US$30 (first class), plus US$5 park entrance and US$4 for bus to the station. It is planned to extend the line to Lapataia. Run by *Ferrocarril Austral Fueguino* with new locomotives and carriages, it uses track first laid by prisoners to carry wood to Ushuaia; tickets from Tranex kiosk in the port, T430709, www.trendelfindelmundo.com.ar Sit on left outbound.

Directory **Airline offices** *Aerolíneas Argentinas*, Roca 126, T421218, airport 421265. *LADE*, San Martín 542, loc 2-B, T/F421123, airport T421700. *LAPA*, 25 de Mayo 64, T432112, F432117. *Tapsa*, agent is *Rumbo Sur*, San Martín 342, T422441/423085. **Banks** Banks open 1000-1500 (in summer). Credit cards useful as difficult to change TCs and very high commission (up to 10%). *Banco de la Nación Argentina*, Rivadavia y San Martín, only bank which accepts Chilean pesos. Cash advance on Mastercard at *Banco de Tierra del Fuego*, San Martín 1044, accepts Amex TCs. Tourist agencies and the *Hotel Albatros* also give poor rates. *Listus* record shop, San Martín 973, or sweet shop next

Isla de los Estados

"This long (75 kilometre) and guarded island lies east of Tierra del Fuego. It is famous in Patagonia as the setting for Jules Verne's novel, The Lighthouse at the End of the World – ruins of the lighthouse remain. Except for the caretakers of the lighthouse and an occasional scientist, few people ever set foot on this cloud-shrouded reserve of Fuegian flora and fauna that no longer exist on the main island. During the 18th and 19th centuries, large numbers of ships were wrecked or lost in the treacherous waters surrounding this island. Much gold, silver and relics await salvage." Robert T Cook.

door, for better rates for cash. **Communications** Internet: *Don Guido Cybercafé*, Godoy 45. US$10 per hr, also offers mailbox facilities for email, 0800-2400. Also *Rivadavia 165*, T430565. US$3.50 per hr, Mon-Fri 0900-2200, Sat 0900-1300, 1500-2200, Sun 1600-2000. *Food Garden*, San Martín 312, internet café. **Post office**: San Martín y Godoy. Mon-Fri 0900-1300 and 1700-2000, Sat 0830-1200. **Telephone**: San Martín 1541, San Martín 1541, also internet service at same address, US$5 per hr. **Embassies and consulates** Chile, Malvinas Argentinas y Jainen, Casilla 21, T421279. Finland, Gobernador Paz y Deloqui. **Germany**, Rosas 516. Italy, Yaganes 75. **Laundry** *Kanip 195*, Mon-Sat 0900-2030, US$3 wash, US$3 dry. *Rosas 139*, between San Martín and Deloqui. Open weekdays 0900-2100, US$8.

Parque Nacional Tierra del Fuego

Parque Nacional Tierra del Fuego

Covering 63,000 ha of mountains, lakes, rivers and deep valleys, the park stretches west to the Chilean border and north to Lago Fagnano, though large areas are closed to tourists to protect the environment. The lower parts are forested; tree species include lenga, ñire and coihue. Birdlife includes several species of geese, as well as ducks, Magellanic woodpeckers and austral parakeets. Introduced species, like rabbits, beavers and muskrats, have done serious environmental damage. Near the Chilean border, beaver dams can be seen and with much luck and patience the beavers themselves. Stand still and down-wind of them: their sense of smell and hearing are good, but not their eyesight.

There are several beautiful walks: the most popular ones are an interpreted trail along Lapataia Bay, good for birdwatching; a 5 km walk along Lago Roca to the Chilean frontier at Hito XXIV; and a 2½-km climb to

Tierra del Fuego

Cerro Pampa Alta which offers fine views. Good climbing on Cerro Cóndor, recommended. There are no recognized crossing points to Chile.

Essentials

In winter the temperature drops as low as -12°C, in summer it goes up to 25°C. Even in the summer the climate can often be cold, damp and unpredictable

The park entrance is 12 km west of Ushuaia. Park administration is at **Lapataia Bay**. Entry US$5. In summer buses and mini-buses, US$5, to the park are run by several companies: *Pasarela*, Fadul 5, T421735, leaving from Maipú y Fadul; *Kaupen*, T434015, leaving from Maipú y 25 de Mayo, and *Eben-Ezer*, T431133, leaving from San Martín y 25 de Mayo. Timetables vary with demand, tourist office has details. Ask at the tourist office about cycling tours in the park, US$65 full day, also 'Eco Treks' available and cultural events. It is possible to hitch as far as Lapataia. *Club Andino* in Ushuaia has a booklet explaining routes in the park (in Spanish) with poor maps. See above for camping possibilities.

Isla Navarino (Chile)

Situated on the southern shore of the Beagle Channel, Isla Navarino is unspoilt and beautiful, with a chain of rugged snowy peaks, magnificent woods and many animals; apart from large numbers of beavers which were introduced to the island and have done a lot of damage, guanacos and condors can be seen inland.

Puerto Williams

Phone code: 061
Colour map 7, grid C2
Population: 1,500

The only settlement of any size on the island is Puerto Williams, a Chilean naval base situated about 50 km east of Ushuaia (Argentina). Puerto Williams is the southernmost permanently inhabited town in the world; 50 km east-south-east is Puerto Toro, the southernmost permanently inhabited settlement on earth. Some maps mistakenly mark a road from Puerto Williams to Puerto Toro – this does not exist, access is only by sea. Due to a long-running border dispute with Argentina here, Puerto Williams is controlled by the Chilean Navy. There is a tourist office near the museum (closed in winter; maps are available); ask for details on hiking.

Museo Martín Gusinde, known as the **Museo del Fin del Mundo** ('End of the World Museum') is full of information about vanished Indian tribes, local wildlife, and voyages including Charles Darwin and Fitzroy of the *Beagle*. A visit is highly recommended. ■ *1000-1300, 1500-1800 (Mon-Thu); 1500-1800 (Sat-Sun), Fri closed (subject to change). US$1.*

Excursions

At **Villa Ukika**, 2 km east of town, the last of the Yámana people live. Sights include beaver dams and waterfalls. A kilometre west of the town is the yacht club (one of Puerto Williams' two night-spots); the wharf is a sunken 1930s Chilean warship. Outside the Naval headquarters you can see the bow section of the *Yelcho*, the tug chartered by Shackleton to rescue men stranded on Elephant Island. For superb views, climb Cerro Bandera which is reached by a path from the dam 4 km west of the town (three- to four-hour round trip, steep, take warm clothes). From here a four- to five-day walking circuit – the *Dientes de Navarino* – begins (information in the tourist office at Puerto Williams). Views of Cape Horn in clear weather; conditions change quickly - it can snow on the hills, even in high summer. No equipment rental on island; buy food in Punta Arenas.

A road leads 56 km west of Puerto Williams to Puerto Navarino. There is little or no traffic and it is very beautiful. There are several smallholdings. Forests of lengas come right down to the water's edge. At **Mejillones**, 32 km from

Shackleton, 'Yelcho' and the rescue from Elephant Island

Shackleton's 1914-16 Antarctic expedition is one of the epics of polar exploration. Shackleton's vessel, Endurance, which left England in August 1914 with 28 men aboard, became trapped in pack-ice in January 1915. After drifting northwards with the ice for eight months, the ship was crushed by the floes and sank. With three boats, supplies and the dogs, the group camped on an ice floe which continued to drift north for eight months. In April 1916, after surviving on a diet largely of seals and penguins, the party took to the boats as the ice broke up. After seven days at sea they reached Elephant Island. From there Shackleton and five other men sailed 1,300 kilometres in 17 days to South Georgia, where there were whaling stations. On reaching the south shore of South Georgia, Shackleton and two men crossed the island (the first such crossing and achieved without skis or snowshoes) to find help. Shackleton, from whom nothing had been heard by the outside world since leaving the island 18 months before, was not at first recognized.

The British government sent a rescue vessel to Elephant Island, but the delays involved led Shackleton to seek help locally. After ice had prevented three rescue attempts - the first from South Georgia, the second from the Falkland Islands/Islas Malvinas, and the third from Punta Arenas - Shackleton persuaded the Chilean authorities to permit a fourth attempt using the tug Yelcho. Leaving Punta Arenas on 25 August 1916, the vessel encountered thick fog, but, unusually for the time of year, little ice, and it quickly reached Elephant Island where the men, who had endured an Antarctic winter under upturned boats, were down to four days of supplies.

Though the expedition failed to cross Antarctica, Shackleton's achievement was outstanding: despite the loss of Endurance, the party had survived two Antarctic winters without loss of life. Shackleton himself returned to the region in 1921 to lead another expedition, but in January 1922, though aged only 47, he suffered a fatal heart attack while in South Georgia.

Puerto Williams, is the graveyard and memorial to the Yámana people. Just before *Estancia Santa Rosa* (10 km further on) a path is said to cross the forest, lakes and beaver dams to Wulaia (four to six hours), where the *Beagle* anchored in 1833; however, even the farmer at Wulaia gets lost following this track. At **Puerto Navarino** there are a handful of marines and an abandoned police post, where you may be allowed to sleep. There are beautiful views across to Ushuaia and west to icebound Hoste Island and the Darwin Massif. A path continues to a cliff above the Murray Narrows; blue, tranquil and utterly calm. If trekking alone in wild parts of the island, beware of sinking mud caused by beaver dams; note also that there is quite a high incidence of rabies among domestic and wild animals (including beavers).

A *Hostería Walla*, on the edge of Lauta bay, T4223571, 2 km out of town (splendid walks). Very hospitable. **D** *Jeanette Talavera*, T4621150, sim@entelchile.net Small dormitories, kitchen and laundry facilities. **D** pp *Pensión Temuco*, Piloto Pardo 224. Also half board, comfortable, good food, hot showers. Overpriced, but recommended. **D** pp *Res Onashaga* (run by Señor Ortiz – everyone knows him). Cold, run down, good meals, helpful, full board available. **E** pp *Hostería Camblor*, T4621033, meals served. You can also stay at private houses. Camping wild is cold but easy. There are several small grocery stores; prices are very high because of the remoteness. Beware drinking water from the rivers without purification. Away from the *Club Naútico*, nightlife in Puerto Williams begins and ends at the *Dientes de Navarino*, a bar in the tiny plaza.

Sleeping and eating

Tierra del Fuego

Transport

Sit on the right leaving Punta Arenas: the flight is beautiful

Air From Punta Arenas by air, *Aerovías DAP*, 3 times weekly, US$160 return. Book well in advance; 20 seater Cessna aircraft and long waiting lists (be persistent). Luggage allowance 10 kg (US$2 per kg extra). Free transport from *DAP* office in Punta Arenas to the airport. Also army flights available (they are cheaper), but the ticket has to be bought through *DAP*. *Aeropetrel* will charter a plane to Cape Horn (US$2,600 for 8-10 people).

Ferry From Ushuaia (Argentina), the *Tres Marías*, once a week in summer, 3-4 hr crossing, US$65 per person, take own lunch; irregular service in winter, and frequent schedule changes. **Boats from Punta Arenas**: *Ñandú* or *Ultragas* leaves on a fixed schedule every 10 days, about midnight, reclining chairs, no food, US$50 one way, including meals, 24-36 hrs. Enquire at the office, Independencia 865, next to service station. The *Navarino* leaves Punta Arenas in third week of every month, 12 passengers, US$150 one way; contact the owner, Carlos Aguilera, 21 de Mayo 1460, Punta Arenas, T228066, F248848 or via *Turismo Pehoé*. The *Beaulieu*, a cargo boat carrying a few passengers, sails from Punta Arenas once a month, US$300 return, 6 days. Navy and port authorities in Puerto Williams may deny any knowledge, but everyone else knows when a boat is due. The Naval vessel *PSG Micalvi* sails once every 3 months from Punta Arenas to Cape Horn via Puerto Williams, and *may* take passengers for approximately US$250 to Cape Horn (letters of recommendation will help) – ask at the *Armada* in Punta Arenas. **To Cape Horn**: ask at the yacht club about hitching a ride on a private yacht to Cape Horn. Luxury cruises around Cape Horn are run by *Tierra Austral* for US$800, 6 days. Captain Ben Garrett offers recommended adventure sailing in his schooner *Victory*, from special trips to Ushuaia to cruises in the canals, Cape Horn, glaciers, Puerto Montt, Antarctica in Dec and Jan. Write to *Victory Cruises*, Puerto Williams (slow mail service); Fax No 1, Cable 3, Puerto Williams; phone (call collect) asking for Punta Arenas (Annex No 1 Puerto Williams) and leave message with the Puerto Williams operator. At Cape Horn there is one pebbly beach on the north side of the island; the ship anchors in the bay and passengers are taken ashore by motorised dinghy. A rotting stairway climbs the cliff above the beach, up to the building where three marines run the naval post. A path leads from here to the impressive monument of an Albatross overlooking the wild, churning waters of the Drake Passage below.

Directory

Airline offices *Aerovías DAP*, *LanChile*, *Ladeco* in the centre of town. **Communications** **Post office**: closes 1900. **Telephone**: *CTC*, Mon-Sat 0930-2230, Sun 1000-1300, 1600-2200.

Chilean Pacific Islands

15

Chilean Pacific Islands

Juan Fernández Islands

Far out in the Pacific are two Chilean island possessions, the Juan Fernández Islands, famed for Alexander Selkirk's enforced stay in the 17th century (the inspiration for Defoe's Robinson Crusoe), and the Polynesian island of Rapa Nui, better known as Easter Island (the most isolated inhabited spot on earth). Both possess dramatic views of the Pacific, and Juan Fernández in particular is famous for the huge cliffs which rise sheer from the ocean. While the cost of getting to these islands is prohibitive for many visitors to Chile, both can be reached relatively easily by air from Santiago.

Juan Fernández Islands

History

Phone code: 032
Colour map 3, grid B2
Population: 500

The islands are named after Joao Fernández, a Portuguese in the service of Spain, who was the first European to visit them in 1574. For the next 150 years, they were frequented by pirates and corsairs resting up before attacking the coast of Spanish America. In 1704, Alexander Selkirk, a Scottish sailor, quarrelled with his captain and was put ashore on what is now Isla Robinson Crusoe, where he stayed alone until 1709 – this became the inspiration for *Robinson Crusoe*. It was not until after 1750 that the Spanish took steps to defend the archipelago, founding San Juan Bautista and building seven fortresses. During the Wars of Independence the islands were used as a penal colony, the Spanish deporting Chilean independence leaders captured after the Battle of Rancagua. In 1915 two British destroyers, HMS *Kent* and *Glasgow* cornered the German cruiser, *Dresden*, in Bahía Cumberland. The German vessel, which was scuttled, still lies on the bottom; a monument on shore commemorates the event and, nearby, unexploded shells are embedded in the cliffs. Some of the German crew are buried in the cemetery.

Geography

Situated 667 km west of Valparaíso, this group of small volcanic islands is a national park administered by CONAF. There are three islands: Isla Robinson Crusoe (4,794 ha) which was the home of Alexander Selkirk; Isla Alejandro Selkirk (4,952 ha) the largest, and Isla Santa Clara (221 ha), the smallest. Selkirk's cave on the beach of Robinson Crusoe is shown to visitors. The only settlement is San Juan Bautista, a fishing village of simple wooden frame houses, located on Bahía Cumberland on the north coast of Isla Robinson Crusoe: it has a church, schools, post office, police station and radio station. The islands are famous for *langosta de Juan Fernández* (a pincerless lobster) which is sent to the mainland. In summer, a boat goes once a month between Robinson Crusoe and Alejandro Selkirk if the *langosta* catch warrants it, so you can visit either for a few hours or a whole month.

Best time for a visit:
Oct-Mar

The islands enjoy a mild climate and the vegetation is rich and varied: the Juan Fernández palm, previously used widely for handicrafts, is now a protected species, but the *sandalo* (sandalwood tree), once the most common tree on the

Isla Robinson Crusoe

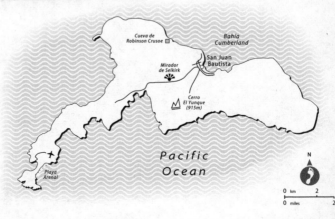

Chilean Pacific Islands

islands, is now extinct owing to its overuse for perfumes. Fauna includes wild goats, hummingbirds and seals. The islands were declared a UN World Biosphere Reserve in 1977. Take insect repellent. There is a CONAF office in San Juan Bautista. ■ *Mon-Fri 0800-1800, with information and advice on the island.*

Sights

The remains of the **Fuerte Santa Bárbara**, the largest of the Spanish fortresses, overlook San Juan Bautista. In the village itself is a Casa de la Cultura, with exhibition rooms. ■ *Mon-Fri 1000-1300 and 1700-2100.* Nearby are the **Cuevas de los Patriotas**, home to the deported Chilean independence leaders. South of the village is the **Mirador de Selkirk**, the hill where Selkirk lit his signal fires. A plaque was set in the rock at the look-out point by British naval officers from HMS *Topaze* in 1868, nearby is a more recent plaque placed by his descendants. Selkirk, a Scot, was put ashore from HMS *Cinque Ports* and was taken off four years and four months later by a privateer, the *Duke*. The mirador is the only easy pass between the north and south sides of the island. A footpath leads further south to the anvil-shaped **El Yunque**, 915 m, the highest peak on the island, where Hugo Weber, a survivor from the *Dresden*, lived as a hermit for 12 years: some remains of his dwelling can be seen. The only sandy beach on Robinson Crusoe is **Playa Arenal**, in the extreme southwest corner, two hours by boat from San Juan Bautista.

Essentials

Sleeping
Lodging with villagers is difficult

San Juan Bautista   AL *Hostería Robinson Crusoe*, T751069. Full board. **B** pp *Alejandro Selkirk*, clean, good food, full board **A** pp. Recommended (Santiago T5313772). **B** *Cabañas Charpentier*, for 4 people, Ignacio Carrera Pinto 256, F751020 (Santiago T2245691). **C** pp *Hostería Cabañas Paulentz*, Ignacio Carrera 120, T751108. With breakfast, comfortable. **C** pp *Hostería Villa Green*, T/F751044. With breakfast, good.

Festival

Each Feb, a yachting regatta visits the islands; setting out from Algarrobo, yachts sail to Isla Robinson Crusoe, thence to Talcahuano and Valparaíso. At this time, Bahía Cumberland is full of colourful and impressive craft, and prices in restaurants and shops double.

Tour operators

Ecoturismo Aventuras, Robinson Crusoe s/n, T751058. Offers horse riding tours. *Endémica Expeditions*, T751077. Offers diving, fishing and trekking. *Marenostrum*, Larraín Alcalde s/n, T751044. Offers underwater excursions. To take a sea tour, it is possible to charter the municipal launch, *Blanca Luz*, which goes to different places and is on Larraín Alcalde 320, T751045. The fishermen's union has 14 launches between them, some of which can be hired.

Transport

Air   Air taxis operate from Santiago (US$370 round trip), by 3 companies: *Transportes Aéreas Isla Robinson Crusoe*, Monumento 2570, Maipú, Santiago, T5314343, F5313772 (leave from Cerrillos, daily in summer if demand is sufficient); *Lassa*, Av Larraín 7941, La Reina, Santiago, T/F2734354, (leave from Tobalaba Aerodrome in Peñalolén, 3 weekly); *Servicio Aéreo Ejecutivo*, Apoquindo 8750, Torre 3, Local 4, T/F2293419. Luggage allowance 10 kg per person, flight takes 2½ hrs. Planes land on an airstrip in the west of the island; passengers are taken by boat to San Juan Bautista (US$3 per person). (1½ hrs, US$10 one way). **Sea**   Boats are operated by *Naviera del Sur* of Valparaíso (Blanco Encalada 1041, of. 18, T594304), leaving in the first week of each month – preference is given to islanders, and passages are sometimes difficult to obtain. Also try some of the following travel agencies: *Agentur*, Huérfanos 757, Of 601,

T337118, Santiago; *Pesquera Chris*, Cueto 622, Santiago, T681-1543, or Cochrane 445 (near Plaza Sotomayor), Valparaíso, T216800, 2-week trips to the island (5 days cruising, a week on the island), from US$200 return. The Chilean Navy have 4 boats a year to the islands, and may take passengers with appropriate credentials – try the Armada at Prat 620 in Valparaíso, T252094.

Directory **Banks** No exchange facilities. Only pesos and US$ cash accepted. No credit cards, no TCs.

Easter Island

History It is now generally accepted that the islanders are of Polynesian origin. Thor Heyerdahl's theories, as expressed in *Aku-Aku, The Art of Easter Island* (New York: Doubleday, 1975), are less widely accepted than they used to be, and South American influence is now largely discounted, see below.

European contact with the island began with the visit of the Dutch admiral, Jacob Roggeven, on Easter Sunday 1722, who was followed by the British navigator James Cook in 1774 and the French sailor Le Perouse in 1786. Between 1859 and 1862 over 1,000 islanders were transported as slaves to work in the Peruvian guano trade. The island was annexed by Chile in 1888. Until 1952 most of Easter Island was leased to a private company which bred sheep on its grasslands: a wall was built around the Hanga Roa area, and the islanders were forbidden to cross.

Geography Isla de Pascua or Rapa Nui lies in the Pacific Ocean just south of the Tropic of
Phone code: 032 Capricorn and 3,790 km west of Chile; its nearest neighbour is Pitcairn Island.
Population 4,000 The island is triangular in shape, with an extinct volcano at each corner. The
original inhabitants called the island Te Pito o te Henua, the navel of the world.
Easter Island is The population was stable at 4,000 until the 1850s, when Peruvian slavers,
always 2 hrs smallpox and emigration to Tahiti (encouraged by plantation owners) reduced
behind the Chilean the numbers. Of the current population about 1000 are from the mainland.
mainland, summer There is one village on the island, Hanga Roa, where most of the population live.
and winter time

Rapa Nui - Easter Island

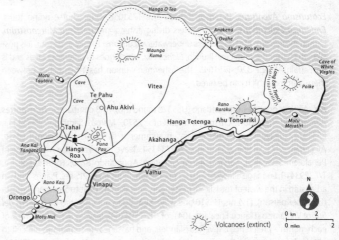

Volcanoes (extinct)

The formation of Easter Island

In geological terms Easter Island is not very old; potassium argon dating shows that its oldest part is under 2.5 million years old. It is located above a tectonic 'hot spot', an active upwelling of liquid rock emerging from beneath the crust of the earth and solidifying. Enough molten rock has poured out to form a mountain nearly 3,000 m high, the altitude of the Easter Island volcano if measured from the sea bed. There are, however, no records of volcanic activity since human occupation of the island began. The three high peaks are all volcanic in origin and consist mainly of basalt. In the cliffs of Rano Kau different layers of basalt can be identified, indicating the existence of distinct lava flows. Caves have been formed where the lava has solidified on the outside but continued to flow downhill on the inside. On Terevaka, where the roofs of some of these caves have collapsed, long caverns up to 10 m high can be seen.

The volcanic nature of the island contributed to the carving of the moai. Extremely hard basalt from Terevaka was used to make some of the hard tools for carving. Sharp edged implements were fashioned using obsidian, volcanic glass formed by lava cooling very rapidly. The moai themselves were carved from tuff, a porous rock much softer than basalt but also volcanic in origin, which can be found at Rano Raruka, a secondary cone on the side of Terevaka.

Unlike most Polynesian islands, Easter Island has no coral reef as winter temperatures are too cold for coral to survive. As a result the coastline has been eroded in parts to form steep cliffs, around Poike, Rano Kao and on the northern side of Terevaka.

Easter Island has no high central plateau and consequently there is little gully erosion which would normally lead to the development of streams and rivers. Moreover much of the island's rainfall drains away underground into the huge caverns formed by the collapse of basalt caves. As a result, although annual rainfall is usually above 1,000 mm, there is always a severe shortage of water and in many years several months of drought.

About half the island, of low round hills with groves of eucalyptus, is used for horses and cattle, and nearly one-half constitutes a national park (■ *US$10, payable at Orongo*). The islanders have preserved their indigenous songs and dances, and are extremely hospitable. Tourism has grown rapidly since the air service began in 1967. Paid work is now more common, but much carving is still done. The islanders have profited greatly from the visits of North Americans: a Canadian medical expedition left a mobile hospital on the island in 1966, and when a US missile-tracking station was abandoned in 1971, vehicles, mobile housing and an electricity generator were left behind.

Average monthly temperatures vary between 15-17°C in August and 24°C in February, the hottest month. Average annual rainfall is 1,100 mm. There is some rain throughout the year, but the rainy season is March-October, with the wettest weather in May. The tourist season is from September-April. **Climate**

Sights

The unique features of the island are the 600 (or so) *moai*, huge stone figures up to 9 m in height and broad in proportion. One of them, on Anakena beach, was restored to its probable original state with a plaque commemorating Thor Heyerdahl's visit in 1955. Other *moai* have since been re-erected. There is an anthropological museum in Hanga Roa, the Museo Antropológico Sebastián Englert, explanations in Spanish only. Most of the

Cultural development

Far from being the passive recipient of external influences, Easter Island shows the extent of unique development possible for a people left wholly in isolation. It is believed to have been colonized from Polynesia about 800 AD: its older altars (ahu) are similar to those of French Polynesia, and its older statues (moai) similar to those of the Marquesas Islands. The very precise stone fitting of some of the ahu, and the tall gaunt moai with elongated faces and ears for which Easter Island is best known were later developments whose local evolution can be traced through a comparison of the remains. Indigenous Polynesian society, for all its romantic idylls, was competitive, and it seems that the five clans which originally had their own lands demonstrated their strength by erecting these complex monuments. The moai were sculpted at the Rano Raraku quarry and transported on wooden rollers over more or less flat paths to their final locations; their red topknots were sculpted at Puna Pau, and then brought to the coast; and the rounded pebbles laid out checkerboard fashion at the ahu all came from the same beach at Vinapu. The sculptors and engineers were paid out of the surplus food produced by the sponsoring family:

Rano Raraku's unfinished moai mark the end of the families' ability to pay. Over several centuries, from about 1400 AD onwards, this stonework slowed down and stopped, owing to the deforestation of the island caused by roller production, and damage to the soils through deforestation and heavy cropping. The birdman cult represented at Orongo is a later development after the islanders had lost their clan territoriality and were concentrated at Hanga Roa, but still needed a non-territorial way to simulate inter-clan rivalry.

The central feature of the birdman cult was an annual ceremony in which the heads of the lineages, or their representatives, raced to the islets to obtain the first egg of the sooty tern (known as the Manutara), a migratory seabird which nests on Motu Nui, Motu Iti and Motu Kao. The winning chief was named Bird Man, Tangata Manu, for the following year. It appears that, in the cult, the egg of the tern represented fertility although it is less clear what the status of the Tangata Manu actually was. The petroglyphs at Orongo depict the half-man, half-bird Tangata Manu, the creator god Make Make and the symbol of fertility, Komari.

objects are reproductions because the originals were removed from the island, but there are good descriptions of island life. ■ US$1.50. Tue-Fri 0930-1230, 1400-1730, Sat/Sun 0930-1230. Sernatur Juumaheke is open from Monday to Friday 0830-1300, 1400-1730.

A tour of the main part of the island can be done on foot, but this would need at least two days, either camping at Anakena or returning to Hanga Roa and setting out again the next day. Most, however, believe that this is far too quick. You could hire a vehicle to see more; horses are also available for hire (for both see below). From Hanga Roa, take the road going southeast past the airport; at the oil tanks turn right to **Vinapu**, where there are two *ahu* and a wall whose stones are joined with Inca-like precision. Head back northeast along the south coast, past **Vaihu** (an *ahu* with eight broken *moai*; small harbour); **Akahanga** (*ahu* with toppled *moai*); **Hanga Tetenga** (one toppled *moai*, bones can be seen inside the *ahu*); **Ahu Tongariki** (once the largest platform, damaged by a tidal wave in 1960, restored with Japanese aid). Turn left to **Rano Raraku** (2 km), the volcano where the *moai* were carved. Many statues can be seen. In the crater is a small lake surrounded by reeds; swimming is possible beyond the reeds. There are good views.

The road heads north past 'the trench of the long-ears' and an excursion can be made to **Poike** to see the open-mouthed statue that is particularly popular with local carvers. Ask the farmer for permission to cross his land. On Poike the earth is red; at the northeast end is the cave where the virgin was kept before marriage to the victor of ceremonies during the birdman cult; ask someone for directions. The road along the north coast passes **Ahu Te Pito Kura** , a round stone called the navel of the world and one of the largest *moai* ever brought to a platform. The road continues to **Ovahe** where there is a very attractive beach with pink sand and some rather recently carved faces and a cave.

From Ovahe, you can return direct to Hanga Roa or continue to **Anakena**, site of King Hotu Matua's village and Thor Heyerdahl's landing place. From Anakena, where there is a white sand beach and palm trees, a coastal path of variable quality runs west, passing interesting remains and beautiful cliff scenery. At **Hanga o Teo**, there appears to be a large village complex, with several round houses, and further on there is a burial place, built like a long ramp with several ditches containing bones. From Hanga o Teo the path goes west then south, inland from the coast, to meet the road north of Hanga Roa.

A six-hour walk from Hanga Roa on the west coast passes **Ahu Tahai** (a *moai* with eyes and topknot in place, cave house, just outside town). Two caves are reached, one inland appears to be a ceremonial centre, the other (nearer the sea) has two 'windows' (take a strong flashlight and be careful near the 'windows'). Further north is **Ahu Tepeu** (broken *moai*, ruined houses). Beyond here you can join the path mentioned above, or turn right to **Te Pahu** cave and the seven *moai* at **Akivi**. Either return to Hanga Roa, or go to Puna Pau crater (two hours), where the topknots were carved.

South of Hanga Roa is **Rano Kau**, an important site where the curious Orongo ruins can be seen. The route south out of Hanga Roa passes the two caves of **Ana Kai Tangata**, one of which has paintings. If on foot you can take a path from the Orongo road, just past the Conaf sign, which is a much shorter route to Rano Kau crater. A lake with many reed islands is 200 m below. On the seaward side is Orongo (■ *US$11*), where the birdman cult flourished, with many ruined buildings and petroglyphs. Out to sea are the 'bird islets', Motu Nui, Motu Iti and Motu Kao. It is very windy at the summit; good views at sunset, or under a full moon. It is easy to follow the road back to Hanga Roa in the dark.

In Hanga Roa is **Ahu Tautira**, next to a swimming area, with cold water, marked out with concrete walls and a breakwater. Music at the 0900 Sunday mass has been described as 'enchanting'. There is a cultural centre next to the football field, with an exhibition hall and souvenir stall.

Recommended reading There is a very thorough illustrated book by J Douglas Porteous, *The Modernization of Easter Island* (1981), available from Department of Geography, University of Victoria, BC, Canada, US$6. See also Thor Heyerdahl's work, details above; *Easter Island, Earth Island*, by Paul Bahn and John Flenley (Thames and Hudson, 1992) for a comprehensive appraisal of the island's archaeology. *Islas Oceánicas Chilenas*, edited by Juan Carlos Castillo (Ediciones Universidad Católica de Chile, 1987), contains much information on the natural history and geography of Juan Fernández and Easter Islands.

Anyone continuing into Polynesia or Melanesia from Easter Island will find David Stanley's *South Pacific Handbook* (Moon Publications Inc, PO Box 3040, Chico, CA 95927, USA, F1-91-63456751) a useful guidebook.

Chilean Pacific Islands

Essentials

Street names are
rarely used. Directions
are given by referring
to local landmarks
such as the church

Food, wine and beer are expensive, often twice the price of the mainland, because of freight charges, but local fish, vegetables, fruit and bread are cheap. Average prices: coffee/tea US$1, meals about US$10 or more, bread US$2 per kilogram, beer/cola US$2 in most bars and restaurants. Bring all you can from the mainland, but not fruit.

Sleeping
■ on map
Price codes:
see inside front cover

Hanga Roa Unless it is a particularly busy season there is no need to book in advance; mainland agencies make exorbitant booking charges. The accommodation list at the airport information desk only covers the more expensive places. Flights are met by large numbers of hotel and *residencial* representatives but it is cheaper to look for yourself. There are even reports of touts approaching passengers at Santiago airport prior to their flight to the island. Accommodation ranges from US$10-200. Room rates, especially in *residenciales* can be much cheaper out of season and if you do not take full board. **L** *Hanga Roa*, Av Pont s/n, T/F100299. Full board, all mod-cons, very luxurious. **L** *Iorana*, Atamu Tekena s/n, Ana Magara promontory, 5 mins from airport, T100312 (Santiago T6332650). Friendly, excellent food, convenient for visiting Ana Kai Tangata caves. **L** *O'Tai*, Te Pito Te Henua s/n, T/F100250. Great location 2 mins from sea, lovely

Hanga Roa

Pacific Ocean

To Market

Ara Roa Rakei

Souvenirs

Av Te Pito Ote Henua

Souvenirs

Caleta Hanga Pilco

Entel

Supermarket

Av Policarpo Toro

Lan Chile

Av Atamu Tekena

Av Apina

Moana Launderette

Av Ngariepua

Insular

Kia Koe Tours

Av Pont

Hertz

Piriti Discotheque

Av Hotu Matua

Mahinatur

Sunoco Service Station

Av Atamu Tekena

N

Not to scale

■ Sleeping	6 Topara	3 Ki Tai
1 Chez Joseph	7 Victoria	4 Kona Koa
2 Hanga Roa		5 Le Pecheur
3 Iorana	● Eating	6 Mama Sabina
4 Orongo Easter Island	1 Ave Rei Pua	7 Pea
5 Otai	2 Cowboy	

gardens, no meals except breakfast. Recommended. **AL** *Chez Joseph*, Avareipua s/n, T/F100281. Full board, or cheaper with breakfast only. **AL** *Poike*, Petero Atamu, T/F100283. Homely, 2-star, hot water. **AL** *Victoria*, Av Pont s/n, T/F100272. Friendly, half board, helpful owner arranges tours. **A** *Orongo Easter Island*, Policarpo Toro. Half board (excellent restaurant), good service, nice garden. T/F100294, or Santiago T2116747. **A** *Topa Ra'a*, Hetereki s/n, T100225, F100353, 5 mins from Hanga Roa. Run down, very helpful, excellent restaurant.

Residenciales AL *Martín y Anita*, T100593, Simon Paoa s/n, opposite hospital in Hanga Roa. With breakfast, clean, good food. Recommended. **AL** *Res Hanga Roa Reka*, T100433, Simon Paoa s/n. Full board, good, friendly, camping available **F** pp. **A** pp *Chez Cecilia*, near Tahai Moai, T100499. With breakfast, speaks English and French, excellent food, camping. **A** *Res Apina Nui*, Hetereki s/n, T223292. With breakfast. **A** *Res El Tauke*, Te Pito Te Henua s/n, T100253. Excellent, airport transfers, tours arranged. **A** *Res Kaipo*, Av Pont s/n, T100340. Small, clean, with breakfast, friendly, with hot water. **A** *Res Pedro Atán*, T100329. With breakfast, Policarpo Toro. **A** *Res Taheta One One*, T100257. Motorbike rental, with breakfast or full board. **B** pp *Res Tahai*, Sector Tahai s/n, T100395. With breakfast, **AL** full board, nice garden. Recommended. Many others, all similar price bracket. Cheapest is **D** pp *Res Maori*, Te Pito Te Henua s/n, T/F100105. With breakfast.

Camping Free in eucalyptus groves near the Ranger's house at Rano Raraku (with water tank), and at Anakena, no water, make sure your tent is ant-proof. Officially, camping is not allowed anywhere else, but this is not apparently strictly enforced. Many people also offer campsites in their gardens, US$5-10 per person, check availability of water first; some families also provide food. Several habitable caves around the coast: for example between Anakena Beach and Ovahe. If you must leave anything behind in a cave, leave only what may be of use to other campers, candles, oil, etc, certainly not rubbish. Camping equipment for hire at shop near the supermarket.

Most *residenciales* offer full board. Coffee is always instant. Beware of extras such as US$3 charge for hot water. It is worth booking a table in advance for evening meals. **Expensive** *Le Pecheur*, French run, unfriendly, seafood speciality, expensive. *Playa Pea*, Av Apina. Pricey but pleasant with fine sea views, seafood. **Mid-range** *Ave Rei Pua*, limited menu, good tuna and lobster. *Cowboy*, nearby, good food, not too expensive. *Ki Tai* for pizzas, snacks. *Kona Koa*, not cheap but good. *Mama Sabina*, Av Policarpo Toro. Clean, welcoming. *Pizzería*, opposite post office. Moderately priced.

Eating
● *on map*
Vegetarians will have no problems on the island

Discos There are 2 in Hanga Roa: *Toroko* (open daily), by the coast in Caleta Hanga Roa, and *Piriti*, near airport (open Thu-Sat). Action begins after 0100. Drinks are expensive: a bottle of *pisco* costs US$9, canned beer US$2. There are also shows of traditional dancing from the island at *Hotel Hanga Roa* (at 2100 hrs), and at *Kona Koa Restaurant* (2200 hrs).

Entertainment

Tapati, or *Semana Rapa Nui*, **end-Jan/beginning-Feb**. It lasts 2 weeks, see box above. Only essential activities continue outside the festival.

Festivals

On Av Policarpo Toro, the main street, there are lots of small shops and market stalls, which close when it rains, and a couple of supermarkets; the cheapest is *Kai Nene* or *Tumukai*. Some local produce can be found free, but ask first. This includes wild guava fruit, fish, 'hierba luisa' tea, and wild chicken.

Shopping

Chilean Pacific Islands

Tapati or Semana Rapa Nui

Held each year in late January/early February, Tapati is organized as a huge competition between groups, many of them families, each of which elects a beauty queen. It begins slowly but keeps on getting better as the fortnight goes on. Families score points by participating in a wide variety of competitions including gastronomy, necklace-making, sculpting moai, body painting, dancing, singing, horse-racing, swimming, modified decathlon. In the most spectacular event, men, dressed only in the traditional thong and with their bodies painted, compete to slide down the side of a volcano, sitting on a kind of sledge made from the trunks of two banana plants. Only for the tough guys!

Lots of tourists, especially from the Chilean mainland, visit at this time. It is best to stay in Hanga Roa, since it is easy to hitch to activities elsewhere.

Cameras Film is readily available but is usually only Kodak 36 print rolls. No film developing on the island. **Handicrafts** Wood carvings, stone *moais*, best bought from the craftsmen themselves, such as Antonio Tepano Tucki, Juan Acka, Hipolito Tucki and his son (who are knowledgeable about the old culture). The municipal market, left of church, will give you a good view of what is available – no compunction to buy. The airport shop is expensive. Good pieces cost between US$30-150. There are several souvenir shops on Av Policarpo Toro including *Hotu Matuu's Favorite Shoppe* where prices have been described as 'top dollar and she will not bargain', but she does have the best T-shirts. Handicrafts are sold at Tahai, Vaihu, Rano Raraku and Anakena. Bargaining is only possible if you pay cash.

Sports **Hiking** Allow at least a day to walk the length of the island, one way, taking in all the sites. It is 5 easy hours from Hanga Roa to Rano Raraku (camp at ranger station); 5 hrs to Anakena (camp at ranger station, but ask first). You can hitch back to Hanga Roa, especially at weekends though there are few cars at other times. Anyone wishing to spend time exploring the island would be well-advised to speak to CONAF first (T223236); they also give good advice on special interests (biology, archaeology, handicrafts, etc). **Horseback** The best way to see the island, provided you are fit, is on horseback: horses, US$35-50 a day (including a guide – cheaper without guides). Tourist office provide a list of people hiring horses. A guide is useful. Try Emilio Arakie Tepane, who also leads horseback tours of the island (Spanish only) T100504, also Ana Rapa, T100540, good value, and Vai Honu, T100935.

Tour operators *Hanga Roa Travel*, T551158, F100153, hfritsch@entelchile.net English, German, Italian and Spanish spoken, good value all inclusive tours. Recommended. *Mahinatur Ltda*, Av Hotu Matua, T100200. Vehicle reservations in advance. Their guide, Christian Walter, is recommended. *Orca*, Caleta Naga Roa, T100375, F100448. Offers diving tours with guides. Maps are sold on Av Policarpo Toro for US$15-18, or at the ranger station at Orongo for US$10. Many agencies, *residenciales* and locals arrange excursions around the island, eg *Aku-Aku Tours*, Krenia Tucki of *Res Kai Poo*, Fernando and Marcelo León (Pai Tepano Rano, recommended). Some go in jeeps, others will accompany tourists in hired vehicles (eg US$110 for 3), prices up to US$50 each per day. The English of tour guides is often poor.

Transport **Local** There are several taxis and in summer a bus goes from Hanga Roa to Anakena on Sun at 0900, returning in the evening (unreliable). **Bicycles**: some in poor condition, are available for rent for US$15 on main street or from *residenciales*. **Motorbike rental**: about US$30 a day plus fuel (Suzuki or Honda 250 recommended because of rough roads). **Vehicle rental**: a high-clearance vehicle is better-suited to the roads than a normal vehicle. If you are hiring a car, do the sites from south to north since travel agencies tend to start their tours in the north. Jeep hire is available from main hotels but hire companies tend to have better vehicles. There are many different companies, so shop around. *Hertz*, Av Policarpo Toro, T100654. *Insular*, Policarpo Toro, T100480. Many other vehicle hire agencies on the same street, eg *Tipanie* (T100577), *Puna Pau* (T100626). Jeep hire US$50-70 per day, US$10 per hour. There is no insurance available, drive at your own risk (be careful at night, many vehicles drive without lights). US$5-10 will buy enough fuel for a one-day trip around the island.

To Easter Island Air: Airport just south of Hanga Roa. The runway has been extended to provide emergency landing for US space shuttles. *LanChile* fly 4 days a week in high season (Thu-Sun), 2 days a week low season (Sun, Thu) 5-5½ hrs. Return to Santiago is Mon, Wed, Fri and Sat (Mon, Fri out of season). Most flights continue to Papeete, Tahiti. *LanChile* office on Av Policarpo Toro, T100279; do not fly to Easter Island unless you have a confirmed flight out (planes are more crowded to Tahiti than back to Santiago) and reconfirm your booking on arrival on the Island. For details of *LanChile* air passes which include Easter Island and which must be purchased outside Chile, see page 44. The fare in 2001 was approximately US$500 return, with occasional special deals available through travel agents. Special deals may be available on flights originating outside Chile, or for those booking in advance. Students studying in Chile are eligible for 30% discount. Don't take pesos to Tahiti, they are worthless in French Polynesia. **Airport tax** Flying from Santiago to Easter Island incurs the domestic tax of US$8. The airport tax for international flights from Easter Island to Tahiti is US$5. **Sea** There are no passenger services to Easter Island. Freight is brought by sea 3 times a year.

Airline office *Lan Chile*, Poilcarpo Toro Y Av Pont. **Banks** US dollars are widely accepted though usually at a poor rate. Buy Chilean pesos on the mainland as local rates are poor. Bank next to tourist office, open 0900-1200 daily, charges US$15 commission on changing TCs, but you can change as many TCs for this fee as you like (and they can be in different names). Cash can be exchanged in shops, hotels, etc, at about 3% less than Santiago. Poor rates on Amex TCs at *Sunoco* service station but no commission. Amex TCs also changed by Kia-Koe Land Operator, *Hanga Roa Hotel*. Prices are often quoted in dollars, but bills can be paid in pesos. Amex credit cards are widely accepted, but cannot be used to obtain cash (but enquire at Sunoco service station). **Communications** Post office: 0900-1700. **Telephone:** *ENTEL* office at Atamu Tekena s/n. Phone calls from the Chilean mainland are subsidized, at US$0.50 per minute, minimum 3 mins. Calls to Europe cost US$10 for 3 mins, cheap rate Sat 1400-1930. **Medical services** There is a 20-bed hospital as well as 3 resident doctors, a trained nurse and 1 dentist on the island. **Directory**

Chilean Pacific Islands

Background

16

Background

History

Archaeology and prehistory

Some 50,000 years ago the very first peoples crossed the temporary land bridge spanning Asia and America at the Bering Straits, and began a long migration southwards. They were hunters and foragers, following in the path of huge herds of now extinct animals, such as mammoth, giant ground sloth, and ancestors of the camel and horse. The first signs that these people had reached South America date from around 14,000 BC, if not earlier.

As sources of game in forested valleys dried up, some groups settled along the coasts, particularly drawn by the abundance of marine life provided by the cold Humboldt current in the Pacific. Some of the earliest evidence of humans in Chile has been found in the north, both on the coast and in the parched Atacama Desert. The coastal people lived on shellfish gathered by the shore, and on fish and sea lions speared from inflated seal-skin rafts.

One such group, the Las Conchas people, migrated from the inland valleys to the coast near Antofagasta around 7,500 BC. They were one of the first peoples in South America to take hallucinogenic drugs. Many graves excavated in this region contained mortars, which may have been used to grind up seeds also found nearby. These seeds contained an alkaloid similar to that found in the ayahuasca plant, which is still used for its hallucinogenic effects by the Shuar in Peru – indeed, the Shuar are believed by some to be descendants of these Atacameño peoples, having migrated to the Amazon in order to hide from the Spanish. Some specialists believe that the many geoglyphs of the Atacama Desert – the most famous ones being the Nazca Lines in Peru – were maps for shamans undergoing the hallucinatory experience of flight after taking hallucinogens such as ayahuasca. Grave goods included bags, trays, and tubes that were used for inhaling the drug in the form of snuff, a method still employed in curing and divination practices in the Andean region and coastal Brazil. Some of the trays and tubes found were decorated with images of supernatural beings and anthropomorphic figures, such as bird-headed angels, styles that are also common in the Andean regions of present-day Peru and Bolivia.

Gradually the settled life of agricultural subsistence took over from the more nomadic hunting lifestyle. Remains of slingshot stones and what seem to be *bolas* (weights attached to cords used to bring down prey by entangling their legs) have been found alongside bones of mastodons in Monte Verde, near Puerto Montt. Other remains found nearby included agricultural tools and medicinal plants, hearths and house foundations, all indications that the site was inhabited for some time by one community. Crop seeds were also found, including those of potatoes, evidence of very early contact with cultures from as far afield as the Central Andes. Some of these remains were found in a remarkable condition, owing to being buried in a peat bog; mastodon bones even had traces of meat on them. Lower levels at Monte Verde have been controversially dated from 34,000 years ago, but it is widely agreed that the site was settled as early as 10,000 years ago.

By about 2,500 BC agriculture was practised throughout much of Chile, as it was across the rest of the continent. Maize, beans, and squash have been found in northern Chile, from as early as 5,000 BC. However, people in the south only turned definitively to agriculture at a much later date. In Araucania, horticulture was not practised until around 500 AD. These people also had unusual burial practices, placing the body in an urn inside a funerary canoe, perhaps reflecting the local dependence on fishing for their livelihood. Elaborate artefacts found in some graves, with stone and copper jewellery as well as ceramic offerings, suggest a stratified society of both rich and poor.

Northern influences

In the north, the extremely dry climate is a great preservative, allowing archaeologists to build up a detailed picture of early life. The people in the Atacama lived in solidly-built adobe houses, arranged in complexes around inner courtyards and corridors, such as can be seen in the village of Tulor near the San Pedro de Atacama oasis. These northern peoples had contacts with neighbouring highland communities, shown by the presence there of plants and other goods found only in the adjacent regions. The important *altiplano* culture of **Tiahuanaco** in present-day Bolivia is thought to have had particularly close links with northern Chile, helping to stimulate the growth of settlements such as at San Pedro de Atacama. Trade with Tiahuanaco, through llama caravans bringing highland goods and produce, boosted the wealth and cultural development of the desert peoples. Some very fine textiles in particular were found in this area, showing distinct design similarities with those of Tiahuanaco. The textiles were hand-spun and coloured with vegetable and cochineal dyes. Clothing and jewellery adornments containing feathers suggested contact even with tropical regions, although these may have been obtained through their *altiplano* intermediaries. Local ceramics were mostly plain and highly polished, but some items decorated with elaborate dragon-like figures had probably been traded with Tiahuanaco.

Mummification was practised from as early as 2,500 BC by coastal peoples, and was also common further north in present-day Peru. The Chinchorro people buried their dead stretched out straight, in contrast to the foetal position used by other Chilean and Peruvian cultures. Internal organs and the brain were removed and the body stuffed with a variety of materials to preserve it. Sticks were attached to the limbs to keep them straight. A mask was placed over the face and a wig of real human hair attached to the head. The body was then coated in a layer of clay and wrapped in animal skins or mats. According to the person's status, they were often buried with their personal possessions, such as clothing, jewellery, musical instruments, and copper items.

In the period 500-900 AD the association between San Pedro de Atacama and Tiahuanaco had become even stronger. In return for trading their agricultural produce and other goods, it is thought that the Tiahuanaco people sought copper, semi-precious stones, and the use of grazing lands in northern Chile. Some graves from this period contained bodies with more elaborate clothing, jewellery, imported ceramics and other valuables, suggesting the existence of a wealthy élite, which was also common in central Andean cultures.

Following the demise of Tiahuanaco in about 1100 AD, a number of cultures arose in the adjacent area bordering southern Bolivia, northern Chile and Argentina, practising derivative agriculture, with terraces and irrigation, and producing ceramics in similar styles. In the Quebrada de Humahuaca in present-day Argentina, several small defensive towns were built with fortified walls and stone houses. Grave remains have revealed that metallurgy was well developed here; some bodies were adorned with pectorals, bracelets, masks, and bells made of copper, silver and gold. Shells from the Pacific and ceramics from present-day Bolivian cultures, such as the Huruquilla, showed the existence of widespread trade links.

Inca expansion

After the demise of Tiahuanaco, the next major empire to touch northern Chile was that of the Incas, which, at the peak of its growth in the 16th century, stretched as far south as the Aconcagua valley. The advancing armies of Inca Topa Yupanqui suppressed resistance in the valleys of the central region, and replaced local structures with their own military administration. They were finally stopped by hostile forest tribes at the Río Maule. This was the southernmost limit of the Inca Empire, some

2,400 miles south of the equator, and the deepest that any imperial movement had penetrated into the southern hemisphere.

One major group, which survived the Inca incursion and resisted conquest by the Europeans right up until the 19th century, was the Mapuche. They were concentrated in the central valley south and east of the Cordillera de Nahuelbuta. The Mapuche were primarily farmers, but also hunted and fished, both inland and along the coasts and lake shores. Their large cemeteries contained a variety of graves, some in canoes or stone chambers, and some in simple earthen graves, suggesting a social hierarchy. Grave goods were plentiful, with elaborate ceramics, wooden and stone artefacts, and jewellery made of copper and semi-precious stones.

Despite the apparently inhospitable conditions these regions were home to a sizeable population of hunting, fishing and gathering peoples from very early times continuously up to the 19th century AD. Bones of horses and extinct giant sloths have been found near to stone arrow heads, in sites such as Fells's Cave and Palli Aike Cave on the Magellan Straits, dating from approximately 8,000 BC, as evidence of the earliest hunters.

The far south

Four distinct cultures developed here: the Haush, Ona, Yámana, and Alacaluf. The oldest of these was the **Haush**, nomadic hunters of the guanaco mainly confined to the farthest southeastern tip of Tierra del Fuego, in present-day Argentina. The Haush hunted with bows and arrows, using guanaco skins for clothing and sometimes for covering their stick-framed houses. They also gathered shellfish and caught fish by the shore, using spears and harpoons.

The **Ona** people also hunted guanaco, ranging on foot across most of the Isla Grande of Tierra del Fuego in family groups. They were strong runners and tall people, some of them 6 ft tall; in fact, all these hunters and gatherers are thought to have been the tallest of the first South American peoples. They wore guanaco skin robes, fur side out, and also guanaco fur moccasins, known as *jamni*. They made open-topped shelters out of guanaco skins, which were weatherproofed with a coating of mud and saliva, and sometimes painted red. The Ona did not use harpoons or spears and only collected shellfish from beaches at low tide.

The **Yámana** were nomadic coastal hunters, travelling in canoes up and down the coasts of the Beagle Channel and around the islands southwards to Cape Horn. They caught otters, fish, and seals, using spears and harpoons, and used slings and snares to catch birds. The Yámana houses were simple, made of sticks and grass, and they wore little clothing, perhaps a small seal skin and skin moccasins in winter.

Like the Yámana, the **Alacalufes** were also nomadic coastal peoples, roaming from Puerto Edén in the Chilean channels, to Yendegaia, in the Beagle Channel. There was some contact with the Yámana, with whom they would sometimes exchange goods and intermarry. The Alacalufes had similar lifestyles to the Yámana, but developed various additions, such as raising a sail on their canoes, and using a bow and arrow in addition to the sling when hunting birds or guanaco.

Colonial history

The first Spanish expeditions to Chile were led by Diego de Almagro and Pedro de Valdivia both of whom followed the Inca road from Peru to Salta and then west across the Andes. Almagro's expedition of 1535-37, which included 100 Spaniards and some thousands of Indians, many of whom perished, reached the heartland, but, bitterly disappointed at not finding gold, returned to Peru almost immediately. Valdivia's expedition carried out what initially appeared to be a swift and successful conquest, founding Santiago in February 1541 and a series of other settlements in the following years. In the 1550s these Spanish settlements were shaken by a

A conquistador with a difference

*Although **Pedro de Valdivia** joined the Spanish army as a young man in 1521, serving in Flanders and Italy, little else is known of his early life. In 1535 he was sent to Venezuela, where he joined an expedition sent to Peru to reinforce Francisco Pizarro. In 1537 he became aide de camp to Pizarro and sided with him in the war between the latter and Diego de Almagro, receiving an award of land and Indians in return. Shortly after he sold his property to finance an expedition southwards to Chile; setting off in 1540 accompanied by 12 white men, one white woman (Inés de Suárez), 1,000 Indians and a few black slaves. Travelling across the Atacama Desert, he reached the Copiapó Valley and then moved south to the*

Mapocho Valley, where he founded Santiago. Receiving further supplies and reinforcements from Peru, he travelled north again, founding La Serena. After a brief expedition to Peru in 1547 where he helped in the defeat of Gonzalo Pizarro by troops sent from Spain, he returned to Chile in 1549, founding the cities of Concepción, Valdivia and Villarrica, before being killed in battle with the Mapuche at Fort Tucapel (sited at the modern town of Carahue, near Temuco).

Although Valdivia's military career was typically bloody and brutal, he is seen by many historians as driven more by the spirit of adventure than by the desire to acquire gold and silver which motivated so many of his fellow conquistadors.

Mapuche rebellion which resulted in the death of Valdivia. These setbacks set the tone for the colonial period in Chile, during which, lacking important resources of precious minerals, inhabited by the warlike Mapuche and never less than four months' journey from Europe, the country was of relatively little importance to Spain except as a frontier zone.

War against the Mapuche was to occupy the Spanish governors who succeeded Valdivia. Known by the Spanish as Araucanians, the Mapuche were fearsome opponents. In 1598 they began a general offensive which destroyed all of the Spanish settlements south of the Río Biobío, revealing the weakness of a colony whose Spanish population was under 8,000. Pushed back into the northern part of the Central Valley, the Spanish were forced to build a string of forts along the Río Biobío, guarded by a frontier army of 2,000 men, the only force of its type in Spanish America, financed by a special subsidy from the viceregal capital of Lima. However, Chile was not important enough to warrant a full scale Spanish assault on the Mapuche and for the rest of the colonial period the Spanish presence south of the river would be limited to the island of Chiloé and to the coastal city of Valdivia.

Situated between the Biobío frontier to the south and the deserts to the north, colonial Chile developed as a compact society; most of its population inhabited the Central Valley and most trade was through Valparaíso. By the end of the 17th century there were few Indians, most having died, intermixed or escaped south of the Biobío. Most of the population was *mestizo* (mixed race), though the society was dominated by a small white élite.

During the colonial period the *hacienda*, or landed estate, was the most important feature of rural society in the Central Valley. In the 17th century Chilean agriculture expanded to meet demands for wheat, tallow, salted beef and cattle hides from Peru while hides were also sent to Potosí and mules to the great fair in Salta. These exports and the need to feed the frontier army led to the development of large scale agriculture. As the *haciendas* grew, small farmers and tenants were gradually forced to become *inquilinos*, a class of peasants tied to the land. The *inquilino* is regarded as the ancestor of the *huaso*, the Chilean cowboy, a figure seen as resourceful, astute, cunning and typically Chilean.

Town planning in the 16th century

Perhaps the most obvious influence of Spanish colonial settlement for a visitor is the characteristic street plan of towns and cities. Colonial cities were founded by means of an official ceremony which included the tracing of the central square and the holding of a mass. A series of Royal Ordinances issued in Madrid in 1573 laid down the rules of town planning. The four corners of the main plaza were to face the four points of the compass 'because thus the streets diverging from the plaza will not be directly exposed to the four principal winds, which would cause much inconvenience'. The plaza and the main streets were to have arcades, and away from the plaza the streets were to be traced out by means of measuring by cord and ruler in the now-familiar grid-pattern. Once this was done building lots near the plaza were distributed, allocated by lottery to the settlers who had rights to be there.

The Ordinances specified the principles underlying the distribution of the major public buildings. Churches were to be distant from the plaza and built on high ground, so that they were easy to see and people had to climb up to them on steps, thereby forcing a greater reverence. The cabildo and the customs house were to be built nearby, while the hospital of the poor and those sick with non-contagious diseases were to be north-facing, planned so that they would enjoy a southern exposure.

The Ordinances also advised settlers on how to deal with local suspicion and hostility: 'While the new town is being built the settlers … shall try to avoid communication and intercourse with the Indians. Nor are the Indians to enter the circuit of the settlement until the latter is complete and in condition for defence and the houses built, so that when the Indians see them they will be filled with wonder and will realize that the Spaniards are settling there permanently and not temporarily.'

Royal Ordinances Governing the Laying Out of New Towns by Zelia Nuttall, Hispanic American Historical Review, May 1922.

Although *haciendas* grew in response to food shortages, they were very self-contained; *haciendas* had their own supplies of food and clothing, their own vineyards, forges and workshops. Ownership of a *hacienda* was one of the clearest marks of upper-class status, although many were the property of religious orders. The *hacienda* remained at the centre of rural life in the Central Valley and social relations between landowners and *inquilinos* changed little until the Agrarian Reforms of the 1960s. Although no colonial *haciendas* remain, a few dating from the 19th century can be visited, notably Villa Huilquilemu, near Talca.

Chile was governed as part of the Viceroyalty of Peru, with its capital in Lima; until the 18th century all trade with Spain had to pass via Lima and trade with other countries was forbidden. This led to uncontrolled smuggling and by 1715 there were 40 French vessels trading illegally along the coast. In 1740 direct trade with Spain was permitted and in 1750 Chile was permitted to mint her own currency.

The War of Independence

Independence came to Spanish America as a direct result of Napoleon's invasion of Spain. As Spanish guerrilla forces fought to drive the French out, these events led to the colonial élites debating where their loyalties lay: to Napoleon's brother Joseph, now officially King? Or to the overthrown king, Ferdinand VII, now in a French prison? Or to the Spanish resistance parliament in Cadiz?

In 1810 a group of leading Santiago citizens appointed a Junta to govern until Ferdinand returned to the throne. Though they protested loyalty to Ferdinand, their

Bernardo O'Higgins

Background

Born in 1778 in Chillán, O'Higgins was the illegitimate son of Ambrose O'Higgins, an Irishman who rose in the Spanish colonial service to become Governor of Chile and Viceroy of Peru, and his Chilean mistress, Isabel Riquelme. At the age of 17 Bernardo was sent to study in London where he met Francisco de Miranda and other South American exiles who were plotting to overthrow Spanish colonial rule. Returning to Chile in 1802 after Ambrose's death, he inherited his father's estate and adopted his surname. After the collapse of Spanish rule, O'Higgins was elected to the first National Congress in 1811. When war broke out between the Chilean Patriots and Royalist forces, O'Higgins recruited his own troops, distinguishing himself in a number of battles and being wounded at El Roble in October 1813. In 1814 he was appointed Commander-in-Chief of the Patriot armies, but defeat at the Battle of Rancagua in October 1814 forced him to retreat with 2,000 men across the Andes to Mendoza. Here he met José de San Martín who was preparing an army to cross the Andes and free Chile from Spanish control as a first step to invading the Spanish stronghold of Peru. Returning to Chile with San Martín, O'Higgins led a risky and unauthorized cavalry charge at the Battle of Chacabuco on 12 February 1817 which assured victory. Four days later the Patriot leaders appointed O'Higgins Supreme Director.

Facing a renewed threat from a Royalist army moving north from Talcahuano, O'Higgins proclaimed Chilean independence in February 1818, but the following month his troops were defeated near Talca and he was badly wounded. A few weeks later, O'Higgins, still recovering,

galloped onto the battlefield at Maipó, at the head of reinforcements and embraced San Martín crying "Glory to the Saviour of Chile." San Martín replied "Chile will never forget the name of the illustrious invalid who, today, presented himself on the battlefield." This episode, known as 'The Embrace of Maipó', is one of the most famous in Chilean history.

As the head of the first Chilean government, O'Higgins remained personally popular, although many of the actions of his government were not. He abolished aristocratic titles and personally sketched the plans for a wide boulevard which was to run along a sheep-track on the outskirts of Santiago and which is now the Avenida Bernardo O'Higgins (or Alameda). Although the Creole élite disliked measures such as the prohibition of burial inside churches and the approval of a Protestant cemetery, opposition to his government was also partly the result of family rivalries. O'Higgins' Constitution of 1822, which allowed for him to remain in office for another 10 years, provoked further opposition. After General Ramón Freire launched a rebellion in Concepción, O'Higgins was forced to resign on 23 January 1823. Six months later a British warship took him to Peru where he accompanied Simon Bolívar on the final campaign against Spanish forces. His final years were lived out on his estate in the Cañete valley, south of Lima. His support for a military insurrection in Chile in 1826 led to the Chilean government stripping him of all his honours, but these were restored to him in 1842, shortly before his death in October of that year. He was buried in Lima, but in 1869 his remains were returned to Chile.

move was seen as a challenge by the viceregal government in Lima, which sent an army to Concepción. War broke out between the Chilean Patriots and these Royalist troops supporting Lima. The defeat of the Patriot army at Rancagua in October 1814 (see page 276) led to a restoration of colonial rule; but, with Bernardo O'Higgins able to escape across the Andes to join forces with Buenos Aires' liberation hero, José de San Martín, the turning point came in 1817 with the invasion of Chile from Mendoza by San Martín's Army of the Andes, a force of 4,000 men which defeated the

Royalists at Chacabuco on 12 February 1817. A Royalist counter-attack was defeated at Maipó, just south of Santiago, on 5 May 1818, putting an end to Royalist power in the Central Valley. The victory of the small Patriot navy led by Lord Cochrane (see box, page 140) at Valdivia in January 1820 helped clear the Pacific coast of Royalist vessels and paved the way for San Martín to launch his seaborne invasion of Peru.

The 19th century

In most of former Spanish America independence was followed by a period of political turmoil, marked by civil wars and dictatorship, which in some cases lasted until the 1860s. Many independence heroes had tragic ends: disgusted at the chaos, San Martín retired to France; Simon Bolívar died penniless and in hiding in a boarding house in Santa Marta, Colombia; and O'Higgins was quickly overthrown. O'Higgins' demise was followed by a brief period of instability, but in 1830 conservative forces led by Diego Portales restored order and introduced the Constitution of 1833, which created a strong government under a powerful president. Portales, a Valparaíso merchant who never became president explained his actions thus: "If one day I took up a stick and gave tranquillity to the country it was only so that the bastards and whores of Santiago would let me get on with my work in peace." Chile became famous throughout Latin America as the great example of political stability: the army was reduced to 3,000 men and kept out of politics; after 1831, four successive presidents served the two five-year terms permitted under the constitution. However, this stability had its other side: civil liberties were frequently suspended, elections rigged, opponents exiled and power lay in the hands of a small landowning élite. Neither was the stability perfect: there were short civil wars in 1851, 1859 and 1891.

The latter half of the 19th century saw Chile's great period of expansion. In 1881, when victory over Peru in the War of the Pacific was assured, the much enlarged army was sent to put an end to Mapuche independence and thus secure continuous Chilean control over the Pacific coastline south of Arica. In the few short years between 1879 and 1883, Chilean territory had expanded both northwards and southwards. However, some Chileans still argue that the victory over Peru and Bolivia came at the price of losing most of Patagonia to Argentina; according to some this should, by dint of colonial land divisions under the Viceroyalty, be Chilean territory.

From the 1860s onwards, conflict between President and Congress became a constant feature of political life. The War of the Pacific brought the Chilean government a new source of income through the tax levied on nitrate exports coming from the new territories of the Atacama, but it also increased rivalry for control of this income. When in 1890 Congress rejected the budget, President Balmaceda announced he would use the 1890 budget for 1891. Congressional leaders denounced this as illegal and fled to Iquique, where they recruited an army which defeated Balmaceda's forces and seized the capital. Balmaceda took refuge in the Argentine embassy, where he committed suicide. His defeat was important: between 1891 and 1924 Chilean presidents were weak figures and real power lay in Congress, ruled by the élite.

The 20th century

In the years before the First World War the income from nitrates helped build a large railway network, roads and ports and the best education system on the continent. However, the collapse of the nitrate industry during the First World War led to worker and student unrest which brought down the constitutional system in 1924 when the military intervened. A new constitution restored the strong presidency which had apparently served Chile so well in the 19th century, but the Great

The War of the Pacific, 1879-83

One of the few major international wars in Latin America since independence, this conflict had its roots in a border dispute between Chile and Bolivia, the frontier between the two in the Atacama Desert being ill-defined at the time of independence. There had already been one conflict: in 1836-39, when Chile defeated Peru and Bolivia. Relations were complicated by the discovery of nitrates in the Atacama in the 1860s: in the Bolivian province of Antofagasta nitrates were exploited by Anglo-Chilean companies; the miners were mostly Chilean.

The War also has to be placed into the wider global context of the late 1870s. The years 1873-1875 saw the worst global recession in the Victorian era, with plunging commodity prices around the world. Recent cutting edge research has shown how this was then followed by one of the most severe El Niño events the world has ever seen, in 1876, leading to the deaths of tens of millions of people around the world owing to severe famine and the inequalities of the colonial economic system. Santiago saw what remains its lowest ever barometric reading in 1877, while there were widespread floods in Peru and droughts in the Bolivian altiplano. In the consequently weak economic system, the imposition of port taxes was both necessary to Bolivia, and the straw that

broke the camel's back for Chile.

In 1878 the Bolivian government, short of revenue, attempted to tax the Chilean-owned Antofagasta Railroad and Nitrate Company. When the company refused to pay, the Bolivians seized its assets. The Chilean government claimed that the Bolivian action broke an 1874 agreement between the two states. When Peru announced that it would honour a secret alliance with Bolivia by supporting her, the Chilean president, Aníbal Pinto, declared war on both states.

None of the three states was prepared for war; they lacked skilled officers and adequate weapons. Control of the sea was vital and the few ironclad ships were far superior to wooden vessels. The Chileans blockaded the Peruvian nitrate port of Iquique with two wooden ships, the Esmeralda and the Covadonga. Peru sent her two best ironclads, the Huáscar and the Independencia, to Iquique. In the Battle of Iquique, 21 May 1879, the Esmeralda was sunk, but in the course of the battle the Independencia ran aground and was captured, thus altering the balance of forces between the two navies. Later in October 1879 off Angamos near Antofagasta, the two Chilean ironclads, Blanco Encalada and Cochrane, cornered the Huáscar and captured her (the Huáscar can be visited in the harbour of Talcahuano).

Depression brought further economic stress which resulted in a series of short-lived governments including a military-led 100-day Socialist Republic in 1932.

As economic conditions recovered in the 1930s, Chile once again became a model of political stability. Between 1932 and 1970 Chile developed a complex multiparty system: two left-wing parties, the Socialists and Communists, representing the urban workers and miners; the Conservative and Liberal parties, dating from the 19th century, representing the landowners; and the Radicals, a centre party representing the middle classes. The Radicals became the key to power, winning the presidency in 1938, 1942 and 1946. However, one major group remained excluded from political life: the peasants, whose votes, controlled by their landlords, gave the Liberals and Conservatives their representation in Congress, and enabled the landlords to block rural reform.

In the 1958 election, the Socialist **Salvador Allende** only narrowly failed to defeat the Conservative Jorge Alessandri. This shook both the right-wing parties and, in the aftermath of the Cuban Revolution, the US government. In 1964, the US and the Chilean right-wing threw their weight behind **Eduardo Frei Montalva**, a

Rather than attack the Peruvian heartland, the Chileans invaded the southern Peruvian province of Tarapacá and then landed troops north of Tacna, seizing the town in May 1880 before capturing Arica, further south. In January 1881 fresh Chilean armies seized control of Lima. Despite these defeats, Peru did not sue for peace, although Bolivia had already signed a ceasefire, giving up her coastal province. Under the 1883 peace settlement Peru gave up Tarapacá to Chile. Although the provinces of Tacna and Arica were to be occupied by Chile for 10 years, it was not until 1929 that an agreement was reached under which Tacna was returned to Peru, while Chile kept Arica.

Chile's relations with her northern neighbours remain sour. There is widespread racism in Chile about the Indian peoples in Peru and Bolivia, and there are signs in Bolivia proclaiming that the Pacific is Bolivian; a Bolivian navy patrols Lake Titicaca. Nevertheless, the war gave Chile a monopoly over the world's supply of nitrates and enabled her to dominate the southern Pacific coast. Some idea of the war's importance in official Chilean history can be gained by the number of streets and squares named after the heroes of the war, especially Arturo Prat and Aníbal Pinto, and after the vessels Esmeralda and Blanco Encalada.

▦ Peruvian province of Tacna, occupied by Chile 1883-1929, restored to Peru 1929

▤ Provinces of Arica & Tarapacá, Peruvian until 1883, now part of Chile

▨ Bolivian province of Antofagasta, before 1879, southern portion of which was claimed by Chile

—··— Present-day frontiers

------- Peru-Bolivia frontier before 1879

—·— Original frontier between Chile & Bolivia

Background

Christian Democrat who promised a 'revolution in freedom'. Frei Montalva's achievements in office were impressive: state ownership of 51% of the copper industry; minimum wage and unionization rights for agricultural workers; the 1967 agrarian reform which began replacing the *haciendas* with family farms. However, these measures raised hopes which could not be satisfied, especially in the country-side where workers now enjoyed rights to push for faster land reform. Hostility from the landowners was reflected in Congress where the National Party, formed in 1966 by the merger of the Conservatives and Liberals, denounced the government. The president's Christian Democrat Party was divided between supporters and opponents of reform. Nevertheless, Frei Montalva has been an enduringly popular President – his memory was widely seen as a key factor in the landslide victory of his son, Eduardo Frei Ruiz-Tagle, in the 1993 Presidential elections.

The 1970 election was narrowly won by Salvador Allende, polling just over 36.3% of the vote, with the electorate split in three. Allende headed a left-wing alliance called Unidad Popular. Allende's government launched an ambitious programme of reforms: banking, insurance, communications, textiles and other industries were

Salvador Allende Gossens

Born in 1908 into an upper- middle-class Valparaíso family, Salvador Allende's childhood ambition was to be a doctor, like his grandfather Ramón Allende Padín, a respected Radical politician who became Serene Grand Master of the Chilean Freemasons. While studying medicine he discovered first-hand the appalling living conditions of the poor and the links between poverty and disease. Even before he qualified as a doctor he became active in politics and was briefly imprisoned during the Ibáñez dictatorship. He was a founder member of the Chilean Socialist party in 1933; at about the same time he became an active freemason.

Elected to Congress for Valparaíso at the age of 29, he served as Minister of Health in Aguirre Cerda's Popular Front government of 1939-42. Elected to the Senate in 1945, he became Senate president in 1965. Allende was a candidate in four presidential elections. In 1952 he gained only 5.45% of the votes, but in 1958 as candidate of the Front for Popular Action, an alliance between the Socialists and Communists, he lost narrowly to the

right-wing candidate, Jorge Alessandri. Easily defeated in 1964 by the Christian Democrat, Eduardo Frei, he finally won the presidency in 1970: in a three-cornered race he gained 36.3% of the vote. Lacking a majority in Congress, heading a broad but divided coalition of eight parties and facing the hostility of much of the Chilean population and of Washington, Allende had increasingly little room for manoeuvre.

When news of the military revolt came through in the early hours of 11 September 1973, Allende went to the Moneda Palace and spoke twice on the radio before communications were cut. Though offered a flight out of the country in return for his resignation, Allende refused, and the Palace was bombed by three Hawker Hunter jets. Most accounts now accept that Allende committed suicide. He was buried in an unmarked grave in Viña del Mar. In September 1990 following the return to civilian rule his body was exhumed and transported to Santiago for a state funeral, thousands of people lining the route from the coast.

taken over in the first year and the nationalization of copper was completed (this last even with the support of the right-wing parties). After that the government ran into major problems: the nationalizations had depleted Chile's currency reserves; hostility by domestic business groups and the US led to capital flight and a US-led boycott on international credit; an alliance between the Christian Democrats and National Party in Congress impeached several ministers; a series of anti-government strikes by truck drivers and professional groups brought the country to a halt in October 1972 and again in August 1973; the supplies in shops were unable to keep pace with the wider purchasing power of many social classes, leading to long queues for foodstuffs; annual inflation rose to over 300% in 1973.

Despite these negative points, Allende's socialist experiment did have a measure of success: agricultural production increased; by 1972 there were 27% more food-stuffs available in Chile than there had been in 1970, but even this increase was out-stripped by the demand caused by the real rises in wages among the poor, a sign that Allende's goal of eradicating poverty was bearing some fruit; per capita food consumption rose for all foodstuffs except red meat, and the lamenting of the queues in the shops was, more than anything, a symbol of upper- and middle-class frustration that their customary position at the head of affairs was being usurped.

Allende's popularity in some quarters was demonstrated by the March 1973 Parliamentary elections, at which the Unidad Popular polled 43.4% of the vote, 7% more than in 1970. Nevertheless, the coup of 11 September 1973, led by **General Augusto Pinochet**, was widely expected, the armed forces having received open

The rise and fall of General Augusto Pinochet Ugarte

Born in Valparaíso in 1915, the son of a customs officer who traced his ancestry to Breton immigrants, Pinochet entered the Escuela Militar (Military Academy) at the age of 17, graduating near the bottom of his class in 1936. His subsequent career included a posting to the Ecuadorean national military academy from 1956 to 1959. In 1964 he became deputy director of the Escuela Militar; among his publications were a history of the War of the Pacific and a textbook on geopolitics.

By 1969 he had risen to the rank of Brigadier General and the following year he became commander of the Santiago garrison, one of the most sensitive and influential postings in the Chilean army. When the Army Commander-in-Chief, General Carlos Prats González, became Minister of the Interior in the Allende government in 1972, Pinochet took over as acting Commander-in-Chief. He took over this post again in August 1973 on the resignation of Prats. Although Pinochet was a relatively unknown figure and was apparently a late convert to the coup plot against Allende, his position as head of the Army made him an automatic choice to become president of the military junta which took over.

In 1974 he became President of Chile, having increased his hold on power by his control over the regime's notorious secret police, the DINA, which was headed by a close colleague, Gral Manuel Contreras. Following his 'election' in 1980 as the only candidate in the first elections held under the new constitution, he began a fresh eight-year term (1981-1989), during which he became the longest serving Chilean president. In 1986 he narrowly escaped an assassination attempt. Following his defeat in the 1988 referendum, he did not stand as a candidate in the December 1989 elections and handed over the presidency in March 1990.

With his stern features enhanced by dark glasses, Pinochet became the stereotype of the South American dictator.

Often seen as a bluff no-nonsense character, he was also noted for his astuteness, his suspicious mind, his ruthlessness and his hatred of democracy and political parties. Furious after his defeat in the 1988 referendum, Pinochet observed that another plebiscite long ago had elected Barrabas. It would be wrong to see his dominance as merely the result of repression and fear. To many Chileans who had hated Allende and feared his policies, Pinochet became a popular figure; the human rights abuses and destruction of democracy were seen by some as a price worth paying.

Despite his advancing years and heart surgery in 1992 Pinochet insisted on remaining Commander-in-Chief of the Army until March 1998 as specified in the 1980 Constitution. He made it clear that he would oppose any moves to bring members of the armed forces to trial for human rights abuses committed during the dictatorship. In December 1990 questions in Congress and in the press about financial scandals involving army officers and his own son-in-law, led him to order all troops to report to barracks. In May 1993 he surrounded the Ministry of Defence with soldiers and ordered generals to wear battle dress to work for a day and in September 1996 he suggested that the armed forces should be prepared to carry out another coup if ever that became necessary.

His subsequent arrest in Britain after an extradition warrant served by Baltasar Garzón, a judge in Spain, the stripping of his immunity in Chile, and the farcical to-ings and fro-ings which characterised his desperate attempts to ward off the Chilean courts and the charges of kidnapping and murder (see main text for full details), have given his notorious career an unexpectedly dramatic denouement. Whatever the final outcome, it is now impossible for Pinochet to end his life with the respect and authority which he spent so long developing.

Background

encouragement from Allende's opponents in Congress, including the Christian Democrats and the opposition on the streets; it later became clear that the CIA had had a major role in fomenting the unrest leading to the pre-coup stand-off. The brutality shocked people who were accustomed to Chile's peaceful traditions. Left-wing activists and people mistakenly identified as leftists were arrested; thousands were executed; torture was widespread; at least 7,000 people were held in the national football stadium; by 1978 there were 30,000 Chilean exiles in Western Europe alone. With political parties and labour unions banned, the government adopted neo-liberal economic policies under the influence of Milton Friedman and the 'Chicago Boys'.

Pinochet installed himself as the undisputed head of a military *junta*. Those who did not approve of his methods often met grisly ends – thus the former head of the Army, Carlos Prats, was assassinated by a car bomb in Buenos Aires in 1974. Under a new constitution, adopted in 1980, Chile became a 'protected democracy' based on the exclusion of political parties and the 'guardianship' of the armed forces who would put forward a single candidate for an eight-year presidential term in 1981. To no one's surprise the candidate was Pinochet, but his bid for a further eight-year term in a plebiscite in 1988 was unsuccessful; nevertheless, in spite of Pinochet's widespread vilification in much of the Western press, he retained popularity among many Chileans, and polled 44% of the vote at this plebiscite, which was widely deemed to be fair.

Even so, when the first results came in, the military government initially tried to maintain that the 'si' (yes to Pinochet) had triumphed. This quickly became untenable, but, under the terms of the constitution of 1980, Pinochet still had 18 months before he had to relinquish power. Eventually, presidential and congressional elections were held in 1989. A veteran Christian Democrat politician, **Patricio Aylwin Azócar**, the candidate of the Coalition of Parties for Democracy (CPD, or Concertación), was elected President and took office in March 1990 in a peaceful transfer of power. General Pinochet remained as Army Commander although other armed forces chiefs were replaced. The new Congress set about revising many of the military's laws on civil liberties and the economy. In 1991 the National Commission for Truth and Reconciliation (the RETTIG Commission) published a report with details of those who were killed under the military régime. The RETTIG commission established that 3,197 people had died as the result of the violation of human rights, but opposition by the armed forces and an amnesty law protecting members of the military prevented mass human rights trials. At this time in Chile's history, prosecution of those guilty of human rights' abuse was widely seen as impossible.

Presidential elections in December 1993 resulted in victory for the Christian Democrat, Eduardo Frei Ruiz-Tagle, candidate of the Concertación coalition, but in congressional elections held at the same time the Concertación failed to achieve the two-thirds majority in Congress required to reform the constitution, replace the heads of the armed forces and end the system of designated senators whose votes enabled the right-wing parties and the military to block reform. As a result Frei's presidency became an exercise in balancing the demands of the parties of the Concertación against the entrenched power of the military and the right-wing parties. Although the Concertación won a comfortable victory in congressional elections in December 1997, they still failed to achieve the majority necessary to break the deadlock and the position of the military was strengthened in March 1998 when General Pinochet retired as Army Commander-in-Chief and, as entitled under the constitution, as a former president who had held office for six years, took up his lifetime seat in the Senate.

The drama began in October 1998, when General Pinochet was arrested in London at a private clinic while recovering from a back operation. The move was on the basis of an arrest warrant issued by a Spanish judge, Baltasar Garzón, for murder and torture of Spanish citizens under the military regime. Pinochet's arrest put the Frei government under great pressure: Pinochet's supporters demanded action while some of the government's supporters, especially in the Socialist party, were privately delighted. These debates were linked to the continuing demands from families of those who had disappeared for news of the whereabouts of the victims' corpses, and prosecutions of those responsible. The events were widely seen as a challenge to Chile's sovereignty, and this, combined with the worsening economic situation and the choice of the first Socialist to head the Concertación into presidential elections (after two Christian Democrats), Ricardo Lagos, made the December 1999 poll unexpectedly close. Fighting against the Mayor of Las Condes, Joaquín Lavín, Lagos won with a tiny majority after a second-round ballot; Lavín had won more votes in the first round of polling.

The ructions caused by the Pinochet affair in Chile show no sign of abating. Having allowed the extradition process to continue, Jack Straw, the British Home Secretary, allowed Pinochet to return to Chile on grounds of ill health in March 2000. However, a legal case started by Judge Juan Guzmán Tapia in the Chilean courts in January 1998 was to mean that Pinochet (born in 1915) could not live out his days in peace. A Supreme Court ruling of July 1999 that, in cases where the fact of death could not be certified, amnesty did not apply, meant that Pinochet and the military were open to charges regarding the 'disappeared'. In June 2000, an Appeal Court ruling stripped Pinochet of his immunity from trial. This decision was confirmed by the Supreme Court in August, and Pinochet was finally indicted by Judge Guzmán on January 29th 2001 on charges of kidnapping and murder related to the infamous 'caravan of death', shortly after the coup in 1973, when many political detainees 'disappeared' in the north of the country. However, in July 2001, the court ruled narrowly that Pinochet's worsening health meant that he was not capable of mounting a proper defence, and thus that the case could not be continued. Judge Guzmán was soon forced to take sick leave as a result of stress induced by the case, but appeals were mounted by the families of victims of the military government. At the time this book went to press, it remained unclear whether Pinochet would face trial in his home country, although the likelihood is that he will not. Even if Pinochet is not tried, the principle that, had it not been for his ill health, he should have been, would have been completely unthinkable prior to the unravelling of the whole Pinochet affair.

Modern Chile

The Pinochet affair has forced Chileans to confront their recent past. Although old wounds have been reopened, the increasing political apathy of the young – which was apparent in the early 1990s, and had been forced by two decades of institutional intolerance and an acute awareness of the failures of their politicians – has been nipped in the bud. While the presidencies of the Concertación have continued with the Pinochetista neo-liberal policies which made Chile such a banker's favourite in the 1980s, this has been accompanied by a genuine attempt at more inclusive government, including significant increases in the National Minimum Wage at rates well above that of inflation. With a pension system on which countries such as Britain have modelled new 'stakeholder' pension schemes, urban Chile is now, for the most part, modern and dynamic.

There are, though, several problems which the government needs to address. While there has been a limited rise in living standards among the inhabitants of Santiago's *callampas* (shanty towns), urban poverty remains widespread. Problems in Santiago are due in large part to the massive centralization of a country in which over a third of the population live in Santiago and the surrounding Región Metropolitana. The unusual geography means that Santiago, with its central position, is a natural focal point. While there has been limited decentralization, Chile is all too dependent on Santiago.

Meanwhile, the newspapers and TV stations are full of talk of Chile's *la crisis económica*. Unemployment in Gran Santiago is up to 15%, and everywhere people are talking about the difficulty of finding – and keeping – work. While this crisis has to be put in the context of the fact that Chile's economy remains the most stable in South America, there is no doubt that the period of constant growth and prosperity of the 1990s has passed. This is largely the result of weaknesses among Chile's main trading partners: the crisis of the Far East had major ramifications in Chile, while the devaluation in Brazil, followed by the July 2001 economic crisis in Argentina, has led to the rise of the US dollar against the Chilean peso. This may well have unfortunate inflationary effects (see box, page 530) for a country in which – uniquely in South America – the local currency held its own against the dollar throughout the 1990s.

Perhaps the most fundamental long-term problem is that Chile's burgeoning wealth depends in part on the ongoing rape of its extensive natural resources, often by multinational companies – industries such as logging and intensive fishing, while successful at present, have the potential to ruin Chile's future. According to one estimate, Chile lost 80% of its marine life in the 1980s; meanwhile the native forests continue to disappear at alarming rates. Clearly, wealth which is based on the destruction of natural resources has a finite shelf life; and the desire of the government to join the North American Free Trade Agreement (expected in 2001), along with the US, Canada and Mexico, is not seen as beneficial in all quarters. There are also moves afoot to extend NAFTA throughout the whole of the Americas.

Nevertheless, this desire is symbolic of Chile's increasingly outward-looking mentality. After four centuries which were often characterized by isolation and insularity, the ramifications of Chile's recent history have put the country into the international eye in an unprecedented manner. Whereas, until recently, Chileans compared themselves to Europeans, they now take increasing national pride in their own achievements – even if Pinochet is not put on trial in Chile, the case and its consequences means that Chile can with justification claim to be in the vanguard of the most significant human rights movement in history, one which in a short space of time has already had repercussions for once repressive heads of state of the Central African Republic and Yugoslavia.

Constitution and government

Chile is governed under the 1980 Constitution, introduced by the military government of General Pinochet and approved in a plebiscite on 11 September 1980, although important amendments were made during the transition to civilian rule in 1989-90. The new constitution provided for an eight-year non-renewable term for the President of the Republic (although the first elected president was to serve only four years), a bicameral Congress and an independent judiciary and central bank. Although Pinochet was not mentioned by name, only one candidate, nominated by the military was to contest the 1981 and 1988 elections. Only after the rejection of Pinochet in the 1988 vote did most of the provisions of the constitution come into operation. In February 1994, the Congress cut the presidential term of office from eight years to six. A two-thirds majority in both houses of Congress is required to reform the constitution.

Congress is composed of a 120-seat Chamber of Deputies and a 47-seat Senate, eight of whose members are nominated rather than elected. Among the nominated

Chilean laws

Chile has a deeply conservative tradition, as is shown by numerous elements in the country's history: it was the first newly independent country in Latin America fully to embrace the Catholic church, and has the most stable 'democratic' (or, until the 1950s, oligarchic) tradition in the region. Nowhere, however, is Chile's conservatism so apparent as in the country's laws. There are numerous examples of this, but some of the most important include the following:

■ The laws governing Chile's income tax system are symptomatic of the country's history and conservatism. Direct income tax is exceptionally low at 1%, and business tax has recently been raised from 15% to 17%, less than half the rate applied in most developed countries; nevertheless, this raise came to the backdrop of vociferous protests from the country's business community, and while Chile's lower and middle classes can clearly not afford to pay more income tax, this is far from true of the country's upper classes. The (socialist) government's inability to tackle this taboo subject is symptomatic both of the oligarchic stranglehold which the Chilean aristocracy retains on the state and of the taboo status of even the slightest economic redistribution – something which goes back to the 'anti-communist wars' waged by the military government in the 1970s and 1980s, and the psychological scars imposed by the real distribution of the Allende government and the events that followed.

■ Until 2000, the rights of a child born out of wedlock were significantly different from those of a child born legitimately to its parents. This meant that the national identity card was stamped with "ilegítimo", ostracizing the child from birth in various important arenas. Schools, for instance, could refuse to take a child, simply because it was illegitimate.

■ Chile is the only country in the world in which divorce does not exist. Couples that want to separate have to go through the farcical process of getting a notary to swear that they were married in the wrong municipality, that their marriage certificate is therefore invalid, and that the couple were never married in the first place – this is manageable for those on reasonable incomes, but the upshot for the rural population who cannot afford to go to notaries is that divorce – and remarriage – are impossible. While a divorce law is currently being prepared, this has been met by attacks in the conservative press, with long articles by Catholic bishops appearing in El Mercurio lamenting this shift to a permissive society – something that perfectly expresses the conflicts between traditions and modernity, and between the poor and the rich, that still find their expression in the Chilean legal system.

senators is one former head of each of the armed forces. Former presidents who have completed a full six-year term are also eligible to join as life senators. In March 1998 Pinochet took up his seat under this provision. The existence of nominated senators has enabled the right-wing opposition parties to block constitutional reform. The abolition of nominated senators has been a major aim of civilian governments since 1990.

Since 1990 the dominant party in Chile has been the Christian Democrats. A centre party which grew rapidly after its foundation in 1957, the Christian Democrats welcomed the overthrow of Allende, but later became the focus of opposition to the dictatorship. Not strong enough to rule on their own, since 1990 they have contested elections in an alliance known as the Concertación. The other members are the Socialists, a centre-left party traditionally split between different factions, the Radicals and the Partido por la Democracía, a new centre-left grouping led by

Rise of the dollar

The year 2001 has been marked by a new and worrying departure in the Chilean economy, namely the rise of the American dollar against the Chilean peso. Those who visited Chile in the 1990s became accustomed to the fact that, while local prices rose steadily, the dollar did not rise to compensate for this, meaning that by 1998 Chile was almost as expensive to visit as Argentina. From a rate of 370 pesos to the dollar in 1992, the peso was at only 430 in 1995 and 470 in 1997.

All that changed in 2001. During the first 6 months alone, the dollar rose from a value of 570 pesos to 680 pesos in August. The rise was due to a combination of external factors, principally the disastrous economic situation in Argentina, which had led to massive strikes in Transandean industry and fears of the devaluation of

the Argentine peso – something which would have disastrous effects on the Chilean economy.

Clearly, on one level, all this is good news for the foreign visitor. As yet, inflation has not followed the rise of the dollar, meaning that, at the time of writing, Chile is cheaper for foreigners than it has been for a decade. However, while many visitors arriving in Chile from Bolivia or Peru complain at the expensiveness of travel here, this is a symbol of the country's prosperity – to wish that a country be cheaper is, in effect, to wish that it be poorer. Should the dollar continue to rise, inflation is bound to follow, and the effects on Chile's already fragile economy would be severe. For this reason, it is to be hoped that the rise of the dollar will soon – to some extent at least – be reversed.

---

ex-socialists. The main opposition to the Concertación has come from the right wing, which is divided into two main parties, Renovación Nacional and the Unión Democrática Independiente. For the 1993 and 1999 elections they formed an alliance called the Unión por el Progreso.

Chile is divided into 13 regions, usually referred to by Roman numerals (although they also have names). The government of each region is headed by an Intendent who is appointed by the President.

Economy

Structure of production Chile's diverse environment allows the production of all temperate and Mediterranean products. Traditional crops, such as cereals, pulses, potatoes and industrial crops, such as sugar beet, sunflower-seed and rape-seed, account for about a third of the value added of agriculture, and vegetables for a quarter. Fruit growing has grown rapidly and fresh fruit now accounts for over US$1 billion in exports a year, making fruit the second most important earner after copper. Another area of expansion is forestry; timber and wood products make up the third place in exports. More than 80% of the 1.6 million ha of cultivated forest is planted with *insignis radiata* pine, a species which grows faster in Chile than in other countries. However, native forest has been declining rapidly, partly because of demand by wood chippers. Chile is the most important fishing nation in Latin America and the largest producer of fishmeal in the world. Industrial consumption absorbs about 93% of the fish catch; fresh fish and fish products contribute about 10% of merchandise exports. Salmon farming is being expanded.

The dominant sector of the economy is mining. Chile has been the world's largest producer of copper since 1982 and also produces molybdenum, iron ore, manganese, lead, gold, silver, zinc, sulphur and nitrates. Chile has a quarter of the world's known molybdenum ore reserves and is believed to have around 40% of the world's lithium reserves. Mineral ores, mostly copper, account for half of total

Mercosur

In June 1996 Chile signed up to become an associate member of Mercosur, the Southern Cone Common Market. Founded in 1991 by Argentina, Brazil, Paraguay and Uruguay, Mercosur is the world's fourth largest integrated international market. Except in aspiration it is not, however, yet a common market. Most goods are tariff-free inside Mercosur, but there is, as yet, no common external tariff, though in December 1995 the four full member states agreed a five-year programme to establish one. Since, however, there is no freedom of movement for workers, a full common market remains a distant aspiration.

As a result of associate membership, Chile and the full members were due to reduce tariffs on trade by 30% with further reductions by the year 2005 eliminating them altogether. A small group of Chilean food and agricultural imports from Mercosur will not be covered by this: tariffs on most of these will be cut between 2006 and 2011, though wheat, flour and sugar will retain their existing tariffs until at least 2014. Within Chile the main opposition to associate membership came from farmers fearing competition from the large-scale meat and grain producers of Mercosur states: to placate their hostility the government offered US$500 million of support for agriculture over the next five years as the Mercosur bill passed through Congress.

export revenue. Fluctuations in world prices for minerals can have a great impact on the balance of payments. Foreign investment is the driving force in mining, which has averaged almost US$900 million a year in the 1990s in exploration and mine development. Copper production is over four million tonnes a year, over 40% of world production, of which 1.4 million tonnes will be produced by the state company, *Codelco*, from its five mines, Chuquicamata, El Teniente, Salvador, Andina and Radomiro Tomic. Privately owned, high-tech mines or joint ventures are responsible for most of the expected growth.

Chile is fortunate in possessing reserves of oil, natural gas and coal, and abundant hydroelectricity potential. Almost all the country's hydrocarbon reserves are in the extreme south, on Tierra del Fuego, in the Strait of Magellan. Two pipelines are planned and up to six new gas-fired power plants may be built in 1998-2002, reducing electricity costs and pollution around Santiago if coal-fired plants are closed.

Manufacturing activity is mostly food processing, metalworking, textiles, footwear and fish processing. The sector has been vulnerable to changes in economic policy: the contribution of manufacturing to total GDP fell from 25% in 1970 to 20% in 1994, but its share of exports rose and the sector grew by over 6% a year in the 1990s.

The policies used to bring inflation down from over 500% at the end of 1973 to less than 10% by the end of 1981 resulted in fiscal balance but an overvalued currency. Freeing the exchange rate in 1982 caused renewed inflation; this was restricted by tight monetary control and a lower public sector borrowing requirement which caused a severe recession and contraction in GDP. In the 1980s Chile negotiated several debt refinancing packages and reduced its foreign debt through schemes which converted debt into equity in Chilean companies. Renewed growth in debt in the 1990s was offset by rising GDP and exports.

Recent trends

The Government follows anti-inflationary policies, accompanied by structural adjustment and reform. Privatization has been widespread, although certain key companies such as *Codelco* remain in state hands. Rising investor confidence brought economic growth throughout the late 1980s and most of the 1990s, and the Chilean model has been held up as an example for other debtor countries to adapt to their own needs.

However, although growth in real GDP averaged 8% during the period 1991-97, it fell to half that level in 1998 because of tight monetary policies implemented to keep the current account deficit in check and lower export earnings – the latter a product of the financial crisis in the Far East. A severe drought exacerbated the recession in 1999, reducing crop yields and causing hydroelectric shortfalls and rationing, and Chile experienced negative economic growth for the first time in more than 15 years. But despite the effects of the recession, Chile maintained its reputation for strong financial institutions and sound policy that have given it the strongest sovereign bond rating in South America. By the end of 1999, exports and economic activity had begun to recover. However, recovery was slow.

In November 2000, the monthly indicator for economic activity increased by an annual rate of 4.6% compared to the same month in 1999, well below the 5.8% expansion registered in October. Activity deteriorated further in December. The sharp drop in unemployment rate was seen as the only positive news at this time, falling to 8.3%. Yet such things are relative: the GDP growth of 5.4% in 2000 was second only to Mexico in Latin America. The Central Bank has forecast growth of 5.6% in 2001 and of 5.9% in 2002.

Culture

Arts and crafts

Chile's traditional crafts are often specific to particular places and all have a long history. Present-day handicrafts represent either the transformation of utilitarian objects into works of art, or the continued manufacture of pieces which retain symbolic value. A number of factors threaten these traditions: the loss of types of wood and plant fibres through the destruction of forests; the mechanization of farm labour, reducing the use of the horse; other agricultural changes which have, among other things, led to reductions in sheep farming and wheat growing; migration from the countryside to the city. On the other hand, city dwellers and tourists have created a demand for 'traditional' crafts so their future is to some degree assured.

The Mapuche Although silverware is one of the traditional crafts of the Mapuche, its production is in decline owing to the cost of the metal. Traditional women's jewellery includes ear-rings, headbands, necklaces, brooches and *tupus* (pins for fastening the *manta*, or shawl). Nowadays, the most common items to be found for sale are *chawai* (ear-rings), but these are smaller and in simpler shapes than those traditionally worn by Mapuche women. It is a matter of debate whether Mapuche silversmiths had perfected their skills before the arrival of the Spaniards; certainly the circulation of silver coins in the 18th century gave great impetus to this form of metalwork. The Universidad Católica in Temuco is in charge of a project to ensure the continuance of the art.

The Mapuche are also weavers of sheep's wool, making ponchos, *mantas*, sashes (*fajas*), reversible rugs (*lamas*) with geometric designs, and bedspreads (*pontros*). The colours come from natural dyes. The main producing areas are around Lago Lanalhue, Chol Chol, Nueva Imperial and other small settlements in the Mapuche heartland between Temuco and the coast (see pages 302 and 313).

Mapuche basketry is made for domestic, agricultural and fishing uses in Lago Lanalhue and the Cautín region. They also make musical instruments: the *trutruca*, a horn 1½ to 4 m long; *pifilka* (or *pifüllka*), a wooden whistle; the *kultrún* drum; *cascahuilla*, a string of bells; and *trompe*, similar to a Jew's harp. Another craft from this region is the carving of horn or antler (*asta*) in Temuco, to make animals, birds, cups, spoons, etc.

The island is famous for its woollen goods, hand-knitted and coloured with natural dyes. With the atrocious weather, clothing (such as sweaters, knitted caps, *mantas*, socks) is very popular; this, and rugs, blankets and patch dolls, are all sold locally and in Puerto Montt. The main knitting centres are Quinchao, Chonchi and Quellón. Other crafts of Chiloé are model boat building, and basketware from Quinchao and Quellón, where mats and figurines such as birds and fish are also made.

Chiloé

Items can be found in any part of the country where there are *huasos*: San Fernando, Chillán, Curicó, Colchagua, Doñihue and also in Santiago. Saddles of leather, wood and iron, carved wooden stirrups in the old style, leather reins, spurs (some of them huge and very elaborate; *huasos* are always proud of their spurs), and hats of straw or other materials are the types of equipment you will see. The clothing comprises ponchos (long, simple in colour and design, often with one or two coloured stripes), *mantas* (shorter, divided into four with a great variety of colour), *chamantos* (luxurious *mantas*, double-sided, decorated with fine patterns of vines, leaves, flowers, small birds, etc) and sashes/*fajas* (either single or tri-coloured, made to combine with *mantas* or *chamantos*).

Cowboy equipment & clothing

The two most famous places for ceramics are Quinchamalí near Chillán, page 290, where the traditional black ware is incised with patterns in white and Pomaire, west of Santiago, page 118), which is renowned for its terracotta household items which are used in many Chilean homes. Less well known is the pottery of the Atacama zone, the clay figures of Lihueimo (Región VI), the household items, clay figurines and model buildings of Pilén de Cauquenes-Maule (Región VII) and the scented pottery of the nuns of the Comunidad de Santa Clara (Convento de Monjas Claras in Santiago and Los Angeles). These highly decorated pieces have been made since colonial times, when they achieved great fame.

Ceramics

Apart from the areas already mentioned, one of the great centres of basket-making is Chimbarongo, just south of San Fernando in the Central Valley. Here weaving is done in almost every household, usually by the men. One of the main materials used is willow, which is collected in June when it is still green and then soaked in water for four months, at the end of which the bark peels off. The lengths of willow are split into four and finished with a knife. Baskets, chairs and lamps are the most common objects made. Willow is not the only fibre used. Many items are made from different types of straw, including the little boxes made of wheat; though the latter are produced throughout the country the most famous are from La Manga, Melipilla. Note also the yawl made for fishing, typical of Chiloé. Other important centres of basket-making are Ninhue-Hualte in Ñuble (Región VIII), Hualqui, 24 km south of Concepción, and San Juan de la Costa, near the coast of Osorno, Región X.

Basketry

The people of the Atacama region edge trays and make little churches out of cactus wood; they also use cactus for drums and bamboo for flutes of various sizes. Different types of wood are used in the construction of guitars, *guitarrones*, harps and *rabeles* (fiddles), mainly in the Metropolitan Region. Villarrica, page 323, is a major producer of wooden items: plates, kitchen utensils, but especially decorative objects like animals and birds, jointed snakes and *picarones* (small figures which, when picked up, reveal their genitals). Another craft in wood is the ship in a bottle, made in Coronel. In Loncoche, south of Temuco, a workshop specializes in fine carvings, in native woods, of country and Mapuche scenes.

Wood

This village, near the Termas de Panimávida, some 25 km northeast of Linares (Región VII), specializes in beautiful, delicate items made from dyed horsehair: bangles and brooches in the shape of butterflies, little hats, flowers, etc.

Rari

Lapis lazuli Mined in the Cordillera de Ovalle, this blue stone, only found otherwise in Afghanistan, is set in silver to make earrings, necklaces and bracelets. Many shops in Santiago sell the gemstone and objects that incorporate it, see page 106.

Fine art and sculpture

The colonial period There was little home-grown art during the colonial period in Chile, but trade with other regions was extensive and Santiago in particular has good collections of non-Chilean colonial art. At this time the Catholic church inevitably dominated the fine arts and sculpture. The many new religious foundations needed images of Christ and the saints to reassure the Christian settlers and also to instruct the new converts, and without a strong local school Chile had to meet this demand from elsewhere. The importation of works from Spain was very costly, so most patrons relied instead on the major colonial artistic centres of Cusco, Potosí and Quito.

The churches and monasteries of Santiago give a vivid sense of the thriving art market in colonial Spanish America: sculptures were shipped down the coast from Lima and from Quito via Guayaquil, canvases carried across the Andes on mule trains from Cusco and Potosí, and occasionally an itinerant Spanish-trained artist would pass through in search of lucrative commissions. Extensive cycles of the lives of Christ, the Virgin and selected saints were popular: a cycle of 40 or 50 large canvases representing the exploits of, say, St Francis, provided instant cover for large expanses of bare plaster, a good clear narrative and an exemplary life to follow.

So, for example, San Francisco in Santiago has a cycle of 53 paintings of the life of St Francis painted in Cusco in the later 17th century. These are based on a similar cycle in the Franciscan monastery in Cusco by the Indian artist Basilio de Santa Cruz Pumacallao which is in turn derived from a series of European engravings. One of the Santiago paintings, the Funeral of St Francis of 1684, is signed by Juan Zapaca Inca, also, as his name suggests, an Indian and follower of Santa Cruz, and the whole series was probably produced under Zapaca's guidance. Wherever possible the artist has introduced bright-coloured tapestries and rich fabrics embellished with lace and gold embroidery, a mark of the continuing importance of textiles in Andean culture. This is a typical pattern for colonial art: a set of European engravings forms the basis for a large painted cycle which in turn becomes the source for further copies and derivatives. The narrative content and general composition remain constant while the setting, attendant figures, costume and decorative detail are often translated into an Andean idiom.

There are, of course, many different categories of colonial art. The big painted cycles were produced more for the educated inhabitants of the monastic establishments than for a lay audience, and were intended for edification rather than devotion. Popular devotion tends to create increasingly decorated and hieratic images. A good example is that of the so-called Cristo de Mayo. Early in the 17th century Pedro de Figueroa, a friar of the Augustinian monastery in Santiago, carved a figure of the crucified Christ which still hangs in the church of San Agustín. This passionate, unusually defiant image was credited with miraculous powers after it survived a serious earthquake in Santiago in May 1647 (hence the popular name *de Mayo*). The only damage was that the crown of thorns slipped from Christ's head and lodged around his neck. A cult quickly grew up around the image, creating a demand for painted copies which are identifiable by the upward gaze, the distinctive necklace of thorns, and the evenly distributed lash marks across the body. The Carmelite convent of San José has a locally produced 18th-century example of the Cristo de Mayo which includes attendant saints and garlands of bright flowers, the latter like pious offerings. The Jesuits established a school of sculpture on Chiloé, where up until the late 19th century, native craftsmen continued to produce boldly expressive Christian images.

In the 19th century, Chile's distance from the old colonial centre of viceregal power worked to its advantage in the field of art. The Lima-born artist José Gil de Castro (died 1841), known as El Mulato Gil, accompanied Bernardo O'Higgins on the campaign for Chilean independence from 1814, working both as an engineer and map-maker and as a portrait painter. His portrait of O'Higgins of 1820 in the Museo Histórico Nacional in Santiago represents him as a towering giant of a man, immovable as the rocky mountains behind him, while in a painting in the Municipalidad of La Serena of 1818 San Martín is shown standing beside a writing desk, his hand inside his jacket in a distinctively Napoleonic pose. The 19th century also brought European traveller-artists to Chile who helped to confirm the Chilean landscape, peoples and customs as legitimate subjects for paintings, including the German Johann Moritz Rugendas who lived in Chile from 1833 to 1845, and the Englishman Charles Wood (in Chile from 1819 to 1852). Examples of both artists' work can be seen in the Museo Nacional de Bellas Artes. The Frenchman Raymond Monvoisin also spent several years in Chile, from 1843 to 1857. His perceptive portraits of members of the government and the literary élite are interesting for the way in which they link the Chilean tradition of Gil de Castro with European sources, and after his return to France he produced the first major painting dedicated to an event from colonial history, the Mapuche hero Caupolicán taken prisoner by the Spaniards (1859, Museo O'Higginiano, Talca). Caupolicán was celebrated in Chile 10 years later in a bronze statue by Nicanor Plaza (1844-1914) erected on the Cerro Santa Lucía in Santiago, and although it originated as an entry for a competition organized by the US government for a statue to commemorate the Last of the Mohicans, it represents the incorporation of the Indian into national mythology.

The Chilean Academy of Painting was founded in 1849 and, although its first presidents were mediocre European artists, they too helped to make Chilean subject matter respectable, while the Academy acted as a focus for aspiring young artists. Antonio Smith (1832-77) rebelled against the rigidity of the academic system, working as a political cartoonist as well as a painter, but his dramatic landscapes grew out of the gradual awakening of interest in Chilean scenery. He transformed the picturesque view into a heroic vision of mountains and valleys, full of air and space and potential. Cosme San Martín (1850-1906), Pedro León Carmona (1853-99), Pedro Lira (1845-1912), Alfredo Valenzuela Puelma (1856-1909) and English-born Thomas Somerscales (1842-1927) extended the range of possible national subjects in the fields of landscape, portraiture, history and genre. The late 19th century saw a number of important commissions for nationalistic public statuary including the peasant soldier 'El Roto Chileno' in Santiago's Plaza Yungay by Nicanor Plaza's pupil Virginio Arias (1855-1941), and several monumental works by Rebecca Matte (1875-1929).

From the later 19th century until well into the 20th century, Chilean painting was dominated by refracted versions of Impressionism. Artists such as **Juan Francisco González** (1853-1933) and **Alfredo Helsby** (1862-1933) introduced a looser technique and more luminous palette to create landscapes full of strong contrasts of sunlight and shadows, a tradition continued by, for example, Pablo Burchard (1873-1964), **Agustín Abarca** (1882-1953), **Arturo Gordon** (1883-1944) and **Camilo Mori** (1896-1973).

The Chilean avant-garde has been dominated by artists who have lived and worked for long periods abroad, many as political exiles. After studying with Le Corbusier in Switzerland and encountering the Surrealists in Paris, **Roberto Matta** (born 1911) moved to New York in 1939 and began painting uniquely unsettling space-age monsters and machines which circulate in a multi-dimensional chaos; he is perhaps the most famous artist to have come from Chile. **Nemesio Antúnez**

(1918-1993) developed more earth-bound abstractions of reality: volcanic land-scapes viewed through flames and falling rocks, or milling crowds, faceless and powerless. The younger generation includes **Eugenio Dittborn** (born 1943) who sends 'Airmail Paintings' around the world in an exploration of ideas of transition and dislocation and, because many contain photographs of victims of political violence, of anonymity and loss. **Alfredo Jaar** (born 1956) creates installations using maps and photographs to document the destructive exploitation of the world's resources, both human and natural – most recently focusing on the aftermath of the Rwandan genocide. In recent years many exiles have returned home and Santiago is now a cultural centre of growing importance, with women particularly well-represented (for example Carmen Valbuena, born 1955, and Bernarda Zegers, born 1951). Chile is the home of an interesting ongoing project called 'Cuerpos Pintados', Painted Bodies, whereby artists from Chile and other Latin American countries are invited to Santiago to paint nude models in the colours and designs of their choice. It is worth watching out for exhibitions of the stunning photographs which are the project's permanent outcome; and also for one-off exhibitions up and down the country of the many very talented local artists (especially in cultural centres such as Concepción and La Serena).

Literature

From colonial times to independence

The long struggle of the Spaniards to conquer the lands south of their Peruvian stronghold inspired one of the great epics of early Spanish American literature, *La Araucana* by **Alonso de Ercilla y Zúñiga** (1533-94). Published in three parts (1569, 1578 and 1589), the poem tells of the victories and defeats of Spaniards. Nothing like an apologia, Ercilla recognizes the brutal work of the Spaniards in a work that has endured. Like a subsequent work, *Arauco domado* (1596), by the criollo **Pedro de Oña** (1570-1643), the point of view is that of the conquering invader, not a celebration of Chilean, or American identity, although Ercilla does show that the people who resisted the Spaniards were noble and courageous. After Ercilla, literature written in what was to become Chile concentrated on chronicling either the physical or the spiritual conquest of the local inhabitants.

Writers in the 18th and early 19th centuries tended to mirror the colonial desire to consolidate the territory which was in Spanish, rather than Mapuche hands. Post-independence, the move was towards the establishment of the new republic. To this end, the Venezuelan **Andrés Bello** (1781-1865) was invited to Santiago from London in 1829 to oversee the education of the new élite. Already famous for his literary journals and strong views on Romantic poetry, Bello made major contributions to Chilean scholarship and law. His main work was *Gramática de la lengua castellana destinada al uso de los americanos* (1847). As Jean Franco says, "He was one of the first of many writers to see that a general literary Spanish could act as an important cohesive factor, a spiritual tie of the Hispanic peoples".

A cultural haven

Chile's relative political stability in the 19th century helped Santiago to become a cultural centre which attracted many foreign intellectuals such as the Argentine Diego Sarmiento and the Nicaraguan Rubén Darío. At this time, Chilean writers were establishing a national literary framework to replace the texts of the colonial era. This involved the spreading of 'buenas costumbres', a republican education for the middle classes and the founding of a national identity. Realist fiction captured the public interest. **José Victorino Lastarria** (1817-1888) wrote *costumbrista* stories, portraying national scenes and characters. **Alberto Blest Gana** (1829-1904) enjoyed two periods of success as a novelist, heavily influenced by Balzac. His most popular novel was *Martín Rivas* (1862), the love story of a young man who wins a wife of a higher class. For some, Blest Gana's presentation of Santiago and its class structure is a worthy imitator of the French *comédie humaine*; for others his realism fails either to unite his themes to his sketches of Chilean life, or to rise above a pedestrian style.

Well into the 20th century, realism was the dominant mode of fiction, but in several guises. **Baldomero Lillo** (1867-1923) wrote socialist realist stories about the coal miners of Lebu: *Sub terra* (1904) and *Sub sole* (1907). Lillo and other regionalist writers shifted the emphasis away from the city to the countryside and the miserable conditions endured by many Chileans. Other novelists concentrated on the crisis of aristocratic values and the gulf between the wealthy and the deprived: eg **Luis Orrego Luco** (1866-1948), and **Joaquín Edwards Bello** (1887-1968).

20th-century prose writing

Another strand was *criollismo*, a movement seeking to portray Chile and the tribulations of Chileans without romanticism, championed especially by short story writers like **Mariano Latorre** (1886-1955), whose main interest was the Chilean landscape, which he described almost to the point of overwhelming his characters. A different emphasis was given to regionalism and *criollismo* by **Augusto d'Halmar** (Augusto Goeminne Thomson, 1882-1950), whose stories in *La lámpara en el molino* (1914) were given exotic settings and were labelled *imaginismo*. D'Halmar's followers, the Grupo Letras (1920s and 1930s), became openly antagonistic towards the disciples of Latorre, eg **Luis Durand** whose books of the 1920s and 1940s described in detail *campesino* life. Another branch of realism was the exploration of character through psychology in the books of **Eduardo Barrios** (1884-1963), eg *El niño que enloqueció de amor* (1915), *El hermano asno* (1922) and *Los hombres del hombre* (1950).

The anti-fascist views of a group of writers known as the Generation of 1938 (**Nicomedes Guzmán**, 1914-65, **Juan Godoy**, **Carlos Droguett**, born 1915, and others) added a politically committed dimension with support for the working class which coincided with the rise to power of the Frente Popular, a socialist movement. At the same time, *Mandrágora*, a journal principally dedicated to poetry, introduced many European literary ideas, notably those of the surrealists. Its influence, combined with a global decline in Marxist writing after the Second World War and the defeat of the Frente Popular, contributed to a new generation in the 1950s whose main drive was the rejection of all the *ismos* that had preceded it. The novelists, short story writers and dramatists were characterized by existential individualism and political and social scepticism. Many writers started publishing in the 1950s, among them **Volodia Teitelboim** (born 1916), a communist exiled to the USSR after 1973, whose novels *Hijo del salitre* (1952) and *La semilla en la arena* (1957) were portrayals of the struggles of the Chilean masses (in 1979 he published *La guerra interna* a mixture of real and imaginary characters in post-coup Chile).

The decline of criollismo

From the 1920s on, a significant development away from *criollismo* was the rise of the female voice. The first such novelist to achieve major recognition was **Marta Brunet** (1901-67), who brought a unique perspective to the rural themes she handled (including the need to value women), but who has also been described as a writer of the senses (by Nicomedes Guzmán). Her books include *Montaña adentro* (1923), *Aguas abajo* (1943), *Humo hacia el sur* (1946) and *María Nadie* (1957). Also born in 1901, **María Flora Yáñez** wrote about the alienation of women, too, with great emphasis on the imagination as an escape for her female protagonists from their routine, unfulfilled lives (*El abrazo de la tierra*, 1934; *Espejo sin imágen*, 1936; *Las cenizas*, 1942). **María Luisa Bombal** (1910-80) took the theme of alienated women even further (*La última niebla*, 1935; *La amortajada*, 1938, and various short stories): her narrative and her characters' worlds spring from the subconscious realm of female experience and are expressed through dreams, fantasies and journeys loaded with symbolic meaning.

Background

Manuel Rojas (1896-1972) was brought up in Argentina, but his family moved to Chile in 1923. His first short stories, such as *Hombres del sur* (1926), *Travesía* (1934) and the novel *Lanchas en la bahía* (1932) were undoubtedly *criollista* in outlook, but he devoted a greater importance to human concerns than his *criollista* contemporaries. By 1951, Rojas' style had changed dramatically, without deserting realism. *Hijo de ladrón* (1951) was perhaps the most influential 20th-century Chilean novel up to that time. It describes the adventures of Aniceto Hevía, the son of a Buenos Aires jewel thief, who crosses the Andes to Valparaíso, ending up, after continually moving on, as a beachcomber. Nothing in his life is planned, or motivated by anything other than the basic necessities. Happiness and intimacy are only brief moments in an unharmonious, disordered life. Aniceto's adventures are continued in *Mejor que el vino* (1958), *Sombras contra el muro* (1963) and *La obscura vida radiante* (1971). To describe the essential isolation of man from the inside, Rojas relaxes the temporal structure of the novel, bringing in memory, interior monologue and techniques to multiply the levels of reality (to use Fernando Alegría's phrase).

The demise of *criollismo* coincided with the influence of the US Beat Generation and the culture epitomized by James Dean, followed in the 1960s by the protest movements in favour of peace, blacks' and women's rights. The Cuban Revolution inspired Latin American intellectuals of the left and the novel-writing 'boom' gained momentum. At the same time, the national political process which led ultimately to Salvador Allende's victory in 1970 was bolstered by writers, folk singers and painters who questioned everything to do with the Chilean bourgeoisie.

To the 1973 coup and beyond

José Donoso (1924-1996) began publishing stories in 1955 (*Veraneo y otros cuentos*), followed two years later by his first novel, *Coronación*. The book describes the chaos caused by the arrival of a new maid into an aristocratic Santiago household and introduces many of Donoso's recurring themes: the closed worlds of old age and childhood, madness, multiple levels of reality, the inauthenticity of the upper classes and the subversion of patriarchal society. The stories in *Charleston* (1960), *El lugar sin límites* (1966), about a transvestite and his daughter who live in a brothel near Talca, and *Este domingo* (1966) mark the progression from *Coronación* to *El obsceno pájaro de la noche* (1970), a labyrinthine novel (Donoso's own term) narrated by a schizophrenic, throwing together reality, dreams and fantasy, darkness and light. Donoso achieved the same status as Gabriel García Márquez, Julio Cortázar and Mario Vargas Llosa with this, his most experimental novel. Between 1967 and 1981 he lived in Spain; in the 1970s he published several novels, including *Casa de campo* (1978), which relates the disintegration of a family estate when the children try to take it over. Back in Chile, he published, among others, *El jardín de al lado* (1981), which chronicles the decline of a middle-aged couple in exile in Spain, *Cuatro para Delfina* (1982), *La desesperanza* (1986) about the return of a left-wing singer from Paris to the daily horrors of Pinochet's regime.

Another writer who describes the bad faith of the aristocracy is **Jorge Edwards** (born 1931). His books include *El patio* (1952), *Los convidados de piedra* (1978), *El museo de cera* (1980), *La mujer imaginaria* (1985) and *Fantasmas de carne y hueso* (1993). His book *Persona non grata* (1973) describes his experiences as a diplomat, including his expulsion from Cuba. **Fernando Alegría** (born 1918) spans all the movements since 1938. His work includes essays, highly respected literary criticism, poetry and novels. He was closely associated with Salvador Allende and was his cultural attaché in Washington in 1970-73. *Recabarren* was published in 1938, after which followed many books, among them *Lautaro, joven libertador del Arauco* (1943), *Caballo de copas* (1957), *Mañana los guerreros* (1964), *El paso de los gansos* (1975), about a young photographer's experiences in the 1973 coup, *Coral de guerra* (1979), also about brutality under military dictatorship, *Una especie de memoria*

Ariel Dorfman

As expressed in the subtitle of his fascinating recent memoir, Heading South, Looking North (1998), the literary and political career of Ariel Dorfman has taken the form of a 'bilingual journey', between the United States and South America, between English and Spanish. Born in Buenos Aires in 1942, his father's political activism saw the family – Russian Jewish immigrants to Argentina – expelled from Argentina in the mid-1940s, when they took up residence in New York, until McCarthyism sent the Dorfmans once more south in 1954, this time to Chile. Here the monolingual, English-speaking adolescent gradually made the Spanish language and Chilean politics and culture his main focus of activity until the military coup of 1973 sent him once again into exile, where he became one of the most articulate, bilingual voices against the military régime.

With the return to civilian government in 1990, he divides his time between Santiago and a professional post at Duke University, writing and broadcasting in both Spanish and English. Dorfman's work, as a poet, novelist, short story writer, essayist, playwright and more recently scriptwriter, is concerned, in his words, with, 'on the one hand, the glorious potential and need of human beings to tell stories and, on the other, the brutal fact that in today's world, most of the lives that should be telling those stories are generally

ignored, ravaged and silenced'. He is perhaps best known for his early critique of US cultural imperialism, How to Read Donald Duck (1971) and his Death and the Maiden (1990), later filmed by Roman Polanski, which deals with torture and resistance.

His prolific output includes the novels Moros en la costa, 1973, (Hard Rain), La última canción de Manuel Sendero, 1982 (The Last Song of Manuel Sendero), Mascara, 1988, Viudas, 1981, (Widows), Konfidenz, 1995 and The Nanny and the Iceberg, 1999; the plays Death and the Maiden, Reader (1995), Widows (1997) and 2 further plays co-written with is son Rodrigo, Mascara and Who's Who (1997); several volumes of essays and many poems (some collected in English as Last Waltz in Santiago and other poems of Exile and Disappearance, (1988). He often adapts his own work to different genres: Widows started as a poem, became a novel and later a play. Much of the work focuses on torture, disappearance, censorship and the exile condition, but also demonstrates staunch rebellion and resistance and optimism for our future.

Most of Dorfman's work is currently in print in English. His memoir Heading North, Looking South is essential reading. The plays, Death and the Maiden, Reader and Widows have been collected in the volume The Resistance Trilogy (1998). His latest novel is The Nanny and the Iceberg (1999).

Background

(1983), Alegría's own memoir of 1938 to 1973, and *Allende: A Novel* (1992). Having been so close to Allende, Alegría could not write a biography, he had to fictionalize it, he said. But the rise and fall of Allende becomes a realization that history and fiction are intimately related, particularly in that Chilean epoch.

The death of Salvador Allende in 1973, and with it the collapse of the left's struggle to gain power by democratic means, was a traumatic event for Chilean writers. Those who had built their careers in the 1960s and early 1970s were for the most part exiled, forcibly or voluntarily, and thus were condemned to face the left's own responsibility in Allende's failure. René Jara says that before 1970 writers had not managed to achieve mass communication for their ideas and 1970-73 was too short a time to correct that. Once Pinochet was in power, the task became how to find a language capable of expressing the usurping of democracy without simplifying reality. Those in exile still felt part of Chile, a country temporarily wiped from the map, where their thought was prohibited.

There are many other contemporary male novelists who deserve mention, but this survey will confine itself to **Antonio Skármeta** (born 1940), another exile, in Germany, until 1980, who writes short stories, novels and directs in the theatre and cinema. His short-story collections include *El entusiasmo* (1967), *Desnudo en el tejado* (1969), *Tiro libre* (1973) and his novels *Soñé que la nieve ardía* (975), *No pasó nada* (1980), *Ardiente paciencia* (1985) and *Match-ball* (1989). *Ardiente paciencia*, retitled *El cartero de Neruda* after its successful filming as *Il postino*, is a good example of Skármeta's concern for the enthusiasms and emotions of ordinary people, skilfully weaving the love life of a postman and a bar owner's daughter into the much bigger picture of the death of Pablo Neruda and the fall of Allende. The most successful Chilean novelist today is **Isabelle Allende** (born 1942). Her book *La casa de los espíritus* (1982) was a phenomenally successful novel worldwide. Allende, a niece of Salvador Allende, was born in Peru and went into exile in Venezuela after the 1973 coup. *The House of the Spirits*, with its tale of the dynasty of Esteban Trueba interwoven with Chilean history throughout much of the 20th century, ends with a thinly disguised description of 1973. It was followed in 1984 by *De amor y de sombra*, a disturbing tale set during the Pinochet régime. The main motivation behind these novels is the necessity to preserve historical reality (see the brief prologue to *Of Love and Shadows*, "Here, write it, or it will be erased by the wind"). The same thing applies in *Paula* (1994), Allende's letter to her daughter in a coma: a possible salvation from the devastation of not being able to contact Paula is through the 'meticulous exercise of writing'. She has also written *Eva Luna* (1987) and *Los cuentos de Eva Luna* (1990), about a fictional Venezuelan storyteller and her stories themselves, *El plan infinito* (1991) and (her most recent novel) *Daughter of Fortune* (1998).

Like her predecessors, Allende employs the marvellous and the imaginary to propose alternatives to the masculine view of social and sexual relations. The same is true of **Lucía Guerra** (born 1942), who published *Más allá de las máscaras* in exile in 1984. Another example might be **Daniela Eltit** (born 1949) who did not leave Chile after 1973 and was actively involved in resistance movements. Her provocative, intense fiction confronts issues of exploitation, violence, the oppression of women and volatile mental states. In *Vaca sagrada* (1991) at least, the protagonist's body becomes the expression of her vulnerability, through her blood, her two lovers' effects upon it, the brutality inflicted upon it and her obsession with her heartbeat. The main characters live out their obsessions and fears in a city in which there are no jobs and no warmth. Three earlier novels, *Lumpérica* (1983), *Por la patria* (1986) and *El cuarto mundo* (1988) maintain the same experimental, challenging approach to contemporary Chilean society.

20th-century poetry In many ways poetry is at some level the lifeblood of Chilean culture; there is a prodigious poetic output, with poetry circles thriving even in remote rural areas. In the first half of the 20th century, four figures dominated Chilean poetry, Gabriela Mistral, Vicente Huidobro, Pablo Neruda and Pablo de Rokha. The three men were all socialists, but in their politics and the expression of their views, each followed a different trajectory. Neruda overshadows all other Chilean poets on an international level, and for this reason he is discussed in the accompanying box, but this should not hide the fact that Chile has had a very strong poetic tradition.

Gabriela Mistral wrote poetry which rejected elaboration in favour of a simple style with traditional metre and verse forms. Her poetry derives from a limited number of personal roots: she fell in love with Romelio Ureta who, for a variety of reasons, blew his brains out in 1909. This inspired the *Sonetos de la muerte* (1914), which were not published at the time. She never lost the grief of this tragic love, which was coupled with her love of God and her 'immense martyrdom at not being a mother'. Frustrated motherhood did not deprive her of tenderness, nor of a deep love for children. The other main theme was her appreciation of nature and landscape, not just Chile, but also other parts of the world which she visited when her diplomatic career led to her representing Chile in North and South America and Europe. Her three principal collections are *Desolación* (1923, but re-edited and amplified frequently), *Tala* (1938) and *Lagar* (1954). She also wrote many poems for children.

If Gabriela Mistral relied on the traditions and her verse alone to present her unique view of a lone woman trying to find a place in a male-oriented world, **Vicente Huidobro** (1893-1948) wanted to break with all certainties and he made grand claims for the poet's role in this. His was nothing short of a quest for the infinite and for the language to liberate it. From Santiago he moved to Buenos Aires, then Paris, where he joined the Cubists, collaborated with Apollinaire and others, began to write in French and got involved in radical politics. Between the 1920s and 1940s he moved from Europe to the USA to Chile, back to Spain during the Civil War, before retiring to Llolleo to confront time and death in his last poems, *Ultimos poemas*, 1948. Huidobro considered himself at the forefront of the avant-garde, formulating *creacionismo*, a theory that the poet is not bound by the real world, but is free to create and invent new worlds through the complete freedom of the word. Nevertheless, all the experimentation and imagery which 'unglued the moon', was insufficient to achieve the language of revelation. So in 1931 he composed *Altazor*, a seven-canto poem which describes simultaneously the poet's route to creation and the ultimate frustration imposed by time and the human condition.

Pablo de Rokha (Carlos Díaz Loyola, 1894-1968) was deeply concerned for the destiny of the Chilean people and the advance of international socialism. His output was an uncompromising, epic search for Chilean identity and through it, for all its political commitment, there runs a deep sense of tragedy and inner solitude (especially true in *Fuego negro*, 1951, written after the death of his wife). *Los gemidos* was his first major book (1922); others included *Escritura de Raimundo Contreras* (1929), a song of the Chilean peasant, *Jesucristo* (1933) and *La morfología del espanto* (1942).

These poets, and Neruda especially, furthered the Chilean poetic tradition, but those who came after Neruda in the 1950s were not necessarily keen to emulate his style or his politics. The new generation of poets was still critical of society but, taking their cue from Nicanor Parra, they did not elevate the writer's role in denouncing inhumanity, alienation and the depersonalization of modern life. Instead writer and reader are placed on the same level; rhetoric and exuberant language are replaced by a conversational, ironic tone. **Parra** (born 1914; see box, page 292), a scientist and teacher, called this attempt to overcome the influence of Neruda *antipoesía* (antipoetry). In the poem 'Advertencia al lector' in *Poemas y antipoemas* (1954), he writes:

According to the doctors of the law this book should not be published:
The word rainbow does not appear in it,
Let alone the word grief,
Chairs and tables, yes, there are aplenty,
Coffins! Writing utensils!
Which fills me with pride
Because, as I see it, the sky is falling to bits.

Obra gruesa anthologizes his work to 1969, followed by *Emergency Poems* (1972, bilingual edition, New York), which contain a darker humour, profound poems, satire, but remain compassionate, socially committed, *Artefactos* (1972) and *Artefactos II* (1982), *Sermones y prédicas del Cristo de Elqui* (1979) and *Poesía política* (1983).

The adherents of *antipoesía* continually sought new means of expression, so that the genre never became institutionalized. There are too many poets to list here, but

Pablo Neruda

Pablo Neruda was born in Parral on 12 June 1904. His real name was Ricardo Neftalí Reyes. Two months after his birth his mother died. His father and stepmother soon moved to Temuco and Neruda's childhood memories were dominated by nature and, above all, rain, "my only unforgettable companion", as he described it in Confieso que he vivido. *Among his teachers in Temuco was Gabriela Mistral. In 1921 he went to study in Santiago, but already he had decided on a literary career. His first book of poems,* Crepusculario *(1923), was published under the pseudonym Neruda, borrowed from a Czech writer; it was postmodernist in style but did not yet reveal the poet's own voice. His next volume,* Veinte poemas de amor y una canción desesperada *(1924) catapulted him into the forefront of Latin American poetry. The freedom of the style and the natural, elemental imagery invoking the poet's two love affairs, with a girl from Temuco and another from the capital, made the collection an immediate success. Three books followed in 1926 before Neruda was sent to Rangoon as Chilean consul in 1927. His experiences in the Orient, including his first marriage, did not alleviate an intense period of solitude and anguish. This inspired one of his finest collections,* Residencia en la tierra *(covering the years 1925-35). The inherent sadness of the* Veinte poemas *becomes despair at the passage of time and human frailty. Reinforcing this overriding theme is a kaleidoscope of images, all seemingly jumbled together and yet deliberately placed to show the chaos and fragmentary nature of man's passage towards death (see particularly 'Arte poética').*

In the 1930s, Neruda moved to Spain, where he edited the review Caballo verde para la poesía *and kept company with many poets. The Civil War, especially the death of Federico García Lorca, affected him deeply and his poetic vision changed radically, away from the subjectivity of his earlier work to a more direct poetry, with a strong political orientation. See 'Explico algunas cosas' in* Tercera residencia *(1947), which explains the move towards militancy.*

Between 1938 and the election of Gabriel González Videla to the Chilean presidency he worked with the Frente Popular, was consul general in Mexico and maintained his membership of the Communist Party. He also composed at this time his epic poem of Latin American and Chilean history, from a Marxist stance, Canto general *(1950). It contains 15 cantos, chronicling the natural and human life of the Americas, the oppression of its peoples, from the conquered pre-Columbian inhabitants to the 20th-century labourers. It celebrates Chile and its campesinos, its anonymous workers in the copper, coal and salt mines and ends with his own testament, 'Yo soy'. One of its most famous sections is "Alturas de Machu Picchu" which mirrors the tone of the whole and his own poetic development: from the universal to the 'minuscule life', from his own introspection to his new-found role as the voice of the*

Gonzalo Rojas (born 1917), Enríque Lihn (1929-88), Armando Uribe (born 1933) and Miguel Arteche (born 1926) are perhaps the best known. Another poetic development of the 1950s onwards was *poesía lárica*, or *de lares*, poetry of one's place of origin (literally, of the gods of the hearth). Its founder and promoter was **Jorge Teillier** (1935-96), whose poems describe a precarious rural existence, wooden houses, fencing, orchards, distant fires, beneath changing skies and rain. The city dweller is an exile in space and time who returns every so often to the place of origin. See especially 'Notas sobre el último viaje del autor a su pueblo natal', which evokes the lost frontier of his youth, the changed countryside and his city life. As for the future, "if only it could be as beautiful as my mother spreading the sheets on my bed", but it is only an unpaid bill; "I wish the UFOs would arrive." In his later poems, the violence of oppressed. Everything now revolves not around futility, but hope and struggle.

Canto general defined Neruda's subsequent enormous output. The political commitment remained, but did not submerge his respect for, and evocation of nature: eg Odas elementales (1954), Nuevas odas elementales (1957) and Tercer libro de odas (1959), which begins with 'El hombre invisible':
"for my life, give me all lives,
give me all the sorrow
of all the world
and I will transform it
into hope ...
give me
the daily
struggle,
because these things are my song
the song of the invisible man
who sings with all men."
(Translated by Margaret Sayers Peden, London: Libris 1991).
Neruda remarried twice and never tired of writing lyric verse, eg Los versos del capitán (1950), Cien sonetos de amor (1959). He also wrote memoirs such as Memorial de Isla Negra (1964), Confieso que he vivido (1974).

Extravagaria (1958), whose title suggests extravagance, wandering, variety, vagaries, is full of memory, acceptance and a kind of world-weary joy; see 'Aquellos días'. Also compare 'Walking around', the most pessimistic poem in Residencia en la tierra ("It happens that I am tired of being a man" ...) with 'A certain weariness':
"I don't want to be tired alone,

I want you to be tired with me ...
"I am tired of the hard sea and the mysterious earth, of the chickens (we never know what they are thinking) ... of getting up ... of going to bed without glory ... of statues, of remembering.
"I want you to grow tired with me
of everything that is well done.
Of everything that makes us grow old.
Of all that lies in wait to wear out other people
Let us tire of what kills
and of what does not want to die."
(Extravagaria has been translated by Alastair Reid, New York: Farrar, Straus and Giroux, 1974.)

Neruda, who was awarded the Nobel Prize in 1971, died of cancer on 23 September 1973, his death hastened by the Pinochet coup and the military's heartless treatment of him when they removed him from Isla Negra to Santiago. The poet's three properties (see pages 91, 135 and 154) were either ransacked or shut up by the dictatorship, but many of the thousands of Chileans to whom and for whom the poet spoke visited Isla Negra to leave their messsages of respect, love and hope until democracy returned. (See Ariel Dorfman's 'Afterword' in The House in the Sand, translation of Una casa en la arena by Dennis Maloney and Clark M Zlotchew, Minneapolis: Milkweed, 1990.) For a bilingual anthology, see Selected Poems of Pablo Neruda, translated and edited by Ben Belitt (New York: Grove Press, 1961); there are many other translations of individual volumes.

---

the city and the dictatorship invade the lares. Among Teillier's books are Para angeles y gorriones (1956), Para un pueblo fantasma (1978), Cartas para reinas de otras primaveras (1985) and Los dominios perdidos (1992). Another poeta lárico, but also an antipoeta, is Floridor Pérez (born 1937). A variation on this type of poetry comes from **Clemente Riedemann** (born 1953), whose Karra Maw'n deals with the Mapuche lands and the German immigration in the area.

Many poets left Chile after 1973 but others stayed to attack the dictatorship from within through provocative, experimental works. In a country with such a strong poetic tradition and such a serious political situation, poets understood that their verses had to mutate in order to reflect and comment on their contemporary reali-ties. A more experimental and opaque poetry developed as a result, dealing with themes such as the reaffirmation of colloquialism, the city developed through the slang of *antipoesía*, and that of poetry itself unravelling contexts and bridging the past and the present. Several of these writers were members of the Grupo Experimental de Artaud: Daniela Eltit (see above), Raúl Zurita, Eugenia Brito, Rodrigo Cánovas. **Zurita** is perhaps the most celebrated poet in Chile today: his verse is a complex and at times difficult union of mathematics and poetry, logical, structured and psychological. *Purgatorio* (1979) had an immediate impact and was followed by *Anteparaíso* (1982), *El paraíso está vacío* (1984), *Canto a su amor desaparecido* (1986) and *El amor de Chile* (1987). 'Pastoral de Chile' in *Anteparaíso* reveals most of Zurita's obsessions: Chilean landscapes, love, Chile's distress, sin and religious terminology. *La Tirana* (1985) by **Diego Maquieira** is a complex, multireferential work, dealing with a Mapuche virgin, surrounded by a culture which oppresses her and with which she disguises herself. It is irreverent, a 'black mass', threatening to the régime. Carmen Berenguer's *Bobby Sands desfallece en el muro* (1983) is a homage to the IRA prisoner and thus to all political prisoners. She also wrote *Huellas del siglo* (1986) and *A media asta* (1988). Carla Grandi published *Contraproyecto* in 1985, an example of feminine resistance to the coup.

Poetry continues to be significant in Chile. There are numerous workshops and organizations for young poets; the *Taller de Poesía de la Fundacion Pablo Neruda* is particularly influencial. There are also important underground literary movements. Interesting young contemporary poets include Carolina Cerlis and Javier del Cerro, both maintaining the experimental and free verse tradition of Zurita and others.

Cinema

Not many months after the first screening organized by the Lumière brothers in Paris in December 1895, moving pictures were exhibited in Chile on 25 August 1896. Initially all the films began to produce imported, but some years later – from 1902 – local artists and entrepreneurs began to produce short documentaries and the first narrative movie, *Manual Rodríguez*, was screened in September 1910. From about 1915, with European production semi-paralyzed by war, the pre-eminence of Hollywood cinema was established. The modern dreams of Hollywood were often more complex, technologically superior and more entertaining than the products of rudimentary national cinemas. The historian of Chilean silent films, Eliana Jara Donoso, quotes a publicity handout for a local movie that read, 'it's so good that it doesn't seem Chilean.'

But despite the overwhelming presence of Hollywood, local film makers in the silent era could still establish a small presence in the market. In the main they made documentaries, for this was a niche that international competitors were not concerned with: regional topics, football competitions, civic ceremonies, military parades. Almost 100 feature films were also made, but these are the domain of the film historian, searching through newspaper articles, for only one such movie has survived (carefully restored by the University of Chile in the early sixties): *El húsar de la muerte* (The Hussar of Death), directed by Pedro Sienna in 1925. It was, like many movies in Latin America at the time, an historical melodrama, exploring the fight for Chilean independence from Spanish rule in the 1810s through the heroic exploits of the legendary Manual Rodríguez. It achieved a great box office success in a year when 16 Chilean films were screened. Never again would so many national movies be produced annually.

The coming of synchronized sound created a new situation in Latin America. In those countries with a large domestic market – in particular Mexico, Argentina and Brazil – investment was made in expensive machinery, installations and rudimentary studios. Elsewhere, and Chile is a telling example, sound devastated local production due to its cost and complexity. Local entrepreneurs were usually unwilling to make the risky capital investment, and the history of Chilean cinema thereafter is littered with tales of self-sacrifice on the part of cast and crew. The first non-silent film made in Chile was *Norte y Sur*, directed by Jorge Délano in 1934, telling the story of a love triangle where a woman is the object of the attentions of a Chilean and an American engineer – flitting between Chile and the US, it was a rare example of sophisticated cinema at a time when the Chilean film output was reverting to often formulaic stories of young men seducing innocent ladies, or the naïve idealization of rural landscapes. Délano stood out in this age – another film of his, *Escándalo* (1940) was almost unique in dealing with the lives of the middle class, rather than those of the aristocracy or the peasantry. Nevertheless, Tobías Barros, an important director of the time, summed up the mood when he sarcastically described his *Río Abajo* as a film "where there are neither illegitimate nor lost children".

An attempt was made in the 1940s to stimulate cinema through state investment. The state agency CORFO saw cinema as an important growth industry and in 1942 gave 50% finance to set up Chile Films. Costly studios were erected, but the plan proved over-ambitious and Argentine film makers ended up using most of the facilities; by 1947 Chile Films had collapsed. In 1959, though, the Universidad de Chile set up a Centre for Experimental Cinema under the direction of a documentary film maker Sergio Bravo, which trained aspirant directors from Chile and elsewhere in Latin America (notably the Bolivian Jorge Sanjinés).

Cinema became intricately involved in the wider political discussions of the 1960s. The years 1968-1969 saw the maturity of Chilean cinema. Five features came out: Raúl Ruiz's *Tres tristes tigres* (Three Sad Tigers); Helvio Soto's *Caliche sangriento* (Bloody Nitrate); Aldo Francia's *Valparaíso mi amor* (Valparaíso My Love); Miguel Littín's *El chacal de Nahueltoro* (The Jackal of Nahueltoro) and Carlos Elsesser's *Los testigos* (The Witnesses). These film-makers came from different ideological and aesthetic tendencies, from the inventive maverick Raúl Ruiz to the sombre neo-realism of Francia, but they can be seen as a group, working with very scarce resources: the films by Ruiz, Elsesser, Francia and Littín were made, consecutively, with the same camera; furthermore, many of the directors sought to break down the traditionally melodramatic themes of Chilean cinema, employing more realistic language and situations more reflective of everyday social problems. Aldo Francia, a doctor by profession, also organized a famous 'Meeting of Latin American Film makers' at the Viña del Mar film festival in 1967. This would be one of the key events in the growing awareness of cineastes across the continent that they were working with similar ideas and methods, producing 'new cinemas'.

The narrow victory of the Popular Unity parties in the election of 1970 was greeted by film-makers with an enthusiastic manifesto penned by Miguel Littín; Littín himself was put in charge of the revived state institution Chile Films. He lasted for only 10 months, tiring of bureaucratic opposition and inter-party feuding, as the different members of Popular Unity all demanded a share of very limited resources. Few films were made between 1970 and 1973; Raúl Ruiz was the most productive film maker of the period, with a number of films in different styles. Littín was working on an historical feature *La tierra prometida* (The Promised Land) when the 1973 coup occurred and post-production took place in Paris. The most ambitious film to trace the radicalization of Chile in 1972 and 1973 was Patricio Guzmán's three part documentary *La batalla de Chile* (The Battle of Chile) which was edited in exile in Cuba. In the first years of exile, this film became Chile's most evocative testimony abroad and received worldwide distribution. Paradoxically, Chilean cinema, which had little time to grow under Popular Unity, strengthened in exile.

Policies following the coup practically destroyed internal film production for several years. Film personnel were arrested, tortured and imprisoned and many escaped into exile. Severe censorship was established: even *Fiddler on the Roof* was banned for displaying Marxist tendencies. It is from the exiled directors that the continuity of film culture can be seen. Littín took up residence in Mexico, supported by Mexican President, Echeverría, and became an explicit spokesman for political Latin American cinema, making the epic *Actas de Marusia* (Letters from Marusia) in 1975 and several other features in Mexico and later in Nicaragua. In the mid-1980s he returned clandestinely to Chile with several foreign film crews to make the documentary *Acta General de Chile* in 1986, a perilous mission documented by Gabriel García Márquez in his reportage *Clandestine in Chile* (1986). Raúl Ruiz took a less visible political role, but since his exile to France, he has produced a body of work that has earned him the reputation of being one of the most innovative directors in Europe, the subject of a special issue in 1983 of France's distinguished journal *Cahiers du Cinéma*. Merely to list his titles to date would overrun the space of this article. He makes movies with great technical virtuosity and often great speed: on a visit to Santiago to celebrate the return to civilian rule in 1990, he shot a film, entitled *La telenovela errante* (The Wandering Soap Opera), in less than a week for US$30,000. Other exile directors to make their mark include Ruiz's wife Valeria Sarmiento, Gastón Ancelovici and Carmen Castillo, all based in France, Patricio Guzmán in Spain, Marilú Mallet in Canada, Angelina Vásquez in Scandinavia, Sebastián Alarcón in the Soviet Union and Antonio Skármeta in Germany.

Inside Chile, the output under censorship varied from maritime adventures such as *El Último Grumete* to Silvio Caiozzi's *Julion comienza en julio* (Julio begins in July, 1979), one of the first films made in the period, set carefully in a turn-of-the-century historical location and self-financed through Caiozzi's work in commercials. It would take him a further 10 years to produce a second feature, *La luna en el espejo* (The Moon in the Mirror), evocatively set in Valparaíso, which was screened in 1990. An example of increased critical debate within Chile in the last years of the Pinochet régime can be found in Pablo Perelman's *Imagen latente* (Latent Image, 1987) which tells of a photographer's search for a missing brother who disappeared after the coup; although the film was not released in Chile until 1990, it was possible to film it in that country in the mid-1980s. Another case is that of *Hijos de la Guerra Fría* by Gonzalo Justiniano (1985), which is replete with metaphors of a society asphyxiated by a repressive system.

The return to civilian rule had some benefits for film-makers, most notably the easing of censorship. The Viña del Mar Film Festival was symbolically reinstated after 20 years, and saw the emotional return of many exiled directors, but that, in itself, could not solve the problems of an intellectual community dispersed around the world and the chronic underfunding and under-representation of Chilean films in the home market. New names have emerged and some internationally successful films have been made, most notably Ricardo Larraín's *La frontera* (The Frontier, 1991), which tells of a school teacher's internal exile in the spectacular scenery of southern Chile in the late 1980s and Gustavo Graef-Marino's *Johnny Cien Pesos* (1993) dealing with violence in Chilean society. The latter was produced by Chile Films, a short-lived production company made up of film directors and producers financed by a State Bank credit loan. The loan was withdrawn, however, when other productions failed at the box office. The last few years have seen the screening of one or two Chilean features a year, the best received being the political thriller *Amnesia* (1994), directed by Gonzalo Justiniano, Andrés Wood's vogue-ish *Historias de Futbol* (1997) and Sergio Castillo's 1997 *Gringuito*, which focuses on the problems of children brought up in exile, returning as foreigners to Chile. This gentle comedy of reintegration has been made to seem somewhat tame by the demonstrations in Chile surrounding the Pinochet extradition process. Larraín's latest feature *El entusiasmo* (Enthusiasms, 1999) did not live up to its title among local audiences, but it garnered international recognition, as did Andrés Wood's new film, *El*

Desquite. With the increasing globalization of the culture industry, the pattern of scarce local production is likely to continue.

Music and dance

At the very heart of Chilean music is the *cueca*, a courting dance for couples, both of whom make great play with a handkerchief waved aloft in the right hand. The man's knees are slightly bent and his body arches back; in rural areas, he stamps his spurs together for effect. Guitar and harp are the accompanying instruments, while hand-clapping and shouts of encouragement add to the atmosphere. The dance has a common origin with the Argentine Zamba and Peruvian Marinera via the early 19th century Zamacueca, in turn descended from the Spanish Fandango. The most tradi-tional form of song is the *tonada*, with its variants the Glosa, Parabienes, Romance, Villancico (Christmas carol) and Esquinazo (serenade) and the Canto a lo Poeta, in common with the custon in Argentina, this may be heard in the form of a Contrapunto or Controversia, a musical duel. Among the most celebrated groups are Los Huasos Quincheros, Silvia Infante with Los Condores and the Conjunto Millaray, all of which are popular at rural dancers, with their poignant combinationof formal singing and rousing accordian music. Famous folk singers in this genre are the Parra family from Chillán, Hector Pávez and Margot Loyola.

In the north of the country the music is Amerindian and closely related to that of Bolivia. Groups called 'Bailes' dance the Huayño, Taquirari, Cachimbo or Rueda at carnival and other festivities and pre-Columbian rites like the Cauzulor and Talatur. Instruments are largely wind and percussion, including *zampoñas* (pan pipes), *lichiguayos*, *pututos* (conch shells), *queñas* (flutes) and *clarines*. There are some nota-ble religious festivals that attract large crowds of pilgrims and include numerous groups of costumed dancers. The most outstanding of these festivals are those of the Virgen de La Tirana near Iquique (see box, page 251), San Pedro de Atacama, the Virgen de la Candelaria of Copiapó and the Virgen de Andacollo.

In the south the Mapuche nation have their own songs, dance-songs and magic and collective dances, accompanied by wind instruments like the great long *trutruca* horn, the shorter *pifilka* and the *kultrún* drum. Further south still, Chiloé has its own unique musical expression: wakes and other religious social occasions include collec-tive singing, while the recreational dances, all of Spanish origin – such as the Vals, Pavo, Pericona and Nave – have a heavier and less syncopated beat than in central Chile. Accompanying instruments here are the *rabel* (fiddle), guitar and accordion.

Wine

Chile is a major producer and exporter of fine wines. The wine-producing area stretches from the valley of the Río Aconcagua in the north to the Biobío Valley in the south. Grapes are also produced outside this area, notably around Ovalle and in the Elqui Valley near La Serena, which is the main production centre for *pisco*, a clear distilled spirit commonly drunk with lemon as *pisco sour* (although the distillery which many hold to be the best is Alto del Carmén, in the upper reaches of the Huasco Valley).

The great majority of Chilean wines come from the Central Valley. The hot, dry summers guarantee exceptionally healthy fruit. Chilean wine is famous for being free from diseases such as downy mildew and phylloxera. As a result growers are spared the costs of spraying and of grafting young vines onto phylloxera resistant rootstocks. Fertilizer is necessary in most regions, especially in Maipo, Aconcagua, Biobío and Maule.

Legislation in 1979 and 1985 established the current system of denominated regions and subregions. There are five denominated wine-growing regions, based around the valleys of the Ríos Aconcagua, Maipo, Rapel, Maule and Biobío. The heartland of Chilean wine production is the Maipo Valley, just south of Santiago, which is home to many of the most prestigious names in Chilean wine. Although the Maipo produces far less wine than the regions to the south, it is considered by many experts to produce the best wines in Chile as a result of the lime content of its soils. For visits to vineyards in this area see page 119.

The main harvest period begins at the end of February, for early maturing varieties such as Chardonnay, and runs through to the end of April for Cabernet Sauvignon, though there are regional variations. Harvest celebrations are often accompanied by two drinks: *chicha*, a partly fermented grape juice and *vino pipeño*, an unfiltered young wine which contains residue from the grapes and dried yeast.

Although the vine was introduced to Chile in the mid-16th century by the Spanish, the greatest influence on Chilean vineyards and wine making has been exerted by the French. In the 1830s one prominent Frenchman, Claudio Gay, persuaded the Chilean government to establish the *Quinta Normal* in Santiago as a nursery for exotic botanical specimens including vines. In the 1970s domestic consumption of wine dropped and wine prices fell, leading to the destruction of many vineyards. In the last two decades, however, large-scale investment, much of it from the United States and Europe has led to increases in wine production, increasingly of quality wines destined for export. Chilean wines are now widely available around the world; they are also very popular within Latin America.

There is a marked distinction between export wines and wines grown for domestic consumption. The most commonly planted grape variety is the dark-skinned *País*, found only in Chile, and thought to be a direct descendant of cuttings imported by Spanish colonists. Many of the vines known in Chile as Sauvignon are not the familiar Sauvignon Blanc, but rather Sauvignon Vert or Sauvignon Gris. Although Chilean wines, especially those produced for export, are typically very clean and fruity, they have only recently developed a full-bodied structure. Most export wines are red Cabernet, and white, Chardonnay.

Four large companies now account for 80% of all the wine sold inside Chile: Concha y Toro, Santa Rita, San Pedro and Santa Carolina. A few others, among them Errázuriz/Caliterra, Undurraga, Cánepa and Manquehue, supply most of the rest of the domestic market. Many of the smaller wineries, however, specialize in exports. Although a few wineries, including Cousiño-Macul, Los Vascos, Montes, Portal del Alto, Santa Monica and Santa Inés, use only their own grapes, this practice is rare and most companies buy in grapes.

Demarcated wine regions

Pacific Ocean

Valparaíso
Río Aconcagua ①
② SANTIAGO
Río Maipo
Río Rapel
Río Cachapoal
○ Rancagua
③ ○ San Fernando
Río Tinguiririca
Río Mataquito ○ Curicó
Río Claro
○ Talca Río Lontué
④ Río Maule
Río Loncomilla
Río Itata
Chillán Río Ñuble
Concepción ○
Río Laja ⑤
ARGENTINA
Los Angeles ○
Río Biobío

N

Temuco ○

Wine Regions	
1 Aconcagua	3 Rapel
2 Maipo	4 Maule
	5 Biobío

0 km 100
0 miles 100

Chilean wine: an aristocratic tradition

The cultivation of grapes in Chile dates back almost to the Spanish conquest, the first recorded vineyard being established in 1551 in La Serena by Francisco de Aguirre. One of the major motives for early vine-growing was to supply wine for the celebration of mass. In the 18th century the efforts of Madrid to restrict the planting of new vines in order to prevent competition with Spanish wines were largely ignored and vineyards became common on haciendas and villages throughout the central valley as far south as the Biobío Valley.

Some of the most famous Chilean wines are closely associated with major names in the Chilean élite of the 19th century, among them the Errázuriz, Cousiño, Subercaseaux and Undurraga families. With the introduction of direct steamship services to Europe, the heads of many of these families travelled to France and returned with French and German grape varieties. New cultivation techniques were also introduced from France. French experts were employed to design the cellars, some of which, with their double walls designed to prevent temperature fluctuations, can be visited today. Some of the largest and most famous of these vineyards were situated just south of Santiago in the floodplains of the Ríos Pirque and Maipo, which were adapted for commercial agriculture by the building of a network of canals. Defended by natural frontiers, the Pacific, the Andes and the Atacama Desert, Chile also benefited by being one of the very few wine-growing areas in the world not to suffer the devastation of the phylloxera louse which destroyed the vineyards of Europe after 1863.

Among the interesting names given to wines, two stand out: '120', one of the most popular wines, commemorates the 120 Patriot soldiers under O'Higgins who hid in the Santa Rita cellars in 1814 after their defeat at Rancagua; *Casillero del Diablo*, one of the best known red wines from Concha y Toro, was one of the favourite wines of the founder Don Melchor de Santiago Concha, who kept intruders away by spreading the rumour that the corner of the cellar where he kept it was haunted by the devil.

People, religion and education

There is less racial diversity in Chile than in most Latin American countries. Over 90% of the population of 14.2 million is *mestizo*. There has been much less immigration than in Argentina and Brazil. The German, French, Italian and Swiss immigrants came mostly after 1846 as small farmers in the forest zone south of the Biobío. Between 1880 and 1900 gold-seeking Serbs and Croats settled in the far south, and the British took up sheep farming and commerce in the same region. The influence throughout Chile of the immigrants is out of proportion to their numbers: their signature on the land is seen, for instance, in the German appearance of Valdivia, Puerto Montt, Puerto Varas, Frutillar and Osorno.

There is disagreement over the number of indigenous people in Chile. Survival International estimate the **Mapuche** population to be one million, but other statistics – including the official ones – put it at much less. For further details see under Temuco. There are also 15,000-20,000 **Aymara** in the northern Chilean Andes and 1200 **Rapa Nui** on Easter Island. A political party, the Party for Land and Identity, unites many Indian groupings, and legislation is proposed to restore indigenous people's rights.

The population is far from evenly distributed: Middle Chile, from Copiapó to Concepción and consisting 18% of the country's area, contains 77% of the total population. The Metropolitan Region of Santiago contains, on its own, about 39% of the whole population. Population density in 1995 ranged from 377 per sq km in the Metropolitan Region to 0.8 per sq km in Región XI (Aisén).

The rate of population growth per annum is lower than most of the rest of Latin America. The cities have higher birth and death rates than the rural areas but infant mortality is higher in the rural areas.

Since the 1960s heavy migration from rural areas has led to rapid urbanization. By 1995, 85.8% of the population lived in urban areas; the most urbanized regions were the Metropolitan Region (96.5% urban) and Región V (90.2% urban). Housing in the cities has not kept pace with this increased population; many Chileans live in slum areas called *callampas* (mushrooms) especially on the outskirts of Santiago.

Religion According to the 1992 census the population is 76.7% Catholic and 13.2% Protestant. Membership of Evangelical Protestant churches has grown rapidly in recent years. The largest of these churches is the Pentecostal Methodist Church. There is also a small Jewish community.

Education Chilean literacy rates are higher than those of most other South American states; according to the 1992 census over 95% of the population above the age of 15 is literate. Census returns also indicated that among the over-25 age population 8% had completed higher education, 42% had completed secondary education, and 44% had only completed primary education. Higher education provision doubled in the 1980s through the creation of private universities.

Land and environment

Geography

Chile is smaller than all other South American republics except Ecuador, Paraguay, Uruguay and the Guianas. It is 4,329 km long and, on average, no more than 180 km wide.

In the north Chile has a short 150 km east-west frontier with Peru. In the far north its eastern frontier is with Bolivia – 750 km long – but from San Pedro de Atacama south to Tierra del Fuego it shares over 3,500 km of frontier with Argentina. In the main this frontier follows the crest of the Andes, but in the far south, where the Andes are lower, there have been frequent frontier disputes with Argentina; these still rumble on. Chilean sovereignty over the islands south of Tierra del Fuego gives it control over Isla Navarino, on which Puerto Williams is the most southerly permanent settlement in the world (apart from scientific bases in Antarctica). Various island archipelagos in the Pacific, including Easter Island/Rapa Nui and the Juan Fernández group, are under Chilean jurisdiction.

Structure The Quaternary Period, 1.6 million years ago, was marked by the advance and retreat of the Antarctic Ice Sheet which, at its maximum extent, covered all of the Chilean Andes and the entire coastline south of Puerto Montt. However, although there are surface remnants of older rock formations, most have disappeared with the dramatic creation of the Andes which started around 80,000 years ago and continues to this day. The South American Plate, moving westwards, meets the Nazca and Antarctic Plates which are moving eastwards and sinking below the continent. These two plates run more or less parallel between 26°S and 33°S and the friction between them creates a geologically unstable zone, marked by frequent earthquakes and volcanic activity. The area of Concepción has been particularly susceptible to both land and undersea quakes and the city was destroyed twice in the 18th century by tidal waves before being moved to its present site.

All of the Chilean Pacific islands were formed by underwater volcanoes associated with fracture zones between the Nazca and Antarctic Plates, Easter Island gaining its characteristic triangular shape from the joining together of three lava flows.

Northern Chile has a similar form to Peru immediately to the north: the coastal range rises to 1,000-1,500 m; inland are basins known as *bolsones*, east of which lie the Andes. The Atacama Desert is, by most measures, the driest area on earth, and some meteorological stations near the coast have never reported precipitation. Water is therefore at a premium as far south as Copiapó; it is piped in from the east, and in the Andean foothills streams flow into alluvial fans in the inland basins, which can act as reservoirs and may be tapped by drilling wells. One river, the Río Loa, flows circuitously from the Andes to Calama and then through the coastal range to the coast, but for most of its length it is deeply entrenched, and unsuitable for agriculture. East of Calama and high in the Andes are the geysers of El Tatio, more evidence of volcanic activity, which are fed by the summer rains which fall in this part of the Andes.

In the past, notably as the ice sheets retreated, there were many lakes in the depressions between the Coastal Range and the Andes. These dried out, leaving one of the greatest concentrations of salts in the world, rich in nitrates: there has been extensive mining activity since the late 19th century. **Northern Desert**

South of Copiapó the transition begins between the Atacama and the zone of heavy rainfall in the south. At first the desert turns to scrub, and some seasonal surface water appears. The Huasco and Elqui follow deep trenches to reach the sea, allowing valley bottoms inland to be irrigated for agriculture. Further south, near Santiago, the Central Valley between the Coastal Range and the Andes reappears, the rivers flowing westwards across it to reach the Pacific. Further south is the Lake District, with its many lakes formed by glaciation and volcanic activity, its attractive mountain scenery, its rich volcanic soils and fertile agricultural land. **Central Chile**

South of Valdivia the Coastal Range becomes more broken until near Puerto Montt it becomes a line of islands as part of a 'drowned coastline' which extends all the way south to Cape Horn. The effects of glaciation can be seen in the U-shaped valleys and the long deep fjords stretching inland. This is a land of dense forests with luxuriant undergrowth which is virtually impenetrable and difficult to clear owing to the high water content. Further south in Chilean Patagonia, coniferous forests are limited in expanse because glaciers have stripped the upper slopes of soil. Some of the remaining glaciers reach sea level, notably the San Rafael, which breaks off the giant icefields of the *Campo de Hielo Norte*. **Southern Chile**

The whole of Chile is dominated by this massive mountain range which reaches its highest elevations in Chile and the Argentine border regions. In the north, near the Peruvian border the ranges which make up the Andes are 500 km wide, but the western ranges which mark the Chilean border, are the highest. Sajama, the highest peak in Bolivia, lies only 20 km east of the border, along which are strung volcanoes including Parinacota (6,330 m). Further south, to the southeast of San Pedro de Atacama, lies the highest section of the Andes, which includes the peaks of Llullaillaco (6,739 m) and Ojos del Salado (altitude from 6,864 m to 6,879 m to 6,908 m depending on your source). Still further south, to the northeast of Santiago and just inside Argentina, lies Aconcagua (6,960 m). **The Andes**

South of Santiago, the Andes begin to lose altitude. In the Lake District, the mountain passes are low enough in several places for crossing into Argentina. South of Puerto Montt, the Andes become more and more inhospitable, and lower temperatures bring the permanent snowline down from 1,500 m at Volcán Osorno near Puerto Montt to 700 m on Tierra del Fuego. Towards the southern end of the Andes are Mount Fitzroy (3,406 m) just over the border in Argentina and the remarkable peaks of the Paine massif.

Climate

It is only to be expected that a country which stretches over 4,000 km from north to south will provide a wide variety of climatic conditions. Annual rainfall varies from zero in northern Chile to over 4,000 mm on the offshore islands south of Puerto Montt. Rainfall is heavier in the winter months (May-August) throughout the country, except for in the northern *altiplano* where January and February are the wettest months.

Variations in the Chilean climate are concentrated by two significant factors: altitude and the cold waters of the Humboldt Current. The Andes, with their peaks of over 6,000 m, are rarely more than 160 km from the coastline. On average temperatures drop by 1°C for every 150 m you climb. The Humboldt Current has perhaps even more impact. The current flows in a northeasterly direction from Antarctic waters until it meets the southern coast of Chile, from where it follows the coastline northwards. Cold polar air accompanies the current on its journey, eventually colliding with warmer air moving in from the southwest. The lighter warm air is forced to rise over the dense cold air, bringing rainfall all year round to the area south of the Río Biobío and rain in winter further north in the Central Valley.

Paradoxically, though, the ocean also has a moderating effect on temperatures. Temperatures are generally moderate and decrease from north to south less than might be expected. As a result of the Humboldt Current temperatures in northern Chile are much lower than they are for places at corresponding latitudes such as Mexico. In the far south the oceans have the opposite effect and temperatures rarely fall below -6°C despite the high latitude. Detailed temperature and rainfall patterns are given in the text.

Flora

The diversity of Chilean flora reflects the geographic length and climatic variety of the country. Although the Andes constitute a great natural barrier, there are connections between the flora of Chile and that of the eastern side of the mountain range, most notably in the far north with the Bolivian altiplano and in the south with the temperate forests of Argentina.

Far North The arid central plain of northern Chile forms one of the driest areas on earth. Vegetation is limited to cacti, among them the *cardon* (Echinopsis atacamensis), and, in the Pampa de Tamarugal around Iquique, the *tamarugo* (Proposis tamarugo), a tree specially adapted to arid climates. On the western slopes of the Andes ravines carry water, which has permitted the establishment of small settlements and the planting of crops. The only native tree of this area, *queñoa* (Polylepis tomentella) – heavily overexploited in the past – grows in sheltered areas, mainly near streams, at altitudes between 2,000 and 3,500 m. Among cacti are the *candelabros* (genus Browningia) and, at higher altitudes (between 3,000 and 4,000 m) the *ayrampus* (genus Opuntia).

The northern *altiplano* supports only sparse vegetation. Many plants found in this area, such as the *llareta* (genus Laretia) and the *tola* (genus Baccharis) have deep root systems and small leaves. Near streams there are areas of spongy, wet salty grass, known as *bofedales*.

To the west of the central plain the Pacific coastal area is almost complete desert, although in places the influence of the Humboldt Current is offset by the

Glacial landscapes

Southern Chile provides some of the best examples of glacial landscapes on earth. One common sign of the region's glacial past are the U-shaped valleys. Good examples can be seen throughout the south, but perhaps one of the best is the Río Simpson between Coyhaique and Puerto Aisén. Sharp mountain ridges can often be seen high above these valleys: these have been caused by the eroding action of the ice on two or more sides. In some places the resulting debris or moraine formed a dam, blocking the valley and creating a lake. This can be seen in several places in the Lake District where glacial moraines formed dammed narrow valleys to form Lagos Calafquén, Panguipulli and Riñihue.

The drowned coastline south of Puerto Montt also owes its origin to glaciation. The ice which once covered the southern Andes was so heavy that it depressed the relatively narrow tip of South America; subsequently once the ice melted and the sea level rose, water broke through, leaving the western Andes as islands and creating the Chilean fjords, glaciated valleys carved out by the ice and now drowned.

camanchaca, an early morning coastal fog which comes off the sea and persists at low altitudes, permitting the growth of vegetation, notably in the Parque Nacional Pan de Azúcar north of Chañaral, and around Poposo, south of Antofagasta, where about 170 flowering plants, including shrubs, bromeliaceae and cacti can be found.

Norte Chico

Lying between the northern deserts and the matorral of central Chile, the Norte Chico is a transition zone: here annual rainfall averages from 30 to 100 mm increasing southwards. In the main dry areas native flora such as *pingo-pingo* (Ephedra andina), *jarilla* (Larrea nitida) and *brea* (Tessaria absinthoides) can be found. On the rare occasions when there is spring rainfall, the desert comes to life in a phenomenon known as the 'flowering of the desert'. The central plain is crossed by rivers; in the valleys irrigation permits the cultivation of fruit such as chirimoya, papaya and grapes.

On the coast near Ovalle sea mists support a forest of evergreen species includ-ing the *olivillo* (Aextoxicon punctatum), *canelo* or winter's bark (Drimys winteri) amd *arrayán* (Luma chequen or Myrtus chequen) in the Parque Nacional Fray Jorge.

Central Chile

The Central Valley, with its dry and warm summers and mild winters, is home to the matoral, a deciduous scrubland ecologically comparable to the chaparral in California and consisting of slow-growing drought-resistant species with deep roots and small spiny sclerophyllous leaves. The original plant cover has been modified by human impact, particularly in the form of livestock agriculture, charcoal-burning and irrigation. In many areas, from the Río Limari in the north to the Río Laja in the south, the result is *espinal* (Acacia cavan), usually considered to be a degraded form of the original matoral and characterized by open savanna scattered with *algarrobo* trees (Prosopis chilensis). Along ravines and on western facing slopes there are areas of evergreen sclerophyllous trees including the *peumo* (Cryptocarpa alba), *litre* (Lithrea caustica) and *boldo* (Peumos boldos) and, along the banks of the great rivers, the *maiten* (Maytenus boaria or Maytenus chilensis) and a local species of willow can be found.

Towards the coast more hygrophilous species grow on hills receiving coastal fogs: among these are *avellano*, *lingue* (Persea lingue), *belloto* or northern acorn (Beilschmiedia miersii) and *canelo* as well as bromeliads and epiphytic lichens and mosses. Species of southern beech (Nothofagus) and the formerly endemic Chilean or ocoa palm (Jubea chilensis), grow under protection in the Parque Nacional La Campana between Santiago and Valparaíso.

Background

☞ Plant pirates

Ever since the first Europeans reached Chile plants have been brought back to the 'old world'; and botanists are still seeking new plant species there. One of the most notable plant hunters was Joseph Banks, who visited Chile on Captain Cook's vessel Endeavour *and documented 125 new plants including the ruby-fruited* Gaultheria mucronata. *Plant hunters were often sent at the request of botanical gardens or commercial nurseries. One of the most famous nurseries was Veitch & Sons who sent William Lobb to Chile in 1840: Lobb returned with seeds of the*

monkey puzzle tree (Araucaria araucana) as well as seedlings which were a huge commercial success. The most famous plant hunter was, of course, Charles Darwin who described many plants and the landscape in great detail. His description of the Ocoa in the Parque Nacional la Campana still holds good today; and the palms he considered ugly can still be seen. Of course botanical travel occurred in both directions: emigrants from Europe took many plants to Chile, notably Spanish broom (Genista hispanica) and vines for viniculture.

Subantarctic temperate forests

As a result of the fragmentation of the great landmass of Gondwana some 120 million years ago, some of the species in these forests (Araucaria araucana, Nothofagus and Podocarpus salingus) share affinities with flora found in Australia and New Zealand as well as with fossils uncovered in Antarctica. Similar affinities of some insect groups have also been established. However the isolation of these subantarctic forests, with the nearest neighbouring forests 1,300 km away in northwestern Argentina, has led to the evolution of many unique endemic species, with volcanic activity also having had an important influence.

Nowadays these forests are mainly of broad-leafed evergreen species; in contrast to temperate forests in the northern hemisphere there are few species of conifers. The dominant genus is the Nothofagus or southern beech, of which eight species are found in Chile. In the Maule area *roble* (Nothofagus obliqua) and *hualo* (Nothofagus glauca) can be found, while further south there is a gradual transitional change via the Valdivian rainforest, see below, to the southern deciduous Nothofagus forests. The latter, which can also be found at higher altitudes along the Andes, include the Patagonian and Magellanic forests. From the Valdivian forest south to the Magellanic forests all species of Nothofagus attract fungis from the genus Cyttaria and, especially in the south, the *misodendron* or South American mistletoe.

Around the Río Biobío, the Valdivian rainforest predominates. This is a complex and diverse environment, which includes ferns, bromeliads, lichens including old man's beard, and mosses, as well as a variety of climbing plants including the *copihue* or Chilean bell flower (Lapageria rosea) the national flower of Chile. Colourful flowering plants which can be easily identified include the firebush or *ciruelillo* (Embothrium coccineum), several species of alstroemeria and berberis and the fuschia. Near the Andes, for example in the Parque Nacional Puyehue, the forests are dominated by two species of Nothofagus, the evergreen *coihue* or *coigüe* (Nothofagus dombeyi) and the deciduous *lenga* (Nothfagus pumilio) as well as by the Podocarpus (Podocarpus salingus) and, near water, myrtle trees like the *arrayán*. The under-storey is dominated by tall *chusquea* bamboos.

In the northern parts of the Valdivian forest at altitudes mainly between 900 m and 1,400 m, there are forests of monkey puzzle trees (Araucaria araucana), Chile's national tree: the most important of these forests are in the Parque Nacional Nahuelbuta in the coastal *cordillera* and in the Parque Nacional Huerquehue in the Andean foothills.

Pablo Neruda on the forest

Under the volcanoes, beside the snow-capped mountains, among the huge lakes, the fragrant, the silent, the tangled Chilean forest... My feet sink down into the dead leaves, a fragile twig crackles, the giant rauli trees rise in all their bristling height, a bird from the cold jungle passes over, flaps its wings, and stops in the sunless branches. And then, from its hideaway, it sings like an oboe... The wild scent of the laurel, the dark scent of the boldo herb, enter my nostrils and flood my whole being... The cypress of the Guaitecas blocks my way... This is a vertical world: a nation of birds, a plenitude of leaves... I stumble over a rock, dig up the uncovered hollow, an enormous spider covered with red hair stares up at me, motionless, as huge as a crab... A golden carabus beetle blows its mephitic breath at me, as its brilliant rainbow disappears like lightning... Going on, I pass through a forest of ferns much taller than I am: from their cold green eyes 60 tears splash down on my face and, behind me, their fans go on quivering for a long time... A decaying tree trunk: what a treasure!... Black and blue mushrooms have given it ears, red parasite plants have covered it with rubies, other lazy plants have let it borrow their beards, and a snake

springs out of the rotted body like a sudden breath, as if the spirit of the dead trunk were slipping away from it... Farther along, each tree stands away from its fellows... They soar up over the carpet of the secretive forest, and the foliage of each has its own style, linear, bristling, ramulose, lanceolate, as if cut by shears moving in infinite ways... A gorge; below, the crystal water slides over granite and jasper... A butterfly goes past, bright as a lemon, dancing between the water and the sunlight... Close by, innumerable calceolarias nod their little yellow heads in greeting... High up, red copihues dangle like drops from the magic forest's arteries... The red copihue is the blood flower, the white copihue is the snow flower... A fox cuts through the silence like a flash, sending a shiver through the leaves, but silence is the law of the plant kingdom... The barely audible cry of some bewildered animal far off... The piercing interruption of a hidden bird... The vegetable world keeps up its low rustle until a storm churns up all the music of the earth.

Anyone who hasn't been in the Chilean forest doesn't know this planet.

From Pablo Neruda, Memoirs, Penguin (1977) page 5-6.

Other species include the giant larch (Fitzroya cupressoides) known as the *alerce* or *lahuén*, which has some of the oldest individual specimens on earth (3,600 years). Athough this conifer grew extensively as far south as the 43° 30′ south, excessive logging has destroyed most of the original larch forest. Some of the best examples of *alerce*, which is now a protected species, can be seen in the Parque Nacional Andino Alerce and in the Parque Pumalin.

The Patagonian and Magellanic forests are less diverse than their Valdivian counterpart, mainly due to lower temperatures. The Magellanic forest, considered the southernmost forest type in the world, includes the evergreen Nothofagus betuloides, the deciduous *lenga* (Nothofagus pumilio) and Nothofagus antarctica, and the *canelo*. Firebush and berberis can also be found, as well as several species of orchids and beautiful species of Calceolaria or slipper plants. Shrubland in the south is mainly characterized by mounded shrubs, usually found in rocky areas. Common species include *mata barrosa* (Mullinum spinosum) a yellow-flowered shrub and *mata guanaco* (Anartrophyllum desideratum), a red-flowered shrub of the legume family.

The Pacific Islands In both the Juan Fernández Islands and Easter Island there are endemic species. In the forests of the Juan Fernández Archipelago at altitudes above 1,400 m important species of ferns can be found as well as tree species such as *luma*, *mayu-monte*, giant naranjillo and the *yonta* or Juan Fernández palm, which, along with the ocoa palm, is one of only two palms native to Chile. The native forests of Easter Island were destroyed, first by volcanic activity and later by human impact, leaving land covered partially with pasture. Although native species such as the *toromiro* can be found, introduced species such as the eucalyptus are more common.

Footnotes

17

558

Footnotes

Basic Spanish for travellers

No amount of dictionaries, phrase books or word lists will provide the same enjoyment as being able to communicate directly with the people of the country you are visiting. Learning Spanish is a useful part of the preparation for a trip to Chile and you are encouraged to make an effort to grasp the basics before you go. As you travel you will pick up more of the language and the more you know, the more you will benefit from your stay. The following section is designed to be a simple point of departure.

If you have been taught the 'Castillian' pronunciation (all z's and c's followed by *i* or *e* are pronounced as *th* as in *think*), be aware that Chilean Spanish is very different. Final s's are missed off and syllables are often omitted.

General pronunciation

The stress in a Spanish word conforms to one of three rules: **1** if the word ends in a vowel, or in **n** or **s**, the accent falls on the penultimate syllable *(ventana, ventanas)*; **2** if the word ends in a consonant other than **n** or **s**, the accent falls on the last syllable *(hablar)*; **3** if the word is to be stressed on a syllable contrary to either of the above rules, the acute accent on the relevant vowel indicates where the stress is to be placed *(pantalón, metáfora)*. Note adverbs take an accent when used interrogatively; ¿*cuándo?*, 'when?'

Vowels

a	not quite as short as in English 'cat'
e	as in English 'pay', but shorter in a syllable ending in a consonant
i	as in English 'seek'
o	as in English 'shop', but more like 'pope' when the vowel ends a syllable
u	as in English 'food', after 'q' and in 'gue', 'gui' **u** is unpronounced; in 'güe' and 'güi' it is pronounced
y	when a vowel, pronounced like 'I'; when a semiconsonant or consonant, it is pronounced like English 'yes'
ai, ay	as in English 'ride'
el, ey	as in English 'they'
oi, oy	as in English 'toy'

Consonants

Unless listed below consonants can be pronounced in Spanish as they are in English.

b, v	their sound is interchangeable and is a cross between the English **b** and **v**, except at the beginning of a word or after **m** or **n** when it is like English **b**
c	like English **k**, except before **e** or **i** when it is the **s** in English 'sip'
g	before **e** and **i** it is the same as **j**
h	when on its own, never pronounced
j	as the **ch** in the Scottish 'loch'
ll	as the 'lli' in 'million'
ñ	as the 'ni' in English 'onion'
rr	trilled much more strongly than in English

x   depending on its location, pronounced as in English 'fox', or 'sip', or
like 'gs'

z   as the **s** in English 'sip'

Pronouns

In the Americas, the plural, familar pronoun *vosotros* (with the verb endings - *áis*, -
éis), though much used in Spain, is never heard. Two or more people, including small
children, are always addressed as *Ustedes* (*Uds*).

Inappropriate use of the familiar forms (*tú, vos*) can sound imperious, condescending,
infantile, or imply a presumption of intimacy that could annoy officials, one's elders,
or, if coming from a man, women.

To avoid cultural complications if your Spanish is limited, stick to the polite forms:
Usted (*Ud*) in the singular, *Ustedes* in the plural, and you will never give offence.

Remember also that a person who addresses you as *tú*, does not necessarily expect
to be *tuteada* (so addressed) in return.

You should, however, violate this rule when dealing with a small child, who might be
intimidated by *Usted*: he/she is, after all, normally so addressed only in admonitions
such as *'¡No, Señor, Ud no tomará un helado antes del almuerzo!'* 'No, Sir, you will not
have ice cream before lunch!'

General hints

Travellers whose names include *b*'s and *v*'s should learn to distinguish between them
when spelling aloud as *be larga* and *v*'s *corta* or *uve*. (Children often say *ve de vaca* and
be de burro to distinguish between the two letters, pronounced interchangeably,
either as *b* or *v*, in Chilean Spanish.)

Greetings, courtesies

excuse me/I beg your pardon	*permiso*
Go away!	*¡Váyase!*
good afternoon/evening/night	*buenas tardes/noches*
good morning	*buenos días*
goodbye	*adiós/chao*
hello	*hola*
How are you?	*¿cómo está?/¿cómo estás?*
I do not understand	*no entiendo*
leave me alone	*déjame en paz/no me moleste*
no	*no*
please	*por favor*
pleased to meet you	*mucho gusto/encantado/encantada*
see you later	*hasta luego/chao*
thank you (very much)	*(muchas) gracias*
What is your name?	*¿Cómo se llama?/¿Cómo te llamas*
yes	*sí*
I speak ...	*Hablo ...*
I speak Spanish	*Hablo español*
I don't speak Spanish	*No hablo español*
Do you speak English?	*¿Habla usted inglés?*
We speak German	*Hablamos alemán*
They speak French	*Hablan francés*
Please speak slowly	*hable despacio por favor*
I am very sorry	*lo siento mucho/disculpe*
I'm fine	*muy bien gracias*
I'm called_	*me llamo_*
What do you want?	*¿Qué quiere?*

I'm called_	*me llamo_*
What do you want?	*¿Qué quiere?*
I want	*quiero*
I don't want it	*No lo quiero*
long distance phone call	*la llamada a larga distancia*
reverse charge phone call	*llamada cobro reverbido*
good	*bueno*
bad	*malo*

Nationalities and languages

American *Norte Americano/a*	Italian *Italiano/a*
Australian *Australiano/a*	Mexican *Mexicano/a*
Austrian *Austriaco/a*	New Zealand *Neozelandés/Neozelandesa*
British *Británico/a*	Norwegian *Noruego/a*
Canadian *Canadiense*	Portuguese *Portugués/Portuguesa*
Danish *Danés/Danesa*	Scottish *Escocés/Escocesa*
Dutch *Holandés/Holandesa*	South African *Sudafricano/a*
English *Inglés/Inglesa*	Spanish *Español/a*
French *Francés/Francesa*	Swedish *Sueco/a*
German *Alemán/Alemana*	Swiss *Suizo/a*
Irish *Irlandés/Irlandesa*	Welsh *Galés/Galesa*
Israeli *Israelito*	

Basic questions

Have you got a room for two people?	-arrive? *-llega-*
¿Tiene habitación para dos personas?	When? *¿Cuándo?*
How do I get to_? *¿Cómo llegar a_?*	Where is_? *¿Dónde está_?*
How much does it cost? *¿ Cuánto vale?*	Where is the nearest petrol station?
How much is it? *¿Cuánto es?*	*¿Dónde está el grifo más cerca?*
When does the bus leave?	Why? *¿Por qué?*
¿A qué hora sale el bus?	

Basics

bank *el banco*	market *la fería*
bathroom/toilet *el baño*	notes/coins *los billetes/las monedas*
bill *la factura/la cuenta*	police (policeman) *la policia (el policia)*
cash *el efectivo*	post office *el correo*
cheap *barato*	supermarket *el supermercado*
church/cathedral *La iglesia/catedral*	telephone office *el centro de llamadas*
exchange house *la casa de cambio*	ticket office *la boletería/la taquilla*
exchange rate *la tasa de cambio*	travellers' cheques *cheques de viajero*
expensive *caro*	

Getting around

aeroplane/airplane *el avión*	second street on the left
airport *el aeropuerto*	*la segunda calle a la izquierda*
bus station *la terminal (terrestre)*	ticket *el boleto*
bus stop *la parada*	to walk *caminar*
bus *el bus/el autobus etc*	Where can I buy tickets?
minibus *el fulgón*	*¿Dónde se puede comprar boletos?*
first/second class *primera/segunda clase*	Where can I park?
on the left/right *a la izquierdo/derecha*	*¿Dónde se puede estacionar?*

Orientation and motoring

arrival *la llegada*
avenue *la avenida*
block *la cuadra*
border *la frontera*
car used for public transport on a
  fixed route *colectivo*
corner *la esquina*
customs *la aduana*
departure *la salida*
east *el este, el oriente*
empty *vacío*
full *lleno*
highway, main road *carretera*
immigration *la inmigración*
insurance *el seguro*
the insured *el asegurado/la asegurada*
to insure yourself against *asegurarse contra*

luggage *el equipaje*
motorway, dual carriageway *autopista*
north *el norte*
oil *el aceite*
passport *el pasaporte*
petrol/gasoline *la gasolina*
puncture *el pinchazo*
south *el sur*
street *la calle*
that way *por allí/por allá*
this way *por aquí/por acá*
tourist card *la tarjeta de turista*
tyre *la llanta*
unleaded *sin plomo*
visa *el visado*
waiting room *la sala de espera*
west *el oeste/el poniente*

Accommodation

air conditioning *el aire acondicionado*
all-inclusive *todo incluído*
blankets *las frasadas*
clean/dirty towels *las toallas limpias/sucias*
dining room *el comedor*
double bed *la cama matrimonial*
guest house *la casa de huéspedes*
hot/cold water *agua caliente/frío*
hotel *el hotel*
Is service included? *¿Está incluído el servicio?*
Is tax included? *¿Están incluidos los
  impuestos?*
noisy *ruidoso*

pillows *las almohadas*
power cut *corte*
restaurant *el restaurante*
room *el cuarto/la habitación*
sheets *las sábanas*
shower *la ducha*
single/double *simple/doble*
soap *el jabón*
to make up/clean *limpiar*
toilet *el sanitario*
toilet paper *el papel higiénico*
with private bathroom *con baño privado*
with two beds *con dos camas*

Health

aspirin *la aspirina*
blood *la sangre*
chemist/pharmacy *la farmacia*
condoms *los preservativos*
contact lenses *las lentes de contacto*
contraceptive (pill) *el anticonceptivo (la
píldora anticonceptiva)*

diarrhoea *la diarrea*
doctor *el médico*
fever/sweat *la fiebre/el sudor*
(for) pain *(para) dolor*
head *la cabeza*
period/towels *la regla/las toallas*
stomach *el estómago*

Time

At one o'clock *a la una*
At half past two/two thirty
  a las dos y media
At a quarter to three *a cuarto para las tres*
It's one o'clock *es la una*
It's seven o'clock *son las siete*
It's twenty past six/six twenty
  son las seis y veinte

It's five to nine *son cinco para
  las nueve*
In ten minutes *en diez minutos*
five hours *cinco horas*
Does it take long? *¿Tarda mucho?*
We will be back at ... *Regresamos a las ...*
What time is it? *¿Qué hora es?*

Days and months

Monday	*lunes*	April	*abril*
Tuesday	*martes*	May	*mayo*
Wednesday	*miércoles*	June	*junio*
Thursday	*jueves*	July	*julio*
Friday	*viernes*	August	*agosto*
Saturday	*sábado*	September	*septiembre*
Sunday	*domingo*	October	*octubre*
January	*enero*	November	*noviembre*
February	*febrero*	December	*diciembre*
March	*marzo*		

Numbers

one	*uno/una*	sixteen	*dieciséis*
two	*dos*	seventeen	*diecisiete*
three	*tres*	eighteen	*dieciocho*
four	*cuatro*	nineteen	*diecinueve*
five	*cinco*	twenty	*veinte*
six	*seis*	twenty one, two	*veintiuno, veintidos etc*
seven	*siete*	thirty	*treinta*
eight	*ocho*	forty	*cuarenta*
nine	*nueve*	fifty	*cincuenta*
ten	*diez*	sixty	*sesenta*
eleven	*once*	seventy	*setenta*
twelve	*doce*	eighty	*ochenta*
thirteen	*trece*	ninety	*noventa*
fourteen	*catorce*	hundred	*cien*
fifteen	*quince*	thousand	*mil*

Family

aunt	*la tía*	husband	*el esposo/marido*
brother	*el hermano*	married	*casado/a*
cousin	*la/el prima/o*	mother	*la madre*
daughter	*la hija*	niece	*sobrina*
family	*la familia*	nephew	*sobrino*
father	*el padre*	single/unmarried	*soltero/a*
fiance/fiancee	*el novio/la novia*	sister	*la hermana*
friend	*el amigo/la amiga*	son	*el hijo*
grandfather	*el abuelo*	uncle	*el tío*
grandmother	*la abuela*	wife	*la esposa*

Key verbs

To go *ir*
I go *voy*
you go (familiar singular) *vas*
he, she, it goes, you (unfamiliar singular) go *va*
we go *vamos*
they, you (plural) go *van*
To have (possess) *tener*
I have *tengo*
You have *tienes*
He she, it have, you have *tiene*
We have *tenemos*
They, you have *tienen*
(Also used as 'To be', as in 'I am hungry' *tengo hambre*)

(NB *Haber* also means 'to have', but is used with other verbs to form the perfect tense, as in 'he hasgone' *ha ido*)
I have gone *he ido*
You have said *has dicho*
He, she, it has, you have done *ha hecho*
We have eaten *hemos comido*
They, you have arrived *han llegado*
Hay means 'there is' and is used in questions such as *¿Hay cuartos?* 'Are there any rooms?'; perhaps more common is *No hay* meaning 'there isn't any'

To be (in a permanent state) *ser*
I am (a teacher) *soy (profesor)*
You are *Eres*
He, she, it is, you are *es*
We are *somos*
They, you are *son*

To be (positional or temporary state) *estar*
I am (in London) *estoy (en Londres)*
You are *estás*
He, she, it is, you are (happy) *está (contento/a)*
We are *estámos*
They, you are *están*

To do/make *Hacer*
I do *hago*
You do *haces*
He, she, it does, you do *hace*
We do *hacemos*
They, you do *hacen*

The above section was compiled on the basis of glossaries by André de Mendonça and David Gilmour of South American experience, London, and the LatinAmerican Travel Advisor, No 9, March 1996

Food

avocado *la palta*
baked *al horno*
bakery *la panadería*
banana *el plátano*
beans *los porotos*
beef *la carne de vawno*
beef steak or pork fillet *el bistec*
boiled *cocido*
boiled rice *el arroz blanco*
bread *el pan*
breakfast *el desayuno*
butter *la mantequilla*
casserole *la cazuela*
chewing gum *el chicle*
chicken *el pollo*
chilli pepper or green pepper *el ají*
clear soup, stock *el caldo*
dining room *el comedor*
egg *el huevo*
fish *el pescado*
fork *el tenedor*
fried *frito*
fritters *las frituras*
garlic *el ajo*
goat *el chivo*
grapefruit *el pomelo*
grill *la parrilla*
grilled/griddled *a la plancha*
guava *la guayaba*
ham *el jamón*
hamburger *la hamburgueso*
hot, spicy *picante*
ice cream *el helado*
jam *la mermelada*
knife *el cuchillo*
lime *el limón*
lobster *la langosta*

lunch *el almuerzo*
margarine *margarina*
meal, supper, dinner *la comida*
meat *la carne*
minced meat *carne molida*
mixed salad *la ensalada mixta*
onion *la cebolla*
orange *la naranja*
pepper *el pimiento*
pasty, turnover *la empanada*
pork *el cerdo*
potato *la papa*
prawns *los camarones*
raw *crudo*
restaurant *el restaurante*
roast *el asado*
salad *la ensalada*
salt *el sal*
sandwich *el sandwich*
sauce *la salsa*
Sausage *la longaniza*
scrambled eggs *los huevos revueltos*
seafood *los mariscos*
soup *la sopa*
spoon *la cuchara*
squash *jugo*
squid *los calamares*
supper *la cena*
sweet *dulce*
sweet potato *la batata*
to eat *comer*
toasted *tostado*
turkey *el pavo*
vegetables *los legumbres/vegetales*
without meat *sin carne, pollo longanizas*

Drink

beer *la cerveza*
boiled *hervido*
bottled *en botella*
camomile tea *la manzanilla*
canned *en lata*
cocktail *el coctel*
coffee *el café*
coffee, small, strong *el cafecito*
coffee, milky *el café con leche*
cold *frío*
condensed milk *la leche condensada*
cup *la taza*
drink *la bebida*
drunk *borracho*
fruit milk shake *el batido*
glass *el vaso*
glass of liqueur *la copa de licor*
hot *caliente*
ice *el hielo*

juice *el jugo*
lemonade *la limonada*
milk *la leche*
mint *la menta*
orange juice *el jugo de naranja*
pineapple milkshake *el batido de piña
con leche*
rough rum, firewater *el aguardiente*
rum *el ron*
soft drink *el refresco*
soft fizzy drink *la bebida*
sugar *el azúcar*
tea *el té*
to drink *beber/tomar*
water *el agua*
water, carbonated *el agua mineral con gas*
water, still mineral *el agua mineral sin gas*
wine, red *el vino tinto*
wine, white *el vino blanco*

Footnotes

Glossary

adobe a sun-dried mixture of silt and clay used as a building material in the country

alfajores flaky biscuits filled with *manjar* (caramelised condensed milk)

almuerzo lunch

altiplano the high plateau found in the northern Andes

cabaña chalet, usually rented out to families in the south and on the coast

cama bed

carabineros police

cerro hill

chicha type of homemade fermented drink, usually made of apples (in the south) or grapes (in the north)

Codec National Petrol Company

Codeff national body campaigning to protect flora and fauna

colectivo a collective taxi

comedor dining room

CONAF national body overseeing the running and administration of Chile's national parks and reserves

congrio not to be confused with conger eel (although Iberian Spanish uses this word to mean this), this is in fact a type of ling

cordillera mountain range

costanera waterfront

cuadra block (in a city)

curanto stew from Chiloé with shellfish, pork and potatoes

estancia sheep farm in the far south of Chile

fundo old-style farm in the Central Valley

huasos chilean cowboys

humitas crushed corn paste stuffed into corn leaves, often sweetened

kuchen cakes in German style (usually found in the south)

pampa flat, desert or semi-desert landscape (found in the Atacama and also in Patagonia)

pebre spicy chilli and tomato sauce found in any restaurant worthy of the name as a relish

peñas restaurant or bar with live folkloric performances

pudu small indigenous deer, very rare, found in the southern Andes

restaurant bailable restaurant with live music and dancing offered to diners. Sometimes it is necessary to pay a cover to enter as well as for the food consumed

Sernatur National Tourist Board, usually very helpful

tábanos horseflies (found in the south)

Index

Footnotes

Footnotes

Shorts

Footnotes

Footnotes

Map index

Footnotes

Advertisers

Will you help us?

We try as hard as we can to make each Footprint Handbook as up-to-date and accurate as possible but, of course, things always change. Many people email or write to us – with corrections, new information, or simply comments. If you want to let us know about your experiences and adventures – be they good, bad or ugly – then don't delay; we're dying to hear from you. And please try to include all the relevant details and juicy bits. Your help will be greatly appreciated, especially by other travellers. In return we will send you details about our special guidebook offer.

email Footprint at:
chi3_online@footprintbooks.com

or write to:

Elizabeth Taylor
Footprint Handbooks
6 Riverside Court
Lower Bristol Road
Bath
BA2 3DZ
UK

Sales & distribution

Footprint Handbooks
6 Riverside Court
Lower Bristol Road
Bath BA2 3DZ England
T 01225 469141
F 01225 469461
discover
@footprintbooks.com

Australia
Peribo Pty
58 Beaumont Road
Mt Kuring-Gai
NSW 2080
T 02 9457 0011
F 02 9457 0022

Austria
Freytag-Berndt Artaria
Kohlmarkt 9
A-1010 Wien
T 01533 2094
F 01533 8685

Freytag-Berndt
Sporgasse 29
A-8010 Graz
T 0316 818230
F 3016 818230-30

Belgium
Craenen BVBA
Mechelsesteenweg 633
B-3020 Herent
T 016 23 90 90
F 016 23 97 11

Waterstones
The English Bookshop
Blvd Adolphe Max 71-75
B-1000 Brussels
T 02 219 5034

Canada
Ulysses Travel Publications
4176 rue Saint-Denis
Montréal
Québec H2W 2M5
T 514 843 9882
F 514 843 9448

Europe
Bill Bailey
16 Devon Square
Newton Abbott
Devon TQ12 2HR. UK
T 01626 331079
F 01626 331080

Denmark
Nordisk Korthandel
Studiestraede 26-30 B
DK-1455 Copenhagen K
T 3338 2638
F 3338 2648

Scanvik Books
Esplanaden 8B
DK-1263 Copenhagen K
T 3312 7766
F 3391 2882

Finland
Akateeminen Kirjakauppa
Keskuskatu 1
FIN-00100 Helsinki
T 09 121 4151
F 09 121 4441

Suomalainen Kirjakauppa
Koivuvaarankuja 2
01640 Vantaa 64
F 09 852751

France
FNAC – major branches

L'Astrolabe
46 rue de Provence
F-75009 Paris 9e
T 01 42 85 42 95
F 01 45 75 92 51

VILO Diffusion
25 rue Ginoux
F-75015 Paris
T 01 45 77 08 05
F 01 45 79 97 15

Germany
GeoCenter ILH
Schockenriedstrasse 44
D-70565 Stuttgart
T 0711 781 94610
F 0711 781 94654

Brettschneider
Feldkirchnerstrasse 2
D-85551 Heimstetten
T 089 990 20330
F 089 990 20331

Geobuch
Rosental 6
D-80331 München
T 089 265030
F 089 263713

Gleumes
Hohenstaufenring 47-51
D-50674 Köln
T 0221 215650

Globetrotter Ausrustungen
Wiesendamm 1
D-22305 Hamburg
T040 679 66190
F 040 679 66183

Dr Götze
Bleichenbrücke 9
D-2000 Hamburg 1
T 040 3031 1009-0

Hugendubel Buchhandlung
Nymphenburgerstrasse 25
D-80335 München
T 089 238 9412
F 089 550 1853

Kiepert Buchhandlung
Hardenbergstrasse 4-5
D-10623 Berlin 12
T 030 311 880
F 030 311 88120

Greece
GC Eleftheroudakis
17 Panepistemiou
Athens 105 64
T 01 331 4180-83
F 01 323 9821

India
India Book Distributors
1007/1008 Arcadia
195 Nariman Point
Mumbai 400 021
T 91 22 282 5220
F 91 22 287 2531

Israel
Eco Trips
8 Tverya Street
Tel Aviv 63144
T 03 528 4113
F 03 528 8269

For a fuller list, see www.footprintbooks.com

Italy
Librimport
Via Biondelli 9
I-20141 Milano
T 02 8950 1422
F 02 8950 2811

Libreria del Viaggiatore
Via dell Pelegrino 78
I-00186 Roma
T/F 06 688 01048

Netherlands
Nilsson & Lamm bv
Postbus 195
Pampuslaan 212
N-1380 AD Weesp
T 0294 494949
F 0294 494455

Waterstones
Kalverstraat 152
1012 XE Amsterdam
T 020 638 3821

New Zealand
Auckland Map Centre
Dymocks

Norway
Schibsteds Forlag A/S
Akersgata 32 - 5th Floor
Postboks 1178 Sentrum
N-0107 Oslo
T 22 86 30 00
F 22 42 54 92

Tanum
Karl Johansgate 37-41
PO Box 1177 Sentrum
N-0107 Oslo 1
T 22 41 11 00
F 22 33 32 75

Olaf Norlis
Universitetsgt 24
N-1062 Oslo
T 22 00 43 00

Pakistan
Pak-American Commercial
Hamid Chambers
Zaib-un Nisa Street
Saddar, PO Box 7359
Karachi
T 21 566 0418
F 21 568 3611

South Africa
Faradawn CC
PO Box 1903
Saxonwold 2132
T 011 885 1787
F 011 885 1829

South America
Humphrys Roberts
Associates
Caixa Postal 801-0
Ag. Jardim da Gloria
06700-970 Cotia SP
Brazil
T 011 492 4496
F 011 492 6896

Southeast Asia
APA Publications
38 Joo Koon Road
Singapore 628990
T 865 1600
F 861 6438

In Hong Kong, Malaysia,
Singapore and Thailand:
MPH, Kinokuniya, Times

Spain
Altaïr
C/Balmes 69
08007 Barcelona
T 933 233062
F 934 512559

Altaïr
Gaztambide 31
28015 Madrid
T 0915 435300
F 0915 443498

Libros de Viaje
C/Serrano no 41
28001 Madrid
T 01 91 577 9899
F 01 91 577 5756

Il Corte Inglés – major
branches

Sweden
Hedengrens Bokhandel
PO Box 5509
S-11485 Stockholm
T 08 611 5132

Kart Centrum
Vasagatan 16
S-11120 Stockholm
T 08 411 1697

Kartforlaget
Skolgangen 10
S-80183 Gavle
T 026 633000
F 026 124204

Lantmateriet Kartbutiken
Kungsgatan 74
S-11122 Stockholm
T 08 202 303
F 08 202 711

Switzerland
Office du Livre OLF
ZI3, Corminboeuf
CH-1701 Fribourg
T 026 467 5111
F 026 467 5666

Schweizer Buchzentrum
Postfach
CH-4601 Olten
T 062 209 2525
F 062 209 2627

Travel Bookshop
Rindermarkt 20
Postfach 216
CH-8001 Zürich
T 01 252 3883
F 01 252 3832

Tanzania
A Novel Idea
The Slipway
PO Box 76513
Dar es Salaam
T/F 051 601088

USA
Publishers Group West
1700 Fourth Street
Berkeley
CA 94710
T 510 528 1444
F 510 528 9555

Barnes & Noble, Borders,
specialist travel bookstores

Footprint travel list

Footprint publish travel guides to over 120 countries worldwide. Each guide is packed with practical, concise and colourful information for everybody from first-time travellers to travel aficionados . The list is growing fast and current titles are noted below. For further information check out the website **www.footprintbooks.com**

Andalucía Handbook
Argentina Handbook
Bali & the Eastern Isles Hbk
Bangkok & the Beaches Hbk
Barcelona Handbook
Bolivia Handbook
Brazil Handbook
Cambodia Handbook
Caribbean Islands Handbook
Central America & Mexico Hbk
Chile Handbook
Colombia Handbook
Costa Rica Handbook
Cuba Handbook
Cusco & the Sacred Valley Hbk
Dominican Republic Handbook
Dublin Handbook
East Africa Handbook
Ecuador & Galápagos Handbook
Edinburgh Handbook
Egypt Handbook
Goa Handbook
Guatemala Handbook
India Handbook
Indian Himalaya Handbook
Indonesia Handbook
Ireland Handbook
Israel Handbook
Jordan Handbook
Laos Handbook
Libya Handbook
London Handbook
Malaysia Handbook
Marrakech & the High Atlas Hbk
Myanmar Handbook
Mexico Handbook
Morocco Handbook

Namibia Handbook
Nepal Handbook
New Zealand Handbook
Nicaragua Handbook
Pakistan Handbook
Peru Handbook
Rajasthan & Gujarat Handbook
Rio de Janeiro Handbook
Scotland Handbook
Scotland Highlands & Islands Hbk
Singapore Handbook
South Africa Handbook
South American Handbook
South India Handbook
Sri Lanka Handbook
Sumatra Handbook
Syria & Lebanon Handbook
Thailand Handbook
Tibet Handbook
Tunisia Handbook
Turkey Handbook
Venezuela Handbook
Vietnam Handbook

Also available from Footprint
Traveller's Handbook
Traveller's Healthbook

Available at all good bookshops

Travellers

Altiplano

Easter Is.

Litoral

CHILE

Araucanía

Los Lagos

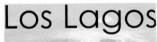

Careterra Austral

Chiloé

Patagonia

Travellers

Ph:+56-65-262099
Fax:+56-65-258555
info@Travellers.cl

www.Travellers.cl

Chile

Pacific Ocean

PERU

BOLIVIA

❶

Iquique □

Antofagasta □

❷

Copiapó □

La Serena □

❸

Valparaíso □   □ SANTIAGO

Rancagua □

Talca □

Concepción □

ARGENTINA

❹

Temuco □

Puert Montt □

❺

Coyhaique □

Atlantic Ocean

❻   ❼

Punta Arenas □

N

0 km   200
0 miles   200

Altitude in metres

4000
3000
2000
1000
500
200
0

Neighbouring Country

——— Major road

——— Unpaved or *ripio* road

——— Railway

- - - - Ferry between Puerto Montt &
         Puerto Natales (Puerto Edén)

· · · · · Ferry between Puerto Montt &
           Puerto Chacabuco/Laguna San Rafael

– · – · Ferry between Quellón & Chaltén

◆ National park

– · – · – International border

– – – Regional border

☐ Salt plains

□ CAPITAL

□ Regional Capital

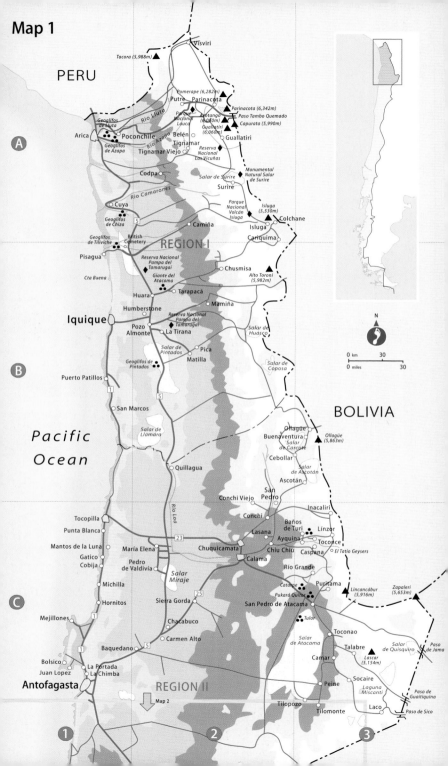

Map 4

Map 6

Map 5

Puerto Edén
Isla
Wellington

ARGENTINA

A

Map 7

Pacific
Ocean

Parque Nacional
Bernardo O'Higgins
Parque Nacional
Torres del Paine

Paso Cancha Carrera

Cerro Castillo

REGION XII

Cueva del Milodón

Paso Dorotea

Balmaceda
(2,035m)

Seno Última
Esperanza

Paso Casas Viejas

Puerto Edén
Ferry Route

Puerto Natales

B

9

Villa Tehuelches

Río Verde

Parque
Nacional
Magallanes

Punta
Arenas

Parque Nacional
Laguna Parillar

Fuerte
Bulnes

Estrecho de Magallanes

C

N

0 km   30
0 miles   30

1   2   3

Map 7

ARGENTINA

Atlantic Ocean

A

Map 6

B

Otway Sound

Isla Isabel

Punta Arenas

Fuerte Bulnes

Estrecho de Magallanes

Isla Dawson

C

Punta Delgada

Punta Espora

Ferry Crossing

255

Cerro Sombrero

Porvenir

Ferry Crossing

Camerón

San Sebastián

San Sebastián

Río Grande

Lago Blanco

Tierra del Fuego

Lago Fagnano

Lago Escondido

Ushuaia

Canal Beagle

Puerto Williams

Isla Navarino

ARGENTINA

Harberton

Isla Wollaston

Cape Horn

N

0 km   30
0 miles   30

1   2   3

Bibliography

Sources for the section on Arts and Crafts are: Artesanía tradicional de Chile, Serie El Patrimonio Cultural Chileno, Ministerio de Educación, 1978; 'Visión estética de la cerámica de Quinchamalí', by Luis Guzmán Molina, Atenea, No 458 (Universidad de Concepción, 1988), pages 47-60; Mapudungun, lengua y costumbres Mapuches, by Orietta Appelt Martín (Temuco: Magin, 1995); Arts and Crafts of South America, by Lucy Davies and Mo Fini (Bath: Tumi, 1994). Tumi, a Latin American Craft Centre in Britain, specializes in Mexican and Andean products and produces cultural and educational videos for schools: at 23/24 Chalk Farm Road, London NW1 8AG, 8/9 New Bond Street Place, Bath BA1 1BH, 1/2 Little Clarendon Street, Oxford OX1 2HJ, 82 Park Street, Bristol BS1 5LA.

A great many sources have been consulted in the preparation of the section on Literature. Apart from those already mentioned, reference is made to: Cedomil Goic, La novela chilena. Los mitos degradados (Santiago: Universitaria, 1991); Kenneth Fleak, The Chilean Short Story. Writers from the Generation of 1950 (New York: Peter Lang, 1989); René Jara, El revés de la arpillera, perfil literario de Chile (Madrid: Hiperión, 1988); Jean Franco, Spanish American Literature since Independence (London: Ernest Benn, 1973); Eugenia Brito, Campos minados. Literatura post-golpe en Chile (Santiago: Mujeres Cuarto Propio, 1990); Poesía chilena de hoy. De Parra a nuestros días, selected by Erwin Díaz (Santiago: Ediciones Documentas, 1989); Lautaro Silva, Vida y obra de Gabriela Mistral (Buenos Aires: Andina, 1967); Gordon Brotherston, The Emergence of the Latin American Novel (1977) and Latin American Poetry. Origins and Presence (Cambridge University Press, 1975); Darío Villanueva y José María Viña Liste, Trayectoria de la novela hispanoamericano actual (Madrid: Austral, 1991); Jason Wilson, Traveller's Literary Companion: South and Central America (Brighton: In Print, 1993); Gerald Martin, Journeys through the Labyrinth (London: Verso, 1989); Poesía Chilena Para el Siglo XXI (Dirección de Bibliotécas, Archivos y Museos, 1996). A key text for English readers is Steven White's Poets of Chile (Unicorn Press, 1986).

Acknowledgements

Many people have helped in making this book as thorough and up-to-date as possible. Janak Jani's work in updating the information on the south of the country was particularly invaluable for its thoroughness of research and detail.

Both Janak Jani and Toby Green would like to give fulsome thanks to all the regional Sernatur offices from Iquique to Punta Arenas who gave their time, expertise and local knowledge to give thorough and complete information on their local area.

Janak would like to thank: Werner and Cecilia Ruf-Chaura of *Casa Cecilia* in Puerto Natales; Andi of *Casa Azul* in Puerto Varas; Hans Liechtiand and Verónica Araneda from *La Tetera* in Pucón; Carlos Grady of the *Hospedaje La Esmeralda* in Chonchi; Patricio Guzmán in Coyhaique; Adrain Turner from *Travellers* in Puerto Montt; Pato Correa and friends in Ancud; and Rebecca Van Someren in Valparaíso.

Toby would like to thank: Emily for coming too; Gregoria Fernandez for helping me through my flu in La Serena; Clark and Manuela from *Hacienda Los Andes* for their help, good company, and a wonderful morning's riding; Miguel Angel and Viviana Olate Rojas in Iquique; the two travelling salesmen from Santiago who got us out of a spot of bother near Illapel; Andrew "Hotel" Chadwick for help, fun and a good party in Santiago; the Chilean Consulate in London; Ben Box, editor of the *South American Handbook*, for help and advice; Charlie Nurse for all his work on previous editions; Sarah Bower for excellent and thorough updates; Rachel Fielding and Stef Lambe for guiding the book through; Tim Burford for a very thorough update; and all the many readers whose letters have helped to make this guide as up-to-date as possible.

Thanks are also due to the following contributors: Jaime Baez; Brian Grady; Robert and Caroline Ely; Robert Terwilliger; Carrie Wittner; Robert Terwilliger; Major JA Valdes-Scott; Arthur Shapiro; RK Headland; Jane Norwich; Francine Audet and Jean Laforest; Gerry Gilmour; Simon Watson Taylor; Huw Clough; Patrick Frehner and Andrea Nicodemus; Luis Guzmán Molina; Steve Cobb; Dr Lyndsey O'Callaghan; John King; Gert Van Lancker and Sandra Van Heyste; Santiago de la Vega; Philip Horton; Nigel Gallop.

About the authors

Toby Green first visited Chile in 1992, when he spent a year teaching English in Santiago, and travelled the country from Arica to Tierra del Fuego. He has returned several times since, while developing a career as a writer and editor. He has written features and reviews for many of the UK national papers, and is the author of two works of narrative travel, 'Saddled with Darwin' (translated into five languages and nominated for two literary prizes) and 'Meeting the Invisible Man'. He lives in Gloucestershire, where he does his best to avoid learning how to drive.

Janak Jani was born in London and spent part of his childhood in France and East Africa. He went on to read Philosophy at Cambridge. He has lived, worked and travelled in over twenty countries in four continents and has had a fascination with Chile for over ten years, stemming from a love affair with *Nueva Canción* music. After spending months in Chile helping to research this book he decided to stay, settling in Valparaìso.